ENCYCLOPEDIA OF MEDIEVAL LITERATURE

Jay Ruud

For Stacey,
My own Beatrice

Encyclopedia of Medieval Literature

Facts On File, Inc.
An imprint of Infobase Publishing
132 West 31st Street
New York NY 10001

Library of Congress Cataloging-in-Publication Data
Ruud, Jay.
Encyclopedia of medieval literature / Jay Ruud.
p. cm.
Includes bibliographical references and index.
ISBN 0-8160-5497-5 (hardcover : alk. paper)
1. Literature, Medieval—Encyclopedias. 2. Literature, Medieval—Bio-bibliography. I. Title.
PN669.R88 2005
809'.02—dc22 2004031066

Facts On File books are available at special discounts when purchased in bulk quantities for businesses, associations, institutions, or sales promotions. Please call our Special Sales Department in New York at (212) 967-8800 or (800) 322-8755.

You can find Facts On File on the World Wide Web at http://www.factsonfile.com

Text design by Rachel L. Berlin
Cover design by Smart Graphics

Printed in the United States of America

VB FOF 10 9 8 7 6 5 4 3 2 1

This book is printed on acid-free paper.

Contents

PREFACE

I owe an important debt of gratitude to the contributors whose expertise helped put this book together. They are listed individually at the end of the volume, but I must specifically acknowledge the work of Albrecht Classen of the University of Arizona and Elisa Narin van Court of Colby College, who gladly contributed a significant number of entries each. I also want to thank the three editorial assistants who helped with the editing of the manuscript and contributed a number of entries themselves: Malene A. Little at Northern State University and Leslie Johnston and Michelle Palmer at the University of Central Arkansas.

I also want to express my gratitude to the University Research Council at the University of Central Arkansas, chaired by Elaine McNiece, for their generous grant that enabled me to hire two of my editorial assistants.

Finally, I want to thank Doubleday, a division of Random House, Inc., for permission to quote extensively from *German and Italian Lyrics of the Middle Ages* and from *The Lyrics of the Troubadours and Trouvères,* two excellent 1973 anthologies translated by Frederick Goldin.

Jay Ruud
Conway, Arkansas
November 2004

INTRODUCTION

To compose an encyclopedia of "medieval literature" of the world is a daunting prospect, since it involves a significant period of time (more than 1,000 years) and a remarkable number of literary traditions (European, Middle Eastern, Persian, Indian, Chinese, Japanese, Korean—and important subcategories of each). Nevertheless, this book is intended to make general sense of that dizzying array of texts and traditions for beginning students of the era, by selecting the foremost texts and writers from each of the major traditions of Europe and Asia. While there are also African and American texts based on oral traditions that may extend back into medieval times, the written texts that we have of these compositions are modern renditions of ancient oral material, and so I have not included them here.

Because this book is written in English for English-speaking students, I have included a greater number of entries from Old English and Middle English than from other literatures. Because English is best understood in the context of European literature, a significant number of texts and writers from French, Provençal, German, Italian, Old Norse, Celtic, Spanish, and Portuguese literature are also included, as well as the most important writers from late classical and medieval Latin literature that formed the basis of early medieval literature in Europe. The following pages also include entries concerning the major writers and texts from classical Arabic and Persian literature, as well as Indian, Chinese, and Japanese, and, to a lesser extent, from the literatures of Korea and of eastern Europe—entries that provide a worldwide context for the more familiar literature in English.

For the most part, the entries included here have been suggested by popular anthologies of world literature, of Western literature, and of English literature. I have included entries from texts that are often used in introductory college or advanced high school classes, since the primary intended reading audience for this book comprises beginning students in these kinds of classes and their instructors who seek some background information. Entries concerning English literature are expanded to include any number of texts that might be taught in courses in medieval English literature or that might shed light on such texts. All entries are followed by a selected bibliography of books and, for more often-studied writers or texts, articles intended as a recommended reading list for those students who want to look further into the topic. A comprehensive bibliography of works on the medieval period in general, and on the most commonly taught writers in particular, appears at the end of the volume.

Before delving into the very specific details of the individual entries that follow, it makes sense to consider first what we mean by the phrase "medieval literature." The term *medieval,* derived from the Latin for "middle period," was an invention of European scholars of the Renaissance, or early modern era, who conceived of themselves as returning to the superior cultural tradition of classical Greece and Rome. Their conception of the 1,000 years that had intervened between classical antiquity and their own time (between roughly 500 and 1500 C.E.) is reflected in the epithet by which they chose to label that span of time—"Middle Ages"—suggesting that the important accomplishments in literature, art, science, philosophy, and culture took place either in antiquity or in the contemporary early modern world, and that little of any consequence had taken place during that intervening millennium. Such a view ignores technological accomplishments such as the invention of the heavy compound plow, the adoption of the stirrup and the horseshoe, the expanded use of the water- and windmill, and the creation of movable type—foundational developments in the history of human civilization (Hollister 1978, 65–67). The view also ignores the monumental aesthetic achievements of the great Gothic cathedrals, as well as, on a lesser scale, the intricate miniatures of illuminated manuscripts. It ignores the primary position of Saint Augustine in Western thought, as well as the complex philosophical arguments of scholastic thinkers such as Thomas Aquinas and William of Ockham, and the invention of the scientific method by Roger Bacon in the 13th century. And of most immediate concern for purposes of this particular book, that view ignores the literary achievements of Dante (the "chief imagination of Christendom," as he has been called), of Chaucer (the acknowledged "father of English literature"), and of such lesser-known figures as Chrétien de Troyes—apparent inventor of the courtly romance, the direct ancestor of the European novel—and the Provençal troubadours, the first poets in western Europe to write poetry in the vernacular, and the inventors of an attitude toward love (often called the "courtly love" tradition) that pervaded Western thought for centuries.

Looking beyond the pejorative connotations of the term *medieval,* however, there is a sense in which the medieval world is in fact a "middle" period. The ancient world had established a body of texts that proved foundational for European culture, and primitive myth had given way to more sophisticated religion, while at the same time the great empire that had united much of the ancient Mediterranean was crumbling. An old world was indeed going through a transition by the fifth century. A modern world was coming into being 1,000 years later, characterized by a more secular and less universally religious outlook, a greater reliance on scientific thought, a more widespread use of the vernacular in literary and other texts, a more mercantile economy, and new and unprecedented connections between and among cultures, including Africa and the Americas, that had not existed before. Many of these trends, of course, had begun earlier, but the Middle Ages form the long transition from the ancient to the modern world.

In this same sense, the term *medieval* has recently come to be used in referring to other literatures as well, so that roughly the same period can be seen in China or in India or the Middle East, for instance, when they all were moving from the ancient world and its foundational texts such as the Bible, the Confucian classics, and the Vedas into a new era from which the modern world would develop. The rise of Islam made Arabic the dominant language of the Middle East, and the Koran the new chief literary inspiration. Japanese culture began to rival that of China, and Japanese literature grew through Chinese models. More vernacular literatures rivaled Sanskrit as the literary language of India, so that regional classics were composed in Tamil, Bengali, and Kannada.

There are some ways in which life in many of these areas of Europe, Asia, or North Africa was similar. Clearly the majority of people everywhere were peasants, usually working the land owned by members of a powerful aristocratic class. Monarchs generally sought support of powerful nobles and gathered the nobility around them, enabling them both to keep an eye on their most powerful vassals and to augment and display their own wealth and glory by the quality and number of their courtiers. Thus the royal courts of Europe, India, China, Japan, Iraq, and Persia were generally sites for the display of pomp and grandeur, where courtiers might feast and obtain valuable gifts and where poets (integral members of the court) might write of the sovereign's virtues, commemorate the martial accomplishments of the king or his vassals, and celebrate the beauties and the loves of the noble courtly women ("The Medieval Era" 2004, 1).

Another aspect of life in medieval times through most of the world is the profound influence of religion on most aspects of everyday life. Christianity survived the fall of the Roman Empire as the one institution that still unified the parts of the defunct empire, and Christianity spread throughout all of Europe during the Middle Ages, with the Roman pope dominating western European culture in a way that transcended national boundaries. In the Middle East, Islam was born and spread rapidly from Arabia east to India and west across North Africa to Spain. Although Hinduism, in a variety of sects, remained the chief religion in India, Buddhism spread from India into China, Korea, and Japan. In those countries it rivaled the native Taoism and Confucianism of China and Shinto of Japan, and literature in these countries often reflects the blending of Buddhism with the native traditions. In Europe, the literature more often reflects clashes between older pagan and newer Christian beliefs. Clarifying and defining the dominant religion as against religions it was coming in conflict with became important to theological writers across Europe, the Middle East, and southern and eastern Asia, and this close attention to theology influenced, as well, much of the writing of poets and storytellers, so that Dante Alighieri, the greatest medieval poet of Europe, constructs in his *Divine Comedy* a detailed picture of the medieval Christian view of salvation and damnation, while the great Persian poet Jalaloddin Rumi writes thousands of mystical verses reflecting ascetic Islamic Sufi mysticism, and in the Bengal region of eastern India the Vaisnava saints (like Vidyāpati and Chandidāsa) were writing allegories of mythic encounters between their god Krishna and earthly women ("The Medieval Era" 2004, 4).

Of course, each regional literature represented in this volume has its own unique aspects as well, and in many cases the literature of this middle period represents a pinnacle of literary achievement for that culture. The classical age of Arabic literature begins with the composition of the Koran, received, as Muslims believe, by Muhammad in the seventh century. The Arabic tribes united under Muhammad's successors, and within 100 years took Syria, Palestine, Egypt, and Libya. Under the Umayyad dynasty, the Islamic caliphate extended from parts of India across the Middle East and northern Africa into Spain to the Pyrenees. It was the largest empire the world had yet seen.

With its new status as a world power and with Arabic as a common language, Islam soon developed a significant literary culture. The Koran itself was written in rhymed prose and provided a model for subsequent writers and poets. The life of the Prophet (Muhammad) also became an important literary subject, initiated by Ibn Ishaq, Muhammad's first biographer. The tradition known as *adab* became the dominant literary style among cultured Muslims. It was an aristocratic style that stressed decorum, learning, and elegance, and used difficult meters and allusions that only the initiated would understand. Among later writers, love became an important theme, as it is in the *Dove's Neckring*, an autobiographical description of the many manifestations of love by the 11th-century scholar Ibn Hazm. Poetry was also abundant, particularly in the form of the *qasída*, an ode that had developed a standard form by the eighth century and survived for hundreds of years, though already by the ninth century its form was being parodied by the remarkable and innovative poet Abu Nuwas. But surely the most popular and influential literary text to come out of medieval Islam is *The Thousand and One Nights*, a huge collection of tales from India, Persia, Egypt, Iraq, and elsewhere, framed by the famous story of Scheherazade. Scorned for centuries in the Islamic world because of its low style, the text has become a classic of world literature.

A number of the best-known Islamic writers of the medieval period are philosophers, like Al-Ghazali and Averroës, whose commentaries on the philosophy of Aristotle became an important influence on scholastic thought in Europe. But with the discouragement of philosophic inquiry under the caliphs of later medieval Islam, Islamic learning and culture began to wane by the 14th and 15th centuries, though the most remarkable world traveler of the period, Ibn Battūta, published the story of his travels at this time.

Islam is not the only world culture that reached its cultural apex in the medieval period. Many scholars consider the Tang (T'ang) dynasty (618–907) to be the high point of Chinese imperial culture. The first half of the period was characterized by political stability and military expansion. Governing the vast empire demanded a huge bureaucracy, which the Tang officials staffed with bureaucrats who earned their positions through civil service examinations, the most prestigious of which included the impromptu composition of a poem. With this kind of cultural emphasis on the art of poetry, every educated Tang bureaucrat was a competent poet, and incidental poems composed for everyday occasions abound in collections of Tang poetry. Thus the major Tang poets reveal a good deal of their own personalities in their poems. The best known of them also illustrate the religious diversity of Tang China: Li Bai (Li Po), the high-spirited Taoist, is perhaps China's best-known poet; his friend, Du Fu (Tu Fu), was a Confucian chiefly concerned with family and with social responsibility; and their contemporary Wang Wei, a high-ranking government official, was a devout Buddhist. Although the last half of the Tang dynasty was characterized by political instability, great Tang poets continued to compose memorable poetry, and the period remains the influential central point of Chinese culture, in painting and the other arts as well as poetry.

Medieval Japan was culturally dominated by China until the Heian period (704–1186), when Japanese literature and culture came into its own. Still influenced by Tang China, Heian Japan was renowned for its refined court culture, where ceremony and religious ritual dominated the lives of the noble class. As in China, the accomplished Heian gentleman was expected to be able to compose poetry as well as master other art forms (such as music, painting, and calligraphy), and to conduct himself according to refined, proper forms of etiquette, a code of behavior (called *miyabi*) not unlike the expectations of courtesy in European courts of the time. Buddhism, which influenced the Heian aesthetic sensibility (called *aware*) concerning the transient beauty of the world, was imported from China and modified by native Shinto beliefs. During this period, the Japanese cultivated simplicity and brevity as aesthetic principles and created the short 31-syllable verse form called the *tanka,* which in modern times developed into the *haiku.* Imperial collections of poetry, most notably the *Kokinshū,* were begun during this period, and Japan's greatest writers were also active: Murasaki Shikibu, author of Japan's most acclaimed work, *The Tale of Genji,* wrote in the early 11th century, as did Sei Shōnagon, whose *Pillow Book* established a new kind of autobiographical prose text. Both of these classical writers were women, an unusual aspect of Japanese literature attributable to the fact that Japanese men of the time wrote in the "official" language of Chinese, leaving women to develop literature in the vernacular.

The subsequent periods of Japanese culture saw the rise of the samurai class that replaced the Heian court, creating a society of noble warriors not unlike the chivalric knights of medieval Europe. The classic *Tale of the Heike* dates from this period. The final centuries of the medieval period in Japan saw the rise of Nō theater under its most important artist, Zeami. These are still considered classical achievements in Japanese literature, but none matches the cherished accomplishments of the Heian era.

The literature of India during the middle period reflects a quite different cultural situation. Though the northern part of the Indian subcontinent was united briefly under the Gupta Empire early in the period, that unity fell apart in the sixth century, and South Asia returned to a collection of independent regional kingdoms that fostered enormous cultural diversity. In this India was somewhat like Europe at the time, and like Europe, the subcontinent had a single traditional common language, Sanskrit, but a large number of vernacular languages that began developing their own literary traditions during this middle period.

Sanskrit was, of course, the traditional language of Hinduism, which was the religion of the vast majority of Indians, despite competition from Buddhism and Islam (which had reached India by the eighth century). But the use of Sanskrit was not limited to religious texts: Sanskrit literature from the second to the 16th century includes every literary genre known at the time. The fourth-century Brahman Kālidāsa is generally recognized as India's greatest dramatist, and most important Sanskrit poet.

But essentially Sanskrit, like Latin in Europe, seems not to have been used in everyday situations, and regional vernaculars became increasingly important for literary expression. Tamil, the language of southernmost India, was the first to develop a vernacular literature. Mystical lyric poetry in the bhakti (or "devotional") tradition was first produced among Tamil poet-saints devoted to the worship of Śiva, such as Campantar, Appar, and Cuntarar. The greatest Tamil poet, however, is generally conceded to be Kampan, who translated the Sanskrit *Ramayana* into Tamil verse in the 12th century.

Regional devotionalism was spurred in part by the influx of Muslim Turks into India in the 12th century, fleeing from the conquests of Central Asia by Genghis Khan. Many of these Muslim refugees were highly educated and formed an elite class that ultimately assumed power in India, establishing the Delhi Sultanate in 1206. Their religion had a strong appeal among the lower castes of Hindu society, since Islam was a classless religion. The bhakti movement, which emphasized personal devotion to the Hindu gods (partly inspired by Sufi mysticism in Islam), spread rapidly among the Indian people as a reaction to the appeal of Islam. In the 11th century, in the southern region of Karnataka, devotees of Śiva (most important, Basavanna and Mahādēviyakka) began writing distinctive poems in the Kannada language. Later, in the 14th and 15th centuries, poets in Bengali dialects of eastern India (notably Vidyāpati and Govindadāsa) were writing devotional songs to Krishna, incarnation of the god Vishnu. The rich variety of Indian literatures is one of the remarkable delights of the middle period.

In Europe, as well, variety is the chief characteristic of the literature. The medieval literature of Europe is most immediately influenced by the Latin classics of late Roman civilization, by the Christian tradition, and by the pagan Germanic tradition of the northern tribes of Europe early in this period. To some degree, Islamic and Jewish traditions, radiating chiefly from multicultural medieval Spain, exerted some influence on European literature as well. From the beginning, Latin was the primary medium of literacy, and the theological works of such church fathers as Saint Jerome and Saint Augustine dominated the early centuries of medieval Europe. Latin remained a language for theological and philosophical texts, but in the north and west of Europe, vernacular languages were becoming more common as literary vehicles. Old English literature became the first major vernacular tradition in Europe, best known for its treatment of earlier Germanic heroic themes in poems like *Beowulf,* but just as characteristically producing Christian texts like *The Dream of the Rood,* a poetic vision of the crucifixion of Christ. This old heroic tradition can be seen influencing later medieval productions such as the French *Song of Roland,* the German *Nibelungenlied,* and all of the literary sagas in Old Norse.

More influential throughout Europe was the development of the vernacular poetic tradition of southern France, or Provençal. Here, poets like Bernart de Ventadorn and Guillaume IX, duke of Aquitaine, developed the poetry of courtly love, perhaps influenced in part by the Arabic poetry of Spain. The courtly love tradition, extolling the virtues of sensual love as the highest pleasure of the physical world and the greatest inducement to noble behavior, spread quickly to northern France, to Spain, Italy, Germany, and England. In northern France, the tradition spawned Guillaume de Lorris and Jean de Meun's highly influential and complex 13th-century love allegory called the *Roman de la Rose.* In addition, courtly love became associated with the chivalric romance, a new literary genre popularized by Chrétien de Troyes in which he recast old Celtic legends of King Arthur. The Arthurian legends spread throughout Europe as well, significantly to

Germany, where poets like Wolfram von Eschenbach and Gottfried von Strassburg composed much-admired romances, and where poets like Walther von der Vogelweide set the standard for lyric love poetry in German.

In Italy, lyric poetry in the courtly tradition became popular in the early 13th century, and from this beginning rose Dante Alighieri, the greatest writer of medieval Europe. Dante's enormously influential *Divine Comedy,* written in the early 14th century, demonstrated that a great work of moral, philosophical, theological, political, and literary significance could be written in the Italian vernacular, and his two disciples of the following generation, Boccaccio and Petrarch (often called the first "humanist"), form with Dante the acknowledged high point of Italian literature.

It was this group of Italian writers (in particular Boccaccio) that influenced the most important English writer of the later Middle Ages, Geoffrey Chaucer. Inspired in the late 14th century to write in his own Middle English vernacular, Chaucer produced such works as the tragic chivalric romance *Troilus and Criseyde* and the comic collection of tales in virtually every late medieval literary genre, *The Canterbury Tales,* demonstrating the narrative possibilities for the English language and earning him the title of "father of English literature."

Thus each of the major traditions of the middle period has its own unique aspects. But one of the remarkable developments of the medieval period was the increasing contact between world cultures. In Spain Christians, Muslims, and Jews lived together, while in India Hindus, Muslims and Buddhists coexisted in a multicultural environment. Viking adventurers from northern Europe traveled through Russia, into Muslim lands of the Mediterranean, and across the Atlantic, making the first European contact with the New World. The Crusades brought western Europeans into contact with Turks and Arabs of the Middle East. From northern Africa Ibn Battūta traveled through dozens of countries, farther than anyone in history had traveled before, and wrote of his wanderings, while Marco Polo visited China and described the lands of the East to an isolated European population. Ultimately Polo's Venice and the ancient Byzantine capital of Constantinople became major trading centers, and a "silk road" was established across Asia to China. By the end of the middle period, Portuguese sailors had explored the coast of Africa and found a sea route to East Asia, while the Spanish had found a route to the New World.

This interconnection of all the world's people is one of the general characteristics of what we might call the modern world—along with an economic system based on trade and capitalism, a reduction of the influence of religion in secular affairs, and a new developing middle class that challenged older notions of class and social stability. Every one of these characteristics has its roots in later medieval developments. The world as it is today grows directly from the medieval period, a lively, varied, eventful era that produced some of the world's greatest artistic achievements, particularly in the area of literature. The following pages explore many of the details of those varied and exciting literatures.

BIBLIOGRAPHY

Caws, Mary Ann, and Christopher Prendergast, eds. *The HarperCollins World Reader: Antiquity to the Early Modern World.* New York: HarperCollins, 1994.

Davis, Paul, et al., comps. *Western Literature in a World Context:* Vol. 1, *The Ancient World through the Renaissance.* New York: St. Martin's Press, 1995.

Hollister, C. Warren. *Medieval Europe: A Short History.* 4th ed. New York: Wiley, 1978.

Lawall, Sarah, and Maynard Mack, eds. *The Norton Anthology of World Literature.* Vol. B, *100–1500.* 2nd ed. New York: Norton, 2002.

"The Medieval Era." In *The Longman Anthology of World Literature:* Vol. B, *The Medieval Era,* edited by David L. Pike, et al., 1–9. New York: Longman, 2004.

Westling, Louise, et al., eds. *The World of Literature.* Upper Saddle River, N.J.: Prentice Hall, 1999.

AUTHORS' TIME LINE

Dates	Author
ca. 345–420	Jerome, Saint
348–aft. 405	Prudentius
354–430	Augustine of Hippo, Saint
ca. 360–ca. 435	Macrobius
365–427	Tao Qian (T'ao Ch'ien or T'ao Yuan-ming)
fl. 375–415	Kālidāsa
5th century	Bhartrhari
ca. 480–ca. 526	Boethius, Anicius Manlius Severinus
ca. 500–ca. 570	Gildas
ca. 530–ca. 609	Fortunatus, Venantius Honorius Clementianus
ca. 538–94	Gregory of Tours
ca. 540–604	Gregory the Great
late sixth century	Taliesin
fl. 560–600	Aneirin
ca. 560–636	Isidore of Seville, Saint
seventh century	Amaru
seventh century	Appar
seventh century	Caedmon
seventh century	Campatar
ca. 600–800	Han Shan (Han-shan)
ca. 673–735	Bede, The Venerable
fl. 698–700	Kakinomoto no Hitomaro
ca. 699–761	Wang Wei
701–762	Li Bai (Li Po)
ca. 704–ca. 767	Ibn Ishaq, Muhammad
712–776	Du Fu (Tu Fu)
ca. 720–799	Paul the Deacon
ca. 721–ca. 757	Ibn al-Muquaffa', Abd Allah
ca. 735–804	Alcuin of York
ca. 756–ca. 814	Abu Nuwas
768–824	Han Yu (Han Yü)
ca. 770–ca. 840	Cynewulf
ca. 770–840	Einhard
772–846	Bo Juyi (Po Chü-i)
779–831	Yuan Zhen (Yüan Chen)
790–816	Li He (Li Ho)
fl. 800	Nennius
ninth century	Cuntarar
805–852	Du Mu (Tu Mu)
ca. 809–849	Walafrid Strabo
ca. 813–ca. 858	Li Shangyin (Li Shang-yin)
ca. 840–912	Notker Balbullus
ca. 849–899	Alfred the Great
882–942	Saadia Gaon
10th century	Dēvara Dāsimayya
ca. 909–984	Aethelwold
ca. 915–990	Eyvind Finson
ca. 932–ca. 1025	Ferdowsi, Abolqasem
ca. 935–aft. 972	Hrosvit of Gandersheim
ca. 955–ca. 1012	Aelfric
ca. 960–1023	Wulfstan
fl. 966–1017	Sei Shōnagon
973–1058	Al-Ma'arri, Abu al-'Ala
fl. 978–1014	Murasaki Shikibu

Dates	Author
994–1064	Ibn Hazm, Abu Muhammad 'Ali ibn Muhammad ibn Sa'id
11th century	Somadeva
fl. 1000–1030	Izumi Shikibu
ca. 1033–1109	Anselm of Canterbury, Saint
1048–1131	Omar Khayyām
1058–1111	Al-Ghazālī
ca. 1071–ca. 1141	Judah Halevi
1071–1127	Guillaume IX, duke of Aquitaine
1079–1142	Abelard, Peter
1083–ca. 1155	Anna Comnena
ca. 1084–ca. 1151	Li Qingzhao (Li Ch'ing-chao)
ca. 1084–1155	Henry of Huntington
1090–1153	Bernard of Clairvaux, Saint
ca. 1095–1143	William of Malmesbury
1095–1188	Ibn Munqidh, Usamah
1098–1179	Hildegard von Bingen
ca. 12th century	Kampan
fl. early 12th century	Philippe de Thaon
12th century	Countess of Dia
12th century	Mahādeviyakka
ca. 1100–1155	Geoffrey of Monmouth
1101–1164	Hëloise
ca. 1105–1150	Marcabru
ca. 1105–ca. 1160	Peter Lombard
ca. 1106–ca. 1167	Basavanna
ca. 1110–ca. 1175	Wace
ca. 1115–1180	John of Salisbury
ca. 1116–ca. 1202	Alanus de Insulis
ca. 1120–1176	Hywel ap Owain Gwynedd
fl. 1125–1148	Rudel, Jaufré
1126–1198	Averroës
ca. 1130–ca. 1165	Archpoet
ca. 1130–1173	Raimbaut d'Orange
ca. 1130–1182	Cyril of Turov
ca. 1130–ca. 1195	Bernart de Ventadorn
ca. 1130–1202	Ralph of Diceto
1132–1197	Ephraim ben Jacob of Bonn
fl. 1135–1148	Cercamon
1135–1204	Maimonides, Moses
ca. 1138–ca. 1212	Giraut de Bornelh
ca. 1140–ca. 1190	Chrétien de Troyes
ca. 1140–ca. 1210	Map, Walter
ca. 1140–1215	Bertran de Born
ca. 1145–ca. 1217	Ibn Jubayr, Abu l-Hussain Muhammad
ca. 1145–ca. 1221	Attar, Faridoddin
ca. 1146–ca. 1223	Giraldus Cambrensis
late 12th century	Der von Kürenberg
late 12th century	Dietmar von Aist
late 12th century	Heinrich von Melk
late 12th century	Layamon
late 12th century	Thomas of Britain
late 12th century	Ulrich von Zatzikhoven
late 12th–early 13th century	Marie de France
fl. 1150–1175	Biket, Robert
fl. 1150–1180	Peire d'Alvernhe
ca. 1150–1190	Béroul
ca. 1150–ca. 1200	Arnaut Daniel
ca. 1150–ca. 1210	Reinmar der Alte
ca. 1150–bef. 1218	Villehardouin, Geoffroi de
ca. 1150–ca. 1220	Conon de Bethune
ca. 1155–ca. 1200	Blondel de Nesle
ca. 1155–ca. 1207	Raimbaut de Vaqueiras
ca. 1160–ca. 1200	Friedrich von Hausen
ca. 1160–ca. 1200	Heinrich von Veldeke
ca. 1160–ca. 1205	Vidal, Peire
ca. 1160–ca. 1210	Hartman von Aue
ca. 1160–ca. 1213	Gace Brulé
ca. 1160–ca. 1216	Innocent III, Pope
ca. 1160–ca. 1231	Folquet de Marseille
fl ca. 1160–1170	Benoît de Sainte-Maure
1165–1240	Ibn al-'Arabi, Muhyi a-Din Abu Bakr Muhammad
ca. 1167–1253	Grosseteste, Robert
ca. 1168–1203	Châtelain de Couci
1168–1241	Yi Kyubo
fl. ca. 1175	Fantosme, Jordan
ca. 1175–ca. 1210	Eilhart von Oberge
ca. 1175–ca. 1230	Walther von der Vogelweide
1179–1241	Snorri Sturluson
fl. 1180–1190	Andreas Capellanus
fl. 1180–1190	Robert de Boron
ca. 1180–ca. 1220	Gottfried von Strassburg

Dates	Author
ca. 1180–ca. 1220	Heinrich von Morungen
ca. 1180–ca. 1220	Wolfram von Eschenbach
ca. 1180–ca. 1240	Neidhart
ca. 1180–1244	Abulafia, Meir ben Todros ha-Levi
ca. 1180–ca. 1252	Garland, John
ca. 1180–ca. 1278	Cardenal, Peire
1181–1226	Francis of Assisi, Saint
ca. 1190–1249	Pier della Vigna
ca. 1196–ca. 1264	Berceo, Gonzalo de
fl. 1200	Geoffrey of Vinsauf
early 13th century	Burkhard von Hohenfels
early 13th century	Giacomino Pugliese
early 13th century	Giacomo da Lentino
early 13th century	Rinaldo d'Aquino
13th century	Fernandez de Santiago, Roi
ca. 1200–ca. 1250	Muset, Colin
ca. 1200–1259	Paris, Matthew
ca. 1200–1270	Sordello
ca. 1200–1275	Ulrich von Liechtenstein
ca. 1200–1292	Sa'di, Moslehoddin
1201–1253	Thibaut de Champagne
ca. 1207–1282	Mechthild von Magdeburg
1207–1273	Rumi, Jalaloddin
ca. 1210–ca. 1290	Guido delle Collone
ca. 1214–1292	Bacon, Roger
fl. 1220–1240	Guillaume de Lorris
ca. 1220–ca. 1297	Bonagiunta Orbicciani da Lucca
ca. 1220–1297	Erceldoune, Thomas
1221–1274	Bonaventure, Saint
1221–1284	Alfonso X
ca. 1224–1274	Thomas Aquinas, Saint
ca. 1224–1317	Joinville, Jean, sire de
fl. ca. 1230	Codax, Martin
ca. 1230–1276	Guinizelli, Guido
ca. 1230–1294	Guittone d'Arezzo
ca. 1230–ca. 1300	Riquier, Guiraut
ca. 1232–1316	Llull, Ramón
ca. 1235–ca. 1280	Davanzati, Chiaro
ca. 1235/40–1305	Jean de Meun
ca. 1236–1306	Jacopone da Todi
ca. 1240–ca. 1288	Adam de la Halle
late 13th century	Der Wilde Alexander

Dates	Author
fl. 1250	Meogo, Pero
fl. ca. 1250–1300	Zorro, Joan
ca. 1250–ca. 1328	Lapo Gianni
fl. 1254–1285	Rutebeuf
ca. 1254–1324	Marco Polo
ca. 1258–ca. 1334	Trivet, Nicholas
ca. 1259–1300	Cavalcanti, Guido
d. 1260	Thomas of Celano
ca. 1260–1300	Robert of Gloucester
ca. 1260–ca. 1313	Angiolieri, Cecco
ca. 1260–1328	Eckhart Meister
ca. 1265–1308	Duns Scotus, John
1265–1321	Dante Alighieri
ca. 1270–ca. 1337	Cino da Pistoia
1270–ca. 1332	Folgore da San Geminiano
ca. 1271–early 14th century	Gianni Alfani
ca. 1271–1316	Frescobaldi, Dino
fl. 1278–1283	Gruffudd ap yr Ynad Coch
1279–1325	Dinis, king of Portugal
fl. 1280–1290	Núñez, Airas
ca. 1281–1345	Bury, Richard de
1282–1348	Manuel, Don Juan
ca. 1283–ca. 1340	Mannyng, Robert, of Brunne
ca. 1283–ca. 1350	Ruiz, Juan
ca. 1283–ca. 1352	Kenkō
ca. 1285–1364	Higden, Ranulph
1287–1367	Yi Chehyon
ca. 1288–1347	Ockham, William
ca. 1290–ca. 1369	Shem Tov
ca. 1300–1349	Rolle, Richard
ca. 1300–1377	Machaut, Guillaume de
1304–1374	Petrarch, Francis
1304–ca. 1377	Ibn Battūta, Abu 'Abdallah
1313–1375	Boccaccio, Giovanni
ca. 1316–1395	Barbour, John
ca. 1320–ca. 1388	Hafez, Mohammad Shamsoddin
ca. 1325–ca. 1380	Dafydd ap Gwilym
fl. 1327	William of Shoreham
ca. 1330–1384	Wycliffe, John
ca. 1330–ca. 1388	Langland, William
ca. 1330–1408	Gower, John

Dates	Author
ca. 1332–1406	Ibn Khaldūn
ca. 1332–1407	López de Ayala, Pedro
bef. 1335–1381	Ball, John
ca. 1337–ca. 1404	Froissart, Jean
ca. 1340–1396	Hilton, Walter
ca. 1341–1391	Clanvowe, John
ca. 1342–ca. 1402	Trevisa, John
1342–ca. 1416	Julian of Norwich
ca. 1343–1400	Chaucer, Geoffrey
ca. 1345–1397	Granson, Oton de
ca. 1346–1407	Deschamps, Eustache
fl. 1350–1380	Chandos Herald
ca. 1350–1388	Usk, Thomas
ca. 1352–ca. 1448	Vidyāpati
ca. 1355–aft. 1414	Mirk, John
fl. 1357	Mandeville, John
ca. 1360–ca. 1419	Epiphanius the Wise
ca. 1361–1407	Scogan, Henry
ca. 1364–1430	Christine de Pizan
ca. 1364–ca. 1443	Zeami
ca. 1366–1456	Shirley, John
ca. 1368–ca. 1426	Hoccleve, Thomas
ca. 1370–ca. 1449	Lydgate, John
ca. 1373–1415	Hus, Jan
ca. 1373–ca. 1440	Kempe, Mergeryca.
1375–ca. 1450 (or 16th century)	Chandidas, Baru
1378–ca. 1465	Hardyng, John
ca. 1379–1471	Thomas à Kempis
ca. 1390–ca. 1475	Ashby, George
1393–1464	Capgrave, John
1394–1437	James I of Scotland
1394–1465	Charles d' Orléans
1398–1458	Santillana, Iñigo López de Mendoza, marqués de
ca. 1395–ca. 1460	Pecock, Reginald
ca. 1395–ca. 1477	Fortescue, Sir John
15th century	Govindadāsa
fl. 1407	Thorpe, William
fl. 1410	Love, Nicholas
ca. 1410–1471	Malory, Sir Thomas
1414–1492	Jami of Herat
ca. 1421–1491	Caxton, William
ca. 1425–ca. 1505	Henryson, Robert
1431–1463	Villon, François
1435–1516	Kanze Kojiro Nobumitsu
ca. 1440–ca. 1492	Henry the Minstrel
1440–1479	Manrique, Jorge
fl. 1447–1486	Lewis Glyn Cothi
fl. ca. 1450	Kabir
1450–1513	Bradshaw, Henry
ca. 1460–ca. 1515	Dunbar, William
ca. 1465–1536	Vicente, Gil
ca. 1475–1522	Douglas, Gavin
ca. 1475–1523	Hawes, Stephen
ca. 1486–ca. 1555	Lindsay, Sir David

Writers Covered, by Language of Composition

ARABIC

Abu Nuwas
al-Ghazālī
al-Ma'arri, Abu al-'Ala
Averroës
Ibn al-'Arabi, Muhyi a-Din Abu Bakr Muhammad
Ibn al-Muquaffa', Abd Allah
Ibn Battūta, Abu 'Abdallah
Ibn Hazm, Abu Muhammad 'Ali ibn Muhammad ibn Sa'id
Ibn Ishaq, Muhammad
Ibn Jubayr, Abul-Hussain Muhammad
Ibn Khaldūn
Ibn Munqidh, Usamah
Judah Halevi
Llull, Ramón
Maimonides, Moses
Saadia Gaon

BENGALI

Chandidas, Baru
Govindadāsa
Vidyāpati

CATALAN

Llull, Ramón

CHINESE

Bo Juyi (Po Chü-i)
Du Fu (Tu Fu)
Du Mu (Tu Mu)
Han Shan (Han-shan)
Han Yu (Han Yü)
Li Bai (Li Po)
Li He (Li Ho)
Li Shangyin (Li Shang-yin)
Li Qingzhao (Li Ch'ing-chao)
Tao Qian (T'ao Ch'ien)
Wang Wei
Yuan Zhen (Yüan Chen)

CZECH

Hus, Jan

ENGLISH

Aelfric
Alfred the Great
Ashby, George
Ball, John
Barbour, John (Scottish)
Bradshaw, Henry
Caedmon
Capgrave, John
Caxton, William
Chaucer, Geoffrey
Clanvowe, John
Cynewulf
Douglas, Gavin (Scottish)
Dunbar, William (Scottish)
Erceldoune, Thomas (Scottish)
Fortescue, Sir John

Gower, John
Hardyng, John
Hawes, Stephen
Henryson, Robert (Scottish)
Henry the Minstrel (Scottish)
Hilton, Walter
Hoccleve, Thomas
James I of Scotland (Scottish)
Julian of Norwich
Kempe, Margery
Langland, William
Layamon
Lindsay, Sir David (Scottish)
Love, Nicholas
Lydgate, John
Malory, Sir Thomas
Mannyng, Robert, of Brunne
Mirk, John
Pecock, Reginald
Robert of Gloucester
Rolle, Richard
Scogan, Henry
Shirley, John
Thorpe, William
Trevisa, John
Usk, Thomas
William of Shoreham
Wulfstan
Wycliffe, John

FRENCH (AND ANGLO-NORMAN)

Adam de la Halle
Benoît de Sainte-Maure
Béroul
Biket, Robert
Blondel de Nesle
Chandos Herald
Charles d'Orléans
Châtelain de Couci
Chrétien de Troyes
Christine de Pizan
Conon de Béthune
Deschamps, Eustache
Fantosme, Jordan
Froissart, Jean
Gace, Brulé
Gower, John
Granson, Oton de
Guillaume de Lorris
Jean de Meun
Joinville, Jean, sire de
Machaut, Guillaume de
Mandeville, John
Marie de France
Muset, Colin
Philippe de Thaon
Robert de Boron
Rutebeuf
Thibaut de Champagne
Thomas of Britain
Trivet, Nicholas
Villehardouin, Geoffroi de
Villon, François
Wace

GERMAN

Burkhard von Hohenfels
Der von Kürenberg
Der Wilde Alexander
Dietmar von Aist
Eilhart von Oberge
Friedrich von Hausen
Gottfried von Strassburg
Hartmann von Aue
Heinrich von Melk
Heinrich von Morungen
Heinrich von Veldeke
Mechthild von Magdeburg
Meister Eckhart
Neidhart
Reinmar der Alte
Ulrich von Lichtenstein
Ulrich von Zatzikhoven
Walther von der Vogelweide
Wolfram von Eschenbach

GREEK

Anna Comnena

HEBREW

Abulafia, Meir ben Todros ha-Levi
Ephraim ben Jacob of Bonn
Judah Halevi
Maimonides, Moses
Saadia Gaon
Shem Tov

HINDI

Kabir

ITALIAN

Angiolieri, Cecco
Boccaccio, Giovanni
Bonagiunta Orbicciani da Lucca
Cavalcanti, Guido
Cino da Pistoia
Dante Alighieri
Davanzati, Chiaro
Folgore da San Geminiano
Frescobaldi, Dino
Giacomino Pugliese
Giacomo da Lentino
Gianni Alfani
Guido delle Collonne
Guinizelli, Guido
Guittone d'Arezzo
Jacopone da Todi
Lapo Gianni
Marco Polo
Petrarch, Francis
Pier della Vigna
Rinaldo d'Aquino

JAPANESE

Izumi Shikibu
Kakinomoto no Hitomaro
Kanze Kojirô Nobumitsu
Kenkō
Murasaki Shikibu
Sei Shōnagon
Zeami

KANNADA

Basavanna
Dēvara Dāsimayya
Mahadeviyakka

KOREAN

Yi Chehyon
Yi Kyubo

LATIN

Abelard, Peter
Aethelwold
Alanus de Insulis
Alcuin of York
Andreas Capellanus
Anselm of Canterbury, Saint
Archpoet
Augustine of Hippo, Saint
Bacon, Roger
Bede, The Venerable
Bernard of Clairvaux, Saint
Boethius, Anicius Manlius Severinus
Bonaventure, Saint
Bury, Richard de
Capgrave, John
Dante Alighieri
Duns Scotus, John
Einhard
Fortescue, Sir John
Fortunatus, Venantius Honorius Clementianus
Francis of Assisi, Saint
Garland, John
Geoffrey of Monmouth
Geoffrey of Vinsauf
Gildas
Giraldus Cambrensis
Gower, John
Gregory of Tours
Gregory the Great
Grosseteste, Robert
Hëloise
Henry of Huntington
Higden, Ranulph
Hildegard von Bingen
Hrosvit of Gandersheim
Hus, Jan
Innocent III, Pope
Isidore of Seville, Saint
Jerome, Saint
John of Salisbury
Llull, Ramón
Macrobius
Map, Walter
Meister Eckhart
Mirk, John
Nennius
Notker Balbullus
Ockham, William of
Paris, Matthew

Paul the Deacon
Petrarch, Francis
Prudentius
Ralph of Diceto
Thomas à Kempis
Thomas Aquinas
Thomas of Celano
Trivet, Nicholas
Walafrid Strabo
William of Malmsbury
Wycliffe, John

NORSE

Eyvind Finson
Snorri Sturluson

PERSIAN

Attar, Faridoddin
Ferdowsi, Abolqasem
Hafez, Mohammad Shamsoddin
Jami of Herat
Omar Khayyām
Rumi, Jalaloddin
Sa'di, Moslehoddin

PORTUGUESE (GALICIAN)

Codax, Martin
Dinis, king of Portugal
Fernandez de Santiago, Roi
Meogo, Pero
Núñez, Airas
Vicente, Gil
Zorro, Johan

PROVENÇAL

Arnaut Daniel
Bernart de Ventadorn
Bertran de Born
Cardenal, Peire
Cercamon
Countess of Dia
Folquet de Marseille
Giraut de Bornelh
Guillaume IX, duke of Aquitaine
Marcabru
Peire d'Alvernhe
Peter Lombard
Raimbaut de Vaqueiras
Raimbaut d'Orange
Riquier, Guiraut
Rudel, Jaufré
Sordello
Vidal, Peire

RUSSIAN

Cyril of Turov
Epiphanius the Wise

SANSKRIT

Amaru
Bhartrhari
Kālidāsa
Somadeva

SPANISH (CASTILIAN)

Alfonso X
Berceo, Gonzalo de
López de Ayala, Pedro
Manrique, Jorge
Manuel, Don Juan
Ruiz, Juan
Santillana, Iñigo López de Mendoza, marqués de
Shem Tov
Vicente, Gil

TAMIL

Appar
Campatar
Cuntarar
Kampan

WELSH

Aneirin
Dafydd ap Gwilym
Gruffudd ap yr Ynad Coch
Hywel ap Owain Gwynedd
Lewis Glyn Cothi
Taliesin

Abelard, Peter (Pierre Abelard) (1079–1142)

Perhaps the most famous man in Europe in his own lifetime, Peter Abelard was a renowned teacher, philosopher, theologian, writer and lover, as famous for his celebrated affair with HELOISE as for his provoking applications of reason to issues of faith.

Abelard was born in the village of Pallet, south of Nantes in Brittany. Eldest son of a noble house, he gave up his inheritance for a life of the intellect. He studied logic in Compiègne before moving to Paris in 1100 to study dialectic under William of Campaux, under whom the cathedral school at Notre Dame had become as famous a center of learning as St. ANSELM's Bec. But Abelard had a penchant for challenging authority, and apparently aroused the resentment of his classmates as well as his teacher as he regularly challenged William. After defeating William in a public debate in 1101, Abelard started his own school at Melun, later moving to Corboeil, southeast of Paris. But by 1105 Abelard had exhausted himself, and returned to Brittany for his health.

But he was back in Paris in 1108, looking for a chair at the cathedral school and studying rhetoric in the meantime with his old master William. He began to teach theology and dialectic at the school of Mont Sainte-Geneviève in Paris, and in 1113 went to Laon to study theology under the well-known Anselm of Laon. Impatient with Anselm's methods—which essentially were exegetical (based on scriptural interpretation) rather than logical—and true to his penchant for challenging older, established authorities, Abelard gave a scandalous public lecture on Ezekiel, raising a number of logical questions.

In 1114 Abelard returned to Paris again, this time to finally take a chair at the cathedral school of Notre Dame. If we are to believe his own words from his autobiography, students flocked to his lectures from all over Europe. Certainly his reputation made him quite wealthy. But it was here, at the height of his reputation, that Abelard was to suffer disaster.

Abelard was living in the home of Fulbert, a canon of the cathedral. He also was given charge of the education of Fulbert's niece, the beautiful Heloise, who was 22 years Abelard's junior. The two became lovers, and when Heloise became pregnant, Abelard married her in secret and sent her to live in Brittany, where she gave birth to their son, whom they named Astrolabe. The affair became publicly known, however, and when Abelard sent Heloise to join the convent of Saint-Argenteuil, Fulbert saw this as Abelard's failure to take responsibility for his actions. One evening in 1118, he hired men to take Abelard in his sleep and castrate him.

After the disgrace of the Heloise affair and his emasculation, Abelard became a Benedictine monk. He entered the monastery of Saint-Denis, but before long had caused resentment among the monks by what they considered his irreverent attitude toward the legend of their patron saint. He was back in Paris teaching again in 1121, but at that time the Council of Soissons brought charges against him for a treatise he had written on the Trinity. He was sentenced to burn his book, and to be imprisoned in the Abbey of St. Medard. Rather than complete a forced residence there, he fled to an out-of-the-way area near Troyes called Nogent-sûr-Seine and set up another school.

In 1125 Abelard's monastic condemnation was lifted, and he was elected abbot of the Abbey of St. Gildas in his native Brittany. Those were difficult years for Abelard, however, since (as might be expected) he aroused a great deal of resentment among the monks there. Allegedly they even tried to poison him. So by 1136, he was back in Paris and teaching again.

But by this time, the opinions expressed in his philosophical treatises, particularly the rationalist approach that seemed to negate the mystery of the Christian faith, had aroused the interest and enmity of the most powerful ecclesiast in Europe, St. BERNARD OF CLAIRVAUX. Bernard denounced Abelard to Pope Innocent II, and Abelard was called to the Council of Sens in 1141. Here Abelard thought he would be given the chance to publicly dispute with Bernard—a debate Abelard would have relished as he had his previous challenges to authority. But he was never given the opportunity to speak in his own defense. He was condemned on several counts of heresy, one of the most serious being his ethical theory, which held that it was the intention of sinning, rather than the act itself, for which we are to be held culpable.

Far from quietly accepting his condemnation, Abelard appealed to the pope (though it was a fruitless appeal since Bernard had already convinced the pope of Abelard's errors). En route to Rome, Abelard was given protection by Peter the Venerable, abbot of Cluny. Peter apparently convinced Abelard to drop his appeal and make peace with Bernard if he could, and to remain at Cluny. Peter was able to obtain authorization from the pope to allow Abelard to spend his remaining days under the protection of Cluny. Abelard died in a Cluniac monastery in 1142.

Abelard influenced the whole subsequent course of medieval scholastic theology—he may have lost the battle with St. Bernard in 1141 but ultimately it was his methods that won out over the next few centuries. Some of his more influential students were Arnold of Brescia, PETER LOMBARD, and JOHN OF SALISBURY. His most influential philosophical work was *Sic et Non* (Yes and no), a text that lists opinions of the most important fathers of the church on both sides of a variety of theological questions. He first wrote the text in 1123 and revised it in 1136. The point of the treatise is that there are respected opinions both for and against most theological points, and that a strict rational approach must be applied to reconcile the various opinions.

Another important text is Abelard's *Dialogus inter philosophum, Judaeum, et Christianum* (*A Dialogue of a Philosopher with a Jew and a Christian*), possibly written at Cluny during the last year of his life, though more recently it has been asserted that it was written during Abelard's years at St. Gildas. In the text, which unlike most such imaginary disputations in the Middle Ages allows the Jew to make a great number of logical points, Abelard presents his final words on the relationship of reason and faith.

But Abelard's most important contributions to literature are his letters to Heloise, written after she had become a nun and he a monk; and his autobiography, entitled *Historia Calamitatum* (*The Story of My Misfortunes*), which tells the story of his life until 1129. Though both of these make interesting reading, particularly since Abelard is the only important medieval philosopher who has left personal letters or an autobiography, one should take care to realize that both are texts Abelard intended for wide circulation, and so present the public face he wanted to be perceived.

Bibliography

Abelard, Peter. *A Dialogue of a Philosopher with a Jew and a Christian.* Translated by Pierre J. Payer. Toronto: Pontifical Institute of Medieval Studies, 1979.

———. *The Letters of Abelard and Heloise.* Translated by Betty Radice. Harmondsworth, U.K.: Penguin, 1974.

———. *The Story of My Misfortunes: The Autobiography of Peter Abelard.* Translated by Henry Adams Bellows. New York: Macmillan, 1972.

Clanchy, M. T. *Abelard: A Medieval Life.* Oxford: Blackwell, 1997.

Robertson, D. W., Jr. *Abelard and Heloise.* New York: Dial Press, 1972.

Abulafia, Meir ben Todros ha-Levi (Ramah) (ca. 1180–1244)

The rabbi Meir Abulafia was the most important Castilian scholar of the Talmud during the first half of the 13th century. Abulafia was born in Burgos, Spain, about 1180, and spent most of his life in Toledo. He was one of three rabbis appointed to the Toledo Jewish court, and helped to establish ritual regulations for the Jews of Spain. He was held in such high regard in Toledo that in 1225, upon the death of his father, Todros ben Judah, he became known by his father's honorary title of *nasi* (prince).

Abulafia's great contributions to scholarship include his substantial Aramaic commentary on the Talmud, called *Peratei Peratim,* of which only the sections on *Bava' Batra'* and on *Sanhedrin* survive. He was also known for his carefully edited Torah scroll (produced after consulting a large number of previous scrolls) that became the definitive edition for Spanish Jewry. His *Masoret Siyag La-Torah,* a manual for Torah writing, was also influential, and he wrote a number of poems in Hebrew that reflect his life and times. The best known of these poems is his "Letter from the Grave." The poem, written in the voice of his deceased sister, was intended as a comfort to his grieving father.

He is most famous, however, for his launching the first Maimonodean controversy. Abulafia was highly orthodox in his views, and defended even the most illogical of the Talmud's *aggadah* (legendary stories) as literally true. But when in his *Guide for the Perplexed* the most esteemed medieval Jewish philosopher, MAIMONIDES, had implied his disbelief in the resurrection of the body, the position shocked and outraged Abulafia. He wrote a series of letters condemning Maimonides, first to the Jewish leaders of Lunel and then to those of northern France. In both cases his letters were dismissed and Maimonides supported. Despite his failure, he remained a staunch antirationalist throughout his life. However, when his younger contemporary Nachmanides sought to revive the controversy over Maimonides 30 years later, Abulafia did not participate in the debate, excusing himself because of his age.

Bibliography

Carmi, T., ed. and trans. *The Penguin Book of Hebrew Verse.* Harmondsworth, U.K.: Penguin, 1981.

Septimus, Bernard. *Hispano-Jewish Culture in Transition: The Career and Controversies of Ramah.* Harvard Judaic Monographs 4. Cambridge, Mass.: Harvard University Press, 1982.

Abu Nuwas (Abu Nuwas al-Hasan ibn Hani al-Hakami) (ca. 756–ca. 814)

Abu Nuwas is the most famous love poet of the Islamic Abbasid dynasty (758–1258). He was called the father of locks, apparently because of his curly hair. Though he wrote in Arabic, he rejected traditional forms and explored new and unconventional subjects for poetry, some of which were considered disreputable or inappropriate by his contemporaries. While he wrote some love poems to women, he is better known for his homoerotic lyrics, and his own preferred practice seems to have been pederasty.

Abu Nuwas was born in Ahwaz in Persia sometime around the year 756. Tradition says his father served in the army of the last Umayyad caliph, Marwan II, while his mother was a Persian who worked as a washerwoman. He was educated at Kufa and in Basra, where he came under the influence of the well-known poet Waliba ibn al-Hubab, from whom he learned the craft of poetry and with whom he is said to have become intimate. After this education, Abu Nuwas followed the conventional route for poets by going to the desert to spend time with the Bedouin tribes and improve his Arabic.

Though he learned his Arabic from the Bedouin, Abu Nuwas refused to accept traditional

Bedouin values, and spurned the conventional literary form of the *QASÍDA*, a genre of poem in which the poet customarily lamented an abandoned campsite and, perhaps, a love he had enjoyed there. Abu Nuwas parodied this theme in a famous poem in which he laments abandoned taverns and the loss of good places to drink.

Abu Nuwas wrote in virtually every genre of Arabic poetry. Another of his more unusual and popular forms was the hunting poem, in which he seems to have emulated the ancient desert hunters. He was the first Arabic poet whose published works include a special section devoted specifically to poems about hunting.

Aside from his hunting and his erotic poems, Abu Nuwas is best known for his bacchic drinking poems. Critics have speculated that his celebration of drunkenness is a symbol in his poetry of the total liberation of the mind and body from the tyranny of logic and of convention. Others have suggested that his focus on the poetry of wine is in fact related to his Persian roots, in that here he continues the hard-drinking tradition of the older Sassanian court of Persia. In any case the Abbasid caliphs, whose relocation of the capital from Damascus to Baghdad helped to bring about a fusion of Semitic Arabic and Persian cultures, were sympathetic to Abu Nuwas's poetry, and he became a favorite of the caliphs al-Amin and Harun ar-Rashid.

Abu Nuwas is said to have even been employed as tutor for the caliph Harun's son, and to have become the boy's lover as well. Most of his life was spent as a courtier in Baghdad, and for his readers across the centuries he has embodied the extravagance and excesses of life as a favored courtier. His life, as celebrated in his poetry, became the stuff of legend for later Arabic writers. In a 13th-century joke book, it is stated that Abu Nuwas claimed he never saw anybody drunk—this was because wherever he was, he was always the first to become intoxicated, and therefore was unable to judge whether anybody else was. Abu Nuwas even appears as a character in the *THOUSAND AND ONE NIGHTS* several hundred years after his death.

Despite the fame he experienced in his life, Abu Nuwas ended in obscurity. Some say he became deeply religious in his old age and abjured his former sins. Some say he died in prison. Some say that he went too far in satirizing a member of a certain clan and that members of the clan beat him to death. Whatever the truth is, Abu Nuwas died sometime around the year 814. He left a body of work remarkable for its variety, its innovation, and its controversial themes. He was sometimes criticized for borrowing too much from other poets (a practice not uncommon in his time), but is praised for his powerful language, his memorable imagery, and his exquisite poetic style. Yet in many ways he remains at least as well known for the legend of his life as for his literary production: His motto was purported to be a line from one of his poems that reads "Accumulate all the sins that you can."

Bibliography

Abu Nuwas. *Selections from the Diwan of Abu Nuwas ibn Hani al-Hakami.* Edited and translated by Arthur Wormhoudt. Oskaloosa, Iowa: William Penn College, 1998.

Kennedy, Philip F. *The Wine Song in Classical Arabic Poetry: Abu Nuwas and the Literary Tradition.* Oxford: Clarendon Press, 1997.

Adam (*Ordo representationis Ade, Le Jeu d'Adam, Le Mystère d'Adam*) (ca. 1170)

The Anglo-Norman play of *Adam* survives in a single 13th-century manuscript found in the French city of Tours. The play, probably produced in England in the mid- to late 12th century, is written (like many late medieval French texts) in octosyllabic (eight-syllable) couplets, and consists of three scenes: The first, and by far the longest (nearly 600 lines), presents the story of the Fall of man and the expulsion from paradise; the second is a brief version of the story of Cain and Abel; the final scene presents a series of Old Testament prophets, repeating passages from the messianic tradition looking forward to the birth of Christ. The play, which is fragmentary, breaks off after the speech of Nebuchadnezzar. The script is interspersed with liturgical chants in Latin that are borrowed from the service of matins for Septuagesima

Sunday, along with other sources. The occasion and manner of the performance of the play are in dispute, but it appears that this vernacular drama must have been intended for a secular audience, that it may have been written to supplement the Latin service and to "bring it to life" for the lay congregation, and that it may have been performed outside the church itself.

The play is lively and sophisticated, and has attracted the interest of scholars studying the history of theater. The elaborate stage directions in the text are of particular interest, as they describe costuming, scenery, and advice on how the actors are to gesture and react. (After they are confronted by God, for instance, Adam and Eve are to be bent over in shame.) The opening stage direction advises the actors that they are to say only what has been written down, and are to add or leave out nothing (suggesting that the writer may have had some experience with ad-libbing actors in the past).

The author takes some liberties himself, though, with the story of Genesis. The plot of the Adam and Eve story owes more to biblical exegesis than to the Bible itself. The play begins with the Second Person of the Trinity ("our Savior"), clad in a "dalmatic" (the sort of outer garment worn by a bishop or abbot), addressing Adam and Eve. Thereafter, he is referred to in the stage directions only as the "Figure." In the play, the Devil character approaches Adam twice before giving up on him and concentrating on Eve. She is swayed, but rebuked by Adam. Then, when a serpent appears, apparently allied with the Devil, she takes the apple (not simply a "fruit" here) and convinces Adam to eat it as well. When the Figure of God confronts them, he not only condemns them to hard work and to the pains of childbirth, but also specifically damns them to hell and everlasting torment, unless, he says, he should relent at some point.

The scene ends with Adam and Eve living outside paradise, the repentant Adam still blaming Eve, and the sorrowing Eve blaming herself and wishing for death. Her last words, though, reveal a note of hope that God will someday relent and save them. The final action of the scene portrays a group of devils snatching Adam and Eve, putting them in chains, and dragging them off to hell. This motif is carried through the subsequent scenes as well: After Cain has slain Abel, devils come and drag them off, treating Abel gently but beating on Cain mercilessly. Even in the scene with the Prophets, each individual prophet is dragged to hell by his own devils after he has spoken his messianic prophecy. Clearly the play's point is that all human beings are damned through Adam's fall, until God commutes his sentence by coming himself in the form of a Savior.

The play *Adam* is sometimes seen as an important link in the evolution of the great MYSTERY PLAY cycles in late medieval England. Certainly the combination and progression of Old Testament scenes leading up to the salvation of humankind mirrors the structure of the mystery cycles. However, the high level of theatrical expertise of the play, as well as the psychology of its characters, seem to be more sophisticated than the later mysteries. Thus the precise relationship between this play and the cycle plays remains unclear.

Bibliography

Le Mystère d'Adam. Edited by P. Studer. Manchester, U.K.: Manchester University Press, 1967.

The Play of Adam (Ordo representationis Ade). Translated by Carl J. Odenkirchen. Medieval Classics: Texts and Studies 5. Brookline, Mass.: Classical Folia Editions, 1976.

Adam de la Halle (Adam le Bossu) (ca. 1240–ca. 1288)

Adam de la Halle was one of the most important of the French TROUVÈRES, as well as a very influential playwright and composer. He was an important innovator in secular theater, and his play *Jeu de Robin et Marion* is sometimes called the first comic opera because of its use of song and dance.

Adam was probably born in Arras in about 1240. He is sometimes called "Adam le Bossu," or "the Hunchback," though he seems not to have had that specific affliction. Perhaps it was a family name referring to one of his ancestors. In any case Adam belonged to the *puy* in Arras—the literary fraternity charged with staging miracle plays, which also sponsored poetic contests, in which he seems to have taken part.

Adam is said to have been educated at the Cistercian Abbey of Vaucelles, after which he apparently went to Paris to continue his schooling—he is often referred to as *maistre,* which would suggest a university education. He probably returned to Arras around 1270, and apparently as part of the *puy* competitions wrote a number of *jeux-partis* (a kind of TENSO or debate poem), many with the poet Jehan Bretel, who died in 1272. At some point in Arras he wrote *Le Jeu de la feuillée* (The play of the greensward), a satirical look at his own life and the citizens of Arras, including his wife, his father (whom he depicts as a miser), and a drunken monk who sells fake holy relics.

In about 1272, Adam entered the service of Robert II, count of Artois. He accompanied Robert on a number of campaigns, and one of his poems, *Le Congé* (The leave-taking), conveys his sorrow at having to leave his wife. It may have been written in 1283, when Adam accompanied Robert to the Angevin kingdom of Naples, where Robert journeyed to help his uncle, King Charles d'Anjou, in the Sicilian war. Adam seems to have become something of a favorite in Charles's court, and he composed a CHANSON DE GESTE, *Le roi de Sicile,* in Charles's honor, though only the opening of the poem has survived. It is likely that Sicily is also where Adam wrote his second important play, *Le Jeu de Robin et Marion* (ca. 1285). This play is a dramatized PASTOURELLE, telling the story of a knight who tries to woo a country maiden. It includes Adam's own lyrics set to what are probably popular folk songs (though they may be Adam's own compositions) sung by the leading actors.

The conventional view is that Adam died in 1288. This is based on the testimony of a scribe who calls himself Jehan Madus and claims to be Adam's nephew, and who in 1288 says that Adam is deceased. However, it has been suggested that the "Maistre Adam le Bosu," who is mentioned as being paid for entertaining at a royal feast in Westminster for the coronation of England's King Edward II in 1307, is Adam de la Halle.

Adam is perhaps best known for his dramatic works, but he wrote a variety of lyrics, including *chansons* (*see* CANSO) and RONDEAUX or dance songs. He is remembered as one of the most important musicians of his time: His *chansons* are all written in the old-fashioned single melody settings, but his *rondeaux* are three-part polyphonic compositions. It seems likely that Adam had learned the new art of polyphony while studying at Paris. Some two dozen manuscripts of his lyrics survive, and it is a testament to Adam's popularity in his own time that one of these manuscripts is a collected edition of his works, arranged by genres—the first such collection for any medieval lyricist—that is now in the National Library of Paris.

Bibliography

Adam de la Halle. *The Lyrics and Melodies of Adam de la Halle.* Edited by Deborah Howard Nelson, and Hendrik van der Werf. New York: Garland, 1985.

Goldin, Frederick, ed. and trans. *Lyrics of the Troubadours and Trouvères: An Anthology and a History.* Garden City, N.Y.: Doubleday, 1973.

Huot, Sylvia. "Transformations of Lyric Voice in the Songs, Motets, and Plays of Adam de la Halle," *Romanic Review* 77 (1987): 148–164.

Marshall, J. H., ed. *The Chansons of Adam de la Halle.* Manchester, U.K.: Manchester University Press, 1971.

Van Deusen, Nancy E. "The Paradox of Privacy in the Love Songs of Adam de la Halle." In *The Cultural Milieu of the Troubadours and Trouvères,* 56–66. Ottawa: Institute of Medieval Music, 1994.

Adam Lay Bound (15th century)

The early 15th-century MIDDLE ENGLISH lyric beginning "Adam lay ybounden" is a fresh and lively lyric expression of the traditional theological concept of the *felix culpa* or fortunate fall. This doctrine held that while our first parents' disobedience brought about the great evil of humanity's fall from grace, it also made necessary the great act of God's love—our redemption through Christ; therefore, paradoxically, the fall was a happy one. In *Adam Lay Bound,* however, the notion of the *felix culpa* is actually carried beyond Christ to Mary, whose glorification the poem celebrates.

The lyric consists of two long, eight-line stanzas of alternating four- and three-foot lines, rhyming *abcbdede.* The stanza bears a striking resemblance to a pair of BALLAD stanzas. This affinity with the popular tradition is also suggested by the poet's use of partial repetition from one line to another, while adding new information—another technique of the ballads—as can be seen in the opening lines of the poem:

Adam lay ibounden
Bounden in a bond.

(Luria and Hoffman 147, ll. 1–2)

The first stanza describes Adam's 4,000 years of imprisonment in limbo before what medieval theologians called the HARROWING OF HELL, when Christ broke the gates of hell on Easter Saturday and carried the souls of the righteous to heaven. The attitude of the poem's speaker seems almost lighthearted and dismissive concerning original sin: "all was for an appil" (l. 5) we are told, as the "clerkes" will find written in their books.

The second stanza turns joyous: If the apple had not been taken, the speaker says, then Mary would never have "ben hevene quen" (l. 13). The image of Mary as the queen of heaven and representations of the "Coronation of the Virgin" were becoming increasingly popular by the 15th century. Certainly the image of Mary as queen ultimately symbolizes her role in mankind's redemption through Christ. But that redemption is never explicitly mentioned in the poem: The lyric ends with the poet's blessing the sin of Adam and exclaiming *"Deo gracias"* (Thanks be to God) because Adam's transgression led ultimately to Mary's glorification.

Bibliography

Luria, Maxwell S., and Richard Hoffman. *Middle English Lyrics.* New York: Norton, 1974.

Aelfric (Ælfric, "the Grammarian") (ca. 955–ca. 1012)

Aelfric was the most important prose writer of the OLD ENGLISH language. He was a Benedictine monk and the greatest scholar of the period known as the "Benedictine Renaissance" in England, a late 10th-century revival of learning begun by St. Dunstan (d. 988) and advanced by the Benedictine monasteries. Aelfric was devoted to education, of both the clergy and the laity, which explains his writing in the vernacular. He wrote scores of sermons, translated the first seven books of the Old Testament into English, produced the first Latin grammar written in a vernacular language, and composed a "Colloquy"—a Latin conversation between a teacher and his students with interlinear Old English translation, intended for teaching.

Born sometime in the mid-10th century, Aelfric was educated at Winchester by St. Athelwold (d. 984), whose Latin biography he later composed. Soon after Athelwold's death, Aelfric joined the new monastery at Cerne Abbas in Dorset, where in 15 years he was to write almost all of his major works. In 1005, Aelfric left Cerne Abbas to become the first abbott of another new monastery, at Eynsham in Oxfordshire, where he seems to have stayed for the rest of his life. As abbot, however, his administrative duties must have given him little time for serious writing, and he produced very little in his last years.

Aelfric wrote more than 100 sermons, most of which were published as "Catholic Homilies" in two volumes. In these sermons, Aelfric deals with a wide variety of theological issues. Often he applies the allegorical interpretation of Scripture advocated by St. AUGUSTINE, whom, along with a variety of other church fathers, Aelfric cites freely. Another collection of homilies dedicated to Aethelweard, patron of Cerne Abbas, is a series of saints' lives (*see* SAINT'S LIFE). It has been speculated that these were intended for private reading, particularly as *exempla,* or illustrative examples of strength and courage in the face of adversity: Aelfric, writing during a period of increasingly dangerous Viking invasions, may have intended these sermons as encouragement to the noble Aethelweard—certainly the sermon on St. Edmund, the Anglo-Saxon king who did battle against an earlier pagan Viking invasion, serves such a purpose.

Though Aelfric probably thought of his sermons as his most important productions, his most popular creation has been his Latin colloquy, a teaching text that shows evidence of humor and glimpses of real life, and that demonstrates Aelfric's dedication to teaching and his understanding of real-life pupils.

The most prolific of Old English writers, Aelfric is famous for the learning and versatility of his writing, as well as his style, which has been admired for its clarity and elegant economy. Writing during an age of turmoil, during which the Danes were devastating England, Aelfric (like many of his contemporaries) seems to have believed he was living in the last days, and made it his mission to educate people, especially concerning basic, orthodox Christian truths—a knowledge absolutely necessary in the coming Apocalypse. His influence continued long after his death, with manuscripts of his works being produced well into the 12th century. His popularity was even revived during the Reformation, when, in 1566, his sermons were republished and he was considered a proto-Protestant because of comments he made in one sermon that apparently denied the doctrine of transubstantiation (the belief in the real presence of the body and blood of Christ in the Eucharist). Aelfric, always scrupulously careful about his orthodoxy, would have been puzzled, perhaps appalled, by such reaction to his work.

Bibliography

Aelfric. *Aelfric's Catholic Homilies.* Edited by Malcolm Godden. Oxford and New York: Oxford University Press for the Early English Text Society, 2000.

———. *Anglo-Saxon Conversations: The Colloquies of Aelfric Bata.* Translated by Scott Gwara. Woodbridge, U.K.: Boydell, 1997.

Grundy, Lynne. *Books and Grace: Aelfric's Theology.* London: King's College Centre for Late Antique and Medieval Studies, 1991.

Hurt, James. *Aelfric.* New York: Twayne, 1972.

Needham, G. I. *Lives of Three English Saints.* London: Methuen, 1966.

Aethelwold (Æthelwold, Ethelwold) (ca. 909–984)

Aethelwold was bishop of Winchester during the reign of the Anglo-Saxon king Edgar and his successors, and with the Archbishops Dunstan and Oswald was one of the chief architects of the widespread ecclesiastical and monastic reform that swept England in the 10th century. For students of literature, Aethelwold is most important as the reputed author of the *Regularis Concordia* (The agreement concerning the rule), a Latin prose document intended to standardize monastic practices in England; and of an OLD ENGLISH prose translation of the Rule of Saint Benedict, intended for novices whose Latin was weak.

Aethelwold is reputed to have been born in Winchester around 909, and to have been a member of the household of King Aethelstan. He was ordained a priest in 938, but when Aethelstan died, Aethelwold decided to enter the monastery of Glastonbury, where Dunstan was abbot. Though inspired by Dunstan and eager to visit the continent to study monastic reforms that were taking place at Cluny and other monastic centers, Aethelwold was asked by King Edred to reestablish the monastic house at Abingdon in 954. He went there as abbot and set about rebuilding and rededicating the buildings. He also sent one of his monks to the reformed continental house of Fleury-sur-Loire to study the new rule and to bring it back to England. Soon he began introducing the reforms at Abingdon. He also established an abbey school at Abingdon, where one of his students was Edgar, the future English king.

Upon Edgar's ascension to the throne, Dunstan was made archbishop of Canterbury and Aethelwold was appointed bishop of Winchester (963). Among his first acts was the dismissal of all the secular clergy attached to Winchester (whom he saw as lax in their discipline), and their replacement with monks. He rebuilt the cathedral at Winchester to make it the greatest church in Europe at the time. He also founded a school that became a center of learning. Among his students were Wulfstan the precentor (not the homilist), who wrote a Latin prose SAINT'S LIFE of Aethelwold, and AELFRIC, the greatest prose writer of the Old English period—who wrote his own life of his master in 1006.

King Edgar's emulation of CHARLEMAGNE may have inspired him to encourage his own monastic reform, as Charlemagne had. Therefore the number of monasteries in England increased rapidly during the early years of Edgar's reign, and as a result there was great diversity in disciplinary practices. To remedy this, the king called a synodical council in 973 at Winchester. With representatives of the reformed houses at Fleury and Ghent in attendance, the council issued a Latin prose supplement to the Benedictine Rule based on the continental model, which became known as the *Regularis Concordia*. It is generally assumed that Aethelwold drafted the Latin text of the document, which regulated monastic life in England. Of interest to literary scholars is the inclusion in the *Regularis Concordia* of the earliest recorded "dramatic" text in English—a trope in the mass performed at Easter matins similar to the famous *QUEM QUAERITAS* TROPE on the continent.

Apparently at the behest of King Edgar, Aethelwold also translated the Benedictine Rule into Old English prose. This translation, extant in two forms (one for monks and one for nuns), was made apparently for the benefit of postulants and novices in the religious orders, whose facility in language was not yet sufficient for them to read and understand the Latin text of the Rule. He also wrote a description of King Edgar's work in reestablishing the English monasteries, of which only a fragment survives. Aethelwold is also famous for having owned the most richly illuminated manuscript known to have been produced in late Anglo-Saxon England: his *Benedictional*, which contains the text of blessings given during the mass illustrated by pairs of illuminations that imply allegorical links between events of Christ's life and Old Testament events on one hand and with eschatological images on the other.

Aethelwold died in 984 after 21 years of visionary administration over the see of Winchester. In 996, his remains were "translated" or moved from their original resting place, and a number of miracles were ascribed to them. Ultimately he was installed as patron saint of Winchester.

Bibliography

The Benedictional of Saint Aethelwold: A Masterpiece of Anglo-Saxon Art: A Facsimile. Introduction by Andrew Prescott. London: British Library, 2002.

Godden, Malcolm. "Biblical Literature: The Old Testament." In *The Cambridge Companion to Old English Literature*, edited by Malcolm Godden and Michael Lapidge, 206–226. Cambridge: Cambridge University Press, 1991.

Greenfield, Stanley B., and Daniel G. Calder. *A New Critical History of Old English Literature.* New York: New York University Press, 1986.

Wulfstan of Winchester. *Life of St. Aethelwold.* Edited and translated by Michael Lapidge and Michael Winterbottom. Oxford: Clarendon Press, 1991.

Yorke, Barbara, ed. *Bishop Aethelwold: His Career and Influence.* Woodbridge, Suffolk, U.K.: Boydell and Brewer, 1988.

Alanus de Insulis (Alain of Lille, Alanus ab Insulis, Alain of Ryssel) (ca. 1116–ca. 1202)

Alanus was one of the leading intellectuals of his time. We hardly know anything about his biography, but we can be certain that he was born in Lille ca. 1116, studied in Paris ca. 1136 (perhaps also in Tours and Chartres), taught at Paris and Montpellier, participated in the Third Lateran Council in 1179, and later joined the Cistercian monastery of Citeaux, where he eventually died ca. 1202 or 1203. Between 1160 and 1165 he wrote his treatises *Regulae caelestis iuris* and *Summa quoniam homines.* His true masterpieces, however, through which he exerted profound influence on poets and philosophers alike throughout the subsequent centuries, were his *Planctus naturae* and the *Anticlaudianus,* the first composed by the end of the 1160s, the latter composed around 1184. Subsequently, perhaps while he lived in southern France, he also wrote a number of theological treatises: *Ars fidei catholicœ, Contra haereticos, Summa quadripartita adversus huius temporis haereticos,* and *Distinctiones,* all exploring the most difficult question for the church: How to deal with heretics and infidels, especially the Muslims and Jews, and the Cathars and Waldensians.

Alanus's contemporaries and posterity harbored great respect for his intellect and called him either Doctor Universalis, Poeta Magnus, or simply Magnus. He was admired for his impressive knowledge of the liberal arts, philosophy, theology, and classical and contemporary literature. Alanus gained most respect for his *Planctus naturae* (*The Plaint of Nature*), in which he deplored man's deviation from the natural course, hence man's turn away from the path of virtue and morality; and his *Anticlaudianus,* in which he projected the principles of how to create the foundation for a new, religiously inspired human existence. The latter consisted of an encyclopedic summary of all learned knowledge available at that time. Alanus also composed a curious poem, *Vix nodosum,* in which he advocated the love for a virgin over an adulterous relationship with a married woman. Among other critical studies, Alanus also wrote *De incarnatione Christi,* which discusses man's inability to comprehend the divine secrets of Christ's incarnation; *De natura hominis fluxa et caduca,* on the semiotic symbolism and temporality of this world; and the *Liber parabolarum,* a collection of elegiacs consisting of proverb-like statements about the contradictory nature of human life. Alanus deeply admired Plato's teachings, but he was also familiar with Aristotle and BOETHIUS. His philosophy is characterized by a certain degree of syncretism, reflected in his tendency to combine mystical with philosophical and rational thought that relied on the logical development of all human understanding and belief systems. Following Boethius, Alanus argued that the entire Christian religion can be confirmed through mathematical-philosophical principles.

The large number of manuscript copies of Alanus's works demonstrate the enormous popularity that he enjoyed throughout the intellectual world of the Middle Ages. The *Vix nodosum* is extant in 27, the *Planctus* in 133, and the *Anticlaudianus* in 110 manuscripts. In the 15th century, Alanus's texts were also among the earliest to be printed. We have one very early edition each (ca. 1460) from his *Vix nodosum* and his *Planctus,* and four editions of his *Anticlaudianus.* Amazingly his rather plain *Liber parabolarum* was printed in at least 29 editions. This vast dissemination of Alanus's texts far into the early modern age is explained chiefly by their use as school textbooks, many of which contain extensive interlinear and marginal glosses by their readers. Some of the best-known 13th-century commentators on Alanus's works were Radulphus of Longchamp, William of Auxerre, Otho of Sankt Blasien, Alberic of Trois-Fontaines, and John of Garland.

Alanus's *Planctus naturae* shows many significant parallels with Matthew of Vendôme's *Ars versificatoria,* the most influential 12th-century textbook for rhetoric and poetry. Walther of Châtillon, in his Latin *Alexandreis,* was one of the first to adapt the allegorical imagery from Alanus's *Planctus,* followed by John of Hauvilla in his *Architrenius* (12th century), and Adam de la Bassé (late 13th century). Not only French and Italian, but also English and German vernacular poets, not to mention the vast number of Latin writers, demonstrate the deep influence which Alanus's rhetorical, didactic, and aesthetic ideals and concepts, especially of nature as an allegorical figure, exerted on them. GOTTFRIED VON STRASSBURG, DANTE ALIGHIERI, and JEAN DE MEUN (13th century), as well as Geoffrey CHAUCER and Hans Sachs (14th and 16th centuries) are some of the most important witnesses of Alanus's influence throughout the ages.

Bibliography

Alanus de Insulis. *Anticlaudianus.* Translated by James J. Sheridan. Toronto: Pontifical Institute of Mediaeval Studies, 1973.

———. *Anticlaudianus.* Edited by R. Bossuat. Paris: J. Vrin, 1955.

———. *Plaint of Nature.* Translated by James J. Sheridan. Toronto: Pontifical Institute of Mediaeval Studies, 1980.

Evans, G. R. *Alan of Lille: The Frontiers of Theology in the Later Twelfth Century.* Cambridge: Cambridge University Press, 1983.

Häring, Nikolaus M., ed. *De Planctu Naturae. Studi Medievali,* 3rd series, 19 (1978), 797–879.

Trout, John M. *The Voyage of Prudence: The World View of Alan of Lille.* Washington, D.C.: University Press of America, 1973.

White, Hugh. *Nature, Sex, and Goodness in a Medieval Literary Tradition.* Oxford and New York: Oxford University Press, 2000.

Albrecht Classen

alba (*aube, aubade*)

The word *alba* means "dawn" in Old Provençal, and refers to a particular type of love poem introduced by the TROUBADOURS that concerned the parting of lovers at dawn. As this "dawn song" trope spread to northern France, it was called an *aubade,* and in Germany became known as a *tagelied.* There are some 11 dawn songs surviving from Provence, six or so from Old French, and well more than 100 from German lyric poetry dating from the end of the 12th century to the end of the 14th. The genre was certainly known in England, where CHAUCER creates a lyrical dawn song within the context of his longer narrative in *TROILUS AND CRISEYDE* and parodies the form in his *REEVE'S TALE.*

The dawn song typically depicts a dramatic situation in which a pair of lovers, having secretly spent the night together, are awakened at dawn, usually by a watchman who is their ally. Sometimes the lady argues that it cannot be dawn and is therefore not time to part. The lovers take turns chiding the night for not staying longer and the day for arriving too soon. There is danger involved because of the lovers' enemies: Talebearers and scandalmongers, or more often the "jealous one" or *gilos* as he is called in Provençal—the lady's husband. The lovers finally part while pledging mutual fidelity and commending one another to God's care. There are usually two speaking voices in the poem—the lover and his lady—but sometimes the watchman has a part as well.

Though this formula may make the dawn songs appear quite conventional, a poet's genius within the convention can make a poem particularly memorable, as, for example, the imagery of the first stanza of WOLFRAM VON ESCHENBACH'S *tagelied* "Sîne klâwen durh die wolken sint geslagen" demonstrates, comparing the rising sun to a great bird of prey:

> *"Its claws have struck through the clouds,*
> *it rises up with great power,*
> *I see it turning gray, like day about to*
> *dawn,*
> *I see day, . . ."*

(Goldin 1973, 147, ll. 1–4)

Bibliography

Goldin, Frederick, ed. *German and Italian Lyrics of the Middle Ages.* Garden City, N.Y.: Anchor, 1973.

Hatto, Arthur T. *EOS: An Inquiry into the Theme of Lovers' Meetings and Partings at Dawn in Poetry.* The Hague: Mouton, 1965.

Kaske, R. E. "The Aube in Chaucer's *Troilus.*" In *Troilus and Criseyde and the Minor Poems: Chaucer Criticism.* Vol. 2, edited by Richard J. Schoeck and Jerome Taylor, 167–179. Notre Dame, Ind.: University of Notre Dame Press, 1961.

Alcuin of York (ca. 735–804)

Alcuin of York was the most influential scholar, teacher, and theologian of the Carolingian renaissance in late eighth-century Europe. In Alcuin the learning of Anglo-Saxon England that had thrived under the Venerable BEDE was disseminated throughout western Europe. As master of CHARLEMAGNE'S Palace School in Aachen, Alcuin was the driving force behind the rebirth of learning for which that era is famous. He established what became the standard liberal arts curriculum of medieval schools, and he was instrumental in preserving and copying ancient patristic and classical books. In addition, Alcuin wrote poetry, theological treatises, textbooks and many letters that have survived.

Alcuin was born in Northumbria and educated at the cathedral school in York, where from an early age his native intelligence drew the attention of his schoolmaster Aelbert (a disciple of Bede) and the archbishop Egbert. In about 766, Alcuin succeeded Aelbert as master of the cathedral school. Over a period of 15 years, Alcuin made York a school with an international reputation. Students from all parts of England as well as the continent came to study at York, and Alcuin also gathered a substantial library, sometimes traveling to the continent to obtain or to copy manuscripts.

In 781, after a trip to Rome, Alcuin met Charlemagne in Parma. The king, intent on reviving learning in his realm, convinced Alcuin to leave York and become the master of his Palace School in Aachen. Here Charlemagne himself became one of Alcuin's pupils, along with the queen and the king's sister and five children. Following this example, most of the highest nobility also attended the school. The school attracted some of the best scholars from Italy, Germany, and Ireland, and became the center for learning in the kingdom.

In 794, Alcuin attended the Synod of Frankfort, a church council at which he was instrumental in the condemnation of the Adoptionist heresy. In his treatise against Felix of Urgel, chief proponent of Adoptionism, Alcuin argued against Felix's idea that Jesus was only human until his baptism, when God adopted him as his son.

In 796, Charlemagne appointed Alcuin abbott of St. Martin's at Tours. It is doubtful that Alcuin, though a deacon of the church, ever was ordained a priest or joined the Benedictine order; nevertheless, he accepted the appointment and proceeded to establish another excellent school at Tours. He died there on May 19, 804.

In his own time, Alcuin's biggest contribution was undoubtedly as an educator. Charlemagne, appalled by the illiteracy among the priests of his kingdom, enacted legislation to ensure that his priests could read and write Latin and understand the Scriptures. He also issued an edict in 802 that the priest in every city and village in his realm should conduct free elementary schools in their parishes. It is certain that Alcuin, as head of the central Palace School, was instrumental in bringing about this educational revolution. The students that Alcuin taught at Aachen went on to instruct priests at liberal arts schools around the country.

One of Alcuin's innovations was the standardization of the LIBERAL ARTS curriculum, consisting of the *trivium* (comprising grammar, logic, and rhetoric) and the *quadrivium* (arithmetic, geometry, music and astronomy)—a curriculum that remained in place throughout the Middle Ages. Alcuin composed textbooks for grammar, logic, astronomy, and rhetoric. These texts, written in the question and answer format of a dialogue, are not particularly original, though the treatise on rhetoric, called *Compendia,* did become widely used. At the same time, Alcuin established scriptoria for the copying of manuscripts, and he is credited for developing the Carolingian minuscule, a clear and standard cursive script that allowed for greater speed in writing.

As a theologian, aside from his treatise against Adoptionism, Alcuin wrote nine scriptural commentaries and a collection of Latin sermons for priests to use. He wrote a very influential missal, and his modification of the Roman liturgy is the direct antecedent of the form in use in the Roman church to this day. In addition, Alcuin was instrumental in the development of a standard text of the Vulgate, the Latin translation of the Bible that, in the 400 years of scribal copying since St. JEROME composed it, had accumulated many copyists' errors.

Many of Alcuin's letters survive, as well as some 170 Latin poems. Of these, two are of particular interest. One is a poem of consolation he wrote on the destruction of the monastery of Lindesfarne by Viking raiders in 793. The other, his longest, is a poem in 1,657 hexameter (six-foot) lines called *On the Saints of the Church of York.* Written presumably upon his leaving York for Aachen, the poem gives a history of the church, an idea of the academic life in Alcuin's school, and a description of the contents of his library.

Bibliography

Bolton, W. F. *Alcuin and Beowulf: An Eighth-Century View.* New Brunswick, N.J.: Rutgers University Press, 1978.

Cantor, Norman F. *Medieval Lives: Eight Charismatic Men and Women of the Middle Ages.* New York: HarperCollins, 1994.

Chase, Colin, ed. *Two Alcuin Letter-Books.* Toronto: Center for Medieval Studies, 1975.

Godman, Peter, ed. and trans. *Poetry of the Carolingian Renaissance.* Norman: University of Oklahoma Press, 1985.

Scott, Peter Dale. "Alcuin as a Poet: Rhetoric and Belief in His Latin Verse," *University of Toronto Quarterly* 33 (1964): 233–257.

Wilbur, Samuel Howell, trans. *The Rhetoric of Alcuin and Charlemagne,* 2nd ed. New York: Russell and Russell, 1965.

Alexanderlied Lamprecht (ca. 1130–1150)

ALEXANDER THE GREAT (356–323 B.C.E.) was one of the most important mythical figures throughout the entire Middle Ages and far beyond. One of the many poets who dealt with Alexander was the Trier priest Lamprecht who composed his *Alexanderlied* sometime between 1130 and 1150 on the basis of a Provençal *Alexander* poem by Alberic de Pisançon. Lamprecht's Middle High German text survived in three manuscripts, the Vorau ms. (fragmentary, but most authentic), the Strasbourg ms. (burned in 1870), and the Basel ms. (abridgement; 15th century).

Basically this epic poem of 7,267 verses retells the story of Alexander's conquest of the Persian Empire and is particularly interesting for us because of the narrative variations and adaptation of the original Hellenistic account by the third-century writer pseudo-Callisthenes. The German version enriches the original chronicle report with many anecdotes about Alexander's youth, his relationship with his father, King Philip, and then his grandiose conquest of the Persian Empire, defeating the mighty ruler Darius. The narrator emphasizes Alexander's intelligence, strategic brilliance, and inventiveness in the battles against his enemies, and embellishes his account with reports about monstrous creatures and also about wondrous flower girls. Alexander and his men spend a long time with them and experience an erotic utopia, but eventually the girls wither away and die as all flowers do. The encounter with the Amazons, on the other hand, represents a major difficulty for Alexander. Their queen reminds him in a letter that his possible victory over the Amazons would be publicly regarded as shameful, insofar as an army of men would have fought young maidens, whereas his defeat at their own hands would result in the complete loss of his honor. Consequently Alexander leaves the Amazons alone and marches further east, until he reaches the wall of Paradise, where he is rejected again. An old man gives him a stone that, as an old Jew reveals to him once he has returned home, teaches him humility and reason. Lamprecht's *Alexanderlied* proves to be entertaining, detailed, and witty in its adaptation of the Graeco-Hellenistic and Provençal sources for his 12th-century German audience.

Bibliography

Classen, Albrecht. "The Amazing East and the Curious Reader: Twelfth-Century World Explorations through a Writer's Mind: Lamprecht's *Alexander*," *Orbis Litterarum* 55, no. 5 (2000): 317–339.

Ruttmann, Irene, ed. *Das Alexanderlied des Pfaffen Lamprecht (Strassburger Alexander). Text, Nacherzählung, Worterklärung.* Darmstadt, Germany: Wissenschaftliche Buchgesellschaft, 1974.

Albrecht Classen

Alexander the Great (356–323 B.C.E.)

The historical Alexander the Great, Macedonian king and world conqueror, was clearly not a medieval figure. However, the character of Alexander became the central figure of a number of medieval ROMANCES, comparable to though less numerous than the cycles of legends surrounding the figures of CHARLEMAGNE and KING ARTHUR.

Historically, Alexander was the son of Philip II, king of Macedon, and in his youth was educated by the great philosopher Aristotle. He became king of Macedonia at the age of 20 upon his father's assassination. In 334 B.C.E., he crossed the Hellespont with 35,000 men to invade the Persian Empire. He conquered Egypt and founded the city of Alexandria. He captured the family of the Persian emperor Darius, then crushed the Persians at the Battle of Arbela in 331. He captured the city of Babylon and the Persian capital of Persepolis, which he burned to the ground in retaliation for the Persian burning of Athens in 480 B.C.E. He married Roxana, daughter of the Bactrian prince Oxytares, and took a second wife, Barsine, the daughter of Darius. Alexander then advanced into India, where he defeated the northern Indian prince Porus in 326 B.C.E. That same year, he contracted a fever and died at the age of 32, having conquered virtually the entire world as he knew it.

The medieval versions of the Alexander legend derive ultimately from a third-century Greek account purported to be by a certain Callisthenes. Latin versions of Callisthenes' story were circulating by the early Middle Ages, and these ultimately were the source of the great 12th-century French *Roman d'Alexandre.* This poem, attributed to Lambert le Tort and Alexandre de Bernay, is a text of some 20,000 12-syllable lines of verse. As the first known poem to use the 12-syllable line, the *Roman* has given its name to that verse form—12-syllable lines are now known as alexandrines. The poem is a fanciful blend of myth and history. Alexander is presented as a king with a retinue of knights and vassals, as if he were Charlemagne, and he visits fantastic lands and enchanted castles, like an Arthurian knight.

Other 12th-century Alexander poems include a Provençal version by Alberic de Pisonçon and the famous German *ALEXANDERLIED*. An Anglo-Norman *Roman de toute chevalrie* was apparently the source of the best-known English version of the legend, the early 14th-century *King Alisaunder*.

King Alisaunder is an anonymous romance of 8,032 verses in octosyllabic (eight-syllable) couplets. Written in MIDDLE ENGLISH in the dialect of London and apparently intended for oral delivery, the poem narrates Alisaunder's mythologized history from his magical conception to his death. In this version, Alexander is not the son of Philip but rather of the Egyptian king Nectanabus, who through magic is able to deceive Philip's wife into sleeping with him. (The scene recalls the legendary events surrounding the conception of King Arthur in the liaison between Uther Pendragon and Igraine, brought about through Merlin's magic.) The first half of the poem relates Alisaunder's youth, succession to the throne, conquest of Carthage, and his Persian war and defeat of Darius. The second half of the poem, focused on Alisaunder in the eastern lands, contains a number of fanciful geographical descriptions and relations of the wonders of those far-off lands. It also tells of Alisaunder's visit with and seduction by Candace, queen of Meroe (historically Ethiopia), and ultimately of Alisaunder's death by poison.

Texts and fragments of other treatments of the Alexander legend survive in Middle English in both verse and prose from the 14th century on. One of these, called the *Alexander Buik*, is a Scottish version once thought to be the work of John BARBOUR. The popularity of Alexander as a romance hero was widespread throughout Europe in the later Middle Ages, and it is not surprising that he, like Arthur and Charlemagne, is consistently represented in late medieval art and literature as among the NINE WORTHIES of the world.

Bibliography

Aertsen, Henk, and Alasdair A. MacDonald. *Companion to Middle English Romance.* Amsterdam: VU University Press, 1990.

Barbour, John. *The Buik of Alexander, or, The Buik of the most noble and valiant conquerour Alexander the Grit.* Edited with introductions, and notes by R. L. Graeme Ritchie. Scottish Text Society New Series 17, 12, 21, 25. 4 vols. Edinburgh: Printed for the Scottish Text Society by W. Blackwood and Sons, 1921–1929.

Kyng Alisaunder. Edited by G. V. Smithers. Early English Text Society 227, 237. 2 vols. London: Published for the Early English Text Society by Oxford University Press, 1952–1957.

Alfonso X (1221–1284)

King of Castile and patron of the arts and sciences, Alfonso X, called El Sabio (the Wise, or the Learned), was also a significant lyric poet and composer in his own right, and in that role is best known as the author of some 400 songs in praise of the Virgin.

Alfonso was the son of Fernando III and Beatrice of Swabia. As a young man he seems to have been well trained in military pursuits and educated in the arts and sciences. He ascended to the throne of Castile and Leon on the death of his father in 1252. Alfonso married Violante, the daughter of King Jaime I of Aragon, with whom he shared an interest in the reconquest of Muslim Spain: Early in his reign he fought a number of Moorish wars and conquered Cadiz in 1262. Meanwhile, he had been elected Holy Roman Emperor in 1254, but the election was disputed and he was never crowned. Generally a weak sovereign, his indecision concerning his succession after his first son Fernando died in 1275 led to diplomatic problems with Aragon and France, and to open revolt at home when his second son, Sancho, led a rebellion in Alfonso's final years, ultimately seizing the throne when Alfonso died in 1284.

Far more successful were Alfonso's efforts to make his court the intellectual and cultural center of Iberia. Calling himself the King of the Three Religions, Alfonso drew to his court Christian, Jewish, and Muslim scholars to work on a program of compilation, translation, and literary creation designed, in part, to encourage the use of the vernacular in learning and in poetry. He sponsored the scholarly production of compilations in various areas. His *Las siete partidas* was an anthology of legal practices going back to Roman times, begun with the hope of standardizing such practices—a hope not realized until the following century. In history, two great collections were begun under Alfonso's patronage: One, the *Crónica general,* is a vernacular history of Spain up to the 13th century; the other, the *Grande e general estoria,* is a vast history of the world up to the time of the Virgin Mary's parents. In science, Alfonso's court made significant contributions to the study of astronomy and astrology, with three important works translated or adapted from Arabic sources by Jewish scholars—one of these, a text of astronomic tables, was a standard reference in Europe for hundreds of years.

In addition, Alfonso's court was famous for his literary contributions, for the king was both a generous literary patron and was himself a poet of some distinction. Many poets had left the repressive court of the Portuguese king Alfonso III (whose long feud with Alfonso X ended when the Portuguese king married Alfonso X's illegitimate daughter—a union that produced another poet-king, DINIS). Thus the Castilian court became the center of Galician-Portuguese poetry, and Alfonso X himself, moved by their lyric productions, chose the Galician-Portuguese tongue as the vehicle for his own verses.

Alfonso's best-known work is a collection of 422 *Cantigas de Santa Maria* or songs in praise of the Virgin Mary. Generally these take the form of brief narratives relating miracles wrought by the Blessed Virgin's intercession. In *Cantiga VII,* for example, an abbess who has slipped in her vows finds herself pregnant and is summoned to appear before the bishop. But Mary is miraculously able to save the nun:

But the lady without delay
Began to call the Mother of God;
And, as from one who was dreaming,
Saint Mary had the child taken
And sent for rearing to Saxony.

(Keller 1962, 304)

Alfonso wrote five other religious poems concerning the life of Christ, in addition to some 45 secular lyrics. A few of these are love poems but most are political lyrics. Of the secular poems, the best known is *Non me posso pagar tanto,* in which he expresses a desire to leave behind the pressures of his world and take to sea as a merchant—a sentiment that any monarch might have felt occasionally, but perhaps would have been particularly fitting during Alfonso's turbulent final years:

Rather, I wish to travel alone
And go like a merchant
In search of a land
Where I cannot feel the sting
Of the black or the spotted scorpion.

(Jensen 1992, 8.3, ll. 48–52)

Bibliography

Burns, Robert I., ed. *Emperor of Culture: Alfonso X the Learned of Castile and his Thirteenth-Century Renaissance.* Philadelphia: University of Pennsylvania Press, 1990.

Jensen, Frede, ed. and trans. *Medieval Galician-Portuguese Poetry: An Anthology.* Garland Library of Medieval Literature 87. New York and London: Garland, 1992.

Keller, John Esten. *Alfonso X: El Sabio.* New York: Twayne, 1967.

———, trans. "Cantigas VII." In *An Anthology of Medieval Lyrics,* edited by Angel Flores, 303–305. New York: Modern Library, 1962.

Alfred the Great (ca. 848–899)

Alfred the Great was king of Wessex from 871 to 899, and was successful in defending his kingdom from Danish invaders and even in expanding his holdings at the expense of the Danes. But beyond preserving an independent Anglo-Saxon kingdom, Alfred was also responsible for an OLD ENGLISH cultural renaissance through his support of learning, and, more specifically, through his own English translations of important Latin texts.

Alfred was born in Wantage in Oxfordshire, the youngest son of Wessex king Æthelwulf. His young adult life, from 865 onwards, was spent constantly embattled by Viking armies. Upon the death of his brother Æthelred in 871, Alfred ascended to the throne. When the Danish chieftain Guthrum invaded Wessex in 878, Alfred was forced to flee to the Athelney marshes in Somerset. One of Alfred's most remarkable accomplishments was being able to rebound from this low point. Within seven weeks he had raised enough of a force to defeat Guthrum decisively at the Battle of Eddington. He subsequently forced Guthrum to accept Christian baptism and to agree to withdraw all his forces from Wessex into East Anglia and Mercia. An official boundary, called Danelaw, was eventually recognized between the Danish and English forces by a treaty in 886. But in 892, a new army of Danes invaded England, and Alfred spent four years fighting them off. He was successful partly because of his institution of the first English navy, and partly because of his establishment of permanent fortifications around his territory. Finally, in 896, a temporary peace was achieved.

Alfred, however, was not content with merely preserving his country. He also wanted to restore it to the heights it had achieved prior to the Viking invasions. He gave the country its first new law code in a century, basing his system on Mosaic law and on previous codes of Wessex, Mercia, and Kent. The law code emphasized protection for the weak, loyalty to one's lord, and restraint of blood-feuds. He also wanted to restore the churches of England to their former glory, and he established a nunnery at Shaftesbury (where his daughter was to become prioress) and a monastery at Athelney. Ambitious, as well, to make his new monastery a true center of learning to help revive letters in his kingdom, Alfred imported scholars from other parts of Europe—from Gaul, Saxony, and Wales. One of the first tasks he set these scholars was the education of the royal household, including the king himself, who began studying Latin in 887.

Alfred's contributions to English literature take the form largely of translations. He believed that the reeducation of his people must begin with books in the vernacular. In addition to encouraging other scholars to translate Latin texts into English—he clearly was behind the translation of BEDE's *Ecclesiastical History* into English—Alfred made several translations of his own, beginning with his rendition of GREGORY THE GREAT's *Cura pastoralis* (Pastoral care). This text, a manual for the spiritual education of the clergy, contained a preface composed by Alfred decrying the decay of English scholarship and expressing his determination to improve that situation. He sent a copy of his translation to every bishop in his kingdom. Later, he translated *Historia adversus pagonos* by Paulus Orosius. This text, a history of the world structured as a series of annals, was expanded by Alfred with up-to-date accounts drawn from contemporary voyages into the far north by Wulstan and by the Norwegian Ohthere. It is possible that the structure of this history influenced the *ANGLO-SAXON CHRONICLES*, which were begun during Alfred's reign, and certainly with his encouragement. Alfred's final literary effort was probably a loose translation of Saint AUGUSTINE's *Soliloquia* (Soliloquies), a kind of commonplace book with quotations about mortality, and a number of everyday examples added by Alfred himself.

Alfred's best-known translation is of BOETHIUS's *CONSOLATION OF PHILOSOPHY*, that vastly popular argument for the uses of adversity in human life. Here and in all of his translations, Alfred used a style of "idiomatic translation," by which he tried to render the sense of his source into idiomatic and vivid English, rather than aiming for a word-for-word imitation of his original.

Much of our knowledge of Alfred's life is contained in *De rebus gestis Aelfredi Magni* (Life of Alfred the Great), a contemporary account by the Welsh monk John Asser, one of the scholars Alfred had brought to Wessex. The biography's objectivity is questionable, effusive as it is in its praise of Alfred, but it would have been difficult not to praise him. An effective and inspirational war leader, as well as a builder, a lawgiver, a supporter of education and the arts and a scholar himself, Alfred is the only English monarch ever given the title "Great."

Bibliography

Abels, Richard Philip. *Alfred the Great: War, Kingship, and Culture in Anglo-Saxon England.* Harlow, U.K.: Longman, 1998.

Asser, John. *The Medieval Life of King Alfred the Great: A Translation and Commentary on the Text Attributed to Asser.* Edited and translated by Alfred P. Smyth. Houndmills, Hampshire, U.K.: 2002.

Duckett, Eleanor Shipley. *Alfred the Great and His England.* London: Collins, 1957.

Sturdy, David. *Alfred the Great.* London: Constable, 1995.

al-Ghazālī (Algazali, Abū Hāmid Muhammad ib Muhammad al'Ghazālī) (1058–1111)

Some 400 titles are attributed to the influential Muslim theologian, philosopher, legalist, and mystic al-Ghazālī. While many of these are false attributions made to him because of his reputation, there is no doubt he was extremely prolific in a variety of genres. His most important works are his spiritual autobiography *The Deliverance from Errord (*Al'Munqidh min al-Dalāl), his theological work reconciling mysticism with orthodox Islam called *The Revival of the Religious Sciences* (*Ihya' 'Ulūm al-Dīn*), and his refutation of the Aristotelian influence so prevalent in Islamic philosophy in the 11th century, The *Incoherence of the Philosophers* (*Tahāfut al-Falāsifah*).

Al-Ghazālī was born in Tūs, Persia. Orphaned as a child, he obtained a good education in his native city, and then in Nishapur, where he was taught by the leading theologian of the time, al-Juwaynī. When his master died he went to study in Baghdad, where he was appointed to a teaching position at the prestigious Nizāmiyyāh school. A popular instructor, he also produced a number of philosophical and theological texts while there. However, in about 1095 he underwent a spiritual crisis, left his family and his prominent position, and spent the next 11 years in Syria as a poor Sufi (the mystical branch of Islam), devoting his time to meditation and mystical devotion. By 1105–06, al-Ghazālī seems to have overcome his personal crisis, and when approached by the son of one of his former patrons to return to teach again at Nishapur, he agreed. Ultimately he retired from Nishapur to return to his home at Tūs, where he taught Sufism, and where he died around 1111.

Al-Ghazālī made lasting contributions to world literature, Islamic theology, and philosophy. His philosophical interest was sparked by the growth of Aristotelianism in Islamic philosophy. He became the main spokesman for the Ash'arite (orthodox philosophers') reaction to Aristotelian doctrines proposed by Alfarabi and Avicenna. He admired the sciences of mathematics, natural science, and especially logic, but thought that in the area of metaphysics the Aristotelians had gone wrong. Al-Ghazālī began his critical attack by writing a summary of the Aristotelian opinions called *The Intentions of the Philosophers* (*Maqāsid al-Falāsifah*), a summary so objective that European scholastic theologians, who knew no other work of al-Ghazālī's, assumed that he was himself an Aristotelian. Al-Ghazālī followed this text with his famous *The Incoherence of the Philosophers* (*Tahāfut al-Falāsifah*), in which he refutes 20 philosophical opinions of the Aristotelians. He singles out three positions for special condemnation as heretical to Islam: The philosophers' denial of the resurrection of the body, a doctrine which al-Ghazālī insisted must be accepted literally; the Aristotelians' belief that God could only know universals, which he thought denied the doctrine of individual providence; and the philosophers' belief in the eternity of the world, which al-Ghazālī thought rejected the notion that God was the direct cause of all effects in the universe. His powerful refutation evoked an equally powerful response from the later 12th-century Islamic philosopher AVERROËS, whose treatise *The Incoherence of the Incoherence* was written specifically to respond to al-Ghazālī 's text.

The Deliverance from Error, al-Ghazālī's autobiographical text, tells of his education and his spiritual and intellectual crisis of 1095, a crisis of doubt that left him unable to teach and forced his resignation from his position at Nizāmiyyāh. He describes as well his years of wandering and the mystical illumination he received as a Sufi that led to the resumption of his faith. Finally, his monumental theological work, *The Revitalization of Religious Sciences,* sought to unify Islamic orthodoxy with the growing Sufi mysticism he had experienced himself. The text strives to eliminate some of the excesses of Sufism while still maintaining that genuine Sufism is the way to find ultimate truth.

Bibliography

Abrahamov, Binyamin. *Divine Love in Islamic Mysticism: The Teachings of Al-Ghazali and Al-Dabbagh.* New York: Routledge-Curzon, 2002.

Al-Ghazālī. *Deliverance from Error: An Annotated Translation of Al-Munqidh min al Dal-al and Other Relevant Works of Al-Ghazali.* Translated by Richard Joseph McCarthy. Louisville, Ky.: Fons Vitae, 1999.

———. *The Incoherence of the Philosophers: A Parallel English-Arabic Text.* Translated by Michael E. Marmura. Provo, Utah: Brigham Young University Press, 1997.

———. *On Disciplining the Soul and On Breaking the Two Desires: Books XXII and XXIII of The Revival of the Religious Sciences.* Translated by T. J. Winter. Cambridge: Islamic Texts Society, 1995.

Hyman, Arthur, and James J. Walsh. *Philosophy in the Middle Ages: The Christian, Islamic, and Jewish Traditions.* 2nd ed. Indianapolis: Hackett, 1983.

Watt, W. Montgomery. *The Faith and Practice of Al-Ghazali.* London: G. Allen and Unwin, 1953.

allegory

Allegory is typically defined as a descriptive or narrative literary text wherein the actions, the objects, and the characters signify ideas or concepts that lie outside the text itself. It might be seen as a kind of extended metaphor in which the literal narrative consistently parallels another level of meaning. In allegory, the writer's main interest is the abstract level of meaning, and the most common technique is the personification of those abstractions. It is thus distinguished from *symbolism,* in which the writer's main interest is the literal action of the story, and an object or person in the narrative suggests some meaning beyond the narrative.

While C. S. Lewis's comment in *The Allegory of Love* that medieval people naturally thought in allegorical terms may be an overstatement, it is certainly true that allegory was a favorite literary form of the European Middle Ages, beginning with PRUDENTIUS's fourth-century poem *PSYCHOMACHIA.* A favorite allegorical genre was the DREAM VISION, wherein the narrator falls asleep and has an enigmatic dream replete with personified abstractions; examples of such dream visions are the French *ROMAN DE LA ROSE,* GOWER's *VOX CLAMANTIS,* and CHAUCER's *PARLIAMENT OF FOWLS.* Sustained allegory also became popular in the MORALITY PLAY genre of the late Middle Ages, with plays like *EVERYMAN.* Like many allegories, *Everyman* manifests a simple and unambiguous relationship between two clear levels of meaning. Other texts, notably LANGLAND's *PIERS PLOWMAN,* consist of complex allegory on several levels.

Allegory was an important tool in medieval biblical exegesis (or scriptural interpretation), in which the habit of reading the Old Testament to find foreshadowings of the New became commonplace, and began to be imitated by readers of literary texts and by writers composing those texts. Beginning in the fourth century, developed by John Cassian and promoted by St. AUGUSTINE, a fourfold method of scriptural analysis was developed consisting of a literal or historical level and three allegorical or "spiritual" levels: A typological level by which the Old Testament events prefigured those of the New Testament; a moral (or "tropological") level in which the events of the narrative were applied to private individual spiritual lives; and the anagogical level, in which the narrative was related to the fate of the soul after death. Such readings influenced creative writers, most especially DANTE, who makes the point (in his famous *Letter to Can Grande*) that he expected his *DIVINE COMEDY* to be read and interpreted as the Scriptures were—on all four levels. Ultimately, the ability to read allegorically is essential to reading medieval literature effectively.

Bibliography

Brittan, Simon. *Poetry, Symbol, and Allegory: Interpreting Metaphorical Language from Plato to the Present.* Charlottesville: University of Virginia Press, 2003.

Hollander, Robert. *Allegory in Dante's Commedia.* Princeton, N.J.: Princeton University Press, 1969.

Lewis, C. S. *The Allegory of Love: A Study in Medieval Tradition.* Oxford: Clarendon Press, 1936.

Meyer, Ann R. *Medieval Allegory and the Building of the New Jerusalem.* Woodbridge, U.K.: D. S. Brewer, 2003.

Nugent, S. Georgia. *Allegory and Poetics: The Structure and Imagery of Prudentius' "Psychomachia."* Frankfurt am Main, Germany: P. Lang, 1985.

Alliterative Morte Arthure
(ca. 1400–1402)

This masterpiece of the ALLITERATIVE REVIVAL survives in a single manuscript, Lincoln Cathedral Library 91, compiled ca. 1440 by the scribe Robert Thornton. Although the date of composition is uncertain (with some scholars putting it as early as ca. 1350), it is now thought to have been composed in the later years of the 14th century. For this particular narrative, date of composition can be key to how it is read: If a later date is accepted, the poem's unromanticized and starkly realistic presentation of warfare and its consequences tends to support those who see the poet's pacifist sympathies and seeming critique of imperialism as combining to create what can only be called an antiwar narrative. (Critiques of war are less common in mid-century when England was celebrating significant victories over France in the Hundred Years' War.) Indeed, even with an earlier dating, it is difficult to read the poem as a conventional Arthurian tale either in its plot or in its characterization. More epic than ROMANCE, the narrative focus is concerned with heroism and tragedy, with battlefields and hubris, and with King ARTHUR as uncommonly central in his role of warrior. The COURTLY LOVE conventions of other Arthurian works in which relations between men and women, and the conventions of idealized chivalric knighthood are thematically central, give place here to a masculinized world, dominated by the warrior Arthur who, in his ambivalent and ambitious characterization, is considered by some to be the most complex Arthur in literature.

The Arthur of the *Alliterative Morte Arthure* is both grand and deeply flawed, in the manner of epic or classical tragic heroes. There are early indications of his pride and rash behavior, and these moments anticipate later events in which Arthur, emboldened by military success, is transformed from defender to aggressor, his military campaigns becoming increasingly imperialistic and unthinkingly aggressive. Breaking from tradition, in the *Alliterative Morte Arthure,* Arthur's hubris and overly ambitious desire for conquest cause his tragic downfall and the failure of the ideals of the Round Table. The poet's direct sources are not known, but the general story line can be found in the chronicles of GEOFFREY OF MONMOUTH and WACE, and in LAYAMON's *Brut.* Nonetheless, the poet embellishes his tale from other sources, most notably in Arthur's character, his dream of Lady Fortune and the inclusion of the NINE WORTHIES as exemplars. The *Alliterative Morte Arthure* is both the source for one of the central episodes in MALORY's *LE MORTE DARTHUR* and probably the most significant English Arthurian work used by Malory for his own complex Arthurian narrative.

There is a finely balanced symmetry to the *Alliterative Morte Arthure*'s plot structure, and the rise-and-fall action is more suggestive of tragedy than romance. In its foreshadowing, also, the narrative has more in common with epic tragedies than with its own tradition of Arthurian romance. The action begins with Arthur refusing to pay homage or tribute to the Roman emperor Lucius and preparing for war. Arthur leads his knights to France, having left England in the care of Mordrede, and en route has a prophetic dream in which a dragon (representing Arthur) defeats a bear (representing either the tyrants who oppress his people or single-handed combat with a giant [823–826]). The dream is taken as an omen of victory and proves true when Arthur, upon arriving in Brittany, kills the giant of St. Michael's Mount. Arthur and his knights then prevail over the forces of the emperor and send as tribute the Romans slain in battle. Emboldened by this military achievement and prompted by his own rash pride, Arthur proceeds to besiege the duke of Lorraine, wins this battle, and continues into Italy conquering towns along the way. The Romans finally offer Arthur the imperial crown and at this pinnacle of success, Arthur dreams of Lady Fortune who, with a turn of her wheel, dashes him down. This dream also proves prophetic: The next morning Arthur learns that Mordrede has taken both crown and queen, and Arthur returns to England where Gawayn's knights are outnumbered and Gawayn himself is killed in a battle scene of uncommon realism. Bitter with sorrow, Arthur kills Mordrede in a final battle in Cornwall but is himself mortally wounded and buried in Glastonbury.

The *Alliterative Morte Arthure* is informed by elegant speeches and vows, detailed descriptions of landscapes and characters, elegiac moments and powerful laments for lost heroes, hubris and heroics, and an unflinching portrayal of the brutalities of war. The characters are developed considerably beyond the conventional superlatives usually invoked and this complexity of character and motivation underlies the whole of the narrative. Heroic and tragic, with a fatally flawed King Arthur at its center, the *Alliterative Morte Arthure* transforms tradition as it portrays both the glory and the horrors of war. If, as some argue, the poet is ambivalent about the consequences of war, and concerned over the sometimes subtle distinction between just and unjust wars, there is also sufficient heroism here to support a reading of Arthur as epic hero engaged in epic feats of arms. As one critic notes, perhaps we need not choose between two thematic interpretations but need to read the poem as holding in unresolved tension conflicting points of view.

Bibliography

The Alliterative Morte Arthure: A New Verse Translation. Translated by Valerie Krishna. Washington, D.C.: University Press of America, 1983.

Benson, Larry D. "The *Alliterative Morte Arthure* and Medieval Tragedy," *Tennessee Studies in Literature* 11 (1966): 75–88.

Göller, Karl Heinz, ed. *The Alliterative Morte Arthure: A Reassessment of the Poem.* Cambridge, U.K.: Brewer, 1981.

Hamel, Mary, ed. *Morte Arthure: A Critical Edition.* New York: Garland, 1984.

Harwood, Britton J. "The *Alliterative Morte Arthure* as a Witness to Epic." In *Oral Poetics in Middle English Poetry,* edited by Mark Amodio, 241–286. New York: Garland, 1994.

Matthews, William. *The Tragedy of Arthur: A Study of the Alliterative "Morte Arthure."* Berkeley: University of California Press, 1960.

Patterson, Lee W. "The Historiography of Romance and the *Alliterative Morte Arthure,*" *Journal of Medieval and Renaissance Studies* 13 (1983): 1–32.

Peck, Russell A. "Willfulness and Wonders: Boethian Tragedy in the *Alliterative Morte Arthure.*" In *The Alliterative Tradition in the Fourteenth Century,* edited by Bernard S. Levy and Paul E. Szarmach, 153–182. Kent, Ohio: Kent State University Press, 1981.

Westover, Jeff. "Arthur's End: The King's Emasculation in the *Alliterative Morte Arthure,*" *Chaucer Review* 32 (1998): 310–324.

Elisa Narin van Court

alliterative revival

The term *alliterative revival* refers to a renewal of interest in ALLITERATIVE VERSE among late 14th-century MIDDLE ENGLISH poets. OLD ENGLISH verse had been governed by strict rules of stress and alliteration, but after the Norman Conquest of 1066 introduced French literature and French tastes into the English courts, alliterative poetry in English became rare, at least in written texts, with many English poets turning to rhymed metrical verse as a result of the French influence.

Still alliterative English verse seems never to have died out completely: LAYAMON used alliteration in his *Brut* (ca. 1200), and the five religious prose texts from the early 13th-century West Midlands known collectively as the KATHERINE GROUP make extensive use of alliterative prose. Judging from these scattered remains, it seems likely that an oral tradition of alliterative verse in English survived into the 14th century.

As written texts in English began to appear in the late 14th century, there was a strong revival of the use of alliterative verse, particularly in the west and the northwest of England. It has been suggested that such poetry was a nationalistic reaction against French poetic forms. Important texts included in this tradition are LANGLAND's *PIERS PLOWMAN* and the anonymous poems *SIR GAWAIN AND THE GREEN KNIGHT, PEARL, WINNER AND WASTER, The PARLEMENT OF THE THREE AGES,* and THE *ALLITERATIVE MORTE ARTHURE,* among others. Although there is much more variation among these poems than in the more strictly rule-bound Old English verses, one still finds lines of four strong stresses, a clear caesura, and alliteration linking the two half lines.

Bibliography

Lawton, David, ed. *Middle English Alliterative Poetry and Its Literary Background: Seven Essays.* Cambridge, U.K.: Brewer, 1982.

Moorman, Charles. "The English Alliterative Revival and the Literature of Defeat," *Chaucer Review* 16 (1981): 85–100.

alliterative verse

All poetry written in Old Germanic languages uses a system of alliterative verse, the best examples of which can be found in the OLD ENGLISH poetic corpus. This form of meter doubtlessly originates among oral poets or SCOPS, who would have recited or sung the verse with the accompaniment of a harp. In Old English poetry, each line is divided by a strong caesura into two half-lines or *hemistichs.* Each hemistich contains two stressed words or syllables and a varying number of unstressed syllables. Thus each line of Anglo-Saxon poetry contains four stressed syllables. The two half-lines are united by alliteration, the repetition of initial sounds.

The key to the alliteration in each line is the first accented syllable of the second hemistich. The second stressed syllable of the second hemistich never alliterated with the first. But at least one and sometimes both of the stressed syllables in the first half-line always alliterated with that initial sound of the second half line. Thus there were three chief types of line in Old English poetry, which might be illustrated by these lines from *Beowulf:*

> *geongum ond ealdum, swylc him God sealde*
> *(his God-given goods to young and old)*
>
> (Heaney 2000, 6–7; l. 72)

Here the first stressed syllable (of *geongum*) alliterates with the first stressed syllable of the second hemistich (*God*)—a line that might be diagrammed as *ab:ac.* Two lines later in *Beowulf* occurs the line

> *wuldres Wealdend, worold-āre forgeaf*
> *(the glorious Almighty, made this man renowned)*
>
> (Heaney 2000, 2–3; l. 17)

This time, both accented syllables in the first half-line alliterate, so that the line could be diagrammed *aa:ac.* The third common type of line can be seen in another line from *Beowulf:*

> *Ne hyrde ic cymlīcorcēol gegyrwan*
> *(I never heard before of a ship so well furbished)*
>
> (Heaney 2000, 4–5; l. 38)

Here the line follows a *ba:ac* pattern, where only the second stressed syllable of the first hemistich alliterates.

Poetic lines could use vowels for alliterative purposes as well as consonants, and when that occurred, any vowel could alliterate with any other vowel. Old English verse was virtually never rhymed, nor were poems arranged into stanzas. The accents in Old English lines were grammatical—

that is, there were no artificially stressed syllables used for the sake of alliteration; rather, the stresses fell on the syllables that would naturally be accented in a word or phrase.

There are significantly more complex rules for classical Old English poetry, but there is a good deal of scholarly controversy about them. The strict rules of Anglo-Saxon poetry seem to have remained relatively unchanged from the earliest written poetry until the Norman Conquest. Very late in the Old English period, however, there seems to have been a relaxing of the rules with some poets, so that in a very late composition like *The* BATTLE OF MALDON, some of the strict rules are broken—for example, on some occasions the final stressed syllable of the second hemistich alliterates. The alliterative tradition disappeared in written verse after 1066, but the tradition was revived—though with much looser rules—in some late 14th-century MIDDLE ENGLISH poetry during a movement called the ALLITERATIVE REVIVAL.

Bibliography

Beowulf: A New Verse Translation. Translated by Seamus Heaney. New York: Farrar, Straus and Giroux, 2000.

Cable, Thomas. *The Meter and Melody of Beowulf.* Urbana: University of Illinois Press, 1974.

Fulk, Robert Dennis. *A History of Old English Meter.* Philadelphia: University of Pennsylvania Press, 1992.

Hoover, David L. *A New Theory of Old English Meter.* New York: P. Lang, 1985.

Pope, John Collins. *The Rhythm of Beowulf: An Interpretation of the Normal and Hypermetric Verse-Forms in Old English Poetry.* Rev. ed. New Haven, Conn.: Yale University Press, 1966.

Russom, Geoffrey. *Old English Meter and Linguistic Theory.* Cambridge: Cambridge University Press, 1987.

al-Ma'arri, Abu al-'Ala (973–1058)

One of the greatest Arab poets of the medieval period, al-Ma'arri was a blind Syrian poet known for his pessimism as well as his originality. Considered heretical by many Muslims, al-Ma'arri is a religious skeptic whose most famous work, nevertheless, is a vision of the afterlife.

Born, as his name implies, in the town of Ma'arrah in Syria, south of Aleppo, al-Ma'arri was stricken with smallpox as a young child. He survived the disease but was blinded for life, yet he compensated for his blindness by cultivating his remarkable memory. Educated at Aleppo, Antioch, and Tripoli, al-Ma'arri is reputed to have memorized the manuscripts he found in those cities, so that he was able to immediately recall vast quantities of prose and verse.

In 1008, thinking to embark on a literary career, al-Ma'arri set off for Baghdad, where he hoped to find a patron. Though well received in literary circles there, he was unable to secure a sponsor, and it was this as well as news of his mother's failing health that convinced him to return to Ma'arrah after 18 months. Here he lived in semi-retirement for the rest of his life. But he produced a collection of early poems called *Saqt al-zand* (*The Spark from the Flint*), a collection that gave him a reputation and inspired a number of young poets to come to Ma'arrah to study with him. Later he produced a larger and more unorthodox volume of 1,592 poems called *Luzum ma lam yalzam* (The constraint of what is not compulsory), the title referring to the constraints he had imposed upon himself with the difficult rhyme schemes of the poems.

Al-Ma'arri's poetry as well as his prose is known for its difficulty, its pessimism, religious skepticism, asceticism, and heterodox ideas. Influenced by Indian thought, al-Ma'arri was a vegetarian, avidly opposed to causing cruelty to animals. He refused even to eat honey, since he saw this as an abuse of bees. He even suggested that animals, who suffered cruelly in this world, would be compensated by a kind of paradise in the afterlife. As for human beings, however, al-Ma'arri seems to have entertained grave doubts about the existence of any kind of immortality, which explains as well his advocating cremation. In addition, though an advocate of social justice, he apparently saw procreation as sinful, since it brought into the world more generations born to suffer. A supreme rationalist, he was skeptical about anything in religion that smacked of myth or absurdity; thus he had no patience with Sufism, the mystic sect of Islam, which he believed to be inspired by the devil. Nor did he have much patience with other poets, most of whom he saw as spinners of lies painting a romantic picture of life instead of telling the truth about life's miseries as he knew them.

Aware of how unorthodox his ideas must seem, al-Ma'arri often cloaked his opinions in obscure language or disguised them as animal fables: One of his more interesting works is a comment on current political events called the *Risalat al'Sahil wa al'Shahij* (Letters of a horse and a mule) in which the animals exchange opinions on the current state of government in Syria. But al-Ma'arri's reputation as a heretic was solidified by the publication of his *Al-Fusul wa al'Ghayat* (Paragraphs and periods), a book that seemed to his contemporaries to be a parody of the KORAN itself.

Al-Ma'arri's most famous work is the prose text *Risalat al-Ghufran* (*The Letter of Forgiveness*), probably written toward the end of his life in about 1033. Here, in a text based on a very literal interpretation of certain sections of the Koran, he gives a fantastic vision of the afterlife (something he did not himself take seriously), presenting many pagan poets in heaven as "forgiven" (thus providing the title). In fact, al-Ma'arri presents both heaven and hell as peopled by poets and philologists who engage in lengthy discussions about the nature of language and poetry. The text may have influenced DANTE.

Bibliography

Al-Ma'arri, Abu al-'Ala. *Risalat al-Gufran: The Letter of Forgiveness.* Translated by Arthur Wormhoudt. Oskaloosa, Iowa: William Penn College, 1997.

———. *Saqt al Zand: The Spark from the Flint.* Translated by Arthur Wormhoudt. Oskaloosa, Iowa: William Penn College, 1972.

Irwin, Robert, ed. *Night and Horses and the Desert: An Anthology of Classical Arabic Literature.* Woodstock, N.Y.: Overlook Press, 1999.

Alysoun (ca. 1300)

The MIDDLE ENGLISH lyric beginning "Bitwene March and Averil," generally entitled *Alysoun* by editors, is one of the best known and most often anthologized of all Middle English poems. One of several important poems known as the HARLEY LYRICS because of their inclusion in the British Museum Ms. Harley 2253, *Alysoun* consists of four stanzas, each with eight lines of three or four metrical feet, rhyming *ababbbbc*. A refrain or "burden" follows each stanza, rhyming *dddc*, where the last word of the refrain is always "Alysoun"—thus the *c* rhyme at the end of each stanza always rhymes with the "Alysoun" that ends the refrain.

The poem describes a succession of the speaker's attitudes and responses to his love for the fair lady Alysoun. The attitudes expressed by the speaker are quite conventional in the COURTLY LOVE tradition, but this particular lyric is admired for its fresh images and lyricism, particularly in the refrain:

An hendy hap ich habbe ihent!
Ichot from hevene it is me sent;
From alle wimmen my love is lent,
And light on Alisoun.

(Luria and Hoffman 1974, 23, ll. 9–12)

The alliteration, especially in the first line, contributes to the rhythmic musicality of the lines. The "hendy hap" is a fortunate destiny, sent to the lover, he believes, "from hevene" itself. His love has been taken away from all other women and has settled on Alysoun alone.

In the first stanza of the poem, the speaker places his love in the traditional season of spring, and says he lives in "love-longinge" for the "semlokest" or fairest of all things. He becomes her servant and hopes she will bring him "blisse"—the first of many religious terms in the poem that give the lady a quasi-divine status.

After the refrain establishes the speaker's joy in his situation, the second stanza moves into a very conventional description of the lady. The speaker praises her hair, her eyes, her countenance, and her figure in a manner similar to that prescribed by medieval rhetoricians like GEOFFREY OF VINSAUF. Alysoun is depicted as cheerful and laughing—not the disdainful and aloof lady more typical of the courtly beloved. At the end of these lines of praise, though, the speaker very predictably declares that he will die of love if he cannot have Alysoun. But this is followed, again, by the rhythmic, affirming refrain.

In the third and fourth stanzas, the speaker describes his sufferings, particularly his lack of sleep and his tormented jealousy and fear of losing his beloved to someone else. What is striking about these stanzas is the speaker's use of memorable, somewhat colloquial alliterative images: Of his insomnia, he says he is "Wery so water in wore" (as weary as water in a troubled pool) (l. 30). When he addresses Alysoun directly, he calls her "Geynest under gore" (kindest under petticoat) (l. 35), an expression some have seen as highly suggestive but that seems more likely to have simply been an earthy expression for "kindest of women," whom he begs in the final stanza to hearken to his song.

One critical crux of the poem is how seriously we are to take the speaker's suffering, particularly since every stanza ends with the upbeat refrain. Some have suggested that the poem is a parody of conventional love poems. It seems more likely that the tone is playful: The speaker goes through the conventional motions of the lover's malady, but cannot really restrain the joy of his love.

Bibliography

Brook, G. L. *The Harley Lyrics: The Middle English Lyrics of Ms. Harley 2253.* 4th ed. Manchester, U.K.: Manchester University Press, 1968.

Fein, Susanna, ed. *Studies in the Harley Manuscript: The Scribes, Contents, and Social Contexts of British Library MS Harley 2253.* Kalamazoo, Mich.: Medieval Institute Publications, 2000.

Luria, Maxwell S., and Richard Hoffman. *Middle English Lyrics.* New York: Norton, 1974.

Ranson, Daniel J. *Poets at Play: Irony and Parody in the Harley Lyrics.* Norman, Okla.: Pilgrim Books, 1985.

Reiss, Edmund. *The Art of the Middle English Lyric: Essays in Criticism.* Athens: University of Georgia Press, 1972.

Amaru (seventh century)

Amaru was a Sanskrit love poet whose "century" (*sataka*) of verses is one of the most admired collections of short love lyrics in the Sanskrit language. Virtually nothing is known of Amaru's life, but he was singled out by the great literary theorist Anandavardhana in the ninth century as the master of the short lyric known as the *muktaka.*

The *Amarusataka,* or "hundred poems of Amaru," has survived in four different versions, ranging in size from 96 to 115 short poems. Only 51 lyrics are common to all four versions, but because of the similarity of style and language, it is virtually impossible to determine which of the extant verses are truly Amaru's.

Amaru's poems are not professions of love addressed to the speaker's beloved, but rather brief vignettes that suggest a single moment in the history of a relationship. Some poems have a male speaker, others a female, still others an objective narrator. But the purpose of all of these poems is to evoke what was aesthetically considered the perfect erotic mood (or *rasa*). In doing so, the poet follows the conventions of the erotic *rasa,* including the presentation of different "types" of women, different emotional states, and various physical aspects of love as described in the *Kamasutra.*

One of Amaru's favorite themes is his depiction of the *manini,* or angry heroine, who chastises her lover for his infidelity. In one poem, the *manini* speaks:

You grovel at my feet
and I berate you
and can't let my anger go.

(Selby 2002, 38, ll. 11–13)

At their most successful, Amaru's poems speak of the universal emotions of love. One such poem expresses the emotion of the lover who is so smitten he can only think of his beloved—a state he compares with mystical notions of divine unity:

O heart,
there is no reality for me
other than she she
she she she she
in the whole of the reeling world.

And philosophers talk about Oneness.

(Selby 2002, 102, ll. 8–13)

Bibliography

Brough, John, trans. *Poems from the Sanskrit.* Harmondsworth, U.K.: Penguin, 1968.

Ingalls, Daniel H. H., trans. *Sanskrit Poetry from Vidyakara's Treasury.* Cambridge, Mass.: Harvard University Press, 1968.

Selby, Martha Ann, trans. "From Amarusataka." In *Norton Anthology of World Literature.* 2nd ed. Vol. B, edited by Sarah Lawall, et al., 1339–1342. New York and London: Norton, 2002.

Ancrene Wisse (*Ancrene Riwle*) (ca. 1190–1220)

Ancrene Wisse, also known as *Rule for a Recluse* and *Guide for Anchoresses,* is a 13th-century text, produced ca. 1190–1220 C.E. It is written in vernacular prose in the West Midlands dialect that Tolkien classified as the "AB language," which is also the dialect of the KATHERINE GROUP and the WOOING GROUP (this language is a standard written—not spoken—dialect, characterized by a significant number of French and Norse loanwords, frequent colloquial expressions, conservative spelling, and syntactical similarities to Old English).

Although *Ancrene Wisse* is a rather straightforward treatise, it contains exempla, brief allegories, biblical allusions, and elaborate descriptions, which all combine to make a lively example of the early English vernacular tradition. Most scholars believe that the Middle English manuscripts MS Cotton Nero A.xiv and MS Cotton Cleopatra C.vi, held by the British Library in London, and MS Corpus Christi 402, held by Corpus Christi College of Cambridge University, contain the least altered and most important versions of the text. Counting fragments, 17 medieval versions exist, 11 in MIDDLE ENGLISH, four in Latin, and two in French, indicating the relative popularity and significance of the work. In some of these versions, the basic text has been revised and adapted for a different audience, such as a larger community or a group of men. It was also interpreted and altered by the LOLLARDS in the late Middle Ages.

Ancrene Wisse, the longest and most complete of the anchoritic rules (ways of life), was sometimes referred to as the *Ancrene Riwle* in the past. *Ancren Riwle* was the title attached to the work by James Morton in his 1853 edition, and has no medieval authority. For some time, the only change was the affixing of the genitive marker *"e"* to *Ancren,* indicating correct usage of the possessive. Today, scholars generally prefer the title *Ancrene Wisse,* which was also assigned in modern times, but is based on a scribal-inscribed colophon found on the first folio of MS Cambridge 402. *Wisse* has been almost universally translated as some variation of "guide," presuming that it is a noun derived from the Middle English verb *wissin,* which means "to guide" or "to direct."

According to the text, *Ancrene Wisse* was written specifically for three sisters at their own behest. These young anchoresses were desirous of a rule to govern their daily routines. The entire manuscript reveals further details concerning the sisters' windows, cells, furnishings, servants, clothing, daily activities, bodily care, and interactions with community members. It also outlines daily devotions, contains exhortations about the care of the soul and regulation of the senses, dispenses advice about sin, penance, and confession, and teaches about the delights of divine love.

The anchoritic vocation was considered to be one of the strictest religious pursuits. Building upon the early desert traditions of the Patristic era, anchorites were individuals who, desiring to spend their entire life in contemplative prayer, withdrew from the world completely. After securing permission from his/her bishop, a prospective anchorite (or female "anchoress") would undergo a formal "burying ceremony," and then be walled up in a small cell attached to a church. This cell, as *Ancrene Wisse* indicates, would have windows built into it for receiving food and other necessary items, for communicating with servants and supplicants, and for observing mass and receiving communion. There were numerous anchorites throughout the Christian West, though England seemingly had the largest number. Moreover, anchoritism was particularly attractive to women, and the majority of practicing anchorites were female. There was no one set Rule that anchorites had to follow, nor did an anchorite have to be a member of a formal religious order. It seems that many anchorites adapted a monastic rule for their own use or asked for one to be created for them to follow. *Ancrene Wisse* is one such creation.

Ancrene Wisse is composed of an introduction and eight parts. The subjects of these are as follows: I. Devotions; II. The Five Senses; III. The Inner Senses; IV. Temptations (external and internal); V. Confession; VI. Penance; VII. Divine Love; VIII. The Outer Rule. Of these, Part I and Part VIII are primarily concerned with external actions, bodily conduct, and daily living. The Inner Rule, found in Parts II through VII, concerns the spiritual comportment of the anchoresses as they wage war against temptation and pursue the love of God.

Ancrene Wisse spends a great deal of textual space detailing the disposition of worldly goods and functions. Adherence to both sets of rules was necessary to vanquish temptation, and even the daily devotions of the anchoresses were framed by their worldly associations. However, it is ultimately the Inner Rule that comprises the substance of the manuscript, and obviously consumed most of the recluse's time. Her primary duty lay in prayer and spiritual development, along with scrupulous monitoring of her own senses.

Scholars have been debating the origins of *Ancrene Wisse* for some time. Suggested sources have included the *Rule of St. Benedict,* which was the basis for the majority of medieval monastic rules, the *Rule of St. Augustine,* and the *Rule of St. Dominic,* as well as the Premonstratensian *Statutes.* Still other scholars suggest that there is no specific tradition to which *Ancrene Wisse* can be tied; rather, these individuals believe it is a composite text that draws on a variety of sources. Whatever the direct source, if indeed there is one, *Ancrene Wisse* clearly draws upon the works of many Patristic theologians, such as St. JEROME and St. AUGUSTINE OF HIPPO, as well as on the Bible.

Much of the early scholarly research about *Ancrene Wisse* was devoted to the search for an author and an audience, as well as direct source material. From these early investigations, the natural progression was to examinations of the linguistic evidence, especially vocabulary and style. More recent scholarship has focused on the relationship between *Ancrene Wisse* and the larger anchoritic tradition, as well as its relationship to the larger field of women's spirituality. Further inquiry into links between *Ancrene Wisse* and the later medieval mystic tradition has also been the subject of recent work on this text.

Ancrene Wisse is a valuable text not only for its glimpse into the anchoritic vocation and its revelations about women's spiritual expression, but also for its preservation of the early English literary tradition. Not many vernacular texts survive from the 13th century, and as such, *Ancrene Wisse* is particularly important in providing both cultural context and key linguistic features, particularly its evidence of the development of the language from OLD ENGLISH into Middle English.

Bibliography

Ancrene Wisse. Edited by Robert Hasenfranz. Kalamazoo, Mich.: Medieval Institute Publications, 2000.

Dobson, E. J. *Origins of Ancrene Wisse.* Oxford: Clarendon Press, 1976.

Georgianna, Linda. *The Solitary Self: Individuality in the Ancrene Wisse.* Cambridge, Mass.: Harvard University Press, 1981.

Grayson, Janet. *Structure and Imagery in Ancrene Wisse.* Hanover, N.H.: University Press of New England, 1974.

Millet, Bella. "The Origins of *Ancrene Wisse:* New Answers, New Questions," *Medium Ævum* 61 (1992): 206–228.

Robertson, Elizabeth. *Early English Devotional Prose and the Female Audience.* Knoxville: University of Tennessee Press, 1990.

Savage, Anne, and Nicholas Watson. *Ancrene Wisse and Associated Works.* Preface by Benedicta Ward. New York: Paulist Press, 1991.

Tolkien, J. R. R. "*Ancrene Wisse* and *Hali Meiðhad,*" *Essays and Studies* 14 (1929): 104–126.

Michelle M. Sauer

Andreas (ca. ninth century)

Andreas is a 1,722-line OLD ENGLISH poem preserved in the VERCELLI BOOK. The extant poem is divided into 15 sections, or fits, and retells a story based on a lost Latin translation of the apocryphal

Acts of Andrew and Matthew, originally written in Greek in the late fourth century. The story focuses on the apostle Saint Andrew and his miraculous rescue of Saint Matthew from a tribe of cannibals whom Andrew is ultimately able to convert to Christianity.

In the poem, the Mermedonians are a fiendish tribe of Ethiopia who eat the flesh and drink the blood of any strangers they capture in their land. The prisoners are blinded and forced to drink a potion that robs them of their reason and reduces them to eating hay like beasts while awaiting their slaughter. Saint Matthew is captured and, though he drinks the potion, remains faithful to God, who rewards his prayers with healing and the promise of rescue.

Andrew is called upon in Achaia, from whence he sets forth somewhat reluctantly with a group of his thanes on a ship captained, as he later learns, by Christ himself. After a stormy voyage he arrives in the land of the Mermedonians, where he is himself captured and tortured for more than three days. But when Andrew miraculously lets loose a great flood from a stone column, the water drowns the Mermedonians in a symbolic baptism. All but 14 of the most wicked of the cannibals are revived and converted to the new faith, while Saint Matthew and the other prisoners are saved.

Andreas was once thought to be the work of the poet CYNEWULF, but that attribution is no longer accepted, and the poem is probably of a later date than that poet's work. Readers have admired *Andreas* for its vivid description of Saint Andrew's stormy sea crossing. Scholars have commented upon resemblances to *BEOWULF* in the text, in things like the sea-voyage to rescue people from man-eating monsters. Some phrases may even be borrowed from Beowulf or other heroic poetry. The heroic language, in fact, seems awkward or even unsuitable to some readers. But the poem is an admirable and effective effort, and seems to invite an allegorical interpretation with Andrew as a type or figure of Christ, harrowing an earthly hell where demonic humans hold captive citizens of God's kingdom. The bondage may suggest bondage to sin, the blindness a spiritual blindness that results in bondage. Ultimately, Andreas is a more sophisticated poem than it may at first appear, and certainly makes for exciting reading, though the story itself was hardly considered orthodox in its time.

Bibliography

Greenfield, Stanley B., and Daniel G. Calder. *A New Critical History of Old English Literature.* New York: New York University Press, 1986.

Kennedy, Charles William, trans. *Early English Christian Poetry.* New York: Oxford University Press, 1963.

Lapidge, Michael. "The Saintly Life in Anglo-Saxon England." In *The Cambridge Companion to Old English Literature,* edited by Malcolm Godden and Michael Lapidge, 243–263. Cambridge: Cambridge University Press, 1991.

Andreas Capellanus (fl. 1180–1190)

Andreas Capellanus is known to us only through his famous Latin treatise *De amore,* or *De arte honeste amandi* (*Art of Courtly Love*), from ca. 1185–90. Both in content and structure based on Ovid's *Ars amatoria* and *Remedia amoris,* this treatise constantly raises expectations about its own sources and its overall intentions, and then disappoints them as well. Although we know nothing concrete about Andreas, we can be certain from the many allusions in his text and its learned character that he was a cleric and a teacher. Although Andreas repeatedly refers to the Countess MARIE DE CHAMPAGNE, and has included in his text fictional judgments promulgated by her about difficult conflicts in love, we can be certain that this represents only part of his literary strategy and that Andreas actually served at the Parisian court of King Philippe Auguste educating the young prince(s). In his prologue he addresses his student Walter (Gualterus) who had asked him to explain to him the secrets of love, and promises to outline for him everything he knows himself about this arcane and complex subject matter: "For I know, having learned from experience, that it does not do the man who owes obedience to Venus's service any good to give careful thought to anything except how he may always be doing something that will entangle him more firmly in his chains" (Andreas

1941, 27). This highly ambiguous statement sets a tone for the entire work that has intrigued and puzzled scholars for centuries. Does Andreas advocate COURTLY LOVE or does he reject it? He confirms himself: "although it does not seem expedient to devote oneself to things of this kind or fitting for any prudent man to engage in this kind of hunting . . . , I can by no means refuse your request" (27).

This treatise, which proved to be one of the most influential critical discussions of (courtly) love throughout the entire Middle Ages, consists, apart from the author's preface, of three books. The first book begins with several definitions of what love is, between what persons love may exist, what the effects of love are, etc. Next Andreas offers a number of dialogues, each between a man and a woman, mostly of different social classes. In all of these dialogues the man woos the lady, but she regularly rejects him, and only once can the man convince her by means of a frightening allegorical tale that love is a noble undertaking if she can find the man to be worthy of the erotic reward (83). These dialogues offer Andreas many opportunities to examine the essential values of courtly love, to experiment with various literary genres, and to explore the basics of courtly love discourse itself. Finally we also learn about what love means for male clerics and nuns, prostitution, and about love among and with peasants who can easily be raped, an act that the narrator does not describe as a crime (150).

Closely following Ovid's model, Andreas subsequently, in his second book, discusses how to retain love. It also confirms the extraordinarily high position assigned to courtly ladies who are treated with greatest respect because of their rhetorical sophistication and impressive knowledge of the rules of love, which are repeated throughout the first two books as absolutely binding for all members of the courtly world. At the end we even hear that many copies of these basic rules were created and disseminated at all courts (186). Moreover, Andreas adamantly confirms that true love is possible only outside of marriage, which is eventually illustrated through a beautiful Arthurian tale of a young Breton knight who has to win a hawk from King Arthur on behalf of his lady.

The third book, however, argues the very opposite, as the narrator now emphasizes that God has forbidden love outside of marriage, and then he moves into a most amazing, perhaps even hilarious misogynistic diatribe in which he ridicules and severely condemns *all* women for their natural vices. The narrator concludes his treatise with serious warnings to Walter to stay away from any form of love, but his conclusions remain surprisingly ambiguous and opaque: "you will see clearly that no man ought to mis-spend his days in the pleasures of love." And: "pass by all the vanities of the world, so that when the Bridegroom cometh to celebrate the greater nuptials . . . you may be prepared to go forth to meet Him" (211). Older scholarship tended to ignore the third book entirely and glorified *The Art of Courtly Love* as the fundamental statement relevant for all of courtly literature. Modern scholars have considered the third book, with its apocalyptic warnings of Christ's second coming that shift gears so radically, and have suggested that Andreas indeed rejected courtly love altogether and used the first two books only as an ironic backdrop for his actual topic. Only most recent scholars have realized the considerable degree of irony and satire throughout the entire treatise and observed Andreas's playful use of traditional literary and scholastic genres, resorting to self-mockery and ridicule of theological literature and also of the pervasive misogyny deeply influencing all of medieval society.

In fact *De amore* proves to be a masterpiece of rhetorical dialectics and illustrates the artistic nature of courtly love literature both in Latin and in the various vernaculars. Undoubtedly, however, the debate about the true meaning of this text will continue, but this phenomenon itself might well have been the author's ultimate purpose. We know that the treatise remained well known throughout the Middle Age because it is documented in Albertanus of Brescia's *De dilectione Dei et proximi* (1238); because it is included in a list of books to be condemned, published by Bishop Etienne of Paris (1277); because it was translated into various vernaculars; and because of the large number of manuscripts and early-modern prints of the text.

Bibliography

Allen, Peter L. *The Art of Love: Amatory Fiction from Ovid to the Romance of the Rose.* Philadelphia: University of Pennsylvania Press, 1992.

Andreae Capellani Regii Francorum. *De Amore, Libri Tres.* Edited by E. Trojel, 1892; Munich: Fink, 1972.

Andreas Capellanus. *The Art of Courtly Love.* Translated with Introduction and Notes by John Jay Parry. New York: Columbia University Press, 1941.

Brown, Catherine. *Contrary Things: Exegesis, Dialectic, and the Poetics of Didacticism.* Stanford, Calif.: Stanford University Press, 1998.

Classen, Albrecht. *Verzweiflung und Hoffnung.* Frankfurt: Peter Lang, 2003.

Albrecht Classen

Aneirin (fl. 560–600)

A single 13th-century Welsh manuscript containing the 1,000-line poem *Y GODODDIN* (*The Gododdin*) is attributed to a sixth-century bard known as Aneirin. In his standard 1938 edition of the poem, the scholar Ifor Williams argued convincingly on linguistic and textual grounds that the bulk of the *Llyfr Aneirin* (*Book of Aneirin*)—now known as MS Cardiff I at the Free Library of Cardiff—dates from the last decades of the sixth century.

Aneirin is mentioned in chapter 62 of NENNIUS's *Historia Brittonum* (ca. 800), where he is said to have been active in the 560s. Internal evidence in his poem suggests that Aneirin was a bard active at the court of the British chieftain Mynyddog Mwynfawr (the Wealthy). He was apparently a contemporary of the poet TALIESIN, and composed his poem in Cumbric, ancestor of modern Welsh and a northern dialect of the Brythonic language, spoken by all the Celtic people in Britain south of the Firth of Forth. Mynyddog was chief of the Gododdin tribe, known to the Romans as the Votadini. Their capital was at Eidyn (modern-day Edinburgh).

The Gododdin is a series of elegies to fallen heroes, all hand-picked by Mynyddog to help defend his kingdom against the Anglian hordes from Northumbria. Mynydogg sends the Gododdin warriors south to meet an overwhelming Anglian force at Catraeth (identified as Catterick in northern Yorkshire), and, fighting boldly, the British army is wiped out almost to the last man. The fact that virtually none of the warriors eulogized is known in other texts suggests that Aneirin was writing close to the events, and that the battle may have been historical and not fiction. It has been suggested that it took place ca. 588–590.

It has been suggested that Aneirin was a younger son of a British king from West Yorkshire, Dunaut Bwr (the Stout) (ca. 505–595), that he was himself present at the Battle of Catraeth, and that in his old age he became a monk at Llancarfan in southern Wales. Such traditions are not really verifiable, and may be merely the stuff of legend.

Bibliography

Aneirin, *The Gododdin: The Oldest Scottish Poem.* Edited by Kenneth H. Jackson. Edinburgh: Edinburgh University Press, 1978.

Breeze, Andrew. *Medieval Welsh Literature.* Dublin: Four Courts Press, 1997.

William, Ifor, ed. *Canu Aneirin.* Cardiff: Gwasg Prifysgol Cymru, 1938.

Williams, Gwyn. *An Introduction to Welsh Poetry: From the Beginnings to the Sixteenth Century.* Freeport, N.Y.: Books for Libraries Press, 1970.

Anelida and Arcite Geoffrey Chaucer (ca. 1378)

One of CHAUCER's most unusual works, *Anelida and Arcite* is a curious and clearly experimental combination of narrative and lyric, in which the English poet seems to have been trying to find an effective way of combining the lyrical love COMPLAINT of his French models, like Guillaume de MACHAUT, with his newfound passion for Italian narrative poetry, particularly as found in BOCCACCIO's *TESEIDA*. Most critics have found the lyric portion of the text far more successful than the narrative.

The poem begins with not one but two epic-style invocations, the first to Mars and Bellona (Roman god and goddess of war), the second to the muses, asking for their help in telling the story of Queen Anelida and her false lover Arcite. A narrative of about 200 lines follows, which Chaucer claims to be taking from Statius, author of the

Latin *Thebaid,* and from an unknown (and probably spurious) poet named Corrine. In fact, he bases the first part of the narrative on the *Teseida,* describing Theseus's triumphant return from battling the Amazons, then switches the scene to Thebes, where Anelida, queen of Armenia, is wooed and then abandoned by the false Arcite—a name Chaucer also borrowed from a completely different character in the *Teseida.* No source has been found for this story, which was probably Chaucer's own invention.

This Chaucer follows with an elaborate "*Complaint,*" nearly as long as the narrative, in which Anelida laments her desertion by the false Arcite. The poem consists of a Proem, a Strophe, an Antistrophe, and a Conclusion. The Proem and Conclusion are in exactly the same verse form, while the Strophe and Antistrophe precisely parallel one another, and the poem ends with a line that echoes its beginning. Praised for its metrical versatility, the "Complaint" has also been admired as a realistic exploration of a mind disturbed by grief.

A final stanza in which Anelida goes to the Temple of Mars follows the complaint, but the poem abruptly breaks off after this. Most critics have therefore assumed that the poem is unfinished, and some have made conjectures about what the poem would have been had Chaucer completed it (James Wimsatt suggests that a long lyric of comfort would have balanced Anelida's lament; Michael Cherniss that the poem would have moved into a DREAM VISION). However, as John Norton-Smith has pointed out, only half of the eight surviving manuscripts of the poem contain the final stanza, and it may well be a later scribal addition. If Chaucer meant to end the poem after the "Complaint," this poem has precisely the same structure as another of Chaucer's short poems, the "Complaint of Mars." Like that poem, Chaucer's concern seems to have been to place the conventional, universal concerns of the traditional lover's complaint into a narrative context that would give it some specificity.

Ultimately most readers have found the poem unsatisfactory. The extremely complex verse form shows Chaucer at his lyrical best, though he never attempts so elaborate a form again in any of his shorter poems. Certainly the brief love narrative is disappointing after the epic machinery that begins it, though it gave Chaucer practice in writing the kind of short tale of a woman abandoned in love that filled his later *LEGEND OF GOOD WOMEN.* The use of lyric within narrative that Chaucer practices here is a technique that Chaucer ultimately perfects in *TROILUS AND CRISEYDE.* If *Anelida and Arcite* is an experiment, it is one that bears valuable fruit later on in Chaucer's career.

Bibliography

Aaij, Michel. "Perverted Love in Chaucer's 'Anelida and Arcite,'" *Medieval Perspectives* 14 (1999): 13–19.

Cherniss, Michael D. "Chaucer's *Anelida and Arcite:* Some Conjectures," *Chaucer Review* 5 (1970): 9–21.

David, Alfred. "Recycling *Anelida and Arcite:* Chaucer as a Source for Chaucer," *Studies in the Age of Chaucer: Proceedings* 1 (1984): 105–115.

Favier, Dale A. "*Anelide and Arcite:* Anti-Feminist allegory, Pro-Feminist Complaint," *Chaucer Review* 26 (1991): 83–94.

Gillam, Doreen M. E. "Lovers and Riders in Chaucer's 'Anelida and Arcite,'" *English Studies* 63 (1982): 394–401.

Minnis, A. J., V. J. Scattergood and J. J. Smith. *The Shorter Poems.* Oxford Guides to Chaucer. Oxford: Clarendon Press, 1995.

Norton-Smith, John. "Chaucer's *Anelida and Arcite,*" in *Medieval Studies for J. A. W. Bennett,* edited by P. L. Heyworth. Oxford: Clarendon Press, 1981, 81–99.

Ruud, Jay. *"Many a Song and Many a Leccherous Lay": Tradition and Individuality in Chaucer's Lyric Poetry.* New York: Garland, 1992.

Wimsatt, James I. "*Anelida and Arcite:* A Narrative of Complaint and Comfort," *Chaucer Review* 5 (1970): 1–8.

Angiolieri, Cecco (ca. 1260–ca. 1313)

The Siena-born lyric poet Cecco Angiolieri was known chiefly for his humorous sonnets, but also for his allegedly profligate lifestyle, though some of that reputation derives undoubtedly from the persona created in his lyrics. A contemporary and acquaintance of DANTE, Cecco devotes much of his poetry to burlesquing the elevated view of love presented in the *DOLCE STIL NOVO* ("sweet new style") practiced by Dante, CAVALCANTI, and other poets of Tuscany.

Very few facts are known of Cecco's life. He was born in Siena, and his family seems to have been wealthy. He is thought to have taken part (as Dante did) in the Battle of Campaldino (1289) with the Sienese troops, allied with the Guelfs of Florence against the Ghibellines of Arezzo (in general, the Guelf party was largely middle class and supported the pope in Italian politics, while the Ghibellines were aristocratic and supported the emperor). Later Cecco probably went to Rome, where he was part of the court of Cardinal Riccardo Petroni. Beyond these things, the only other facts we know are that in 1291, Cecco was sued for criminal assault and was acquitted; and that, upon his death, all five of his sons renounced their inheritance because it would have meant being responsible for Cecco's substantial outstanding debts. His reputation for wild living was so widespread that BOCCACCIO included a story about him in *The DECAMERON* (ninth day, fourth story), in which he loses his money, shirt, and horse to a gambler he has taken on as a servant.

This reputation is only enhanced by many of the 128 extant sonnets attributed to Cecco, in which he presents a persona who devotes himself to carousing, brawling in taverns, chasing loose women, and complaining that his stingy father won't give him enough money. Not all of his poems are in this vein: In some, he shows the influence of the Sicilian school of love poetry established by GIACOMO DA LENTINO, who first brought to Italy poetry in the COURTLY LOVE style of the Provençal TROUBADOURS, and also shows his familiarity with the more fashionable *Dolce Stil Novo* of Florence. But his best-known sonnets are his humorous ones.

Cecco might be considered with FOLGORE DA SAN GEMINIANO as one of the earliest Italian poets in the popular realistic humorous vein. Both poets give a vivid picture of everyday life, though Cecco certainly differs from Folgore in his raucous, burlesque manner. In his most popular poems, Cecco replaces the angelic woman, bringer of blessings, characteristic of the *Dolce Stil Novo,* with Becchina, a cobbler's daughter who seems to bring more of a curse than a blessing to Cecco's persona. His sonnets present his love spats with Becchina, his complaints about his rich but stingy parents, and his outrage at his own resulting poverty. His frustration comes out as bitterness against all of creation in his most famous poem, *"S'i' fosse foco, arderei 'l mondo"* ("If I were fire, I would burn the world").

The tendency of scholars has often been to read these sonnets autobiographically. More recent critics, however, have pointed out the profound influence of earlier Latin GOLIARDIC VERSE on Cecco's comic poetry, and thus the persona Cecco creates owes much to the *golias* persona. Perhaps Cecco's three poems addressed to Dante may also be read in this light. In all three sonnets, Cecco disputes with Dante in some way: One poem draws attention to an inconsistency in the last sonnet of Dante's *VITA NUOVA;* another abuses him for suggesting that Cecco should not write poems about Becchina; a third, addressed to Dante in exile at Verona, suggests that his lot is not much different from that of the impoverished Cecco. While these might be read as evidence of enmity between the poets, it is certainly possible that they are the voice of Cecco's irascible persona and are intended humorously.

Cecco, long obscure to English readers, was made somewhat more accessible in Victorian England when Dante Gabriel Rossetti (who called Cecco the "scamp" of Dante's circle) translated several of his poems into English.

Bibliography

Angiolieri, Cecco. *The Sonnets of a Handsome and Well-Mannered Rogue.* Translated by Thomas C. Chubb. New York: Archon, 1970.

Bondanella, Peter E. "Cecco Angiolieri and the Vocabulary of Courtly Love," *Studies in Philology* 69 (1972): 55–71.

Rossetti, Dante Gabriel, trans. *The Early Italian Poets.* Edited by Sally Purcell. Berkeley: University of California Press, 1981.

Anglo-Saxon Chronicle

The term *Anglo-Saxon Chronicle* refers not to a single text but to a group of anonymous texts written in OLD ENGLISH prose compiled at various places around England and all deriving ultimately from an original core text. The *Chronicle* is the chief written source for the history of Anglo-Saxon England, particularly from the reign of King ALFRED THE GREAT (871–899) through the Norman Conquest and in some manuscripts somewhat later. Linguistically, the *Chronicle* is important also because it was written in the vernacular rather than Latin. The construction of such a chronicle was probably initially inspired by the keeping of "Easter tables," which were lists of years used by clergy to compute the dates of Easter, and often included brief notations in Latin of the major events that took place each year. The author or authors of the original compilation seem to have used material from existing annals in Kent, Mercia, and Saxony, from available "universal histories," and from ninth-century Frankish annals, as well as from the Venerable BEDE's *Ecclesiastical History of the English People.* Following Bede's example, the chroniclers reckon dates from the birth of Christ, using *anno Domini* or "the year of our Lord" to designate years. The original material in the *Chronicles,* sometimes called the common stock, covers the period from about 60 B.C.E. (from the Roman conquest of Britain) until the year 891, apparently the year in which the first compilation was completed under King Alfred, and probably at his command. Perhaps the text was intended to provide a common history for the English peoples and help to unite them during Alfred's wars against Norse invaders.

The *Anglo-Saxon Chronicle* survives in seven complete manuscripts and one fragment. The manuscripts vary in precisely what they record. But each records the common stock. It seems likely that the original manuscript, produced under Alfred's patronage, was distributed from his capital at Winchester to significant regional centers, where clerics and sometimes laymen continued to add to them. There seems to have been some attempt to update them systematically, probably with royal "continuations" sent out periodically from Winchester. But in addition, most of the regional centers began to include matters of local interest in their versions of the *Chronicle,* and after about 915 the different manuscripts diverge from one another significantly.

The chroniclers follow the examples of the earlier Easter tables and Latin annals for the years up until 449. But beginning with that year, and the arrival of Hengest and Horsa, the first Saxon invaders of Britain, the chroniclers begin to record more substantial entries. The entry for 755, relating the story of Cynewulf and Cyneheard, has been called the first "short story" in English. The entries concerning Alfred's wars against the Danes from 893 to 897 are very important as a historical source. The death of King Edward in 975 and of Prince Alfred in 1040 and the martyrdom of Bishop Aelfheah in 1011 are memorable entries. The histories of the reigns of Ethelred and of King Edward the Confessor in the earlier 11th century are told in the most detail. But perhaps the most significant entry of all is the memorable Old English heroic poem called *The* BATTLE OF BRUNANBURH, which serves as the entry for the year 937.

Only one version of the *Anglo-Saxon Chronicle* extends past the year 1080, and that is the text called the PETERBOROUGH CHRONICLE, which extends the history through the reign of King Stephen until 1154. That individual text is valuable in its own right, though in general the *Anglo-Saxon Chronicle* remains the most important source for the history of England between the time of Bede in the eighth century and the Norman Conquest in the 11th, and was the main source for that period in later Anglo-Norman histories of England.

Bibliography

The Anglo-Saxon Chronicle. Translated and edited by M. J. Swanton. New York: Routledge, 1998.

The Anglo-Saxon Chronicle: According to the Several Original Authorities. Edited, with a translation, by Benjamin Thorpe. Rolls Series. 2 vols. London: Longman, Green, and Roberts, 1861.

The Anglo-Saxon Chronicle: A Revised Translation. Edited by Dorothy Whitelock, David C. Douglas, and Susie I. Tucker. New Brunswick, N.J.: Rutgers University Press, 1962.

Anna Comnena (Anna Komnena) (1083–ca. 1155)

Anna Comnena was the daughter of the Byzantine emperor Alexis I Comnenus, and is often considered the world's first female historian. She is best known as the author of the *Alexiad,* a 15-book history of her father's reign that is a major source for details about daily life in the Byzantine court, and for the Byzantine reactions to the Latin armies of the First Crusade.

Anna was the oldest child of Alexis and his empress, Irene Doukas. Alexis, whose claim to the throne was tenuous, made Anna his heir and betrothed her to Constantine Doukas (whose father and grandfather had both been emperors). But when Anna's brother John was born in 1087, the emperor changed his mind. In 1082 he disinherited Anna in favor of her brother. Anna turned to her studies and received a superior education in Greek literature, philosophy, history, theology, rhetoric, mathematics, and even medicine. When her husband Constantine died in 1097, she was remarried to another scholar, historian, and military leader, Nikephoros Bryennios, whose father had been a pretender to the throne.

Upon her father's death in 1118, Anna conspired with her mother to seize the throne from her brother John. But when her husband Bryennios refused to take part, the plot was discovered. The new emperor was lenient and spared his sister's life, but confiscated her property. Anna, disappointed in her husband, reportedly cursed God for making her a woman. She had four surviving children and apparently lived with Bryennios until his death in 1137, after which she was confined to the convent Kecharitomene, which her mother Irene had founded. Here, she consoled herself with writing her *Alexiad,* which traced the history of her father's rise to power, beginning in 1069, and the story of his reign (1081–1118). She is known to have still been writing the history in 1148, but certainly died before 1156, when a funeral oration was given in memory of her.

Anna's goals in writing the history were, first, to continue her husband's composition, "Historical Materials," that ended in 1079, and second, to ensure that her father's accomplishments were not forgotten. She was able to rely to some extent on her own experiences and observations, but sought out other written sources and witnesses. Because of her family connections she had access to diplomatic correspondence and sometimes she quotes imperial decrees in full in the text of her history.

The *Alexiad* is valued for its attention to detail and use of the best available sources, as well as for its contemporary account of the Byzantine attitude toward the greedy, "barbarous" Frankish crusaders. The text is also admired for its use of lively anecdotes, its detailed picture of Byzantine life, and its portrayal of characters, particularly of women. Anna's own strong personality constantly comes through in her text, especially her intelligence, her family pride, her religious orthodoxy, and her hatred of the crusaders. Sometimes she appears as a character in her own text, traveling with her father or nursing him as he lies dying. But the hero of the text is clearly her father, who comes across as a near-epic figure, fighting to save his empire from crises fomented by disloyalty inside the empire and pressure from the outside. Alexis is called the 13th apostle and the luminary of the universe. Anna's language—a classical Attic Greek rather than the colloquial language of Byzantium—recalls her infatuation with Homer, and reinforces the epic quality of her text. But ultimately Anna's learning and access to detailed information make her text invaluable to scholars and entertaining to readers of all kinds.

Bibliography

Buckler, Georgiana Grenfell. *Anna Comnena: A Study.* 1929. Reprint, London: Oxford University Press, 1968.

Dalven, Rae. *Anna Comnena.* New York: Twayne, 1972.

Sewter, E.R.A., trans. *The Alexiad of Anna Comnena.* Harmondsworth, U.K.: Penguin, 1969.

Annales Cambriae (444–977)

The *Annales Cambriae* (or *Welsh Annals*) are a chronicle covering some 533 years, beginning around the year 444 C.E. and ending in 977. For some of the years, important events are briefly noted. The earliest extant version of the chronicle, written in Latin, is appended to NENNIUS's *Historia Britonium* in the Harley manuscript of that text. There are two later manuscript versions as well.

The text was probably compiled between 960 and 980, and relies on some older chronicles, some of them probably Irish. Of most interest in the *Annales* are two entries that concern the history or legend of the British hero Arthur (not yet referred to as "King"). For the year 516, the entry reads "The Battle of Badon, in which Arthur carried the Cross of our Lord Jesus Christ for three days and three nights on his shoulders and the Britons were the victors" (Morris 45). It has been suggested that "shoulders" is a mistranslation of "shield," so that the cross would be a symbol on the shield Arthur carried into battle. But the date of 516 seems late for the Battle of Badon, since GILDAS says it took place in the year of his birth, around 500.

The second Arthurian entry is for the year 537. It reads "The Battle of Camlann, in which Arthur and Medraut fell: and there was plague in Britain and Ireland" (Morris 45). This is the first recorded mention of Arthur's final battle and of a "Medraut," i.e., "Mordred." The entry is cryptic, and it is impossible to tell whether Medraut fought on Arthur's side or against him in the battle. But this appears to be the kernel of the legendary battle between King Arthur and his son/nephew that ended in their mutual destruction at the Battle of Camlann.

Bibliography

Bengle, Richard L. *Arthur King of Britain: History, Chronicle, Romance and Criticism.* New York: Appleton-Century-Crofts, 1964.

Morris, John, ed. and trans. *Nennius: British History and The Welsh Annals.* London: Phillimore, 1975.

Anne of Bohemia (1366–1394)

Anne of Bohemia was the daughter of the Holy Roman Emperor Charles IV and in 1382 became the wife of King RICHARD II of England. She became popular among her English subjects and seems to have been a steady and calming influence upon the king, who was said to be inconsolable when she died of the plague in 1394. As queen, Anne was apparently a patron of such literary artists as Geoffrey CHAUCER, and the connections between England and Prague she brought were instrumental in creating the channel by which the ideas of the English theologian John WYCLIFFE were able to reach the Czech reformer Jan HUS.

Anne was born in 1366 and married Richard when she was 15. She was less than a year older than her husband. By all accounts she was an intelligent, cultured, pious, and well-read woman. Because of her family background, she was well connected with aristocratic families across Europe. By the time of her marriage her brother Wenceslas (or Václav) IV was emperor, but, despite his lofty title, he had little money and could give her no dowry. The marriage agreement, however, specified that England would lend Wenceslas 15,000 pounds. These arrangements, added to her reputed lack of beauty, initially made Anne and her large Czech entourage unpopular in England. Over time, however, her charm won over the people, and endeared her to her husband. In particular she impressed the people of London by pleading their case to the king when, in 1392, he revoked the city's charter because they had offended him. Most historians believe she was a calm and rational influence on Richard's short-tempered and sometimes unstable personality. She was married to him for 12 years before dying of the plague at the age of 27. She never bore him any children. The spring after her death, Richard gave orders to destroy the royal manor at Sheen, where Anne had died.

There are a number of traditions about Anne that are difficult to prove. One is that she owned copies of the gospels in Latin, German, and Czech. Another is that she possessed a Wycliffite or "LOLLARD" Bible. Still another claims that at one time she interceded for Wycliffe himself. These stories are not considered particularly reliable. It is certain, though, that through her connections there were scholarship opportunities for students from the University of Prague to attend Oxford and thereby to gain access to Wycliffe's writings. Jerome of Prague, close friend and disciple of Jan Hus, is known to have been at Oxford in 1398 and to have brought manuscripts of some of Wycliffe's treatises back to Prague.

As a patroness of the arts, Anne's reputation may be more deserved. John CLANVOWE dedicated his *Book of Cupid* to her. Chaucer pays her a compliment in *TROILUS AND CRISEYDE* when he speaks of England's "first letter" being an "A," and a famous frontispiece of one of the *Troilus* manuscripts portrays Chaucer reading the poem to Anne, Richard, and their court. It is also believed that Alceste in the prologue to *The LEGEND OF GOOD WOMEN* is an allegorical representation of Anne, who may have asked him to write the poem in 1386. In the original prologue, Chaucer asks that the poem be delivered to Queen Anne at the palace at Sheen. After her death, those two lines were removed from the prologue. Anne now lies buried with Richard in the tomb he commissioned in 1395 at Westminster Abbey.

Bibliography

Saul, Nigel. *Richard II.* New Haven, Conn.: Yale University Press, 1997.

Taylor, Andrew. "Anne of Bohemia and the Making of Chaucer," *Studies in the Age of Chaucer* 19 (1997): 95–119.

Thomas, Alfred. *Anne's Bohemia.* Minneapolis: University of Minnesota Press, 1998.

Wallace, David. *Chaucerian Polity: Absolutist Lineages and Associational Forms in England and Italy.* Stanford, Calif.: Stanford University Press, 1997.

Anselm of Canterbury, Saint

(ca. 1033–1109)

Saint Anselm of Canterbury is often called the first scholastic. That is, he is considered by many to be the first medieval Christian theologian to apply philosophical argument in the classical sense to spiritual matters. In his *Proslogion,* he calls this "faith seeking understanding"—he never believed that one should use reason to decide what to believe, but rather that one should believe first and then seek to find rational explanation. He was a successful abbot, a political figure embroiled in the controversies of his time, and most important, a profoundly influential thinker and writer who influenced the course of philosophical and theological discussion for generations.

Anselm was born to noble parents in Piedmont around 1033. After some youthful trauma, the nature of which we do not know, he traveled to France in 1059 seeking to further his education, and entered the newly founded monastery at Bec in Normandy. Here he quickly became the protégé of the prior lanfranc, later archbishop of Canterbury. Anselm became a monk in 1060 and rose quickly in the order, becoming prior in three years' time. By 1078 he was abbot of Bec, and under his leadership Bec developed into a very successful monastic school.

The Norman aristocracy, of course, had conquered England while Anselm was at Bec, and in 1093 his reputation was such that he was asked to become archbishop of Canterbury. At first Anselm refused, giving the excuse that he was too old to assume the position, though it is likely he saw the appointment as politically precarious and foresaw difficulties in dealing with the Norman king of England, William Rufus.

If that was the case, his anxiety was well grounded. Quarreling with the king over whether he as archbishop owed his loyalty first to the pope or the king and over who had the right to appoint bishops (an act called "investiture"), Anselm left England in 1097 for Rome, wishing to give up the see of Canterbury. Pope Urban II, however, refused to allow him to do so.

While in exile, Anselm demonstrated and enhanced his widespread reputation by taking a leading role in the Church Council at Bafri in 1098, the main purpose of which was to explore reconciliation with the Greek church, which had separated from the western church just a few decades before. Urban had asked Anselm to be the chief apologist for the western church at the council. One item on the council's agenda was the excommunication of William Rufus, a process that Anselm was able to defer to a later date.

Still archbishop of Canterbury but still in exile at Laon in 1100, Anselm received word of William's death in a hunting accident on August 2. William's brother Henry, now the new king, asked Anselm to return. However, when Anselm refused to take an oath of allegiance to Henry, he was again obliged to leave England for another three years of exile. This problem of investiture was a difficult one at that time: In 1073 Pope Gregory VII had outlawed lay investiture (that is, investiture by secular authorities rather than the church), but had encountered stiff opposition from the Holy Roman Emperor, Henry IV. Finally in 1107, Anselm and the English Henry agreed to a compromise in which the king gave up the right of investiture as long as Anselm allowed bishops to swear homage to the king in secular matters. Anselm returned to Canterbury, where he died in 1109.

Anselm's best-known texts include the *Monologion,* a work intended as a theodicy or justification of God, in which he argues that all good things have their origin in God; and the better-known *Proslogion.* It is in the latter text that he makes his famous "ontological argument" for the existence of God: I have a concept in my head, the argument goes, of a being than which nothing greater can be conceived. Such a being must exist of necessity, Anselm argues, because something that exists in reality is greater than something that exists only in the mind, and if the being in question did not exist, then anything that exists would be greater, and this is a logical contradiction. This argument was revived in the 17th century by Descartes, and has been debated ever since Anselm first made it.

Anselm had written the latter two texts at Bec, but perhaps even more influential was his treatise *Cur deus homo,* or *Why God Became a Man,* written during his exile in 1098. In it Anselm explains that God's incarnation in Jesus Christ was necessary as a part of God's plan for the atonement for human sin. Dissatisfied with the earlier "Devil's Rights" theory of atonement current in the earlier Middle Ages, which said that the Devil had rights to human beings because of the Fall and thus had to be paid off to release his claim, Anselm offered a new "satisfaction" theory of atonement. In Anselm's version God's justice required satisfaction from sin that man was responsible for making. But human beings were not able to make adequate satisfaction to meet the demands of justice—only God himself could do so. Since man must satisfy justice but only God was able to, it was necessary for God to become man and sacrifice himself. The argument can be seen influencing a number of medieval texts, perhaps most impressively in the "HARROWING OF HELL" sequence in Passus 18 of *PIERS PLOWMAN,* as well as other texts in which Christ and the Devil debate about their relative rights to human souls.

Anselm's written texts show a profound knowledge of the church fathers, especially AUGUSTINE—he was called "Augustine redivivus." He also shows a familiarity with Aristotelian logic, probably derived secondhand through BOETHIUS. His work ushered in a whole new age of rational debate among Christian theologians, a debate that was to include such thinkers as Peter ABELARD, Albertus Magnus, Thomas AQUINAS and William of OCKHAM, and to dominate Christian theology in the high Middle Ages.

Bibliography

Evans, G. R. *Anselm.* London: Geoffrey Chapman, 1989.

Hopkins, Jasper. *A Companion to the Study of St. Anselm.* Minneapolis: University of Minnesota Press, 1972.

Hopkins, Jasper, and Herbert Richardson, trans. *Complete Philosophical and Theological Treatises of Anselm of Canterbury.* Minneapolis: A.J. Banning Press, 2000.

Southern, R. W. *Saint Anselm: A Portrait in a Landscape.* Cambridge: Cambridge University Press, 1990.

Appar (Tirunavukkaracar) (seventh century)

With CAMPATAR and the later CUNTARAR, Appar is one of the three major poet-saints of the Saivist (devotees of Śiva) bhakti sect of the Tamil language region of southern India. The bhaktis emphasized a personal relationship with Śiva, one of the three chief gods of Hinduism. Appar's poems, like those of the other two saints, are in the traditional lyrical form called *patikam,* which consisted generally of 10 verses, though sometimes of 11. Appar's poems, glorifying Śiva and the shrines sacred to him, form books IV to VI of the sacred bhakti text *Tevarum* (Garland of God).

Tradition says that Appar was raised in a Saivist family, but that he lost his parents early in life and, as a young man, converted to Jainism and became an ascetic monk in that religious movement. Later in life he rejoined his Saivist faith. He says in his poetry that he was suffering from a severe illness that Jain medicine could not cure. But it is said that through the prayers and urging of his sister, Tilagavati, he turned to Śiva for help, and his disease was cured.

Once reconverted, Appar became an ardent bhakti activist. He is reputed to have lived well into his 80s despite suffering religious persecution under the Jainist king Mahendravarman of the Pallava dynasty (reigned 600–630). Appar is reputed to have converted the king to Saivism. He spent the rest of his life establishing monasteries and combating Jainism, Buddhism, and the ritualistic Brahmanism as well, stressing the individual spirituality of Saivism.

Known also as Thirunavukkaracar ("Lord of divine speech"), Appar writes ecstatic poetry that expresses regret for his former Jainist life, praise of Śiva's temples and holy places, and a close, loving relationship with his God, whom he calls "Lord sweet as honey."

Bibliography

Peterson, Indira Viswanathan. *Poems to Śiva: The Hymns of the Tamil Saints.* Princeton, N.J.: Princeton University Press, 1989.

Archpoet (ca. 1130–ca. 1165)

One of the best-known of the 12th-century Latin poets known collectively as "goliards" (because of their tongue-in-cheek devotion to a mythical patron of vagabonds named Golias) is known only by his title *Archpoet.* Like the other poets in GOLIARDIC VERSE, the Archpoet satirizes the church and praises the delights of the flesh, especially gambling, food and drink, and sex.

Ten poems attributed to the Archpoet survive in 35 manuscripts (comprising some 714 lines), and from the poems details of his life can be gleaned. In one poem he claims to be of knightly birth. The poet's patron was the noble and wealthy Reinald von Dassel, archbishop of Cologne and archchancellor of the Emperor Frederick Barbarossa (whom the Archpoet praised in one of his poems). Reinald was made archbishop in 1159 and died in 1167, so the Archpoet must have been active at that time. Dassel apparently had to use his influence more than once to bail the poet out of trouble, for which the Archpoet showed his gratitude in his poem "In Praise of Archbishop Reinald von Dassel."

The Archpoet's best-known poem is his "Confession of Golias," in which he confesses to the sins of gambling, drinking, and sexual excesses. Apparently the poem was written in response to complaints about his excesses made to his patron—complaints he dealt with by freely and comically admitting to them. Another poem, the "Confession of Jonah," seems to have been written after he was dismissed from Dassel's service because of some ill-advised sexual escapade. In the poem he compares himself to Jonah, who refused God's command, and now from exile begs for a second chance.

Several of the Archpoet's poems are begging poems, asking his patron for money. In some poems he writes in quantitative verse—the long and short syllables of classical Latin; sometimes he writes in rhythmic verse—the stressed and unstressed syllables typical of vernacular Germanic poetry. His poems are full of allusions to classical Latin and to Christian texts, and sometimes border on the sacrilegious. His best-known lines, from stanza 12 of his poem X ("The Confession of Golias"), sum up his themes and his attitude:

> *I propose to die in a tavern,*
> *So that wine may be near my mouth as I*
> *die.*
> *Then choruses of angels will happily sing:*
> *"May god be kind to this drinker."*
>
> (qtd. in Hardin and Hasty 1994, 9)

Bibliography

Dronke, Peter. "The Archpoet and the Classics," in *Latin Poetry and the Classical Tradition,* edited by Peter Godman and Oswyn Murray. Oxford: Clarendon Press, 1990, 57–72.

———. "The Art of the Archpoet: A Reading of 'Lingua balbus.' " In *The Interpretation of Medieval Lyric Poetry,* edited by W. H. T. Jackson, 22–43. New York: Columbia University Press, 1980.

Hardin, James, and Will Hasty, eds. "German Writers and Works of the Early Middle Ages: 800–1170," Vol. 148, *Dictionary of Literary Biography.* Detroit: Gale Research, 1994, 8–9.

Watenpuhl, Heinrich, and Heinrich Krefeld, eds. *Die Gedichte des Archipoeta.* Heidelberg, Germany: Carl Winter, 1958.

Arnaut Daniel (Arnaud) (ca. 1150–ca. 1200)

Arnaut Daniel was one of the most esteemed of the TROUBADOUR poets, admired particularly for his technical skill and virtuosity. His verses are written in the *TROBAR RIC* style, which involved intricate rhyme schemes, elaborate ornamentation, and the use of rare words selected mainly for their sound. Arnaut was even known to create words if they fit his purposes. His *VIDA* tells us that his songs were difficult to learn and to comprehend.

Arnaut's *vida* also says that he was born in Ribérac on the Dordogne river in the bishopric of Périgueux in the Aquitaine. Apparently he was of the noble class. Arnaut's fellow troubadours BERTRAN DE BORN and GIRAUT DE BORNELH came from this same general area, and it is likely that Arnaut was well acquainted with them. Like many troubadours, Arnaut traveled between many courts. He claims to have been present at the coronation of the French king Philippe-Auguste in 1180, and it has been suggested that he was at one time in the entourage of RICHARD I Lionheart.

While Arnaut wrote some rather bawdy verse, most of his poetry exalts the notion of true love. For Arnaut, love and art are one: Love inspires and directs his song, and it also spurs him toward moral perfection. As Linda Paterson puts it, for Arnaut "the joy of love, moral worth, and artistic perfection were bound together" (Paterson 1975, 189).

Arnaut's reputation, though, rests mainly on his skill as a technician of verse. While some earlier troubadours debated the merits of different styles, Arnaut generally speaks of polishing and embellishing his verse, which he refers to in one song as *trobar prim,* designating a highly polished style. He is generally credited with inventing the verse form called the sestina, a poem of six six-line stanzas and a concluding three-line stanza called a *congedo.* The same six rhyme words are repeated in each six-line stanza, in an order determined by their placement in the first stanza. The rhyme word of the first line of each stanza begins with the rhyme word from the last line of the previous stanza, and the other rhyme words all move down a line in order. All six words are used in the *congedo,* with half the words used as internal rhymes.

Another of Arnaut's songs, *"L'aur'amara"* ("The Rough Wind"), is lauded by DANTE as one of the best examples of a love poem in the vernacular. In the poem where each long stanza repeats the same rhymes *abcdefgbhhicjklcm,* nearly a third of all the syllables in the poem are part of the rhyme scheme, and the words of the poem are otherwise held together by alliteration and assonance. It is a remarkable technical achievement.

Arnaut was highly admired by PETRARCH, and even more highly by Dante, who considered Arnaut the greatest of the troubadours. He mentions Arnaut several times in *De VULGARI VLOQUENTIA,* and introduces him as well in the 26th canto of the *Purgatorio.* In that canto, Dante has the great Italian poet Guido GUINIZELLI refer to Arnaut as *miglior fabbro del parlar materno,* that is, the "better craftsman in the mother tongue." The use of the term "craftsman" suggests that Dante admired Arnaut particularly for his technical virtuosity. When Dante has Arnaut speak for himself, it is in his native Occitan language. Arnaut is the only character in the DIVINE COMEDY allowed to speak in any language other than Italian—a sign of Dante's respect for Arnaut as the ideal vernacular poet. In the 20th century, Arnaut was also admired by Ezra Pound and T. S. Eliot, and when Eliot dedicated his *Waste Land* to Pound, he used Dante's tribute to Arnaut to do so, calling him *il miglior fabbro:* "the better craftsman."

Bibliography

Arnaut Daniel. *The Poetry of Arnaut Daniel.* Edited and translated by James J. Wilhelm. New York: Garland Press, 1981.

Goldin, Frederick, ed. and trans. *Lyrics of the Troubadours and Trouvères: An Anthology and a History.* Garden City, N.Y.: Doubleday, 1973.

Paterson, Linda M. *Troubadours and Eloquence.* Oxford: Clarendon Press, 1975.

Arthur, King

King Arthur was the legendary king of Britain who became the central figure in a literary tradition that spanned centuries and included hundreds of texts in the later Middle Ages and beyond, even into the 21st century. Over the course of the medieval period, the literary figure of Arthur developed from a Romanized Celtic "leader of battles" to a refined king presiding over the world's most glamorous court, and surrounded by the greatest, most chivalric of knights.

It is possible that Arthur was an historical figure. According to NENNIUS, the purported author of the early ninth-century *Historia Britonium,* Arthur was the *dux bellorum* or leader of battles who led the Britons to success in 12 battles against the Saxons, culminating in a decisive victory at Mount Badon, where he killed 960 of the enemy in one charge. Mount Badon was apparently a historical battle—it is mentioned by the contemporary chronicler GILDAS, though Gildas does not mention Arthur. The *ANNALES CAMBRIAE* (*Welsh Annals*) put Arthur at the Battle of Badon in 516, and say that Arthur and someone named "Medraut" fell at the Battle of Camlann in 537.

After the ultimate Saxon victory, Arthur as the last great Celtic hero became a major figure in Welsh legend and folklore. In the seventh-century poetic lament *GODODDIN,* Arthur is alluded to as a great warrior. In *The SPOILS OF ANNWFN,* he leads an army to the Celtic Otherworld to bring back a magic cauldron. In the complex narrative *CULHWCH AND OLWEN,* Arthur is the center of a court full of heroes—including Kay and Bedivere—who perform miraculous deeds and kill giants.

Arthur grew from a national British hero to a major figure in world literature with the publication of GEOFFREY OF MONMOUTH's *HISTORIA REGUM BRITANNIAE* (ca. 1136), a "History of the Kings of Britain" in Latin prose in which Arthur figures as Britain's greatest king. In Geoffrey, Arthur is the product of an adulterous union between King Uther Pendragon and Ygerne, duchess of Cornwall, after a tryst arranged by the seer Merlin, who transforms Uther into the likeness of Ygerne's husband. Geoffrey extols Arthur as the vanquisher of the Saxons, but also makes him a world conqueror. His wife is Guanhumara, his sword is Caliburn, and his greatest knight is his nephew Gawain. His other nephew, Mordred, betrays him by usurping Arthur's kingdom and his queen. In a final battle at Camlann, Mordred is killed, but Arthur is taken to Avalon, from whence he will return when his wounds are healed. Geoffrey's story provided the basic outline of Arthur's supposed history for the rest of the Middle Ages. In about 1155, WACE translated Geoffrey's story into Anglo-French poetry, adding details like Arthur's round table, a wedding gift from Guenevere's father. In the early 13th century, LAYAMON freely adapted and expanded Wace's story into early MIDDLE ENGLISH verse, the first version of the Arthurian legend in English.

The Arthurian tradition took a different turn in the hands of the late 12th-century French creators of the ROMANCE tradition, MARIE DE FRANCE and CHRÉTIEN DE TROYES. In their texts, Arthur himself moves into a secondary role as his court provides the background for the adventures of some of his individual knights (Gawain, Yvain, Lancelot), and the newly fashionable concept of COURTLY LOVE becomes central to most tales. Chrétien introduces Lancelot as Arthur's greatest knight, who also replaces Mordred as the queen's more sympathetic lover. In his *Le Conte du Graal* (The story of the grail), Chrétien introduces the naïve knight Perceval and the mysterious vessel, the Grail, which becomes a staple of the Arthurian tradition.

In the 13th century, a series of lengthy French prose romances known collectively as the VULGATE CYCLE attempted to pull together and unify a number of elements in the Arthurian tradition, and to fill in the gaps in the story of the mysterious Grail, which becomes in these romances the Holy Grail, the cup from which Christ drank at the Last Supper. The Grail becomes the object of a quest by all of Arthur's knights, but only Sir Perceval, Sir Bors, and Sir GALAHAD are able to achieve the quest. The Vulgate Cycle introduces Merlin into Arthur's reign as his early adviser, and the motif of the sword in the stone by which Arthur proves his legitimacy as king. In these romances, Arthur unwittingly sleeps with his own half sister, Morgause, and begets the traitor Mordred as his own son.

By the 13th century, the popularity of Arthurian romance had spread into most of the vernacular literatures of Europe. Important German versions of some of Chrétien's stories were produced by WOLFRAM VON ESCHENBACH and HARTMAN VON AUE. Versions in Spanish, Portuguese, Italian, Dutch, Norwegian, and Icelandic were composed in the 13th and 14th centuries, and a number of Middle English romances of Arthur appeared in the 14th and 15th centuries.

As the Middle Ages drew to a close, the English knight Sir Thomas MALORY chose to write his own version of the Arthurian legend. He attempted to tell, in a single book, the whole story of King Arthur, from his conception to his mysterious end after the Battle of Camlann. His work, known as *Le MORTE DARTHUR* (ca. 1470), uses the Vulgate Cycle and some English romances as its major sources, and introduces as well the story of TRISTAN AND ISOLDE, making Tristram one of Arthur's knights. Malory's book is the culmination of the medieval legend of King Arthur, and when it was printed by CAXTON in 1485, it brought the Arthurian story to a wider audience than it had ever reached before. Not only did Malory's text provide a summative compilation of the medieval Arthurian tradition, but it also served as the basis of all later versions of the legend, including Tennyson's *Idylls of the King,* T. H. White's *The Once and Future King,* Steinbeck's *Acts of King Arthur and His Noble Knights,* and Thomas Berger's *Arthur Rex.* It is largely to Malory, to Geoffrey of Monmouth, and to Chrétien de Troyes that the legend of King Arthur owes its position as the most widespread and influential literary tradition in Western literature.

Bibliography

Baswell, Christopher, and William Sharpe, eds. *The Passing of Arthur: New Essays in Arthurian Tradition.* New York: Garland, 1988.

Braswell, Mary Flowers, and John Bugge, eds. *The Arthurian Tradition: Essays in Convergence.* Tuscaloosa: University of Alabama Press, 1988.

Fenster, Thelma S., ed. *Arthurian Women: A Casebook.* New York: Garland, 1996.

Fries, Maureen, and Jeanie Watson, eds. *Approaches to Teaching the Arthurian Tradition.* New York: Modern Language Association, 1992.

Lacy, Norris J., and Geoffrey Ashe. *The Arthurian Handbook.* New York: Garland, 1988.

Lagorio, Valerie M., and Mildred Leake Day, eds. *King Arthur through the Ages.* 2 vols. New York: Garland, 1990.

Loomis, Roger Sherman. *The Development of Arthurian Romance.* New York: Norton, 1963.

Ashby, George (ca. 1390–ca. 1475)

Like Geoffrey CHAUCER and Thomas HOCCLEVE, George Ashby was a government employee who also became known as a poet. For more than 40 years, by his own testimony, Ashby worked as clerk of the signet under King Henry VI and his queen, Margaret of Anjou (his job was to write out bills to be sent to the secretary of state for signature). A Lancastrian during the turbulent Wars of the Roses, Ashby's fortunes rose and fell with those of his royal patrons: He wrote his *Prisoner's Reflections* while imprisoned at Fleet, and wrote *The Active Policy of a Prince* while charged with the education of Henry and Margaret's son, Edward of Lancaster, the prince of Wales.

Ashby's early life is obscure, but he implies in his poetry that he was associated with the royal household from an early age, and that he was educated there by royal tutors (rather than in the church). He is known to have owned land in Middlesex. He was a favorite of Queen Margaret, and after the resounding defeat of her army by the Yorkist Edward IV at Towton in 1461, Ashby was incarcerated. While at Fleet Prison (ca. 1461–63), he wrote a poem of some 50 RHYME ROYAL stanzas, displaying the influence of Chaucer not only in its verse form, but also in the reflection of BOETHIUS in the tone of the consolation.

He acknowledges this debt to Chaucer in his other major poem, *The Active Policy of a Prince,* in which he calls himself an "apprentice" of Chaucer, GOWER, and LYDGATE. That poem, also in rhyme royal, is intended as a book of instruction in the art of statecraft for Prince Edward. Writing in about 1470, the 80-year-old Ashby addresses the 17-year-old prince as the hope of the realm. In it Ashby emphasizes Edward's lineage (likely a reaction to Yorkist rumors of the prince's bastardy). He then advises Edward to study the examples of history to learn what kinds of behavior to emulate and what to eschew. He chides the contemporary noble class for its greed, and advises Edward to keep the common people prosperous to avoid rebellion, not to allow other nobles to become richer than the king, and not to show mercy to traitors. Much of this advice, as Scattergood points out, seems to be designed to keep Edward from committing the same mistakes his father had made (1971, 284).

The single manuscript version of *The Active Policy of a Prince* is followed by a long series of rhyme royal stanzas (1,260 lines) that loosely translate Latin maxims. Generally entitled the *Dicta et opinions deversorum philosophorum* (Sayings and opinions of diverse philosophers), this has generally been considered a separate text. Scattergood, however, considers it an appendix to *The Active Policy*, comprising further advice for the young prince.

Prince Edward, killed the following year in the Battle of Tewkesbury, was never given a chance to put any of Ashby's advice into practice. After this final Lancastrian defeat, the aged Ashby must certainly have lost his position in government, and doubtlessly died shortly afterward. His poetry has been generally abjured as dull, pedestrian, and uninspired, though it does give us an interesting view of the mind of a middle-class bureaucrat during a tumultuous time in English history.

Bibliography

Bateson, Mary, ed. *George Ashby's Poems.* London: Published for the Early English Text Society by the Oxford University Press, 1965.

Green, Richard Firth. *Poets and Princepleasers: Literature and the English Court in the Late Middle Ages.* Toronto: University of Toronto Press, 1980.

Scattergood, V. J. *Politics and Poetry in the Fifteenth Century.* New York: Barnes and Noble, 1971.

———. *Reading the Past: Essays on Medieval and Renaissance Literature.* Blackrock, Ireland: Four Courts Press, 1996.

Athelstan (Aethelstan) (ca. 895–939)

Son of King Edward the elder and grandson of ALFRED THE GREAT, King Athelstan was perhaps the most powerful monarch of all the royal house of Wessex, and indeed the first who could legitimately claim to be king of all England. His greatest triumph was the major victory he won over the combined forces of the kings of Scotland and Strathclude (in Wales) and the Norse king of Dublin who claimed the throne of Northumbria—a victory that ensured Northumbria would be part of a united England, and provided the matter for one of the great OLD ENGLISH heroic poems, *The BATTLE OF BRUNANBURH.*

Athelstan was probably the illegitimate son of King Edward, and was raised in the household of his aunt, Athelfled, at Gloucester in Mercia. He became king upon the death of his father in 924, and quickly began to extend his power over the Celts and Britons in the west and over the Viking lords of the north. The Norse king Sitric Caech of York did recognize Athelstan's sovereignty almost immediately, and to strengthen their alliance Athelstan gave Sitric the hand of his sister Eadgyth in marriage in 926, and Athelstan marched into York as their king when Sitric died the next year.

Athelstan was adept at creating alliances through marriage and diplomacy. Four other sisters were married to European princes, including Charles III ("the Simple") of France and Otto I of Germany. He was also foster father to Hakon the Good, later king of Norway. When diplomacy failed, Athelstan found that the threat of force could be a valuable tool. He forced the Welsh to accept a boundary of his making, and stopped Welsh raids on Mercia while exacting tribute from their leaders. He defeated the Cornish and established a boundary with them, taking their King Hoel hostage. He reached an alliance with the Scots that lasted for seven years. During the peace, Athelstan strengthened his power through new law codes and regulated currency. He also was a collector of holy relics and works of art and a generous patron of a number of religious houses, no doubt to consolidate their support.

The crisis of Athelstan's reign occurred when Constantine II, king of Scotland, married his daughter to Olaf Guthfrithsson, future king of Dublin and potential heir of his kinsman Sitric Caech's Northumbrian throne. Perceiving this as a threat to his power, Athelstan invaded Scotland and devastated Constantine's army. In response, Olaf brought his Norse army from Dublin, joined forces with Constantine and the Welsh king of Strathclude, and began raiding in Mercia. Athelstan and his brother Edmund met this enemy alliance in 937 at a place called Brunanburh and won the most decisive battle of his time, virtually ensuring a unified England. The battle passed into legend, and Athelstan's courage and leadership were celebrated in Old English verse within a few years of the battle. The poem, *The Battle of Brunanburh,* was inserted into *The* ANGLO-SAXON CHRONICLE as the entry for the year 937.

Athelstan died in Gloucester two years later. He was buried in Malmesbury Abbey, one of the religious houses he had generously supported. Unmarried and childless, Athelstan was succeeded on the throne by his brother, Edmund.

Bibliography

Campbell, Alistair, ed., *The Battle of Brunanburh.* London: W. Heinemann, 1938.

Muir, Bernard James, ed., *Leoð: Six Old English Poems: A Handbook.* New York: Gordon and Breach, 1989.

Rodrigues, Louis J., trans., *Three Anglo-Saxon Battle Poems.* Felinfach, U.K.: Llanerch Publishers, 1996.

Atsumori Zeami (ca. 1400)

ZEAMI's play *Atsumori* is the most anthologized and probably the most performed drama of medieval Japanese Nō theater. Like many Nō plays, *Atsumori* is based on an incident in classical Japanese literature—in this case the ninth chapter of *The* TALE OF THE HEIKE—in which the ghost of Atsumori, a 16-year-old warrior killed in battle, confronts his slayer years later, obsessed with revenge.

Atsumori is what is known as a "warrior play"—one of five basic categories of Nō drama. In a warrior play, the protagonist (or *shite*) of the drama is the ghost of a warrior killed in battle. In warrior plays prior to Zeami, these ghosts were shown as suffering in a Buddhist afterlife where they cannot achieve transcendence, where they are still consumed by the frenzy of battle and passion for bloodshed, and continue to fight one another rather than finding peace. Zeami, whose plays were performed before a cultured courtly audience, altered the direction of the warrior play to reflect the kind of beauty and elegance appreciated by his patrons.

The story of Atsumori was well known from the *Tale of the Heike.* Near the end of a battle at Icho-no-tani on Suma Bay between the Heike and their archenemies, the Genji, the Heike are driven into the sea. But the young warrior Atsumori, more at home in the refined court setting of the capital than on the battlefield, has left his flute, and returns to retrieve it. But before he can escape, the battle-hardened Genji veteran Kumagai no Naozane engages him in battle. Having overcome Atsumori, Naozane removes his helmet and realizes the young Heike is only a boy of 16, about the age of his own son. After an internal struggle, Naozane kills the young warrior, knowing that his approaching comrades will do so in any case. Naozane then finds the flute, an emblem of noble refinement, under Atsumori's armor. Unable to reconcile himself to the brutality of his act and the warrior's way of life, Naozane rejects his warrior life and becomes a Buddhist priest.

No doubt Zeami's audience would have been familiar with this classic story. His play opens, as a warrior play conventionally does, with the entrance of the *waki,* or secondary actor, usually a monk or priest. In this case, the priest identifies himself as Naozane, now called Renshō. He reveals his remorse over killing Atsumori, and announces that he is on his way back to Icho-no-tani, scene of the battle, in order to pray for the dead boy. Atsumori himself (the *shite* or lead actor) now enters from the other direction. He is in the guise of a young grass cutter or reaper, and sings an entrance song that does not reveal his true identity. He plays the flute, which surprises Renshō, who did not expect to find such courtly refinement in such a pastoral setting. The priest now questions the young reaper, who, as a sign of his emotional agitation, begins to dance. The disguised Atsumori now leaves the stage.

Between the first and second acts of a Nō drama, an interlude occurs. In this case, a villager passes by and, in response to Renshō's questioning, relates the "backstory" of the play—the familiar tale of Atsumori's death. This intermission, as the audience considers it, leads into the climactic act of the play, the *kyū*. After Renshō sings a "waiting song" in which he expresses his desire to perform holy rites for Atsumori's soul, the ghost of the boy enters again, this time in the garb of a warrior so that there can be no doubt about his identity.

Now Atsumori rehearses his obsession with his death, the passion that will not allow him to achieve transcendence and enlightenment. The chorus, acting as an extension of his own mind, helps recite Atsumori's thoughts as his frenzy forces him to dance again, reliving his final battle with Naozane. As the dance reaches its climax, Atsumori raises his sword to Renshō. But he ultimately sees in Renshō not an enemy but rather a Buddhist priest. He lets go of his passion, and as the play draws to a close, Atsumori asks Renshō to pray for him, and walks off, we assume to his salvation.

What allows *Atsumori* to transcend the pattern of previous warrior plays is Zeami's brilliant twist of making the priest not simply a random character but rather the ghost's own killer. The confrontation is profound: Not only was Atsumori devastated by his violent death in the bloom of his youth, but Naozane, too, was emotionally scarred by the brutal act he was forced to commit. Both characters are tormented by their obsessions, and each realizes that he needs the help of the other to transcend that torment. In the end, Naozane is able to pray for the soul of the man he killed, and Atsumori is able to forgive the man who killed him.

Bibliography

Hare, Thomas. Blenman. *Zeami's Style: The Noh Plays of Zeami Motokiyo.* Stanford, Calif.: Stanford University Press, 1986.

Japanese Nō Dramas. Edited and translated by Royall Tyler. London: Penguin, 1992.

Rimerr, J. Thomas, and Yamazaki Masakazu, trans. *On the Art of Nō Drama: The Major Treatises of Zeami.* Princeton, N.J.: Princeton University Press, 1984.

Terasaki, Etsuko. *Figures of Desire: Wordplay, Spirit Possession, Fantasy, Madness, and Mourning in Japanese Noh Plays.* Ann Arbor: Center for Japanese Studies, University of Michigan, 2002.

Attar, Faridoddin (Farid ud-Din) (ca. 1145–1221)

Attar was a Persian poet, Sufi mystic, and biographer. Some 30 of his works survive, including long narrative poems, biographies of saints, and short mystical lyrics.

Very little is known of Attar's life beyond what can be found in his works. He seems to have been born in Nichapur, an important center of Sufi mysticism in northeast Iran near what today is the city of Meshed. The name *Attar* means "druggist," which at the time referred to anyone working as a physician; in his poetry, Attar describes working with patients. Attar was little known in his own time, but his reputation has grown steadily over the years and he has been very influential on later writers. Most scholars believe he was killed in 1221, when the Mongol army destroyed Nichapur and slaughtered the population.

Attar's most influential work is *Manteq al-Tayr* (*The Conference of the Birds*), an epic-length allegory in rhyming couplets. In it Attar creates a new form of frame tale—a continuous narrative in which other shorter narratives are embedded. In the narrative, a large congregation of birds meets in preparation for a pilgrimage to find the mythical Simurgh, whom they regard as their king, though they have never seen him. The birds choose the Hoopoe as their guide, and he immediately sets about strengthening their resolve, arguing the birds out of various attachments to the world through a series of exemplary tales.

To convince them of the need to give up all worldly impediments, the Hoopoe tells the story of Sheikh Sam'an, the longest of the 100 or so tales in the poem. In it Sheikh Sam'an abandons his faith for love of a Christian girl who convinces him to burn the KORAN, drink wine, ignore the true faith (Islam), worship idols, and ultimately to tend a herd of pigs. Sam'an is saved through the prayers of his disciples and returns to the true faith. His Christian girlfriend, realizing the error of her ways, follows him and converts to Islam on her deathbed.

It was common in Middle Eastern literature to tell moral tales using animals and birds, and traditionally a bird was symbolic of the soul. The allegory of *The Conference of the Birds* seems clearly to indicate that the soul must give up worldly attachments if it seeks God, here represented by the Simurgh. In the tale the Hoopoe finally leads the birds on an arduous journey through seven valleys to the palace of Simurgh. Of the thousands who start the journey, only 30 birds (or *si murgh* in Persian) arrive at the palace, and they find only a set of mirrors in which they look upon themselves: By ridding themselves of worldly encumbrances, they have become the God they seek—God, it turns out, is to be sought within ourselves.

Attar's other works include a collection of 97 biographies of Sufi saints, *Tazkerat ol-ouliya*. In the collection Attar includes a good deal of romantic elaboration of his sources. One of his best-known biographies in this collection is his story of Hallaj, a mystic-martyr to whom Attar was especially devoted. Also fairly well known is *Mosibatname* (The book of affliction), which, like *The Conference of the Birds,* is made up of a frame story containing a number of embedded parables and tales. In it a Wayfarer requests 40 special powers to cure his affliction, but is refused all of them. In the end he casts himself into the Ocean of Soul only to recognize that he himself is the essence of God. In *Oshtoname* (The book of the camel), Attar's protagonist commits suicide, suffering and dying for the sake of love. Attar's other significant works include *Elahiname*, a conversation among a king and his six sons, *Pandname* (The book of counsel), and a number of ecstatic lyric poems.

Attar focuses on several Sufi themes in his poetry. Like all mystics, Sufis emphasize the need for direct personal experience of God, and often describe visions during which God speaks directly to the mystic. Again as with most mystics, the experience of God transcends time and space, and in eternity souls are permanently united with God. Specifically Attar focuses on two important Sufi themes: First, that the soul is in great pain when it is apart from God; and second, that to find God one must eliminate worldly distractions and seek God within oneself.

Ultimately, Attar's work is interesting in its use of the frame narrative, a device later used in the *THOUSAND AND ONE NIGHTS* as well as by CHAUCER and by BOCCACCIO. But his poetry also has a universal appeal to any reader interested in the way of the mystic, and in this sense Attar has been particularly admired by Sufi writers.

Bibliography

Arberry, Arthur John. *Muslim Saints and Mystics: Episodes from the Tadhkirat al-Auliya.* London: Routledge and Kegan Paul, 1979.

Attar, Farid ud-Din. *The Conference of the Birds.* Translated by Afkham Darbadi and Dick Davis. New York: Penguin, 1984.

Rypka, Jan, et al. *History of Iranian Literature.* Dordrecht, Netherlands: D. Reidel, 1968.

Aucassin et Nicollette (either ca. 1230 or ca. 1270)

This anonymous verse narrative has come down to us in only one manuscript, Paris, Bibliothèque Nationale fr. 2168, but it easily proves to be one of the most charming and intriguing medieval French tales about the love of two young people, one of whom is a Christian (he), and the other originally a Muslim (she). Formally the text consists of 21 verse sections alternating with 20 sections in prose, which makes it a *chantefable,* a term coined by the poet. The author might have originated in the Picardie, and, if we can believe an allusion to himself at the beginning of the text (I, 2), he was already an old man when he composed this charming poem. Despite many scholarly debates about this line, the possibly ironic element of this self-reference has hardly ever been mentioned.

The date of *Aucassin et Nicolette* is very unclear. Some scholars argue for the first half of the 13th century because of an allusion to a 20-year war that could refer to the Albigensian Crusade, which would definitely place the text beyond 1229. Others suggested a date around 1270 on paleographical grounds and because of a reference to a new kind of coin minted only after 1266.

The author demonstrates an extraordinary sense of humor mixed with a remarkable contempt for the church's teachings, such as when he mentions that harpists and JONGLEURS provide entertainment to the evil sinners in hell, which to Aucassin, kept in prison by his father because of his love for Nicolette, seems much preferable to paradise. Whereas the latter is a place where "old priests go, and old cripples, and the maimed who grovel day and night in front of altars and in old crypts . . . dying of hunger, thirst, cold, and misery," hell to him appears much more appealing: "That is where beautiful courtly ladies go, because they have two or three lovers as well as their husbands . . . I want to go with them, provided I have with me Nicolette, my very sweet friend" (Burgess 1988, VI). Nicolette, however, who quickly proves to be the main character in this tale—obviously the only one truly active and competent enough to strategize how to realize her love for Aucassin—had been kidnapped from her royal parents in Carthage and sold as a slave girl by some Saracen traders. The viscount of Beaucaire had bought and baptized her, and taken her on as his godchild. Aucassin's father, the Count Garin of Beaucaire, is involved in a war with Count Bougar of Valence, and he desperately wants to convince his son to be knighted and lead his troops. He strikes a deal with Aucassin, offering him permission to talk with his beloved and kiss her once if he takes up arms for his father. But the latter breaks his promise once his son has defeated the opponent and imprisons Aucassin because he insists on his love for Nicolette. Nicolette manages to escape and hides in a forest where she creates a bower where Aucassin (now released from prison by his father) eventually finds her with the help of a group of children. The lovers depart together and travel across the sea until they reach the curious country of Torelore where everything has turned to its opposite: The king lies in childbed while his wife wages war using rotten crab-apples, eggs, and fresh cheeses. When Aucassin gets involved and kills many of the enemies, the king of Torelore stops him, saying: "It is not our custom to kill each other" (XXXII). But when a Saracen pirate ship arrives, they are all taken prisoner, and the lovers are placed on two different ships. Aucassin accidentally returns to Beaucaire, where he is liberated and entrusted with the land because his parents have died three years earlier. Nicolette, in the meantime, is taken to Carthage, where her parents no longer recognize her until she reveals the secret to them. In order to find her lover, she soon dons a minstrel's garb and secretly returns to Provence, disguised as a man. After she has tested Aucassin's love for her, she recovers her true appearance, and the two lovers marry.

Although the narrative seems to be very light, facetious, even nonsensical entertainment, the satirical author offers profound criticism of military operations, explores the significance of gender roles, seriously critiques the medieval practice of marriage arrangements according to social, financial, and political criteria in total disregard of the young people's feelings and desires, and also examines the possibility of interracial marriages. This *chantefable* also proves to be interesting because it operates with both prose and verse, opens up many different perspectives toward the new money-based economy (Nicolette pays five sous to the children in return for their help to direct Aucassin to her hiding place in the woods; Aucassin also gives money to a man in the woods), discusses the danger of piracy and kidnapping, and emphasizes the significance of truthfulness and keeping promises (consider Aucassin's father). Finally, the poet also sheds light on the life of minstrels and jongleurs.

Bibliography

Aucassin et Nicolette. Edited by Jean Dufournet. Paris: Garnier-Flamarion, 1984.

"Aucassin et Nicolette. English & French," edited by Anne Elizabeth Cobby, translated with an introduction by Glyn S. Burgess, in *Voyage de Charlemagne à Jérusalem et à Constantinople: English & French.* New York: Garland, 1988.

Vance, Eugene. "The Word at Heart: *Aucassin et Nicolette* as a Medieval Comedy of Language," *Yale French Studies* 45 (1970): 33–51.

Gilbert, Jane. "The Practice of Gender in *Aucassin et Nicolette*," *Forum for Modern Language Studies* 33, no. 3 (1997): 217–228.

Krueger, Roberta L. "Beyond Debate: Gender in Play in Old French Courtly Fiction Author(s)." In *Gender in Debate from the Early Middle Ages to the Renaissance,* edited by Thelma S. Fenster and A. Clare Lees, 79–95. New York: Palgrave, 2002.

Albrecht Classen

Augustine of Hippo, Saint (354–430)

Saint Augustine of Hippo is perhaps the most influential of the fathers of the western Christian church. He wrote voluminously, helping to establish what became orthodox Christianity as distinguished from what are now seen as heretical sects of Manichaeism and Pelagianism. For literature, his most important contributions are probably his CONFESSIONS (his spiritual autobiography telling the story of his early life and his eventual conversion to Christianity) and his development of a fourfold method of reading Scripture—an exegetical approach that became important in the writing and interpretation of later medieval literature.

Augustine was born in the North African city of Thagaste on November 13, 354. His father was a pagan but his mother, Monica, was Christian, so he grew up acquainted with the Christian faith. He received a classical Roman education in nearby Madaura and, in 371, traveled to Carthage to continue his instruction. He became devoted to philosophy, especially that of Cicero, and while studying the Christian Scriptures was appalled by the immoral behavior of the patriarchs and by the anthropomorphic depictions of God. He turned to Manichaeism, with its idea of a finite God and warring good and evil principles, as a rational alternative and remained a member of that sect for nine years.

In 375 Augustine returned to Thagaste to teach, but he quickly went back to Carthage and, in 383, to Rome in search of better students. He became disenchanted with Manichaeism and became a skeptic for several years. But in Rome, he met Bishop Ambrose of Milan, who showed him a different, spiritual way to read the Scriptures, and ultimately he was converted to Christianity and baptized by Ambrose in 387. He then returned to Africa to found a monastery and to write. It was about this time that he wrote what is still his most popular work, his *Confessions,* a spiritual autobiography describing his journey to embrace the Christian faith. In 396, he was made bishop of Hippo, and his fame as a theologian and champion of orthodox Christianity was spreading throughout the Roman Empire.

In his early years as bishop, Augustine's efforts were spent chiefly in writing against the Manichean heresy he had himself been part of. Since the Manicheans rejected the Old Testament, particularly the book of Genesis, Augustine felt he had to rescue Genesis from the absurdities of a literal reading. His major text in this debate, *The Literal Meaning of Genesis,* was begun and abandoned in about 393, and finally published in 413. In the earlier version Augustine speaks of the spiritual understanding of Scripture, and details three spiritual levels of reading beyond the literal level. While Augustine's categories—allegorical or figurative, analogical (which saw Old Testament figures as prefiguring New Testament ones), and etiological (which deals with causes)—are not quite identical with the categories later used by Thomas AQUINAS and DANTE, Augustine here does set the groundwork for that kind of reading of Scripture and, by extension, of literature.

Augustine turned to the Donatist sect next. A sect of the church claiming that sacraments performed by sinful priests were null and void, the Donatists outnumbered orthodox Christians in Hippo when Augustine first arrived in the city. He argued that the sacrament is holy in itself, and that it did not depend upon the holiness of the priest. Eventually the Donatists were outlawed by the Roman emperor.

After this the Pelagian heresy demanded much of Augustine's attention until about 430. The controversy with the Pelagians was over the nature of grace. Pelagius had claimed that human beings, by their own free will, could perform good works and thereby be saved. Augustine argued that no good deed could be done without God's grace. He proposed that humans were predestined by God to receive grace—no one could merit the gift of grace, and no one could fail to be saved if he had received God's grace. The doctrine became important for John Calvin during the Protestant Reformation.

In the meantime, however, the classical world was shaken by Alaric the Visigoth's sacking of Rome in 410. Looking for a scapegoat, many Romans blamed the downfall of the empire on Christianity. Augustine took it upon himself to defend the church against these charges, and in response wrote his most influential book, *De civitate Dei,* or *The* CITY OF GOD. Finally finished in 427, the book argues that the world has always been divided into two cities: the City of God and the earthly city. The City of God is eternal, and peopled by all those God has saved through his grace. The earthly city is the city of the damned. The cities exist simultaneously in the world, but only the inhabitants of the one are destined for salvation.

Saint Augustine died in Hippo on August 28, 430, even as another Germanic tribe, the Vandals, were besieging his own city. He left nearly 120 major treatises, as well as hundreds of sermons and letters. His powerful writing, his profound thought, and his skillful rhetoric made him the dominant voice in the formative years of Latin Christendom. No less a figure than St. JEROME, author of the Vulgate translation of the Bible, called Augustine "the second founder of the faith."

Bibliography

Augustine. *City of God.* Edited by David Knowles and translated by Henry Bettenson. New York: Penguin, 1984.

———. *Confessions.* Translated by Philip Burton. London: Everyman, 2001.

Brown, Peter Robert Lamont. *Augustine of Hippo: A Biography.* Rev. ed. Berkeley: University of California Press, 2000.

Fitzgerald, Allan D., et al., eds. *Augustine through the Ages: An Encyclopedia.* Grand Rapids, Mich.: William B. Eerdmans, 1999.

Auto de los Reyes Magos (1150–1200)

The *Auto de los Reyes Magos* (Play of the three wise kings) constitutes the one and only example of a 12th-century liturgical play in Castilian—the romance "dialect" that is now modern Spanish. While there was a significant tradition of liturgical drama in Latin, the emergence of such a tradition in the vernacular is noteworthy because Castilian was not adopted as the official language of the administration until the reign of Alfonso the Learned (1252–84). Since its modern publication in 1863 by Amador de los Ríos, however, the play has remained at the center of a critical controversy over the very existence of a vernacular liturgical tradition west of Catalonia. Early critics asserted the existence of such a tradition and claimed that the lack of examples is predicated on the destruction of so many Castilian manuscripts during the many wars that engulfed medieval Castile. Subsequently, opinion has begun to change and since the 1950s, critics have come to acknowledge that the lack of a manuscript record may attest to the fact that medieval Castile did not possess a tradition of religious drama.

Comprising only 147 poetic lines of varying syllabic length, the *Auto de los Reyes Magos* that we know today may be only a fragment of what was originally a much longer work. Some critics have nevertheless suggested that the surviving version of the play may indeed be complete. Structurally, the play is divided into five scenes that focus on the soliloquies by Gaspar, Baltasar and Melchor, their journey on the road to Bethlehem, their visit with King Herod, a soliloquy by Herod, and the rabbinical response in Herod's court.

Aside from being composed in vernacular romance, the play is remarkable for the realism of its characters and several dramatic innovations. The responses of King Herod and the three kings forge the central conflict between belief in Christ's birth and non-belief. For his part, Herod is skeptical and cannot believe in the existence of a king more powerful than himself. The reactions of the three kings reveal a preoccupation with verisimilitude—or believability. While each of them ultimately accepts the validity of the sign, their responses vary and model a variety of plausible human responses.

While Gaspar is the most skeptical of the three, Baltasar immediately accepts the star as a sign of the Messiah's birth. Melchor initially doubts the veracity of the star but ultimately accepts it.

The play is also unique in that the gifts that the kings bring to Bethlehem do not function simply as signs but as tests of whether the baby is an earthly king, a mortal man or, indeed, the Messiah. Another noteworthy innovation is the final scene in which the rabbinical authorities disagree on how to respond to Herod's appeal for guidance and ultimately denounce themselves for not speaking the truth. These innovations reveal the degree to which early vernacular drama was free to experiment in ways not possible in the liturgical Latin tradition.

Certainly another area of experimentation centers on the use of the vernacular dialect Castilian and multiple metric forms. In attempting to examine possible sources of the *Auto de los Reyes Magos,* critics have dedicated considerable effort to the cultural identity of the author. Was he a Gascon, a Catalan, a Mozarab—a Christian living in Muslim Spain—or someone else? To answer this question, one must examine word choices, the presence of (im)perfect rhyme, and the manner in which short Latin vowels become diphthongs—two vowels forming a single syllabic unit.

Bibliography

Donovan, Richard B. *The Liturgical Drama in Medieval Spain.* Toronto: Pontifical Institute of Mediaeval Studies, 1958.

Hardison, O. B. *Christian Rite and Christian Drama in the Middle Ages: Essays in the Origin and Early History of Modern Drama.* Baltimore: Johns Hopkins University Press, 1965.

Regueiro, José. "El *Auto de los reyes magos* y el teatro litúrgico medieval," *Hispanic Review* 45 (1977): 149–164.

Shergold, N. D. *A History of the Spanish Stage from Medieval Times until the End of the Seventeenth Century.* Oxford: Clarendon Press, 1967.

Sturdevant, Winifred. *The "Misterio de los Reyes Magos": Its Position in the Development of the Mediaeval Legend of the Three Kings.* Baltimore: The Johns Hopkins Studies in Romance Literaturas and Languages, 1927.

Wardropper, Bruce W. "The Dramatic Texture of the *Auto de los Reyes Magos,*" *MLN* 70 (1955): 46–50.

John Parrack

Averroës (Ibn Rushd) (1126–1198)

The most important Muslim Aristotelian philosopher and the most renowned scholar of Islamic Spain was Ibn Rushd, known in the West as Averroës the Commentator for his influential commentaries on Aristotle. Averroës was a jurist, a physician, an astronomer, and a prolific writer whose commentaries, through translations into Hebrew and Latin composed by Andalusian Jews, exerted an influence on medieval Jewish philosophy and Latin scholasticism even greater than he had on Muslim philosophy.

Averroës was born in Córdoba in 1126 to a family of learned jurists. Details of his early education are unknown, but he clearly had excellent training in law, grammar, literature, medicine, and theology in his early years. He is known to have been in Marrakesh in 1153, and seems to have met 'Abd al-Mu'min, the first Almohad ruler of Spain. He returned to Marrakesh in 1163 and became acquainted with the court vizier and physician Ibn Tufayl, who introduced Averroës to the new Almohad ruler, Abū Ya'qūb Yūsuf, whose interest in philosophy led him to ask Averroës to compose Arabic commentaries on some of Aristotle's more obscure works. Averroës's first commentary appeared in 1169, the same year he was appointed to a judgeship in Seville.

In 1171 Averroës returned to Córdoba, where according to some sources he became chief judge. Then in 1182, upon the retirement of his old sponsor Ibn Tufayl, Averroës became court physician, a position he kept after Abū Ya'qūb Yūsuf was succeeded by his son Abū Yūsuf Ya'qūb in 1184. But in 1195, for reasons that remain obscure, Averroës was disgraced and exiled to Lucenna (near Córdoba). It seems likely that the dismissal from court was prompted by conservative religious authorities' objections to some of his philosophical arguments, since all of his philosophical and theological texts were burnt in conjunction with his exile. At some point, however, Averroës was pardoned and allowed to return to Marrakesh, where he lived in retirement until his death in 1198.

Averroës wrote 38 commentaries on Aristotle, of which 28 are extant in Arabic, 36 in Hebrew, and 34 in Latin. He considered it his primary task to correct the erroneous interpretations of Aristotle made by earlier philosophers, in particular the 10th-century eastern Muslim philosopher Avicenna. The commentaries—on such texts as Aristotle's *Physics, Metaphysics, Rhetoric, Poetics, De anima,* and others—are of three types: *major* (which contain the text as well as commentary), *middle* (an extensive interpretive essay), and *epitome* (a shorter interpretation). For some Aristotelian texts, he wrote all three types of commentary. In addition Averroës wrote commentaries on Plato's *Republic,* Porphyry's *Isagoge,* Ptolemy's *Almagest,* and other classical Greek texts. In addition, he wrote influential works on Islamic law (*Bidāyat al-mujtahid*) and on medicine (*al-Kulliyyāt*). He also wrote works defending the study of philosophy against those who considered it incompatible with strict Islamic law. His best-known work in this vein is the *Tahāfut al-Tahāfut* (*The Incoherence of the Incoherence*), a direct response to the Muslim attack on Aristotelianism (*The Incoherence of the Philosophers*) by the Persian scholar AL-GAZĀLI (d. 1111).

Averroës's influence on medieval and Renaissance European thought cannot be overstated. Through his commentaries, the texts and interpretations of Aristotle's works made available in Europe stimulated philosophers in the Latin West and in Judaism. Some of the doctrines with which he became associated in the West were the idea of the eternity of the world, the denial of individual providence, and most important (following from his discussion of divine and human intellect), the denial of individual immortality. All of these doctrines were condemned by orthodox Christian theologians. Latin "Averroists," however, developed what became known as the doctrine of the double truth, by which they claimed that philosophy and theology could reach truths that are mutually contradictory. Averroës himself never made such a claim—he argued that his views were compatible with Islamic faith—but the doctrine of the double-truth seems to have become popular at the University of Paris in the 13th century.

Bibliography

Averroës. *Tahafut al-Tahafut (The Incoherence of the Incoherence).* Translated by Simon van den Bergh. 2 vols. London: Luzac, 1954.

Butterworth, Charles E., ed. and trans. *Averroes' Middle Commentaries on Aristotle's Categories and De interpretatione.* Princeton, N.J.: Princeton University Press, 1983.

———, ed. and trans. *Averroës' Three Short Commentaries on Aristotle's "Topics," "Rhetoric," and "Poetics."* Albany: State University of New York Press, 1977.

Davidson, Herbert A. *Alfarabi, Avicenna, and Averroes on Intellect: Their Cosmologies, Theories of the Active Intellect, and Theories of Human Intellect.* New York: Oxford University Press, 1992.

Hyman, Arthur, and James J. Walsh. *Philosophy in the Middle Ages: The Christian, Islamic, and Jewish Traditions.* 2nd ed. Indianapolis, Ind.: Hackett, 1983.

Leaman, Oliver. *Averroes and His Philosophy.* Oxford: Clarendon Press, 1988.

Rosenthal, E. I. J., ed. and trans. *Averroës' Commentary on Plato's Republic.* Reprint with corrections. Cambridge: Cambridge University Press, 1969.

Awntyrs off Arthure at the Terne Wathelyne, The (ca. 1375–1425)

The Awntyrs off Arthure at the Terne Wathelyne, a poem written in MIDDLE ENGLISH, is an important contribution to the ALLITERATIVE REVIVAL. The poem is an Arthurian ROMANCE but, interestingly, does not detail the adventures of King ARTHUR as its title suggests. Instead, it tells two separate stories, and Sir GAWAIN is the only character with an active role throughout the poem.

Scholars have estimated the date of composition of *The Awntyrs off Arthure at the Terne Wathelyne* to be from the late 14th century to early 15th century, although recent scholarship narrows this time frame to the first quarter of the 15th century. The 715-line poem is written in ALLITERATIVE VERSE in the Northwest Midland dialect, with 13-line stanzas comprising nine four-stress long lines, rhyming *ababababc*, and a four-line "wheel" rhyming *dddc*. Four extant manuscripts of the poem are found in the text of Oxford, Bodleian Library: MS Douce 324, the "Ireland-Blackburne" MS, the Lincoln Cathedral Library MS 91 (the "Thornton Manuscript"), and the Lambeth Palace Library MS 491.

The poem is separated into two distinct sections. The first half depicts the visit and prophecy of a ghost, Gaynour's (Guenevere's) mother's spirit, and the advice the ghost gives to Gaynour and Gawayn. Although the ghost's soul is tortured because of her adulterous life, and Gaynor's character in Arthurian literature is also typically adulterous, this is not the emphasis of the ghost's speech to Gaynour. For example, when Gaynour asks what prayers she should perform to help the ghost's soul, she advises Gaynour to be charitable to the poor, as if that is more valuable to the salvation of her soul. The ghost holds up an ideal of the common good for the commonwealth, a relevant issue in medieval society in which it is incumbent upon the rich to have mercy upon the poor, and the powerful to pity the weak. The poem also addresses contemporary issues such as the common practice of usurping lands during battles, and criticizes the covetous ways of King Arthur, advising that pride offends God the most. The discourse regarding lands evolves into a prophecy about the fall of Arthur's kingdom, and in Awntyrs, Arthur's fall is attributed primarily to his pride and his covetous nature rather than to the betrayal of Guenevere and Mordred, as traditionally depicted in Arthurian literature.

The second half of the poem begins at approximately line 339 after the ghost has exited and Queen Gaynour returns to the hall to advise Arthur of the encounter. The text abruptly abandons the exchange with the ghost after Gaynour's report and introduces the character of Galeron, who addresses King Arthur and demands the return of his land, which was confiscated subsequent to Galeron's defeat in battle. Gawayn offers to fight Galeron on the court's behalf, most appropriate since Gawayn was the recipient of Galeron's lands after Arthur conquered and confiscated them. The remainder of the poem focuses primarily on the battle between the two knights. Ultimately, Galeron yields to Gawayn and kneels before King Arthur. Arthur subsequently declares that he will appoint Gawayn a duke of other properties if Gawayn releases his claim on Galeron's lands and returns the same to him. Gawayn agrees, Galeron's lands are restored, and Galeron is made a knight of the Round Table. In the last stanza, Gaynour fulfills her promise made to the ghost during the first half and writes to men in religious orders to read prayers and sing masses.

The two halves of the poem may initially appear to lack any significant connection, with the first half of the poem depicting the exchange with the ghost, and the second half, a typical chivalric story. However, the two parts can be reconciled. One link between the two is the theme of charity. The ghost warns of the importance of the nobility to be merciful to the commonwealth and in response to Gawayn's question of how the confiscator of lands will fare, indicates that the king's covetous nature will lead to his misfortune. In the second half, Galeron's lands are restored to him in what may be argued is responsive to the ghost's admonishments. Another way to connect the two halves is to view the poem's structure as influenced by the popular artistic form of the diptych. A diptych is a painting comprising two panels connected by a hinge that folds, and it is the viewer's responsibility to look at the halves and determine their relationship, as in the famous 14th-century portrait of Richard II known as the Wilton Diptych, a work either predating or possibly contemporary with the writing of this poem. More extensive arguments for this connection are made by A. C. Spearing.

The poem also addresses issues related to contemporary religion. The ghost's sole opportunity for redemption from purgatory is afforded by the payment of funds to the church, which is essential to the immediate salvation of the soul. The ghost could also represent the Christian perspective with the emphasis on generosity, while Arthur and his

Round Table may represent the court attempting to live up to the ideal.

In addition to the moral lessons and practical advice that the poem afforded contemporary readers, *The Awntyrs* is also of interest to students of medieval literature because of its role within the alliterative revival and contribution to Middle English. The decisions to write in English by two prominent courtly writers of the 14th century, GOWER and CHAUCER, the address in 1363 to Parliament in English by Edward III, and the composition of *The Awntyrs* and related texts all reflect the revival of English as a literary language in the later 14th century.

Bibliography

Phillips, Helen. "*The Awntyrs off Arthure:* Structure and Meaning. A Reassessment," *Arthurian Literature* 12 (1993): 63–89.

———. "The Ghost's Baptism in *The Awntyrs off Arthure,*" *Medium Ævum* 58 (1989): 49–58.

Shepherd, Stephen H. A., ed. *Middle English Romances.* New York: W. W. Norton, 1995.

Spearing, A. C. "*The Awntyrs off Arthure.*" In *The Alliterative Tradition in the Fourteenth Century,* edited by Bernard S. Levy and Paul E. Szarmach, 182–202. Kent, Ohio: Kent State University Press, 1981.

———. "Central and Displaced Sovereignty in Three Medieval Poems," *Review of English Studies* 33 (1982): 247–261.

Michelle Palmer

Ayenbite of Inwyt Dan Michel of Northgate (1340)

The devotional manual *Ayenbite of Inwyt*—that is, "again-bite" (remorse) of the "inner wit" (conscience)—is a devotional manual in MIDDLE ENGLISH produced in Kent by a Benedictine monk named Dan Michel of Northgate and completed in 1340.

Of Dan Michel himself little is known. He was a monk of Saint Augustine's Abbey in Canterbury, and he writes in *Ayenbite* that he produced the manuscript in his own hand when he was 70 years old and his faculties were growing dim. The text is a translation of a French moral tract called *Le somme des vices et des vertues* (Treatise on the vices and virtues) by the Dominican frère Loren of Orleans. The French treatise, written in 1279, was also called *Le somme le roi* (The treatise of the king), since it was originally composed for the French king Philip III (1245–85). It has been suggested that the French original was one of the sources for CHAUCER'S *PARSON'S TALE,* and some have suggested that Chaucer also knew the English version. There is, however, no proof of this.

Ayenbite of Inwyt is written to teach its reader how to live a good Christian life. It is made up of several discourses, each of which is itself subdivided into separate components. The treatise covers each of the 10 commandments, the 12 articles of the creed, the seven deadly sins, as well as the virtues. There are also sections on the knowledge of good and evil, and advice on how a Christian should face death. Unlike similar kinds of manuals (as, for example Robert MANNYNG of Brunne's *Handlyng Sinne*), *Ayenbite of Inwyt* does not illustrate its points with exemplary anecdotes. Nor does it use a great deal of ALLEGORY, as would have been common to Dan Michel's contemporaries.

Dan Michel does not follow his original French source precisely, and he has sometimes been faulted for making simple translating errors. Some scholars have even questioned whether Dan Michel was in fact the translator or was merely a copyist in the monastery, producing a fair copy of someone else's translation. But what has most interested scholars about *Ayenbite of Inwyt* is its language. As a rare example of the Kentish dialect of Middle English in the 14th century, Dan Michel's text is extremely valuable to linguists studying the characteristic features of that dialect.

Bibliography

Dan Michel's Ayenbite of Inwyt or Remorse of Conscience. Edited by Richard Morris. Introduction, notes, and glossary by Pamela Gradon. EETS 278. Oxford: Published for the Early English Text society by the Oxford University Press, 1979.

Francis, W. Nelson. "The Original of the 'Ayenbite of Inwyt,' " *PMLA* 52 (1937): 893–895.

B

Bacon, Roger (ca. 1214–1292)

It is generally believed that Roger Bacon was born in ca. 1214, in Ilchester, Somersetshire, to a wealthy family of minor nobility. Bacon received a first-rate education based on the LIBERAL ARTS curriculum of the *trivium* and *quadrividium* (grammar, rhetoric, and logic; arithmetic, music, geometry, and astronomy). He began university studies at Oxford at the age of 13, and there he studied under Robert GROSSETESTE, the university's first chancellor. Grosseteste's influence on Bacon is evident from the scholar's experiments in the field of optics and study of Aristotelian ideas. Bacon traveled to France in ca. 1234, where he received the master of arts degree from the University of Paris sometime before 1239. At the university, he worked as a *magister regens* (regent master) of the Faculty of Arts where he focused on the currently unpopular works of Aristotle and was nicknamed *Doctor Mirabilis,* or Wonderful Teacher. Bacon soon resigned from teaching and returned to Oxford in ca. 1247, where he devoted his time to scientific study and experimentation.

Shortly after his return, Bacon joined the Franciscan order. His reasons for becoming a friar are dubious—some say he was a holy person and that joining naturally suited Bacon's character and temperament; others say he joined because of financial difficulties that made it necessary for him to gain patronage for his research. At first Bacon seemed content in the Franciscan order; however, when the order decreed that no Franciscan be allowed to publish without permission, Bacon was appalled. Bacon openly criticized his contemporary theologians and felt the world needed his revolutionary religious knowledge. Many members of the church disagreed with Bacon's scholarly pursuits, and he disagreed with their disregard for philosophical, scientific, and other nontheological knowledge. Like St. AUGUSTINE, Bacon believed that Christians must learn from and make use of the teachings of pagan philosophers and other secular fields of scholarship. The Franciscans, known for their scholarly tradition, tolerated Bacon's radical theological ideas for a while, but ultimately exiled him to a friary in Paris in ca. 1257 under the charge of heresy.

By this time Bacon had produced the *Communia naturalium,* on science, and the *Communia mathematicae,* which recorded contemporary mathematical knowledge; however, he was forbidden from writing and publishing any new work while in exile. Determined to write and publish a massive encyclopedia including information on all of the then-current sciences, Bacon contacted Cardinal de Foulkes, who shortly became Pope Clement IV, and proposed the work. The pope mistakenly believed that Bacon had already written this text, and he asked Bacon to send him the *scriptum principale,* or comprehensive work on philosophy. When the work was not received, the pope issued a papal mandate for the work, a document that is still extant. In response to the pope's requests, Bacon rapidly produced his greatest works: the *Opus majus* (Great work), the *Opus minus* (Smaller work), and the *Opus tertium* (Third work). Bacon's 1272 *Compendium philosophiae* attacked the vices and ignorance of the clergy and the failings of the Franciscan and Dominican orders. But then in approximately 1278, Bacon was again imprisoned in a convent in Italy by the Franciscans under the charge that there were suspected novelties in his teaching.

Bacon was ahead of his time: He was one of the first to predict explosives, automobiles, airplanes, submarines, and powered boats; he explained the principles of light, used a camera obscura to observe solar eclipses, conducted experiments in the field of optics and observed the refraction of light through lenses (which eventually led to the development of eyeglasses), and pointed out the need for calendar reform. He studied many fields extensively, including Greek and Hebrew, mathematics and science, magic and alchemy, astronomy and astrology, philosophy and theology. Roger Bacon's health failed before he could finish his *Compendium Studii Theologia,* a work intended to stress the need to know Greek and Hebrew for the study of the Bible; nevertheless, his endeavor to finish the work shows that the scholar continued his passion for and devotion to the pursuit of knowledge until he died in 1292. The brilliance of Bacon's avant-garde, unconventional ideas was not recognized until long after his death.

Bibliography

Bacon, Roger. *Compendium of the Study of Theology.* Edited and translated with introduction and notes by Thomas S. Maloney. Leiden: E. J. Brill, 1988.

———. *Opus Majus.* Translated by Robert Belle Burke. 2 vols. New York: Russell and Russell, 1962.

———. *Roger Bacon's Philosophy of Nature: A Critical Edition, with English Translation, Introduction, and Notes, of De multiplicatione specierum and De speculis comburentibus.* Edited by David C. Lindberg. South Bend, Ind.: St. Augustine's Press, 1998.

Clegg, Brian. *The First Scientist: A Life of Roger Bacon.* New York: Carrol and Graf, 2003.

Easton, Stewart C. *Roger Bacon and His Search for a Universal Science: A Reconsideration of the Life and Work of Roger Bacon in the Light of His Own Stated Purposes.* New York: Columbia University Press, 1952; Westport, Conn.: Greenwood Press, 1970.

Leslie Johnston

Ball, John (bef. 1335–1381)

John Ball was an English priest and one of the leaders of the PEASANTS' REVOLT of 1381, during which Ball, known as the "mad priest" of Kent, advocated a radical equality and the elimination of church property. Through his letters and sermons, he helped incite tens of thousands of rebels to storm London. When the rebellion was put down, Ball escaped but was captured at Coventry, brought before the boy-king Richard II, and executed for his role in the revolt.

Virtually nothing is known of Ball's early life. He was ordained a priest probably in York, where he served at the Abbey of St. Mary. From here, he seems to have moved to Colchester, where in 1366 he was first arrested for heretical preaching. Forbidden to preach by the archbishop of Canterbury, Ball seems to have taken little notice of the reprimand and continued his radical sermons, in which he condemned the wealth of the church and advocated equality between social classes. In 1376, he was arrested again by the new archbishop of Canterbury, Simon of Sudbury. Again he had been preaching heresy, declaring that one need not pay tithes to an unworthy priest and that property should be shared in common among all people.

Ball was in jail again at the outbreak of the Peasants' Revolt in June of 1381. He was not forgotten by his supporters, however, and when Wat Tyler's men began their march on London, they freed Ball from the archbishop's prison at Maidstone in Kent. As the throng swelled and threatened the city, Ball gave an inspirational sermon at Blackheath on the text "When Adam delved and Eve span, who was then the gentleman?"—a text emphasizing the essential equality of all people under God. Eager to bring down the lords of church and state who oppressed them, the rebels stormed the city. At one point they assailed the Tower, where they captured and murdered Ball's old enemy, Archbishop Sudbury. The appearance of 10-year-old Richard II at Smithfield ultimately quelled the revolt. Ball fled London and went into hiding, but was captured at Coventry. On July 15, he appeared before Richard II at St. Albans, where he was hanged, drawn, and quartered before the nobility he had sought to overthrow.

Ball's significance for literary scholars comes chiefly from two extant letters written to inspire his followers and exhort them to stand together against the established powers. Russell Peck (1992) has noted that Ball's letters deliberately employ certain characteristics of St. Paul's epistles, including typically Pauline greetings and an evangelistic tone suggesting the simple equality of the early church. The fact that Ball, like Paul, was writing from prison was exploited as well. Most important, however, is Ball's use of the figure of *PIERS PLOWMAN* in one of his letters: The Plowman symbol of LANGLAND's great poem was clearly familiar to Ball, who tells the rebels to stand firm and let Piers Plowman do his work—apparently the work of reforming society. He alludes to other characters in the poem as well, including Dowel and Dobet. Ball's reference to Langland's poem was seen by some chroniclers as an indictment of the poem itself, and many scholars believe that the C-text of *Piers Plowman* was a later revision by Langland that consciously attempted to remove any possibility of radical interpretation of the poem.

Ball himself was linked by his accusers and by early chroniclers with the heretical views of John WYCLIFFE and his LOLLARD followers. But Ball does not appear to have been a disciple of Wycliffe, and the attempt to link the rebellion to the Lollards seems to have been born of the chroniclers' desire to make all dissidents part of a single movement. Modern scholars believe that Wycliffe's connection with Ball, and probably Ball's influence on the leaders of the rebellion, have both been somewhat exaggerated by early historians.

Bibliography

Bowers, John M. "*Piers Plowman* and the Police: Notes Toward a History of the Wycliffite Legend," *Yearbook of Langland Studies* 6 (1992), 1–50.

Dean, James, ed. *Medieval English Political Writings.* Kalamazoo: Published for TEAMS (the Consortium for the Teaching of the Middle Ages) in association with the University of Rochester by Medieval Institute Publications, Western Michigan University, 1996.

Green, Richard Firth. "John Ball's Letters: Literary History and Historical Literature." In *Chaucer's England: Literature in Historical Context,* edited by Barbara Hanawalt, 176–200. Medieval Studies at Minnesota 4. Minneapolis: University of Minnesota Press, 1992.

Justice, Steven. *Writing and Rebellion: England in 1381.* The New Historicism: Studies in Cultural Poetics 27. Berkeley: University of California Press, 1994.

Peck, Russell A. "Social Conscience and the Poets." In *Social Unrest in the Late Middle Ages,* edited by Francis X. Newman, 113–148. Binghamton, N.Y.: Medieval and Renaissance Texts and Studies, 1986.

ballad

Ballads, specifically folk ballads (also called traditional or popular ballads), are narrative folk songs transmitted orally among the common people in preliterate or partially literate societies. While ballads are known to have existed throughout Europe, the ballads composed in the remote areas along the English-Scottish border beginning in the 13th century are among the best known and most studied. These songs are simple and direct. They focus chiefly on plot, and most commonly present a single incident, beginning at a crucial turning point that moves the plot toward disaster. Action is presented impersonally—that is, the poet leaves out all personal feeling or commentary on the action—and dramatically—we are shown rather than told about events, and there is a great deal of dialogue at crucial points.

The oral nature of the popular ballads is clear from a number of stylistic characteristics: stock epithets or formulas are used often (terms like *blood-red wine* or *milk-white steed,* for example); there is a good deal of parallelism and repetition—sometimes the repetition of a refrain, for example, but most often the use of "incremental repetition," wherein the poet repeats a line or part of a line, but with an addition that helps advance the narrative.

Other typical elements of folk ballads include the use of the supernatural; the concentration on love, courage, or domestic situations; the focus on common people; the absence of transitional devices between episodes; and the use of a summary closing stanza. Further, English traditional ballads are most often composed in what has become known as the ballad stanza: a four-line iambic stanza of alternating four- and three-foot lines, rhyming *abcb*. Rhyme in the ballads was not always exact rhyme.

The well-known ballad "The Wife of Usher's Well" might serve as an example of a "typical" folk-ballad. It begins with two stanzas that introduce a middle-class family and the sudden death of a widow's three sons:

There lived a wife at Usher's Well,
And a wealthy wife was she;
She had three stout and stalwart sons
And sent them o'er the sea.

They hadna' been a week from her,
A week but barely ane,
When word came to the carlin wife
That her three sons were gane.

The verse form is clearly a ballad stanza. There is a use of the stock epithet "stout and stalwart sons," as well as the incremental repetition in lines five and six, repeating the detail of "a week" with the emphasis that it was only *ane* (one). And the sons' sudden deaths are narrated without any comment by the narrator.

As the ballad progresses, the sons return and spend the night at their mother's home. They sleep in the bed she has made them, but when the cock crows, they must return to their graves. The eerily supernatural climax of the story is reached mainly through incremental repetition and the use of dialogue:

Up then crew the red, red cock,
And up and crew the gray.
The eldest to the youngest said,
"'Tis time we were away."

The cock he hadna' crawed but once,
And clapped his wings at a',
When the youngest to the eldest said,
"Brother, we must awa'.

"The cock doth craw, the day doth daw,
The channerin' worm doth chide:
Gin we but missed out o' our place,
A sair plain we maun bide."

(Child, no. 79)

The last three lines might be translated, "The fretting worm chides: if we are missed out of our place [i.e., the grave], a sore pain we must abide."

The modern interest in folk ballads dates from the publication in 1765 of Bishop Percy's *Reliques of Ancient English Poetry.* Francis Child created a five-volume standard edition in the late 19th century called *The English and Scottish Popular Ballads.* Child's edition contains 305 different ballads, some of them with up to 25 different versions. Though the earliest literary reference to ballads is a disparaging remark in the 14th-century poem *PIERS PLOWMAN* regarding ballads of ROBIN HOOD, it is likely that some of Child's ballads date as far back as 1200. Child's most recent examples are probably as modern as 1700.

At one time there was a scholarly debate about the origins of popular ballads. Some scholars claimed that the ballads were composed communally by the "folk," probably at common public events like dances. Others argued that the ballads must have been the work of individual poets, adopted by the community because they were delivered orally. Modern criticism favors the idea of individual composition, though certainly once the ballads were passed on by word of mouth, each individual singer would be likely to alter the text as well as the music of any particular ballad. Such a phenomenon would certainly explain why there are so many variant versions of individual ballads.

Many modern scholars are interested in the ballads as the expressions of the common working-class people of the late Middle Ages. In the ballads, according to this point of view, we hear the voices of the common laborers and tradespeople, as opposed to those with a stake in the power structure, like the nobility or the church. Thus many popular ballads depict some inadequacy in the social structure, in the feudal system, or in the church. This is generally subtext, though, with love, heroism, and the supernatural remaining the chief overt themes of the popular ballads.

Bibliography

Bronson, Bertrand Harris. *The Traditional Tunes of the Child Ballads: With Their Texts, According to the Extant Records of Great Britain and America.* Princeton, N.J.: Princeton University Press, 1959–72.

Child, Francis. *The English and Scottish Popular Ballads.* 5 vols. Boston: Houghton Mifflin, 1882–98.

Fowler, David C. *A Literary History of the Popular Ballad.* Durham, N.C.: Duke University Press, 1968.

Harris, Joseph, ed. *The Ballad and Oral Literature.* Cambridge, Mass.: Harvard University Press, 1991.

Morgan, Gwendolyn. *Medieval Balladry and the Courtly Tradition.* New York: Peter Lang, 1993.

Percy, Thomas. *Reliques of Ancient English Poetry. 1765.* Reprint, London: Bickers and Sons, 1876.

ballade

The *ballade* was one of the major fixed forms of late medieval French lyric poetry. The name seems to have come from the Old Provençal *ballada,* which was a dance song. Guillaume de MACHAUT is generally credited with inventing and developing the form, which became popular in the 14th and 15th centuries in France as well as England. Typically the ballade consisted of three stanzas of the same rhyme scheme, usually with three rhymes. Each stanza ends with an identical line, which acts as a refrain.

For Machaut, the *ballade* was not only a poetic but also a musical form (*see* Laidlaw 54–57). Machaut's ballades had seven or eight lines, and each stanza was divided into three parts. A two-line opening (the *ouvert*) was answered by a two-line close (the *clos*), both sung to the same short musical phrase, so that the first four lines of each stanza rhymed *abab.* The rhyme scheme shifted with the continuation of the stanza (the *outrepassé*), which was also sung to a different musical phrase and might be two or three lines long. A concluding refrain provided a general focal point for the poem and the individual stanza. Thus the final lines of the ballade might rhyme *cbc,* or perhaps *cbcb.*

After Machaut, the ballade became more exclusively a poetic rather than a musical form, but the stanzas kept their three-part structure, although the *outrepassé* sections of many French ballades became longer. Eustache DESCHAMPS generally used at least a four-line *outrepassé,* but at times he used an *outrepassé* up to 10 lines.

Another later development in the *ballade* was the use of an *envoi,* a concluding address that summed up the poem or dedicated it to someone. The *envoi* was usually a truncated final stanza appended to the three stanzas of the *ballade* proper, and usually addressed directly to a "prince" or "princes." This seems to have been a development that occurred during literary competitions (called *puy*) at which the presiding judge was addressed as "Prince." Some *envois* might be addressed to a literal prince, the poet's patron.

Deschamps and Jean FROISSART popularized the *ballade* form in the late 14th century, and CHRISTINE DE PIZAN and CHARLES D'ORLÉANS perfected the form in the early 15th. It reached its culmination in French poetry with the lyrics of François VILLON later in the 15th century. Ultimately the most common *ballades* in French poetry consisted of octasyllabic lines arranged in three eight-line stanzas with a four-line envoi, rhyming *ababbcbC ababbcbC ababbcbC bcbC,* where the capital *C* represents the refrain.

The ballade also became a popular verse form in late 14th-century courtly poetry in England, and was used by both GOWER and CHAUCER. Many of Chaucer's lyric poems are *ballades,* though he does change the lines to decasyllabic and often uses a complete final stanza as an *envoi.* Chaucer's philosophical poem *Lak of Stedfastnesse* might serve as an example of an English ballade. The first stanza reads

> *Somtyme the world was so stedfast and*
> *stable*

That mannes word was obligacioun,
And now it is so fals and deceivable
That word and deed, as in conclusion,
Ben nothing lyk, for turned up-so-doun
Is al this world for mede and wilfulnesse,
That al is lost for lak of stedfastnesse.

(Benson 1987, 654)

The *ababbcc* rhyme scheme is clear (the same scheme that Chaucer uses for his RHYME ROYAL stanza), and one can see three basic parts to the stanza: the two-line *ouvert* talks about how people used to be faithful and reliable, and the *clos,* which spills over into the fifth line, contrasts those times with the contemporary world, where there is no relation between word and deed. The *outrepassé* generalizes that the world is now turned upside down, and the refrain, which reappears at the end of the following two stanzas, declares that all is lost through lack of steadfastness.

The poem's envoi is addressed to a real prince—in this case, to King Richard II:

O prince, desire to be honourable,
Cherish thy folk and hate extorcioun.
Sufre nothing that may be reprievable
To thyn estat don in thy regioun.
Shew forth thy swerd of castigacioun,
Dred God, do law, love trouthe and
worthinesse,
And we thy folk agein to stedfastnesse.

(Benson 1987, 654)

Chaucer's *envoi* uses the same *ababbcc* pattern as the rest of the *ballade,* but serves as a tool to assert the kinds of values that Chaucer sees as necessary to return the world to "steadfastness," and the final line echoes the refrain but alters it to express hope. Thus, in the hands of a master like Chaucer, or Villon or Christine de Pizan, the *ballade* could be a very effective vehicle for lyric expression.

Bibliography

Benson, Larry, et al., eds. *The Riverside Chaucer.* 3rd ed. Boston: Houghton Mifflin, 1987.

Laidlaw, James C. "The *Cent balades:* The Marriage of Content and Form." In *Christine de Pizan and Medieval French Lyric,* edited by Earl Jeffrey Richards, 53–82. Gainesville: University Press of Florida, 1998.

Barbara Allen (15th century)

The anonymous *Barbara Allen* (sometimes *Barbara Allan*) is one of the most famous traditional ballads and dates at least as far back as the 16th century. The ballad follows the traditional pattern of an unyielding woman and her starry-eyed lover. Barbara Allen is unusual in that the practical heroine finally does succumb to irrational love and thus meets her own demise.

The oral tradition inherent in ballads has given us several extant versions of this song. The story varies, but the constant aspects are that a man who is in love with Barbara Allen requests that she come to his deathbed. She complies, but denies his love. His death causes her to die the next day from remorse over her hardheartedness.

The name of the young man varies from one version to the next. In some he is known as "Sweet William." In Child's 84-A version, he is "Sir John Graeme, in the West Country"; in Child's 84-B version, he is known only as a "young man" (Morgan 1996, 31–32).

Another of the poem's variants is Barbara Allen's motivation for denying the love of the dying man. In Child's 84-A version, the man insulted Barbara Allen by not buying her drinks at the tavern.

"O didn't ye mind, young man," said
she,
"When ye was in the tavern a-drinking,
That ye made the healths go round and
round,
And slighted Barbara Allen?"

(Morgan 1996, 31)

Barbara Allen denies his love as retaliation for this affront.

Child's 84-B version shows Barbara Allen to be less emotional and instead pragmatic:

"If on your death-bed you be lying,
What is that to Barbara Allen?
I cannot keep you from your death;
So farewell," said Barbara Allen.

(Morgan 1996, 32)

In this version she finds no logical purpose to give him her love since he will die soon, so she instead withholds it.

The ballad also varies in the song of the death-knell. Barbara Allen purportedly hears a message in the ringing and it is alternately, "Woe to Barbara Allen," "Unworthy Barbara Allen," and "Hard-hearted Barbara Allen."

In some versions Barbara Allen sees the corpse of the young man. Her reaction is different depending on the version one reads. In Child's 84-B version, her response is abhorrent:

She turned herself round about,
And she spied the corpse a-coming:
"Lay down, lay down the corpse of clay,
That I may look upon him."

And all the while she looked on,
So loudly she lay laughing,
While all her friends cried out amain,
"Unworthy Barbara Allen!"

(Morgan 1996, 32)

Her actions in this version make her death in the following lines appear to be retribution for the dead lover rather than her reformed heart causing her to die in sorrow. "When he was dead and laid in grave/ Then death came creeping to she" (Morgan 1996, 32).

Contrastingly, Child's variant 81 reveals Barbara Allen's change of heart, and her resulting sorrow-filled death seems sincere.

She looked to the east, she looked to the
west,
She saw the corpse a-coming—
"Lay down, lay down that deathly frame
And let me look upon it."

The more she looked, the more she wept,
Until she burst out crying:
"I might have saved one young man's life
If I'd a done my duty. . . ."

(Cartwright 1985, 241)

This version clearly shows Barbara Allen's compassion and we feel sympathy not only for the young man, but also for her as she realizes her own culpability in his death. Further deserving of our sadness is Barbara Allen's mother who, in this version, ". . . died for love of both/ She died on Easter Monday," which in this text is the day following Barbara Allen's Easter death (Cartwright 1985, 241).

Even the death of the heroine does not bring an end to the variations of her tale. In at least one version, the couple finds love after death.

Barbara Allen was buried in the old
churchyard;
Sweet William was buried beside her.
Out of Sweet William's heart grew a rose;
Out of Barbara Allen's a briar.

They grew and they grew in the old
churchyard
Till they could grow no higher.
At the end they formed a true-lover's knot,
And the rose grew round the briar.

(Wilhelm 1971, 371–372)

The use of the sympathetic grave plants predates the ballad and was first linked with the TRISTAN AND ISOLDE romance. The plants symbolize "the transcendence of true love" (Morgan 1996, 29). Here they give a peaceful end to the otherwise sad tale.

Throughout its many variations, *Barbara Allen* remains a mournful ballad of the sorrows of unrequited love.

Bibliography

Cartwright, Christine A. " 'Barbara Allen': Love and Death in an Anglo-American Narrative Folksong," in *Narrative Folksong New Directions: Essays in Appreciation of W. Edson Richmond,* edited by Carol L. Edwards and Kathleen E. B. Manley. Boulder, Colo: Westview Press, 1985, 240–265.

Child, Francis James, ed. *The English and Scottish Popular Ballads.* New York: Cooper Square Publishers, 1965.

Morgan, Gwendolyn A., ed. and trans. *Medieval Ballads: Chivalry, Romance, and Everyday Life, A Critical Anthology.* New York: Peter Lang, 1996.

Wilhelm, James J., ed. and trans. *Medieval Song: An Anthology of Hymns and Lyrics.* New York: E.P. Dutton, 1971.

Malene A. Little

Barbour, John (ca. 1316–1395)

John Barbour was a 14th-century Scottish poet, known chiefly for his patriotic 13,000-line verse chronicle *The* BRUCE (1375), an account of the reign and military victories of the Scottish King Robert the Bruce and his disciple James Douglas, and their role in gaining Scottish independence from English domination. For this contribution he has often been called the father of Scottish poetry.

Barbour was probably born in Aberdeen, and aside from his university education, lived most of his life in that city. He was made archdeacon of Aberdeen in about 1357, and in 1364, 1365, and again in 1368, he is thought to have studied in Oxford and in Paris, and possibly to have taught there as well. In 1372, King Robert II appointed Barbour auditor of the Exchequer, a position to which he was reappointed in 1382 and again in 1384.

The Bruce became an instant popular success and a symbol of Scottish unity and independence, and has remained so over the years. Although it has been suggested that John Ramsay, the scribe who composed both extant manuscripts of *The Bruce* (from 1487 and 1489), made substantial alterations to the poem, most scholars still consider it to be Barbour's, and it is the only poem attributed to him with any certainty. Two other works—*The Brut* (an account of the legendary history of Britain, based ultimately on GEOFFREY OF MONMOUTH), and *The Stewartis Original* (a pedigree of the Stewart family from the time of their founder, Banquo)—are mentioned as Barbour's in *Andrew of Wyntoun's Original Cronykil,* but neither of these texts has survived. Three other works have at one time or another been attributed to Barbour: The *Troy Book* (which has been proven on linguistic grounds not to be Barbour's), *The Lives of the Saints* (50 legends that are contemporary with Barbour), and *The Alexander Buik* (a Scottish rendition of the life of Alexander the Great). There is no certainty that any of these are Barbour's.

Bibliography

Barrow, G. W. S. *The Kingdom of the Scots.* London: Edward Arnold, 1973.

———. *Robert the Bruce and the Community of the Realm of Scotland.* Los Angeles: University of California Press, 1965.

Boitani, Piero. *English Medieval Narrative in the 13th and 14th Centuries.* Cambridge: Cambridge University Press, 1982.

Ebin, Lois A. "John Barbour's *Bruce:* Poetry, History, and Propaganda," *Studies in Scottish Literature* 9 (April 1972): 218–242.

Kinghorn, Alexander M. "Scottish Historiography in the 14th Century: A New Introduction to Barbour's *Bruce,*" *Studies in Scottish Literature* 6 (January 1969): 131–145.

Mainster, Phoebe A. "How to Make a Hero: Barbour's Recipe: Reshaping History as Romance," *Michigan Academician* 29 (Spring 1988): 225–238.

Skeat, W. W., ed. *The Bruce.* 4 vols. EETS e.s. 11, 21, 29, 55. London: Published for the Early English Text Society by N. Trübner, 1870–89.

Barlaam and Josaphat Rudolf von Ems (ca. 1220–1223)

Rudolf von Ems composed one of many medieval versions of the *Barlaam and Josaphat* story sometime between 1220 and 1223. He descended from a family of lower nobility in Hohenems in Vorarlberg (today western Austria) and was a *ministerialis* (servant in the lower courtly administration), perhaps in the service of the bishop of Constance. Apart from the *Barlaam and Josaphat* (47 manuscripts),

Rudolf also wrote the merchant-romance *Der guote Gêrhart* (two manuscripts), an *Alexander* romance (three fragmentary manuscripts), the courtly love romance *Willehalm von Orlens* (29 manuscripts), and a major world chronicle (more than 100 manuscripts).

The account of *Barlaam and Josaphat* originated in India sometime in the third century C.E. and spread both to the Far East and to Europe. Translations and adaptations of this *Stoff* (literary material) exist in Persian, Aramaic, Turkish, Hebrew, Greek, Latin, and then in practically all medieval European languages. Basically, *Barlaam and Josaphat* derives its narrative material from the legendary account of the life of Siddhartha Gautama (Buddha).

In Rudolf's version, which does not differ much from his sources, the Indian king Avenier cruelly persecutes the Christians. When his son Josaphat is born, prophets foretell that his son will be a great king one day, but will convert to Christianity. To avoid this, Avenier has Josaphat raised in total isolation to keep away all signs of human misery. Nevertheless the young man eventually observes a leper, a sick man, and then a dead man. The Christian hermit Barlaam becomes his teacher and subsequently baptizes him. When the father learns of this, he solicits the help of two sorcerers to cure Josaphat of his illusion, but both fail and convert as well. Finally King Avenier divides his realm in two and gives one to Josaphat. Immediately Josaphat's kingdom prospers, whereas his father's land severely declines. Now Avenier converts to Christianity himself and becomes a pious hermit. Soon after, the protagonist abdicates from his throne and joins Barlaam in the desert. There he dies and is buried next to his teacher. As the vast number of translations of this text from all over medieval Europe tells us, the ancient account of Buddha, rephrased in Christian terms, deeply stirred the various audiences and made this into one of the most successful "best sellers" of its time.

Bibliography

Calomino, Salvatore. *From Verse to Prose: the Barlaam and Josaphat Legend in Fifteenth-Century Germany.* Scripta Humanistica 63. Potomac, Md.: Scripta Humanistica, 1990.

Rudolf von Ems. *Barlaam und Josaphat.* Edited by Franz Pfeiffer, Mit einem Anhang aus Franz Söhns, *Das Handschriftenverhältnis in Rudolfs von Ems 'Barlaam',* einem Nachwort und einem Register von Heinz Rupp. Deutsche Nachdrucke. Reihe: Texte des Mittelalters. 1843; Berlin: de Gruyter, 1965.

Albrecht Classen

Basavanna (Basavesvara) (ca. 1106–ca. 1167)

Basavanna is generally considered to be the leader of the group of poet-saints of the bhakti sect of Vīraśaivism. In the 11th and 12th centuries, the Vīraśaivis ("militant devotees of Śiva") shaped a religious movement in the Karnataka region of southern India devoted to Śiva, one of the three chief gods of Hinduism. The group, also called the Lingayats, formed a reformist religious community that opposed unthinking ritualistic religious practice as well as the traditional Hindu caste system. Hence the bhakti were committed to radical ideas of equality and social justice.

Like other Vīraśaivist saint-poets, Basavanna composed short poems called *vacanas* (literally "sayings" or "utterances") in Kannada, the language of Karnataka. Thus Kannada is the oldest literary language in southern India, with the exception of Tamil. The *vacana* were composed in the colloquial language of everyday speech, but typically contain arresting natural imagery and occasionally radical ideas.

Many of the poets involved in the Vīraśaivist movement tended to be from the lower castes and were illiterate. However Basavanna, reputed leader of the movement, was actually born into the Brahman caste, from which came priests and scholars. He went through a brahmanical initiation in 1114. His parents apparently died when he was a child. His foster father, Madiraja, was apparently a scholar and from a young age Basavanna seems to have been involved in Sanskrit learning. As a youth, Basavanna is reputed to have come under the influence of a bhakti guru or spiritual teacher, and was initiated into the sect. Tradition says he spent some time wandering before becoming minister to King Bijjala of Kalyana, whom Śiva told Basavanna in a dream to visit. Bijjala may have been married to the daughter of Basavanna's foster father, and so would have known Basavanna as a young man. Despite being the king's treasurer, he devoted his efforts to building a spiritual community focused on religious and caste reform.

Bijjala, spurred on by conservatives to oppose the egalitarian sect, sentenced some of them to death after an inter-caste marriage ceremony. When extremists among the new community failed to listen to his pleas against violent retaliation, Basavanna left Kalyana for Kappadisangama, where he died shortly thereafter. In the meantime Vīraśaivist extremists assassinated King Bijjala and ultimately were scattered by retaliatory persecution.

Basavanna is known to have written more than 900 *vacanas,* in which he advocates the ideals of his movement. In some, he denigrates ritualistic practice in favor of a religion of the heart: "I worship with my hands,/the heart is not content./What else shall I do?" (Ramanujan 1973, #487, ll. 7–9), he asks in one poem. In other *vacanas,* he asserts ideals of social justice, rejecting the caste system as a vehicle for the rich to dominate the poor: "The rich will make temples for Śiva./ What shall I,/a poor man,/ do?" (Ramanujan 1973, #820, ll. 1–5), he asks.

The colloquial nature of Basavanna's poems, their striking imagery, and their militant ideals place them among the most interesting and readable literature of medieval India.

Bibliography

Ramanujan, A. K., ed. and trans. *Speaking of Śiva* Harmondsworth, U.K.: Penguin, 1973.

Battle of Brunanburh, The (10th century)

The Battle of Brunanburh is an OLD ENGLISH poem of 73 lines celebrating the great victory of Athaelstan, king of Wessex (and grandson of ALFRED THE GREAT), with his brother Edmund, over the combined forces of Olaf Guthfitharson, the Norse king of Dublin (called Anlaf in the poem), and Constantine II, king of Scotland. Unlike the rather inconsequential engagement similarly celebrated in *The BATTLE OF MALDON,* Athelstan's victory over the Danes and Scots was a turning point in English history—it ensured that Northumbria, which had sworn allegiance to Anlaf, would ultimately remain a part of a unified England.

The poem is preserved in four manuscripts of the *ANGLO-SAXON CHRONICLE,* where it is inserted as the entry for the year 937. Whether it was produced specifically for the *chronicle,* or whether the chronicler found a copy of the poem separately and elected to include it, is unknown. In either case, the poet treats the subject matter with high seriousness, in a strict traditional heroic verse that by the 10th century was somewhat archaic.

An independent account of the battle, largely fictionalized, occurs in the Old Norse *EGIL'S SAGA,* where Egil is described as taking part in the battle on Athelstan's side. But despite the multiple historical sources, the location of the battle has been the subject of some controversy. The poem merely records that the battle took place "around Brunanburh" (that is, Brown's fort), near a "Sea of Storm." The 12th-century chronicler Florence of Worcester claimed that the battle had occurred near the mouth of the Humber River on England's east coast. But modern scholars favor a site in the west, probably north of Chester and perhaps as far north as the Scottish lowlands.

The poem begins with generous praise of the valor and warlike qualities of Athelstan and his brother Edmund and of the whole royal house of Wessex. The battle is then described, with the grim slaughter of Viking and Scottish nobility and the ignominious flight from the battlefield by the Norsemen and the Scots. The poet jeers ironically as the Vikings return in their ships to Dublin, while their fallen sons and kinsmen await the devouring ravens and wolves.

The ending is perhaps the most unusual part of the poem, for here the poet goes beyond praising the reigning noble house for its victory and conceives of the battle as a triumph for the entire English nation. It reflects a new national consciousness, one that must have been building since the loose confederation of seven Anglo-Saxon monarchies had first united under Alfred the Great.

Perhaps it was this nationalistic tone that caught the attention of Tennyson, who published his own modern translation of the poem in 1876. Doubtless the poem's attraction for him was that here, for the first time, a national poet speaks with authority and confidence about the aspirations of the English nation as one people.

Bibliography

Campbell, Alistair, ed. *The Battle of Brunanburh.* London: W. Heinemann, 1938.

Muir, Bernard James, ed. *Leoð: Six Old English Poems: A Handbook.* New York: Gordon and Breach, 1989.

Rodrigues, Louis J., trans. *Three Anglo-Saxon Battle Poems.* Felinfach, U.K.: Llanerch Publishers, 1996.

Battle of Maldon, The (ca. 1000)

The Battle of Maldon is an OLD ENGLISH poem in ALLITERATIVE VERSE, composed shortly after the 991 battle between local English forces and Viking invaders. The anonymous poet wrote in the style of traditional heroic poetry about a contemporary, local event, thereby transforming an ignominious English defeat into a memorable representation of the Germanic warrior code.

The historical setting of the poem is the England of King Ethelred the Unready (that is, ill-advised). During Ethelred's reign (978–1016), after a generation of peace, Norsemen had once more begun raiding the English coast. The *ANGLO-SAXON CHRONICLE* tells of Danish invaders bringing 93 ships to raid the southeastern coast of England in 991. After plundering several coastal towns, the Vikings came to Maldon, sailing up the estuary of the River Blackwater and setting up a base on the island of Northey near the river's mouth. The island was an ideal sanctuary, being approachable from the mainland only by a narrow causeway that was accessible only at low tide. On August 11, Byrhtnoth, ealdorman (or earl) of Essex, led a group of his own loyal retainers and an army of untrained local peasants and farmers drafted into service for the occasion. Byrhtnoth was killed and his retainers slaughtered in the ensuing battle.

In his own lifetime, Byrhtnoth was well known not only as a warrior but also as a protector of monasteries, so that he could be a natural hero for the Christian poet seeing him as a defender of the faith against the pagan Viking invaders. In the poem, which seems to depict actual events quite accurately, the English control the causeway, thus preventing the Norsemen from crossing to the mainland. But here Byrhtnoth makes what proves to be a fatal error. In order to break the stalemate and force a battle, Byrhtnoth allows the Vikings to cross over from the island—it is a rashness or overconfidence typical of the Germanic epic hero, like BEOWULF's refusal to use his sword against Grendel.

In the ensuing battle, Byrhtnoth is killed, at which point the majority of the English home guard flee from the battle. Only the earl's personal retainers—his noble aristocratic retinue—adhered to the old Germanic heroic tradition and refused to leave the battlefield after their lord had fallen. The poem becomes a series of courageous speeches from the English nobles, followed by single combat with the enemy. Ultimately, the old retainer Byrhtwold delivers the most famous speech of all, a memorable summation of the heroic code:

Hige sceal þē heardra, heorte
þē cēnre,
Mōd sceal þē māre þē ūre
mægen lytlað.

(Cassidy and Ringler 1971, ll. 312–13)

[Courage shall grow the harder, heart the
keener,
Spirit the greater, as our strength lessens.]

The end of the poem is missing, and so the poet has not left any description of the ultimate slaughter of the English defenders. But the solemn tone of the poem makes it clear that such an end was certain. The manuscript of the poem (British Museum Cotton Otho A xii) was destroyed in 1731 in the same fire that damaged the *Beowulf* manuscript. Fortunately for modern readers and scholars, a transcript had been made of the poem by librarian John Elphinston about 1724, and all modern editions of the poem are based on that transcription.

Bibliography

Alexander, Michael, trans. *The Earliest English Poems.* Harmondsworth, U.K.: Penguin, 1966.

Cassidy, Frederic G., and Richard N. Ringler. *Bright's Old English Grammar and Reader.* 3rd ed. New York: Holt, Rinehart and Winston, 1971.

Pope, John Collin, ed. *Eight Old English Poems.* 3rd ed. Prepared by R. D. Fulk. New York: Norton, 2001.

Scragg, Donald G., ed. *The Battle of Maldon, AD 991.* Oxford: Blackwell, 1991.

beast epic (beast fable, *Tierdichtung*)

Medieval beast epics, like the earlier fables of Aesop and others, were linked series of tales revolving around animals that talked and behaved like human beings. Often they were written in a mock-epic style that parodied the conventions of other literary genres, like epics and romances. The tone might range from low comedy to bitter satire, but often beast epics had a didactic purpose, usually to satirize the contemporary court or the church.

The origin of the beast epic genre has been a matter of scholarly debate. Some have held that the stories were shaped by TROUVÈRES and monastic scholars out of popular traditions. Others believe that scholastic Latin writers originated the tradition. In any case, the first text with features of a beast epic was composed in Latin between 782 and 786 by a cleric of CHARLEMAGNE's court known as Paulus Diaconus. In about 940, an anonymous German monk from Lorraine composed a 1,226-line Latin poem called *Edbasis captivi* that featured a runaway calf that is caught by a wolf and eventually saved by a bull, dog, and fox. A later Latin beast poem from the late 12th century was the witty *Speculum stultorum* (by the Canterbury monk Nigel Wireker), which recounts the adventures of the donkey Burnellus.

But the first fully developed beast epic is probably the 6,500-line Latin poem *Ysengrimus,* composed about 1150 by the Flemish poet Nivardus. This text introduces the wolf Ysengrimus, the fox Reinardus, who engages in an affair with the wolf's mate, and the cock Sprotinus, who has a dispute with the fox.

Nivardus's text was the chief source for the most important and influential beast epic, the *ROMAN DE REYNART.* Begun about 1173 by the French poet Pierre de St. Cloud, the *Roman* chronicles the adventures of the fox introduced by Nivardus, the popular "Reynard the fox." The affair of the fox and the wolf's wife in particular helped inspire several other "branches," or groups of stories, added to the Reynart cycle by mainly anonymous writers between 1178 and 1250. These ultimately swelled the *Roman de Reynart* to some 27,000 lines of octosyllabic French verse. These included 27 branches of stories, containing characters like the lion, badger, camel, ant, cat, and hare, in addition to the wolf, fox, and cock.

From this source developed other versions of the Reynart beast epic. The Alsatian poet Heinrich der Glicherzare wrote *Reinhart Fuchs* in Middle High German about 1200. The story of Reynart's trial from the *Roman* inspired a number of other beast epics through the 13th and 14th centuries, including the French *Couronnement de Renart, Renart le Nouvel,* and *Renart le Contrefait,* as well as the Dutch *Van der Vos Reynaerde* and *Reynaert's Historie.* The popular Dutch versions inspired more Reynart stories in German, Danish, Swedish, and English.

The best-known text inspired by the *Roman de Reynart* is Geoffrey CHAUCER's *NUN'S PRIEST'S TALE,* which relates the story of the fox's failed attempt to trick the cock Chaunticleer into becoming his dinner. Beast fables, particularly those inspired by Reynart, remained in fashion through the 15th century, culminating in Caxton's printed prose text in 1481.

Bibliography

Best, Thomas W. *Reynard the Fox.* Boston: Twain, 1983.

Blake, N. F., ed. *The History of Reynard the Fox; translated from the Dutch original by William Caxton.* Early English Text Society. London: Oxford University Press, 1970.

Needlen, Howard. "The Animal Fable Among Other Medieval Literary Genres," *New Literary History* 22, no. 2 (Spring 1991): 423–439.

Ziolkowski, Jan M. *Talking Animals: Medieval Latin Beast Poetry, 750–1150.* Philadelphia: University of Pennsylvania Press, 1993.

Becket, Thomas (Thomas à Becket) (1118–1170)

Born in London in 1118 on the Feast of Saint Thomas Aquinas, Saint Thomas à Becket lived a dramatic life that continues to inspire Christians and artists even in the 21st century. His parents were Norman settlers: His father was Gilbert, a knight turned businessman, and his mother was a pious lady who ingrained her Christian principles into her son's character. During his early years Becket was educated at Merton priory in Surrey and later at Paris. He returned to London to work as a financial clerk for a relative for three years, but in 1141, having lost both of his parents by the age of 24, Becket went to live at the house of Theobald, the archbishop of Canterbury.

With his energetic and charming personality, Becket won the regard of his master, and Theobald sent Becket to study law at Bologna and Auxerre. Thus when the position of chancellor opened in 1154, Theobald recommended his favorite student, and in 1155, King HENRY II made Becket chancellor of England. Becket carried out his duties as chancellor with pomp, efficiency, energy, and unequalled quality, providing the young king (12 years his junior) with advice and friendship. After Theobald died in 1161, King Henry, against Becket's warnings, recommended Thomas as his successor, an appointment Henry assumed would give him an ally and agent in the church who would aid him in fulfilling his endeavor to gain complete control of his kingdom, including power over the church. Although as chancellor Becket had generally proceeded according to the wishes of the king even if they were disagreeable to the church, he knew that if he became archbishop his conscience would force him to act in favor of the church's rather than the king's interests, and that therefore a break in his friendship with Henry was inevitable. Becket was reluctantly ordained a priest and then a bishop and was consecrated as archbishop of Canterbury, ultimately relinquishing his office as chancellor.

After Becket was consecrated he underwent a great deal of change, going from a brazen, irascible, pompous man to an archbishop of austere, devout, and temperate lifestyle, while retaining his brilliance, generosity, and authoritative personality. He began doubling the alms to the poor, personally examining the candidates to the priesthood, regularly visiting the monks in their cloister, and wearing a penitential hair shirt. Thomas protected the church from the changes King Henry wished for it and resisted all royal assaults on religious liberty. By 1163 St. Thomas and Henry had experienced conflicts, and dissension between the two former friends reached its peak in the matter of "criminous clerks." At a council at Westminster, Henry demanded that the bishops accept all of the ancient customs of the realm. The bishops refused, but Thomas later submitted in privacy. In 1164 King Henry II demanded consent to the *Constitutions of Clarendon,* a written document outlining the ancient customs, contrary to the law of the church, that Henry wished to reinstate. One of the main ambitions of the *Constitutions* was to transfer the trials of clerics to secular courts (at the time they could only be tried in church courts). The bishops, including Thomas, submitted, but then the archbishop quickly repented and opposed the king.

Thomas fled threats of death and imprisonment to France. During this time the king harassed and exiled Thomas's relatives and allies and the archbishop excommunicated and suspended Henry's allies. Peace negotiations between the two former friends repeatedly failed, and in 1170, Henry excluded Becket, the one man who could crown kings in England, from his son's coronation and got the archbishop of York, Becket's enemy, to perform the ceremony, thus defying the rights of the See of Canterbury. Thomas sent papal letters of suspension to the bishops who had assisted at the ceremony and refused to absolve the bishops unless they swore obedience to the pope. The king realized he must try to restore peace with the archbishop, and a resolution was reached. Becket returned from France—he was joyful to be back in Canterbury and enthusiastically received; however, he immediately provoked Henry by excommunicating those bishops who supported the king during his own exile. Henry became furious, and when the archbishop of York told the king that while Thomas lived he would never have peace, Henry angrily responded, "Who will rid me of this meddlesome priest?" Four knights heard these words and believed they would gain the king's favor by getting rid of the archbishop. On December 29, 1170, they murdered Becket in front of the main altar of Canterbury Cathedral after Becket refused to relent to the king, saying, "It is useless to threaten me.... You will find my foot set against yours in God's fight." Becket's final words were, "I accept death in the name of Jesus and for the church."

The murder shocked the continent, and soon pilgrims began to flock to his grave, and miracles were attributed to him. King Henry II was excommunicated by the pope, and he suffered much public shame as a result of the murder. Two years later, on February 21, 1173, Becket was canonized by Pope Alexander III, and on July 12, 1174, King Henry did public penance at the Shrine of St. Thomas of Canterbury. Becket's remains were kept in the choir of Canterbury Cathedral, the Trinity Chapel, and there his shrine remained one of the most frequently visited pilgrimage sites until Henry VIII, while destroying the Catholic religion in his realm, ordered the destruction of the shrine and demanded that wherever Becket's name appeared it should be scratched out.

Becket has been memorialized in all forms of art, particularly literature, and most notably in *Policraticus* and *Metalogicus,* philosophical treatises dedicated to Becket by JOHN OF SALISBURY, Becket's intimate friend and secretary while archbishop of Canterbury; in *Murder in the Cathedral* by T. S. Eliot, a modern dramatization of Becket's murder; and in *The CANTERBURY TALES,* by Geoffrey CHAUCER, a group of stories that, combined, make up the greatest work of English medieval literature and one of the most influential literary works of all time. *The Canterbury Tales,* in which a story collection is framed by the larger story of a group of pilgrims from all walks of life who are traveling from London to Canterbury to pay homage at Becket's shrine, reveals the awe and passion English Christians have continually felt for their martyr, Thomas à Becket.

Bibliography

Barlow, Frank. *Thomas Becket.* Berkeley: University of California Press, 1986.

Butler, John. *The Quest for Becket's Bones: The Mystery of the Relics of St. Thomas Becket of Canterbury.* New Haven, Conn.: Yale University Press, 1995.

Duggan, Anne. *Thomas Becket: A Textual History of His Letters.* Oxford: Clarendon Press, 1980.

Jones, Thomas M., ed. *The Becket Controversy.* New York: Wiley, 1970.

Knowles, David. *Thomas Becket.* Stanford, Calif.: Stanford University Press, 1970.

Staunton, Michael, trans. *The Lives of Thomas Becket.* Manchester, U.K.: Manchester University Press, 2001.

Warren, W. L. *Henry II.* Berkeley: University of California, 1973.

Leslie Johnston

Bede, The Venerable (ca. 673–735)

The Venerable Bede was an English monk who, though he never traveled beyond the boundaries of his native Northumbria, gained an international reputation as perhaps the most learned man of his age. Though he wrote some 40 books on theology, hagiography, rhetoric, and science, his best-known work, on which most of his modern reputation depends, is the *Historia ecclesiástica gentis Anglorum* (*The ECCLESIASTICAL HISTORY OF THE ENGLISH PEOPLE*), completed in 731. The *Historia* tells the history of Britain from the time of Julius Caesar's conquest of the island through the Saxon invasions to the arrival of Saint Augustine, the first Roman missionary, in 597, and the squabbles of the petty kingdoms of Saxon England.

Appended to the last chapter of his *Historia,* Bede gives an account of his life, which is the chief source of our knowledge about him. He relates that he was born in the vicinity of Wearmouth, where he was taken by his relatives to the nearby monastery of St. Peter at the age of seven. There he was put in the care of the abbot, Benedict Biscop, to be educated. He became a deacon at the age of 19 and a priest at 30. After completing his education, he moved to the sister monastery of St. Paul in Jarrow, where he spent the rest of his life.

Bede seems to have been a much-loved member of the Wearmouth and Jarrow communities. A letter from one of his students, Cuthbert, describes the Venerable Bede on his deathbed: During his last illness, according to Cuthbert, his students still came in to read by his bedside. Even to the last, Bede was working on translating the Gospel according to John into Old English, and is reputed to have expired immediately after completing it, with a pious prayer and a peaceful acceptance of his end. He died on May 27, 735.

The libraries at Wearmouth and Jarrow must have been magnificent for their time. It is from them that Bede gleaned his vast knowledge of such a wide variety of subjects, from astronomy to theology. He wrote chiefly in Latin, the universal language of his age, but he also knew Greek and Hebrew well and was familiar with the writings of the church fathers and of classical writers.

Bede's remarkable scholarship shows in a number of ways. He is the first scholar to have written that the calendar in use in his own time was inaccurate because the solar year was slightly longer than 365 days—a mistake that was not corrected until the establishment of the Gregorian calendar hundreds of years later. Bede was also the first scholar to write in the English language, though only fragments of his English writings survive. He wrote hymns as well, and was one of the first in England to use the style now called Gregorian. He wrote the first martyrology that included historical notes.

But he is best known and remembered as a historian, chiefly for his *Historia.* Here his innovations are equally impressive. He was the first historian to date events from the year of the incarnation, and so it is to him we owe the convention of A.D. and B.C. dating. He put his history together from a large variety of sources, written and oral, and was careful to note in his text what he had borrowed from other writers. He was also careful to sort fact from hearsay when he reported something. For these reasons, Bede is often referred to as the first modern historian.

But Bede's motives for writing history were different from most modern historians. He says at one point that if history records the actions of good men, then the reader will be inspired to do likewise; and if it records the deeds of evil men, then the reader will be compelled to shun their example. Everything he did or wrote, Bede says, was subordinate to his study of Scripture, and the underlying theme of his *Historia Ecclesiastica Gentis Anglorum* is the providential unfolding of Christianity's growth in England.

Bede's reputation was widespread in his own day and became even greater in the generations that followed. More than 150 manuscripts of the *Historia* are still extant, attesting to its wide popularity, and King ALFRED THE GREAT had the book translated into English in the ninth century. Bede was called "Venerable" to acknowledge his great learning within a few generations of his death—he is so called by ALCUIN and others in the early ninth century, and in 853 the Council of Aachen formalized the title. The Venerable Bede was named a doctor of the church by Pope Leo XIII in 1899, and May 27 was declared his feast day.

Bibliography

Bede. *Bede's Ecclesiastical History of the English People.* Edited by Beretram Colgrave, and R. A. B. Mynors. Oxford: Clarendon Press, 1969.

———. *The Ecclesiastical History of the English People; The Greater Chronicle; Bede's Letter to Egbert.* Edited by Judith McClure, and Roger Collins. Oxford: Oxford University Press, 1994.

Blair, Peter Hunter. *The World of Bede.* Cambridge: Cambridge University Press, 1990.

Ward, Benedicta. *The Venerable Bede.* Kalamazoo, Mich.: Cistercian Publications, 1998.

Benoît de Sainte-Maure (ca. 1160–1170)

Medieval audiences were fascinated by the many accounts of the siege and fall of Troy (ca. 1250 B.C.E.) and Aeneas's escape from the burning city after the Greeks had conquered it with the help of Ulysses' trick, the Trojan horse. According to the ancient Roman poet Virgil (70–19 B.C.E.), and also according to many medieval authors, Aeneas subsequently founded Rome, but on his way to Italy he reached many other shores and so became the forefather of various royal houses, such as of England (*see* SIR GAWAIN AND THE GREEN KNIGHT, late 14th century). The Old French cleric Benoît de Sainte-Maure composed one of earliest of these large epics dealing with this history, the *Roman de Troie,* dedicated to the English queen ELEANOR OF AQUITAINE, wife of the English king HENRY II since 1152. Benoît followed a long-standing tradition of bringing back to life this highly popular narrative material, but his *Roman* itself subsequently spawned a whole new generation of Latin and vernacular narratives about the history of Troy that extended far into the 15th century. He identifies himself in line 132 as Beneeit de Saint-More, and as Beneit in lines 2065, 5093, and 19,207.

As was to become common practice in the entire Middle Ages, Benoît mostly relied on the pseudo-historiographical accounts of the Trojan history written by Dares Phrygius (*De excidio Troiae historia,* late fifth century C.E.) and Dictys Cretensis (*Ephemeris belli Troiani,* third century C.E.), whereas he disregarded the original epic by Homer, which was known to the Middle Ages only through the short Latin version by Baebius Italicus (before 68 C.E.). Benoît vastly expanded his chronicle sources and created an extensive new account which closely resembles a courtly romance; this in turn deeply influenced many subsequent poets interested in the "matter of Troy," especially Herbort von Fritzlar (*Das Liet von Troye,* ca. 1195–1200), Guido de Columnis (*Historia destructionis Troiae,* 1287), and Konrad von Würzburg (*Trojanerkrieg,* ca. 1281–87), and then also a number of chronicle authors, such as Jans of Vienna (end of the 13th century), not to mention Giovanni BOCCACCIO (*IL Filostrato*), Geoffrey CHAUCER (TROILUS AND CRISEYDE), and Shakespeare (*Troilus and Cressida*).

Benoît followed Dares and Dictys very closely, but he also added much fictional material, especially in the description of love affairs, battle scenes, weapons, and buildings. His *Roman de Troie* is divided into three major sections: Following a prologue (verses 1–144) and an overview of the entire text (verses 145–714), the poet first discusses the origins and history, then the causes of the Trojan War (verses 715–4936). In the second section Benoît turns to the actual Trojan War leading up to the destruction of Troy (verses 4937–26590); the third section deals with the conflicts and bickering among the victors, and their own tragic destinies, including Aeneas's and Ulysses' (verses 26591–30300). The romance concludes with a brief epilogue by the poet (verses 30301–30316).

In his prologue Benoît explains that he composed his *Roman* because he wanted to preserve the knowledge of these ancient events which were "wrongly" told by Homer, whereas he himself intended to present nothing but a factual and "true" account. Nevertheless, he adapted his historiographical material to the medieval tastes of his courtly audience, but the outcome of the Trojan War, according to Benoît, still remains the total destruction of the world of Troy. Surprisingly, his evaluation of knighthood ultimately proves to be negative as well, since even the Greek victors are not able to enjoy the fruits of their labor, and since the various love relationships mentioned here regularly result in betrayal, suffering, and tragedy (this historical perspective finds one of its best reflections in the anonymous Middle High German *Moriz von Craûn* [ca. 1220], which was obviously influenced by Benoît's text). The *Roman,* despite its massive volume, has been preserved in more than 30 manuscripts, a fact that testifies to Benoît's enormous popularity.

Benoît also composed, on behalf of King Henry II of England, the *Chronique des ducs de Normandie,* where the author is identified, albeit in a summary passage, as Beneit from Touraine. The extensive *Chronique* consists of 44,542 lines in octosyllabic (eight-syllable) rhymed couplets and offers a world history taking us from Creation through the time of King Henry I (1135). Benoît obviously drew much material for his vernacular chronicle from the Latin chronicles by Dudo de Saint-Quentin and Guillaume de Jumiège, but his own contribution consisted of many fictionalized dialogues and countless proverbs. The *Chronique* has been preserved in two manuscripts.

Bibliography

Beckman, Gustav Adolph. *Trojaroman und Normannenchronik. Die Identität der beiden Benoît und die Chronologie ihrer Werke.* Munich: Hueber, 1965.

Benoît de Sainte-Maure. *Chronique des ducs de Normandie.* Edited by Carin Fahlin. 3 vols. Uppsala: Almqvist and Wiksell, 1967. Vol. 4 with notes by Sven Sandqvist: Almqvist and Wiksell, 1979.

Gordon, R. K., trans. *The Story of Troilus as told by Benoît de Sainte-Maure, Giovanni Boccaccio, Geoffrey Chaucer, Robert Henryson.* Toronto: Toronto University Press, 1978.

Kearns, Carol Bubon. "Influence of the Trojan Myth on National Identity as Shaped in the Frankish and British Trojan-Origin Myths and the *Roman de Brut* and the *Roman de Troie.*" Ph.D. diss., University of Florida, 2002.

Kelly, Douglas, ed. *The Medieval "Opus": Imitation, Rewriting and Transmission in the French Tradition: Proceedings of the Symposium Held at the Institute for Research in the Humanities, October 5–7 1995, the University of Wisconsin–Madison.* Amsterdam: Editions Rodopi, 1996.

Albrecht Classen

Beowulf (eighth–10th century)

The best-known and most admired text in OLD ENGLISH literature, *Beowulf* is an epic poem in 3,182 lines of ALLITERATIVE VERSE recreating the heroic age of Germanic culture, an age in which the lord—"ring-giver" or "gold-friend"—distributed treasure to his retainers from his gift-stool in a mead hall, and the retainers pledged their loyalty and their support in the lord's wars, even to the point of dying with him on the battlefield. It was also a world in which vengeance for the death of one's kinsman or lord was a sacred obligation. And it was a world that the Christian poet responsible for the poem seems both to value and to criticize. The poem survives in a single manuscript in the British Library (COTTON VITELLIUS A.XV), and presents its protagonist in three great battles against monstrous foes, separated by some 50 years.

This first great English poem has no scenes set in England. It begins with a genealogy of Danish kings, going back to Scyld Scefing, a good king who subjugated the Danes' neighbors and left a good treasure for his heirs. His descendent Hrothgar builds Heorot, the greatest mead hall ever seen. Here the order of civilization reigns, and the SCOP or bard, sings a song of creation. But in the outer darkness, Grendel, a monster of the dark and the chaos, is maddened by the song of the scop. Grendel attacks Heorot at night. He kills 30 of Hrothgar's warriors, and makes the mead hall a place of fear for the Danes. After 12 years Beowulf, a young warrior of the Geatish nation in southern Sweden, hears of Hrothgar's troubles and comes with a band of warriors to win fame by ridding Heorot of the monster. Over the drinking of mead, his credentials are challenged by the Danish retainer Unferth, but Beowulf makes his *beot* (his boast or vow) to destroy Grendel. That night, Beowulf and his men sleep in Heorot. The monster skulks in and devours one of the sleeping Geats, after which Beowulf, scorning to use armor against a monster that has no knowledge of such things, battles Grendel hand-to-hand. Ultimately Beowulf overpowers the monster and tears off his arm. Grendel slinks home to die, and the Danes make a great celebration of Beowulf's victory. The Danish scop composes a song in praise of Beowulf, and Grendel's arm is hung up in Heorot as a sign.

But the Geatish hero has little time to rest. Grendel's mother, seeking to avenge her son, attacks Heorot that night and kills one of the Danes. Beowulf must seek the new monster in the dark mere where she lives. He swims under the surface in full battle gear, tracking her to her home in an underwater cave. His sword proves useless against her, and he is nearly killed as she pins him to the ground and brandishes a knife, but he finds a magic sword hanging in the cave and kills the monster. He also finds the body of Grendel, and cuts offer the monster's head to bring back to Heorot.

Beowulf bids farewell to Hrothgar, who gives him many gifts and much advice, and Beowulf sails back to Geatland and reports on his activities to his own king, Hygelac. Beowulf's final battle occurs 50 years later. Hygelac and his heirs having been killed, Beowulf has become the Geatish king. His own people are being threatened by a fire-breathing dragon, who has been stirred to vengeance after sleeping for hundreds of years when a luckless intruder steals part of the dragon's cursed treasure. Beowulf, taking 11 retainers, says he will fight the dragon alone and enters the lair while all his men except a certain Wiglaf run off to the woods. In the ensuing battle, Beowulf, aided by his young kinsman, is able to defeat the dragon, but is mortally wounded himself, burned by the dragon's fire. He dies of his wounds, and Wiglaf chastises the Geats for leaving their king, predicting that they will now be destroyed by neighboring tribes because of their failure to support their gold-friend. The poem ends with Beowulf's burial.

A brief summary of the poem does not capture one of the most remarkable aspects of the narrative, which is the background of Germanic history constantly put before the audience through the so-called digressions in the poem. The two longest of these are the story of the Danish king Hnaef, who, despite the marriage of his sister Hildeburh to Finn, king of the Frisians, is caught up in a feud with Finn's tribe that ends finally in the deaths of Hnaef, of Hildeburh's son, and of Finn; and a story from Beowulf's own lips concerning the disastrous marriage of Hrothgar's daughter Freawaru to Ingeld the Heathobard, another unsuccessful attempt to settle a tribal feud through marriage. These tales, plus the allusion to the murder of Hrothgar's son by the boy's own uncle, and the ultimate fiery destruction of Heorot, may be suggestions by the Christian poet that the monstrous vengeance of Grendel's mother, a monster from outside of Germanic society, is in fact a destructive force within the society itself.

This is certainly a question for critical dispute. A number of other points have proven matters of debate for scholars, not the least of which is the question of oral composition. Beowulf clearly is in the style of Anglo-Saxon heroic poetry that predates the first written compositions in English in the seventh century. Early in the 20th century many scholars believed that the poem was a pure Germanic heroic oral composition, made up of poems similar to the one that the scop in the poem sings after Beowulf's first victory. These scholars believed that Christian elements in the poem were interpolations from a monkish scribe. It was later suggested that the poem was composed extemporaneously in oral-formulaic fashion similar to that of Yugoslav oral poets in the 20th century, and written down by a scribe. Few scholars hold these views any longer: It seems likely that *Beowulf* is a text whose author was literate, but who used the traditional language of oral heroic poetry to create his own epic-length poem.

The other most hotly debated issue in *Beowulf* criticism has been its date. It is known, from GREGORY OF TOURS's *History of the Franks,* that the Geatish king Hygelac was killed in a raid on the Frisians in 521; therefore, the action of the poem must take place in the sixth century. Early scholars assumed an early date for the poem's composition: Some claimed it was as early as the late seventh century, attributing it to the golden age of Northumbrian culture at the time of the Venerable BEDE. Some suggested a later date, in the later eighth century, during the reign of the powerful King Offa of Mercia. More recent criticism, however, has argued for an even later date, one closer to the date and place of the Wessex manuscript itself in the late 10th century. While some of the language of the text would be archaic, these critics argue that it is deliberately so because of the conservative word stock that was conventional in heroic poetry.

The sublime tone of the poem, its sustained epic grandeur, and the power of its presentation of a characteristic hero of Anglo-Saxon heroic age, all serve to make *Beowulf* the most important poem in Old English. In addition, it is highly significant as the first major poem in a vernacular European language.

Bibliography

Brodeur, Arthur G. *The Art of Beowulf.* Berkeley: University of California Press, 1959.

Fry, Donald K. "Old English Formulas and Systems," *English Studies* 48 (1967): 193–204.

Goldsmith, Margaret. *The Mode and Meaning of Beowulf.* London: Athlone Press, 1970.
Heaney, Seamus. *Beowulf: A New Verse Translation.* First bilingual ed. New York: Farrar, Straus, and Giroux, 2000.
Hill, John M. *The Cultural World in Beowulf.* Toronto: University of Toronto Press, 1995.
Huppé, Bernard F. *The Hero in the Earthly City: A Reading of Beowulf.* Binghamton: Medieval and Renaissance Texts and Studies, State University of New York at Binghamton, 1984.
Irving, Edward, Jr. *Rereading Beowulf.* Philadelphia: University of Pennsylvania Press, 1989.
Klaeber, Friedrich, ed. *Beowulf and the Fight at Finnsburg.* 3rd ed. Boston: D.C. Heath, 1950.
Niles, John D. *Beowulf: The Poem and Its Tradition.* Cambridge, Mass.: Harvard University Press, 1983.
Orchard, Andy. *A Critical Companion to Beowulf.* Rochester, N.Y.: D. S. Brewer, 2003.
Sisam, Kenneth. *The Structure of Beowulf.* Oxford: Clarendon Press, 1965.
Tolkien, J. R. R. "*Beowulf:* The Monsters and the Critics," *Proceedings of the British Academy* 22 (1936): 245–295.
Whitelock, Dorothy. *The Audience of Beowulf.* Corrected ed. Oxford: Clarendon Press, 1958.

Berceo, Gonzalo de (ca. 1196–ca. 1264)

Gonzalo de Berceo is significant as the first Castilian poet whose name we know. He was a priest attached to the Benedictine monastery of San Millán de la Cogolla, probably as notary to the abbott. His extant works include nine devotional poems of some length (about 13,000 verses survive): Four are hagiographies or saints' lives, two are poems concerned with orthodox doctrine, and three are poems of devotion to the Virgin Mary. One of Berceo's important contributions is his use of the *cuaderna vía* (known as the clerical meter), consisting of single-rhymed stanzas of four 14-syllable lines, a form that Berceo helped popularize.

Berceo says that he was raised in the monastery of San Millán, and that he was born in San Millán's hometown of Berceo. He may have studied at the Estudio General in Palencia between 1210 and 1214. By 1221, Berceo had been ordained a deacon, and by 1237 he was a priest.

Berceo's earliest works, probably written during the 1230s, are two saints' lives about local Spanish saints. His *Vida de San Millán* was apparently written to encourage contributions to the monastery. In the text San Millán appears in the sky with Saint James before a battle between Christians and Moors. Once the Christians have secured the victory, the king of León orders that all of his subjects pay alms to St. James at Compostela, while the Castilian hero Fernán Gonzalez decrees that all his countrymen should pay tribute to San Millán.

Berceo was probably also familiar with the nearby monastery of Santo Domingo de Silos, and his *Vida de Santo Domingo de Silos* was a translation of Grimaldus's 11th-century Latin prose life of the saint. Less successful are Berceo's two doctrinal studies, written in rhymed prose, the *Sacrificio de la Misa* (The sacrifice of the mass), which popularized several Latin commentaries on the mass, and the *De los Signos que Aparesçeran ante del Juiçio* (Visible signs preceeding the Last Judgment), which is largely a translation of a Latin poem.

But Berceo's best-known work is his *Milagres de Nuestra Señora* (*Miracles of Our Lady*), a collection of some 25 miracle tales, all but one from a Latin collection—the other tale, set in Spain, most likely came to Berceo from an oral source. The theme of this text, probably written later in Berceo's career (ca.1260), seems to be the power of the Virgin to save her devotees from any obstacles or calamities, despite their sins, and to inspire profound devotion to her. Two other Marian texts are the *Loores* (Praises) *de Nuestra Señora,* and the *Duela de la Virgin* (Grief of the Virgin), an account of the crucifixion of Christ from Mary's point of view.

In his last years Berceo returned to hagiography, producing a *Vida de Santa Oria,* the life of an 11th-century Spanish recluse, and the *Martiro de San Lorenzo,* an account of the martyrdom of Saint Lawrence, whom tradition associated with the northeastern Spanish province of Huesca.

Ultimately Gonzalo de Berceo's contribution to literature was his ability to combine the ecclesiastical Latin tradition with the popular conventions of the Castilian minstrels. His style has been called simple and popular, though he clearly was a learned priest. Perhaps his most significant accomplishment is his ability to retell the learned tales in a popular, uncomplicated way.

Bibliography

Berceo, Gonzalo de. *Miracles of Our Lady.* Translated by Richard Terry Mount, and Annette Grant Cash. Lexington: University of Kentucky, 1997.

Keller, John Esten. *Gonzalo de Berceo.* New York: Twayne, 1972.

Perry, Theodore Anthony. *Art and Meaning in Berceo's Vida de Santa Oria.* New Haven, Conn.: Yale University Press, 1968.

Suszynski, Olivia C. *The Hagiographic-Thaumaturgic Art of Gonzalo de Berceo: Vida de Santo Domingo de Silos.* Barcelona: Ediciones Hispam, 1976.

Bernard of Clairvaux, Saint (1090–1153)

Bernard of Clairvaux was the most important and influential figure of the mid-12th-century Latin church. He is best known as the maker and confidante of popes, the opponent of Peter ABELARD, and the major force behind the Second Crusade. His literary legacy includes hundreds of letters and a number of sermons, the most important an influential series of sermons on the Song of Songs in which he allegorized the text to portray the mystical union of Christ and the soul.

Born of noble parents in 1090 near Dijon in France, Bernard studied the *trivium* at a local school as a boy. When his mother died in 1107, however, Bernard seems to have experienced a spiritual crisis that, in 1111, led him to withdraw from the world. Ultimately he became a monk at the abbey of Citeaux, where he so distinguished himself that after three years he was chosen to found a new Cistercian house as its abbot. He and 12 companions chose an isolated valley near the Aube river in France and named it Clairvaux. Bernard's reputation as a preacher brought crowds of pilgrims to Clairvaux to hear him, and his personal charisma also brought many new monks into his order. In a short time, the extraordinary growth of Clairvaux and the Cistercian order generally made Bernard famous throughout the western church.

Bernard was involved in a number of controversies in his time. Already in 1119, he was embroiled in a debate with the Cluniac monks, charging them with lax discipline, though ultimately he befriended the abbot of Cluny, the famous Peter the Venerable. In 1130, when the traditional cardinals of the church elected Anacleus II pope while the monastic party supported Innocent II, Bernard threw all of his influence behind Innocent, who ultimately was recognized. In the mid-1140s, Bernard opposed the preaching of Arnold of Brescia, who was inciting rebellion by condemning the wealth of the church.

Most famously, Bernard challenged the controversial Abelard in 1140 at the Council of Wens. Bernard, who believed in the primacy of faith and held a mystical view of man's relationship with God, believed that the rational approach of Abelard was a true threat to the church. It is said that at the council, Bernard defended his own position so passionately that Abelard had no chance to offer a defense, and left the council—though an alternative account suggests that there was never any intention of allowing Abelard to speak. He was subsequently condemned.

In 1145, Bernard's influence reached its apex when Eugenius III, one of his own disciples, was elected to the papacy. When Eugenius called for western Europe to mount a crusade after the Muslims captured the city of Acre in the Holy Land, Bernard became the official preacher of the Second Crusade. He traveled extensively to preach the crusade and successfully inspired an army that launched a disastrous campaign into the Near East. Widely blamed for the failure of the crusade, Bernard spent his final years in the shadow of that failure. He died at Clairvaux on August 20, 1153.

Despite reputed chronic illness and constant pain, Bernard traveled and preached extensively; he was constantly called—often by the pope—to combat perceived threats to the church, so that he came to be known as "the Hawk of Rome." He was charismatic, impulsive, passionate, and often (in his writing) eloquent. Some of his hymns are still sung today, but his most important literary contributions are his sermons on the Song of Songs. These seem to indicate a genuine mystical experience on Bernard's part—at least their imagery inspired later mystical writers. In these sermons, the soul longs desperately for God:

> a holy soul ardently desires the presence of *Christ,* he endures the deferment of the kingdom painfully.
>
> (Bernard 1971, Sermon 59, 3.125)

But Christ will come as the bridegroom in a mystical marriage with the soul, whom he loves with all his heart:

> anyone who is united to the Lord becomes one spirit with him. . . . Hence he lays claim to our land for himself. . . . From there is his bride, from there his bodily substance, from there the Bridegroom himself, from there the two become one flesh.
>
> (Bernard 1971, Sermon 59, 3.121–22)

With imagery like this, Bernard's influence on subsequent Christian writers, mystical or otherwise, was pronounced. A century and a half later, DANTE thought so highly of him that he placed Bernard in the highest regions of paradise in his *DIVINE COMEDY.*

Bibliography

Bernard of Clairvaux. *On the Song of Songs.* Translated by Killian Walsh. *The Works of Bernard of Clairvaux.* 4 vols. Cistercian Fathers Series 4. Spencer, Mass.: Cistercian Publications, 1971.

Billy, Dennis J. "Redemption and the Order of Love in Bernard of Clairvaux's 'Sermon 20' on 'The Canticle of Canticles,' " *Downside* Review 112, no. 387 (April 1994): 88–102.

Botterill, Steven. *Dante and the Mystical Tradition: Bernard of Clairvaux in the Commedia.* Cambridge: Cambridge University Press, 1994.

Evans, G. P. *Bernard of Clairvaux.* New York: Oxford University Press, 2000.

Bernart de Ventadorn (Bernard of Ventadour) (ca. 1130–ca. 1195)

The most popular and influential of all the Provençal TROUBADOURS was almost certainly Bernart de Ventadorn. Some 45 of his lyrics survive (18 of them with music), which is more than any other troubadour. The number of manuscripts of his work and the widespread imitations of and allusions to his poetry reinforce Bernart's status as the best known of the Provençal poets.

We have no real facts about Bernart's life. His *VIDA* repeats a number of legends about him, including his humble origins (his mother was purportedly a serf and his father a baker), his birth in the castle of Ventadour near Limoges in the province of Limousin, his love affair with his lord's wife and later with Queen ELEANOR OF AQUITAINE, and his death in the monastery of Dalon. Much of this is simply legend inspired by his poetry and, in part, by a stanza in PEIRE D'ALVERNHE's satiric poem about his fellow troubadours that speaks of Bernart's low-born parents.

Bernart clearly had a long association with the castle of Ventadour, and he may have been born there. In one of his poems he mentions the "school" of Ebles. Ebles II was viscount of Ventadour from 1106 to ca. 1147, and was well known as a poet himself, though none of his lyrics are extant. Bernart may mean he learned poetry from his patron Ebles, or that in his poetry he follows the *TROBAR LEU* style of Ebles, idealistically extolling COURTLY LOVE, rather than the darker and more pessimistic *TROBAR CLUS* style. But the details of Bernart's life are so sparse that it is not clear whether he refers to Ebles II or his son and successor Ebles III, both of whom were known to be patrons of troubadours.

It seems certain that Bernart was associated with Eleanor of Aquitaine, to whom he alludes several times in his poems. Probably he was attached to her court in the early 1150s, and very likely he traveled to England in 1154 for the coronation of HENRY II, Eleanor's husband. But Bernart seems to have returned to southern France shortly thereafter. Many of his poems mention Raymond V, count of Toulouse, and it is likely he was a member of Raymond's court, perhaps, as tradition says, even until

Raymond's death in 1194. There is no evidence that he joined a monastery upon Raymond's death.

Of the 45 lyrics attributed to him, all but three *TENSOS* (debate poems) are love poems in the *CANSO* form, and all seem to date from between 1150 and 1180. He was widely admired in his own day and remains the most popular of troubadours. Frederic Goldin praises Bernart for his skillful playing on the variety of perspectives among his immediate audience (the lady herself, sympathetic lovers in the group, and enemies of the lovers). Others admire Bernart for the beauty and clarity of his language and for the varied range of the emotions he expresses. In one poem, he is the helpless lover, overcome by the power of love:

> *Whenever I see her, you can see it in me,*
> *in my eyes, my look, my color,*
> *because I shake with fear*
> *like a leaf in the wind.*
> *I don't have the good sense of a child,*
> *I am so taken over, ruled by love;*
> *and when a man is overcome like this,*
> *a lady may let herself feel great pity.*
>
> (Goldin 1973, 129, ll. 41–48)

In another, reacting to his lady's disdain, he expresses his disillusionment and skepticism about love and about women in general:

> *This is how she shows herself a woman*
> *indeed,*
> *my lady, and I reproach her for it:*
> *she does not want what one ought to want,*
> *and what is forbidden to do, she does,*
> *I have fallen in evil grace,*
> *I have acted like the madman on the bridge,*
> *and how this came about I cannot say,*
> *except that I climbed too high on the*
> *mountain.*
>
> (Goldin 1973, 147–149, ll. 33–40)

Bernart is the most important practitioner of the *trobar leu* style, and certainly much of his popularity was the result of his having composed in this very clear and natural language. The sheer number of musical settings that have survived suggest that Bernart was as popular as a musician as he was as a poet. Finally Bernart's association with courts of northern France and England in the 1150s suggest that he is to a large extent responsible for spreading the art and style of the vernacular Occitan poets into northern Europe and for stimulating the beginning of the *TROUVÈRE* tradition in France.

Bibliography

Bernart de Ventadorn. *Songs: Complete Texts, Translations, Notes and Glossary.* Edited by Stephen G. Nichols, Jr., et al. Chapel Hill: University of North Carolina Press, 1962.

Goldin, Frederick, ed. and trans. *Lyrics of the Troubadours and Trouvères: An Anthology and a History.* Garden City, N.Y.: Anchor, 1973.

Treitler, Leo. "The Troubadours Singing Their Poems." In *The Union of Words and Music in Medieval Poetry,* edited by Rebecca A. Baltzer, Thomas Cable, and James I. Wimsatt, 15–48, Austin: University of Texas Press, 1991.

Wilhelm, James J. *Seven Troubadours: The Creators of Modern Verse.* University Park: Pennsylvania State University Press, 1970.

Béroul (ca. 1150–1190)

This Anglo-Norman writer, whose identity is mostly shrouded in mystery, is credited with the creation of a unique French *Tristan* romance that seems to have drawn from an oral-literary source (*estoire*) lost today. We know Béroul's name from two self-references in the text (Berox, vv. 1268 and 1790), and he might have composed his verse narrative for his patron, Richard de Lucy, duke of Cornwall (d. 1179). It has come down to us only in one fragmentary manuscript of 4,485 lines in octosyllabic couplets, written in the second half of the 13th century. The romance sets in at that point when the two lovers (*see* TRISTAN AND ISOLDE) meet on a moonlit night in the garden under a pine tree from which King Marc is spying on them. They recognize the king, however, because of his shadow, and skillfully deceive him in pretending to have met for political and social reasons only. Later the lovers are caught by King Marc and three of his barons because blood stains on his bed and on Yseut's (Isolde's) betray them. The lovers are bound and thrown into prison, and are supposed to be burned alive, but on the way to the stake, Tristan escapes through a chapel and awaits an opportunity to free his beloved as well.

Before Yseut can be burned, the leper Yvain suggests to King Marc that turning the queen over to him and his fellow lepers as a sex object for their enjoyment would be a more severe penalty than burning her at the stake. King Marc agrees, and while the lepers lead Yseut away, Tristan rushes up to them, frees his beloved, and seeks refuge with her in the Morrois forest. The couple, however, lead a miserable existence there, only ameliorated by their love for each other. One day Marc discovers them in their wooden cabin, but since he observes them sleeping partly clothed, not in loving embrace, and particularly being separated by a sword, he is suddenly convinced of their innocence. While the lovers realize that they have been discovered without being killed, the effect of the love potion is waning (being exhausted after three years), so they desire to return to the court. Marc announces that he will allow Yseut to come home, though he banishes Tristan from his country. But Marc forces Yseut to swear an oath to prove her alleged innocence, which allows Tristan to appear in the disguise of a leper and to carry his beloved on his shoulders across a swamp to the site of the ceremony. This represents the intended opportunity for her to declare that no man other than the king and the poor leper has ever lain between her thighs. King Arthur, who is present at the scene, intervenes and forces Marc to accept this oath as valid. Tristan's worst enemies, three barons at Marc's court, continue to plot against the protagonist and try to catch him *in flagrante,* but Tristan kills them all. At this point in the account, Béroul's narrative breaks off.

Bibliography

Béroul. *Tristan et Yseut: les premières versions européennes.* Edited by Ch. Marchello-Nizia. Paris: Gallimard, 1995.

———. *Roman de Tristan.* Translated by Norris Lacy. The Garland Library of Medieval Literature 36. New York: Garland, 1989.

Burch, Sally L. " 'Tu consenz lor cruauté:' The Canonical Background to the Barons' Accusation in Beroul's *Roman de Tristan,*" *Tristania* 20 (2000): 17–30.

Grimbert, Joan Tasker, ed. *Tristan and Isolde: A Casebook.* New York: Routledge, 2002.

Pensom, Roger. *Reading Béroul's Tristran: A Poetic Narrative and the Anthropology of Its Reception.* Bern: Lang, 1995.

Reid, T. B. W. *The Tristran of Beroul: A Textual Commentary.* Oxford: Blackwell, 1972.

Albrecht Classen

Bertran de Born (ca. 1140–1215)

Bertran de Born was a TROUBADOUR poet and a minor nobleman who was born in Limoges and is associated with the continual petty wars between King HENRY II and his sons. Some 44 extant lyrics are attributed to him, though five of these are of disputed authorship. Bertran is best known for his *SIRVENTES* dealing with war, and for DANTE's immortal picture of him in the *DIVINE COMEDY.*

Bertran is remembered largely as an opportunist and a mercenary, a *"vavasour,"* whose fortunes depended largely upon the success of whichever side he happened to be fighting on. His livelihood depended on war, and therefore many of his poems glorify battle and the plunder of battle in a way that seems brutal to modern tastes.

To a large extent, many of Bertran's martial exploits have to do with his attempts to gain sole possession of his family's property, the castle of Hautefort, which he owned jointly with his younger brother Constantine from at least 1169. He seems to have taken part in an uprising against RICHARD I Lionheart, then duke of Aquitaine, because of Richard's support of his brother in a quarrel over Hautefort. Bertran then supported Richard's older brother, Henry, known as the Young King, in an unsuccessful rebellion against Henry II; the rebellion ended when the 28-year-old Young King died of a fever July 11, 1183.

Following the collapse of the rebellion, Richard besieged Bertran at Hautefort, ultimately taking the castle and imprisoning Bertran. However, Richard eventually pardoned Bertran and restored his property, so that Bertran was able to bequeath it to his sons. Thereafter, Bertran supported Richard, and two of his surviving songs are *sirventes* honoring Richard on his return to Aquitaine in 1194 after his imprisonment.

Bertran was married twice and had five known children, one of whom was also a troubadour, known as Bertran de Born lo Fils. The elder Bertran was associated with the Abbey of Dalon late in his life, and tradition says he became a monk there. He died in 1215.

Bertran's political poetry reflects the military events he was involved in and sometimes depicts realistic aspects of battle, though often with a remarkable wit. He also wrote some CANSOS, or love poems, two of which flatter Mathilda, daughter of Henry II and ELEANOR OF AQUITAINE. But his most famous poem (though it is of questionable authenticity) is his *planh* or COMPLAINT on the death of the Young King, which opens

If all the grief and sorrow, the strife,
The suffering, the pains, the many ills
That men heard tell of in this woeful life
Assembled, they would count as nil
Compared to the death of the young English
  king,
Who leaves behind youth and worth in
  tears
In this dark world beset with shadowy
  fears,
Lacking all joy, abounding in doleful spite.

(Wilhelm 1970, 170)

Dante names Bertran the model composer of war poetry in *De VULGARI ELOQUENTIA*. But he also places Bertran in hell in canto 28 of the *Inferno*, where for his role in inciting the Young King to rebellion he inhabits circle eight with the "sowers of discord" and, in a memorable image, is pictured carrying his disembodied head like a lantern. Dante's portrait owes something to a scene in an early biography of Bertran, in which Bertran says to Henry II: "the day the valiant young King, your son, died, I lost my wit, and my knowledge, and my understanding."

Bibliography

Goldin, Frederick, ed. and trans. *Lyrics of the Troubadours and Trouvères: An Anthology and a History.* Garden City, N.Y.: Doubleday, 1973.

Paden, William D., Jr., Tilden Sankovitch, and Patricia H. Stäblein. *The Poems of the Troubadour Bertran de Born.* Berkeley: University of California Press, 1985.

Wilhem, James J. *Seven Troubadours: The Creators of Modern Verse.* University Park: Pennsylvania State University Press, 1970.

bestiary

Bestiaries were popular medieval collections of descriptions and anecdotes of both real and mythical animals, accompanied by moral commentary that gave a Christian interpretation to the animal's stated qualities. The view behind the format of the bestiary was that one could learn of God through the book of his word (the Scriptures) or through the book of his works (his Creation.). Thus God's creatures were formed in a manner that taught human beings Christian truths.

Later medieval bestiaries were based ultimately on the Greek *Physiologus.* A text produced between the second and fourth centuries C.E., the *Physiologus* contained about 50 anecdotes drawn from nature, followed by a "moralization" of the anecdotes. It was based on animal lore from much older traditions—from Indian, Hebrew, and Egyptian authorities, as well as from classical Greek students of natural philosophy like Pliny and Aristotle. The animals described in the Greek text are generally to be found in northern Africa or the Mediterranean region. By the sixth century, the Greek text had been translated into several languages—Ethiopian, Syriac, Armenian, and, most important, Latin. The Latin *Physiologus* was popular in western Europe, and by the 12th century writers began to expand the text, adding animals from northern Europe, for example, drawing material from ISIDORE OF

SEVILLE's popular seventh-century Latin encyclopedia, the 20-volume *Etymologiae.* Later bestiaries could contain as many as 150 entries—three times as many as the original *Physiologus.*

Bestiaries also began to appear in the European vernacular, the earliest of which survives as an OLD ENGLISH fragment in the 10th-century EXETER BOOK, containing verse descriptions of a panther and a whale. Bestiaries became popular in French in the 12th and 13th centuries, with works by PHILIPPE DE THAON, Gervaise, Guillaume le Clerc, and Pierre de Beauvais. English bestiaries appear beginning in the 12th century; the most famous of these is known as the Aberdeen bestiary. Bestiaries from the 12th and 13th centuries are often richly illustrated with imaginative and sometimes humorous illustrations, apparently intended to teach those who could not read. Illuminated bestiaries were immensely popular, and many show similarities in some of their particular illuminations. It is possible that model books existed from which illustrators drew on exemplars for various beasts. The illuminated bestiaries also seem to have influenced other manuscripts' illuminations, as well as animals depicted in frescoes or sculptures in church decoration.

Bestiaries included accurate descriptions of real animals, but at the same time contained fantastic descriptions of completely imaginary animals, or myths about genuine animals, all presented with the same authority. Thus entries were included for unicorns, phoenixes, cockatrices, or manticoras (man-eating creatures with lions' bodies, human faces, and scorpions' tails). Some observations about actual animals may have been distortions of earlier real observations that were repeated over and over again, even, one would think, after people must have known they were inaccurate: The "fact" that the swan sings beautifully before it dies, or that the barnacle goose was hatched from an egg that hung in a tree. At the same time, the elephant might be described accurately, but the description would include an anecdote that the elephant had no knees, and therefore slept leaning against a tree. This was moralized to apply to fallen human beings, who had to rely on Christ for their support. The pelican was purported to feed its young with blood from its own breast, thus symbolizing Christ himself, who gives his children eternal life through his own sacrificial blood. Animal lore from medieval bestiaries continued to influence myths and legends about various animals through the early modern period and even into contemporary times, from the notion of the "swan song" to the popularity of mythical beasts like the phoenix or the unicorn.

Bibliography

Barber, Richard, trans. *Bestiary: Being an English Version of the Bodleian Library, Oxford MS. Bodley 764.* With original miniatures reproduced in facsimile. Woodbridge, U.K.: Boydell Press, 1993.

Clark, Willene B., and Meradith T. McMunn, eds. *Beasts and Birds of the Middle Ages: the Bestiary and Its Legacy.* Philadelphia: University of Pennsylvania Press, 1989.

Curley, Michael J., trans. *Physiologus.* Austin: University of Texas Press, 1979.

Hassig, Debra, ed. *The Mark of the Beast: The Medieval Bestiary in Art, Life, and Literature.* New York: Garland, 1999.

McCulloch, Florence. *Mediaeval Latin and French Bestiaries.* University of North Carolina Studies in the Romance Languages and Literatures 33. Chapel Hill: University of North Carolina Press, 1962.

Mermier, Guy R., trans. *A Medieval Book of Beasts: Pierre de Beauvais' Bestiary.* With illustrations by Alexandra Eldridge. Lewiston, N.Y.: E. Mellen Press, 1992.

White, T. H., ed. and trans. *The Book of Beasts: Being a Translation from a Latin Bestiary of the Twelfth Century.* New York: Dover, 1984.

Yamamoto, Dorothy. *The Boundaries of the Human in Medieval English Literature.* Oxford: Oxford University Press, 2000.

Bevis of Hampton (ca. 1324)

Bevis of Hampton belongs to the category of MIDDLE ENGLISH verse ROMANCES referred to as "Matter of Britain," because of its setting in Britain itself, unconnected with the French romances of CHARLEMAGNE or those utilizing classical material or legends of King ARTHUR. Thus it is usually mentioned with romances like *GUY OF WARWICK* and *HAVELOK*. Like *Guy, Bevis of Hampton* survives in the famous early 14th-century Auchinleck manuscript, and its five other extant manuscripts and early printed edition attest to the story's popularity, though the texts are different enough to be separate romances, perhaps based on separate MINSTREL versions of the story. The most accepted (Auchinleck) version of the text is a sprawling and episodic narrative of 4,320 lines, the first 474 of which are composed in six-line TAIL RHYME stanzas, and the remainder in octosyllabic (eight-syllable) couplets. The story itself is not unique to *Bevis,* but is popular throughout Europe in a variety of languages. The immediate source for Bevis was an Anglo-Norman French CHANSON DE GESTE from the 12th century called *Boeuve de Haumton.*

The romance is chiefly an adventure story, structured into five sections, each of about 900 lines, perhaps reflecting portions of the story broken up for piecemeal recitation by a minstrel. In the first section of the poem, Bevis's father, Guy, Earl of Hampton, is murdered by his wife's lover, the emperor of Germany, whom she quickly marries. When the seven-year-old Bevis attacks his new stepfather, his mother sells him to merchants, who sell him as a slave to Ermin, the Saracen king of Armenia, under whom he is trained as a warrior. The king's daughter Josian falls in love with Bevis, sparking the jealousy of others in the king's court.

In the second part of the poem, King Brademond threatens to destroy Ermin's kingdom if he is not permitted to marry the king's daughter. Ermin knights Bevis, giving him the sword Morgeli and the magnificent horse Arondel, and Bevis leads an army against Brademond, defeating him and forcing him to swear allegiance to King Ermin. Josian can no longer resist, and declares her love to Bevis, promising to convert to Christianity for him. But Ermin, convinced by Brademond that Bevis has deflowered his daughter, orders Brademond to destroy Bevis, and Brademond has Bevis thrown into a pit to be fed on bread and water. Meanwhile the king marries Josian to King Yvor. But Bevis, after seven years' imprisonment, is able to escape, ultimately diving with his horse into the sea and swimming for his life.

The third section of the romance begins as Bevis, en route to Armenia, finds time to defeat a giant who is besieging a town. When he gets to King Ermin's court, he discovers that Josian has been married to King Yvor, and that Yvor has also been given his sword Morgeli and his steed Arondel. Bevis enters Yvor's castle disguised as a beggar, but his horse Arondel immediately recognizes him, and Josian convinces him that she has remained a virgin for seven years. After drugging Yvor's regent Garcy, they escape from the castle, but Garcy sends the giant Ascopard after them. Josian is able to reconcile Ascopard to Bevis and the giant becomes his page. The giant then transports Bevis and Josian to Cologne, where Bevis's uncle is a bishop. Bevis asks both Josian and Ascopard to be baptized by his uncle, and while Josian accepts baptism, the giant refuses. While in Cologne, Bevis is faced with a dragon that is terrorizing the city, and agrees to do battle with the monster.

In a battle that goes on for days beginning the fourth section of the romance, Bevis ultimately kills the dragon and saves the city. Afterward, he speaks with his uncle about his usurped patrimony, and the bishop advises him to return to England and fight for his inheritance. Bevis leaves, putting Josian under the protection of the giant Ascopard. An evil earl named Miles tricks Ascopard into leaving Josian unguarded, then forces her to marry him. Josian kills the earl on their wedding night, and is condemned to death, but is rescued at the last minute by Bevis and Ascopard. They all journey to England, and Bevis enters Hampton disguised as a French knight. He is secretly reunited with his old mentor, Saber, and a battle ensues with Bevis's stepfather, the emperor of Germany. Ascopard captures the emperor, takes him to Saber's castle, and throws him in a pot of molten lead. Seeing this, Bevis's mother throws herself from a tower and dies, leaving Bevis in possession of Hampton. He sends for Josian and marries her, and visits England's King Edgar to have his claim to his estates recognized. But when his horse Arondel kills the king's son, Bevis is forced to forfeit his lands and leave England with a pregnant Josian and a small group of followers, including his old friend Terri, whom he makes his new page.

As part five begins, Ascopard, angered at being displaced as page, abducts Josian for King Yvor, taking her from her infant sons Miles and Guy. Bevis and Terri go in search of Josian. She has convinced Yvor that she is a leper, and has been confined to a castle guarded by Ascopard. Meanwhile Saber, warned in a dream of Bevis's misfortune, begins a search of his own, and kills Ascopard in battle, rescuing Josian. The two of them search and ultimately find Bevis and Terri. The couple reclaim their children, and they all make their way to Armenia, where they help King Ermin battle Yvor. Bevis defeats Yvor in combat and sends him to Ermin, who ransoms him.

It would seem that the romance should end here, but more action postpones any closure. King Ermin names Bevis's son Guy his heir before his death. Bevis helps Guy convert Armenia to Christianity. Bevis's horse Arondel is stolen by members of Yvor's court, and Saber, regaining the horse, is rescued from several of Yvor's knights by Bevis's sons. Bevis confronts Yvor again, defeats him, and gains his kingdom of Mombraunt. Saber gets word that King Edgar has taken his lands, and he and Bevis go back to England, where Bevis appeals to the king, but the king's steward calls Bevis a traitor, and a street battle ensues, in which Bevis and six men must fight the entire population of London in the streets of Cheapside. Bevis is rescued by his sons and reconciled with the king. King Edgar gives his daughter to Bevis's son Miles, and Bevis returns to Mombraunt with Josian, where he rules for 20 years. At that point Arondel dies, and Bevis and Josian follow shortly after. Guy has them buried in a new chapel, and founds a religious house where he commissions songs to be sung for the soul of the horse Arondel.

While the plot of the poem seems lengthy and repetitious, it is easy to see how popular audiences were drawn to the adventure of the story, and its exotic as well as its realistic English settings. Perhaps the characters of the hero and heroine are the most appealing aspect of the poem: Bevis is rash and sometimes misguided, pious but flawed. Josian is assertive, resourceful, and bold. They are a refreshing change from the perfectly pious hero and his helpless, distant lady.

Bibliography

Barron, W. R. J. *English Medieval Romance.* London: Longman, 1987.

Baugh, A. C. "The Making of *Beves of Hampton.*" In *Bibliographical Studies in Honor of Rudolf Hirsch,* edited by William E. Miller and Thomas G. Waldman, 15–37. Philadelphia: University of Pennsylvania Press, 1974.

"Bevis of Hampton." In *Four Romances of England,* edited by Ronald B. Herzman, Graham Drake, and Eve Salisbury. Kalamazoo, Mich.: Medieval Institute Publications, 1999.

Brownrigg, Linda. "The Taymouth Hours and the Romance of *Beves of Hampton,*" *English Manuscript Studies 1100–1700* 1 (1989): 222–241.

Jacobs, Nicolas. "*Sir Degarré, Lay le Freine, Beves of Hamtoun,* and the 'Auchinleck Bookshop,' " *Notes and Queries* 227 (Aug. 1982): 294–301.

Mehl, Dieter. *The Middle English Romances of the Thirteenth and Fourteenth Centuries.* London: Routledge and Kegan Paul, 1968.

Weiss, Judith. "The Major Interpolation in *Sir Beues of Hamtoun,*" *Medium Aevum* 48 (1979): 71–76.

Bhartrhari (fifth century)

Bhartrhari was a Hindu philosopher, linguist, and poet whose linguistic philosophy has in recent decades been of great interest to Western thinkers, who have compared him with Wittgenstein, Saussure, and Derrida. His three "centuries" of verse survive in a large number of manuscripts, and were influential on writers of lyric poetry (*muktaka*) not only in Sanskrit but also in all regional Indian dialects in later centuries.

Legends surrounding Bhartrhari say that he was of noble birth, that he was attached for a time to the court of the king, and that he tried seven times to renounce the world before ultimately becoming a recluse and living in a cave. But nothing is certain about his life, not even when he lived (which has been estimated as late as the seventh century), nor is it certain that the same Bhartrhari that wrote the collection of poetry was also the philosopher. We do know that the Chinese Buddhist pilgrim I Ching, who traveled to India in the seventh century, mentions Bhartrhari as a legendary figure at that time.

Bhartrhari's poems, collected in the *Śataka-trayam,* are divided into three "centuries" or groups of 100 poems. The three groups comprise poems of ethical or political wisdom (*nīti*), poems of love (*śrngāra*), and poems of renunciation of the world (*vairāgya*). The hundreds of extant manuscripts are full of discrepancies, and among them contain some 700 poems—clearly most of these are poems of a later date that became attributed to Bhartrhari. Modern editors have identified some 200 poems that appear in virtually all manuscripts, and that are therefore attributed to Bhartrhari with some degree of confidence.

The voice that comes through in these poems is often that of a somewhat embittered court poet who resents having to rely on an arrogant but intellectually inferior monarch for survival, and resents the avarice and hypocrisy of other members of the court. "Wise men are consumed by envy," he says in one poem, and "kings are defiled by haughty ways" (Miller 1978, no. 4). It is also the voice of one who, though wishing to renounce the world in favor of the unchanging ultimate reality beyond the senses, is hopelessly charmed by the beauty of women:

a heady fragrance,
then the touch of her breasts.
I whirl in sensations
which veil what is real.
I fall deceived by senses
cunning in seduction's art.

(Miller 1978, no. 102)

No doubt it is the philosophical tone of many of these poems, and their rich linguistic texture, that leads a majority of scholars (though by no means all) to identify the poet Bhartrhari with the famous linguistic philosopher and author of the *Vākyapadīya.* Here, Bhartrhari explains his theory of language, called *sphota-vada.* Basically his theory is concerned with the relationship of language, meaning, and reality. In Bhartrhari's theory, no individual syllable contains the whole or a part of the meaning of a word; rather the word's meaning appears suddenly after all the syllables have been pronounced. Meaning is revealed in a flash of insight or intuition (*Pratibhaa*). This indivisibility of meaning in the word Bhartrhari equates to the indivisibility of meaning in the universe: Ultimate reality (Hindu *Brahman*) is meaning, and it is one and indivisible.

Bibliography

Coward, Harold G. *Bhartrhari.* Boston: Twayne, 1976.

Hamilton, Sue. *Indian Philosophy: A Very Short Introduction.* Oxford: Oxford University Press, 2001.

Miller, Barbara Stoler, trans. *The Hermit and The Love Thief: Sanskrit Poems of Bharitrihari and Bilhana.* New York: Columbia University Press, 1978.

Biket, Robert (Robert Biquet) (fl. 1150–1175)

Robert Biket is known only as the author of a late 12th-century Anglo-Norman poem called *Lai du cor* ("The Lai of the Horn"). The poem is a 580-line text of the type known as a Breton *LAI*—a short ROMANCE of the sort promulgated by Breton MINSTRELS and made popular by MARIE DE FRANCE. After Marie, Robert is one of only two other writers of Breton *lais* whose names we know.

Like many extant Breton *lais,* Robert's is set in the court of King ARTHUR. In the story Arthur is hosting a great feast at Caerleon, and each king, great baron, or knight present is accompanied by his lady or his wife. A youth enters bearing a highly ornate ivory drinking horn that he presents to Arthur as a gift of the king of Moraine. An inscription on the horn declares that an "evil fay" had cast a spell on the horn such that no man could drink from it unless his wife was completely true to him, and had never even thought about being with another man. The horn would empty its contents all over anyone whose wife was unfaithful.

The king immediately attempts to drink from the horn, and is soaked with wine down to his shoes. He makes a move to attack Guenevere with a knife before he is restrained by GAWAIN and others who reason with him that no woman alive could pass such a test, since all women would at least have thought about another man. The queen convinces Arthur that the cause of his failure with the horn is a small ring she gave a boy many years earlier.

Arthur is appeased, but to avoid being the only one shamed insists that all the men present be made to drink from the horn. All try to drink, and all are drenched with wine, so that Arthur laughs and forgets his wrath. Finally the horn comes to a knight named Caradoc, whose wife encourages him to drink and fear not. He stands and drinks down the entire horn full of wine, at which all present are astonished. Arthur rewards him by giving Caradoc the territory of Cirencester to hold perpetually and by making him a gift of the precious horn.

Lacy points out that the *Lai du cor* is remarkable because of its verse form—hexasyllabic (six-syllable) rhymed couplets—and because of its "humorous irreverence toward Arthur" (Lacy 1991). One finds this sort of "chastity test" in several Arthurian romances, but "The Lai of the Horn" is the earliest and best-known occurrence of it.

Bibliography

Biket, Robert. *The Anglo-Norman Text of Le Lai du Cor.* Edited by C. T. Erickson. Oxford: Blackwell, 1973.

Lacy, Norris J. "Robert Biket." In *The New Arthurian Encyclopedia,* edited by Norris J. Lacy, 38. New York: Garland, 1991.

Black Death (1347–1352)

The advent of the Black Death followed hard upon the Great Famine (1315–22), the worst famine in the history of Europe, in which at least 10 percent of the population died over the course of seven years. The Black Death itself was a combination of three related diseases: bubonic plague, pneumonic plague, and septicemic plague. The name "black death" probably originates from one of the common signs of infection: The lymph nodes of victims, usually those in the groin, would swell and darken. These swellings were also called buboes, hence the term "bubonic." The plague was extremely contagious, particularly the pneumonic variety, which could be contracted by inhaling the droplets produced when an infected person coughed or sneezed. The third and rarest form, septicemic plague, was the most horrifying because the plague bacteria entered the bloodstream directly, causing death in mere hours. A person might go to bed seemingly hale and hearty, only to be found dead in the morning after what must have been a night spent in agony. Mortality rates for bubonic plague were between 60 percent and 90 percent, while pneumonic plague was usually fatal within a matter of days. All three forms of the plague originated with rats and the fleas they carried, and rats were absolutely everywhere in medieval Europe.

These plague-infested rats arrived in Europe on merchant vessels, appearing first in Sicily and Sardinia by way of the Asian steppes and the Crimea. The population of Europe had been greatly weakened through malnutrition as a result of the Great Famine, and under such circumstances, weakened immune systems were no match for the virulent plague. The Black Death advanced across Europe at a terrifying pace, carrying off one-third of the population and as many as half of the residents of towns, where the effects of malnutrition were further exacerbated by the cramped living conditions and general lack of sanitation. Those who cared for plague victims often succumbed themselves, and monasteries and convents had a high mortality rate as monks, priests, and nuns contracted the disease from those in their care. Coffins for the dead could not be manufactured quickly enough, and often corpses were consigned to large mass graves.

While the causes and transmission of the plague bacillus are understood today, in the Middle Ages the process of infection was a terrifying mystery. Many contemporary theories were formed as to how this catastrophe might have been caused. Some attributed the onset of the Black Death to the configurations of the stars or other natural phenomena, such as earthquakes or even thick fogs. However, these causal theories were not restricted to nature, and marginal groups might also be blamed. Jews were accused of poisoning wells, while in Spain, the blame was placed on Arabs. The Jewish communities of the Rhineland paid a particularly high price as Jews in Strasbourg, Frankfurt, Mainz, and Cologne were massacred in 1349. Most considered the plague an expression of God's wrath and believed that the only way to escape the plague was to live in perpetual quarantine or flee. *The* DECAMERON by Giovanni BOCCACCIO (1313–73) is set during the plague years and details the attempt of a group of young Italian nobles to avoid the contagion rampant in Florence by quarantining themselves in a country villa and then passing the time by inventing a series of tales.

Despite attempts to avoid the effects of plague, outbreaks recurred throughout the remainder of the 14th and 15th centuries. The recurrence in 1361–62 was notable for the number of children who were killed and is often called the children's plague. Having been born after the main onslaught of the Black Death, these children lacked the immunity that came from prior exposure. The unpredictable but ever-present threat of plague, which claimed both peasant and noble, meant that levels of anxiety remained at a constant high from one generation to the next.

While the Black Death itself was a horrific event in the history of Europe, its onset acted as a catalyst for developments in medieval society. The Black Death acted as an impetus for the development of Christian spirituality as an increasing number of people sought to understand the seemingly arbitrary nature of the Black Death as well as their own mortality and purpose in life. On a more practical level, greater resources, such as land and food, were available for those who survived, and laborers could expect higher wages as a result of the shortage of manpower. For landowners, hiring the workers necessary for the cultivation of their demesne lands became prohibitively expensive. This, in turn, led to a decline in serfdom and the onset of several popular peasant rebellions, notably the Jacquerie in France and the PEASANTS' REVOLT of 1381 in England.

Bibliography

Jordan, William C. *The Great Famine: Northern Europe in the Early Fourteenth Century.* Princeton, N.J.: Princeton University Press, 1996.

Nirenberg, David. *Communities of Violence: Persecution of Minorities in the Middle Ages.* Princeton, N.J.: Princeton University Press, 1996.

Shrewsbury, J. F. D. *A History of Bubonic Plague in the British Isles.* Cambridge: Cambridge University Press, 1970.

Swanson, R. N. *Religion and Devotion in Europe c. 1215–1515.* Cambridge: Cambridge University Press, 1995.

Ziegler, Philip. *The Black Death.* Stroud, U.K.: Sutton Publishing, 2003.

Diane Korngiebel

Blickling Homilies (ca. 1000)

Most likely compiled sometime in the late 10th century, the collection known as the *Blickling Homilies* is a series of 18 sermons in OLD ENGLISH, all dealing with major feast days or saints' days of medieval Christianity and arranged roughly to correspond with the Christian calendar. The author or authors of the sermons are unknown, but in Sermon 11, for Ascension Day, the author—or perhaps the scribe—purports to be writing in 971. It is possible the entire collection was written at approximately that time.

Such a date would be consistent with one of the chief thematic concerns of the sermons—that is, the imminence of Judgment Day. There was widespread anxiety throughout Christian Europe concerning the approaching end of the millennium, interpreted by many as the date that would usher in the end time. While the author(s) of these homilies make orthodox statements to the effect that only God knows the day and hour of the end, he or they seem obsessed by the topic and bring it into the sermons of the collection at every opportunity. Some of the better-known homilies are Sermon 7, on Easter Sunday, which contains a HARROWING OF HELL episode, a dialogue between Christ and Adam and Eve, and in the second half, like so many of the homilies, a sermon concerning signs of the end of the world. Sermon 10, for Rogation Wednesday (preceding Ascension Day), is concerned specifically with the coming day of judgment. Sermon 16, on Michaelmas, is of particular interest to students of *BEOWULF* because the sermon contains an account of St. Paul's Vision of Hell that echoes the description of Grendel's mere and suggests a possible knowledge of the poem by the homilist.

The style of the sermons in the Blickling collection is more colloquial, more popular, and more manifestly intended for oral delivery than the later, more polished and scholarly sermons of AELFRIC and WULFSTAN. They contain fantastic elements and eschatological urgency that is likely to have appealed to the average citizen more than the scholar. This is not to say that the sermons evince no knowledge of learned sources, both secular and nonsecular. In addition to *Beowulf* and the *Vision of St. Paul,* the homilist(s) apparently knew the *Gospel of Nicodemus,* the *Apocalypse of Thomas,* and the *New Testament of James* as well as a number of saints' lives, to mention only a few apparent sources.

The manuscript of the homilies seems to have been produced in Mercia, and it has been conjectured that it was compiled for a monastic foundation in the vicinity of Lincoln. From at least the late 13th century, the book belonged to the Corporation of the City of Lincoln. In its margins are recorded lists of Lincoln city officials over a period of some 400 years, well into the 17th century. In 1724 the city gave away the manuscript, and for about 200 years it was in the library of Blickling Hall in Norfolk, from which it received the name by which it is now known. In 1932 the manuscript was auctioned, and now belongs to the John H. Scheide library in Princeton. It is the most important and valuable Old English manuscript currently situated in the United States.

Bibliography

Dalby, Marcia. *The Old English Homily and Its Background.* Albany: State University of New York Press, 1978.

Gatch, Milton McCormick. *Eschatology and Christian Nurture: Themes in Anglo-Saxon and Medieval Religious Life.* Aldershot, U.K.: Ashgate, 2000.

Jeffrey, Elizabeth J. *Blickling Spirituality and the Old English Vernacular Homily.* Studies in Medieval Literature 1. Lewiston, N.Y.: Edwin Mellen, 1989.

Morris, Rev. R., ed. *The Blickling Homilies of the Tenth Century.* London: Early English Text Society, 1874.

Swanton, Michael, ed. *Anglo-Saxon Prose.* London: Dent, 1975.

Blondel de Nesle (ca. 1155–ca. 1200)

Blondel de Nesle was one of the most important of the early TROUVÈRES, the northern French poets following in the tradition of the Provençal TROUBADOURS. Some 20 of Blondel's lyrics are extant, all written during the last quarter of the 12th century. His lyrics show considerable variety in their stanza structure and their musical composition. The poems include a number of themes adopted from the COURTLY LOVE tradition of the troubadours, including the poet's complaint to the god of love, the mistress's indifference to the lover, and the poet's dying for love. In the following verses from his lyric "Se savoient mon tourment," Blondel expresses his suffering for love:

It makes me grieve
That she is so gentle
Who turns into my agony
What is meant to be the whole world's
pleasure.

(Goldin 367, ll. 10–14)

Nothing is known of Blondel's life other than what can be gleaned from his poetry. None of the surviving manuscripts refers to him as "Messire," so it may be assumed that he was either the younger son of a noble family, or a commoner. Nesle is apparently his place of birth—a town likely in Picardy judging by the language of his lyrics. He seems to have known other poets, as he dedicates lyrics to both GACE BRULÉ and CONON DE BÉTHUNE, though he is not mentioned in the poetry of his contemporaries.

The best-known incident in Blondel's life never actually happened. A legend grew about him in the 13th century that he was minstrel to RICHARD I Lionheart, and that when Richard was captured and imprisoned by Leopold V of Austria upon his return from the Third Crusade in 1193, Blondel roamed Europe searching for his master. He sang the first part of a song they had composed together, and, when Blondel sang the song at Dürrenstein fortress where Richard was being kept, the king sang the last part of the song. Blondel was then able to take the news of Richard's whereabouts back to England and have him ransomed.

The legend is of course completely fictional, but it does demonstrate how well-known Blondel was in his own time and in the following century, and suggests that he was traditionally associated with

Richard I, who could well have been his patron. His poems were particularly widespread, some of them surviving in 10 or more manuscripts—a large number of individual trouvère lyrics.

Bibliography

Goldin, Frederick, ed. and trans. *Lyrics of the Troubadours and Trouvères: An Anthology and a History.* Garden City, N.Y.: Anchor, 1973.

Lavis, G. *Les Chansons de Londel de Nesle.* Liège: Faculté de philosophie et lettres de l'Université de Liége, 1970.

Tischler, Hans, ed. *Trouvère Lyrics with Melodies: Complete Comparative Edition.* Neuhausen, Germany: Hänssler-Verlag, 1997.

Boccaccio, Giovanni (1313–1375)

Boccaccio was an Italian poet and writer of prose fiction, largely influenced by DANTE and his close friend PETRARCH, and with those two is considered one of the three great writers of the Italian *trecento* (i.e., 14th century). His *DECAMERON* is one of the seminal works of world literature, and the most important work of prose fiction to come out of the Italian Middle Ages.

Giovanni Boccaccio was the illegitimate son of a Florentine merchant named Boccaccino di Chelo and an unknown mother, probably of humble origin. He was born, probably in Florence or his father's native town of Certaldo, in 1313, and some time before 1320 his father recognized and legitimized him and brought him to live in his household. Boccaccio was trained in mathematics, accounting, and general business practices, and in 1327 he accompanied his father as his apprentice to the city of Naples. Here his father was a councillor and chamberlain in the court of King Robert of Anjou, representing the interests of the great Bardi banking house of Florence.

The young Boccaccio was unhappy as a banker, and later in life he expresses his regret at his early education's ignoring rhetoric and the great classical poets. He did prevail upon his father to allow him to attend the University of Naples from about 1331 to 1336 in order to study canon law. Here Boccaccio studied under Dante's friend CINO DA PISTOIA, a connection that must have contributed to his lifelong reverence for his great Tuscan predecessor. Having made some connections at court, Boccaccio was also able to explore the substantial Royal Library in Naples, an opportunity that may have filled some of the earlier gaps in his education. In the meantime, Boccaccio's father left Naples in 1332 to pursue business interests in Paris, leaving the young Boccaccio on his own.

About this time Boccaccio began his poetic career. His earliest work, *Caccia di Diana* (*Diana's Hunt,* ca. 1334), was written in TERZA RIMA in emulation of Dante. His first major work, *FILOCOLO* (Love's labor, ca. 1336), is significant as the first prose ROMANCE in Italian, and it retells the French story of FLOIRE ET BLANCHEFLOR (whom Boccaccio calls Florio and Biancofiore). In the first book of *Il Filocolo,* Boccaccio describes his first meeting with the woman he calls Fiametta (Maria d'Aquino) in the Church of San Lorenzo on Easter Saturday. He depicts her as the love of his life and his inspiration (like Dante's Beatrice or Petrarch's Laura). She appears in many of his later works including the *Teseida* and the *Elegia di Madonna Fiametta,* and she is one of the storytellers in the *Decameron.* But no historical verification of the existence of such a person has been found, and it is possible that she was simply a literary fiction.

Before 1341, Boccaccio also wrote *Il FILOSTRATO* (The Love-struck). Written in eight-line stanzas of OTTAVA RIMA, the poem tells the story of the love affair of the Trojan prince Troiolo and his beloved Creseida, and was the chief source for Chaucer's *TROILUS AND CRISEYDE* (ca. 1385). It was certainly Boccaccio's major achievement thus far, but soon after its composition, financial crisis changed Boccaccio's life. In 1341, with the Bardi company in dire financial straits, Boccaccio was forced to leave Naples and return to Florence.

In Florence Boccaccio faced his own economic difficulties. He was never able to obtain the support of a wealthy patron, as Dante and Petrarch had been able to do. On the brink of poverty, he finished his *Teseida* (*Book of Theseus*), an epic-length romance in ottava rima concerning the love of Arcita and Palemone for the beautiful Emilia that was the source of Chaucer's *KNIGHT'S TALE.*

But ultimately Boccaccio, recognizing that courtly romances of the sort he had been writing were not appropriate for the bourgeois audience of Florence, began to write didactic allegories. His *Commedia delle ninfe* (Comedy of the Florentine nymphs, ca. 1341–42) is an allegory of virtues with alternating prose and lyrical sections, similar to Dante's VITA NUOVA, while his *Amorosa Visione* ("Vision of Love," ca. 1343) depicts love as an ennobling force. Composed in terza rima, the verse recalls the DIVINE COMEDY. Boccaccio followed this with his *Elegia di Madonna Fiametta* ("Elegy of Lady Fiametta," ca. 1343–44), a narrative made up of letters purported to be from the pen of Fiametta, jilted by her lover. It is a work with a legitimate claim to be the world's first epistolary novel.

But Boccaccio's greatest achievement in these years was his *Decameron*, a collection of 100 short stories or *novelle* told over a period of 10 days by seven Florentine ladies and three gentlemen who have fled from Florence to the hills of Fiesole to escape the BLACK DEATH. The work is justly famous for its grim and realistic firsthand account of the plague in Florence in its prologue. But the *Decameron* has remained popular and readable largely because of its great variety of tales and styles, from FABLIAUX to romances and moral tales. Boccaccio began the text shortly after 1348 and finished in roughly 1350–52.

The year 1350 marked a significant turning point in Boccaccio's life, for it was then that he began his friendship with Petrarch, having convinced his idol to stop in Florence on his way to Rome for the jubilee of 1350. Over the next 24 years, they corresponded regularly. Boccaccio also traveled to see Petrarch three times. Petrarch's influence changed the direction of Boccaccio's literary development: He became more devoted to humanistic scholarship and didactic purpose, and began to write almost exclusively in Latin. He wrote *De casibus virorum illustrium* (The fates of illustrious men, ca. 1355–60), which influenced Chaucer's MONK'S TALE, and *De claris mulieribus* (*Famous Women*, ca. 1361), which was a source both for Chaucer's *LEGEND OF GOOD WOMEN* and CHRISTINE DE PIZAN'S *BOOK OF THE CITY OF LADIES*. At the same time he worked on *Genealogia deorum gentilium* (The genealogy of the gentile gods, ca. 1350–65), a study of classical mythology. Boccaccio's new passion for humanistic letters was fed at the same time by the scholar Leontius Pilatus, whom he met in Milan while visiting Petrarch in 1359. Pilatus taught Boccaccio Greek, and Boccaccio was able to secure an appointment for him as professor of Greek at the University of Florence—the first such appointment since antiquity.

By this time the commune of Florence had recognized Boccaccio's usefulness, and he was being sent on diplomatic missions, to Ludwig of Bavaria in 1351, to the papal court at Avignon in 1354 and 1365, and at Rome in 1366. He also served in the Condotto, the department of military funding. Such appointments mitigated to some extent his financial situation; he is also known to have taken minor orders in the late 1350s. Sometime in the late 1360s, however, Boccaccio's health began to decline. He made a final trip to his old home in Naples in 1370, but returned ill and exhausted in 1371. Scholars have suggested that his prolonged illness may have been a case of dropsy or scabies, or a combination of both. He was severely ill in 1372, but late that year began a series of lectures on Dante sponsored by the commune of Florence. Boccaccio's interest in Dante had never wavered, and he had already written his *Trattatello in laude di Dante* (In praise of Dante) in two different versions published in 1351 and 1360. He was to revise the text one more time in conjunction with his lectures in 1373.

Petrarch died in 1374, and Boccaccio himself, worn out by long illness, followed on December 21, 1375. His contribution to the study of the classics, including Greek, his efforts in recovering and preserving the reputation of his beloved Dante, his influence on important fellow writers like Chaucer and Christine de Pizan, and most important, his own literary contributions, especially to the development of prose fiction with his *Decameron*, make Boccaccio a major figure in the history of world literature.

Bibliography

Bergin, Thomas G. *Boccaccio.* New York: Viking Press, 1981.

Boccaccio, Giovanni. *The Book of Theseus.* Translated by Bernadette McCoy. New York: Medieval Text Association, 1974.

———. *The Decameron: A Norton Critical Edition.* Edited and translated by Mark Musa, and Peter E. Bondanella. New York: Norton, 1977.

———. *Famous Women.* Edited and translated by Virginia Brown. Cambridge, Mass.: Harvard University Press, 2001.

———. *The Filostrato of Giovanni Boccaccio.* Translated by N. E. Griffin, and A. B. Myrick. New York: Biblo and Tannen, 1967.

Branca, Vittore. *Boccaccio: The Man and His Works.* Translated by Richard Monges. Cotranslated and edited by Dennis J. McAuliffe. Foreword by Robert C. Clements. New York: New York University Press, 1976.

Boethius, Anicius Manlius Severinus (ca. 480–ca. 526)

Boethius was a late Roman statesman, philosopher, and poet. He is best known for his CONSOLATION OF PHILOSOPHY, written while he languished in prison at Pavia awaiting his eventual execution under Theodoric the Ostrogoth. The *Consolation,* an attempt to justify the ways of God to men and to reconcile God's foreknowledge with human free will, was one of the most-read texts in the Western world for more than 1,000 years. In addition, Boethius's treatises on logic, on music, and on arithmetic were authoritative textbooks in European education for hundreds of years, and his theological tracts provided a model for what became the scholastic method of high medieval philosophy.

Boethius was born into one of the most respected patrician families of late Rome. When his father died, the child Boethius was raised by Quintus Aurelius Memmius Symmachus, one of the richest and most powerful men in Rome. Boethius was always close to Symmachus, and married his daughter Rusticiana. Aside from introducing him to orthodox Christianity, Symmachus gave Boethius a thorough education in the major Greek philosophers. It is possible he studied with some of the Neoplatonic teachers of Athens or Alexandria, but there is no way to know with certainty. In any case, his Greek was proficient enough that at an early age he set himself the goal of translating all of Plato and Aristotle into Latin. He was quite probably the most educated Roman of his generation.

Sometime after 500 Boethius entered the service of the Ostrogothic emperor of Rome, Theodoric. Theodoric had conquered Rome in 493 and was crowned emperor of the West at Ravenna, ostensibly with the support of the Byzantine emperor, to whom he owed nominal allegiance. Boethius rose under Theodoric's rule and became a consul in 510, when he began to serve in the Senate. By 522, the year he saw both his sons made consuls, Boethius had been named *magister officiorum* (master of offices) by Theodoric, in effect functioning as the emperor's prime minister. But in 524, for reasons that remain controversial, Boethius fell out of favor with Theodoric and was imprisoned.

It is clear that by this time, Theodoric had broken with Constantinople and its emperor, Justin (519–527). A Roman senator, Albinus, was charged with conspiring with Justin to overthrow Theodoric. Boethius rose to Albinus's defense, which raised suspicions about his own loyalty. It has been suggested that prior to this time, Boethius had been instrumental in helping heal a schism between the Roman and Byzantine churches, and this may have raised Theodoric's suspicions as well. Add to this the fact that Theodoric was a strong proponent of the Arian sect against orthodox Christianity, and there seems to have been plenty of reason for Theodoric to have been suspicious about Boethius's loyalty. Arrested and accused of treason, Boethius was imprisoned at Pavia in 523, and after a long confinement, was condemned without a trial, and was ultimately tortured to death sometime between 524 and 526.

Aside from the *Consolation,* composed in prison, Boethius's works fall into three categories. Most numerous are his logical treatises. Of these, his translation and commentary on Porphyry's *Isagoge* (itself an introduction to Aristotle's *Categories*) was especially influential. In his commentary, Boethius began the discussion of universals that became one of the most hotly debated questions in late medieval philosophy: Do universals have an existence apart from bodies themselves, Boethius asks. His answer, that universals exist not solely in sensible bodies but are understood apart from them, sparked a debate between Realists and Nominalists that lasted for centuries. Further, Boethius's translations of Aristotle's *Prior* and *Posterior Analytics* were the main sources for the study of Aristotelian logic in the Middle Ages. Collectively, Boethius's were the most important texts on logic before the 12th century, and were known as the *logica vetus* (old logic).

Boethius's next-largest group of texts are his instructive works on mathematical disciplines. Dedicated to his father-in-law Symmachus and apparently written at his request, these four texts, mainly translations of Greek originals, deal with the four chief mathematical disciplines as conceived by the Neoplatonists: Arithmetic, Music, Geometry, and Astronomy. Named the *quadruvium* by Boethius, these four disciplines ultimately became known as the *quadrivium,* the scientific and mathematical branch of the seven LIBERAL ARTS in the medieval education system, and Boethius's works became the standard texts for some of these subjects. In particular his *Instituione musica* was the chief musical textbook in schools for 1,000 years.

Boethius is also generally credited with the composition of five short treatises on theology, known as the *Opuscula sacra.* Scholars question the authenticity of the fourth of these treatises (on the "Catholic Faith"). The others, dealing with such subjects as the Trinity and Christology, show the influence of St. AUGUSTINE, but also show a good deal of originality, especially in the way that Boethius uses philosophical terms and methods in solving theological questions, his scrupulous use of logic, and his distinction between faith and reason. This method of dealing with theological issues served as a model for later medieval philosophers, and has led some scholars to name Boethius the first "scholastic" philosopher.

Finally, Boethius's *Consolation of Philosophy* became the book for which he is chiefly remembered. Written in the ancient classical form of Menippean satire, in which sections of prose and poetry alternate, the text is essentially a dialogue between the character Boethius and Lady Philosophy, who through her arguments leads Boethius from despair to confidence and consolation. The text begins with Boethius bewailing his own innocent suffering, and questioning why God would allow the good to suffer and evil to go unpunished. Philosophy shows him that the wicked are always unhappy, that virtue is always its own reward, that Fortune is fickle and anyone trusting in her gifts is bound to lose them, that Divine foreknowledge is not the same as predestination, and that humans do possess free will. The book, virtually unknown in its own time, went on to become very popular over the next few centuries, not only in its original Latin but also in several vernacular languages of Europe, into which it became one of the first texts to be translated. King ALFRED THE GREAT himself made a translation of the text into OLD ENGLISH in the ninth century, and CHAUCER made his own MIDDLE ENGLISH translation in the 14th, while JEAN DE MEUN translated it into French in the 13th.

After St. Augustine, Boethius must be regarded as the most influential Latin thinker in the earlier medieval period, acting as the vehicle through which a great deal of classical thought was transmitted to the Latin Middle Ages. The *Consolation*'s focus on the traditions of Greek thought with which Boethius was conversant make it essentially the last great record of classical antiquity passed on to Latin Europe. And its huge popularity made its influence on European literature enormous.

Bibliography

Boethius. *The Consolation of Philosophy.* Translated by P. G. Walsh. Oxford: Oxford University Press, 2000.

Chadwick, Henry. *Boethius: The Consolations of Music, Logic, Theology and Philosophy.* Oxford: Clarendon Press, 1981.

Gibson, Margaret, ed. *Boethius: His Life, Thought, and Influence.* Oxford: Blackwell, 1981.

Marenbon, John. *Boethius.* Oxford: Oxford University Press, 2003.

Reiss, Edmund. *Boethius.* Boston: Twayne Publishers, 1982.

O'Daly, Gerard. *The Poetry of Boethius.* Chapel Hill: University of North Carolina Press, 1991.

Bo Juyi (Po Chü-i) (772–846)

One of the best-known poets of the Middle TANG DYNASTY, Bo Juyi was a successful government official who believed that poetry should be accessible to all, and that it should be used for the betterment of society. He was the most prolific of all Tang poets, leaving a legacy of more than 2,800 poems.

Bo was born in China's Shaanxi (Shensi) province. His father was a scholar, and at 29, Bo passed the JINSHI—the national civil service examination—and entered a life of public service. He had a successful political career, being appointed to a succession of positions in various parts of the Tang empire. Perhaps it was this broad experience that made him more keenly aware of the plight of the common people in the empire. In any case he became an advocate for the poor and the disenfranchised. With his friend YUAN ZHEN, Bo developed a theory of literature that called for a poetry that was both straightforward and socially conscious. The ideal Confucian poet, in his view, was one that used his literary talent to persuade those in power to cure social ills. In his *xin yuefu,* or "new *yuefu,*" Bo used a traditional form, not unlike a *BALLAD* or folk song in Western tradition, to dramatize the abuses suffered by the common people. In his poem "Watching the Reapers," for example, he expresses his feeling of shame at how well he is paid as a government bureaucrat at the same time that government policies are causing others to starve:

They lost in grain-tax the whole of their crop;
What they glean here is all they will have to eat. . . .
At the year's end I have still grain in hand.
Thinking of this, secretly I grew ashamed
And all day the thought lingered in my head.

(Waley 1941, "Watching the Reapers," ll. 19–26)

In this poem and others like it, Bo deliberately aimed for a style of verbal simplicity. According to one old legend, he read all of his poems to an old peasant woman before publishing them, and he reworked any parts of the poem that she did not understand. Such a story is probably apocryphal, but it does indicate how important Bo thought it was to make his poems accessible to all.

While Bo thought his poems of social commentary were his most important, the majority of his readers over the centuries have preferred some of his other productions. His most popular poem has probably been "A Song of Unending Sorrow," which tells the story of a tragic love affair, based on the historical liaison between the Emperor Xuanzong (Hsuan-tsung) and a young concubine named Yang Guifei (Yang Kuei-fei). But critical appreciation has been most kind to his personal poems. Like his great predecessor Du Fu, Bo used small incidents in his own life to reflect in poetic form on his inner responses. He writes of little things—gardening, eating, family concerns—often with humor, but sometimes with great poignancy, as in the following poem where he remembers the death of his three-year-old daughter, jarred into remembering her when by chance he runs into her nurse on the street:

There came a day—they suddenly took her from me;
Her soul's shadow wandered I know not where.
And when I remember how just at the time she died
She lisped strange sounds, beginning to learn to talk,
Then I know that the ties of flesh and blood
Only bind us to a load of grief and sorrow.

(Waley 1941, "Remembering Golden Bells," ll. 7–10)

With his colloquial diction, his outspoken social criticism, and his autobiographical poems that provided a model for a number of later poets in the genre, Bo Juyi, is a unique figure among the Tang poets. Though not of the stature of Du Fu or

Li BAI, he is one of the more important voices of the era.

Bibliography

Waley, Arthur. *The Life and Times of Po-Chü-i, 772–846 A.D.* London: Allen and Unwin, 1940.

———, trans. *Translations from the Chinese.* New York: Knopf, 1941.

Watson, Burton, trans. *Po Chü-i: Selected Poems.* New York: Columbia University Press, 2000.

Bonagiunta Orbicciani da Lucca (ca. 1220–ca. 1297)

The only verifiably certain fact about Bonagiunta Orbicciani da Lucca's life is that he was a notary whose official documents were produced between 1242 and 1257. He seems to have lived into the later part of the century, since one of his poems takes Guido GUINIZELLI to task, and a few poems attributed to him are addressed to DANTE.

Bonagiunta seems to have been a well-known orator as well as a poet. He also apparently had something of a reputation as a heavy drinker, and, as a result, Dante places him in purgatory among the gluttons in his *DIVINE COMEDY.*

Dante also refers to Bonagiunta in *De VULGARI ELOQUENTIA,* where he is mentioned along with GUITTONE D'AREZZO as writing in a "plebeian" rather than a courtly style, and is there associated with the Tuscan school of poetry. Most scholars associate Bonagiunta more with the earlier Sicilian school of GIACOMO DA LENTINO, and in fact he was accused at one point by another poet, probably Chiaro Davanzati, of plagiarizing from Giacomo. Ultimately Bonagiunta seems to have drawn from both the Sicilian and Tuscan poets and from those of Dante's group, the *stilnovisti,* but was not necessarily a close follower of any tradition. The technical proficiency of his poetry is acknowledged, but Bonagiunta is not known for any stylistic or thematic innovations—he simply uses the conventions he inherited. He is best known not for any of his poems but rather for the use Dante makes of him in the *Purgatorio,* where in canto XXIV he is made to recognize that neither he nor Giacomo nor Guittone had been able to achieve the loftiness of expression evident in the *DOLCE STIL NOVO* ("sweet new style") of Dante and his group.

Bibliography

Goldin, Frederick, trans. *German and Italian Lyrics of the Middle Ages: An Anthology and a History.* New York: Doubleday, 1973.

Miller, Kenneth W. "A Critical Edition of the Poetry of Bonagiunta Orbicciani da Lucca," Ph.D. diss., Indiana University, 1973.

Bonaventure, Saint (1221–1274)

Saint Bonaventure was born Giovanni, son of the physician Giovanni di Ritella, in Bagnorea near the city of Viterbo in 1221. According to legend, he was healed of an illness at the age of 10 through the intercession of St. FRANCIS OF ASSISI. He studied with the Franciscans as a young man and was sent to complete his education at the University of Paris in 1235, where he studied under the English scholar Alexander of Hales. He joined the Franciscans in Paris after receiving his master of arts degree in 1243. By 1254 he was master of theology at the Franciscan school at Paris. As a student and later an instructor in Paris, Bonaventure was a colleague of the Dominican scholar Thomas AQUINAS. When in 1256 the secular priest William of St. Amour attacked both orders of friars as false apostles, it was Aquinas and Bonaventure who wrote the defenses of their respective orders, and later in his life, Bonaventure upheld the Franciscan order once more against similar attacks from Gerard of Abbeville.

In 1257, in part because of his recent strong defense of the order, Bonaventure was chosen minister general of the Franciscans, a position he held for 16 years. In this office, Bonaventure dealt with the severe internal division among the Franciscans between the Spiritualists, who called for the strict observance of St. Francis's original Rule, and the *Relaxati,* who sought relaxation of the Rule. Bonaventure wrote the first constitution of the order, reforming the organization in the true spirit of St. Francis, and regularly visited Franciscan houses throughout Europe to see that the constitution was being implemented. He resolved the conflict so successfully that he was called the Second Founder of the Franciscan order.

When the general chapter of the Franciscans met in 1260, it commissioned Bonaventure to write a new, more authentic, life of Saint Francis. Bonaventure used THOMAS OF CELANO's biography as a guide, but also did a good deal of original research by speaking with the companions of St. Francis who were still alive, and by visiting places frequented by the saint. By the general chapter meeting in 1263, Bonaventure had completed two forms of his Life: the *Legenda maior,* giving a complete biography, and the *Legenda minor,* to be used for liturgical readings on Francis's feast day. Later that year, Bonaventure recodified the Rule for the Franciscan-affiliated Poor Ladies of St. Clare.

By 1266, philosophers at the University of Paris, following arguments of the Islamic philosopher AVERROËS (Ibn Rushd), had begun teaching what became known as the doctrine of the double-truth: Natural reason, it was claimed, must accept things as true that are contrary to the truth of divine revelation. Moving to Paris early in 1267, Bonaventure gave a series of sermons opposing the unorthodox teachings of the philosophers, particularly attacking the philosophers' arguments for the eternity of the world (a notion that denied God's Creation) and for the existence of a single active intellect for all human beings (a notion that denied individual immortality). Bonaventure gave two more series of sermons against the philosophers in September of 1267 and February of 1268.

In Rome for the coronation of Pope Gregory X in 1272, Bonaventure was recruited by the new pope to organize an ecumenical council to meet on reforming the church, reunifying the Roman church with the Greek, and ensuring the safety of the Holy Land. While working on this task, Bonaventure was also back in Paris by March 1273, giving another series of sermons against the philosophers. But he never completed this series, being called back to Italy at the end of May at the request of the pope, who wanted to appoint him cardinal bishop of Albano, and also wanted him to prepare for the Council of Lyons to take place in 1274. At that council, Bonaventure resigned as minister general of the Franciscans. But shortly after preaching a sermon celebrating a "reunification" with the Greeks who attended the council, Bonaventure fell ill and died on July 15. He was buried at Lyons the same day.

In addition to his myriad sermons and his *Life of Saint Francis,* St. Bonaventure left a number of scriptural commentaries and theological works. These include a commentary on Ecclesiastes that emphasizes God as the eternal good; one on the Gospel of Luke concerned with the role of the preacher; and one on the Gospel of John focused on the dual nature of Christ. Bonaventure's commentary on PETER LOMBARD's *Sentences* deals with the science of theology itself as faith made understandable by reason, but subordinated to the divine authority of Scripture. In his theological texts, Bonaventure relied most heavily on the writings of St. AUGUSTINE, rather than on the philosophy of Aristotle, on which his Dominican contemporaries so heavily relied.

But even more than these texts, Bonaventure's mystical writings may be his greatest literary contribution. The best known of these is *Itinerarium mentis in Deum* (*The Mind's Road to God*), which he wrote in 1259 on a pilgrimage to Alverna, the site where St. Francis had received the *stigmata* (the five wounds of Christ) 35 years before. The tract visualizes a seven-stage journey from contemplation of the created world to mystical contemplation of the Trinity. Bonaventure's other mystical works include *De triplici via* (concerned with reflection, prayer, and contemplation as the "threefold way" to God), *Soliloquium* (a "soliloquy" in which the soul speaks as the voice of God), and *Lignum vitae* (in which Christ's cross is the "Tree of Life"). In these tracts, Bonaventure follows the mystical lead initiated by St. Francis, and stresses the importance of love over intellect in the individual's relationship with God.

Aside from Aquinas and Pope Gregory, Bonaventure was personally acquainted with many of the other major figures of his time. He wrote an office on the Passion of Christ for the French king Louis IX (St. Louis), and wrote other treatises for the royal family. He was revered for his saintliness in his own lifetime, and DANTE places Bonaventure in paradise in his *DIVINE COMEDY* (1321), where the poet has Bonaventure chastise corrupt members of his own order. Bonaventure was canonized in 1482 and was named a doctor of the universal church"by Pope Sixtus V in 1587. He was called the Devout Doctor in the 14th century, and ever since the 15th has been known as the Seraphic (that is, Angelic) Doctor.

Bibliography

Bonaventure, Saint. *Bonaventure: The Soul's Journey into God, The Tree of Life, The Life of St. Francis.* Translated by Ewert Cousins. New York: Paulist Press, 1978.

———. *The Journey of the Mind to God.* Translated by Philotheus Boehner. Edited, with introduction and notes by Stephen F. Brown. Indianapolis: Hackett, 1993.

———. *What Manner of Man? Sermons on Christ by St. Bonaventure.* A translation with introduction and commentary by Zachary Hayes. Chicago: Franciscan Herald Press, 1974.

———. *The Works of Bonaventure: Cardinal, Seraphic Doctor, and Saint.* Translated by José de Vinck. Paterson, N.J.: St. Anthony Guild Press, 1960.

———. *Works of Saint Bonaventure.* Edited by Philotheus Boehner and Sr. M. Frances Laughlin. 2 vols. St. Bonaventure, N.Y.: The Franciscan Institute, 1955–1956.

Bougerol, Jacques G. *Introduction to the Works of Bonaventure.* Translated by José de Vinck. Paterson, N.J.: St. Anthony Guild Press, 1964.

Hayes, Zachary. *Bonaventure: Mystical Writings.* New York: Crossroad, 1999.

Book of Dede Korkut, The (*Kitabi Dada Gorgud*) (14th century)

The Book of Dede Korkut is generally regarded by the Turkish people as their national epic. The text is not an epic in the general sense of a unified heroic narrative. It does, however, in 12 separate and self-contained stories, illustrate the values, character, and identity of the Turkish nation. The written text originated in the oral traditions of the Oghuz tribes, which had migrated to the area around the Caspian Sea from somewhere in East Central Asia in the ninth and 10th centuries. The book bears the name of its narrator, Korkut; "Dede" is a title meaning "grandfather" or "white-bearded one," that is, a wise and respected member of the community. He is a sage and storyteller who inserts a moral summation at the end of each story.

The Book of Dede Korkut survives in two 16th-century manuscripts. One is in the Royal Library of Dresden and the other in the Vatican. But the original tales seem to have been composed at a time when the Orghuz people had very recently been converted to Islam, and thus the tales reflect an earlier period, and although they allude to Islamic beliefs, they reflect a pre-Islamic era. For example, the text generally invokes Allah, but occasionally the ancient sky-god Tanri is referred to. The 12 tales are connected to members of the family of the Great Khan Bayinder.

The tales are typically composed of prose passages alternating with poetic speeches. They include a variety of genres, from realistic tales of the Great Khan to philosophical meditations (in the "Dali Domrul") to fantastic folktales like "Basat and Tapagoz," which tells the story of the aristocratic Basat and his battle with the one-eyed monster Tapagoz—a tale that is likely derived from an ancient analogue of Odysseus's battle with the Cyclops Polyphemous. There are also tragic stories of rebellion and internal conflict within the tribes, so that treachery becomes a common motif in the stories. Still, Dede Korkut ends each tale on a note of hope and benediction.

Bibliography

The Book of Dede Korkut. Translated with an introduction and notes by Geoffrey Lewis. Harmondsworth, U.K.: Penguin, 1974.

Nerimanoglu, Kamil Veli. *The Poetics of "The Book of Dede Korkut."* Maltepe, Ankara: Atatürk Culture Center Publications, 1999.

Book of Doctrines and Beliefs Saadia Gaon (933)

The most important work of the Jewish philosopher SAADIA GAON is his monumental *Book of Doctrines and Beliefs.* Writing at a time when many of his fellow Jews were questioning their own beliefs in the face of convincing rationalist

Muslim treatises demonstrating the compatibility of Islam with classical Greek philosophy, Saadia wrote in Arabic aimed at his semi-assimilated contemporaries, defending Judaism in rational terms that demonstrated how the Torah could be defended by arguments compatible with Plato and Aristotle. Like his Arab contemporaries, Saadia's method was to deal with individual scriptural problems through rational analysis, rather than to construct an elaborate philosophical system. Thus he borrows from Plato, Aristotle, the Stoics, and the Neoplatonists as seems appropriate to him.

His book is divided into a section on the Divine Unity and a section on Divine Justice. The first part begins with four proofs demonstrating the Creation of the world, and asserts a distinction between the creator and the world created, leading to a conviction of Creation *ex nihilo* (i.e., out of nothing). He follows this by a refutation of 12 other theories of creation that differ from his own. From here Saadia begins his discussion of the creator, particularly stressing the unity of God and including a refutation of Dualism and of the Christian doctrine of the Trinity. Saadia completes the first section of his book with a discussion of Scripture and law. Here he underscores the authority of prophets and divides the commandments of the Torah into those of reason and of revelation, a distinction later rejected by other Jewish philosophers, most notably MAIMONIDES.

The section on Divine Justice begins with a discussion of human free will. In contrast to his Muslim models whose system, called *Kallah,* ascribed all power to Allah and held human free will to be an illusion, Saadia argued that the law would mean nothing without free will, since one could not freely choose whether to follow it. God has freely chosen to grant human free will, and his foreknowledge does not cause human choice. Saadia goes on to discuss human merit and demerit, the nature of the soul (refuting other theories like the doctrine of metampsychosis), the resurrection of the dead, and the subsequent reward and punishment of the human soul in the afterlife. He also deals with the teachings concerning the Messiah and redemption, interpreting passages from the book of Daniel regarding the coming of the Messiah, and refuting Christian claims regarding Jesus as Messiah. The teachings regarding Messianic redemption are based almost entirely on statements of the Bible and the Talmud, the definite year of salvation being fixed by an interpretation of well-known passages in the book of Daniel. In the concluding portion the author refutes those who assume that the messianic prophecies refer to the time of the Second Temple; and he argues also against the Christian doctrine of the Messiah. The book concludes with an appendix presenting a system of ethics.

Bibliography

Efros, Israel Isaac. *Studies in Medieval Jewish Philosophy.* New York: Columbia University Press, 1974.

Helm, Paul, ed. *Referring to God: Jewish and Christian Philosophical and Theological Perspectives.* New York: St. Martin's Press, 2000.

Hyman, Arthur, and James J. Walsh, eds. *Philosophy in the Middle Ages: The Christian, Islamic, and Jewish Traditions.* 2nd ed. Indianapolis: Hackett, 1983.

Book of Good Love, The Juan Ruiz (1343)

Juan RUIZ's *The Book of Good Love,* perhaps the most important long poetic text surviving from medieval Spain, is a miscellany of 12 poems, each focused on a different love affair. The book opens with a prose sermon, or parody of a sermon, in which Ruiz claims to be presenting many examples of *loco amor* (that is, carnal love) in order to demonstrate the sort of sinful love that his readers must learn to eschew in favor of God's spiritual love or *buen amor,* the "good love" of the title. The tone of this sermon, and indeed of the entire work, which juxtaposes so abruptly coarse or ribald sexual exploits with sententious moralizing, makes it difficult for readers or scholars to determine the author's intent. Is he satirizing the moralistic attitude toward art so popular in his day? Is he satirizing the clerics, who, like the "Ruiz" of the book, engage in *loco amor* against their vows of chastity? Is he perhaps serious in his own moralizing? There is no consensus among readers.

The narrative portion of the text begins with two unsuccessful love affairs undertaken by "Ruiz."

The hapless narrator then consults the personified Don Amor, who gives him advice borrowed from Ovid and then sends him to Venus, who reiterates much of the same advice. This is followed by the story of the affair of Don Melón's wooing of Doña Endrina, a tale based on a 12th- or 13th-century Latin comedy called *Pamphilus*, which was written to show how Ovid's teachings might be applied in real life. In Ruiz's tale Melón is able to win the girl through the aid of a go-between, an old bawd named Trotaconventos. This crone is one of the first great comic characters in European literature, and is a prototype of the even more famous and admired bawd in Rojas's later 15th-century classic *La* CELESTINA.

Trotaconventos attempts to help the narrator in subsequent episodes: First she advises him to seek the love of a nun, and accosts one named Faroza. The outcome of this affair is ambiguous, but after the death of Faroza, Trotaconventos tries to obtain the favors of a Moorish girl for the Archpriest, but the girl spurns her suit. Ultimately Trotaconventos dies, and the narrator denounces death and, after expressing a number of further opinions, ends with some rather ambiguous advice on how to understand his *Book of Good Love*.

Ultimately only two of the 12 love stories end successfully for the wooer—a fact that might suggest something about Ruiz's final intent. But its ambiguity aside, the text is entertaining, witty, ironic, and boisterous, and presents a vivid and humorous picture of social life in 14th-century Spain. Ruiz displays a familiarity with a wide range of medieval and classical sources, including Ovid, contemporary sermons, French fabliaux, GOLIARDIC VERSE and perhaps the *CARMINA BURANA*, possibly the *ROMAN DE LA ROSE*, and *The Dove's Neckring* by the Moorish scholar *IBN* HAZM. A puzzling and uneven work, the *Book of Good Love* remains one of the founding classics of Spanish literature.

Bibliography

The Book of True Love. Old Spanish edited by Anthony N. Zahareas. Translated by Saralyn Daly. University Park: Pennsylvania State University Press, 1978.

Burkard, Richard. *The Archpriest of Hita and the Imitators of Ovid: A Study in the Ovidian Background of the Libro de buen amor*. Newark, Del.: Juan de la Cuesta, 1999.

Dagenais, John. *The Ethics of Reading in Manuscript Culture: Glossing the Libro de buen amor*. Princeton, N.J.: Princeton University Press, 1994.

Lida de Malkiel, Maria Rosa. *Two Spanish Masterpieces: The Book of Good Love and The Celestina*. Urbana: University of Illinois Press, 1961.

Book of Invasions, The (*Book of the Taking of Ireland, Leabhar Gabhála Éireann*)

The *Leabhar Gabhála Éireann* is a collection of narratives that are part of Ireland's "mythological cycle." They present a fairly systematic set of etiological myths concerning the origins of a number of Ireland's features (the lakes and shaping of the land, for example) and for a number of mainly agricultural human practices (such as plowing or churning). More important, the book presents the Irish traditions concerning the settlement of their own land as a series off invasions by a succession of mythic or legendary peoples, including the Partholians, the Nemedians, the Fir Bolg, the divine Túatha Dé Danann, and ultimately the Gaelic Milesians. The text was begun perhaps in the eighth century, and as many as five different versions were produced, all from relatively late manuscripts (though the ancient origin of much of the material has been demonstrated), the most important being the Book of Leinster (ca. 1150).

The Book of Invasions is made up of 10 sections. The first section deals with the Creation of the world, followed by an account of the first settlers of Ireland, identified as a son of Noah named Bith and his daughter Cessair with her husband and a number of others who, denied a place on Noah's ark, built their own boat and sailed for seven years before landing in Munster. They are ultimately wiped out by rising flood waters. It seems clear that medieval Irish Christians, perhaps the monks who produced the earliest manuscript, edited the Celtic mythological material to make it conform to biblical history.

Parts three through seven of the *Book of Invasions,* which have been shown to be the earliest parts of the book, detail several more waves of invasions. The first of these, the Partholians, come to Ireland from the eastern Mediterranean. They are said to have cleared four plains and created seven lakes. The story says that they also introduced cattle, milling, and the brewing of beer into Ireland. They are said to have fought with the Fomorians, a demonic race of underworld monsters. But the Partholians are wiped out by a plague. The Partholians are followed by the Nemhedhains, who find Ireland by chance while sailing from Scythia. They also fight the Fomorians, and are cruelly subjugated by the monsters, forced to pay a huge tribute to them—two-thirds of their goods—each Samhain (the Irish fall festival that is precursor to modern Halloween). Eventually the Nemhedhains leave Ireland. The fourth invasion of Ireland described in *The Book of Invasions* is by the people called the Fir Bolg. They are said to be descended from the Nemhedhains. The Fir Bolg are credited with dividing Ireland into its five traditional provinces, and established a monarchy connected with the goddess of the land, a "marriage" that insures the fertility of land and people.

The most important invasion of the mythological cycle is that of the Túatha Dé Danann (the "People of the Goddess Danu"), who arrive, the text says, from an island in the north. Many scholars have seen these beings as rationalizations of older Celtic deities. At first they coexist peacefully with the Fir Bolg. But the Túatha Dé Danann wish to rule the island, and they have significant powers, including Druidical knowledge and four powerful treasures: The Stone of Destiny (that cried out in the presence of the rightful king), the Spear of Lugh (the Celtic god of light and one of the Túatha Dé Danann), the Sword of Nuadha (the first king of the Túatha Dé Danann), and the Cauldron of Dagda (a magic cauldron that was never empty—perhaps an early Celtic precursor of the HOLY GRAIL). The Túatha Dé Danann battle the Fir Bolg, kill their king Eochaidh, capture Tara (the seat of sovereignty), and rule all of Ireland. Later, however, the Túatha Dé Danann are subjugated by the monstrous Fomorians. Nuadha is killed by Balor of the Baleful Eye, a Fomorian whose single eye strikes his enemies dead. Lugh ultimately kills Balor with a slingshot that strikes his eye, and the Túatha Dé Danann eventually exile the Fomorians from Ireland.

The eighth section of the *Book of Invasions* concerns the coming of the Milesians, the Celtic people who are the legendary (and perhaps even the historical) precursors of the Irish people. Their leaders, Ebor and Eremon, defeat the Túatha Dé Danann at the battle of Tailtu, and divide the land between them. The seven Milesian wives give names to various parts of the island, and the book ends as a Túatha Dé Danann woman, Macha, marries Crunniuc mac Agnoman, the prince of Ulster. Mach is scorned by the Ulstermen and gives birth to twins at Emhain Macha, after which she curses the Ulstermen.

The last two sections of the *Book of Invasions* are simply rolls of kings. Although the book was considered authoritative by native Irish historians until the 17th century, just how much of the *Book of Invasions* can be considered actual history has been a matter of scholarly debate for over a century. It is probably unwise to claim that anything in the book is historical fact: Even those aspects of the book that might contain a kernel of historical truth are blurred with myth and legend.

Bibliography

Carey, John. *A New Introduction to Lebor Gabála Érenn, the Book of the Taking of Ireland.* London: Irish Texts Society, 1993.

MacAlister, Robert Alexander Stewart, ed. *Lebor Gabála Érenn: The Book of the Taking of Ireland.* 5 vols. Early Irish Text Society 34, 35, 39, 41, 44. Dublin: Published for the Irish Text Society by the Educational Company of Ireland, 1938–1956.

Book of the City of Ladies, The (*Le Livre de Cité des dames*) Christine de Pizan (1405)

In one of her most famous treatises, *The Book of the City of Ladies,* the French "feminist" writer Christine de Pizan (1364–1429 or 1430) powerfully responded to the vitriolic mockery of women initiated by Jean de Montreuil, royal secretary and provost of Lille, after he had read JEAN DE MEUN'S *ROMAN DE LA ROSE* in 1401 and had written an enthusiastic essay defending this late-medieval encyclopedic and allegorical ROMANCE initially begun by GUILLAUME DE LORRIS. Jean was supported by the brothers Gontier and Pierre Col, who also admired Jean de Meun's erudition. The conflict turned into a veritable *querelle des femmes* (quarrel about women), in which, however, Christine was not alone in her defense of women, since the influential chancellor of the University of Paris, Jean Gerson, defended her position.

After having written a number of poems and letters defending women, Christine finally composed her *Book of the City of Ladies* (1405), which was deeply inspired by the French translation of BOCCACCIO'S *De Claribus Mulieribus* (*Concerning Famous Women*, ca. 1375). Christine reiterates the numerous examples of virtuous and admirable ladies from the past and present, and also adds many modern personalities to support her case for women. As early as 1399, in her poem *L'Epistre au dieu d'amours* (Letter of the god of love), Christine had unmistakably stated that misogynous opinions about women dominated the literary world only because a vast majority of men were responsible for the production of literature. The *Book of the City of Ladies,* composed virtually at the end of the public quarrel, obviously appealed to a wide audience, as documented by 27 surviving full French manuscripts and fragments, as well as by a Flemish (1475) and an English translation (1521).

The *Book of the City of Ladies* drew its fundamental imagery from St. AUGUSTINE'S *CITY OF GOD* and specifically attacked the highly popular, but vehemently misogynist *Liber lamentationum Matheolulu* (ca. 1295) by Matheolus (or Mathieu of Boulogne) and translated into French by Jeahn le Fèvre, ca. 1371–72. Christine argues that all people—both men and women—are subject to human sinfulness and can find salvation only by striving toward virtue and by fleeing the bodily prison. Employing the use of ALLEGORY, Christine utilizes a trope from the New Testament (Luke 1:38), the annunciation to the Virgin Mary, for a legitimization of her own writing, which associates her with God's mother. Three figures, Lady Reason, Lady Rectitude, and Lady Justice, appear to the narrator and commission her to build a literary city where women can find a refuge from male persecutions, or misogyny. In highly learned dialogues, these ladies answer Christine's questions as to why men criticize the female sex. Reason, for instance, points out that some men are "themselves steeped in sin, some because of a bodily impediment, some out of sheer envy, and some quite simply because they naturally take delight in slandering others" (Christine 1999, 18). Christine also learns that Ovid, among many others, was driven to slandering women because "he was so licentious, both in the way he carried on and in the encouragement he gave to others to do the same, he was finally sent into exile" as a castrated criminal (Christine 1999, 21). In subsequent chapters the question is raised why women have regularly and systematically been unjustly excluded from public service and official roles. Reason points out that there have always been women who acquired the highest degree of learning, and women who displayed the most advanced degree of good judgment. For each aspect of women's ability equal to that of men we are given a number of examples, both from mythology and antiquity, demonstrating that the notion of women's total limitation to the domestic sphere is entirely erroneous considering many ruling women both past and present.

In the second book, Lady Rectitude instructs Christine how to erect the houses and buildings within the City of Ladies, and illustrates this with a long and detailed list of virtuous, honorable, and loving women, again drawing the examples from antiquity and the early Middle Ages. In the third book, Lady Justice describes what religiously inspired women inhabit the City of Ladies, beginning with the Virgin Mary and Mary Magdalene, then turning to female martyrs such as Saint Catherine, Saint Margaret, and Saint Lucy, and to many other female saints. In her conclusion, Christine admonishes all married women to accept their status and to love their husbands, whether they are kind or cruel, good-natured or sinful. She also advises girls to be "pure and modest, timid and steadfast," and to arm themselves "with strength and virtue against the deceitful ways of seducers" (Christine 1999, 239). Addressing widows and all other women, she urges them to guard their honor and to protect their virtues against attacks by men. This City of Ladies will be populated only by women who "pursue virtue and shun vice" (Christine 1999, 239).

Far removed from modern feminist approaches, Christine idealizes the demure but steadfast lady who understands the limits of her political, economic, and hence public influence, but also knows how to defend herself against male seductions and denunciations and to stake her own sphere at home. Nevertheless, Christine insists on women's equality with men in intellectual, artistic, and literary terms. Moreover, she claims that women in their roles as wives and royal consorts would be fully entitled to assume highly responsible political functions as rulers and judges, but also, by the same token, as heads of their families at every level of life. Christine also uncovers deep-seated patriarchal prejudice against women as heirs to a family line and exposes unjustified male objections to women's education and leadership. The *Cité des dames* proves to be a masterpiece of medieval feminist writing, which successfully deconstructed most contemporary misogynist positions and became a beacon of women's liberation.

Bibliography

Altmann, Barbara K., and Deborah L. McGrady. *Christine de Pizan: A Casebook.* New York: Routledge, 2003.

Blamires, Alcuin. *The Case for Women in Medieval Culture.* Oxford: Clarendon Press, 1997.

Blumenfeld-Kosinski, Renate, and Kevin Browlee, trans. *The Selected Writings of Christine de Pizan.* Edited by Renate Blumenfeld-Kosinski. New York: Norton, 1997.

Christine de Pizan. *The Book of the City of Ladies.* Translated with an introduction and notes by Rosalind Brown-Grant. London: Penguin, 1999.

———. *Le livre de la cité des dames.* Edited by Eric Hicks and Thérèse Moreau. Paris: Stock, 1996.

Hult, David R. "The Roman de la Rose, Christine de Pizan, and the querelle des femmes." In *The Cambridge Companion to Medieval Women's Writing,* edited by Carolyn Dinshaw and David Wallace, 184–194, Cambridge: Cambridge University Press, 2003.

Willard, Charity Cannon. *Christine de Pizan: Her Life and Works.* New York: Persea Books, 1984.

Albrecht Classen

Book of the Duchess, The Geoffrey Chaucer (ca. 1370)

CHAUCER's first extant sustained literary effort, *The Book of The Duchess* is a DREAM VISION in octosyllabic couplets that is concerned with the death of Blanche, duchess of Lancaster and wife of Chaucer's very powerful patron, JOHN OF GAUNT. The poem, a narrative of some 1,334 lines, was purportedly written at the request of the bereaved widower. Whether it was written shortly after the duchess's death from the plague in 1369 or sometime later is a matter of some scholarly debate.

In the poem an insomniac narrator is finally able to fall asleep after reading the tale of Ceys and Alcyone from Ovid's *Metamorphoses.* He dreams that he is awakened by the song of birds to find himself within a chamber adorned with stained glass windows that tell the story of the fall of Troy, and frescoes that depict scenes from the *ROMAN DE LA ROSE.* From his chamber, he rides out with a group of hunters to seek the "hert"—a pun on "hart" and "heart." While in the wood, he encounters a knight dressed in black. The mourning knight speaks to the poet about his sorrow, which he describes figuratively as a chess match during which his opponent Fortune has destroyed his happiness by taking his queen. The literal-minded narrator sees no great sorrow in this loss, and the Black Knight goes on to describe at great length the beauty of "fair White," the woman he loved (*White* is the English translation of "Blanche"), and how he met and wooed her. The apparently slow-witted narrator still cannot understand the knight's grief until the frustrated lover blurts out plainly "She ys ded!" (Benson 1987, l.1309), at which the narrator expresses his own pity and thus ends the "hert-hunting." The knight returns to his "long castle" (a pun on Gaunt's title, the duke of Lancaster—that is, long castle), and the dreamer awakens.

While no extant manuscript of the poem attributes it to Chaucer, it is clearly his work, and he refers to it both in the prologue to the *LEGEND OF GOOD WOMEN*, where he calls it "the Deeth of Blaunche the Duchesse" (l. F 418; G 406) and in his *Retraction* to the *CANTERBURY TALES*, where he calls it "the book of the Duchesse" (X, 1086). Scholars have noted that Chaucer owes much to courtly French sources, including the *ROMAN DE LA ROSE;* Jean FROISSART's *Paradys d'amour;* Guillaume de MACHAUT's *Dit de la Fonteinne amorese* and *Remede de Fortune;* and in particular Machaut's *Jugement dou Roy de Behainge*, in which a noble woman mourns the death of her lover. The consolation for the lady's death in the poem has been compared to that offered in BOETHIUS's *CONSOLATION OF PHILOSOPHY*, though Chaucer's translation of that work was probably not made until well after he wrote *The Book of the Duchess.*

Critics have focused on a number of aspects of the poem. The relationship of the Ceys and Alcyone story to the knight's grief is unclear, though it certainly sets an appropriate mood for the poem. The question of the poet's own troubled mind that prevents his sleeping is another area of critical concern. Chaucer's use of the allegory of the chess game has interested some critics, while others have debated whether or not the knight in the poem is intended to represent John of Gaunt. But most important is the question of whether the dreamer is naïve and therefore blunders into the knight's final declaration or is a subtle psychologist whose naïve pose deliberately draws the knight out. In any case the realistic psychology of the poem has particularly impressed modern readers of the poem.

The most significant aspect of *The Book of the Duchess* is Chaucer's deliberate decision to write a courtly elegy in English. It was the first time that English had been used for serious poetry of the court, and Chaucer's success in the genre—his poem, dealing as it does with a serious event of real significance, is much more widely admired than any of his French models—ensured the establishment of a true, serious literary tradition in English.

Bibliography

Adams, Jenny. "Pawn Plays with Knight's Queen: Playing with Chess in the *Book of the Duchess*," *Chaucer Review* 34 (1999): 125–138.

Boardman, Phillip C. "Courtly Language and the Strategy of Consolation in the *Book of the Duchess*," *English Literary History* 44 (1977): 567–579.

Bolens, Guillemette, and Paul Beekman Taylor. "The Game of Chess in *Chaucer's Book of the Duchess*," *Chaucer Review* 33 (1998): 325–334.

Butterfield, Ardis. "Lyric and Elegy in *The Book of the Duchess*," *Medium Aevum* 60 (1991): 33–60.

Bronson, Bertrand H. "The *Book of the Duchess* Re-opened," *PMLA* 67 (1952): 863–881.

Clemen, Wolfgang. *Chaucer's Early Poetry.* Translated by C. A. M. Sym. London: Methuen, 1963.

Shoaf, R. A. "Stalking the Sorrowful H(e)art: Penitential Lore and the Hunt Scene in Chaucer's *The Book of the Duchess*," *JEGP* 78 (1979): 313–324.

Travis, Peter. "White," *SAC* 22 (2000): 1–66.

Wimsatt, James. *Chaucer and the French Love Poets: The Background of the Book of the Duchess.* Chapel Hill: University of North Carolina Press, 1968.

Bradshaw, Henry (ca. 1450–1513)

Henry Bradshaw was a Benedictine monk and English poet of the 15th century. Bradshaw was attached to St. Werburgh's monastery in Chester, and his most significant literary contribution is his *Chronicon and a Life of St. Werburgh*, an epic-like text in rather crude RHYME ROYAL stanzas extolling the life of the patron saint of his monastery.

Bradshaw was born in Chester where, in his youth, he was received into St. Werburgh's Abbey. After a customary period of study at Gloucester College in Oxford when he was a novice, Bradshaw returned to spend the rest of his life in the monastery in his native Chester. As a young man he wrote a Latin treatise praising his home city, *De antiquitate et magnificentia Urbis Cestricie* (The ancient and magnificent city of Chester), which no longer survives.

Bradshaw's second work, the English *Chronicon and a Life of St. Werburgh*, was finished, according to a dedicatory *BALLADE* at the end of the manuscript, in 1513, the year Bradshaw died. It contains passages on the founding of the city of Chester, a chronicle of the kings of Mercia, and also a life of St. Werburgh. Bradshaw describes her as the daughter of King Wulfere of Mercia. St. Ermenilde and St. Sexburge, abbesses at Ely, are Werburgh's mother and grandmother. Bradshaw narrates the founding of Chester by a legendary giant named Leon Gaur, he tells of the Norse invasions of 875, and he relates the great fire of 1180 that threatened Chester until it was miraculously quenched when St. Werburgh's shrine was carried into the streets.

Little of Bradshaw's work is original. Among others, he cites BEDE, WILLIAM OF MALMESBURY, GIRALDUS CAMBRENSIS, and Ranulph HIGDEN as sources; but his most important source was a Latin text called the *True or Third Passionary,* an anonymous life of the saint that Bradshaw found in St. Werburgh's library.

Bradshaw's poem was printed in 1521. It has since been both praised and derided by critics. Some have seen in the poem a refreshing kind of naïve or folk genius. Others have decried Bradshaw's apparent lack of any sense of meter. In any case Bradshaw wrote not for a courtly but for an unsophisticated audience, and none of his critics has questioned the sincere piety evident in his work.

Bibliography

Horstmann, Carl, ed. *The Life of Saint Werburge of Chester.* 1887. Reprint, Millwood, N.Y.: Kraus Reprint, 1988.

Bricriu's Feast (*Fled Bricrenn*) (ca. eighth century)

Bricriu's Feast is one of the longest tales in the group of early Irish narratives known as the ULSTER CYCLE, the cycle containing the exploits of the great Irish mythological hero CUCHULAIN. The story, which survives in several versions, probably dates back to the eighth century, though the earliest manuscript containing the tale is the *Book of the Dun Cow* from about 1100. Of special interest to students of medieval ROMANCE because of its relationship to the MIDDLE ENGLISH poem *SIR GAWAIN AND THE GREEN KNIGHT, Bricriu's Feast* makes entertaining reading in itself because of its comic as well as heroic elements.

The plot of the tale revolves around the notion of the "hero's portion": It was customary among ancient Celtic peoples to present a "champion's portion" of any feast to the acknowledged greatest warrior present—a custom that occasionally caused spontaneous battles among rival claimants at the feast. In this story Bricriu "of the poison tongue"—the Irish trickster figure—invites the heroes of Ulster to a feast at his newly built palace, but before the day of the feast he promises the hero's portion to three different warriors (Lóegaire Buadach, Conall Cernach, and Cuchulain). When the feast day arrives, the three warriors rise to do battle in the hall in dispute over the portion. The Ulstermen's King Conchobar stops them, and it is decided to submit the question to Ailill, king of Connacht. In the meantime Bricriu has stirred up a rivalry between the wives of the heroes as well, saying that the first one to enter the doors to the feast will be considered the preeminent woman in Ulster. The three women tuck up their skirts and race to the palace, while their husbands demolish Bricriu's house trying to let the women in.

A series of tests follows: Ailill looses wild cats upon the heroes, and while Cuchulain alone stands his ground, Lóegaire and Conall refuse to accept the judgment that he receive the champion's portion because it was not earned in battle against men. Ailill's wife Medb gives the heroes trophies, the most valuable going to Cuchulain, but again the others refuse to accept the outcome. Finally they decide to submit the dispute to Cu Roi, a legendary wizard from the south of Ireland (probably not originally part of the northern Ulster cycle at all). At Cu Roi's castle, the three warriors stand guard on successive nights. A giant easily defeats Lóegaire and Conall the first two nights, but on the third Cuchulain conquers the giant as well as a monstrous beast and nine other warriors. Cu Roi awards the prize to Cuchulain, but when the three arrive back at Conchobar's court, Lóegaire and Conall again refuse to accept Cuchulain's victory.

After this a large, hideous churl (or *bachlach*) appears at court carrying a great axe. The churl challenges the heroes of the court to a game: He will allow one of them to cut off his head with his axe so long as the warrior agrees to return the following night to allow his own head to be cut off. When Lóegaire takes up the challenge and beheads the intruder, the churl simply picks up his head and walks off. Lóegaire fails to appear the following night, and Conall takes up the challenge. But he has similar success and, like Lóegaire, does not appear the following night to take the churl's return blow. Next Cuchulain, like the others, beheads the churl. But unlike anyone before him, Cuchulain has the courage to return the following night to receive the churl's blow. When Cuchulain puts his own head on the chopping block, the churl tells him to rise up, declaring that there is no warrior in all Ireland that can match him, and awards him the hero's portion—and awards his wife precedence over all other women in Ulster—forever after. The churl then disappears, and it is revealed that he was in fact Cu Roi in disguise, who had come to see that the Ulstermen adhered to his original judgment.

While the story has been criticized at times for being repetitious and rambling, it remains a fascinating look at an ancient Celtic custom. It has long been recognized that the "beheading game" of *Bricriu's Feast* is a close analogue to that in *Sir Gawain and the Green Knight.* Even the Green Knight's name, Bercilak, seems clearly related to the *bachlach* in *Bricriu's Feast.* Thus the tale is important not only in its own right but also for its relationship to the Arthurian tradition.

Bibliography

Dillon, Myles. *Early Irish Literature.* Chicago and London: University of Chicago Press, 1948.

Cross, Tom Peete, and Clark Harris Slover. *Ancient Irish Tales.* 1936. Reprinted with a revised bibliography by Charles W. Dunn. New York: Barnes and Noble, 1969.

Bruce, The John Barbour (1375)

The Bruce (1375), by John BARBOUR, a 14th-century Scottish poet, is a patriotic 13,000-line poem chronicling the reign and military victories of the Scottish king Robert the Bruce and his disciple, James Douglas, and describing their role in gaining Scottish independence from English domination. *The Bruce* is composed in octosyllabic (eight-syllable) couplets, and so marks a break from the older ALLITERATIVE VERSE tradition that had dominated Scottish poetry in previous centuries. The story is introduced as the "true" record of the history of Robert the Bruce's reign (1306–29), though clearly it is historical fiction by a highly partisan Scottish writer. For example, for reasons that are unclear, Barbour fails entirely to mention the role of William Wallace in the Scottish fight for independence, but spends a great deal of time relating the exploits of the relatively less important Douglas, possibly because of the importance of Douglas's family in the Scotland of Barbour's own day. In fact, *The Bruce* is less a true chronicle than a ROMANCE, in the tradition of the romances concerning the martial exploits of CHARLEMAGNE or ALEXANDER THE GREAT, popular at the time.

The 20 books of *The Bruce* are impossible to summarize in a brief space. The poem opens with the death of King Alexander III (1286) and of his granddaughter, the "Maid of Norway" (1290), events that threw the Scottish succession into turmoil. The Bruce faction disputes the claims of John Baliol, and the Scottish barons entrust the question of succession to their "friendly" neighbor, England's King Edward I. The Bruce refuses Edward's condition—that he rule Scotland as vassal to Edward. When Baliol accepts those conditions, Edwards moves quickly to imprison him and to set about conquering all of Scotland. From that point, Robert the Bruce sets out to become king of an independent Scotland. He kills his rival John Comyn and proclaims himself king, and is supported by Douglas, whose lands have been seized by the English. At the Battle of Methven, Robert is defeated and by the third book has become a fugitive. But Edward I dies, and Edward II is slow to continue his father's attempts to subjugate Scotland. Meanwhile the Bruce continues to elude the English, and in book eight he wins the Battle of Loudoun Hill. He captures numerous castles, and by book 11, Edward II is prepared to bring his full force against Robert. Books 11 through 13 depict, in vivid detail, the apex of the Bruce's military achievements, the Battle of Bannockburn. Barbour includes an account of 15,000 common folk who join the battle and help rout the English army. After his success at Bannockburn, Robert the Bruce can announce that all landholders in Scotland must swear him allegiance.

In the later books of the poem, Robert's brother Edward Bruce strikes out on his own to win Ireland from English domination. Edward is presented as a foil to Robert—he is a bold warrior but rash and headstrong, and his designs often end in disaster. When, in book 18, he attacks the English against the advice of his council, his army is overwhelmed and he is killed. The more prudent Robert works toward peace with the English. The young English king Edward III is persuaded by his counselors to accept peace, agrees to a treaty that grants Scotland complete independence, and marries his seven-year-old sister, Joan of the Tower, to the Bruce's five-year-old son, David.

In book 20, the ailing Bruce enacts an ordinance that establishes his line of succession through David and Joan if they have a male child, and through his grandson Robert Stewart (Barbour's own patron, King Robert II) if that line fails. In dying, the Bruce expresses a wish that his heart might go on a crusade against the enemies of Christ. His body is buried at Dunfermline, but the faithful Douglas carries Bruce's heart in an enameled box, and takes it into battle in Spain against the Saracens. Douglas dies in the battle, but the Bruce's heart is brought back to Scotland and buried at Melrose Abbey.

Burkhart von Hohenfels (early 13th century)

This poet is mentioned in numerous historical documents between 1212 and 1242 as a member of a south German family of lower nobility (*ministeriales*) from the area of Lake Constance. He seems to have been in the service of Emperor Frederick II (1216) first and then of King Henry VII between 1222 and 1228. The famous manuscript *Grosse Heidelberger Liederhandschrift* (*Manessische Liederhandschrift*) contains a fictional portrait of the poet (fol. 110r) who is conversing with a courtly lady and passes a manuscript scroll to her.

Burkhart composed 18 COURTLY LOVE songs that are characterized by highly unusual imagery and motifs derived from hunting, falconry, bird-snaring, bestiary, warfare, and feudalism. In four dance songs the poet specifically reflects the influence of NEIDHART by adapting and also modifying the summer and winter motifs. But Burkhart does not allow the peasant theme to enter his poetry, as Neidhart does. The experience of winter only means that the courtly dance has to take place indoors (song no. I). If birds could properly perceive the beauty and virtues of his lady, they would declare her the mistress of the entire summer (no. III). In no. V, the poet describes his symbolic attempt to escape the snares of love by fleeing into a foreign country because his lady denies him her favor, but then he consigns himself to the noble power of her virtues and courtly honor. Burkhart here also envisions what he would do if he were a woman and were wooed by a lover, namely, open his heart and give the gift of love to him. As Neidhart does, the poet also has two young women discuss with each other the meaning of love in its social context (no. VII), but again without Neidhart's aggressive and satirical tone.

Burkhart obviously enjoyed developing innovative nature images to reflect upon love (no. XI), and he also created a remarkable woman's song (no. XIII) where the female voice ponders how she can pursue a virtuous life and at the same time follow her heart's desires. In no. XII the poet describes the effect of love in terms of personal bondage ("nu bin ich eigen," 4, 5). His lady's love is so powerful that it chases all other thoughts out of his heart, but if only once he could be allowed to enter her heart chamber, all his worries and doubts would disappear (no. XVI). Subsequently Burkhart describes his innermost feelings of love as a desire to enter a feudal contract with his lady (no. XVII). Finally, the poet states that no falcon returned faster to his master than his thoughts of love would fly to his lady (no. XVIII).

Bibliography

Goldin, Frederick, ed. and trans. *German and Italian Lyrics of the Middle Ages: An Anthology and History.* Garden City, N.Y.: Anchor Press, 1973.

Kornrumpf, Gisela, ed. *Texte,* 2nd ed. Vol. 1, *Deutsche Liederdichter des 13 Jahrhunderts,* edited by Carl von Kraus, 33–51. Tübingen, Germany: Niemeyer, 1978.

Sayce, Olive. *The Medieval German Lyric 1150–1300: The Development of Its Themes and Forms in Their European Context.* Oxford: Clarendon Press, 1982, 299–302.

Worstbrock, Franz Joseph. "Verdeckte Schichten und Typen im deutschen Minnesang um 1210–1230." In *Fragen der Liedinterpretation,* edited by Hedda Ragotzky, Gisela Vollmann-Profe, and Gerhard Wolf, 75–90. Stuttgart, Germany: S. Hirzel, 2001.

Albrecht Classen

Bury, Richard de (ca. 1281–1345)

Richard de Bury was an English bishop and statesman, who is remembered as a scholar and a lover of books who authored the Latin autobiographical text *Philobiblon,* describing his love of manuscripts and his passion for collecting them.

Richard was the son of Sir Richard Aungerville, and is occasionally known by that surname, but he came to be called de Bury because of his birthplace at Bury St. Edmunds in Suffolk. He was educated at Oxford, became a Benedictine, and was appointed tutor to the young prince of Wales, Edward of Windsor, son of King Edward II and Queen Isabella. He apparently supported Isabella's actions to depose her husband and put her son on the throne as Edward III, and after that occurred in 1327, Richard was appointed to a number of important offices, including bishop of Durham in 1333, lord chancellor of England in 1334, and lord treasurer in 1336. He also served the king on diplomatic trips to the court of Pope John XXII at Avignon in 1330 and 1333, and on the earlier trip he seems to have met PETRARCH. He was also a leading figure, particularly in his later years, in England's peace negotiations with Robert the Bruce of Scotland and with King Philip of France. Worn out by a prolonged illness, Richard died at his manor at Aukland and was buried in Durham Cathedral.

One of Richard's most lasting contributions to English culture was his founding of Durham College at Oxford. To the library of Durham College, he bequeathed his large collection of books, and one of the purposes of his *Philobiblon* was to give some direction to those charged with managing the library at the college. He also addresses himself to contemporary clergy, and as bishop tries to instill in them the love of books and of learning that was his own passion. At the same time, he wished to explain why he himself had spent so much of his life and fortune in amassing what was, for his time, a huge collection of manuscripts.

Richard wrote at least two other works—his *Epistolae Familiarium* and *Orationes ad Principes*—but is remembered primarily for the *Philobiblon.* That text was first printed in Cologne in 1473, and subsequently was published in Germany, in France, and in England in 1598. It was not translated into English until 1832. As for Richard's book collection, it remained intact at the Durham College Library until Henry VIII dissolved the college in the 16th century, after which the library was broken up and scattered.

Bibliography

Bury, Richard de. *The Philobiblon.* Introduction by Archer Taylor. Berkeley: University of California Press, 1948.

———. *Philobiblon.* Text and translation by E. C. Thomas, edited and with a foreword by Michael Maclagan. Oxford: Published for the Shakespeare Head Press by B. Blackwell, 1960.

Caballero Cifar, El (*Caballero Zifar*) (ca. 1299–1305)

El Caballero Cifar is the earliest full-length indigenous chivalric ROMANCE in Spanish, written in Castilian prose in about the year 1300. While its author is anonymous, he was clearly familiar with the *LAIS* of MARIE DE FRANCE and with the romances of CHRÉTIEN DE TROYES, and possibly with the prose romances of the 13th-century French VULGATE CYCLE as well. Evidence suggests that the author may have been a cleric, and some scholars have suggested Ferrán Martínz, archdeacon of Madrid, as a possible author, but such conjectures are impossible to prove. The romance survives in two extant manuscripts, one preserved in Madrid at the National Library of Spain, the other in Paris at the National Library of France. An early printed version, published at Seville in 1512, is also extant.

The structure of the *Caballero Cifar* is rambling and, by modern standards, somewhat incoherent. It has been compared to the loose narrative style of late Greek or Byzantine tales. The plot follows the adventures of the knight Cifar and his wife, Grima, as well as the later chivalric adventures of his sons Garfín and Roboán. These, along with an episode concerning the Lady of the Lake, suggest the influence of the popular romances of King ARTHUR. In addition, the text combines a secularized adaptation of the life of St. Eustache, other popular tales, and didactic matter and exempla.

The most admired and discussed character in the *Caballero Cifar* is the peasant squire of Cifar's son Roboán, known as El Ribaldo. The last part of the romance focuses chiefly on the adventures of Roboán and his squire, and scholars have seen in El Ribaldo a predecessor of the picaresque hero of later, Golden Age Spanish literature—embodying a sort of realism uncharacteristic of most chivalric literature. Also, in El Ribaldo scholars have seen the original forerunner of Cervantes's immortal Sancho Panza.

Bibliography

Burke, James F. *History and Vision: The Figural Structure of the* Libro del Cavallero Zifar. London: Tamesis, 1972.

Nelson, Charles L., trans. *The Book of the Knight Zifar.* Lexington: University of Kentucky Press, 1983.

Olsen, Marilyn A., ed. *Libro del Cauallero Çifar.* Madison, Wisc.: Hispanic Seminary of Medieval Studies, 1984.

Walker, Roger M. *Tradition and Technique in* El libro del Cavellaro Zifar. London: Tamesis, 1974.

Webber, E. J. "The Ribaldo as Literary Symbol." In *Florilegium Hispanicum,* edited by John S. Geary 131–138, Madison, Wisc.: Hispanic Seminary of Medieval Studies, 1983.

Caedmon (seventh century)

Caedmon, according to the Venerable BEDE, is the author of the first Christian poetry in English. In his *Historia ecclesiastica gentis Anglorum* (*Ecclesiastical History of the English People*), Bede tells the story of Caedmon's inspiration, which includes a nine-line poem known as "Caedmon's Hymn." The OLD ENGLISH version of this poem survives in an English translation of Bede, and demonstrates Caedmon's adaptation of the form and structure of Old English ALLITERATIVE POETRY to a new Christian subject matter. While early scholars enthusiastically attributed a number of religious poems to Caedmon, including several in the JUNIUS MANUSCRIPT, serious modern scholarship doubts any of these attributions except for the nine lines of Caedmon's original hymn.

In Book IV, chapter 24 of his *Ecclesia,* Bede says that Caedmon, employed as a laborer at the monastery of Whitby, was at a feast one night while a harp was being passed from person to person, and the guests were sharing songs. Since Caedmon knew nothing about poetry, he left the party and went out to the stable to tend the cattle. Bede reports that as Caedmon slept, a heavenly figure appeared to him in a vision and told him to sing. When Caedmon complained that he had left the feast because he couldn't sing, the heavenly visitor told him to sing a song of Creation. Caedmon responded with what is known as *Caedmon's Hymn.* It begins

Nu sculon herigean *heofan-rices weard,*
Meotodes meahte *and his*
mod-geþanc,

That is, "now we must praise the kingdom of heaven's warden, the Creator's might, and the thoughts of his mind." A glance at the style of the verse quickly reveals the use of the same style and meter common to Germanic heroic poetry. Each line of *Caedmon's Hymn* contains two half-lines, or *hemistiches.* Each half-line contains two stressed syllables. The hemistiches are linked by alliteration: The first stressed syllable of the second half-line determines the alliteration for the line; that syllable alliterates either with the first, the second, or both stressed syllables of the first half-line. The lines contain a series of parallel attributes, as is common in all Anglo-Saxon poetry—here, only two parallel concepts are listed: *heofan-rices weard* and *Meotodes meahte.* Yet it is clear that Caedmon has followed a typical pattern of Germanic epic or heroic poetry, but substituted the subject matter of Latin Christianity.

Bede's story continues as Caedmon visits the abbess and a group of learned monks the following morning, and they agree that Caedmon has received a divine gift. The abbess convinces Caedmon to enter the monastery, and he devotes the rest of his life to composing Christian verse in the Germanic style. In the end, Bede describes Caedmon's saintly passing.

Bibliography

Fry, Donald K. "The Memory of Caedmon." In *Oral Traditional Literature: A Festschift for Albert Bates Lord,* 282–293, Columbus, Ohio: Slavica, 1981.

Hieatt, Constance B. "Caedmon in Context: Transforming the Formula," *JEGP* 84 (1985): 485–497.

O'Keefe, Katherine O'Brien. "Orality and the Developing Text of Caedmon's Text," *Speculum* 62 (1987): 1–20.

Calila e Digna, El libro de (*Calila y Dimna*) (1251)

The *Libro de Calila e Digna* is the earliest example of Castilian Spanish prose fiction. It is an anonymous collection of moral beast-fables that was commissioned by ALFONSO X (called *el Sabio* or "the Wise") in 1251, before he became king, based on the Arabic collection by Abdulla ibn al-Muqaffa, the *Kalila wa-Dimna.* The Arabic text was in turn a translation of a lost Persian collection by a certain Barzuya. Ultimately, the collection stems from the Sanskrit *Panchatantra,* a third-century Hindu compilation that had been made for an Indian king.

Like most collections of animal fables, *Libro de Calila e Digna* is didactic in intent, satirizing human behavior through the tales of animals. The title of the book comes from the names of two jackals whose story forms the frame narrative for the collection. Digna is a power-hungry schemer who brings about his own downfall and ultimately his death after he causes the estrangement of the bull and the lion. Within this frame many other characters who are part of the main action temporarily take on the role of narrator and tell stories of their own. In addition, the whole story of Digna is placed within a larger frame of a conversation between a philosopher and a king, so that the structure of the narrative includes tales within tales, a popular Oriental and Middle Eastern technique that lies behind such collections as the *THOUSAND AND ONE NIGHTS.*

The *Libro de Calila e Digna* stands at the head of the long tradition of Spanish prose fiction. It directly influenced the collection of 51 tales called *El conde Lucanor* (or the *Libro de Patronio*) by Alfonso X's nephew, Juan MANUEL (1282–1348). It also influenced the episodic structure of later picaresque novels that culminate in Cervantes's *Don Quixote.* The *Libro de Calila e Digna* was ultimately translated into Latin by Raymond de Bézier in 1313, a translation that made the text popular throughout Europe.

Bibliography

Calila e Dimna. Edited with an introduction and notes by Juan Manuel Cacho Blecua y María Jesús Lacarra. Madrid: Editorial Castalia, 1984.

Parker, Margaret. *Didactic Structure and Content of El Libro de Calila e Digna.* Miami, Fla.: Ediciones Universal, 1978.

Picerno, Richard A., ed. *Medieval Spanish Ejempla: A Study of Selected Tales from "Calila y Dimna," "El libro de los engaños de las mujeres" and the "Libro de los exemplos por A.B.C."* Miami, Fla.: Ediciones Universal, 1988.

Campatar (seventh century)

Campatar is one of the three "masters" or "saintlords" of the bhakti religion popular in the Tamilspeaking region of southern India. *Bhakti* was a sect of Hinduism particularly devoted to the god Śiva and emphasizing personal spiritual experience above priestly ritual.

With APPAR and CUNTARAR, Campatar is the author of the Tamil *Tevaram* (Garland to God), a collection of hymns for worship that are considered sacred texts by devotees of Śiva. The poems are all composed in a traditional musical form called a *patikam* (or "decad"), a lyric of generally 10 verses, though occasionally there are 11. The songs relate to the mythological deeds of Śiva, or to sacred places where Śiva dwells—most of them refer to specific temples, and tradition says that the three masters traveled from temple to temple composing these hymns. They continued to be sung at shrines devoted to Śiva or in private worship. Characteristic of the hymns is their emphasis on a personal relationship with the god. Campatar's poems form books I-III of the seven books of the *Tevaram.*

We know only legends about Campatar. One such legend says that the goddess Parvati, consort of Śiva, suckled the baby Campatar, and in response he sang his first hymn. A more likely tradition says that the Pandya queen Mankaiyarkkaraci sent Campatar into southern India to save it from the Jainist "heresy." He is said to have reconverted the king Arikesari Maravarman to Saivism (the worship of Śiva). The zealous young saint is also reputed to have encouraged the slaughter of thousands of Jains who would not be reconverted.

Campatar's emphasis on the personal relationship with Śiva is captured in these lines from a hymn dedicated to the temple in Pulamankai:

> *Pure gold, first being,*
> *living in grove encircled Pulamankai*
> *he is my own.*

(Peterson 1989, no. 18; ll. 3–5)

Bibliography

Peterson, Indira Viswanathan. *Poems to Śiva: The Hymns of the Tamil Saints.* Princeton, N.J.: Princeton University Press, 1989.

Canon's Yeoman's Tale, The Geoffrey Chaucer (ca. 1395)

Well into *The CANTERBURY TALES,* CHAUCER presents his readers with a surprise. Breaking from the pattern that gives each of the original pilgrims introduced in the GENERAL PROLOGUE a turn to tell a story, Chaucer suddenly introduces a dramatic variation when he depicts a Canon (a cleric bound by the Augustinian rule) and his servant Yeoman riding hard to catch up to the group of pilgrims to join them on their route to Canterbury.

After the Yeoman has greeted the company, he begins to boast about his master's skill and knowledge, saying the Canon could pave the road to Canterbury with gold if he desired. When the Host asks why, if that is true, the Canon is dressed in such ragged clothes, the question seems to draw the Yeoman into a true revelation of how his master's obsession with alchemy has destroyed him. The Canon tries to stop the Yeoman's tongue, but when this proves impossible, he rides off, leaving the company. The Yeoman, now released from any inhibitions, tells all his master's frustrated attempts to find the Philosopher's Stone. The Yeoman also chastises his own foolishness for sharing the Canon's obsessions.

In the second part of his tale, the Yeoman tells the story of a different canon (he swears it is not his own master) who uses alchemy to dupe ignorant and greedy people. In the story the canon convinces a priest in London that he has actually found the secret of turning base metals into silver (though in fact it is all a trick). He sells the "secret" to the unwitting priest for 40 pounds, and the priest never sees him again. The Yeoman ends by admonishing his audience to leave the black art before it destroys them. Only divine revelation, not alchemy, will reveal ultimate truth.

There are no specific sources for Chaucer's tale, and his portrait of the dishonest alchemist was an unusual one for his time. Early critics thought the vehemence of the Yeoman's condemnation of alchemy to be evidence of Chaucer's personal antipathy toward the subject. Other scholars have discussed thematic parallels and contrasts between *The Canon's Yeoman's Tale* and *The* SECOND NUN'S TALE, which always precedes it in Fragment VIII of *The Canterbury Tales*—particularly the contrast of God's Creation with the pseudo-creation of the alchemist, and the parallel between the hellish fire of the alchemist and the divine fire of St. Cecilia in *The Second Nun's Tale.* Other scholars have focused on explaining the relationship between the first, autobiographical part of *The Canon's Yeoman's Tale* and the second part concerning the devious canon and the London priest, a relationship that depicts a kind of degeneration from obsession to deliberate deception.

Bibliography

Cowgill, Bruce Kent. "Sweetness and Sweat: The Extraordinary Emanations in Fragment Eight of the *Canterbury Tales,*" *Philological Quarterly* 74 (Fall 1995): 343–357.

Duncan, Edgar H. "The Literature of Alchemy and Chaucer's *Canon's Yeoman's Tale:* Framework, Theme, and Characters," *Speculum* 43 (1968): 633–656.

Grennen, Joseph. "Saint Cecilia's 'Chemical Wedding': the Unity of the *Canterbury Tales,* Fragment VIII," *JEGP* 65 (1966): 466–481.

Harwood, Britton J. "Chaucer and the Silence of History: Situating the *Canon's Yeoman's Tale,*" *PMLA* 102 (1987): 338–350.

Patterson, Lee. "Perpetual Motion: Alchemy and the Technology of the Self," *Studies in the Age of Chaucer* 15 (1993): 25–57.

canso (*canzo, chanso, chanson*)

The *canso* was the most important poetic genre among the Provençal TROUBADOURS: a love lyric. It was through the *canso* that the vernacular poets of Occitan influenced the entire subsequent course of Western literature by introducing the conventions of *fin amor* or COURTLY LOVE into the European literary tradition. In addition, the troubadours passed on through their *cansos* a practice of technical virtuosity and lyrical innovation that was characteristic of their songs.

The word *canso* means "song" in Provençal, and it is important to remember that troubadour lyrics were performed as music. Poets strove for originality of form both in music and versification, and ideally each *canso* was expected to have a unique tune and verse form. Such an expectation led to incredible variety and virtuosity among the lyrics: At one end of the spectrum is the relatively simple eight-line stanza in regular octosyllabic lines of BERNART DE VENTADORN's poem "Non es mervelha s'eu chan" ("Of course it's no wonder that I sing") (Goldin 1973, 127), which has a rather straightforward *abbacddc* rhyme scheme; at the other end is something like the 10-line stanza from PEIRE D'ALVERNHE's lyric "Rossinhol, el seu repaire" ("Nightingale, you will go for me") (Goldin 1973, 163) that intersperses lines of seven, three, and six syllables in a complex *ababccdccd* rhyme scheme.

As for the tradition of *fin amor* that the troubadour *cansos* establish, one convention is that the lady is described in such general terms in the poetry that all are essentially interchangeable. Bernart describes his lady thus:

I do not think you can see a nobler body in
the world:
she is beautiful and white, young and gay
and soft,

(Goldin 1973, 135, ll. 16–17)

Of his lady, CERCAMON says:

The most beautiful lady a man ever saw
is not worth a glove next to her;
when the whole world grows dark,
where she is—see, there is light.

(Goldin 1973, 97, ll. 19–22)

And ARNAUT DANIEL says:

When I look at her golden hair, her soft,
young spirited body,
if someone gave me Luserna, I'd still love
her more.

(Goldin 1973, 217–19, ll. 19–21)

The women in these three poems are indistinguishable enough that all three poets could easily be in love with the same person.

Typically, though, the *canso* focuses not on the lady but on her effects on the poet. When Bernart sees his beloved, he says:

I shake with fear
like a leaf in the wind.
I don't have the good sense of a child,

(Goldin 1973, 129, ll. 43–45)

Cercamon is similarly overcome by love:

I start, I burn, I tremble all over,
sleeping and waking, for love of her.

(Goldin, 1973, 97, ll. 25–26)

But Arnaut stresses the ennobling effect love has on the lover:

Each day I am a better man and purer,
for I serve the noblest lady in the world,
and I worship her, I tell you this in the
open.

(Goldin 1973, 217, ll. 8–10)

These are the conventions typically communicated in the *canso*. In form, the *canso* generally contained five or six stanzas in identical rhyme scheme, and ended in a *tornada* or shorter closing verse (called an *envoi* in northern France). The *tornada* often made a direct address by the author to the audience, and sometimes revealed the *senhal*, or pseudonym for the lover's lady, as in this *tornada* from one of Arnaut Daniel's songs, where he simply makes the adjective "Desired" the secret name for his lady:

Arnaut sends his song of the nail and the
uncle,
to please her who rules his soul with her
rod,
to his Desired, whose glory in every
chamber enters.

(Goldin 1973, 223, ll. 37–39)

Bibliography

Goldin, Frederick, ed. and trans. *Lyrics of the Troubadours and Trouvères: An Anthology and a History.* Garden City, N.Y.: Anchor, 1973.

Cantar de Mío Cid (1140–1207)

The *Cantar de Mío Cid,* or *Poema de Mío Cid* as it is also known, serves as the only remaining literary manifestation of an essentially complete epic poem in Castilian. Like classical epic poems such as *The Odyssey* or *The Iliad,* the *Cantar de Mío Cid* is a narrative poem that recounts the challenges, successes, and failures of Rodrigo de Vivar—the epic hero. Rodrigo, also known as the Cid—meaning *lord* in Arabic—lived from 1043–99 and gained the epithet *campeador,* or "great warrior," for his bravery in establishing the border between Navarre and Castile in the early 1060s. The epic story of Rodrigo was immortalized by Hollywood in 1961 with *El Cid,* starring Charlton Heston as Rodrigo and Sophia Loren as his wife, Jimena. Unlike many cinematic adaptations, *El Cid* substantially relies on the epic poem for its plot, characters, and themes.

The poem itself consists of 3,730 poetic lines and is divided in three parts or *cantares.* Rodrigo's epic struggle has two aspects: the Cid's political estrangement from King Alfonso; and the personal crisis related to the dishonor of his daughters by their husbands—the Infantes de Carrión. One of the many artistic achievements of the *Cantar de Mío Cid* is the manner in which the poem intertwines such different plot lines, creating a tapestry in which Rodrigo reveals himself both as a brave soldier and military strategist as well as a father and husband. The first *cantar* centers on King Alfonso's decision to give credence to those members of the court who are jealous of Rodrigo and have accused him, in his absence, of having stolen much of the Moorish tribute that he was charged with collecting. Accepting the king's order for his exile from Castile and León, Rodrigo visits his wife, Jimena, and his two young daughters, Elvira and Sol, to say good-bye. Rodrigo cries openly (v. 277) and appeals to God to allow him successfully to marry his daughters. The remainder of the first *cantar* centers on Rodrigo's need to survive and provide for his entourage of vassals. He achieves this by conquering Moorish lands and finally capturing the count of Barcelona, whom he frees after three days of imprisonment.

In the second *cantar,* the Cid's military victories continue with the conquest of Mediterranean lands, including the city of Valencia. Additionally, Rodrigo gains considerable wealth through the defeat of the king of Seville and King Yucef of Morocco. In each case, he sends a portion of this new wealth to Alfonso to whom he continues to remain faithful even in exile. At Alfonso's court, jealousy of the Cid and his success grows to the point that the noble but cowardly Infantes de Carrión offer to marry the Cid's daughters in order to enrich themselves. Unaware of their true motives, the king agrees to the marriages and pardons the Cid. The second *cantar* concludes with the marriage of Elvira and Sol—the Cid's daughters—in Valencia.

The final *cantar* brilliantly interweaves the Cid's heroism in battle with his love and concern for his family. The Cid's sons-in-law repeatedly reveal their cowardice both in the Cid's household in Valencia and in battle against King Búcar. Confronted with the Cid's growing wealth and power as well as the mockery of their behavior, the Infantes decide to take revenge on the Cid through their marriages to Elvira and Sol. They request to take their leave of Valencia in order to show Elvira and Sol their homeland in Carrión. Upon arriving in Corpes, they spend the night and make love to their wives. But the following morning, they instruct their entourage to go ahead while they brutally beat Elvira and Sol, leaving them for dead. The Cid's reaction to this dishonor is significant in that he does not immediately take revenge. Rather, he demands justice of King Alfonso, who calls all the parties to court in Toledo. At court, the Cid requests the return of his prized swords—given as gifts to the Infantes—as well as the dowry that he had bestowed on them. In addition, he demands an explanation from the Infantes as to why they dishonored his daughters. When they boast of their behavior, the Cid requests that his family's honor be restored through battle. At this moment, two messengers arrive at court asking for the marriage of the Cid's daughters to the princes of

Aragon and Navarre, of which they will be queens. This proposal will bring much additional power, wealth, and honor to the Cid, and King Alfonso accedes to the proposal. As scheduled, three weeks later, the representatives of the Cid not surprisingly defeat the Infantes de Carrión. The poem closes with the remarriage of Elvira and Sol, a symbolic act that genetically connects all future kings of Spain to the Cid—the national epic hero.

This connection between the Cid and the kings of Spain has contributed to the nationalist interpretation of the *Cantar* advocated by the great Hispanist Ramón Menéndez Pidal (1869–1968). In His "traditionalist" conception of the origins of the *Cantar,* Menéndez Pidal sought to free the poem from any foreign influence—especially the French epic tradition—and he asserted that the poem emerged from a process of collective authorship around 1140. This theory has been countered by the British Hispanist Colin Smith, who has proposed an "individualistic" interpretation of the poem's origins. He has suggested that a man named Per Abad wrote the poem around the year 1207—the date with which the poem closes. For Menéndez Pidal, Abad is not the author but the scribe, or copyist, and the date is not the date of the poem's original composition but rather of the creation of the sole existing manuscript.

Aside from its nationalist implications and the competing theories of authorship, the *Cantar de Mío Cid* is distinguished by its realism. In contrast to the *Chanson de Roland* (SONG OF ROLAND) in France, the *Cantar de Mío Cid* is "veristic" epic. The Cid is not a superhuman figure but a man who does heroic deeds as he loves and cares for his family. He does not seek conflict with King Alfonso or the Moors but harmony on both a political and personal level. At the same time, the *Cantar* contains moments of humor and irony. Just as a nine-year-old girl can show bravery when the people of Burgos hide in their homes, the Infantes can show their cowardice when a lion escapes its cage in the Cid's household.

Bibliography

Chasca, Edmund de. *El arte juglaresco en el* Cantar de Mío Cid. Madrid: Editorial Gredos, 1967.

———. *The Poem of the Cid.* Boston: Twayne, 1976.

Montaner, Alberto, ed. *Cantar de Mío Cid.* Barcelona: Crítica, 1993.

Menéndez Pidal, Ramón. *Cantar de Mío Cid.* 3 vols. Madrid: Bailly-Baillière, 1908–1911.

———. *En torno al* Poema del Cid. Barcelona: E.D.H.A.S.A., 1963.

Smith, Colin. *The Making of the Cid.* Cambridge: Cambridge University Press, 1983.

John Parrack

Canterbury Tales, The Geoffrey Chaucer (1386–1400)

The Canterbury Tales, composed by Geoffrey CHAUCER, is the most celebrated literary work of the English Middle Ages. The book is a collection of stories purportedly told by a diverse company of English men and women on pilgrimage to the shrine of St. Thomas BECKET at Canterbury Cathedral. Left unfinished on Chaucer's death in 1400, the volume includes a prologue and 24 tales of varying length.

Chaucer was a popular author in the 15th century, and *The Canterbury Tales* survives in whole or in part in 82 manuscripts. None of these manuscripts is in Chaucer's handwriting, and none was transcribed during his lifetime. The two earliest, the HENGWRT MS (owned by the National Library of Wales in Aberystwyth) and the ELLESMERE MS (owned by the Huntington Library in San Marino, California), were copied in part by the same scribe. Hengwrt is the earlier of the two and its text is thought by some scholars to be the more accurate. Ellesmere is a luxurious volume with fine illustrations of the individual pilgrims, and its text may reflect a correction of errors in the earlier manuscript. The Ellesmere MS is used as the base text for most modern editions of the *Tales.*

The language of *The Canterbury Tales* is a MIDDLE ENGLISH dialect spoken in London and southeast England in the last quarter of the 14th century. Chaucer's decision to write his book in the English vernacular perhaps reflects his appreciation of DANTE and BOCCACCIO, who composed their most important works in Italian, and of the many French poets who crafted lyrics and ROMANCES in the French vernacular. Unlike his friend John GOWER, who wrote major works in English, French, and Latin, and unlike Dante, Boccaccio, and PETRARCH, who crafted lengthy works in Latin as well as in the vernacular, Chaucer, so far as we know, composed significant narratives in English only.

All but two of the tales are in verse, the two exceptions being lengthy prose treatises on moral and spiritual matters (*The TALE OF MELIBEE* and *The PARSON'S TALE*). Chaucer's characteristic poetic line in *The Canterbury Tales* contains 10 syllables, five of them stressed: Along with Gower, he seems to have invented the iambic pentameter, which was to become the dominant line in English narrative poetry. It is this line that he employs so brilliantly in the flexible rhymed couplets of the GENERAL PROLOGUE and 16 tales.

Chaucer composed *The Canterbury Tales* over a stretch of at least 20 years, but the date of no tale is known exactly; it is unclear in what year he started work on the tales, and even the relative chronology of the tales is uncertain. A few works (*The KNIGHT'S TALE, The PHYSICIAN'S TALE, The MONK'S TALE,* and *The SECOND NUN'S TALE*) appear to have been written relatively early, but they may well have been revised for inclusion in the *Tales.* The four texts using the seven-line RHYME ROYAL stanza (*The MAN OF LAW'S TALE, The CLERK'S TALE, The PRIORESS'S TALE,* and *The SECOND NUN'S TALE*) are often assumed to have been composed as a group, but this is conjectural. A few stories respond to earlier ones (*The MILLER'S TALE, The REEVE'S TALE, The MERCHANT'S TALE, The PARDONER'S TALE, The NUN'S PRIEST'S TALE,* and *The CANON'S YEOMAN'S TALE*) and therefore appear to have been written relatively late. It is often speculated that *The SHIPMAN'S TALE* was assigned initially to the Wife of Bath, and that the General Prologue was revised in conjunction with the writing of individual tales, but there is no sure knowledge of this. What does seem certain is that Chaucer did not write the tales in the order in which they appear in any manuscript or printed volume, and that when he died he left behind a collection of fragments including as few as one tale (Fragment II) and as many as six (Fragment VII), without clear indication of how they were to be joined together.

The premise underlying *The Canterbury Tales* is that when Chaucer, on springtime pilgrimage to Canterbury, arrived at the Tabard Inn in Southwark, he encountered a group of pilgrims making the same trip. Chaucer joined the merry company, whom he describes individually in the General Prologue. At the suggestion of innkeeper Harry Bailly, the pilgrims agreed to a storytelling contest so as to make the route seem shorter. Each pilgrim would "telle tales tweye / To Caunterbury-ward" (Benson 1987, 36, I 792–93) and two more on the way home. This plan is not fulfilled—only one pilgrim, Chaucer himself, tells two tales, and some do not tell any—and it may not in fact represent Chaucer's ultimate intention. At one point Chaucer talks of each pilgrim telling a tale or two, and in the prologue to the final tale Harry Bailly tells the Parson that "every man, save thou, hath toold his tale" (Benson 1987, 287, l. 25). As we do not know when these three passages were written, we cannot determine which of them—if any—represents Chaucer's final word. In any event, *The Canterbury Tales* claims to be the accurate record of the stories recounted by the pilgrims in their contest.

Chaucer used this liminal setting of pilgrimage as the vehicle for an unprecedented exploration of the social, economic, and political world of late 14th-century England. The pilgrims' occupations span the social classes of his time, including military vocations from knight to yeoman; religious vocations from monk and prioress to pardoner and parson; countrymen from franklin to plowman; professionals from lawyer to manciple; entrepreneurs from merchant to sea captain; and tradespeople from weaver to miller to the clothmaking Wife of Bath. The tales widen the frame both chronologically and spatially, stretching from ancient Greece and Rome at the one extreme, to contemporary London, Bath, Oxford, and Cambridge at the other, and incorporating settings as diverse as Lombard towns and countryside, the coast of Brittany, a suburb of Paris, "Asie," the realm of Genghis Khan, a poor widow's farm, and hell.

The tales span a wide range of genres, from idealistic romance to bawdy FABLIAU to devout SAINT'S LIFE to philosophical meditation, with many tales mixing genres in unexpected ways. A connection may often be found between the character or social position of a narrator and the type of story assigned to that narrator, though some connections are loose. The texts where the linkage is most fully developed are *The* WIFE OF BATH'S TALE, *The* PARDONER'S TALE, and *The Canon's Yeoman's Tale*, each of which has a substantial prologue.

A limited range of occupations were available to women in medieval England, which may explain why only three of the 30-odd pilgrims are female. Chaucer overcomes this gender constraint by having women play large roles in many of the tales, often as a story's protagonist. Chaucer's women range from children to wives to aged widows, from virgins to flirts to prostitutes. Two mothers-in-law are wicked, and some of the wives are adulterous, but an equal number of women serve as moral foci.

In the General Prologue and in the prologue to *The Miller's Tale* Chaucer apologizes for the bawdy language in some of his writing, attributing it to the churlish character of particular pilgrims. He invites a discriminating reader to "Turne over the leef and chese another tale" (Benson 1987, 67, l. 3177). In the *Retraction* that closes *The Canterbury Tales* he revokes his many "translacions and enditynges of worldly vanities" (Benson 1987, 328, l. 1085) and asks forgiveness for having written them. Whether one takes these apologies as earnest or dismisses them as rhetorical artifice, readers who have immersed themselves in the brilliance of Chaucer's unfinished book cannot help but be glad for every page that he did write, both the earthy and the sublime, and to wish that he had lived to write still more. Harry Bailly declares in the General Prologue that the finest story is one "of best sentence and moost solace" (Benson 1987, 36, I 798). The phrase defines Chaucer's accomplishment in *The Canterbury Tales.*

Bibliography

Benson, Larry D., gen. ed. *The Riverside Chaucer.* 3rd ed. Boston: Houghton Mifflin, 1987.

Cooper, Helen. *Oxford Guides to Chaucer: The Canterbury Tales.* 2nd ed. Oxford: Oxford University Press, 1996.

Patterson, Lee. *Chaucer and the Subject of History.* Madison: University of Wisconsin Press, 1991.

Pearsall, Derek. *The Canterbury Tales.* London: George Allen and Unwin, 1985.

Whittock, Trevor. *A Reading of the Canterbury Tales.* Cambridge: Cambridge University Press, 1968.

David Raybin

Cantigas de Amigo

The *Cantigas de Amigo* (or "songs to a friend") are Galician-Portuguese lyrics written between the 12th and 14th centuries. In this kind of lyric, a female persona sings to or about her lover. Generally the subject is the suffering the woman felt at her lover's absence and her longing to be happily reunited with her beloved. These lyrics are less likely to express the conventions of COURTLY LOVE than they are to emphasize the pain of separation and the importance of loyalty in love. Peter Dronke points out that most of the best *cantigas de amigo* focus on a single memorable image, and he quotes a song of Pero MEOGO to illustrate:

Hinds on the hillside, tell me true,
my love has gone, and if he lingers there,
fair ones, what shall I do?

Hinds on the hillside, I'm telling you:
My love has gone, and I long to know,
fair ones, what I shall do.

(Dronke 1996, 104)

While the majority of such poems are written, like this one, by male composers using a female persona (as in the case of Martin CODAX, for example), it seems clear that such poems come from a very old folk tradition. The *KHARJAS* that form the concluding stanzas in the romance vernacular of Hebrew and Arabic *muwashshah* poetry bear a close resemblance to *cantigas de amigo:* They are generally lyric outcries on love from a female perspective. It seems likely that these snatches of colloquial songs are traditional, probably associated with folk dances. Written between 1000 and 1150, these *kharjas* predate the *cantigas de amigo,* and suggest an oral tradition behind the genre.

That tradition seems to have been common far beyond the Iberian Peninsula. Dronke points out that between the sixth and ninth centuries, church councils across Europe regularly condemned the composition of licentious songs, specifically *puellarum cantica* or the songs of girls. Charlemagne, in 789, expressly forbade nuns in his kingdom to write or send *winileodas* (that is, "songs for a friend"—essentially the same term as *cantigas de amigo*), and Dronke identifies the Old English lyric *WULF AND EADWACER* as an example of what this early Germanic analogue to the *cantigas de amigo* was like (Dronke 1996, 86–92).

Bibliography

Dronke, Peter. *The Medieval Lyric.* 3rd ed. Woodbridge, U.K.: Boydell and Brewer, 1996.

Klinck, Anne L., and Ann Marie Rasmussen, eds. *Medieval Woman's Song: Cross-Cultural Approaches.* Philadelphia: University of Pennsylvania Press, 2002.

canzone (plural: *canzoni*)

The *canzone* was a late medieval lyric form popular in Italy among poets influenced by the Provençal TROUBADOURS. Derived largely from the Occitan *CANSO,* particularly as practiced by the troubadour GIRAUT DE BORNEIL, the *canzone* was usually a poem of five to seven stanzas with an identical rhyme scheme. Stanzas could range from seven to 20 lines, generally of 11 syllables, often ending with a *commiato* (similar to the *envoi* of a French *BALLADE*)—a short stanza half the length of the others, serving as a summary or closing.

In *De VULGARI ELOQUENTIA,* DANTE calls the *canzone* the noblest form of Italian verse, and says it is the ideal genre for dealing with the three highest subjects of poetry: valor, virtue, and love. But in practice, the chief subject of the *canzoni* that survive from late medieval Italy is love. The form seems to have been used first by GUITTONE D'AREZZO, chief poet of the Sicilian School, and then by his followers, most notably Guido GUINIZELLI and poets of the new style of Tuscan poetry, the *DOLCE STIL NOVO,* including Guido CAVALCANTI and DANTE himself.

Perhaps most influential of all were the *canzoni* composed by PETRARCH in his *Canzoniere.* Petrarch's *canzoni,* always five or six stanzas with a *commiato,* established a fixed form for the genre and influenced Italian poets well into the Renaissance. The standard Italian *canzone* came thus to be called the *canzone petrarchesca.*

The most influential structural aspect of the *canzone* is described by Dante in *De vulgari eloquentia.* Dante describes the *canzone* as having a three-part structure within a two-part structure: The form, he says, is divided into two parts, the *fronte* (or *frons* in Latin), or head, and the *sirma* (*cauda* in Latin), or tail. However, the *frons* is further subdivided into two *piedi,* or feet, which are identical in structure. The *cauda* might contain a final *commiato.* Thus the structure of the *canzone* might be described as AA/B. This structure was to influence the development of the sonnet (with its subdividable *octave* followed by a *sestet*), and therefore the whole history of European poetry.

Bibliography

Barber, Joseph A. "Rhyme Scheme Patterns in Petrarch's *Canzoniere,*" *MLN* 92 (1977): 139–145.

Wilkins, Ernest Hatch. "The Canzone and the Minnesang," in *The Invention of the Sonnet, and Other Studies in Italian Literature.* Roma: Edizioni de Storia e letteratura, 1959.

Canzoniere (*Rime sparse, Rerum vulgarium fragmenta*) Francis Petrarch (ca. 1330–1374)

Although PETRARCH assumed that his great lasting fame would come from his works in Latin, in particular his epic *Africa* on the exploits of his favorite hero, Scipio Africanus, his reputation today rests chiefly on his lyric poetry in the vernacular, a collection of short poems he referred to as "trifles" in a letter two years before his death. Petrarch never gave this collection of 366 Italian lyrics a proper title, referring to them as *Rerum vulgarium frag-*

menta (Fragments of things in the vernacular), but they have become known to modern readers by the name *Rime sparse* (Scattered verse), or more often by the title *Canzoniere* (Song book). The chief theme of the collection is Petrarch's love for the beautiful Laura, though the real subject of the poems is Petrarch's own psyche: his emotions and aspirations as revealed in his expressions of love—in particular the inner conflict between his desire for worldly greatness and fame and his desire for heavenly reward.

Of the 366 poems in the standard edition of the *Canzoniere,* 317 are SONNETS. Petrarch also includes 29 longer *canzoni,* as well as three more elaborate forms—nine *sestinas,* seven *ballatas,* and four *madrigals.* Of these poems, the vast majority are essentially love poems to the lady Laura, the paragon of beauty and excellence. Some 37 poems take other subjects, including the virtue of fame, religious and moral issues, political themes including Petrarch's love of Italy and desire to resurrect the glory of the city of Rome, and matters concerning his friends or patrons. Other themes run through all of the poems, as Petrarch muses on the transience of earthly things, the ravages of time, and the virtues of peace and tranquillity.

Petrarch underscores this transience by relating the death of his beloved Laura. He first met her, he tells us, on Good Friday, April 6, 1327, and she died on Easter Sunday, the same date 21 years later, probably during the BLACK DEATH. Manuscript tradition as old as the 16th century divides the *Canzoniere* into the first 263 poems, referred to as *In vita di Madonna Laura* (*The Lady Laura in Life*) and the last 103, called *In morte di Madonna Laura* (*The Lady Laura after Death*). While the titles and specific divisions were not made by Petrarch, they do reflect his own careful ordering of the poems.

Despite Petrarch's protestations to the contrary, he seems to have been keenly interested in the texts of his "trifles," as evidenced by his own manuscript copy of the poems, still extant in the Vatican library. This manuscript contains a significant number of notes and corrections to the poems, as well as marginal annotations that reflect a meticulous concern for the precise ordering of the 366 lyrics. Scholars have determined that the text of the *Canzoniere* went through at least nine revisions over a 30-year period, indicating that each poem in the collection has been placed where it is in the final ordering with a particular purpose in mind. The poems of the first part concern the poet's love for the living Laura, epitome of all that is admirable. They focus, however, not on her but on the poet's reactions to her—the paradoxical effects of a love that is both pleasurable and painful at the same time:

. . . blessed be the first sweet agony
I felt when I found myself bound to Love,
the bow and all the arrows that have
pierced me;
the wounds that reach the bottom of my
heart.

(Petrarch 1985, 35, ll. 5–8)

In poem 264, the *canzone* that begins the second part of the text, Petrarch wonders how after Laura's death he can go on with his own life, drawn to the eternal reward of Christian love but still earthbound through his love of Laura:

for with death at my side
I seek new rules by which to lead my life,
and see the best, but still cling to the worst.

(Petrarch 1985, 63, ll. 134–136)

As the collection ends (poem 365), the poet asks God to forgive his soul for straying from the eternal good to the mortal, earthly good that was Laura:

I go my way regretting those past times
I spent in loving something which was
mortal
instead of soaring high, since I had wings
that might have taken me to higher levels.

(Petrarch 1985, 77, ll. 1–4)

Just what Laura represents in the text is a matter of some debate. Since few details of Laura's life are ever revealed, some critics have suggested that she is purely a symbol, specifically of the laurel, the tree whose branches served as the symbol of fame and glory. A number of early poems in the collection use the imagery of Apollo and Daphne, whom the god turned into a laurel tree, suggesting that this connection was intended. Whether she existed or not, love for Laura is, in the text, a love for worldly glory, and Petrarch's poems to her are the means by which that glory can be achieved. The reader finds, even in the second part of the collection, self-conscious references to the act of writing, expressing the paradox that Laura's death has rendered him unable to write, but his love forces him to write; ultimately writing of his love causes him suffering, but also soothes his pain. The poems also preserve his love, and in doing so preserve the poet's worldly reputation, gaining fame for both the poet and his inspiration.

Throughout his Italian poems, Petrarch reveals the influence of DANTE as well as other vernacular poets like CAVALCANTI and CINO DA PISTOIA. One can also see echoes of classical poets like Ovid, Virgil, and Catullus, as well as TROUBADOURS like ARNAUT DANIEL and BERNART DE VENTADORN. But Petrarch's own influence on subsequent centuries was more profound than that of any of these poets. Although ultimately the poet of the *Canzoniere* rejects worldly endeavors in favor of Christian salvation, the tension between the two desires and the paradoxes caused by his attempt to reconcile worldly and heavenly love struck a responsive chord in the Renaissance and led to Petrarch's huge popularity throughout Europe during that time.

Bibliography

Bloom, Harold, ed. *Petrarch.* Introduction by Harold Bloom. New York: Chelsea House, 1989.

Mann, Nicholas. *Petrarch.* Oxford: Oxford University Press, 1984.

Petrarch, Francis. *The Canzoniere, or, Rerum vulgarium fragmenta.* Translated with notes and commentary by Mark Musa. Introduction by Mark Musa with Barbara Manfredi. Bloomington: Indiana University Press, 1996.

———. *Selections from the Canzoniere and Other Works.* Translated with an introduction and notes by Mark Musa. Oxford: Oxford University Press, 1985.

Roche, Thomas P., Jr. *Petrarch and the English Sonnet Sequences.* New York: AMS Press, 1989.

Trinkaus, Charles. *The Poet as Philosopher: Petrarch and the Formation of Renaissance Consciousness.* New Haven, Conn.: Yale University Press, 1979.

Capgrave, John (1393–1464)

John Capgrave was a 15th-century English Augustinian friar who wrote theological texts, saints' lives (*see* SAINT'S LIFE), poetry, and historical works in both Latin and English. He had a wide reputation throughout Europe as a learned scholar in his own day, and rose to the position of provincial (that is, the ecclesiastical governor) of his order in England.

Capgrave was born at Lynn in Norfolk, and most likely entered the Augustinian order at a young age. He was probably university educated, and there is reason to believe that he received a doctorate degree from Oxford. He was ordained a priest in 1417 or 1418, and at some point before 1456 he was made provincial of his order. He went on pilgrimage to Rome at least once, but he spent most of his life in the King's Lynn friary, and died there in 1464 at the age of 71.

Capgrave's Latin writings include theological texts, biblical commentary, historical texts, and lives of saints. Among his Latin works are the *Vita Humfredi Ducis Glaucestriae,* a life of Humphrey, the duke of Gloucester, who was Capgrave's patron and to whom he dedicated a number of his works; the *Liber de Illustribus Henriciis* (Book of the illustrious Henries), a book on the lives of English kings, German rulers, and other famous men named Henry; and the *Nova Legenda Angliae,* perhaps his most significant Latin text, a collection of the lives of English saints, which is a revision of an earlier collection by John of Tinmouth called the *Sanctilogium.*

In English, Capgrave wrote a few poems, a guide to the pilgrimage sites of Rome, a life of the English saint Gilbert of Sempringham, and a verse biography of St. Catherine of Alexandria. But Capgrave's best-known English work is his *Chronicle of England from the Creation to AD 1417.* The *Chron-*

icle is a compilation of many earlier sources and of Capgrave's own perceptions. The history is admired for its lucid style as well as its concrete details, especially in the later sections concerned with Capgrave's own lifetime. The *Chronicle* is still an important source for historical information about the reign of Henry IV.

Bibliography

Lucas, Peter J., ed. *John Capgrave's Abbreuiacion of Cronicles.* Oxford: Published for the Early English Text Society by the Oxford University Press, 1983.

Munro, J. J., ed. *John Capgrave's Lives of St. Augustine and St. Gilbert of Sempringham, and a Sermon.* 1910. Reprint, Milwood, N.Y.: Kraus Reprint, 1987.

Nova Legenda Anglie: As Collected by John of Tynemouth, John Capgrave, Others, and First Printed, with New Lives. Oxford: Clarendon Press, 1901.

Winstead, Karen A., ed. *The Life of Saint Katherine.* Kalamazoo, Mich.: Medieval Institute Publications, 1999.

Cardenal, Peire (ca. 1180–ca. 1278)

Peire Cardenal was the most important poet of the Albigensian period in southern France. He is best known for his moral SIRVENTES, many of which are bitter satires and attacks on the clergy and the French nobility.

Tradition says that Peire was the child of a noble family from Puy-en-Velay, and that he was educated for a career in the church but chose instead to become a TROUBADOUR. His chief patrons were Raimon VI and Raimon VII, counts of Toulouse and leaders of the Provençal resistance to the invaders from the north during the Albigensian Crusade.

Pope INNOCENT III had called for the Crusade against the Catharist heretics in the Languedoc region in 1209, a cause that was taken up enthusiastically by northern French nobility under the command of Simon de Montfort. Montfort destroyed the city of Béziers in 1209, and, with the support of the clergy, slaughtered the entire population. He defeated the combined armies of Peire's patron Raimon VI and Pedro II of Aragon at Muret in 1213 and occupied Toulouse itself in 1215. When Raimon took back the city in 1217, Montfort laid siege to the city.

Peire is said to have fled from Narbonne and later from Toulouse to escape Montfort's armies. For awhile he was under the protection of Jacme I, king of Aragon, after Pedro fell at Muset. The crusade ended in Languedoc when Raimon VII surrendered in 1229, virtually ceding the entire region of Occitan to the French king. The Catharist heresy continued, however, for the rest of the century until the Inquisition ultimately succeeded in wiping it out.

Peire was never a heretic, but was rather deeply devout. His song to Mary, the first such poem in Provençal, is a very orthodox praise of the Virgin. But he did clearly resent the war, the cruelty of the French nobility, and the venality of the clergy and monastic orders during and after the crusade. One of his poems begins:

> *Buzzards and vultures*
> *do not smell out stinking flesh*
> *as fast as clerics and preachers*
> *smell out the rich.*
>
> (Goldin 1973, 301, ll. 1–4)

Later in the same poem, he declares:

> *Frenchmen and clerics win praise*
> *for their felonies, because they succeed;*
> *usurers and traitors*
> *take the whole world that way,*
>
> (Goldin 1973, 301, ll. 9–12)

In his moral outrage and his righteous vituperation, Peire is a worthy heir to the troubadour tradition begun by MARCABRU. Tradition says he lived to be nearly 100 years old. Ninety-six of his songs are still extant.

Bibliography

Goldin, Frederick, ed. and trans. *Lyrics of the Troubadours and Trouverès: An Anthology and a History.* Garden City, N.Y.: Anchor, 1973.

Wilhelm, James J. *Seven Troubadours: The Creators of Modern Verse.* University Park: Pennsylvania State University Press, 1970.

Carmina Burana (early 13th century)

The *Carmina Burana* is a famous collection of love songs, religious songs, drinking songs, political songs, gambling songs, and also of moral songs and religious drama, mostly written in Latin, but to some extent also in a mixture of Latin and Middle High German (called "macaronic poetry"). This collection was created sometime in the early 13th century and copied down in a manuscript, today housed in the *Bayerische Staatsbibliothek München* (Bavarian State Library of Munich; MS. Clm 4660 and Clm 4660a [single leaves that had been separated from the original manuscript at some time]). We do not know for sure where this collection was originally put together since the manuscript itself does not provide us with any specific clues, but the *Carmina Burana* were certainly copied in a south German or, more likely, Austrian convent, such as in Seckau (near Graz, Styria), Murnau (southern Bavaria), or Neustift/Brixen (south Tyrol). The main section, consisting of 228 songs, was systematically put together by a group of scribes, and later scribes added a group of another 26 songs. Since a few songs in this collection can be dated more precisely (NEIDHART's song CB 168 [ca. 1217–19] and WALTHER VON DER VOGELWEIDE's "Palästinalied" [ca. 1220–25]), and since we can draw solid conclusions from paleographical, art-historical evidence—the manuscript is richly illustrated—and musicological evidence, it seems most reasonable to date the *Carmina Burana* at ca. 1230.

Following the sweeping secularization process in which most convents were dissolved in 1803, the manuscript was transferred from the Benedictine Abbey of Benediktbeuern near Bad Tölz (southern Bavaria) to the State Library in Munich. The collection, however, kept the name *Carmina Burana,* or "Songs from Benediktbeuern," and the manuscript itself is known today as *Codex Buranus.* Because Benediktbeuern had always entertained close cultural and economic contacts with southern Tyrol, and keeping in mind the fairly open-minded intellectual milieu at the Augustinian convent of Neustift/Brixen, recent scholarship has increasingly argued that the *Carmina Burana* were copied there.

The redactor(s) obviously relied on older song collections and had them copied either entirely or in parts. Thematically the *Carmina Burana* offer a wide range of topics, both religious and secular: greed and simony, jealousy, fortune, virtues, religious conversion, sermons for various groups of clergy, criticism of the Holy See in Rome, pilgrimage to the Holy Land, erotic love, unconventional and perverse forms of love (including homosexuality, adultery, rape, and prostitution), love laments, political, ethical, and moral laments, including laments about undesired pregnancy, about approaching death, the poverty of a student, and even the parodic lament by an already fried swan about its own death (CB 130). Moreover, there are songs about the evils at the court, wine, gambling, drinking, gluttony, and the other seven deadly sins, and about the life of goliards (*see* GOLIARDIC VERSE). Many times the poets grotesquely parodied religious genres. Some of the best-known poems such as "*Estuans intrinsecus*" resort to the traditional confession of a churchgoer, but in reality the songs offer nothing but frank acknowledgments of earthly delight in pleasure and sensuality. Not surprisingly, a number of songs prove to be openly obscene, but most of them display an outstanding poetic skill in the employment of rhetorically sophisticated language and music (43 of the poems are accompanied by lineless neumes, that is, notation systems for the general melody, but not for the intervals and the rhythm). The poets were obviously members of a university-trained group of people, both students and teachers, such as Gautier de Châtillon, Giraldus of Bari, Hugo Primas of Orleans, Gottfried of Saint Victor, the ARCHPOET, Peter of Blois, Philipp the Chancellor, and Marner, but the majority of songs have come down to us anonymously. The poets not only display a remarkable disrespect of the church and its sacred texts, they also proudly demonstrate their thorough familiarity with classical Roman literature. Although there are many allusions to the life of minstrels and poor students, most songs seem to have been composed by well-established poets, probably in leading positions at universities and cathedral schools, not afraid of satirizing many of the holiest institutions and ideals of the Catholic Church, freely playing with the cruder human instincts and desires—which would explain the general anonymity of the poets. These highly liberal songs, however, are framed by very serious moral-ethical songs and by Christian dramas. One of the earliest songs, *"Postquam nobilitas seruilia cepit amare"* (CB 7), deserves closer examination here. The poet criticizes the decline of the aristocracy that has assumed crude and boorish behavior. Nobility without inner virtues is worth nothing, and man's true nobility rests in his mind and in his being an image of God: *"Nobilitas hominis mens et deitatis imago"* (3, 1). The poet defines this nobility even further, mentioning the ability to control one's temper, the willingness to help those in need, the understanding and acceptance of the limits for man set up by nature, and the absence of fear of anything in this world, except for fear of one's own moral decrepitude. True nobility is characterized by virtues, whereas the person who is lacking in virtues is a degenerate being: *"Nobilis est ille, quem uirtus nobilitauit, / Degener est ille, quem uirtus nulla beauit"* (4, 1–2).

Many of the songs are contrafactures, that is, they are using the melody of other songs for their own purposes. The individual songs have often come down to us in scores of other manuscripts (a total of 502 at the latest count), and only a few of the songs are unique to the *Codex Buranus.* The *Carmina Burana* have always enjoyed great respect among medievalists, but they gained true popularity among the wider audience only when the German composer Carl Orff (1895–1982), in 1937, set to his own music 25 songs selected from this collection in the form of a scenic oratorio or cantata, originally accompanied with ballet and divided into the three themes of Spring, Tavern Life, and Love.

Bibliography

Carmina Burana. Edited by Alfons Hilka and Otto Schumann. Heidelberg: Carl Winter, 1930–1970.

Lehtonen, Tuomas M. S. *Fortuna, Money, and the Sublunar World: Twelfth-Century Ethical Poetics and the Satirical Poetry of the Carmina Burana.* Helsinki: Finnish Historical Society, 1995.

Peterson, Jeffrey. "Writing Flowers: Figuration and the Feminine in *Carmina Burana* 177," *Exemplaria* 6 (1994): 1–34.

Sayce, Olive. *Plurilingualism in the Carmina Burana: A Study of the Linguistic and Literary Influences on the Codex.* Göppingen: Kümmerle, 1992.

Walsh, P. G., ed. and trans. *Love Lyrics from the Carmina Burana.* Chapel Hill: University of North Carolina Press, 1993.

Albrecht Classen

Castle of Perseverance, The (ca. 1405–1425)

The Castle of Perseverance is the oldest complete extant MORALITY PLAY in English. There is an earlier play called *The Pride of Life,* but it survives only in a fragment. Like other morality plays, *The Castle of Perseverance* addresses the salvation of the individual human soul, and does so in the form of ALLEGORY. It is written predominantly in 13-line stanzas rhyming *ababcdcdeffe,* in a form similar to that used by the so-called Wakefield Master of the TOWNELEY CYCLE of plays. At 3,649 lines and containing 33 characters, the play is also the longest and most complex of the extant moralities, and it is the only one that contains all three conventional morality-play themes: the battle between the Vices and Virtues for the human soul; the summoning of Death; and the debate of the four Daughters of God.

The play survives in a single manuscript in Washington's Folger Library, a manuscript named for its earliest known owner, Cox Macro. With *Mankind* and *Wisdom, The Castle of Perseverance* is therefore referred to as one of the Macro plays. The manuscript copy of *The Castle of Perseverance* dates from about 1440, and is clearly of East Anglian origin. The text includes banns that an actor was supposed to have read, summarizing the play and declaring that it will be performed a week later at some central location in the town. These banns make it clear that the play was performed by a traveling troupe of actors who must have performed it at various locations throughout East Anglia.

The manuscript also contains a crude diagram that shows us how the play was meant to be staged. According to the drawing, the action would be performed in a round playing area bordered by a ditch, around which the audience would be seated. At the center of the playing space was a tower on stilts, representing the Castle. Five scaffolds would be erected at various points at the circumference of the circle: To the East was the scaffold of God, to the north was the Devil (or Belial), to the west the World (*Mundus*), and to the south the Flesh (*Caro*). A fifth scaffold was inserted somewhat asymmetrically in the northeast for Covetousness, presented in the play as a lieutenant of the World. Beneath the Castle itself was a bench representing a bed, on which the protagonist *Humana Genus* (Mankind) is born at the beginning of the play and on which he dies some 3,000 lines later. No doubt the acting troupe needed the week's time proclaimed in the banns in order to construct their elaborate set. Stage directions in the text of the play indicate that props and costumes were also elaborate and important to the production: In his temptation, for example, Mankind is proffered a robe covered in golden coins; Belial's costume apparently included pipes of burning gunpowder that appeared to shoot from his ears, hands, and backside. Such stage directions suggest a lively production, with a good deal of physical action and movement and, it seems likely, interaction with the audience sitting in the round among the five scaffolds, each of which at certain times in the production became the focus of action.

The action of the play follows a four-part structure that falls into a rough pattern of temptation, repentance, further temptation and fall, and final salvation. In the beginning of the play, the newly born Mankind is accompanied by his Good Angel and his Bad Angel. The Bad Angel seduces him to come and meet the World, the Flesh and the Devil, along with the Seven Deadly Sins. Mankind promises them his friendship when Penitence suddenly pierces him with a lance representing his distress over his sins. Repenting, Mankind asks mercy, and through God's grace, Confession and Repentance show him where he can be safe: In the Castle of Perseverance—a term that in this context seems to denote a kind of Christian patience in the face of adversity and temptation.

With Mankind safely lodged within the Castle and defended by seven Virtues, the forces of evil, led by the Devil and the Seven Deadly Sins, lay siege to the Castle. The individual combats that occur between the Vices and Virtues are clearly based on PRUDENTIUS's famous fifth-century *PSYCHOMACHIA*, but ultimately the Vices are defeated when the Virtues toss roses at them: The roses, traditional Christian symbols of Christ's passion and sacrifice, wound the Vices and drive them off.

But Covetousness (or Greed), more clever than his fellow Vices, avoids battle with the Virtues and approaches Mankind directly, tempting him out of the Castle with material objects that will give him comfort and security. Obtaining Mankind's promise always to desire more and never to share with others, Covetousness succeeds in drawing Mankind away from God. Just then, unexpectedly, Death appears, describing his function as the great leveler who draws all (rich and poor) to the same end. He strikes Mankind, who is immediately deserted by the World. Though Mankind has hoped to leave his goods to his own kin, they are all claimed by a page sent by the World, named "I Wot Neuere Whoo": Thus in the play, "I never know who" inherits one's goods upon his death.

Mankind realizes his grave error at the last moment and prays for mercy, and this initiates the debate among the four Daughters of God: Truth and Righteousness on the one hand—both of whom argue the justice of Mankind's damnation, and Mercy and Peace on the other—who assert God's merciful nature. The four daughters bring the case before the throne of God himself, who opts for mercy. Mankind is admitted to heaven, but God has the last speech in the play, advising the audience members to repent of their sins and to follow virtue.

Aside from the influence of Prudentius, scholars have noted that the play may owe something to the Anglo-Norman ROMANCE *Chasteau d'Amours* (attributed to Robert GROSSETESTE), which among other things includes a debate among the four daughters of God. It has also been suggested that the play—whose action moves among the various areas of the playing circle—

owes much to the traditional medieval motif of life as a journey from birth to death, from innocence to experience, a pilgrimage to our ultimate heavenly home, if we remain faithful on the journey.

Bibliography

Bevington, David, ed. *The Macro Plays: The Castle of Perseverance, Wisdom, Mankind.* New York: Johnson Reprint, 1972.

Kelley, Michael R. *Flamboyant Drama: A Study of "The Castle of Perseverance" and "Wisdom."* Carbondale: Southern Illinois University Press, 1979.

King, Pamela M. "Morality Plays." In *The Cambridge Companion to Medieval English Theatre,* edited by Richard Beadle, 240–264, Cambridge: Cambridge University Press, 1994.

The Macro Plays: The Castle of Perseverance, Wisdom, Mankind. Edited by Mark Eccles. EETS 262. London: Published for the Early English Text Society by the Oxford University Press, 1969.

Potter, Robert A. *The English Morality Play: Origins, History, and Influence of a Dramatic Tradition.* London: Routledge and Kegan Paul, 1975.

Southern, Richard. *The Medieval Theatre in the Round: A Study of the Staging of "The Castle of Perseverance" and Related Matters.* 2nd ed. London: Faber and Faber, 1975.

Cavalcanti, Guido (ca. 1259–1300)

The true founder of the *DOLCE STIL NOVO* ("sweet new style") school of poetry and DANTE's closest friend, the poet Guido Cavalcanti was, more than anyone else, the person responsible for the "sweet new style" that Dante followed and then transcended in his *DIVINE COMEDY.* The style, characterized by a philosophical approach and learned imagery, is represented most manifestly in Cavalcanti's great *CANZONE, DONNA ME PREGA* (A lady asks me).

Guido was born in 1259 or before—he is known to have been at least six years Dante's senior—to a wealthy merchant family of Florence. His father, Cavalcante de' Cavalcanti, was a prominent Guelf (a member of the party that supported the pope in Italian politics). He betrothed his son to Bice, daughter of the Ghibelline captain Farinata (the Ghibellines were the aristocratic party that supported the emperor) to help seal the peace between the two factions in the late 1260s, and in 1280 Guido was named as a guarantor of the peace arranged by Cardinal Latini. A prominent public figure, Guido was elected a member of the General Council of the Commune of Florence in 1284, and was reelected in 1290. But by this time a split had occurred within the Guelf party of Florence, and bitter, even violent, political feuds were raging between the Blacks (generally representing the old money, banking, and imperial interests) and the Whites (who represented trade interests and the peace faction). Corso Donati, leader of the Blacks (and Dante's brother-in-law), was an unscrupulous politician: Cavalcanti, an outspoken White, was the target of an assassination attempt while he was on a pilgrimage to Santiago de Compostela.

On June 24, 1300, in an attempt to deal with the violence in the city, the six priors of the commune (who were the chief magistrates of the city) decided to sentence the leaders of both sides to exile. Cavalcanti, along with Donati and other prominent citizens, was forced to go into exile at Sarzana. It was a particularly bitter pill to swallow since Dante himself was serving as one of the priors at the time. Cavalcanti's sentence was revoked the following month, but Cavalcanti was not to return—he died in Sarzana at the end of August.

Dante's friendship with Cavalcanti dates certainly from at least the early 1280s. Dante was influenced strongly by Guido's poetry, and thought of him as the "father" of modern love poetry in the vernacular. He and Cavalcanti exchanged several sonnets on a variety of topics, and Dante dedicated the *VITA NUOVA* to him, calling Cavalcanti *"primo amico,"* that is, "my first friend." Dante's puzzling lack of reference to Cavalcanti in the *Divine Comedy,* however, has caused some scholars to wonder whether their friendship had cooled before Cavalcanti's death: The only reference to Guido is in canto X of the Inferno, when Dante speaks with Guido's father in the circle of heretics, and mentions that *perhaps* Guido held Virgil "in scorn." Possibly Dante's part in Guido's banishment had strained their friendship. Or perhaps Dante was simply writing a new kind of poetry that went beyond Guido's, and therefore does not invoke him.

In any case, while he was alive, Guido's influence over Dante, and over Italian lyric poetry in general was tremendous. He has left 52 poems (*SONNETS*, *canzoni*, songs, and other genres). All display his characteristic style, which was forged largely in contrast with the Tuscan style of GUITTONE D'AREZZO, which Cavalcanti saw as vulgar and overwrought rhetorically. He returned to a simpler and more direct lyric style rhetorically, but at the same time introduced very difficult imagery drawn from philosophy, science, psychology, medicine—a variety of learned traditions.

Cavalcanti's influence has been admired even into modern times. The 20th-century American poet Ezra Pound thought Cavalcanti a brilliant psychologist regarding love and its effects, and translated a number of his poems into English.

Bibliography

Anderson, David. *Pound's Cavalcanti: An Edition of the Translations, Notes, and Essays.* Princeton, N.J.: Princeton University Press, 1983.

Ardizzone, Maria Luisa. *Guido Cavalcanti: The Other Middle Ages.* Toronto: University of Toronto Press, 2002.

Goldin, Frederick, trans. *German and Italian Lyrics of the Middle Ages: An Anthology and a History.* New York: Doubleday, 1973.

Nelson, Lowry, Jr., ed. and trans. *The Poetry of Guido Cavalcanti.* New York: Garland Press, 1986.

Shaw, James E. *Guido Cavalcanti's Theory of Love: The "Canzone d'Amore" and Other Related Problems.* Toronto: University of Toronto Press, 1949.

Valency, Maurice. *In Praise of Love.* New York: Macmillan, 1958.

Caxton, William (ca. 1421–1491)

Businessman, critic, writer, translator, and printer, William Caxton is most celebrated for establishing the first printing press in England. Caxton was born in Kent sometime between 1415 and 1422, most likely in 1422. Besides the information he documents in the prologues and epilogues to his manuscripts, little is known of Caxton's life or ancestry; however, his parents are thought to have been influential because they gained an apprenticeship for their son to Robert Large, a wealthy silk mercer who became sheriff in 1430 and lord mayor of London in 1439. After Large's death in 1441, Caxton moved to Bruges, capital of Flanders, seat of the Burgundian government and thriving center for manufacturing and trade. In Bruges the prosperous merchant traded in textiles, particularly silk and wool, as well as luxury goods such as manuscripts, and he was appointed governor of the English Nation of Merchant Adventurers. Here he met Margaret of York, the sister of England's King Edward IV and the wife of Charles the Bold, duke of Burgundy. The duchess hired Caxton to become her financial adviser and to acquire and translate books for her. The first book she asked Caxton to translate was the *Le Recueil des Histoires de Troyes,* a popular French ROMANCE. Sometime between the years 1470 and 1474, Caxton traveled to Cologne where he met Ulrich Zell, a priest from Marinz, the town where Johann Gutenberg had established the very first printing press. Zell had established the first printing press in Cologne and is probably responsible for teaching Caxton the skill. Caxton, who by this time had translated *The History of Troy* and made several copies of the book, returned to Bruges and, under the duchess of Burgundy's sponsorship, set up his own printing press and hired calligrapher, bookseller, and translator Colard Mansion. Together, in 1474, they printed copies of *The History of Troy,* the first book to be printed in the English language, and dedicated the book to the duchess. The next year the duo printed *The Game and Play of Chess Moralized.* The printer returned to England in 1476, and set up a printing press at Westminster, where, in 1477, he printed Earl Rivers's translation of the *Dictes and Sayings of the Philosophers,* the first book to be printed in England.

During his career Caxton translated many works from French, Latin, and Dutch into English; printed many small, usually religious, documents such as indulgences; and printed approximately 100 texts, most notably CHAUCER's *CANTERBURY TALES* and *TROILUS AND CRISEYDE,* MALORY's *MORTE D'ARTHUR,* Godfrey of Bouillon's *The Order of Chivalry,* Ranulph HIGDEN's *Polychronicon,* GOWER's *CONFESSIO AMANTIS,* Virgil's *Aeneid,* many poems by LYDGATE and, perhaps his most ambitious task, Jacobus de Voragine's *GOLDEN LEGEND*. Caxton's texts included prologues and epilogues that he wrote, which included his opinion of the work; therefore, he is not only remembered as the first printer of English literature, but also as the first critic of the same.

Caxton's body of work gave his peers access to contemporary literature in their own language and gives modern scholars an idea of the tastes, politics, and culture of the later medieval society he lived in. The materials Caxton printed were both a response to and an influence on the reading public, and, although Chaucer is ultimately responsible for the success of his writing, Caxton is to be credited with making Chaucer's work more rapidly and readily available to the general reading public of the time than it would have been otherwise, thus accelerating Chaucer's influence and eminence.

Until recently, people assumed that Caxton lived a life of celibacy as a bachelor because there is no mention of any wife in his writing. However, the discovery of medical records proving that he unquestionably had a legitimate daughter, Elizabeth, has led scholars to believe that he had a wife and that his wife was most likely Maude Caxton, who was buried at St. Margaret's in Westminster around the time William Caxton was buried there after his 1491 death, which allegedly occurred on the very day he completed the lengthy translation of the *Vitas Patrum*, or *Lives of the Fathers*. Trainees Robert Copeland and Wynkyn de Worde succeeded Caxton; the latter is responsible for printing the *Lives of the Fathers* after Caxton's death. Many of Caxton's original manuscripts are currently housed in London's British Museum.

Bibliography

Blake, Norman Francis. *Selections from William Caxton.* Oxford: Clarendon Press, 1973.

———. *William Caxton and English Literary Culture.* London: Hambledon Press, 1991.

Painter, George D. *William Caxton: A Biography.* New York: Putnam, 1977.

Penninger, Frieda Elaine. *William Caxton.* Boston: Twayne, 1979.

Leslie Johnston

Celestina, La Fernando de Rojas (ca. 1490–1502)

La Celestina is the name popularly given to the famous Spanish prose dialogue originally published in 1499 as the *Comedia de Calisto y Melibea.* The anonymous first edition consisted of 16 *auctos* or acts, but a second edition in 1502 (rechristened a *Tragicomedia*) added five more acts between the original acts 14 and 15, and also revealed (in an acrostic) the author to be one Fernando de Rojas. A prefatory letter to the later editions claims that Rojas discovered the first act and part of the second act, written by an unknown author, and completed the text in just two weeks. Rojas, a converted Jew who is known to have practiced law and who died in 1541, was apparently a law student at the University of Salamanca between 1494 and 1502, and scholars believe that the work was intended for reading aloud to students at the university (a custom of the time). The first reading of the original 16-act version of the text is believed to have taken place in 1497.

The text tells the story of the noble youth Calisto who, pursuing a hawk, enters the garden of a Jew named Pleberio. There he meets and falls in love with the Jew's beautiful daughter Melibea, but she rebuffs him. Calisto's unsavory servant Sempronio suggests that his master employ the services of an aged bawd, La Celestina, who is practiced in all the arts of seduction and will be able to win the girl's love for Calisto. After a complex dialogue, the devious Celestine is able to persuade the virtuous Melibea to answer Calisto's suit.

The grateful Calisto pays Celestina in cash and a gold necklace. But when the wicked Sempronio and his fellow servant Pármeno hear of this, they decide they deserve a share of the profit. They await Celestina at her hut near the river, along with their whores, Celestina's friends Elicia and Areusa, but when Celestina returns home, she refuses to share her fee and is stabbed to death by the two servants. Apprehended by the authorities, Sempronio and Pármeno are hanged the following day.

In the first version of the text, these events are followed by Calisto's tryst with Melibea in her garden, where he successfully seduces her but is killed when he falls from the garden's high wall. The lamenting Melibea responds by throwing herself from a tower, and the dialogue ends with Melibea's grieving parents, Pleberio and Alissa, responding with moral sentiments to their daughter's death and dishonor.

In the revised, 21-act version of the story, a new character is introduced after act 14. Centurio, a *miles gloriosus* or "braggart soldier" character, is persuaded by the harlots Elicia and Areusa to help them avenge Celestina and their lovers Sempronio and Pármeno on Calisto, whom they blame for the deaths. Calisto has not died but continues to visit Melibea for several weeks after their first time together, and thus Centurio is able to set a trap for Calisto at Melibea's house. When Calisto is within, Centurio's gang attacks Calisto's followers awaiting him outside, and when Calisto rushes to aid his friends, he falls from his ladder and dies. The final acts follow the plot of the earlier version.

Rojas's chief sources for his text seem to have been the medieval Spanish writers Juan RUIZ and Martínez de Toledo, but he clearly also used the Bible, Homer, Virgil, PETRARCH, and the Roman playwrights Plautus (the source of the *miles gloriosus*) and Terence (from whom he seems to have borrowed the device of the servants' love affairs paralleling the protagonists'). The book contains scenes of frank sexuality, verbal obscenity, and thinly veiled social criticism that seem not to have run afoul of the authorities. In fact, its huge popularity led to the printing of 63 editions in Spain in the 16th century alone. In addition, translations of *La Celestina,* as it came to be known after its most popular character, were made into Italian in 1506, German in 1520, French in 1527, and English before 1530. Further, there were six different sequels to the book published in 16th century Spain. *La Celestina* proved inspirational and profoundly influential on other Spanish writers, including Cervantes and Lope de Vega, who considered it a national treasure.

Reasons for the text's popularity are not hard to find. The romantic "Romeo and Juliet" love story appeals to many readers. Others are moved by Melibea's grieving parents. Rojas's brilliant use of dialogue to explore the complex relationships and psychological interplay of characters is much admired by scholars. The realistic, picaresque-type scenes involving the low-class characters in particular are celebrated for the vivid picture they give of late 15th-century Spanish society. Further, many critics have been intrigued by the embittered voice of social criticism beneath the overt morality of the text. Written during the decade of grand historical events of Spanish history (the discovery of the New World, the conquest of Granada, the expulsion of Jews from Spain), *La Celestina* gives voice to a great deal of bitterness and alienation—perhaps giving vent to the disenchantment with his society Rojas felt as the son of a forced Jewish convert to Christianity.

But without doubt the largest reason for the book's long-lived popularity is the character of Celestina herself. Often called one of the great characters of Spanish (if not European) literature, the old crone is a fascinating comic embodiment of evil—a shrewd, hypocritical, malign, and cunning panderess and sorceress who nevertheless comes across as completely human.

Bibliography

Cohen, J. M., trans. *The Spanish Bawd: La Celestina, being the tragi-comedy of Calisto and Melibea.* Harmondsworth, U.K.: Penguin, 1964.

Gilman, Stephen. *The Spain of Fernando de Rojas: The Intellectual and Social Landscape of La Celestina.* Princeton, N.J.: Princeton University Press, 1972.

Severin, Dorothy Sherman, ed. *Celestina.* With the translation of James Mabbe (1631). Warminster, Wiltshire, U.K.: Aris and Phillips, 1987.

———. *Tragicomedy and Novelistic Discourse in Celestina.* Cambridge: Cambridge University Press, 1989.

Cent Ballades Christine de Pizan (1399–1402)

Throughout her lifetime, CHRISTINE DE PIZAN (ca. 1364–ca. 1431) composed hundreds of *BALLADES* and other short poems, especially between 1393 and 1412. A major collection, her *Cent Ballades* (One hundred *ballades*), written between 1399 and 1402, appeared in 1402 as part of her *Livre de*

Christine, perhaps under the influence of the admired and publicly highly esteemed poet Eustache DESCHAMPS, who had also written a collection of *Cent Ballades.* Another collection with the same title by the poet Jean le Sénéchal seems to have provided an additional model. Christine focused on specific themes such as widowhood, the development of a love relationship as seen from a woman's perspective, debates between man and woman, moral and ethical instruction through the utilization of ancient mythology, accusation of false lovers, criticism of current political events, or praise of patrons. In ballade no. 50, in which the purpose of her poetry is identified as *esbatement* ("entertainment"), Christine explicitly distances herself from the poetic "I" in her other poems, emphasizing the fictional nature of this pronoun and the literary sources from which she drew her material for her love poetry.

By contrast, the opposite seems to be the case in many of her other ballades. In her various poems on widowhood, for example, the autobiographical element emerges quite clearly because she strongly foregrounds her personal suffering resulting from a great loss in her life, the death of her husband, Etienne de Castel, in 1389. This finds additional confirmation in her *L'Avision-Christine* (Vision of Christine, 1405), where she reflects upon her life and emphasizes that she used her poetry to console herself in her early widowhood. In many other ballades Christine deals with the unfortunate ending of love relationships, either because the man proves to be unfaithful, or because of his death. Fortune itself, as a force of nature, plays a major role in Christine's work, obviously as a result of her close study of BOETHIUS's *CONSOLATION OF PHILOSOPHY* (ca. 523). In a number of her poems Christine indicates her intellectual interests, especially her reading of Ovid's *Metamorphoses* and the history of the Trojan War in one of the many medieval renderings.

Christine's later fame heavily rests on her active participation in the acclaimed intellectual debate about the role of women within courtly society, in which she sharply defends women's individuality and innocence against the vicious misogyny formulated in JEAN DE MEUN's continuation of GUILLAUME DE LORRIS's *ROMAN DE LA ROSE* (ca. 1370–80). This interest in women's rights is already noticeable in her early ballades.

In one poem Christine appeals to the duke of Orleans to find a place in his household for one of her sons, Jean. In another case, the poet laments the April 1404 death of Philip the Bold, duke of Burgundy, who had commissioned her to write his brother's biography, *Faits et Bonnes Meurs du Sage Roi Charles V* (The deeds and good character of King Charles V). In other poems Christine experiments with formal elements, such as in her *Ballades d'Estrange Façon* (Ballades in a curious form), varying verse and stanza structures. At other times Christine allows her humor to come through, such as in *Jeux a vendre* (Songs for sale), or she reflects on moral teachings, as in *Enseignements* (Instructions). In her later ballades, Christine experiments with traditional love relationships involving figures such as a wooing young man, a jealous husband, and the lady herself. In these poems, although the wife wants to grant the lover his wishes, eventually gossip forces the man to depart from the court and to leave his lady behind, which makes him complain bitterly about his loneliness. Christine also reflects her solid education in the classics, as documented by her reference to Ovid (no. XLII). In her final ballade, no. 100, Christine underscores her authorship of all of these poems and incorporates an anagram of her name in the refrain.

Bibliography

Cent Ballades d'Amant et de Dame. Edited by Jacqueline Cerquiglini. Paris: Union générale d' éditions, 1982.

Laidlaw, James C. "The *Cent ballades:* The Marriage of Content and Form." In *Christine de Pizan and Medieval French Lyric,* edited by Earl Jeffrey Richards, 53–82, Gainesville: University Press of Florida, 1998.

The Selected Writings of Christine de Pizan. Translated by Renate Blumenfeld-Kosinski and Kevin Brownlee. Edited by Renate Blumenfeld-Kosinski. New York: Norton, 1997.

Albrecht Classen

Cercamon (fl. 1135–1148)

Cercamon was one of the early TROUBADOUR poets. Tradition says he was born in Gascony, like his friend and fellow troubadour MARCABRU. His *VIDA* says that Cercamon was Marcabru's teacher, but the scholarly consensus today is that more likely Cercamon learned from Marcabru. At the very least, his poems seem to owe a great deal to Marcabru's, as they do also to those of William IX, the first troubadour. From Guillaume, Cercamon seems to have learned his smooth and simple technique—his songs are examples of the *TROBAR LEU* style of troubadour poetry. Like Marcabru, Cercamon focuses on the theme of true love, which he distinguishes from adulterous love.

We have no specific knowledge of Cercamon's life. His pseudonym, the only name by which he is known, means "vagabond" in Provençal, suggesting he spent some of his life wandering. But William X of Aquitaine, son and heir of the first troubadour, was briefly his patron, as the lament he wrote on William's death suggests. Cercamon also alludes in one poem to the marriage of the 15-year-old Eleanor of Aquitaine, his patron's daughter, to the future Louis VII of France in 1137. In another poem Cercamon seems to allude to Eleanor's scandalous behavior with her uncle Raymond of Antioch in 1148, during the Second Crusade.

Cercamon celebrates true love, and condemns the kind of behavior that Eleanor was accused of. For him love was pure, and promiscuity represented the corruption of love. The true lover should serve his beloved and earn her attention through years of service:

> *I start, I burn, I tremble, all over,*
> *sleeping and waking, for love of her.*
> *I am so afraid of dying,*
> *I dare not think of asking her;*
> *however, I shall serve her two years or*
> *three,*
> *and then, maybe, she will know the*
> *truth.*

(Goldin 1973, 97, ll. 25–30)

Seven of Cercamon's songs survive. An eighth is of questionable authorship. According to his *vida*, he also wrote "pastorals," but if this is true none are extant. The pastoral form did ultimately become popular in the south of France, as did Cercamon's depictions of the trembling, humble lover.

Bibliography

Goldin, Frederick, ed. and trans. *Lyrics of the Troubadours and Trouvères: An Anthology and a History.* Garden City, N.Y.: Anchor, 1973.

Wolf, George, and Roy Rosenstein, ed. and trans. *Poetry of Cercamon and Jaufre Rudel.* New York: Garland, 1983.

Chandidas, Baru (Chandidasa)
(ca. 1375–ca. 1450, or 16th century)

Chandidas is the name of one of the most important saint-poets of the *Vaisnava* sect (those devoted to worship of Vishnu as god), who wrote lyric poetry in the early Bangali dialect of northeastern India. He is presumed to have written his *Shrikrsnakirtan* in the late 14th or early 15th century, though some scholars have placed him as late as the 16th century.

One of the difficulties of saying anything definitive about Chandidas is that there may well be more than one poet by that name. The *bhanita* (poetic lines mentioning the poet's name) of a number of poems give four different names: Baru Chandidas, Dwija Chandidas, Dina Chandidas, and simply Chandidas. Scholars have debated whether these names reflect four different poets or are different names for the same poet—a dilemma known among scholars as the "Chandidas mystery." Tradition says that Baru Chandidas was born in the small village of Nannur in the Birbhum district, some 24 miles east of Suri. He was, according to the same tradition, the son of the Brahman Durgadas Bagchi, and he ultimately renounced Brahmanism, some say because of a love affair with a woman of a lower caste—though this latter is most likely a fictionalized detail borrowed from his own poetry. Whatever the details of his life, he became much admired, and certainly a good number of poets tried to exploit his name by attaching it to their own compositions, so that now more than 1,000 extant poems are attributed to him.

What is certain about Chandidas is his association with *bhakto* (i.e., "sharing [in god]"), the spiritual movement that swept India between the 12th and 18th centuries. The movement stressed a passionate devotion to god, but a devotion independent of traditional Hindu rituals or social values. In some ways, bhakti literature might serve as a way of expressing social or economic discontent, though in a way that urged its audience to recognize the unreality of the physical world rather than to protest. The movement produced a large number of poems composed in local dialects rather than in classical Sanskrit, so that Chandidas's lyrics are among the earliest composed in the Bangali dialect. The poems might take the form of fervent devotion to a particular god or sometimes of an expression of zeal for an abstract divine principle whose attributes are inexpressible.

In the case of Chandidas, the poems focused on devotion to the god Vishnu, particularly in his most popular incarnation as Krishna. Chandidas's *Shrikrsnakirtan* (meaning "the dalliance of Krishna") consists of 412 songs in the meter of Bangali folk songs. These are divided into 13 separate sections. The poems concern an incident in the mythology surrounding Krishna that involves his love affair with a *gopi* (or herdswoman) named Rādhā. The incident itself is mentioned as early as the sixth century in the Tamil region of India, but becomes in the bhakti songs of Chandidas a metaphor for the love and longing of the soul for god, and of god for the soul.

The manuscript of Chandidas's *Shrikrsnakirtan* was discovered by the scholar Basantaranjan Vidvadvallabh at Bankura early in the 20th century, and was published in 1916. A classic Indian film entitled *Chandidas* was made in 1932, focused on protesting the caste system and celebrating the bhakti movement through the legendary biography of the poet. His songs remain popular to this day, and his traditional birthplace at Nannur is a popular tourist destination for thousands of admirers annually.

Bibliography

Dimock, Edward C., and Denise Levertov, trans. *In Praise of Krishna.* Edited by Edward C. Dimock. Garden City, N.Y.: Doubleday, 1967.

Chandos Herald (fl. 1350–1380)

The herald of the English knight Sir John Chandos wrote one of the most important firsthand accounts of the early years of the Hundred Years' War, a verse chronicle in French called *La Vie du Prince Noir* (*The Life of the Black Prince*). Focusing on Edward, the Black Prince, eldest son of Edward III and hero of the Battle of Poitiers, Chandos Herald's poem was one of the sources Froissart used for the second edition of his *Chronicles.*

We know virtually nothing of Chandos Herald, not even his name. His lord, Sir John Chandos, was one of the great friends of Prince Edward. Sir John had saved Edward's life at Poitiers and was a hero in the prince's Spanish wars. King Edward made him one of the founding members of the Order of the Garter before he was killed at the bridge of Lussac near Poitiers on New Year's Day, 1370.

His herald may have been a Fleming from Valenciennes, like Froissart himself. He probably entered Chandos's service around 1360. Froissart mentions the herald twice in his *Chronicles,* once as carrying a message from Chandos to Prince Edward in 1369. It is unknown what happened to the herald after Chandos's death, but it seems likely that this was when he completed his poem, sometime before about 1380.

The herald's poem presents the Black Prince as an ideal chivalric hero, valiant, pious, and comparable to Arthur and Roland, though the poem contains little in the way of personal realistic detail. It seems that the Herald may not have known Prince Edward well personally. He does, however, make his own master, Chandos, a secondary hero of the poem. The text gives an account of the Battle of Poitiers, but is most valuable for its firsthand account of the Black Prince's Castilian campaign of 1366–67, particularly the details of the Battle of Najera, where he describes fleeing Castilian knights leaping into and dying in a river red with blood.

The English victory is the high point of the herald's poem, but he also describes the death of his master and the declining health and ultimate death of the Black Prince himself in 1376. The poem thus ends not with an optimistic tone after the victory, but with rather an elegiac tone of nostalgia over the loss of the flowers of chivalry.

Bibliography

Barber, Richard W., ed. and trans. *The Life and Campaigns of the Black Prince: From Contemporary Letters, Diaries, and Chronicles, Including Chandos Herald's "Life of the Black Prince."* London: Folio Society, 1979.

Gransden, Antonia. *Historical Writing in England: c. 1307 to the Early Sixteenth Century.* Vol. 2. Ithaca, N.Y.: Cornell University Press, 1982.

Tyson, Diana B. *La Vie du Prince Noir by Chandos Herald.* Beihefte zur Zeitschrift für Romanische Philologie, cxlvii. Tübingen: M. Niemeyer, 1975.

chansons de geste

The chansons de geste (or "songs of great deeds") are heroic or epic poems in Old French written chiefly in the 12th and 13th centuries. The poems celebrate the martial deeds of historical or pseudohistorical French heroes (the word *geste* has a secondary meaning of "history") and at the same time glorify the ideals of chivalric feudal society. Although the chansons de geste provide some of the raw material (the "matter of France") for later medieval romances, their main focus is on war, and love has little or nothing to do with their stories.

There are some 120 extant chansons de geste, many of which concern the emperor CHARLEMAGNE and his retinue. This cycle of epics is called the *Geste du Roi,* and the best-known of these, the *Chanson de Roland* or *SONG OF ROLAND,* is also one of the earliest (ca. 1100). A larger and more unified cycle of 24 poems revolves around the career of William d'Orange (also known as Guillaume de Toulouse), another important historical figure from the time of Charlemagne. Some chansons de geste are written about the exploits of Christian knights against Saracens. A fourth group of poems is concerned with feudal barons from northern France who revolt against their sovereign lords as a result of some injustice.

The typical verse form used among the chansons de geste, at least in the earlier examples, is a 10- or 11-syllable line marked by a strong caesura after the fourth syllable. The lines are grouped into stanzas (called *laisses*) of varying length, united by assonance—that is, repetition of identical vowel sounds—in the final word of each line of the *laisse.*

One area of scholarly contention regarding the chansons de geste has to do with their origin. There are clearly passages of formulaic diction in the existing poems, which suggests that they have an origin in oral tradition. But it is also clear that the prevailing worldview of the songs seems more that of the period of the Crusades than that of the Carolingian era in which most of the narratives are set. Some scholars believe that the stories originated at Charlemagne's time and were passed down and added to in oral tradition for hundreds of years. Another theory is that the songs originated much closer to the time of the written versions and were composed by wandering JONGLEURS who picked up historical facts and traditions in their wanderings. Either way it can be said with some certainty that the kernel of the story in each chanson de geste is much older than the written text, and that the individual texts do contain some elements of oral tradition.

Bibliography

Calin, William. *The Epic Quest: Studies in Four Old French Chansons de Geste.* Baltimore: Johns Hopkins University Press, 1966.

Daniel, Norman. *Heroes and Saracens: An Interpretation of the Chansons de Geste.* Edinburgh: Edinburgh University Press, 1984.

Ferrante, Joan M., trans. *Guillaume d'Orange: Four Twelfth-Century Epics.* New York: Columbia University Press, 1991.

Kay, Sarah. *The Chansons de Geste in the Age of Romance: Political Fictions.* Oxford: Clarendon Press and New York: Oxford University Press, 1995.

chansons de toile (chansons d'histoire)

Thirteenth-century sources use the term *chansons de toile* (or occasionally *chansons d'histoire*), or "spinning songs," to refer to a small but distinct group of French poems that present brief narratives with female protagonists, often a noble lady mourning the absence of her knightly lover. These short poems are memorable for their ability to create a scene with a few vivid images and for their lively dialogue.

These songs usually begin by naming the heroine—Bele Doette, for example, or Bele Yolande. Then the poem describes what the heroine is doing—it may be spinning or embroidering, it might be sitting alone in a tower window, it might be reading. But from this standard beginning, a number of different kinds of narratives might ensue. In Bele Doette's song, for example, the protagonist hears of her lover's death and ends by becoming a nun at Saint-Pol. Bele Yolande, on the other hand, gives herself to her lover at the end of her song, and we are told:

> *fair Yolande clings to him with kisses,*
> *and in France's sport she pins him fast.*
>
> (Dronke 1996, 98)

These songs consist of several short stanzas united by a single rhyme and separated by a substantial refrain. In "Fair Yolande," for example, there are six four-line stanzas and a two-line rhyming refrain in Yolande's own voice that translates " 'God, how the name of love is sweet: I never thought it would bring me grief!' " (Dronke 1996, 97).

Altogether there are 20 extant *chansons de toile,* most of which are anonymous. Nine of these appear in one *chansonnier* (or songbook manuscript) attached to St. Germain-dez-Pres. Six songs have survived because they were included in longer works—five of these in one text, the *Roman de Guillaume de Dole* (ca. 1210) by Jean Renart. The other five poems are attributed to the 13th-century poet Andefroi le Bastart.

It has been suggested that all of the anonymous *chansons de toile* are the work of a single 13th-century poet (perhaps Andefroi himself). But there are some significant differences between the poems attributed to Andefroi and the other lyrics: Musically, the anonymous lyrics are in a minor mode while Andefroi's are in a major. Andefroi's poems use 12-syllable lines while the anonymous poems generally use much shorter lines, sometimes six or eight syllables. Andefroi's songs also usually have more stanzas than the typical anonymous *chansons de toile.* It seems likely that the anonymous poems are much earlier than Andefroi's—most likely 12th century at the latest, and that Andefroi's poems are a revival and reworking of the earlier genre.

Bibliography

Dronke, Peter. *The Medieval Lyric.* 3rd ed. Cambridge, U.K.: Brewer, 1996.

Lewis, C. B. "The Origin of the Weaving Songs and the Theme of the Girl at the Fountain," *PMLA* 37 (1922): 141–181.

Tischler, Hans, ed. *Trouvère Lyrics with Melodies: Complete Comparative Edition.* Neuhausen, Germany: Hänssler-Verlag, 1997.

Charlemagne (Charles I, Charles the Great) (742–814)

One of the most important figures of the medieval world, Charlemagne was king of the Franks and ultimately emperor of the West. Renowned for his military strength, which enabled him to expand his empire from the North Sea to the Pyrenees, Charlemagne's more important contribution to Western civilization includes the revival of learning and the arts that was encouraged and that flourished under his reign. In addition, the legend of Charlemagne provided material for many popular literary treatments in the centuries that followed.

Born in 742, the son of King Pepin the Short and Berthe (daughter of Caribert, the count of Laon), Charlemagne became joint ruler of the Frankish Kingdom with his brother Carloman in 768. His early reign was strongly influenced by his virtuous mother (d. 783), even after Charles ruled in his own right following his brother's death in 771. His first major war occurred in 773, when he invaded Lombardy in response to a threat to the pope. Charlemagne crushed the Lombards, put their king into a monastery, and assumed the crown of Lombardy himself.

For some 10 years after this, Charlemagne fought the Saxons and finally defeated them, forcing their leader, Wildukind, to be baptized and adding their territory to his growing empire. In 788, Tassilo, the duke of Bavaria and technically one of Charlemagne's vassals, defied the king and was subsequently defeated. Like the Lombard king before him, Tassilo was pressured into entering a monastery, thus adding Bavaria to Charles's empire. Shortly thereafter, in 791, Charles became embroiled in a long war with the Avars, who ruled an area along the Danube. Ultimately, in 799, he defeated them as well and expanded his hegemony once again.

About this time Pope Leo III was under attack again, and he was deposed in 800. Charlemagne once again crossed the Alps and restored the pope to his position, after which, on Christmas Day 800, the pope, seeing Charlemagne as the true protector of the faith, crowned him emperor of the West—the first to be crowned since the sixth century.

Charlemagne continued to reign until his death in 814, after which his empire was divided among his sons. He maintained good relations with the eastern, or Byzantine emperor, as well as with the caliph of Baghdad, Haroun-al-Raschid, who not only sent him a white elephant but agreed to protect pilgrims en route to Jerusalem, deep in Muslim territory.

Charlemagne built a great imperial palace at Aachen, a wonder in its day, and was interested not only in conquest but also in establishing order and promoting learning in his empire. During what became known as the "Carolingian renaissance," schools were set up across the empire, the arts flourished, and monasteries began building up great libraries, preserving manuscripts and making multiple copies of older texts in their scriptoria, thus preserving many classical texts that might otherwise have been lost. He convinced the great Anglo-Saxon scholar ALCUIN to become priest of the imperial chapel and to help reform education in his realm. Alcuin headed the palace school and standardized the LIBERAL ARTS curriculum, composing textbooks for use in studying grammar, logic, astronomy, and rhetoric. Alcuin also is credited for developing the Carolingian minuscule—a form of cursive script that allowed for clear and rapid transcription.

In addition to his influence on learning, Charlemagne himself became the subject of literary texts. EINHARD (a student of Alcuin's) wrote an early biography of him, *Vita Caroli Magni* (*Life of Charlemagne*), published in about 830. Written in imitation of Suetonius, Einhard's biography contains a good deal of firsthand, personal detail, and has often been admired for its fidelity to truth. A second idealized biography, *Gesta Caroli* (The deeds of Charles), is believed to have been written by NOTKER BALBULUS in 883–84. Composed for Charlemagne's great-grandson Charles the Fat, Notker's biography helped to establish Charlemagne as a legendary hero.

Many legends developed around Charlemagne, glorifying him as the defender of the faith (which could be said with some truth), particularly against Saracens (which was entirely apocryphal). Charlemagne and his knights became the focus of a cycle of heroic poems known as the *geste du roi,* a group of some 20 epic poems of the sort known as CHANSONS DE GESTE. Charlemagne is the central figure of these poems, but they general involve the exploits of his "12 Peers," the chief warrior knights or "paladins" that owe him allegiance. The list varies, but in the earliest and most important poem in the cycle, the *Chanson de Roland,* or *SONG OF ROLAND,* the list includes Roland, Oliver, Gérin, Gérier, Bérengier, Otton, Samson, Engelier, Ivon, Ivoire, Anséis, and Girard.

In the end Charlemagne's contributions to Western culture are among the most significant in history, but ultimately his legend became popular enough to rival his actual accomplishments.

Bibliography

Bullough, Donald. *The Age of Charlemagne.* 2nd ed. New York: Exeter Books, 1980.

Halphen, Louis. *Charlemagne and the Carolingian Empire.* 1949. Translated by Giselle de Nie. New York: North Holland, 1977.

James, Edward. *The Franks.* New York: Basil Blackwell, 1988.

Riché, Pierre. *Daily Life in the World of Charlemagne.* 1978. With expanded footnotes and translated with an introduction by Jo Ann McNamara. Philadelphia: University of Pennsylvania Press, 1988.

Thorpe, Lewis, trans. *Two Lives of Charlemagne.* Harmondsworth, U.K.: Penguin, 1969.

Charles d'Orléans (1394–1465)

In the Battle of Agincourt, 1415, the English, by means of their superior longbows that effectively defeated the enemy knights on horseback, won a major victory over the French, butchering masses of their opponents and taking many peers as prisoners. One of the prisoners was Charles d' Orléans. Charles's mother was Valentina, daughter of the duke of Milan (house of the Visconti), and his father was Louis, duke of Orléans and the brother of King Charles VI. He spent his childhood in Chateaudun, 20 miles south of Orléans, where he acquired a solid education in the liberal arts under his tutor, Nicholas Garbet. His father was assassinated in 1407 by a band of men hired by his political enemy, Jean-sans-Peur, duke of Burgundy, and his mother died the following year. Already in 1406, as a 12-year-old, Charles had married Isabelle, widow of King RICHARD II of England. After her death in 1409, Charles married Bonne d'Armagnac. However, since Charles was not released from his imprisonment for 25 years, after 1415 he never again saw his wife, who died before his return in 1440. In 1428 English troops invaded and largely destroyed his estates. Only Orléans held out and was relieved on May 8, 1429, with the help of JOAN OF ARC. This, however, reconfirmed the English decision to keep Charles as long as possible, irrespective of the payment of the ransom, which had become more difficult to put together than ever before, although ironically Joan's military achievements eventually led to the liberation of France from English occupation.

After Charles's ransom had finally been paid in 1440, he returned to France and married Marie de Clèves, niece of Philip of Burgundy, who had contributed to the ransom. Charles made major efforts to bring about peace negotiations to end the Hundred Years' War between England and France, and a peace settlement was finally signed on May 28, 1444, in Tours. In 1447 Charles tried in vain with some military troops to recapture the Duchy of Asti, an Italian property he had inherited from his mother. But he had too few resources to hold on to Asti and left again in 1448, only to renounce his claim on Asti entirely in 1450, allowing the new duke of Milan, Francesco Sforza, to take control of the duchy. Thereafter, despite some expectations that Charles would be a political leader, he basically retired to Blois for the rest of his life and refrained from getting involved in political conflicts with the French royalty despite his close family relations. His wife bore him two daughters and one son who later rose to the French throne as King Louis XII. Charles died on January 4, 1465.

During his 25 years in England Charles was highly active in writing meditative and allegorical poems in English, 141 of which are found in British Library MS Harley 682. Recent scholarship has even identified him as one of the leading 15th-century English poets. Back in France, Charles continued composing poetry and quickly gained a great reputation among his contemporaries. In Blois he created a kind of literary court with poetry contests. One of his many visitors was the rather notorious François VILLON who wrote three poems, most famously his *"Je meurs de suif auprés de la fontaine"* ("I die of thirst beside the fountain"), during his stay there. Other well-known poets also joined Charles, such as Jean Meschinot, René d'Anjou, Olivier de la Marche, and Georges Chastelain. Charles set up the practice of giving his guests the first line for a ballad and asking them to write the rest. Many of these poems have been preserved in a manuscript (Paris, Bibliothèque Nationale, fr. 25458) that served Charles as a poetry album for his own poems and those of his visitors.

Composing verse was a common element in the education of medieval nobles, but Charles demonstrated a powerful poetic gift from early on. Throughout his life he published volumes with his poetry, beginning with *Retenue d'amours,* composed prior to his capture at Agincourt, followed by the *Complainte de France* (1433), then a 550-line sequel to *Retenue,* then *Songe en complainte* (1437); in total he composed 89 chansons, five COMPLAINTS, 123 *BALLADES,* four carols, and 435 RONDEAUX. He wrote 125 poems in English, many of which have French counterparts. His entire *œuvre* includes more than 13,000 verses and sheds significant light on the poet's concept of self, his melancholic perception of life, and his contempt for man's hypocritical nature.

Charles's major themes were of a melancholy and introspective character, focusing on his destiny in exile, solitude, the idle passage of time, the various experiences of love, life as a prison, old age, religious experiences, and death. But he also reflects a certain degree of humor, especially in his many love poems offering advise to unhappy lovers.

Bibliography

Arn, Mary-Jo, ed. *Charles d'Orléans in England (1415–1440).* Cambridge, U.K.: Brewer, 2000.

———. *Fortunes Stabilnes. Charles of Orleans's English Book of Love. A Critical Edition.* Binghamton, N.Y.: Medieval and Renaissance Texts and Studies, 1994.

Charles d'Orléans. *Poésies.* Edited by Pierre Champion. 2 vols. Paris: Champion, 1923–1927.

Classen, Albrecht. *Die autobiographische Lyrik des europäischen Spätmittelalters.* Amsterdam and Atlanta: Editions Rodopi, 1991, 269–345.

Coldiron, A. E. B. *Canon, Period, and the Poetry of Charles of Orleans. Found in Translation.* Ann Arbor: The University of Michigan Press, 2000.

Fein, David. *Charles d'Orléans.* Boston: Twayne, 1983.

Spence, Sarah, ed. and trans. *The French Chansons of Charles d'Orléans with the Corresponding Middle English Chansons.* New York: Garland, 1986.

Albrecht Classen

Châtelain de Couci (ca. 1168–1203)

One of the most popular of the late 12th-century TROUVÈRES is known only as the Châtelain de Couci, that is, the governor of the castle of Couci. He has been identified by historians as Guy de Thourette, or Guy IV de Couci, who was one of the most powerful barons in France, a well-known crusader, and châtelain from 1186 until his death in 1203.

Guy is known to have taken part in the Third Crusade, and may have been at Acre in 1191. He was one of the leaders of the Fourth Crusade, but died and was buried at sea in May or June of 1203. His death is recorded in *The Conquest of Constantinople* by his fellow crusader Geoffroi de VILLEHARDOUIN, the marshall of Champagne.

The Châtelain de Couci follows closely in the tradition of vernacular love poetry handed down from the Provençal TROUBADOURS. Much of what he writes is conventional, though he is admired for his skillful use of rhyme schemes, and is most admired for his depiction of the pain experienced by the mournful lover who must leave his lady. In his best-known poem, beginning "A vous, amant," Couci depicts the lover who must leave his lady to go on a crusade, and expresses the agonizing feeling of being torn between loyalty to God and his beloved:

Love, pity! If ever God did something base,
He has, like a brute, broken true love in two:
I cannot put this love away from me,
And yet I must leave my lady.

(Goldin 1973, 351, ll. 29–32)

The châtelain's reputation made him the subject of a sensationalized fictional romance of the late 13th century, composed by an otherwise unknown author named Jakemes. In the *Roman du Châtelain de Coucy et la dame de Fayel,* the hero (here called Renaud) loves the Lady de Fayel and wins her love in return through his service and his poetry. The Lady's jealous husband tricks Renaud into going on a crusade, where he is killed by a poisoned arrow. In accordance with Renaud's wishes, his heart is sent back to his lady, along with a love letter and the strands of her blonde hair she had given him as a love token. But when the jealous husband intercepts the package with its incriminating letter, he takes his revenge by cooking the heart and serving it to his wife as a meal. When the Lady Fayel discovers what she has done, she collapses in a dead faint.

Renaud includes six poems in his romance. Four of these are certainly the châtelain's genuine work, while the other two are of doubtful authorship. Altogether some 33 extant poems are attributed to Guy, though most of these are probably not his. Most critics accept about 15 poems as genuine.

Bibliography

Goldin, Frederick, ed. and trans. *Lyrics of the Troubadours and Trouverès: An Anthology and a History.* Garden City, New York: Anchor, 1973.

Lerond, Alain, ed. *Chansons attribuées au Chastenlain de Couci.* Vol. 7, Publications de la Faculté des lettres et sciences humaines de Rennes. Paris: Presses Universitaires de France, 1964.

van der Werf, Hendrik. *The Chansons of the Troubadours and Trouvères: A Study of the Melodies and Their Relation to the Poems.* Utrecht: A. Oosthoek, 1972.

Chaucer, Geoffrey (ca. 1343–1400)

Geoffrey Chaucer was the most admired and influential writer of the English Middle Ages. Known chiefly as a narrative poet, particularly for his varied collection of *CANTERBURY TALES* (ca. 1387–1400) and his tragic verse ROMANCE, *TROILUS AND CRISEYDE* (1385), Chaucer was also an accomplished lyric poet, the author of prose texts, and an admired translator (having rendered the very influential French ALLEGORY the *ROMAN DE LA ROSE* and BOETHIUS's popular *CONSOLATION OF PHILOSOPHY* into MIDDLE ENGLISH).

Chaucer was born in London between 1340 and 1345, son of the wine merchant John Chaucer and his wife, Agnes. As a child, Geoffrey would have heard of England's great victory at Crécy in the Hundred Years' War, and he lived through the BLACK DEATH, which killed half of his countrymen. Though a member of the bourgeois class, John Chaucer must have had influential friends, because by 1357, his son Geoffrey was serving as a page in the household of Countess Elizabeth of Ulster, wife of Prince Lionel, second son of King EDWARD III. Three years later, he was in France, perhaps with Prince Lionel, fighting in the war. He was taken prisoner and ransomed, King Edward himself contributing 16 pounds to the ransom—evidence that he was considered a valuable courtier by the royal family. A truce was arranged in 1360 that led to a nine-year hiatus of hostilities between England and France, during which some scholars believe Chaucer may have been studying law at the Inner Temple, one of the Inns of Court. In 1366, Chaucer married Philippa Pan Roet, a minor aristocrat and lady-in-waiting to the queen (and thus Chaucer's social superior). Their son Thomas (who later became one of the wealthiest and most influential men in England) was born in 1367. Chaucer also traveled to Spain in 1366, and is known to have been on the continent in 1368 as well, in the "king's service." In 1367 he was made "valettus," and later esquire, in the household of the king, who granted him an annual salary of 20 marks. It is possible that Chaucer's 1368 trip was to meet with Prince Lionel, who was in Milan for his wedding to a daughter of the powerful Visconti family—a marriage whose celebratory feasting across Europe led to Lionel's death from food poisoning before his return to England.

Chaucer, in the meantime, had apparently become close to Lionel's brother, JOHN OF GAUNT, who would soon become the most powerful man in England. Chaucer wrote his first important poem, *The BOOK OF THE DUCHESS,* apparently as an elegy on the death of Gaunt's first wife, Blanche of Lancaster. This and other early poems indicate a strong French influence, particularly of the poet Guillaume de MACHAUT, on Chaucer's verse at this time. In 1369 and again in 1370, Chaucer was fighting in France, this time with Gaunt's army. In 1372, his wife Philippa became lady-in-waiting in the household of Gaunt's new wife, Constance of Castile. This relationship may have led to Gaunt's longtime affair with Philippa's sister, Katherine Swynford. But also in 1372, Chaucer was sent on the first of his diplomatic missions to Italy, to negotiate an English port for Genoese ships. Scholars believe Chaucer also visited Florence, and have speculated that he may have met PETRARCH on this trip, or that he may have witnessed one of BOCCACCIO's public lectures on the poetry of DANTE begun in 1373. Neither of these conjectures can be proven, and neither is very likely, but it is true that Chaucer's poetry began increasingly to show the influence of Italian poetry through the 1370s and 1380s.

In 1374, Chaucer was given the significant position of controller of customs for wool at the Port of London, and in addition to his £10 salary, received the grant of a daily gallon of wine for the rest of his life (a grant he later converted to 20 marks annually in cash). He also leased a house over Aldgate in London. In his unfinished DREAM VISION poem *The HOUSE OF FAME,* Chaucer provides a comic caricature of himself, going over his account books all day at work and then going home to bury his face in another book, having no interaction with other people and living like a hermit—but without the abstinence. Still, Chaucer was kept busy as well with diplomatic tasks. He made a number of trips to France in 1376–77, negotiating for peace with France and a marriage for the young Prince Richard, son of Edward, the Black Prince (eldest son of King Edward III), and, upon the death of the Black Prince in 1376, heir to the English throne. In 1377, Edward III died and the 10-year-old prince became King RICHARD II.

Chaucer was in Italy once again in 1378, on a diplomatic mission to the Viscontis in Milan, during which he gave his friend, the poet John GOWER, his power of attorney. The Italian influence on Chaucer's work increased significantly after this second (or possibly third) visit, and is apparent in his *PARLIAMENT OF FOWLS* (ca. 1381, perhaps written to celebrate Richard's betrothal to ANNE OF BOHEMIA), his *KNIGHT'S TALE* (ca. 1382, based on Boccaccio's *TESEIDA*), and his *Troilus and Criseyde* (ca. 1385, based on Boccaccio's *Il FILOSTRATO*).

In 1380, a woman named Cecily Chaumpaigne signed a document releasing Chaucer from all legal actions in the case of what she calls "my rape." This incident has been a matter of some controversy among Chaucer scholars. Since others are also named in her charges, and since "rape" could have meant "abduction" at the time, the precise nature of the charges brought against Chaucer and then dismissed remains a mystery. That same year, Chaucer's second son Lewis was born, to whom in 1391 Chaucer addressed his *Treatise on the Astrolabe,* a technical manual on how to use the complicated astronomical device with which he seems to have been fascinated. In the early 1380s, Chaucer also translated Boethius, and concepts and images popularized by the *Consolation of Philosophy* began to find their way into his poetry, especially *Troilus,* the *Knight's Tale,* and some shorter lyric poems like *TRUTH, Gentilesse,* and *Lak of Stedfastnesse.* Perhaps some of the consolation Chaucer sought from Boethius was from the political turmoil of the times: The PEASANTS' REVOLT shook the aristocracy to its core in 1381. A few years earlier, the Western church had split into two factions (an event called the Great Schism), with a pope in Rome and a rival pope in Avignon. And in England, the doctrine and writings of John WYCLIFFE had been officially condemned in 1380, leading to the emergence of a sect of heretical Wycliffite followers called LOLLARDS.

Besides, the pressures of the controllership seem to have been increasing for Chaucer. He was allowed to appoint a deputy in 1382, and that deputy became permanent in 1385. By this time, Chaucer's international reputation as a poet seems to have become significant, as he received a complimentary poem from the French poet Eustache DESCHAMPS, who called him the "great translator." But in 1386, Chaucer lost his position altogether with the ascendancy of Gaunt's younger brother, the Duke of Gloucester, who led a faction that deposed and ultimately executed several of Richard II's closest advisers. Chaucer gave up his house at Aldgate and moved to Kent, where he was justice of the peace from 1385–89, and also served in Parliament. But without his controllership, he seems to have had time to begin significant new projects. About 1386 he began, and apparently soon abandoned, his *LEGEND OF GOOD WOMEN,* a tribute (in parody of the *GOLDEN LEGEND*) to martyrs of the God of Love. He also began his greatest and most ambitious work, *The Canterbury Tales,* around 1387—the year that records indicate his wife, Philippa, died.

When Richard reached his majority and, with Gaunt's support, began to rule in his own right in 1389, Chaucer was appointed to the responsible position of clerk of the king's works, responsible for maintenance of all the royal estates. But when he was robbed in Surrey in the performance of his duties (it appears he may have been robbed three times in the space of four days), he resigned his post, later becoming deputy royal forester for

Petherton in Somerset. In his last decade, as Chaucer continued to work on his *Canterbury Tales,* Richard continued to favor Chaucer, granting him an annuity of £20 a year in 1394 and a tun of wine a year in 1398, but the king's own position was growing more and more untenable as his actions, particularly after the death of Anne of Bohemia in 1394, became more and more irrational. In 1399, Gaunt's son Henry of Derby deposed Richard and became king himself. Meanwhile, apparently in financial straits (most likely as Richard's government failed to pay his salary), Chaucer leased a home in the garden of Westminster Abbey for a period of 53 years in 1399. Chaucer's last datable poem, the *COMPLAINT TO HIS PURSE,* was written to the new king Henry IV, essentially begging for some compensation. Henry confirmed and even increased Chaucer's royal annuities, but the poet did not live to enjoy them long. He died, according to tradition, on October 25, 1400, and was buried in what was to become Poet's Corner at Westminster Abbey.

Chaucer has been called the father of English literature—probably an inflated title, but it is certainly true that more than anyone else, Chaucer made English a respected literary language among his own countrymen and throughout Europe. Every subsequent English or Scottish writer for two centuries was directly influenced by Chaucer, and even Shakespeare turned to him for the plots of at least two of his plays. Chaucer's East Midland dialect became the standard for written English, and the decasyllabic line he popularized became the standard English iambic pentameter line. His influence on English literature is immeasurable, and his contributions, particularly the memorable characters and entertaining variety of genres contained in his *Canterbury Tales,* continue to engage readers to this day.

Bibliography

Benson, Larry D., et al., eds. *The Riverside Chaucer.* 3rd ed. Boston: Houghton-Mifflin, 1987.

Chaucer Life-Records. Edited by Martin M. Crow and Clair C. Olson from materials compiled by John M. Manly and Edith Rickert, with the assistance of Lilian J. Redstone and others. Oxford: Clarendon Press, 1966.

Howard, Donald R. *Chaucer: His Life, His Works, His World.* New York: Dutton, 1987.

Pearsall, Derek. *The Life of Geoffrey Chaucer: A Critical Biography.* Oxford: Blackwell, 1992.

Chester Cycle

The Chester Cycle was a collection of 25 MYSTERY PLAYS performed in the city of Chester in the late medieval and early Tudor periods. Like other mystery play cycles, the Chester plays were first performed at the festival of CORPUS CHRISTI in late May or June, and indeed the first recorded mention of the plays is in a civic document of 1422 in which they are referred to as the "Play of Corpus Christi."

The 1422 reference implies that the plays were even then a long-standing tradition. Celebration of Corpus Christi, which became widespread in England after 1311, consisted of a long procession involving the entire city. Eventually it seems that the city guilds became concerned with staging plays as part of the celebration—plays that told the story of God's divine plan for humankind from Creation to Doomsday. It appears that in Chester, the original procession traveled from the church of St. Mary on the Hill to the Church of St. John's outside the city walls, and it is likely that the plays were put on at St. John's originally. However, eventually the plays themselves were performed in procession, being mounted on movable stages called pageant wagons and performed at various sites around the city. With this development, costs seem to have soared, since each play needed a separate wagon, actors, props, and sets. But the plays involved the entire community and were a source of pride for the guilds. If the expense was too great for one guild, several might join together to fund a production.

With the Protestant Reformation, the mystery plays came under fire because of their traditionally Catholic theology and their association with the Roman Catholic festival of Corpus Christi, established to celebrate the real presence of the body and blood of Christ in the Eucharist. By 1521 the plays were being performed on Whitsunday (Pentecost) and took three days (Monday through Wednesday of Whitsunday week) to perform. It appears that the first nine plays, from the Creation and the Fall of Lucifer through the Gifts of the Magi, were performed on the first day; the next eight plays, from the Massacre of the Innocents through the HARROWING OF HELL, were performed on the second day; and the last six plays, from the Resurrection through Judgment Day, were performed the final day.

Despite strong governmental and ecclesiastical disapproval, the plays continued into the reign of Elizabeth. Civic pride and tradition often outweighed official disapproval. During this time, legends grew that the plays were originally written by the Chester monk Henry Francis around 1380, or even by the well-known monk Ranulph HIGDEN (1299–1364), and were established under Chester's first mayor, but these stories probably were intended to justify the performance of the plays as a vital part of Chester's history. In 1575, despite the disapproval of the archbishop of York, the city corporation approved the performance of the cycle, though Sir John Savage, the mayor, was afterwards brought before the Privy Council to explain himself. That was the last time the plays were performed, until they were revived in 1951.

The continued popularity of the plays is evident from the fact that eight manuscripts have survived, five of them containing the full cycle. Each of these copies was produced between 1591 and 1607—long after the plays had ceased to be performed.

Whether there was a single original author for the plays is impossible to know, and, in any case, it was certainly not likely to be Higden or Francis. Certainly the cycle has been revised significantly over the years, but a number of aspects of the plays give them a kind of unity and suggest a single mind—writer, reviser, producer—behind the text we now have. For example, some 80 percent of the total lines in the plays are written in what has come to be called the Chester stanza—an eight-line stanza rhyming *aaabaaab* or *aaabcccb,* where the *a* and *c* lines have four metrical feet and the *b* lines have three, as in this stanza from the first play:

I, God, most of majesty,
in whom beginning none may be;
endless, also, most of posty [power]
I am and have ever been.
now Heaven and Earth is made through me
the earth is void only, I see;
therefore light for more lee [greater happiness]
through my might I will kever [secure]

(Mills 1992, 26–27, ll. 1–8)

There is also a symmetry to the entire production, which begins with a long speech by God addressed to the audience, and ends with set speeches from the four Evangelists, also to the audience. Further, many plays have an "Expositor" character, who comments on the action and interprets it for the viewers.

Other aspects of the Chester cycle that make it unique are the plays of Abraham and Melchizadek and the play of the Coming of Antichrist, neither of which has a counterpart in the other extant cycles. Further, the Chester plays seem to have used a good deal of music, including an angel choir and a sung "Magnificat," probably performed by a chorister soloist.

Bibliography

Beadle, Richard, ed. *The Cambridge Companion to Medieval English Theatre.* Cambridge: Cambridge University Press, 1994.

Kolve, V. A. *The Play Called Corpus Christi.* Stanford, Calif.: Stanford University Press, 1966.

Mills, David. *The Chester Mystery Cycle: A New Edition with Modernised Spelling.* East Lansing, Mich.: Colleagues Press, 1992.

Salter, Frederick Millet. *Medieval Drama in Chester.* 2nd ed. New York: Russell and Russell, 1968.

Travis, Peter. *Dramatic Design in the Chester Cycle.* Chicago: University of Chicago Press, 1982.

chōka

The *chōka* or "long poem" (sometimes called a *nagauta*) is one of the two forms of poetry used by the Japanese poets whose work was collected in the eighth-century anthology called *The* MAN'YŌSHŪ (the other form being the *TANKA,* or "short poem"). The *chōka* could be composed in any number of verses—though in practice, the longest *chōka* in the

Man'yōshū is 149 lines. The *chōka* alternates lines of five and seven syllables, and ends with a final couplet of two seven-syllable lines. In effect, the last five lines of a *chōka* are identical in form to the more popular *tanka:* 31 syllables in five lines of five, seven, five, seven, and seven syllables. Further, the *chōka* was typically followed by one or two (or even more) short poems called *hanka*—a word from the Chinese meaning "a verse that repeats." These *hanka,* usually in the five-line form of the *tanka,* acted as envoys, detailing, enlarging, or summarizing the theme of the longer main body of the poem.

Of the 4,516 poems anthologized in *The Man'yōshū,* only 265 are *chōka.* These, however, are generally the most memorable poems in the collection, particularly those attributed to the acclaimed poet HITOMARO Kakinomoto, called the "Saint of Poetry." One of his best-known poems is the *chōka* "On leaving his wife as he set out from Iwami for the capital." The main body of the poem consists of 24 lines and ends with these verses:

Farther and farther my home falls behind,
Steeper and steeper the mountains I have crossed.
My wife must be languishing
Like dripping summer grass.
I would see where she dwells
Bend down, O mountains!

(Nipon Gakujutsu Shinkokai 1965, 32)

The poem is accompanied by two *tanka*-like *hanka,* the last of which reads:

The leaves of bamboo grass
Fill all the hill-side
With loud rustling sounds;
But I think only of my love,
Having left her behind.

(Nipon Gakujutsu Shinkokai 1965, 32)

The effective but understated emotion that gives the poem its lyrical appeal is characteristic of the *chōka* in the *Man'yōshū.* Although *chōka* continued to be composed after the collection in *the Man'yōshū,* none of these is particularly effective, and the *chōka* was soon virtually completely displaced by the *tanka* among Japanese poets.

Bibliography

Keene, Donald. *Seeds in the Heart: Japanese Literature from Earliest Times to the Late Sixteenth Century.* Vol. I, *A History of Japanese Literature.* New York: Columbia University Press, 1999.

Miner, Earl, Hiroko Odagiri, and Robert E. Morrell. *The Princeton Companion to Classical Japanese Literature.* Princeton, N.J.: Princeton University Press, 1985.

Nipon Gakujutsu Shinkokai, trans. *The Manyoshu.* With a new foreword by Donald Keene. 1940. New York: Columbia University Press, 1965.

Chrétien de Troyes (ca. 1140–ca. 1190)

Chrétien de Troyes, writing in French in the late 12th century, may be the inventor of the genre of chivalric ROMANCE. He is certainly the poet most responsible for shaping the form and style of Arthurian literature as it developed through the high Middle Ages. Basing his narratives in part on tales told by wandering Breton MINSTRELS, and building on the currency of GEOFFREY OF MONMOUTH's pseudo-historical *HISTORY OF THE KINGS OF BRITAIN* (ca. 1136), Chrétien adapted the legends of King ARTHUR and his knights to the current vogue of COURTLY LOVE and created a new kind of literature, more focused on the interior development of individual knights than on the nationalistic stories of war available in the established narrative CHANSONS DE GESTE. Five Arthurian romances are attributed to Chrétien: *ÉREC ET ÉNIDE* (ca. 1170); *CLIGÈS* (ca. 1176); *YVAIN* (or *Le Chevalier au Lion, The Knight with the Lion*) and *LANCELOT* (or *Le Chevalier de la Charrette, The Knight of the Cart*), which he worked on simultaneously between ca. 1177 and 1181; and finally *PERCEVAL* (or *Conte du Graal, The Story of the Grail*), which he left unfinished upon his death, sometime before 1191. His works survive in some 30 manuscripts, two of which contain all five romances.

Little can be said about Chrétien's life other than what can be gleaned from the comments, particularly the prologues, to his extant romances. He dedicates his *Lancelot* to the Countess MARIE DE CHAMPAGNE, daughter of ELEANOR OF AQUITAINE, who had married Count Henry the Liberal sometime between 1159 and 1164. Chrétien claims to have gotten both the subject matter and themes of his poem from Marie, implying that he was likely a court poet at Troyes, the capital of Champagne, during Marie's time there. The dedication of *Perceval* to Philip, count of Flanders, suggests that Chrétien found a new patron in Philip in the 1180s, and the unfinished state of *Perceval* may indicate that Chrétien died before the count's death in 1191.

In *Cligès*, Chrétien declares that he is the author of *Érec et Énide*, and that he has also translated Ovid's *Commandments* and *The Art of Love* into French, along with parts of the Latin poet's *Metamorphoses.* He also claims to have written a poem of King Mark and Isolde the Blond—a contribution to the famous medieval legend of TRISTAN AND ISOLDE that is no longer extant. This prologue establishes a fairly clear chronology of *Érec* as Chrétien's first romance and *Cligès* as his second, the other three following since they are not yet mentioned. It also suggests that Chrétien was a writer educated in the seven LIBERAL ARTS, familiar with Latin, but working in the vernacular for nobles at court—and therefore likely a cleric, like his contemporary in Marie's court, ANDREAS CAPELLANUS.

Chrétien's romances are written in the traditional verse form of Old French, octasyllabic (eight-syllable) couplets. They average about 7,000 lines (except for *Perceval*, which is unfinished at 9,000). The five poems explore similar themes, and in that sense complement one another. *Érec et Énide* explores the marriage of a knight who prefers to spend all of his time at home with his new wife, and his lady who urges him to engage in the kind of adventure that will bring him honor and shore up his sagging reputation. His subsequent struggle to prove his chivalric worth, and his wife's struggle over whether to keep quiet and obey her husband or to warn him when danger approaches, makes a fascinating narrative of mutual growth in nobility. In the comic romance *Cligès*, the plot focuses on the importance of maintaining technical purity and innocence, and on the heroine's not becoming like the adulterous Isolde. Fénice is loved by Cligès and returns his love, but will not be unfaithful to her husband. Therefore she takes a potion that makes her appear to be dead, and once she is legally dead, she is free to indulge her love for Cligès—thus by the end of the romance her morality is just as questionable as Isolde's.

In *Yvain*, Chrétien reverses the situation of *Érec*, for the protagonist, after winning his lady, is granted leave to go forth and win his reputation, but forgets his promise to return to his wife in a year. After she forsakes him, Yvain must go through grief and madness before he works his way back to his beloved through acts of charity and service to others. In Lancelot, the situation of *Cligès* is reversed, and Lancelot and GUENEVERE engage in precisely the kind of affair that Tristan undertook with Isolde, and Lancelot's willingness to perform any task, even if it means his public dishonor, is a sign of his perfect private devotion to his beloved.

In Chrétien's final romance, *Perceval*, the protagonist is depicted in a long process of maturation, learning about knighthood, about love, about religion, and ultimately about charity, since he learns it was his lack of charity that prevented him from achieving some of the tasks set before him, including asking the question about the nature of the Grail procession that will cure the Fisher King.

Chrétien is also the author of two extant lyric poems, and has occasionally been suggested as the author of the pseudo-hagiographical *Guillaume d'Angletree*, though most scholars dispute his authorship of this text. Although recognized as a pioneer, Chrétien has not always been appreciated as an artist. In the early 20th century, the scholar Joseph Bédier called him "not so much a creative artist as a clever compiler." But he is responsible for introducing the Lancelot-Guenevere story and the theme of the Holy Grail into the Arthurian tradition—two of the tradition's most enduring themes. His use of the romance influenced popular and courtly literature for some 400 years, and his courtly style was adopted by GUILLAUME DE LORRIS in the highly influential 13th-century *ROMAN DE LA ROSE*. His stories influenced Middle

High German texts like WOLFRAM VON ESCHENBACH's *PARZIFAL*, on the later French VULGATE CYCLE, on MIDDLE ENGLISH romances like *YWAIN AND GAWAIN* and *SIR PERCEVAL OF GALLES*, and even texts in Italian or in Old Norse. Chrétien's influence on subsequent literature has been enormous, and it might be argued that his focus on the growth and maturity of characters and on their interior lives begins the development that leads to the modern novel.

Bibliography

Chrétien de Troyes. *Arthurian Romances.* Translated by William W. Kibler and Carleton W. Carroll. Introduction and notes by William W. Kibler. New York: Penguin, 1991.

Frappier, Jean. *Chrétien de Troyes: The Man and His Work.* Translated by Raymond J. Cormier. Athens: Ohio University Press, 1982.

Holmes, Urban Tigner. *Chrétien de Troyes.* New York: Twayne, 1970.

Kelly, Douglas, ed. *The Romances of Chrétien de Troyes: A Symposium.* Lexington, Ky.: French Forum, 1985.

Mullally, Evelyn. *The Artist at Work: Narrative Technique in Chrétien de Troyes.* Philadelphia: American Philosophical Society, 1988.

Pickens, Rupert T. *The Welsh Knight: Paradoxicality in Chrétien's Conte del Graal.* Lexington, Ky.: French Forum, 1977.

Topsfield, L. T. *Chrétien de Troyes: A Study of the Arthurian Romances.* Cambridge: Cambridge University Press, 1981.

Christ and Satan (eighth century)

The text now known as *Christ and Satan* is an OLD ENGLISH work in three distinct sections forming the fourth and final poem in the JUNIUS MANUSCRIPT. The poem, probably written in eighth-century Anglia, comprises 730 extant lines in ALLITERATIVE VERSE (some lines are missing from the last section of the poem).

The unity of the poem is questionable. Certainly the style and language are consistent throughout the text, but there is no continuous narrative, which has led some scholars to suggest that the text is actually made up of three separate poems. The manuscript's editor, however, has proposed that *Christ and Satan* is not intended primarily to be a narrative but rather a number of lyrical passages on related biblical and theological themes.

Part I, the longest section of the text at 364 lines, depicts the lament of Satan after his fall from heaven. Notable in this section is the use of language recalling Old English ELEGAIC POEMS, a vocabulary that speaks of Satan as an outlawed wanderer, bereft of his Lord's mead hall. Part II of the poem is concerned chiefly with the HARROWING OF HELL, though it also touches on the deeds of the Risen Christ and on Judgment Day. An interesting part of this section is Eve's prayer to Christ as he enters hell—she laments her part in the Fall and reminds Christ that he was born of one of her own daughters, and so pleads for deliverance from hell. The third and shortest part of the poem retells the story of Satan's temptation of Christ in the wilderness. This part of the manuscript is apparently incomplete, however, leaving out Satan's urging of Christ to test God by throwing himself off the tower.

There is no single source for the Old English poem. The first part is drawn from earlier Christian legends of Lucifer's fall. The second draws largely from the apocryphal Gospel of Nicodemus and from the Gospels, and the final part from the temptation stories in the Synoptic Gospels. At one time, it was customary to attribute all of the poems of the Junius manuscript to CAEDMON or his school, but modern scholars make no such claim, though it has been suggested that *Christ and Satan* has elements of both the Caedmon and Cynewulf "schools" of poetry.

Bibliography

Krapp, George Philip. *The Junius Manuscript.* Anglo-Saxon Poetic Records, I. New York: Columbia University Press, 1931.

Christine de Pizan (ca. 1364–1430)

Often known as the first professional woman of letters, Christine de Pizan (or Pisan) was born in Venice but as a child moved to the court of Charles

V of France, where her father was invited to be court physician and astrologer. Under her father's tutelage, Christine was taught to read and write, and was schooled in the arts of rhetoric and philosophical discourse. She was uncommonly well educated for a woman at this time, and her learning supported her later in life when her father's death in the 1380s, followed by her husband's death in 1390, left her to care for three children, her widowed mother, and a niece. After working for some years as a copyist for manuscript workshops in Paris, in the late 1390s Christine chose to earn her living by writing her own original works commissioned by various members of the aristocracy and royal family. While her skill at writing lyric verse first brought her renown and reputation, her later works concerning moral issues, the position of women in society, politics and government, chivalry, and a well-received biography of Charles V, established her as the foremost female writer of her time, and one of the most remarkable literary figures, male or female, in medieval Europe.

Christine was an essential part of the intellectual and literary culture in late 14th- to early 15th-century Europe, yet she remained essentially French and wrote only in that language. Her works were translated into other languages and sometimes ascribed to male authors by those who could not, for example, accept that a woman could write so knowledgeably about the arts of chivalry (*Le Livre des fais d'armes et de chevalrie,* 1410). After her early success with lyric poetry for the aristocracy, she turned her attention to works of moral, social, and political import until civil war in France forced her retreat to a convent in 1418, where she died sometime in the 1430s. The extant manuscripts of her work testify to her popularity and influence as they range from the most sumptuously illuminated, commissioned by the aristocratic patronage she enjoyed, to considerably less elegant manuscripts intended for a broader audience. Christine's *L'Avision* or *The Vision* (1405) is an important source of biographical information framed in a DREAM VISION and peopled with allegorical figures.

Christine's literary endeavors were vast and various in genre and subject matter: She produced courtesy and devotional books, literary debates, biographies, lyric poetry, chivalric manuals, dream visions, and defenses of women. This last, in particular, marks Christine's bold vision and her lifelong concern with the pervasive literary and social anti-feminism of her time and culture. Interestingly, the first full, written expression of her attempts to revise literary and cultural understandings of women are in the form of an exchange of letters debating the merits of the *ROMAN DE LA ROSE,* an exchange that came to be known as the *quarelle,* and may have been the first literary quarrel of its kind.

The *Roman de la Rose* was a widely read and extraordinarily influential dream ALLEGORY in which the dreamer Amant (the lover) goes in quest of a forbidden "rose," and allegorical figures help or hinder his "pilgrimage." Begun by GUILLAUME DE LORRIS around 1230 and greatly expanded and completed by JEAN DE MEUN more than 40 years later (it is generally around the often sexually explicit Jean de Meun section that the *quarelle* revolved), the *Roman de la Rose* influenced most dream narratives that followed it, including CHAUCER's, who also translated the allegorical vision into MIDDLE ENGLISH. Variously read as Christian allegory, secular ROMANCE, or a combination of the two genres, the allegorical characters personify or introduce ideas such as sex outside of marriage, sensual love, clerical hypocrisy, and instructions concerning relations between the sexes. One aspect of Jean de Meun's poem that disturbed Christine was the author's pervasive and generally negative view of women and his portrayal of them as fickle, untrustworthy, immoral, debauched, bestial, and legitimate prey for men who are justified in using even physical force to fulfill their pursuit. These and other misogynist views of women were ubiquitous in medieval literature and culture, but it was not only the anti-feminist misrepresentation of women that offended Christine.

Christine's strongest criticisms of Jean de Meun's narrative concerned what she saw as the author's immoral and un-Christian view of marriage and the relations between the sexes. Christine's concerns with virtue, morality, rationality, and the soul, and the ways in which the sexes share vices and virtues, are the basis for her critique of the poem's misogynist representation of women. The actual debate or *quarelle* began with Christine's disagreement with Jean de Montreuil's (provost of Lille) favorable opinion of the poem. The disagreement developed into an exchange of letters that included, among others, Jean Gerson (chancellor of the University of Paris), Gontier Col (first secretary and notary to Charles VI), and Pierre Col (canon of Paris and Tournay). Literary and political leaders alike joined in the debate, but Christine easily held her own with literate and articulate arguments concerning Jean de Meun's moral perversities, his attacks on sacred institutions such as marriage, and his condemnation of all women on the basis of a few examples.

After the *quarelle* Christine wrote what would be the first and most famous of her book-length defenses of women against literary and cultural misogyny, *The* BOOK OF THE CITY OF LADIES, in which she challenges male authors' misogynistic generalizations about women. Responding again to texts such as the *Roman de la Rose* and authors as diverse as Matheolus, Ovid and BOCCACCIO, Christine's *City of Ladies* is a sustained allegorical vision in which she is enlisted by three Virtues—Reason, Rectitude, and Justice—to build a city in which all virtuous women will live free from the constraints of misogyny. Modeled on Boccaccio's *Concerning Famous Women*, the *City of Ladies* contains stories of famous women and in true allegorical fashion, their stories are the bricks and mortar, the walls and foundations, the towers and the inhabitants of the city itself. Radical in its revision and selective readings of famous women's lives and deeds, Christine's work directly challenges male authorities and their misrepresentations of women. Nonetheless, modern reception of the *City of Ladies* is varied and contentious, and in this, it represents modern critical response to Christine's work in general.

While Christine de Pizan's stature as a learned woman of letters is unassailable, her feminist credentials have been variously supported, contextualized, and challenged. Some critical writings (mostly early feminist movement writings) laud Christine's corrective writings and her overt challenge to patriarchal definitions of female roles and behaviors. Later critics are slightly more cautious, and locate Christine's feminist ideology in the contexts of medieval European culture. Critical writings in this category generally credit Christine for writing against tradition, and for giving voice to female perspective and erudition. The ideological position of many of these assessments is that given the prevailing wisdom and cultural strictures of the medieval period, Christine does much to revise misogynist views of women. Finally, those who challenge Christine's status as "feminist" writer generally acknowledge her erudition and literary productivity, yet they charge her with a form of social conservatism that belies "true" feminist ideologies. There is much evidence, indeed, for Christine's conservatism: She believes in a hierarchical social structure, advocates wifely obedience to husbands, and espouses the ideology of separate spheres of endeavor for men and women. Indeed, Christine's *The Book of the Three Virtues* (1405), a sequel text to the *Book of the City of Ladies*, is a "courtesy book" for women, in which she seeks to instruct and advise them in moral and appropriate behaviors, and much of the advice is conservative in tone and substance. Yet these aspects of Christine's thinking and writing are less severely judged by some who argue that we cannot evaluate her in 21st-century contexts, that her historical and social contexts of a necessity inflect her thinking and writing, and that to expect her writings to reflect modern feminist sensibilities is to misinterpret and devalue what she does accomplish in her work. It is only fitting that the author who began a literary *quarelle* over one of the most influential works of the medieval period should herself be the subject of an ongoing and lively debate. Christine's extraordinary career as a woman of letters, her productivity and originality, her rhetorical and moral acuity, continue to intrigue and excite all who read her works.

Bibliography

Brown-Grant, Rosalind. *Christine de Pizan and the Moral Defense of Women*. Cambridge: Cambridge University Press, 1999.

Christine de Pizan. *The Writings of Christine de Pizan*. Edited by Charity Cannon Willard. New York: Persea Books, 1994.

———. *The Book of the City of Ladies.* Translated by Rosalind Brown-Grant. London: Penguin Books, 1999.

———. *The Book of the City of Ladies.* Translated by Earl Jeffrey Richards. New York: Persea Books, 1981.

Delany, Sheila. " 'Mothers to Think Back Through': Who Are They? The Ambiguous Example of Christine de Pizan," in *Medieval Texts and Contemporary Readers,* edited by Laurie A. Finke and Martin B. Shichtman. Ithaca, N.Y.: Cornell University Press, 1987, 177–197.

Desmond, Marilyn, ed. *Christine de Pizan and the Categories of Difference.* Minneapolis: University of Minnesota Press, 1998.

McLeod, Enid. *The Order of the Rose: The Life and Ideas of Christine de Pizan.* London: Chatto and Windus, 1976.

Quilligan, Maureen. *The Allegory of Female Authority: Christine de Pizan's Cité des Dames.* Ithaca, N.Y.: Cornell University Press, 1991.

Elisa Narin van Court

Chronicles Jean Froissart (1369–1404)

The most important work of French prose from the 14th century, Jean Froissart's *Chroniques* ("Chronicles") provide a vivid account in four books of roughly the first half of the Hundred Years' War between England and France. Froissart, a poet and courtier at the English court until the death of his patron, Queen Philippa of Hainault (wife of King EDWARD III), was with their son, the Black Prince, during the prince's campaign in Gascony, and therefore could give a firsthand account of many of the events he describes. When Queen Philippa died, Froissart took service with Robert de Namur of the royal family of Flanders, for whom he began Book I of what became his *Chronicles.* Froissart later gained a new patron, Guy de Châtillon, count of Blois, through whose influence he was made a parish priest at Estinnes-au-Mont in Brabant. For Guy and a third patron, Wenceslaus of Luxembourg, Froissart wrote Book II of the *Chronicles.*

Froissart was able to rely on his own experiences and on the secondhand eyewitness accounts of people he knew for much of the story of the war, but for events prior to 1360, he relied on an earlier version by a knight named Jean Le Bel, who had fought in the war under John of Hainault. Thus most of the first part of the *Chronicles* is simply a redaction of Le Bel's work. The first version of Froissart's Book I, written for the pro-English Robert de Namur, is clearly biased on the side of the English. But Froissart revised his first book at least twice, expunging the English partisanship, presumably to please his new pro-French patrons Guy de Châtillon and Wenceslaus of Luxembourg. Still, only a few passages of Book I are truly Froissart's own composition, most famously the account of the Black Prince's stunning victory over the French—and capture of the French king Jean II—at the Battle of Poitiers in 1356.

Book I is the longest of the four books, and covers the years from 1322 to 1378. It contains accounts of Edward III's ascension to the throne, his establishment of the Order of the Garter, the great English victory at the Battle of Crécy, the BLACK DEATH, the peasants' *Jacquerie* revolt in France, the death of Pedro the Cruel of Castile, the Black Prince's brutal sack of Limoges, and other events. It is important to remember when reading Book I, though, that for the most part you are actually reading Le Bel's account of events.

Book II of the *Chronicles* was probably written between 1387 and 1388, and covers the years of 1375–85. In it Froissart relates the Great Schism of the Western church, in which rival popes were established at Rome and Avignon. He gives his famous account of the PEASANTS' REVOLT OF 1381 in England, relates the affairs of Flanders and the disastrous Flemish defeat by the French at the Battle of Roosebeke, and describes the marriage of the French king Charles VI to Isabella of Bavaria in 1385.

Froissart's Book III covers the period 1386–88, and was likely composed about 1391 and revised a few years later. Here, Froissart describes the splendor of the famous court of Gaston Phoebus of Foix, which he had visited himself. He also describes plans made for a French invasion of England, the campaign of JOHN OF GAUNT in Spain, and the beginning of RICHARD II's difficulties with his uncle, the duke of Gloucester. It contains Froissart's account of the 1388 Battle of Otterburn, in which the Scots defeated the English forces and captured their leader, Harry Percy (Hotspur). This book also contains a fascinating account of a trial by combat in which Sir Jean de Carrouges killed Jacques Le Gris after Carrouges's wife accused Le Gris of raping her.

The final book of the *Chronicles* was completed in about 1400, and deals with events from 1389 to 1400, including the death of the count of Foix, the madness of Charles VI, and, most famously, Froissart's detailed account of the downfall and deposition of Richard II by his cousin, Henry Bolingbroke. The *Chronicles* end with Richard's death and the progress of his hearse through London.

Although Froissart's goal was doubtless to record the most important events of his lifetime, particularly military but also political and cultural events, historians are reluctant to take Froissart's narratives at face value. Although he has the general outline of events right, he is often demonstrably wrong about details. In part the reason for this is his desire to create a very readable narrative, which leads him to depict events with dialogue that brings his narrations to life—but which presents conversations he cannot possibly have overheard. In part Froissart's unreliability stems as well from his clearly aristocratic bias. As a spokesman for chivalry and the noble class (who were, after all, his audience), he cannot be expected to give an objective account of the peasant uprisings in France or in England, although his account of John BALL's sermon to the peasants in 1381 is in fact surprisingly fair. It is best to see Froissart as a social historian, giving a clear sense of the attitudes, motivations, and material world of the nobility of his day. He is also a popularizer of history, presenting memorable narratives of the greatest events of his time. His *Chronicles* survive in some 100 manuscripts, and the magnificent illuminations of some of them manifest the respect in which his narratives were held by the aristocratic audiences who read them.

Bibliography

Ainsworth, Peter F. *Jean Froissart and the Fabric of History: Truth, Myth, and Fiction in the* Chroniques. Oxford: Clarendon Press, 1990.

Brereton, Geoffrey, ed. and trans. *Froissart: Chronicles.* New York: Viking, 1978.

Figg, Kristen Mossler. *The Short Lyric Poems of Jean Froissart: Fixed Forms and the Expression of the Courtly Ideal.* New York: Garland, 1994.

Wimsatt, James I. *Chaucer and His French Contemporaries: Natural Music in the Fourteenth Century.* Toronto: University of Toronto Press 1991.

Cino da Pistoia (ca. 1270–ca. 1337)

Cino da Pistoia was a jurist by vocation, but his posthumous reputation rests on his fame as a lyric poet. He was admired by both DANTE and PETRARCH, and is sometimes seen by scholars as an intermediary between the two, in some ways following the former and anticipating the latter.

Cino was born to a wealthy Pistoian family. He studied law, first in Pistoia and then at the University of Bologna, and subsequently taught law in Siena, Naples, Florence, and in Perugia. Cino, a member of the party of Blacks Guelfs (a group generally made up of bankers and old-money interests), became embroiled in the sometimes turbulent politics of his day and, from 1303 to 1306, was under a sentence of exile from Pistoia. He was, like Dante, a supporter of the cause of the Holy Roman Emperor Henry VII. He became well known as a jurist through his influential legal treatises, particularly his commentary on the first nine books of Justinian's *Codex* entitled *Lectura in codicem* or "Readings in the Codex," published in 1314. In 1324 he was made an honorary citizen of Florence. He died in Perugia in about 1337.

Today, Cino is remembered chiefly as a poet. Dante praises his lyrics several times in *De VULGARI ELOQUENTIA*. His poetry displays some of the features of the *DOLCE STIL NOVO* ("Sweet new style"), the school of Dante and CAVALCANTI: Like theirs, his poetry focuses on an internalized image of his lady. But he is known for very personal poetry—he wrote a sonnet of sympathy to Dante upon the death of his beloved Beatrice. And Cino's own best-known poetry concerns his grief over the loss of his own lady, Selvaggia. In the SONNET *"Io fui 'n su l'alto e 'n sul beato monte"*

("I was on the high and blessed mountain"), he describes himself at his lady's tomb:

> *There I called in this manner on Love:*
> *"Let Death draw me to himself,*
> *my sweet god, for here lies my heart."*
>
> (Goldin 1973, 435, ll. 9–11)

This personal focus, and his characteristic theme of grief and longing, appealed to Petrarch who, like Dante, knew Cino personally and who paid Cino tribute both in a *CANZONE* (LXX) about his predecessors and in a SONNET (XCII) written upon Cino's death.

Bibliography

Cino da Pistoia. *The Poetry of Cino da Pistoia.* Edited by Christopher Kleinhenz. New York: Garland, 1985.

Goldin, Frederick, ed. and trans. *German and Italian Lyrics of the Middle Ages: An Anthology and a History.* New York: Doubleday, 1973.

Tusiani, Joseph, ed. *The Age of Dante: An Anthology of Early Italian Poetry.* New York: Baroque Press, 1974.

ci (tz'u) poetry

The term *ci* (or *tz'u*) meant "song lyric." *Ci* poetry was a form of Chinese verse in which a poet composed a lyric poem that could be sung to a popular melody. It was a form that had its origin in popular music, but developed into a vehicle for serious poetry during the ninth and 10th centuries (late TANG DYNASTY), and reached its full flowering during the Sung dynasty (960–1279).

Popular music in China had been revolutionized during the eighth and ninth centuries by new influences from Central Asia, and new song forms were developed with prescribed numbers of lines, syllables per line, rhyme schemes, and the like. The songs were popular not in the sense of being folk lyrics sung by the masses, but rather in the sense of songs performed for the entertainment of a sophisticated urban audience by courtesans. Given their origin in such performances, it is not surprising that the subject matter of early *ci* lyrics was inevitably love—most often the songs dealt with a woman who grew old waiting for her absent lover, who never returned.

As serious poets began to experiment in the *ci* form, they assigned their lyrics to existing tunes. They also adopted the persona of the forlorn, waiting woman in most of their lyrics. Few poems exist with their musical notations, but the earliest *ci* poems have only one stanza. Some later *ci* contain three stanzas, but most commonly the *ci* were made up of two stanzas in identical or nearly identical form. Such two-part *ci* naturally presented ideas that contrasted or complemented one another, such as a description of a scene and a reaction to it, or a dream and then the reality. As the *ci* form became more and more popular, large handbooks (known as *cipu*) were compiled containing model lyrics corresponding to each popular *ci* melody. Generally the same 800 or so melodies were used over and over again in the hundreds of thousands of *ci* poems produced in Sung China by some 4,000 poets.

The ninth century saw the earliest known *ci* poets: Wen Tingyun (812–870) and Wei Zhuang (836–910). The best known *ci* poet of the 10th century was Li Yu (937–978), the last southern Tang emperor. Imprisoned after his overthrow, Li Yu spent a good deal of his time during his final years composing poetry, much of it concerning the loss of his kingdom and of his beloved wife. Such themes echoed the forlorn sadness of the waiting woman bereft of her lover in the conventional *ci* poems. LI QINGZHAO, China's most celebrated woman poet, was renowned as a composer of *ci* lyrics in the 12th century, generally evoking that same mood of forlorn sadness, in her case often over her dead husband.

The range of subject matter open to the *ci* poet remained relatively narrow until the 11th century, when the poet Su Shi (1037–1101) began to compose *ci* on a wide variety of subjects previously treated only in the more traditional *shi* form. Despite criticism that he was disregarding the essential quality of the *ci,* Su Shi developed a new approach that was called *haofang pai* or "heroic" style, intended to directly express the poet's own feelings rather than those of a persona.

Bibliography

Idema, Wilt, and Lloyd Haft. *A Guide to Chinese Literature.* Michigan Monographs in Chinese Studies, 74. Ann Arbor: University of Michigan, 1985.

Landau, Julie, trans. *Beyond Spring: Tz'u Poems of the Sung Dynasty.* New York: Columbia University Press, 1994.

City of God, The Augustine of Hippo (413–427)

Still considered St. AUGUSTINE OF HIPPO's magnum opus, *De Civitate Dei*, or *The City of God*, details the great theologian's view that all human beings are citizens either of the City of God or the earthly city—one group predestined to eternal bliss in the heavenly city, the other doomed to spend eternity with the devil.

What prompted Augustine to write this text was one of the most severe calamities of the classical world: In 410 the city of Rome was sacked by the armies of Alaric the Visigoth. Though the city was no longer the imperial capital, it still symbolized the power of the empire and the classical world, and its fall struck deep in the psyches of late classical Romans. Refugees from Rome fled to North Africa, where Augustine was bishop of the city of Hippo. Many of these Romans were patricians who had never converted to Christianity, and their contention was that Rome had fallen because it had abandoned the old gods in favor of the Christian one, and therefore the Christians were to blame for the disaster.

Thus Augustine began the *City of God* to refute these claims. The book is divided into two major parts, as Augustine himself describes. The first 10 books deal with the pagan gods: In books 1 through 5, Augustine demonstrates that the pagan gods are powerless to distribute either rewards or punishments in this world. In books 6 through 10, he describes the gods' further inability to provide for human beings' happiness in the life to come.

The second part of *The City of God* deals more specifically with the two cities. Having demolished the charges that by ceasing to worship pagan gods, the people of Rome had brought destruction upon themselves, Augustine begins to make his own case for what exactly Christians can expect. He says at one point that Christians are merely pilgrims in this physical world. Their true home is in the heavenly city. For there are two branches of human beings, characterized by two loves: *caritas* and *cupiditas*—that is, divine and earthly love. The first branch belongs to the City of God, the second to the earthly city. The first live by God's law, the second according to the standards of the world. All of human history, in Augustine's view, evinces a tension between these two cities. Thus the second part of Augustine's text is divided into three parts of four books each: In the first, Augustine deals with the origin of the two cities; in the second, he discusses the course of their history; and in the third, he discusses their final destiny—for the City of God, eternal happiness with God, and for the earthly city, ultimate damnation.

The work was important enough for Augustine to keep at work on it for some 14 years, during years when he was distracted by many other controversies, including his combating the Pelagian heresy, which held that human beings could save themselves through their free will to produce good works. In some ways *The City of God* answers the Pelagians as well, since it indicates that human beings are predestined for one or the other of the cities. The City of God is not, Augustine makes clear, an earthly place. Thus not all in the church will be saved, Augustine says, and there are some who, by individual acts of grace, belong to the City of God—he uses Job as an example.

Though it took him a long time to finish, the controversy Augustine was dealing with needed an answer; therefore, he brought out *The City of God* in installments, as he finished individual books. Thus the first three books were published by 414, the fourth by the following year, the next five by 416, the next three by 420, and the final eight between 420 and 426. He then polished the whole work so that it was complete in 427.

Augustine's vision of the two cities, of the two kinds of love that motivated humankind, and of this world as a place of pilgrimage for the Christian wayfarer on his way to the heavenly Jerusalem were to have a profound influence on European thought and art for the next thousand years. *The City of God* is one of the first truly seminal texts for the European Middle Ages.

Bibliography

Augustine of Hippo. *Augustine: The City of God.* Translated by Henry Bettenson. Introduction by David Knowles. Harmondsworth, U.K.: Penguin, 1972.

Donnelly, Dorothy F., ed. *"The City of God": A Collection of Critical Essays.* New York: Peter Lang, 1995.

O'Daly, Gerard. *Augustine's City of God: A Reader's Guide.* Oxford: Clarendon Press, 1999.

Clanvowe, John (ca. 1341–1391)

John Clanvowe was a poet, a diplomat, a knight, and a member of the household of King RICHARD II. He was also a friend and contemporary of Geoffrey CHAUCER, and it was Chaucer more than anyone who seems to have influenced Clanvowe's style, particularly in his best-known work, *The Cuckoo and the Nightingale,* or *The Book of Cupid.*

Clanvowe is believed to have been born in Hergest in Herefordshire near the Welsh frontier. Apparently of Welsh ancestry himself, Clanvowe inherited an estate near the border. He became a knight in the service of Sir Humphrey de Bohun, the 11th Earl of Hereford, and fought in France, taking part in the Battle of Lussac Bridge in 1369. When Hereford died in 1373, Clanvowe entered the service of King EDWARD III. Later he was knight of Richard II's household. Like Chaucer, he was a supporter of JOHN OF GAUNT, and is included among the so-called LOLLARD knights, a group of high-ranking laymen in Richard's court who were followers of John WYCLIFFE's heresy. A lover of the pageantry of chivalry, Clanvowe was known for taking part in the famous monthlong tournament of Saint Inglevert in 1389, in which three French knights challenged all comers.

Clanvowe's relationship with Chaucer may have begun when both were being sent on similar diplomatic missions under both Edward III and Richard II. Their relationship was close enough for Chaucer to ask Clanvowe to be one of the witnesses to his 1380 release from the charge of *raptus* by Cecily Champain.

Clanvowe died near Constantinople in 1391, where he may have gone on a crusade, or, more likely, a pilgrimage with his friend and fellow "Lollard knight," Sir William Neville, admiral of the King's Fleet. It is reported that after Clanvowe's death, Neville refused food and died a few days later. The two were buried in a single grave, and many now believe that the two were longtime companions in a homosexual relationship.

Clanvowe is the author of a pacifist religious tract entitled *The Two Ways.* In this prose treatise Clanvowe condemns worldly excess and encourages his readers to love God and to follow his commandments. He is believed to also be the author of a more accessible poem in a Chaucerian style entitled *The Cuckoo and the Nightingale, or The Boke of Cupid* (although his son, Thomas Clanvowe, has been thought by some to be the author). This poem, written for St. Valentine's Day, was attributed to Chaucer for more than three centuries, until manuscript evidence led the great 19th-century Chaucerian scholar W. W. Skeat to link it to Clanvowe.

The Cuckoo and the Nightingale is a courtly poem of 290 lines, written in stanzas of five octosyllabic (or eight-syllable) lines rhyming *aabba.* The poem is both a DREAM VISION and a DEBATE POEM. Cupid sends the poet into the woods, where he hears a nightingale singing praises of love, while a cuckoo ridicules his song. The poet chases the cuckoo away and comforts the nightingale, and in the end a parliament of birds is called for, to take place on St. Valentine's Day. The poem's debt to Chaucer's *PARLIAMENT OF FOWLS* is clear, and Clanvowe also refers at one point to Chaucer's "Palamon and Arcite," the early version of *The KNIGHT'S TALE.* These relationships suggest that Clanvowe's poem was produced in the mid-1380s.

Clanvowe's two very different works and the fascinating variety of his life, in addition to the rather recent attribution to him of a text long thought to be Chaucer's, make him and his work an inviting subject for further study.

Bibliography

Clanvowe, John. *The Works of Sir John Clanvowe.* Edited by V. J. Scattergood. Cambridge: U.K. Brewer, 1975.

Patterson, Lee. "Court Politics and the Invention of Literature: The Case of Sir John Clanvowe." In *Culture and History, 1350–1600,* edited by David Aers, 7–42. Detroit: Wayne State University Press, 1992.

Cleanness (*Purity*) (ca. 1375)

Cleanness is a MIDDLE ENGLISH poem included in the famous Cotton Nero A.x manuscript along with *SIR GAWAIN AND THE GREEN KNIGHT, PEARL,* and *PATIENCE,* and is generally believed to have been written by the same author as the other three poems. All are in a similar North West Midland dialect, and all are written in alliterative lines characteristic of the so-called ALLITERATIVE REVIVAL of the late 14th century. At 1,812 lines, *Cleanness* is second only to *Sir Gawain* in length in the manuscript. It has a number of features in common with *Patience:* It is a narrative homily or sermon, using biblical stories to illustrate a particular virtue. Like *Patience, Cleanness* seems to be written in four-line units similar to stanzas, though lacking any rhyme. Although *Patience* occurs first in the manuscript, scholars have speculated that *Cleanness* may be the earliest of the four poems, perhaps because in its generally rigorous morality it shows less of the poet's characteristic sense of humor and playfulness.

The theme of the poem is the virtue of spiritual cleanness, and God's abhorrence of impurity. It begins by attacking impure priests, who profane the sacrament if they come to it with impure hands. The poet notes the beatitude "Blessed are the pure in heart," and then considers the parable of the wedding guest from the Gospels: The filthy wedding garment, the poet says, denotes the filthy state of the guest's soul. Allegorically our deeds are our garments, and when we approach the feast in the heavenly kingdom, God wants our garments to be clean. After a long list of a wide variety of sins, the poet focuses on sins of the flesh as particularly abominable to God. *Cleanness* illustrates its theme with three stories from the Scriptures: the stories of the Flood and of the destruction of Sodom and Gomorrah from Genesis, and the episode of Belshazzar's feast from the book of Daniel. The poet retells the stories in vivid detail, and his descriptions of the fall of Sodom and the destruction of Babylon are memorable and justly admired. In a typically medieval interpretation, the Flood is seen as God's punishment for unnatural or perverted sexual practices in which the sons of God mate with the daughters of men in Genesis 6. The destruction of Sodom and Gomorrah is described specifically as punishment for what the poet sees as the scorn of nature in the homosexual practices of Sodom.

The retelling of the tale of Belshazzar's feast is the longest exemplum in the poem. It begins with a description of the Babylonians' excesses in the sacking of Jerusalem, their killing of women, children, and priests, and their theft of the holy vessels of the Temple, which they take to Babylon. Belshazzar himself is pictured as a glutton, an idolater, and a lustful keeper of concubines. His feast, it has been noted, is described much like that of a 14th-century English nobleman. But his defiling of the Jewish holy vessels at the feast ultimately dooms him and the entire city of Babylon to God's vengeance.

Scholarly interest in the poem has sometimes focused on the apparently significant break between the section on Sodom and Gomorrah and that on Belshazzar's feast. The last section seems to be added on to what was a complete poem of the Sodom episode. Further, the Belshazzar narrative is presented less dramatically than the earlier parts of the poem. These differences have led some to speculate that a second poet may have added the last section of the poem. Other critics have been interested in the poet's sources: The main source for *Cleanness* was, of course, the Bible, and of the four poems in the Cotton Nero manuscript, this is the only one that also uses apocryphal books as source material. The poet also alludes specifically to JEAN DE MEUN and uses his section of the *ROMAN DE LA ROSE* at one point in the text. He also used a French version of the travels of John MANDEVILLE in describing the Dead Sea.

Bibliography

Brewer, Derek, and Jonathan Gibson, eds. *A Companion to the Gawain-Poet.* Woodbridge, U.K., and Rochester, N.Y.: D. S. Brewer, 1997.

The Complete Works of the Pearl Poet. Translated with an introduction by Casey Finch; Middle English texts edited by Malcolm Andrew, Ronald Waldron, and Clifford Peterson. Berkeley: University of California Press, 1993.

Gardner, John, trans. *The Complete Works of the Gawain-Poet.* Woodcuts by Fritz Kredel. Chicago: University of Chicago Press, 1965.

Kelley, T. D., and John T. Irwin. "The Meaning of *Cleanness:* Parable as Effective Sign," *Medieval Studies* 25 (1973): 231–260.

Morse, Charlotte. "The Image of the Vessel in *Cleanness,*" *University of Toronto Quarterly* 40 (Spring 1971): 202–216.

Clerk's Tale, The Geoffrey Chaucer (ca. 1390)

CHAUCER's Clerk of Oxford, a theology student, tells one of the most controversial and disturbing of the *CANTERBURY TALES.* Told partly in response to the WIFE OF BATH's assertion that it is impossible for a cleric to speak well of women, the *Clerk's Tale* recounts the story of Patient Griselda, a saintlike wife who endures her husband's cruelty for years but ultimately receives her just reward. The story was well known in the 14th century, since BOCCACCIO had included it as the last tale of his *DECAMERON,* and PETRARCH had so admired it that he wrote a version of the story in Latin and sent it to Boccaccio, and it is to Petrarch that the Clerk narrator attributes the story. The trial and testing elements suggest folktale origins for the Griselda story, since it resembles tales with a "beauty and the beast" sort of plot.

Walter, the marquis of Saluzzo in Lombardy, is implored by his people to take a wife and beget an heir. The carefree bachelor is reluctant, but agrees on the condition that the people accept whomever he chooses to marry. They agree, and Walter surprises everyone by choosing Griselda, daughter of the peasant Janicula, one of the poorest of his subjects.

Prior to their marriage Walter makes Griselda swear to conform her will to his: She must never question or disobey him in anything, or even complain about any of his decisions. In the course of time, Griselda gives birth to a daughter. But Walter, desiring to test Griselda's obedience, tells Griselda that his subjects resent her and her daughter, and sends a servant to take the child from her mother, apparently to put it to death. Griselda does not complain.

Four years later Griselda gives birth to a son. When the child is two, Walter is taken again by the desire to test his wife, and he tells her that his people are angry that the descendant of the peasant Janicula is now heir to the throne. Once more Walter sends the same servant to Griselda to take her child from her, presumably, again, to put it to death. Again, Griselda raises no objection, save only to beg that the child be buried properly so that he will not be torn apart by beasts.

Some years later, Walter decides to put Griselda to the ultimate test. He claims that his people are insisting he divorce her and take a new wife, and sends Griselda back to her father, wearing only a shift to cover her nakedness. In the meantime he sends word to his sister in Bologna, to whom he has sent the children, that his son and daughter should be sent home. Walter tells Griselda that the girl, now 12 years old, is to be his new bride, and orders Griselda to make preparations for his new wedding. Griselda agrees to do so, with the small caveat that Walter should not test the new bride as he did Griselda, since the girl is too tender to stand it.

Finally Walter declares that "it is enough," and tells Griselda she has passed the test. He reveals that the boy and girl are Griselda's children, alive and well, and he welcomes Griselda back as his wife. Griselda, hearing the news, falls into a faint and grips the children so tightly that they can be released from her grasp only with great difficulty. The tale ends with Griselda's son succeeding Walter as marquis. The Clerk moralizes at the end, saying that it would be intolerable if wives actually acted like Griselda, and that the point of the story is that people should be "constant in adversity." He then adds an envoi, addressed specifically to the Wife of Bath, advising women not to act like

Griselda but to take the reins of the marriage themselves.

Like most of Chaucer's other religious or moral tales, *The Clerk's Tale* is written in RHYME ROYAL stanzas. Otherwise it is in a rather plain style and follows Petrarch's story fairly closely. Chaucer's variations from Petrarch either emphasize the pathos or emotions in the story (such as the detail of Griselda's fierce grip on her children); or add biblical allusions to stress the parallels between Griselda and Christ; or provide moral commentary, as when the narrator lashes out at Walter with frustration over his obsessive need to test his wife.

Critical commentary on the tale has focused on the motives for Walter's behavior and for Griselda's patience. Since Chaucer makes both Walter and Griselda more human, it is more difficult to accept an allegorical reading of the tale. It is also difficult to accept the moral that we should be patient in adversity, since this puts Walter into the position of God—a position few are comfortable with. The allegorical interpretation is more palatable if one sees Griselda not as a mortal human but as the figure of Christ, softening the Father's stance toward humanity. Some, however, have discussed the relationship of the tale to the philosophy of nominalism, which held that God's absolute power meant he was not subject to human concepts of morality.

Bibliography

Benson, C. David. "Poetic Variety in the 'Man of Law's and the 'Clerk's Tales.' " In *Chaucer's Religious Tales,* edited by C. David Benson and Elizabeth Robertson, 137–144. Cambridge, U.K.: Brewer, 1990.

Georgianna, Linda. " 'The Clerk's Tale' and the Grammar of Assent," *Speculum* 70 (1995): 793–821.

Grudin, Michaela Paasche. "Chaucer's 'Clerk's Tale' as Political Paradox," *Studies in the Age of Chaucer* 11 (1989): 63–92.

Kirk, Elizabeth. "Nominalism and the Dynamics of the 'Clerk's Tale': 'Homo Viator' as Woman." In *Chaucer's Religious Tales,* edited by C. David Benson and Elizabeth Robertson, 111–120. Cambridge: D. S. Brewer, 1990.

Lynch, Kathryn L. "Despoiling Griselda: Chaucer's Walter and the Problem of Knowledge in 'The Clerk's Tale,' " *Studies in the Age of Chaucer* 10 (1988): 41–70.

Middleton, Anne. "The Clerk and His Tale: Some Literary Contexts," *Studies in the Age of Chaucer* 2 (1980): 121–150.

Steinmetz, David C. "Late Medieval Nominalism and the 'Clerk's Tale,' " *Chaucer Review* 12 (1977): 38–54.

Cligès Chrétien de Troyes (ca. 1176–77)

The ROMANCE of *Cligès* is thought to be the second of CHRÉTIEN DE TROYES's extant romances because the author begins the poem with "The poet who wrote of Erec / And Enide" (*"Cil qui fist d'Erec et d'Enide"*) (1–2), and refers to works he has translated (including Ovid's *Art of Love*), but does not mention his three other romances (*YVAIN*, *LANCELOT*, and *PERCEVAL*). The patron for *Cligès*, like the patron for the earlier *EREC AND ENIDE*, may have been a member of the Plantagenet family, and the poem was most likely presented to a courtly audience in expectation of a reward. Unlike *Erec and Enide,* with its various and related chivalric romance adventures centered around the titular couple, *Cligès* is a complexly structured romance in which the character of the title does not even appear until line 2365; the first third of the almost 7,000-line poem is concerned with the story of Cligès's parents, Alexander and Sordamour. In this first part of the romance, Alexander, the son of the emperor of Greece, travels to King ARTHUR's fabled court in Britain to "better understand honor" (86) and win fame and renown.

The first section of the romance engages to the full the literary convention of a knight seeking arms and adventure and finding love. In this case the love interest is the queen's companion, the beautiful Sordamour, who had always "laughed at love" (443), until she sees Alexander. After pages of love laments and feats of arms, the lovers are joined and Sordamour gives birth to a son, Cligès. The narrative then employs a device to connect the two plots: Upon the death of Alexander's father (the emperor of Greece), Alis, the younger brother of Alexander, takes the title of emperor (he is told that his brother has died in a shipwreck). When

Alexander hears of this he sets out for Greece where, rather than openly challenge his brother for the throne, for the sake of peace comes to an agreement with him whereby Alexander rules the country but Alis retains the crown and the title of emperor. Alexander is not entirely happy with this arrangement and makes Alis promise that he will never marry and that in time both title and crown will go to Alexander's son, Cligès. Through this compromise peace is achieved.

Years pass (in a few poetic lines), and on his deathbed Alexander tells his now grown son that to discover his worth and be tested in courage and virtue, he must go to King Arthur's court. Alexander and Sordamour are quickly dispatched into death's arms, and the story now turns to Alis, who is persuaded by evil barons to break his promise to his brother and marry the daughter of the German emperor. Unfortunately for Alis, he takes Cligès with him to claim his bride in Germany where Fenice (Alis's intended) and Cligès fall in love at first sight. Fenice and Alis marry, but with the aid of a potion, Alis only dreams that the marriage is consummated. After pages of expressive and extensive love laments, punctuated with feats of arms, Cligès and Fenice declare their love for one another and plan the means by which they can be together.

If this begins to sound familiar, it should, because the romance of *TRISTAN AND ISOLDE* is inscribed into this romance both literally and thematically. And if the reader does not immediately recognize the parallels, the poet draws attention to the romances' shared issues with the lovers, and particularly Fenice, repeatedly claiming that the love of Tristan and Isolde is what their love is *not*. Indeed, the poet repeatedly offers his romance as the antithesis or anti-*Tristan and Isolde* story. The reasoning behind this authorial claim seems to be that while Tristan and Isolde commit adultery against Isolde's husband, King Mark, the lovers in *Cligès* do not commit adultery because Fenice's marriage to Alis has never been consummated, and that the lovers are justified in their actions (whatever they may be) because Alis broke his promise to his brother. This justification may seem somewhat spurious (Tristan and Isolde, after all, fall in love only after mistakenly drinking a love potion), and the very insistence that this love is not the immoral love of Tristan and Isolde acts more to emphasize the similarities than to make clear moral distinctions. And, like their romance counterparts, the lovers do manage to escape Fenice's husband and enjoy an idyllic interlude before they are discovered. After they flee to Britain, news comes that Alis has died and the lovers return to Greece to claim the scepter and orb. Nonetheless, the happily-ever-after conclusion does not extend past the reign of Cligès and Fenice: In the concluding lines the poet tells us that from that time forward the empresses are kept locked away because of Fenice's deceit and tricks, and that no uncastrated men are admitted to their seclusion.

Cligès may be Chrétien's most enigmatic romance. While the diptych structure of two stories of paired lovers becomes popular in 13th-century romances, the structure itself is based on the *Tristan and Isolde* story. This structural influence, coupled with the constant refrain in the second part of the diptych that they are *not* Tristan and Isolde, suggests a tripart or triptych structure in which the *Tristan and Isolde* romance is the necessary background to the two central narratives. As such, and given the narrative's insistent moral condemnation of the adulterous affair of Tristan and Isolde, the narrative seems overwhelmingly concerned with complexly confused issues of morality and immorality. This narrative division, so evident in the structure of the poem, is paralleled in the thematics of the poem with its excess and literalization of conceits from PETRARCH; its focus on the bodily, material aspects of what are more commonly romance figures and metaphors (arrows through eyes, two hearts becoming one, etc.); and in the poem's insistence upon the fragmentation of bodies, which occurs both during the love laments and during the battle scenes, which are some of the most violent (dismemberment, beheadings, etc.) in Chrétien's works. The romance of *Cligès* is disturbing in its details and thematically complicated; in turn parodic and didactic, moralistic and indulgent, the romance invites a full range of critical responses, which are becoming increasingly important to the study of Chrétien de Troyes's works. In common with other romances, *Cligès* promotes ideals of right kingship, the importance of legitimate inheritance, and the liberal conduct of the "true" knight. Nonetheless, the moral problems with which the romance is concerned and its seeming inability to reconcile the varied models of adultery and deceit leave the reader with more questions than answers, with moral uncertainties and the failure of perfect resolution.

Bibliography

Chrétien de Troyes. *Cligès.* Translated by Burton Raffel. With an afterword by Joseph Duggan. New Haven, Conn.: Yale University Press, 1997.

———. *Sir Cleges.* Edited by Anne Laskaya and Eve Salisbury, in *The Middle English Breton Lays,* TEAMS Middle English Text Series. Kalamazoo: Western Michigan University, Medieval Institute Publications, 1995, 367–408.

Duby, Georges. *The Knight, the Lady, and the Priest: The Making of Modern Marriage in Medieval France.* Translated by Barbara Bray. New York: Pantheon Books, 1983.

Freeman, Michelle A. *The Poetics of Translatio Studii and Conjointure: Chrétien de Troyes's Cligès.* French Forum Monographs 12. Lexington, Ky.: French Forum, 1979.

Haidu, Peter. *Aesthetic Distance in Chrétien de Troyes: Irony and Comedy in Cligès and Perceval.* Geneva, Switzerland: Droz, 1968.

Kelly, Douglas. *Medieval French Romance.* Twayne's World Authors Series 838. New York: Twayne, 1993.

Noble, Peter S. *Love and Marriage in Chrétien de Troyes.* Cardiff: University of Wales Press, 1982.

Polak, Lucie. *Chrétien de Troyes, Cligès.* Critical Guides to French Texts 23. London: Grant and Cutler, 1982.

Elisa Narin van Court

Cloud of Unknowing, The
(ca. 1350–1400)

One of the best-known mystical treatises in MIDDLE ENGLISH, *The Cloud of Unknowing* is a prose work in a North East Midland dialect from the later 14th century. Its anonymous author seems to have been familiar with the works of Richard ROLLE (d. 1349), with whom he disagreed, and to have been known by Walter HILTON, whose *Scale of Perfection* (1395) is written, at least in part, as an answer to the *Cloud.* The *Cloud* author is concerned with the process of preparing the mind and soul for contemplation that may lead to mystical union with God—thus the "cloud" referred to in the title is the gulf that separates human from divine. The *Cloud* author's method for crossing this gulf, derived essentially from the influential early Christian mystic known as Pseudo-Dionysius the Areopagite, involves negation (what mystics call the apophatic method): The negation of the self, the senses, even the intellect—since none of these can experience God—and the elevation of love alone as the faculty that can penetrate the cloud.

The *Cloud* author belongs to a tradition dating back to the fourth-century theologian Gregory of Nyssa, who discussed the mystical experience as encompassing three stages—purgation, illumination, and unity. The first two stages must involve the mystic's intellect as he prepares himself for the experience, but the final stage eliminates the activity of reason, and the mystic—through love and a kind of negation of our common ways of knowing—is aware of the presence of God in an engulfing darkness. The Pseudo-Dionysius, whom the *Cloud* author calls Denis (originally thought to be the follower of Saint Paul mentioned in Acts 17.34, but apparently in fact a sixth-century Syrian monk) also emphasizes the importance of the mystic's rising beyond reason in the final stage of unity with God, and emphasizes the negation of all physical categories in that stage of unity.

The *Cloud* author, who was probably a priest and well-read in church fathers and medieval theologians, seems to have been particularly influenced by Gregory and especially Dionysius. The text consists of 75 chapters, and does not proceed in any linear kind of argument; rather, its mode of organization has been compared to a spiral, in which the author keeps returning to his thesis, first stated explicitly in chapter 3: The mystic must focus on God in love, and must expunge from his mind any of God's creations or anything associated with them, so that nothing remains but the stark will toward God alone. To this point the author returns again and again, spending some time clarifying and illustrating this necessity, explaining pitfalls, acknowledging the importance of intellect and imagination in the first stages of contemplation (that is, purgation and illumination) and the necessity for building on them, but always returning to the apophatic stage of unity with the Godhead.

One of the aspects of the *Cloud* that critics have found fascinating is the author's pervasive use of bodily imagery to make his readers better able to follow the abstract argument about the negation of bodily senses. The climax of the book, occurring in the brief description of actual union in chapters 67 and 68, juxtaposes the physical desire to play with *something* and physically *everywhere* with the spiritual union occurring physically *nowhere* and with a physical *nothing.* For the *Cloud* author, the mystic must transcend the reliance on the senses, by which we know through seeing, hearing, smelling, tasting, feeling, because spiritual realities have no such qualities; rather by the very elimination of the senses, we become cognizant of the spiritual.

Ultimately, *The Cloud of Unknowing* presents its readers with a method by which those seeking contemplation might prepare for a mystical experience, rise above the intellect and all physical images and concepts, and pierce through the nothingness that is the cloud. The treatise seems to have been well known in its own day, as 17 extant manuscripts of the text survive. On the basis of style, subject matter, and manuscript association, the author of *The Cloud of Unknowing* is also believed to be the author of six other late medieval mystical texts: *The Book of Privy Counseling, The Epistle of Prayer,* the *Denis* [i.e., Dionysius] *Hid Divinity* (the *Cloud* author's own version of one of Dionysius's texts), *Benjamin Minor, The Epistle of Discretion in Stirrings,* and *Of Discerning Spirits.* None of these minor texts has achieved the popularity, the readability, or the simple fresh appeal of the *Cloud,* which remains a classic of Western and mystical spirituality.

Bibliography

Burrow, J. A. "Fantasy and Language in *The Cloud of Unknowing,*" in *Essays in Criticism* 27 (1977): 283–298. Reprinted in *Essays on Medieval Literature.* Oxford: Clarendon Press, 1984, 132–147.

Clark, John P. H. "*The Cloud of Unknowing.*" In *An Introduction to The Medieval Mystics of Europe,* edited by Paul E. Szarmach, 273–291. Albany: State University of New York Press.

The Cloud of Unknowing. Edited by Patrick J. Gallacher. Kalamazoo, Mich.: Medieval Institute Publications, 1997.

Emery, Kent, Jr. "The *Cloud of Unknowing* and Mystica Theologia." In *The Roots of the Modern Christian Tradition,* edited by E. Rozanne Elder, 46–70. Kalamazoo, Mich.: Cistercian Publishing.

Englert, Robert William. *Scattering and Oneing: A Study of Conflict in the Works of the Author of The Cloud of Unknowing.* Analecta Cartusiana 105. Salzburg: Institut für Anglistik und Amerikanistik, Universität Salzburg, 1983.

Hodgson, Phyllis, ed. *The Cloud of Unknowing.* EETS e.s. 218. London: Oxford University Press, 1944.

Johnston, William. *The Mysticism of the Cloud of Unknowing: A Modern Interpretation.* 2nd ed. St. Meinrad, Ind.: Abbey Press, 1975.

Lees, Rosemary Ann. *The Negative Language of the Dionysian School of Mystical Theology: An Approach to the Cloud of Unknowing.* Analecta Cartusiana 107. 2 vols. Salzburg: Institut für Anglistik und Amerikanistik, Universität Salzburg, 1983.

Wolpers, Clifton, trans. *The Cloud of Unknowing.* Baltimore: Penguin Books, 1961.

Codax, Martin (fl. ca. 1230)

Nothing is known of the life of the 13th-century Galician TROUBADOUR and JONGLEUR Martin Codax outside of the seven extant lyrics attributed to him. These songs are important as the earliest secular songs in Spain to survive with music. They are in the Galician-Portuguese dialect, which was the dominant language for secular literature in 13th-century Spain.

Martin Codax seems to have been from the city of Vigo in Galicia, the area in that corner of northwestern Spain just north of Portugal. It has been suggested that he may have been connected with the court of Dom DINIS of Portugal. He is admired for writing feelingly about the sea of the Galician coast, but mainly his poems are good examples of the genre known as *CANTIGAS DE*

AMIGO—poems in which male poets speak in the persona of a female speaker who yearns for her absent lover. A good example of the combination of these elements is the first stanza of the poem beginning *Ondas do mar de Vigo* ("Waves of the Bay of Vigo"):

Waves of the bay of Vigo,
tell me whether you have seen my friend?
and, oh God, whether he will come soon?

(Jensen 1992, 31.1, ll. 1–3)

Seven of these love poems survive, and most scholars agree that the poems are intended to work together as a cycle. Six of the seven lyrics survive with music in the unique Vindel manuscript—a single folded page discovered in Madrid in 1914 and now, since 1977, in the possession of the Pierpont Morgan Library in New York.

The poems consist of short stanzas with refrains, and make extensive use of parallelism. Musically, they are said to show some similarities to Galician folk songs as well as to Mozarabic hymns. They are of paramount significance to musicologists because of their early date and their unique status as examples of Spanish secular music.

Bibliography

Ferreira, Manuel Pedro. *The Sound of Martin Codax: On the Musical Dimension of the Galician-Portuguese Lyric, XII–XIV Centuries.* Lisbon: UNISYS, Impr. Nacional-Casa da Moeda, 1986.

Jensen, Frede, ed. and trans. *Medieval Galician-Portuguese Poetry: An Anthology.* Garland Library of Medieval Literature, 87. New York and London: Garland, 1992.

Pope, Isabel. "Medieval Latin Background of the Thirteenth-Century Galician Lyric," *Speculum* 9 (1934): 3–25.

Colloquy of the Old Men (*Colloquy with the Ancients, Acallam na Senórech*) (12th century)

The earliest and most significant compilation of stories in the old Irish FENIAN CYCLE of heroic tales is the *Acallam na Senórech* or the *Colloquy of the Old Men.* The text survives in three manuscripts—two from the 15th century and one late one from the 17th century. Linguistic evidence, however, indicates that the text was composed in the 12th century. Unfortunately, all three manuscripts break off before any conclusion is reached. Incomplete as it is, though, the extant text runs to some 8,000 lines, making it the longest of all old Irish works save only the TÁIN BÓ CUAILGNE.

The text takes the form of a frame narrative, not unlike the Arabic *Thousand and One Nights.* The frame itself tells the story of a meeting between Saint Patrick and the last surviving members of the *fian* warrior band of the great mythic hero Finn mac Cumaill. It begins as Oisín (Finn's son) and Cailtre, last of the Fenians, are wandering with a small band a century and a half after the great battles in which Finn and the other Fenians perished. Soon after the narrative begins, Oisín separates from Cailtre to seek his mother, who is one of the Tuatha de Danann, the gods of pagan Ireland. Cailtre and the others continue south toward Tara, and on the way they meet with Saint Patrick. Cailtre and his companions accept Christianity, and Saint Patrick begins to travel with Cailtre. As they travel, the saint asks Cailtre questions about the landscape, and Cailtre relates several tales about the place names of the woods and hills they pass through.

When Patrick asks about Finn mac Cumaill, Cailtre tells about hunting with Finn in Arran, between Scotland and Pictland, and sings a lay about Arran and its many stags. He tells Patrick how the hill Finntulack ("Whitemound") in Munster got its name from Finn himself when he and the Fenians left that hill on the morning of their last battle. He tells the story, too, of Cael's Strand, so named for a young Fenian warrior who also fell in the ensuing battle, but whose quest for his beloved Créde had delayed the fight. After Cael's death, Créde had sung a lament while lying beside him on the shore where his body had washed up.

When they arrive at Tara, Cailte, Patrick, and their companions find Oisín already there, at the court of Diarmuid mac Cerbaill, and the ancient heroes continue to tell tales. Some of the stories are concerned with mythological or historical themes, but for the most part they are tales of the Fenian bands, many of them unique to this text.

It seems likely that a single compiler put together the text of the *Acallam na Senórech*, gathering, perhaps from oral sources or from written sources long since lost, as many legends of old Ireland as he could find. Whether the author was a cleric or a layperson, the most remarkable thing about his text is Saint Patrick's interest in and respect for ancient Irish lore. Such a relationship is rare indeed at this point in time. In a later ballad version of the frame narrative, Saint Patrick condemns the pagan Fenians, declaring that Finn is in hell, while the Fenians defiantly declare that if such is the case, God is a poor judge of character, and they would rather be in hell with Finn than in heaven with such a lord.

Bibliography

The Colloquy of the Old Men (Acallam na senórach). Translated with introduction and notes by Maurice Harmon. With a preface by Seán Ó Coileáin. Dublin: Maunsel, 2001.

Dillon, Myles. *Early Irish Literature.* Chicago: University of Chicago Press, 1948.

Stories from the Acallam. Edited by Myles Dillon. Dublin: Dublin Institute for Advanced Studies, 1970.

complaint

A complaint is a genre of lyric poem in which a speaker bemoans his own lot or the general condition of society. The late Middle Ages saw four different varieties of complaint: In one type the speaker lamented the depravity of the world or of his current political situation, as ALANUS DE INSULIS does in his *De planctu naturae* (The complaint of nature). A second type of *complaint* involves cautionary tales about the fickleness of Fortune, involving the downfall of eminent persons, as BOCCACCIO writes in his *De casibus virorum illustrium* (The fall of illustrious men.) Third, some complaints deal with the cruel tricks that Fortune may have played on the speaker himself, such as penury or exile. The best-known poem in this category is certainly CHAUCER'S *COMPLAINT TO HIS EMPTY PURSE*, in which the poet parodies the conventions of the amatory complaint by applying them to his empty purse.

The amatory complaint was the most common type. In this kind of lyric, the speaker decries his cruel treatment at the hands of his beloved: She may be unfaithful to him, or unreasonable with him, or most typically will not "pity" him or accept his love. In the amatory complaint, the speaker most often describes his sorry state, explains the causes of it, and appeals to the lady to remedy the situation. Such poems were especially popular in late medieval France. MACHAUT had written complaints in the mid-14th century, often using them within narrative poems or *dits*, in order to heighten the emotional impact of the scene. Poets after Machaut, such as CHRISTINE DE PIZAN and later François VILLON, wrote numerous complaints. Chaucer was the first to use the French term *complainte* in English, and wrote a number of complaints himself.

Taking his cue from Machaut, Chaucer sometimes created narrative frames for lyric complaints as a way of contextualizing them, as he does in *The* Complaint *of Mars* and in ANELIDA AND ARCITE (the latter from a woman's point of view). But Chaucer also wrote conventional *complaints* such as *The Complaint unto Pity* and (again with a woman speaker) *The Complaint of Venus.*

Unlike the so-called fixed forms of the *ballade*, *rondeau*, and *virelai*, the complaint was characterized by its subject matter rather than its form. Thus it was a much more flexible type of lyric that might be written in a rather loose form (as Chaucer does in his *Complaint to his Lady*) or might even be written in one of the fixed forms (as Chaucer does in *The Complaint to His Purse*, which takes the form of a *ballade*). The complaint remained a popular lyric genre well into the Renaissance.

Bibliography

Davenport, W. A. *Chaucer: Complaint and Narrative.* Woodbridge, Suffolk, U.K.: Brewer, 1988.

Complaint of Chaucer to His Empty Purse (*Complaint to His Purse*) Geoffrey Chaucer (ca. 1399)

One of Chaucer's best-known lyrics, the *Complaint to His Empty Purse* may be the last poem Chaucer completed. The *Complaint,* addressed to King Henry IV (who had deposed his cousin RICHARD II in 1399), is essentially a begging poem, calling upon the new king to pay Chaucer the annuities or annual salary he had been granted during Richard's time. Characteristically, however, Chaucer turns the request into an entertaining joke, a playful parody of poetic convention: He addresses his empty purse as if it were a lady in a COURTLY LOVE poem, to whom the lover addresses a COMPLAINT at being treated so badly by the lady. In Chaucer's case it is the purse that, by being empty, has not kept faith with him.

The *Complaint* is in the form of a *BALLADE,* with three *RHYME ROYAL* stanzas followed by an *envoi* addressed to King Henry. The stanzas all end with the refrain, addressed to the Purse, "Beth hevy ageyn, or elles mot I dye" (Benson 1987, 656, ll. 7, 14, 21)—a refrain that plays upon the traditional motif of the lover's dying if he cannot win Lady's love in return. The five-line envoi, however, addresses the king himself, indicating the poet's loyalty by calling Henry king by royal descent, by free election, and by conquest (the three validations by which Parliament had recognized his sovereignty), then ends by asking that Henry "Have mynde upon my supplicacion" (l. 26).

Chaucer had known Henry, the son of his former patron John of Gaunt, nearly all his life, and must have understood the kind of poem that would appeal to the new king's tastes. At any rate, we know that Henry did in fact grant Chaucer a generous new annuity of 40 marks per year over and above the 20 marks that King Richard had granted him, probably (according to scholars' best guesses) in February of 1400 (though the proclamation is backdated to October 13, 1399). Chaucer, who died later that year, was not able to benefit long from the King's generosity.

Bibliography

Benson, Larry D., et al. *The Riverside Chaucer.* 3rd ed. Boston: Houghton Mifflin, 1987.

Ferris, Sumner. "The Date of Chaucer's Final Annuity and of the 'Complaint to His Empty Purse,' " *Modern Philology* 65 (1967): 45–52.

Ruud, Jay. *"Many a Song and Many a Leccherous Lay": Tradition and Individuality in Chaucer's Lyric Poetry.* New York: Garland, 1992.

Scattergood, V. J., ed. *Oxford Guides to Chaucer: The Shorter Poems.* Oxford: Oxford University Press, 1995.

Confessio amantis John Gower (ca. 1390)

Confessio amantis (*The Lover's Confession*) is the last major work by the English poet John GOWER. Completed in about 1390, the poem is Gower's only major text in English, consisting of some 33,000 lines in octosyllabic (eight-syllable) couplets, a verse form popular in medieval French narrative poetry. Among the many tales included in the text are the "Tale of Sir Florent" (an analogue of CHAUCER'S WIFE OF BATH'S TALE), the "Tale of Custance" (an analogue of Chaucer's MAN OF LAW'S TALE), and "Apollonius of Tyre" (the source of Shakespeare's *Pericles*).

In his prologue to the poem, Gower describes a meeting with King RICHARD II, who commissions him to compose a work for him. Gower decided that in writing for the English court, he would write in English (his previous works had been in French and Latin), and would make use of the fashionable COURTLY LOVE tradition to structure the poem. Playing on the poetic metaphor of the "religion of love," Gower organized his book as a confessional manual for a lover. The narrator, the unhappy lover Amans, confesses his sins against Love to Genius, represented here as the Priest of Venus (Gower takes this notion from the *ROMAN DE LA ROSE,* in which Genius is the priest of Nature). The confession follows the order of seven deadly sins, and during the confession Genius questions Amans, demonstrating for him the nature of each sin through illustrative stories.

But the *Confessio amantis* is only superficially concerned with courtly love. As Gower says in the prologue, he intends to take a middle way between instruction and pleasure in the composition of the poem. The instruction is always present beneath the pleasurable frame of the love story. The prologue is a long complaint about the corrupt state of society, and most readers have seen it as irrelevant to the rest of the poem. In fact, throughout the text Gower is chiefly concerned with his favorite themes: the decay of human society because of human beings' lack of moral integrity and abandonment of reason, brought about by a deficiency of love—not the love personified by Venus in the poem, but rather *caritas,* the divine principle that brings unity to all creation.

While Genius focuses on showing Amans the need to govern his passion by his reason, his tales almost never have anything to do with romantic love. More commonly they follow the pattern of the "Tale of Constantine and Sylvester" (in book 2), in which Constantine rejects the idea of being healed by the sacrifice of infant children as a violation of the universal principle of *caritas,* the natural law of God. In other tales it is clear that human beings' abandonment of this kind of moral responsibility is the cause of society's problems.

Other aspects of Gower's text illustrate his basic human compassion, even in extreme cases: His notorious "Tale of Canace" (in book 3) describes the title character's incest with her brother, but Gower's moral condemnation in the tale is saved for her father Eolus, who in a rage kills Canace and her child. Later the poignant ending of Gower's text also reflects this compassionate tone. The lover is revealed as too old for love—a twist through which Gower emphasizes the transient nature of mundane love, and by contrast recommends *caritas,* the love that supports the common profit.

Thus the *Confessio amantis* deals chiefly with moral responsibility and with divine love, but because its chief audience is intended to be the king, Gower adds book 7, a book on the education of Alexander intended to be a guide for King Richard. Again this book appears to be a digression from the love theme. But more than any individual, the king must follow natural law, must be a responsible moral agent, and that is the ultimate theme of the poem.

It is possible that *Confessio amantis* was conceived as a companion piece for Chaucer's LEGEND OF GOOD WOMEN which may also have been a royal commission and which, like this poem, plays on the religion of love motif and is constructed as a parody of the GOLDEN LEGEND extolling the saints of Love. Perhaps alluding to this connection, Gower has Venus refer to her servant Chaucer at the end of his text. The *Confessio amantis* survives in 49 manuscripts and was printed by CAXTON. Manuscript evidence indicates that Gower revised his poem at least twice. The first version of 1390 praises Richard II. Within two years Gower revised the poem and left out the praise of Richard. By 1393 he had written another version, this time dedicating the poem to the future Henry IV, a prince in whom Gower had perhaps grown to have more confidence than he had in Richard.

Bibliography

Bullón-Fernández, María. *Fathers and Daughters in Gower's Confessio amantis: Authority, Family, State, and Writing.* Cambridge: D. S. Brewer, 2000.

Echard, Sian. *A Companion to Gower.* Cambridge, U.K.: Brewer, 2004.

Fisher, John H. *John Gower: Moral Philosopher and Friend of Chaucer.* New York: New York University Press, 1964.

Lewis, C. S. *The Allegory of Love: A Study in Medieval Tradition.* Oxford: Clarendon Press, 1936.

Macauley, G. C., ed. *The Complete Works of John Gower.* 4 vols. Oxford: Clarendon Press, 1899–1902.

Peck, Russell A., ed. *Confessio amantis.* With Latin translations by Andrew Galloway. Kalamazoo: Published for TEAMS (The Consortium for the Teaching of the Middle Ages) in association with the University of Rochester by Medieval Institute Publications, Western Michigan University, 2000.

Confessions, The Augustine of Hippo (ca. 400)

St. AUGUSTINE's most popular and most discussed book is his *Confessions,* a spiritual autobiography that traces his spiritual journey through several stages until his ultimate conversion and embracing of the faith for which he was to become the most notable of all theologians.

The book has been one of the most influential in European history. Some have called it the world's first autobiography. Certainly it tells the saint's life story, and in an introspective and individualized manner that sets it apart from earlier "self-representations" in literature. Augustine focuses on motives and on doubts and uncertainty as he covers his somewhat passionate youth and his attraction to philosophy, Manichaeism, and skepticism until his ultimate conversion brought about partly by St. Ambrose of Milan and partly by his own inspired reading of the book of Romans. His frustrations and his emotions are powerfully portrayed in a style that combines biblical quotations, philosophy, allusion, and classical rhetoric.

The Confessions has also been called the world's first "modern" book. Certainly it is a monument to self-awareness and to the power of language in shaping memory and thought, and, by Augustine's creation of this book, in self-fashioning. Language is shown to be powerful, and it is, in fact, through reading another text, the book of Romans, that Augustine is converted.

The first nine chapters concern Augustine's early life. The 10th chapter, a longer section perhaps added late in the composition, discusses memory and the conscious mind while it brings the reader up to the present of Augustine's writing, some 13 years after his conversion and his mother's death, with which the narrative ends. The last three chapters are somewhat confusing to modern readers, since they abandon the autobiography and deal with theological points, but perhaps Augustine, having shown how he reached his present acceptance of Christianity through the grace of God, intends to end by explaining just what that faith consists of.

Augustine says that his motive in writing the book is to answer his critics, both inside and outside the Catholic Church, now that he is bishop of Hippo and a respected ecclesiast—critics who may well remember his misspent youth. But *The Confessions* is not addressed to those critics, but to God himself. Thus he offers his confession of sin as well as faith to God, and offers his readers a concrete example of the change that the grace of God can work in an individual life: his own.

Bibliography

Augustine. *Augustine: The Confessions.* Translated by Gillian Clark. Cambridge: Cambridge University Press, 1993.

Hawkins, Anne Hunsakeer. *Archetypes of Conversion: The Autobiographies of Augustine, Bunyan, and Merton.* Lewisburg and London: Bucknell University Press and Associated University Presses, 1985.

Kennedy, Robert Peter, and Kim Paffenroth. *A Reader's Companion to Augustine's Confessions.* Westminster, U.K.: John Knox Press, 2003.

Morrison, Karl F., ed. and trans. *Conversion and Text: the Cases of Augustine of Hippo, Herman-Judah, and Constantine Tsatsos.* Charlottesville: University of Virginia Press, 1992.

Conon de Béthune (ca. 1150–ca. 1220)

Conon de Béthune was one of the earliest French TROUVÈRES to compose vernacular verse in the style of the Occitan TROUBADOURS. He may have known the troubadour BERTRAN DE BORN—certainly his poetry shows the influence of Bertran, as three of his 10 extant lyrics follow the pattern of one of Bertran's poems. He may have known GACE BRULÉ, as he dedicates one of his poems to Guillaume V. de Garlandce, one of Gace's friends. It is likely Conon also knew the trouvère Le CHÂTELAIN DE COUCI, who like Conon is known to have participated in the Third Crusade (1189–93).

Conon came from a noble family of Artois, being the fifth son of Robert V, seigneur of Bethune, and of Alix de Saint-Pol. As a young man he is reputed to have spent some time in the French court. Two of his lyrics allude to his taking part in the Third Crusade, and in one he names the poet Huon d'Oisi as his mentor. Huon died at the siege of Acre in 1191, and in one of his own poems he chastises Conon for abandoning the crusade early.

Conon was a major figure, however, in the Fourth Crusade (1202–04). He took part in the siege of Constantinople and attended the coronation of the first Latin emperor of Constantinople, Baldwin IV, to whom Conon was related. He stayed on after the coronation to take part in political events in the city and engaged in a number of military and political negotiations under his cousin the emperor. In 1217 he became seneschal and in 1219 regent of the empire. He died about a year later in Constantinople.

Not many of Conon's poems survive, but there is a wide variety and consistent quality among those that do. Conon's poetry was well known in his own day and continues to be among the most admired among the trouvères. His best known lyric, "Ahi, amors," demonstrates vividly his knowledge of the conventions of COURTLY LOVE as well as his crusading fervor:

Alas, Love, what hard leave
I must take from the best lady
a man ever loved and served.
May God in his goodness lead me back to
her
as surely as I part from her in grief.
Alas, what have I said? I do not part from
her at all.
If my body goes to serve our Lord,
my heart remains all in her power.

(Goldin 1973, 339, ll. 1–8)

Bibliography

Goldin, Frederick, ed. and trans. *Lyrics of the Troubadours and Trouvères: An Anthology and a History.* Garden City, N.Y.: Doubleday, 1973.

van der Werf, Hendrik. *The Chansons of the Troubadours and Trouvères: A Study of the Melodies and Their Relation to the Poems.* Utrecht: A. Oosthoek, 1972.

Consolation of Philosophy, The (*Consolatio Philosophiae*) Boethius (524–526)

BOETHIUS's *Consolation of Philosophy* is a short philosophical tract composed when the author was in prison, awaiting execution for treason by Theodoric the Ostrogoth. The text deals with the basic question of why, in a universe governed by divine providence, innocent people suffer and the wicked go unpunished. Boethius, an orthodox Christian, never alludes to a Christian God or Christian doctrine in his text, choosing instead to try to work out the problem strictly through human reason. The sentiments and teachings of the *Consolation*, however, proved compatible to medieval Christianity, and the book became one of most popular texts in Europe for 1,000 years.

The form Boethius uses in the *Consolation* is an ancient classical genre called Menippean satire, which consists of alternating sections of prose and poetry. In the *Consolation* the poems generally either sum up points that Philosophy has argued or give Boethius a chance to reflect upon whatever point has just been made. In effect the poems also enable the reader to ponder and digest the rather dense prose arguments. Structurally, the text is a dialogue between Philosophy and the persona Boethius has created of himself. As such, it is not unlike a Platonic dialogue, with Philosophy taking the part of Socrates and Boethius in the position of the character whom the philosopher draws out in order to instruct. In fact, the text of the *Consolation* owes a great deal to Plato—whose work Boethius knew well—though it also draws significantly from Aristotle, as well as from the Stoics, Plotinus, Cicero, and St. AUGUSTINE.

The *Consolation* opens with the character Boethius in his prison cell, lamenting his downfall. Lady Philosophy enters and, seeking to cure him, begins questioning him to find the nature of his mental distress. He complains to her that God's providence seems to govern all things except the affairs of human beings. She responds that he is the cause of his own misery, having strayed too far from her wisdom, his true country.

In Book II Philosophy reminds Boethius that he should not complain about Fortune's treatment of him, since it is her nature to be fickle. Nothing on earth actually belongs to us, Philosophy argues, and therefore Fortune can take nothing that is truly ours. Wealth, power, honor, fame—all of these are transient. Bad fortune, in fact, is advantageous, since it teaches us not to depend on the things of this world and shows us who our true friends are.

It is the nature of all human beings to seek the Highest Good (i.e., God), Philosophy continues in Book III, and true happiness lies in attaining what we truly seek. Those things in the power of Fortune are partial goods, and cannot bring true happiness. But Boethius stresses the question, in Book IV, of why good people suffer and why evil goes unpunished. Philosophy's answer is that the wicked are weak and unhappy, since true happiness lies in seeking the Good, and power is defined as attaining what one seeks. The Good, therefore, are happy, since they have what they desire. Further, what seems unjust from our earthly perspective can be seen as justice from the eternal perspective of divine providence.

In his fifth book Boethius addresses chance, free will, and providence. Boethius cannot reconcile human free will with God's foreknowledge. Philosophy explains that God sees all from eternity—defined as timelessness rather than endless time. From the eternal view, past, present, and future are witnessed as a single instant. The temporal vantage point sees things as changing, sees moments as occurring one after another. Since God sees all things as we see the present, he does not cause all things—the actions of human free will are seen but not caused by him.

Boethius was executed in prison, shortly after he completed his text of the *Consolation,* and the work was little known in the decades immediately following. However, it became hugely popular in the succeeding centuries. A large number of Latin manuscripts and commentaries by scholars like William of Conches, Nicholas TRIVET, and Pierre d'Ailly were made. In addition the text was one of the first Latin texts to be translated into vernacular European languages. King ALFRED THE GREAT made a translation into OLD ENGLISH, believing it to be, after the Bible, the one book he thought his people should read. Translations were also made into German, Dutch, and Italian. Later JEAN DE MEUN translated it into French, and Maximus Planudes into Greek. In the 14th century Geoffrey CHAUCER translated it into MIDDLE ENGLISH, and the *Consolation* proved to be a significant influence on his subsequent works, in particular *THE KNIGHT'S TALE* and *TROILUS AND CRISEYDE.* Through the prestige of its being perhaps the last document of classical antiquity passed on to western Europe, as well as its sheer popularity evidenced by the plethora of manuscripts, commentaries and translations, the *Consolation of Philosophy* exerted a profound influence on medieval European literature, and, ultimately, on the entire Western literary tradition.

Bibliography

Boethius. *The Consolation of Philosophy.* Translated by P. G. Walsh. Oxford: Oxford University Press, 2000.

Chadwick, Henry. *Boethius: The Consolations of Music, Logic, Theology and Philosophy* Oxford: Clarendon Press, 1981.

Gibson, Margaret, ed. *Boethius: His Life, Thought, and Influence.* Oxford: Blackwell, 1981.

Marenbon, John. *Boethius.* Oxford: Oxford University Press, 2003.

Reiss, Edmund. *Boethius.* Boston: Twayne Publishers, 1982.

O'Daly, Gerard. *The Poetry of Boethius.* Chapel Hill: University of North Carolina Press, 1991.

Convivio (*The Banquet*) Dante Alighieri (1304–1307)

DANTE's *Convivio* is an unfinished work in alternating verse and prose commentary that was apparently intended to bring the wisdom of philosophy to readers of vernacular Italian. Conceived metaphorically as a *Convivio,* or *Banquet,* the text was to offer separate courses in wisdom gleaned from the wisest of philosophers, in which a *CANZONE* of Dante's was to be the "meat" of the meal, while his prose commentary on the poem was the meal's "bread." Dante originally planned 14 courses of alternating *canzone* and discussion, but completed only four books—an introductory tract and three "courses"—before he abandoned the text to focus on his *DIVINE COMEDY.*

Dante worked on the *Convivio* between 1304 and 1307. He includes *canzoni* that appear to be conventional love poems, but that, in his commentary, he interprets allegorically as being concerned with love for the personified Lady Philosophy. He asserts that, after the death of his beloved Beatrice as related in his *VITA NUOVA* (1292), the "gentle lady" he describes as consoling him was in fact the Lady Philosophy to whom these poems are addressed. Certainly the *Convivio's* structure combining alternating passages of verse and prose owes something to the scheme for the *Vita Nuova,* but it also suggests the influence of *The* CONSOLATION OF PHILOSOPHY by the fifth-century Roman philosopher BOETHIUS. That influence is also apparent in the personified Lady Philosophy and, of course, the philosophical subject matter itself.

The extant text of the *Convivio* begins with an introductory book explaining his intent for the work, declaring that the vernacular language is appropriate for topics of moral and ethical significance—a point Dante argues more extensively in *De* VULGARI ELOQUENTIA and that he demonstrates conclusively in the *Divine Comedy.* He does mention that he is writing in an elevated style to give the text sufficient gravity to discuss these topics in Italian. In the second book, he discusses his *canzone* beginning *Voi che 'ntendendo* (You who through intelligence move the third sphere) in a 16-chapter commentary, and in the third he includes a 15-chapter discussion on his poem *Amor, che ne la lente* (Love, that speaks to me within my mind). These first two "courses" focus on the praise of Lady Philosophy. The fourth book, commenting on the *canzone Le dolci rime d'amor* (The tender rhymes of love), spends 30 chapters addressing the question of true nobility. It was a subject that Boethius had discussed. But Dante is clearly interested in other classical authors, including, most significantly Virgil.

Why Dante abandoned the *Convivio* is a matter of some debate. But it is a significant question, since the *Convivio* as projected would have been a huge work, judging from the length of the first four books. Perhaps his study of Virgil had inspired him to focus on his own epic-length poem. Perhaps the tacit rejection of the values of his *Vita Nuova* and his love for Beatrice in favor of philosophical discourse was not as interesting for Dante as his spiritual *Comedy,* in which Beatrice played a central role. Indeed, there are places in the *Comedy* in which Dante seems to reject his earlier work: In Canto II of the *Purgatorio,* for example, while Dante and others are listening to a recitation of the poem *Amor, che ne la lente* (second *canzone* of the *Convivio*), he is chastised by Cato and urged to run toward the mountain to begin his ascent of Purgatory. In the *Paradiso,* Beatrice twice corrects mistaken notions Dante had expressed in the *Convivio* (first, in Canto II, on the cause of spots on the moon; second, in Canto XXVIII, on the hierarchy of angelic orders). And there are other similar instances. Perhaps these passages imply that Dante had grown beyond his earlier work. Still, Dante's readers have found the *Convivio* worthwhile. There are 30 extant manuscripts of the text, six of them from the 14th century. In addition, there was an early (1490) printed edition of the text in Florence, and three editions printed in Venice. *The Convivio* remains, for Dante scholars, the most interesting and significant transitional work between the *Vita Nuova* and the *Divine Comedy.*

Bibliography

Dronke, Peter. *Dante's Second Love: The Originality and the Contexts of the Convivio.* Exeter: Society for Italian Studies, 1997.

Lansing, Richard H., trans. *Dante's Convivio (The Banquet).* New York: Garland, 1990.

Cook's Tale, The Geoffrey Chaucer (ca. 1390)

The Cook's Tale immediately follows the REEVE'S TALE in all manuscripts of CHAUCER'S *CANTERBURY TALES.* In the prologue to the tale, the London Cook, Roger of Ware, commends the Reeve for his tale and sets about to match it with one of his own. Though Chaucer seems to have broken off after only 58 lines of the tale, it is clear from the contemporary setting, the working-class characters, and the gambling and prostitution in the story that it would have been another FABLIAU, like the preceding REEVE'S and MILLER'S TALES.

In the fragment a miscreant apprentice named Perkyn Revelour robs from his master to pay for his gambling and other vices. His master dismisses him, and he moves in with a fellow dissolute, whose wife runs a shop. In the final couplet of the fragment, we are told that the shop is merely a front for the woman's real livelihood, which is prostitution.

We cannot know what Chaucer intended with this tale: whether he left it unfinished on purpose or intended to finish it but never got around to it, or whether in fact he completed it but most of it has not survived. Whatever the case, there are a number of 15th-century continuations of the story by scribes or lesser poets who wanted to complete the tale. None of these "continuations" seems in any way to reflect Chaucer's intent for the text.

Bibliography

Benson, Larry, et al., ed. *The Riverside Chaucer.* 3rd ed. Boston: Houghton-Mifflin, 1987.

Kolve, V. A. *Chaucer and the Imagery of Narrative: The First Five Canterbury Tales.* Stanford, Calif.: Stanford University Press, 1984.

Partridge, Stephen. "Minding the Gaps: Interpreting the Manuscript Evidence of the Cook's Tale and the Squire's Tale," in *The English Medieval Book: Studies in Memory of Jeremy Griffiths,* edited by A. S. G. Edwards, Vincent Gillespie, and Ralph Hanna. London: British Library, 2000, 51–87.

Scattergood, V. J. "Perkyn Revelour and the 'Cook's Tale,' " *Chaucer Review* 19 (1984): 14–23.

Woods, William F. "Society and Nature in the 'Cook's Tale,' " *Papers on Language and Literature* 32 (1996): 189–205.

Corpus Christi

The feast of Corpus Christi celebrates the real presence of the Body of Christ in the sacrament of the Eucharist or Holy Communion. According to the doctrine, through a miracle brought about as the priest says the Mass, the consecrated host (communion wafer) is transformed into the real body of Christ in a process known as transubstantiation. The festival celebrating this miracle is observed annually on the Thursday after Trinity Sunday.

The festival was a medieval institution, established in 1264 by Pope Urban IV. The doctrine itself had developed in the 12th century and was defined by the Fourth Lateran Council in 1215. In the 1220s St. Juliana of Comnillion, prioress of a convent near Liege, was granted a vision that convinced her of the need to establish a festival to honor the sacrament. In 1246 a local festival was established in Liege, and when Pope Urban, former bishop of Liege, became pope, he issued a bull establishing the festival for the entire western church, with no less a man than Thomas AQUINAS himself authoring a new office for the festival. However, the feast does not seem to have been generally celebrated until Pope Clement V reissued Urban's bull in 1311.

From that time, the festival became increasingly popular until, in many parts of Europe, it was the most important church festival of the year. The celebration took the form of an elaborate procession, one whose splendor increased as time went on. The Eucharist was carried by priests—whose power was particularly underscored by the doctrine of transubstantiation—and by civic leaders, followed by members of the trade guilds of the town. In later 14th-century England, the procession would be followed by cycles of MYSTERY PLAYS, staged and performed by the guild members, that became a source of civic pride. Four manuscripts containing these types of plays have survived, generally referred to as the CHESTER, YORK, TOWNELEY and N-TOWN CYCLES, all of which present a series of plays depicting God's intervention in human affairs from Creation until Doomsday.

In England, the conversion of the country to Protestantism, and the hostility of Protestantism to the doctrine of transubstantiation, led to a suppression of the Corpus Christi plays in their various cities. The last public performance of the plays is recorded in Chester in 1575. The festival itself, however, remained popular in Catholic areas of Europe as a manifest symbol of Catholicism against the incursion of Protestantism.

Bibliography

King, Pamela M. "Corpus Christi, Valencia," *Medieval English Theatre* 15 (1993): 103–110.

Kolve, V. A. *The Play Called Corpus Christi.* Stanford, Calif.: Stanford University Press, 1966.

Rubin, Miri. "Corpus Christi: Inventing a Feast," *History Today* 40, no. 7 (1990): 15–21.

Corpus Christi Carol (15th century)

The memorable but mysterious *Corpus Christi Carol* is one of the best-known but most difficult of the late medieval English lyrics. Early carols like this one were not necessarily connected with any particular season, but were rather songs of joy, particularly of religious joy. The "Lully, lullay, lully, lullay . . ." refrain is the aspect of this poem that characterizes it technically as a "carol." Some versions have this burden after each stanza, while others only include it as a prelude to the rest of the poem.

The earliest extant version of the lyric appears in the Balliol College MS 354, the commonplace book of Richard Hill compiled 1503–36. Hill was a London grocer who delighted in lists and riddles; thus the enigmatic carol's appeal to him is obvious.

The Corpus Christi Carol has been interpreted in numerous ways. Some believe it relates to the ancient fertility myth of "The Fisher King," which was Christianized and modified in Arthurian literature as part of the Holy Grail legend. "The Fisher King" is the story of a man who is constantly dying and never reaches death, and his ultimate redemption by the Grail Knight—a redemption suggested in the final stanza, where the Eucharist, the celebration of Corpus Christi or the body of Christ, is suggestive of the Holy Grail.

That the poem is a description of Holy Communion is suggested by the "hall/That was hanged with purpill and pall" (Davies 1964, no. 165, ll. 5–6), which signifies curtains around the altar. "And in that bed ther lythe a knight/ His woundes bleding day and night" (ll. 9–10) could be the communion wafer bleeding from being dipped into the communion wine (Parker 1992, 8).

Another interpretation is that the carol is an analogue of two other lyrics, *The Three Ravens* and *The Twa Corbies*. That argument interprets the knight in *The Corpus Christi Carol* to be Christ himself and a parallel to the knight in *The Three Ravens* and *The Twa Corbies*. It also infers that the crying maiden in *The Corpus Christi Carol* parallels the doe of the other two poems.

Because of the line "The fawcon hath born my mak away" (l. 2), some think the song refers to Anne Boleyn since her ancestral badge was the white falcon. R. L. Greene argues for this interpretation and asserts the narrator is Catherine of Aragon. An interpretation that combines this with the focus on Holy Communion addresses the Act of Supremacy Henry VIII issued to separate the Church of England from the Holy Roman Church in 1534. If the line "By that beddes side ther kneleth a may" (l. 11) is taken to be a female communicant, the church could be the "mak" that the "fawcon [Anne Boleyn] hath born . . . away"—particularly with the emphasis on "Corpus Christi," the "real presence" of the body of Christ in the Eucharist denied by Protestant reformers (Parker 1992, 9).

Although there may never be an interpretation that satisfies all analysts of the *Corpus Christi Carol*, it has already proven to be an enduring work that leaves the reader with a sense of solemnity and reverence.

Bibliography

Davies, R. T., ed. *Middle English Lyrics: A Critical Anthology*. Evanston, Ill.: Northwestern University Press, 1964.

Greene, R. L. "The Meaning of the Corpus Christi Carol," *Medium Aevum* 29 (1960): 10–21.

Kane, George. *Middle English Literature: A Critical Study of the Romances, the Religious Lyrics,* Piers Plowman. London: Methuen, 1951.

Parker, David A., "The Act of Supremacy and The Corpus Christi Carol," *English Language Notes* 30 (December 1992): 5–10.

Malene A. Little

Cotton Vitellius A.xv

The sole manuscript containing the Old English epic poem *Beowulf* is the British Museum manuscript Cotton Vitellius A.xv. It is thus designated because it was from the collection of the antiquarian Sir Robert Bruce Cotton (1571–1631), and was found in the bookshelf beneath a bust of the Roman emperor Vitellius. It was the 15th book on the first shelf, hence "A.xv."

Nearly all of the approximately 30,000 lines of Old English poetry survive in four manuscripts (the Exeter Book, the Junius Manuscript, and the Vercelli Book are the other three). In addition to Beowulf, the Cotton manuscript contains the Old English poem *Judith* and some prose works.

The manuscript was donated to the English people along with the rest of Cotton's collection in 1700. It was moved shortly thereafter because of the deterioration of Cotton's estate, and barely escaped disaster when it was tossed from a window when its new home, Ashburnham House in Westminster, caught fire in 1731. The fire did damage the edges of the manuscript, however, and some passages of the texts were lost. The Cotton collection was moved to the British Museum after the fire, where it still resides. The manuscript was rebound in 1845 with paper frames added in an attempt to slow the deterioration of the fire-damaged vellum pages.

Scholars generally agree that the Cotton Vitellius A.xv manuscript was produced roughly in the year 1000, and in Wessex. It is likely, however, that *Beowulf* was written much earlier (most scholars favor the eighth century, but other guesses range into the 10th) and probably in Mercia or Northumberland.

Bibliography

Beowulf and the Fight at Finnsburg. Edited by Friedrich Klaeber. 2nd ed. Boston: Heath, 1950.

Beowulf: A Verse Translation. Translated by Seamus Heaney. Edited by Daniel Donoghue. Norton Critical Edition. New York: Norton: 2001.

Countess of Dia (12th century)

The best-known of the 20 or so women TROUBADOURS (or *trobairitz*) who have left extant poems or fragments, the Countess of Dia has long been admired for her direct and passionate verse and for her technical skill in composing in the clear and natural *TROBAR LEU* style used by popular troubadours like BERNART DE VENTADORN. James Wilhelm has called her "the Sappho of the Rhone."

Virtually nothing is known about the countess's life. Her title tells us that she was of noble descent and that she was from the town now called Die, southeast of Valence in the valley of the Drôme River. One tradition says that she was Beatriz, the daughter of Guigne VI of Viennois, and that she married William I, the count of Valentinois. Thus the countess is often referred to as "Beatriz." But there is, in fact, no reason to believe this tradition, and for that matter this Beatriz was certainly not the countess of Dia.

Nor is there any reason to believe the information contained in her *VIDA*, which claims that she was the wife of Guilhèm de Poitiers (we know of five contemporaries known by this name) and lover of the famous troubadour RAIMBAUT D'ORANGE. While it is tempting to associate her with Raimbaut (the city of Orange is fairly close to the town of Die), it has also been suggested that her lover may have been Raimbaut IV, the poet's nephew. But the point is probably moot, since the affair is almost certainly fictional.

In the absence of any real biographical data, it is necessary to allow the countess's four surviving lyrics to speak for themselves. It has been common for scholars to remark upon the directness of the female voice in the countess's lyrics, so unexpected from the woman portrayed in conventional COURTLY LOVE lyrics as distant, aloof, passive, and idealized. So it is surprising and refreshing when the countess says:

> *I'd like to hold my knight*
> *in my arms one evening, naked.*
>
> (Bruckner 1995, 11, ll. 9–10)

Like other troubadours, the countess also plays on the various perspectives of her audience, but again her method is quite straightforward:

> *And you, foul-tongued, jealous man,*
> *don't think that I'll be slow*
> *to please myself with joy and youth*
> *just because it may upset you.*
>
> (Bruckner 1995, 13, ll. 17–20)

At times the countess expresses the same kinds of love-longing and distress at her lover's cruelty that male troubadours articulate:

> *I would like to know, my fine, fair friend,*
> *Why you are so fierce and cruel to me.*
> *I can't tell if it's from pride or malice.*
>
> (Bruckner 1995, 9, ll. 33–35)

It may be a valuable corrective to remember, however, that the songs of the Countess of Dia are written for public performance, presumably by a JONGLEUR, and that though the voice sounds quite personal, there is really nothing individualizing in the texts: The countess, like other poets of the time, is creating a persona that speaks her lines. Part of her skill as a poet is in getting us to respond to the immediacy of the voice.

Bibliography

Bogin, Meg. *The Women Troubadours.* Scarborough, U.K.: Paddington Press, 1976.

Bruckner, Matilda Tomaryn. "Fictions of the Female Voice: The Women Troubadours," *Speculum* 67 (1992): 865–891.

Bruckner, Matilda Tomaryn, Laurie Shepard, and Sarah White, eds. and trans. *Songs of the Women Troubadours.* New York: Garland, 1995.

Paden, William D., Jr., ed. *The Voice of the Trobairitz: Perspectives on the Women Troubadours.* Philadelphia: University of Pennsylvania Press, 1992.

Wilhelm, James J. *Seven Troubadours: The Creators of Modern Verse.* University Park and London: The Pennsylvania State University Press, 1970.

courtly love

The term *courtly love,* generally used to describe a group of literary conventions common in western Europe in the later medieval period, was in fact never used in the Middle Ages. It was coined by the scholar Gaston Paris in 1883 to denote an attitude toward love called *fin amors* by the Provençal TROUBADOUR poets, among whom it originated at the end of the 11th century. It is likely that the new treatment of love owed something to the poetry of Muslim Spain, as well as to Ovid's *Ars amatoria.* Its elevation of women may have been influenced, as well, by the Cult of the Virgin (the new veneration of the Virgin Mary in the high Middle Ages), and its refinement of love to a spiritual rather than merely a physical ideal may also owe something to the Catharist movement in southern France.

From Provence, the new convention spread through Europe. French poets adapted the lyric expression of love to the new narrative ROMANCE genre. The German poets called the new notion of refined love *minne.* The Italian poets of the *DOLCE STIL NOVO* school elevated the lady to angelic status, while the English love poets downplayed the adulterous aspects of their French sources. In short, the concept of a refined love and its effects on the one who loves spread through Europe, with a great variety of manifestations, and became a dominant theme in late medieval vernacular literature for hundreds of years.

C. S. Lewis wrote the first truly significant study of the idea of courtly love, and while his book *The Allegory of Love,* has been superseded it still provides a good starting point for discussion. Lewis considers four aspects of courtly love: humility, nobility, adultery, and the Religion of Love. The lover (nearly always assumed to be the male in courtly love poetry) must be humble and must serve the lady. In an adaptation of feudal imagery that becomes conventional, his mistress is described as his sovereign and he her vassal. He is unworthy of her and can only win her love through long service and faithful adherence to her wishes and commands, even if they are unreasonable: In CHRÉTIEN DE TROYES' *LANCELOT,* for example, the queen tells the protagonist to "do his worst" at a tournament, at which he immediately begins losing deliberately.

In fact, though, this humility is an outward show. One of the chief conventions of courtly love is that only the truly noble can love. Thus GOTTFRIED VON STRASSBURG dedicates his romance of *TRISTAN* to the "noble hearts" in his audience, since only they can understand true love. Conversely, love is also ennobling—the lover becomes more noble as a consequence of his love, and as a result of serving his lady. In order to become worthy of her, he must refine his courtly virtues: He must become more generous, more courteous to all ladies, and a finer practitioner of knightly arms. The lady herself is the image of these qualities, the mirror of those perfections that the lover wants to see in himself—the ideal that will refine his character. Thus in CHAUCER's *TROILUS AND CRISEYDE,* for example, the hero becomes Troy's "Hector the Second" in the war with the Greeks in order to impress his lady, Criseyde.

Third, the early courtly love lyric, as practiced in Provençal, does indeed glorify adultery. Most likely this is a reaction to the nature of medieval marriage among the nobility: If a woman had virtually no voice in choosing her husband, she had complete freedom in choosing her lover. And although in practice her actions were probably closely guarded to ensure the legitimacy of her lord's offspring, her fantasies might find an outlet in courtly love poetry. Thus according to the conventions of the genre, love must always be kept secret. The lovers may have a go-between, but must always be on guard against the "talebearers" who are constantly watching, and must beware of the "jealous one"—the husband. This is the typical situation in the erotic *ALBA* or "dawn song," where the lovers must part in the morning after a night of love, so that they are not found together by the "jealous one." In the great romances that appeared later, the most popular lovers—TRISTAN AND ISOLDE, LANCELOT and GUENEVERE—all engage in adulterous affairs.

Lewis's fourth aspect, the "Religion of Love," refers to the metaphorical treatment of the powerful force of love as a deity in courtly love poetry. With love defined as Venus, or Cupid, or more typically the "God of Love," a sort of playful parody of orthodox religion becomes common in some courtly love literature. The emphasis of medieval clerical writers on the extreme importance of virginity, and their prevailing attitude about the evils of the sex act itself (an attitude to be expected from a class of males sworn to celibacy), certainly encouraged secular love poets to burlesque the church with a burlesque "religion" that made sexual love its focus. Thus John GOWER, for example, in his *CONFESSIO AMANTIS*, writes of a lover confessing his sins against the God of Love to Love's priest, Genius. Or in the prologue to Chaucer's LEGEND OF GOOD WOMEN, the God of Love chastises the poet for writing of Criseyde's betrayal of her lover, and assigns him the penance of writing a series of lives of women who were "Love's martyrs," in parody of the popular *GOLDEN LEGEND* and other collections of SAINTS' LIVES.

Scholars after Lewis did much to refine, modify, and challenge his notions. Maurice Valency made it clear that to assume, as Lewis apparently had, that courtly love was a real social phenomenon was unreasonable, and that courtly love conventions must be assumed to apply only to literary texts. However, it does appear that the courtly audience of love poetry and romances saw those texts as relating in some ways to their own lives. Certainly the singers of the early love lyrics saw themselves as addressing various perspectives of their courtly audiences through the expression of different attitudes in their lyrics (*see* Goldin 1975). More recent critics have challenged the notion that the idea of courtly love has any practical value at all in discussions of literature. Certainly it is true that a text like Andreas CAPELLANUS's *Art of Courtly Love,* with its numerous "rules" about how a love affair must be conducted, cannot be taken seriously. But it is also obvious that widespread literary conventions concerning the nature of love and the characteristics of the true lover did indeed exist in medieval Europe. Images like the lover suffering from a malady that can only be cured by the medicine of the lady's love, or the lover in prison from which only the lady's love can release him, abound in late medieval texts. Illustrations of the psychology of love through the interaction of personified abstractions like Reason and Pity, or Beauty, Wealth, and Generosity in love ALLEGORIES also became popular after GUILLAUME DE LORRIS's influential first part of the extremely popular 13th-century poem the *ROMAN DE LA ROSE.*

Perhaps the best way to consider courtly love as a tradition is to think about it as a rather elaborate and stylized game of flirtation that was played in the noble courts of later medieval Europe. Such playful behavior was apparently encouraged at courts like those of ELEANOR OF AQUITAINE and her daughter, the Countess MARIE DE CHAMPAGNE, who may have set the fashion for the rest of Europe. Courtly love literature is best appreciated as one aspect of that game—the production of texts that provided food for discussion among the lovers in the court, and those who fancied themselves so.

Bibliography

Boase, Roger. *The Origin and Meaning of Courtly Love: A Critical Study of European Scholarship.*

Manchester, U.K.: Manchester University Press, 1977.

Burns, E. Jane. *Courtly Love Undressed: Reading Through Clothes in Medieval French Culture.* Philadelphia: University of Pennsylvania Press, 2002.

Goldin, Frederick. "The Array of Perspectives in the Courtly Love Lyric," In *In Pursuit of Perfection: Courtly Love in Medieval Literature,* edited by Joan M. Ferrante and George D. Economou, 51–100. Port Washington, N.Y.: Kennikat Press, 1975.

———. *The Mirror of Narcissus in the Courtly Love Lyric.* Ithaca, N.Y.: Cornell University Press, 1967.

Kelly, Douglas. *Medieval Imagination: Rhetoric and the Poetry of Courtly Love.* Madison: University of Wisconsin Press, 1978.

Lewis, C. S. *The Allegory of Love: A Study in Medieval Tradition.* New York: Oxford University Press, 1936.

Newman, F. X., ed. *The Meaning of Courtly Love.* Albany: State University of New York Press, 1968.

O'Donaghue, Bernard. *The Courtly Love Tradition.* Manchester, U.K.: Manchester University Press, 1982.

Shaw, J. E. *Guido Cavalcanti's Theory of Love.* Toronto: University of Toronto Press, 1949.

Valency, Maurice. *In Praise of Love: An Introduction to the Love-Poetry of the Renaissance.* New York: Macmillan, 1958.

Crowned King, The (ca. 1415)

The Crowned King is a MIDDLE ENGLISH poem of 144 lines of ALLITERATIVE VERSE. The poem survives in a single manuscript, Bodleian MS Douce 95. Like other late 14th- and early 15th-century alliterative poems, such as *MUM AND THE SOTHSEGGER* and *RICHARD THE REDELES, The Crowned King* is clearly influenced by William LANGLAND's *PIERS PLOWMAN,* in particular recalling the prologue to that poem. Like *Piers, The Crowned King* is a DREAM VISION. Like the other aforementioned poems, *The Crowned King* is a topical poem concerned with particular contemporary events, in this case the English king Henry V's preparations to invade France in 1415.

The poet begins by praising Christ, the Crowned King, for sending meaningful dreams, then goes on to describe how recently, on Corpus Christi Day, he had been celebrating in Southampton, when he fell asleep and had a dream. He describes how in his dream he was on a hill looking down into a deep dale, where he saw a crowned king asking an assembled multitude of his people for money to conduct a war. An unnamed clerk knelt before the king and asked permission to speak. When the king granted permission, the clerk ran through a long list of proverbial admonitions in the manner of many conventional poems that give "advice to princes." In his catalogue of proverbs, the clerk recommended that the king devote himself to justice, and treasure the people that are true to him. He should value the labor of his subjects, and should beware of flatterers. He should be kind to the clergy and should comfort the poor. In particular he should avoid any appearance of greed. Ultimately he should emulate Christ, the Crowned King of Heaven, and give to his subjects prosperity and peace.

In 1415, Corpus Christi Day fell on May 29. Henry V left London on June 8 for Southampton, from which he set sail for France in August. These facts probably explain the details in the beginning of the poem. Henry had secured from Parliament a very large grant for his war on the previous November 19. The poet's attitude toward the resumption of hostilities with France is not completely clear, but he certainly is not writing a poem of unthinking propaganda in support of the invasion. His advice to the king has nothing to do with King Henry's rightful claim to the French throne, but rather focuses on the effects of new taxation on the English people. The good will of his subjects will profit Henry more than wealth, the poet asserts, and he appears to be admonishing the king that dealing with the welfare of his subjects at home is more important than seeking adventures abroad. The end of the poem, encouraging a comparison between the earthly king and Christ, the king of heaven, asserts unequivocally that the goodness of Christ's kingship consists of the peace and prosperity he brings. Thus *The Crowned King* makes a pacifist statement in a time of war—and specifically at a time when Henry V himself was engaged in an effort to sway public opinion in favor of his

French campaign (he had, for example, just commissioned John LYDGATE to write his *TROY BOOK* specifically for this purpose). This may explain the poet's use of an unnamed figure of authority within a dream as his spokesman, rather than directly questioning the king's choices.

Bibliography

Barr, Helen, ed. *The Piers Plowman Tradition: A Critical Edition of Pierce the Ploughman's Crede, Richard the Redeless, Mum and the Sothsegger, and The Crowned King.* London: Dent, 1993.

Lawton, David, ed. *Middle English Alliterative Poetry and Its Literary Background.* Cambridge: Cambridge University Press, 1982.

Cuchulain

Cuchulain was the greatest hero of medieval Ireland. The stories of his deeds belong to the ULSTER CYCLE of Irish tales, where Cuchulain is presented as the nephew of Conchobar, king of Ulster. Cuchulain was reputed to possess great personal beauty as well as incredible strength and courage, and when he went into his battle-frenzy, was a virtually invulnerable killing machine. His greatest feats are described in the Irish prose epic *TÁIN BÓ CUAILNGE* (The cattle raid of cooley), in which he single-handedly holds off an invading army on the border of Ulster.

Cuchulain was said to be the son of Dechtire, Conchobar's sister, and the Irish god Lugh. His childhood name was Setanta, and he was raised as a foster child in the house of his uncle the king. His reputedly famous beauty consisted of his having seven fingers on each hand and seven toes on each foot, with seven pupils in each eye. He was also supposed to have four moles (a blue, a red, a green, and a yellow one) on each cheek. At the age of six, Setanta fought and killed the ferocious watchdog of Culann the Smith, after which he became known as "Cu Chulain," or "The Hound of Culann."

A number of boyhood deeds are attributed to Cuchulain, and when he was still a young man he invaded the fortress of Forgall the Wily, leaping over the fortress wall to ask for the hand of Forgall's daughter Emer. Forgall had forbidden Emer to marry before her older sister, and denied Cuchulain's suit, sending his warriors to challenge the youth. But Cuchulain had no trouble killing all 20 of his attackers, and Forgall himself was killed when he fell while fleeing from the scene. Returning home to Emain Macha, the Ulster capital, Cuchulain was attacked again, this time by Emer's aunt and her supporters. Cuchulain, in his battle frenzy, killed so many attackers that the river ran red with blood.

Shortly after his marriage to Emer, Cuchulain becomes involved in the adventure told in the tale *BRICRIU'S FEAST.* In this story, Bricriu of the Poison Tongue invites the great warriors of Conchobar's court to a feast, at which the "champion's portion" was to go to the greatest warrior in Ulster. Cuchulain, Loegaire, and Cuchulain's kinsman Conall all vie for the title, and after several tests, they are challenged to a beheading contest by a terrible stranger with an axe. Each hero, in turn, strikes off the head of the stranger, but only Cuchulain returns the following night to accept the stranger's return blow. It is his courage that ultimately gains him recognition as the warrior deserving of the champion's portion.

In the *Táin bó Cuailnge,* often simply called the *Táin,* Cuchulain must protect Ulster from an invasion by Queen Mebd of Connacht and her allies. A strange illness debilitates all the adult warriors of Ulster, and the 17-year-old Cuchulain guards a ford that forms the border between the two territories, defeating a Connacht warrior each day in single combat. Ultimately he is forced to fight his own foster brother, Ferdiad, who battles him for three days before Cuchulain finally kills him with his secret weapon, the dreaded *gae bolga,* a spear that makes 30 wounds.

Cuchulain's death comes about through deception and misfortune. The 27-year-old Cuchulain, once again called upon to face an entire army single-handed, rides into battle fully conscious that his end is near. He is tricked into breaking a number of *geis* or taboos, on which his life depends, and he is distracted by satirists—poets who threaten to deride Ulster if he does not toss his spears to them. Lugaid, king of Munster, who fights Cuchulain to avenge his father's death at Cuchulain's hands, throws back one of the spears and disembowels Cuchulain with it. Obtaining a truce from his enemies to get a drink of water from a lake, Cuchulain then ties himself to a pillar so that he will not die lying down, and Lugaid lifts up Cuchulain's head and strikes it off. Yet even in death, Cuchulain will not surrender easily—his sword comes down and cuts off Lugaid's hand.

Cuchulain's exploits survive in numerous medieval tales, and interest in his legendary exploits was revived during the Irish literary renaissance at the turn of the 20th century. The great Irish poet William Butler Yeats wrote several poems and plays on the deeds of Cuchulain. A symbolic figure of indomitable Irish manhood during the Irish cultural revival, Cuchulain's statue at the Dublin General Post Office commemorates the Easter Rising of 1916.

Bibliography

Dillon, Myles. *Early Irish Literature.* Chicago: University of Chicago Press, 1948.

Kinsella, Thomas, trans. *The Táin.* With brush drawings by Louis Le Brocquy. London: Oxford University Press, 1970.

Mallory, J. P., ed. *Aspects of the Táin.* Belfast: December Publications, 1992.

Tymoczko, Maria. *Two Death Tales from the Ulster Cycle.* Dublin: Dolmen Press, 1981.

Culhwch and Olwen (ca. 1100)

Culhwch and Olwen is the oldest of the Welsh tales included in manuscripts of *The* MABINOGION, and the earliest extant narrative concerning the court of King ARTHUR. A complete text survives in the *Red Book of Hergest* (ca. 1400), and a fragmentary version in the *White Book of Rhydderch* (ca. 1325), but linguistic evidence suggests that the tale was composed hundreds of years before these manuscripts were assembled.

The tale encompasses a number of traditional folklore motifs and is at the same time a compendium of British tradition. Culhwch is the son of the British king Cilydd, and is cursed by his stepmother so that he can never marry unless he wins Olwen, daughter of the chief of giants, Ysbaddaden. Consumed with love for Olwen (even though he has never seen her), Culhwch goes to the court of his cousin, King Arthur, to seek help in winning the giant's daughter. He is first confronted by Arthur's porter, Glewlwyd Gafaelfawr, who speaks of having been with Arthur in Scandinavia, India, Greece, and other kingdoms, including mythical ones—thus Arthur is presented as a major figure on the world stage, rather than simply as a Celtic hero. It is a picture that anticipates GEOFFREY OF MONMOUTH's presentation of Arthur in the 12th century.

Arthur's chief lieutenant is Cei (who later is Sir Kay in Arthurian legends), and next to him Bedwyr (Sir Bedivere) is his best knight. When Culhwch requests Arthur's help, the king agrees, and sends seven of his best men, led by Cei and Bedwyr, to help Culhwch achieve his love. When Culhwch approaches Ysbaddaden, the giant imposes 40 seemingly impossible tasks on Culhwch that he insists must be accomplished before Culhwch may wed his daughter. Many of these have to do with the preparations for the wedding feast, including the shaving of the giant. For instance, the giant insists that a great thicket be uprooted and burnt, plowed, planted, and harvested all in one night; he requires that the divine Mabon, son of Modron, be freed from a secret watery prison in which he is being held; and he wants blood obtained from the Black Witch from the Valley of Grief in the uplands of Hell.

Arthur himself joins his men for some of the more difficult tasks, in particular the hunting of Twrch Trwyth, a great magic boar who holds between his ears the razor, comb, and sheers that must be used to shave the giant. Arthur and his men chase Twrch Trwyth from Ireland to Wales and into Brittany, finally catching him and taking the comb from him in Cornwall after a great battle. The boar then charges into the sea and is never seen again. Ultimately, the tasks accomplished, Culhwch kills the giant and marries the beautiful Olwen.

The tale is interesting for its many folklore elements—the jealous stepmother, for instance, or the beautiful maiden who is loved from afar and who must be won through the performance of difficult tasks. Another folklore motif is the legend of the "oldest animal": In the search for Mabon, Arthur's men inquire about him of a number of animals, each of which directs them to an older animal who is more likely to know the answer. Thus they ask a blackbird, a stag, an owl, and an eagle before they learn the answer from the salmon, the oldest animal of all. The story has parallels in Irish, Persian and Sanskrit folklore.

More specifically Celtic elements have also been the object of scholarly study of *Culhwch and Olwen.* The hunt of the magic boar may be related to the fact that swine were considered sacred animals by the ancient Celts, and loomed large in their mythology. It has even been suggested that embedded in the narrative of Culhwch is an ancient Celtic myth of the birth of the swine god. This kind of conjecture, of course, is impossible to prove. More obviously related to old British legend is a catalogue of some 200 names that appears in the text. This is purportedly a list of all of Arthur's retainers, warriors, and attendants, but seems to list a number of legendary British figures. Another area of scholarly debate concerns the authors' familiarity with Ireland. It was once believed that the story was originally an Irish one, retold in Welsh, but more recent studies have suggested that the author knew almost nothing about Ireland itself, thus the author and the tale seem almost certainly native Welsh in origin.

Bibliography

Breeze, Andrew. *Medieval Welsh Literature.* Dublin: Four Courts Press, 1997.

Bromwich, Rachel, A. O. H. Jarman, and Brynley F. Roberts, eds. *The Arthur of the Welsh: The Arthurian Legend in Medieval Welsh Literature.* Cardiff: University of Wales Press, 1991.

Foster, Idris Llewelyn. "*Culhwch and Olwen* and *Rhonabwy's Dream.*" In *Arthurian Literature in the Middle Ages,* edited by Roger Sherman Loomis, 31–41. Oxford: Clarendon Press, 1959.

Loomis, Richard M., trans. "The Tale of Culhwch and Olwen." In *The Romance of Arthur,* edited by James J. Wilhelm and Laila Zamuelis Gross, 27–55. New York: Garland, 1984.

Cuntarar (ninth century)

Cuntarar, with APPAR and CAMPATAR, is one of the three major poet-saints of the bhakti sect from the Tamil language area of southern India. The *bhakti* were a reformist sect of Śaivism, the religion devoted to Śiva, one of the three great gods of Hinduism. With Appar's and Campatar's, Cuntarar's hymns to Śiva are included in the sacred text called *Tevaram,* of which Cuntarar's hundred extant songs form the last book. Written in a traditional 10-verse lyric form called *patikam,* Cuntarar's songs praise Śiva and his holy temples, the shrines where singing the hymns of the *Tevaram* became a sacred tradition.

Cuntarar was reputedly born in the Arcot district of India. He was a member of the priestly Brahmin caste, but married two very low-caste women. The bhakti sect in general called for the social reform of the Brahmin caste system. The sect also emphasized a personal relationship with God and eschewed the priestly rituals of Brahmin Hinduism.

This personal relationship might not always be completely pleasant. Tradition says that, because of his failure to keep a promise made in the god's name to one of his wives, Cuntarar was struck blind by Śiva. This results in some bitter poetry concerning Śiva's harsh treatment of the poet. But Cuntarar's sight was restored, and he writes a great deal about the love of God in personal language (the term *bhakti,* in fact, means "love of God"). Cuntarar's songs consistently emphasize the mutual love between human beings and their God, and he shows God's love for his people as never wavering, even if the people sin. To emphasize this loving relationship, in his poetry Cuntarar sometimes pictures himself as a woman married to Śiva. He pledges his devotion to God that will last as long as he lives:

I will think of the day on which
I should forget you
as the day of my death,
the day when the senses fail,
the day life leaves the body.

(Peterson, 1989, no. 148)

Cuntarar is said to have died at the young age of 32, a fact that might explain why his poetic output is only about a third that of the other two Tamil poet-saints, Appar and Campatar.

Bibliography

Peterson, Indira Viswanathan. *Poems to Śiva: The Hymns of the Tamil Saints.* Princeton, N.J.: Princeton University Press, 1989.

Shulman, David Dean, trans. *Songs of the Harsh Devotee: The Tevaram of Cuntaramurttinayanar.* Philadelphia : University of Pennsylvania, 1990.

Cursor Mundi (ca. 1300)

The *Cursor Mundi* sets out to "run round the world" by paraphrasing the historical material of the Bible in combination with other legendary and religious material to produce a history of the world from Creation to the final judgment. Composed in the north of England early in the 14th century, the *Cursor* survives in nine manuscripts that preserve two distinct versions of the poem. Although the poem is consistent in its overall design, it has been described by literary historians as an "open text," one into which scribes frequently inserted new material. For instance, the four earliest manuscripts, all copied in the north, show an accretion of new material regarding the life of the Virgin Mary and more recent history. A fifth northern manuscript preserves only a fragment of the poem. Later in the 14th century, the "southern" version of the *Cursor* was created when a scribe translated the work into the dialect of the Midlands and eliminated some of the nonbiblical material that had been added to the later northern manuscripts. The southern version survives in the remaining four manuscripts, which were copied in the late 14th and 15th centuries.

The poet of the *Cursor* constructed his poem in keeping with the practice of dividing human history into seven ages. This scheme, developed fully by St. AUGUSTINE in his *CITY OF GOD,* was designed to clarify God's redemptive plan for humanity as described by Christian doctrine. The first age is the period from Creation to Noah's flood, the second from Noah to the Tower of Babel, the third from Abraham to David, the fourth from David to the Babylonian exile of the Israelites, the fifth from the exile to John the Baptist, the sixth from the baptism of Jesus to the Last Judgment, and the seventh is the eternal age of the new Heaven and Earth. The first, second, and fourth ages all end with precursors of the Last Judgment, while Noah, David, and John all prefigure the coming of the Christ.

In the *Cursor* the first four ages largely follow the historical books of the Hebrew Scriptures but also include legendary material regarding the life of Seth and the history of the wood of the cross. The account of the fifth age, however, utilizes different materials. Beginning with a selection of Christological prophecies from the Hebrew Scriptures, it turns to an ALLEGORY of incarnation and redemption taken from Robert GROSSETESTE's *Le Chateau d'Amour* and to legends of the life of the Virgin Mary and the childhood of Jesus. More than a third of the *Cursor,* however, is devoted to the sixth age, which includes a life of Jesus and the acts of the apostles taken from the New Testament and apocrypha, but also a history of the cross and a description of the Last Judgment. The poem concludes with several prayers, additional material regarding the Virgin, and a guide to confession and repentance.

The *Cursor Mundi* is one of several paraphrases of the Bible composed in Middle English during the 13th and 14th centuries. Perhaps the most famous of these are the MYSTERY PLAY cycles of biblical drama, but anonymous poets produced *Genesis and Exodus* (ca. 1250) and the *Metrical Paraphrase of the Old Testament* (ca. 1400), and the printer William CAXTON created a comprehensive paraphrase in his *GOLDEN LEGEND* (1483). These works and many others appear to be the result of both the efflorescence of English poetry that produced the works of Geoffrey CHAUCER, William LANGLAND, and the *PEARL* poet, and a resurgence of piety in the wake of the Fourth Lateran Council. Many take as their basis the *Historia Scholastica,* a Latin paraphrase of the Bible composed in the 13th century by the Parisian professor Peter Comestor. Most, like the *Cursor,* have twin goals of explaining the divine plan of redemption in human history and of providing an engaging but morally unassailable alternative to the chivalric ROMANCES popular in late medieval society.

Bibliography

Fowler, David C. *The Bible in Early English Literature.* Seattle: University of Washington Press, 1976.

Horrall, Sarah M., ed. *The Southern Version of the Cursor Mundi.* 5 vols. Ottawa: University of Ottawa Press, 1978–2000.

Morey, James. *Book and Verse: A Guide to Middle English Biblical Literature.* Urbana: University of Illinois Press, 2000.

Morris, Richard, ed. *Cursor Mundi: A Northumbrian Poem of the XIVth Century, edited from British Museum Ms. Cotton Vespasian A.3, Bodleian Ms. Fairfax 14, Göttingen University Library Ms. Theol, 107, Trinity College Cambridge Ms. R.3.8.* 7 vols. Early English Text Society, Original Series 57, 59, 62, 66, 68, 99, 101. 1874–93. London: Published for the Early English Text Society by the Oxford University Press, 1961–1966.

Thompson, John J. *The Cursor Mundi: Poem, Texts and Contexts.* Medium Aevum Monographs, New Series 19. Oxford: Society for the Study of Medieval Languages and Literature, 1998.

Timothy S. Jones

Cynewulf (ca. 770–ca. 840)

Cynewulf was an OLD ENGLISH poet active in the late eighth and early ninth centuries. Four works are attributed to him by modern scholars: *The Fates of the Apostles* and *Elene* (both preserved in the VERCELLI BOOK), and *Juliana* and the *Ascension*—sometimes called *Christ II* (both preserved in the EXETER BOOK). In these texts Cynewulf utilized a powerful new idea: writing about Christian subject matter in the oral style of Old English ALLITERATIVE VERSE.

Nothing certain is known about Cynewulf beyond his name. That name occurs as a kind of signature in the epilogues of the four poems attributed to him: In each of these works, the author inserts runes, embedded in the texts, that spell out his name. In *The Fates of the Apostles,* this even takes the form of an acrostic, creating a playful tone not unlike the Old English RIDDLES.

Cynewulf was a very common name in Old English, and attempts to identify the writer with some known historical personage, like Bishop Cynewulf of Lindesfarne (737–780), have been unsuccessful. Equally unproductive have been attempts to look at the four poems' epilogues as autobiographical statements. All four present the poet as a sinful man requesting the prayers of his readers. In *Elene* he says that he is an aged man who, after leading a sinful life, has received God's grace and the gift of poetic inspiration in his old age. But such declarations are typical of this kind of religious verse, and there is no reason to take them as anything but convention. The one thing that can be said with some certainty about Cynewulf is that he was from either Northumbria or, more likely, Mercia, based on his language. It is even possible that no single poet named Cynewulf existed, and that the runic inscriptions are a poetic game creating a fictional narrator for the four poems.

The poems themselves share a kind of typological style that examines the lives of Christ, his apostles, and his saints, and sees in them examples of how to live a moral life in the face of coming judgment, both individual and universal. Each poem ends with Cynewulf anticipating his own judgment. *The Fates of the Apostles* is his shortest poem, at 122 lines. In it Cynewulf juxtaposes the apostolic virtues with his own life. *Juliana* is a SAINT'S LIFE of 731 lines, in which Juliana's virtues are extolled, and readers are asked to pray to St. Juliana for Cynewulf's soul. *The Ascension* (426 lines) is a poem about the Ascension of Christ that was placed in the Exeter Book between two other poems on Christ, the first on the Incarnation and the last on the Second Coming. Originally thought to be three sections of a single poem, the texts are all related in subject matter and style, and Cynewulf's *Ascension* (or *Christ II*) provides a bridge between the first and last sections. It is unknown whether Cynewulf himself inserted his poem here, or whether the anonymous compiler of the Exeter Book had the idea to link the other poems with Cynewulf's. In either case it was an inspired idea.

Cynewulf's most admired work is *Elene*, the story of the finding of the True Cross by Elene, the mother of the Emperor Constantine. Also his longest work at 1,321 lines, the poem enumerates a number of conversion experiences associated with the cross, including Constantine's vision of the cross before the Battle of Milvian Bridge. The epilogue depicts a final conversion: that of Cynewulf himself.

Over the years Cynewulf has been put forward as the author of many other poems in the Old English corpus, including *The Phoenix*, *The* DREAM OF THE ROOD, and ANDREAS, all of which are similar in style to the four signed poems. Modern scholars no longer accept such attributions, though, and there is even some doubt, as mentioned earlier, that a poet by the name of Cynewulf actually existed. We have no way of knowing the truth. However, as Olsen points out (1994), the important thing is that, among his contemporaries, Cynewulf "was conceived as an individual in the modern sense."

Bibliography

Anderson, Earl R. *Cynewulf: Structure, Style, and Theme in His Poetry*. Rutherford, N.J.: Fairleigh Dickinson University Press, 1983.

Calder, Daniel C. *Cynewulf*. Boston: Twayne, 1981.

Greenfield, Stanley B., and Daniel C. Calder. *A New Critical History of Old English Literature*. New York: New York University Press, 1986.

Gordon, R. K., trans. *Anglo-Saxon Poetry*. London: Dent, 1970.

Sisam, Kenneth. "Cynewulf and His Poetry," *Proceedings of the British Academy* 18 (1932): 1–28.

Cyril of Turov (Kirill of Turov) (ca. 1130–1182)

Cyril was a 12th-century bishop of Turov, in the northwestern part of the Russian principality of Kiev. He was a writer and a renowned preacher, whose sermons are among the most popular in Old Russian, and they are included in sermon anthologies dating from the 15th century, though he based much of their content on Byzantine models. Many of the works attributed to him are considered dcoubtful by scholars, but most agree that Cyril is the author of two parables, eight sermons on various church feasts, between 22 and 30 prayers (known for their asceticism, and some still used today), and two Canons of the Mass (or hymn cycles in honor of saints).

According to a SAINT'S LIFE dated well after his death, Cyril was born into a noble family and was well educated, but renounced his wealth and position at an early age and entered Borisoglebsk monastery in Turov. Legend says that Cyril, desiring a more ascetic life, left the monastery to become a recluse, but that the prince of Turov, with the townspeople, were so struck by his faith that they pleaded with him to become bishop of Turov. Whether or not this is all true, Cyril was consecrated as bishop sometime after the mid-12th century.

Among Cyril's more interesting works is *The Parable of the Soul and the Body*, written sometime between 1160 and 1169. The tale was intended to satirize the bishop of Rostov, Theodore, who was attempting through devious means to establish an independent episcopal seat in Rostov, not subject to the Metropolitan in Kiev. The parable is really an ALLEGORY based on a local folktale of a blind man and a lame man. In the tale the blind man convinces the lame man to help him rob a vineyard. In Cyril's allegory, the blind man is the soul, who is also the spiritual leader Bishop Theodore. The lame man is the body, also representing Prince Andrew Bogolyubsky, that the secular leader Theodore had convinced to champion his ultimately unsuccessful cause.

The topical nature of this parable is unusual for Cyril, who deals more typically with theology. His sermons are his best-known works. They are characterized by the elaborate use of rhetorical devices, particularly parallelism and antithesis, metaphor and simile, amplification and the use of dramatic dialogue: Cyril typically takes a scriptural text for his sermon and adds details, particularly speeches put into the mouths of biblical characters. In his sermon on the Deposition, Cyril puts a long lament into the mouth of the Virgin Mary as she witnesses Christ's death on the cross. In his sermon on Easter, Cyril includes a long description of the return of spring, including several details drawn from nature. But each item in the description is part of an ellaborate allegory, in which the renewal of the world of nature parallels the spiritual renewal within human beings. The spring represents faith, the lambs represent the meek, the calves represent the unbelievers, and so on.

Cyril's sermons are dramatic, vivid, and figurative, but they are also clearly inspired by Byzantine models, which Cyril certainly read in the original. He was familiar with the art of Greek rhetoric, and Moser (1989) suggests that his sermons follow the structure recommended for declamatory speeches in Greek rhetorics: They follow a three-part structure of a proem, a narrative or exposition of the subject matter, and an epilogue, consisting of a eulogy ending with a prayer.

Saint Cyril is said to have died on April 28, 1182, of natural causes. His literary and historical influence, particularly through his popular sermons, is felt not only in Russian, Ukrainian, and Byelorussian literature, but in that of the South Slavs of the Balkans as well. Respected for his mastery of Greek rhetoric and Byzantine theology in medieval Russia, Cyril is sometimes known as "the Russian Chrysostom," after the most influential of saints in the Orthodox Church.

Bibliography

Likhachev, Dmitry, ed. *A History of Russian Literature: 11th–17th Centuries.* Translated by K. M. Cook-Horujy. Moscow: Raduga Pub., 1989.

Lunde, Ingunn. *Verbal Celebrations: Kirill of Turov's Homiletic Rhetoric and Its Byzantine Sources.* Wiesbaden, Germany: Harrassowitz, 2001.

Moser, Charles A., ed. *The Cambridge History of Russian Literature.* Cambridge: Cambridge University Press, 1989.

Dafydd ap Gwilym (ca. 1325–ca. 1380)

Dafydd ap Gwilym is universally acknowledged to be the greatest medieval Welsh poet, perhaps the greatest Welsh poet of all time. While eminently conscious of the old Welsh bardic tradition that preceded him, Dafydd was also familiar with the COURTLY LOVE conventions practiced by the French poets who were popular among the new Anglo-Norman aristocracy in Wales. He borrowed from those conventions to forge a new kind of Welsh poetry that Dafydd, through his wide travels and reputation, brought into the mainstream of European literature.

Tradition says Dafydd was born in southern Wales at Brogynin in Cardiganshire, five miles northeast of Aberystwyth. His father was Gwilym Gam ap Gwilym, and his family was apparently of the *uchelwyr* (that is, part of the native Welsh aristocracy). Dafydd spent part of his youth with his uncle, Llywelyn ap Gwilym, who was constable of Newcastle Emlyn (and himself a poet), and seems to have been influential in Dafydd's education.

Wales had lost its independence in 1282, and Dafydd belonged to a family of some wealth with a history of serving the Norman aristocracy. Dafydd himself seems to have had no fixed occupation but a comfortable fortune. He may have qualified early in his life for minor religious orders, but spent a good deal of his life traveling around Wales—to Bangor, to Anglesey, even to Chester (to which he alludes in one of his poems), though he seems not to have gone any further beyond the borders of his home country. In his travels he apparently visited the houses of the Welsh and Norman gentry and the taverns of the Norman towns, where he entertained all with his poems in the Welsh tongue. His travels and his aristocratic education probably brought him into contact with the young wandering poets from France and from Provence, whom the Welsh called *Y Gler,* and from whom he may have learned the courtly conventions of love poetry.

Dafydd also seems to have lived for a time with his patron, Ifor ap Llewelyn, on his estate in Glamorganshire. Dafydd seems to have seen his relationship with Ifor as similar to the bards' relationships with their princes before 1282. He dedicated a number of poems to Ifor, and may have been responsible for giving Ifor his epithet *Hael* (the generous).

Dafydd died in about 1380. According to tradition, he was buried at the Cistercian abbey of Strata Florida, not far from his birthplace. Though the abbey is now in ruins, a slate memorial on the grounds is dedicated to Dafydd ap Gwilym. Two of his fellow poets (Iolo Goch and Madog Benfras) wrote elegies for him, calling him "the nightingale of Dafed" and "the pillar of song of the southland."

About 160 of Dafydd's songs are extant, in addition to a number of doubtful poems sometimes ascribed to him. Among them are satires, praise poems, elegies, as well as poems concerning nature and love, two themes that before him were not generally the subjects of serious poetry in Welsh. At times, particularly when writing traditional kinds of lyrics like songs of praise for his patrons, Dafydd used the traditional form from the previous century, called *awdl.* But for most of his poems, especially his lyrics of love and nature, Dafydd utilized the new *cywydd* verse-form. This was a very difficult form consisting of seven-syllable lines arranged in couplets and employing *cynghanedd,* an intricate system that included assonance, consonance, and internal rhyme as well as parenthetical commentary. Such elaborate effects make his lyrics incredibly difficult to translate.

Dafydd called himself *"den Ofydd"* (that is, "Ovid's man"). His most characteristic poems focus on love themes, especially in idealized natural settings where physical love is an escape from the strictures of society. Often he utilizes the fanciful device of the *llatai* ("love messenger")—a friendly bird or animal that takes his love message to his lady. The lady is generally one of two favorites: the fair-haired Morfudd or the dark Dyddgu. Many scholars speculate that these women are simply types for the poet, though it is possible he may be addressing some of his love poems to noble ladies in his audience.

Dafydd's love poetry is atypical, however, for two reasons. First, it makes no pretensions of being spiritual—his poems are sensual and celebrate physical love exclusively. Second, he writes with humor and with a colloquial style that adds to the freshness and immediacy of his lyrics. In what is perhaps his best-known poem, *Merched Llanbadarn* (The girls of Llanbadarn), he presents the speaker of his poem attending church for the sole purpose of ogling the women, and when one woman points out to her friend that the young man is staring at her, the lady replies

> *'Is that how it is with him?'*
> *The other, by her, asks her*
> *'Whilst this world lasts, it's no response*
> *To him; to hell with him, the ponce!'*

(Thomas 2001, 101, ll. 31–34)

Dafydd ap Gwilym is a major medieval poet. In some ways, his writing in a difficult meter in an obscure language has prevented him from having a wider reputation than he currently has. But his innovations in form and in content revolutionized poetry in Welsh, and his use of the *cywydd* verse-form made it the most popular poetic form among Welsh poets for at least 300 years.

Bibliography

Bell, H. Idris, and David Bell, ed. and trans. *Dafydd ap Gwilym: Fifty Poems.* London: The Honourable Society of Cymmrodorion, 1942.

Bromwich, Rachel, trans. *Dafydd ap Gwilym: A Selection of Poems.* Cardiff: University of Wales Press, 1982.

———. *Tradition and Innovation in the Poetry of Dafydd ap Gwilym.* Cardiff: University of Wales Press, 1987.

Loomis, Richard M. *Dafydd ap Gwilyn: The Poems.* Binghamton, N.Y.: Center for Medieval and Early Renaissance Studies, 1982.

Thomas, Gwyn. *Dafydd ap Gwilym: His Poems.* Cardiff: University of Wales Press, 2001.

Dalimil's Chronicle (ca. 1310)

The so-called *Dalimil's Chronicle* is the first verse chronicle in the Czech language, dating probably to the beginning of the 14th century. The name Dalimil is traditionally given to the author of this text, but it seems unlikely that any such person ever existed. Based largely on the 12th-century Latin *Chronica bohemica* (*Bohemian Chronicle*) by a canon named Cosmas, *Dalimil's Chronicle* gives the story of Czech history from its mythic beginnings to about the year 1310.

Some scholars have suggested that the unknown author of the chronicle was a high-ranking clergyman; others that he was a minor aristocrat. In either case, he is quite outspoken in his views. There is a good deal of moralizing in the chronicle, which is doubtlessly why a cleric has been proposed as its author. But more significant is the chronicler's vehement condemnation of foreign influences in Bohemia. Certainly the impact of Italian and French power had been felt in the region, but most especially the chronciler resents German hegemony. With a nationalistic fervor unusual in medieval Europe, he fiercely condemns German influence, foreign knights and their customs, and any Czech rulers who grant privileges to foreigners. The chronicler's evaluation of past Bohemian rulers is based chiefly on their attitude toward Germans: Those who showed favor to Germans are invariably categorized as bad kings.

On the positive side, the chronicler expresses a real affection for the Czech land, traditional Czech customs, and the Czech language. His choice to write a chronicle in the vernacular Czech language is in itself a nationalistic gesture, paralleling in its own way DANTE's choice to write in Italian or CHAUCER's in English. At one point in his poem, the chronicler depicts the princess and seer Libuše prophesying that if the Czechs allow themselves to be ruled by foreigners, their language will disappear. In part, the chronicler's apparent xenophobia may stem from the end of the native Przemyslid dynasty in Bohemia with the death of Wenceslas (Vaclav) III and the ascension of the 14-year-old John of Luxembourg to the Czech throne. The chronicler's chief goal was to advocate for an independent Czech state with its own native language.

Written at the beginning of what is known as the Čzech Gothic period, *Dalimil's Chronicle* is written in irregular rhymed verse. The author made rather uncritical use of his sources and, as a result, mixes myth and legend quite freely. For example, he tells the story of a man named Čech, who killed a man in Croatia and was forced to flee with his six brothers. After a time they came through a forest and climbed a hill called Říp. From that high vantage, he saw that the land was good and claimed it for his own and his descendants. For more recent events, those covering the period 1230–1310, *Dalimil's Chronicle* is far more reliable.

Bibliography

Thomas, Alfred. *Anne's Bohemia: Czech Literature and Society, 1310–1420.* Minneapolis: University of Minnesota Press, 1998.

Dame Sirith (ca. 1272–1283)

The only extant FABLIAU written in English before CHAUCER, *Dame Sirith* is a poem of 450 lines composed in a mixed meter—predominantly in six-line TAIL RHYME stanzas rhyming *aabccb* (similar to Chaucer's *TALE OF SIR THOPAS*), but sometimes switching to octosyllabic (eight-syllable) couplets—a fact that some scholars have proposed suggests the poet was trying to convert an earlier text into stanzas. Composed in a southern West Midland dialect of MIDDLE ENGLISH, the poem is written almost completely in dialogue, and the single surviving manuscript of the poem has marginal notes indicating several speakers: Wilekin, Margeri, and Dame Sirith, with other unmarked lines for a narrator. These details indicate that the poem was intended for some sort of dramatic performance, either one involving four actors or, perhaps more likely, a dramatic reading by a minstrel who might assume different voices for the various characters.

Like all fabliaux, *Dame Sirith* is concerned with sex and trickery: a lustful clerk (student) who in the end tricks a gullible wife into an act of adultery. As the poem opens, the clerk Wilekin visits Margeri, and after some hesitancy reveals to her that he has loved her for many years, and, now that her husband is out of town, pleads that she grant him his desire. Margeri is scandalized and refuses him, swearing by the King of Heaven never to be unfaithful. She continues to refuse even when Wilekin promises to be secret, and begs her to have mercy. Wilekin's language parodies the conventional terms of COURTLY LOVE—the long service of the lady, the secrecy of the affair, the purity of his intentions, the danger of dying from love, and the need for the lady's mercy. But it is clear that his motivation is pure lust.

Advised by a friend to ask help of the old bawd Dame Sirith, Wilekin visits her and tells Sirith of his need. At first she feigns not to know anything about such matters, but when Wilekin offers her a large reward and promises to keep her role secret, Sirith agrees to help him. She takes her dog and feeds it mustard and pepper to make tears flow from its eyes, telling the confused Wilekin that this will win his lady. She takes the dog and visits Margeri, whom she convinces that the dog is Sirith's own daughter, transformed into a bitch by a vengeful cleric whose love she refused. The terrified Margeri begs Sirith to run and find Wilekin before the same fate befalls her, and Sirith quickly fetches the clerk, telling him coarsely as he goes in to Margeri to "till" her well and stretch her thighs. The poem ends as Sirith addresses the audience directly, offering her services to anyone who may need them—for a fee.

The fabliau was a popular form in France between 1150 and 1320, with some 150 examples of the genre surviving from that period. But Dame Sirith is the only English fabliau to survive. However, its existence, plus the fragment of an analogue called the *Interludium de Clerico et Puella* (Interlude of the cleric and the girl) from about 50 years later, and the survival of several later ballads that seem to be based on fabliau plots, have led some scholars to conjecture that fabliaux existed in oral form in England, but were not typically written down until after Chaucer's tales gave them some legitimacy.

Bibliography

Busby, Keith. "*Dame Sirith* and *De Clerico et Puella*," in *Companion to Early Middle English Literature*, edited by N. H. G. E. Veldhoen and H. Aertsen. Amsterdam: Free University Press, 1988, 69–81.

Furrow, Melissa. "Middle English Fabliaux and Modern Myth," *English Literary History* 56 (1989): 1–18.

Hines, John. *The Fabliau in English.* London: Longman, 1993.

Lewis, Robert E. "The English Fabliau Tradition and Chaucer's 'Miller's Tale,' " *Modern Philology* 79 (1982): 241–255.

Salisbury, Eve, ed. *The Trials and Joys of Marriage.* Kalamazoo, Mich.: Medieval Institute Publications, 2002.

Von Kreisler, Nicholai. "Satire in *Dame Sirith* and the *Weeping Bitch.*" In *Essays in Honor of Esmond Linworth Marilla,* edited by Thomas Austin Kirby and William John Olive, 379–387. Baton Rouge: Louisiana State University Press, 1970.

Daniel (eighth–ninth century)

Daniel is an OLD ENGLISH alliterative poem of 764 lines appearing in the Bodleian Library's JUNIUS MANUSCRIPT. The poem is based mainly on the Vulgate version of the Old Testament book of Daniel, chapters 1 through 5. But far from being a simple paraphrase, the Old ENGLISH text is unified by its homiletic tone and the theme of pride and its accompanying fall, interpreted as the working out of divine retribution.

The poem begins with a description of the prosperity the Jews experienced for as long as they followed God's law and the destruction and captivity they were faced with when they turned from God. This introduction presages the hard-hearted pride of Nebuchadnezzar, who falls ignominiously when he will not acknowledge God even after witnessing the miracle of the three youths in the furnace. The poem climaxes with the feast of Belshazzar and his prideful insolence in profaning the holy vessels of the Jews, ensuring his own fall. But the chief focus of the poem (for most of the first 485 lines) is the story of the youths Hannaniah, Azariah, and Mishael and their miraculous salvation from the furnace. Daniel himself does not appear until after Nebuchadnezzar's first dream, and he does not assume a major role as seer and prophet until after Nebuchadnezzar's second dream. After Belshazzar's feast, Daniel begins to interpret the writing on the wall, but the poem breaks off abruptly. Clearly the poem is unfinished as we have it, but it is likely that the completed poem would have depicted the downfall and death of Belshazzar, since that would have fittingly paralleled the other two downfalls in the poem. It is unlikely that the poem was ever intended to include any version of the second, apocalyptic half of the biblical book of Daniel.

A difficult structural problem in the poem is caused by two lyrical passages—the prayer of Azariah and the song of the three youths (lines 279–439). For one thing, Azariah's prayer for deliverance appears after that deliverance has already occurred in the poem. Second, that deliverance is narrated twice. And finally, the prayer of Azariah, along with another longer version of the song of the three youths, occurs independent of this text in another Old English manuscript, the EXETER BOOK. Scholars generally agree that the passage in question was interpolated into the original text of *Daniel*, though it is possible to read the prayer as a communal prayer for the deliverance of the Hebrew people. But the precise relationship between this passage and the independent poem in the Exeter Book is complex and uncertain. It is unclear which may have borrowed from which, whether both are by the same poet or whether there was some collaboration between two writers. The coincidental survival of both poems in different manuscripts may result from the popularity in the liturgy of the two biblical passages from which these two lyrics derive.

The date of *Daniel's* composition is also uncertain. Malcolm Godden notes the poem's "pervading sense of human vulnerability," underscored by the false security of the walled cities of Jerusalem and Babylon, neither of which can stave off disaster when it comes (Godden 1991, 224). Uncertainty and the constant danger of heathen attack would make the poem relevant at nearly any time during dangers of Viking intrusion.

Bibliography

Godden, Malcolm. "Biblical Literature: The Old Testament." In *The Cambridge Companion to Old English Literature,* edited by Malcolm Godden and Michael Lapidge, 206–226. Cambridge: Cambridge University Press, 1991.

Greenfield, Stanley B., and Daniel G. Calder. *A New Critical History of Old English Literature.* New York: New York University Press, 1986.

Krapp, George Philip. *The Junius Manuscript.* Anglo-Saxon Poetic Records, I. New York: Columbia University Press, 1931.

Dante Alighieri (1265–1321)

Dante Alighieri is universally admired as one of the greatest writers in Western culture. His *DIVINE COMEDY* stands as perhaps the most significant text in medieval European literature.

Dante was born in Florence at the end of May in 1265, during the internecine strife between the Italian parties known as the Guelfs and the Ghibellines. While there are certainly complex differences between the two parties, in general the Guelfs supported the power of the pope in temporal matters, while the Ghibellines supported the supremacy of the Holy Roman Emperor. The year after Dante's birth, the Ghibellines suffered a decisive defeat at Benevento, and the Guelfs gained control of Florence. Dante's was a family of modest means, but he was very proud of his noble heritage: His great-great-grandfather Cacciaguida had been knighted by Conrad III and had died in the Second Crusade.

In 1274, the nine-year-old Dante met Bici Portinari, a girl his own age who later became the wife of a Florentine banker named Simone de Bardi. Dante claimed to have loved her from that moment, and called her "Beatrice," that is, "bringer of blessings." He speaks of meeting her again in 1283. But in that same year, Dante's father died, and shortly thereafter he married Gemma Donati. The marriage had been arranged by Dante's father in 1277. The couple eventually had two sons and, probably, two daughters as well.

Around this time, too, Dante met the poet Guido CAVALCANTI, and, with Cavalcanti, became the center of a group of poets who practiced the *DOLCE STIL NOVO*—that is, the "sweet new style"—a movement in Italian poetry that relied on complex, learned imagery in place of the clichéd love conventions of earlier Italian writers.

About 1287 Dante went to Bologna to study at the university. In 1289, he joined the Florentine cavalry. His passion for his own noble ancestry led him to enlist in what was considered the aristocratic branch of the military. While in the cavalry, Dante took part in the battle of Campaldino between Florence and Arezzo, and later the siege of the Pisan fortress of Caprona.

The first great crisis of Dante's life occurred in 1290, when, on June 8, the woman he called Beatrice died. His grief over her death caused him to compose the *VITA NUOVA,* or "new life," his first important literary accomplishment. It consists of 31 lyric poems, interspersed with narrative settings that describe the context in which the poem was composed, and sometimes relate Dante's intent in writing the poem. Dante's grief over the loss of Beatrice is clear, but ultimately the text culminates in an interest in the attributes of the now heavenly form of Beatrice. The *Vita nuova* ends with Dante's vow to write no more about her until he can "write of her that which has never been written of any woman" (chapter 62)—a vow he keeps when he makes the figure of Beatrice his guide through the heavenly realm in his *Divine Comedy.*

Dante entered the political life of Florence by enrolling in the Apothecaries' Guild in 1295. In 1299, he was appointed to fill a minor ambassadorship, and then, in June through August of 1300, served as one of the six priors of Florence. About this time, the Guelf party that had ruled Florence since 1266 split into two rival factions: the Whites, consisting mainly of merchants interested in peaceful trade, and the Blacks, made up of bankers and old money interested in empire and supported by the reigning pope, Boniface VIII. The hostility between Whites and Blacks had reached such ferocity by the summer of 1300 that Dante and the other priors were forced to exile leaders of both parties, including Dante's brother-in-law Corsa Donati of the Black faction and Dante's friend and fellow poet Guido Cavalcanti of the Whites.

Pope Boniface, however, took the opportunity to interfere in Florentine politics, and, in 1301, summoned Charles of Valois to "pacify" Florence—that is, essentially, bring it under papal control by force. As Charles's armies approached, the Florentine government sent Dante to Boniface in October to formally protest the invasion. Charles marched into Florence in November, and set the Blacks—Boniface's party—in control. Dante himself was tried *in absentia* and sentenced to exile for two years on spurious charges of graft and embezzlement. He was ordered to appear before the Florentine court to answer the charges against him or to pay a fine, but, when Dante refused to appear, he was sentenced on March 10, 1302, to permanent exile, and charged never to return to Florence on pain of death.

Dante took refuge at first with Bartolommeo della Scala in Ravenna in 1302. When Bartolommeo died in 1304, Dante began a long life of wandering, moving from one town or one noble patron to another. He probably visited Bologna in 1304, the Malaspina family in Lunigiana in 1306, and then the mountains of Casentino on the upper Arno. It has been suggested that he may have visited Paris in 1307–09. By 1314, he was staying with the Ghibelline captain Can Grande della Scala in Verona. In about 1318, he returned to Ravenna to live with Guido Novella da Polenta.

Now no longer involved directly in political life, Dante was free to write his most significant works. In 1303–04 he wrote a Latin treatise entitled *De* VULGARI ELOQUENTIA (On the vulgar tongue), in which he defends the use of the vernacular language, Italian, in serious literature. At the same time he outlines principles of poetic composition in Italian.

Between 1304 and 1308, Dante was working on his next major project, called the CONVIVIO (*The Banquet*). This text was to be a metaphorical banquet of some 14 courses, structured in alternating passages of poetry and prose in a manner similar to the *Vita Nuova,* with the avowed goal of introducing philosophy to the layman. It seems likely that Dante abandoned the *Convivio* to devote himself more fully to his masterpiece, what he called his *Comedy,* to which later admirers have added the epithet *Divine.* Dante began work on the Inferno about 1307, and had finished that first installment of the *Comedy* by about 1314.

He did interrupt his work on the *Inferno* to write the treatise *De* MONARCHIA (On monarchy) in about 1312–13. The occasion that inspired this work seems to have been the unsuccessful invasion of Lombardy by the Holy Roman Emperor Henry VII of Luxembourg. Henry's intent was to pacify northern Italy and force the rebellious Italian cities to submit to his authority. Dante saw him as a savior, and asserts in his pro-Ghibelline argument that the emperor received his authority directly from God, and not through any intermediary in the church. Not surprisingly, the pope condemned Dante's treatise.

After Henry's untimely death ended his dream of a universal monarchy, Dante devoted the remainder of his life to the completion of his life's work. Settled relatively permanently in Ravenna, he completed the *Purgatorio* in 1319 and the *Paradiso* in 1321, shortly before his death. He died in Ravenna on September 13 or 14, and his tomb remains there, rather than in the city of his birth that exiled him.

Dante's influence on Italian culture and on Western literature has been immense. His choice of his native Tuscan dialect for the *Comedy* demonstrated that the vernacular could be an appropriate vehicle for serious literature and established Tuscan as the standard literary language of Italy. CHAUCER acknowledged his debt to Dante in such works as *The HOUSE OF FAME* and *The MONK'S TALE*. During the Renaissance, Dante's influence was eclipsed by PETRARCH's, but his preeminence was rediscovered by the English Romantic poets, and the 20th century saw his reputation rise to equal those of Shakespeare and Homer as a pillar of Western literature. William Butler Yeats called Dante "the chief imagination of Christendom," while T. S. Eliot wrote that "Dante and Shakespeare divide the modern world between them. There is no third."

Bibliography

Dante Alighieri. *The Divine Comedy.* Edited and translated by Charles Singleton. 3 vols. Bollingen Series, 80. Princeton, N.J.: Princeton University Press: 1970–1975.

———. *Inferno.* Translated by Jean Hollander and Robert Hollander. New York: Doubleday, 2000.

———. *Purgatorio.* Translated by Jean Hollander and Robert Hollander. New York: Doubleday, 2003.

———. *Dante's Vita Nuova.* Translated by Mark Musa. Bloomington: Indiana University Press, 1973.

Jacoff, Rachel, ed. *The Cambridge Companion to Dante.* Cambridge: Cambridge University Press, 1993.

Davanzati, Chiaro (ca. 1235–ca. 1280)

There are two Florentines of the late 13th century named Chiaro Davanzati. One of them died in 1303; the other was married with five sons and died in 1280. While the second candidate is more often identified with the prolific poet of that name, that identification is by no means certain. It is clear that the poet fought in the famous battle of Monaperti in 1260, in which Florence and the Guelfs (the party supporting the papacy) were soundly defeated by the Ghibellines (the party supporting the emperor).

Davanzati left some 200 poems dealing with a wide array of themes from love to politics to moral and ethical issues. Many are *CANZONI*, but there are also two *SONNET* cycles inspired by medieval lapidaries and bestiaries. In his early poetry, Chiaro manifests the influence of GIACOMO DA LENTINO's "Sicilian school" of poetry and the earlier Provençal TROUBADOURS, particularly those like BERNART DE VENTADORN who wrote in the popular TROBAR LEU style. Later, however, his focus on political and spiritual themes suggests the influence of GUITTONE D'AREZZO and the Tuscan school. In his latest poetry Davanzati seems to have adopted the method of GUIDO GUINIZELLI, emphasizing the "gentle heart" of the lover, and the lady as God's representative on earth. Thus in his last poems Davanzati might be seen as one of the forebears of the *stilnovisti*, the school to which DANTE belonged.

Davanzati was a prolific poet and one who seems to have been well acquainted with most of the other major poets of his time, yet he does not seem to have been an influential poet in his own day and has not attracted much attention from literary historians or critics.

Bibliography

Goldin, Frederick, trans. *German and Italian Lyrics of the Middle Ages: An Anthology and a History.* New York: Doubleday, 1973.

debate poetry

Debate poetry was a medieval tradition characterized by an argument or discussion between two opposed parties. The issue of the debate might be a serious philosophical, theological, or moral tradition, or it might concern some question of COURTLY LOVE or of poetry itself. Some scholars have traced the roots of the debate form to the pastoral contest represented in the classical poets Theocritus and Virgil. But the most likely model for medieval debates was BOETHIUS's extraordinarily popular *CONSOLATION OF PHILOSOPHY*, in which the allegorical figure of Lady Philosophy engages in a philosophical debate with the persona of Boethius himself—a dialogue form ultimately based on Plato.

The earliest type of debate poetry in the vernacular was the *TENSO* (discussion), a form popular among the Provençal TROUBADOURS. A famous *tenso* between GIRAUT DE BORNEIL and RAIMBAUT D'ORANGE saw the two troubadours debating the relative merits of the TROBAR CLUS, or difficult style of poetry, against the TROBAR LEU, or easy style of troubadour lyric. Other related forms in Provençal were the *partimen* (a philosophical debate) and the *jeu parti* (a love debate).

At the same time, there were secular Latin poems in a debate format, and in the 12th century, St. BERNARD OF CLAIRVAUX and Hugo of Saint Victor composed a debate among the four "daughters of God"—Peace and Righteousness, Justice and Mercy—who argue among themselves the fate of sinful humankind. This theme was to become popular in later medieval MORALITY PLAYS.

This sort of ALLEGORY was not uncommon in the popular French form of the 12th and 13th centuries, the *débat.* Here the two participants might be people but might also be birds or animals who are representative, frequently personifications, of opposed qualities. The *débat* might concern love or morality, or might be political allegory or satire. Generally the debate was inconclusive, and in the end was submitted to a third party, often a prince, though sometimes a fictitious judge or the audience itself as arbitrator.

In England, debate poems tended to be focused on themes of morality and religion, and debate poems might take the form of an allegorical argument between Body and Soul or between Virtues and Vices or Reason and Will. The 14th-century poem in ALLITERATIVE VERSE *WINNER AND WASTER* is a political satire in which the merits of accumulating and spending are weighed. But the earliest and best known of MIDDLE ENGLISH debate poems is the 13th-century *The OWL AND THE NIGHTINGALE,* in which the two birds may represent two kinds of poetry—didactic religious and secular love poetry—and argue about the benefits they bring to humanity. Bird debates became particularly popular in England in the following two centuries, including John CLANVOWE's *The Thrush and the Nightingale* and CHAUCER's *PARLIAMENT OF FOWLS*—such a "parliament" was a debate among more than two participants, like the earlier Middle English *PARLIAMENT OF THE THREE AGES.*

Chaucer's purest debate poem is his short poem *Fortune,* a debate of alternating *BALLADES* spoken by a "Plaintiff" and the allegorical figure of Fortune, whose themes are drawn directly from the second book of Boethius's *Consolation.* In the end of *Fortune,* the combatants (as in the French *débat*) submit their case to a group of unnamed "Princes," in what seems to be a direct appeal by the poet for remuneration.

Thus the debate poem was extremely flexible, could take many forms, and was used for many purposes across a number of countries in the later Middle Ages, No doubt this flexibility helped make the form as popular as it was.

Bibliography

Altmann, Barbara K. *The Love Debate Poems of Christine de Pizan.* Gainesville: University Press of Florida, 1998.

Bossy, Michel-André, ed. and trans. *Medieval Debate Poetry: Vernacular Works.* New York: Garland, 1987.

Conlee, John W. *Middle English Debate Poetry: A Critical Anthology.* East Lansing, Mich.: Colleagues Press, 1991.

Reed, Thomas L., Jr. *Middle English Debate Poetry and the Aesthetics of Irresolution.* Columbia: University of Missouri Press, 1990.

Decameron, The (1350–1352)

The Decameron is the most widely read and highly acclaimed work of Giovanni BOCCACCIO. Consisting of 100 short stories or *novelle* told within a frame story set in Florence during the BLACK DEATH of 1348, *The Decameron* is famous for its humor, its vitality, its realism, and its variety of tone and subject. The text is universally revered as the most significant contribution to prose fiction from the European Middle Ages, and influenced the development of narrative for centuries.

Like CHAUCER's *CANTERBURY TALES* and the Arabic *THOUSAND AND ONE NIGHTS,* Boccaccio creates a frame for his story collection. After a famous detailed and horrifying description of plague-ridden

Florence (a city that lost 70 percent of its population to the plague in 1348), Boccaccio describes how seven young Florentine ladies of good family meet three gentlemen by chance in a church, and how the 10 decide to leave the city for a country estate in the hills of Fiesole above Florence. As an antidote to the moral and political anarchy and stress of the disease-ridden city, the 10 young people resolve to pursue a daily regimen of orderly activity and entertainment at the estate, with the idea that the pleasure and recreation will restore their spirits (and therefore make them less susceptible to the pestilence). As part of the schedule, each of the characters will tell one story daily for 10 days. A king or queen is chosen for each day, and that person declares a theme to which all stories for the day must conform—all but those of the character Dineo, who reserves the right to tell the final story each day, and to be exempt from the theme.

The beginning, in addition to the introductions and epilogues for individual tales and days, provides a frame and direction for the huge variety of narratives in the text. In addition some scholars have noted a thematic pattern to the tales. These seem to deal first with outside forces like fate or destiny that overwhelm human beings, and are then defeated by the efforts of human will; second, the tales present internal forces, in particular love, and how love causes both unhappiness (on Day Four) and joy (on Day Five); third, the use of human wit or cleverness to overcome obstacles or to trick others becomes the focus. All of the themes are reprised on the Ninth Day, when the theme is left open. After a good deal has been said about human vice and folly for the first nine days, the stories of the 10th Day are to tell of "those who have acted generously or magnificently in affairs of the heart or other matters" (Musa and Bondanella, 1982, 602). These tales contrast with the earlier ones in their emphasis on heroic virtue, generosity, and patience. In the end the great variety of the tales creates a complete human comedy, showing life as a whole, with all of its contradictions and diversity.

A few brief examples of the variety of stories included in the text will suffice: The 10th story of the third day, for example, is a FABLIAU involving a religious hermit named Rustico, who is approached by an innocent young convert named Alibech who seeks to learn the best way to serve God. Rustico convinces her that putting the devil back into hell (his euphemistic description of sexual intercourse) pleases God most—but the jest backfires when he is unable to keep up with Alibech's religious zeal. The ninth story of the fifth day is a ROMANCE involving the unrequited love of Federigo for the lady Monna Giovanna. After Federigo squanders his entire fortune in vain pursuit of his lady, he is left with only a falcon. The lady has a son who falls ill and tells his mother that obtaining Federigo's falcon will make him happy. Giovanna goes to Federigo to make the request, but Federigo, having nothing else to offer her, kills his falcon and serves it to her as a meal before she makes the request. This final act of generosity ultimately wins the lady's love.

Perhaps the most influential tale in the text is the 10th story of the 10th day, the moral tale of Patient Griselda. This is a story of a poor woman married to the marquis of Sanluzzo, whose husband tests her fidelity and obedience by pretending to have her two children killed, professing to divorce her to marry a younger girl, and ultimately forcing her to prepare the house and welcome the new bride. In the end he reveals that the new "bride" is their daughter and that he has kept the children safe for 12 years, and he praises Griselda for her patient steadfastness. The tale was translated into Latin verse by Boccaccio's friend and mentor PETRARCH, and retold by Chaucer as *The CLERK'S TALE.*

Boccaccio's interest is in lively storytelling. He spends little time on the psychology of his characters, but rather shows us what they are like by what they do. Nor are his tales didactic in the sense of much medieval literature. Although Boccaccio greatly admired DANTE'S *DIVINE COMEDY* with its moral thrust, in many ways his *Decameron* seems particularly intended to answer Dante: The 100 tales specifically echo the 100 cantos in the *Comedy,* and in addition Boccaccio specifically alludes to Canto V of Dante's *Inferno,* where the adulterers Paolo and Francesca refer to the book they were reading (apparently the French prose *Lancelot*) as their "Galeotto," the go-between in Lancelot and

Guenevere's love affair. Dante's implication seems to be that reading for pleasure may be morally precarious. Boccaccio subtitles his book "Prince Galeotto," asserting thus that his book is to be read for pleasure, and that such reading is appropriate—even, as in the case of the 10 members of his *brigata* (the young narrators of the tales), restorative both physically and emotionally.

Bibliography

Bergin, Thomas G. *Boccaccio.* New York: Viking Press, 1981.

Branca, Vittore. *Boccaccio: The Man and His Works.* Translated by Richard Monges. Cotranslated and edited by Dennis J. McAuliffe. With a foreword by Robert C. Clements. New York: New York University Press, 1976.

Musa, Mark, and Peter Bondanella, trans. *The Decameron.* With an introduction by Thomas G. Bergin. New York: New American Library, 1982.

Olson, Glending. *Literature as Recreation in the Later Middle Ages.* Ithaca, N.Y.: Cornell University Press, 1982.

Wallace, David. *Giovanni Boccaccio: Decameron.* Cambridge: Cambridge University Press, 1991.

Deor (*Deor's Lament*) (ca. eighth century)

Deor is an OLD ENGLISH poem from the 10th-century EXETER BOOK manuscript, a large compilation of Anglo-Saxon poetry. The poem is probably somewhat older than the manuscript; certainly its subject matter is much older, dating back to the fifth century and beyond to incidents from Germanic mythology.

Deor is a 42-line poem divided into six strophes of unequal length, each followed by a common refrain. Such a structure was highly unusual in Old English poetry (only the lyric *WULF AND EADWACER* evinces a similar form), though it was not so uncommon in Old Norse verse—a fact that has led some to conjecture that *Deor* could be a translation. Like the much longer and better-known poem *WIDSITH*, *Deor* deals in large part with the life of a MINSTREL or SCOP in the courts of Anglo-Saxon nobles.

Each strophe of the poem presents a different case of adversity suffered and ultimately lived through. The first strophe refers to the imprisonment of Weland, the Old Norse goldsmith-god, by his enemy King Nithhad, who had fettered him and forced Weland to work for him. The second strophe speaks of Beaduhild, Nithhad's daughter whom Weland raped and impregnated after killing her brothers as revenge for his imprisonment. *The* PROSE EDDA contains a full account of the story alluded to in these two strophes.

The third strophe mentions Geat and Maethild, alluding to Maethild's fateful dream of her own death that comes true when she drowns in a river. Theodoric (presumably the Ostrogoth) is mentioned in strophe 4, and the cruel reign of another Ostrogothic king, Ermanaric, is described in strophe 5. Each of these strophes ends with the refrain *þæs ofereode, þisses swa mæg!* ("that passed over, this may also!").

All of this leads into a meditative section (lines 28–34) that some have considered a scribal interpolation. The lines add a Christian tone to the poem, suggesting that God gives grace to some but hardship to others, but these generalizations seem somewhat out of keeping with the rest of the poem and particularly with the refrain.

In the final section of the lyric, the poet introduces himself as Deor (a name meaning "wild animal"), and describes his own misfortune: Once the court poet or scop for the Heodenings, Deor has been replaced by another singer, Heorrenda, who has also been granted lands that his lord had originally intended for Deor. The poem gives the impression of having been written, perhaps, to comfort the displaced poet as he reminds himself that great figures of the past have also suffered, and—through his refrain—that ultimately time puts an end to all troubles. But many scholars consider the poet's own story to be fictional, and suggest that the poem was written to console a patron suffering from some unnamed misfortune.

Bibliography

Banjeree, Jacqueline. " 'Deor': The Refrain," *Explicator* 42 (1984): 4–7.

Malone, Kemp, ed. *Deor.* Rev. ed. Exeter: University of Exeter, 1977.

Risden, E. L. "*Deor* and the Old English Ode and Gnomic Compassion," *In Geardagum* 11 (1990): 57–70.

Der von Kürenberg (late 12th century)

Der von Kürenberg was one of the earliest German COURTLY LOVE poets. His songs were copied in the famous early 14th-century *Manessische Liederhandschrift* (Manesse song manuscript), also known as *Grosse Heidelberger Liederhandschrift* (ms. C), one of the most important collections of the earliest Middle High German courtly love songs (*Minnelieder*). These songs, composed between 1170 and 1200, today are collectively called *Des Minnesangs Frühling* (Spring of courtly love songs).

Der von Kürenberg originated in lower Austria. His songs, composed between 1150 and 1175, have the same poetic structure as the one utilized by the *NIBELUNGENLIED* poet (ca. 1200), that is, three- or four-beat half-lines, two of which regularly make up a rhyming couplet. In contrast to most courtly poets, Kürenberg's poems are clearly divided into separate stanzas, 15 in total. In some of these a female voice speaks (*Frauenstrophen*), and in others we hear a man speak (*Männerstrophen*), and sometimes the stanza consists of a dialogue between man and woman (*Wechsel*). Kürenberg discusses the fundamental problems of courtly love, such as the physical distance between the lovers, misunderstandings, loneliness and longing, and domestication through love. The latter aspect is most beautifully expressed through the image of a preying falcon whom the lady has raised for more a year, but who then flies away into distant lands (6). In the following stanza (7) the poetic voice says that she or he saw a falcon flying high, with bands of silk attached to his foot, which could represent either the soft but firm bonds between two lovers, or the loss of the beloved. In one stanza the male voice expresses his anger because his lady has ordered him to leave her country (10), and in another stanza he admits that he stood next to her bed one night but did not dare to wake her up (3), to which she responds that there was no reason for his hesitation. As in most other courtly love songs, Kürenberg formulates that love and sorrow are intimately entwined.

Bibliography

Moser, Hugo and Helmut Tervooren, ed. *Des Minnesangs Frühling.* 38th ed. Stuttgart, Germany: Hirzel, 1988.

Sayce, Olive. *The Medieval German Lyric 1150–1300. The Development of Its Themes and Forms in Their European Context.* Oxford: Clarendon Press, 1982.

Willson, H. B. "Wooing in Some Poems of Der von Kürenberg," *Journal of English and Germanic Philology* 83, no.4 (1984): 469–481.

Albrecht Classen

Der Wilde Alexander (late 13th century)

Not much is known about this south German GOLIARDIC poet who flourished in the late 13th century. The epithet "wild" might signify that he lacked, as a dependent poet, a stable social status and moved, like many contemporary singers, from court to court to seek support for his art. The innovative elements in some of his didactic and erotic songs could have been another reason for the label "wild." The Jena song manuscript J, which also offers the music for the songs, identifies him as "meister" (master), so he was not of aristocratic background, though in his poetry he maintained the traditional ideals that characterized 12th-century courtly poetry. He composed seven songs with didactic, erotic, and political content. The last one belongs to the category of the *Leich* (lay), a song with a highly complex rhyming scheme, whereas the other songs follow more traditional types. His first song is a Christmas song. In the following, mostly didactic, songs, Alexander discusses many different religious, moral, and ethical aspects. He also addresses material problems of wandering singers (II, 16), refers to the Arthurian tradition (II, 24), sings a song of praise of his beloved lady (III), criticizes selfish and vicious behavior displayed by courtiers (II, 14–15), returns to the topic of COURTLY LOVE and the ensuing pain because the lovers cannot meet (IV), and explores the role of letter writing to reach out to his beloved (VI). In his *Leich* (VII) Alexander identifies himself as an armored knight fighting on the side of Lady Love and describes the process of wooing for love using the imagery of a knightly battle, evoking the Homeric account of the defeat of Troy at the hands of the Greeks.

Alexander's most important and innovative poem is his "Strawberry Song," "Hie vor dô wir kinder wâren" (V; "Erstwhile when we were children"). The song describes the innocence of children who are playing in a meadow, until a forester calls them and warns them of snakes. One of the children is bitten, and they all lament that the wound will never heal. The man admonishes them to leave the forest, otherwise they would suffer the same destiny as the five foolish virgins in the New Testament. The intricate combination of erotic with religious themes, the symbolic employment of the strawberry motif, the obviously biblical reference to the forester, and the image of the children playing on the meadow, which in the poet's presence has been transformed into a pasture, makes this text one of the most charming and enigmatic 13th-century German courtly songs.

Bibliography

Kraus, Carl von, ed. *Deutsche Liederdichter des 13. Jahrhunderts.* 2nd ed. Revised by Gisela Kornrumpf. Tübingen, Germany: Niemeyer, 1978.

McDonald, William C. "A Pauline Reading of Der Wilde Alexander's 'Kindheitslied,' " *Monatshefte* 76, no. 2 (1984): 156–175.

Albrecht Classen

Deschamps, Eustace (ca. 1346–1407)

Eustace Deschamps was a prolific French poet who wrote hundreds of lyrics and wrote, as well, a satire on women called the *Mirour de Mariage* and a prose treatise on versification called the *Art de dictier* (Art of writing poetry). Deschamps held positions in the government of Charles V, and was a close friend and disciple of the most influential French poet of his age, Guillaume de MACHAUT. He was well-acquainted with the Savoyard poet and knight Oton de GRANSON, and he also dedicated poems to his two most famous contemporaries, Geoffrey CHAUCER and CHRISTINE DE PIZAN.

Deschamps, also called Moreal, was born in about 1346 in Champagne, in the town of Vertus near Reims. He received a typical early education in Latin grammar and logic, and as a young man apparently studied law, perhaps at the school in Orléans. He does not seem to have received a degree, but apparently entered the service of King Charles V in about 1367. For the last 40 years of his life, he worked in various capacities for the king and for his sons, Louis of Orléans and Charles VI. A number of his poems are highly partisan, anti-English lyrics stemming from Deschamps' experiences in the Hundred Years' War, in particular after 1380 when the English burned his boyhood home in Vertus. He was, however, not without sympathy for some individual Englishmen: He was a personal friend of Lewis Clifford (member of the English Privy Council and later well-known as one of the "LOLLARD knights"), and his poetry acknowledges his admiration for the English hero Guiscard d'Angle. His *BALLADE* addressed to Chaucer praises the English poet as the "grand translator," and extols his translation of the *ROMAN DE LA ROSE.* Playing on the imagery of the *Rose* itself, Deschamps says that Chaucer has sown his works in the soil of England, and made it a garden—the garden of the *Rose.*

Deschamps learned the art of poetry from Machaut, who he says "educated" him. One early source claims that Machaut was Deschamps's uncle, though there is no independent verification of that assertion. Apparently he began a relationship with the older poet that continued until Machaut's death in 1377. At that point he wrote a double *ballade* in praise of Machaut, expressing his admiration and affection for the master and his poetry, and describing Machaut as the "flower of all flowers" of poets.

Deschamps's *ballade* addressed to Christine de Pizan seems to have been written in response to a complimentary letter he had received from her in

1403. In his reciprocal letter of praise to her, he refers to her as an "elegant Muse," and praises her for her "philosophy," although he avoids saying anything about her skill as a poet.

These short occasional poems are probably Deschamps's best known compositions, but his most ambitious work is certainly his *Mirour de mariage,* the anti-feminist satire that, like Chaucer's *WIFE OF BATH'S TALE,* relies on St. JEROME's letter *Adversus Jovinianum,* Matheolus's *Lamentations,* and Ovid's *Ars amatoria.* This unfinished allegorical poem of 12,103 lines focuses on a young man named *Franc Vouloir* ("Free Will") and the question of whether he should marry. The young man's false friends, with names like "Desire," "Folly," and "Servitude," are quick to advise marriage. But Free Will decides to discuss the matter with his true friend, *Repertoire de Science* ("Wisdom"), who argues a marriage of the spirit is far superior to a marriage of the flesh, and convinces Free Will not to marry.

Deschamps's *Art de dictier* describes the various "fixed forms" of French poetry—*ballades, VIRELAIS,* RONDEAUX, *LAIS*—and, more important, introduces the idea of poetry as "natural music." Deschamps argues that poetic texts do not need musical accompaniment, but can stand alone because poetry in itself is a form of music. This was not a revolutionary idea, but it was not characteristic of medieval literary theorists. It was more typical to think of poetry as a branch of rhetoric, as DANTE does in *De VULGARI ELOQUENTIA.*

Deschamps even tried his hand at dramatic poetry, including a farce called the *Farce de Maîrtre Trubert et d'Antroignart,* concerning the defeat of a cunning lawyer, and the *Dit de quatre offices de l'Ostel du Roy,* a morality play. But of the some 80,000 lines of verse Deschamps produced, the vast majority constitute lyric poetry, including 1,017 *ballades,* 171 rondeaux, 139 *chansons royals* (a form descended from the earlier CHANSON), 84 *virelais,* and 14 *lais.* In addition, he wrote 12 lyric poems in Latin. Deschamps does not limit himself to conventional love poetry, but writes on a variety of topics—moral, comic, satiric, patriotic, and often personal, as he alludes to particular circumstances in his own life. Deschamps was an important poet, prolific and interesting, though in terms of quality and influence his verse has been overshadowed by the major contemporary poets with whom he was associated: Machaut, Christine, and Chaucer.

Bibliography

Deschamps, Eustace. *Selected Poems.* Edited by Ian S. Laurie and Deborah M. Sinnreich-Levi. Translated by David Curzon and Jeffrey Fiskin. New York: Routledge, 2003.

Laurie, I. S. "Deschamps and the Lyric as Natural Music," *Modern Language Review* 59 (1964): 561–570.

Olsen, Glending. "Deschamps' *Art de Dictier* and Chaucer's Literary Environment," *Speculum* 48 (1973): 714–723.

Wimsatt, James I. *Chaucer and His French Contemporaries: Natural Music in the Fourteenth Century.* Toronto: University of Toronto Press, 1991.

Dēvara Dāsimayya (Jedara Dāsimayya) (10th century)

Dēvara Dāsimayya was one of the poet-saints of the Vīraśaiva reform movement within Hinduism. He seems to have lived a century before the other two most famous poets in the tradition, BASAVANNA and MAHADEVIYAKKA. Like them he wrote in the Kannada language of southern India, and wrote chiefly *vacanas*—short poems in a colloquial and direct language that communicated spiritual ideas to common people. The reformist Vīraśaivas eschewed the highly ritualistic practices of the Hindu priesthood, and called for the breakdown of the traditional Hindu caste system, thus many of their members were from the lower castes.

Tradition says that Dēvara Dāsimayya was born in Mudanuru. In the village was a Rāmanātha temple—one dedicated to Śiva as worshipped by the epic hero Rāma, known as an incarnation of the god Vishnu. Thus all of Dāsimayya's *vacanas* are addressed to "Rāma's lord."

There are many legends concerning Dāsimayya. One says that he was in the forest mortifying his flesh when Śiva appeared to him and told him that working in the world was a more acceptable means of worship, after which Dāsimayya returned to Mudanuru and became a weaver (thus he is sometimes called "Dāsimayya of the weavers" or "Jedara Dāsimayya"). Other legends depict Dāsimayya winning debates with Brahmins, Jains, and others. He was apparently a well-known teacher in the territory ruled by the Jain king Jayasimha, whose wife Sugale was converted by Dāsimayya. Legend says he ultimately converted the king and 20,000 of his subjects. Whether the legends are true or not, clearly Dāsimayya had a reputation as a great Vīraśaivist missionary.

Dēvara Dāsimayya's spirituality was mystical, like that of Mahadeviyakka after him. The Vīraśaivist rejection of ritual was meant to stress individual, personal spirituality that aimed for a oneness with God, or Śiva (one of the three major gods of Hinduism). In part, this meant transcending the barrier between body and soul, as Dāsimayya suggests in one poem: "You know the secret of my body/I know the secret of your breath./That's why your body/is in mine" (Ramanujan 1973, 106).

It meant, as well, blurring other distinctions in the physical world, such as that between male and female. In another poem, Dāsimayya says:

If they see
breasts and long hair coming
they call it a woman

If beard and whiskers
they call it a man:

but, look, the Self that hovers
in between
is neither man
nor woman.

(Ramanujan 1973, 110)

Such a blurring of distinctions, of course, ultimately implies a breakdown of castes as well, as Dāsimayya's successor Basavanna realized. Dāsimayya is distinguished from the other poet-saints of Virasaivism by the direct nature of his language, sometimes verging on coarseness. But like the other poet-saints, he evinces a mystical outlook and radically reformist ideals.

Bibliography

Ramanujan, A. K., ed. and trans. *Speaking of Śiva.* Harmondsworth, U.K.: Penguin, 1973.

Dietmar von Aist (late 12th century)

Dietmar von Aist hailed from the Austro-Bavarian region and wrote some of the earliest Middle High German courtly love poems, preserved in the famous *Manesse Manuscript* (ms. C; see DER VON KÜRENBERG) and the contemporary *Weingartner Liederhandschrift* (ms. B). Some historical documents refer to a Dietmar von Aist between 1139 and 1171, but it is difficult to say whether he was identical with this poet. He is, along with Der von Kürenberg, one of the earliest contributors to the so-called *Des Minnesangs Frühling* (Spring of courtly poetry) collection, and he composed 16 songs. Dietmar, however, develops the COURTLY LOVE themes further and employs many different poetic genres. He explores the meaning of sorrow resulting from love (I), addresses a messenger whom he is sending to his lady (II), develops the first Middle High German spring poem in praise of love (III), and utilizes the falcon motif for a discussion of how a lady chooses a lover for herself (IV). Dietmar also wrote two winter songs (VIII, XI), and experimented with the genre of *Wechsel* (XII, XIV, XV) where man and woman exchange opinions about love in separate stanzas. Most important, Dietmar also composed one of the earliest Middle High German dawn songs (XIII) (*see* ALBA) in which the two lovers wake up early in the morning, alerted by a bird sitting on a linden tree outside their window, and lament that he has to depart before anybody can discover them. The woman cries and begs him to return as soon as possible because he is taking all her happiness with him.

Bibliography

Groos, Arthur. "Modern Stereotyping and Medieval Topoi: The Lovers' Exchange in Dietmar von Aist's

'Ûf der Linden obene,' " *Journal of English and Germanic Philology* 88, no. 2 (1989): 157–167.

Moser, Hugo, and Helmut Tervooren. *Des Minnesangs Frühling.* 38th ed. Stuttgart, Germany: Hirzel, 1988.

Albrecht Classen

Dinis (King Diniz) (1279–1325) *king of Portugal*

Dom Dinis was the sixth king of Portugal, a significant patron of the arts, and the most influential poet of his day. His poetry, written in the Galician-Portuguese language, owes something to the native tradition of Portugal, but more clearly displays the influence of some of the greater Provençal TROUBADOURS, like BERNART DE VENTADORN and Jaufré RUDEL. His was also the last royal court to patronize Portuguese lyric poets, and the tradition soon died out after flowering in Dinis's court.

Dinis was son of Alfonso III, whom he succeeded as king in 1279. He was knighted by his grandfather, ALFONSO X of Castile and Leon, and he married Isabel of Aragon. With Isabel, Dinis worked to improve the lives of the poor in his country, often through the founding of new social institutions like orphanages and other shelters. Largely because of such activity, Isabel was named a saint after her death. Dinis also made and enforced new criminal and civil law codes that, by reducing the power of the nobility, protected the lower classes from abuses. Dinis also sought to reduce the amount of land held by the church, setting off a conflict with the papacy that was only resolved by a special concordat with the pope in 1290.

Dinis was a hard-working and peaceful monarch in a time of war and unrest. He promoted economic and commercial development as well as improving agriculture (he was nicknamed the "farmer king"). He built the Portuguese navy, mainly to protect sea commerce, and he founded the first university in Portugal, at Lisbon (later Coimbra) in 1290. He signed a treaty with Castile defining the border between the two countries—an agreement that still stands today. He protected the property holdings of the Knights Templars in Portugal when Pope Clement V dissolved the order in 1312, founding a new Order of Christ that was essentially a continuation of the older order.

King Dinis's last years were marred by a rebellion by his son Alfonso. His wife Isabel is purported to have made peace between the two. Dinis died on January 7, 1325, in Santarem, and was succeeded by his son, who became Alfonso IV.

Of all Dinis's great accomplishments, he may be best remembered for his cultural interests, particularly in literature. He wrote several books himself, on hunting, science, and administration, but most memorably he composed poetry. His extant poems number 137. Of these, 73 are *cantigas de amor* (songs of love), which deal mainly with the pains of unrequited love. All but a few of these are in the same basic form, with three stanzas of seven lines each. They are also characterized by the use of a good deal of verbal and semantic parallelism and a great diversity of rhyme. Music for seven of his love songs has survived on a single fragmentary page from a songbook of about 1300, discovered in Lisbon in 1990.

Dinis's compositions include 51 *CANTIGAS DE AMIGO*, or songs from a woman's point of view. These tend to be more flexible in form and lighter in tone than his *cantigas de amor,* possibly because ultimately they spring from the popular tradition. But during Dinis's reign and in his hands, the genre became more stylized and formal. Dinis is probably the best-known author of *cantigas de amigo* in Portuguese. One example is the poem beginning *Non chegou, madr', o meu amigo* ("Mother, my friend did not arrive"), in which the speaker complains to her mother that her lover has failed to keep his promise to return to her:

That the traitor lied
grieves me, for he broke his
  promise deliberately.
Oh mother, I am dying of love!

(Jensen 1992, 10.8, ll. 13–15)

Dinis is important not only because of his own literary output, but also for his support of poetry in his court. He encouraged the translation of Spanish, Latin, and Arabic texts into Portuguese, and he welcomed troubadours and JONGLEURS from Castile, Aragon, Leon, and elsewhere to become part of his brilliant court. He may have personally overseen the compilation of the *Cancioneiro da Ajuda,* and his influence certainly was the spirit behind the assembling of two other major anthologies of the period, the *Cancioneiros da Vaticana* and the *Cancioneiros Colocci-Brancuti* (or *da Biblioteca Nacional de Lisboa*). Among these three compilations, 200 poets and some 2,000 poems are preserved, an accomplishment that ranks as one of King Dinis's most important.

Bibliography

Ackerlind, Sheila R. *King Dinis of Portugal and the Alfonsine Heritage.* New York: Peter Lang, 1990.

Bell, Aubrey F. G. *Portuguese Literature.* Reprinted with new bibliography. Oxford: Clarendon Press, 1970.

Jensen, Frede, ed. and trans. *Medieval Galician-Portuguese Poetry: An Anthology.* Garland Library of Medieval Literature 87. New York and London: Garland, 1992.

Vidigal, B. ed. *The Oxford Book of Portuguese Verse: XIIth Century–XXth Century.* Chosen by Aubrey F. G. Bell. 2nd ed. Oxford: Clarendon Press, 1972.

Divine Comedy, The (*Commedia*) Dante Alighieri (1307–1321)

Italian poet DANTE ALIGHIERI's *Divine Comedy* is one of the seminal works of Western culture and the unrivaled greatest literary text of the European Middle Ages. The poem is epic in scope, telling the story of a lost traveler who, to find his way back to his true home, must journey through the three realms of the medieval Christian afterlife—Hell, Purgatory, and Heaven. The pilgrim Dante's trek is also an ALLEGORY of the soul journeying toward God, and of the political Everyman groping toward social stability and peace. Dante called the work the *Commedia,* a reference to its happy ending as well as to its use of the Tuscan vernacular as opposed to Latin, the language his contemporaries would have expected in a text dealing with such weighty issues and demanding a sublime style. Dante's deliberate choice of the vernacular made the bold declaration that classic literary art could be composed in the everyday languages of Europe. It was Dante's disciple BOCCACCIO who first called the *Commedia* "Divine," and it has been known by that epithet ever since.

Born in Florence in 1265, Dante began his poetic career under the influence of his friend Guido CAVALCANTI as a love poet in the school of the *DOLCE STIL NOVO* ("sweet new style"). Most of his love poetry was intended for a woman he called Beatrice ("bringer of blessings") who, beyond his reach and married to another, was the perfect object of the idealized form of love characteristic of the *stilnovist* lyric. When Beatrice died young, in 1290, Dante composed the *VITA NUOVA* in her memory, poetically tracing the progress of his love from the purely sensual to, after her death, the purely spiritual. In this way, the heavenly Beatrice was positioned to become Dante's guide through Paradise in his *Commedia.* In the years after Beatrice's death, Dante became embroiled in the political life of Florence, a life characterized by bitter civil struggles between Dante's White party and the rival Blacks. In 1301, while Dante was away from the city on a diplomatic mission, the Blacks staged a coup assisted by Pope Boniface VIII and his ally, Charles of Anjou. In his absence, Dante was charged with political graft and exiled for life from his native city. He never returned, spending his last 20 years wandering among the cities of Italy, staying with various nobles willing to shelter him, and finally dying in Ravenna in 1321. The theme of the lost wanderer trying to get home that frames the *Commedia* poignantly mirrors Dante's own situation.

Perhaps the first remarkable aspect of the poem is its structure. Sometimes compared to a Gothic cathedral or an elaborate scholastic system like that of Thomas AQUINAS, the structure of the *Commedia* is both vast in its conception and intricate in its detail. In effect a celebration of the ordered harmony of the universe as well as a reflection of the mystery of the holy Trinity, the entire poem is built on the numbers 3 and 1, and the number 9 (the square of 3). The poem is divided into three large sections or *canticles—Inferno, Purgatorio,* and *Paradiso.* Each canticle contains 33 cantos, except the first, which contains an introductory canto, bringing the total number of cantos in the poem to a perfect 100. This same numerological concern is reflected in the verse form Dante created for the poem, called *terza rima* ("third rhyme"), which rhymes *aba bcb cdc* and so on, so that each tercet (three-line stanza) is interlocked with the preceding and succeeding group. Each line of the tercet contains 11 syllables, for a total of 33—thus the number of syllables in each tercet is the same as the number of cantos in each canticle. Further, the inner structure of each canticle is based on the number 9: There are nine circles of sinners in the Inferno; nine sites in Purgatory, including ledges for each of the Seven Deadly Sins in addition to an ante-Purgatory and, at the summit, the earthly Paradise; and nine spheres in Heaven representing the spheres of the planets and fixed stars of medieval astronomy. But within these structures, each canticle is also organized according to a threefold pattern. In Hell, the sins represented in the nine circles are of three types, symbolized by the three beasts who threaten the pilgrim narrator in the first canto: sins of the She-wolf (representing incontinence), sins of the Lion (representing violence), and sins of the leopard (representing fraud and malice). Purgatory, as Dante's guide Virgil explains in Canto XVII, is divided according to three ways in which love (the motivating force for all human actions, including sin) can be defective—thus love may be misdirected (in the case of lust, gluttony, and greed), insufficient (in the case of sloth), or perverted (into self-love, in the case of wrath, envy, and pride). In Heaven the blessed souls participate in a vision of God according to their own qualities or limitations, so that their vision may be incomplete, it may come through obtaining the four cardinal virtues, or it may be perfect like that of the angels. The whole structure of the *Commedia* strives to embody the textual equivalent of the Holy Trinity.

Dante's geography is conventionally medieval: He depicts Hell as a great funnel-shaped cavern created when Lucifer fell from heaven. The land displaced as a result of the formation of Hell became Mount Purgatory, rising from the otherwise landless southern hemisphere. The earthly Paradise, humankind's original home, is at the top of Mount Purgatory, and from there Dante ascends into the interlocked spheres of the astronomers' heavens. Thus on one level Dante presents a journey through what his contemporaries would have conceived of as the literal world of the afterlife, specifically dated from Good Friday to Easter Sunday of the year 1300. On another level, however, the journey is the allegorical journey of the human soul to moral perfection. In the beginning, the pilgrim Dante has wandered from the path of virtue into a dark wood of sin. Just as the sacrament of penance involves a three-step process—confession, penance, and absolution—so the pilgrim Dante moves through the Inferno (suggesting Prevenient Grace, or the conviction of sin), Purgatory (Justifying Grace, or the assurance of forgiveness), and Paradise (Sanctifying Grace, or the movement toward holy living).

This is only one level of the allegory Dante invites his readers to discover in his text. In a famous letter to one of his patrons, Can Grande Della Scalla of Verona (a letter of uncertain authenticity), Dante encouraged readers to interpret his *Commedia* in three different allegorical senses in addition to the literal sense. Thus people and events in the text all have several meanings. Dante's guide Virgil is the literal Latin poet who described the underworld in Book VI of his *Aeneid,* but he also suggests human reason, and therefore can take Dante only through Purgatory and not into Heaven. For a guide in Paradise Dante must rely on Beatrice, who is not only Dante's historical lover but also the divine love and grace that has saved him. The punishments of the *Inferno* are ordered according to the retributive justice of the Old Testament "eye for an eye" ethic and are often admired for their perfect *contrapasso* or "counterpenalty," so that the lustful are blown about by winds, as in life they were at the mercy of their own tumultuous passions. But the individual sinners also represent allegorically the sin itself. And on another level the reader ultimately becomes aware that morally, the sinners are in hell merely what they were on earth: They still engage in the sin that damned them, and, in fact, the sin is ultimately to be seen as its own punishment. Morally, sin and hell are identical.

One may read *The Divine Comedy* for a variety of reasons: Politically, Dante develops a theme throughout the *Commedia* of the need for the Holy Roman Emperor to restore order to the ravaged cities of Italy and for the Popes to cease their interference in the internal secular affairs of the Italian states. Morally, one can trace the spiritual development of the pilgrim narrator from seeing things with worldly eyes to understanding, in the end, God's moral vision. But most readers find most memorable the variety of characters—biblical, classical, historical, and contemporary—with whom Dante peoples his afterlife. Paolo and Francesca's moving defense of their adultery (*Inferno* V), BERTRAN DE BORN's appearance holding his severed head like a lantern (*Inferno* XXVIII), Ugolino's pathetic tale of starvation and the cannibalization of his children (*Inferno* XXXIII), these and many other individuals have become indelible images in the European consciousness.

The Divine Comedy was vastly popular in the 14th century and continued to be so in subsequent generations. Twelve commentaries on the poem appeared by 1400, and Boccaccio gave public lectures on the poem in Florence in 1373–74. The poem influenced poets from PETRARCH and CHAUCER to Pound and Eliot, went through more than 400 editions in the centuries after the printing press arrived in Italy, and has been translated into dozens of languages, including numerous English translations in recent years. Clearly the poem, in its infinite variety, still speaks to contemporary readers.

Bibliography

Bergin, Thomas G. *Perspectives on the Divine Comedy.* New Brunswick, N.J.: Rutgers University Press, 1967.

Bloom, Harold, ed. *Dante's Divine Comedy.* New York: Chelsea House, 1987.

De Gennaro, Angelo A. *The Reader's Companion to Dante's Divine Comedy.* New York: Philosophical Library, 1986.

Gallagher, Joseph. *To Hell and Back with Dante: A Modern Reader's Guide to the Divine Comedy.* Liguori, Mo.: Triumph Books, 1996.

Jacoff, Rachel, ed. *The Cambridge Companion to Dante.* Cambridge: Cambridge University Press, 1993.

Mandelbaum, Allen, trans. *The Divine Comedy.* With an introduction by Eugenio Montale and notes by Peter Armour. New York: Knopf, 1995.

Musa, Mark, ed. and trans. *The Divine Comedy.* 3 vols. Harmondsworth, U.K.: Penguin, 1984–1986.

Grandgent, C. H., commentary. *Companion to the Divine Comedy.* Edited by Charles S. Singleton. Cambridge, Mass.: Harvard University Press, 1975.

Dojoji Kanze Kojirô Nobumitsu (ca. 1500)

The Japanese dramatist NOBUMITSU was one of the last important producers of Nō plays. His most famous play is *Dojoji,* so called beause it is set in the Dojoji temple in the Wakayama prefecture in western Japan. Based on an 11th-century Buddhist tale of a priest pursued by a lustful widow, the Nō play substitutes an innocent young girl for the widow and thereby alters the effect of the story. In Nobumitsu's version a huge bell becomes central to the action (this integral use of such a prop is very unusual in Nō drama). The play begins with a ceremony held at the Dojoji temple to celebrate the installation of the bell. The priest performing the ceremony gives orders that no women are to be allowed to enter the temple grounds during the service. But a female dancer approaches the temple, convinces a servant to allow her to enter, and dances around the bell. Her dancing lulls the servants to sleep, at which she rushes to the bell, leaps into it, and pulls it down so that it crashes to the ground around her, awakening the servants. They rush to the bell, but it is hot to the touch. After some trepidation, they reveal to the priest what has happened, and he relates to them the story of the bell.

According to the priest, once long ago a young ascetic mountain recluse made an annual pilgrimage to Kumano. Each year he stayed with the same steward and his daughter on the pilgrimage route. When the girl was a child, the ascetic would bring her a gift every time he stayed with her father. In jest, the father told the girl that perhaps the holy man would marry her some day, and she grew up believing in this fantasy. When she was grown, she approached the pilgrim and asserted that he should marry her and take her away with him. But the pilgrim refused, and fled from the girl. He fled to the temple where he hid from the girl in a great bell. The girl, pursuing the young man, turned into a serpent in her wrath. Spying the bell, she wrapped herself around it and stung it with her venomous tail. The bell became so hot that it killed the pilgrim hiding inside.

Now the priest, recognizing that the dancer hiding within the bell is the same woman as before, performs a kind of exorcism on the bell: Without being struck, it begins to peal, and a serpent, rather than a girl, emerges from the bell. The serpent engages in a spiritual battle with the priest. Flames engulf the serpent and she rushes off to fling herself into the river.

Dolce Stil Novo

The *Dolce Stil Novo* ("sweet new style") is the name generally given by scholars to a style of Italian love poetry prevalent in the last quarter of the 13th century. Lyric poetry in this style is characterized by a reverential attitude toward women, presented as angelic creatures who might lead their lovers to the love of God, and by a new poetic language, rhetorically direct but making use of difficult imagery drawn from a variety of learned traditions.

It is unclear whether the *stilnovisti* (those who wrote in the *Dolce Stil Novo*) ever formed a "school" in any sense. The term is borrowed from DANTE, who, in the 24th canto of his *Purgatorio* depicts the earlier poet BONAGIUNTA ORBICCIANI of Lucca praising Dante's poem *Donne, ch'avete intelletto d'amore* ("Ladies, who have intelligence of love"). He recognizes Dante's lyric style as having surpassed his own and that of the two earlier schools of Italian poetry—the Sicilian (founded by GIACOMO DA LENTINO) and the Tuscan (led by GUITTONE D'AREZZO, "the Notary")—and calls it the "sweet new style." Based on the similarity of theme and style, most scholars include a small number of mainly Florentine poets in the group, including Guido GUINIZELLI, Guido CAVALCANTI, LAPO GIANNI, Dino FRESCOBALDI, GIANNI ALFANI, CINO DA PISTOIA, and Dante himself. Others have suggested that Dante intended the term to apply only to himself.

It was the earliest of these poets, Guinizelli, who is considered the father of the movement. His seminal *CANZONE* called *Al cor gentil* (The gentle heart) introduces many themes that became common in *stilnovist* lyrics. Guinizelli declares that an individual's value lay not in birth or wealth but in character, the "gentle heart," and that it was in the power of the Beloved Lady to activate the virtue inherent in the gentle heart of her lover. The woman, as embodiment of God's beauty and truth, may lead her lover to divine love by refining his earthly desires and turning them toward heaven.

Cavalcanti saw Guinizelli as an inspiration for his own conscious rejection of the earlier Tuscan school, which Cavalcanti faulted for being rhetorically overwrought. He sought a less embellished style himself, but in his major *canzone, Donna me prega* (A lady asks me), he introduced difficult imagery taken from scholastic philosophy, physics, astronomy, and particularly psychology and medicine. He presents love as an overwhelmingly negative force because of the psychological suffering it causes, but, with Guinizelli, asserts that only the genuinely noble in heart are able to understand love or the true poetry of love.

Although Dante borrowed a good deal from his friend Cavalcanti, especially in his earlier lyrics, he ultimately rejected the older poet's focus on the negative psychological effects of love, and presented love as an overwhelmingly positive force. The turning point in his development is the lyric *Donne, ch'avete intelletto d'amore*, mentioned by Bonagiunta in the *Purgatorio*. That lyric, the first *canzone* in Dante's VITA NUOVA, abandons the presentation of the lover himself and his anguish, and turns instead to a focus on the perfections of his lady, Beatrice, whom the angels desire to complete the perfection of heaven, and who ennobles her admirers and brings them to the love of God.

It may be that Dante refers only to his own achievement by his term "sweet new style." But characteristics generally associated with the term—the elevation of the woman to angelic status and the refinement of the true lover who, unlike the ignoble masses, can comprehend the learned and exclusive imagery of love poetry—are evident in Guinizelli,

Cavalcanti, and several of Dante's other contemporaries. Though Dante ultimately moves beyond his peers, his early association with them in a *stilnovist* "school" makes historical sense.

Bibliography

Goldin, Frederick, trans. *German and Italian Lyrics of the Middle Ages: An Anthology and a History.* New York: Doubleday, 1973.

Jacoff, Rachel, ed. *The Cambridge Companion to Dante.* Cambridge: Cambridge University Press, 1993.

Shaw, James E. *Guido Cavalcanti's Theory of Love: The "Canzone d'Amore" and Other Related Problems.* Toronto: University of Toronto Press, 1949.

Valency, Maurice. *In Praise of Love.* New York: MacMillan, 1958.

Donna me prega Guido Cavalcanti (ca. 1290)

Guido CAVALCANTI's *Donna me prega,* (A lady asks me) is one of the most often anthologized and discussed poems in Italian literature. In the poem, Cavalcanti says he is writing the poem at the request of a lady in order to define the phenomenon of love. In his first stanza, he outlines the poem, announcing the specific aspects of love he intends to "demonstrate":

where it dwells, and who created it,
its influence and potency,
its essence, its effects,
the pleasure which gives it the name of love,
and whether it is visible.

(Goldin 1973, 325, ll. 10–14)

In addition, Cavalcanti expresses three other themes that become characteristic of his poetry: First, love, as pictured here and elsewhere in his poetry, is an overwhelming and often negative force; second, only the truly noble in heart are able to understand love or its poetry; and third, the terms he will use to describe love will come from learned sciences. Love is, he says:

an accident that is often cruel,
and so unmerciful, it is called love:
. . .
and now I speak to those who understand,
for I do not think that one whose heart is base
can follow such an argument:
because unless I can use the methods of natural philosophy
I am unwilling to demonstrate
where it dwells and who created it,

(Goldin 1973, 323–25, ll. 2–10)

These last two themes Cavalcanti took and refined from his great predecessor, Guido GUINIZELLI. But the extent of Cavalcanti's learned allusions was never approached by Guinizelli. In the remainder of *Donna me prega,* Cavalcanti goes on to discuss love in familiar terms to scholastic philosophers like Albertus Magnus or Thomas AQUINAS, or perhaps a more direct influence would be the Muslim philosopher AVERROËS. Love becomes destructive because a man mistakes the image of his beloved, held within his memory, for the highest good, and seeks to attain it though, in the woman, it is unattainable. Here and elsewhere, he uses terms drawn from medieval psychological and medical theory, developing a doctrine of "spirits" that dominate the internal landscape of the mind, in which most of the drama of Cavalcanti's love affairs occurs.

While Dante borrowed much from Cavalcanti, including the psychological imagery and the spirits, the exclusive attitude about lovers, and the internalization of the love story, for Dante love was a very positive force, and one that ultimately leads him to Paradise in the *Divine Comedy.* Nevertheless, Cavalcanti's influence, through this and other poems, was tremendous.

Douglas, Gavin or Gawin (ca. 1475–1522)

Gavin Douglas was a late medieval Scottish poet. Douglas, Robert HENRYSON and William DUNBAR have often been referred to as the "Scottish Chaucerians" because they evince the profound influence of Geoffrey CHAUCER. Douglas is primarily remembered for his translation of the *Aeneid* and for three allegorical poems: *The Palice of Honour, King Hart,* and *Conscience,* all of which were written between 1501 and 1513.

Douglas was born into a noble family. He was the third son of Archibald Douglas, the fifth earl of Angus, known as "Bell-the-Cat." Douglas was educated in St. Andrew's and earned his master of arts in 1494. It is probable he also studied in Paris. He held various ecclesiastical offices including a benefice in East Lothian, the deanery of Dunkeld, and the position of abbot of Arbroath. In 1501, he was appointed provost of the St. Giles Cathedral in Edinburgh. His final position as bishop of Dunkeld was awarded in 1515.

War and politics changed the focus of Douglas's life. In 1513, the Battle of Flodden resulted in the devastating defeat of the Scots and the death of James IV. Douglas's two brothers were also killed in the battle. Queen Margaret Tudor (widow of James IV and sister of Henry VIII) married Douglas's nephew, the sixth earl of Angus. Thereafter, Douglas was enmeshed in their political agendas and was unable to concentrate on his religious writings.

Numerous events tarnished Douglas's career. In 1515, with the queen's intervention, he was granted the bishopric of Dunkeld. There was strong political opposition and Douglas was accused of irregularities in obtaining benefices. He was imprisoned for nearly a year and only released after intercession by the pope. Douglas subsequently became further entrenched in the politics of his brother and sister-in-law, and thus a part of what was known as the "English party" in Scotland. In 1521, he requested aid from Henry VIII. The next year, the Scottish Lords of Council accused Douglas of high treason and he permanently lost his position as bishop of Dunkeld. He was sentenced to exile and died of the plague in England in September 1522.

Douglas's *Palice of Honour* was an allegorical piece modeled on Chaucer's HOUSE OF FAME. Although it was probably finished in 1501, it was not printed until ca. 1553 in London; another printing took place in Edinburgh in 1579. The piece is dedicated to James IV and was designed for a courtly audience. This DREAM VISION depicts the narrator entering on a pilgrimage to the "Palice of Honour." On the way he learns about moral governance. He is also given a book to translate from the goddess Venus.

Douglas's other two major poems are less significant and there is some question as to whether Douglas authored them. *King Hart* was first printed in 1786 and is similar to the allegory *EVERYMAN*. King Hart surrounds himself with his five servitors (the senses) as well as Queen Plesaunce and Foresight. After being taken hostage by Queen Plesaunce, he is forced to recognize his own humanity. The other poem attributed to Douglas, called *Conscience,* is a four-stanza conceit about the avarice of churchmen.

Douglas's most important work was his translation of Virgil's *Aeneid*. Douglas was the first to translate classical poetry into the English vernacular. Additionally, he used colloquial Scottish phrases along with the poetic language. The translation itself is in heroic couplets and each book is prefaced by an original prologue complete with discussions of Virgil's poetry and style. In three of the books, he also provides passages of seasons and landscape descriptions.

Gavin Douglas's three allegorical poems along with his brilliant translation of the *Aeneid* make him a significant figure in medieval literature.

Bibliography

Douglas, Gavin. *Selections from Gavin Douglas.* With an introduction, notes, and glossary by David F. C. Coldwell. Oxford: Clarendon Press, 1964.

Bawcutt, Priscilla J., ed. *The Shorter Poems of Gavin Douglas.* 2nd ed. Edinburgh: Scottish Text Society, 2003.

Gray, Douglas. "Gavin Douglas and 'The Gret Prynce Eneas,' " *Essays in Criticism* 51 (2001): 18–35.

Parkinson, David. "The Farce of Modesty in Gavin Douglas's 'The Palis of Honoure,' " *Philological Quarterly* 70 (1991): 13–26.

Scheps, Walter, and Looney, J Anna. *Middle Scots Poets: A Reference Guide to James I of Scotland, Robert Henryson, William Dunbar, and Gavin Douglas.* Boston: G. K. Hall, 1986.

Malene A. Little

Dream of Rhonabwy, The (*Breudwyt Rhonobwy*) (ca. 1220)

The Dream of Rhonabwy is an early 13th-century Welsh prose tale found among the tales of the *MABINOGION* in the 14th-century manuscript known as the *Red Book of Hergest.* Other manuscripts of the *Mabinogion* do not contain the tale. *The Dream of Rhonabwy* is a satirical look at contemporary Welsh society, contrasting the warriors of Rhonabwy's time with the gigantic heroes of the age of King ARTHUR. Its structure follows the illogical structure of an actual dream.

The tale is set during the reign of Madog ap Maredudd, prince of Powys (ca. 1160). It begins when Iorweth, Madog's brother, is outlawed, and a band of warriors is sent off to find him. Rhonabwy is among this band. They spend the night in the house of Heilyn Goch ("the Red"), but the filthy bedding he is given makes it impossible for Rhonabwy to sleep. He chooses to lie on a yellow oxskin instead, and during the night has a DREAM VISION of King Arthur. Rhonabwy finds the giant Arthur at his court at Rhuyd-y-Groes on the Severn. The king is amused at the thought that Britain in later days is in the care of fellows as puny as Rhonabwy. Arthur is reminded that he is due to fight the Battle of Badon at noon. Rhonabwy goes with the armies to Badon, where Arthur proceeds to play a game of *gwyddbwyll* (a Welsh board game related to chess) against Owain, son of Urien. A group of squires enter to complain that Arthur's men are killing Owain's ravens. When Arthur refuses to stop them, Owain gives orders that his standard be raised, and another group of squires complains that now the ravens are killing Arthur's troops. The battle ends when Arthur crushes the golden game pieces. Arthur then grants his enemies a two-week truce, and a group of bards sings Arthur's praise in an incomprehensible language. Arthur decides to spend the night in Cornwall, and as the army prepares to follow him there, the noise they make awakens Rhonabwy, who has been asleep for three days and nights.

The Dream of Rhonabwy is an enigmatic poem, and seems to satirize the Arthurian age as well as the writer's contemporaries. Perhaps it also satirizes literary conventions, in particular bardic poetry. The writer was a literary man who consciously composed the story as a written text: He ends the poem with a colophon stating that the tale was never recited aloud (as traditional tales were), but must instead be read. Scholars have proposed that the dream on the oxhide may suggest the writer's familiarity with Virgil or with GEOFFREY OF MONMOUTH. Others have related it to the Irish tradition of the *tarbhfheis* or "bull-sleep," illustrated in the Irish tale of *Dá Derga's Hostel.* According to this custom, a man sleeps on a bull's hide and has a spell of truth chanted, and whoever he sees in his dream is destined to be the next king of Tara. Through the Norman and Welsh connections with Ireland after their invasion of the country in 1169, the author of *The Dream of Rhonabwy* may have become aware of such customs. This Irish connection also suggests a later date for the composition of the tale than immediately after the reign of Madog, even though the satirical effect would be diminished the later the tale was composed.

Bibliography

Breeze, Andrew. *Medieval Welsh Literature.* Dublin: Four Courts Press, 1997.

Jones, Gwyn, and Thomas Jones, trans. *The Mabinogion.* 2nd ed. London: Dent, 1974.

Richards, G. M., ed. *Breudwyt Rhonabwy.* Cardiff: University of Wales Press, 1948.

Dream of the Rood, The (ca. eighth century)

Perhaps the best-known of the religious poems and sermons that make up the 10th-century OLD ENGLISH manuscript called the VERCELLI BOOK, *The Dream of the Rood* is a DREAM VISION (the oldest such poem in English), in which a speaker relates a remarkable dream wherein the *rood,* the cross on which Christ was crucified, takes life and speaks.

The poem begins as the narrator describes his vision of a gold-bedecked cross that tells the dreamer its life story: Born in a forest, the cross was cut down and transformed into an instrument of torture. Christ, depicted in the poem as a bold young warrior who mounts the cross of his own will as an act of courage, is hung upon it. The cross describes its desire to defend Christ against those who want to kill him, but is prevented from doing so. It laments bitterly the way the crowd mocked both of them—himself and Christ. Thus Christ is pictured as an Anglo-Saxon warrior lord, and the cross as one of his retainers, bound by Germanic custom to defend his lord and avenge his death.

Christ is buried, as is the cross, but it is later found, resurrected as it were, by St. Helene, and now it has its place in glory. Just as Mary redeemed womankind after Eve's fall, so the cross has redeemed all trees after the first tree's fruit damned mankind. And now, the cross tells the dreamer, all may be saved because of him who suffered on the rood. It commands the dreamer to tell others of his vision.

The poem ends as the speaker, inspired by the good news of the dream, prays joyfully and with new hope to the King of Glory, with whom he hopes to spend eternity because of what the cross has told him.

It appears that *The Dream of the Rood* was a well-known poem in its own day, and that it likely predates the manuscript in which it is preserved. Parts of the rood's speech appear carved in runic letters on the famous Ruthwell Cross, now at Dumfries in southern Scotland, a cross produced in the early eighth century. The silver reliquary known as the Brussels Cross, made to hold a piece of the true cross sent to Alfred the Great by Pope Marinus in 884, also is inscribed with a quotation from *The Dream of the Rood.* These references suggest that the poem may have been known and circulating as early as the eighth century. Alternatively, they may suggest that the poem was a redaction of an earlier original quoted in the runic inscription, or that the poet incorporated the earlier inscribed verses into his own work.

Having an inanimate object speak is a device typical of Old English RIDDLES. The Germanic elements of the poem also extend, as mentioned, to the depiction of Christ and of the cross itself, which ironically, as a Germanic retainer, can only obey its lord by *not* defending him. But the poem is thoroughly Christian as well, and may be the best available illustration of the blending of the two cultures in Anglo-Saxon England.

Bibliography

Alexander, Michael. *The Earliest English Poems.* 3rd ed. New York: Penguin, 1991.

Clemoes, Peter. "King and Creation at the Crucifixion: The Contribution of Native Tradition to the 'Dream of the Rood' 50-6a," in *Heroes and Heroines in Medieval English Literature,* edited by Leo Carruthers. Cambridge: Brewer, 1994, 31–43.

Fleming, John. "*The Dream of the Rood* and Anglo-Saxon Monasticism," *Traditio* 22 (1966): 43–72.

Krapp, George E., ed. *The Vercelli Book.* Anglo-Saxon Poetic Records 2. New York: Columbia University Press, 1932.

Pigg, Daniel. " 'The Dream of the Rood' in Its Discursive Context: Apocalypticism as Determinant of Form and Treatment," *English Language Notes* 29, no. 2 (June 1992): 13–22.

dream vision (dream allegory)

The dream vision was a favorite genre of medieval narrative poetry, in which a narrator falls asleep and dreams what becomes the main body of the story. Often the dream was in the form of an ALLEGORY, or was otherwise enigmatic, and called for interpretation on the part of the reader. Dream visions might be serious moral or religious tracts like ALANUS DE INSULIS's *Complaint of Nature* (ca. 1165), or might be comic or romantic secular love poems like CHAUCER's *HOUSE OF FAME* (ca. 1379), or allegorical political debates like the 14th-century MIDDLE ENGLISH poem in ALLITERATIVE VERSE *WINNER AND WASTER,* or perhaps even satirical, like the third book of *The Lamentations of Matheolus* (ca. 1295), containing a vision of heaven where married men receive the highest honor because of the great travail they have in this world. But within this wide variance of form and content, medieval dream visions generally have certain important elements in common.

First, dream visions are written in the first person. The narrator becomes the dreamer, and relates the story as his own dream experience. Sometimes the dreamer is the protagonist of the dream fiction, but sometimes he is merely an observer, as is the dreamer of Chaucer's *BOOK OF THE DUCHESS* (ca. 1369). Second, the dream itself depicts what Katherine Lynch calls a liminal experience (1988, 47), one in which the dreamer crosses a border into a supernatural or mystical realm that reflects in some way on the world he has left and must return to. Thus the narrator of Chaucer's *Parliament of Fowls* (ca. 1382) visits the Temple of Venus and the garden of the goddess Natura, and the dreamer of *Pearl* has a paradisal vision of his lost Pearl's participation in the train of the Virgin Mary. Third, the dream contains an important lesson or is in some way instructive for the dreamer: Often the dreamer is presented in a state of melancholy or some other mental confusion before he falls asleep, suggesting that he has some unresolved difficulty that the dream will help him work out. Thus the dreamer in *The Parliament of Fowls* begins by reading a book in order to learn a "certain thing," but falls asleep, and the dream seems intended as an answer to his problem.

Many dream visions include other common elements. Often the dreamer is naïve or obtuse, as the narrator of Chaucer's *Book of the Duchess* is unaware of the implications of the things he hears from the Black Knight in his dream, or the narrator of *The Parliament of Fowls* goes back to reading after his vision, oblivious to his dream's message. Many times the dreamer is accompanied by a guide or mentor, as, for example, Chaucer's narrator is carried away by a talkative Eagle in *The House of Fame,* or guided by Scipio Africanus in *The Parliament of Fowls.*

The dream serves at least two significant functions for the poet. First, it provides a frame for the narrative, and thereby allows the writer to explore different levels of narration, and, further, to examine the role of the narrator and his relationship with the narration. It becomes a self-reflexive genre, as at the end of Machaut's *Fonteinne Amoureuse* (ca. 1360–62), when the narrator says he will go back and write down the dream he has just had. On a deeper level, the dream itself acts as a real dream might for a modern psychoanalyst—it explores the interiority of the narrator's mind, suggesting perhaps that the troubled narrator must look inside himself to find the solutions to the dilemmas that plague him. Nowhere is this more manifest than in Langland's *Piers Plowman* (ca. 1377), where, in the middle passūs, the dreamer (Will) engages in debates with allegorical figures of Wit, Study, Reason, and Imaginitive—attributes of his own mind.

While the significance of dreams is attested to in ancient literature, and Joseph's interpretations of Pharoah's dreams in the book of Genesis would have been familiar to medieval writers, the more direct inspiration for dream vision narratives is surely Cicero's *Somnium Scipionis,* or "The Dream of Scipio," popular in the Middle Ages through the fourth-century commentary on the text by Macrobius. Indeed, Chaucer acknowledges this inspiration at the beginning of *The Parliament of Fowls,* when his narrator falls asleep reading Cicero's text. Macrobius delineates three meaningful kinds of dreams: the vision (*visio*) or prophetic vision, in which what we dream actually comes true; the oracular dream (*oraculum*), in which an authority figure appears and gives us a message; and the enigmatic dream (*somnium*), which reveals a truth but in a veiled manner that must be interpreted. This last, the *somnium,* became the perfect model for the dream vision, since poets could create an ambiguous narrative that required some thoughtful interpretation by the reader or audience. This explains in part why many dream narratives are open-ended or, in Chaucer's case, unfinished, like *The House of Fame.* In particular if the narrator is presented as obtuse, the author was inviting the reader to complete the understanding of the poem.

The other most significant textual influence on the dream narrative was the very popular 13th-century *Roman de la Rose* by Guillaume de Lorris and Jean de Meun. While most previous dream visions had been philosophical or religious, the *Roman de la Rose* initiated the vogue for love-visions in the form of dreams. Typically these were set in a spring landscape, where the narrator falls asleep to the singing of the birds or the babbling of a brook, and awakens, perhaps in another beautiful garden. Chaucer's love visions, more introspective than most, present the dreamer falling asleep while reading a book.

Other dream visions of note are the 14th-century English *Parliament of the Three Ages,* and two poems by so-called Scottish Chaucerians

Gavin DOUGLAS (*The Palace of Honor*) and William DUNBAR (*The Thrissil and the Rois*). There is even an early example in OLD ENGLISH—*The DREAM OF THE ROOD*. With the possible exception of the ROMANCE, the dream vision was probably the most popular genre in medieval Europe.

Bibliography

Hieatt, Constance B. *The Realism of the Dream Vision: The Poetic Exploration of the Dream-Experience in Chaucer and His Contemporaries.* De Proprietatibus Litteraum, Series Practica 2. The Hague: Mouton, 1967.

Lynch, Kathryn. *The High Medieval Dream Vision.* Stanford, Calif.: Stanford University Press, 1988.

Quinn, William A., ed. *Chaucer's Dream Visions and Shorter Poems.* New York: Garland, 1999.

Russell, J. Stephen. *The English Dream Vision: Anatomy of a Form.* Columbus: Ohio State University Press, 1988.

Spearing, A. C. *Medieval Dream Poetry.* Cambridge: Cambridge University Press, 1976.

Du Fu (Tu Fu) (712–770)

By general consensus Du Fu has been recognized as China's greatest poet since the ninth century, though he was unsuccessful both as a poet and as a civil servant during his own lifetime. Often called the "poet-historian," Du Fu delineates, in realistic detail, Chinese life during and after the disastrous An Lushan (An Lu-shan) rebellion of 755. More serious and socially conscious than his contemporary and friend LI BAI (Li Po), Du Fu presents a devout Confucian view in his poetry, in contrast with the Taoism of Li Bai.

Du Fu was born in Xianyang (Hsianyang), in what is now the Henan (Honan) province. He was the grandson of an important court poet (Du Shenyan), and so received the Confucian education that would have been afforded a member of a scholarly family. However he failed the imperial civil service examination in 736, and spent the following years in poverty, wandering about China's northern provinces. In 745, during his wanderings, he met Li Bai, and was much taken with the older poet. The two remained lifelong friends, despite their temperamental differences, as poems like Du Fu's "Dreaming of Li Bai" attest.

Du Fu returned to Xi'an (Chang-an), the imperial capital, in 746, to try again to achieve an official post, but once more failed the examinations. In 755, the northeastern provinces rose in rebellion, led by the general An Lushan. The emperor, Xuanzong (Hsuan-tsung), was driven from the capital, and Du Fu was trapped behind enemy lines. Some of his early poems describe his waiting for news of the war and hearing only of the defeats of the imperial forces. Eventually he was able to make his way through the lines to the temporary capital at Fengxiang (Feng-hsiang). After the emperor abdicated in favor of his son Suzong (Su Tsung), Du Fu, in the breakdown of the imperial civil service system, was finally given an official court post by the new emperor.

When the emperor succeeded in retaking the capital, however, Du Fu was given a minor post in one of the provinces, at Hua-zhou—a post he was very unhappy with. Ultimately he resigned and returned, with his family, to a life of traveling, first to the northwest and then to Chengdu, the capital of Sichuan (Szechuan), where he settled for a while in 760 and seems to have enjoyed the patronage of Yen Wu. After 765, however, Du Fu went back to a life of wandering. He traveled down the Yangtze River and finally to the lakes region of central China in the final year of his life. It was during these last years of traveling that he produced most of his poetry.

Du Fu's poetry stems from his own experiences of poverty, war, and disappointment, and the tone and emotional range of the individual poems tend to reflect the stage of his life during which they were written. Indeed Du Fu encouraged such an interpretation, publishing his poems in chronological arrangements in their earliest editions—a practice continued in subsequent printings of his poetry. In general the poems display the Confucian ethical emphasis on family, society, and the state, and, in particular, Du Fu is known for his sympathetic depiction of the human suffering caused by the An Lushan revolt. There is also a tremendous variety and range in Du Fu's poems both in style (he ranges from the colloquial to the formal) and subject matter (he may write about gardens, about paintings, about his family, about the defeat of imperial armies). But one likely reason for Du Fu's continuing appeal is his portrayal of the details of personal life, as in his poem "Jiang Village," which describes his reunion with his family during the time of war and of his service of the emperor:

From west of the towering ochre clouds
The sun's rays descend to the plain.
In the brushwood gate birds raise a racket:
From a thousand miles the traveler comes
home.

Wife and children are amazed I survived,
When surprise settles, they wipe away
tears . . .

(Owen 1996, 423)

Unappreciated during his own life, the depth and complexity of Du Fu's poetry and the keen intellect behind it began to be recognized in the early ninth century. His influence on subsequent Chinese poetry was immense, even greater than that of Li Bai, and his work is considered much more representative of the classic poetry of the TANG DYNASTY than that of his great contemporary.

Bibliography

Chou, Eva Shan. *Reconsidering Tu Fu: Literary Greatness and Cultural Context.* Cambridge: Cambridge University Press, 1996.

Hawks, David. *A Little Primer of Tu Fu.* Oxford, U.K.: Oxford University Press, 1967.

Owen, Stephen, ed. and trans. *An Anthology of Chinese Literature: Beginnings to 1911.* New York: Norton, 1996.

Du Mu (Tu Mu) (803–852)

One of the leading poets of the late TANG DYNASTY, Du Mu was best known for his *jueju*—brief quatrains that generally focused on sensual descriptions that were popular in the second half of the Tang dynasty. Sometimes called *Xiao Tu* (Little Tu) to distinguish him from the more famous DU FU, Du Mu wrote a range of longer poetry as well, and also wrote prose essays. He was a successful bureaucrat, a painter, and a calligrapher, but the image he creates for himself in his poetry is that of an epicurean, enjoying drink, women, and the beauties of nature.

Du Mu was born in the Tang city of Xi'an (Changan). His father was a historical scholar, and Du Mu was well educated in the Confucian classics. He passed the *JINSHI* civil service examination in 827, and held a long series of minor posts. The political intrigues of his time no doubt contributed to his inability to attain any higher appointments in the bureaucracy, but that failure frustrated Du Mu, and he often shows his dissatisfaction in his poetry, and also in letters that he wrote to high-ranking officials in the government, criticizing military and domestic policy. He was appointed to his highest post, secretariat drafter, in 852, shortly before his death.

Du Mu is particularly famous for his *jueju.* These were poems of four lines of either five or seven syllables. The form was particularly suited to express a brief, fleeting emotion, or to depict the very essence of an experience or a scene. As such, it has been compared to the later Japanese form, the TANKA. Each line, at least according to later practitioners of the form, had a specific function: The *jueju* contained an opening line, a second line to develop the opening, a turning point in the third line, and a conclusion in the fourth. Thus in one of Du Mu's quatrains, "Sent in Parting," the first line makes an opening generalization, the second sets that concept in a specific scene, the third focuses on a new mood created by the personified candle, and the last leaves a final impression of sorrow:

Great love may seem like none at all:
Wine before us, we only know that smiles
won't come.
The tallow candle has a heart—it grieves at
parting,
In our place drips tears until the break of day.

(Burton 1990, 286)

It has been suggested that the beautiful images Du Mu created in his poetry were something of an escape from the bleak situation of the late Tang imperial government. In a world where provincial generals were beyond imperial control and the court was dominated by the deception of those in power, the art of poetry had an appealing permanence and truth for late Tang poets. Du Mu, in brief lyric utterances, creates a beauty that transcends the reality of his official life.

Bibliography

Burton, R. F., trans. *Plantains in the Rain: Selected Chinese Poems of Du Mu*. London: Wellsweep, 1990.

Graham, H. C., trans. *Poems of the Late T'ang*. Harmondsworth, U.K.: Penguin, 1965.

Watson, Burton, ed. and trans. *The Columbia Book of Chinese Poetry: From Early Times to the Thirteenth Century*. New York: Columbia University Press, 1984.

Dunbar, William (ca. 1460–ca. 1515)

Perhaps the most notable of the Scottish "makars" or poets writing under the influence of CHAUCER, Dunbar was a master of a great variety of poetic forms, themes, and styles, varying his technique from the formal, courtly, and rhetorically ornate in a poem like *The Golden Targe,* to the colloquial, coarse, or vulgar in a poem like *The Tretis of the Tua Mariit Wemen and the Wedo.* A cleric as well as a courtier, Dunbar left some 80 short poems displaying a remarkable versatility and stylistic virtuosity.

William Dunbar was born in Lithian in Scotland, apparently related to some branch of the family of the earls of Dunbar and March. He attended St. Andrews University where he received a master's degree in 1479. We know nothing of the years immediately following his completion of this degree. It has been suggested that Dunbar may have been a friar, though there is little sound evidence of that. He does seem to have moved in court circles and have traveled in connection with the court: In 1492 he is known to have been on a diplomatic mission to Denmark. He seems also to have begun making a reputation for himself as a poet as well. One of his most scurrilous poems, his poem of mutual abuse called *FLYTYNG* that he wrote with Glasgow scholar Walter Kennedy, was probably written about 1500.

By 1500 Dunbar was a fixture at the court of King James IV, the first Scottish king to act as patron of the arts. James granted Dunbar an annual salary in 1500, and Dunbar remained at court, not only as a court poet but also as a royal secretary and diplomat (as his trip to Denmark would suggest). He traveled to London in 1501 in connection with the marriage being arranged between James and Margaret Tudor, daughter of English king Henry VII—a marriage Dunbar formally commemorated with his courtly allegorical poem *The Thrissill and the Rois.* Dunbar also most likely served the court as a chaplain—he received holy orders in 1503 and is known to have presided over his first mass in 1504. Dunbar served James faithfully until 1513. The last record we have of Dunbar is from May of that year, when he drew out his annual pension for the last time. In September of 1513, James was killed at the Battle of Flodden in his ill-advised attack on England. Some have suggested that Dunbar may have fallen with his sovereign in the battle, though his age would have made that unlikely. Still, there is no record of him after Flodden. He has been suggested as the author of a poem written to James's widow in 1517, but this is merely conjecture. He was certainly long dead by 1530 when Sir David LINDSAY lamented him in *The Testament of the Papyngo.*

The variety of Dunbar's poetic output is remarkable. His best-known courtly poems include his early ornate poem *The Golden Targe,* written in the complex nine-line stanza borrowed from the COMPLAINT in Chaucer's *ANELIDA AND ARCITE.* At the end of the poem Dunbar praises Chaucer, as well as LYDGATE and GOWER. Another poem in the high courtly style and owing a great deal to Chaucer is *The Thrissill and the Rois* (1503), an epithalamium (a poem celebrating a wedding) on the marriage of James and Margaret. The poem uses Chaucerian RHYME ROYAL stanzas, and begins with the poet being awakened by May, who forces him to get up and takes him to an allegorical garden of love, where he witnesses three parliaments (of beasts, birds, and flowers), all presided over by the goddess Natura and each including an allegorical representative of the king himself, who in each case receives advice from Nature. The poem owes a great deal to Chaucer's *PARLIAMENT OF FOWLS*, as well as to the prologue to his *LEGEND OF GOOD WOMEN*.

Dunbar's comic poems owe something to Chaucer as well, but also to the everyday life of the Scottish court, for Dunbar often includes real courtiers in his poetry. One of his well-known poems, "Sir Thomas Norny," burlesques a courtly style by presenting the court jester as if he were a knight. The poem, written in TAIL RHYME stanzas, is a send-up of Chaucer's *TALE OF SIR THOPAS*. Dunbar's longest poem, *The Tretis of the Tua Mariit Wemen and the Wedo* (*Treatise of the Two Married Women and the Widow*), also owes something to Chaucer, especially *The WIFE OF BATH'S TALE* and *The MERCHANT'S TALE*. The poem tells the story of a man who, from a hiding place in a garden, is able to overhear a conversation among three women, each of whom discusses the difficulties of marriage in colloquial, frank, and sometimes obscene language.

Some 20 of Dunbar's extant poems are begging poems, at least one of which seems directly inspired by Chaucer's popular *COMPLAINT TO HIS EMPTY PURSE*. Only a few of the poems are religious—surprisingly few considering the fact that Dunbar was a priest. But his trilogy of poems on Christ's nativity, passion, and resurrection are memorable—particularly the last poem, which, like LANGLAND or the MYSTERY PLAYS, presents the conquering Christ triumphantly harrowing hell. The first stanza proclaims Christ the champion after battle with the "dragon black," breaking the gates of hell, causing the devils to tremble, and ransoming us with his blood:

Done is a batell on the dragon blak;
Our campion Chryst confoundit hes his force:
The getis of hell ar brokin with a crak,
The signe triumphall rasit is of the croce,
The divillis trymmilles with hiddous voce,
The saulis ar borrowit and to the bliss can go,
Chryst with his blud our ransonis dois indoce:
Surrexit Dominus de sepulchro.

(Kinsley 1979, 11)

The stanzas are Chaucerian rhyme royal, with a Latin refrain: Repeated at the end of each stanza, the refrain means simply "The Lord has risen from the tomb."

Some of Dunbar's poems are presented as moral or philosophical reflections. His most famous poem, often called *Lament for the Makars*, is a case in point. That title is inadequate, since the poem deals with a number of other subjects, but does include a lament for departed poets. The poem is a meditation on mortality. Nothing on earth is secure, and all earthly estates, power, and fame are transient. Knights, clerks, and yes, poets as well, all go down to death—each four-line stanza ends with the refrain *Timor mortis conturbat me* ("The fear of death troubles me"). Significantly, "the noble Chaucer" appears in line 50 of the 100-line poem, the emphatic midpoint of the text, a tribute to Dunbar's most important poetic influence.

Dunbar left poems in a great variety of styles, though he seems to have generally written in a plainer style as he grew older. His legacy is rich, diverse, and complex, and he remains one of the most engaging of medieval Scottish poets.

Bibliography

Bawkutt, Priscilla. *Dunbar the Makar.* Oxford: Clarendon Press, 1992.

Kinsley, James, ed. *The Poems of William Dunbar.* Oxford: Clarendon Press, 1979.

Reis, Edmund. *William Dunbar.* Boston: Twayne, 1979.

Ross, Ian Simpson. *William Dunbar.* Leiden: E. J. Brill, 1981.

Duns Scotus, John (ca. 1265–1308)

Known as the Subtle Doctor, the Franciscan friar Duns Scotus was one of the most influential and significant philosophers and theologians of the later Middle Ages. His elaborate and nuanced discussions promoted the importance of love and of will at the expense of reason; of philosophical "realism" that stressed the objective existence of universals; and of "intuitive cognition" through which human beings understood individuals. Scotus also was instrumental in putting forth the doctrine of the Immaculate Conception of the Virgin Mary, a position that earned him his other popular nickname—the "Marian Doctor."

John Duns Scotus was born in Scotland, probably in or near the village of Duns close to the English border. He entered the Franciscan friary at Dumfries in 1278, and in 1281 took his friar's vows. Between 1281 and 1291, he may have been attending universities in Scotland and England. Some have suggested that he attended Oxford and even Paris during this interval, but no one really knows. In 1291 he was ordained a priest. It may have been after this that he began his studies at Oxford. At some point in the 1290s it seems likely he was studying in Paris with the well-known scholars James of Quarcheto and Gonsalvus of Spain. He may have been lecturing at Cambridge between 1297 and 1300, but he is known to have lectured at Oxford between 1300 and 1302, specifically on the very influential *Sentences* of PETER LOMBARD. He produced his most important work, the *Oxford Commentary* (the *Opus Oxoniense*) sometime between 1297 and 1300. Probably by the autumn of 1302, he was in Paris, where he continued his lectures on the *Sentences.* A shorter commentary survives from this period: The *Reportata Parisiensia* (ca. 1304) continues his commentary on Peter Lombard, but this briefer and sketchier text is not in his own hand. Rather, it is a "report" in the sense of being apparently compiled from his students' lecture notes.

In June of 1303 Scotus and some 80 other foreign scholars were forced to leave Paris when they refused to sign a petition condemning Pope Boniface VIII and supporting the French king Philip the Fair in his dispute with the pope. Allowed to return to the university in the autumn of 1304, Scotus was named *magisterium* or master, recommended by his old mentor Gonsalvus. In 1307, however, Scotus was sent to Cologne to teach at the Franciscan school there. Some have speculated that Scotus's views on the Immaculate Conception made him a figure of controversy; he was also later condemned for an emphasis on human freedom that verged on the Pelagian heresy, and those views may have made him unpopular. In any case, Scotus left Paris in 1307 to teach in Cologne, and never returned. He died there on November 8, 1308.

In addition to the two commentaries on the *Sentences,* Scotus is credited with a large number of other works, but many of these texts are thought to be spurious by modern scholars. It is fairly certain that Scotus wrote the commentaries on Aristotle and Porphyry attributed to him. The complexity of his thought, the uncertainty of the manuscripts attributed to him, and his intricate, convoluted sentences (which go on at great length, and are built from qualifications within qualifications) make it extremely difficult to determine or to understand the system of his thought. The chief source for our understanding is his *Oxford Commentary.* From this it is clear that his ideas about epistemology and metaphysics are chiefly Aristotelian, but influenced by the Arabic commentator Avicenna. However, Scotus's emphasis on voluntarism, on the primacy and freedom of the will, is directly opposed to Avicenna. Some of his thought is based on that of Thomas AQUINAS, including his defense of the "realist" position about universals. But his theory of intuitive cognition, by which the mind may directly know individual things rather than knowing them only through indirect "abstractive" cognition, is in direct contrast with Aquinas, and anticipates later "nominalist" philosophers like WILLIAM OF OCKHAM.

Significant in his own right but also as a transitional figure between the great systematizing philosophers of the 13th century, like Aquinas, and the skeptics of the 14th century, like Ockham, Scotus may be best remembered unjustly for being the inspiration of Milton's coinage of the word Dunce. In later centuries, Scotus's subtle metaphysics inspired the poetry and philosophy of Gerard Manly Hopkins. And in 1854, his argument for the Virgin's special status finally won the day as Pope Pius IX declared the Immaculate Conception an official doctrine of the Catholic Church.

Bibliography

Cross, Richard. *Duns Scotus.* Oxford: Oxford University Press, 1999.

Frank, William A., and Allan B. Wolter. *Duns Scotus: Metaphysician.* Lafayette, Ind.: Purdue University Press, 1995.

Williams, Thomas, ed. *The Cambridge Companion to Duns Scotus.* Cambridge: Cambridge University Press, 2003.

Wolter, Allan B. *Duns Scotus on the Will and Morality.* Washington, D.C.: The Catholic University of America Press, 1986.

———. *Duns Scotus: Philosophical Writings.* Indianapolis: Hackett Publishing Company, 1987.

———. *The Philosophical Theology of John Duns Scotus.* Edited by Marilyn McCord Adams. Ithaca, N.Y.: Cornell University Press, 1990.

E

Earl of Toulouse, The (*Erl of Tolous*) (ca. 1350–1400)

The *Earl of Toulouse* is a late 14th-century verse ROMANCE written in the dialect of the northern East Midlands. The narrator identifies the text as a "Breton *LAI*," though it has been suggested that the narrative has little in common with those MIDDLE ENGLISH texts typically thought of as Breton *lais*—*SIR LAUNFAL*, *SIR ORFEO*, and CHAUCER's *WIFE OF BATH'S TALE* and *FRANKLIN'S TALE*. Although nothing is known of the poem's author, the moralistic tone and language of the romance have led some to suggest he was a cleric. The poem is written in 102 12-line stanzas rhyming *aabccbddbeeb*, in tetrameter (four-beat) lines, except for the b-rhyme lines, which are trimeter (three-beat)—a form known as the TAIL-RHYME stanza, parodied by Chaucer in his *TALE OF SIR THOPAS*.

The poem tells the story of Sir Barnard, the earl of Toulouse, and his love for Dame Beulybon (her name combines belle and bon—"beautiful" and "good"), the wife of Emperor Dyoclysyan. The poem opens as the emperor unjustly seizes some of Sir Barnard's lands. Dame Beulybon tries unsuccessfully to mediate the dispute, and in the ensuing battle, Sir Barnard kills 60,000 of the emperor's troops and takes prisoner his favorite, Sir Trylabas. Sir Trylabas negotiates his freedom by agreeing to arrange a meeting between Sir Barnard and Dame Beulybon, with whom the earl has fallen in love. Disguised as a hermit, Sir Barnard meets with the lady and obtains a ring as a token of her regard. Returning from the tryst, Sir Barnard is ambushed by Trylabas and two other knights, but he is able to kill them.

Now the tale moves toward its crisis. The emperor is away, and leaves Dame Beulybon under the protection of two of his knights, who attempt to seduce her. When they are rebuffed, they connive to dishonor the empress. They convince a young "carver" named Sir Antore, presumably a squire, to hide naked in the empress's bedchamber. When they subsequently burst in and find him, they slay him immediately and accuse the empress of adultery. When the emperor returns, he is forced by the demands of justice to burn his wife at the stake unless a champion can be found to defend her in a trial by combat.

Sir Barnard, of course, answers the call. But first, disguised as a monk, he visits the empress and hears her confession, to be assured that she is, in fact, not guilty of the charges. Convinced of her innocence, Barnard champions her in the lists, defeats her accusers, and the two wicked knights burn at the stake in her stead. The emperor, grateful for his wife's reprieve, returns Barnard's lands and makes him the royal steward. After three years, the emperor dies, Barnard is elected his successor, marries Dame Beulybon, and, over the next 23 years, has 15 children with her.

More than simply an entertainment, *The Earl of Toulouse* also examines the chivalric code, showing the Emperor in particular as falling short of the ideal, and in so doing creating an atmosphere in which his knights' corruption reflects that of their leader. But truth prevails, and ultimately the true chivalry of Barnard and the empress return the kingdom to righteousness.

The story has analogues in several languages, and the folklore motif of the "accused Queen" has been shown to be widespread. Some scholars have suggested a relationship between this story and that of the apocryphal scriptural tale of *Susanna and the Elders,* of which there was a contemporary Middle English version. In addition a number of historical analogues have been cited as possible sources for the tale, the most convincing of which is the case of Empress Judith, second wife of Louis the Pious. In 831, Judith was accused of adultery with Bernard I, count of Barcelona and Toulouse. She was to be tried by combat, but no accuser appeared at her trial, and she was, therefore, acquitted. The names and circumstances of Judith's story make it not unlikely that this historical incident provided the ultimate source for the romance.

Bibliography

Cabaniss, Allen. "Judith Augusta and Her Time," *University of Mississippi Studies in English* 10 (1969): 67–109.

Fellows, Jennifer, ed. *Of Love and Chivalry: An Anthology of Middle English Romance.* London: Everyman, 1992.

Laskaya, Anne, and Eve Salisbury, eds. *The Middle English Breton Lays.* Kalamazoo: Published for TEAMS in association with the University of Rochester by Medieval Institute Publications, Western Michigan University, 1995.

Reilly, Robert. "*The Earl of Toulouse:* A Structure of Honor," *Mediaeval Studies* 37 (1975): 515–523.

Ecclesiastical History of the English People The Venerable Bede (731)

The *Historia ecclesiastica gentis Anglorum (Ecclesiastical History of the English People)* is the most important work by the Anglo-Saxon scholar, the Venerable BEDE, a learned eighth-century Northumbrian monk. Writing the five books of his history in Latin, the universal language of Europe at the time for scholarly texts, Bede traces the history of Britain from the time of the Roman invasion through the invasion of the tribes of Angles, Saxons, and Jutes, which Bede dates to 449 C.E., up until Bede's own time.

Bede is most interested in the fortunes of Christianity in Britain, and therefore focuses the early part of his text on the conversion of the Britons, dealing at some length with the Pelagian heresy that was the focus of much of St. AUGUSTINE's polemical writing, and whose founder, Pelagius, was a Briton. Bede then describes the invasion of the pagan Anglo-Saxons (basing this section largely on the work of the sixth-century monk GILDAS), and then begins to relate the fortunes of the seven petty kingdoms of Anglo-Saxon England (Wessex, Sussex, Essex, East Anglia, Mercia, Kent, and Northumbria). This is the low point of the history of the church on the island, until the arrival of a later Saint Augustine, an emissary of Pope GREGORY THE GREAT, who is charged with establishing a church in England. Augustine succeeds in converting King Ethelbert of Kent, and the success of the English church grows steadily from that point.

Perhaps the best-known section of Bede's history is his description of the cowherd CAEDMON, who, divinely inspired to compose a hymn of praise for God's Creation, is the first recorded poet in the English language. A number of manuscripts of Bede's history include the Old English text of Caedmon's hymn alongside Bede's Latin rendition of it.

While Bede was in many ways the first "modern" historian—he questioned the authenticity of his sources and strove to use eyewitness accounts when possible—he also had a clearly didactic purpose, focusing on morality and including a number of SAINTS' LIVES as a part of his text, whose miracles served as evidence of the divinely ordained mission of the English church. Bede is the first historian to date events from the birth of Christ, thereby creating the "B.C." and "A.D." dating system.

In all, more than 150 manuscripts of Bede's history survive, a testament to its widespread popularity and early recognition as a masterpiece. It was translated into OLD ENGLISH at the behest of King ALFRED THE GREAT in the ninth century, and it continues to be the most important historical source for the early Anglo-Saxon period in England.

Bibliography

Blair, Peter Hunter. *The World of Bede.* Cambridge: Cambridge University Press, 1990.

Colgrave, Beretram, and R. A. B. Mynors, eds. *Bede's Ecclesiastical History of the English People.* Oxford: Clarendon Press, 1969.

McClure, Judith, and Roger Collins, ed. *The Ecclesiastical History of the English People; The Greater Chronicle; Bede's Letter to Egbert.* Oxford: Oxford University Press, 1994.

Ward, Benedicta. *The Venerable Bede.* Kalamazoo, Mich.: Cistercian Publications, 1998.

Eckhart, Meister (ca. 1260–1328)

The Dominican teacher Eckhart was one of the most influential thinkers and preachers of his time. Because of his profound spirituality and visionary language, he has often been identified as a mystic, but the label of philosopher and theologian would be more appropriate for him. Between 1275 and 1280, he joined the monastic order of the Dominicans in Erfurt in eastern Germany, studied at Cologne and Paris, and began teaching in Paris in 1293. Shortly before 1298, he was elected prior of the Convent in Erfurt and vicar of the Province of Thuringia. In 1300 Eckhart returned to Paris and gained his master's degree, which allowed him to assume a teaching position (hence the honorary name under which he has been known ever since). In 1303, the members of the Saxon province of his order elected him as their first provincial, or governor, and in 1307, he was appointed vicar of the province of Bohemia. Both appointments required extensive traveling throughout northern Europe. In 1310 the province of Alemannia elected him as their provincial, but the General Chapter of Naples rejected this decision to avoid the accumulation of too many responsibilities on one person. Instead he was sent to Paris again to teach, a very rare honor for any member of the Dominican Order. Two years later Eckhart assumed a position as preacher in Strasbourg where he gained tremendous influence, and where he also came into contact with some important mystical writers, such as Henry Suso, and a number of Dominican nuns in southwest German women's convents. After a series of various posts, Eckhart was sent to teach at the Dominican school in Cologne in 1322, continuing the famous tradition established by his immediate forerunners there, Albertus Magnus and Thomas AQUINAS.

In Cologne, however, Eckhart soon faced serious opposition to his mystical sermons, especially by Archbishop Henry of Virneburg, who opened a lengthy inquisitional trial against him for heresy in 1326. The following year Eckhart appealed to the pope in defense of his case, but in 1328, he died in Avignon at the papal court while awaiting a decision. In 1329 the pope issued the bull *In agro dominico,* in which 28 of 108 propositions by Eckhart, for which he had been accused of heresy by the archbishop of Cologne, were condemned as either heretical, suspicious, or dangerous. The bull, however, also stated that before his death, Eckhart had recanted everything in his writing that might have been construed as heretical in the minds of his readers.

Eckhart is famous for his deeply spiritual sermons, lectures, and treatises, written both in German and in Latin. He exerted a tremendous and long-lasting influence on contemporary philosophers and theologians, and on numerous 19th- and 20th-century thinkers and writers. Many of his thoughts bear surprising similarity with fundamental Buddhist ideas, especially as he deeply probed the meaning of human life and human dignity, and investigated the role of the soul, free will, humility, and of man's relationship with the Godhead. Other questions pondered by Eckhart pertained to the relationship between time and eternity, the issue of transcendentalism and the absolute nothingness, the religious ideal of poverty in spirit, and, above all, the idea of negative theology (God is beyond all human comprehension and can only be approached in negative terms).

Bibliography

Clark, James M. *Meister Eckhart: An Introduction to the Study of His Works with an Anthology of His Sermons.* London: Thomas Nelson and Sons, 1957.

Classen, Albrecht. "Meister Eckhart's Philosophy in the Twenty-first Century," *Mystics Quarterly* 29, no. 1–2 (2003): 6–23.

Meister Eckhart. *Werke.* 2 vols. Text and Translation by Josef Quint. Editing and commentary by Niklaus Largier. Bibliothek des Mittelalters 20. Frankfurt am Main: Deutscher Klassiker Verlag, 1993.

Tobin, Frank J. *Meister Eckhart: Thought and Language.* Philadelphia: University of Pennsylvania Press, 1986.

Albrecht Classen

Edward (ca. 15th–16th century)

The old Scottish folk BALLAD *Edward* is, like many similar ballads (*LORD RANDALL,* for example), a brief and suggestive narrative of domestic tragedy. Structured, like *Lord Randall,* as an increasingly tension-filled dialogue between a mother and son, *Edward* tells the story of the son's murder of his father—an act apparently suborned by the mother herself.

The ballad begins with the mother's question "Why dois your brand sae drap wi bluid,/Edward, Edward,"—why, she wants to know, is there blood on Edward's sword. He evades her question by first claiming that it is his hawk's blood, then that it is the blood of his chestnut horse. When the mother refuses to believe either evasion, Edward reveals that the blood is his father's.

Asked what penance he will perform for the murder, Edward replies that he will sail over the sea. He will leave his towers and his hall, and, as for his wife and children, Edward says that they will have to beg through life. Surprise and shock underscore the climax of the ballad, where, in the powerful final stanza when the materialistic mother asks what he will leave to her, Edward answers that she will have from him only the curse of hell, because of the "counseils" that she gave him—implying that she herself has incited him to the bloody patricide.

Edward was included in Bishop Thomas Percy's *Reliques* (1765). Percy calls the poem a "Scottish ballad" and says that he received it in manuscript from Sir David Dalrymple. It was subsequently included as #13 in Francis Child's great edition of *English and Scottish Popular Ballads* (1882). Variants of the ballad exist in Swedish, Danish, Finnish, and German, but none rivals the English version for suspense, artistic brevity, or shock value.

Bibliography

Child, Francis James, ed. *The English and Scottish Popular Ballads.* 1882–98. Reprint, New York: Cooper Square Publishers, 1965.

Percy, Thomas, ed. *Reliques of Ancient English Poetry.* 3 vols. 1765. Edinburgh: James Nichol, 1858.

Edward III (1312–1377)

Born to King Edward II and his queen, Isabelle of France, at Windsor Castle on November 13, 1312, Edward III reigned for 50 eventful years. The years were filled with both disasters—most notably the losses that occurred with the Hundred Years' War and the tragedy of the BLACK DEATH—and triumphs—most notably improvements to the monarchy, including constitutional developments such as adding a House of Commons to the Parliament, and the military victories experienced at the Battles of Crécy and Poitiers.

In 1325 Edward's mother returned home to France to fulfill diplomatic duties to her brother, the French king Charles IV. While in France she became engaged in an affair with Roger Mortimer of Wigmore, an English baron in exile. The paramours invaded England in September of 1326 and captured Edward II in 1327 (they eventually had the king murdered). In January of 1327 Edward II formally relinquished his reign to his son, Edward III, who was 14 at the time. During the first several years of Edward's reign, he was known as king, but his mother and her lover were *de facto* rulers of England. Their administration was poorly governed and hardly better than that of Edward II. By the end of 1330, however, Edward III had Mortimer arrested, tried, convicted, and executed—all within the span of six weeks; he had his mother confined to her home, but treated to all of the luxuries she had been accustomed to, until her death. Finally Edward could personally rule his kingdom.

Just one year after becoming king, Edward (fulfilling his mother's wishes) married Philippa of Hainault in gratitude for the count of Hainault's assistance to his mother. She was a popular and devoted queen, and together they had many children, including JOHN OF GAUNT and Edward the Black Prince. Philippa died in 1369, and after her death, Edward withdrew from public life and enjoyed the companionship of his young mistress, the despised Alice Perrers, formerly one of Queen Philippa's maids.

When Edward's uncle, Charles IV, died in 1328, Edward, the only surviving grandson of Charles IV's father, Philip IV the Fair, contested Philip of Valois's right to rule France. Edward invaded France and laid claim to the throne, thus beginning what we know as the Hundred Years' War.

Under Edward's reign governmental reforms gave more power to the rising middle class, or Commoners, in Parliament. Parliament formally divided into two houses—the upper house representing the nobility and high clergy and the lower representing the middle class. Edward III established the office of justice of the peace. Chivalric idealism was at its height—as a prince Edward III was educated at his mother's court (his tutor was the famous bibliophile Richard de BURY), where among other things he learned to be a valorous knight, establishing the Order of the Garter in 1348. The tragedy of the bubonic plague, or the Black Death, struck during Edward's reign, killing roughly one-third of England's population during its first occurrence between 1348 and 1350, and striking several more times in the latter half of the century. The plague sparked unpredictable social and economic changes.

The year after the Black Prince died, Edward, who was still grieving, died of a stroke on June 21, 1377, at the age of 65, and was buried at Westminster Abbey. His grandson, RICHARD II, son of the Black Prince, succeeded him. Edward's rule may be considered a success not only because of his victories and valor, but because he overcame obstacles from the preceding administration created by his father and mother, and he restored dignity to the English monarchy.

Under Edward's reign, the English language flourished. For the first time, in 1362, English (rather than French) was formally used in Parliament. Two of the greatest MIDDLE ENGLISH literary works, William LANGLAND'S *PIERS PLOWMAN* and at least two of Geoffrey CHAUCER'S *CANTERBURY TALES* (*The SECOND NUN'S TALE* and *The MONK'S TALE*) appeared during this period. Some of this literary flourishing was the direct result of Edward's patronage: Chaucer received a royal annuity in 1367 and another (in the form of a daily gallon of wine) in 1374. In June of 1374, Edward appointed Chaucer controller of customs, a job he held for 12 years. Chaucer also served in the war in France under the leadership of King Edward (and after his capture was ransomed with the king's contribution), worked as an esquire in Edward III's household, and made several diplomatic trips to the continent during Edward's reign.

Bibliography

Ormrod, W. M. *The Reign of Edward III: Crown and Political Society in England 1327–1377.* New Haven, Conn., and London: Yale University Press, 1990.

Waugh, Scott. *England in the Reign of Edward III.* Cambridge Medieval Textbooks. Cambridge: Cambridge University Press, 1991.

Leslie Johnston

Egil's Saga Snorri Sturluson? (ca. 1230)

One of the longest and most acclaimed of the Icelandic family SAGAS, *Egil's Saga* tells the story of an enigmatic protagonist, Egil, son of Skallagrim. One of Iceland's most famous SKALDIC poets, Egil was a Viking adventurer who at different times in the saga is a drunkard, a killer and warrior, a wanderer, a farmer, and a miser. Narrated, like most of the sagas, in a plain and objective style, the saga creates in its title character one of the most memorable individuals in Old Norse literature.

Many scholars attribute *Egil's Saga* to medieval Iceland's most famous writer, SNORRI STURLUSON (1179–1241), author of *HEIMSKRINGLA* and the

PROSE EDDA. If this is true, then *Egil's Saga* is the only Icelandic saga whose author is known. Snorri was said to have been descended from Egil himself, and, between 1201 and 1206, lived at Borg, where Egil had his farm. Like most Icelandic family sagas, *Egil's Saga* evinces a serious interest in the history of Iceland during its early years, and features a prolonged feud between the protagonist and another character, though the feud in Egil's saga has a unique twist: It is waged against members of the Norwegian royal house.

Historically the narrative spans 150 years. It is set against the background of King Harald Fairhair's unification of Norway, a unity achieved through war and tyranny, and the killing or expulsion of any noble rivals to Harald's power—generally to Iceland. The scope of the saga extends throughout the Viking world—from Norway, the rest of Scandinavia, and Iceland to Finnmark, the Baltic, and northern England. It also spans the history of Egil's family from the time of his grandfather Kvedulf to that of his grandson Grim, and establishes a pattern: Members of the family belong to one of two contrasting types, generally characterized as "dark" or "light." Egil, an ugly and incorrigible child, takes after his father as one of the "dark" individuals; his handsome and exemplary brother and rival, Thorolf, is on the "light" side.

Egil's story is complex and sometimes outrageous, alternating between the treachery of Egil's enemies and his own ruthless responses, often motivated by his resistance to any kind of authority. Egil kills his first rival at the age of six over a ballgame. His feud with Eirik Bloodaxe, son of Harald Fairhair, begins when he kills Eirik's son and one of Eirik's friends whom he had tried to bring to court. At one point he joins the retinue of the English king ATHELSTAN and takes part in the famous BATTLE OF BRUNANBURH. He later finds himself stranded in York, where Eirik has become king, but is able to escape with his life by composing a poem for Eirik to "ransom" his head. Ultimately he inherits his father's land in Iceland and becomes a respectable farmer, at one point presenting an impressive legal case in court defending his son Thorstein's land claims. But even in his old age, the blind Egil retains some of his dark mood, and one night disappears with two slaves and two money chests. When he is discovered the next morning near the farm, neither slaves nor chests are to be found. He has buried the money and killed the slaves so that no one will ever find his treasure. Indeed, even after death, he remains a puzzling character: His skull is discovered buried beneath the altar of a church built by his niece's husband. The thick, solid skull cannot be broken, even with an axe.

The saga is also sprinkled with bits of Egil's verse, and contains, as well, three of his major poems. As skaldic poems made up of elaborate metaphors, or KENNINGS, these are very difficult to interpret and even more difficult to translate, but they do illustrate Egil's skill as a poet. Most admired is his lament for his drowned son. Determined to end his own life, the grieving Egil is convinced by his daughter to write a poem for his son. In it he expresses his helplessness over his loss, and blames his god Odin, who has deprived him of his child, but grudgingly still worships the god for giving him the art of poetry that allows him to express his grief. Egil's "Head-Ransom" poem to Eirik Bloodaxe is unusual in that it uses both alliteration and rhyme, and praises the king in a clearly ironic tone that Eirik must have misinterpreted. His other major poem is a eulogy for his blood-brother, patron, and protector Arinbjorn, repaying his friend's kindness as Arinbjorn leaves Iceland to reclaim his lands in Norway.

Egil's Saga survives in two vellum manuscripts from the middle of the 14th century, as well as several fragments dating from as early as 1250. It has been translated into English at least six times, and remains one of the most popular works of medieval prose fiction, mainly because of its fascinating title character.

Bibliography

Andersson, Theodore M. *The Icelandic Family Saga: An Analytic Reading.* Cambridge, Mass.: Harvard University Press, 1967.

Palsson, Hermann, and Paul Edwards, trans. *Egil's Saga.* Harmondsworth, U.K.: Penguin, 1976.

The Sagas of Icelanders: A Selection. With a preface by Jane Smiley and an introduction by Robert Kellogg. New York: Viking, 2000.

Turville-Petre, E. O. G. *Scaldic Poetry.* Oxford: Clarendon Press, 1976.

Eilhart von Oberg (ca. 1175–ca. 1210)

Eilhart was the first Middle High German poet to introduce the Tristan material to his audience, probably borrowing from a now-lost Old French source, the *Estoire de Tristan* from ca. 1170. Eilhart, who is named in 11 documents between 1189 and 1207, composed his *Tristrant und Isalde* about 1190, probably at the court of the duke of Brunswick, Henry the Lion. Henry was married to Mathilde, daughter of the English king HENRY II and his wife, ELEANOR OF AQUITAINE, famous patroness of the arts. It is quite likely that Mathilde brought a French version of the original poem with her, giving Eilhart access to this exciting new literary material. His text, preserved in three fragmentary manuscripts from around 1200 and in three complete 15th-century paper manuscripts, obviously exerted tremendous influence on subsequent generations. GOTTFRIED VON STRASSBURG referred to Eilhart when he composed his *TRISTAN* in ca. 1210, and most of the late medieval *Tristan* versions, especially the 15th-century prose novel *Tristrant und Isalde* (printed 14 times between 1488 and 1664), were influenced by him as well. The 15th-century Czech *Tristram* is directly based on Eilhart's text.

As in all other *Tristan* versions, Eilhart's romance describes the love triangle involving the Irish Princess Isalde and her husband Marke, the king of Cornwall, and, above all, Isalde's secret lover, Marke's own nephew Tristrant. Their illicit affair is brought about by a love potion concocted by Isalde's mother who had destined it for her daughter and her future son-in-law, Marke, but, by chance, Tristrant and Isalde drink it. Its power forces the two to stay together for four years, and their love continues thereafter (in Gottfried's *Tristan* there is no time limitation). Eilhart follows the lovers' story until the bitter end, when Tristrant already has married another woman and is mortally wounded from battle. His true beloved, trained in medical sciences, comes to his rescue, but his wife pretends to him that the opposite is the case, whereupon he dies, immediately followed by Isalde's own death. The role of Fortune and the narrator's irony characterize Eilhart's version, which, though lacking in intellectual depth, broadly appealed to a wide audience throughout the centuries, especially because several humorous scenes based on grotesque misunderstandings and violence offer fairly coarse entertainment. Significantly, Eilhart also includes the Arthurian world in his text, whereas Gottfried entirely concentrates on the court of Cornwall.

Bibliography

Eilhart von Oberg. *Tristrant.* Edited by Danielle Buschinger. Göppinger Arbeiten zur Germanistik 202. Göppingen, Germany: Kümmerle, 1976.

Schulz, James A. "Why Do Tristan and Isolde Leave for the Woods? Narrative Motivation and Narrative Coherence in Eilhart von Oberg and Gottfried von Strassburg," *Modern Language Notes* 102, no. 3 (1987): 586–607.

Thomas, J. W., trans. *Eilhart von Oberge's Tristrant.* Lincoln and London: University of Nebraska Press, 1978.

Albrecht Classen

Einhard (ca. 770–840)

The life of the Frankish emperor CHARLEMAGNE is best recorded by the Benedictine monk Einhard in his biography, *Vita Karoli Magni Imperatoris* (ca. 830). Einhard was born around 770 in Seligenstadt in the area of the Maingau as the son of an East Frankish aristocratic family. He received his education in the famous monastery of Fulda, which had been founded by St. Boniface in 744. Working in the scriptorium, between 788 and 791, Einhard copied a number of manuscripts. To further his education, Einhard was sent to the court of Charlemagne, where he became the student of ALCUIN who gave him the nickname Nardulus (Little Nard) because of his small stature. His outstanding abilities in the areas of architecture and painting were soon recognized since he was put in charge of building palatial residences in Aachen and elsewhere, and accepted into the group of the king's intimate advisers in 996 or 997. Charlemagne also employed him as his spokesperson and diplomat. For instance, in 813 Einhard went to Rome to get the pope's approval for the elevation of Charlemagne's son Louis the Pious, who had been his own student, to the rank of co-emperor. After Charlemagne's death in 814, Einhard continued to serve in his highly esteemed functions at court and received from Louis, together with his wife Imma (who died in 836), an estate in Michelstadt in 815. In 827 he had the relics of the saints Marcellinus and Peter transferred from Rome to his abbey in Michelbach in the Odenwald, and later to Mühlhaim (today east of Frankfurt). This transfer, which basically amounted to theft, Einhard discussed in 830 in his *Translatio et Miracula S. Marcellini et Petri* (The translation of the saints Marcellinus and Peter). Einhard also seems to have composed a number of poems while he studied under Alcuin, but none has survived.

Einhard is most famous for his *Vita Karoli Magni Imperatoris,* which he based on the *Annales royals* (The royal annals), diplomatic, and juridical writings, and, of course, on his personal experiences with the emperor. This *Vita* was the first of its kind in the Middle Ages and was highly praised by Einhard's contemporaries WALAFRID STRABO and Lupus of Ferriore, and was copied throughout the entire Middle Ages. Einhard glorifies Charlemagne and praises him above all for his *magnanimitas* (generosity) and *constantia* (constancy). The author drew much rhetorical material from classical sources, such as Suetonius's lives of the emperors, but the *Vita* still offers a detailed and more or less realistic portrait of Charlemagne and his life, discussing his military accomplishments, his family, his hospitality to foreigners, his personal lifestyle, his patronage of the liberal arts, his religiosity, charity, building programs, his coronation as emperor in 800, and finally Charlemagne's death in 814, along with his last will.

Einhard also composed many letters, 58 of which have survived, the earliest dating from 823. He continued to write treatises and other texts until his old age, such as his *Questio de adoranda cruce* (On worshiping the cross). He died in 840 in Seligenstadt.

Bibliography

Einhard. *Charlemagne's Courtier: The Complete Einhard.* Edited and translated by Paul Edward Dutton. Readings in Medieval Civilizations and Cultures 3. Peterborough, Ontario: Broadview Press, 1998.

Tischler, Matthias M. *Einharts Vita Karoli: Studien zur Entstehung, Überlieferung und Rezeption.* 2 vols. Monumenta Germaniae Historica, Schriften 48. Hannover, Germany: Hahnsche Buchhandlung, 2001.

Albrecht Classen

Eiriksson, Leif (Leif Ericsson) (ca. 975–ca. 1025)

The Norse explorer Leif Eiriksson was the leader of the first recorded European expedition to the mainland of North America. His story is told in two 13th-century Icelandic SAGAS called *Grœnlendnga saga (The Greenlanders' Saga)* and *Eiríks saga rauða (Eric the Red's Saga),* known collectively as the *VINLAND SAGAS,* after the name the Norsemen gave to the land they had discovered.

Leif was the son of Eirik the Red, who, in about 985, led an expedition of 25 ships from Iceland to found a new colony in southwest Greenland. Only 14 ships arrived, but the Norse established a settlement that lasted for several centuries. Eirik became leader of the new colony, and had an estate at Brattahlid. Leif, Eirik's oldest child, was probably born at his father's farm in Iceland between 970 and 980, and sailed to Greenland with Eirik, where he grew up at Brattahlid.

The sagas give two different versions of Leif's discovery of Vinland. The earlier *Greenlanders' Saga* says that the Norse captain Bjarni Herjófsson went off course while trying to sail to Greenland to visit his father. Bjarni sighted lands to the west, but did not explore them. When he reached Greenland and told his story, he was criticized for his lack of curiosity. Leif set off with a ship and 35 men to explore the new lands. In the later and probably less reliable *Eirik's Saga,* Leif sails from Greenland to Iceland and then to Norway in 999, and spends time with King Olaf Tryggvason, who converts him to Christianity and sends him back to Greenland to convert Eirik's settlement. On his return trip to Greenland, Leif is blown off course and lands in Vinland. Most scholars doubt the accuracy of the second version.

In either case Leif and his men discover three new lands: One is a barren island of level stone, which Leif names Helluland ("Flat Rock Land"). The second is a strand of evergreen forest that Leif calls Markland ("Forestland"). The third is a place where wheat fields and grape vines grow naturally, and where Leif's men make wine from the grapes. Leif names the place Vinland ("Wineland"). Leif and his men spend the winter in Vinland, where they build a large house and a shelter for their ship. They also cut down a number of trees to bring back a cargo of lumber to Greenland, where there are virtually no trees. Returning to Greenland, Leif rescues a group of 15 survivors from a shipwreck, an act that earns him the nickname "Leif the Lucky." His cargo makes Leif the wealthiest man in Greenland upon his return.

These are the events as related in the sagas. Both sagas also tell of members of Leif's family, most notably his sister-in-law Gudrid and her third husband, Thorfinn Karlsefni, who make their own subsequent voyages to Vinland. Leif himself never returned, at least not according to the sagas. His father Eirik died shortly after his return from Vinland, and Leif became leader of the Greenland settlement. Of Leif's later years, not much is known. He was the most renowned man in Greenland and lived at Brattahlid, presumably until he died. His son Thorkell is documented as head of the household at Brattahlid in 1025, so it seems likely that Leif was dead by that time.

The *Vinland Sagas* were written some 250 years after Leif Eiriksson's expedition to the North American continent, and they represent two distinct oral traditions into which a number of fantastic or romanticized elements have been introduced over the two centuries that had intervened. As a result, many assumed that the tales of Norse voyages across the Atlantic were mere fabrications, until Norwegian archeologist Helge Ingstad discovered a genuine Norse site in northern Newfoundland at a place called L'Anse aux Meadows. It is now an accepted fact that Norsemen did visit the Americas around the year 1000. Thus it seems reasonable to conclude that at least the basic facts of Leif's voyage to North America recorded in the sagas may be accurate.

Bibliography

Ingstad, Helge. *Westward to Vinland: The Discovery of Pre-Columbian Norse House-sites in North America.* Translated by Erik J. Friis. London: Cape, 1969.

Jones, Gwyn, trans. *Eirik the Red and other Icelandic Sagas.* Oxford: Oxford University Press, 1980.

———. *The Norse Atlantic Saga: Being the Norse Voyages of Discovery and Settlement to Iceland, Greenland, and North America.* 2nd ed. Oxford: Oxford University Press, 1986.

Magnusson, Magnus, and Hermann Palsson. *The Vinland Sagas.* Harmondsworth, U.K.: Penguin, 1965.

The Sagas of Icelanders: A Selection. Preface by Jane Smiley and introduction by Robert Kellogg. New York: Viking, 1997.

Eleanor of Aquitaine (ca. 1122–1204)

Both admired and maligned, Eleanor of Aquitaine was one of the most influential and powerful queens in the entire Middle Ages. Born ca. 1122 in Poitiers or Belin near Bordeaux as the daughter of Duke William X of Aquitaine, she grew up within the context of Occitan TROUBADOUR poetry and became an important patron of this literary culture herself. In 1137 her father died on a Crusade to Santiago de Compostella, but before his death he had expressed his wish that his daughter marry Louis, son of the French king Louis VI. Once the wedding was concluded in July of that year, the relatively small royal house of the Capetians acquired the wealthy territory of Aquitaine. The king died in August, and so the newlyweds entered Paris as the successors to the French throne. Although the marriage seems to have been a happy one, Eleanor strongly supported the secular courtly culture of the south, whereas her husband was highly religious and yet got into a number of conflicts with the church. In 1144 the couple attended the dedication of the new Gothic choir of St. Denis.

After the dukedom of Edessa in modern-day Macedonia had been occupied by a Turkish ruler, Louis VII, together with the German Hohenstaufen king Konrad III, went on a crusade from 1147 to 1149. Eleanor accompanied her husband, but a deep conflict between the couple threatened their marriage because of differences about the course of the crusade and an open power struggle between them. After their return to Paris, Eleanor, who had in the meantime delivered a second daughter (not a son, who would have been important for the royal succession), insisted on divorce, based on allegedly too close family ties between them. This divorce was granted in 1152, and only two months later Eleanor remarried, exchanging rings with Duke Henry of Normandy, the future HENRY II. In 1153 Eleanor's two daughters married brothers of the house of Blois, and in the same year Eleanor delivered a boy, named William, who died in infancy in 1156. But William was followed by four brothers and three sisters. In 1154 Henry was elected king of England, and Eleanor soon became actively involved in the government of the new country where she strongly promoted the arts and literature. BENOÎT DE SAINTE-MAURE dedicated his *Le Roman de Troie* to a "riche dame de riche rei," which could only have meant Eleanor. In 1155 or 1157 WACE sent a copy of his French translation of GEOFFREY OF MONMOUTH's *HISTORIA REGUM BRITANNIAE* to the queen. THOMAS OF BRITAIN seems to have dedicated his *Tristan and Yseult* to the queen sometime before 1173. The troubadour poet BERNART DE VENTADORN (ca. 1125–ca. 1200) spent time at the British court, enjoying her patronage and, as rumors have it, her love. Numerous contemporaries and scandal-hungry posterity often claimed that Eleanor had many erotic relationships, as reflected in the Middle High German stanza "Were diu werlt alle min" contained in the *CARMINA BURANA* (early 13th century, no. 108 a., fol. 60), but these were probably the result of envy, jealousy, and fear of this resolute, highly intelligent, and independently minded queen who was fascinated by the newest developments in courtly literature which, by her time, began to focus on COURTLY LOVE.

Henry and Eleanor married their children off to various European noble houses to establish a network of family connections strengthening the British position, but it seems that Eleanor had less to say about it than Henry. She was likewise not involved in the political conflict between the king and the archbishop, Thomas BECKET of Canterbury, leading to Becket's murder at the hands of some French knights, who committed their act more or less on behalf of the king on December 29, 1170. On a more personal level, Eleanor also seems to have lost her direct influence on Henry, especially because her husband kept a concubine, Rosamund de Clifford, from 1165 until her death in 1176. Between 1168 and 1172 Eleanor set up her own court in Poitiers, where she also began her patronage of CHRÉTIEN DE TROYES, who dedicated his *Lancelot* to her daughter Marie. The latter is also mentioned in ANDREAS CAPELLANUS's treatise *De amore* (The art of courtly love, ca. 1185–90). Eleanor is also documented as the patron of several major art works in Poitiers, such as a stained glass window in the cathedral. In 1173 Henry II's sons began a rebellion against their father, in which they were openly supported by their mother. Eleanor especially leaned on her son, the future RICHARD I Lionheart, who ruled over his mother's dukedom of Aquitaine until he was crowned king of England in 1189. But in 1173 Eleanor was captured by her husband's troops and thrown into prison in England for 10 years, while her sons had to submit to their father's authority and could not stay in touch with their mother. Eventually she was freed again and participated in various political events. At the same time the conflicts between Henry II and his sons continued until 1187 when the king joined a crusade, but he died on July 6, 1189 before he could depart. Eleanor, who now had free rein, secured the English throne for Richard who was crowned on September 3, 1189. The following year Richard went on a crusade, while Eleanor arranged his marriage with Berengaria, daughter of King Sanchez of Navarra. Eleanor brought the bride to Richard, who was awaiting them in Messina, Sicily, and they were married in Cyprus. The queen mother then returned to Aquitaine and then to England. When Richard was taken prisoner by the Austrian duke Leopold while on his way home from the crusade,

Eleanor eventually collected the huge ransom and so made possible the release of her son in 1194. But he died soon after, in 1199. In her old age, Eleanor withdrew to Fontevrault, and died on April 1, 1204, either there or in Poitiers.

Bibliography

Boyd, Douglas. *Eleanor: April Queen of Aquitaine.* Thrupp, Stroud, Gloucestershire, U.K.: Sutton Publishing, 2004.

Carmina Burana: Lateinische und deutsche Gedichte einer Handschrift des XIII. Jahrhunderts. 1847. Amsterdam: Rodopi, 1966.

Owen, D. D. R. *Eleanor of Aquitaine: Queen and Legend.* Oxford: Blackwell, 1993.

Weir, Alison. *Eleanor of Aquitaine by the Wrath of God, Queen of England.* London: Jonathan Cape, 1999.

Albrecht Classen

elegaic poetry

By modern definition, an *elegy* is a poetic meditation on mortality occasioned by the death of an individual close to or important to the poet, such as Milton's *Lycidas* or Tennyson's *In Memoriam.* In classical Greek or Latin, however, the term *elegy* referred only to a particular verse form that naturally lent itself to a serious of somber mood. Thus in classical times it came to refer to almost any grave or solemn personal meditation in lyric form. It is in this more general sense that the term *elegiac* is used to describe the mood of a collection of OLD ENGLISH poems found chiefly in The EXETER BOOK, including particularly *The WANDERER, The SEAFARER, The WIFE'S LAMENT,* and *The RUIN.*

Most often in these poems, the somber meditative mood is occasioned by exile or loneliness. The speaker may be a *wraecca,* or wandering exile, who cannot participate in the communal life of the mead hall, where the unity of the tribe under the lord was celebrated. A man without a lord in Germanic society was outside the sphere of normal human activity, and could only feel lonely, isolated, and vulnerable. Speakers in Old English elegaic poems meditate upon the sense of loss this condition of exile brings. Sometimes the speaker's vision expands to include a meditation upon the transient nature of the world in general. The emotional suffering occasioned by this sense of loss is sometimes relieved in the elegy by some sort of consolation, usually the Christian consolation that contrasts the permanence of heavenly eternity with the transience of the physical world.

Aside from the strong sense of pain and loss that these poems share, they are also characterized by difficulty of language and structure. These difficulties have often led to differences of opinion concerning the interpretation of these poems. A significant question, for example, is whether the Christian consolations that can be found at the ends of certain elegies are truly part of the poems or are scribal interpolations. But to take *The Wanderer* as perhaps the most complete example of an Old English elegy, one can see the progression from personal loss to universal loss to final consolation. It is difficult to believe this is not the poet's intent.

Bibliography

Green, Martin, ed. *The Old English Elegies: New Essays in Criticism.* Rutherford, N.J.: Fairleigh Dickinson University Press, 1983.

Klinck, Anne. "The Old English Elegy as a Genre," *English Studies in Canada* 10, no. 2 (1984): 129–140.

Mora, María José. "The Invention of the Old English Elegy," *English Studies* 76, no. 2 (1995): 129–139.

Morgan, Gwendolyn. "Essential Loss: Christianity and Alienation in the Anglo-Saxon Elegies," *Geardagum: Essays on Old and Middle English Literature* 11 (1990): 15–33.

Ellesmere manuscript

The Ellesmere manuscript (Huntington Library MS. Ellesmere 26.C.9) is the most famous literary manuscript from the English Middle Ages. It is one of the two earliest manuscripts of Geoffrey CHAUCER's *CANTERBURY TALES* (the other being the HENGWRT MANUSCRIPT), and is probably composed by the same scribe that produced that text. The Ellesmere was produced within the first decade after Chaucer's death in 1400, probably within a few years of the Hengwrt. Unlike the Hengwrt, however, the Ellesmere is a beautifully produced and finished manuscript, essentially giving the impression that *The Canterbury Tales* is a finished work when it is not. Prior to the early 20th century, editors tended to use the Ellesmere as the base text of editions of Chaucer, until modern editors established the earlier authority of the Hengwrt.

Still in many ways the Ellesmere is superior to the Hengwrt: It is a complete version of the *Tales* (the Hengwrt lacks *The CANON'S YEOMAN'S TALE* as well as the prologue to *The MERCHANT'S TALE* and the ending of *The PARSON'S TALE*). Furthermore, the Ellesmere places the tales into a logical and coherent order that has become standard in editions of Chaucer.

What has truly made the Ellesmere so famous is its beautiful illuminations. Clearly the text was produced for a wealthy patron. The 464 pages of the manuscript are decorated with illuminated initials, floriated borders, and most famously 23 miniature portraits of the Canterbury pilgrims, including one of Chaucer himself. Each individual tale is illustrated with a portrait of its teller placed in the border at the beginning of the story.

The manuscript became part of the Bridgewater House Library, a collection founded by Queen Elizabeth's Lord Keeper of the Great Seal, Sir Thomas Egerton, who later became Baron Ellesmere. The collection was in the possession of the earls of Ellesmere until Henry Huntington bought the entire library in 1917. Huntington brought the manuscript back to San Marino, California, where it is the centerpiece of the Huntington Library collection in that city.

Bibliography

Hanna, Ralph, III. Introduction to *The Ellesmere Manuscript of Chaucer's Canterbury Tales: A Working Facsimile.* Woodbridge, U.K.: Brewer, 1989.

Stevens, Martin, and Daniel Woodward, eds. *The Ellesmere Chaucer: Essays in Interpretation.* San Marino, Calif.: Huntington Library, 1995.

Woodward, Daniel, and Martin Stevens, eds. *The New Ellesmere Chaucer Monochromatic Facsimile.* San Marino, Calif.: Huntington Library/Yushodo, 1997.

Emaré (ca. 1350–1400)

Emaré is an anonymous 14th-century MIDDLE ENGLISH verse ROMANCE identified by its author as a "Breton *LAI*." The text survives in a single manuscript in a North East Midland dialect. Like many vernacular romances of the time, the 1,035-line poem is written in 12-line TAIL RHYME stanzas. The poem is of particular interest as a version of the popular story of the abused Constance, told by the author's contemporaries John GOWER in his *CONFESSIO AMANTIS* and Geoffrey CHAUCER in *The MAN OF LAW'S TALE.*

The heroine of the tale is the young and patient Emaré. Born the daughter of a widowed emperor, the beautiful Emaré unwittingly becomes the object of her father's incestuous lust. The emperor makes her a gift of an elaborately embroidered robe that has the power to amplify her beauty, but when he attempts to seduce his daughter, she rebuffs him. The emperor retaliates by setting the maiden (still wearing her ornate robe) adrift in a rudderless boat. Eventually she lands in Galys (Wales), where she is loved by King Cador. The king marries Emaré despite his mother's protests, and when Cador is away in battle, Emaré gives birth to his son Segramour. Through the machinations of her malevolent mother-in-law, Emaré is once again set adrift, this time with her infant son. This time she ends up in Rome, where a kindly merchant befriends her and takes care of Emaré and her child. Ultimately, she and Segramour are reunited with both King Cador and the emperor, whom they find again by chance when the two men make pilgrimages to Rome.

Whether the text is, in fact, based on a Breton *lai* as the author claims is impossible to know. There is no extant French version of the tale, though the name Emaré may indeed be a form of the French word for "troubled." One possible source for the story, particularly considering the North East Midland dialect of the tale, is an earlier 14th-century analogue by Nicholas TRIVET, who was the first to name the heroine Constance.

Bibliography

Gibbs, A. C., ed. *Middle English Romances.* Evanston, Ill.: Northwestern University Press, 1966.

Mills, Maldwyn, ed. *Six Middle English Romances.* London: Dent, 1973.

Osborn, Marijane, ed. and trans. *Romancing the Goddess: Three Middle English Romances About Women.* Urbana: University of Illinois Press, 1998.

Ephraim ben Jacob of Bonn (1132–1197)

The Jewish poet and exegete (interpreter of Scripture) Rabbi Ephraim ben Jacob was born in Bonn in the Rhineland in 1132, where he was raised and educated. He became head of the rabbinical court in Bonn, and his decisions are looked upon as important interpretations of the Talmud. But he is best remembered today as a chronicler and poet of the Second Crusade.

Rabbi Ephraim's *Book of Historical Records* documents the accusations of ritual murder brought against the Jews of the city of Blois in France in 1171. This was the first instance of the so-called blood libel in continental Europe: the charge that Jews make use of the blood of Christian children for their Passover ritual. Rumor spread that such an act had been committed in Blois, and that the body of the slaughtered child had been cast into the Loire. Ephraim ben Jacob describes the burning of more than 30 Jews of Blois in retaliation.

Such stories are, unfortunately, not uncommon during the period of the Crusades, when Christians, roused to fight the Muslim infidels in the Holy Land, by extension might well turn their wrath against the Jewish infidel living among them in Europe. During the First Crusade in Germany, communities of Jews, faced with death or conversion, were prompted to kill their own children to prevent them from falling into the hands of Christians and being forcibly converted. Ephraim ben Jacob's best-known poem, his *Akedah,* or "The Sacrifice of Isaac," was written in response to these events. It retells the story of Abraham's sacrifice of his son, but describes Abraham as actually slaying Isaac before the Angel can stop him. The child is brought back to life, but the text clearly reflects recent history for Rabbi Ephraim.

Ephraim ben Jacob's *Sefer Zekhirah* (Book of remembrance) contains liturgical poems as well as a chronicle of the times of the Second and Third Crusades. He also wrote a legend of the martyr Amnon of Mainz. His poetry and prose serve as a major primary historical source for study of the Ashkenazic Jews (those of Germany and northern Europe) of the 12th century.

Bibliography

Baron, Salo Wittmayer. *A Social and Religious History of the Jews.* Vol. 6. 2nd ed. New York: Columbia University Press, 1983.

Chazan, Robert. "Ephraim ben Jacob's Compilation of Twelfth-Century Persecutions," *Jewish Quarterly Review* 84 (1993–94): 397–416.

———. *European Jewry and the First Crusade.* Berkeley: University of California Press, 1987.

Marcus, Jacob. *The Jew in the Medieval World: A Sourcebook, 315–1791.* New York: JPS, 1938.

Epiphanius the Wise (Epifanii Premudryi) (ca. 1360–ca. 1419)

Epiphanius, called the Wise, was a Russian monk best known for writing SAINTS' LIVES based on the life stories of two other monks with whom he may have been acquainted. His works are among the best examples of a new elaborate prose style popular in 15th-century Russia and the Balkans, called *pletenie sloves,* usually translated as "word weaving."

Little is known of Epiphanius' early life, but he apparently joined the monastery of Gregory the Theologian in Rostov as a young man. The monastery had a good reputation as an academic center during the earlier 14th century. At Gregory the Theologian Epiphanius may well have met St. Stefan of Perm (d. 1396), who was to become a well-known missionary and the subject of Epiphanius's first biography. Later Epiphanius became a resident at Trinity Monastery, a house founded by Sergius of Radonezh. Epiphanius's residence at the monastery probably began before the 1391 death of Sergius, who was to become the subject of Epiphanius's second biography.

In the monasteries Epiphanius would have learned manuscript copying, icon painting, and, most important, writing. He also had learned

Greek and was familiar with the Greek tradition of hagiography or saints' lives. According to some sources, Epiphanius spent some time in Moscow between 1390 and 1415. He is also believed to have traveled at some point to Mount Athos, Constantinople, and Jerusalem. He seems to have become spiritual adviser to his fellow monks before his death around 1419.

Epiphanius's *Zhitie Stefana Permskogo* (The life of Stefan of Permia), composed in the late 1390s, is, perhaps, his most characteristic work. It describes Stefan's missionary work among the Permians (a people now known as Zyrians living to the east of Muscovy). Epiphanius uses Stefan's mission to elevate the status of Russia as a center for the promulgation of Christianity. Also unusual in Epiphanius's text is his presentation of the events of Stefan's life as paralleling important events in church history, thereby presenting Stefan as a new and important part of that history. But the most important aspect of this text is Epiphanius's ornate prose style, word weaving: Epiphanius makes abundant use of parallelism—verbal pairs, parallel phrases and clauses, and frequent repetition create a rhythmic, almost poetic tone to the prose. Traditionally, this particular style, the *pletenie sloves,* was associated with a current monastic movement called *hesychasm. Hesychasm,* propounded by Epiphanius's master Sergius Radonezh, concerned the inner, ascetic prayer life of the monastic recluse. A part of this prayer of the heart was the search to find the perfect words of inspiration, words that ultimately became part of the word-weaving technique.

Epiphanius's other major work, *Zhitie Sergiia Radonezhskogo* (The life of Sergius Radonezh), concerns the saintly founder of Epiphanius's Trinity Monastery. Unfortunately, no extant manuscripts of Epiphanius's work survive—only abbreviated redactions of the text in Serbian or other languages. Still, the conclusion of the text as we have it makes a masterful use of the same sort of word weaving Epiphanius had used in his life of Stefan.

Since the 19th century, critics have attempted to attribute other texts to Epiphanius: Most notable of these have been "The Tale of Monk Epiphanius on His Journey to Jerusalem" and "The Life and Death of the Grand Prince Dmitry Ivanovich." Neither of these attributions is universally accepted by scholars, and the only grounds for such attributions is a similarity in style to Epiphanius's extant works.

Bibliography

Børtnes, Jostein. *Visions of Glory: Studies in Early Russian Hagiography.* Atlantic Highlands, N.J.: Humanities Press, 1988.

Kitch, Faith C. M. *The Literary Style of Epifanij Premudryj: "plentenie sloves."* Munich: Sagner, 1976.

Wigzell, Faith. "Epifanii Premudryi." In *Reference Guide to Russian Literature,* edited by Neil Cornwell and Nicole Christian, 272–274. London: Fitzroy Dearborn, 1998.

Erceldoune, Thomas (Thomas the Rhymer) (ca. 1220–1297)

Thomas of Erceldoune, sometimes called Thomas Rhymer (that is, MINSTREL), was a Scottish poet of the late 13th century who attained a reputation as a seer or prophet in the centuries after his death. Although certain texts have been attributed to him over the years, no surviving poetry is currently considered to be his, and he is best known to literary scholars as the subject of a well-known ROMANCE (*The Romance and Prophecies of Thomas of Erceldoune*) and of a popular BALLAD, *Thomas Rhymer,* printed in Francis Child's collection (no. 37).

Virtually nothing is known of the life of the historical Thomas, other than the mention of his name in a registry of the trinity House of Soltra, recording that he had inherited property in Erceldoune, a village in Berwickshire on the English border. According to the *Romance and Prophecies* (ca. 1401), Thomas was visited by the queen of the elves while he sat under a tree in the Eildon Hills. He falls in love with the lady and she carries him off to Elfland, where he is granted visions of heaven, hell, and purgatory. Thomas lives there in bliss with the lady for seven years, after which she returns him to the Eildon tree. Before the queen leaves him, Thomas asks her for the gift of some wonder or "ferly" as a token of her love. In response she recites for him a "prediction" of 14th-century history, including details of the wars between Scotland and England, the last identifiable event being the invasion of Scotland by England's King Henry IV. The elf-queen adds to these several much more obscure prophecies regarding later events. Because of his insight into the future, Thomas becomes known as "True Thomas." He is last seen following a hart and hind into a forest, from whence he never returns. The romance, particularly the motif of the protagonist snatched off to fairyland from beneath a tree, is reminiscent of the MIDDLE ENGLISH romance of *SIR ORFEO*.

A similar story, without the specific prophecies, is told in the ballad *Thomas the Rhymer*. Here, when the beautifully attired lady approaches Thomas under the tree, he bows down to her and calls her queen of heaven. The lady reveals that she is the queen of elfland, and invites him to love her, after which she says he must be her servant for seven years. She rides off with him, and en route to her home she shows him three paths: the neglected and overgrown path of righteousness, the broad road to wickedness, and the winding road to Elfland, separate from either. They wade through a river of blood and enter a garden, where the queen gives Thomas an apple to eat, and tells him that it will give him a tongue that never lies. He stays seven years in Elfland, though because of the magic apple it is implied that he is indeed "True Thomas" when he returns to the world.

Thomas became known for his prophecies, and was considered a kind of Scottish "Merlin" well into the 19th century. He is reputed to have predicted the death of Scottish king Alexander III in 1286, the decisive Battle of Bannockburn in 1314, as well as the ascension of the Scot James VI to the English throne in 1603. His prophecies were continually being revised and updated, well into the 16th century.

At one point Thomas was thought to have been the author of *The Romance and Prophecies of Thomas of Erceldoune*, but it is clear that the romance was composed at least 100 years after the historical Thomas's death. The Middle English romance called *Sir Tristrem* was attributed to Thomas by Sir Walter Scott when Scott edited the poem from the Auchenlick manuscript in 1804, but that attribution is unlikely. At one time Thomas was also thought to be the author of the English *SIR LAUNFAL*, but that poem is now attributed to Thomas Chestre. Thus no surviving poetry can be attributed with confidence to Thomas, but his reputation continues to make him the best-known Scottish poet of his time.

Bibliography

Child, Francis James, ed. *The English and Scottish Popular Ballads*. 5 vols. 1882–1898. New York: Cooper Square Publishers, 1965.

The Romance and Prophecies of Thomas of Erceldoune. Edited by James A. H. Murray. 1875. Millwood, N.Y.: Kraus Reprint, 1987.

Erec and Enide Chrétien de Troyes (ca. 1170)

The first of five extant Arthurian ROMANCE poems by the French poet CHRÉTIEN DE TROYES, *Erec and Enide* is a sophisticated poetic narrative thought to be one of the earliest romances of Arthur in the courtly French tradition. (*CULHWCH AND OLWEN*, a Welsh Arthurian prose tale, is dated almost a century earlier but has little in common with the courtly French productions that influenced English and continental writers). The French poem is filled with elaborate and detailed descriptions of clothing, castles, characters, and jousts, with characters, in particular, described in superlatives (the noblest knight, the loveliest of ladies), as Chrétien writes for his aristocratic audience in a style we now associate with courtly romance. As in most Arthurian romances, the central character is not King ARTHUR, but a knight of the Arthurian court, yet in this case, the Arthurian knight unusually shares center stage with his wife. Indeed, *Erec and Enide*, like Chrétien's other poetic romances, does far more than entertain the aristocracy and it is in the pairing of Erec and Enide that the poet, in keeping with the rhetorical injunction to entertain and to teach, provides a lesson in moderation and balance between individual and social responsibilities.

The poem opens with Chrétien's distinctive authorial address to his audience and the invocation of his own name as storyteller of this tale that "poets usually ruin." Chrétien commonly begins his romances with an interjection of some sort in which his name and the story's origins are announced, gestures that were fairly uncommon for a 12th-century poet. Having established his narrative claim, the poet launches into his tale with the now traditional romance setting of the Arthurian court. Erec is a knight of the Round Table and, as befits an Arthurian knight, excels at knightly jousts and games. However, once he is married to Enide, a lovely young woman he meets on a quest early in the romance, Erec leaves off knightly feats of arms and is content to spend his hours and days only with Enide. There is much grumbling among his fellow knights about Erec's new lack of interest in knightly affairs, and it is Enide who tells him that the court thinks it is shameful that he has lost all interest in fighting and chivalry. The opinion of the court, which shapes the way one is perceived, is central to this and other courtly romances, and Enide pays dearly for being the bearer of bad tidings as Erec orders her to precede him as he sets out on horseback for adventures unknown. Erec prohibits Enide from speaking a word during their travels, but time and again when they are faced with some danger from a recreant knight or thieves or some other foe, Enide (who seems to see the dangers before Erec) disobeys Erec's command and warns him of their danger. With each act of disobedience, Erec becomes increasingly enraged with Enide, even as he successfully deals with the dangers.

In the course of their shared adventures, Erec is clearly testing Enide, but even as he repeatedly proves himself as a knight, his motivation for testing his wife is never expressed. The poet tells us what Enide is thinking throughout, often in highly rhetorical detail, but Erec remains a mystery and the poet's handling of his characters invites the audience to supply their own interpretation of Erec's actions. The lovers are finally reconciled when Erec almost dies, and we are assured that both have been tested and proved their love. In a manner of speaking, Enide's disobedience proves her love, just as Erec's testing his knightly prowess in a way that interferes with his marital obligations proves his love. In the final scenes, Erec and Enide are enthroned on identical thrones and crowned with identical crowns: Neither is higher nor more elaborately jeweled than the other. Having undergone shared adventures and having learned to balance marital with martial demands and personal desires with social responsibilities, the couple is now prepared to rule as king and queen.

Even though Erec's precise motivation for the testing of his wife is never quite clear, the outcome is more than clear. The romance represents immoderate behavior as a negative value, which threatens the social order even as it destroys personal relations. Both Erec and Enide need to find the balance between their public and their private responsibilities, and once they have they can participate as equals both in the bedroom and in the court.

Chrétien recounts with great imaginative power concerns that were both literary and real in the 12th century. Romance, as a genre, focuses on the individual in conflict with his or her social and cultural environment; romance, as a mirror for real-life conflicts between personal and public duties, focuses on the resolutions available, as improbable as they may appear. In *Erec and Enide* we witness the conflict, the testing, and the resolution, in a poem that serves as a finely crafted, if fantastical, mirror for princes.

Bibliography

Chrétien de Troyes. *Erec and Enide.* Translated by Burton Raffel. Afterword by Joseph J. Duggan. New Haven, Conn.: Yale University Press, 1997.

Burgess, Glyn. *Chrétien de Troyes, Erec and Enide.* Critical Guides to French Texts 32. London: Grant and Cutler, 1984.

Kelly, Douglas. *The Art of Medieval French Romance.* Madison: University of Wisconsin Press, 1992.

Maddox, Donald. *The Arthurian Romances of Chrétien de Troyes: Once and Future Fictions.* Cambridge Studies in Medieval Literature 12. Cambridge: Cambridge University Press, 1991.

Elisa Narin van Court

estates satire

The term *estates satire* applies to a satirical tradition in medieval literature that might occur in any number of genres (from sermon to moral tract to

DREAM VISION) and in most languages of western Europe, in particular Latin, French, and English. The form seems to have originated in the 12th century, but it became particularly popular in the 13th and 14th centuries, culminating in CHAUCER's use of the form in the GENERAL PROLOGUE to his *CANTERBURY TALES*.

In medieval political and social theory, society was divided into three "estates" or classes. One of the earliest expressions of this ideal is in the work of the English Benedictine monk AELFRIC at the beginning of the 11th century: Society was made up of three estates, according to Aelfric and other conventional theorists—that is, the clergy (those who pray), the aristocracy (those who fight), and the peasants (those who work). The clergy were expected to care for the souls of all members of the Christian society. The laborers were supposed to care for the physical needs of all members of the society, making sure all were fed and clothed. The nobles were needed to defend the society from dangers from without and disruption from within. Each estate relied upon the others in a mutually dependent relationship. Thus if all the estates performed their tasks properly, society would thrive in peace and justice, and its individual members would be content and happy.

Of course in practice, society did not function so smoothly. For one thing, the estates were not static, and after Aelfric's time, the estate of the clergy became more complex, as new orders of friars were formed and recognized in the 13th century—friars who by the 14th century would become notorious for corrupt practices. A growing number of new occupations and an economy that was shifting gradually from land to money were making the laboring estate more complex by creating a growing middle class in the cities. Power struggles between the nobility and high-ranking clergy also manifested the discrepancy between reality and the ideal of the good society.

Like most satire, estates satire starts with a notion of the ideal and demonstrates how far it is from reality as expressed in the text. Estates satire usually involves more than the three basic estates, but examines a number of more specific occupations, including popes, bishops, priests, kings, knights, monks, friars, burghers, merchants, farmers, and so on. Sometimes women were seen as a separate category within society, or might be divided into wives, widows, and maidens. The satire would delineate the duties of the particular "estate," and discuss the characteristics of, for example, friars in general. Most important, the satire would then focus on the failings of the members of that occupation. Specifically, the vices and abuses most commonly associated with each occupation were dealt with. Often those failings would be presented as the cause of the generally decayed state of human society. When the estates fail to fulfill their functions, they fail to support society as they should.

Estates satire flourished in the difficult times of the later 14th century. In England, the opening vision of LANGLAND's *PIERS PLOWMAN*, describing a "fair field full of folk," is a survey of the various estates of English society and of their various failures. John GOWER's Latin DREAM VISION poem called *VOX CLAMANTIS* ("The Voice of One Crying") begins with a scathing diatribe against the peasants who revolted against what Gower saw as the natural order of society in 1381; it is an earnest estates satire that does not spare the other estates for their failure to perform their proper functions to preserve the unity and peace of the Christian society of England.

Chaucer's General Prologue is a text that relies heavily on the estates satire tradition. But Chaucer expands the tradition by creating portraits that are not simply representatives of different estates (a Nun, a Friar, a Miller), but are also individuals (Madame Eglantine, Huberd, Robin), and Chaucer—emulating JEAN DE MEUN's treatment of personified abstractions in the *ROMAN DE LA ROSE*—has them speak for themselves, so that the reader gets an ambiguous picture of the character's actions since they are seen from the character's own point of view. Fraud, greed, and hypocrisy are common, but the irony of the situation is how unaware of their own faults the pilgrims are when they speak for themselves.

Bibliography

Cooper, Helen. "Langland's and Chaucer's Prologue," *Yearbook of Langland Studies* 1 (1987): 71–81.

Leicester, H. Marshall. "Structure as Deconstruction: 'Chaucer and Estates Satire' in the 'General Prologue,' " *Exemplaria* 2 (1990): 241–261.

Mann, Jill. *Chaucer and Medieval Estates Satire: The Literature of Social Classes and the General Prologue to the Canterbury Tales.* Cambridge: Cambridge University Press, 1973.

Strohm, Paul. *Social Chaucer.* Cambridge, Mass.: Harvard University Press, 1989.

Everyman (ca. 1485)

Generally conceded to be the finest example of the type of late medieval drama known as a MORALITY PLAY, *Everyman* (or, more properly, *The Summoning of Everyman*) was produced between 1485 and 1500. As is the case with all moralities, *Everyman* concerns the moral life of an individual human being, representative of all people (hence the name Everyman), and depicted through the use of personified abstractions, or ALLEGORY.

Although the ultimate source of the story seems to be an allegorical tale of Death's messenger contained in the much earlier work *BARLAAM AND JOSAPHAT,* more immediately *Everyman* may be an English translation of a Dutch play called *Elckerlijc,* known to have been produced for a festival in Antwerp in the 1490s. Some scholars, however, believe that the Dutch play is a translation of the English one. Though *Everyman* survives in four early printed versions, none is dated, so it is difficult to establish the priority of either text. Whichever was first, the plays have some differences but both seem to show the influence of a late 15th-century ascetic movement popular on the continent called *Devotio moderna.*

The play begins with a personified Prologue who describes the audience as "sinners" and exhorts them to pay close attention. Next comes a monologue by God, who laments the fact that human beings have turned away from him and prefer worldly goods. God sends his messenger, Death, to summon Everyman to come to him and make an accounting of his life. Everyman, stunned by Death's unexpected approach, first tries to bribe the messenger with money. He then asks for leave to find someone to accompany him on the journey. Death allows this, but one by one, when they learn where he is bound, Everyman's friends desert him: Fellowship, Kindred, Cousin, and Goods all fall away. Goods responds to Everyman's charge that he was led astray with the observation that the man has misled himself. Now at his lowest point, Everyman finds Good Deeds so weak and weighed down as to be nearly buried. But Good Deeds agrees to accompany him, and Knowledge shows Everyman how to strengthen Good Deeds: He must go to confession and perform penance for his sins. This done, Good Deeds is strong enough to make the journey. Other friends that Knowledge has made known to Everyman—Strength, Beauty, Discretion, and Five Wits (his five senses)—stay with Everyman only to the edge of the grave, but will go no further. Nor can knowledge stay with Everyman beyond Death (for Knowledge is only a guide through this life), but Good Deeds does go into the grave with him. In the end a learned Doctor of Theology addresses the audience, expressing optimism that Everyman will be saved.

The play is brief and builds inexorably toward its conclusion as, one by one, Everyman's fair-weather friends desert him. Its structure follows commonplace medieval religious ideas, as the first group of abstractions (Fellowship, Goods and the like) were considered to be gifts of Fortune, while the last group (Strength, Beauty and others) were considered gifts of Nature. But only gifts of Grace are eternal, and those came through the sacraments Everyman performs before his death. The play thus reflects orthodox doctrine, as set out by St. AUGUSTINE, that salvation cannot come from good deeds alone, but only through grace—and the vehicle of grace is the church.

The play uses the extended metaphor of a journey, playing on the conventional metaphor of life as a pilgrimage. It also incorporates the biblical Parable of the Talents, in which the servant who has buried his single talent is condemned when his master comes for an accounting. The mercantile, accounting motif must also have been particularly effective among the burghers of a city like Antwerp.

While the play lacks some of the broad humor created by characters such as the VICE in other morality plays, and while the versification (in tetrameter couplets irregularly interspersed with quatrains) is sometimes weak, *Everyman* remains, even today, a powerful play, driving home its stark warning about the inevitable end of life and about the human need for preparedness.

Bibliography

Conley, John. "The Doctrine of Friendship in *Everyman*," *Speculum* 44 (1969): 374–82.

King, Pamela M. "Morality Plays." In *The Cambridge Companion to Medieval English Theatre*, edited by Richard Beadle, 240–64. Cambridge: Cambridge University Press, 1994.

Kolve, V. A. "Everyman and the Parable of the Talents," in *Medieval English Drama: Essays Critical and Contextual*. Chicago: University of Chicago Press, 1972, 316–40.

Van Laan, Thomas F. "Everyman: A Structural Analysis," *PMLA* 78 (1963): 465–75.

Exeter Book, The (ca. 970–990)

The Exeter Book is the common name given to the Exeter Cathedral Chapter Library, MS. 3501. The manuscript is the largest of the four collections of OLD ENGLISH poetry still in existence. It was written by a single hand, almost certainly that of a monastic scribe, during the last part of the 10th century—roughly between 970 and 990.

The manuscript consists of 130 folios. Its front cover bears the marks of having been used as a cutting board as well as a beer coaster. Its back cover and the final 14 pages of the manuscript have been damaged by fire.

The manuscript has been in the possession of Exeter Cathedral since roughly the year 1070. It is listed as one of the donations made to the cathedral by Leofric, bishop of Cornwall and Devon, who died in 1072. Scholars believe that the manuscript was copied in the West Country, perhaps near Devon. The catalogue describes it as *i mycel Englisc bok be gehwilcum thingum on leothwisan geworht* (that is, "one great English book about every kind of thing, composed in the verse"). Whether the scribe put the collection together from poems that came to him individually, or whether (as some scholars believe) he was making a copy of a poetic anthology put together at the time of Alfred the Great or his immediate successors, is a matter of some debate but probably unsolvable.

About half the poems in the Exeter Book are on Christian themes, while the other half are concerned with secular matters. The latter include most of the best-known examples of Old English ELEGAIC POETRY. Some of the important poems included in the Exeter Book are *The* WANDERER, *The* SEAFARER, WIDSITH, DEOR, WULF AND EADWACER, *The* WIFE'S LAMENT, *The* HUSBAND'S MESSAGE, *The* RUIN, and 95 Anglo-Saxon RIDDLES—though these are all modern names for the poems, which are untitled in the manuscript.

Bibliography

Jebson, Tony, ed. "The Exeter Book." Available online. URL: http://www.georgetown.edu/labyrinth/library/oe/exeter.html. Accessed on January 30, 2005.

Krapp, George Philip, and Elliott van Kirk Dobbie, eds. *The Exeter Book*. Vol. 3, *Anglo-Saxon Poetic Records*. New York: Columbia University Press, 1936.

Exile of the Sons of Uisliu (*Story of Deirdre*) (eighth–ninth century)

Perhaps the best-known of all ancient Irish tales, the *Exile of the Sons of Uisliu*, or, as it is perhaps more popularly known after its haunting heroine, the *Story of Deirdre*, is a part of the Ulster Cycle of Irish legends, the cycle concerning the deeds of the great Irish mythical hero CUCHULAIN. Deirdre's story is one of the "pre-tales" attached to the chief story in the Ulster cycle, the Irish national epic called the *TÁIN BÓ CUAILNGE* (*The Cattle-Raid of Cooley*). In the *Táin*, the kingdoms of Ulster and Connacht go to war over ownership of a miraculous bull. The *Exile of the Sons of Uisliu* is told, in part, to show why the great Ulster heroes Fergus, Dubthach, and Cormac fight on the side of Connacht in the *Táin*.

Conchobar, king of Ulster, is generally presented in a sympathetic manner as the uncle and lord of the great hero Cuchulain. In the *Exile of the*

Sons of Uisliu, however, Conchobar is depicted as a cruel tyrant and an enemy of the lovers who are the tale's protagonists. The story begins with the birth of Deirdre (Irish *Derdriu*) in Conchobar's court. She is daughter of Conchobar's court storyteller, or *scelaige,* but a dire prophecy—that she will bring evil—surrounds her birth. Despite the warning, Conchobar raises her in his court and, when she is old enough, takes her to his bed.

Deirdre chafes at her position as Conchobar's concubine, and turns to Noisiu, son of the Ulster warrior Uisliu, to be her deliverer. She accosts him one day while he is tending cattle and, threatening him with shame and mockery, she obtains his oath that he will marry her. The situation is a difficult one for Noisiu: He is bound by blood ties and other obligations to Conchobar as his lord, and the only way to have Deirdre is to elope with her and flee the court. Noisiu's brothers throw in their lot with the two lovers, and leave Conchobar's fortress with them.

After some time the sons of Uisliu sue for peace with Conchobar, and the king gives his word that he will accept them back at his court. He sends three of his greatest retainers, Fergus, Dubthach, and his own son Cormac, as guarantors of the brothers' safety on their return. But secretly, he plots their destruction. First he makes use of an ancient Irish taboo called a *geis* against Fergus. It is a peculiar *geis* of Fergus that he must never refuse an invitation to eat or drink, and so the king causes Fergus to be delayed by a meal while the rest of the travelers, who have sworn not to eat or drink until they arrive at Conchobar's court, move on. With Fergus out of the way, Conchobar convinces his former retainer, Eogan mac Durthacht, that killing the sons of Uisliu would regain him Conchobar's friendship. Eogan does so, killing Fergus's son, along with Noisiu and his brothers. In the battle that follows, Fergus, Dubthach, and Cormac join the fight against Conchobar. Later, of course, they will fight against him in the *Táin.*

But the story of Deirdre is not over. Conchobar again takes her captive after Noisiu is slain, and for a year, she mourns her husband and refuses to yield to Conchobar's attempts to seduce her. But she despises being a captive of the man she hates. In the end as Conchobar and Eogan mac Durthacht are driving her to a fair in a chariot, she kills herself by dashing her head against a block of stone.

Deirdre has been called the Irish Helen since, like Helen of Troy, she helps bring on the destruction of a kingdom. She has also been compared to Isolde, spurning the king who wants her in favor of one of his retainers. But her tale has also become an archetypal myth of the defiant woman who will not be defined or imprisoned by the tyranny of social convention. Her story of resistance inspired a number of 20th-century retellings, most important William Butler Yeats's 1906 play *Deirdre* and John Millington Synge's *Deirdre of the Sorrows,* first produced at Ireland's National Theater, the Abbey, in 1911.

Bibliography

Dillon, Myles. *Early Irish Literature.* Chicago: University of Chicago Press, 1948.

Gantz, Jeffrey, trans. *Early Irish Myths and Sagas.* Harmondsworth, U.K.: Penguin, 1981.

Kinsella, Thomas, trans. *The Táin.* London: Oxford University Press, 1970.

Exodus (ca. eighth century)

Exodus is an OLD ENGLISH poem of 590 lines, preserved as the second poem in the JUNIUS MANUSCRIPT in Oxford's Bodleian Library. The poem is not a mere paraphrase of the biblical Book of Exodus; rather, it is conceived as an epic with Moses as hero, both in the sense of a leader of battles and of a speaker of wisdom familiar in Old English heroic poetry. Focusing chiefly on chapters 13 and 14 from the book of Exodus, the poem concentrates on the central episodes of the Hebrews' flight from Egypt, the miraculous parting of the Red Sea, and the subsequent destruction of the Egyptians that ensures their escape.

The poem begins by introducing Moses as lawgiver. It moves into the description of the 10th plague of Egypt—the killing of the first-born—and to the release of the Hebrews. A pillar of cloud leads and protects the people as they flee toward the sea. The Israelites' escape from Egypt and crossing of the Red Sea are presented largely as heroic military operations, with Moses being described in vocabulary suited for a military commander. The armor and weapons of both the Hebrews and the Egyptians are described in a manner consistent with heroic poetry, and after the Egyptians have been drowned, the Hebrews are described plundering the bodies as they would after a victorious battle.

Thematically, the poem focuses on God's protection of his chosen people, as a long digression (considered an interpolation by some critics) concerning God's protection of Noah and of Abraham follows the vivid description of the Egyptian defeat. The Anglo-Saxon church would have seen itself as similarly in need of God's protection, and as dealing, like Moses, with a wayward people needing constantly to be brought back to God. Further, they would have seen the Exodus story as allegorical: Traditionally, the Hebrews fleeing Egypt were interpreted as representing Christians leaving the prison of this life for their eternal home (the Promised Land). Pharaoh in this reading represents the devil, and the crossing of the Red Sea the baptism by which the devil is defeated. Such an allegorical reading is invited in the poem, as are other symbolic readings. The poet's use of nautical imagery, for example, to describe the Hebrews' movement over the desert may relate to Old English poems like *The* SEAFARER and *The* WANDERER, where traveling on the sea is seen as a metaphor for the pilgrimage of this life as the Christian looks for safe haven in the eternal, promised paradise—an interpretation that would underscore the traditional allegorical interpretation of the poem's events.

Exodus is a poem of epic grandeur. Particularly admirable is the vivid description of the converging forces of Egyptians and Israelites—a description involving the shifting of points of view between the two armies in a style Greenfield and Calder describe as "cinematic" (1986, 213). Though the poem is difficult, such passages make *Exodus* one of the most exhilarating of all the poems in the Old English canon.

Bibliography

Godden, Malcolm. "Biblical Literature: The Old Testament." In *The Cambridge Companion to Old English Literature,* edited by Malcolm Godden and Michael Lapidge, 206–226. Cambridge: Cambridge University Press, 1991.

Greenfield, Stanley B., and Daniel G. Calder. *A New Critical History of Old English Literature.* New York: New York University Press, 1986.

Krapp, George Philip. *The Junius Manuscript.* Anglo-Saxon Poetic Records, I. New York: Columbia University Press, 1931.

Eyvind Finson (*Skáldaspillir*) (ca. 915–990)

The SKALDIC poet Eyvind Finson was one of the last, but one of the most important, skaldic court poets of Norway. Of his personal life, not much is known. But he was of the family of King Harold Fairhair, and thus related to Harold's son, Hacon the Good (ca. 933–960), the first of three kings in whose courts Eyvind served. Eyvind is best known for two long poetic works, *Hákonarmál* and *Háleygjafal,* as well as for some 14 shorter skaldic poems, or *lausavísur.* Eyvind's nickname, *skáldaspillir* ("plagiarist"), implies that he borrowed quite heavily from earlier writers.

King Hacon's crown was contested by his nephews, the sons of Harold Fairhair's brother, Eirik Bloodaxe, whom Hacon had overthrown. Hacon fought several battles with these brothers, until he was killed in 960 in battle on the island of Stord and succeeded by his nephew Harold Greycloak. Eyvind's *Hákonarmál* was written to commemorate this battle. Twenty-one stanzas of this text are preserved in the *HEIMSKRINGLA,* and three stanzas are also quoted in the *PROSE EDDA.* Eyvind's poem vividly retells the king's last battle. In the climax of the poem, the chief Norse god Odin sends two of his Valkyrie to ferry Hacon's soul to Valhalla. There is an eight-stanza conversation between Odin, Hacon and the Valkyrie about the appropriateness of his acceptance into the pagan Valhalla, since Hacon was in fact a Christian. But he is praised for not violating any of the pagan Norse temples, and is welcomed into Odin's great hall after all. According to the end of Eyvind's poem, Hacon's equal will not be seen before the end of the world.

Under the reign of Harold Greycloak (ca. 960–970), Eyvind is purported to have written the bulk of his 14 extant *lausavísur*. Some of these deal with the Battle of Stord. Others deal with famine and cold summers that accompanied the reign of Harold and his brothers. Never on good terms with the sons of Eirik Bloodaxe, Eyvind constrasts the poverty under the miserly Harold with the days of plenty under his old patron, Hacon. Eyvind is at his most playful and his most scathing in these poems, making witty and elaborate use of the KENNINGS that so prominently characterize Old Norse poetic style.

Harold was succeeded by Hacon, the earl of Lade and the last pagan king of Norway (ca. 970–995). Eyvind's second major poem, *Háleygjafal*, was composed for Earl Hacon. In it Eyvind traces the earl's family tree back to the Norse god Frey (or *Yngvifreyr*) himself, giving the new monarch as impressive a lineage as his predecessors in the older Ynglingar line of kings. The poem ends with a celebration of Earl Hacon's great victory in 986 in the naval battle of Hjórunga Bay, in which he routed an invading fleet of Jómsvikings (a Danish warrior community). Only nine full stanzas and seven half-stanzas of this poem survive, mostly, once again, in the *Heimskringla* and a few only in the *Prose Edda*.

Bibliography

Poole, Russell Gilbert. *Viking Poems on War and Peace: A Study in Skaldic Narrative*. Toronto: University of Toronto Press, 1991.

Turville-Petre, E. O. G. *Scaldic Poetry*. Oxford: Clarendon Press, 1976.

Fables Marie de France (ca. 1160–1215) Although currently less popular than her *LAIS*, particularly her well-known *LANVAL*, the *Fables* of MARIE DE FRANCE were her best-known work in the Middle Ages, with some 25 extant manuscripts dating from the 13th through 15th centuries. This collection of 102 fables—short didactic narratives ending with explicit moral lessons in the manner of Aesop—is the first such collection surviving in a vernacular European language. In her 40-line prologue, Marie claims that Aesop translated his fables from Greek into Latin for King Romulus, who intended them for the edification of his young son. In her 20-line epilogue, she reveals that she has translated the fables into French from an earlier English version by King Alfred. She says that (like Aesop) she is making the translation at the behest of a noble patron, one Count William (a claim that has led some critics to suggest that the collection was intended as a "mirror for princes," such as, for example, Thomas HOCCLEVE's 15th-century *Regiment of Princes*). Marie also asserts in the epilogue her own authorship for the fables, ending the whole collection with a moral to the effect that "only a fool will allow himself to be forgotten."

There is no evidence that King ALFRED THE GREAT ever produced a collection of fables (though a number of PROVERBS were attributed to him), so that allusion is puzzling. It appears that 40 of Marie's fables were translated from the fourth-century Latin text known as *Romulus Nilantinus,* but the remainder of the fables are gathered from a variety of other sources, including Arabic collections, and it appears that Marie was the first to present the collection in this particular form. The majority of Marie's fables—about 60 of them—use human-like animals as the sole characters, and in a manner that recalls the popular ROMAN DE RENART cycle, Marie's beasts inhabit a feudal society, in which the Lion is the king—though sometimes greedy and prideful. The Wolf is presented as a breaker of oaths, and the Fox as a trickster who, in Fable 60, is outsmarted by a Cock in a story that may have been one of the sources for CHAUCER's *NUN'S PRIEST'S TALE.* In about 20 other tales, human beings relate to talking animals in the narratives, while 18 of the fables contain only human characters. There is even one fable in which the characters are all inanimate objects that interact with one another.

Marie relates her fables in witty octosyllabic (eight-syllable) couplets, and they range in length from a scant 10 lines to more than 100. Most of the tales are between 20 and 60 lines long. Marie frames her *Fables* with two stories (Fable 1 and Fable 102) in both of which the protagonists fail to take advantage of something offered to them: in the first, a cock ignores a precious stone that he finds in his barnyard; in the last, a hen spurns the food given her by a woman. It is as if Marie frames her collection with a warning that the wisdom offered by these fables must be recognized as valuable by the readers, or it will go to waste.

Fables were in general popular texts in medieval education, and Marie succeeds in making them available to a more vernacular audience, including women like herself. Indeed, critics have noted how sensitive Marie is to the gender of her animal characters, such as a pregnant sow in one fable or a raped she-bear in another. She even softens the antifeminist morals of some traditional fables, as when she shows sympathy for the usually maligned and inconstant Widow of Ephesus (Kruger 2003, 178). Taken as a whole, the *Fables* do not give a single simple formula for moral living, but reflect a more complex and thoughtful morality. In general, though, they do reflect the feudal ethos of the 12th century, condemning oath-breaking, bad masters, greed, pride, envy, and the self-seeking of members of the nobility.

Bibliography

Jambeck, Karen. "The *Fables* of Marie de France: A Mirror of Princes." In *In Quest of Marie de France, a Twelfth-Century Poet,* edited by Chantal E. Maréchal, 59–106. Lewiston, N.Y.: Edwin Mellen Press, 1992.

Kruger, Roberta L. "Marie de France." In *The Cambridge Companion to Medieval Women's Writing,* edited by Carolyn Dinshaw and David Wallace, 172–183. Cambridge: Cambridge University Press, 2003.

Marie de France. *Les Fables.* Edited and translated by Charles Bruckner. 2nd ed. Louvain, Belgium: Peeters, 1998.

Mickel, Emanuel J., Jr. *Marie de France.* New York: Twayne, 1974.

fabliaux

Fabliaux were a kind of comic tale in verse that flourished in northern France beginning in the late 12th century. There are about 160 extant fabliaux, written typically in octosyllabic couplets and written in a plain, direct style appropriate to their contemporary realistic settings and lower or middle class characters. Fabliaux tend to use a good deal of dialogue, more than is common in other medieval poetic genres. Although the term means "little fable," fabliaux are characterized by their general lack of moral purpose and their bawdy subject matter.

Most fabliaux were about 300–400 lines or fewer, though there are some that exceed 1,000 lines. Though the names of a few writers have been associated with fabliaux, including Philippe de Beaumanoir, Gautier le Leu, Jean Bodel, and most significantly RUTEBEUF, fabliaux were almost always anonymous. Scholars once debated whether the fabliaux were of a courtly or bourgeois origin, but modern scholarship favors the assumption of a literate audience familiar with the conventional plots of the courtly ROMANCES that many fabliau plots parody. Thus it is likely that both the author and audience of the fabliaux were members of the aristocratic class and the literate upper middle class. Because the poor student or cleric is so often portrayed sympathetically in the tales, one conjecture is that many of the authors were members of that group.

Fabliaux were chiefly satirical, and their main targets were the clergy (especially priests and monks), foolish husbands, and women in general, who are likely to be portrayed as scheming, unscrupulous, and promiscuous. Accordingly fabliaux have often been accused of being antifeminist, though it might be noted that the women in the tales are presented as clever and intellectually superior to their stupid, cuckolded husbands. It may be that the characterization of women in the fabliaux is a reaction against the elevation of women in the COURTLY LOVE tradition characteristic of the romances that the fabliaux were parodying.

In the fabliau the chief virtues are ingenuity, toughness, practicality, and a willingness to take chances and to do whatever is necessary to take advantage of someone else for one's own advancement. The main transgressions of the fabliau world are gullibility, softness, conceit (which is always going to be exploded), and idealism (which is always going to crash on the stones of reality).

The action of the fabliau usually revolved around the sexual exploits of a woman bent on tricking and cuckolding her foolish husband, who may deserve his cuckolding because he was foolish enough to marry a woman far younger than he, or because he ignores or otherwise abuses his wife. Inevitably it is a priest, monk, or poor divinity student who helps the wife plan her husband's cuckolding. In the end of a fabliau, there is often a kind of rough justice that is meted out to the characters—the foolish and gullible are penalized, and the trickster figure (usually the priest or monk) is also punished, often for carrying the joke too far. This is a motif called the trickster tricked, common to many fabliaux.

The latest fabliau in French is found in a manuscript from 1346. But by the 14th century the interest in fabliaux had spread to Italy and England. BOCCACCIO includes a number of fabliau tales (in prose) in his *DECAMERON*. In England, CHAUCER included several fabliaux in his *CANTERBURY TALES:* Written in decasyllabic English couplets, Chaucer's fabliaux include some of his most admired tales, written at the peak of his creative career. They differ from the Old French fabliaux in the complexity of their plots, their use of realistic descriptive detail, and their detailed development of character. Chaucer's fabliaux include *The MERCHANT'S TALE, The REEVES' TALE, The SHIPMAN'S TALE,* and the particularly widely admired *MILLER'S TALE.*

Bibliography

Benson, Larry D., and Theodore M. Andersson. *The Literary Context of Chaucer's Fabliaux.* Indianapolis: Bobbs-Merrill, 1971.

Bloch, R. Howard. *The Scandal of the Fabliaux.* Chicago: University of Chicago Press, 1986.

Hellman, Robert, and Richard O'Gorman, ed. *Fabliaux: Ribald Tales from the Old French.* New York: Thomas Y. Crowell, 1965.

Muscatine, Charles. *The Old French Fabliaux.* New Haven, Conn.: Yale University Press, 1986.

Fantosme, Jordan (fl. ca. 1175)

Jordan Fantosme was an Anglo-Norman poet and historian whose *Chronicle* provides a history of the young King Henry's first rebellion against his father, HENRY II, and of the ensuing war between the older Henry and the Scottish king William the Lion. These events of 1173–74 are described in a lively monorhymed poem divided into *laisses,* after the fashion of the CHANSONS DE GESTE.

Fantosme was most likely the clerk of Elias, the bishop of Winchester, and previously had been a student of Gilbert de la Porrée, bishop of Poitiers and a well-known scholastic philosopher. He claims to have been eyewitness to many of the events he describes. That claim cannot be verified, but it is certainly true that Fantosme seems to have had access to good information from both sides of the conflict, so that his *Chronicle* is generally a reliable and historically valuable text, written possibly within a year of the war itself. It is also a significant literary text, dramatic and colorful. Its most recent editor (R. C. Johnston) examines Fantosme's versification and determines that he uses five different meters in his poem, suggesting as well that the lines are arranged, like ALLITERATIVE VERSE, into half-lines with two stresses each.

Fantosme begins his story with the young Henry's decision to rebel and his obtaining the support of powerful French nobles and the French king Louis VII. The Scottish king William the Lion, against the advice of some of his nobles, decides to support the rebellion and invades Northumbria. At the same time, an army of Flemings, whom Fantosme satirizes as weavers rather than soldiers, attacks East Anglia. The old King Henry's powerful speech before launching his army into battle is a memorable part of the poem (though it is most likely formulaic rather than historical), and ultimately the rebellion is put down, and King William is defeated and captured at Aluwich in 1174. Henry then invades France to lift the siege of Rouen, and Fantosme's text ends with the king facing new challenges. Fantosme explicitly compares his hero, Henry II, to CHARLEMAGNE—a parallel often encouraged by Henry himself.

Perhaps the most memorable scene in the *Chronicle* concerns the Battle of Fornham, a significant turning point in the rebellion. Here after Peronelle, the countess of Leicester, has incited her husband to join the rebellion against Henry, she dons armor herself and rides beside the earl into the decisive battle. Overthrown and nearly drowned in a ditch where she loses her jewelry, the countess and the earl, her husband, are defeated and taken prisoner.

Fantosme's *Chronicle* is lively and readable. While the author seems a supporter of the old king's cause, he does seem to have deliberately left out details about the young Henry's culpability and that of his younger brothers, perhaps out of wide-ranging loyalty to the royal family. Nevertheless, the story that Fantosme presents is accurate, entertaining, and valuable.

Bibliography

Fantosme, Jordan. *Chronicle.* Edited and translated by R. C. Johnston. Oxford: Clarendon Press, 1981.

Fenian Cycle (Finn Cycle, Ossianic Cycle)

The Fenian Cycle is one of the major cycles of heroic stories to come out of medieval Ireland (the other being the ULSTER CYCLE). The name comes from the Irish word *fiana,* meaning "bands of warriors." Such *fiana* apparently did exist in early Irish history: One such group is known to have traveled to Britain to aid Aedán mac Gabráin, the Irish king of Scotland, in his war against the Angles in 603. Such *fiana* were evidently a recognized element in early Irish society. According to tradition, a Fenian initiate was required to know the 12 conventional forms of Irish poetry, and had to endure certain physical trials before being admitted to the band, after which they forsook their own families, becoming technically "kinless" men.

The chief hero of the Fenian Cycle is Finn mac Cumaill, leader of the Fenian company Clann Baiscne. Finn and his companions, particularly his son Oisín ("Little Deer," the poet laureate of the group) and his grandson Oscar, are the perpetual rivals of another Fenian company, Clanna Morna, led by Finn's nemesis Goll mac Morna, who had killed Finn's father Cumaill at the battle of Cnucha (identified with Castleknock, near Dublin). In many ways, however, Finn is like King ARTHUR, since most of the tales told about him concern members of his band rather than Finn himself. Historically, Finn and his men are purported to have lived in the third century of the Christian era, and are traditionally associated with the high King Cormac mac Art (ca. 227–ca. 283). Their tales are set in Leinster and Munster—thus the Finn tales are a southern and eastern tradition, as opposed to the Ulster legends, which are set in Ulster and Connacht in the north. The Fenian tales also seem to have been written down later than those of the Ulster cycle: Linguistic evidence suggests that virtually none of the extant tales of Finn were written down before the 12th century. Perhaps the earliest great compendium of Fenian lore is the *Acallam na Senórach* (*The* COLLOQUY OF THE OLD MEN), and Finn's exploits continued to be sung throughout the Middle Ages and even down to the 19th century. In this the Fenian tales differ, again, from those of Ulster, which were fewer and less likely to continue into modern folklore. It appears that from their beginning, perhaps the eighth century, the Ulster tales were the stories of the aristocracy, while the Finn tales began and continued as a folk tradition.

Finn himself is depicted as a national hero, either a supporter of the high King of Ireland or a defender of Ireland against all foreign invaders, particularly Vikings. He is traditionally said to have been descended from supernatural beings. He is characterized as just, generous, truthful, loyal, and nearly invincible in battle. He was also raised to be a druid and a seer. One story of his early life depicts him being raised by a druid in the woods. The druid is able to catch the great Salmon of Knowledge that swam in the River Boyne—anyone who ate the salmon would be granted knowledge of all the future of Ireland. Finn was told to prepare the fish for the druid to eat, but as the salmon cooked, some fat splattered onto Finn's thumb. When Finn licked his burned thumb, he immediately gained the power of second sight, and was able to foresee the invasion of the Vikings.

The most typical stories in the Finn Cycle are told in the poetic form called *laoidh,* a genre similar to the English BALLAD. These poems, ranging in length from a few lines to dozens of stanzas, are generally written in rhymed quatrains of seven-syllable lines, and are put into the mouths of some participant in the action of the story. A typical *laoidh* tells how Finn and his men are challenged by a supernatural blacksmith, whom they are able to defeat and win a prize of excellent weapons. The most significant collection of these short narrative poems is the *Duanaire Finn* (The poem book of Finn), a manuscript compiled, possibly by Irish Franciscan friars, in 1626–27.

A few prose tales survive as well, and the most famous of these is generally known as "The Pursuit of Diarmaid and Gráinne," a narrative that bears a striking resemblance to the Deirdre story in *The Exile of the Sons of Uisliu* from the Ulster Cycle. In the Fenian story, Finn is betrothed to the much younger Gráinne, daughter of the high King Cormac mac Art. At the wedding feast, Gráinne falls in love with the handsome Diarmaid, one of Finn's band. After drugging most of the assembly, she declares her love for Diarmaid, who somewhat reluctantly agrees to elope with her. Finn and his band spend 16 years chasing the couple, who constantly elude them with the magical help of Diarmaid's foster-father Aonghus, until eventually they are reconciled to Finn.

One night, however, a hound bays, and Diarmaid rises in the morning to investigate. He finds Finn at the foot of the mountain Ben Bulben in Sligo, who reveals to Diarmaid that he has lost 30 of his men that morning hunting the great Boar of Ben Bulben. Finn also reveals that Diarmaid has a *geis* or taboo against hunting the Boar. It is possible that Finn has deliberately lured Diarmaid to his death. When the Boar reappears, Diarmaid fights it, but is mortally wounded as he kills the Boar. Diarmaid asks Finn to save his life by giving him a healing draught of well-water from his own hands (one of Finn's magical powers), but Finn taunts Diarmaid and delays offering the water long enough for Diarmaid to die. Eventually, after Diarmaid's death, Gráinne marries Finn after all.

While it is well known, this tale is atypical in depicting the darker side of the hero Finn. The great number and variety of Fenian tales make it difficult to survey them in brief space, but the popularity and longevity of the tales and ballads must be noted as remarkable.

Bibliography

Dillon, Myles. *Early Irish Literature.* Chicago and London: University of Chicago Press, 1948.

MacKillop, James. *Fionn mac Cumhaill: Celtic Myth in English Literature.* Syracuse, N.Y.: Syracuse University Press, 1986.

Tóruigheacht Dhiarmada agus Ghráinne: The pursuit of Diarmaid and Gráinne. Edited and translated by Nessa Ní Shéaghdha. Dublin: Published for the Irish Texts Society by the Educational Company of Ireland, 1967.

Ferdowsi, Abolqasem (Firdowsi) (ca. 932–ca. 1025)

Abolqasem Ferdowsi is famous as the author of the Iranian national epic, the *Shāh-nāmah,* or "Book of kings." Working from one known written source and doubtlessly several other sources, both written and oral, Ferdowsi put together the traditional stories that had been building for centuries into a single text of some 50,000 couplets of remarkable poetic power. Ferdowsi chose to write in Persian, even though court poets of his time wrote almost exclusively in Arabic, in order to better render the pre-Islamic past of Iran and to preserve the tales and the culture that he thought might otherwise be forgotten.

Little is known with certainty about Ferdowsi's life. He was born in eastern Iran, near Tus. His family was of modest means, though they were landowners. He completed his great work around the year 1000. He wrote the poem for a sophisticated court culture, and his patron was the Soltan Mahmud of Ghazna (d. 1030). Given the fact that the Soltan and all his court were Muslim, and that Ferdowsi certainly was as well, the decision to write in Persian is interesting, as is the clearly Zoroastrian religious outlook that pervades the text. The choice of Zorastrianism, the pre-Islamic religion of Iran, is a part of the nationalistic flavor of the epic, though Ferdowsi was careful to remove any references to Zoroastrian rituals or prayers, leaving only the dualistic conflict between cosmic good and evil in the poem.

The 50,000 lines of the poem are organized into an introduction and 50 chapters, each concerned with a particular king. Indeed, one thread that helps unify the massive form of the epic is the theme of the divinely ordained monarchy.

The chapters are arranged chronologically, beginning with the creation, moving in the first two-thirds of the poem through mythical and legendary characters, through the conquest of Alexander the Great and a fictionalized history of the dynasties—the Parthian and Sassanian kings (247 B.C.E. through 652 C.E.)—who reigned in Iran in the centuries after Alexander. The *Shāh-nāmah* ends with the last Sassanian shah who died in a futile attempt to stem the Arab conquest of Iran in 652.

Thus, like the OLD ENGLISH *BEOWULF,* the story ends on tragic note: the ruin of the nation. This tragedy is reflected in the tone that seems to dominate the epic. The best-known section of the *Shāh-nāmah* is that dealing with the traditional Iranian tales known as the Seistan cycle. The great hero of this section is the noble Rostám, a superhuman warrior who is compelled by an irresistible fate to unwittingly kill his only son, the devoted Sohráb, in combat. The moving story has been popular in Western literature since the mid-19th century, when Matthew Arnold retold it in English verse.

Like the Bible or the epics of Homer in Western culture, the *Shāh-nāmah* has been the cornerstone document of Iranian national literature, serving as the foundational text of modern Iranian culture and the source of allusion and artistic inspiration from the Middle Ages to the present. Ferdowsi, as its author, is a revered, almost legendary figure within Iranian letters.

Bibliography

Davis, Dick. *Epic and Sedition: The Case of Ferdowsi's Shāhnāmeh.* Fayetteville: University of Arkansas Press, 1992.

Ferdowsi, Abolqasem. *Fathers and Sons.* Translated by Dick Davis. Washington, D.C.: Mage Publishers, 2000.

———. *In the Dragon's Claws: The Story of Rostam and Esfandiyar, from the Persian Book of Kings by Abdolqasem Ferdowsi.* Edited and translated by Jerome W. Clinton. Washington, D.C.: Mage Publishers, 1999.

———. *The Legend of Seyavash.* Translated by Dick Davis. London and New York: Penguin, 1992.

———. *The Shâhnâma of Firdausi.* Translated by Arthur George and Edmond Warner. London: K. Paul, Trench, Trübner and Co., Ltd, 1905–1915.

———. *The Tragedy of Sohráb and Rostám: From the Persian National Epic, the Shahname of Abol-Qasem Ferdowsi.* Translated by Jerome W. Clinton. Rev. ed. Seattle: University of Washington Press, 1996.

Yar-shater, Ehsan. *The Lion and the Throne: Prose Rendition.* Translated by Dick Davis. Washington, D.C.: Mage Publishers, 1998.

Fernandez de Santiago, Roi (Roi Fernandez *clérigo*) (13th century)

There is some question as to whether Roi Fernandez de Santiago is the same person as the poet who signs himself Roi Fernandez *clérigo,* but most scholars believe this to be the case. Assuming they are correct, 25 extant poems are attributed to this Galician poet, 18 of which are *cantigas de amor,* or love poems, while seven are *CANTIGAS DE AMIGO,* songs with female speakers. He was likely a priest (hence the title *clérigo*), and he is sometimes associated with the court of Alfonso X (known as "the Wise"), the Spanish king of Castile from 1221 until 1284.

Roi Fernandez's best-known lyric is a *marinha* or "sea poem" beginning *Quand' eu vejo las ondas* (When I see the waves). Here the pounding of the waves is answered by the pounding of the speaker's heart as he thinks of his beloved, with the implication that it is the sea that separates them:

When I see the waves
and the very steep cliffs,
then suddenly waves begin pounding
in my heart for the pretty lady:
cursed by the sea,
which does me such great harm!

(Jensen 1992, 52.2, ll. 1–6)

In the original, scholars have seen a correspondence between the rhythm of the poem and cadence of the waves themselves. The last two lines of the stanza curiously recall the refrain of an Italian song quoted in BOCCACCIO'S *DECAMERON* (ca. 1350): "the wave does me great harm."

Fernandez's love lyrics tend to include fairly traditional COURTLY LOVE motifs, particularly the idea of the speaker's suffering for love of his lady. In one fairly unusual poem, though, beginning *Ora começa o meu mal* (Now my grief begins), Fernandez reverses expectations; he replaces the convention of the "god of love" with a devil, and describes the speaker's suffering after finding a new love to supplant the old:

For the demon of love
Made me choose another lady!

(Jensen 1992, 52.1, ll. 5–6)

Similar occasional innovative touches appear in some of Fernandez's *cantigas de amigo.* Some of these lyrics are in the form of dialogues between a girl and her mother, with the mother generally taking the role of spokesperson for conventional societal restraints on the girl's love for her *amigo.* In the lyric *Madre, quer' oj eu ir veer* (Mother, today I wish to go see), though, the girl's mother supports her daughter's determination to follow her amigo to Sevilla:

—My daughter, go, and I will come with you.

—This will give me great pleasure,
for I do not know when I shall see him.

(Jensen 1992, 52.3, ll. 5–7)

These original touches to his lyrics make Roi Fernandez de Santiago one of the more enjoyable lyric poets of the rich 13th-century Galician-Portuguese tradition.

Bibliography

Flores, Angel, ed. *An Anthology of Medieval Lyrics.* New York: Modern Library, 1962.

Jensen, Frede, ed. and trans. *Medieval Galician-Portuguese Poetry: An Anthology.* Garland Library of Medieval Literature, 87. New York: Garland, 1992.

Ferumbras (Fierabras, Firumbras)

Although today the best-known *CHANSON DE GESTE* is *The SONG OF ROLAND,* the numerous surviving manuscripts about Fierabras (Ferumbras in MIDDLE ENGLISH) point to this CHARLEMAGNE ROMANCE epic character as the most popular during the Middle Ages. The *Fierabras* cycle conflates two separate stories. In the first, the Destruction of Rome, Fierabras, who is the son of the sultan and a formidable warrior, leads the Saracen (Muslim) attack on Rome and the theft of the relics of Jesus Christ. In the second episode, the Song of Fierabras, Charlemagne's forces follow the Saracens into Spain. Fierabras converts to Christianity after losing a fight with Oliver, the most famous of Charlemagne's Peers after Roland. Fierabras then assists the Franks in defeating the Saracen army of his father. Meanwhile, his sister, Floripas, frees Roland and other Peers imprisoned by her father because of her love for Guy of Burgundy, one of Charlemagne's knights. By the conclusion, Floripas and Fierabras are baptized while their father is killed for rejecting Christianity. Fierabras returns the stolen relics to Charlemagne, and Floripas marries Guy, who will become king of Spain (de Mandach 1987, 129–30).

Three Middle English manuscripts of the Fierabras cycle survive: *Sir Ferumbras, Firumbras,* and *The Romance of the Sowdone of Babylone and of Ferumbras His Sone Who Conquered Rome.* Of the three, the last receives the highest praise of the Middle English Charlemagne romance poems because it is the most complete—the other two omit the Destruction of Rome, for example—and because critics consider it the most original and inventive of the translations. Dorothee Metlitzki has categorized the stereotypical Saracen characters found in these romances, such as the converted knight (Ferumbras, who at one point saves the life of Charlemagne), the defeated sultan (Laban, the sultan of Babylon, and father of Ferumbras and Floripas, who began the war by ordering the destruction of Rome after Romans had robbed his ships), the enamored princess (Floripas, whose use of magic and murder on behalf of her lover and father's enemy, Guy of Burgundy, makes her a medieval amplification of Medea), and the Saracen giant (the fiercest opponents the Christians face in battles with the Saracens; they include the Ethiopian monsters Estragot and his wife Barrok) (Metlitzki 1977, 160–197). Metlitzki contends that "the romantic Saracens of the military encounters are stereotypes petrified in a literary convention which served as a vehicle of propaganda and psychological warfare" (188). Jeffrey Jerome Cohen specifically connects *The Romance of the Sowdone of Babylone* to English involvement with the final failed Crusades of the Middle Ages. This Charlemagne romance's incorporation of Chaucerian phrases helps date it after the 1390 Crusade in Tunis and to the first half of the 15th century.

Interest in the Fierabras cycle continued into the Early Modern era. For instance, in 1484 William CAXTON printed his translation of a French prose adaptation of Fierabras, which he entitled the *History and Lyf of the Noble and Crysten Prince Charles the Grete* (de Mandach 1987, 136). Apparently Caxton was interested in employing the Matter of France (romance epics about Charlemagne and his Peers) as a model the English should follow in reacting to the rising threat of the Islamic Ottoman Empire.

Bibliography

Cohen, Jeffrey Jerome. "On Saracen Enjoyment: Some Fantasies of Race in Late Medieval France and England," *Journal of Medieval and Early Modern Studies* 31, no. 1 (2001): 113–146.

Hausknecht, Emil, ed. *The Romance of the Sowdone of Babylone and of Ferumbras His Sone Who Conquered Rome.* 1881. EETS ES 38. London: Oxford University Press, 1969.

Herrtage, Sidney J. *The English Charlemagne Romances.* Part I: *Sir Ferumbras.* 1879. EETS ES 34. London: Oxford University Press, 1966.

Mandach, Andre de. "The Evolution of the Matter of Fierabras: Present State of Research." In *Romance Epic: Essays on a Medieval Literary Genre,* edited by Hans-Erich Keller, 129–139. Studies in Medieval Culture, 24. Kalamazoo, Michigan: Medieval Institute, 1987.

Metlitzki, Dorothee. *The Matter of Araby in Medieval England.* New Haven, Conn.: Yale University Press, 1977.

O'Sullivan, M. I. *Fierumbras and Otuel and Roland.* 1935. EETS OS 198. Suffolk, U.K.: Boydell and Brewer, 2002.

Barbara Stevenson

Filocolo, Il Giovanni Boccaccio (ca. 1336)

One of BOCCACCIO's earliest works, composed during the young writer's first years of independence in Naples between 1336 and 1338, the lengthy prose ROMANCE *Il Filocolo* (Love's labor) has been called the first Italian novel. The text has been criticized by many readers as overly pedantic, full of learned allusions and digressions included by the 23-year-old poet as a demonstration of his newly acquired knowledge. In addition, the plot is rambling and circuitous. Boccaccio uses a combination of sources, mainly two short poems in French but including Dante, Ovid, Virgil, and other short French and Italian texts, in retelling the popular medieval story of *FLOIRE ET BLANCHEFLOR* (here called Florio and Biancifiore).

Boccaccio's text begins with an introduction, set at Easter, in which the narrator is urged by Fiammetta (Boccaccio's name for a beautiful married Neapolitan woman he claims to be in love with him) to retell the story of Florio and Biancifiore in the Italian vernacular. This is followed by the five books of Boccaccio's romance, beginning with the births—on the same day—of Florio (the son of the pagan king Felice of Spain) and Biancifiore (posthumous child of Lelio, a descendant of the Roman hero Scipio Africanus, and his wife, Giulia—a descendant of Julius Caesar—who dies in childbirth). The children are raised in the same royal household and fall in love, but the king, unaware that Biancifiore is not of low birth, tries to separate the couple. He sends Florio off to be raised by an uncle, and sells Biancifiore to merchants who in turn sell her to an Egyptian sultan in Alexandria. King Felice tells Florio that the girl has died, but when he threatens suicide, his mother tells him the truth. At that point Florio sets off to recover his lost love, adopting the name Filocolo ("Love's Labor") as appropriate to his task.

After many adventures along the way, Filocolo arrives in Naples, and takes part in a festival at which Fiammetta herself reigns as queen and must provide a solution to 13 questions of love. Although a digression, this episode became the most famous section of the *Filocolo.*

From Naples Filocolo ultimately reaches Alexandria, where he learns that Biancifiore is imprisoned in a castle. He befriends the governor of the castle during a chess game, and with his help and that of Biancifiore's nurse, attains the chamber of his beloved. After a pagan marriage ceremony of their own devising, Filocolo and Biancifiore consummate their love. Though they are discovered, they survive being burnt at the stake through the magic of Filocolo's ring, and are ultimately married publicly. Following more adventures, including a stop in Rome to be converted to Christianity, Filocolo and Biancifiore return home, where Filocolo receives his dying father's blessing and is crowned king with Biancifiore as his queen. The Roman priest Ilario, who had converted the couple, attends their coronation and writes the tale of their adventures in Greek, and from this imaginary source Boccaccio claims to have translated his own version of the story.

Though overblown and in many ways unsatisfactory, *Il Filocolo* is important as (most likely) Boccaccio's earliest significant work, and as containing his first mention of Fiammetta (identified as the lady Maria d'Aquino), whom he purports to love, but may well have simply made up as a literary device, since no record survives of the existence of such a person.

Bibliography

Bergin, Thomas G. *Boccaccio.* New York: Viking Press, 1981.

Boccaccio, Giovanni. *Il Filocolo.* Translated by Donald Cheney with the collaboration of Thomas G. Bergin. New York: Garland, 1985.

Branca, Vittore. *Boccaccio: The Man and His Works.* Translated by Richard Monges. Cotranslated and edited by Dennis J. McAuliffe. Foreword by Robert C. Clements. New York: New York University Press, 1976.

Kirkham, Victoria. *Fabulous Vernacular: Boccaccio's Filocolo and the Art of Medieval Fiction.* Ann Arbor: University of Michigan Press, 2001.

Filostrato, Il ("The Love Struck") Giovanni Boccaccio (ca. 1338)

The second major work of the great Italian poet, Boccaccio's *Il Filostrato* tells the story of what he calls the "ill conceived" love affair between the Trojan prince Troiolo and the beautiful but fickle Creseida. Based on what is essentially a subplot in the *Roman de Troie* of BENOIT DE SAINTE-MAURE (ca. 1160), *Il Filostrato* became the inspiration for CHAUCER's most important ROMANCE, *TROILUS AND CRISEYDE,* and ultimately Shakespeare's tragicomedy on the same subject.

Il Filostrato was probably the last important work Boccaccio completed during his stay in Naples, before the financial crisis of 1341 forced his return to Florence. Its dedication by the fictionalized narrator calling himself Filostrato (a word with a Greek etymology suggesting one vanquished or prostrated by Love) is addressed to a lady he calls Filomena. The narrator will, he says, relate his suffering "in the guise of another," suggesting that Troiolo's pain is a reflection of his own. For centuries readers have felt the dedication to be autobiographical, but there is no particular reason to think so, or to believe that any actual lady of Florence corresponded to the Filomena of the dedication. Boccaccio is seeking to recreate the context for the suffering passion of the young lover extolled by the youthful DANTE and his friend Guido CAVALCANTI. He does so in the historical setting of ancient Troy, a city ultimately destroyed by the love of Paris for the beautiful Helen—a popular subject in late medieval romances such as Benoit's. Boccaccio, however, probably did not use Benoit's text directly; he most likely knew either Binduccio dello Scelto's Italian translation or Guido delle Colonne's Latin version, the *Historia troiana* (1287). He also chose to write the poem in the eight-line stanzas known as OTTAVA RIMA, a form used in popular Italian romances called *cantari.*

In Boccaccio's story, Troiolo is a young Trojan prince (the son of King Priamo) who mocks the silly excesses of lovers, and Creseida is a young widow whose father, Calcas, a Trojan seer, deserts the besieged city and joins the Greek camp when he foresees the certain destruction of Troy. When

Troiolo sees Creseida, he is completely overcome by love, and suffers more than those he had previously mocked. His friend Pandaro, Creseida's cousin, becomes his go-between, and soon brings the two lovers together. A period of joy and peace for the lovers ensues, until the war encroaches on their lives. After one skirmish, an exchange of prisoners is declared. At this point, Calcas convinces the Greeks to sue for the exchange of his daughter Creseida. At the news that she is to be sent to the Greek camp, Creseida and Troiolo are devastated. Although Pandaro tries to convince Troiolo to seize Creseida and flee the city, Troiolo fails to act, and Creseida leaves, vowing to return to Troiolo within 10 days.

The Greek warrior Diomede escorts Creseida to the Greek camp, where he woos her and wins her love. Meanwhile the unsuspecting Troiolo tries to wait out Creseida's absence by passing time with Sarpidone, but his longing cannot be assuaged. When Creseida does not return to Troy, his grief becomes unbearable. Then, when his brother Deifobo seizes Creseida's golden brooch from Diomede in battle, Troiolo is finally certain Creseida has betrayed him. He storms into battle, bent on avenging himself on the seducer Diomede, but he is struck down by the fierce Achille before he can take his revenge. Boccaccio's narrator closes his story with an admonition to all young men to control their passions and not to fall in love with fickle young ladies, despite their beauty and their charms.

Il Filostrato, notwithstanding its roots in the medieval romance tradition that extolled the refined behavior of the noble class, is in fact very popular in tone and colloquial in language, and is intended, as Boccaccio's earlier works generally are, for a sophisticated middle-class audience rather than a noble one. Though of less consequence in itself than Boccaccio's later epic *TESEIDA* or his famous frame narrative *The DECAMERON, Il Filostrato* may be just as significant in its influence on later writers, especially in the English tradition.

Bibliography

Bergin, Thomas G. *Boccaccio.* New York: Viking Press, 1981.

Boccaccio, Giovanni. *Il Filostrato.* Italian text edited by Vincenzo Pernicone. Translated with an introduction by Robert P. apRoberts and Anna Bruni Seldis. New York: Garland, 1986.

———. *The Filostrato of Giovanni Boccaccio.* Translated by N. E. Griffin, and A. B. Myrick. New York: Biblo and Tannen, 1967.

Hanly, Michael G. *Boccaccio, Beauvau, Chaucer; Troilus and Criseyde: Four Perspectives on Influence.* Norman, Okla.: Pilgrim Books, 1990.

Findern Manuscript (Findern Anthology) (ca. 1456)

Cambridge University Library MS. Ff. 1.6 is commonly known as the "Findern Manuscript" because it is believed to have belonged to the Findern family and to have been produced at their country house in Derbyshire in the middle of the 15th century, perhaps around the year 1456. The text is an anthology containing a number of poems by GOWER, by CHAUCER (including *The PARLIAMENT OF FOWLS* and *The LEGEND OF GOOD WOMEN* as well as the short lyrics *The Complaint of Venus, The Complaint Unto Pity,* and *The COMPLAINT TO HIS PURSE*) and by other authors copied by various hands. The manuscript also contains what are probably original compositions by a variety of poets.

Of particular interest to scholars have been the names of women appearing mainly in the margins of the manuscript: names like "Anne Schyrley," "Margery Hungerford," "Fraunces Crucker," "Elisabeth Coton," and "Elisabeth Frauncys." All are surnames of well-known families living in the immediate vicinity of the Findern household, suggesting that a number of women from the area were united in their literary interests, and that the manuscript was a cooperative production of a group of women who were the audience as well as the scribes of the poems. It is possible that the Anne Schyrley (or "Shirley") mentioned is the daughter of the well-known copyist and book lender John SHIRLEY (1366–1454). Many of the patrons of John Shirley's bookshop were women, and scholars have conjectured that the Findern manuscript was produced by a group of women who gathered together to share poetry, and that they copied into the book favorite poems that they came across in borrowed manuscripts. The manuscript is thus evidence of the literacy and taste of women in the 15th century.

Perhaps more important, it is quite possible that the poetic interests of the women who produced the Findern manuscript was not limited to the reading of other people's verse, but that many of the lyric poems preserved in the manuscript were composed by the women themselves to share with one another. Though not unlike COURTLY LOVE poems by male authors who assume a female persona, some 15 lyrics from the Findern manuscript have been proposed by scholars as the work of women poets. If this attribution is true, these poems would be among the earliest in English written by women poets. The best-known of these poems occur on folio 135r of the manuscript: Here is a cycle of four lyrics beginning "Come home, dere herte, from tareing," expressing a woman's lamenting the absence of her lover and ultimately rejoicing when he returns. Each poem of the cycle uses a 13-line structure, with stanzas of five, three, and five lines, rhyming *aabba aab aabba.* The situation is certainly one that would have been common to women of the time, and the formal aspects of the poem suggest the poet's sophistication, but it should be noted that without other evidence, it is impossible to be certain that the author was one of the women that produced the manuscript, or even that the author was female. That attribution remains an interesting but unproven theory.

Bibliography

Beadle, Richard and A. E. B. Owen, eds. *The Findern Manuscript: Cambridge University Library ms. Ff. 1. 6.* New York: British Book Centre, 1977.

Hanson-Smith, Elizabeth. "A Woman's View of Courtly Love: The Findern Anthology," *Journal of Women's Studies in Literature* 1 (1979): 179–194.

McNamer, Sarah. "Female Authors, Provincial Setting: The Re-Versing of Courtly Love in the Findern Manuscript." *Viator* 22 (1991): 279–310.

Robbins, Rossell Hope. "The Findern Anthology," *PMLA* 69 (1954): 610–642.

Finnsburh Fragment (*The Fight at Finnsburh, The Battle at Finnsburh*) (ca. 700–1000)

The Fight at Finnsburh is the name commonly given to a fragment of 48 lines of an OLD ENGLISH poem discovered on a single parchment manuscript page in the 18th century and subsequently lost. The fragment survives only in a faulty transcription made and printed by George Hickes in 1705. The fragment has been of significant interest to *BEOWULF* scholars because it deals with the Danish-Frisian feud that also forms the subject of the SCOP's song recited in lines 1063–1159 of *Beowulf,* after Beowulf kills the monster Grendel.

The longer story from which both the fragment and *Beowulf's* Finn episode are taken involves an attempt to settle the long-running feud between the Frisians (and their King Finn) and the Danes (under King Hnaef) through Finn's marriage to Hnaef's sister Hildeburh. During the ensuing peace, Hnaef and 60 of his retainers visit Finn and Hildeburh at the Frisian stronghold, Finnsburh. For unexplained reasons, the peace is broken and the Frisians attack Hnaef and his men at night in their hall, killing Hnaef and many of his followers and losing a number of their own men in the process, including the son of Finn and Hildeburh. A truce is declared during which the Danes, now under the leadership of Hengest, are to put aside the Germanic obligation to avenge their fallen lord and to remain with the Frisians through the winter, acting as the retainers of Finn, their king's killer. The truce breaks down in the spring as the Danes, awakened to their obligation to their fallen lord, take up arms, slaughter Finn, and return home with Hildeburh and with the Frisian treasure.

The fragment begins in mid sentence, as one of the Danes has noticed a flash of light outside the hall, perhaps torchlight glistening on armor, that warns the Danes of the Frisians' treachery. The Danes post warriors at both doors to the hall and fight heroically, holding out for five days without losing a single man. But several are wounded and their armor is wearing out. Here the fragment breaks off. The remainder of the story we know from the scop's version of events in *Beowulf,* which begins with Hildeburh looking upon the devastation after the end of the battle in the hall.

Critical interest in the *Finnsburh Fragment* has been concerned chiefly with its relationship to the Finn episode in *Beowulf.* Some scholars have argued that the fragment is the only surviving example of a kind of short narrative *lay* supposed to have been popular in Anglo-Saxon courts between the sixth and 10th centuries. Such short narratives, intended for oral delivery (like *Beowulf's* scop's song), were supposed to narrate, in a concise and unadorned style, events concerned with the Germanic heroic age, the period of Germanic migrations including the Anglo-Saxon invasion of Britain in the fifth century.

More recent criticism, however, no longer considers the fragment to be an example of a genuine *lay* of this kind. For one thing, little can be said with certainty about an imperfect copy of a fragment whose original page has been lost. Second, it is not known how long the original poem was that contained this fragment: If, as earlier scholars thought, the fragment lacks only a few lines at the beginning and a few at the end, then it could conceivably be an early *lay.* But the style of the surviving fragment is not concise and terse but somewhat discursive, suggesting it may in fact be part of a much longer poem. If the fragment tells only a very small part of a much larger narrative (as seems more likely now), then earlier hypotheses are not valid. Still, the fragment remains interesting as one of the few surviving scraps of Germanic heroic legend in Old English, scraps that tantalizingly suggest a far richer tradition, perhaps irrevocably lost.

Bibliography

Beowulf and the Fight at Finnsburg. 2nd ed. Edited by Friedrich Klaeber. Boston: Heath, 1950.

Fry, Donald K. *Finnsburh Fragment and Episode.* London: Methuen, 1974.

Tolkien, J. R. R. *Finn and Hengest: The Fragment and the Episode.* Edited by Alan Bliss. Boston: Houghton Mifflin, 1983.

Floire et Blancheflor (ca. 1160 and 13th century)

This Old French idyllic verse ROMANCE exists in two different versions, the earlier one, sometimes called aristocratic, composed ca. 1160 (Manuscript A), and the later, called "popular," composed sometime in the 13th century. The early version has come down to us in four manuscripts (A, B, C, V), the later is preserved as a fragment in one manuscript and contains a number of additional accounts about the male protagonist's chivalric adventures, such as defending Babylon for the Emir, which gains him his favor and the privilege to marry Blancheflor.

Nothing is known about the original author. The narrative is based on a long literary tradition apparently harkening back to ancient Arabic literature, such as the account of "Neema and Noam" in *THOUSAND AND ONE NIGHTS.* Some scholars have also postulated ancient Persian or Indian sources, but we have no proof for that. The Old French version, in turn, spawned many translations into other European languages, especially Middle Dutch (Diederic van Assenede's *Floris eende Blanceflor*), Middle High German (the *Trierer Floyris,* ca. 1170, and Konrad Fleck's *Flore und Blancheflur,* ca. 1220), MIDDLE ENGLISH (*Floris and Blanchefleur,* 13th century), Old Italian, and Old Spanish. We also know of Norwegian (*Flóres saga ok Blankiflúr,* ca. 1300), Swedish (*Flores och Blanzeflor,* ca. 1311), and Danish versions (15th century). The 13th-century Old French version inspired BOCCACCIO to write his *Il Filocolo* (ca. 1340–50). A recently discovered 14th-century Spanish *Crónica de Flores y Blancaflor* confirms the universal popularity of this narrative. The 15th century witnessed a steady growth of additional translations and recreations into Early New High German, Yiddish, Czech, Greek, and Spanish (one version, today lost, was printed in 1512, the other ca. 1530).

Basically the narrative relates the story of two children who are born on the same day, one to a heathen queen, the other to a Christian captive from the Galician coast (today, the northwest of Spain). The two children are brought up and are, upon the insistence of Floire, educated together. Soon enough they fall in love. When the heathen

King Fénix—who in the 13th-century version is called Galerïn—observes their profound affection, he sends his son to a school far away from home, promising to let Blancheflor follow him in a fortnight. When this does not happen, Floire pines away and so is allowed to return home. Upon his wife's advice, however, Fénix quickly sells Blancheflor to some Babylonian merchants who in turn sell her to their emir. To make up an explanation, the parents deceive their son into thinking that his beloved has died, which they prove with an elaborate tomb for the girl. In his despair Floire is about to commit suicide, but his mother quickly intervenes and later reveals the truth to him. This sets the young man on the search for his beloved, now supported and richly equipped by his father. Eventually Floire tracks down Blanchefloire and manages to enter the tower where she is kept along with all the other female slaves. Eunuchs guard the building tightly, but the young man bribes one of them into letting him enter hidden in a basket of flowers. Servants carry him up, but take him not to his beloved's room, but to the room where a German princess, Claris, lives. Since Claris is Blancheflor's friend, she helps Floire reunite with his beloved. After several days of happiness, however, Floire is discovered, and the emir orders a court date for them at which one of them shall be executed. Because of their deep love, Floire and Blancheflor plead to die for each other. When the emir observes their absolute dedication, and hears his councilors strongly advise him to show mercy and set them both free, he kind-heartedly consents and weds them as well. At the same time, upon Floire's urging, the emir takes Claris as his wife. Soon news arrives that Floire's father has died, so the young couple returns to his land and the new king, Floire, for his wife's sake, embraces Christianity and makes his people convert as well.

Remarkably, despite the fleeting reference to the Christian religion at the beginning (Blancheflor's mother is a Christian) and the end (Floire's baptism), the entire narrative is predicated on a surprisingly open-minded attitude toward Muslims. The only conflicts concern love and the disagreement between the older and the younger generation. Moreover, all female figures in this tale prove to be highly intelligent and admirable, and often serve as the most trustworthy advisers. *Floire et Blancheflor* shows intriguing parallels with *AUCASSIN ET NICOLETTE,* although there are no direct connections between the two verse narratives.

Bibliography

Le Conte de Floire et Blancheflor. Edited by Jean-Luc Leclanche. Paris: Librairie Honore Champion, 1980.

Grieve, Patricia E. *Floire and Blancheflor and the European Romance.* Cambridge: Cambridge University Press, 1997.

Hubert, Merton Jerome, trans. *The Romance of Floire and Blanchefleur: A French Idyllic Poem of the Twelfth Century.* Chapel Hill: University of North Carolina Press, 1966.

Albrecht Classen

Floure and the Leaf, The (ca. 1460–1480)

The Floure and the Leaf is a 595-line MIDDLE ENGLISH poem in RHYME ROYAL stanzas that was formerly attributed to Geoffrey CHAUCER, but is certainly too late to be his. The great Chaucerian scholar W. W. Skeat included it in his volume of *Chaucerian and Other Pieces,* and argued forcefully that it was written by the author of another anonymous Middle English poem, *The Assembly of Ladies,* but Skeat's opinion has not found a consensus. The title comes from an aristocratic game in the French and English courts of the late 14th century, in which members of the court took sides in love debates, in particular those associated with the celebration of May, in which the courtiers supported either the party of the Flower or of the Leaf. Chaucer alludes to this court fad in the Prologue to his *LEGEND OF GOOD WOMEN,* and GOWER makes a similar allusion in his *CONFESSIO AMANTIS.* The French poet Eustace DESCHAMPS wrote three *BALLADES* on the subject, taking the side of the Flower in two of them, and of the Leaf in the third.

In the poem, a female narrator rises early to walk in a grove, from which, on a wide meadow beyond, she sees two parties of noble men and women. The first group, dressed in white and led by Diana, goddess of chastity, and including nine worthy knights later identified as the NINE WORTHIES, is the company of the Flower. The company of the Leaf arrives dressed in green, and led by Flora, goddess of the flowers. The parties sing and dance, and the knights joust, but the party of the Flower suffers from the heat, and when a great hailstorm comes up they suffer again, from the buffets of hail and from the cold. The adherents of the Leaf are safe from these extremes of temperature as they take shelter under the laurel tree, and they comfort the Flower party after the storm.

The ALLEGORY of the two parties seems obvious. The Flower may look beautiful but is transient and delicate, and if the poem is related to a love debate, the flower suggests impermanence, a fickleness that is easily affected by passions that may blow hot and cold. The sturdier, more enduring Leaf suggests fidelity. In the poem, the narrator meets another Lady who acts as her guide, and who explains the allegory of the two parties, condemning those of the Flower for their idleness. The guide then asks the narrator which faction she herself would support, and the narrator opts for the Leaf, a decision for which she is praised.

The condemnation of the "hot and cold" fickleness of lovers recalls Thomas MALORY's comments about love in his *Le MORTE DARTHUR*, with which this poem is roughly contemporary. But the love-vision genre owes a great deal to Chaucer's DREAM VISION poems like *The Legend of Good Women* and *The PARLIAMENT OF FOWLS*. Echoes of LYDGATE, Deschamps, and the *ROMAN DE LA ROSE* are also apparent in the text. The female narrator is unusual, and some have speculated that the poet was a woman, though there is no way to prove such a theory.

No manuscript version of the poem is extant. The earliest text of the poem is a printed version in Thomas Speght's 1598 edition of Chaucer's works. John Dryden, ironically admiring the work as one of Chaucer's best, composed a modernized version of the poem in his *Fables Ancient and Modern* (1700).

Bibliography

Barratt, Alexandra A. T. " 'The Flower and the Leaf' and 'The Assembly of Ladies': Is There a (Sexual) Difference?" *Philological Quarterly* 66 (1987): 1–24.

The Floure and the Leafe. In *The Floure and the Leafe; The Assembly of Ladies; The Isle of Ladies*, edited by Derek Pearsall. Kalamazoo, Mich.: Medieval Institute Publications, 1990.

Harrington, David V. "The Function of Allegory in *The Flower and the Leaf*," *Neuphilologische Mitteilungen* 71 (1970): 244–253.

Skeat, W. W., ed. *Chaucerian and Other Pieces*. Vol. 7, *The Works of Chaucer*. Oxford: Oxford University Press, 1897.

flyting

From the obscure word *flite*, meaning to quarrel or dispute, the term *flyting* is most properly applied to a genre of Scottish poetry that seems to have originated in the late 15th or early 16th century, in which two poets exchanged vigorous, scurrilous, and often vulgar and profane invective. It has remained a feature of Scottish poetry even through the 20th century, but its origins are more difficult to trace.

Some scholars point out a tradition within heroic poetry of boasting matches between leaders prior to battle—a kind of exchange that can be seen, for example, in the OLD ENGLISH poem *The BATTLE OF MALDON*, where the leader of the Viking warriors engages in an insulting exchange with Byrhtnoth, the English commander. Similar verbal sparring occurs as well in some of the CHANSONS DE GESTE. Other scholars point to poetic debates like the Provençal *TENSO* as influential on the *flyting*. Still others attribute the Scottish *flyting* to the tradition of the Celtic bards, whose heirs the Scottish poets may have felt themselves to be.

The best-known example of a *flyting* is the 552-line *Flyting of Dunbar and Kennedie*. The type of invective common to such poems can be seen in a few lines that close Dunbar's first harangue of Kennedie:

Muttoun dryver, girnall river, gadswyver—
fowl fell the;
Herretyk, lunatyk, purspyk, carlingis pet,

Rottin crok, dirtin dok—cry cok, or I sall quell the.

(Kinsley 85, ll. 246–48)

(That is, "mutton driver, granary plunderer, mare-buggerer—fowl strike you down; heretic, lunatic, pickpocket, darling of old women; old ewe with sheep-rot, filthy arse—admit defeat, before I shall slay you.")

Bibliography

Kinsley, James, ed. *The Poems of William Dunbar.* Oxford: Clarendon Press, 1979.

Folgore da San Geminiano (Folgore San Gimignano, Giacomo da Michele) (ca. 1270–ca. 1332)

The real name of this early popular 14th-century poet was Giacomo da Michele, but he is known to posterity as "Folgore," a name that means "splendor." Little is known of his life. He may have been the man of that name noted for his military deeds in 1305 and 1306 and ultimately made a knight in 1332, though many believe he died before that date. Certainly his poetic output, the 32 sonnets that have survived, dates only from about 1309 until 1317. His poems are in what has been called the "realistic-comical" style, and seem to have been produced as entertainment for the wealthy middle class citizens of Florence and of Siena.

Folgore's best-known work is a sonnet series called *Sonetti de' mesi,* or "Sonnets of the months." The series consists of 14 sonnets—one for each individual month plus a dedicatory sonnet and a concluding one. The sonnets for each month explore the pleasures and pastimes appropriate to each month, and at the same time give modern readers a realistic glimpse into the daily lives and the social customs and pursuits of wealthy Tuscans of the 14th century. Folgore dedicated these sonnets to Niccolò de' Nisi of Siena, and praised him and his circle for being more courteous than Lancelot—a line suggesting that in the cities of Italy, wealth was creating a new "courtly" class of bourgeoisie, whose elegant tastes Folgore reflects and also refines with his verse. It was once believed that the Niccolò addressed in Folgore's sonnet is the same Niccolò of Siena chastised as a notorious spendthrift by DANTE in canto XXIX of the Inferno (in the *DIVINE COMEDY*), but that view is no longer seriously held by scholars.

Folgore wrote another, lesser known sonnet sequence called *Sonetti de la semana* or "Sonnets of the Week," a series of eight poems on individual days of the week along with a dedicatory sonnet. These are dedicated to a Guelf nobleman and describe, again, the social gatherings of the wealthy. Five other extant poems seem to have been part of a projected series of 17, and deal with the qualities of knighthood in an allegorical style.

Folgore, a strong advocate of the Guelf party (the Italian party made up mainly of the middle class that generally supported the pope in Italian politics), does express his political sentiments in at least four of his extant sonnets, including his chagrin at the Guelfs' 1315 military defeat by the Ghibellines (the party supported by the aristocracy that generally supported the emperor in Italian politics). Since Folgore's latest extant poems seem to be dated not long after this defeat, perhaps political fortunes influenced his abandonment of poetry. Or perhaps he died about this time, and was in fact not the same man knighted in 1332. We can only speculate. But interest in Folgore's poetry was revived in the 19th century when new English translations of his "Sonnets of the months" were made by Dante Gabriel Rossetti, and Folgore's value as a poet continues as people see in his poetry the realistic depiction of his times.

Bibliography

Aldington, Richard. *A Wreath for San Gemignano.* New York: Duel, Sloan and Pearce, 1945.

Rossetti, Dante Gabriel, trans. *The Early Italian Poets.* Edited by Sally Purcell. Berkeley: University of California Press, 1981.

Folquet de Marseille (ca. 1160–1231)

One of the more unlikely of the Provençal TROUBADOURS, Folquet de Marseille was the son of a Genoese merchant from whom he is said to have inherited a good fortune, and by 1178, he was a wealthy merchant himself, living in Marseille.

Within a few years, however, Folquet had become a troubadour. Allusions in his poems suggest he was in the court of Alfonso II of Aragon by around 1180, and over the next 15 years seems to have been associated with several other courts of southern France and Spain.

Folquet wrote all of his extant poems in these years. Of the 29 lyrics attributed to him, 13 have music that has survived. Many are fairly conventional COURTLY LOVE poems. Folquet seems to have become known for his amorous exploits. He was one of the first troubadours to use the *coblas esparas*—individual stanzas intended to stand alone. One such stanza is addressed to his JONGLEUR, Vermillion, and concerns a certain woman who he felt had ruined one of his *CANSOS*:

> *Vermillion, I am complaining to you about*
> *an evil, stupid, painted lady who has*
> *destroyed and ruined my song by saying*
> *that I composed it about her . . .*
>
> (Paden 2000, 71)

In some of his poems, though, Folquet suggests a more spiritual passion. One of his better-known poems, beginning "Vers Dieus, el vostre nom," is a prayer to God in the form of a dawn song (*see* ALBA).

Such poems were an indication of the direction Folquet's life was about to take. Sometime around 1200, he withdrew from the world—according to his *VIDA* along with his wife and two sons—and entered the Cistercian abbey of Thoronet in Provence, where in 1201, he was made abbot. By 1205, he had become bishop of Toulouse. It was as bishop that Folquet gained real notoriety. He became a supporter and protector of St. Dominic, and in 1215, was a cofounder of the Dominican order. He also was instrumental in founding the University of Toulouse in 1229. But he is best known for his role in the Albigensian Crusade, preached against the heretical Catharist sect that was widespread in Provence and the rest of southern France. Folquet was chief prosecutor of heretics during the Crusade, and was renowned for his cruelty: He is said to have sent hundreds to their deaths, and a contemporary poem names him as the Antichrist.

Nevertheless Folquet is the only troubadour to appear in paradise in DANTE's *DIVINE COMEDY*. The great Italian poet places Folquet in the third circle of heaven, the circle of Venus, in Canto IX of *Paradiso*. Here Folquet explains to Dante how his amorous early life eventually led him into a passion for God. Dante never mentions Folquet's role in the Crusade.

Bibliography

Goldin, Frederick, ed. and trans. *Lyrics of the Troubadours and Trouvères: An Anthology and a History.* Garden City, N.Y.: Anchor, 1973.

Paden, William D. *Medieval Lyric: Genres in Historical Context.* Urbana: University of Illinois Press, 2000.

Stronski, Stanislaw. *Le troubadour Folquet de Marseille.* Cracow: Académie des sciences, 1910.

Fortescue, Sir John (ca. 1395–ca. 1477)

Sir John Fortescue was a constitutional lawyer who wrote in both Latin and English. Because of his forthright writing style, his works were significant in the development of English prose. He was immersed in politics and his writing is a reflection of that. His most famous works are *De laudibus legum Angliae* (1468–1470, published in 1546), *De natura legis naturae* (1431–1433), and *The Governance of England* (ca. 1473).

Fortescue was born into an ancient Devonshire family in Norris, Somerset. He was admitted to Lincoln's Inn (ca. 1415) and later graduated from Exeter College, Oxford. He spent the majority of his life in service of the house of Lancaster. He was appointed as a Member of Parliament in 1421, sergeant-at-law in 1430, and chief justice of the king's court in 1442, and was knighted in 1443.

Fortescue faithfully served under Henry VI even to the point of joining him in exile in 1461 after his defeat by the Yorkist faction during the Wars of the Roses. While in exile with the king, Queen Margaret, and Prince Edward, Fortescue aided in the prince's education. He wrote two of his most famous works for this purpose: *De Natura legis natura* and *De laudibus legum Angliae.* In the Battle of Tewkesbury (1471), Prince

Edward was killed, Henry VI was defeated, and Fortescue was taken prisoner. As a result of the battle, Edward IV of the House of York was the irrefutable king. Fortescue was pardoned and his property returned to him only after he recanted his pro-Lancastrian arguments with the work *A Declaration upon Certain Writings* (1471–73). He was also admitted to the king's council as a result of the retraction. He spent his final years in Ebrington, during which time he wrote *Understanding and Faith.*

Based on his history, it is not surprising that Fortescue's most famous works are political. Fortescue had spent time abroad and studied the governments of both Scotland and France. *De natura legis naturae* was translated into English as *Monarchia: or, The Difference between an Absolute and a Limited Monarchy.* It was one of the works written for Prince Edward's education and concerned the forms of "natural" government.

De laudibus legum Angliae (In praise of the laws of England) was also for Edward's instruction. In it Fortescue favorably compared England's *jus politicum et regale* government to France's *jus regale* government. The former is a government in which the king rules by laws to which the people have assented; in the latter, the king has absolute rule by laws he has made for himself.

The Governance of England was a work originally written for Henry VI, but rewritten and presented to Edward IV after the Yorkist success at Tewkesbury. Its substance was very similar to *De laudibus legum Angliae,* but also included practical recommendations—for example, that the king rely only on guaranteed revenues and that the council be composed of paid appointees. This would ensure impartial advisement by the council.

Clearly, Fortescue's political involvements influenced his major works: *De laudibus legum Angliae, De natura legis naturae,* and *The Governance of England.* As a result, his work was also an influence on the politics of his time.

Bibliography

Fortescue, John. *On the Laws and Governance of England.* Edited by Shelley Lockwood. Cambridge and New York: Cambridge University Press, 1997.

Gill, Paul E. "Politics and Propaganda in Fifteenth-Century England: The Polemical Writings of Sir John Fortescue," *Speculum* 46 (April): 333–347.

Gross, Anthony. *The Dissolution of the Lancastrian Kingship: Sir John Fortescue and the Crisis of Monarchy in Fifteenth-Century England.* Stamford, U.K.: P. Watkins, 1996.

Kekwech, M. L. " 'Thou Shalt Be under the Power of the Man': Sir John Fortescue and the Yorkist Succession," *Nottingham Medieval Studies* 42 (1998): 188–230.

Malene A. Little

Fortunatus, Venantius Honorius Clementianus (ca. 530–ca. 609)

Fortunatus, sometimes called the last of the classical poets, was a Latin poet who became bishop of Poitiers in Frankish Gaul. He was a prolific versifier and author of SAINTS' LIVES, and is still remembered today through hymns that continue to be sung in Christian worship.

Fortunatus was born in Trevizo, near Venice, about 530. He was brought up in Aquileia and converted to Christianity at an early age, and later received a classical education in Ravenna (at that time capital of the Western Empire), studying grammar and rhetoric as well as Roman law. Sometime around 565, in his early 30s, he contracted an eye disease. When the disease was cured, Fortunatus believed it had been cured through the intercession of St. Martin of Tours, and in gratitude, he undertook a pilgrimage to Tours in order to worship at St. Martin's shrine.

Fortunatus's route to Tours took him through modern-day Germany, a journey that took him two years to complete. According to one legend, he repaid hospitality on his route across Europe by composing poems and songs, sometimes extemporaneously. In any case, he apparently made his reputation as a poet during this trip, which can be traced by reference to poems that he wrote in Mainz, Cologne, Metz, Rheims, and Paris before coming to Tours. After arriving in Gaul, Fortunatus became attached to the Frankish king of Austrasia, Sigebert I. Fortunatus became court poet to

Sigebert, and is said to have traveled with the king throughout Gaul.

In approximately 567, Fortunatus visited Poitiers, where, in the convent of the Holy Cross, he met Queen Radegunda, who had founded the convent after leaving her husband, King Clotaire I of the Franks. Fortunatus eventually became an adviser to Radegunda and her daughter Agnes, the abbess. He served as steward and financial adviser for the convent of 200 nuns and eventually, after he was ordained, as their chaplain, until the abbess and the former queen died in 587. Some of his best-known verses come from this period: In 568 the convent was given a sacred relic—a piece of the true cross from Byzantine emperor Justin II. Fortunatus celebrated the gift by writing a series of hymns. Of these, the hymns *Vexilla regis prodeunt* (The royal banners forward go) and *Pange lingua gloriosi lauream certaminis* (Sing my tongue the glorious battle) were adopted as part of the liturgy for Holy Week for the medieval church.

After Radegunda's death, Fortunatus spent some time visiting some of the most important spiritual leaders in Gaul, and was particularly befriended by GREGORY OF TOURS. It was Gregory who encouraged Fortunatus to publish his poetry, and apparently to compose a four-book, 2,243-line hexameter verse biography of St. Martin of Tours. In 599, Fortunatus was elected bishop of Poitiers, a position he kept for only a short time, for he was dead by 609, possibly earlier.

Fortunatus published 10 books of his verse during his lifetime, and one more was published posthumously. Besides his verse life of St. Martin, he published a number of other saints' lives, including biographies of St. Radegunda as well as St. Hilary of Poitiers and St. Germain of Paris. His great variety of poems includes panegyrics, elegies, verse letters to friends, patriotic poems, epigrams and occasional poems, in addition to his hymns. Most contemporary critics are unimpressed by the quality of Fortunatus' verse, though it is the most important poetry to come out of the rather bleak period of Merovingian Gaul. But in general his poetry avoids ALLEGORY, and often gives concrete details of everyday life. Other than his surviving hymns, his works are admired chiefly for the light they throw on Christian life during that era.

Bibliography

George, Judith, ed. and trans. *Venantius Fortunatus: Personal and Political Poems.* Liverpool: Liverpool University Press, 1995.

———. *Venantius Fortunatus: A Latin Poet in Merovingian Gaul.* Oxford: Clarendon Press; New York: Oxford University Press, 1992.

Raby, Frederic James Edward. *A History of Latin Poetry in the Middle Ages.* 2nd ed. Oxford: Clarendon Press, 1957.

Francis of Assisi, Saint (1181–1226)

Francis was born at Assisi in Umbria in 1181 or 1182. His father, Piero Bernardone, was a prosperous cloth merchant who had plans for Francis to follow him in his trade, or perhaps become a knight. In 1201 he was taken hostage for a year after an attack on Perugia, and in 1205 his father again outfitted him for a military expedition, this time to Apulia. But he quickly returned home after a vision in which God called him to his service. When Christ, in another vision, told Francis to repair his church, he resolved to become a hermit and dedicate himself to repairing the church of San Damiano, near Assisi. His father, angry at Francis's use of family funds and embarrassed by Francis's behavior, imprisoned him and brought him before the bishop. In a famous scene, Francis stripped himself before the bishop and embraced the life of poverty. In 1211, when he had 11 followers, Francis gave them a short *rule* (now lost) and subsequently received approval from Pope Innocent III to found the Friars Minor. Clara Sciffi, a girl from a noble family of Assisi, joined Francis and founded the Poor Clares. In 1219 Francis journeyed to Egypt to preach to the sultan; it was there he contracted an eye ailment that plagued him the rest of his life. After a new official *rule* of the Friars Minor was approved November 29, 1223, Francis gave up leadership of the order and went to the mountains to live in secluded prayer. On the mountain of La Verna he received the Stigmata (marks resembling Christ's crucifixion wounds) from a crucified, winged seraph. In declining health because of illness and self-deprivation, he died at the Porziuncula, the site of many important early events of his order, on October 3, 1226. Within two years of his death, he was canonized by Pope Gregory IX.

Francis called for simplicity of life, poverty, and humility before God. He worked to care for the poor, and one of his first actions after his conversion was to care for lepers. By seeking to make himself an image of Christ—to serve as an exemplar for his followers—he created a transparent self that has made the accurate reconstruction of his life and vision very difficult. The legend of Francis as it has come down to us is represented in two types of the literature. First, of course, are his own writings. Francis was not a prolific writer, but by the middle of the 13th century, the friars had begun to collect his works. The most popularly anthologized of these was the *Admonitions.* This work reveals the depth and clarity of his visions as well as the limits of his education and simplicity of his vocabulary. Francis's writings, however, were largely ignored in the development of his legend and were seldom used by subsequent hagiographers. In 1971, Esser and Oliger published the first attempt at identifying and classifying the earliest manuscripts of Francis's writings.

Hagiographical materials (SAINTS' LIVES) are the most voluminous category of literature concerning Francis. These early biographies and devotional works evolved into layers of historical accretions. In preparation for the canonization of Francis, THOMAS OF CELANO prepared the first official account of his life. This text has two missions: to honor the new saint and instruct readers about the importance of Francis's particular path of holiness. In addition, Thomas prepared a series of readings based on the saint's life for the liturgical celebration of the divine office. Within a short time other portraits of the new saint began to emerge. In 1232 Henri d'Avranches used Celano's portrait as the foundation for a *Versified Life of St. Francis* which represents a courtly approach to the life. Celano's second life of Francis, *The Remembrance of the Desire of a Soul* (1247), reflects a much fuller portrait of the saint. In response to the rapid growth of the order the general minister, BONAVENTURE of Bagnoreggio, produced in 1260 *The Legenda major.* This important work has two sections, the first describing Francis's life and virtues, the second describing his miracles. Bonaventure also authored *The Legenda minor,* a liturgical piece. In 1266, the order sought to curtail the proliferation of materials about Francis and decreed that all versions of the life of Francis except that by Bonaventure should be removed. This decree had little effect, and new versions and amplifications of Francis's life continued for centuries.

Bibliography

Armstrong, Regis J., J. A. Wayne Hellman, and William Short, eds. *Francis of Assisi. The Early Documents.* 3 vols. New York: New City Press, 2001.

Esser, Kajetan, and Remy Oliger. *La tradition manuscrite des opuscules de saint François d'Assise: préliminaires de l'édition critique.* Rome: Institut historique O.F.M.C.A.P., 1972.

Cook, William R. *Images of St. Francis of Assisi: In Painting, Stone, and Glass: From the Earliest Images to ca. 1320 in Italy.* Florence (Firenze): S. Olschki, 1999.

House, Adrian. *Francis of Assisi.* Mahwah, N.J.: HiddenSpring, 2001.

Cynthia Ho

Franklin's Tale, The Geoffrey Chaucer (ca. 1395)

The Franklin's Tale is one of the most admired and discussed of CHAUCER'S *CANTERBURY TALES.* The tale is based chiefly on the folklore motif of the "rash promise," though there is no specific source or close analogue to Chaucer's story. The Franklin narrator says it comes from a Breton *LAI,* and certainly it has elements of medieval ROMANCE narrative. However, the trials of the female protagonist, Dorigen, also suggest elements of some of Chaucer's tales of pathos in which the heroine, like Constance in *The MAN OF LAW'S TALE* or Griselde in *The CLERK'S TALE,* finds happiness after a series of tribulations.

The tale concerns the Breton knight Arveragus, who wins the love of the beautiful Dorigen. When the two marry, they agree that neither shall have complete sovereignty in the marriage—that Dorigen shall be subject to Arveragus as his wife, but he shall be subject to her as her lover. When Arveragus goes over the sea to enhance his knightly reputation, Dorigen spends each day fretting over the rocks that line the shore, fearful that they will wreck her husband's ship when he returns. When a young squire, Aurelius, expresses his love for her, Dorigen rejects him by swearing to grant him her love only if the rocks along the shore disappear. Following the conventions of COURTLY LOVE, Aurelius takes to his bed and seems about to die of love, when his brother proposes a possible solution to him. They visit a learned clerk who, by means of magic, promises to make the rocks vanish in exchange for a huge fee, which Aurelius agrees to pay.

When the rocks disappear, Aurelius finds Dorigen and asks her to keep her promise: The rocks being gone, she must give him her love. The horrified Dorigen, after considering a number of women who had committed suicide rather than commit adultery, goes to Arveragus (now safely returned) to reveal her dilemma. Arveragus insists that "Trouthe is the hyeste thing that man may kepe" (Benson 1987, 187, l. 1479) and sends her to Aurelius to keep her word. Aurelius, impressed by Arveragus's noble gesture, emulates the knight by performing a generous action of his own: He releases Dorigen from her pledge. The clerk, in his turn, demonstrates his own generosity by forgiving Aurelius his debt. In the end the Franklin poses a *demande d'amour*—that is, a question for the audience to consider. He asks, Which character was the most "fre"—that is, most generous?

A good deal of criticism has considered the crucial place of *The Franklin's Tale* in what George Lyman Kittredge called Chaucer's "Marriage Debate"—a debate begun by the WIFE OF BATH and continued in *The CLERK'S TALE* and *The MERCHANT'S TALE*, concerning sovereignty in marriage. The Franklin's depiction of a marriage of mutual sovereignty seems to be the solution to the question. Another aspect of the tale explored by many scholars is the focus on "gentilesse," or true nobility, displayed by the knight, the squire, and the clerk in the tale. In this view the Franklin, a rich landowner but not a member of the noble class, wants to make a case for his own innate gentility to be recognized.

More recent criticism has seen both of these views as oversimplified. Few contemporary scholars accept the concept of the "marriage debate" quite as Kittredge presented it, though clearly Chaucer is concerned in many of his tales with marriage and male/female relations. But the marriage in the Franklin's tale is far from ideal, and Arveragus's assertion of his sovereignty by compelling his wife to "keep her word," which was never intended seriously, seems a profoundly flawed notion of "trouthe." Nor is the Franklin's enumeration of the three men's "generosity" ultimately convincing: None of the three men gives away anything that he was entitled to to begin with, all having been gained through deceit and subterfuge. It has seemed clear to most recent critics that Chaucer has created a far more complex tale than previously thought.

Bibliography

Benson, Larry, et al. *The Riverside Chaucer.* 3rd ed. Boston: Houghton Mifflin, 1987.

Collette, Carolyn. "Seeing and Believing in the *Franklin's Tale*," *Chaucer Review* 26 (1992): 395–410.

Crane, Susan. "The Franklin as Dorigen," *Chaucer Review* 24 (1990): 236–252.

Kittredge, George Lyman. "Chaucer's Discussion of Marriage," *Modern Philology* 9 (1911–1912): 435–467.

Mann, Jill. "Chaucerian Themes and Style in the Franklin's Tale," in *New Pelican Guide to English Literature.* Vol. 1, Part 1. *Medieval Literature: Chaucer and the Alliterative Tradition,* edited by Boris Ford. Harmondsworth: Penguin, 1982–1988, 133–153.

Raybin, David. " 'Women, of kynde, desiren libertee': Rereading Dorigen, Rereading Marriage," *Chaucer Review* 27 (1992): 65–86.

Frescobaldi, Dino (ca. 1271–1316)

Dino Frescobaldi came from a family of poets. His father, a prominent Florentine banker named Lamberttuccio di Ghino, was also a poet who followed the Tuscan school of GUITTONE D'AREZZO. His son, Matteo (ca. 1300–48), also wrote poetry, like Dino, in the manner of the *DOLCE STIL NOVO* ("sweet new style"), followers of Guido CAVALCANTI.

Frescobaldi seems to have been more admired in his own day and in immediately subsequent generations than he has been in more modern times. BOCCACCIO, for example, describes him as an intelligent man and a well-known poet, who at least, according to Boccaccio, was responsible for the rediscovery of the first seven cantos of DANTE's *Inferno.* Boccaccio says he sent two recovered cantos to Moroello Malaspino, with whom Dante was staying, in exile from Florence. Whether the story is true or not, it demonstrates that Frescobaldi was famous in the 14th century, and that his name was associated with Dante and, presumably, other members of the school of *Dolce Stil Novo.*

In Frescobaldi's lyrics, love often brings anguish and despair. The torments of love are a favorite theme of Cavalcanti's works, and much of Frescobaldi's work echoes Dante and Cavalcanti, as, for instance, this passage from his SONNET beginning "Donna, da gli occhi":

Lady, from your eyes it seems a light
comes forth and enters my soul:
and this light, when it is with her, often
  seems
to unite with the desire already there.

(Goldin 1973, 417, ll. 1–4)

The scientific description of the physical sight of the lady in this poem seems to derive directly from Cavalcanti's verse.

Yet Frescobaldi strove to be more than an imitator, and sought to stretch the boundaries of *stilnovist* imagery. In the same poem, he compares the lady to a "she-wolf" who torments him. Such images may have been considered improper by Cavalcanti or Dante, and some modern critics have suggested that Frescobaldi goes too far or tries too hard for something new in his images. Others think of him as an innovative poet whose attempts to rejuvenate the conventions of the *Dolce Stil Novo* helped keep the style alive.

Bibliography

Goldin, Frederick, trans. *German and Italian Lyrics of the Middle Ages: An Anthology and a History.* New York: Doubleday, 1973.

Friar's Tale, The Geoffrey Chaucer (ca. 1390)

The Friar's Tale is one of Chaucer's comic *CANTERBURY TALES.* Told by the pilgrim Friar, the quintessence of venality himself, the tale satirizes the abuses of summoners (officers of the ecclesiastical court) and is essentially a moral tale attacking the sin of simony (the abuse of church offices through bribery and graft). The Friar, a mendicant preacher, employs what is basically a sermon element, an *exemplum* or short anecdote illustrating a moral point, condemning the sin of greed. As such, the tale is partly intended to insult the pilgrim Summoner, who responds with a vicious attack on friars in *The SUMMONER'S TALE.*

In the tale a greedy and corrupt Archdeacon employs an equally avaricious Summoner, who is also a thief and a "bawd," or pimp. The Summoner sets out to extort money from an innocent old woman by means of a false summons. On the way he meets a Yeoman dressed in a jacket of green. As the two fall in together, the Yeoman introduces himself as a bailiff, and the Summoner, ashamed of his true occupation, claims to be a bailiff as well. They get along so well that they swear brotherhood and make a pact to share everything they obtain on their ride. As the Summoner presses to know more about the Yeoman, he finally reveals that he is a Fiend and that his dwelling is in Hell—and that he roams the earth in search of souls.

Far from being put off by this revelation, the Summoner becomes very curious about what things are like in Hell, and is fascinated by the Devil's ability to change shape. He never recognizes that he might be in some danger himself. As they ride, they pass by a carter whose horses are stuck in the mud. When the carter curses the horses, the Summoner tells the Devil to take them, since the carter has given them to the devil. But the Fiend tells him that the curse is not heartfelt, and, therefore, he cannot touch the animals. When the two arrive at the old woman's house and the Summoner attempts to extort money from her, she curses him, and because the curse is truly from her heart, the Devil carries the Summoner off to hell. Important to the story is the often-repeated word "intent": As it is the widow's heartfelt *intent* that the Summoner go to the Devil unless he will repent of his sins, it is the Summoner's avowed *intent* never to repent, and that is what ultimately damns him.

While several analogues to *The Friar's Tale* exist, making use of the folk motif of the "heartfelt curse," Chaucer's is especially notable for its characterization of the obliviously corrupt Summoner and for the lively dialogue between the characters. The satire of the blackmail and extortion rampant in ecclesiastical courts is also something unique to Chaucer.

Bibliography

Bloomfield, Morton W. " 'The Friar's Tale' as a Liminal Tale," *Chaucer Review* 17 (1983): 286–291.

Hahn, Thomas. "Text and Context: Chaucer's 'Friar's Tale,' " *Studies in the Age of Chaucer* 5 (1983): 67–101.

Kline, Daniel T. " 'Myne by Right': Oath Making and Intent in The Friar's Tale." *Philological Quarterly* 77 (1998): 271–293.

Ridley, Florence H. "The Friar and the Critics." In *The Idea of Medieval Literature: New Essays on Chaucer and Medieval Culture in Honor of Donald R. Howard,* edited by James M. Dean and Christian Zacher, 160–172. Newark: University of Delaware Press, 1992.

Williams, David. "From Chaucer's Pan to Logic's Fire: Intentionality in Chaucer's 'Friar's Tale.' " In *Literature and Ethics: Essays Presented to A. E. Malloch,* edited by Gary Wihl and David Williams, 77–95. Kingston and Montreal: McGill-Queen's University Press, 1988.

Friedrich von Hausen (ca. 1160–ca. 1200)

Friedrich von Hausen was one of the few Middle High German COURTLY LOVE poets whose biography is relatively well known. He seems to have been active between 1171 and 1190 and was the son of Walther von Hausen, a man of lower nobility located somewhere in the area between Bingen on the Rhine and the Palatinate. Friedrich was in the service of powerful German bishops and kings and participated in the Third Crusade, during which he died on May 6, 1190, after a fall from his horse, shortly before the death of Emperor Frederick Barbarossa, near Philomelium in Asia Minor. Friedrich was the leading Rhenish love poet of his time and is credited with having introduced the concept of esoteric, unrequited love to his German contemporaries. Friedrich drew inspiration both from Provençal and northern French poetry, creating *contrafacta* (adaptations of music from other songs for his own text), and drawing from native German sources. His 17 songs, primarily preserved in the famous *Weingartner Liederhandschrift* (MS. B) and the *Grosse Heidelberger Liederhandschrift* (MS. C), consist of wooing songs and crusade songs. The latter genre treats a lover's painful decision to go on a crusade although he has to leave his beloved behind. Here, cast in the image of a struggle between body and heart, courtly love competes with love for God. Whereas nature motifs are mostly missing, Friedrich heavily relies on introspection, reflection, and the critical examination of emotions. Some of the characteristic themes in his poetry are his lady's kiss as the highest reward for the man; love that began in childhood; his songs as messengers for his lady; the heart as a hermit's cell; the comparison of his love for his lady with the love between Dido and Aeneas; and military metaphors for love.

Bibliography

Bekker, Hugo. *Friedrich von Hausen: Inquiries into His Poetry.* Chapel Hill: University of North Carolina Press, 1977.

Des Minnesangs Frühling. Edited by Hugo Moser and Helmut Tervooren. 38th ed. Stuttgart: Hirzel, 1988.

Sayce, Olive. *The Medieval German Lyric 1150–1300: The Development of Its Themes and Forms in Their European Context.* Oxford: Clarendon Press, 1982.

Albrecht Classen

Froissart, Jean (ca. 1337–ca. 1404)

Jean Froissart was a courtier and poet in the tradition of Guillaume de MACHAUT, but is best known as perhaps the most important prose writer in 14th-century Europe. His *Chroniques*, or *Chronicles*, present a vivid and detailed narrative of, roughly, the first half of the Hundred Years' War, and the 100 extant manuscripts of the text, some expensively illuminated, testify to the *Chronicles'* popularity among the aristocratic patrons and audience for which Froissart intended them. The text remains popular today, and Froissart's descriptions of some of the contemporary events—the Battles of Crécy and Poitiers, for example, and the PEASANTS' REVOLT of 1381—are the best-known images we have of those monumental events.

Froissart was born in Valenciennes in the independent county of Hainault in the Low Countries. He seems to have come from a family of businessmen, whose primary interest was moneylending, but Froissart's talent for poetry enabled him to garner a position in the noble house of John of Hainault, the count's uncle. At some point he drew the attention of his countrywoman Philippa of Hainault, queen of EDWARD III, who invited him to be a part of the English court in 1361. He says in Book IV of the *Chronicles* that he entertained the queen with love poetry in the courtly fashion of the time, some of which has survived. In the queen's court he became acquainted with some of England's most important military officers as well as captive French nobility, awaiting ransom after England's decisive victory at the Battle of Poitiers five years earlier.

He also traveled extensively as a part of Queen Philippa's court. He visited Scotland and the court of David II, and toured the Welsh marches. In 1366, he was with Edward the Black Prince in his campaign in Gascony. With the Black Prince in Bordeaux in 1367, Froissart was in his service at the birth of the prince's son, the future King RICHARD II. In 1368, he was with the large retinue that attended Prince Lionel, second son of the king, on his journey to Italy to marry Violante Visconti of Milan. In the same entourage was another young English poet named Geoffrey CHAUCER.

Returning from Milan in 1369 by way of Brussels, Froissart received word that Queen Philippa had died. Assuming there would be nothing for him if he returned to England, Froissart entered the service of Robert de Namur of the royal family of Flanders. It was for Sir Robert that Froissart began his *Chronicles.*

The Hundred Years' War had begun the year of Froissart's birth. Thus, while he was able to write much of the history based on his own observations and the eyewitness reports of people he knew, he had to base the first part of the *Chronicles* on an earlier source: a chronicle composed by the knight Jean Le Bel, who had served in the war under John of Hainault. Froissart based the first version of his Book I almost word-for-word on Le Bel. Later he revised his first book at least twice before he died, but in his earliest version, only a few passages—like the description of the Battle of Poitiers—are truly Froissart's composition.

Le Bel's text ends with events of about 1360, and here Froissart takes up the narrative on his own. By this time Froissart had taken holy orders and been made a parish priest at Estinnes-au-Mont in Brabant, an appointment he owed to a new patron, Guy de Châtillon, count of Blois. Under the patronage of Guy and of Wenceslaus of Luxemburg, Froissart labored on Book II of his *Chronicles,* but with a new point of view: Whereas Robert de Namur had been pro-English concerning the war, both Guy and Wenceslaus were pro-French. This may have prompted Froissart's revision of his first book, which may have appeared partisan as it stood.

For Wenceslaus, Froissart also wrote a verse ROMANCE called *Méliador,* in which Froissart embedded a number of Wenceslaus's own lyric poems. That work has not impressed scholars. After Wenceslaus's death, Froissart continued to work on the *Chronicles,* and with Guy of Blois as his sole patron, he was appointed canon of Chimay, near Liege. In his later years, Froissart traveled to the court of Gaston Phoebus of Foix, the brilliance of which he describes in Book III of the

Chronicles. Later, in the mid-1390s, he made a visit to England, where he met Richard II. Five years later he was to write of Richard's deposition in Book IV of the *Chronicles.*

Froissart's *Chronicles* end in the year 1400. Of Froissart's own end, nothing definite is known. He is said to have survived until at least 1404, possibly as late as 1410, and to have been buried at Chimay. He left a body of lyric poetry that, to some extent, influenced Chaucer's own lyric production, but he is best remembered for his vivid recreation of 14th-century life in his lively and entertaining *Chronicles.*

Bibliography

Ainsworth, Peter F. *Jean Froissart and the Fabric of History: Truth, Myth, and Fiction in the* Chroniques. Oxford: Clarendon Press, 1990.

Brereton, Geoffrey, ed. and trans. *Froissart: Chronicles.* New York: Viking, 1978.

Figg, Kristen Mossler. *The Short Lyric Poems of Jean Froissart: Fixed Forms and the Expression of the Courtly Ideal.* New York: Garland, 1994.

Wimsatt, James I. *Chaucer and His French Contemporaries: Natural Music in the Fourteenth Century.* Toronto: University of Toronto Press, 1991.

Gace Brulé (ca. 1160–ca. 1213)

Gace Brulé was one of the earliest of the TROUVÈRES, northern French vernacular lyric poets of the high Middle Ages. It is likely that he was born in Champagne. His name is simply a corruption of the word *burelé,* meaning "banded" or "barred," describing the blazon of red and silver bands he wore on his shield. Gace Brulé was a knight and is known to have owned property in Grusliere (in Dreux). The future King Louis VIII seems to have been his patron late in his life, but his poetry suggests that he had several other patrons among the highest ranks of the nobility. At one point he seems to have been attached to the court of Geoffrey II, count of Brittany (through whom Gace may have been acquainted with the famous TROUBADOUR, BERTRAN DE BORN). The Countess MARIE DE CHAMPAGNE was also among Gace's patrons, and through her court he may have met some of the other well-known literary figures attached to her, including CHRÉTIEN DE TROYES.

Gace also is thought to have known many other poets among the first generation of trouvères, including BLONDEL DE NESLE, CONON DE BÉTHUNE, and perhaps Le CHATELAIN DE COUCI. Accompanying one of his many noble patrons, he seems to have taken part in either the Third or the Fourth Crusade, or perhaps both. A document from late in his life suggests that he also had some dealings with the Knights Templar.

Gace was one of the most prolific of the trouvères, as well as one of the best known. Quotations and allusions to his poetry appear in the texts of several other poets, and one of his lyrics, *Ire d'amors,* is cited by DANTE in *De VULGARI ELOQUENTIA,* though Dante mistakenly attributes the poem to THIBAUT DE CHAMPAGNE.

Gace is known for faithfully following the conventions of the vernacular lyric established by the troubadours. Goldin compares him to GUILLAUME IX in his explicitly categorizing his songs according to their intended audience, often beginning them with *Compaignons* or *Seigneurs* (for his strictly male audience). Gace has also been compared with BERNART DE VENTADORN, and many of his songs resemble the love songs of that prolific troubadour. His song "Li pluseur ont d'Amours chanté," for example, begins with a sentiment quite common in Bernart—that the true lover's song rises above those of the false, for love ennobles the singer:

> *Most have sung of Love*
> *as an exercise and insincerely;*
> *so Love should give me thanks*
> *because I never sang like a hypocrite.*
> *My loyalty kept me from that,*
> *and Love, which I have in such abundance*
> *it is a miracle if I hate anything,*
> *even that crowd of pests.*

(Goldin 1973, 385, ll. 1–8)

Bibliography

Mayer-Martin, D. J. "The Chansons of Gace Brulé: A Stylistic Study of the Melodies," in *Literary and Historical Perspectives of the Middle Ages: Proceedings of the 1981 SEMA Meeting,* edited by Patricia W. Cummins, Patrick W. Conner, and Charles W. Connell. Morgantown: West Virginia University Press, 1982, 93–103.

Rosenberg, Samuel N., and Samuel Danon, eds. and trans. *The Lyrics and Melodies of Gace Brulé.* Music edited by Hendrik van der Werf. New York: Garland, 1985.

Galahad

Sir Galahad was one of the most important of the knights in the legendary ROMANCES of King ARTHUR. He is the son of Arthur's greatest knight, Sir LANCELOT, and Elaine, daughter of King Pelles. Most important, Galahad's goodness and purity make him chief of the knights who achieve the quest of the HOLY GRAIL. The Grail, originally a mysterious Celtic vessel of myth, had by the 13th century come to be identified with the vessel Christ drank from at the Last Supper, and a perfect Christian knight was needed to be worthy of its quest. Galahad's name may be derived from the Old Testament place name Gilead, or it may come from an ancient Welsh hero called Gwalhafed.

Galahad first appears as a character in the 13th-century VULGATE CYCLE, specifically in the *Queste del Saint Graal* (Quest of the Holy Grail), where he is the perfect knight foreordained to achieve the Grail. Lancelot (whose own baptismal name was Galahad), thinking that he is going to the bed of Queen Guenevere, is tricked by King Pelles into sleeping with the king's daughter, Elaine. Pelles's questionable behavior stems from his knowledge of the prophecy, first brought to light in the opening romance of the Vulgate Cycle, the *Estoire del saint Graal* (History of the Holy Grail): Elaine will give birth to the destined Grail knight, who will be of the ninth generation from Nascien, the king baptized by Josephus (son of Joseph of Arimathea, who in legend brought Christianity to Britain). Lancelot, the king knows, is the eighth in line from King Nascien.

If Galahad's illegitimate birth is a spot on his character, the fact that he remains a virgin his entire life erases that blemish. It also makes him worthy of the Grail. His companions on the Grail quest—Sir Perceval (whom he replaces as the chief Grail knight in literary history) and Sir Bors (Lancelot's kinsman)—are also renowned for their chastity. Lancelot himself, the greatest of the earthly knights, fails on the quest because of his adultery with the queen.

As the adventure of the Grail begins, Galahad, raised in a nunnery where his aunt is prioress, is knighted by his father and makes his way to Arthur's court. Here he fulfills the signs that establish his identity as the Grail knight: He sits in the Perilous Seat and, from a stone floating in the river, he pulls a sword reserved for the greatest knight. Galahad is present when the Holy Grail appears to the knights of the Round Table, and all swear to seek it. Galahad obtains a white shield on which a red cross has been painted with the blood of King Evelake (or Mordrains, brother-in-law of Nascien). His adventures all tend to have allegorical significance: One of his earliest challenges, for example, is a battle he undertakes with seven knights who prove to be the Seven Deadly Sins. Later, after joining Bors and Perceval, he acquires the sword of King David himself (from whom he is also descended). Perceval's sister gives Galahad a belt for the sword made from her own hair, and this pure maiden becomes for Galahad the chaste and holy equivalent of the knight's lady in a more conventional courtly romance. The sister dies after her pure blood has cured a leprous noblewoman, and Galahad leaves his companions for a while, spending some time traveling with his father, Lancelot. Afterward, he comes upon an abbey where the paralyzed King Mordrains lies—the king has been allowed to live long enough to see the Grail knight, of his own blood, come to fulfill the prophecy. Once healed, Mordrains dies. Ultimately reunited with Bors and Perceval, Galahad makes his way to the Castle Corbenic, where he heals the maimed king and sees the Grail. Informed that he will find the Grail in the country of Sarras, the three Grail knights travel to that land. Although imprisoned upon their arrival, the three knights are fed in their captivity by the Grail, and eventually Galahad becomes king of the country. His reign lasts for only a year, however. At the end of that time, Joseph of Arimathea and the Grail appear to Galahad. After hearing mass, Galahad is able to gaze into the mysteries of the Grail, and after what is described as an ecstatic mystical experience, Galahad desires to enter permanently into heavenly bliss. He prays to be able to die, and is granted his request.

Galahad is the perfect knight, not only in virtue but in his beauty and in his physical prowess as well. No other knight can defeat him in battle or joust. Thomas MALORY keeps the story as told in the Vulgate Cycle essentially unchanged in his 15th-century *Le MORTE DARTHUR*, and thus it became a part of the English Arthurian tradition. For many more modern writers, like Tennyson or T. H. White, Galahad's character has been less central to the story—it is difficult to make purity and perfection interesting to modern readers. But Galahad's legacy remains what it was from the beginning: The ideal culmination of the medieval propensity to combine Christianity with chivalry.

Bibliography

Barber, Richard. *The Holy Grail: Imagination and Belief.* Cambridge, Mass.: Harvard University Press, 2004.

Lacy, Norris J., general ed. *Lancelot-Grail: The Old French Arthurian Vulgate and Post-Vulgate in Translation.* 5 vols. New York: Garland Publishing, 1993–1996.

Malory, Sir Thomas. *Le Morte Darthur, or the Hole Book of Kyng Arthur and of His Noble Knyghtes of the Rounde Table.* Edited by Stephen H. A. Shepherd. New York: Norton, 2004.

gap

The term *gap* was applied to a particular genre of TROUBADOUR lyric poetry popularized by GUILLAUME IX, the first troubadour. Essentially the *gap* was a boasting song, in which the singer presents himself as a master in his field—either the greatest poet, or the noblest courtier, or the truest lover, or, more commonly, all of these, since the convention in the COURTLY LOVE tradition was that love ennobled the lover, and gave him the skills to sing. The best in any one of these areas must also be the best in the others, since they are interconnected.

In Guillaume's poem "Ben vuelh que sapchon li pluzor," the poet boasts:

I want everyone to tell
whether there's good color to this vers
that I have brought out of my workshop:
because I'm the one that gets the flower in
this craft,
and that is the truth.

(Goldin 1973, 33, ll. 1–5)

As the poem goes on, the "crafts" of which he is master turn out to be not only poetry, but courtliness and physical lovemaking as well.

Another early troubadour, MARCABRU, wrote a well-known *gap*, "D'aisso lau Dieu," in which he satirizes the attitude of the lustful man who boasts of his ability to fool the *gilos* or jealous husband and have any woman he wants:

In another man's woods
I go hunting every time I feel like it,
and I set my two little dogs barking,
and my third, my hound,
thrusts forward,
all bold and fixed on the prey.

(Goldin 1973, 59, ll. 37–42)

But the true lover could boast as well, and a more common kind of *gap* from that point of view is BERNART DE VENTADORN's "Non es meravelha s'eu chan," which begins

Of course it's no wonder I sing
better than any other troubadour:
my heart draws me more toward love,
and I am better made for his command.

(Goldin 1973, 127, ll. 1–4)

The true lover's humility was a tenet of the courtly tradition, so Marcabru's poem displays the lust of the false lovers that he condemned. But the ennobling power of love to raise the lover to the heights of noble behavior and poetic skill was also a tenet of courtliness, so that one could speak as Bernart does and still maintain humility, because the praise would go to the power of love.

Bibliography

Goldin, Frederick, ed. and trans. *Lyrics of the Troubadours and Trouvères: An Anthology and a History.* Garden City, N.Y.: Anchor, 1973.

Garland, John (Johannes de Garlandia) (ca. 1180–ca. 1252)

John Garland was a Latin poet and grammarian who was born in England and taught at the University of Toulouse as well as the University of Paris. He was the author of five major works in Latin verse, as well as several pedagogical texts, including a *Parisiana poetria* discussing the various styles of versification.

In his own verses, Garland informs us that he was born in England and studied at Oxford before moving on to the University of Paris in about 1202, where he mentions that one of his instructors was ALANUS DE INSULIS. He also declares that, having spent most of his life in France, he prized that country over the land of his birth. In 1229, after teaching for some time at Paris, Garland was chosen as one of the instructors to be sent to the newly founded university in Toulouse in the Languedoc region in the south of France, where he was made master of grammar. Thus Garland was thrust into hostile territory during the Albigensian Crusade. While in Toulouse, he began his epic poem *De triumphis Ecclesiae* (The triumph of the church), a poem celebrating the victories of the church in the Crusades and its triumphs over heresy, including three chapters on the Albigensian Crusade itself. By 1232 or 1233, however, the orthodox professors at the university were becoming increasingly unpopular in that region, and Garland fled to Paris, where he spent the remainder of his life.

Back at the University of Paris in 1234, Garland wrote a poem in 1,426 hexameter (six-syllable) lines on the Latin laws of accent called, appropriately, *Accentuarium.* He wrote an *Epithalamium beatae Mariae Virginis* (Wedding song for the blessed Virgin Mary) and *Carmen de Ecclesia*—a poem on the liturgy that he dedicated to Fulk, the bishop of London. He also composed the *Integumenta Ovidii,* a mythographic commentary on Ovid's *Metamorphoses.* A number of his verses were written as teaching texts or to help his pupils: He wrote a *Compendium totius grammatices* (Compendium of grammar) in verse, as well as a verse treatise entitled *Equivoca,* which is basically a list of homonyms. His *Dictionarius cum commento* (Dictionary with commentary) is a glossary for use by his students, and he wrote, in addition, a rhetorical tract called *Exempla honestae vitae* (Moral examples)—assuming, in the classical sense of Cicero, that the rhetorician was a good man expressing the truth. His *Parisiana poetria* (ca. 1233), was probably intended as a textbook for his students at Paris. As mentioned above, it was a kind of poetic handbook containing illustrations of the various styles of Latin versification, to which is added an interesting section of the "vices" of poetry, such as digression, obscurity, and faulty diction. Garland relies on Horace and on GEOFFREY OF VINSAUF.

Other works have been attributed to John Garland, many erroneously. He has often been confused with another John Garland who wrote two important musical treatises in the later 13th century. He also was the purported author of an alchemical study actually composed by the 14th-century author Martin Lortholain. His grammatical works were popular in England in the later Middle Ages, but his pedantic and uninspired verse did not find an audience in the Renaissance.

Bibliography

Garland, John. *Morale Scolarium.* Edited, with an introduction, by Louis John Paetow. Berkeley: University of California Press, 1927.

Johannes de Garlandia. *Compendium grammaticae.* Edited by Thomas Haye. Cologne (Köln): Böhlau, 1995.

———. *De triumphis ecclesiæ libri octo.* Edited by Thomas Wright. London: J. B. Nichols and Sons, 1856.

Gawain (Gauvin, Gawein, Gwalchmei, Walewein, Walwanus, Gawen)

Gawain is a knight of King ARTHUR's court and a central character in the Arthurian tradition, but throughout the ROMANCES, his strengths and weaknesses vary as, depending upon the time period, the geographical location, and the author, he is alternately depicted as the loyal knight and nephew of King Arthur or a fickle libertine and troublemaker.

Gawain appears in MIDDLE ENGLISH literature early on, as Gwalchmei in the Welsh *CULHWHC AND OLWEN* (ca. 1100), and in GEOFFREY OF MONMOUTH's *HISTORIA REGUM BRITANNIAE* (*History of the Kings of Britain*, ca. 1136). The English treatment of the character traditionally tends to feature Gawain as a central figure in the plot. As the son of King Lot of Orkney and Arthur's sister Morgause, Gawain is King Arthur's nephew, and would probably succeed him should Arthur and Queen GUENEVERE produce no heir. He is typically portrayed as Arthur's most loyal and supportive knight who embarks on a quest in Arthur's name or intercedes in a challenge on his behalf, such as the beheading test in *SIR GAWAIN AND THE GREEN KNIGHT* and the marriage to the loathly lady in *The WEDDYNG OF SYR GAWEN AND DAME RAGNELL*. However, the 15th-century treatment by Sir Thomas MALORY incorporates more negative aspects of Gawain's character, as Malory borrows from the French tradition.

In the 12th century, CHRÉTIEN DE TROYES introduced LANCELOT into Arthurian literature in *LANCELOT, or the Knight of the Cart*, and although Gawain is putatively prominent in the French romances, Chrétien makes Lancelot the ideal Arthurian knight, and Gawain's character suffers through his quests somewhat comically, often depicted as a foil to the hero, and negatively portrayed as a frivolous lover and philanderer. In the continuations of *Perceval* (a continuation of Chrétien's unfinished work), Gawain replaces Perceval in his quest for the HOLY GRAIL but he is posited as a counter to the more virtuous Perceval who appears, even in the unfinished work, destined to complete his quest.

The VULGATE CYCLE goes further in its treatment of the Gawain character as a knight unable to complete the quest. In the *Quest of the Holy Grail*, Gawain is the first knight to vow to go on the quest. But his pledge saddens King Arthur, who predicts that with the departure of Gawain and the other knights, they will never be reunited at the Round Table again. As Gawain embarks on the quest, we see how spiritually bankrupt he is because his interpretation of the quest is limited to the secular conquests and adventures. Both a monk and a hermit reveal his faults to him but he is unwilling to undertake the necessary penance. While Gawain, Hector, and many other knights on the quest complain of no adventure, these knights do not encounter Lancelot, Galahad, Perceval, and Bors because those four are on the true quest. When Gawain's vision of the dissolution of the Round Table is interpreted by a holy man, Gawain determines the quest is pointless for him and departs to return to King Arthur. His reluctance even to stay and speak further with the holy man is indicative of his inability to embrace the spiritual aspect of his life. Later, in *The Death of King Arthur* of the Vulgate, Gawain is even vilified when Lancelot kills Gawain's brother, Gaheriet (in error), and Gawain's repetitive refusal to entertain peace with Lancelot leads to Arthur's war with him to achieve vengeance for Gawain. Ultimately, Gawain is defeated by Lancelot and dies later as a result of a head wound inflicted by Lancelot from which he never recovers, and although Gawain, on his deathbed, urges Arthur to solicit Lancelot's help in defeating the usurper Mordred, Arthur refuses because of all that has passed. Gawain's thirst for vengeance, then, ultimately results in the destruction of Arthur's kingdom. This treatment of Gawain in the French tradition continues in Malory's *Le MORTE DARTHUR*, as he casts not Gawain but Lancelot as the ideal knight.

The range of depictions of the Gawain character is unique among the major characters of the Arthurian tradition. Rather than having one particular theme or purpose always attached to Gawain's role, he is involved in a variety of plots, allowing his character to be more malleable for the writer's intent. In some texts, the purpose of his character is to endure a test and prove a moral. One example of this is his participation in the beheading game in *Sir Gawain and the Green Knight* and subsequent travel to find the Green Knight to live up to his pledge and demonstrate his courtesy. In others, his character serves Arthur by performing vows. In *Weddyng*, for example, Gawain promises to wed the hideous hag, Dame Ragnell, so that Arthur will be given the answer to a riddle that will save his life. Still yet in *Weddyng* and loathly lady stories, he functions as a vehicle for commentary on aristocracy and definitions of nobility. The transformation of Gawain's character may render him more complex, but he is continually utilized by romance writers throughout the tradition and even enjoys popularity today, as evidenced, for example, by his role as Welsh narrator Gwalchmai in Gillian Bradshaw's 1980 *Hawk of May*.

Bibliography

Busby, Keith. *Gauvain in Old French Literature*. Amsterdam: Rodopi, 1980.

Michelle Palmer

General Prologue, The (ca. 1386)

Geoffrey CHAUCER's *CANTERBURY TALES* opens with one of the most famous introductions in literary history, the narrative poem commonly known as the General Prologue. Composed in rhyming couplets of iambic pentameter lines, the poem divides into three main parts, each of which helps to establish a context for the events of the *Canterbury Tales*. The first part, just five sentences long, indicates that the story takes place in the springtime, when people go on pilgrimages; introduces the narrator's distinctive voice; and locates the collection's opening scene in the Tabard Inn in Southwark, across the River Thames from London (Benson 1987, 23, ll. 1–42), where English pilgrims gather to journey to Canterbury. A central section provides descriptions of 27 pilgrims who will be the narrator's companions (Benson 1987, 23–34, ll. 43–714). The final part is the most disparate: It opens with an apology in which the narrator disclaims responsibility for any off-color content, adds the character description of the Host who will lead the company, and closes by introducing Chaucer's central narrative device—the pilgrims will participate in a storytelling contest (Benson 1987, 34–36, ll. 715–858).

The 18-line opening sentence is as moving as it is syntactically brilliant: *When* April's sweet showers pierce the drought of March and Nature awakens, *then* people yearn to go on pilgrimage, and in England this means a trip to St. Thomas's shrine in Canterbury Cathedral. In this intensely lyrical sentence Chaucer articulates the spiritual frame for his book: The journey to Canterbury replicates the passage from drought to moisture, from winter to spring, from sickness to health. The following sentences are typical of Chaucer's technique as they do three important things at once: They indicate the narrative's spiritual and spatial movement from tavern to cathedral, they introduce the narrator's self-deprecating voice, and they announce the presence of a congenial company of "sondry folk" (Benson 1987, 23, l. 25), the assorted travelers whom Chaucer will now introduce.

The heart of the General Prologue is a descriptive list of the pilgrims who will travel together and tell stories. Twenty-seven pilgrims are portrayed in terms of their profession ("whiche they weren"), rank ("of what degree"), and appearance ("in what array that they were inne") (Benson 1987, 24, ll. 40–41). The company comprises members of the three estates that traditionally categorized medieval social classes—those who fight, those who pray, and those who plow—along with a large group of those new people whom Chaucer apparently found fascinating: tradesmen and professionals.

The general ordering of the pilgrims is loosely hierarchical. A Knight is pictured first, along with his son, a Squire, and his servant, a Yeoman. A group of major ecclesiastical figures are described next: a Prioress accompanied by a Nun and three priests, followed by a Monk and a Friar. Then come four high-level professionals (Merchant, Clerk, Lawyer, and Franklin), followed by five guildsmen (Haberdasher, Carpenter, Weaver, Dyer, and Tapestry weaver) and their Cook. The list continues with three more modest professionals (Shipman, Physician, and Wife) and two men from the countryside: a Parson and a Plowman. The final group of portraits includes five disreputable clerics and tradesmen (Miller, Manciple, Reeve, Summoner, and Pardoner).

The genre of the portraits is that of ESTATES SATIRE, a form in which writers satirize the various occupations by highlighting characteristic failings and abuses. Chaucer recasts the genre by individualizing the pilgrims' activities and appearance, and by relaying the portraits in a deadpan voice that makes it unclear whether a particular pilgrim is being mocked, praised, or simply described.

The closing section of the General Prologue opens with an apology: Chaucer disingenuously asks readers not to blame him for the vulgar language that some pilgrims will employ in their tales. In this disclaimer of responsibility for the realistic voices and characters that he has created, Chaucer blurs the line between fiction and fact, as it is the quality of Chaucer's mimetic artistry that makes the *Canterbury Tales* such an effective evocation of the variety of life and thought in late 14th-century England.

The final character introduced in the General Prologue is the Host, later identified as Harry Bailly. Having a tavernkeeper lead the pilgrimage accents Chaucer's audacious intermingling of serious spiritual concerns and playful worldly matters. A similar fusing of the thoughtful and the pleasurable underscores the rules Harry proffers for a storytelling contest to entertain the pilgrims as they travel. The pilgrims are asked to tell "Tales of best sentence and moost solaas" (Benson 1987, 36, l. 798), that is, stories offering both the most valuable message and the greatest enjoyment. The balance between delight and instruction mirrors that between the tavern in Southwark and the cathedral in Canterbury, the two poles in the pilgrims' journey. Fashioning a narrative that engages a reader even as it raises complex and politically sensitive issues is Chaucer's accomplishment in the General Prologue, as it is in the *Canterbury Tales* as a whole.

Bibliography

Benson, Larry D., et al., ed. *The Riverside Chaucer.* 3rd ed. Boston: Houghton Mifflin, 1987.

Mann, Jill. *Chaucer and Medieval Estates Satire.* Cambridge: Cambridge University Press, 1973.

Morgan, Gerald. "Moral and Social Identity and the Idea of Pilgrimage in the General Prologue," *Chaucer Review* 37 (2003): 285–314.

Nolan, Barbara. " 'Poet Ther Was': Chaucer's Voices in the General Prologue to *The Canterbury Tales,*" *PMLA* 101 (1986): 154–169.

Wallace, David. "The General Prologue and the Anatomy of Associational Form." In *Chaucerian Polity: Absolutist Lineages and Associational Forms in England and Italy,* 65–82. Stanford, Calif.: Stanford University Press, 1997.

David Raybin

Genesis (*A*, ca. 700; *B*, mid-ninth century)

The OLD ENGLISH *Genesis* is a poem of 2,935 lines, surviving in the Junius manuscript in Oxford's Bodleian library. Based on the first book of the Bible, the poem is divided in the manuscript into 41 sections or *fitts.* But most significantly, lines 235–851 of the text are written in a different style and tone from the rest of the poem, and are clearly an interpolation of later origin than the rest of the poem.

The earlier *Genesis,* usually called *Genesis A,* is a relatively faithful rendition of the biblical text from the Creation through the story of the sacrifice of Isaac in Genesis 22.13. Part of the manuscript is missing after the third day of the creation story, after which the text jumps to the creation of Eve. The chief modification in the story is the poet's addition of the non-biblical story of the fall of Satan and his rebel angels. More than half the text of *Genesis A* is concerned with the story of Abraham, who at least at some points—the section narrating Abraham's rescue of his nephew Lot, for example—is described like an Anglo-Saxon warrior.

Most scholars, however, have been more interested in *Genesis B,* the interpolated poem. *Genesis B* focuses on the story of the fall of the rebel angels (for the second time in the manuscript) and on the Fall of Man. Since the leaves containing the story of the fall in *Genesis A* have apparently been lost, it seems that the manuscript was "completed" by the insertion of *Genesis B*. This section is later than the poem into which it has been inserted—probably from the mid-ninth century as opposed to the early eighth century for *Genesis A*. The 19th-century German scholar Edward Sievers suggested that *Genesis B* was based on a continental Old Saxon original—a conjecture that was verified when a fragment of the original Saxon poem was found in a manuscript in the Vatican library in 1894.

Genesis B begins in the midst of God's speech to Adam and Eve, instructing them not to eat of the forbidden tree. This is followed by a long flashback describing the fall of Lucifer. Most fascinating about this text is the characterization of Lucifer, who is presented as a tragic fallen warrior who refused to submit to God, still struggling against his defeat while chained in hell. He urges one of his "thains," another fallen angel, to go to earth and corrupt God's Creation. In the Old English poet's version, the devil speaks first to Adam, saying that God has sent him with new instructions, allowing Adam and Eve to eat of the forbidden tree. When Adam is not fooled, the devil approaches Eve. He convinces her that Adam will incur God's wrath if he does not follow the new commandment to eat of the tree, and out of concern for her mate, Eve eats the apple and persuades Adam to do so. Thus in this poem, in an unusual reading of the story, the Fall is seen as the deception of pure innocence by wicked guile, rather than as willful sin.

One question that has fascinated literary scholars has been the relationship of *Genesis B* with Milton's *Paradise Lost.* Milton was acquainted with Franciscus Junius, owner of the manuscript, and therefore may have known of *Genesis B* and its portrayal of Satan. On the other hand, both depictions may have been based on a fifth-century Latin text (the *Poematum de Mosaicae historiae gestis libri quinque* of Avitus).

Bibliography

Godden, Malcolm. "Biblical Literature: The Old Testament." In *The Cambridge Companion to Old English Literature,* edited by Malcolm Godden and Michael Lapidge, 206–226. Cambridge: Cambridge University Press, 1991.

Greenfield, Stanley B., and Daniel G. Calder. *A New Critical History of Old English Literature.* New York: New York University Press, 1986.

Kennedy, Charles William, trans. *Early English Christian Poetry.* New York: Oxford University Press, 1963.

Krapp, George Philip. *The Junius Manuscript.* Anglo-Saxon Poetic Records I. New York: Columbia University Press, 1931.

Geoffrey of Monmouth (ca. 1100–1155)

Geoffrey of Monmouth was the author of the 12th-century *HISTORIA REGUM BRITANNIAE* (*History of the Kings of Britain*), a pseudo-history in Latin prose that popularized the legendary monarchs of pre-Saxon Britain. Geoffrey's history is one of the most important and influential texts of the European Middle Ages because it introduced the story of King ARTHUR, previously known only in Welsh and Breton legend, into the mainstream of European literature.

Little is known of Geoffrey's life. Probably he was born at Monmouth in southern Wales. He may have been Welsh, but some scholars believe that his pro-Breton bias evident in the *Historia* suggests he was of Breton descent. This is not unlikely, since many Bretons came to England during the Norman Conquest and immediately thereafter.

Some time before 1129, Geoffrey was living near Oxford. His signature appears on six different charters between 1129 and 1151, all related to religious houses in or near Oxford. Twice after 1139, Geoffrey added the title *magister* after his name, which could imply that he was in some kind of teaching capacity in Oxford. There was not yet a university there, but it was already a center for scholars.

In 1151, Geoffrey was named bishop elect of the see of St. Asaph. He was ordained a priest in 1152, but it is unlikely he ever actually visited St. Asaph. The area was a hotbed of animosity between the English and the Welsh, and probably would have been unsafe. In 1153, he was one of the bishops to witness the Treaty of Westminster that named Henry of Anjou the heir of King Stephen and ended the civil war that had marred most of Stephen's reign. According to the *Welsh Chronicles* (not necessarily known for their accuracy), Geoffrey died in 1155, probably having lived his last four years in London.

The three literary works attributed to Geoffrey were all written during the 23 years he was at Oxford, and seem, at least in part, to have been written to curry the favor of powerful nobles and win Geoffrey some political appointment—a goal that was realized when he was made bishop. His earliest work (ca. 1130–35) was *Prophetiae Merlini* (The prophesies of Merlin), a long series of cryptic prophecies that were later incorporated into the *Historia Regum Britanniae* as Book VII. Geoffrey had appropriated the Welsh tradition of Myrddin, a seer who was said to have foretold the overthrow and destruction of the Saxon power in Britain. Geoffrey invented most of the undecipherable oracles, though they provided fuel for generations of commentators who sought to decipher them. These were originally dedicated to Alexander, bishop of London, and were apparently written at his request.

Geoffrey's greatest work followed shortly thereafter. Though he calls it a "history," and claims that he took the stories from "a certain very ancient book in the Celtic tongue" that he received from Walter, archdeacon of Oxford, it is clear that Geoffrey is mainly repeating oral legends or simply exercising his imagination through most of the *Historia Regum Britanniae.* The book tells the story of the legendary kings of Britain before the Anglo-Saxon invasion, beginning with Brutus, great-grandson of the Trojan Aeneas, who names the island "Britain" after himself. Here also is the story of King Lear; of Belinus (who sacks Rome); of Vortigern, who loses the island to the Saxons; and most important, of King Arthur, who drives the Saxons out of Britain, then becomes a world conqueror, and is about to take Rome itself when he hears of his wife's betrayal of him with his nephew Mordred, whom he has left as regent of the kingdom. He is wounded in battle while defeating Mordred, and is borne away to the Isle of Avalon.

Geoffrey's *Historia* was completed around 1138. Several different dedications are preserved for the *Historia* in various manuscripts, and these seem to reflect the changing political climate of the time: Most of the manuscripts dedicate the work to Robert of Gloucester, illegitimate son of Henry I and thus half-brother of the Empress Matilda, whose claim to the throne had begun the civil war in 1138, and lasted until her son, Henry of Anjou, was named Stephen's heir. Some manuscripts dedicate the work to King Stephen and Robert of Gloucester together: Robert had supported Stephen's claim to the throne in 1135 but withdrew his support in favor of Matilda in 1138. A third dedication is to Waleran Beaumont, count of Meulen, one of Stephen's chief supporters after Robert's defection. Clearly Geoffrey was attempting to position himself as a supporter of the king in the changing political climate of the late 1130s.

Geoffrey's final work was the *Vita Merlini* (Life of Merlin), a 1,500-line poem in Latin hexameters dedicated to Robert de Chesney, the new bishop of London, and completed about 1150. The Merlin Geoffrey presents in this poem is not at all like the character of the earlier *Historia.* Rather it seems that in the intervening years, Geoffrey had become better acquainted with the Welsh Myrddin legends, and makes his Merlin a wild man of the woods who has lost his reason in battle and now lives in the forest, where he meets the bard Taliesin, who describes life in the isle of Avalon, where King Arthur has been taken to have his wounds healed by the sorceress Morgen.

But it is his *Historia* on which Geoffrey's fame rests. Geoffrey gave the legend of King Arthur the coherent form that it took throughout the high Middle Ages in Europe, and for that, his importance in the European literary tradition cannot be overemphasized. The creators of ROMANCE later in the 12th century, like CHRÉTIEN DE TROYES and MARIE DE FRANCE, created narratives set against what they perceived as Geoffrey's historical account. Later writers added characters, expanded incidents, and elaborated situations, but the basic outline of the Arthurian story begins with Geoffrey.

Bibliography

Geoffrey of Monmouth. *The Historia Regum Britanniae of Geoffrey of Monmouth.* Edited by Neil Wright. Cambridge: Brewer, 1985.

Parry, John Jay, ed. and trans. *Vita Merlini.* Urbana: University of Illinois Press, 1925.

Tatlock, J. S. P. *The Legendary History of Britain.* Berkeley: University of California Press, 1950.

Thorpe, Lewis, trans. *The History of the Kings of Britain.* London: Penguin, 1966.

Geoffrey of Vinsauf (fl. 1200)

With his *Poetria nova,* composed between 1200 and 1202, with last additions and revisions probably from ca. 1215, Geoffrey of Vinsauf was, with Matthew of Vendôme (*Ars versificatoria,* late 12th century), Eberhard (Evardus) the German (*Laborinthus*), Gervase of Melkley (*Ars poetica*), and John of Garland (*Parisiana poetria*), one of the most influential authors of theoretical studies on poetry, rhetoric, and the arts. We know very little about Geoffrey, except that he is identified in the various manuscripts as "Galfridus Anglicus," which indicates that he originated in England. He studied in Paris and taught at Hampton in England; in his dedication to Pope Innocent III (1198–1216) he mentions that he had once been sent from England to Rome.

The *Poetria nova* begins with the image of a house to be built, which needs first to be visualized before the actual construction can begin, as the basic metaphor to be followed by a poet or artist: "construct the whole fabric within the mind's citadel; let it exist in the mind before it is on the lips" (Nims 1967, 17). Subsequently, Geoffrey lays out his art of poetics and teaches his reader how to approach the task first by ordering the material, then developing the structure of a poem, exploring modes of description, considering elements of amplification and abbreviation, adding rhetorical ornaments, experimenting with the linguistic aspects, and so forth. Finally, Geoffrey concludes his treatise with some comments on how to create a good memory and train the mind to retain as much as possible.

He also outlines the principles of good delivery of a speech, emphasizing the mouth, the countenance, and the gestures. Geoffrey recommends to his audience: "let a voice controlled by good taste, seasoned with the two spices of facial expression and gesture, be borne to the ears to feed the hearing" (Nims 1967, 91). At the end of his treatise the author dedicates his work to a certain William, who might have been William of Wrotham, archdeacon of Taunton who held important political posts in England between 1204 and 1215, or William de Sancta Matre Ecclesia, bishop of London (1199–1221), a close adviser to the kings HENRY II, RICHARD I, and John.

Geoffrey's major sources were the pseudo-Ciceronian *Rhetorica ad Herennium* and Horace's *Ars poetica* (*Poetria*). His treatise has come down to us in more than 200 manuscripts, a majority of which originated in England. Apart from his *Poetria nova,* he also wrote a prose *Documentum de modo et arte dictandi et versificandi,* a *Summa de coloribus rhetoricis,* and a short poem, *Causa magistri Guafredi Vinesauf.* Geoffrey's *Poetria* was undoubtedly the most influential textbook in late-medieval Europe because it proved to be so adaptable to teaching poetry, the art of letter writing (epistolarity), and the art of preaching sermons.

Bibliography

Gallo, Ernest, ed. *Poetria Nova and Its Sources in Early Rhetorical Doctrine.* De proprietatibus litterarum. Series maior 10. The Hague: Mouton, 1971.

Geoffrey of Vinsauf. *Documentum de Modo et Arte Dictandi et Versificandi.* Translated by Roger P. Parr. Milwaukee, Wisc.: Marquette University Press, 1968.

Nims, Margaret F., trans. *Poetria Nova of Geoffrey of Vinsauf.* Toronto: Pontifical Institute of Mediaeval Studies, 1967.

Albrecht Classen

Geraint and Enid (13th century)

Geraint and Enid is a Welsh prose ROMANCE included in some manuscripts of the *MABINOGION.* One of what are known as the "three romances" in Welsh (the others being OWAIN and PEREDUR), *Geraint*, like the other two texts, is essentially a retelling of one of the 12th-century courtly romances of the French poet CHRÉTIEN DE TROYES. In this case the French analogue is Chrétien's *EREC ET ENIDE*. The Welsh writer's "Geraint" is the name of a traditional Celtic hero of Cornwall and Devon, and also the name of a seventh-century Cornish king.

In terms of plot, *Geraint* is the closest of the three Welsh romances to its French counterpart. Beginning at Whitsuntide (i.e., Pentecost) at King ARTHUR's court at Caerleon on Usk, the story tells of a mysterious white stag that leads Arthur, Guenevere, and Geraint into the forest. Here, Geraint's adventure begins: He comes to a town where he is persuaded to help the lord, Earl Ynywl, gain back sovereignty over his realm from his usurping nephew, the "Knight of the Sparrowhawk," whom Geraint defeats in a tournament. In doing so, he wins the hand of the earl's beautiful daughter, Enid.

After their marriage, Geraint becomes ruler of his father's kingdom, but he falls into a kind of sloth, neglecting his knightly duties because of his excessive doting on his wife. One morning she inadvertently reveals to him what the courtiers are saying about his dereliction of duty, and when she sheds tears in her account, Geraint inexplicably begins to suspect her of being unfaithful to him. He rather brusquely forces her to leave the court and ride forth with him. After a number of trials in which Geraint proves his prowess (including defeating three giants and a mysterious enemy shrouded in a magic mist), Enid is able to convince him of her faithfulness and her love for him. The story ends with Enid restored to her husband's good graces, Geraint restored to his reputation, and the two of them ruling their kingdom in peace and prosperity.

Geraint and Enid is generally conceded to be the best of the three Welsh romances, and at the same time is probably closest of the three to the story as told by Chrétien. The beginning of the text shows a familiarity with Welsh geography, though the remainder of the story is, like many Arthurian romances, set in a vague countryside, a setting of adventure. The beginning of the narrative is well constructed, though the later part of the story becomes rambling. It is a matter of debate whether Chrétien's poem is the source of *Geraint and Enid*, or whether the two romances had an earlier common source, though the chivalric concerns of the story might suggest that the Welsh writer was familiar with the French poem. But the sympathy built for the guiltless Enid, and the vivid descriptions included in the narrative, make the Welsh romance worthwhile reading. Indeed, when Tennyson retold the story for his *Idylls of the King*, he entitled his version "Geraint and Enid" (1857).

Bibliography

Breeze, Andrew. *Medieval Welsh Literature.* Dublin: Four Courts Press, 1997.

Jarman, A. O. H., and Gwilym Rees Hughes. *A Guide to Welsh Literature I.* Swansea: Davies, 1976.

Jones, Gwyn, and Thomas Jones, trans. *The Mabinogion.* 2nd ed. London: Dent, 1974.

Gest of Robyn Hode, A (*A Lytel Geste of Robin Hode*) (ca. 1450)

A Gest of Robyn Hode is the longest medieval poem about the heroic English outlaw. It survives in five early printed books, including two from approximately 1510. However, the poem itself contains references and allusions that suggest it was composed in the middle of the 15th century. This was a period when the BALLAD emerged as a form of popular literature. Like ballads, the *Gest* is written in four-line stanzas with an *abcb* rhyme scheme. It also includes many phrases like "Lyth and lystyn, gentilmen, / All that nowe be here" that give the illusion of oral performance. The *Gest*, however, is much longer and more complex than most ballads, making it a difficult work to categorize.

The structure of the *Gest* suggests that the poem may have been created by combining several shorter poems about ROBIN HOOD into a more complex narrative. The printed texts are divided into eight sections called *fitts* and most of these correspond to shifts in action in the narrative itself. In the first fitt, Robin sends a party of his men out of Barnesdale forest to look for traffic on Watling Street. They encounter an impoverished knight and bring him home to Robin, who promptly loans him the money to pay off his debt to the abbot of St. Mary's Abbey. In the second fitt, the knight goes to the abbot, pays his debt, and then goes home for a year to raise the funds to repay Robin. His return to Barnesdale, however, is delayed when he stops at a wrestling match to sort out an injustice. The third fitt turns to Little John, who, under the name Reynolde Grenelefe, has won a shooting contest and impressed the Sheriff of Nottingham and joined his retinue. One day on a hunting expedition in Barnsdale, John promises to lead the Sheriff to "a right fayre harte, / His coloure is of grene." This marvelous deer turns out to be Robin Hood and the Sheriff is relieved of his property, forced to spend a night sleeping in the forest, and then sent home humiliated. Fitt four returns to the story of the knight, who fails to turn up at the appointed time to repay his loan. Discouraged, Robin sends his men out to search the countryside. They return with a party of monks from St. Mary's Abbey, whom they relieve of 800 pounds. When the tardy knight arrives, Robin tells him that his debt has been paid and gives him an extra 400 pounds as well.

A new plot thread begins in the fifth fitt when Robin and his men enter an archery contest in Nottingham, where they are ambushed by the Sheriff. Robin escapes and takes refuge at the castle of the knight, now identified as Sir Richard at the Lea, whom he had helped. The Sheriff complains to the king in the sixth fitt and Edward promises to come deal with Robin Hood and Sir Richard himself. Meanwhile, Robin and his men return to the forest, but the Sheriff manages to surprise and capture Sir Richard. Alerted by the knight's wife, Robin and his men ride to Nottingham, kill the Sheriff, and rescue Sir Richard. At the same time, King Edward arrives and begins to search the county for Robin Hood and Sir Richard. When a straightforward military approach fails, the king disguises himself as an abbot and rides through the forest with a party of knights disguised as monks. When Robin Hood waylays the group, the king is impressed with his loyalty, generosity, and sense of justice. Revealing his true identity to the outlaws, Edward grants them pardon and invites Robin Hood to join his court. In the final fitt, Robin lives at court for 15 months but longs for the greenwood. Begging leave for a seven-day pilgrimage from Edward, he returns to Barnesdale and takes up again with his band of men. For 22 years Robin lives in the forest until he is betrayed and murdered by the prioress of Kirkley Abbey and Sir Roger of Donkesly.

The distinct stories of tricking the Sheriff, the archery contest, the disguised king, and Robin Hood's death do not survive in manuscripts or books contemporary with the *Gest,* but similar stories are recorded later, and episodes like the disguised king are widespread in medieval folklore and literature. Only the substantial involvement with the distressed knight is out of keeping with the early ballads. Aside from the Sheriff, Robin generally encounters tradesmen and other members of the commercial class. In aiding Sir Richard, the outlaw moves outside his social group and, at the same time, undermines the nobility's presumption of superiority. By asserting that a yeoman could rescue a knight from financial ruin, the *Gest* makes a case for the superiority of wits and skill over an inherited title. This social ideology suggests that the audience for the *Gest* was neither discontented peasants nor rural gentry but the newly affluent and socially empowered mercantile classes of the towns. By the early 16th century, the publishing industry was printing many devotional, historical, and literary works for this new market, and the multiple printings of the *Gest* by several publishers suggests that it was a success with these new readers.

Bibliography

Dobson, R. B., and John Taylor, eds. *Rymes of Robin Hood: An Introduction to the English Outlaw.* 3rd. ed. Stroud: Sutton, 1997.

Knight, Stephen, and Thomas Ohlgren, eds. *Robin Hood and Other Outlaw Tales.* Kalamazoo, Mich.: Medieval Institute Publications, 1997.

Ohlgren, Thomas H. "The 'Marchaunt' of Sherwood: Mercantile Ideology in *A Gest of Robyn Hode.*" In *Robin Hood in Popular Culture,* edited by Thomas Hahn, 175–190. Cambridge, U.K.: Brewer, 2000.

Ohlgren, Thomas H., ed. *Medieval Outlaws: Ten Tales in Modern English.* Stroud: Sutton, 1998.

Timothy S. Jones

ghazal

The *ghazal* is a very common verse form in medieval Arabic, Persian, and Turkish poetry. Scholars have traced the origin of the *ghazal* to 10th-century Persia, where it developed out of the older form called the QASÍDA that had come into Persia from Arabia. The *qasída,* often a panegyric in praise of a ruler or nobleman, might run to a length of 100 or more couplets in monorhyme. The *ghazal* developed out of the *tashbib,* or opening couplet of the *qasída,* in which the poet would talk more generally about some universal theme like love, life, death, beauty, or nature. The *ghazal,* which became the most popular form of poetry in Persia, usually did not exceed 12 couplets and, more often, contained about seven. The *ghazal* was given its definitive form about the 13th century by writers like the Persian SA'DI.

In its classical form, each couplet (or *bayt*) of the *ghazal* is completely self-contained. The sense of one *bayt* should not run over into the next. In addition the *bayt* itself should have a turn, or *volta,* moving from one line to the next, so that the second line gives a new twist to what was introduced in the first line, and each couplet is like a separate poem in itself.

The first *bayt* of a *ghazal* is called the *matla,* which sets the mood and tone of the poem. The *matla* is a rhymed couplet, and the rhyme subsequently appears as the second line of each succeeding couplet, so that the rhyme scheme of the *ghazal* is *aa ba ca da ea* etc. In addition the *matla* usually introduces a refrain, or *radif,* consisting of a word or short phrase that follows the rhyme in each *bayt.*

Further, each *bayt* of the *ghazal* must follow the same meter, or *beher.* There are technically 19 different meters available for *ghazals,* but generally these can be categorized as short, medium, or long. Thus the only requirement of the first line of each couplet is that it follow the same *beher* as the rest of the poem.

The concluding couplet of the *ghazal* is usually called the *maqta.* This is essentially a signature *bayt,* in which the poet includes his pen name (*taknhallus*). This *bayt* tends to be more personal than the rest of the poem, and the poet may consider his own state of mind, or talk about his personal faith or love, or even engage in self-praise.

At first, *ghazals* were strictly love poems—hence the name, which is an Arabic word meaning "talking to women." As the form developed, it came to include a number of themes, including philosophical, mystical, religious, and social topics, usually with a tone of longing. In post-medieval times, the *ghazal* was introduced in the West, particularly in Germany, largely through admiration for the poet HAFEZ, and continues to be a very popular form in modern Urdu poetry.

Ghazali, al-

See AL-GHAZALI.

Giacomino Pugliese (early 13th century)

Giacomino Pugliese was a lesser-known poet of the Sicilian school of Italian poetry (*see* GIACOMO DA LENTINO), who was active in the first half of the 13th century. Eight of his *CANZONI* are extant. We know nothing of his life at all save what might be gleaned from his poems, and all attempts to identify him have been unsuccessful. Giacomino does have his admirers, however: Though his poetry tends toward a loose structure, it has been praised for going beyond the COURTLY LOVE conventions to include a fresh use of language, perhaps inspired by popular poetic tradition or by realistic detail.

Some critics have suggested that Giacomino's eight poems be arranged to follow the chronology of a love affair: They describe the passion of the lovers, their parting, and ultimately the death of the lady. In any case, his best-known poem is the one dealing with the beloved's death, entitled "Morte, perchè m'ài fatta sì gran Guerra" (Death, why have you made so great a war against me?). The poem has been praised for what seems a realistic (rather than conventional) expression of personal emotion. In this poem Giacomino also deals with the theme of memory, alluding to the memory of the lady's voice and its effects on his emotions:

I remember and go over the time when she
was with me,
she often called me Sweet Friend—
she does not do it now,

(Goldin 1973, 247, ll. 55–57)

It was a theme that PETRARCH was to pick up with great success in the following century.

Bibliography

Goldin, Frederick, trans. *German and Italian Lyrics of the Middle Ages: An Anthology and a History.* New York: Doubleday, 1973.

Tusiani, Joseph, ed. *The Age of Dante: An Anthology of Early Italian Poetry.* New York: Baroque Press, 1974.

Giacomo da Lentino (Iacopo da Lentini, "the Notary") (early 13th century)

Generally recognized as the first writer of courtly lyric poetry in Italian, Giacomo da Lentino was a notary in the court of the Emperor Frederick II of Sicily. He is credited with founding the Sicilian school" of Italian poetry, which introduced into Italian many of the forms and themes of the lyrics of the Provençal TROUBADOURS. Giacomo, no mere imitator, is also credited with inventing that most versatile and adaptable of lyric forms, the SONNET.

Giacomo's name appears in legal records between 1223 and 1240. In one of the latest of such documents, he refers to himself as notary of the lord emperor. In his own poems, Giacomo calls himself "the Notary" and says that he was born in Lentino (now Lentini, a city north of Syracuse in Sicily). Other poets refer to him with respect, the most important DANTE himself, who lists Giacomo in *Purgatorio* XXIV at the head of the leading poets of the previous generation. Two of Giacomo's *tenzone* or debate poems (*see* TENSO), one with Frederick's chancellor, PIER DELLA VIGNA, and one with the abbot of Tivoli, present Giacomo as a recognized expert on the definition and nature of love.

Giacomo's poems do evince a clear debt to Provençal lyrics. In form his 17 extant *CANZONI* are clearly adopted from the Provençal *CANSO*. In content Giacomo borrows most of the COURTLY LOVE themes of the troubadours: The lover is the lady's servant; she acts toward him as a feudal lord. The lover will do anything to prove his worthiness and nobility to the lady, but is apprehensive about declaring his love to her. Partly, of course, this is because of the tale-mongers around the couple and often the jealousy of the lady's husband. Certain conventional troubadour images appear in Giacomo as well, including the lover as a ship lost at sea, or the lady's beauty as a rose.

Giacomo's audience, however, was more narrow than the entire court that served as the troubadour audience. Giacomo was writing for a group of other bureaucrats—at once more learned and less diverse than the Provençal court. It is important to note that Frederick II's court was also significant for its contribution to the transmission of Aristotle to the West, along with his Arabic commentators. In this atmosphere Giacomo and his fellow poets, as well as their audience, looked at love from a more philosophical and intellectual standpoint. Thus Giacomo's most famous canzone, "Maravigliosamente/un amor mi distringe," examines the poem as an imperfect expression of the perfect form of love that exists, in response to the lady's image, in the lover's mind:

> *Like a man who keeps his mind*
> *on a distant thing and paints*
> *the likeness of his thought:*
> *O Beautiful, I do the same:*
> *inside my heart*
> *I bear your image;*

(Goldin 1973, 211, ll. 4–9)

But Giacomo's most original contribution is his invention of the sonnet. Some 25 of his roughly 40 extant lyrics are sonnets, and they are the earliest we possess. Therefore Giacomo is generally credited with inventing the form. In the spirit of intellectualizing love poetry, Giacomo set out to create a poem in which there could be a logical relationship between the structure of the poem and its theme. His sonnets display this sort of logical order, and it is this idea of the intellectual nature of love that takes root later in the Italian tradition of love poetry.

Unfortunately none of Giacomo's lyrics survives in its original Sicilian. Scribes who copied his poems regularly altered his language to conform to Tuscan after that dialect had become standard in Italy.

Bibliography

Goldin, Frederick, trans. *German and Italian Lyrics of the Middle Ages: An Anthology and a History.* New York: Doubleday, 1973.

Jensen, Frede, ed. and trans. *The Poetry of the Sicilian School.* New York: Garland, 1986.

Kleinhenz, Christopher. "Giacomo da Lentino and the Advent of the Sonnet: Divergent Patterns in Early Italian Poetry," *Forum Italicum* 10 (1976): 218–232.

Langley, Ernest, ed. *The Poetry of Giacomo Da Lentino.* Cambridge, Mass.: Harvard University Press, 1915.

Gianni degli Alfani (ca. 1271–early 14th century)

Gianni degli Alfani was a minor Florentine poet in the manner of the DOLCE STIL NOVO style popularized by Guido CAVALCANTI. Seven of his poems are extant, and they tend to be largely derivative, echoing poems of Cavalcanti and DANTE.

Very little is known of Alfani's life, and, indeed, he has not been definitively identified, though it is likely he was a silk merchant and that, like Dante, he was exiled from Florence during the bitter political struggles between the Black and White Guelfs. He seems to have traveled extensively, but circumstances of his death are unknown.

Of Alfani's seven surviving poems, six are *ballate*—a kind of traditional dance song with a refrain that had become popular among the *stilnovisti.* The other is a sonnet specifically addressed to Cavalcanti. Like Cavalcanti, Alfani focuses on the pain and anguish of love, and does use some of the medical imagery (such as the psychology of the "spirits") that characterized the poetry of his master. But Alfani tends to focus on the moment of anguish itself, rather than examining the inner psychological effects of that moment as the lover contemplates it after the fact. At the end of one of his *ballate,* for instance, he sends the poem to "Guido" (Cavalcanti). Alfani's admiration of Guido, his use of scientific imagery, and his concentration of the moment of pain (the "scream of anguish") are all present:

Then find your way into the mind of
Guido,
for only he sees Love,
and show him the spirit that draws forth
a scream from the anguish of my shattered
heart.

(Goldin, 1973, 413, ll. 18–21)

Critics of the past often dismissed Alfani as a slavish adherent of the style Cavalcanti initiated. However, some recent critics have seen him, with his focus on the lover's pain and the lady as cause of that pain, as a precursor of the next major force in Italian poetry, PETRARCH.

Bibliography

Goldin, Frederick, trans. *German and Italian Lyrics of the Middle Ages: An Anthology and a History.* New York: Doubleday, 1973.

Tusiani, Joseph, ed. *The Age of Dante: An Anthology of Early Italian Poetry.* New York: Baroque Press, 1974.

Gildas (Sapiens ["The Wise"], Badonicus) (ca. 500–ca. 570)

Gildas was the author of *De excidio et conquestu Britanniae* (ca. 540), that is, "The ruin and conquest of Britain," the earliest historical account of the Anglo-Saxon invasion of Britain. His work was used as a source by both BEDE and ALCUIN. Tradition says that Gildas was the son of a British chief from the area of Clyde (now in Scotland), and that he attended a Welsh school founded by St. Illtud. He was certainly a cleric, probably a monk. According to the later historian William of Malmsbury, Gildas spent some time in the community at Glastonbury. He is also reputed to have later founded the monastery of Rhuys in Brittany. *The Welsh Annals* place his death about 570.

His purpose in writing *De excidio* was not historical but moral: He condemns, in the strongest language, the five petty kings of the Britain of his time, and implies that the Saxon conquest was divine retribution for their sins. At the same time he condemns the priests of his time for sloth and simony. But Gildas is important particularly for contributions to the preservation of the legend of King ARTHUR: His text describes the utter defeat of the Britons by the Saxons, until the rise of a British hero named Ambrosius Aurelianus, whom Gildas calls a "moderate man" who had survived from the Roman nation. This Ambrosius Aurelianus, according to Gildas, rallied the Britons and led them in victorious battle against the Saxons. The 26th chapter of *De excidio* also describes the Battle of Mount Badon, in which the "hangdog" Saxons were defeated utterly. Gildas says that this battle took place the year of his birth, 44 years earlier (giving him the surname Badonicus).

Gildas never mentions Arthur by name. One might conclude that this is evidence that there was, in fact, no historical Arthur. The mention of the Battle of Mount Badon, however, is made without any mention of the leader of the British forces. Welsh tradition has always associated Mount Badon with Arthur. It is possible that Gildas, whose purpose was not historical but moral, doesn't mention Arthur because he simply knows that all of his readers know who the hero of Mount Badon is.

In ca. 1130, another Welshman, Caradoc of Llancarfan, wrote a life of Gildas that explains the omission: According to this saint's life, Gildas's brother, Hueil, was a rebel put to death by Arthur. Gildas became Arthur's enemy, but the two were later reconciled. According to the historian GIRALDUS CAMBRENSIS, Gildas originally had written about Arthur, but destroyed those sections of *De excidio* after Hueil's death. There is no evidence that Caradoc's life is anything but legend.

Bibliography

Alcock, Leslie. *Arthur's Britain.* London: Penguin, 1971.

Brengle, Richard L. *Arthur King of Britain: History, Chronicle, Romance, and Criticism.* New York: Appleton-Century-Crofts, 1964.

Giraldus Cambrensis (Gerald of Wales) (ca. 1146–ca. 1223)

Gerald of Wales, or Giraldus Cambrensis, was a priest, a courtier, a scholar, and historian whose numerous Latin works established him as an important man of letters in 12th- and 13th-century England and Wales. Known for a tumultuous official career that saw him twice rejected in his bid to be bishop of St. David's, Gerald is best known for his influential *Itinerary through Wales* and *Description of Wales,* both written in about 1188.

Gerald was born in Pembrokeshire in southern Wales, the youngest son of an Anglo-Norman knight named William of Barri and a Welsh princess called Anharad. He received his early education at St. Peter's in Gloucester and then attended the University of Paris, where he studied and also taught rhetoric in the 1160s. By 1174 he was a priest, with benefices in both England and Wales. He was also serving Archbishop Richard of Canterbury as his legate, or ecclesiastical ambassador, to the diocese of St. David's in Wales, where Gerald's uncle David fitz Gerald was bishop. Appointed Archdeacon of Brecon by his uncle, Gerald sought the bishopric when David died in 1176, but his nomination was rejected by King HENRY II, perhaps because of Gerald's Welsh ancestry. Following this failure Gerald returned to Paris for further study in law and theology. In 1184, the king appointed him to the position of court chaplain.

In that capacity he accompanied Prince John to Ireland in 1184. This proved the occasion of his writing the *Topographia Hibernica,* a description of the geography, the animal life, and the early history and legends of Ireland. He is reputed to have read the text aloud to scholars at Oxford University in about 1185. About the same time he wrote *Expugnatio Hibernica,* which tells the story of the Norman conquest of Ireland from 1169–85. In 1188, Gerald spent five weeks with Baldwin, then the archbishop of Canterbury, traveling thoughout Wales preaching the Third Crusade. From this experience, Gerald composed the *Itinerarium Cambriae* and *Descripto Cambriae* (*The Itinerary through Wales* and *The Description of Wales*), which remain his best-known works.

In 1194, after 10 years of royal service, Gerald retired from court life and returned to the life of a scholar, spending time at Oxford and at Lincoln. When the bishopric of St. David's became open once again in 1198, Gerald was elected to the post, but the new archbishop of Canterbury, Hubert Walter, blocked his appointment and was supported by Prince John, who became king in 1189. Unwilling to have his ambition thwarted a second time, Gerald tried to rally support among the Welsh for his appointment. He also made three separate trips to Rome to appeal directly to the pope to intervene. His defiance aroused the royal and pontifical wrath, and Gerald was outlawed and forced to flee England, only to be imprisoned eventually at Châtillon. Ultimately, though, Gerald was reconciled with King John and the archbishop, and in 1203 accepted his failure to achieve the see of St. David's. He spent his last 20 years pursuing his literary career. When he died, he was buried at St. David's.

Gerald wrote several works about the disputed bishopric, as well as an autobiographical work called *De rebus a se gestis.* In addition he composed two theological works, seven SAINTS' LIVES, and a collection of poems and short pieces called *Symbolum electoram,* assembled toward the end of his life. In his *De principis instructione* (ca. 1193), Gerald recounts the discovery and reinterment, in 1191, of the bodies of King ARTHUR and Queen Guenevere at Glastonbury Abbey. Of particular interest to Arthurian scholars, Gerald refers to Arthur and to Merlin in several of his works, repeating the traditions that Arthur was visited at Caerleon by ambassadors from Rome and that the kings of Ireland paid tribute to King Arthur. Gerald also respected Merlin's famous prophecies, though he expresses serious reservations about the account of history given by the first Arthurian chronicler, GEOFFREY OF MONMOUTH.

Bibliography

Bartlett, Robert. *Gerald of Wales, 1146–1223.* Oxford: Clarendon Press, 1982.

Giraldus Cambrensis. *The Historical Works of Giraldus Cambrensis.* Containing *The Topography of Ireland,* and *The History of the Conquest of Ireland,* translated by Thomas Forester; *The Itinerary through Wales,* and *The Description of Wales,* translated by Sir Richard Colt Hoare. Revised and edited by Thomas Wright. 1863. Reprint, New York: AMS Press, 1968.

O'Meara, John J., trans. *The History and Topography of Ireland.* Harmondsworth, U.K.: Penguin, 1982.

Richter, Michael. *Giraldus Cambrensis: The Growth of the Welsh Nation.* Rev. ed. Aberystwyth: National Library of Wales, 1976.

Roberts, Brynley F. *Gerald of Wales.* Cardiff: University of Wales Press, 1982.

———, ed. *Itinerary Through Wales.* Newtown, Wales: Gwasg Gregynog, 1989.

Rutherford, Anne, ed. *I, Giraldus: The Autobiography of Giraldus Cambrensis (1145–1223).* Based on the translation by H. E. Butler. Cambridge, Mass.: Rhwymbooks, 2002.

Giraut de Bornelh (Guiraut de Borneil) (ca. 1138–ca. 1212)

Called by his contemporaries the "master of the TROUBADOURS," Giraut de Bornelh was an influential Provençal poet whose 77 extant lyrics are the largest number to have survived from any individual troubadour of the 12th century.

Giraut was born in the region of Dorgogne, apparently to parents of modest means. He was, however, able to obtain an excellent education. His *VIDA,* or early biography, claims that he spent his winters in scholarly pursuits and his summers traveling about to the various courts of the Occitan and northern Spain, accompanied by two singers who performed his songs. The *vida* says that he never married. In his later life, he was known as a benefactor of the church in St. Gervais, and it is likely that is where he lived out his final years.

Giraut's lyrics confirm that he traveled widely, and reveal that, as a professional troubadour, he was connected at one time or another with virtually every important nobleman in the area, including Alfonso VIII of Castile, Raymond V of Toulouse, and Ferdinand II of Leon. He knew Alfonso II of Aragon well enough to have composed a *TENSON,* or debate poem, with him on the subject of whether it is better for a lady to love a king or a knight. His association with Adémar V of Limoges was particularly close, since he is thought to have accompanied Adémar to Jerusalem during the Third Crusade in 1192, and one of his poems from that period praises Richard I of England.

Giraut also seems to have been acquainted with many of his contemporary troubadours. He is satirized in a famous *SIRVENTES* by PEIRE D'ALVERNHE, who says that Giraut "looks like a goatskin dried out in the sun" (Goldin 1973, 171, l. 14). But Giraut seems to have been particularly close to RAIMBAUT D'ORANGE, whose death he mourns in a lyrical lament, and with whom he composed a *tenson* concerning the relative merits of the two chief styles of troubadour poetry, the *TROBAR CLUS* and the *TROBAR LEU*.

Giraut is the poet most often considered in discussions of style in the troubadour lyric, partly because he uses stylistic terms, like *clus* and *leu*, in his poetry. He is best remembered as a defender of the *trobar leu*, the clear and easy style, in his famous *tenson* with Raimbaut. But Giraut also composed in the *trobar clus*, the obscure and complex style, and defends that mode in another of his lyrics, "La flors el vergan." Some critics believe that he composed in the *trobar clus* early in his career, but abandoned it for the *trobar leu* later on. Others argue that Giraut most likely adapted his style to fit the tastes of whatever patron he happened to be composing for at the time.

While Dante did not concur with the high opinion Giraut's contemporaries had of him, he did admire the moral content of many of Giraut's verses, and called Giraut the "poet of rectitude." Despite this morality in some of his poetry, Giraut was not without humor and irony. About half of his extant lyrics are *CANSOS*, or love songs, but these are not highly original and he is more admired today for his efforts in other genres, like the *tenson* with Raimbaut. Giraut's *ALBA*, or "dawn song," "Reis glorios, verais lums e clartiatz" may be the best known of all troubadour songs. It is sung by the watchman, who warns the lover that he must leave his mistress's side. In the final stanza, the watchman comes to realize that his efforts on behalf of the lover are not appreciated, especially now that he is telling the lover to leave his lady:

Fair friend, how you begged me not to fall
asleep outside there on the steps
but watch all night till daybreak; now
you wish my song away, and me,
and soon the dawn will rise.

(Goldin 1973, 197, ll. 26–30)

Bibliography

Gaunt, Simon. *Troubadours and Irony.* Cambridge: Cambridge University Press, 1989.

Goldin, Frederick, ed. and trans. *Lyrics of the Troubadours and Trouvères: An Anthology and a History.* Garden City, N.Y.: Anchor, 1973.

Sharman, Ruth Verity. *The Cansos and Sirventes of the Troubadour Giraut de Borneil: A Critical Edition.* Cambridge: Cambridge University Press, 1989.

Gita-govinda (Song of the cowherd)
Jayadeva (12th century)

The *Gita-govinda* is a collection of Indian pastoral lyric verses dramatizing the love affair of Krishna (an incarnation of the god Vishnu) with the cowherdess Rādhā, a love that was interpreted as an ALLEGORY of the love of the human soul for god. The dramatic poem was one of the last important Indian devotional works (or bhakti) written in Sanskrit, and proved highly influential on the later development of literature in regional languages of India, particularly in Bengal, where it fired the imagination of later Vaishnavist poets (devotees of the lord Vishnu) such as VIDYĀPATI.

Tradition associates the poem's author, Jayadeva, with a temple of the god Jagannath in the city of Puri in eastern India. Padmavati, Jayadeva's wife, was purportedly a dancer in the temple, and the *Gita-govinda* has been sung and interpreted in dance at the Jagannath temple for at least five centuries.

The text of the *Gita-govinda* tells the love story in 24 cantos. The romantic tale is introduced in the beginning, but the next few cantos make it clear that Krishna is no mortal lover, but divine. The poem returns to its romantic love theme, creating an appropriate mood by invoking images of the spring. But when Krishna spreads his love among several other cowherd girls, Rādhā becomes jealous and reacts with fury to Krishna's approach. Realizing her desire to have him exclusively to herself, Krishna eases Rādhā 's anger and persuades her that he loves her truly. The reconciled couple passionately reunite in their love, and the poem ends as Krishna seems set on granting Rādhā 's every wish.

Clearly Jayadeva's intent is for the poem to be read on two levels at once. On the literal level, the poem is a satisfying love story. On the allegorical level, one sees the ecstasy of mystical union with the divine, and then, in Rādhā, the intense desire for the god's exclusive love wins him to her. The human desire for god is presented as not simply one-sided: The god, too, needs and desires unity with the human soul, indeed is not complete without the devotion of human love. And ultimately god's love for the human soul is unrestrained and manifest in the desire to give human beings all their desire. The poem is a classic of spiritual longing and bliss, and remains, especially among modern Vaishnavists, a popular expression of spirituality.

Bibliography

Ayengar, N. S. R., ed. and trans. *Sacred Profanities: A Study of Jayadeva's Gitagovinda.* Original Sanskrit text with English translation. Delhi: Penman Publishers, 2000.

Miller, Barbara Stoler, ed. and trans. *Love Song of the Dark Lord: Jayadeva's Gitagovinda.* New York: Columbia University Press, 1977.

Pathy, Dinanath, Bhagaban Panda, and Bijaya Kumar Rath. *Jayadeva and Gitagovinda in the Traditions of Orissa.* New Delhi: Harman Publishing House, 1995.

gnomic verse

The term *gnomic* (meaning "sententious" or "aphoristic") was originally applied to ancient Greek poets like Solon and Theognis, who wrote short moralistic poems in the sixth century B.C.E. By extension, it has been applied to similar kinds of short aphoristic passages in medieval Germanic languages, in particular two Old English compilations (also called "Maxims I" and "Maxims II"), the first of which appears in the EXETER BOOK, and the second of which is included as part of a prologue to the ANGLO-SAXON CHRONICLE in the British Museum manuscript Cotton Tiberius B.i. They seem to have been recorded in their present form sometime in the 10th century.

These maxims usually express a generalized observation concerning the world or about human beings' behavior in it. Most of these generalizations include verbs like *shall* or *must.* As such, the gnomic verses express something about *wyrd*—about the way things are fated to be in this world. When the poet says that

Frost shall freeze
fire eat wood

(Alexander 1966, 88)

he expresses the inevitability of these natural laws. When he says:

Courage must wax
war-mood in the man,
the woman grow up
beloved among her people,
be light of mood
hold close a rune-word

(Alexander 1966, 88)

he expresses the expectations society has for the two genders, expectations that should presumably be seen as just and inviolable: This is how people *should* behave.

The intent of the Old English gnomic verses is to express natural, moral, and social truths in a brief, solemn, authoritative manner.

Bibliography

Alexander, Michael, trans. *The Earliest English Poems.* Harmondsworth: Penguin, 1966.

Williams, Blanche Coulton, ed. *Gnomic Poetry in Anglo Saxon.* New York: Columbia University Press, 1914.

Gododdin, Y (*The Gododdin*) Aneirin (ca. 600)

Y Gododdin is a poem in the ancient Brithonic dialect of Cumbric (an ancestor of modern Welsh), spoken by the tribe known to the Romans as

Vōtadīnī, but to themselves as the Gododdin. From their capital at Eidyn (modern-day Edinburgh), they dominated that region from the Firth of Forth south to around Durham. The poem is attributed to the bard ANEIRIN, and survives in a single 13th-century manuscript called *Llyfr Aneirin* (*Book of Aneirin*), now located at the Free Library of Cardiff.

The textual tradition of *The Gododdin* is a complex puzzle, but evidence does suggest that the bulk of the poem was composed originally in the late sixth century (though some scholars support a date some 300 years later). As it now exists, the poem comprises some 1,000 lines divided into 103 stanzas of varying length. Generally these stanzas consist of a number of lines united by a common end rhyme (*unodle*), probably the oldest poetic form in Welsh. The lines are usually about nine or 10 syllables long, and sometimes contain internal rhyme or alliteration. Some scholars have suggested close parallels between the Gododdin and OLD ENGLISH heroic poetry, another detail that suggests an early date for the poem.

The poem is made up of a series of laments for fallen British warriors, killed at the Battle of Catraeth (ca. 588–90). No continuous narrative emerges from the text, but the story of the battle can be pieced together. The Gododdin king Mynyddog Mwynfawr (the Wealthy) assembles at his court in Eidyn a group of 300 great warriors and their retinues, gathered from the areas of Scotland, Yorkshire, and northern Wales. For a year the young men train while eating and drinking mead and wine at Mynyddog's court. After the year has ended, the men are sent to attack an overwhelming army of Northumbrian Anglians from Berenicia and Deira. Mynyddog does not seem to have led the operation himself, perhaps due to advanced age. But the vastly outnumbered British army engages the enemy at Catraeth (now identified as Catterick near Richmond in North Yorkshire). The battle rages for an entire week, with truces called on Friday and Sunday to count the dead. Ultimately all of the Gododdin are slaughtered, with the exception of three men—in some stanzas—or just one, the poet himself, in others.

That Aneirin was in fact a survivor of the battle seems far-fetched, and it may be simply a poetic device. But the majority of scholars believe that most of his stanzas were, in fact, written shortly after the battle. There are, to be sure, a few later interpolations in the poem: one refers to the death in ca. 642 of Domnall Brecc, a well-known king of Dál Riada in Scotland; another is a cradle song for the child of Dinogad, sung while his father is hunting near the falls of the river Derwent. But with regard to stanzas directly concerned with the fallen heroes of Catraeth, the fact that virtually none of the warriors mentioned are known from other sources is regarded as evidence that the battle was, in fact, historical and that the verses were written shortly thereafter, since it seems unlikely that a poet writing 300 years after the fact would bother to commemorate men who were by that time unknown.

Like most heroic poetry, *The Gododdin* seems written chiefly to extol the warrior virtues of courage and fidelity to one's word and to the lord whose mead you have drunk. In the poem the British heroes kill many times their own number of the enemy, though in a hopeless cause. The description of one warrior is famous in the Arthurian tradition as being the first mention of King ARTHUR in literature: The hero Gwawrddur is said to have "glutted the ravens"—that is, killed so many of the enemy that the ravens had more than enough to eat—though, we are told, "he was not Arthur." In other words he was not the equal of the greatest warrior of all—Arthur—whose name had become (in British thought) proverbial for the ideal of heroic prowess. Certainly it is possible that the line concerning Arthur is a later interpolation, but there is no real evidence to dismiss it. The Gododdin, fighting a losing battle against the Angles, are seen as making war in the tradition of Arthur, the last great defender of the British against the Anglo-Saxon invaders just a few generations earlier.

Bibliography

Breeze, Andrew. *Medieval Welsh Literature.* Dublin: Four Courts Press, 1997.

Jackson, Kenneth H., ed. *The Gododdin: The Oldest Scottish Poem.* Edinburgh: Edinburgh University Press, 1969. Reprinted in 1978.

William, Ifor, ed. *Canu Aneirin.* Cardiff: Gwasg Prifysgol Cymru, 1938.

Williams, Gwyn. *An Introduction to Welsh Poetry: From the Beginnings to the Sixteenth Century.* 1954. Freeport, N.Y.: Books for Libraries Press, 1970.

Golagros and Gawane (*The Knightly Tale of Golagros and Gawain*) (ca. 1450–1500)

Golagros and Gawane is a late 15th-century ROMANCE written in Middle Scots (closely related to the Northern dialect of MIDDLE ENGLISH). The 1,362-line poem, composed in the same complex, 13-line stanza (utilizing rhyme as well as alliteration) as the better-known *AWNTYRS OFF ARTHURE AT THE TERNE WATHELYN*, is adapted from two episodes from what is called the "First Continuation" of CHRÉTIEN DE TROYES's chivalric romance *PERCEVAL*. No manuscript version of *Golagros and Gawane* has survived, but the first Scottish printers, Walter Chepman and Andrew Myllar, published the poem in 1508 with the title *The Knightly Tale of Golagros and Gawain.* A single copy of this early printed edition is extant, and is now in the National Library of Scotland.

Like *The Awntyrs off Arthure, Golagros and Gawain* falls into two loosely related parts. In the first, the boorish Sir Kay is, as in so many romances, contrasted with the courteous Sir GAWAIN. King ARTHUR and his knights, on pilgrimage to the Holy Land, run out of supplies one night after a long march through Tuscany. Noting a city in the distance, Arthur sends Kay to obtain provisions. But the vulgar Kay instead tries to seize a brace of roasted birds from a dwarf. He is beaten soundly for his behavior by the knight who is lord of the castle, and sent back to Arthur with nothing. Gawain decides to attempt the mission himself, and, through his courteous behavior that acknowledges the foreign knight's rights, succeeds where Kay had failed.

The second, longer part of the poem begins after Sir Spynagros, lord of the Tuscan castle, has feasted Arthur and his men for four days. He then serves as guide for the knights as they start on their way. As they come to the Rhône, they see a castle that Spynagros explains belongs to a knight, Golagros, who pays homage to no lord. Arthur, appalled by the anarchic implications of such an arrangement, declares that he will deal with Golagros when he returns from Palestine.

When Arthur returns, he besieges the castle, and after four days of indecisive combat, Sir Golagros comes out of the castle to challenge Arthur's champion, Sir Gawain, to single combat. Gawain defeats Golagros, and spares his life. But to save face, Golagros asks Gawain to come with him into his castle and act as if Golagros has vanquished him. In an unprecedented act of courtesy, Gawain agrees. In the castle, Golagros ultimately explains the truth to his people, who wish to keep him as their lord but to do homage and fealty to the perfectly courteous Gawain and his lord Arthur. The poem concludes with Golagros pledging his allegiance to the king as his liege lord. After a celebration of nine days, Arthur and his knights leave Golagros—and Arthur courteously releases Golagros from his fealty.

The poem's second episode (four times the length of the first) repeats and enlarges the theme of the first. In both episodes, following the code of knightly behavior with perfect courtesy ultimately produces only honor to all involved. The discourteous knight, Kay, is shamed, but Gawain's generosity produces generous behavior in Sir Spynagros, the Tuscan knight, just as it later inspires Golagros to high courtesy, and finally leads to Arthur's own courteous gesture in the end.

Admired for its complex verse form, its vivid and elaborate descriptions of the battle scene between Golagros and Gawain, and its interesting structural strategy, *Golagros and Gawane* is a poem that deserves to be better known than it is. It compares well with most Middle English verse romances, and is clearly the product of a skilled artist, composing at the very end of the medieval Arthurian tradition.

Bibliography

Barron, W. R. J. "*Golagros and Gawain:* A Creative Redaction," *Bibliographical Bulletin of the International Arthurian Society* 26 (1974): 173–185.

Mathewson, Jeanne T. "Displacement of the Feminine in *Golagros and Gawane* and *The Awntyrs off*

Arthure," Arthurian Interpretations 1, no. 2 (1987): 23–28.

Sir Gawain: Eleven Romances and Tales. Edited by Thomas Hahn. Kalamazoo, Mich.: Medieval Institute Publications, 1995.

Golden Legend (*Aurea Legenda*) Jacobus de Voragine (ca. 1265)

Jacobus (or James) de Voragine composed the *Golden Legend* as a collection of writings centered on the lives of the saints and their celebrations (*see* SAINTS' LIVES). The text is composed largely of miraculous tales concerning popular saints and brief expositional notes about specific liturgical feasts linked to the cult of saints. James was a member of the Dominican Order, becoming vicar of the order ca. 1283. He was appointed archbishop of Genoa, ca. 1292. James created the text as a source for ecclesiastical preaching, but the *Golden Legend* was more popular within the vernacular culture of the day—a wider contemporary trend that is witnessed by a similar passion among the laity for other liturgical works such as the medieval books of hours. Hundreds of manuscripts containing the *Golden Legend* remain extant in numerous languages. Frequently, these manuscripts exhibit the special hagiographic interests of their individual audiences through the inclusion or emphasis of local saints. The text's popularity was considered dangerous during the 16th century with both Catholic and Protestant writers condemning the fantastic nature of the *Golden Legend* and its ability to lead the rustic believer into superstition.

The *Golden Legend* begins with a series of exegetical notices discussing the symbolic and historical meanings of common Catholic celebrations such as Easter, Pentecost, and the Circumcision of Our Lord. These discussions reflect a traditional approach to Christian Scripture that assumed Scripture to have a literal, symbolic and spiritual message. For instance, the entry for *epiphany* is constructed around the symbolic interpretations of earlier church authorities such as John Chrysostom, Remigius, and Jerome. James's next section of entries outlines the careers of biblical heroes. These sections, entitled "histories," cover the period from Adam to Job and are very close synopses of the biblical texts. The *Legend* demonstrates a preference for personal stories, however, that better provide material for sermons. Joshua is merely listed as having fought many battles for the Lord, while the more intimate story of Samuel's miraculous birth and his calling is produced in full.

After Job, the *Legend* shifts—providing accounts of Christian saints from late antiquity. Christian martyrs and saints such as St. Martin and St. Benedict who are found in most early medieval martyrologies appear alongside more modern saints such as St. FRANCIS OF ASSISI and St. Louis of France. Each of these entries emphasized the miraculous power, absolute purity, and single-minded devotion of the saint, as well as how these characteristics affected the lives of others around them. Much of the text is dedicated to affirming traditional Christian goals such as asceticism, poverty, chastity, and charity.

The *Legend*'s contents are arranged according to relative importance and calendar order. Christ and the saints mentioned in biblical texts come first with the later saints following behind. The biblical heroes are listed in the order they appear within the Bible, but the days they should be celebrated within Christian worship are listed in each notice. Later martyrs and saints are placed in order as they appear throughout the Christian calendar year. This layout emphasizes the importance of Christ and the biblical text, while simultaneously strengthening the *Legend*'s role as a source for daily devotions. The result is a continuous chain of sanctity that links Adam through Jesus to James's own period. Moreover, since saints were held to be alive in heaven and capable of wielding power on earth, James's text introduced his audience to a powerful set of patrons.

The *Legend* ends with a list of 12 criteria for correct belief, a sort of creed that instructs the reader on the fundamentals of Christianity. Much of the creed is written in the first person, as a confessional prayer. This may indicate James's hope that readers would be drawn to Christianity through utilizing his collection. A grand history of Christian sanctity and its miraculous workings is presented for the reader's edification. James's other works include various series of sermons as well as a chronicle concerning the history of Genoa.

Bibliography

"Golden Legend." In *Oxford Dictionary of the Christian Church,* edited by F. L. Cross. Oxford: Oxford University Press, 1997.

Gorlach, Manfred. *The South English Legendary: Gilte Legende and Golden Legend.* Manfred, Germany: Technische Univ. Carolo-Wilhelmina, Inst. für Anglistik und Amerikanistik, 1972.

"James of Voragine." In *Oxford Dictionary of the Christian Church,* edited by F. L. Cross. Oxford: Oxford University Press, 1997.

Jeremy, Mary. "Caxton's *Golden Legend* and Varagine's *Legenda Aurea,*" *Speculum* 21 (1946): 212–221.

Medieval Sourcebook: "The Golden Legend (*Aurea Legenda*)." Compiled by Jacobus de Voragine, 1275. Translated by William Caxton, 1483. Available online. URL: http://www.fordham.edu/halsall/basis/goldenlegend/index.htm. Accessed February 1, 2005.

Reno, Christine M. "Christine de Pisan's use of the *Golden Legend* in the *Cite des dames,*" *Les Bonnes Feuilles* 3 (1974): 89–99.

Chris Craun

Golestan (*Gulistan*) Sa'di (1258)

SA'DI of Shiraz composed the second of his major works, *Golestan* (*The Rose Garden*), in Shiraz after a 30-year career as a traveling scholar. Part of a longstanding Persian literature of advice and moral counsel, the text is a collection of prose passages and short lyrics aimed at instructing the reader in moral behavior in a variety of situations. Like most Muslim classics, *Golestan* is written in the *adab* tradition (a word that implies etiquette or appropriate behavior). In literature *adab* refers to an ideal of literature combining erudite intellectual knowledge and polished literary style with moral and ethical instruction. In this, the *Golestan* has succeeded so well that over the centuries it has been perhaps the classic literary model of prose style in Persian.

The text of the *Golestan* begins with a preface, in which Sa'di describes how he came to write the *Golestan:* he was, He says, living a life of contemplation when a friend came to visit him. The friend encouraged him to share his wisdom, for the sake of others. Later, as the two of them strolled through a park and his friend gathered flowers, Sa'di announced that flowers would all fade, but that he would compose a book, a "Rose Garden," that would never wither. At that, the friend threw away his flowers and promised to take in the flowers of wisdom that Sa'di would compose.

The *Golestan* proper comprises eight books, each with a general organizational topic (although anecdotes sometimes are only distantly related to the purported topic of the book in which they appear). The titles of the books include "On the Character and Conduct of Kings," "On the Ethics of Dervishes," "On the Virtues of Contentment," "On the Advantages of Silence," "On Love and Youth," "On Feebleness and Old Age," "On the Effect of Education," and "On the Conduct of Society." The topics Sa'di covers in these books range from mystical devotion to political justice to erotic love, and on all these topics Sa'di provides commonsense wordly wisdom. Each anecdote ends with a moral, provided either by Sa'di or by one of the characters in the story. Sa'di's main emphases are the virtues of charity, humility, industry, prudence, and acceptance, but the world he presents is clearly a real contemporary world where moral choices must sometimes be practical and expedient. The first anecdote of the *Golestan,* for instance, involves a shah who has condemned an innocent man to death. As the prisoner begins to curse the shah, the ruler asks his ministers what the man is saying. The first minister tells him that the man was quoting the KORAN's admonition against showing anger. But as the shah begins to relent, the second minister informs him of what the man is truly saying. The shah's conclusion is that the lie was better than the truth, since it promoted peace and goodwill.

This kind of practical worldly wisdom appears also in anecdotes demonstrating self-interest and an attitude of "what goes around comes around": In the 35th anecdote of Book I, Sa'di recounts being in a boat and watching two men drowning. The boatman dives in to help, but in his eagerness to save one man, he is forced to allow the other to drown. He then reveals that the man he saved had helped him years earlier when he was stranded in the desert. The one that drowned had flogged him when he was a child.

The most admired books of the *Golestan* are the first two, on the conduct of shahs and the behavior of dervishes. Since these two groups represented the political and the spiritual exemplars of society, it was natural that their behavior would be of particular interest to readers. The ideal shah, of course, was one who treated his people justly and compassionately. That such was not always the case is clear from a number of Sa'di's anecdotes. In the sixth anecdote of Book I, for instance, a Persian shah oppresses his people and appropriates their wealth, until many of his subjects flee his realm. His court minister advises him that generosity and mercy are the things that give a ruler his people's support, and that the shah has displayed none of these qualities. The minister is thrown in prison, but soon after, the shah is deposed by a rebel army.

Dervishes, too, need to be models of spirituality, humility, and generosity, and many of Sa'di's anecdotes illustrate those behaviors. But dervishes might fall short of expectations as well: In the sixth anecdote of Book II, a dervish visits the house of a king, where in order to appear holy he eats very little of the banquet set before him, and spends more time praying than he typically would. When he returns to his home, he orders a large meal, and his son asks why he didn't eat at the king's dinner. The dervish says that he acted as he had in order to serve his purposes. The son tells him that now he needs to go back to praying, since what he has done has served no purpose in heaven.

In general, fiction is not considered appropriate in classical Muslim literature, but since the *Golestan* uses fiction for didactic purposes, it is acceptable. Certainly the characters of Sa'di's anecdotes never rise above conventional types, but the appeal of the work has always been its commonsense moral instruction and the eloquence of its language. In addition, the book makes use of Sufi mystical thought, and recent criticism has noted that beneath the popular reading of the text is a more complex allegory discernable only to Sufi initiates. In particular, the sensual erotic love described in the text, particularly in book 5 on "Youth and Love," refers metaphorically to a desire for unity with God, who is the beloved.

The huge popularity of the *Golestan* among Persian readers, for whom, like Shakespeare in English, it pervades everyday speech in the form of proverbs, led to its early popularity in the West as well. The text was translated into Turkish in the 14th century, and in the 17th century into German, French, English, Dutch, and Latin. Sa'di's work is said to be the most popular text of Muslim literature, after the Koran itself.

Bibliography

Rehatsek, Edward, trans. *The Gulistan, or Rose Garden, of Sa'di.* London: Allen and Unwin, 1964.

Ali-shah, Omar, trans. *Saadi: The Rose Garden (Gulistan).* Paris: Tractus, 1997.

Yohannan, John D. *The Poet Sa'di: A Persian Humanist.* Lanham, Md.: University Press of America, 1987.

goliardic verse

With the rise of the medieval university system, secular learning also gained in importance. Many student scholars who had to learn the Latin language and ancient Roman literature turned to imitating the love poetry by Horace, Propertius, and Ovid, among others, and also composed many drinking songs, satirical songs ridiculing the church authorities, erotic songs, but also religious songs in Latin. At times in central Europe they also composed in Middle High German or combinations of Latin and German. Most goliards tended to be vagrant students (*vagantes*), but many of them were also learned and highly esteemed scholars. Some scholars have tried to distinguish between the social classes of the goliards, *vagantes*, and gleemen, called *ioculatores* or *histriones* (courtly fools or actors), but since we do not know a great deal about any of these poets, we can continue using the terms interchangeably.

The earliest representative of goliardic poetry was the ninth-century Irish scholar Sedulius Scotus who settled at the Carolingian court and gained fame for his satirical poetry. The name *goliard* has often been connected with a certain Golias, a legendary, learned bishop, although many goliardic songs were highly irreverent and rebellious, emphasizing a hedonistic enjoyment of life. GIRALDUS CAMBRENSIS (1146–1223) related the term "goliards" to the Latin *gula* (gluttony), but the most common etymological explanation today relies on the biblical name Goliath, who represented monstrous wickedness in the Middle Ages.

Most goliardic poetry has come down to us anonymously, collected in such famous manuscripts as *Arundel* 384 and *Harleian* 913 and 978 in the British Museum; *Rawlinson* G109 in the Bodleian Library, Oxford; the *Cambridge Songbook* (Ff. 1.17, 11th century); and the famous *CARMINA BURANA* (early 13th century), today in the Staatsbibliothek Munich. Some goliardic poetry has been attributed to famous poets, teachers, and clerics such as Gauthier de Châtillon, the Primas of Orléans, the ARCHPOET, the Marner, Otloh of St. Emmeram, Marbod of Rennes, Geoffrey of Winchester, Hugh of Orléans, Hilarius, Philip the Chancellor, Geoffrey of St. Victor, and Peter of Blois. The Goliards, when they did not deal with the themes of wine, women, and song, deftly satirized the moral and political decline in the church and attacked vices among the lay audience. Most of them seem to have been students and teachers especially at French universities of the 12th and 13th centuries, but they could be found in other parts of Europe as well. Through wordplay, poetic strategies, skillful rhyme schemes, and other literary elements the goliards demonstrated their command of classical Latin poetry and language and at the same time turned their criticism against the church and the worldly authorities, exposing a wide range of sinful behavior and moral depravity. A number of goliardic poems utilized well-known religious songs and replaced their texts with erotic verses (a process called *contrafactum*). Most goliardic verses have come down to us without musical notation, but the *Carmina Burana* contains a number of neumes or early musical notations that indicate the melodies at least in rough terms.

Bibliography

Breul, Karl, ed. *The Cambridge Songs: A Goliard's Song Book of the XIth Century.* 1915. New York: AMS Press, 1973.

Parler, David, trans. *Selections from the Carmina Burana.* Harmondsworth, Eng.: Penguin, 1986.

Waddell, Helen. *Songs of the Wandering Scholars.* 1927. London: The Folio Society, 1982.

Whicher, George Frisbe, ed. and trans. *The Goliard Poets: Medieval Latin Songs and Satires with Verse Translations.* Norfolk, Conn.: New Directions, 1965.

Zeydel, Edwin H. *Vagabond Verse: Secular Latin Poems of the Middle Ages.* Detroit: Wayne State University Press, 1966.

Albrecht Classen

Gottfried von Strassburg (ca. 1180–ca. 1220)

Although we know next to nothing about the Middle High German poet Gottfried von Strassburg, he certainly enjoys the greatest respect for his *TRISTAN* ROMANCE (ca. 1210), which easily proves to be the best version of the entire medieval TRISTAN tradition. In the fictionalized portrait of Gottfried in the famous *Manessische Liederhandschrift* (ms. C, early 14th century), the poet is identified as *meister* (master), which signals his learned background. By the same token, he was probably not of noble origin. Apart from his *Tristan,* Gottfried also composed a number of COURTLY LOVE songs, contained in the *Manessische Liederhandschrift* (ms. C) and in the *Kleine Heidelberger Liederhandschrift* (ms. A). His *Tristan* enjoyed tremendous popularity, as documented by 11 complete manuscripts and 17 fragments. Many contemporary and subsequent poets expressed profound respect for Gottfried and his literary accomplishments. Based on his name and his language, we know that he hailed from Strassburg (Strasbourg) or its vicinity, where he obviously received a solid education in the *trivium,* the *quadrivium,* classical literature, rhetoric, and theology. He is one of the first medieval poets to reflect critically on his predecessors and to identify some of the best contemporary poets within the literary excursus of his *Tristan.* A rather obscure and negative comment in his review of other Middle High German poets might be aimed at his competitor, WOLFRAM VON ESCHENBACH, whose writing style and poetic art he obviously disliked very much.

Gottfried mentions in the prologue to his text that he searched far and wide for the best source for his *Tristan,* examined many libraries, and studied many books in French and Latin until he found the version by the Old French poet THOMAS OF BRETAGNE (ca. 1170). He then translated this text and expanded it considerably. As was common in the Middle Ages, poets such as Gottfried were not much interested in developing an original story; instead they were proud of their ability to create literary variations and adaptations of their sources. Gottfried's prologue is important also for his teaching about "noble hearts," as only true lovers would be allowed to join the community of those determined by true spiritual nobility. Gottfried created the remarkable image of readers of love stories who enjoy these texts like bread, almost in a eucharistic sense of the word, implying that true lovers need stories of true love.

In his *Tristan,* Gottfried develops a number of new concepts regarding the love between Tristan and Isolde. First we learn about the history of Tristan's parents, Rivalin and Blanscheflor, whose son is born illegitimately, which causes severe military and political problems with Rivalin's inheritance, the kingdom of Parmenie. Consequently, the young hero Tristan, by now an orphan, has to grow up in hiding, but he receives tremendous learning, especially in languages and music. Later he kills his deceased father's opponent, King Morgan, but then departs for the court of his uncle, King Mark of Cornwall. Similarly as in EILHART VON OBERG's *Tristrant,* the young hero wins the Irish princess Isolde the Fair as a bride for his uncle Mark, but accidentally both drink the love potion brewed by Isolde's mother, also called Isolde, who had intended it for her daughter and her future husband to guarantee happiness in their marriage. The effect of the love potion, however, is quite different from Eilhart's version, as their newfound love will last forever, and they cannot survive a day without seeing each other. The adulterous couple struggles hard to defend themselves against the courtly spies and Mark's suspicions, and at one point, Isolde has to undergo a trial by ordeal with the hot iron. Significantly, here we observe the young woman emerging as the true protagonist as she secretly orchestrates a deceptive game. She officially professes never to have lain in the arms of a man except her husband and the poor pilgrim who had carried her from the ship to the shore, and then had fallen under her weight. This pilgrim, however, was Tristan, and subsequently Isolde's oath is accepted, as the narrator states, by God who, like a windswept sleeve, ignores her outrageous lie as he supports the lovers against the jealous husband.

Isolde demonstrates her intellectual maturity and mastership of love again in the Petitcrîu scene. Petitcrîu is a little dog who wears a magical bell around its neck, and anybody who listens to the bell's music immediately experiences complete happiness and forgets all his sorrows. Tristan wins this dog for his beloved by killing a giant, which then allows him to claim the dog as his prize, causing enormous misery to his previous owner. Contrary to his expectations and limited understanding of the nature of love, however, Isolde tears off the bell and thus destroys the musical "drug," as she does not want to enjoy happiness without Tristan. In fact, here Isolde proves to possess a truly "noble heart," whereas Tristan seems to think only of material happiness.

At the end of his narrative Gottfried has the lovers taking refuge in a magical cave in the midst of a forest after they have been discovered by the king *in flagrante* and were expelled from the court. In the cave they enjoy each other and live their love in a utopian setting, without need for any food and drink. One day Mark happens to find the cave and sees, to his surprise, a sword strategically placed between the two young people while they are sleeping in bed. This erroneously convinces him that Tristan and Isolde are innocent—he does not know that Tristan heard him arrive at the cave and intends to deceive him with the sword. Full of love for both his wife and his nephew, Mark allows them to return to his court. Yet when Mark catches them in tender embrace once again, Tristan must depart for good, leaving Isolde behind full of grief. In distant lands he meets another young woman, also called Isolde (Whitehand), who falls in love with him, whereas he is still longing for Isolde the Fair. Before the narrative can develop this intricate situation further, the text breaks off, whereas in Eilhart's version and in many subsequent *Tristan* romances, Tristan and his true beloved Isolde eventually meet their death just when she is coming to rescue him from a mortal wound.

Not one of the many manuscripts containing Gottfried's *Tristan* offers a conclusion, which forces us to accept that the poet left his text as a fragment, either because he died too early, or because he could not or did not want to complete his romance. Gottfried not only composed a highly intriguing romance of adulterous love, but also incorporated much scholastic learning, reflected intensively on ancient classical literature, such as Ovid and Cicero, and combined religious concepts with amazingly unorthodox concepts of love.

Bibliography

Des Minnesangs Frühling. Edited by Hugo Moser and Helmut Tervooren. 38th ed. Stuttgart: Hirzel, 1988.

Gentry, Francis, trans. *Tristan and Isolde.* New York: Continuum, 1988.

Gottfried von Strassburg. *Tristan und Isolde.* Edited by Karl Marold. 3rd rev. ed. 1906. Berlin: de Gruyter, 1969.

Hasty, Will, ed. *A Companion to Gottfried von Strassburg's "Tristan."* Rochester, N.Y.: Camden House, 2003.

Albrecht Classen

Govindadāsa (15th century)

Govindadāsa is the name of one of the best-known poet-saints of the Vaishnava sect (those devoted to worship of Vishnu as god), a part of the Hindu spiritual movement called *bhakto* ("sharing [in god]"). In general these bhakti poets expressed a passionate devotion to god, independent of the strict Brahmanical tradition, and wrote their poetry for people largely uneducated in classical Sanskrit. Thus the lyrics of the bhakti poems were written in the language of everyday people, in Govindadāsa 's case in the early Bengali dialect of northeastern India.

Like his fellow Bengali Vaishnava poet-saints Chandidas and Vidyāpati, Govindadāsa chose as the subject for his lyrics the Hindu myth of Krishna, most popular incarnation of the god Vishnu, and his love affair with the *gopī* or herding woman named Rādhā. But with all of these poets, the question of authorship is a complex one for two main reasons. First, later poets would sometimes ascribe their own poems to a prestigious earlier poet to give their own religious views the authority that name provided. In addition bhakti devotees generally assumed a new religious name, and many people might therefore choose the same name, especially a name that ended in the suffix -dāsa (that is, "servant"). Since *Govinda* was a name frequently used to address Krishna, particularly in his role as lover of *gopī*, since it meant, essentially, "herdsman," the name Govindadāsa means "servant of Krishna"—a name almost certain to be popular with bhakti devotees of Vishnu.

Thus we cannot be sure that the Govindadāsa whose name appears in the signature lines (or *bhanitās*) of many lyric poems is always the same poet. The poems themselves, however, are simple, vivid, and memorable. They tend to be written in the conventional bhakti style called *mādhurya-bhāva,* a style that speaks of Krishna in the role of divine lover. In these poems the narrator conventionally speaks in the voice of Rādhā, who represents, metaphorically, the human soul longing for god. The yearning for sexual unity by the lovers becomes the vivid image of a passionate spiritual longing. In one of Govindadāsa's poems, the speaker's longing for unity with her love is expressed in images that dissolve her own identity into his:

> *Let the water of my body join the waters*
> *of the lotus pool he bathes in.*
> *Let the breath of my body be air*
> *lapping his tired limbs.*

(Dimock and Levertov 1967, 58)

In another the pain of her lover's imminent departure is too much to bear, and in the *bhanita* that ends the poem, Govindadāsa takes on the persona of *gopī* companions of Rādhā, who, abashed by the intimacy of the scene, softly steal away:

> —*Where has he gone? Where has my love gone?*
> *O why has he left me alone? . . .*
> *Taking her beloved friend by the hand,*
> *Govinda-dāsa led her softly away.*
>
> (Dimock and Levertov 1967, 23)

Bibliography

Dimock, Edward C., and Denise Levertov, eds. and trans. *In Praise of Krishna.* Garden City, N.Y.: Doubleday, 1967.

Gower, John (ca. 1330–1408)

John Gower was a friend and contemporary of fellow poet Geoffrey CHAUCER. He enjoyed a literary reputation second only to Chaucer's in his own lifetime and throughout the 15th century, and Shakespeare himself borrowed the plot of his *Pericles* from Gower's *Apollonius of Tyre.* His body of work has not been as palatable to more modern tastes as Chaucer's has; thus Gower's reputation has suffered since the 17th century. Still Gower is remarkable for having written major poetic compositions in three different languages: French (the *MIROUR DE L'OMME*), Latin (*VOX CLAMANTIS*), and English (*CONFESIO AMANTIS*), a feat no other English poet can match.

Gower was born in Kent, and his English verse shows characteristics of the 14th-century Kentish dialect. He seems to have been from an upper-middle-class family, and may have been educated as a lawyer. He wrote some early love poems in French that were collected in the *Cinkante Ballades* before 1374. But he turned to more serious literary endeavors in the mid-1370s, perhaps due to his friendship with Chaucer, which must have developed about this time since, when Chaucer left on a trip to Italy in 1378, he gave Gower his power of attorney.

Between 1376 and 1379, Gower wrote a long moralizing poem in French called *Mirour de l'omme* (Mirror of man). In this text Gower stresses the decline of society because of man's turning from right reason. Not unlike his contemporaries LANGLAND and Chaucer, he includes a long section of ESTATES SATIRE, that is, satire of the three "estates" (nobility, clergy, and commoner), including satires of individual professions within those estates.

By this time Gower seems to have been a major benefactor of the Priory of St. Mary Overeys in Southwark. He may have contributed to its 1377 restoration. By the 1390s, Gower was living in an apartment at the priory. It has been suggested that some of the manuscripts of his works were actually produced at the priory under Gower's own supervision.

He followed the *Mirour de l'omme* with his Latin work *Vox clamantis* (The voice of one crying), a poem that begins with a powerful description of the PEASANTS' REVOLT OF 1381 as a frightening example of the chaos into which society falls when its members neglect the rational strictures of natural law. Gower goes on to criticize the three estates again, and then adds a section addressing the duty of the king to uphold the law and remain morally responsible. It was these two works chiefly that led Chaucer to call him "the moral Gower" in his dedication to *TROILUS AND CRISEYDE* (ca. 1385).

Gower's last major work, written between 1386 and 1390, has always been his most popular. The *Confessio amantis,* apparently commissioned by RICHARD II to be written in English, is organized as a confessional manual in which a lover is examined by a priest of Venus and confesses his sins against love. Yet Gower begins his English poem with another description of moral corruption and the decay of society because of man's turning from Reason. The tales that follow, in fact, have little to do with the kind of COURTLY LOVE the king seems to have had in mind when he gave Gower the commission, but have more to do with *caritas,* or universal love, and with moral responsibility.

Gower spent a good deal of time in his later years revising his major works, partly to make them more closely complement one another, and partly to reflect his growing disenchantment with Richard II. He had praised Richard's rule in the first version of the *Confessio amantis* in 1390, but in a revision shortly afterward, he omitted the flattery of Richard, and in 1393, Gower revised the poem again, rededicating it to Henry Bolingbroke (later King Henry IV). Later still he revised the earlier *Vox clamantis,* replacing lines that had excused the young king with lines that condemned the state of English society. When Henry deposed Richard in 1399, Gower wrote a partisan history of the events in the *Cronica Tripertita,* for which Henry granted him an annuity.

By this time Gower was in ill health. He married his nurse, Agnes Groundolf, on January 25, 1398, and apparently went completely blind in 1401. He died in October of 1408, leaving his goods to Agnes and the priors of St. Mary's, where he was buried. His effigy in Southward Cathedral depicts his head lying on three large volumes representing his three major works.

All of Gower's major poetry expresses his moral theme, and it seems clear that he wished to be remembered more as a moralist than as a poet. Still he was technically an admirable craftsman of verse, and his French and English verses are smoothly metrical octosyllabic couplets. It was largely this technical virtuosity that made him most admired in the generations immediately following his death. Today his work seems unattractively didactic to many readers. Of all his works, *Confessio amantis* is Gower's most entertaining and therefore currently the most likely to be read, and includes not only the source for Shakespeare's *Pericles,* but also the "Tale of Florent" and the "Tale of Constance" (analogues of Chaucer's WIFE OF BATH'S TALE and MAN OF LAW'S TALE, respectively).

Bibliography

Burrow, J. A. *Ricardian Poetry: Chaucer, Gower, Langland.* New Haven, Conn.: Yale University Press, 1971.

Fisher, John H. *John Gower: Moral Philosopher and Friend of Chaucer.* New York: New York University Press, 1964.

Gower, John. *Confessio amantis.* Edited by Russell A. Peck. Toronto: University of Toronto Press, 1980.

Macaulay, G. C., ed. *The Complete Works of John Gower.* 4 vols. Oxford: Clarendon Press, 1899. Reprint, Grosse Pointe, Mich.: Scholarly Press, 1968.

Granson, Oton de (Othe de Grandson) (ca. 1345–1397)

Oton de Granson was a French soldier, courtier, an occasional poet, and a contemporary and friend of Geoffrey CHAUCER. Granson, a landed knight of Savoy, fought on the English side in the Hundred Years' War, and kept up a long friendly relationship with Chaucer, with whom he traded poetic correspondence and whose poetry was a major influence on his own, along with that of the dominant French poet of his time, GUILLAUME DE MACHAUT.

Granson became attached to the English court around 1369, when he probably met Chaucer. By that time he was probably already quite familiar with Machaut's poetry, and was practiced in the various conventional genres of French lyric poetry (the so-called fixed forms): *BALLADES*, RONDEAUX, VIRELAIS, and the like. He was with the earl of Pembroke in 1372, fighting at La Rochelle. Between 1372 and 1374, he was held as a prisoner in Spain, and is believed to have written a good deal of his early poetry there. In 1374, Granson entered the service of JOHN OF GAUNT. He returned to his native Savoy in 1376, but by 1379 was back serving with the English garrison at Cherbourg. He is known to have been in Portugal on a diplomatic mission for King RICHARD II in 1382, and was taking part in peace negotiations between the English and French in 1384. Upon the death of his father in 1386, Granson returned to Savoy to deal with his inheritance, but he was in England again in 1392, and was on campaign with Gaunt's son, the future Henry IV, shortly after his return. In the early 1390s he was again part of negotiations to end the war with France, and Richard II considered him valuable enough to grant him a 100-mark annuity. Granson returned to Savoy again in 1396, and it was there that he died in August 1397, defending himself in a judicial duel against the charge of having been complicit in the murder of the count of Savoy.

The bare facts of his life tell us little about the man, but those who knew Granson all testify to his personal charm. FROISSART speaks well of him in describing the battle at la Rochelle. CHRISTINE DE PIZAN speaks of his chivalric and courtly qualities in two of her poems. Eustache DESCHAMPS writes a humorous *ballade* about a joke Granson played on him in the 1384 peace negotiations. But Chaucer's praise is the most effusive: In the envoi to his *Complaint of Venus,* he calls Granson "the flour of hem that make in France."

Indeed if it were not for Chaucer's *Complaint of Venus,* many current readers would not have heard of Granson. Chaucer's poem is a triple *ballade* that translates three of the five poems in Granson's sequence called *Les Cinq balades ensievans.* Chaucer follows Granson's original verses very closely, but changes the speaker of the poems to a woman, which obliges him to make some changes in the English version. It seems clear that one of Chaucer's motives in the translation is to flatter his friend.

That flattery may in part be the returning of a compliment. A number of Granson's poems, in particular his two longest works (likely composed when he was in Savoy between 1386 and 1392), show a strong influence of Chaucer's poetry. In the *Songe Saint Valentin,* Granson presents a DREAM VISION in which the dreamer visits a garden in search of a lost gem, but finds a group of birds choosing their mates on Valentine's Day. A lone falcon refuses to choose, saying he has lost the best of all mates. In the end he flies off alone, and the narrator spends 130 lines in a meditation on love and lovers, presenting himself, in the meantime, as an inept lover. The poem shows the influence of Chaucer's *PARLIAMENT OF FOWLS* in particular, but also *The BOOK OF THE DUCHESS* and *TROILUS AND CRISEYDE.*

Granson's longest extant work (at 2,495 lines) is another dream vision, *Livre Messire Ode.* The poem is influenced largely by Machaut's *Voir-Dit,* and, like all Machaut's *dits,* it contains an episodic narrative interspersed with love lyrics. In the text a narrator, dressed in black as an emblem of his sorrow in love, meets a stranger who also feels love's pains, and promises to help him. After a long interview with the stranger, the poem moves into an allegorical debate between the narrator's heart and body, then ends with some 800 lines of the lover's complaint, including a more general meditation of the nature of love itself. Throughout, the lover's lady, called the best lady in all of France, is identified with "Isabel," almost certainly Isabel of Bavaria, the queen of France. Thus the poem, in some sense, is intended as a compliment to the queen. But it also owes something to Chaucer's *Book of the Duchess* (whose lover dresses in black) as well as *Troilus and Criseyde.*

One other aspect of Granson's career worth noting is his involvement in the literary invention of St. Valentine's Day. Seven of Granson's 122 extant poems are on the occasion of Valentine's Day, the earliest being the *Balade de Saint Valentin double,* probably written before 1374. In this and in subsequent poems, he develops the notion of St. Valentine as an appropriate saint for lovers to pray to. It was Chaucer that seems to have invented the idea of birds choosing their mates on St. Valentine's Day, and that motif became a part of the tradition as developed by Granson and Chaucer and continued by later medieval writers. Indeed Granson's complicity with Chaucer in inventing the myth that connected St. Valentine's Day with romantic love is probably Granson's most lasting legacy.

Bibliography

Braddy, Haldeen. *Chaucer and the French Poet Graunson.* Baton Rouge: Louisiana University Press, 1947.

Kelly, Henry A. *Chaucer and the Cult of St. Valentine.* Davis Medieval Texts and Studies, 5. Leiden, Netherlands: Brill, 1986.

Piaget, Arthur, ed. *Oton de Grandson: sa vie et ses poesies.* Mémories et documents publiés par la Société de la Suisse Romande, 3rd series, Vol. 1. Lausanne, Switzerland: Payot, 1941.

Wimsatt, James I. *Chaucer and His French Contemporaries: Natural Music in the Fourteenth Century.* Toronto: University of Toronto Press, 1991.

Gregory of Tours (ca. 538–594)

Gregory of Tours was a sixth-century Gallo-Roman bishop, historian, and writer of SAINTS'

LIVES, whose *Historia Francorum* (History of the Franks) is our most important source for the history of early Merovingian France.

Gregory was born Georgius Florentius to a distinguished Roman family in Avernus (now called Clermont-Ferrand) in Gaul. Six of his relatives served as bishops, and his father was descended from a second-century Christian martyr named Vectius Epagatus. After his father's death, the young Gregory lived with his uncle Gallus, who was bishop of Clermont, and who educated him as a churchman of the time. When Gallus died in 554, the Clermont priest Avitus took over Gregory's education, schooling him in the Scriptures. In 573, he was appointed bishop of Tours upon the death of Bishop Euphronius, another uncle, and upon his ascension to the see he changed his name to Gregory to honor Gregorius of Langres (507–540) a sainted ancestor of his mother. When he went to Rome for his consecration, the poet FORTUNATUS wrote an enthusiastic poem to celebrate the event.

It appears that Fortunatus's confidence was well-placed. Gregory was an effective and memorable bishop, all the more impressive considering the circumstances under which he served: Rival factions of Frankish warriors were fighting each other for control of Gaul, and his see of Tours was the scene of battle and pillaging on more than one occasion during his episcopate. He traveled widely and met with many of the most powerful leaders of the Franks to protect his people and the rights and property of the church in his district.

These firsthand experiences of some of the most important events and people of his age gave him the raw material of his famous and influential *History of the Franks.* In 10 books, Gregory gives a universal history, focusing largely on contemporary events, for which his history is invaluable. In Book 1 Gregory presents the history of the world from Adam to the Frankish conquest of Gaul, and in Book 2 he focuses on Clovis, the first Merovingian king of the Franks. In Book 3 he brings the history down to 548 and the reign of King Theodebert, and in Book 4 he goes through the reign of Sigebert (575). Beginning with Book 4, Gregory is relating events of which he had personal knowledge, and he depicts himself as playing an important role in many of the major events. Books 5 through 10 seem to have been written very close to the time of the events they record, at intervals between 575 and 591. For the most part Gregory tells a simple, unadorned story, and attempts to do so in an impartial manner. But he also was especially interested in the unusual or extraordinary—crimes, wars, and other unusual events—particularly miracles, in which, as an officer of the church, he had a tremendous interest.

Certainly Gregory's religious attitudes deeply influenced his historical masterpiece, but they were even more apparent in his other literary productions. His see of Tours was one of the holiest sites in Gaul, since it housed the remains of St. Martin, the fourth-century bishop of Tours whose tomb was visited by numerous ailing pilgrims annually, and the stories of their miraculous cures inspired Gregory's imagination. His first literary effort was a book concerning the miracles of St. Martin in 575. He continued to document Saint Martin's miracles in two more books finished in 581 and 587, and in a fourth book that he never completed. After 581, he wrote a life of another Gallic saint, Julian the Martyr, who had died near Gregory's hometown of Clermont-Ferrand. In 587, Gregory began writing his *Liber in gloria martyrum* (Book of the glories of the martyrs), which tells of more miracles accomplished by the Gallic martyrs who died during Roman persecutions.

Ultimately, Gregory's contribution to early medieval letters was significant. His history was enormously influential and is still the chief source of political, spiritual, and cultural history of the Frankish kingdom of the sixth century. His saints' lives, as early examples of the genre, were circulated widely and helped influence the development of that literary form. His late Latin language is also interesting to linguistic scholars. But in his own heart, his literary output served to further his religious aims: to tell the story of how Christianity survived and even thrived in the turbulence of his time, and to present a view of history that demonstrated God rewarding the virtuous and punishing the wicked.

Bibliography

Gregory of Tours. *Life of the Fathers.* Translated with an introduction by Edward James. Liverpool, U.K.: Liverpool University Press, 1985.

Heinzelmann, Martin. *Gregory of Tours: History and Society in the Sixth Century.* Translated by Christopher Carroll. Cambridge: Cambridge University Press, 2001.

Mitchell, Kathleen, and Ian Wood, eds. *The World of Gregory of Tours.* Leiden, Netherlands: Brill, 2002.

Riché, Pierre. *Education and Culture in the Barbarian West from the Sixth through the Eighth Century.* Translated by John J. Contreni. With a foreword by Richard E. Sullivan. Columbia: University of South Carolina Press, 1978.

Thorpe, Lewis, trans. *The History of the Franks.* Harmondsworth, U.K.: Penguin, 1974.

Gregory the Great (Pope Gregory I) (ca. 540–604)

The son of a Roman senator, the young Gregory had wealth, position, and learning. He was named prefect of Rome in his early 30s (ca. 573), and seemed well on his way toward a secular political career. Despite these prospects, Gregory chose to liquidate his property as a means of benefiting the poor. Aside from charitable donations, he founded a number of monasteries on his Sicilian estates before becoming a monk himself in Rome. His star, however, was too bright to remain behind monastic walls, and Gregory soon became one of the seven deacons of Rome that served the pope. In 578, he appeared at the imperial court of Constantinople as the pope's representative. After a few years of service, he returned to his monastic life in Rome, apparently intending to live out his life in peace and asceticism (that is, religious self-denial). His selection to the papacy in ca. 590 (which Gregory appears to have resisted) denied him this opportunity.

Indeed, Gregory's preference for an ascetic life is not hard to understand given the many challenges facing Italy at the time of his ascension. Repeated invasions by the Lombard kingdom had reduced large areas to famine and pestilence. Severe poverty abounded. Moreover, the imperial authority at Constantinople had little concern for the Roman plight, and greater desire to establish the religious primacy of the Eastern patriarch over the Roman pope. The representative of imperial power in the West had pointedly been established in the north Italian city of Ravenna, which considered itself a political and religious rival to old Rome. Gregory understood very well the predicament of his new office.

Yet Gregory proved an able administrator, capable of balancing political realities with spiritual ideals. Using the papacy's wealth in a large number of charitable projects for the public good, he ensured social stability for the short run while developing the agricultural production of papal property into a support for the long haul. Bypassing the complicated task of accessing imperial power, Gregory treated with the Lombards separately, establishing that his statesmanship was as accomplished as his administrative skill. While this may have angered the imperial establishment, Gregory's success and his closer relationship with the Lombards insulated him from reprisal. Politically, Gregory's time as pope was clearly successful.

Gregory's energy and skill, however, exceeded his political abilities. He worked hard to establish Roman primacy in the face of repeated imperial assertions suggesting that this authority should rest with the patriarch of Constantinople. His many acts of charity and energetic writings did much to portray the pope as bishop of the West, caretaker of the poor and defender of orthodoxy—at a time when the actual power of the papacy was particularly low. He was responsible for organizing the first official missionary delegation to Britain—a fact that was never forgotten by the Anglo-Saxon church. Gregory's reputation as a church leader is best represented by his near-immediate elevation to sainthood after his death.

Gregory's writings illustrate his practical role as the leader of the Western church. His focus is frequently educational in nature, as opposed to theological speculation. He is widely held to have developed liturgical singing such as Gregorian chant, but his direct contributions remain indistinct. Historians also link the training of Roman liturgical chanters in a *Schola Cantorum* to Gregory's papacy.

Similarly, his name is traditionally linked with the *Gregorian Sacramentary,* a guide for the liturgical year that was widely used after the ninth century; proving his direct involvement has proved difficult. Aside from liturgical concerns, Gregory also wrote a guide for pastoral bishops, the *Liber regulae pastoralis,* which emphasizes the responsibility of local churchmen for the souls in their care. Gregory, himself, preached to the local populace; a collection of sermons entitled *Homilies on the Gospels* remains extant. A large number of his letters also survive, providing important insight into Gregory's world and his concerns as pope—particularly his view of Christianity outside Rome. His *Dialogues,* a collection of Italian SAINTS' LIVES, remained popular throughout several centuries after his death, becoming a model for similar hagiographical collections.

Gregory's main literary activity was exegetical in nature. He wrote formal commentaries on several biblical texts, the most famous of which is his *Moralia in Job.* These didactic works utilized the traditional tripartite style of exegesis in which each passage is dissected for a literal, mystical and moral sense. These commentaries would gain a popular following during the Carolingian and later periods based upon the authority of Gregory's authorship. Overall, Gregory's sense of religion was mildly ascetic and contemplative, and he encouraged the cult of saints with some cautions. His general demeanor appears to hold to his self-designation as *Servus servorum Dei:* Servant of the servants of God.

Bibliography

Cavadini, John C., ed. *Gregory the Great: A Symposium.* Notre Dame, Ind.: University of Notre Dame Press, 1995.

Evans, G. R. *The Thought of Gregory the Great.* Cambridge: Cambridge University Press, 1986.

Grégoire le Grand. Colloques internationaux du Centre National de la Recherche Scientifique, 101. Paris: Editions du Centre national de la recherche scientifique, 1986.

Gregory the Great. *Forty Gospel Homilies.* Translated by Dom David Hurst. Kalamazoo, Mich.: Cistercian Publications, 1990.

———. *Life and Miracles of St. Benedict: Book Two of the Dialogues.* Translated by Odo J. Zimmermann and Benedict R. Avery. 1949. Westport, Conn.: Greenwood Press, 1980.

———. *Pastoral Care.* Translated and annotated by Henry Davis. Westminster, Md.: Newman Press, 1950.

Markus, R. A. *Gregory the Great and His World.* Cambridge: Cambridge University Press, 1997.

Moorhead, John. *Gregory the Great.* London: Routledge, 2005.

Patrologia Latinae. Edited by. J. P. Migne. Vols. 75–78. Paris, 1844–1864. CD-ROM ed. Alexandria, Va.: Chadwyck-Healey, 1995.

Chris Craun

Grosseteste, Robert (ca. 1167–1253)

Robert Grosseteste was an English cleric, statesman and scholar. He was the first chancellor of Oxford University and, later, bishop of Lincoln. He was also a prolific writer, producing sermons, commentaries on the Bible and on Aristotle, translations, an ALLEGORY on the salvation of man from the Fall through Christ's resurrection *(The Castle of Love),* and, most famously, scientific treatises. In his time, Grosseteste was considered one of the most important clerics in Europe.

Grosseteste was born in the village of Stradroke in Suffolk in about 1167 or shortly thereafter. Not much is certain about his life before about 1214, but it seems probable that he attended Oxford and, later, the University of Paris. In 1215, he returned to Oxford as chancellor of the university, a post he held until about 1221. He made Oxford one of the vital intellectual centers of Europe, and was instrumental in enhancing the role of the sciences in the university curriculum. When the Franciscan Order came to England in 1221, Grosseteste felt an intellectual and spiritual affinity with them, one that lasted his whole life, though he never joined the order himself. He founded the Oxford Franciscan School and beginning in about 1224, he served as lecturer in theology for the Franciscans in Oxford.

In addition to his affiliation with the university, Grosseteste held a number of ecclesiastical positions between 1214 and 1232, but resigned from most of them, citing ill health as his reason. But when the bishopric of Lincoln, England's most populous see, became available in 1235, Grosseteste was elected the new bishop and accepted the position, an appointment he kept until his death in 1253. He immediately began a program to reform clerical abuses in his diocese, beginning with visits to monasteries under his authority. He also contended with King Henry III over the king's right to make ecclesiastical appointments, and even supported the reforming efforts of the most powerful, and rebellious, English baron, Simon de Montfort (1208–65). He also defended the independence of the English clergy from domination by the pope and the curia, and decried the papal appointments of alien clergy in England. In 1250 he even traveled to the papal court at Lyon and presented Pope Innocent IV and his cardinals with a complaint attributing to the curia all the evils of the church. His protest had no effect, but his position as one of the most respected clerics in the world allowed him to escape censure. In his last years, Grosseteste vigorously opposed a new tax on the English clergy, imposed by the allied king and pope, to support a new Crusade.

In his own day, Grosseteste was best known as a writer and scholar. He translated texts of Aristotle and other Greek writers (including the so-called Pseudo-Dionysus) into Latin, providing Europe with translations apparently going back to the original Greek, as opposed to the translations made from Arabic. He also wrote commentaries on Aristotle, and composed scientific studies of geometry, physics, astronomy, and, most important, optics: His best-known treatise is probably *De Luce* (On light). His insistence that experiments must be used to test the truth of hypotheses has led modern admirers to see Grosseteste as one of the formulators of the modern scientific method—along with his most famous pupil, Roger BACON.

In addition to Bacon, Montfort, Henry III, and Innocent IV, Grosseteste was acquainted with other significant figures of his time, including GIRALDUS CAMBRENSIS, who apparently sponsored him for his first ecclesiastical appointment, and Matthew PARIS, who includes a number of anecdotes about Grosseteste in his *Chronicle.*

Bibliography

Ginther, James R. *Master of the Sacred Page: A Study of the Theology of Robert Grosseteste, ca. 1229/30–1235.* Aldershot, U.K.: Ashgate, 2004.

McEvoy, James. *Robert Grosseteste.* Oxford: Oxford University Press, 2000.

Southern, Richard William. *Robert Grosseteste: The Growth of an English Mind in Medieval Europe.* Oxford: Clarendon Press, 1986.

Thomson, S. Harrison. *The Writings of Robert Grosseteste.* Cambridge: Cambridge University Press, 1940.

Gruffudd ab yr Ynad Coch (Gruffudd son of the Red Judge) (fl. 1278–1283)

One of the last great poets writing in the bardic tradition of the Welsh courts was Gruffudd ab yr Ynad Coch. Although he is also generally credited with having written five or six religious odes focused on Judgment Day, Gruffudd is remembered today chiefly for his celebrated lament on the death of Llywelyn ap Gruffydd, the last native prince of Wales. The lament, famous for the magnitude of its grief, has been faulted by some for its apparently uncontrolled personal emotion, but others consider it to be "the most powerful poem in Welsh literature" (Breeze 1997, 58).

During the high Middle Ages, a courtly culture not unlike that of the rest of western Europe flourished in the three independent kingdoms of Wales (Gwynedd, Powys, and Deheubarth). This culture included patronage of poets, who were a highly trained and exclusive order of professional bards with specific duties addressed in the law codes of the time. But the elegant poetry of this age of princes came to a close with Llywelyn's death on December 11, 1282.

Llywelyn, last prince of Gwynedd, had been acknowledged prince of Wales by the English king Henry III in 1267. But his territorial ambitions had strained his relations with the nobles of southern Wales, and later with King Edward I. When Llywelyn's younger brother David made a foolish, unprovoked attack on the English in 1282, Llywelyn came to David's support and war began. While trying to rally support in southern Wales, Llywelyn was ambushed and killed near Cilmeri on the banks of the river Irfon by forces under the command of Roger Mortimer. His body was ultimately buried in the abbey of Cwm Hir, but the English beheaded his corpse and his head was taken to be paraded through the streets of London.

With Llywelyn died the last hope for Welsh independence, a catastrophe suitably lamented in Gruffudd's ode on the death of the prince. In 104 monorhymed lines, making extensive use of parallelism and powerful visual imagery, Gruffudd expresses his grief in passionate and personal language, with, as he says, "Heart cold in the breast with terror" (Clancy 1977, l. 1). He extols Llywelyn's generosity, describes his wounds, and expresses his rage at the English who killed him. He describes the widows, orphans, and burnt and pillaged homes that he foresees for the Welsh without Llywelyn as their protector, comparing the situation to the British loss of King ARTHUR at the Battle of Camlan hundreds of years before:

Many a wretched cry as at Camlan,
Many a tear rolling down a cheek,
With my prop cut down, gold-handed prince,
With Llywelyn's death, gone is my mind.

(Clancy 1977, ll. 57–60)

For Gruffudd the future holds no consolation. In words reminiscent of the Apocalyptic passage of Luke's Gospel, Gruffudd foresees cosmic consequences for Llywelyn's death, which has disturbed the natural order of the universe:

See you not the ocean scourging the shore?
See you not the truth is portending?
Have you no belief in God, foolish men?
See you not that the world is ending?

(Clancy 1977, ll. 67–70)

The poem ends with a reference to Llywelyn's severed head, followed by 12 parallel lines honoring that head of his lord that had been taken to London to be dishonored.

Gruffudd's "Lament for Llywelyn ap Gruffudd" survives in a single manuscript known as the Red Book of Hergest (1375–1425) in Oxford's Jesus College. It is still highly admired by students of Welsh poetry, and is also important for marking a turning point in literature. With the death of Llywelyn, the status of the Welsh bard, the poet of princes, had to change irrevocably, and with it the forms and subjects of Welsh poetry.

Bibliography

Breeze, Andrew. *Medieval Welsh Literature.* Dublin: Four Courts Press, 1997.

Clancy, Joseph P., trans. "Lament for Llywelyn ap Gruffudd." In *The Oxford Book of Welsh Verse in English,* edited by Gwyn Jones, 31–33. Oxford: Oxford University Press, 1977.

Conran, Anthony, and J. E. Caerwyn Williams, trans. *The Penguin Book of Welsh Verse.* Harmondsworth, U.K.: Penguin, 1967.

McKenna, Catherine. "The Religious Poetry Attributed to Gruffudd ab yr Ynad Coch," *Bulletin of the Board of Celtic Studies* 29 (1981): 274– 284.

Williams, Gwyn. *An Introduction to Welsh Poetry: From the Beginnings to the Sixteenth Century.* 1954. Freeport, N.Y.: Books for Libraries Press, 1970.

Guenevere (Guinevere, Gwenhwyfar, Gaynour, Guenhumare)

Guenevere is the wife and queen of King ARTHUR and in most texts the lover of Arthur's greatest knight, Sir LANCELOT du Lac, in the vast body of medieval literature belonging to the Arthurian legend. While throughout the Arthurian tradition, Guenevere is depicted as unfaithful to her husband, the treatment of her character varies significantly depending upon the object of and the motivation for her illicit love.

In GEOFFEY OF MONMOUTH's influential chronicle *HISTORIA REGUM BRITANNIAE* (*History of the Kings of Britain,* ca. 1136), Guenevere is described as the most beautiful woman in the land, and as belonging to a noble old Roman family in Celtic Britain (in later texts she is the daughter of Arthur's ally, King Leodegraunce of Camiliard). In

Geoffrey's story, however, which provided the frame for all subsequent versions of the legend, Arthur leaves both his realm and his queen in the care of his nephew Mordred when he goes to the continent to make war on the Roman emperor. While Arthur is out of the country, Mordred usurps his throne, and Geoffrey tells us that Guenevere is living adulterously and out of wedlock with her husband's nephew, having forsaken her marriage vows. When Arthur returns to Britain to make war on the traitor, Guenevere enters a convent out of despair.

Geoffrey's immediate followers, WACE and LAYAMON, took different directions in their depictions of the queen. In his *Roman de Brut* (ca. 1155), a verse chronicle in French written for English king HENRY II, Wace admits that Guenevere had given her love to a noble knight with many virtues, though the fact that he is her husband's nephew is a problem for Wace. Wace also describes her motive for entering the convent as sorrow for the sin she had committed. A harsher picture of Guenevere appears in Layamon's English ALLITERATIVE VERSE *Brut* (ca. 1200). Layamon never mentions love as a motivation for Guenevere, and Arthur vows to burn the queen when he catches her. GAWAIN, Mordred's brother, follows his uncle by vowing to hang Mordred and to pull the queen apart with horses. The chronicle tradition influences the famous tragic 14th-century *ALLITERATIVE MORTE ARTHURE,* in which Guenevere is said to have married Mordred. When Arthur returns to fight his nephew, Mordred writes a letter to Guenevere telling her to flee along with their children. It is the only English text in which Guenevere is not barren. In the *Alliterative Morte,* she flees to a nunnery in fear of her true lord, Arthur.

In the Welsh tradition, Guenevere does have children with Arthur, and the queen is depicted as a fallen and despicable woman fairly universally in Welsh texts. In MARIE DE FRANCE's 12th-century *LAI* of *LANVAL,* probably based on Breton sources related to the Welsh traditions, Guenevere (called simply "the Queen") is lustful and treacherous, propositioning the noble Lanval, and then lying to Arthur and accusing Lanval of indecency when he rejects her advances.

It is in the French ROMANCE tradition that Guenevere's reputation begins to soften, first and most significantly in CHRÉTIEN DE TROYES's romance of *LANCELOT,* or *The Knight of the Cart* (ca. 1175). This text introduces Lancelot as Arthur's invincible knight, whose love for the queen reaches nearly religious heights and spurs him to remarkable feats of arms, of self-deprivation, and of fidelity (to his lady). While the queen, like most courtly mistresses, is shown as somewhat haughty and capricious, her love for Lancelot is unquestioned, and, the text implies, perfectly justifiable because of the knight's worthiness, according to the COURTLY LOVE tradition.

As the romance tradition develops, the contrasting representations of Guenevere combine to make her a far more complex character. In the lengthy *Prose Lancelot,* part of the series of early 13th-century French prose romances known as the VULGATE CYCLE, the Lady of the Lake reassures the queen that her love for Lancelot, the noblest knight in the world, cannot be wrong. But in a later romance of the Vulgate Cycle, the more ascetically Christian *Quest of the Holy Grail,* it is Lancelot's illicit love for the queen that causes his failure to achieve the Grail. In the final romance of the cycle, the *Mort Artu,* the affair of Guenevere and Lancelot is one of the causes of the fall of Arthur's Round Table. Guenevere herself, however, is strong in defense of her virtue against the traitor Mordred. When Arthur leaves England in his charge, she is angry because she knows Mordred cannot be trusted. When he usurps the throne and attempts to marry the queen, she takes refuge in the Tower of London and sends a message to Arthur herself, warning him of Mordred's treachery.

Thomas MALORY's picture of Guenevere in his *MORTE DARTHUR* is the culmination of the medieval legend, and provided the model of the character of Guenevere for all modern treatments of the legend. Malory used both the *Alliterative Morte* and the Vulgate Cycle as sources, but chose to accept the Vulgate attitude toward the queen's love. In Malory, Guenevere's love is clearly ennobling, and she seems to move from the haughty and selfish mistress to a more generous and courageous character in the end as she resists and thwarts Mordred's designs. Malory declares that the queen was a true lover all her life, and that as a result she had a good end. Her end in Malory's text comes, as usual, in a nunnery. But she is a true nun, not simply one who has fled for sanctuary out of fear. In Malory, she rejects the vanities of the world, admits her culpability in causing the fall of Arthur's kingdom, and embraces true Christian charity, inspiring Lancelot to lead a life of prayer, and dying a holy and respected abbess. In Malory, Guenevere has come as far as possible from the traitress of Geoffrey of Monmouth or the lustful wench of Marie de France. After Malory, it was no longer possible to depict Guenevere as an uncomplicated adulteress, and much more difficult to make her a villain.

Bibliography

DiPasquale, Pasquale, Jr. "Malory's Guinevere: Epic Queen, Romance Heroine and Tragic Mistress," *Bucknell Review* 16 (1968): 86–102.

Ruud, Jay. "Teaching the 'Hoole' Tradition through Parallel Passages." In *Approaches to Teaching the Arthurian Tradition,* edited by Maureen Fries and Jeanie Watson, 73–76. New York: Modern Language Association, 1992.

Wheeler, Bonnie, and Fiona Tolhurst, eds. *On Arthurian Women: Essays in Memory of Maureen Fries.* Dallas: Scriptorium, 2001.

Guide for the Perplexed Maimonides (1190)

MAIMONIDES is widely regarded as the most important Jewish philosopher of all time, and it was his *Guide for the Perplexed* that made him famous throughout the world. Influenced chiefly by Aristotle and by Arabic commentators, especially al-Fārābi and Ibn Sīanā (Avicenna), Maimonides set out to show how Aristotelian philosophy could be shown to inform the beliefs of traditional Judaism. The book purports to be a personal answer to one of Maimonides' former students, a certain Joseph ben Judah. Joseph is presented as one who believes in the law, but is confused by the literal meaning of certain phrases and parables that appear in Scripture. Thus Maimonides cautions that his *Guide* is only for the educated, not for the simple masses who have no interest in philosophic inquiry. He begins by interpreting the Scriptures, and eschews the literal interpretation of certain anthropomorphic descriptions of God. He then moves to a discussion of Divine attributes generally, arguing that no positive attributes whatever could be ascribed to God—one could only accurately use negative attributes (such as "God is not unloving"), since anything else put limits on the deity. Aquinas later atttacked this famous "doctrine of negative attributes."

Maimonides moves on to argue for God's existence, his unity, and his incorporality, and argues that God is the creator of the world. He discusses miracles and prophecy, and then moves to the problem of evil. Moral evil, according to Maimonides, is the product of human choice, while natural evil (earthquakes, disease, and the like) comes about because of a privation or lack of good. And divine providence, while it governs the universe through natural laws, acts on human beings to a degree proportional to the person's intellect. Finally Maimonides discusses the law, which he argues is not established by divine caprice but follows wisdom. Human beings, says Maimonides, can determine the logical reasons for many of these laws.

The text of the *Guide* was translated into Hebrew, and a medieval Latin translation was made from one of the Hebrew translations, so the text was widely read. But Maimonides' rational approach to religious questions led many conservative Jews of his day to condemn his works. In some parts of Europe, Jews were forbidden to read his compositions. Elsewhere only those mature in the faith were allowed to read the *Guide for the Perplexed.* In France three leading rabbis denounced Maimonides' works to the Dominican friars in charge of the Inquisition, and through the efforts of those rabbis Maimonides' books were burned. When eight years later those same Dominicans began burning texts of the Talmud itself in France, at least one of the complaining rabbis repented in the belief that God was punishing the Jews of France for their condemnation of Maimonides. The rabbi, Jonah Gerondi, traveled to Maimonides' grave in Tiberias to ask forgiveness. History has seen Maimonides' reputation continue to triumph over his contemporary rivals' animosity.

Guido delle Collone (ca. 1210–ca. 1290)

One of the members in the "Sicilian school" of Italian poetry, which followed the lead of GIACOMO DA LENTINO, Guido delle Collone was a judge located in Messina, where his name appears on some 15 legal decisions between 1243 and 1280. DANTE admired his *CANZONI*, but Guido is probably better known for his Latin prose *Historia destructionis Troiae*, which was popular throughout Europe and was translated into several languages.

Not much is known about Guido's life, other than his career as a jurist. It is unknown whether he had any connection with the important Roman family with the same surname. Only five of his *canzoni* are extant, and they display a debt to the Provençal TROUBADOURS as well as his fellow Sicilians, though his poetry is admired for displaying a more polished style than that of his Italian predecessors. At least that is Dante's judgment as he alludes to two of these poems in his *De VULGARI ELOQUENTIA*. In one of his more striking *canzoni*, "Anchor che l'aigua per lo foco lassi," Guido uses natural imagery to parallel experiences of love. In one passage, he uses the image of a magnet:

> *The magnet, so the learned say,*
> *could not attract iron with such force,*
> *if the air between them did not permit it.*
> . . .
> *Just so, my lady, Love understood*
> *he could not*
> *draw me to himself except through you.*
>
> (Goldin 1973, 253, ll. 53–61)

This application of scientific imagery to explain the nature of love is taken up later by the important Tuscan poet Guido GUINIZELLI.

Guido completed his *Historia destructionis Troiae* ("History of the Destruction of Troy") in 1287, apparently at the request of the bishop of Salerno. While Guido claimed that his text was a true historical account, based on eyewitness reports from a certain Dictys of Crete and Dares the Phrygian, it is in fact a Latin prose adaptation of the French verse ROMANCE by BENOÎT DE SAINT-MAURE entitled the *Roman de Troie* (ca. 1160). Guido's text did much to popularize the legend of Troy in medieval Europe. In its turn, it became the source for BOCCACCIO's romance *Il FILOSTRATO* (1335–36) and, with Boccaccio, for CHAUCER's *TROILUS AND CRISEYDE* (ca. 1385). It was included in the *Recueil des Histoires de Troie* by Raoul le Fèvre, a text translated into English in 1475 by William CAXTON, who printed it the following year, making it the first book printed in England.

Bibliography

Benson, C. David. *The History of Troy in Middle English Literature: Guido delle Colonne's Historia Destructionis Troiae in Medieval England.* Woodbridge, U.K.: D. S. Brewer, 1980.

Goldin, Frederick, trans. *German and Italian Lyrics of the Middle Ages: An Anthology and a History.* New York: Doubleday, 1973.

Guido delle Collone. *Historia Destructionis Troiae.* Edited by Nathaniel Edward Griffin. Cambridge, Mass.: Mediaeval Academy of America, 1936.

———. *Historia Destructionis Troiae.* Translated by Mary Elizabeth Meek. Bloomington: Indiana University Press, 1974.

Jensen, Frede, ed. and trans. *The Poetry of the Sicilian School.* New York: Garland, 1986.

Guillaume IX (William IX, duke of Aquitaine, seventh count of Poitiers) (1071–1127)

At the age of 15 Guillaume IX ruled an area greater than that of the king of France. He was excommunicated for his promiscuous personal life, and was defeated soundly in his crusading adventures, but he was also the author of the earliest vernacular love poems in the European Middle Ages. This colorful figure is known as the first Provençal TROUBADOUR, and his 11 extant poems contain motifs that became conventional in the COURTLY LOVE tradition that came ultimately to dominate the European literary scene in the later Middle Ages.

Guillaume succeeded his father as the seventh count of Poitiers and the ninth duke of Aquitaine in 1086. At the age of 15, he ruled a huge realm, mainly through advisers until his twenties. He married Phillipa, niece of Guillaume's neighbor Raymond, the lord of Toulouse. When Pope Urban II proclaimed the First Crusade in 1095, Guillaume did not respond, but Raymond of Toulouse did, and in 1097, citing his wife's claims, Guillaume marched into Toulouse and annexed the territory of the absent Raymond.

After the success of the First Crusade, Guillaume decided to join the Crusade of Stephen of Blois in 1101. He raised a huge army from Aquitaine and Gascony and set off for the Middle East, but was crushed by the Turkish army at Heraclea (in modern-day Turkey). His army was massacred, and he was lucky to escape with his life. But by October of 1102, he was back in his court in Poitiers, entertaining both clergy and courtiers with stories and songs of his exploits.

In Poitiers Guillaume established a dazzling court and patronized poets and singers, of which he was himself the premier representative. Contemporary accounts attest to his personal charm, his wit, his flouting of ecclesiastical authority, and his licentious behavior, which he celebrates openly and with great delight in his poetry. His best-known adulterous affair was with the Vicomtesse Aimeric of Châtellerault, with whom he consorted openly after moving his wife Phillipa to a separate castle. The story goes that when a bald papal legate told him he must end this affair, Guillaume responded "the hair on your head will curl before I give up the Vicomtesse."

Guillaume was excommunicated in 1114, partly for his earlier annexation of Toulouse but largely, as well, for his profligate lifestyle. The censure does not seem to have had much effect on the duke, though after it was lifted in 1117, Guillaume did take part in another crusade, joining King Alfonso of Aragon (called "the Battler") in a successful war against the Spanish Moors in 1120.

In 1121, in one of his more outrageous acts, Guillaume married his son (the future Guillaume X, b. 1099) by his wife, Phillipa, to Anor, the daughter by her previous marriage of his mistress, the Vicomtesse. Out of this unlikely union was born ELEANOR OF AQUITAINE. Guillaume died on February 10, 1126, at the age of 54.

There is a fascinating variety of tone among Guillaume's 11 extant songs. Six of them might be called burlesque poems, and they reflect the character of Duke Guillaume, the reprobate. One of these songs, "Farai un vers, pos mi somelh" ("I shall make a *vers,* since I am sleeping"), recounts a FABLIAU-like encounter with two highly promiscuous noblewomen. Another, "Companho, tant ai agutz d'avols conres" ("My companions, I have had so much miserable fare"), underscores his disdain for the church, as it includes a blasphemous prayer asking God why He did not destroy the first man who guarded his wife's chastity.

In other poems Guillaume creates the persona of the courtly lover who becomes the servant of the lady he desires, though she is difficult to attain. These and other motifs, like the springtime opening or *REVERDIE,* the extolling of *joy* and *youth,* and the inherent nobility of one who truly understands love, all become conventional in the later poetry of courtly love. The metrical forms Guillaume used also influenced the music of the later troubadours; many of these Guillaume seems to have borrowed from the music of the church, and this may have been an aspect of his flaunting of church convention as well. In any case it is impossible to overestimate Guillaume IX's influence on the later development of secular, vernacular lyric poetry in Europe.

Bibliography

Bond, Gerald A., ed. and trans. *The Poetry of William VII, Count of Poitiers, IX Duke of Aquitane.* New York: Garland, 1982.

Goldin, Frederick, ed. and trans. *Lyrics of the Troubadours and Trouvères: An Anthology and a History.* Garden City, N.Y.: Anchor, 1973.

Jensen, Frede. *Provençal Philology and the Poetry of Guillaume of Poitiers.* Odense, Denmark: Odense University Press, 1983.

Wilhelm, James J. *Seven Troubadours: The Creators of Modern Verse.* University Park: Pennsylvania State University Press, 1970.

Guillaume de Lorris (fl. 1220–1240)

In about 1237, Guillaume de Lorris wrote the first part (4,058 verses) of probably the most important and most influential 13th-century allegorical romance, the ROMAN DE LA ROSE. The text breaks off as a fragment, and was later continued by JEAN DE MEUN about 40 years later (between 1264–74). Jean's continuation more than doubled the text and brought the account to its close at verse 21,780. Whereas Guillaume does not introduce himself, Jean identifies his source by name. Guillaume originated from Lorris near Orléans, but we know nothing else about him. His portion of the *Roman de la Rose,* however, proved to be of greatest inspiration for the entire Middle Ages and beyond, basically creating the literary foundation of allegorical poetry.

The *Roman* begins with the poet dreaming a dream of significant truth for him, for which he finds confirmation in MACROBIUS's (fl. 400 C.E.) commentary on Cicero's *Somnium Scipionis* (Dream of Scipio). He intends his account to be a literary treatment of the art of love, an art that was indeed teachable for medieval philosophers and writers (*see* ANDREAS CAPELLANUS's *Art of Courtly Love*). Immediately following, Guillaume begins to relate his dream that he had had five years earlier in which he wandered through a beautiful meadow in spring, observing birds, flowers, and a lovely stream. When he comes to a garden surrounded by a high wall, he observes figures and inscriptions engraved in it. These are all allegorical figures, representing the wide range of human emotions, all of them concerning those factors that are detrimental to love: Hate, Felony, Villainy, Covetousness, Avarice, Envy, Sorrow, Old Age, Pope Holy (Hypocrisy), and Poverty. When the narrator tries to enter the garden, he finds the gate locked. After he knocks, a graceful woman (Idleness) opens the door to him. She mentions her friend, Mirth, and allows the Narrator to enter. The garden proves to be like Paradise, and naturally the young man meets Lady Gladness and Lady Courtesy who introduce him to the God of Love.

The narrative now leads us directly to an allegorical explanation of how a person is smitten by love, since the God of Love holds 10 arrows in his hands that reflect two radically opposed aspects of love: first Beauty, Simplicity, Independence, Companionship, and Fair Seeming; then Pride, Villainy, Shame, Despair, and Faithlessness. The God of Love is accompanied by such ladies as Beauty, Wealth (along with Hospitality), Largesse (accompanied by King ARTHUR), Franchise, Gentility, Courtesy, and finally Youth. The garden itself is described again as the most idyllic place ever conceived, anticipating in a way early-modern utopian images. Nevertheless the young man (the Lover) gets to read the story of Narcissus, the letters carved into the wall of a fountain, obviously as a warning to those who fall in love with themselves. But once the dreamer has caught sight of a rose, he falls in love with her. This process is also described in allegorical terms: The God of Love shoots an arrow through the dreamer's eye that enters his body and goes to his heart, making him a loyal servant of Love. Guillaume casts these events in straight feudal terms, transferring the imagery of giving one's pledge to the liege-lord to the area of love: "with joined hands I became his man" (Dahlberg 1971, 57). Subsequently the lover learns the Commandments of Love, which have strong similarities to Andreas Capellanus's rules in his *Art of Courtly Love* (ca. 1180–90). But he also has to experience the Pains of Love before he is informed about the Remedies for the Pains. The dialectics of love are illustrated in the following sections where the lover is encouraged by Fair Welcome and frightened away by Danger. Then Reason appears and advises the Lover to abjure the God of Love altogether, warning him of the emotional passions of love that make him lose his rationality.

At this point a Friend arrives and provides support for the Lover, soon aided by Franchise and Pity, so that he finally can kiss the Rose, the allegorical goal of all his desires. As quickly as this first success has been achieved, however, failure immediately sets in because Evil Tongue marshals Jealousy against the Lover, building a wall around the rose. At this point, Guillaume's part of the verse romance breaks off, only followed by 78 additional lines of a sort of conclusion by an anonymous poet.

Guillaume's section of the *Roman de la Rose* proves to be most delightful in its gracious exploration of budding love and in its allegorical illustration of the various emotions and passions a lover experiences and the problems that arise in the development of a love relationship. Guillaume elegantly incorporates many elements from classical Latin literature, but the entire framework and specific set-up of his allegorical romance is fully representative of the Middle Ages.

Bibliography

Arden, Heather. *The Romance of the Rose.* Boston: Twayne, 1987.

Brownlee, Kevin, and Sylvia Huot. *Rethinking the "Romance of the Rose": Text, Image, Reception.* Philadelphia: University of Pennsylvania Press, 1992.

Dahlberg, Charles, trans.: *The Romance of the Rose.* Princeton, N.J.: Princeton University Press, 1971.

Guillaume de Lorris and Jean de Meun. *Le Roman de la Rose.* Edited by Félix Lecoy. 3 vols. Paris: Champion, 1965–1970.

Nouvet, Claire. "Reversing Mirror: Guillaume de Lorris' *Romance of the Rose*," in *Translatio Studii. Essays by His Students in Honor of Karl D. Uitti for His Sixty-Fifth Birthday,* edited by Renate Blumenfeld-Kosinski, Kevin Brownlee, Mary B. Speer, Lori J. Walters. Amsterdam: Rodopi, 2000, 89–205.

Robbins, Harry W. *The Romance of the Rose.* New York: E. P. Dutton, 1962.

Albrecht Classen

Guinizelli, Guido (ca. 1230–1276)

Guido Guinizelli, a Bolognese jurist, was one of the most influential lyric poets in medieval Italian literature. His seminal CANZONE, "Il cor gentil" (The gentle heart) was regarded by DANTE and his circle as something of a manifesto for the *DOLCE STIL NOVO,* the "sweet new style" that they believed they had brought to vernacular poetry in Italy.

There has been some disagreement about the identity of the poet (since we know of two contemporaries by that name), but most scholars now agree that he was the son of Guinizzello da Magnano and Guglielmina di Ugolino Chisleri. Guido became a judge in Bologna in about 1266, and was active in support of the Ghibelline party (the political party supporting the Holy Roman Emperor), controlled in Bologna by a powerful family called the Lambertazzi. But the Ghibellines were defeated by the Guelfs (the party supporting the pope) in 1274, and Guinizelli was forced to go into exile at Monselice. He died in Padua in 1276.

Only a small number of Guinizelli's poems survive: Some five *canzoni* and 15 sonnets are extant, plus fragments of two other songs. It seems clear that early in his career, Guinizelli wrote in the manner of the Tuscan school, after GUITTONE D'AREZZO, whom at one point he calls his "father." Indeed some scholars have suggested a date later than 1230 for Guinizelli's birth, since they believe he must have been younger than Guittone to have venerated him so much. But in "Al cor gentil," Guinizelli went in a new poetic direction.

In his great *canzone,* Guinizelli says first that true love is found only in the gentle (or "noble") heart, and that only such a heart can be perfected by love. His lady, he contends, is like one of God's angels inhabiting the earth, and so is in that manner divine herself. Most important, Guinizelli brings imagery from medieval astronomy into the poem, comparing his love to the "intelligences," those angels whose task is to move the planets in their heavenly spheres in accordance with the divine will. As the intelligences follow God's will, his will is in tune with the lady's.

Guinizelli's learned vocabulary introduced a new category of imagery and a new poetic language into vernacular poetry. For Guittone and for other poets like BONAGUINTA ORBICCIANI DA LUCCA, such rhetoric was unsuitable for poetry, and they condemned Guinizelli's practice in their own verse. But for Dante and his circle, Guinizelli had rejuvenated the old clichés of COURTLY LOVE poetry, and had initiated a poetic revolution. After Guinizelli, learned, scientific images and intellectual vocabulary drawn from sources like Aristotle and Averroës were the new language of poetry, and those who were unable to understand that language were not worthy to be part of that new revolution.

In the *DIVINE COMEDY,* Dante pays tribute to Guinizelli as the founder of the new poetry in canto 26 of the *Purgatorio.* He praises him in *DE VULGARI ELOQUENTIA* and in the *CONVIVIO* as well, and alludes to Guinizelli's great poem as something familiar to all in one of his sonnets, "Amore e'l cor gentil sono una rosa." It is unlikely that Guinizelli had any intention of starting such a revolution. He was only interested in writing a love poem in a different manner than the tradition called for. Dante, CAVALACANTI, and the other *stilnovisti,* on the other hand, *were* looking for a break from the past, and they found their inspiration in "Al cor gentil."

Bibliography

Goldin, Frederick, ed. and trans. *German and Italian Lyrics of the Middle Ages: An Anthology and a History.* New York: Doubleday, 1973.

Guinizelli, Guido. *The Poetry of Guido Guinizelli.* Edited and translated by Robert Edwards. New York: Garland, 1987.

Tusiani, Joseph, ed. *The Age of Dante: An Anthology of Early Italian Poetry.* New York: Baroque Press, 1974.

Guittone d'Arezzo (ca. 1230–1294)

Guittone d'Arezzo was the leading figure in the Tuscan school of poetry, the second important poetic movement in vernacular Italian in the Middle Ages. A group of followers calling themselves *guittoniani* emulated his style and created a thriving poetic tradition to replace the earlier Sicilian school, whose source of inspiration had dissolved as the imperial court at Naples declined. As the most important poet of the immediately preceding generation, Guittone came under harsh criticism from DANTE, who at first followed but later abjured Guittone's style.

The facts we know of Guittone's life are few. He was born near Arezzo and his father was a public official of some kind. Guittone himself was apparently involved in commercial ventures and did a good deal of traveling. He is also known to have been a member of the Guelf party (the party that initially supported the pope in Italian politics)—he wrote a poem lamenting the 1260 defeat of the Guelfs of Florence at Montaperte. When the Ghibellines (the party that supported the emperor) controlled Arezzo after 1256, Guittone was exiled. His travels throughout Italy, to Bologna, Pisa, and ultimately Florence, put him in touch with powerful people and with other writers.

In 1266, apparently after a sincere spiritual crisis, Guittone left his secular life, including his wife and three children, to enter the religious order of the Knights of the Blessed Virgin Mary, known as the merry friars. From this point on, he forsook the COURTLY LOVE poetry of his earlier life, and focused on religious, moral, and political themes. He died in Florence in 1294, in a monastery to which he had donated a large sum of money the previous year on the condition that they would care for him until his death.

Dante faulted Guittone for what he called his excessive rhetoric and common language, and claimed that only the ignorant and vulgar were impressed by his poetry. In fact Guittone's language was filled with a greater number of terms borrowed from Provençal and Latin than that of his forerunners in the Sicilian school. He also used more complex rhetorical figures and sentence structures than his predecessors. Dante at first emulated Guittone's style, then rejected it in favor of the simpler and clearer manner of the Sicilians. In fact all subsequent Italian poets owed a debt to Guittone: The sophisticated court of Frederick II at Naples was a likely heir to the TROUBADOUR tradition, which flourished in the great courts of southern France. But with a new audience of middle-class citizens of the great Italian cities, Guittone needed to fashion something new. He kept the older forms of the troubadours, but needed to turn away from the values of a landed aristocracy to those of the municipal citizen. His poems extol the virtues of personal energy, self-sufficiency, ambition, merit and the earning of reward. His lyric "Gioia ed allegranza," for example, ends with the lines

> *But to suffer, if he has to,*
> *to gain by his own worth and manliness—*
> *that is a man's way.*

And I have a right to say
that by great manliness
I have won something great which so
pleases me
that any other joy I have isn't worth a fifth
of that which, for this reason, my heart
feels.

(Goldin 1973, 267, ll. 26–33)

In this love poem, the poet sees the achieving of success in love, or any other matter, as dependent on personal energy and hard work. It was this sort of attitude that Dante saw as plebeian, and he sought a new kind of exclusiveness in his own poetic movement, the DOLCE STIL NOVO, or "sweet new style," which ultimately replaced the Tuscan school of poetry.

Guittone was a very prolific writer: 50 of his *canzoni* are extant, along with some 251 sonnets in addition to other poems. His reputation has been dimmed by Dante's judgment of him, but a more objective view will admit his important contribution to poetry in the Italian vernacular.

Bibliography

Goldin, Frederick, trans. *German and Italian Lyrics of the Middle Ages: An Anthology and a History.* New York: Doubleday, 1973.

Moleta, Vincent. *The Early Poetry of Guittone d'Arezzo.* London: Modern Humanities Research Association, 1976.

Guy of Warwick (ca. 1300)

Guy of Warwick is a ROMANCE in MIDDLE ENGLISH verse, first composed very early in the 14th century. It is one of a group of romances (including *HAVELOK, BEVIS OF HAMPTON,* and *KING HORN*) associated with what was called the "Matter of England," because of its English setting and origins. But the legend is based ultimately on an Anglo-Norman French source, *Gui de Warewic* (ca. 1240). The English text survives in several versions, the oldest of which is the version in the Auchinleck manuscript. In its complete form, the romance runs to some 12,000 lines. The sprawling legend of Sir Guy, involving his winning of the earl of Warwick's daughter, his saving England from the Danes by defeating the giant Colbrand, and his saintly last days, was extremely popular (judging from the number of manuscripts and early printed versions of the story), and remained popular even into the 19th century.

Most modern readers find the poem to be rambling and lacking in unity. One of the reasons for this is that the text as preserved in the Auchinleck manuscript is in fact a compilation of what were probably originally three separate romances: The first, in about 7,000 lines written in octosyllabic (eight-syllable) couplets, concerns Guy's feats of chivalry undertaken to win his beloved Felice. The second, in some 3,500 lines composed in TAIL-RHYME stanzas, deals with Guy's forsaking worldly chivalry to become a soldier of Christ. The final section, concerning the romantic adventures of Guy's son Reinbrun, includes about 1,500 lines, also in tail-rhyme stanzas.

In part 1, Guy is introduced as the son of Siward, the steward of Earl Rohand of Warwick. Guy, a lowly cupbearer, is in love with the earl's daughter Felice, but the lady is the traditional haughty heroine of the COURTLY LOVE tradition, and spurns Guy three times because of his low status and his lack of knightly honor. Motivated to become the world's greatest knight in order to win his love, Guy spends seven years abroad, making a name for himself. He fights in a tournament for the daughter of the emperor of Germany, whom he also saves. He later breaks the emperor's siege of Duke Segwin. He travels to Constantinople, where he saves Emperor Ernis from the Saracens and slays the sultan. He rescues Lady Ozelle from being married against her will, and helps Sir Tyrry to win her hand, as well as her kingdom. In each case, Sir Guy hears of some wrong that needs righting, and steps in to see that justice is done. When he finally returns to England, he battles a dragon and wins the gratitude of King ATHELSTAN, as well as the hand of his beloved Fenice.

Thus the first section of *Guy of Warwick* is essentially a self-contained chivalric romance in itself. Part 2, however, owes as much to the SAINT'S LIFE genre as it does to romance. After a mere 50 days of marriage to Fenice, Guy leaves her, and their unborn child, to go on pilgrimage to the Holy Land, hoping to atone for the sins he committed on his previous adventures. He becomes the soldier of God and fights a number of battles against the enemies of God and of the right, appearing as the answer to a prayer to fight for his friend Sir Tyrry, a battle in which he is described as an angel. When he returns to England this time, it is in disguise as a beggar. King Athelstan, whose kingdom is threatened by the Danes and their champion, an African giant named Colbrond, prays for a savior, and in response is told in a dream where to find a beggar who will save England—the disguised Guy. In the ensuing battle, Sir Guy turns down a bribe, overcomes the giant, and saves England from the Danes. Afterward, he goes off to live in a hermitage. Here, he is fed by Fenice, who does not recognize him until he reveals himself to her by sending her his ring shortly before he dies. After Guy's death, there are conventional signs of sainthood, such as the odor of sanctity from his body, and the establishment of a church on the site of his death. If the first part of the text was a typical courtly romance, the second suggests that saintliness is not the sole province of those in religious orders, and that knighthood itself may be a religious calling.

The third part of the text implies that the chivalric tradition continues in new generations. This brief tail-rhyme romance concerning Sir Guy's son Reinbrun follows the boy through a kidnapping by Russian pirates at the age of seven and a shipwreck on the shores of Africa, where he is given to the daughter of King Argus. Sir Guy's own teacher, Sir Harrad, comes in search of Reinbrun, but is imprisoned by King Argus. Harrad is made to do battle against King Argus's warriors. When he discovers that the one knight he cannot defeat is Reinbrun himself, the two are reunited and travel back to England.

The romance of *Guy of Warwick* attained a huge popularity, probably because of the patriotic overtones of Guy's fight with the giant Colbrond and his association with Athelstan. John LYDGATE wrote a version of the legend (ca. 1450), and it was accepted as genuine by chroniclers and historians for centuries. In the Renaissance Michael Drayton told the story of Sir Guy's battle with Colbrand in his *Poly-Olbion.*

Bibliography

Dannenbaum, Susan C. "Guy of Warwick and the Question of Exemplary Romance," *Genre* 17 (1984): 351–374.

Mehl, Dieter. *Middle English Romances of the Thirteenth and Fourteenth Centuries:* New York: Barnes and Noble, 1968.

Richmond, Velma B. *The Legend of Guy of Warwick.* New York: Garland, 1996.

Wiggins, Alison, ed. *Stanzaic Guy of Warwick.* Kalamazoo, Mich.: Medieval Institute Publications, 2004.

Zupitza, J., ed. *The Romance of Guy of Warwick: The Second or 15th-Century Version.* Edited from Cambridge University Library ms. ff. 2.38. London: Published for the Early English Text Society by Oxford University Press, 1966.

Hafez, Mohammad Shamsoddin (Hafiz) (ca. 1320–ca. 1388)

Hafez is one of the best-known poets of medieval Persia, known particularly as the master of the classical form of the *GHAZAL*. Little is known with certainty about his life. His biography is gleaned from what is found in his poetry and from traditions that grew around him after his death. We do know that the name *Hafez* means "one who has memorized the KORAN." He is also known to have lived in the city of Shiraz in what is now south-central Iran, and it seems likely he was attached to a mystical Sufi order.

Hafez wrote over 500 *ghazals,* in addition to other poems. Collectively his poetry is known as the *Divan-e Hafez.* Hafez himself, however, was not responsible for compiling his own collected verse. Two separate compilations were made the generation after his death by his admirers, Mohammad Golandaam (who wrote a preface to his collection of Hafez's work) and Sayyid Kasim-e Anvar (whose collection comprises 569 *ghazals* attributed to Hafez).

Tradition says that Hafez was born in Shiraz to a coal merchant, and that he had memorized the Koran, as well as poetry by his idols SA'DI and ATTAR, by the time he was in his teens. But at that point his father died, and Hafez became apprenticed to a baker. Legend has it that while delivering bread to the wealthy section of Shiraz, Hafez met the incomparably beautiful Shakh-e Nabat. Though his poetry suggests he was married and had at least one child, he continued to address a number of spiritual poems to Shakh-e Nabat, seeing the young woman as a physical symbol of the beauty of her creator.

In any case Hafez does seem to have gained some reputation as a poet during the reign of Abu Eshaq Inju (1343–53). However, when Abu was succeeded by the bigoted tyrant Mobarezoddin (1353–58), Hafez was cast out of favor. The sensuality of his early poems was unwelcome in Mobarezoddin's puritanical court, and Hafez's "protest" poetry of this period often indirectly refers to Mobarezoddin by the code name *mohtaseb* (the "secret police").

With Mobarezoddin's successor, Shah Shoja, an enlightened ruler who appreciated poetry, Hafez returned to favor. He wrote a number of panegyrics about the new shah, and seems to have been the ruler's drinking companion. But he fell out of favor with Shah Shoja about 1368, possibly through the enmity of the religious establishment, which seems to have considered Hafez a somewhat heretical freethinker. Hafez remained in exile for six years, during which he found new poetic inspiration in a woman named Dordane.

Hafez was invited back to Shiraz by the shah in 1374, his reputation now having reached its greatest heights: He was invited to Baghdad and to Bengal to the courts of the princes there. But at about the age of 60, according to tradition, Hafez was overcome with a longing for a mystical experience of God, and fasted for 40 days within a circle of his own making. Reputedly, he achieved his vision on the 40th day, and from that time until his death wrote nearly half of his *ghazals* on mystical subjects, while continuing to teach a small group of disciples. He is said to have gone into retirement when Shah Shoja died in 1385.

Hafez was buried in Musalla Gardens on the Roknabad River in Shiraz, a place now called Hafezieh. His tomb is frequented by many visitors, and it is an Iranian custom to open the *Divan-e Hafez* at random with a question, and divine the answer through Hafez's verse.

Hafez is an acknowledged master of lyric poetry that is both original, subtle, and multilayered, with his sensual poetry often being interpreted in mystical ways. The ultimate meaning of his verse is often disputed, but one of his great admirers, Goethe, saw Hafez's sensuality and mysticism as a unique "harmony of opposites."

Bibliography

Hafez, Mohammed Shamsoddin. *The Divan of Hafez: Persian-English.* Translated by Reza Saberi. Lanham, Md.: University Press of America, 2002.

———. *The Gift: Poems by Hafiz, the Great Sufi Master.* Translated by Daniel Ladinsky. New York: Penguin, 1999.

———. *Fifty Poems of Hafiz.* Translated by Arthur J. Arberry. Cambridge University Press, 1970.

———. *Poems from the Divan of Hafiz.* Translated by Gertrude Lowthian Bell. London: W. Heinemann, 1928.

Hali Meidenhad (*Hali Meiðhad*) (ca. 1200)

The prose tract entitled *Hali Meidenhad* (*Holy Maidenhood*) is a homily intended chiefly to encourage young women to enter religious life by dissuading them from matrimony. The treatise, written in the West Midlands in England between about 1190 and 1225, survives in two manuscripts, both of which also contain the text of the piece known as *SAWLES WARDE,* and some of the SAINTS' LIVES that belong to what is known as the KATHERINE GROUP.

The sophisticated style of *Hali Meidenhad,* characterized by the use of native phrases and alliterative passages, has been compared to that of the *ANCRENE WISSE,* but unlike that moderate and humane text, *Hali Meidenhad* reflects an extreme and abusive tone that is contemptuous of the very idea of marriage. As such it is in the tradition of JEROME's fifth-century tirade *Against Jovinian,* who had dared argue that the celibate life was not necessarily superior to matrimony.

The author bases his homily on a single text, Psalm 45.10: "Hearken, O daughter, and consider, and incline thine ear; forget also thine own people, and thy father's house." From here, he fashions his argument as a struggle against the devil himself, who hates virginity because it was through the Virgin Mary that he lost his sovereignty over humankind. Young women should not pursue earthly marriage, but rather the much more spiritually satisfying marriage with Christ, the fruit of which will be virtue rather than children. The author paints a sometimes sardonically humorous, sometimes disgusting picture of marriage, from the woman's suffering indignities in bed to the discomfort of pregnancy to the annoyances of housework. Most striking is the author's description of a woman's plight in an abusive relationship, which he seems to regard as not atypical:

> His looking at you terrifies you; his hateful merriment and his rude behavior make you shudder. He chides you and bickers with you and scolds you shamefully; he mocks you as a lecher does his whore; he beats you and mawls [sic] you as his purchased slave and his family servitor. Your bones ache, and your flesh smarts; your heart swells within you from sore mortification, and your face flushes outwardly from anger.
>
> (Dunn and Byrnes 1973, 101)

The homily holds out one escape from this kind of life: the convent—marriage to Christ, the perfect spouse.

The blessed maiden who as God's daughter and the spouse of his Son has excluded herself completely from such servitude need not endure anything like this. So, blessed maiden, forsake all such sorrow in exchange for an exceptional reward, as you ought to do without any payment.

(103)

Bibliography

Bennett, J. A. W. *Middle English Literature.* Edited and completed by Douglas *Gray. Oxford History of English Literature,* Vol. 1, part 2. Oxford: Clarendon Press, 1986.

Corpus of Middle English Prose and Verse. "Hali Meidenhad, an Alliterative Homily of the Thirteenth Century." Available online. URL: http://www.hti.umich.edu/cgi/c/cme/cme-idx?type=header&idno=HMaid. Accessed February 2, 2005.

Dunn, Charles W., and Edward T. Byrnes, eds. *Middle English Literature.* New York: Harcourt, 1973.

Furnivall, F. J., ed. *Hali Meidenhad.* Revised by Oswald Cockayne. Early English Text Society 18. 1866. Oxford: Oxford University Press, 1922.

Millett, Bella, ed. *Hali Meiðhad.* Early English Text Society 284. London and New York: Published for the Early English Text Society by the Oxford University Press, 1982.

Han Shan (Han-shan, Master of Cold Mountain) (ca. 600–800)

The name *Han Shan* literally means "cold mountain," and it is unclear whether the eccentric Zen recluse traditionally associated with that name was in fact a real person or a legendary figure around whose name the 300 poems attributed to him were assembled during the TANG DYNASTY of medieval China. Regardless of their author, however, the poems themselves have come to be much admired outside of China, particularly in Japan and the United States.

The poems seem to have been originally collected sometime late in the Tang dynasty. A preface to the collection purports to be written by a Tang official named Yin Luqiu (Yin Lü-ch'iu), who describes his meeting with the strange hermit Han Shan and his fellow recluse, Shide (Shih-te). According to Yin Luqiu, no one knew anything about where Han Shan came from, but he lived a reclusive life at a place known as Cold Mountain in the Tiantai (T'ien-t'ai) Mountains, from which he occasionally visited the nearby Guoqing (Kuo-ch'ing) Temple. After relating stories of Han Shan's unusual behavior, Yin Luqiu describes how both Han Shan and Shide disappear into a cave. After this, Yin Luqiu says, he gathered together poems that the two recluses had carved into trees, or written on rocks or the walls of houses, and he presents the collection as those very poems.

Yin Luqiu's preface is suspicious for a number of reasons, not the least of which is that there is no record of any Tang bureaucrat of that name. It seems likely that the entire story is the product of a fertile literary imagination. It is even uncertain whether anyone existed by the name of Han Shan, though there are several mountains by that name, and one does have a temple. Nor do we have a date for the poems: Yin never gives a date, and estimates of dates for the poems' production range from the late sixth to the early ninth centuries.

Nevertheless, though the quality is uneven, many of the poems themselves make worthwhile reading. They are written in a simple, often colloquial language, and most are in a traditional Chinese eight-line form with five characters to a line, where even lines rhyme. The lyrics cover a wide range of topics: Some satirize greed, pride, or the corruption of the Buddhist clergy; some complain of poverty, of life's brevity, or of the difficulties of official Chinese bureaucracy in the Tang dynasty. Some of the most effective, and the basis of Han Shan's popularity, involve vivid descriptions of Cold Mountain itself, or of the natural world around it, often with an application to individual spiritual life. One such poem is the following:

Here is a tree older than the forest itself;
The years of its life defy reckoning.
Its roots have seen the upheavals of hill and valley,
Its leaves have known the changes of wind and frost.

The world laughs at its shoddy exterior
And cares nothing for the fine grain of the wood inside.
Stripped free of flesh and hide,
All that remains is the core of truth.

(Watson, 1970, 111)

The poems are available in several English translations, including some by award-winning American poet Gary Snyder. They speak to a modern environmentalist mood, but also to a spirituality that sees in nature a way of expressing the inexpressibility of the transcendent God.

Bibliography

Han Shan. *Cold Mountain: 100 Poems by the T'ang Poet Han-shan.* Edited and translated by Burton Watson. New York: Columbia University Press, 1970.

Henricks, Robert G. *The Poetry of Han-shan: A Complete, Annotated Translation of Cold Mountain.* Albany: State University of New York Press, 1990.

Snyder, Gary. *Riprap and Cold Mountain Poems.* San Francisco: Grey Fox Press, 1965.

Han Yu (Han Yü) (768–824)

One of the better-known poets of China's Middle TANG DYNASTY, Han Yu was also a very important prose stylist who advocated a change from the prevailing "parallel prose" style of his day in favor of a more organic prose structure. He is best remembered, however, for his eloquent protest of a memorial to a relic of the Buddha, in which he condemned both Buddhism and Taoism as irrational and barbarian religions inevitably conflicting with traditional Confucian values.

Han Yu was born into a family of scholars in Nanyang in modern-day Henan. He was orphaned at a young age, but embarked, like most of his contemporary poets, on a career in the imperial bureaucracy. He passed the JINSHI (*chin-shih*) exam in 792, and subsequently, after serving some time with two military governors, he obtained a post as instructor at the Imperial University in 802. He held other posts in a career with several ups and downs. However, in 819 he jeopardized his career by writing the *Jian ying Fogu biao* (Memorial against the welcoming of the Buddha bone), in which he condemned the imperial reception and devotion to a relic of the Buddha's finger bone that had arrived at the palace. In the early Tang dynasty, Buddhism had flourished, and the imperial court had enthusiastically patronized the growth of the new religion. Han Yu was at the forefront of a Confucian counterattack on Buddhism, as well as Taoism. The emperor, however, was so angry at Han Yu's "Memorial" that he wanted the writer executed. Instead, after his wrath abated, he demoted Han Yu and sentenced him to exile in the south, in Chaozhou.

As a poet, Han Yu began by writing rather simple didactic lyrics that were not much admired by his contemporaries. His best poetry was written during the years of his demotion and exile—these were much more complex and technically accomplished. His best-known poem of this period may be "*Nanshan shi*" (Poem of the Southern Mountains), though many believe that his less ostentatious "Autumn Meditations" is his poetic masterpiece. During his later years, after he had regained some status in the bureaucracy (he was ultimately appointed rector of the university, among other positions), Han Yu's poetic output was somewhat reduced, and he wrote only rather uncomplicated occasional verse. Beyond his own verse, Han Yu's contribution to Chinese poetry includes his "discovery" and championing of the young and wildly imaginative LI HE, author of haunting supernatural verse that has been particularly appealing to Western readers.

Han Yu's larger contribution is in literary prose. He was a chief spokesman for the *guwen yundong* (ancient style prose movement), which called for a reform in the style and content of prose. Han Yu opposed the artificiality of the "parallel prose" style popular in his time, a style that required every pair of lines in a prose composition to be strictly parallel or antithetical. In such compositions, form was allowed to dominate content, according to Han Yu, and he advocated a style that grew more organically out of the content, a style he saw as a return to the traditional, ancient prose style. Initially praising originality in the content of prose texts, Han Yu later decided that content should be judged according to its adherence to correct Confucian doctrine—in particular, he revived interest in the neglected scholar Mengzi (Mencius) and promoted what became known as "Neo-Confucianism." Thus his prose, like his early poetry, took on a didactic purpose.

Beyond the very famous *Jian ying Fogu biao,* Han Yu's best-known prose texts are his *Yuandao* (Inquiry into the way), in which he condemns Buddhism and Taoism and discusses the correct Confucian teachings. His *Song Meng Dongye Xu* (Preface to Meng Dongye's "farewell") is an exploration of the tradition of poetry. On the less serious side, and to the chagrin of some of his friends, Han Yu also wrote a number of fables and parodies. One such parody is *Mao Ying Zhuan* (Biography of hair point), in which Han Yu relates the "official career" of a hair point, or writing brush, in the style of a traditional biography of some important bureaucrat. Of all his voluminous output, such occasional comic pieces might have a particular appeal to a contemporary reader. In his own day, he was so respected a writer that he became known as the Prince of Letters.

Bibliography

Hanson, Kenneth O., trans. *Growing Old Alive: Poems by Han Yü.* Port Townsend, Wash.: Copper Canyon Press, 1978.

Hartman, Charles. *Han Yu and the T'ang Search for Unity.* Princeton, N.J.: Princeton University Press, 1986.

Idema, Wilt, and Lloyd Haft. *A Guide to Chinese Literature.* Ann Arbor: Center for Chinese Studies, University of Michigan, 1997.

Owen, Stephen. *The Great Age of Chinese Poetry: The High T'ang.* New Haven, Conn., and London: Yale University Press, 1981.

———. *The Poetry of Meng Chiao and Han Yü.* New Haven, Conn.: Yale University Press, 1975.

Hardyng, John (1378–ca. 1465)

John Hardyng was a soldier, spy, and poet, who authored a verse history of England known as *The Chronicle of John Hardyng.* The chronicle exists in two versions: The first version, dedicated to Henry VI, narrates English history from the legendary founding of the nation by the Trojan Brutus, through the year 1437. Its chief aim seems to be to make a case for the claims of the English kings to sovereignty over Scotland. The second version of the poem (carrying the history to 1464) was revised in the interests of the Yorkist faction, and reflects Hardyng's change of loyalties during the War of the Roses.

Hardyng was born in Northumbria in 1378, and at the age of 12, became part of the household of Sir Harry Percy (called "Hotspur"). Under Percy, son of the earl of Northumberland, Hardyng learned the profession of arms, and fought behind his lord in border skirmishes against the Scots. He was under Percy's command when the latter was killed at the Battle of Shrewsbury (1403), in rebellion against King Henry IV. Pardoned by the king, Hardyng next entered the service of Sir Robert Umfraville. Under Umfraville, Hardyng took part in Henry V's campaign in France, fighting in the Battle of Agincourt in 1415.

It was about this time that Henry V took an interest in Hardyng, and recruited him to help create a case for the English king's right to govern Scotland. Henry sent Hardyng to Scotland in 1418 to help scout the best way to invade the country and to gather evidence for Henry's claim to Scotland. Hardyng was in Scotland for three years, and returned to present Henry with "evidence" (in the form of documents he apparently forged himself) in 1422. In gratitude Henry promised Hardyng the Northamptonshire manor of Geddington in payment for services rendered—at least Hardyng always claimed so. But Henry died later that year, and Hardyng never received his promised manor. Nevertheless, he had always remained in Umfraville's service, and had been well rewarded by his lord, being made constable of the castle of Warkworth and later of Kyme, a castle he maintained as his home until his death.

But when Umfraville died in 1436, Hardyng stepped up his efforts to support the English claim to Scotland and to press his own claim to his promised manor. He began writing the first version of his verse chronicle about this time. In 1440, he presented King Henry VI with more "evidence" for English sovereignty. Henry did grant Hardyng an annuity of 10 pounds per year, but no manor was forthcoming. In 1457, Hardyng again presented forged documentary evidence to Henry, and presented him, as well, with the completed chronicle, containing a Proem addressed to the king. In it Hardyng presses Henry to reconquer Scotland like his predecessor, Edward I, and even includes maps to assist the invasion. For his services Hardyng's annuity was increased to 20 pounds.

As the War of the Roses progressed (between supporters of Henry and the Lancaster line and those of the king's cousin, the Duke of York), Hardyng decided to throw his support behind the Yorkist faction, and decided to rewrite his chronicle to present to York. It was not a great shift for him; he had, after all, supported Percy's rebellion against the first Lancaster, Henry IV. In revising his history, Hardyng inserted lines rejecting Henry IV's claim to the throne. He also removed a eulogy praising Henry V, and called Henry VI a man "of small intelligence." Further, he pressed York's claim to the throne through the female line by Lionel of Clarence, second son of EDWARD III (the Lancasters claimed descent through John of Gaunt, Edward's third son). Richard, duke of York, had died in 1360, and Hardyng presented his second chronicle, with events through 1464, to York's son, Edward IV—along with more evidence of his Scottish claims.

The *Chronicle* survives in 12 manuscripts, and was first published, with a continuation, by Richard Grafton in 1543. As a historian, Hardyng used a number of sources, including BEDE, NENNIUS, the *Brut,* as well as primary documents (genuine ones) from the Percies and others. Still, Hardyng's chronicle has never been admired as a literary work. It is of interest as an eyewitness account of Agincourt, as a tribute to Hardyng's patrons, particularly Percy and Umfraville, and for Hardyng's didactic advice to his royal audience on good government. He provides a picture of the lawless conditions during the War of the Roses in order to extol the importance, and the princely responsibility, of keeping an ordered society and the rule of law.

Bibliography

Gransden, Antonia. *Historical Writing in England II: c. 1307 to the Early Sixteenth Century.* Ithaca, N.Y.: Cornell University Press, 1982.

Hardying, John. *The Chronicle of John Hardying.* Edited by Henry Ellis. New York: AMS Press, 1974. Originally published 1812.

Harley Lyrics, The (ca. 1300–1350)

The Harley Lyrics are a collection of 32 MIDDLE ENGLISH lyric poems contained in the British Museum MS. Harley 2253. The manuscript was produced in the West Midlands (most likely Hereford or Leominster) some time in the first half of the 14th century, though the poems themselves appear to be from various parts of England. In addition to the lyrics, the manuscript contains a variety of material, including Anglo-Norman lyrics, SAINTS' LIVES, and FABLIAUX, as well as Latin verse and prose, mainly of a religious nature. The 32 English poems are the earliest collection of lyrics in Middle English assembled in one manuscript, and contain more than half of the extant secular lyrics from prior to the 15th century. They include some of the most admired short poems of the English Middle Ages.

The collection comprises a wide variety of poems gathered from several authors and forms. They show both a native English and a French influence. Their prosody displays remarkable range, from complex rhymed stanzas to ALLITERATIVE VERSE to TAIL-RHYME stanzas. In subject matter they show no less diversity. There are political poems, such as the one on the Battle of Lewes (1264) and one on the famous Battle of Bannockburn (1314). There are love songs, including the well-known *ALYSOUN,* which praises the beauty of the speaker's lady, and the equally admired *LENTEN IS COME WITH LOVE TO TOUNE,* which is essentially a *REVERDIE* rejoicing in the spring that brings love to the world. Another famous Harley lyric, *Blow, Northern Wind,* uses the foul weather of winter to convey the feelings of the lover who cannot win his lady.

These and other poems in the manuscript show the influence of the COURTLY LOVE conventions popular in continental lyric poetry of the time. There are also religious lyrics, including prayers and songs of praise to the Virgin, as well as a kind of love song to Christ called *Suete Iesu, King of blysse.* Finally, there are poems that defy classification, like the humorous *Man in the Moon* that takes a comic look at the mythic creature of the heavens. Considered as a whole, the lyrics are lively and fresh, rising above the conventionality of much continental verse, yet the lyrics also show an aesthetic sophistication suggesting a highly literate group of authors.

Robert Harley, first Earl of Oxford (1661–1724), apparently acquired the manuscript shortly before his death. It passed to his son, Edward Harley, the second Earl, who was a well-known book collector and a friend of Alexander Pope. When the second earl died, his collection of 7,639 manuscripts was sold to the British nation, and became the cornerstone of the manuscript collection in the British Library. Of these, the best-known and arguably the most important manuscript is number 2253, because of its invaluable collection of lyrics.

Bibliography

Brook, G. L., ed. *The Harley Lyrics: The Middle English Lyrics of Ms. Harley 2253.* 4th ed. Manchester, U.K.: Manchester University Press, 1968.

Facsimile of British Museum MS. Harley 2253. With an introduction by N. R. Ker. Early English Text Society, o.s. 255. London: Published for the Early English Text Society by the Oxford University Press, 1965.

Ransom, Daniel J. *Poets at Play: Irony and Parody in the Harley Lyrics.* Norman, Okla.: Pilgrim Books, 1985.

Harrowing of Hell (*Anastasis,* Descent into Limbo)

In medieval Christian tradition, the soul of Christ was believed to have descended into hell after his crucifixion and before his resurrection, and to have delivered from their imprisonment the souls of the righteous held there from the beginning of time. The tradition, popular in art and literature, commemorates Christ's victory over death. In the Byzantine Church, this event was called the *Anastasis* (meaning "resurrection"), and was a standard theme of Byzantine iconography. In OLD ENGLISH and MIDDLE ENGLISH, the event was called the Harrowing of Hell, and was a popular theme in homilies, poems, and particularly in the CORPUS CHRISTI cycles of MYSTERY PLAYS.

The doctrine of the Harrowing of Hell seems to have its roots in the early church. Two passages from the first letter of Peter (probably a second-century text) allude to Christ preaching to the souls that were disobedient in the time of Noah (1 Pet. 3.19–20), and later, to the Gospel being preached among the dead (1 Pet. 4.6). So pervasive was the tradition that it was adopted as part of the Apostle's Creed, the earliest extant universal statement of orthodox Christian belief, in which is included the phrase *descendit ad inferos* ("he descended into hell"). The story is first told unambiguously in the apocryphal *Gospel of Nicodemus* (possibly from the third or fourth century), chapters 17 through 27 of which describe Christ's descent into hell. Here, Satan and a character called Hades engage in a dialogue, during which the King of Glory enters hell to rescue the souls of the righteous who, until his crucifixion, had no path to salvation. He leads the Old Testament "saints" into heaven, and casts Satan himself into Tartarus.

Some Christians had difficulty dealing with the notion that Christ would enter hell, since it was assumed only those who sinned would do so, and they would suffer torments while there. The orthodox medieval view of the Harrowing was expressed by Thomas AQUINAS, who explained that Christ did not descend in order to suffer punishment, nor to convert unbelievers in hell, but rather as a part of his triumph over death: Before his sacrifice none could enter heaven, but now he descended to deliver all those who before his death had lived in faith and in charity—those, technically, who dwelt in Limbo, that region pictured by DANTE as the topmost circle of hell where the only punishment was separation from God.

In early Christian and Byzantine art, Christ is usually shown surrounded by a mandorla and reaching out, grasping Adam and/or Eve by the arm to raise them from a grave or tomb. As time went on, other pre-Christian figures were added, including John the Baptist, Abel, David and Solomon, and many of the prophets, and Christ is depicted trampling on the fallen gates of Hell or, sometimes, on Satan himself. In later medieval art, he might be shown entering a wide-open monstrous mouth, symbolizing the Mouth of Hell as Leviathan, to take hold of our first parents entrapped there.

The Latin text of the *Gospel of Nicodemus* was known in England from early times. The Venerable BEDE seems to have been acquainted with the text, and there are early Old English poems alluding to Christ's descent into hell. The first use of the term Harrowing appears in one of the sermons of AELFRIC. The story is paraphrased in the MIDDLE ENGLISH poem called the *CURSOR MUNDI*, but the fullest development of the theme appears in the mystery plays. All four of the extant cycles (the YORK CYCLE, the CHESTER CYCLE, the N-TOWN PLAYS and the TOWNELEY CYCLE) include a separate pageant depicting the Harrowing, in vivid and dramatic detail, generally depicting the devils as comic in their overconfidence and subsequent confusion.

Probably owing something to these dramatic scenes, the great Harrowing of Hell passus from William LANGLAND's *PIERS PLOWMAN* (ca. 1377) is certainly the most colorful and memorable of all medieval literary presentations of the story. Here Christ enters hell, and debates with the devil over the justification for his depriving the devil of the souls that had been his for thousands of years. The devil claims rights to the souls because of Adam's fall, but Christ claims he has paid any outstanding debt by his death, and argues (in terms reminiscent of St. ANSELM's argument for "Why God became man") that he has also made satisfaction to God, and thereby saved humanity. He ultimately leads all human souls into salvation.

Bibliography

Butler, Michelle M. "The York/Towneley Harrowing of Hell?" *Fifteenth-Century Studies* 25 (2000): 115–126.

Howard, John S. "Dialectic and Spectacle in the Harrowing of Hell," *Essays in Literature* 21 (1994): 3–13.

Langland, William. *The Vision of Piers Plowman: A Critical Edition of the B-Text Based on Trinity College Cambridge MS B.15.17.* 2nd ed. Edited by A. V. C. Schmidt. London: Dent, 1995.

Meredith, Peter. "The Iconography of Hell in the English Cycles: A Practical Perspective." In *The Iconography of Hell,* edited by Clifford Davidson and Thomas H. Seiler, 158–186. Kalamazoo, Mich.: Medieval Institute, 1992.

Mullini, Roberta. "Action and Discourse in *The Harrowing of Hell:* the Defeat of Evil," *Medieval English Theatre* 11 (1989): 116–128.

Simpson, James. *Piers Plowman: An Introduction to the B-Text.* London: Longman, 1990.

Tamburr, Karl. "From Narrative to Drama: The Transformation of the Gospel of Nicodemus in Middle English," *Medieval Perspectives* 16 (2001): 135–150.

The York Plays. Edited by Richard Beadle. London: Arnold, 1982.

Hartmann von Aue (ca. 1160–ca. 1210)

The Southwest German (Allemanic) poet Hartmann von Aue introduced the genre of the Arthurian ROMANCE to German literature. He translated, or adapted, CHRÉTIEN DE Troyes's Old French romance *EREC* (ca. 1160) into Middle High German in about 1180 (one complete manuscript from the early 16th century survives, and three fragments). At the end of his life he also translated Chrétien's *YVAIN* as *Iwein,* ca. 1203 (15 complete manuscripts and 17 fragments). His earliest text, however, was the didactic dialogue poem *Die Klage* (ca. 1175; one manuscript) in which a heart and body discuss the nature of love. Two other major works by Hartmann are the religious verse legend *Gregorius* (ca. 1187; six complete manuscripts and five fragments) and the erotic verse novella *Der arme Heinrich* (*Poor Henry,* ca. 1191; three manuscripts). In between he also composed 18 COURTLY LOVE songs, so-called *Minnelieder,* copied in the famous *Manessische Liederhandschrift* (ms. C, early 14th century) and two other manuscripts. Manuscript C also contains a fictionalized portrait of Hartmann, but it does not tell us anything about the historical poet.

We know that Hartmann hailed from Swabia, which is confirmed by his language and his association with the ducal family of Zähringen. However, there are many locations in southwest Germany with the suffix *au* or *aue*, or a corresponding word compound, so we cannot identify Hartmann's origin any further. As he relied heavily on Chrétien's works, he obviously had a very good command of French.

In his two Arthurian romances, Hartmann pursues a fairly identical narrative model centered on the court of King ARTHUR. Early in the narratives the protagonist leaves the court to pursue chivalric adventures and quickly achieves triumphant success, which then allows him to marry in the presence of Arthur. In *Erec* the young husband too passionately embraces marital life with Enite and neglects his duties as a ruler and knight. In *Iwein* the opposite is the case, as the hero departs from his wife, Laudine, soon after their marriage, promising her to return from his tournament journey within one year. But he forgets his promise and is subsequently rejected by Laudine. Erec embarks on a brutal quest for his recovery as an honorable knight and forces his wife to accompany him. Although he forbids her to speak to him, she repeatedly warns him of oncoming dangers and so saves his life, but he punishes her for disobeying him with increasing intensity. Ultimately, however, he learns to accept his wife as an equal partner which then gives him enough strength to win the most dangerous battle against a hostile knight, and thus he reestablishes the *joie de la curt* ("joy of courtly life"). Iwein, on the other hand, once he has lost his wife, loses his mind and roams the forest naked, until a maiden rescues him by means of a magic salve. Now he goes on his true quest, accompanied by a lion whom he had protected against a dragon, and finally demonstrates that he has learned the fundamental values of knighthood and chivalry, involving compassion, empathy, protection of women and orphans, and service for the poor and needy. Iwein also wins back his wife, Laudine, and returns to King Arthur.

In *Gregorius* Hartmann traces the life of his young hero, the product of a brother's rape of his sister. Although he is raised in a convent and could easily succeed the abbot, who treats him like his son, Gregorius is anxious to learn about his noble origin and soon unwittingly marries his mother (like Oedipus in Greek myth). When the truth comes out, he is so deeply grieved that he has a fisherman lock him to a rock in the middle of a lake and is then abandoned. God, however, keeps him alive, and after 17 years, he is chosen as the new pope because he has proven to be the true penitent and hence a model Christian.

In *Der arme Heinrich,* a young knight contracts the deadly disease of leprosy and can only await his death until a young peasant woman offers herself as sacrifice for his recovery, according to the advice of a famous medical doctor in Salerno (near Naples). Although Henry at first agrees, he quickly changes his mind when he peaks through a hole in the wall separating him from the operation room where he observes the naked woman on the table and is deeply moved by her beauty. Renouncing his original plan and respecting God's intentions for him, he terminates the preparations for the surgery to remove her heart. The woman expresses deep frustration because she had hoped to gain quick salvation for her soul, but in the end, she has to accept Henry's decision. At this point, God, who has observed Henry's change of mind, helps him to recover, and once he has returned home and resumed his leadership, he elevates the woman and her family to the status of free peasants, which then allows him to marry her. Despite its seemingly simplistic religious framework and similarity to a fairy tale, this verse novella invites many different interpretations as an ALLEGORY of human frailty and dependency on God's will, as a symbolic tale of true love, and as a psychological account of an individual's quest for his or her identity.

In his 18 courtly love poems (four of them of questionable authenticity), Hartmann pursues traditional themes representative of classical Middle High German *Minnesang* (courtly love poetry). He formulates, above all, complaints about unfulfilled love, yet he also idealizes the pursuit of love for ethical reasons. In his *Tristan* (ca. 1210), GOTTFRIED von Strassburg praises Hartmann as one of the leading poets of his time.

Bibliography

Clark, Susan L. *Hartmann von Aue: Landscapes of Mind.* Houston, Tex.: Rice University Press, 1989.

Hartmann von Aue. *Arthurian Romances, Tales, and Lyric Poetry: The Complete Works.* Translated by Frank Tobin, Richard Lawson, and Kim Vivian. University Park: Pennsylvania State University Press, 2001.

Albrecht Classen

Havelok (*Havelok the Dane*) (ca. 1275–1303)

The Middle English *Havelok* (*Incipit vita Havelok quondam rex Angliae et Danemarchie*) was probably composed sometime between 1275 and 1303, during the reign of Edward I, although the precise date is uncertain. The single extant copy of the romance is found in a collection of pious and didactic narratives (MS. Laud Misc. 108, Bodleian) including *The Life and Passion of Christ* and *The Sayings of St. Bernard,* and occurs in the last part of the manuscript along with, among other works, another early Middle English romance, *King Horn.* The romance of *Havelok* contains elements of hagiography (or a saint's life), yet its primary focus seems to be political and social and may, indeed, be connected with the reign and person of Edward I. The romance may have been in origin pro-Danish propaganda (there are two earlier 12th-century versions of the story: Geoffrey Gaimer's Anglo-Norman *Estorie des engles,* and the Old French *Lai d'Havelok*), but the anonymous poet seems more engaged with the narrative as a mirror or handbook for princes in which ideal kingship, lawful succession, law and order, and the private and public aspects of the exemplary king are canvassed.

After an invocation to Christ (ll. 15–22), the romance opens in England with an extended passage of praise for the reign of King Aflelwolde, and goes on to relate his impending death and the provisions he makes for his only child, a daughter named Goldeboru. Aflelwolde leaves the care of his daughter and heir to one of his barons, Godrich of Cornwall, who promises to guard her and, when the time comes, aid her in her succession to the throne. Not unexpectedly Godrich reconsiders his oath to the king and decides to supplant Goldeboru with his own children. The action then moves to Denmark, where a parallel tale of treachery unfolds when the king of Denmark dies, leaving his son and heir, Havelok, and his two daughters to the care of his friend and noble, Godard. Godard immediately abrogates his oath to the king, imprisons the children, and kills the two daughters. He arranges for the death of Havelok, but this is fortuitously avoided when Grim, the man commissioned to undertake the murder, discovers the kyne-mark on Havelok's shoulder that reveals him to be the divinely appointed heir to the throne. Grim and his family escape with the child Havelok to England where the two plots of lost inheritance are joined together, literally: Goldeboru is forced into marriage with Havelok, whom Godrich believes to be a commoner, and this marriage below her state, or "disparagement," legally discounting her from succeeding to the throne. (The use of "disparagement" is only one of many medieval legalisms with which this romance is informed).

Goldeboru's despair about the marriage below her rank is transformed when one night in bed, she notes a light coming from Havelok's mouth and the kyne-mark—a birthmark attesting to royal descent (from Old English *cynemearc*)—on his shoulder. She concludes that her "common" husband is, in fact, of royal birth, and her conclusion is confirmed when an angel tells her that Havelok will be king of England and Denmark. Havelok awakes to tell her of a dream that has perplexed him, which she interprets for him on the basis of her own conjectures and the angel's confirmation. Goldeboru advises they set out for Denmark, where Havelok is successful in regaining his throne; after which they return to England and secure the English throne. The good are rewarded, the bad are punished, and the romance ends with a brief summary of wrongs put right and the conventional authorial request for a prayer to be said for "hym that haueth the rym maked" (2999).

Havelok is both conventional *and* remarkable as a medieval romance: the concern with lost inheritance; a hero who grows up in lowly circumstances but reveals himself (through his courtesy, his beauty, or his treatment of others) to be more than circumstances suggest; the quest for identity and social status; all these themes are common to medieval romance. Yet even while *Havelok* shares many elements and motifs with other Middle English romances, the extent to which it is concerned with politics and policy, kingship and commonwealth, rightful succession and just rule, is rare in contemporary narratives and considerably heightened from its sources. *Havelok* is also extraordinarily realistic for a romance and its realism (in addition to its emphasis on just rule) is one of the primary sites for critical commentary concerning its political significance. Variously called a romance of nation or a romance of kingship, most recent critical commentary tends to focus on the national, political, and judicial aspects of the romance. Critical readings also include explorations of the popular hero as exemplary king, and the ways in which the title (*Vita Havelok*) anticipates the hagiographical elements in the romance and Havelok's status as a secular Christian hero. Amusing and edifying, *Havelok* fulfills with a flourish the medieval literary injunction to instruct and entertain.

Bibliography

Barnes, Geraldine. *Counsel and Strategy in Middle English Romance.* Cambridge: Brewer, 1993.

Crane, Susan. *Insular Romance: Politics, Faith, and Culture in Anglo-Norman and Middle English Literature.* Berkeley: University of California Press, 1986.

Delany, Sheila. "The Romance of Kingship: *Havelok the Dane.*" In *Medieval Literary Shapes of Ideology,* 61–73. Manchester, U.K.: Manchester University Press, 1990.

Field, Rosalind, ed. *Tradition and Transformation in Medieval Romance.* Cambridge, U.K.: Brewer, 1999.

Meale, Carol, ed. *Readings in Medieval English Romance.* Cambridge, U.K.: Brewer, 1994.

Mehl, Dieter. *The Middle English Romances of the Thirteenth and Fourteenth Centuries.* London: Routledge and Kegan Paul, 1969.

Smithers, G. V., ed. *Havelok.* Oxford: Clarendon Press, 1987.

Staines, David. "*Havelok the Dane:* A Thirteenth-Century Handbook for Princes," *Speculum* 51 (1976): 602–623.

Stuart, Christopher. "*Havelok the Dane* and Edward I in the 1390s," *Studies in Philology* 93 (1996): 349–364.

Turville-Petre, Thorlac. "*Havelok* and the History of the Nation." In *Readings in Medieval English Romance,* edited by Carol Meade, 121–134. Cambridge, U.K.: Brewer, 1994.

Elisa Narin van Court

Hawes, Stephen (ca. 1475–ca. 1523)

Stephen Hawes was an English poet at the dawn of the Tudor age whose poetic inspirations were his major medieval predecessors in English poetry: CHAUCER, GOWER, and the dominant 15th-century poet, John LYDGATE. Hawes, who was groom of the chamber to King Henry VII, is best known for his allegorical love poem *The Pastime of Pleasure, or The Historie of Graunde Amoure and La Belle Pucel* (ca. 1506).

Little is known with certainty of Hawes's life. Probably he was born in Suffolk. He seems to have been educated at Oxford, and to have learned languages visiting universities on the continent, but much of what is assumed of his life is conjecture. Tradition says that Henry VII was attracted by Hawes's learning, particularly his prodigious memory that allowed him to recite by heart long passages from Chaucer and from Lydgate. Henry gave him a position in his household, making him groom of the chamber.

Hawes's surviving poems all tend to be moral or love allegories in a medieval courtly style reminiscent of Lydgate and, ultimately, the *ROMAN DE LA ROSE*. His *Example of Virtue* (ca. 1504) is written in the RHYME ROYAL stanzas popularized by Chaucer, and is a conventional moral allegory concerning a life spent seeking purity. *The Comfort of Lovers* (first printed 1510) is a love allegory, while *The Conversion of Swearers* (printed 1509) is a condemnation of blasphemy, particularly the typically medieval custom of swearing by the body of Christ. In 1509, Hawes also wrote *A Joyful Meditation,* his celebration of Henry VIII's coronation.

But Hawes is known mainly for his *Pastime of Pleasure,* which was first printed by Wynkyn de Worde in 1509, and went through several subsequent editions in the 16th century. The poem is dedicated to Henry VII, and is conceived as a chivalric romance in an allegorical landscape, in which the knight Graunde Amoure strives to win the fair Lady La Belle Pucel. Written, like his *Example of Virtue,* in rhyme royal stanzas, Hawes's poem runs to 45 chapters and almost 6,000 lines. Some half of these describe Graunde Amoure in the Tower of Doctrine, where he receives a grounding in the seven Liberal Arts to make him worthy of his beloved. From here he moves to the Tower of Chivalry and learns what he will require to battle the allegorical forces he needs to conquer in order to win his lady's love.

Most critics see Hawes as chiefly medieval in his allegorical style and his emphasis on such things as Fortune's wheel and earthly life as a pilgrimage, but see his interest in the education of a prince and worldly accomplishments as looking forward to poets of the Renaissance. Indeed Hawes's text certainly must have influenced Spenser's *Faerie Queene.* But Hawes was not optimistic about the future of poetry in English: In section 14 of his *Pastime of Pleasure,* he depicts himself as the only remaining devotee of true poetry—certainly he was the last English poet in the Chaucerian courtly tradition.

Bibliography

Edwards, A. S. G. *Stephen Hawes.* Boston: Twayne, 1983.

Gluck, Florence W., and Alice B. Morgan. *Stephen Hawes: The Minor Poems.* EETS, no. 271. London: Published for the Early English Text Society by the Oxford University Press, 1974.

Mead, William Edward, ed. *Pastime of Pleasure.* EETS, o.s. 173. London: Published for the Early English Text Society by H. Milford, Oxford University Press, 1928.

Heian period (794–1186)

The HEIAN period refers to the epoch in Japanese history extending from 794 to 1186, when the capital city was located in Heiankyō (modern-day Kyoto). This early medieval period began when the emperor moved the capital from NARA, and it ended after the Genpei War, when the victorious Minamoto clan transferred the capital to KAMAKURA.

The Heian period is distinguished for its refined, artistic court culture. Although the emperor's court served as the cultural center, the real political power lay with dominant clans, in particular the Fujiwaras. The aristocracy—making up less than 1 percent of Japan's approximately 5 million inhabitants—was divided into 10 ranks, with rank determining a person's job. We know about this aristocracy through the writings of its members, but little is known of the lower classes.

The aristocracy resided in *shinden* palaces, typically one-story wooden structures consisting of wings joined by corridors, surrounded by gardens. Living arrangements were fluid. The principal wife, for instance, might live with her family and have her husband visit. The nobleman could have his own mansion and assign his wives to various wings. Aside from the official wife, the aristocrat may have secondary wives. Though aristocrats practiced polygamy (along with casual affairs), monogamy was the norm for the lower classes who lacked the funds and leisure time for multiple partners.

Heian Japan looked back to the Chinese TANG DYNASTY of the 600s to 900s as a model, much in the same way that medieval Europe was inspired by the earlier Roman Empire. Fusing native Japanese characteristics with this borrowed Chinese culture, Heian aristocracy devoted itself to what Ivan Morris calls the "cult of beauty in art and nature" (194). Court ceremonies and religious rituals (*eiga*) ruled aristocratic life. The refined nobleman was expected to compose poetry and compete in literary contests, play musical instruments and sing, dance, paint (calligraphy was especially cultivated), and master etiquette forms for conducting love affairs and other social interactions. Such a code resembles the *sprezzatura* ("artful artlessness") of Europe's ruling class during the early modern period.

The prevailing sensibility was *aware*, intense emotion stemming from the Buddhist realization of the ephemeral beauty of this world, and expressed in the arts through principles of elegant aesthetics (*miyabi*). Although Buddhist ideas were imported from China, they were modified by native Shinto thought. For instance the belief in spirits and demons was based in Shinto, but exorcists were frequently Buddhist clerics.

Given the focus upon aesthetics, it is not surprising that the Heian era is the Japanese golden age for the arts and produced the country's greatest authors: MURASAKI SHIKIBU, author of Japan's most treasured classic, *The* TALE OF GENJI (*Genji Monogatari*), classified as the world's first novel and one of the finest; SEI SHŌNAGON, whose *Pillow Book* (*Makura no Sōshi*) is a complex piece of autobiographical writing that defies easy categorization and description; and IZUMI SHIKUBU, Heian Japan's foremost poet.

The above-mentioned authors were all women living circa 1000, and their presence in the canon of Japanese literature from their time to the present is unusual for literary canons. In contrast, medieval women writers from Europe had to be "recovered" in recent decades. The reasons for this dominance by women writers are much discussed, but, in short, come from the fact that, as in medieval Europe, where men dominated the official language of Latin, so, too, in medieval Japan, men tended to write in the official language of Chinese. Subsequently, Heian women developed the script of *onna-de* ("woman's hand") to write in the vernacular language of Japanese. Secluded behind screens from the prying eyes of men, women writers such as Murasaki Shikibu would entertain such royal patrons as Empress Shōshi with romance prose narratives interspersed with poetry (*monogatari*), *waka* poetry reflecting the Shinto appreciation of nature, and autobiographical writings, such as diaries (*nikki*).

Once the Heian era ended, however, the number of women writers with their refined elegant style declined, as the emperor and the aristocracy in Heiankyō began to lose power to provincial military rulers and as more austere Confucian and Buddhist attitudes began to dominate during the Kamakura era.

Bibliography

Miner, Earl, Hiroko Odagiri, and Robert E. Morrell. *The Princeton Companion to Classical Japanese Literature.* Princeton, N.J.: Princeton University Press, 1985.

Morris, Ivan. *The World of the Shining Prince: Court Life in Ancient Japan.* New York: Knopf, 1969.

Stevenson, Barbara, and Cynthia Ho, eds. *Crossing the Bridge: Comparative Essays on Medieval European and Heian Japanese Women Writers.* New Middle Ages Series, edited by Bonnie Wheeler. New York: Palgrave/St. Martin's, 2000.

Barbara Stevenson

Heimskringla (The Disk of the World)

Snorri Sturluson (ca. 1235)

Heimskringla is a vast compilation of Old Icelandic SAGAS concerning the kings of Norway, from their beginnings in myth and legend and the advent of King Harald Fairhair around 850 through the death of King Eystein in 1177, some 50 years before SNORRI STURLUSON began his work on the text. Snorri, Iceland's most important medieval writer, was also the author of the PROSE EDDA (a kind of handbook of Norse mythology and SKALDIC POETRY), and perhaps of *EGIL'S SAGA* (one of the most admired of Icelandic family sagas concerning a skaldic poet who may have been Snorri's ancestor). Snorri, a powerful chieftain and poet himself, lawspeaker of the Icelandic Althing and the wealthiest man in Iceland during his prime, ends his history of the kings of Norway a generation before the Norwegian king with whom he himself was acquainted—Hakon Hakonarson, who likely ordered Snorri's murder in 1241.

The title *Heimskringla* is not Snorri's but was given to the text by an early editor, who simply derived it from the first two words of the manuscript, *kringla heims* ("the circular world"). The collection begins with *Ynglinga Saga,* which traces the descent of the Norwegian kings back to Odin himself. After this mythic beginning, Snorri includes 15 more sagas devoted to the Norwegian kings Halfdan the Black; Harald Harfager (Harald Fairhair); Hakon the Good; Harald Grafeld and Earl Hakon, son of Sigurd (in a single saga); Olaf Trygvason; Olaf Haraldson (St. Olaf); Magnus the Good; Harald Hardrade; Olaf Kyrre; Magnus Barefoot; Sigurd the Crusader (and his brothers Eystein and Olaf); Magnus the Blind and Harald Gille (in a single saga); the sons of Harald (Sigurd, Inge, and Eystein, in a single saga); Hakon Herdebreid (Hakon the Broad-shouldered); and Magnus Erlingson. It is possible that Snorri's compilation owes something to previous histories of Norwegian and Danish kings—the relatively brief Latin text *Historia Norwegiæ* and *Saxonis Gesta Danorum*—Saxo's significant Latin history of the Danes. Like Snorri, the authors of these texts traced the ancestry of the Scandinavian monarchs to Norse pagan gods. However, there is no evidence that Snorri was aware of or had read these texts.

The sagas may be read as fascinating and sometimes romantic historical narratives. One of the most entertaining is the *Saga of Harald Hardrade,* who travels to Constantinople and dies in battle against King Harold of England shortly before the Norman Conquest. But more than simple tales of adventure, the sagas of *Heimskringla* are composed with certain common thematic concerns. Snorri's focus on the history of Norwegian kings was not disinterested: As a major participant in the political turmoil that characterized his age (the "Sturlung Age" in Iceland, known for its widespread lawlessness and civil unrest), Snorri was aware of the impending annexation of Iceland by the Norwegian crown, an act deemed necessary to "pacify" the country and that indeed took place in 1262, bringing to an end four centuries of Icelandic independence. In his *Heimskringla,* Snorri contemplates the positive and negative aspects of Norwegian kingship. The political unity and national identity it brought to Norway are clear benefits of the monarchy. However, the thirst for power and the suppression of personal liberties were common destructive characteristics of the kings, and were the forces that compelled Iceland's pioneer settlers to leave Norway in the first place.

Thus one of the most famous passages in the *Heimskringla* is in the *Saga of Saint Olaf,* where, in a speech before his fellow nobles, the petty chieftain Hroerek warns them against offering the kingdom to Olaf. Reviewing Norwegian history, he argues that every king they have had (with the exception of Hakon the Good) was so concerned with consolidating his own power that the Norwegians themselves suffered. Hroerek is later proven correct when Olaf has him blinded and kills off some of the other petty kings who object to his power. The tale seems an illustration of Snorri's basic theme.

Another impressive characteristic of Snorri's text is his scrupulous standard of historical veracity, so unusual for his time. He tried to find trustworthy eyewitness accounts, and depended a good deal on the *Íslendingabók* (*The Book of the Icelanders*), the first vernacular history of Iceland up to the year 1120, written by the exceptionally reliable Ari Thorgilsson the Learned. Snorri also relied very heavily on skaldic poems: The skalds were court poets for the various kings, and wrote verse commemorating significant events of the kings' reigns. Skalds were often present at battles, and since excessive flattery was not characteristic of skaldic poetry (except as satire), the poems that survived, and that he included in the texts of the sagas, were trustworthy sources for Snorri's research.

The *Saga of Saint Olaf* was the first of Snorri's kings' sagas, and ultimately forms the centerpiece of *Heimskringla.* In the case of Olaf, Snorri had a vast amount of legendary material to sift through concerning the king's biography. Previous treatments of Olaf's life had been hagiographical—essentially SAINTS' LIVES—that depicted the king as saintly from his early days on. But Snorri knew that Olaf was much more complex, and depicts him, more accurately, as a vindictive and ambitious monarch who used Christianity as a means to achieve his goal of power. In Snorri's tale, Olaf only becomes saintly—ethically and spiritually—once he has been defeated and lives in exile in Russia, and particularly when he suffers his final defeat in battle.

Although scholars differ as to how accurate Snorri's narratives are, the sagas still provide one of the most important sources for early Norse history. Snorri's text is remarkable for its objectivity, for the psychological realism of its characters, and the plausible cause-effect relationships of its events as Snorri presents them.

Bibliography

Bagge, Sverre. *Society and Politics in Snorri Sturluson's Heimskringla.* Berkeley: University of California Press, 1991.

———. "From Sagas to Society: The Case of *Heimskringla.*" In *From Sagas to Society: Comparative Approaches to Early Iceland,* edited by Gisli Palsson, 61–75. Enfield Lock, U.K.: Hisarlik, 1992.

Bermann, Melissa A. "*Egil's Saga* and *Heimskringla,*" *Scandinavian Studies* 54 (1982): 21–50.

Carroll, Joseph. "The *Prose Edda,* the *Heimskringla,* and *Beowulf:* Mythical, Legendary, and Historical Dialogues," *Geardagum: Essays in Old and Middle English Literature* 18 (1997): 15–38.

Ciklamini, Marlene. "The Folktale in *Heimskringla,*" *Folklore* 90 (1979): 204–216.

———. *Snorri Sturluson.* Boston: Twayne, 1978.

Kuhn, Hans. "Fabulous Childhoods, Adventures, Incidents: Folktale Patterns within the Saga Structure of *Heimskringla,*" *Journal of Folktale Studies* 41 (2000): 76–86.

Sturluson, Snorri. *Heimskringla: History of the Kings of Norway.* Translated by Lee Hollander. Austin: University of Texas Press, 1964.

Heinrich von Melk (late 12th century)

This religious author who wrote in Middle High German composed two verse narratives, *Von des todes gehugde* (On the remembrance of death) and *Priesterleben* (On the life of priests). He identifies himself in the epilogue to the former as "Häinrîchen, dînen armen chnecht" (Henry, God's lowly servant, v. 1031), and he also begs God for the salvation of Abbot Erkenfried (Erchennenfride) of Melk in Upper Austria, who governed from 1122 to 1163 (v. 1033). Heinrich characterizes himself as a lay person, a *conversus* who had not taken the vows to join the convent as a monk and was associated with the monastery of Melk only indirectly.

Both of Heinrich's texts are preserved in the Vienna miscellany manuscript cod. 2696, *Von des todes gehugde* without any text loss (1,042 verses), but *Priesterleben* only in fragmentary form (746 verses, probably a loss of 1,900 verses). In the first poem Heinrich addresses a lay audience and reminds them of their imminent death, admonishing them to change their lives now to meet God's demands and to save their souls. His religious appeals address people of all social classes, but above all, he is concerned with the clerics who have failed in paying attention to God's words. According to Heinrich bishops tend to assign church offices and parishes to the highest bidder (a sin called *simony*); priests, when preaching, would attack only the poor and spare the rich; and all of them would lead an almost secular lifestyle. Moreover Heinrich criticizes knights for their blood feuds, he attacks ladies and their lovers for their decadence and arrogance, and finally, he laments the loss of all virtues and values at his time, especially since money and material wealth dominate the world. The second part of *Von des todes gehugde* consists of a gloomy lament about the temporality of human life and the worthlessness of external, secular glories (a theme called *memento mori*).

In his *Priesterleben,* Heinrich intensifies his attacks on the ethical and moral decay of the clergy, and emphasizes, for instance, their disregard of celibacy. His criticism also targets those women who become priests' concubines. Insofar as Heinrich refers to the common practice of COURTLY LOVE songs that did not emerge until after 1163, Abbot Erkenfried could not have been the poet's patron. Both Heinrich's poetic language and the content suggest that he wrote his poems in the 1170s or 1180s.

Bibliography

Egert, Eugene. "Notes on Heinrich von Melk's *Priesterleben,*" *Amsterdamer Beiträge zur älteren Germanistik* 19 (1983): 147–157.

Gentry, Francis G., ed. *A Companion to Middle High German Literature to the 14th Century.* Leiden, Netherlands: Brill, 2003.

Heinrich von Melk. *Von des Todes gehugde. Mahnrede über den Tod.* Mittelhochdeutsch/Neuhochdeutsch.

Edited and translated by Thomas Bein and Susanne Kramarz. Stuttgart, Germany: Reclam, 1994.

Maurer, Friedrich, ed. *Die religiösen Dichtungen des 11. und 12. Jahrhunderts. Nach ihren Formen besprochen.* Vol. 3. Tübingen, Germany: Niemeyer, 1970.

Mitchell, Earl Douglas. *Heinrich von Melk: A Diplomatic Edition. A Translation, and a Commentary.* Ph.D. diss., University of Texas at Austin, 1967, 1969.

Albrecht Classen

Heinrich von Morungen (ca. 1180–ca. 1220)

Historical documents from 1217 and 1218 identify the Middle High German poet Heinrich von Morungen, who was in the service of Margrave Dietrich von Meissen. The famous Manesse manuscript (C; early 14th century) contains a fictional portrait of Heinrich. He composed fairly traditional courtly love poems, resorting to a wide range of themes and topoi (commonly used poetic images). Heinrich reflects some influence from Old French courtly love poetry (TROUVÈRE and TROUBADOR poetry), but his work is firmly anchored in traditional German *Minnesang.* In his 35 songs he utilizes nature introductions, verbal exchanges between man and woman, and he often laments about the pain resulting from unrequited love. In song no. 32, he compares himself to a child who looks into a mirror and then destroys the image when he tries to grab the picture in the mirror, breaking it in the process, representative of the futile sufferings of a lover. Heinrich tends to intensify the emotional dimension of his wooing and formulates rather aggressive complaints about his distant lady. In song no. 3, for instance, he announces that he hopes his son will acquire outstanding physical beauty and, thus, would produce heavy love pangs in his cold-hearted lady in retaliation for the father's failure. In song no. 5, the poet presents COURTLY LOVE as a magical force that allows his lady to come to him through walls, and in song no. 22, she appears to him in the form of Lady Venus. Moreover, when his beloved lady talks to him, he loses all his wits (song no. 26). Heinrich's general advice to his male audience is to woo honorable ladies, as this would implant *hohen muot* ("high spirits"; song no. 28, 2, 5) in the male lovers. Many of his love songs associate the experience of courtly love with the brilliance of the sun, the moon, the stars, and jewels. Heinrich demonstrates concrete influences from classical antiquity, as he utilizes motifs borrowed from Ovid, the topos of the swan song, the Narcissus motif, the fable of Procne and Philomela, and the nymph Echo.

Bibliography

Des Minnesangs Frühling. Edited by Hugo Moser and Helmut Tervooren. 38th ed. Stuttgart, Germany: Hirzel, 1988.

Sayce, Olive. *The Medieval German Lyric 1150–1300. The Development of Its Themes and Forms in Their European Context.* Oxford: Clarendon Press, 1982.

Albrecht Classen

Heinrich von Veldeke (ca. 1160–ca. 1200)

Originating from the Limbourg area, today in eastern Belgium, Heinrich von Veldeke became the "father" of Middle High German literature when he translated the famous French *Roman d'Eneas.* His romance *Eneit* basically introduced secular literature informed by classical antiquity to his German audiences. He completed about three-fourths of his work (10,934 verses) by 1174, and presented the poem during wedding celebrations at the court of Cleve (in northwestern Germany). After he had lent the manuscript to Countess Margarete of Cleve, Count Heinrich, the brother of the Thuringian landgrave Ludwig III, stole it and took it with him. Only in 1183 did Heinrich von Veldeke regain the manuscript from Hermann, count of the Palatinate Saxony and successor of Ludwig III, and complete his work upon Hermann's and his brother Friedrich's invitation. Whereas in Virgil's classical version the narrative became the basis for a national-Roman epic, both the French author and Heinrich transformed it into an early courtly romance. The ancient source emphasized the historical, military, and religious aspects, making Aeneas into the true founder of the Roman Empire.

By contrast the medieval text versions focus more on the erotic elements without excluding the important battle scenes that eventually lead to Eneas's victory and allow him to marry Lavinia, the *ur*-mother of the Roman Empire. Heinrich carefully elaborates the monologues and dialogues, providing us with important insight into his protagonists' fears, aspirations, and motifs. The author also spends much time describing details of their clothing, weapons, fortifications, and other typical aspects of courtly culture. Heinrich's *Eneas* has been preserved in seven complete manuscripts and in five fragments.

During his early life Heinrich also composed 37 COURTLY LOVE poems, one of which criticizes the TRISTAN motif (song no. 4), stating that he, the poet, would be in no need of the love potion as he fell in love with his lady all by himself and yet would experience even more intense love than Tristan. For Heinrich courtly love represents the highest ethical ideal and provides people with pure and high spirits (no. 12). Moreover, around 1165, he also composed a hagiographical text, *Servatius* (Life of the saint Servatius). Heinrich was highly praised by many Middle High German poets who admired him as the master of courtly love.

Bibliography

Des Minnesangs Frühling. Edited by Hugo Moser and Helmut Tervooren. 38th ed. Stuttgart: Hirzel, 1988.

Heinrich von Veldeke. *Eneit*. Translated by J. W. Thomas. Garland Library of Medieval Literature, Series B, no. 38. New York: Garland, 1985.

Cormier, Raymond. "Classical Continuity and Transposition in Two Twelfth-Century Adaptations of the Aeneid," *Symposium* 47, no. 4 (1994): 261–274.

Sayce, Olive. *The Medieval German Lyric 1150–1300: The Development of Its Themes and Forms in Their European Context*. Oxford: Clarendon Press, 1982.

Albrecht Classen

Heloïse (1101–1164)

Heloïse is best known as one half of the Middle Ages' most celebrated couple. The romantic correspondence she shared with Pierre Abélard makes up what is, perhaps, the most legendary account of passionate, romantic love. Having been orphaned at a young age, Heloïse was the ward of her uncle Fulbert, a cleric and canon of Notre Dame in Paris. She was the pride and joy of her uncle, who acknowledged Heloïse's intellectual capabilities and ensured she received a proper education; Heloïse quickly became known as one of the most learned young ladies of the day. Fulbert happened to move in the same circle as Peter ABÉLARD, a brilliant French philosopher who was a master at the school of Notre Dame and known as one of the most intelligent men of his time. Having heard of Heloïse's reputation, Abélard persuaded Fulbert to trust him with Heloïse's education, and, moreover, to let him move in with the unsuspecting Fulbert and his beautiful niece. In *The Letters of Abélard and Heloise*, Abélard schemingly comments, "I was amazed by his simplicity—if he had entrusted a tender lamb to a ravening wolf it would not have surprised me more" (Abélard 2004, 11). During this time, when Abélard was 40 and Heloïse was 18, the pair fell in love and engaged in a passionate affair, which soon rendered Heloïse pregnant.

When Abélard found out Heloïse was expecting a child, he abducted her and carried her away to live at his sister's home, and there she gave birth to their child, Astrolabe, in 1118. When Heloïse's Uncle Fulbert found out about the pregnancy and about the abduction of his niece, he was furious. To appease Fulbert, Abélard offered to marry Heloïse, although he wished to keep the marriage a secret in order to retain his status as a cleric, canon, and theology teacher, and, although Heloïse opposed the marriage because she preferred to be known as Abélard's lover rather than his wife, the couple wed in a secret ceremony. Uncle Fulbert was infuriated—because of the secrecy of the wedding, he was suspicious that the couple did not actually marry and that Abélard was plotting to abandon Heloïse to a convent. Thus, in 1118, he had Abélard castrated. The public shame Abélard experienced led him to join the Benedictine monastery St. Denis. At this time, at Abélard's request, Heloïse joined the convent Argenteuil, just outside of Paris.

As a nun and a monk, the lovers developed their own separate lives and did not communicate for some time. During this period Abélard recorded his misfortunes in a letter written to console a troubled friend, and this letter became known as his *Historia Calamitatum* (*The Story of My Misfortunes*). By chance (according to tradition), Heloïse saw Abélard's account, which centered on their life together, and responded to him in a letter explaining that although she was a nun, she lived an unsatisfied life of longing over her past with Abélard. Abélard, however, felt that the religious life had saved the pair from an affair that would have inevitably turned catastrophic. Through the ongoing correspondence, Heloïse was eventually convinced monastic life was, indeed, the answer to her and Abélard's problems. In 1129, when the Abbot Suger of St. Denis established his abbey's ownership of Argenteuil and expelled all the nuns, Heloïse and her nuns joined Abélard at Le Paraclet, where Abélard acted as magister (master) of the house and Heloïse served as prioress and later abbess of the spiritual community.

While Heloïse is distinguished for her education and knowledge, she is also known, perhaps better, as a monastic administrator who was honored by popes and other religious figures, such as Peter the Venerable. She published no other work besides her correspondence to Abélard, and the authenticity of even this work has been questioned—many believe the letters were all written by Abélard, while others think they were all written by an outsider (particularly since no known manuscripts date before 1350)—although today most scholars believe that they are, certainly, genuine.

Abélard and Heloïse were both 63 years of age when they died. Abélard was buried at Le Paraclet after his death in 1142, and in accordance with his wishes, Heloïse was buried next to him after she died in 1164. Legend has it that when she was buried there, Abélard reached out from his grave to embrace her. Their remains were reinterred at Père Lachaise Cemetery in Paris in 1817, where there is a monument celebrating the couple.

This legendary relationship of passion, revenge, steadfastness, spirituality, and even obsession has become a prominent theme in European literature. Their romance been immortalized by JEAN DE MEUN in the *ROMAN DE LA ROSE*, Francis PETRARCH, Alexander Pope, François VILLON, and Jean-Jacques Rousseau, among others.

Bibliography

Abélard, Pierre. *The Letters of Abélard and Heloïse.* Rev. ed. Translated with an introduction by Betty Radice. New York: Penguin, 2004.

Radice, Betty. "The French Scholar-Lover: Héloïse." In *Medieval Women Writers,* edited by Katharina M. Wilson, 90–108. Athens, Ga.: University of Georgia Press, 1984.

Townsend, David, and Andrew Taylor, eds. *The Tongue of the Fathers: Gender and Ideology in Twelfth-Century Latin.* Philadelphia: University of Pennsylvania Press, 1998.

Leslie Johnston

Hengwrt manuscript

The Hengwrt manuscript (National Library of Wales Ms. Peniarth 392 D) is the earliest surviving manuscript of Geoffrey CHAUCER's *CANTERBURY TALES,* and is therefore of prime significance in helping scholars establish Chaucer's intent for his text. The scribe responsible for the manuscript appears to be the same one that produced the more famous ELLESMERE MANUSCRIPT of the *Tales,* though the less finished nature of Hengwrt suggests that it is almost certainly an earlier production. The manuscript is usually dated to the first decade after Chaucer's death in 1400, though recent studies of the manuscript by modern editors have revealed the presence of a second hand in the composition, which some have suggested is the hand of a supervisor for the project. It has been suggested that Chaucer himself may have supervised part of the manuscript's production. If that were true, then the traditionally accepted date of the manuscript would be pushed back to the last decade of the 14th century.

However, the Hengwrt manuscript has certain defects. It would seem that the scribe received the text in small pieces rather than all at once (and some parts of the text seem never to have reached him at all). As a result the sequence of the tales is not logical. In addition, when the manuscript was bound, some fragments were put out of order. The Hengwrt manuscript is missing *The* CANON'S YEOMAN'S TALE completely, as well as the prologue to *The* MERCHANT'S TALE, and the end of *The* PARSON'S TALE. These problems would suggest that Chaucer was not alive, or was incapacitated, when the final manuscript was put together. Thus it makes sense to date the Hengwrt manuscript to about the time of Chaucer's death.

There are additions to the manuscript that were made in the 16th and 17th centuries. It seems to have belonged to one Fouke Dutton, a draper of Chester, by the mid-16th century, and by the 1570s was associated with a family called Banestar, who brought it to Wales. It was acquired by the collector Robert Vaughan of Hengwrt, Meirionnydd, who died in 1667. Vaughan's library was bequeathed to W. W. E. Wynne of Peniarth in 1859, in whose possession it began to be studied by Chaucer scholars. Wynne sold the Vaughan manuscripts to Sir John Williams in 1904, who, in turn, donated them to the newly founded National Library of Wales in 1909, where it has resided ever since.

Bibliography

Ruggiers, Paul G., ed. *The Canterbury Tales: A Facsimile and Transcription of the Hengwrt Manuscript, with Variants from the Ellesmere Manuscript.* Norman: University of Oklahoma Press, 1979.

Stubbs, Estelle, ed. *The Hengwrt Chaucer Digital Facsimile.* Leicester, U.K.: Scholarly Digital Editions, 2000. CD-ROM.

Henry II Plantagenet (1133–1189)

Henry II was one of the most influential monarchs in English history. Renowned as the ruler of the vast Angevin empire that included most of France as well as England, Henry revolutionized the English legal system but became notorious for his role in the murder of Thomas BECKET, his archbishop of Canterbury. With his wife, ELEANOR OF AQUITAINE, Henry was an important patron of the arts. His final years, however, were troubled by wars with his own rebellious sons.

King Henry II of England was born in Le Mans, France, the son of Geoffrey of Anjou and Empress Matilda, daughter of Henry I. During Henry's childhood, Geoffrey was fighting to secure Normandy as a part of his son's heritage at the same time that his mother was fighting a civil war with King Stephen over the English throne. He became duke of Normandy upon the death of his father in 1151 and went to Paris to do homage for his fief to King Louis VII. Louis's queen, Eleanor, fell in love with the young duke. Shortly thereafter her marriage to Louis was annulled, and almost immediately she married Henry, bringing with her the duchy of Aquitaine, which she held in her own right.

In 1153, Henry took a large force to England, where he intended to do battle with Stephen. But Stephen, disillusioned by the death of his own son, Eustace, agreed to the Treaty of Winchester, recognizing Henry as his heir. The following year, upon Stephen's death, Henry became king of England. Within just six weeks, he had pacified the country. He then set about to reform the English legal system, using itinerant justices and other royal officials to control local sheriffs and other courts. He instituted trial by jury in England, and also introduced grand juries to indict those accused of certain types of crimes. These legal reforms are what led to his conflict with his old friend and former chancellor, Thomas Becket, who, as archbishop of Canterbury, opposed legal reforms by which Henry seemed to encroach on the rights of the church. When in frustration Henry wished for someone to rid him of the "meddlesome priest," four of his knights murdered Becket in Canterbury Cathedral on December 29, 1170. That same year, he had crowned his eldest son Henry III in his own lifetime, hoping to avoid any question about succession after his death.

Blamed for Becket's murder, Henry traveled to Ireland the following year and subjugated it to Norman rule, ostensibly to extend the authority of the church but, in fact, to extend his own hegemony. In his absence, however, Queen Eleanor was conspiring with his sons Henry, Geoffrey, and Richard (the future RICHARD I) to usurp his throne, the newly crowned heir finding it difficult to wait to assume real power. Aided by King Louis, the three sons attacked Normandy in 1173. Henry imprisoned Eleanor and put down the rebellion, pardoning his sons. In the meantime, combating the sense that his misfortunes were the "revenge of Becket," Henry decided in July 1174 to do public penance at Becket's tomb, allowing himself to be scourged by an assemblage of bishops, abbots, and monks.

In 1186, the young Henry rebelled again, this time with the encouragement of the new French king, Philip II Augustus, but young Henry died of dysentery, and with him died the rebellion. With the intent of naming his youngest son, John, his new heir, Henry demanded that Richard give over control of Aquitaine, which his mother had ceded to him. Richard, who had been heir apparent after his older brother's death, now in 1188 began his own rebellion, aided by Philip. A very ill Henry was forced to give in to all of their demands, at the same time learning that John had also joined the rebellion. He died in 1189, cared for by his bastard son Geoffrey, the only one who had remained loyal to him.

In addition to his accomplishments of centralizing royal power and reforming the court system, Henry, with his wife Eleanor, was an important patron of literary artists. The *LAIS* of MARIE DE FRANCE are addressed to Henry. The Anglo-Norman poet WACE seems to have written his *Roman de Brut* (1155) for Henry and Eleanor's court, and Henry is known to have also commissioned Wace to write his *Roman de Rou* (1160–74), though he ultimately withdrew the commission. The TROUBADOUR BERNART DE VENTADORN is known to have written verse for Eleanor, and another troubadour, BERTRAN DE BORN, is known to have been involved in the young Henry's rebellion.

Bibliography

Appleby, John Tate. *Henry II: The Vanquished King.* New York: Macmillan, 1962.

Barber, Richard. *Henry Plantagenet: A Biography.* New York: Roy Publishers, 1967.

Gillingham, John. *The Angevin Empire.* 2nd ed. London: Arnold, 2001.

Warren, W. L. *Henry II.* Berkeley: University of California Press, 1973.

Henry of Huntingdon (ca. 1084–1155)

Henry was the archdeacon of Huntingdon who, at the request of Alexander, bishop of Lincoln, composed a history of the English people from early Anglo-Saxon times through the accession of King HENRY II in 1154. His *Historia Anglorum* (*History of the English People*) first ran up to the year 1129, but its popularity was such that Henry revised the text three more times before his death, ending his final version with the end of Stephen's reign in 1154. He seems to have died about 1155, when a new archdeacon was appointed.

Henry was probably born near Ramsey in Huntingdonshire sometime before 1085. His father, Nicholas, was himself archdeacon of Huntingdon. Henry may have been educated in the household of Robert Bloet, bishop of Lincoln from 1093–1123. Upon the death of Nicholas in 1110, Bishop Bloet appointed Henry to his father's post as archdeacon, a fact that suggests Henry was already a priest by this time. It should be noted that clerical celibacy was not enforced in England prior to the early 12th century, so that Henry's inheriting his father's position as archdeacon was not particularly unusual. Henry was apparently married himself, and his son Aristotle also became a cleric. In his *Historia,* Henry derides the English church councils of his time that sought to ban clerical marriage.

It was Bishop Bloet's successor, after 1123, who asked Henry to write his *Historia.* The only other recorded fact of Henry's life concerns his trip to Rome with Archbishop Theobald, undertaken in 1139. Stopping at the Abbey of Bec en route to the papal city, Henry became acquainted with the Norman historian Robert of Torigni, who at the time was in charge of the abbey's large manuscript collection. Robert apparently showed Henry a new Latin history by GEOFFREY OF MONMOUTH, the *HISTORIA REGUM BRITANNIAE* (*History of the Kings of Britain*), with its elaborate treatment of the King ARTHUR legend as "history." In a letter written to a Briton friend named Warinus, Henry summarizes Geoffrey's text, and includes in his summary a number of details about Arthur's last battle that are not in any extant manuscripts of Geoffrey's *Historia.* Henry adds, as well, a note about how the Bretons claim that Arthur is not dead, and are waiting for his return.

In his own *Historia,* Henry relied particularly on BEDE and the *ANGLO-SAXON CHRONICLE* for the earlier sections, and seems also to have been familiar with the work of WILLIAM OF MALMESBURY. Thus Henry's history, up until the year 1126, is of little independent value. However, the material after that date, for the last part of the reign of King Henry I and for all of King Stephen's reign, in Henry's *Historia* is a valuable contemporary account. There are, however, some difficulties with the text. For one thing, Henry had a tendency to change his opinions of people as he wrote subsequent revisions of his text, so that in his earliest characterization of Henry I, for instance, he condemns the king for cruelty, lust, and avarice, but in a later revision, he omits his criticism, except to say that the king needed money in order to govern effectively. Another difficulty is that Henry's often entertaining anecdotes are generally untrustworthy as historical fact, even though many of them are quite memorable, such as the story of how Henry I died when he refused to listen to his doctor's warning against eating lampreys. A third aspect of the *Historia* that might affect its reliability is Henry's tendency to use events as opportunities to moralize, particularly about the downfall of the rich and powerful as examples of the vanity of worldly success.

Henry is the author of a number of other works, including the gloomy and moralistic *Epistola ad Walterum de contemptu mundi* (Letter to Walter on contempt for the world) and eight volumes of epigrams in Latin. But by far his most important work is his English history.

Bibliography

Henry of Huntingdon. *Epistola ad Warinum,* in *Chronicles of the Reigns of Stephen, Henry II, and Richard I,* edited by Richard Howlett. London: Longman, 1885.

———. *Historia Anglorum: The History of the English People.* Edited and translated by Diana Greenway. Oxford: Clarendon Press, 1996.

———. *The History of the English People, 1000–1154.* Translated from the Latin, with an introduction and notes by Diana Greenway. Oxford: Oxford University Press, 2002.

Partner, Nancy F. *Serious Entertainments: The Writing of History in Twelfth-Century England.* Chicago: University of Chicago Press, 1977.

Henryson, Robert (ca. 1425–ca. 1505)

Robert Henryson was the outstanding Scottish poet of the 15th century, and author of one of the finest late medieval narrative tragedies, *The Testament of Cresseid.* For centuries Henryson was classified among a group of poets known as the "Scottish Chaucerians," a group that included King JAMES I, Gavin DOUGLAS, David LINDSAY, and William DUNBAR. That term is no longer used with Henryson, since it implies his poetry is derivative, which it is not, and ignores his originality, which is significant.

For such a well-known poet, Henryson's biography is almost a complete mystery. We know that he was dead by 1508, when Dunbar mourned his death in his elegiac *Lament for the Makars.* He probably was born in the 1420s or early 1430s. He lived in Dunfermline, where he is believed to have been a schoolmaster at the grammar school in the Benedictine abbey in that city. It has also been suggested that he was a notary with some legal training, which would mean that he had studied at one of the Scottish universities (possibly Glasgow) or, as some have proposed, in Italy at Bologna. The only thing that is certain is that he was well read in the church fathers, in BOETHIUS, and in Aristotle, a fact that is evident in his poetry.

Henryson's first major work was *The Morall Fabillis of Esope the Phrygian,* a collection of 13 beast fables in the manner of Aesop, written probably in the 1480s. It is the oldest collection of fables in the Scots language, and is probably based chiefly on a 13th-century collection attributed to a certain Walter the Englishman. In this work, Henryson's morals are far more complex than Aesop's, and encourage his readers to think carefully about the implications of the tales. At the center of the collection is the fable of "The Lion and the Mouse," which Henryson introduces with a DREAM VISION prologue in which Aesop visits the dreamer to discuss the importance of fables. In the tale, the trapped Lion is saved by the Mice who gnaw on the ropes that have snared him. In his moral, Henryson argues that the fables should be interpreted politically, suggesting that the Lion signifies the king, and the Mice the common people, so that the fable indicates the mutual dependence of all segments of society. In the significant fable that follows, called "The Preaching of the Swallow," the birds are all warned by the Swallow that the Fowler is growing flax to snare them, but they ignore the warning and follow their own immediate passions. The citizens of the commonwealth, the fable seems to say, must be prudent. Henryson's *Moral Fables* are based on the common medieval assumption that in the created world in general, and in animals in particular, are lessons for human behavior. In Henryson's case, he is most interested in lessons for the political realm, which in Henryson's Scotland was beginning to disintegrate.

Some of Henryson's other poems include *Orpheus and Eurydice,* a retelling in RHYME ROYAL stanzas of the classical legend, based on Book 3, meter 12 of Boethius's *CONSOLATION OF PHILOSOPHY.* Like the *Fables,* the story ends with a moral, which Henryson sets off by composing it in couplets. He interprets the tale allegorically, equating Orpheus with the intellect and Eurydice with the appetite. Orpheus's journey to hell to rescue Eurydice is an image of the intellect trying to recover the passions enticed by the physical world. Of his 12 other shorter poems, one that stands out is the poem called *The Bludy Serk,* a poem in BALLAD-like stanzas that narrates the story of a knight who is killed while rescuing a maiden from a giant, and who gives the maiden his bloody shirt as a memento. Henryson interprets the story as an ALLEGORY of Christ's sacrifice. Another allegory is *The Garmont of Gud Ladeis,* in which the allegorical garment is constructed of a variety of virtues. Another minor poem, *Robene and Makyne,* is a pastoral poem in eight-line stanzas. But Henryson's most important poem by far is his *Testament of Cresseid,* an alternative ending to Chaucer's *TROILUS AND CRISEYDE.*

Henryson's poetry is fresh, vivid, witty, and sometimes powerful. As an artist, he owes a great deal to Chaucer, but was skilled himself in the use of dramatic irony and in the use of colloquial dialogue to create a sense of immediacy. As a Scotsman in a period of discord between the king and barons, conflict with England, economic and social turbulence, and political uncertainty, Henryson was also particularly interested in morality, politics, and the good society.

Bibliography

Benson, C. David. "O Moral Henryson," in *Fifteenth-Century Studies,* edited by Robert F. Yeager. Hamden, Conn.: Archon, 1985, 215–236.

Fox, Denton, ed. *The Poems of Robert Henryson.* Oxford: Clarendon Press, 1981.

Gray, Douglas. *Robert Henryson.* Leiden: Brill, 1979.

MacQueen, John. *Robert Henryson: A Study of the Major Narrative Poems.* Oxford: Clarendon Press, 1967.

Patterson, Lee. "Christian and Pagan in *The Testament of Cresseid,*" *Philological Quarterly* 52 (October 1973): 696–714.

Powell, Marianne. *"Fabula Docet": Studies in the Background and Interpretation of Henryson's Fables.* Odense, Denmark: Odense University Press, 1982.

Henry the Minstrel (Blind Harry) (ca. 1440–ca. 1492)

Henry the Minstrel was a 15th-century Scottish poet who, sometime between 1460 and 1480, wrote the famous historical poem *Wallace.* An epic in 12 books and nearly 12,000 lines of rhymed couplets, *Wallace* relates the story of William Wallace, Scottish hero of the wars against the English, who was executed by Edward I in 1305.

Little is known about Henry himself, and the information we do have may be largely myth. He may have been born in Lothian; he certainly shows a good deal of knowledge of the geographic details of central Scotland. There are records of payments to Henry for services as a minstrel in the court of King James IV of Scotland between 1473 and 1492. He claims to have based his story of Wallace on a lost work by John Blair, a chaplain who served Wallace. Henry is often known as "Blind Harry," and was reputedly blind from birth. Vivid visual images in his descriptions in the poem, however, make that unlikely. If Henry was indeed blind, he must have been sighted at one time. It is also certainly possible that the myth of his blindness was simply a means of establishing his credentials as Scotland's epic poet, as the Greek Homer was purportedly blind.

The poem is strongly anti-English in its sentiments. The first two books introduce Wallace as the patriotic Scottish hero. Books 3 to 6 recount his several battles with the English and his becoming guardian of Scotland. Ultimately this epic hero of the Scots is betrayed to the English and executed in the final book.

The only extant manuscript of Blind Harry's *Wallace* was produced in 1488 by the scribe John Ramsay, who had also copied the text of that other Scottish national epic, John BARBOUR's *The Bruce.* The *Wallace* manuscript is currently held by the Scottish national library. Henry's poem clearly glorifies Wallace with sometimes exaggerated and sometimes completely fabricated incidents, but remains, essentially, an important source for the story of Wallace's life. Blind Harry's story remained popular for centuries, particularly when it was rewritten and modernized by William Hamilton of Gilbertfield in the 18th century. Robert Burns, William Wordsworth, and others found inspiration in the story of Wallace—as, of course, did the 20th-century filmmaker Mel Gibson, who used Wallace's story for his acclaimed film *Braveheart* (1995).

Bibliography

Goldstein, R. James. *The Matter of Scotland: Historical Narrative in Medieval Scotland.* Lincoln: University of Nebraska Press, 1993.

Henry the Minstrel. *The actis and deidis of the illustere and vailzeand campionn Schir William Wallace, knicht of Ellerslie.* Edited by James Moir. 1889. New York: AMS Press, 1976.

———. *The Wallace: Selections.* Edited by Anne McKim. Kalamazoo, Mich.: Medieval Institute Publications, Western Michigan University, 2003.

Higden, Ranulf (Ralph Hikedon) (ca. 1285–1364)

Ranulf Higden was a Benedictine monk of Saint Werburgh's Abbey in Chester, who wrote several theological texts but is best known for his *Historia polychronica,* or *Polychronicon*—a universal history in Latin prose.

Higden entered the monastery in 1299. During his long tenure at Werburgh's, he wrote *Speculum curatorum* (Mirror of curates) in 1340, a book on Latin grammar (*Paedagogicon grammatices*) and one on theology (*Distinciones theologicae*), and, about 1346, *Ars componendi sermons* (Art of preaching). This last text has gained some scholarly attention recently as a readable and concise manual for medieval preachers, owing much to contemporary rhetorical texts. By 1352, Higden had the position of keeper of the abbey library and head of St. Werburgh's scriptorium. His death is recorded in 1364.

Higden's major literary contribution was his *Polychronicon.* The book is a compendium of the scientific, geographical, and historical knowledge of its time, and aims to be both instructive and entertaining. In its first edition Higden gives a history of the world, with a particular focus on Britain, down through the year 1327. It was written in seven books, the first of which concentrated on geography. The early version was circulated locally. Higden subsequently revised the text to bring the history down to 1352, and this later, longer version of the text gained widespread popularity through the 14th century. There were manuscripts in many religious houses, where the material was regularly updated.

Higden's text was translated into MIDDLE ENGLISH by John TREVISA in 1387. In this form it became even more popular. Trevisa's translation was printed by William CAXTON in 1482, and went through two more printed editions by 1527. Higden's fame as author of the *Polychronicon* led to the attribution of other texts to him that he almost certainly did not write. The best-known example of this is the popular myth that Higden, sometimes known as Ranulf of Chester, was the author of the CHESTER CYCLE of MYSTERY PLAYS. But there is no real evidence of this.

Bibliography

Higden, Ranulf. *Ars componendi sermons.* Translated by Margaret Jennings and Sally A. Wilson, with an introduction and notes by Margaret Jennings. Paris: Peeters, 2003.

———. *Polychronicon Ranulphi Higden monachi Cestrensis: Together with the English translations of John Trevisa and of an unknown writer of the fifteenth century.* Edited by Rev. Joseph Rawson

Lumby. Published by the authority of the Lords commissioners of Her Majesty's Treasury, under the direction of the Master of the rolls. 9 vols. London: Longman and Co., 1865–86.

Jennings, Margaret. *Higden's Minor Writings and the Fourteenth-Century Church.* Leeds, U.K.: Leeds Philosophical and Literary Society, 1977.

Taylor, John. *The "Universal Chronicle" of Ranulf Higden.* Oxford: Clarendon Press, 1966.

Hildegard von Bingen (1098–1179)

Medieval mysticism found one of its earliest and best representatives in Hildegard of Bingen. She was born in 1098, as the 10th child of the nobleman Hildebert of Bermersheim and his wife Mechthild, near Alzey in the vicinity of the Rhine. When she was eight, her parents oblated her to monastic life (i.e., committed her, as a child, to the church), handing her over to the hermit Jutta of Spanheim, who lived next to the Benedictine convent of Disibodenberg. After Jutta's death, Hildegard became the leader (*magistra*) of the women's convent and gained considerable reputation as a prophetess (*"prophetissa teutonica"*), attracting to Disibodenberg many people who sought Hildegard's advice and help. When Hildegard tried to establish her own convent, she experienced severe conflicts with the abbott, who was afraid of losing the financial income resulting from the considerable landholdings of the nuns and from the money donated by the streams of pilgrims who wanted to see Hildegard. After bitter struggles with the abbott, the local authorities, and the Mainz canons, Hildegard moved, with a small group of nuns, to a new location and built the women's convent at Rupertusberg near Bingen in 1147 (destroyed by Swedish forces in 1632). Financially this proved to be highly risky, and the new women's convent gained a solid foundation only when they reached an agreeable settlement with the community of Disibodenberg in 1158.

Hildegard had experienced mystical visions—live experiences with the Godhead—since her early childhood, but she began to write them only in about 1141, when she was 42. She was assisted in her massive enterprise by the monk Volmar of Disibodenberg and the convent sister Richardis of Stade. During a church synod in Trier in 1147–48, Hildegard received official recognition as a mystic by Pope Eugen III, who acknowledged that God had revealed Himself to her. Hildegard particularly enjoyed the support of the famous Cistercian scholar, theologian, and politician BERNARD OF CLAIRVAUX, who also believed in her mystical visions. Despite a series of long illnesses throughout her life, Hildegard became a major public figure and was consulted by people all over Europe for religious, political, and medical advice. Between 1158 and 1161 she went on her first major preaching tour (unheard of for a medieval woman), followed by a second tour in 1160, a third one between 1161 and 1163, and a fourth one between 1170 and 1171. She died on September 17, 1179, when she was 82 years old.

Hildegard went through many political and personal conflicts and fought on many fronts during her life, but this did not diminish the extraordinary admiration she enjoyed as abbess, mystical visionary, political adviser, and medical scholar. Shortly before her death she faced her most serious challenge by the Mainz Cathedral canons because she had allowed a repentant nobleman to be buried in sacred ground next to their convent, whereas the church had excommunicated him before his death and did not recognize his final confession. Mainz then imposed a strict interdict on the convent, which banned the singing of the divine office and receiving of communion, but eventually Hildegard, who had appealed to the Mainz archbishop in 1179, managed to achieve a repeal of this interdict, which restored the regular church service.

Hildegard's followers tried to initiate a canonization process during the 13th century, which received the support of the popes Gregory IX and Innocent IV, but never reached the desired goal. Nevertheless, since the 15th century Hildegard has been venerated locally as a saint.

Hildegard wrote major mystical and medical-scientific texts: *Scivias* (Know your way; 1141–51); *Liber simplicis medicinae* (The book of simple medicine) and *Liber compositae medicinae* (The book of compound medicines; both before 1158); *Liber vitae meritorum* (The book of life's merits;

1158–63); and *Liber divinorum operum* (The book of the divine works; 1163–73/74). She also composed a liturgical play for her nuns, *Ordo virtutum* (The order of virtues), and more than 70 hymns, collected in her *Symphonia armoniae celestium revelationum* (Symphony of the harmony of celestial revelations). Moreover, Hildegard is famous for her nearly 300 finely crafted letters to popes and kings, bishops, and many other dignitaries. Most curiously the abbess developed a secret language for her convent, *Lingua ignota* (ca. 1150; contains approx. 900 words), wrote the *Vita Sancti Disibodi* (1170; Life of Saint Disibodus), the *Vita Sancti Ruperti* (ca. 1173; Life of Saint Rupertus), and some other theological texts.

Hildegard formulates, in her *Scivias,* the most amazing mystical visions of the universe, presenting the image of the universal egg as its center. Here she observes the incarnation of Christ and traces world history in 26 visions, beginning with the fall of Lucifer and taking us up to the Day of Judgment. The first book represents God as the creator, the second Christ as salvation, and the third the Holy Ghost. As the title of this text indicates (Know your ways), Hildegard intended her text as a guidebook for the spiritual seeker, as the evil in this world is caused by an imbalance of the cosmic harmony. Hildegard's almost scientific-mathematical visions explicitly insist on the equality of men and women in God. In her *Liber divinorum operum* the author portrays in ALLEGORY virtues and vices, who discuss with one another the cosmic correlation between man and the Godhead.

In her medical tracts, Hildegard emphasizes, above all, gynecological issues, herbal medicine, and the healing power of the elements; jewels, animals, and metals seen in light of humoral pathology (the medieval theory of the humors); and human sexuality, and advocates a mystical anthropology embedded in medical sciences.

Bibliography

Bowie, Fiona, and Oliver Davies, ed. *Hildegard of Bingen: An Anthology.* With new translations by Robert Carver. London: SPCK, 1990.

Flanagan, Sabina. *Hildegard of Bingen, 1098–1179: A Visionary Life.* London: Routledge, 1989.

Maddocks, Fiona. *Hildegard of Bingen: The Woman of Her Age.* New York: Doubleday, 2001.

Newman, Barbara. *Voice of the Living Light: Hildegard of Bingen and Her World.* Berkeley: University of California Press, 1998.

Albrecht Classen

Hilton, Walter (ca. 1340–1396)

Walter Hilton was an English mystical author best known for his spiritual guidebook *The Scale of Perfection.* Numerous other treatises and letters in Latin as well as MIDDLE ENGLISH have been attributed to Hilton, but aside from the *Scale,* only the *Epistle on the Mixed Life* and the brief tract *Of Angels' Song* are indisputably Hilton's work, and all three of his extant treatises were written between 1380 and 1395.

Not much is known about Hilton's life. He seems to have attended Cambridge, and it is believed that after his graduation he spent some time as a contemplative hermit, since his familiarity with that lifestyle is clearly evident in his writing. He is known to have become an Augustinian canon at the priory of Thurgarten in Nottinghamshire. In addition to his responsibilities as canon, he also seems to have become the spiritual adviser of a number of devout souls, to whom in particular he addresses his spiritual treatises. Hilton died at Thurgarton on March 23, 1396.

Hilton addresses his *Scale of Perfection,* a text that became immensely popular for two centuries, to a "sister," probably a female recluse at the beginning of her contemplative life. But with a potentially wider audience in mind, he warns that the book is intended only for those who have devoted themselves to the contemplative lifestyle. The lengthy treatise is divided into two books. The first, in 93 chapters, deals in part (as the title implies) with a discussion of the ascending stages of contemplation. But the main theme of book 1 is the discussion of man's soul as the image of God, corrupted by sin. Restoring the true image of God in the soul through the obliteration of sin and the meditative union with God is the focus of the book. Book 2, apparently written some time after the first book, consists of 46 additional chapters concerned essentially with more of the same kind of thing, though in somewhat greater detail. Readers have sometimes criticized Hilton for being repetitious, but recent scholars have defended the structure of the *Scale,* relating it to the scholastic method of breaking each question into parts and then dealing with each part in detail (Sargent 1982).

Of Hilton's other compositions, the best known is the *Epistle on the Mixed Life,* a treatise in the form of a letter addressed to a pious nobleman. Hilton advises that the contemplative life is not possible for those involved in the active life of the world, but that the mixed life can be spiritually satisfying (Christ himself led a mixed life) since work should be performed as a duty to God, and works of charity can only be performed in the world. The treatise *Of Angels' Song* is addressed to a "brother" who has reached an advanced stage of contemplation, and focuses on how to distinguish a true mystical experience from a false one. Hilton has occasionally been suggested as the author of the anonymous contemporary meditative text *The* C*LOUD OF* U*NKNOWING,* but most scholars believe that, though Hilton seems to have been familiar with that text, he is probably not the author.

Hilton's style is consistently didactic, but not austere. His tone is friendly, accessible, and humane. This is what makes his *Scale of Perfection* a more comfortable and readable text than some of the other 14th-century mystics, like Richard ROLLE. He advises the contemplative that he or she must be humble, must learn the nature of prayer, and must turn away from transient worldly goods toward God. But he is careful to advise the contemplative not to go to extremes in physical asceticism.

This warm personal approach no doubt contributed to making Hilton's book very popular in its own time and in succeeding centuries, evidenced by the 47 extant manuscripts of the text, and its early printing by Wynkyn de Worde in London in 1494. The recent renewal of interest in late Middle English mystics like Rolle, JULIAN OF NORWICH, and Margery KEMPE has helped make Hilton fashionable once more.

Bibliography

Hilton, Walter. *The Stairway of Perfection.* Edited and modernized by M. L. Del Mastro. Garden City, N.Y.: Doubleday, 1979.

Knowles, David. *The English Mystical Tradition.* London: Burns and Oates, 1961.

Milosh, Joseph E. *The Scale of Perfection and the English Mystical Tradition.* Madison: University of Wisconsin Press, 1966.

Sargent, Michael G. "The Organization of the Scale of Perfection," in *The Medieval Mystical Tradition in England,* edited by Marion Glascoe. Exeter, U.K.: University of Exeter Press, 1982, 231–61.

Historia Regum Britanniae Geoffrey of Monmouth (ca. 1138)

The *Historia Regum Britanniae* (*History of the Kings of Britain*) is a pseudo-history in Latin prose that relates the legends of the pre-Saxon kings of Britain. Written by GEOFFREY OF MONMOUTH in about 1138, the *Historia* is highly significant in the Western literary tradition because it is the text that first introduced King ARTHUR to the mainstream of European literature.

Geoffrey was born in Monmouth in southern Wales in about 1100. He may have been Breton rather than Welsh. In either case he would have been familiar with the legendary Celtic British hero Arthur, renowned for having defeated the Saxons at the Battle of Badon. Three different dedications to the *Historia*—one to Robert, earl of Gloucester, one to King Stephen along with Robert, and one to Count Waleran Beaumont—suggest Geoffrey's attempts to gain favor with the king and his supporters for purposes of preferment: Robert had first supported Stephen for the crown, then shifted allegiance to his half-sister, Matilda, who invaded England in 1139, and precipitated a civil war. Waleran was one of Stephen's loyal supporters. Geoffrey's shifting dedications suggest the shifting alliances of those troubled times. Ultimately, Geoffrey's efforts paid off when he was named bishop of St. Asaph in 1151.

But in the *Historia,* Geoffrey had produced a work of tremendous appeal. Some 200 Latin manuscripts of the *Historia* are still extant, attesting to the popularity of the text in the late Middle Ages. Geoffrey clearly was familiar with GILDAS and BEDE, whom he mentions in his introduction. He also drew material from NENNIUS, particularly in his descriptions of some of Arthur's battles and of some of the "marvels" of Britain. But he says in his dedication that Walter, archdeacon of Oxford, had given him a "certain most ancient book in the British language" that told the history of all the British kings. The consensus among modern scholars is that such a book never existed, that Geoffrey drew most of his material from legend and some from his own vivid imagination. The citation of that "ancient book" is likely the result of medieval writers' tendency to cite authorities to lend credibility to their work. Most readers saw Geoffrey's *Historia* as factual history even through the Renaissance, during which it provided source material for playwrights, such as Shakespeare, looking for familiar historical incidents to dramatize. Most modern readers, however, have no difficulty reading the *Historia* as fiction.

The *Historia* begins with the life of Brutus, great-grandson of the Trojan Aeneas. Exiled from Italy for accidentally killing his father, Brutus becomes leader of a group of Trojan captives in Greece. He leads them out of captivity, eventually to settle on the island of Albion, which is renamed Britain after him. Thus for hundreds of years, through their mythical founder Brutus, the British people traced their lineage to the Roman nation founded by Aeneas, and, ultimately, back to Troy itself.

The Brutus story is followed by brief histories of a series of kings without much to distinguish them, until the detailed and romantic story of King Lear and Cordelia. Another series of kings follows (containing the story of Gorboduc). The next major story concerns Belinus and Brennius, two brothers who contend for the British throne, are eventually reconciled, and end by conquering Gaul and ultimately capturing Rome itself.

After another series of kings, Geoffrey deals with the invasion of Britain by Julius Caesar and the exploits of later Romans, and includes the story of Cymbeline. Book 5 of the text provides another long series of kings, culminating in Constantine, who becomes emperor of Rome.

The longest, most detailed, and most important part of the *Historia* occurs in books 6 to 11. The story here begins with Vortigern, who usurps the British throne from its rightful heir, Aurelius Ambrosius. Vortigern foolishly invites Saxons into Britain as mercenaries, but they slaughter the British nobility at a conference and desolate the country. Vortigern flees and is ultimately overthrown by Aurelius Ambrosius and his brother Uther Pendragon. Aurelius is able to stop the Saxons but is killed, and Uther becomes king. With the aid of the seer and sorcerer Merlin, Uther begets Arthur.

When Arthur becomes king at the age of 15, he defeats the Saxons and then subdues the Picts and Scots. He invades Ireland and conquers it as well as Iceland. He becomes a great emperor, defeating Norway and Denmark and then all of Gaul. Required by a Roman emissary to pay tribute to Rome, Arthur rejects the demand and invades the Roman Empire. He defeats the Roman Lucius and is poised to take Rome itself when he receives word that his kingdom has been usurped in his absence by his nephew Mordred, who has allied himself with the Saxons and has also betrayed him with his wife, Guenevere.

Arthur has no choice but to return to Britain and fight the usurper. He defeats Mordred at the River Camel but is mortally wounded. He is carried off from the battle to the Isle of Avalon, where his wounds will be "attended to." With such an end, Geoffrey gives some credence to the "Breton hope"—the legendary belief among the Welsh and Bretons that Arthur was not dead but would come again.

Geoffrey's book ends anticlimactically with the pathetic history of the last British king, Cadwallader, the ultimate collapse of the British monarchy, and the victory of the Saxons.

The climactic story of Arthur was what made the *Historia* popular, and it must be acknowledged that Arthur became popular through the *Historia*. In Geoffrey, Arthur is an epic hero who falls through the turning of Fortune's Wheel. He is also a messianic hero as he had been to the British people for hundreds of years. The chief outline of Arthur's career—his "miraculous" birth, his achievement of the crown, his creation of a world-renowned kingdom, his betrayal by his wife and nephew, his wounding and admittance to Avalon—all is created by Geoffrey's story. In Geoffrey's text, Arthur wields a sword called Caliburn, holds court in the city of Caerleon, is associated with the magic of Merlin, and has a heroic and rash nephew named GAWAIN. All of these details form a backdrop for the later ROMANCE writers like CHRÉTIEN DE TROYES and MARIE DE FRANCE to fill in with details of Arthur's knights and further adventures. But the outline of the whole history of Arthur remains essentially the same even through Thomas MALORY's great compendium of Arthurian tradition at the end of the 15th century.

Bibliography

Geoffrey of Monmouth. *The Historia Regum Britanniae of Geoffrey of Monmouth.* Edited by Neil Wright. Cambridge: Brewer, 1985.

Tatlock, J. S. P. *The Legendary History of Britain.* Berkeley: University of California Press, 1950.

Thorpe, Lewis, trans. *The History of the Kings of Britain.* London: Penguin, 1966.

Hoccleve, Thomas (Occleve) (ca. 1368–ca. 1426)

A poet and disciple of CHAUCER, Thomas Hoccleve is best known as the author of the *Regement of Princes* (ca. 1409–12), a book of advice for Prince Hal, the future King Henry V of England. Recently, critics have been interested in Hoccleve's candid discussion of his mental breakdown of 1417, the only such discourse in MIDDLE ENGLISH.

Perhaps Hoccleve received his name from Hockliffe, a village in Bedfordshire where he may have been born around 1368. He seems to have received a good education, and he says in one poem that he sought to become a priest, but being unable to receive a benefice, he opted to marry in about 1411. In another poem he speaks of leading a dissolute life as a youth, drinking, gambling, and chasing women—a situation that seems to have turned around with his marriage. Whether these things are true or simply a part of Hoccleve's poetic persona is impossible to determine. We do know that at about the age of 19, Hoccleve became a clerk in the Office of the Privy Seal, and that he continued in that office for some 35 years. In 1399, Hoccleve was granted an annuity of 10 pounds per year for life, a grant that was increased to 20 marks (something over 13 pounds) in May of 1409. Despite this income Hoccleve complains in a number of poems about his difficult financial situation. Still records show that he was paid regularly on a semiannual basis. He was also, at this point, at the height of his literary career, beginning his composition of the *Regiment of Princes.*

Sometime around 1417, Hoccleve suffered an emotional disorder, which he says made him lose the substance of his memory. He never says how long his illness lasted, but in his *Complaint* (1422), he describes his efforts to readjust to normal life, and tells of the actions of his friends, at the Privy Seal and elsewhere, who mistrust his recovery and try to avoid him. The last official references to Hoccleve in government documents come in 1426, and it is likely that he died shortly after that.

Hoccleve's earliest poem, *The Letter of Cupid* (1402), is based on a French poem by CHRISTINE DE PIZAN called *Epistre au Dieu d'Amours.* Other minor poems include a controversial *Address to Oldcastle* (1415)—a poem supporting orthodoxy against the LOLLARD heresy addressed to the famous Lollard knight (and eventually martyr) Sir John Oldcastle; an admired poem in praise of the virgin entitled *The Mother of God;* and a number of "begging" poems, like *The Balade to King Henry V for Money,* bewailing his financial straits.

Hoccleve's major works begin with *La Male Règle* (1406), a didactic poem in which he describes his misspent youth. The *Regement of Princes* (1409–13) follows, describing do's and don'ts for rulers and addressed to Prince Henry. Then, after his mental illness, appears a group known as the "Series" poems (1422): These include the aforementioned *Complaint* as well as the *Dialogue with a Friend, Jereslaus Wife, Learn to Die,* and *The Tale of Jonathas.* These five poems are linked by dialogues between a speaker and a friend who gives literary advice.

For many readers Hoccleve is most important as a follower of Chaucer. Indeed, the best-known passages of the *Regement of Princes* are Hoccleve's lament for Chaucer's death and praise of Chaucer as his "maister." Particularly important is the portrait of Chaucer that appears in the British Museum Harley manuscript of the poem, which Hoccleve says he has included so that people will not forget what his master looked like. The Hoccleve portrait seems to have been the model for all subsequent portraits of Chaucer that have come down to us. Whether Hoccleve actually knew Chaucer or simply revered him as his greatest poetic predecessor is a matter of some debate. However, Hoccleve clearly uses Chaucer as the model for his verse. Most of his poetry, including the *Regement,* is in Chaucerian RHYME ROYAL stanzas. His first major work, *La Male Règle,* is in eight-line stanzas rhyming *ababbcbc*—a stanza form Chaucer invented for *The MONK'S TALE.* Hoccleve alludes to *The LEGEND OF GOOD WOMEN* in *The Letter of Cupid* and to *The WIFE OF BATH'S TALE* in his *Dialogue with a Friend.*

Hoccleve's poetry is generally regarded as conventional and uninspired. It is, however, quite representative of its time, and Hoccleve is important as a link between Chaucer and his Tudor successors such as Skelton. But for readers the most interesting aspects of Hoccleve's poetry are his autobiographical passages, with his frank discussions of his youthful transgressions and his ill health, which make him an individual in the readers' eyes.

Bibliography

Blyth, Charles R., ed. *Thomas Hoccleve: The Regiment of Princes.* Kalamazoo: Western Michigan University for TEAMS, 1999.

Knapp, Ethan. *The Bureaucratic Muse: Thomas Hoccleve and the Literature of Late Medieval England.* University Park: Pennsylvania State University Press, 2001.

Mitchell, Jerome. *Thomas Hoccleve: A Study in Early Fifteenth-Century English Poetic.* Urbana: University of Illinois Press, 1968.

Holy Grail

The concept of the Holy Grail is intimately associated with the world of courtly culture, chivalry, and Christianity. While it may have its origins in Celtic mythology, the earliest references to the Grail can be found in medieval Latin sometime around 718 when the Grail was described as a kind of serving dish. The word appears in medieval courtly literature first in the decasyllabic (10-syllable lines) *Roman d'Alexandre* (1165–70) and in CHRÉTIEN DE TROYES's *PERCEVAL,* or the *Conte du Graal* (The story of the Grail, ca. 1180). Here the young hero, Perceval, appears in the castle of his uncle, the wounded Fisher King, but he does not understand the situation there and does not ask his uncle, whom he does not even recognize as a relative, about his ailments or about who is served with the Grail, because of instructions about proper behavior at court that he had received prior to this encounter. Because Perceval fails to ask the crucial question, both the Grail and the entire company of Grail knights has disappeared the next morning. This failure forces Perceval to embark on a long and arduous quest for the true meaning of the Grail and of life. After a long quest, Perceval meets a hermit (another relative) who explains the Grail to him as the cup from which Christ drank at the Last Supper—apparently by this point he has acquired sufficient maturity and ethical understanding to receive this knowledge. But Chrétien's text is incomplete. Perhaps it would have ended with Perceval assuming the throne of the Grail, as occurs in the third "continuation" of Chrétien's text.

After Chrétien, many reworkings of the Grail account appeared in the courts of both France and of Germany. Almost the same sequence of events as in Chrétien's *Perceval* occur in WOLFRAM VON ESCENBACH's *PARZIVAL* (ca. 1205), although here the criticism raised against Parzival has more to do with the social decline in communication, courtly mores, and the social contact among people. The quest for the Grail thus represents a quest for the healing of the rift between the misery of social reality and the ideals of knighthood. In France, ROBERT DE BORON (fl. 1180s–1190s) fully developed the Grail myth in his *Joseph d'Arimathie,* or *Roman de l'estoire dou Graal,* connecting it for the first time with Avalon at Glastonbury Abbey in Somerset, where a grave marked as King Arthur's was purportedly discovered around 1190. The Grail, often in conjunction with a bleeding lance identified as the spear of Longinus, thus became an icon of medieval utopia, intimately connected with Christ's passion and the notion of salvation from human suffering. The association of the Grail with the Last Supper is quite obvious, as is the association of the religious component with the secular aspect of medieval knighthood.

In Robert's text, the Grail, as a holy object, is the center piece of the Grail community established by Joseph of Arimathie and continued by a series of ideal knights. The Grail provides happiness for those who behold it and inspires them to accept the task of spreading Christianity in the world. Many other subsequent writers incorporated the Grail motif in their works, such as the authors of the *Didot-Perceval* (ca. 1195–1215), the First and the Second Continuator of Chrétien's *Conte du Graal,* the authors of the VULGATE CYCLE, the prose *Perlesvaus* (ca. 1191–1212), the prose Welsh *PEREDUR,* the Old French prose *Queste del Saint Graal* (ca. 1215–30) with GALAHAD as its protagonist—which was later translated into Middle High German as the *Prosa-Lancelot*—then Heinrich von dem Türlin with his Middle High German composition in verse, *Diu Crône* (ca. 1220–40), and Claus Wisse and Philipp Colin with their *Nüwe Parzefal* (1331–36). One of the most ambitious Grail romances might have been Albrecht's *Jüngere Titurel* (ca. 1250–70), consisting of 6,207 stanzas.

Irrespective of its actual shape and form, either as an object or as an idea, the Grail symbolized the highest goal of late-medieval knighthood and represented the perfect union of the secular with the spiritual. Some historians have argued that the chalice today preserved in the cathedral of Valencia, Spain, which originated from Mont Salvador (1076–1399), might represent the original object venerated by medieval knighthood. More important, though, the *Queste del Saint Graal* and other versions of the Grail myth represent the attempt by representatives of the Cistercian order to integrate worldly knighthood into a religious quest for God and the defeat of evil.

Bibliography

Barber, Richard. *The Holy Grail: Imagination and Belief.* Cambridge, Mass.: Harvard University Press, 2004.

Groos, Arthur, and Norris J. Lacy, eds. and introduction. *Perceval/Parzival: A Casebook.* Arthurian Characters and Themes. New York: Routledge, 2002.

Lacy, Norris J. "The Evolution and Legacy of French Prose Romance." In *The Cambridge Companion to Medieval Romance,* edited by Roberta L. Krueger, 167–182. Cambridge: Cambridge University Press, 2000.

Owen, D. D. R. "From Grail to Holy Grail," *Romania* 89 (1968): 31–53.

Albrecht Classen

Horn Childe (ca. 1300)

The Northern MIDDLE ENGLISH verse ROMANCE *Horn Childe* is a poem of 1,136 lines written in TAIL-RHYME stanzas sometime between about 1290 and 1340. The story of *Horn Childe* is essentially the same as that of the better-known romance *King Horn,* though most readers consider *King Horn* the more successful work. *Horn Childe,* however, is notable because it is a poem that was probably known, and parodied, by Geoffrey CHAUCER.

The protagonist of the poem is a prince named Horn, son of King Hatheolf, who rules northern England. Hatheolf is killed by invading Irish marauders led by Malkan, but Horn is able to escape through the help of his faithful mentor Arlaund. Arlaund manages to bring Horn to southern England and places him in the care of the king, Houlac. But when Houlac's daughter, Rimnild, falls in love with him, Horn is denounced before the king by his envious companions, Wikard and Wikel. The king, angered at the seduction of his daughter, beats the princess, but Rimnild convinces Horn to flee for his life to Wales, giving him a magic ring as a token of her love and vowing to wait seven years for his return.

In Wales, Horn adopts the name "Godebounde," and enters the service of the Welsh king, Snowdon. From Wales he crosses the sea to Ireland and serves Finlak of Youghal, the Irish king. In the service of Finlak, Horn does battle with his father's murderer, Malkan, who is also Finlak's enemy. Horn is able to kill Malkan and thereby avenge his father's death. But he leaves Ireland after Finlak's daughter falls in love with him. Horn returns to Houlac's kingdom, where Rimnild is about to be given in marriage to Moging. Horn, wearing a beggar's disguise, attends the wedding banquet. He makes himself known to Rimnild by placing her ring in a cup she serves him. The poem ends as Horn defeats the groom Moging in a wedding tournament. He then kills the traitor Wikard and blinds Wikel. He finally marries Rimnild and returns to the north to claim his own kingdom.

In his *TALE OF SIR THOPAS,* Chaucer composes a rollicking parody of tail-rhyme romances, and specifically compares Sir Thopas to great heroes like King Horn. It seems likely that Chaucer was thinking of *Horn Childe,* a romance that uses the tail-rhyme stanza itself, when he made the allusion. The famous Auchinleck manuscript, which contains *Horn Childe,* was produced in London in the 1330s and has been thought by some scholars to have been known by Chaucer himself.

Bibliography

Horn Childe and Maiden Rimnild. Edited from the Auchinleck MS, National Library of Scotland, Advocates' MS 19.2.1 by Maldwyn Mills. Heidelberg, Germany: C. Winter Universitätsverlag, 1988.

House of Fame, The Geoffrey Chaucer (ca. 1379)

A DREAM VISION by CHAUCER, *The House of Fame* is a poem of three books in octosyllabic couplets. Most scholars believe that it was written after *The BOOK OF THE DUCHESS* but before *The PARLIAMENT OF FOWLS.* The verse form and focus on love put the poem, like *The Book of the Duchess,* in the tradition of French love visions that begins with the *ROMAN DE LA ROSE.* Like the *Parliament,* though, *The House of Fame* shows the strong influence of the major Italian writers, particularly DANTE, but also, to a lesser extent, BOCCACCIO. In book 2 of the poem, Chaucer refers to his work as customs officer, which indicates that the poem must have been written after his appointment to that post in 1374. But the influence of BOETHIUS in book 3 of *The House of Fame* suggests a date of 1378–80, when Chaucer was likely working on his translation of *The CONSOLATION OF PHILOSOPHY.* Thus a date around 1379 seems most likely for the poem.

Like Dante in the *DIVINE COMEDY,* Chaucer divides his poem into three parts. The poem begins with allusions to Virgil, describes a fabulous journey, and utilizes a guide ordained by heaven. But Chaucer's comic tone contrasts with Dante's high seriousness, even to the point of including mock-heroic invocations to the gods and the muses.

Like Chaucer's other dream visions, *The House of Fame* begins with allusions to classical literature, but instead of reading a text that puts him to sleep (as he does in the *Book of the Duchess* and *The Parliament of Fowls*), this time the Dreamer sees the text of Virgil's *Aeneid* reenacted within his dream, as paintings on the wall of a temple in which his dream begins. It is the story of Aeneas's desertion of Dido, presented as an illustration of a false lover. After viewing the frescoes, the Dreamer leaves the temple to find himself standing in a desert wasteland, wondering what to do next, when suddenly a huge golden eagle swoops down and snatches him up, carrying him into the heavens. The desert may suggest the wasteland in which Dante finds himself at the beginning of the *Comedy,* while the eagle almost certainly is drawn from canto 9 of the *Purgatorio,* where an eagle carries Dante to the first ledge on the mountain of Purgatory.

Book 2 of *The House of Fame* is justly the most admired and popular part of the poem. Certainly it is the most humorous. The Eagle, we learn, has been sent from Jupiter, who has taken pity on the Dreamer's long and fruitless service of Cupid and Venus. The bird has been sent as a guide to teach the Dreamer about love, and he is to bring the Dreamer to the House of Fame, where he will hear tidings of love, both true and false. The humor in the vision lies partly in the Eagle, who comes across as a pedantic and irrelevant lecturer, and partly in the characterization of the Dreamer: The Eagle calls him "Geffrey," and paints a picture of him as a bureaucrat buried in his books at the office, and at home holed up in his study writing, a hermit with no sense of what goes on out in the world. It is an amusing self-caricature, and the most detailed autobiographical passage in Chaucer's poetry.

In book 3, the Eagle deposits Geffrey at the castle of Fame. He finds great classical poets as well as popular entertainers at the castle. Suddenly a great crowd bursts in, and much of the third book is taken up by seven groups of petitioners who approach the throne of the goddess Fame to make requests. The goddess grants or denies their requests for no apparent reason, demonstrating, apparently, how completely random is her distribution of respectable or dishonorable reputations—as such, she is reminiscent of the fickle goddess Fortune in Boethius, and indeed, in that work, fame is one of the areas within the control of Fortune.

Ultimately a stranger approaches Geffrey to ask him if he has come seeking fame himself. When Geffrey denies the suggestion, the stranger leads him into another house, the house of Rumor, telling him he will hear what he desires here. From this spinning house, truth and falsehood are emitted, all mingled together. Geffrey is told that a man "of gret auctoritee" is about to make an announcement. At this point, the poem breaks off.

Just what this announcement would have been has been the object of a good deal of conjecture by critics, in particular those trying to date the poem by internal evidence. Some have held that the announcement pertained to the marriage of King RICHARD II to ANNE OF BOHEMIA. Others have proposed it may have been intended as a greeting for Queen Anne when she arrived in England. Still others have suggested it concerned the pending betrothal of John of Gaunt's daughter Philippa. All of these might be appropriate if the date of the poem were 1379. Some who believe the poem is earlier have suggested the announcement may concern Richard's anticipated engagement in 1377 to Marie, the young princess of France. Twice the poem specifies the date of December 10, but no one has satisfactorily explained the significance of this date. If the poem was intended to commemorate some important occasion, there is no consensus as to what that occasion was.

Nor is it clear whether the ending of the poem has been lost or the poem was simply left unfinished. Since only three manuscripts of the poem are extant, it seems unlikely the poem was well known in its own time (although Thomas USK may allude to it in his *Testament of Love*). It may be that whatever anticipated event was to be announced by the man of "great authority" never occurred.

Beyond the occasion for the poem, it has been suggested that Chaucer may be facing in *The House of Fame* a turning point in his own development as a poet. Certainly after this poem he turned to Italian influences in his poetry far more than French. Perhaps, for himself, he saw that as the route to lasting fame.

Bibliography

Amtower, Laurel. "Authorizing the Reader in Chaucer's *House of Fame*," *Philological Quarterly* 79 (2000): 273–291.

Bennett, J. A. W. *Chaucer's Book of Fame*. Oxford: Clarendon Press, 1968.

Boitani, Piero. *Chaucer and the Imaginary World of Fame*. Cambridge: D. S. Brewer, 1984.

Delany, Sheila. *Chaucer's House of Fame: The Poetics of Skeptical Fideism*. Chicago: University of Chicago Press, 1972.

Hrafnkel's Saga (late 13th century)

The Saga of Hrafnkel, the priest of Frey, is one of the best known of the Old Icelandic family sagas dealing, as most such sagas, with a feud. *Hrafnkel's Saga* is unusual in its directness and its simple, straightforward structure that focuses directly on the feud and eliminates all matters extraneous to it, thus emphasizing the tragic inevitability of its conclusion. Set in eastern Iceland during the first half of the 10th century, the saga was probably written late in the 13th century, though some have suggested it may be more recent, since the earliest surviving manuscript fragment of the saga dates from about 1500.

Since the plot of *Hrafnkel's Saga* revolves around a lawsuit, an understanding of the Icelandic General Assembly, the Althing, is necessary background for the story. In the 10th century, the Althing met annually to make laws and to judge suits in an open-air legislature. Each of Iceland's four administrative quarters had its own court at the Althing, and each quarter was represented by at least nine *godi,* who were both chiefs and priests, and appointed the judges for their own quarters. All men of standing put themselves under the protection of the *godi* of their district, and according to law could be sued only in the court of their *godi's* district. If for some unforeseen reason a man wanted to sue his own *godi,* his only hope would be to find another *godi* to whom he could shift his loyalty, if that *godi* would accept him.

The saga tells of Hrafnkel, a *godi* with a rich farm called Adalbol. His most prized possession is his horse Freyfaxi. Hrafnkel vows that he will kill anyone who rides Freyfaxi. He hires a shepherd named Einar who, though warned not to touch the horse, rides him one day when some sheep have escaped. Hrafnkel, bound by his oath, calmly kills Einar with an axe. When Einar's father, Thorbjorn, asks Hrafnkel for compensation, Hrafnkel refuses but makes a counter offer which Thorbjorn rejects. Hrafnkel also refuses to meet the father in court since that would imply they were equals.

Thorbjorn turns to his nephew Sam, a skilled lawyer, for help against Hrafnkel. Since Hrafnkel is their own *godi,* Sam and Thorbjorn search for another *godi* who will give them protection and support their suit at the Althing. This proves nearly impossible, for since Hrafnkel is such a formidable foe no other *godi* is willing to offend him. At last they succeed in convincing the *godi* Thorgeir to help them, and through his power and influence they manage to get Hrafnkel convicted at the Althing and sentenced to outlawry.

With the help of Thorgeir and his followers, Sam surprises Hrafnkel at Adalbol and conducts a legal confiscation of his property while Hrafnkel is bound and tortured. Ignoring Thorgeir's advice to kill Hrafnkel, Sam allows him to live when he agrees to turn over his farm and position of *godi* to Sam. Hrafnkel and his family are then summarily turned out of their home.

But Sam has not seen the last of Hrafnkel. He and his family move to the region called Lagarvatn, where he buys a rundown farm on credit. Through hard work and persistence, Hrafnkel builds up the farm and becomes wealthy again. He also obtains the sworn loyalty of all those who move into the area, and becomes *godi* there. Some time later Sam's brother Eyvin is killed by Hrafnkel when he passes close to his farm. Before Sam can gather forces to avenge the matter, Hrafnkel descends on Adalbol with 70 men, captures Sam, and gives him the same choice Sam had given him earlier. Sam moves back to his old farm, and though he tries to mount support to avenge himself on Hrafnkel again, he is unable to do so.

Scholars have been interested in a number of themes suggested by the saga. One, of course, is the danger of pride—something that leads to the fall of both Hrafnkel and Sam. The political implications of the story are also important: Are powerful nobles to be considered above the law? Can justice only be achieved through the use of force? Another question scholars have been concerned about is the historical accuracy of the saga. While Hrafnkel and his family are mentioned in the *Landnámabók* (*Book of Settlements*), a number of other characters seem to be fictitious. The story is thus generally regarded as historical fiction, based on some independent strands of oral historical tradition. However, its traditional objective but dramatic style coupled with its simple structure and brisk narrative pace make it a good introduction to saga literature.

Bibliography

Jones, Gwyn, trans. *Eirik the Red and Other Icelandic Sagas.* Oxford: Oxford University Press, 1999.

Palsson, Hermann. *Art and Ethics in Hrafnkel's Saga.* Copenhagen: Munksgaard, 1971.

———, trans. *Hrafnkel's Saga and Other Icelandic Stories.* Harmondsworth, U.K.: Penguin, 1971.

The Sagas of Icelanders: A Selection. Preface by Jane Smiley; introduction by Robert Kellogg. New York: Viking, 2000.

Hrotsvit of Gandersheim (Hroswitha) (ca. 935–after 972)

In 1494 the German humanist and crowned poet laureate Conrad Celtis, while teaching and researching in Regensburg, discovered a medieval manuscript in the convent library of the St. Emmeran monastery (today Bayerische Staatsbibliothek München, Clm 14485 1–150), which contained the works of the 10th-century Gandersheim nun Hrotsvit. He immediately hailed her as a literary wonder who proved to him and his contemporaries that Germany also had had a glorious, intellectually highly developed past that could even compete with classical Roman literature. Hrotsvit has enjoyed superior respect for her Latin dramas, religious tales, and historiographical poems ever since because she appears to have been the first and only Saxon (or generally, German) woman playwright in the early Middle Ages who endeavored to try her hand at such a sophisticated literary genre. Hrotsvit's oeuvre (the complete body of her texts) was printed in Nuremberg in 1501, accompanied by six woodcuts for the dramas: two by Albrecht Dürer and four by Wolfgang Traut. Additional manuscripts containing Hrotsvit's works were not found until the 20th century.

Although we have no biographical material about the poet, references in the texts—especially the *Primordia coenobii Gandeshemensis*—and circumstantial evidence allow us to draw a fairly clear picture of Hrotsvit's life. She was the daughter of a high-ranking Saxon noble family and joined the Benedictine convent of Gandersheim as a canoness under the rule of the abbess Gerberga II (born ca. 940). Her *Primordia* Hrotsvit also states that she was born long after the death of Emperor Otto II (Nov. 30, 912). She was obviously proud of her literary achievements, since she explains her own name in the introduction to her dramas as "*Clamor Validus Gandeshemensis.*" As Jacob Grimm observed (*Lateinische Gedichte*, 1898, 9), her Old Saxon name derived from two compounds, *hruot*, meaning "voice" (in Latin: *clamor*), and *suid*, meaning "strong" (in Latin: *validus*). Katharina Wilson offers the following explanation: "Seen as allegorization of her name, 'Clamor Validus' could be best rendered as 'Forceful Testimony' (that is, for God), or 'Vigorous (valid) Attestation' (that is of Christian truth)" (1998, 4).

The convent of Gandersheim, founded in 852 in northern Germany near the Harz mountains by Count Liudolf and his wife, Oda, admitted only daughters of noble families and educated them in the classical arts, music, theology, and probably also some philosophy. Although Emperor Otto I had freed the convent from royal rule and allowed the abbess to administer every aspect of her convent all on her own, he and his own family maintained close ties with Gandersheim. The convent soon grew into a major center of intellectual and spiritual education. Hrotsvit demonstrates with her large oeuvre that 10th-century convent women were fully capable of making their own voices heard and could participate in the literary activities of their time. She seems to have begun writing already during her school years, a regular aspect of medieval educational principles, but those texts have not come down to us.

Hrotsvit composed eight religious tales (legends), first on the Virgin Mary, then on the Saints Ascensio, Gongolfus, Pelagius, Theophilus, Basilius, Dionysius, and Agnes. Subsequently she wrote seven religious dramas: *Gallicanus* (I and II), *Dulcitius, Calimachus, Abraham, Pafnutius,* and *Sapientia.* Finally, she created two historical verse epics, the *Gesta Ottonis* (Deeds of Otto) and *Primordia coneobii Gandeshemensis* (The origins of the Gandersheim abbey). Not surprising for a convent woman, Hrotsvit repeatedly glorified the life and suffering of martyred virgins who lived and died in the time of the late Roman Empire and of the early Middle Ages as witnesses of the power of Christ. Although her heroines often reflect women's physical weakness, their oaths to keep their virginity, the hope to join the chorus of divine virgins in the afterlife, and their hope that Christ would welcome them as his heavenly brides signal these women's courage and spiritual dedication. Surprisingly, many of Hrotsvit's texts are characterized by a quite earthy humor and prove to be considerably entertaining even for modern tastes. For her religious tales and the historical poems Hrotsvit heavily drew from the Roman poets PRUDENTIUS (348–405 C.E.) and Virgil (70–19 B.C.E.), among many other late antique and early medieval writers. Most important, however, proved to be the dramatist Terence (195–159 B.C.E.), whose comedies seem to have exerted a considerable influence on the early-medieval convent schools. But Hrotsvit rejected his secular outlook with its often highly erotic allusions, and decided to create her own dramas to replace Terence in the reading (or performance) canon within her convent. In the preface to her dramas, Hrotsvit states that many nuns "frequently read Terence's fiction,/and as they delight in the sweetness of his style and diction,/they are stained by learning of wicked things in his depiction." Her own religious dramas served as powerful substitutes with which she hoped to convert her audiences back to virtuousness and Christian piety: "Therefore I, the Strong Voice of Gandersheim, have not refused to imitate him in writing/whom others laud in reading,/so that in that selfsame form of composition in which the shameless acts of lascivious women were phrased/the laudable chastity of sacred virgins be praised within the limits of my little talent." Although Hrotsvit tends to utilize humility topoi (standard phrases) about her unworthiness (see the preface to the religious legends), she emerges not only as a most powerful Latin author, but also as a highly self-conscious personality fully aware of her abilities to write in various learned genres.

Bibliography

Brown, Phyllis Rugg, Katharina M. Wilson, and Linda A. McMillin. *Hrotsvit of Gandersheim: Contexts, Identities, Affinities, and Performances.* Toronto: Toronto University Press, 2004.

Hrotsvithae Opera. Edited by H. Homeyer. Munich: Ferdinand Schöningh, 1970.

Hrotsvit of Gandersheim: A Florilegium of Her Works. Translated with Introduction by Katharina M. Wilson. Cambridge: D. S. Brewer, 1998.

Wilson, Katharina M., ed. *Hrotsvit of Gandersheim: "Rara Avis in Saxonia"?* Ann Arbor, Mich.: Medieval and Renaissance Collegium, 1987.

Albrecht Classen

Hus, Jan (John Huss) (ca. 1373–1415)

Jan Hus was a Czech religious reformer who challenged abuses in the church and supported the growing Czech nationalist movement in the early 15th century. Hus was accused of heresy because of his criticism of the papacy and the church, and was burned at the stake at the Council of Constance. But Hus's followers ultimately became the Moravian Church, and in his beliefs he was a forerunner of the Protestant Reformation.

Hus was born at Husinec in southern Bohemia (now the Czech Republic) in about 1373. In 1390, he enrolled in the faculty of arts at the University of Prague (now Charles University), receiving his master's degree in 1396 and subsequently lecturing there on philosophy, becoming dean of the arts faculty in 1401. That same year, in addition to his university duties, he was ordained a priest and began his ministry preaching fiery sermons (calling for church reform) in the Czech language at Bethlehem Chapel in Prague. His conducting services in Czech rather than the customary Latin contributed significantly to the movement for Czech nationalism, and he attracted a large number of followers.

Hus came to prominence during a period of severe disorganization in the church hierarchy. After a disputed election in 1378, two rival popes vied for power, one in Rome and the other in Avignon—a situation known as the Great Schism. After an attempt to rectify the problem through an election by an international church council at Pisa in 1409, a third pope was named, but neither of the other two would accept his claim to the papacy. In questioning papal authority, Hus was giving voice to the doubts and frustrations of much of Europe. In condemning the practices of bishops, Hus was striking a blow as well for Czech nationalism, since many Bohemian bishops were appointees from Germany, and had little regard for their Czech parishioners.

Hus was also influenced to some extent by the writings of the English reformer John WYCLIFFE, who had died in 1384. Through the marriage of ANNE OF BOHEMIA to the English king RICHARD II, an alliance and easy correspondence had arisen between the two countries, and Hus's closest disciple, Jerome of Prague, had spent some time in London in the 1390s and had brought back to Prague several manuscripts of Wycliffe's writings. Hus was less radical than Wycliffe, but agreed with the English reformer in his attacks on some of the worst abuses of the church: Priests, Hus said, must be held to a higher level of morality, and avoid drunkenness as well as sexual and financial abuses. Preaching and Bible lessons should be conducted in the language of the people, as Hus was doing at Bethlehem Chapel. All Christians should receive full communion in the Mass (at this time, only the priests were allowed to receive the wine at communion). Hus objected strongly to the sale of indulgences (personal pardons blessed by the pope and sold ostensibly for charitable purposes). Finally, Hus asserted that the authority of the Bible must be seen as overriding decisions by popes or church councils if those decisions were contrary to Scripture—thus the new notion of "papal infallibility" was, for Hus, unsupportable.

In 1403, 45 of Wycliffe's propositions were condemned by the German masters of the University of Prague, who formed a majority of the university faculty. Despite this official condemnation, Hus translated Wycliffe's *Trialogus* into Czech, and supported a number of Wycliffe's views from the pulpit. In 1405, on orders from Pope Innocent VII (the one in Rome), Archbishop Zbyněk issued a decree condemning Wycliffe's "errors" and forbidding any further attacks on the clergy. In 1408, upon the urging of the new Roman pope Gregory XII, both the university and Bohemia's King Wenceslas took measures to collect all Wycliffite writings in Prague, an order with which Hus complied.

At the same time, the king was advancing the Czech nationalist movement. The University of Prague had been dominated by Germans since its founding in 1348, but in 1409, they gave control of the university over to the Czech masters, at which the German students and faculty (at least 1,000 of them) left the university. Hus was chosen rector of the university that same year. Later in 1409, the archbishop forbade any preaching in Prague except at the cathedral and at collegiate, parish, and cloister churches (thus in effect outlawing worship at Bethlehem Chapel), and in 1410 he ordered Wycliffe's writings burned. When Hus and his associates protested to John XXIII, the pope elected from the Council of Pisa, the archbishop excommunicated Hus. The people of Prague greeted this news with riots in protest. With the support of the populace and of King Wenceslas, Hus continued his advocacy of church reform, protesting in particular against a new program of indulgences, and when he refused to appear before Pope John in 1411, his excommunication was affirmed by the pope. Prague was placed under interdict, and the pope ordered the arrest of Hus and the destruction of Bethlehem Chapel. Hus fled to Austi in 1412, and here wrote his most important works: *De ecclesiâ* (*The Church*), a Latin exposition of Wycliffite ideas; and *On Simony*, a Czech attack on clerical greed and monetary abuses. When the king refused to obey the pope's demands, Hus returned to Prague in 1414 and continued to preach.

Later in 1414, an international church council was convened at Constance, mainly to settle the question of papal succession. Hus was called to appear before the council to defend his teachings. When Sigismund, the Holy Roman Emperor, guaranteed his safety, Hus answered the summons and agreed to appear before the council. But when he arrived in Constance, he was immediately arrested and put on trial for heresy. He was tried, found guilty, and was burned at the stake on July 6, 1415. His chief lieutenant, Jerome of Prague, suffered the same fate the following year.

Having turned Hus and Jerome into martyrs, the church now had to deal with open rebellion in Bohemia and Moravia. Hus's followers formed what was essentially a national church, the Hussites, and a period of "Hussite Wars" followed. Five crusades were proclaimed against the Hussites, but the Roman Church was never able to completely subdue them. The "Unity of Brethren," the last Hussite denomination, was the first group to publish hymnals and the Bible in the vernacular, 60 years before Luther organized his Protestant Church. Luther certainly admired Hus, and adopted a number of his positions, though Luther's doctrine that salvation depended on "faith alone" and "Scriptures alone" was more radical than anything Hus had advocated.

Bibliography

Hus, Jan. *The Church.* Translated, with notes and introduction by David S. Schaff. 1915. Westport, Conn.: Greenwood Press, 1974.

———. *The Letters of John Hus.* Translated by Matthew Spinka. Manchester, U.K.: Manchester University Press, 1972.

Peter of Mladonovice. *John Hus at the Council of Constance.* Translated with notes and introduction by Matthew Spinka. New York: Columbia University Press, 1965.

Spinka, Matthew. *John Hus: A Biography.* Princeton, N.J.: Princeton University Press, 1968.

———. *John Hus and the Czech Reform.* 1941. Hamden, Conn.: Archon Books, 1966.

Husband's Message, The (*The Lover's Message*) (10th century)

The Husband's Message is an OLD ENGLISH lyric poem preserved in the 10th-century manuscript known as the EXETER BOOK, a large collection of Anglo-Saxon poetry. The poem is often paired with *The* WIFE'S LAMENT, because like that poem it deals with the separation of a husband and wife. Whereas the speaker of *The Wife's Lament* is a woman expressing anguish over her husband's absence, *The Husband's Message* is sent by a man giving his wife reassurances of their coming reunion. Despite the coincidental similarities, though, there is no reason to believe that the two poems were intended to be companions.

Although the poem has been damaged by a fire that scorched the later pages of the manuscript, enough is intact to clarify the poem's situation. One of the remarkable aspects of the poem is that its speaker is, in fact, a staff that the husband has sent, carved with runes that reveal his message to her. Giving voice to inanimate objects was a familiar device in Old English RIDDLES. The first part of the poem, where most of the fire damage has occurred, is clearly the personal history of the staff, in which it establishes its credentials as a messenger, speaking of how it has traveled with its lord (the woman's husband) in many foreign lands and has come by ship to bring her a message from him.

The message describes the husband's state: Though a feud has driven him from his home and wife to live in exile, he has found a new home among strangers and now has accumulated some wealth and property. Therefore he is sending for his wife, and the signal for her to board ship and come to him will be the first cry of the cuckoo.

In the last section of the poem, the husband gives a runic signature, which is his pledge to keep the promises he made to her in their youth. The runic message has been the subject of some critical speculation, but the point seems to be that only the wife receiving the message would understand it.

Bibliography

Alexander, Michael, trans. *The Earliest English Poems.* Harmondsworth, U.K.: Penguin, 1966.

Krapp, George Philip, and Elliott Van Kirk Dobbie, eds. *The Exeter Book.* Vol. 3, The Anglo-Saxon Poetic Records. New York: Columbia University Press, 1936.

Hywel ap Owain Gwynedd (ca. 1120–1170)

Hywel, the son of Owain Gwynedd—the powerful and effective prince of northern Wales, was a poet as well as a prince and warrior. His literary efforts include eight extant poems, including five love lyrics that are unique in 12th-century Welsh court poetry.

Hywel was Owain's oldest son, a natural child by an Irish woman called Pyfog. In 1136–37, with his brother Cadwaladr, Owain raided the English stronghold of Ceredigion in south Wales, and established his own power there. When his father died in 1137, Owain claimed the throne of Gwynedd in the north, and he put Hywel in command of south Ceredigion in 1139. Hywel skirmished with his uncle Cadwaladr, trying to establish his own authority throughout the region, but ultimately he was expelled from Ceredigion by his uncle in 1153. At the same time, he was helping his father consolidate his power in the north. He supported his father against the English king HENRY II as Henry tried to reassert English authority in the region. Though suffering a setback in 1157, Owain fomented a general Welsh revolt against the English in 1165, after which he was able to expand and protect his own holdings until his death in 1170.

Upon Owain's death, Hywel was engaged in a brief power struggle with his two half-brothers, Dafyddd and Rhodri, who defeated and killed him at Pentraeth in Anglesey in 1170. One of his supporters, Peryf ap Cedifor, wrote an elegy expressing the grief all of Hywel's retainers felt at his passing.

It is as a poet himself that Hywel is best remembered today. His compositions show that he had studied the formal process of versification under someone well versed in Welsh poetic traditions. Perhaps his instructor was Gwalchmai, Owain Gwynedd's court poet, who was older than Hywel and whose poem entitled *Gorhoffedd* (that is, "Boast") bears the same title as Hywel's longest and best-known poem. Hywel's "Boast" focuses on three major themes: his prowess in battle (a theme quite common for a court poet); his love of his native land, expressed in his descriptions of nature; and his love of women—eight in all that he mentions in his poem, described in a kind of self-mocking tone. Two of his short poems are fairly conventional celebrations of battle. Five of his other lyrics are specifically love poems. Hywel speaks in one breath of the seashore, the green wood and the nightingale, and in the next of a childlike waif of a girl whose footstep barely disturbs the rush she walks upon.

Scholars have speculated that Hywel's position as prince allowed him a certain freedom from following conventions, thus enabling him to write the nature poetry and love lyrics that are unique in Welsh court poetry. Or it may simply be that when poets of lower social rank wrote personal poems of this type, they were not thought of by contemporaries as important enough to preserve. In either case, his self-mockery, his love poetry, and his love of nature are elements that influenced subsequent Welsh poetry, looking forward in some ways to the lyrics of DAFYDD AP GWILYM.

Bibliography

Williams, Gwyn, trans. *Welsh Poems, Sixth Century to 1600.* London: Faber and Faber, 1973.

Williams, John Ellis Caerwyn. *The Poets of the Welsh Princes.* Cardiff: University of Wales Press, 1994.

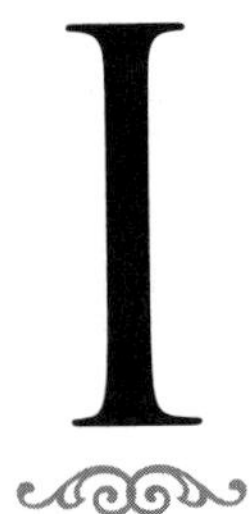

Ibn al-'Arabi, Muhyi a-Din Abu Bakr Muhammad (1165–1240)

Ibn al-'Arabi is one of the most important medieval mystical writers of the Sufi sect of Islam. He is sometimes called al-Shaykh al-Akbar (The Greatest Shaykh), while Muhyi a-Din, his honorific name, means "reviver of religion." Ibn al-'Arabi was born in Murcia, in Andalusia, and moved to Seville with his family after the Almohads conquered southern Spain. He was educated in Seville, and having been introduced to Sufi mysticism, became a wandering scholar through Spain and northern Africa for some years, seeking out Sufi masters. Making his pilgrimage (*hajj*) to Mecca in 1201, he is said to have fallen in love with a young Persian woman who became for him his inspiration, the physical manifestation of the beauty of God's universe (this story may be apocryphal, since falling in love on pilgrimage was a common motif in Arabic literature).

Ibn al-'Arabi's monument to this woman, whom he calls by many names, is his *Tarjuman al-Aschwag* (The interpreter of desires), a collection of 61 QASÍDAS (conventional love poems) that express allegorically his love of God through his expressions of love for the woman. The collection was misunderstood, and Ibn a-'Arabi wrote a "Treasury of Lovers," an explanation of the mystical allegory in his poems, to clarify their spiritual intent: The young girl represents the perfect soul, the longing for her is the longing of the soul that seeks union with God.

After his experiences in Mecca, Ibn al-'Arabi traveled further throughout the Middle East, and finally settled in Damascus in 1223. Here he did much of his writing. More than 900 works are attributed to him, but most, of course, cannot be his. His most famous mystical treatise is *al-Futūhāt al-Mikkiyya* (The Meccan revelations). This is largely a prose work, though it contains many poems. Chiefly it attempts to explain the hidden, mystic meaning of much of the universe. In one chapter of this text, "The Alchemy of Happiness," Ibn al-'Arabi describes a trip through hell and the heavens. Another text, describing Mohammad's night journey through the seven heavens, is Ibn al-'Arabi's *Shajarat al-Qawm* (The Tree of existence). For Ibn al-'Arabi, the Prophet's journey is an allegory for the journey of the heart of the mystic, seeking reunion with God. Ibn al-'Arabi's other better known works are *Fuses al-Hiram* (*Bezels of Wisdom*), in which each chapter is presented as a "bezel," or jewel, of spiritual wisdom; and *Divan*, a substantial collection of some 900 poems, some mystical, a few personal.

In Ibn al-'Arabi's thought, the unity of all Being was essential to religion, and seeking union with the Godhead, with sheer Being, was the goal. For Ibn al-'Arabi, all religions sought this same goal, and therefore, all faiths were ultimately one faith.

His enemies cursed him for heretical pantheism (a belief in the divinity of the whole universe), but Ibn al-'Arabi defended himself by reference to sacred and orthodox texts.

Ibn al-'Arabi said that he was driven by God to write and that his texts were responses to God's urging rather than his own productions. Still one of the most influential of medieval Sufis, his tomb in Damascus continues to be an important pilgrimage center for that city.

Bibliography

Ibn al-'Arabi. *The Bezels of Wisdom.* Translated by R. W. J. Austin. New York: Paulist Press, 1980.

Ibn al-'Arabi. *The Tarjumán al-ashwáq: A Collection of Mystical Odes.* Edited by Reynold A. Nicholson. London.: Theosophical Publishing House, 1978.

Irwin, Robert, ed. *Night and Horses and the Desert: An Anthology of Classical Arabic Literature.* Woodstock, N.Y.: Overlook Press, 1999.

Ibn al-Muqaffa', Abd Allah (ca. 721–ca. 757)

One of the first and most influential writers of prose fiction in Arabic, Ibn al-Muqaffa' was of Persian descent and devoted much of his energies to translating important Persian texts into Arabic in the years following the Muslim conquest of Persia. His best-known work, *Kalilah wa-Dimnah,* is a collection of instructive animal fables that is still used throughout the Middle East as a model of exemplary prose.

Ibn al-Muqaffa's father was tortured by the despot Hajjaj, and his hand shriveled up as a result, hence his son was called Ibn al-Muqaffa' (or "son of the shriveled"). Originally a Zoroastrian, Ibn al-Muqaffa' converted to Islam, though his enemies always questioned the sincerity of his conversion, and he was, at one point, accused of heresy because one of his texts imitates a part of the KORAN.

Ibn al-Muqaffa' worked in Basra (a major port city in what is modern-day Iraq) as a government secretary, part of a middle class of scribes and bureaucrats. He also worked as a translator, rendering into Arabic the history of the kings of Persia. In addition he wrote *Kitab Adab al-Kabir* (The grand book of conduct), with advice on statesmanship including the importance of generosity and the danger of flattery, and *Risala al Sahaba* (A letter on the entourage), which was a political text discussing the caliph and segments of his court.

But Ibn al-Muqaffa's most important contribution to Arabic literature was his *Kalilah wa-Dimnah.* Originally a collection of Indian fables for princes, the text had been translated in the sixth century from Sanskrit into Old Persian, and Ibn al-Muqaffa' reworked the Persian collection into Arabic and changed it enough to make it a new creation. He wrote his own prologue and a section expressing religious skepticism, and he set the collection in a frame narrative in which a pre-Islamic sage called Burzoe travels to India in search of a famous book of wisdom that he copies. The fables themselves contain a good deal of practical wisdom—advising appropriate conduct for government bureaucrats more than for the princes for whom the Indian collection was originally intended—and also display a common theme of storytelling as a way of getting out of life-threatening situations. In addition the text is structured in a way that embeds tales within tales, so that in telling one story as a way out of a difficult situation, a narrator may have a character within his tale begin telling a tale of his own. Both of these motifs—the life-ransoming stories and the embedded stories—appear later in the more famous Arabic collection, *The* THOUSAND AND ONE NIGHTS.

The intent of Ibn al-Muqaffa's work seems to have been largely didactic. In part he wanted to introduce the refined pursuits and sensibilities of the *dihqan* (the traditional Persian country gentleman) to the new Muslim Abbasid court in Basra. In addition he wanted his *Kalilah wa-Dimnah* to be a model for Arabic grammar and literary style, and wrote it simply enough so that schoolchildren or nonnative speakers of Arabic could use it as a model. He hoped they would commit the text to memory.

These concerns helped Ibn al-Muqaffa' become instrumental in helping to develop the concept of *adab*—a social and ethical code and cultural refinement expected of the genteel or of one who wanted to advance in society, later applied especially to literary style.

Ibn al-Muqaffa' died young—he was apparently murdered (possibly in a fire) by political enemies before he was 40. But his animal fables remained extremely popular throughout the Middle Ages, and were translated into Persian, Turkish, Latin, and Hebrew. They continue to be popular today, and still serve as a model of refined Arabic prose. No definitive edition of the *Kalilah wa-Dimnah* exists, however, and versions of the text differ.

Bibliography

Irwin, Robert, ed. *Night and Horses and the Desert: An Anthology of classical Arabic Literature.* Woodstock, N.Y.: Overlook Press, 2000.

Younes, Munther Abduffatif. *Tales from Kalila wa Dimna: An Arabic Reader.* New Haven, Conn.: Yale University Press, 1989.

Ibn Battūta, Abu 'Abdallah (1304–ca. 1377)

Though less famous in the West than his predecessor MARCO POLO, Ibn Battūta is almost certainly the most inexhaustible traveler in the medieval world. In his *Rihlah* (*Book of Travels*) he narrates his 27-year trek of some 75,000 miles across Africa, the Middle East, Asia Minor, Central Asia, India, and into China. More than any other traveler in the premodern world, Ibn Battūta fulfilled the pledge he is said to have made to himself: That he would never travel the same road twice.

Ibn Battūta was born in Tangier in Morocco in 1304. He was raised and educated in a family of legal scholars until, at age 21, he decided to fulfill one of the five pillars (spiritual requirements) of Islam and make his pilgrimage to Mecca. Moreover he hoped to further his education by studying with some of the eastern sages. He set out in 1325 and, after crossing North Africa, Egypt, Palestine, and Syria, he arrived in the holy city of Mecca a year and a half later.

His journey had apparently instilled in him a passion for travel, and from a base in Mecca, Ibn Battūta explored both coasts of the Red Sea and traveled down the East African coast as far south as modern-day Tanzania. He returned through the Persian Gulf and Oman, ultimately returning to Mecca by an overland caravan route that took him through central Arabia.

His wanderlust undiminished, Battūta conceived (about 1330) a plan to visit the Muslim ruler of Delhi, and he set out on a new journey to India. But rather than traveling to Delhi directly, Battuta took ship for the Byzantine capital of Constantinople and then pressed on across Asia Minor, crossing the Black Sea and exploring the Crimea and some of Central Asia. He journeyed through the Asian steppes and Afghanistan, and finally arrived at Delhi in 1333. Here, making use of his legal education, Battūta served the sultan for eight years as a jurist, ultimately becoming the chief justice of Delhi. Then in 1341, the sultan chose Battuta to act as emissary to the Chinese emperor.

Doubtlessly relishing this new opportunity for travel, Ibn Battūta started out for Beijing, but quickly suffered a setback when he was shipwrecked. Undeterred, Battuta visited Ceylon (Sri Lanka) and the Maldive Islands. From southern India he set out again for China, exploring Bengal, Burma, Sumatra, and Canton on the way to the Chinese city of Quonzhou (Zaytun) and, possibly, Beijing. In any case he then decided to make another pilgrimage to Mecca, where he returned in 1347. From here he finally made his return trip to Morocco, arriving home in 1349–24 years after he had left.

Even after such a prodigious journey, however, Ibn Battūta was not content, and he was curious to see the celebrated Muslim culture of Andalusian Spain. In 1350, he visited Granada. In 1353, he took his final trip—a caravan across the Sahara to visit the Muslim empire of the Mandingos in Mali, in the area of the Niger River.

It was apparently upon his return to Morocco in 1354 that the Marinid Sultan, Abu 'Inan, commissioned the Andalusian scribe Ibn Jazayy to help Battuta write his memoirs. Battuta dictated the story of his adventures to the young literary scholar, who completed his text in 1357. After that date Ibn Battūta fades into obscurity, probably acting as a judge in a town somewhere in Morocco. No one knows the details of his final years, but he is purported to have died in either 1368 or 1377.

The story of Ibn Battūta's travels was very popular in the Arab world, and was copied and reproduced regularly over the four centuries following its first appearance. In the 19th century, translations made the book popular in the West as well as in Japan and Iran. It is clear at times that Ibn Battūta, relying on his memory of events sometimes long past, occasionally embellishes or gets things muddled, and it is sometimes difficult to put his journeys into a proper chronological sequence. It is also clear that sometimes Ibn Jazayy uses his own imagination and may exaggerate certain accounts. Still Ibn Battūta's record provides an invaluable historical source for everyday life in virtually every Muslim society in the 14th century, including everything from the Ottoman Empire to Muslim India to sub-Saharan Africa.

Bibliography

Dunn, Ross. *The Adventures of Ibn Battuta: A Muslim Traveler of the 14th Century.* Berkeley: University of California Press, 1989.

Gibb, H. A. R., trans. *The Travels of Ibn Battuta, A.D. 1325–1354.* Cambridge: Published for the Hakluyt Society at the University Press, 1971.

Hamdun, Said, and Noel King. *Ibn Battuta in Black Africa.* Princeton N.J.: M. Wiener, 1994.

Ibn Hazm, Abu Muhammad 'Ali ibn Muhammad ibn Sa'id (994–1064)

Ibn Hazm was an Andalusian writer, jurist, and Muslim theologian active in the early 11th century. His times were turbulent—he lived through a civil war that ended the Umayyad caliphate as well as destructive wars between Arabs and Berbers. A failed politician, Ibn Hazm became an influential spokesman for strict literalist interpretation of the KORAN, and was also the author of one of the best-known treatises on sensual love ever written.

Ibn Hazm's father was vizier under the Umayyad caliph at Córdoba, and Ibn Hazm was raised in the harem of the palace of Madinat al-Zahira, where until the age of 14, he was educated by the women of the harem in the Koran and in poetry. When the Caliph Hisham II fell, Ibn Hazm's father was deposed and disgraced, and the family moved to Córdoba. But in 1013, their home was destroyed when the Berbers attacked the city, and Ibn Hazm began a wandering existence. He did study history, theology, and law, and he served as vizier at least twice. But he was also persecuted for his support of the Umayyad party, and was imprisoned, banished, and at times forced to flee for his life. Disappointed in the political situation of his time, Ibn Hazm seems to have withdrawn from public life and retired to devote the last 30 years of his life to his writing.

Ibn Hazm's most popular text, *Tawq al-Hamama* (*The Dove's Neckring* or *Ring of the Dove*), was one of his earlier works, written in 1027. The title alludes to the practice among lovers of using pigeons to send messages back and forth. The book was purportedly written at the request of a friend who asked Ibn Hazm to discuss the nature of love. It is a collection of prose passages on various aspects of love, illustrated by short poems and also by fascinating autobiographical details reflecting a good deal about life in Umayyad Córdoba. While the treatment of love was a fairly conventional theme in medieval Arabic literature, one is struck in this text by Ibn Hazm's psychological insights. Also fascinating are the parallels with the European COURTLY LOVE tradition apparent in this text: Though the object of the male lover's affections in Ibn Hazm's text is often a beautiful slave girl (rather than the noble lady of the courtly lover's songs), the lover still becomes the lady's servant, and the lover's nobility was refined by his service to his beloved:

It is not just to disapprove
A meek servility in love:
For Love the proudest men abase
Themselves, and feel it no disgrace.

(qtd. in Irwin 1999, 255)

Ibn Hazm seems to have revised the text of *The Ring of the Dove* later in his life. The last two sections of the book, "The Vileness of Sinning" and "The Virtue of Continence," are quite out of keeping with his earlier tales of sensual love. Their tone, however, is consistent with the older Ibn Hazm's concerns. In his later years he condemned love poetry and claimed it promoted immorality. He also came to support the views of the Zahirites, who believed in a strict literalist interpretation of the Koran.

It was in this spirit that Ibn Hazm composed his other well-known text, *Kitah a'-Fisal fi al-Milal wa al-Ahwa' al-Nihal* (The book of religious and philosophical sects). In legal theory Ibn Hazm thought that all law must conform to a very narrow literalist interpretation of the Scriptures. In this book Ibn Hazm examines—and condemns—all forms of religion that he was aware of. Christianity and Judaism receive especially harsh treatment in the book, but worst of all is Ibn Hazm's condemnation of any sect of Islam (including Sufis, Shi'ites, and others) that does not follow the true Zahirite principles of scriptural literalism.

Such a stance put Ibn Hazm at odds with most of the Islamic sects of his time, and many of his later religious texts were publicly burned as heretical. But Ibn Hazm remains famous for his contributions to literature in Arabic. He is said to have written some 400 books, though fewer than 40 are extant. Of these, the youthful work on love that Ibn Hazm rejected has become the work for which he is best remembered.

Bibliography

Arberry, A. J., trans. *The Ring of the Dove.* London: Weatherby, 1953.

Irwin, Robert, ed. *Night and Horses and the Desert: An Anthology of Classical Arabic Literature.* Woodstock, N.Y.: Overlook Press, 1999.

Ibn Ishaq, Muhammad (ca. 704–ca. 767)

Ibn Ishaq was the grandson of a slave who was given his freedom upon converting to Islam. His father and two uncles were professional traditionists—preservers of the oral traditions that had been passed down concerning the life of Muhammad. Based originally in Medina, Ibn Ishaq himself became an expert on Muhammad, specifically on the prophet's military career. Accused of too rationalist an approach in his study of Muhammad's life, Ibn Ishaq left Medina in 733. He studied in Alexandria and eventually traveled to Baghdad, collecting all of the traditional stories he could find and compiling them into a single narrative, *Sirat Rasul Allah* (The biography of God's prophet). Written about a century after the death of the prophet, Ibn Ishaq's text was the earliest biography of Muhammad. His original work is no longer extant, but the text was revised in the ninth century by one Ibn Hisham, and that version has survived, along with extensive quotations and allusions to Ibn Ishaq's text in other historical works.

Oral tales, memories, and legends about Muhammad's life began to circulate immediately after the prophet's death, and these were preserved (sometimes orally, sometimes in writing) by professional traditionists like Ibn Ishaq's father and uncles. These scholars preserved not only the stories but also their sources, so that it was known which eyewitness had passed his or her version of the event down to which storyteller. In this way, the authority of the tales could be verified.

When Ibn Ishaq collected these tales, he preserved their attributions as well, so that his text is filled with phrases like "Abdullah told me that . . ." Thus Ibn Ishaq felt free to at least imply his own doubts about certain stories that had been passed down: He begins one section with the disclaimer "It is alleged in popular stories (and only God knows the truth)." As such, the biography provides a helpful insight into how medieval narratives grew out of oral sources. But for the most part the biography is valuable particularly to Muslims, because it is the chief source for detailed information about the life of God's messenger.

Ibn Ishaq's biography preserves a far more detailed picture of Muhammad than we have for the founders of any other major religious traditions. The text is a collage of short anecdotes, genealogy, poems, long lists of supporters or opponents of Muhammad, and more detailed narratives. It begins by tracing Muhammad's descent from Adam through Abraham and his son Ishmael. Ibn Ishaq then relates the history of Arabia until the time of Muhammad. He then includes stories concerning the prophet's birth, his visions in the desert, his preaching and building his community of believers, his exile to Medina and triumphant return to

Mecca, and subsequent religious wars, concluding with Muhammad's death and details of the burial of the prophet.

In addition, Ibn Ishaq is careful to show Muhammad's life in the context of the community of faith he established, so that other members of the community, such as Salman the Persian, the first non-Arab convert to Islam, are given prominent stories of their own within the larger arc of the prophet's life-story.

Little more is known of Ibn Ishaq's life or the circumstances of his death (in Baghdad), but his legacy is the biography that is still the best authority we have for the life of one of the world's most significant religious figures.

Bibliography

Guillaume, Alfred, ed. and trans. *The Life of Muhammad: Translation of Ishaq's Sirat Rasul Allah.* 1955. Karachi: Oxford University Press, 1997.

Newby, Gordon Darnell. *The Making of the Last Prophet: A Reconstruction of the Earliest Biography of Muhammad.* Columbia: University of South Carolina Press, 1989.

Ibn Jubayr, Abu l-Hussain Muhammad (Ibn Jubair) (ca. 1145–ca. 1217)

Ibn Jubayr, late 12th-century secretary to the governor of Granada, made his pilgrimage (*hajj*) from Spain to Mecca in 1183. He kept a detailed journal of his travels, including his visits to various cities in addition to Mecca, and published an account of his journey when he returned to Granada in 1185. *The Travels of Ibn Jubayr* is a vivid account of the Mediterranean world and the Middle East of the 12th century.

Ibn Jubayr was born in Valencia to an old and distinguished family. He was educated in the KORAN as well as Islamic law, literature, and tradition, and composed poetry as well. Having gained a reputation for his learning and his piety, he was made secretary to the Moorish governor of Spain's wealthiest city, Granada. Although the pilgrimage to Mecca is a sacred obligation for all Muslims of sufficient means to undertake at least once in their lifetimes, Ibn Jubayr decided to make his in 1183 as a kind of penance for having drunk seven glasses of wine that had been forced upon him by his superior, the governor. He took as his companion on his journey a physician from Granada named Ibn Hassan.

Ibn Jubayr seems to have kept his journal on a daily basis, noting his impressions and details about places, people, and unusual customs immediately, while they were fresh in his mind. He describes at length Mecca and Medina, Islam's holiest cities. But he is also impressed by Alexandria, and describes its famous lighthouse. He is also interested in the government of the sultan of Egypt, particularly his generosity to students and to the poor. In Sicily he remarks upon the volcanoes and the beauty and wealth of Palermo. He describes, in addition, his visits to Jerusalem, Baghdad, Cairo, and Syria, and speaks with great admiration of Saladin.

Although Ibn Jubayr is known to have traveled extensively on other occasions, he left a record only of his 1183–85 journey. He later is said to have taught at Fez, and to have accumulated a significant fortune, though tradition says that, out of piety, he gave up his riches.

Bibliography

Broadhurst, R. J. C., trans. *The Travels of Ibn Jubayr.* London: J. Cape, 1952.

Ibn Khaldūn (1332–1406)

Islam's most admired historian, ʿAbd-ar-Rahmān Abū Zayd ibn Muhammad ibn Muhammad ibn Khaldūn—generally known simply as Ibn Khaldūn—is chiefly remembered as the author of the *MUQADDIMAH* (literally, "Introduction," namely to a work of universal history). But Ibn Khaldūn's life was politically active as well as contemplative and intellectual.

Born to a family of politically influential scholars and scribes in the North African city of Tunis, Ibn Khaldūn received an extensive early education in the KORAN, in Arabic, in Muslim law, and in the sciences of mathematics and logic as well as philosophy (particularly the Islamic Aristotelians). He later studied Arab mysticism (Sufi). Thus Ibn Khaldūn was trained to take the position of a court scribe, in the tradition of his family. The BLACK DEATH of 1349 killed his parents and many of his teachers, and the young Ibn Khaldūn soon left Tunis for the position of scribe at the court of Fez, the center of political power of the Merinid dynasty in North Africa at the time. But Ibn Khaldūn was restless and temperamental, and he moved restlessly from court to court, always seeking more influence. In 1362 he was in the court of Muhammad V in Granada, and in 1365 he was appointed *hajib* (the head of the government) in the Hafsid city of Bougie, though his career was in ruins after the emir of Constantine occupied Bougie the following year, sending Ibn Khaldūn into a decade of minor appointments and uncertainty.

By 1375, Ibn Khaldūn was worn out by his political career and by the constant strife between the Merinid and Hafsid dynasties of northwest Africa, and he retired to the fortress village of Qal'at Ibn Salāmah in what is now Algeria, where, in seclusion between 1375 and 1379, he began what was to be a history of the Arabs and the Berber people, but which developed into a new philosophy of history, his *Muqaddimah.* In it, he argues that the laws of God can be demonstrated to be the foundation of the good society, both economically and socially. The state is established to defend the community against aggression and violence from within and without, to protect private property, to prevent fraud and theft, and to protect the currency. But more generally, his study of history led him to postulate that empires rise and fall according to a three-stage pattern, during the first stage of which empires are established because human beings seek civilization and its economic and cultural benefits as a good. But in the second stage, the dynasty inevitably becomes corrupt and exploits its citizens, the state weakens, and, in the third stage, a new and vital society overthrows them and creates a new empire.

Perhaps it was the perspective given him by his study of history that reinvigorated Ibn Khaldūn to reenter public life. In 1384 he accepted an appointment as a judge in Cairo, where he was also appointed an instructor in Islamic law at the Qamhîyah College. From that point until his death in 1406, Ibn Khaldūn was (off and on) chief judge at the Malikite school of law, and at times administrator of Sufi institutions in Egypt. He continued his interest in historical scholarship and in Islamic law and its application in everyday life.

Aside from his *Muqaddimah,* Ibn Khaldūn is known for his *History of the Berbers,* our chief source of information about the history of North Africa and the Berber people during this turbulent period. Some of his earlier works made him famous in his own time even as a young man: philosophical treatises on logic, on arithmetic, and on law; a commentary on a well-known poem in praise of Muhammad called the *Burda,* and a summary of the work of AVERROËS. He also met with the famous Tatar conqueror Tamerlane in 1400, and left an important historical account of that meeting. But the wide-ranging social, economic, and historical philosophy of his *Muqaddimah* has ensured Ibn Khaldūn his own place in the history of civilization.

Bibliography

Al-Azmeh, Aziz. *Ibn Khaldûn: An Essay in Reinterpretation.* London: Routledge, 1990.

Baali, Fuad. *Social Institutions: Ibn Khaldûn's Social Thought.* Lanham, Md.: University Press of America, 1992.

Ibn Khaldûn. *The Muqaddimah: An Introduction to History.* Translated by Franz Rosenthal, abridged and edited by N. J. Dawood, with a new introduction by Bruce B. Lawrence. Princeton, N.J.: Princeton University Press, 2005.

Mahdi, Muhsin. *Ibn Khaldûn's Philosophy of History: A Study in the Philosophic Foundation of the Science of Culture.* London: G. Allen and Unwin, 1957.

Ibn Munqidh, Usamah (1095–1188)

Usamah Ibn Munqidh was a Syrian nobleman and military leader who fought as the ally of the great Muslim leader Saladin in the Third Crusade against the European invaders. He was also a learned man of letters—a student of the KORAN and of Arabic poetry who wrote a book on rhetoric (*al-Badi*) and a book of his own poems (*Diwan*), but he is best known for his autobiography, *Kitāb al I'tibār,* which he wrote when he was nearly 90 years of age.

Usamah was born into a noble family—his family castle still stands in the western part of Syria—in the year that Pope Urban II called for the First Crusade. He was raised to be a courtier and a warrior, and was admired in his time for his physical and mental prowess. He lived in the area around Palestine and so was acquainted with crusaders who had made a home there, and counted some among his friends. He also fought bravely alongside Saladin against both Frankish armies and against enemy Arabs. He witnessed the fall of the Fatimid caliphate in Egypt. In 1174, when Usamah was 79 years old, Saladin gave him a permanent residence in the palace in Damascus. It was during his residency there that Usama wrote his famous memoirs.

For Western readers, the most interesting parts of the autobiography deal with Usamah's encounters with, and views of, the Franks and other Europeans. Most interesting are his views of western medicine—at one point he is brought in to help two European patients (as a learned man he knew a good deal about Muslim medicine) and begins to treat them, only to be overruled by a Frankish doctor who quickly kills both patients. Usamah also comments on marital relations among the Franks, whom he sees as being strangely without jealousy regarding their spouses.

But in Usamah's text, the Europeans are only a sidelight. He writes of his home life, of his military victories and defeats, and of military strategy. He includes anecdotes about hunting and about animals, as well as some poetry. Looking back at his life, Usamah does not understand all that has happened to him, but sees life and the world as governed by an overall divine plan. Usamah's book makes fascinating reading for its picture of life in 12th-century Syria and its presentation of a Muslim view of the Crusades.

Bibliography

Hitti, Philip, trans. *An Arab-Syrian Gentleman and Warrior in the Period of the Crusades: Memoirs of Usamah Ibn-Munqidh.* Records of Western Civilization. 1929. New York: Columbia University Press, 2000.

Innocent III (ca. 1160–1216) *pope*

Innocent III was the most powerful and influential pope of the high Middle Ages, and in terms of political power as well as spiritual authority, his pontificate marks the historical apex of papal influence. He succeeded in persuading the sovereigns of several European nations to recognize him as their secular lord, he launched both the Fourth Crusade and the Albigensian Crusade, he recognized the new mendicant orders of Saint Dominic and Saint Francis, and he convoked the Fourth Lateran Council (the most important church council of the Middle Ages). In addition, he was the author of one of the most popular spiritual treatises of all time. More than anyone else, Innocent was responsible for building the papacy into the prestigious institution it had always been in theory.

Innocent was born Lothario dei Segni, a member of one of the highest ranking of noble Roman families. His early education took place in Rome, after which he studied theology in Paris and law in Bologna. In 1187, Pope Gregory VIII appointed him a subdeacon, and at the papal court his brilliance, particularly in canon law, so impressed Clement III that he was made a cardinal at the age of 30. When the 90-year-old Celestine III died, Lothario was elected pope at the age of 37, taking the name of Innocent III.

Innocent had three major objectives in his pontificate: first, to make real the doctrine of *plenitudo potestasis* (fullness of power) that the pope could theoretically exercise as the successor of Peter and hence, essentially, the vicar of Christ; second, to eliminate heresy within the church's dominions; and third, to win back the Holy Land for the Christian church.

Innocent wasted no time in acting on the first of these objectives. Taking advantage of the death of the Holy Roman Emperor Henry VI in 1198, Innocent reorganized the government of Rome in order to exercise secular authority over the Papal States surrounding the city. Claiming as justification the "Donation of Constantine" (a spurious document by which Emperor Constantine was purported to have given secular control of the Roman Empire over to the pope), Innocent strove to influence the election of the new emperor. His main objective was to prevent the new emperor from reuniting Germany with Sicily and thereby surrounding the Papal States with a single powerful empire. He first threw his support to Otto of Brunswick against the Hohenstaufen candidate Philip of Swabia, but after Philip was murdered in 1208 and Otto invaded Sicily in defiance of the pope, Innocent swung his support to the young Hohenstaufen heir, Frederick II—the king of Sicily and Innocent's ward. Innocent did not live to see Frederick act upon his own ideas about a universal empire, thus initiating a clash between church and state.

In other secular matters, Innocent was involved in a conflict with the French king Philip II over the king's attempt to divorce his wife, Ingeborg of Sweden. Innocent also clashed with King John of England when the king refused to accept the papal appointee, Stephen Langton, as archbishop of Canterbury. Ultimately, having been excommunicated and pronounced deposed by the pope and threatened with invasion from France, John sued to be reconciled with the church, and in 1213 agreed to become the feudal vassal of the pope, making England a papal fief. The kings of Portugal, Aragon, and Hungary were also persuaded to become the pope's vassals. Thus Innocent was able to realize the idea of a feudal theocracy.

Innocent's efforts to eliminate heresy involved, first, his peaceful reconciliation of splinter groups to the Catholic Church. The Humiliati had been previously condemned, but Innocent approved them in 1201 and organized them into three orders. He also welcomed two Waldensian groups in 1208 and 1210, and approved the Hospitaliers of the Holy Spirit, whom he brought to Rome in 1201 to run his hospital for the poor. Most significantly, he approved the rule of St. Francis in 1210, and particularly encouraged the preaching activities of St. Dominic and his followers, whom he wanted to employ to preach against the dualist Catharists of southern France.

Innocent was unable to convert the Catharists through preaching, and when his legate, Peter of Castelnau, was murdered in 1208, he launched a war against them, the Albigensian Crusade. He vested the Dominicans with the power to act as Inquisitors, and legitimized a bloody campaign that destroyed the civilization of Provence and the entire Langedoc region and allowed the French, led by Simon de Montfort, to turn the Crusade into a war of conquest and annex the region after the defeat of the Albigensians at Muret in 1213.

Innocent also spent a good deal of energy on the idea of a Crusade to recapture Jerusalem. He called for a Crusade immediately upon his election to the pontificate in 1198, but a conflict between England and France delayed the raising of an army until 1204. Innocent, having established the first tax on the clergy to fund the Crusade, persuaded the Venetians to build a fleet to transport the crusader army. But Innocent quickly lost control of the Crusade, and partly through the influence of the Venetians, the army ignored the Holy Land and was diverted to a conquest of the Christian cities of Zara and Constantinople instead. His war with the Catharists occupied Innocent for some time, and it was not until their defeat that he could begin planning another crusade. He died suddenly in Perugia while making preparations for the Fifth Crusade—which ultimately failed miserably. It seems fair to say that Innocent's crusading goals were the least successful aspect of his pontificate.

Innocent's biggest successes, on the other hand, were almost certainly achieved with the Fourth Lateran Council in November 1215. After nearly three years of preparation, the council comprised more than 1,200 representatives, 412 of them bishops and archbishops, 800 of them abbots, priors, and other lay and ecclesiastical representatives. The council approved 70 canons or decrees, including a number that shaped Roman Catholicism for the next 750 years. The Inquisition was essentially established by measures against heresy contained in canon 3. Priests were banned from participating in any trial by ordeal or combat by canon 18. Canon 21 required, for the first time, that all Christian laypersons confess their sins to a priest at least once a year. And canon 1 defined the doctrine of transubstantiation, whereby the real presence of the body and blood of Christ in the Eucharist was affirmed. It was Innocent's highest achievement, and he died suddenly shortly after the council, in 1216.

Innocent's contribution to literature includes more than 6,000 surviving letters, and collections of the sermons he preached as pope. He was also the author of several spiritual treatises during his time as cardinal, the most important of which was his *De miseria humanae concitionis* (The misery of the human condition), better known as *De contemptu mundi* (Contempt for the world). Written in 1195, the tract became enormously popular, surviving in more than 600 manuscripts. It was also translated into a number of languages, including apparently an English version by CHAUCER, who alludes to it in his prologue to *The LEGEND OF GOOD WOMEN,* and quotes from it in the prologue to his *MAN OF LAW' TALE.*

Innocent was a sincere reformer, and was renowned and respected for his skills as a preacher and theologian, as well as for his piety, his intelligence, his efficiency, and his energy. Posterity has sometimes condemned his secular ambitions and his conduct of the Albigensian Crusade, but it is impossible to deny his success in achieving for the papacy its highest status of power and influence.

Bibliography

Innocent III, Pope. *The Letters of Pope Innocent III (1198–1216) Concerning England and Wales: A Calendar with an Appendix of Texts.* Edited by C. R. Cheney and Mary G. Cheney. Oxford: Clarendon Press, 1967.

———. *On the Misery of the Human Condition (De miseria humane conditionis).* Edited by Donald R. Howard. Translated by Margaret Mary Dietz. Indianapolis: Bobbs-Merrill, 1969.

Packard, Sidney Raymond. *Europe and the Church under Innocent III.* Rev. ed. New York: Russell and Russell, 1968.

Powell, James M., ed. *Innocent III: Vicar of Christ or Lord of the World?* Rev. ed. Washington, D.C.: Catholic University of America Press, 1994.

Sayers, Jane. *Innocent III: Leader of Europe, 1198–1216.* London: Longman, 1994.

Ipomadon (ca. 1390)

The title *Ipomadon* refers most often to an anonymous late 14th-century MIDDLE ENGLISH chivalric ROMANCE in 12-line TAIL-RHYME stanzas, probably produced originally in the area of northwest Yorkshire. At 8,890 lines *Ipomadon* is the longest of the tail-rhyme romances, and is also in many ways the most sophisticated in its concern with the psychology of its characters, its depiction of the details of court life, and its preservation of some of the finer points of the COURTLY LOVE tradition. This literary sophistication may derive in part from the poet's source, an admirable Anglo-Norman romance by the poet Hue de Rotelande called *Ipomédon* (ca. 1190).

The story revolves around the love of Ipomadon for La Fière, princess of Calabria. The princess has vowed to marry the greatest knight in the world. Ipomadon is prince of Apulia, but visits the Calabrian court in disguise. He earns no reputation in arms, but devotes most of his time to hunting, and thus is rebuffed by the princess and must leave Calabria in disgrace, determined to make a name for himself through valorous deeds in foreign lands. He returns (in disguise) to Calabria to compete in a tournament to win his beloved, though after he has won the tournament, he leaves without claiming La Fière. Later, after other adventures at the court of Sicily and after becoming king of Apulia upon his father's death, he returns to Calabria disguised as a fool to defend his Lady from her enemies who besiege her, overcomes all adversaries, and ultimately weds the princess.

Rotelande wrote his Anglo-Norman poem in the wake of CHRÉTIEN DE TROYES's groundbreaking romances, and seems particularly influenced by Chrétien's EREC ET ENIDE. The anonymous 14th-century poem preserves in English something very close to the spirit of those original French courtly romances. The story contains a good deal of humor and deals sympathetically with the lovers' emotions, which are often expressed in the form of soliloquies. Although the story has been criticized for the apparent lack of motivation for Ipomadon's constant disguises, its use of the "fair unknown" motif (in which the noble youth in disguise proves his true nobility through deeds) may have been influential on later adaptations of that theme, including the "Tale of Sir Gareth" in MALORY's *Le MORTE DARTHUR.*

Two other versions of the Ipomadon story in Middle English are extant: One is an earlier 14th-century prose version called *Ipomedon,* and the other a shorter rendering in rhyming couplets called *The Lyfe of Ipomydon,* preserved in a 15th-century manuscript. The four very different extant versions of the story are clear indications of its widespread popularity in England in the later Middle Ages.

Bibliography

Calin, William. *The French Tradition and the Literature of Medieval England.* Toronto: University of Toronto Press, 1994.

Purdie, Rhiannon, ed. *Ipomadon.* EETS 316. Oxford: Oxford University Press for the Early English Text Society, 2001.

Schmidt, A. V. C., and Nicolas Jacobs. *Medieval English Romances.* New York: Holmes and Meier, 1980.

Ise Monogatari (*Tale of Ise*) (ninth century)

Ise Monogatari is a ninth-century HEIAN Japanese collection of 125 short, sequential episodes. Each episode contains both prose and poetry that illustrate the life and times of an unnamed ideal man, perhaps Ariwara no Nirihira, a middle-ranking bureaucrat of imperial descent who died in 880. The collection begins with an anecdote about a young nobleman recently come of age, who has his first youthful infatuation with two sisters. This elicits his first famous love poem:

> The man caught a glimpse of them through a fence. His heart was taken immediately by the fact of such beauty going to waste in such an outdated place. He knew not what to do. Tearing off the sleeve of his hunting garment, he used it to write a poem to send to the ladies. He was wearing a pattern of disordered leaves and ferns:
>
> *"Like young shoots of murasaki growing on*
> *the Kasuga Plain,*
> *I suddenly come upon you;*
> *My heart is as confused and unknowing as*
> *The random pattern of my sleeve.*
> *Is it hiding something?"*
>
> (Keene 1955, 67–68)

As a fictional autobiography of an amorous hero, the work is an important formative step in the creation of Japanese prose fiction. The life portrayed is expressed through emotion, and thus *Ise* is not a biography or a diary, but an evocation of the moods and sentiments that represent the exemplary male aristocratic lifestyle in the Middle Heian period. Important themes of the work include how to achieve courtly elegance, how to be a successful lover, and how to be a good poet.

Considerable critical debate exists about authorship of the work. Despite claims for Narihira, critics now generally agree that the work in its present form represents the accumulated labors of several authors (including Narihira, his sons, and his friends) who drew their materials from existing poetry collections and orally circulating tales. An interesting theory speculates that one of Narihira's lovers, the poet and priestess Ise, either wrote or heavily edited the text. What is certain is that in its present form, *Ise Monogatari* is the result of a centuries-long process of accretion as copyists and editors added explications and poems, and rearranged the structure of the existing ones.

Ise Monogatari, a classic from the time it was written, has been enormously influential in the development of Japanese literature by serving as a touchstone for Japanese taste for centuries. In addition *Ise* has provided the subject matter for numerous illustrations and decorative motifs throughout the history of Japanese painting.

Bibliography

Keene, Donald, ed. *Anthology of Japanese Literature from the Earliest Era to the Mid-Nineteenth Century.* New York: Grove Press, 1955.

Konishi, Jinichi. *A History of Japanese Literature.* Translated by Aileen Gatten. Princeton, N.J.: Princeton University Press, 1984.

Vos, Fritz. *A Study of the Ise-Monogatari with the Text According to the Den-Teika-Hippon and an Annotated Translation.* The Hague: Mouton, 1957.

Cynthia Ho

Isidore of Seville, Saint (ca. 560–636)

Considered the last of the Latin church fathers, Isidore was born about 560 and died in Seville on

April 4, 636. Isidore was important in his own day as an enlightened prelate and for his influence at important church councils in Visigothic Spain, but remains best known for the written legacy he left, most notably his encyclopedic texts. His 20-volume *Etymologiae* was the most comprehensive encyclopedia in the West until the 18th century.

The youngest child of a Hispano-Roman family that had settled in Visigothic Seville, Isidore was raised by his elder brother, Leander. Leander, who was archbishop of Seville, saw to it that Isidore received a solid education, especially in the Latin fathers like St. AUGUSTINE, GREGORY THE GREAT, St. JEROME, and St. Ambrose, among others. It has also been suggested that Isidore was acquainted somewhat with the Mishnah or with some other rabbinic texts.

In the year 600, Isidore succeeded his brother as archbishop. In his new position, he promoted education and scholarship, producing himself more than 20 major texts. He was a close adviser to King Sisebut (612–621) and King Sisenand (631–636). As such he presided over the Fourth Council of Toledo, convoked by Sisenand on December 5, 633. Some scholars have remarked that Isidore seems to have tried to stem the tide of increasingly harsh anti-Jewish legislation that characterized subsequent church councils in Visigothic Spain—indeed, one of the pronouncements of the Fourth Toledo Council specifically condemns forced baptism of Jews. However the same ruling also upholds the sanctity of baptism as a sacrament, and thus holds that Jews already forcibly baptized, as apparently many had been under King Sisebut, must remain Christian. The legislation also fails to distinguish between "converted" Jews and others, labeling all as "Jews." This ambiguity may have opened the way for some of the harsher actions of later councils.

Isidore's literary production includes a number of exegetical works. He was also interested in historical commentary. His *Chronicon* is concerned with the rise and fall of empires, while his *Historia regibus Gothorum* tells the history of the Goths, reinterpreting their story as a part of salvation history as they convert from the Arian heresy to the true faith. *De natura rerum* deals with explanations of natural phenomena. His three-volume *Sententiae* is the first of what became a common medieval genre, a book of sentences—that is, the teachings of patristic writers, most notably Augustine and Gregory, arranged according to subject.

But Isidore's most famous work is his great encyclopedia, the *Etymologiae.* Here, organized topically and hierarchically, is a compendium of thousands of topics, summing up classical knowledge of science, art, and geography, and dealing with many topics other medieval writers never comment on. The text survives in more than 1,000 manuscripts, an indication of its huge popularity throughout the Middle Ages.

Ultimately Isidore is remembered for his vast encyclopedic writings that leave us a compendium of early medieval knowledge. His writings reveal an overriding interest in the establishment of a strong, centralized monarchy in Spain, to protect the church and to maintain order; and in a centralized authority within the church itself, especially to combat threats like the Macedonian and the Acephalite heresies, and especially the Arian heresy (which denied the divinity of Christ), from which the Visigoths had so recently been converted.

Bibliography

Donini, Guido, and Gordon B. Ford, trans. *Isidore of Seville's History of the Kings of the Goths, Vandals, and Suevi.* Leiden, Netherlands: Brill, 1970.

Macfarlane, Katherine Nell. *Isidore of Seville on the Pagan Gods.* Vol. 70, pt. 3. Transactions of the American Philosophical Society. Philadelphia: American Philosophical Society, 1980.

McGinn, Bernard. *The Doctors of the Church: Thirty-three Men and Women Who Shaped Christianity.* New York: Crossroad Publishing, 1999.

"I Sing of a Maiden" (ca. 15th century)

The anonymous 15th-century MIDDLE ENGLISH lyric that begins "I sing of a maiden that is makeles" is perhaps the best known of all late medieval lyrics in praise of the Virgin Mary. Two couplets in the poem are borrowed from an inferior 13th-century lyric that seems to have served as a source for the poet. "I Sing of a Maiden" is found in a manuscript of miscellaneous lyrics, ballads, carols, and Latin poems, both religious and secular. Some have suggested that the collection was the repertoire of a traveling MINSTREL or entertainer.

"I Sing of a Maiden" is a deceptively simple poem in its structure and vocabulary, though quite complex in its theology and its imagery. The lyric consists of five four-line stanzas. The prevailing meter is a three-stress line, though some lines have only two metrical feet. The rhyme scheme is *abcb* in the first and last stanzas, *abab* in the second through the fourth. This slight variance in rhyme scheme follows the sense of the poem, which has a three-part structure: In the first stanza, the poet introduces his theme. In the middle three he develops it in three parallel stanzas. In the last stanza, he sums up and reinforces his theme.

The theme of the poem revolves around the term makeles used to define Mary. The word has the double meaning of both "matchless" (that is, without peer) and "mateless" (that is, without a mate—a virgin). This peerless woman, we are told, chose to be the mother of God. The middle three stanzas explore just how this paradox of the virgin mother could occur. The momentous incarnation of God is pictured in the poem through the simple and natural image of the falling of dew:

He cam also stille
Ther his moder was
As dew in Aprille
That falleth on the gras.

He cam also stille
To his moderes bowr
As dew in Aprille
That falleth on the flour.

He cam also stille
Ther his moder lay
As dew in Aprille
That falleth on the spray.

(Luria and Hoffman 1974, 170, ll. 5–16)

The "repetition with variation" technique of these stanzas suggests the poet's familiarity with the BALLAD tradition. The "dew" of these lines has rich symbolic associations in theology and biblical interpretation, being a common symbol of the Holy Spirit, as well as of Christ descending to earth. April, the season of spring, is the time of renewal and rebirth, both spiritually and physically. For April is also associated with love, and God (the "he" of these lines) is seen as approaching Mary gently like a lover, becoming closer and more intimate as the stanzas progress—first he comes to where she is, then to her bower, then specifically to her bed. The flower of the middle stanza is also rich with connotations, since Mary was often symbolized by a flower, a sign of purity. The progressive movement from grass to flower to spray (or branch) is an expansion that possibly suggests the swelling of Mary's womb.

In the final stanza, the poet sums up the overall theme of the lyric by stressing again Mary's matchlessness and matelessness and her unique qualifications ("Was never non but she") to be the Mother of God. The fresh and vivid imagery and the complex ideas embodied in the poem's simple lines have made "I Sing of a Maiden" one of the most admired of late medieval poems. Stephen Manning has said that this poem "represents the supreme achievement of the Middle English lyric" (Manning 1960, 12).

Bibliography

Luria, Maxwell S., and Richard Hoffman. *Middle English Lyrics.* New York: Norton, 1974.

Manning, Stephen. " 'I Syng of a Mayden,' " *PMLA* 75 (1960): 8–12.

Oliver, Raymond. *Poems Without Names: The English Lyric, 1200–1500.* Berkeley: University of California Press, 1970.

Izumi Shikibu (fl. 1000–1030)

Like many HEIAN female writers, Izumi Shikibu is not known by her birth name but rather by a sobriquet (or pen name) taken from a famous male member of her family. In this case she is known by the title of her first husband, the governor of Izumi. She is celebrated for her diary and her many *waka* poems (*see below*), which appeared in later imperial collections. In the second half of the 10th century, female members of the middle aristocracy serving as ladies-in-waiting at court developed the prose *hiragana* (vernacular diary or *nikki*). Izumi Shikibu's diary, *Izumi Shikibu Nikki,* records her romance (begun in 1003) with Prince Atsumichi, the brother of her deceased former lover. Prince Atsumichi died in 1007, and in 1010, Izumi remarried and retired to the provinces to write poetry until her death. *Izumi Shikibu Nikki* is a combination of short prose sections intermingled with lyric insertions. The work blends the third-person omniscient narrator of the *monogatari* (the vernacular Japanese novel) with the personal revelations of the *nikki.*

Izumi is also a master of *waka* poetry. This classical verse form uses 31 syllables in a five-line poem in a 5-7-5-7-7 syllable pattern. More than 240 of her poems were anthologized together with her prefaces, which demonstrate her individuality and distinctive voice. Her most famous *waka,* written when she was quite young, is an expression of Buddhist piety:

Out of the darkness
on a dark path,
I now set out.
Shine on me,
moon of the mountain edge

(Rexroth 1982, 18)

Bibliography

Cranston, Edward, trans. *The Izumi Shikibu Diary: A Romance of the Heian Court.* Cambridge, Mass.: Harvard University Press, 1969.

Miner, Earl, trans. "The Diary of Izumi Shikibu." In *Japanese Poetic Diaries,* 95–153. Berkeley: University of California Press, 1969.

Rexroth, Kenneth. *Women Poets of Japan.* New York: New Directions, 1982.

Cynthia Ho

Jacopone da Todi (Jacopo Benedetti or Bennetti) (ca. 1236–1306)

The Italian Franciscan Jacopone da Todi was an ascetic and poet who wrote more than 100 lyric poems, or *LAUDA,* on religious themes, though stylistically somewhat influenced by the love songs of the TROUBADOURS. He is said to have gone through a cataclysmic conversion upon the death of his wife, becoming a strict Spiritualist Franciscan, whose opposition to Pope Boniface VIII resulted in his excommunication and life imprisonment.

Tradition says that Jacopone was born into the noble family of Benedetti in Todi sometime in the 1230s. He trained for the law and possibly studied at Bologna. According to legend Jacopone was a successful advocate until 1268, when his young wife was killed by the collapse of a building during a festival in Todi. Rushing to his dying wife, Jacopone loosened her rich dress to discover a hairshirt she was wearing beneath it. Shocked by her death and struck by the evidence of her ascetic piety, Jacopone is said to have abandoned his law practice, given his goods to the poor, and spent 10 years as a penitent hermit, determined to live in absolute poverty.

In about 1278, Jacopone joined the Franciscan order as a lay brother or Tertiary at the convent of San Fortunato, at Todi. Among the Franciscans of this time there were two factions: The Spiritualists advocated a strict adherence to St. FRANCIS's original rule of absolute poverty; the Conventuals favored a laxer interpretation of the rule. Jacopone, like the other friars of San Fortunato, was a strict Spirtualist and wrote a number of poems condemning the corruption of the Franciscan order under the Conventualists, accusing them of hypocrisy and pride in their desire for worldly honor. He also wrote a number of poems praising the spiritual value of poverty.

The Franciscan Spiritualists gained a great victory when the poor hermit Pier da Morrone became Pope Celestine V in 1294. Jacopone was among a group of Spiritual friars who petitioned the new pope for the right to live apart from other Franciscans in order to observe the Rule absolutely. Celestine granted the request, thus giving the Spiritualists some autonomy, and they began to be known as "the poor hermits of Celestine." Celestine, however, abdicated the papal seat after only five months, only to be replaced by the unapologetically worldly Boniface VIII. Boniface revoked the privileges Celestine had granted the Spiritual friars, and in return incurred their active opposition. In 1297, Jacopone signed a manifesto at Lunghezza that declared Celestine's resignation and Boniface's election invalid. In retaliation Boniface excommunicated the Spiritualists who had signed the document, and when they fled to the stronghold of Palestrina, besieged them with papal troops. The rebels surrendered in 1298, and Jacopone was imprisoned for life in the nearby fortress of Castel San Pietro.

From his prison cell Jacopone wrote numerous lyrics, some attacking Boniface as the "new Lucifer," others pleading with the pope for absolution. In one of his better-known poems, *"Que farai, fra Jacopone?"* ("And what now, Fra Jacopone?"), the poet begins by bewailing his imprisonment, but ends with a recognition that the hardship and deprivation have helped lead him to his ascetic ideal.

In October 1303, Boniface died, and the succeeding pope, Benedict XI, lifted Jacopone's excommunication and released him from his prison. Now a broken old man, Jacopone lived out his last few years at the convent of San Lorenzo in Collazzone near his native Todi, and it was there he died in 1306. His tomb is in the Franciscan Church of San Fortunato.

Jacopone's lyrics, simple, vivid, emotional, and sometimes ardently mystical, were nearly all written in his native Umbrian dialect. His poetry enjoyed widespread popularity, evidenced by the many manuscripts of his songs that survive (often in other regional Italian dialects) in addition to seven early printed editions. His most admired poem in the vernacular is a *lauda* in dialogue form called *"Donna del paradiso"* (Lady of paradise). The poem, admired for its realism and emotion, depicts the torments of Christ (related to the Virgin Mary by a messenger), a lament spoken by the Virgin, and a final scene of farewell between Christ and Mary. But the most famous poem attributed to Jacopone (though without certainty) is the Latin sequence called the *Stabat Mater dolorosa* ("The Mother stood grieving"), a poem of 60 lines portraying the Virgin standing in sorrow at the foot of the cross. The poem became one of the most widespread and popular hymns in the medieval church.

Bibliography

Dronke, Peter. *The Medieval Lyric.* New York: Harper, 1969.

Hughes, Serge, and Elizabeth Hughes, trans. *Jacopone da Todi: The Lauds.* Classics of Western Spirituality. New York: Paulist Press, 1982.

Peck, George T. *The Fool of God: Jacopone da Todi.* Tuscaloosa: University of Alabama Press, 1980.

Underhill, Evelyn. *Jacopone da Todi, Poet and Mystic 1228–1306: A Spiritual Biography.* Italian text translated into English verse by Mrs. Theodore Beck. 1926. Freeport, N.Y.: Books for Libraries Press, 1972.

James I of Scotland (1394–1437)

James I, king of Scotland, is the purported author of the early 15th-century ROMANCE called *The KINGIS QUAIR* (The king's book), a poem owing a great deal to CHAUCER. Thus James (if he is indeed the poem's author) is one of the earliest and most accomplished of the poets called the "Scottish Chaucerians." As king, James was popular, especially with the common people, but he made enemies among the nobility and was assassinated on February 20, 1437.

James was born at Dunfermline in Fife. He was the second son of King Robert III and Annabela Drummond, but became heir apparent when his older brother was murdered, allegedly by the Duke of Albany, his own uncle. As the boy James was traveling to France in 1406, he was kidnapped by English pirates and delivered to the English king Henry IV. Henry imprisoned the young Scottish prince, who soon became king when his father died shortly after James's abduction.

James was an English prisoner for 18 years. He apparently received a good education in captivity, and perhaps was acquainted with the French nobleman and poet CHARLES D'ORLEANS, who was being held prisoner at the same time as James. Upon his release from prison in 1424, James married Lady Joan Beaufort, who was the daughter of John Beaufort, earl of Somerset, and the granddaughter of JOHN OF GAUNT and Chaucer's sister-in-law, Katherine Swynford. Joan is, purportedly, the heroine of *The Kingis Quair.*

In James's absence, his uncle Albany served as Scottish regent, and upon Albany's death in 1420, his son Murdoch became governor. When James returned, it was to a country in serious disorder. James acted quickly to eliminate rivals to his authority and to suppress the nobility, with the support of the clergy and the middle class. Murdoch and his family were executed. James concerned himself with the proper administration of justice for the commons, he promoted and kept peaceful relations with both England and France, he was a patron of the arts, and he asserted his direct control over the state treasury. But a group of dissident nobles, led by Sir Robert Graham and Walter Stewart, the earl of Atholl, assassinated him in Perth in 1437.

There is some question as to whether *The Kingis Quair* was in fact written by James. There is no contemporary reference to his being a poet, and it is only in the 16th century that he is mentioned as the author of *The Kingis Quair.* He is named the author in a manuscript colophon (a scribal addition at the end), where it is asserted that he wrote the poem for Joan Beaufort. Certainly the imprisoned king in the poem who falls in love seems clearly autobiographical, and there is no compelling reason to deny James's authorship of the poem. Other poems that have been attributed to him over the years—"The Ballad of Good Counsel," "Christis Kirk on the Green," and "Peblis to the Play"—seem to have no real claim to his authorship.

Bibliography

Balfour-Melville, E. W. M. *James I, King of Scots, 1406–1437.* London: Methuen, 1936.

James I of Scotland. *The Kingis Quair.* Introduction, notes and glossary by John Norton-Smith. Oxford: Clarendon Press, 1971.

The Kingis Quair of James Stewart. Edited by Matthew P. McDiarmid. Totowa, N.J.: Rowman and Littlefield, 1973.

Scheps, Walter, and J. Anna Looney. *Middle Scots Poets: A Reference Guide to James I of Scotland, Robert Henryson, William Dunbar, and Gavin Douglas.* Boston: G. K. Hall, 1986.

Jami of Herat (Nur al-Din 'Abd al-Rahman ibn Ahmad al-Jami) (1414–1492)

Known as the last great Persian classical poet, Jami was a Sufi mystic and saint in the tradition of SA'DI and HAFEZ. He was born at Jam, near the city of Herat, in what is now Afghanistan. He was said to have been well educated, but legend has it that he was disliked by other poets of his time because of his lack of humility. He was a member of a mystical order of dervishes, but was also attached to the court of the Timurid (the dynasty descended from Tamerlane) ruler of Heart, where he had a good friend in the vizier. His influence was significant, and he wrote in a variety of literary genres, both poetry and prose, as well as commentaries on the KORAN and treatises on rhetoric, grammar, music, and Sufism. Some 40 extant texts are attributed to him with some degree of confidence. He is best known for his *Haft Aurang* (The seven thrones, the Persian name for the constellation Ursa Major). These are poems of epic length with romantic plots that are frequently ALLEGORIES of mystical themes.

One of the best-known tales from The Seven Thrones is his allegory of sacred and profane love called Salaman and Absal, a text that became well known in Europe through Edward FitzGerald's 19th-century translation. He also retells the story of the lovers Layla and Majnun, the Persian Romeo and Juliet made famous by the 12th-century poet Nizami. But the best-known tale from *The Seven Thrones* is the story of Yusuf and Zuleika. This is a retelling of the familiar story of Joseph and Potiphar's wife, in which Zuleika, daughter of the king of Mauretania, falls in love with Joseph in a dream before she ever sees him. She travels to Egypt and marries Potiphar, but declares her passion for Joseph when he comes into her service. He flees from her, and she ultimately repents. In the end of the story, she is betrothed to Joseph.

In addition to *The Seven Thrones,* some of Jami's better-known works include *Bhararistan* (The abode of spring), a collection of stories, and *Nafahat al-Uns* (Zephyrs of tranquility), a Sufi biographical dictionary. He has at times been faulted for the use of elaborate figures of speech or rhetorical flourishes, but his style was influential on Persian literature for centuries.

Bibliography

FitzGerald, Edward, trans. *Rubaiyat of Omar Khayyam and the Salaman and Absal of Jami: Rendered into English Verse.* London: Bernard Quaritch, 1879.

Pendlebury, David, ed. and trans. *Yusuf and Zulaikha: An Allegorical Romance.* London: Octagon Press, 1980.

Yohannan, John D., ed. *Joseph and Potiphar's Wife in World Literature: An Anthology of the Story of the Chaste Youth and the Lustful Stepmother.* New York: New Directions, 1968.

Jean de Meun (Jehan de Meung) (ca. 1235/40–1305)

Jean de Meun, who continued GUILLAUME DE LORRIS's fairly short first part of the *ROMAN DE LA ROSE* (ca. 1237), created one of the most influential, but also most provocative allegorical poems in the late Middle Ages. He was borne at Meung-sur-Loire as Jean Chopinel (or Clopinel) and gained his master of arts degree, probably at the University of Paris. He is documented as residing at the Hôtel de la Tourelle in the Faubourg Saint-Jacques (Paris) from at least 1292 to his death. Apart from his work on the *Roman,* he translated from Latin into French such famous works as Vegetius's *De re militari* (ca. 385–400 C.E.), BOETHIUS's *De consolatione philosophiae* (*The CONSOLATION OF PHILOSOPHY,* ca. 525/526 C.E.), and the well-known correspondence of ABELARD and HELOISE (ca. 1120–40). Jean also claims to have translated GIRALDUS CAMBRENSIS's *De mirabilibus Hiberniae* and Aelred of Rievaulx's *De spirituali amicitia,* neither of which has been preserved, and he also seems to have authored the satirical *Testament maistre Jehan de Meun* and *Codicile maistre Jehan de Meun.*

Jean is, however, best known for his portion of the *Roman de la Rose,* which he wrote between 1264 and 1274. Its enormous popularity is documented by more than 250 manuscripts and 21 printed editions from 1481 to 1538. We know of one Dutch, two Italian, and three English translations, the earliest of which was written by Geoffrey CHAUCER. Jean deeply influenced the greatest writers in Italy, France, and England from the 13th through the 16th century, such as DANTE, BOCCACCIO, GUILLAUME DE MACHAUT, Chaucer, John GOWER, Thomas HOCCLEVE, John LYDGATE, Thomas USK, Gavin DOUGLAS, Jean FROISSART, Jean Molinet, and Clément Marot. CHRISTINE DE PIZAN, enraged about the misogyny in Jehan le Fèvre's French translation (ca. 1371–72) of the *Liber lamentationum Matheoluli* (original ca. 1295) and in Jean de Meun's portion of the *Roman,* participated in a large open debate about gender issues, the *querelle de femmes.* In 1401 Jean de Montreuil, royal secretary and provost of Lille, wrote an enthusiastic defense of the *Roman* (today lost), to which Christine responded with a vehement attack on Jean de Meun's derogatory treatment of women. An exchange of letters followed involving two other royal secretaries, Pierre and Gontier Col, defending Montreuil's perspective. But Jean Gerson, chancellor of the University of Paris, supported Christine's argument, particularly since he had already preached a sermon against Jean de Meun in 1401 and subsequently wrote a poem in the form of a vision against the *Roman* in 1402. Christine published her correspondence with her opponents in 1402, which ignited further debates, stretching to the end of the year when those involved turned toward other interests. Christine, however, continued her energetic defense of women in her subsequent writings. The influence of the *Roman de la Rose* on medieval German literature seems to have been minuscule, since we know of no translations and direct allusions, apart from some didactic love debates. The Styrian poet Hugo von Montfort (1357–1423), however, seems to have adapted some of the allegorical elements in his poem *"Ich gieng ains morgens auss durch aventewr"* (no. 28).

Although Jean de Meun purported to continue and complete Guillaume's *Roman,* his almost 18,000 verses represent a highly innovative and independent allegorical treatise containing a multitude of philosophical and pragmatic reflections. His portion of the *Roman* begins with the Lover despairing over his chances to win the Rose, when Reason appears and advises him against love altogether, since it is nothing but "A treasonous loyalty, disloyal faith—/A fear that's full of hope, a desperate trust—/A madman's logic, reasoned foolishness" (Robbins 1962, vv. 4272–74). Reason also offers teachings about spiritual, religious friendship as an alternative to erotic love, about the effects of Fortune, and what constitutes true happiness—a reflection of Boethius's *De consolatione philosophiae*—then about the irrelevance of wealth and the corruption of justice. Reason illustrates her arguments with references to the lives of famous people in the Roman Empire, such as Seneca and Nero, Croesus and Phanie, but she also refers to the destiny of the king of Sicily, Manfred, and other kings who had been victims of misfortune. At this point, however, the Lover decries Reason as lewd and irresponsible, and turns to a Friend who advises him to use bribery and deceit to win his Rose. Again the Lover vehemently rejects this avenue, but he has to listen to the Friend's lengthy discussion of how to use gifts and largesse to achieve his goal. This suddenly gives way to a *laudatio temporis acti,* a lament about the depravity of the present time and a praise of the golden past. Next the Friend explains how jealous husbands abuse their wives, and the Jealous Husband defends his position by relating the story of Heloise and Abelard, which then leads to a misogynistic diatribe, quickly interrupted again by the Friend's teachings of the art of love, which motivates the Lover to visit Fair Welcome. Hereupon the God of Love forgives the Lover for listening to Reason and promises help.

The following sections represent an allegorical battle plan of how to win the Rose, particularly involving False Seeming and Forced Abstinence. False Seeming kills Evil Tongue and enters the castle, where they win the Duenna as go-between, which allows the poet to have her outline her life of lewdness, to develop a theory of love, to tell stories of unhappy female lovers in antiquity (Dido, Phyllis, Oenone, and Medea), and of how women gain men's love. She illustrates this strategy with the stories of Vulcan, Venus, and Mars. Although the Lover then gains entry into the Castle of Jealousy, Danger still blocks his way to the Rose. Subsequently the various allegorical figures fight against each other until a truce is declared. Venus then agrees to come to Love's aid, and the battle begins anew. Both here and earlier the poet interpolates short digressions, once offering an apology for having written his book (using the modesty topos, a conventional medieval rhetorical motif), then examining the relationship between art and nature, the question of destiny and free will, the influence of the stars on human life (astrology), explaining the properties of mirrors and glasses, dreams and frenzies, the true nature of nobility, finally turning to a general complaint about man's abuse of nature and his breaking of all natural rules. Nevertheless Nature sends Genius to encourage the God of Love, and Genius expounds the absolute relevance of sexuality and love for Nature to continue through the creation of progeny. Genius also describes the life of the blessed in paradise, and argues, drawing from Roman mythology and literature (particularly Virgil), that Jupiter ordered man to enjoy his life and to make full use of all the resources supplied by nature. Inspired by this long speech, Love's barons prepare the final assault on the castle of Jealousy. In the meantime Venus attacks the tower of Shame, while the poet quickly tells the stories of Pygmalion and of Cinyras and Myrrha to demonstrate that man ought to love and enjoy sexuality. Once Venus has set fire to the tower of Shame, the Lover succeeds in gaining entrance into the Ivory Tower and finally wins the Rose. This last section is nothing but a thinly veiled, almost pornographic description of the sexual act of deflowering the Rose (v. 21,736). The *Roman de la Rose* concludes with the poet admitting that he entirely forgot Reason's exhortations and enjoys his rose. With this the Lover awakens from his dream and ends his account.

Scholarly opinions about Jean's intentions and strategies vary widely, particularly because of the poet's unique form of irony and satire and the sophisticated differentiation between the narrator figure and the actual author, not to mention the numerous allegorical figures. Moreover Jean's portion is characterized by highly contradictory discourses determined by various voices, and it would be impossible to determine which of these truly win the debates. The obvious didacticism is undermined at every turn of the narrative, and lofty ideals deftly clash with highly truculent and erotic images. The traditional ideal of *fin'amors* (or COURTLY LOVE), as defended by Guillaume, still lingers in the background, but Jean makes every effort to deconstruct it without truly offering an alternative, except for crude sexuality. Undoubtedly the *Roman de la Rose,* with all its contradictions, fragmentary nature, distorted discourse, and encyclopedic character (see the wide range of sources from classical antiquity to the 12th century), proves to be one of the masterpieces of medieval French literature. The 13th- and 14th-century manuscripts containing the *Roman de la Rose* were some of the best and most richly illustrated manuscripts of their time.

Bibliography

Arden, Heather. *The Romance of the Rose.* Boston: Twayne, 1987.

Brownlee, Kevin, and Sylvia Huot. *Rethinking the "Romance of the Rose": Text, Image, Reception.* Philadelphia: University of Pennsylvania Press, 1992.

Classen, Albrecht. "Hugo von Montfort: A Reader of the *Roman de la Rose,*" *Monatshefte* 83, no. 4 (1991): 414–432.

Dahlberg, Charles, trans. *The Romance of the Rose.* Princeton, N.J.: Princeton University Press, 1971.

Fleming, John F. *The Roman de la Rose: A Study in Allegory and Iconography* Princeton N.J.: Princeton University Press, 1969.

Le Roman de la Rose. Edited by Félix Lecoy. 3 vols. Paris: Champion, 1965–1970.

Robbins, Harry W., trans. *The Romance of the Rose.* New York: E. P. Dutton, 1962.

White, Hugh. *Nature, Sex, and Goodness in a Medieval Literary Tradition.* Oxford: Oxford University Press, 2000.

Albrecht Classen

Jerome, Saint (ca. 345–420)

Eusebius Hieronymus, the Roman biblical scholar better remembered as St. Jerome, was born in the important port city of Aquileia, located on the northernmost shore of the Adriatic Sea. Aquileia was a substantial center of Christianity during the late Roman Empire; its bishop oversaw several churches throughout the surrounding region. Jerome's genius was recognized early and as a young man he studied both secular and clerical subjects at Rome, where he was eventually baptized as a Christian. This period laid the foundation for his lifelong devotion to scholarship and Christianity.

Jerome openly embraced the growing Roman fascination with Christian asceticism (that is, the practicing of religious self-denial), first returning to Aquileia to join a small ascetic community of personal friends, and then beginning a pilgrimage to the Holy Land, ca. 374. On his way to Palestine, however, Jerome diverted to the Syrian Desert, where he remained as an ascetic hermit for six years. During this time, Jerome came into contact with a Jewish community from which he learned to read Hebrew. At the end of this period, Jerome was ordained as a priest before traveling to the imperial capital of Constantinople. He then returned to Rome where he became a papal secretary for Pope Damasus.

Aside from his secretarial duties, Jerome's second visit to Rome (ca. 382–385) was spent preaching the merits of asceticism to urban Romans. His message was well received—particularly by young noblewomen. Since the ascetic life required abstention from marriage, many noble families were less than thrilled with Jerome's influence on their daughters. The removal of an eligible daughter meant losing an important family asset for the building of alliances and the shoring up of family position. Furthermore, asceticism itself was still not completely accepted by many of Rome's upper classes, and Jerome's efforts to spread its ideals were viewed as a threat. When one of his young female pupils died while practicing an ascetic lifestyle, Jerome found his welcome in Rome to be wearing thin. The death of his protector, Pope Damasus, suggested that it was a suitable time for Jerome to renew his interest in pilgrimage.

After visiting the ascetic centers of Antioch, Egypt, and Palestine, Jerome became the abbot of his own male monastery in Bethlehem ca. 386. This institution not only served the spiritual development of its members, but also provided a convenient hostel for the steady number of Roman pilgrims seeking to visit sites associated with the life of Christ. From this stable setting, Jerome was able to devote the rest of his life to the study of biblical texts while maintaining a presence within powerful church circles back in the West.

Jerome's writings attest to his impressive scholarship, his biting wit, and his fierce concern for the Roman church. His most famous and influential work was his revised Latin edition of the biblical corpus. Pope Damasus requested the project as part of his broader campaign to codify and authorize biblical material. Jerome began by translating the individual Gospel books from the Greek, but his knowledge of Hebrew convinced him to translate the books of the Torah and the Prophets directly from Hebrew examples. Composed and translated as individual books, these biblical texts were gathered together sometime around the early seventh century into a single format known as the Vulgate. This Latin edition became the most popular medieval biblical text, though it is important to realize that the contents of these medieval collections often differ from one another. Jerome did not translate what would be considered the entire New Testament; other anonymous writers filled in these gaps. Medieval changes in the construction of Latin and later translations of Jerome's work into vernacular languages such as Old High German added to the variety and mistakes common in medieval Scriptures. Nor did each "biblical" collection contain all the same texts. The standardization of biblical collections into an orthodox set of texts would take several centuries; a final critical edition of the Vulgate as a whole would not emerge until 1528. The Catholic Church pronounced the Vulgate as authoritative during the Council of Trent, ca. 1560—a gathering largely influenced by the Counter-Reformation.

Jerome's other important works include translations of texts by African Christian teachers such as Origen, as well as Jerome's continuation of the historical *Chronicle* began by Eusebius of Caesarea. More popular, however, was Jerome's catalogue of worthy ecclesiastical authors and their works entitled *De viris illustribus.* This extended bibliography would become an authoritative list of orthodox Christian writers and their works during the Middle Ages, creating a shopping list for ecclesiastical libraries across Europe. Aside from these works of literature, existing portions of Jerome's personal correspondence provides a welcome insight into the turmoil and debate within Christianity during the fourth and fifth centuries. His opinionated nature and biblical knowledge led Jerome to engage with most of the disputes of his day: Arianism, Pelagianism and Origenism. He was also involved with leading Christian figures such as Rufinus, Melania and St. AUGUSTINE.

Finally, it should be noted that Jerome's reputation for scholarship lent his name an authority in later periods that was only matched by that of the English scholar BEDE. Many medieval texts would appear that falsely claimed to be the work of Jerome. The most influential of these works was the *Martyrologium Hieronymianum,* or the *Martyrology of St. Jerome.* This list of saints was widely held to be the work of Jerome during the Middle Ages and at least one manuscript contained an attached letter in which Jerome referred to a list of martyrs. This link between the manuscript and Jerome was forged specifically to make use of Jerome's authority, and highlights his importance in the medieval world.

Bibliography

Corpus Christianorum Series Latina. Vols. 72–80. Turnholti, Belgium: Brepols, 1953 ff.

Early Church Fathers. "Ante-Nicene Fathers." Available online. URL: http://www.ccel.org/fathers2/. Accessed February 4, 2005.

The Homilies of Saint Jerome. Translated by Marie Liguori Ewald. Washington, D.C.: Catholic University of America Press, 2001.

Kelly, J. N. D. *Jerome: His Life, Writings, and Controversies.* London: Duckworth, 1975.

"Jerome, St." In *Oxford Dictionary of the Christian Church,* edited by F. L. Cross, 867–868. Oxford: Oxford University Press, 1997.

On Illustrious Men. Translated by Thomas P. Halton. Washington, D.C.: Catholic University of America Press, 1999.

Patrologia Latinae. Edited by J. P. Migne. Vols. 22–30. Paris, 1844–1864. CD-ROM ed. Alexandria, Va.: Chadwyck-Healey, 1995.

Rebenich, Stefan. *Jerome.* London: Routledge, 2002.

Saint Jerome: Dogmatic and Polemical Works. Translated by John Hritzu. Washington, D.C.: Catholic University of America Press, 1965.

Selected Letters of St. Jerome. Translated by F. A. Wright. Cambridge, Mass.: Harvard University Press, 1933.

Chris Craun

jinshi (*chin-shih*)

The *jinshi* examination in imperial China was the most prestigious of the civil service exams, the approximate equivalent of a doctorate degree, but more selective. Passing the exam guaranteed the candidate power and prestige within the complex Chinese imperial bureaucracy. Since the examination emphasized poetic composition, it encouraged the intelligentsia of medieval China to study poetry and cultivate talents in poetic composition. It is no accident that most of the important poets of medieval China (such as WANG WEI, LI HO, BO JUYI, and YUAN ZHEN) made their careers as government employees.

The elaborate Chinese civil service system was established theoretically to draw the best minds in the empire into government service, without regard to birth or wealth. In effect, the time and intense study that a candidate had to spend preparing for the examinations probably precluded all but a very few candidates from the lower classes. There were three tiers of exams: first at the county level, next at the provincial level, and finally at the national level, in the capital. The most prestigious of these national exams was the *jinshi;* those who passed it were called "presented scholars," and were presented to the emperor. But it is estimated that the pass rate for the *jinshi* exam was only 2 to 3 percent of the thousand or so scholars who took the exam each year. It is easy to see that this state of affairs led to lives of bitter frustration among those who were never able to pass the exam despite years or even decades of preparation.

There were three sections to the *jinshi* exam as it developed after its introduction in the early TANG DYNASTY in 680: First, the candidate had to demonstrate rote knowledge of a memorized portion of the acknowledged Confucian classics. Second, the candidate was required to compose a poem and a piece of rhymed prose on an assigned topic and according to an assigned rhyme scheme. Third, the candidates were required to write "dissertations" or essays on contemporary problems—there were five main questions to be dealt with, and each of these could be divided into several sub-questions, all of which the candidate had to address in his dissertation.

Bibliography

McMullen, David. *State and Scholars in T'ang China.* Cambridge: Cambridge University Press, 1998.

Owen, Stephen. *The Great Age of Chinese Poetry: The High T'ang.* New Haven and London: Yale University Press, 1981.

Joan of Arc (Jehanne d'Arc) (ca. 1412–1431)

Joan of Arc, also called the Maid of Orléans, was a peasant girl who became a national heroine and the patron saint of France. At a crucial period of the Hundred Years' War, she led the French resistance to English invaders and turned the tide of the war. A mystic visionary, Joan was ultimately captured and imprisoned by the English and condemned by an ecclesiastical court to be burned at the stake in 1431. She was 19 years old.

The France of Joan's youth was torn by civil war. The Treaty of Troyes (1422) had recognized the claim of England's Henry V to the French throne, and his heir, supported by the duke of Burgundy, was accepted as king in all parts of France controlled by England and Burgundy. The dauphin Charles, last heir of the Valois line, had no rights under the treaty but was supported by the Armagnac party, and controlled part of France south of the Loire River.

Joan was born into a peasant family in the village of Domrémy in Lorraine about 1412. By the age of 13 she began to hear what she described as her "voices," whom she later identified as the Archangel Michael and Saints Catherine and Margaret. Over the next few years these voices urged Joan to find an escort to the dauphin, from whom she was to receive an army and drive the English out of France. She resisted the voices until 1428, when she first approached the Armagnac captain Robert de Baudricourt at nearby Vaucouleurs. Baudricourt refused her at first, but her persistence finally convinced him to give her an armed escort to the dauphin's court at Chinon in February 1429. By then the English had laid siege to Orléans, the strategic gateway across the Loire into the dauphin's territory.

When Joan met the dauphin, she was able to convince him of her divine mission (some say by relating to him a private prayer he had made to God). After having her examined by a group of clerics and advisers at Poitiers to ensure her orthodoxy, Charles gave her titular command of an army. She was given armor and her own banner (reading "Jesus, Mary"), and brought to the army at Blois, 35 miles southwest of Orléans. She is said to have expelled prostitutes and forced her men to go to confession, give up foul language, and swear to refrain from looting civilians. Her army lifted the siege of Orléans on May 8, 1429, and pushed on to victories in several other cities to arrive at Rheims, where, in accordance with tradition, the dauphin was crowned King Charles VII of France on July 17. After the coronation Joan begged the king to deliver Paris from the English, but Charles was uninterested, preoccupied with trying to negotiate peace with Burgundy. While Joan was fighting on the outskirts of Paris, the king withdrew his forces, and Joan spent a restless winter at court.

In May Burgundy renewed the war, laying siege to Compiègne. Determined to help, Joan led a small army of additional troops into the city on May 23. That afternoon she led a sortie outside the city and was ambushed by Burgundian troops. Staying in the rear guard, Joan was trapped outside when the gates of the city were prematurely closed, and was captured. Philip the Good, duke of Burgundy, refused to ransom her and sold her to the English for 10,000 francs. Pierre Cauchon, the bishop of Beauvais and a longtime supporter of the Anglo-Burgundian party, was charged with organizing an ecclesiastical court in Rouen (deep in English territory) to try Joan for witchcraft and heresy. Yet against inquisitorial custom, she was held in an English military prison with male guards, a situation that put her in constant danger of rape.

Joan's trial lasted five months, and is well documented, including her often witty and confident replies to her interrogators. Ultimately, however, threatened with execution and torture, she signed a document abjuring her voices on May 24, and assumed female attire as the court directed her. But by May 28, condemned to perpetual imprisonment, she had resumed her male clothing and recanted her abjuration. She was immediately considered "relapsed" by members of the tribunal. She had a quick "Relapse Trial" May 28–29 and was convicted of "idolatry" for her cross-dressing, and of refusal to submit to the authority of the church, and on May 30, 1431, was turned over to the secular English authorities and burned at the stake at Rouen as a relapsed heretic.

Peace was concluded between France and Burgundy in 1435, and in 1436, the Armagnacs recovered Paris. They regained Rouen in 1449, and early in 1450, King Charles initiated an investigation into Joan's trial and condemnation. The church began its own inquiry into Joan's trial in 1452. In 1453, the Hundred Years' War ended, and in 1455, a rehabilitation trial opened for Joan. In 1456, the Inquisition announced her rehabilitation at Rouen, in a document read publicly declaring her trial to have been tainted with fraud and errors of law, therefore rendering the Condemnation Trial null and void. Her innocence was proclaimed and her good name restored. In 1920, Joan was canonized, and her feast day, July 10, declared a national holiday in France. She remains the only figure in history ever to be both condemned and canonized by the Catholic Church.

Joan has been of particular interest to literary scholars for a number of reasons. Her mystic "voices" have invited comparisons between her and other, more literary, female mystics of the late medieval period, like JULIAN OF NORWICH and Margery KEMPE. Further, Joan was the subject of CHRISTINE DE PIZAN's last poem, *Le Ditié de Jehanne d'Arc.* Written while Christine, an ardent Armagnac partisan, was sheltered at the abbey of Poissy, the poem is the only literary text written about Joan during her lifetime. Composed two weeks after Charles VII's coronation, it displays unbridled optimism, and sees Joan as the contemporary embodiment of the examples of courageous women Christine provided in her *BOOK OF THE CITY OF LADIES.* A host of later writers turned to Joan's life for inspiration: Maligned in Shakespeare's *Henry VI, Pt. 1,* she fares better in the hands of Voltaire, Friedrich Schiller, Mark Twain, Jean Anouilh, Bertolt Brecht, and Bernard Shaw. In addition the text of her trial itself has recently been read as a literary text in its own right (for instance, in Sullivan 1999).

Bibliography

Astell, Ann, and Bonnie Wheeler, eds. *Joan of Arc and Spirituality.* New York: Palgrave Macmillan, 2003.

Fraioli, Deborah A. *Joan of Arc: The Early Debate.* London: Boydell and Brewer, 2002.

Gordon, Mary. *Joan of Arc.* Penguin Lives. New York: Viking, 2000.

Margolis, Nadia. *Joan of Arc in History, Literature, and Film: A Select, Annotated Bibliography.* New York: Garland, 1990.

Pernoud, Régine. *Joan of Arc: By Herself and Witnesses.* Translated by Edward Hyams. Lanham, Md.: Scarborough House, 1982.

Sullivan, Karen. *The Interrogation of Joan of Arc.* Minneapolis: University of Minnesota Press, 1999.

Warner, Marina. *Joan of Arc: the Image of Female Heroism.* New York: Knopf, 1981.

Wheeler, Bonnie, and Charles T. Wood, eds. *Fresh Verdicts on Joan of Arc.* The New Middle Ages 2. New York: Garland, 1996.

John of Gaunt (duke of Lancaster) (1340–1399)

John of Gaunt, so-called after the mispronunciation of his birthplace, Ghent, was born in 1340 as the fourth son of King Edward III and Queen Philippa of England. As an infant Gaunt was declared earl of Richmond and was admitted into the Order of the Garter through that title. In 1359 Gaunt married Blanche of Lancaster, the younger of two daughters and coheiresses of Henry, duke of Lancaster (the most prominent and wealthy man in the kingdom next to the king). His marriage to Blanche made him the earl of Derby, Lincoln, Leicester, and Lancaster, and steward of England. Following the deaths of his father-in-law in 1361 and his sister-in-law in 1362, Gaunt became duke of Lancaster and recipient of one the largest English inheritances of all time. The duke and duchess had three children: Henry, duke of Hereford and Lancaster, earl of Derby, and eventually King Henry IV; Philippa, who married King John I of Portugal; and Elizabeth, who married John Holland, duke of Exeter, and Sir John Cornwall, Lord Fanhope.

When Blanche died of the plague in 1369, the duke was deeply heart-broken, but perhaps he found comfort in the commemorative *BOOK OF THE DUCHESS,* which Geoffrey CHAUCER intended as both a tribute to Blanche and a source of consolation for Gaunt, his patron. In *The Book of the Duchess,* Chaucer describes Blanche as beautiful, kind, and gentle. The poem's combination of a "love-vision" and an elegy made Chaucer's first major poem a truly unique work of literature. Besides providing Chaucer's financial livelihood (Gaunt bestowed a life pension upon him), John of Gaunt had a fairly close relationship to Chaucer: The poet's wife, Philippa, was governess to John of Gaunt's children when she married Chaucer and remained in the service of Gaunt's household, favored by the duke of Lancaster for years into her marriage. Philippa was also the sister of Katherine Swynford, who later became Gaunt's third wife. John of Gaunt is also distinguished in literature as a major character in Shakespeare's *Richard II,* in which (as in real life) he is the uncle to the king and the father to Richard's rival Henry Bolingbroke.

After Blanche's death, Lancaster married Constance of Castile, the daughter and heir of Pedro the Cruel, and the couple shared a strictly political marriage that made Gaunt king of Castile and Leon. Constance died in 1394, leaving John with one daughter by her, whom he married to Juan of Portugal's son. Eventually Gaunt's son-in-law became Henry III, king of Castile and Leon. The descendants of this alliance ruled Spain until the death of King Charles II in 1700.

After Constance died Gaunt married Katherine Swynford and had the pope and the king legitimize his four children with her, known as the Beauforts (Swynford had been Gaunt's mistress for most of Gaunt's marriage to Constance of Castile, perhaps as long as 20 years). This marriage made Chaucer and Gaunt lawfully related as brothers-in-law. The Beaufort children were John Beaufort, earl of Somerset and marquis of Dorset; Henry Beaufort, cardinal and chancellor of England; Thomas Beaufort, duke of Ester; and Joan Beaufort. The Beauforts were active in Henry Tudor's rise to the throne.

Although he was never king, John of Gaunt exercised nearly royal power during the last year of Edward III's reign and during Richard II's minority. He was unpopular with the public (his London home, the Savoy, was destroyed in 1381 during the PEASANT'S REVOLT as a mob cried, "We will have no king called John") because of his demonstrations of power, his defense of his elderly father's government, his attacks upon the church and on the privileges of London, and the people's suspicion that he had sinister ambitions.

Gaunt was without a doubt one of the most influential and important political figures during the latter half of the 14th century. He is remembered for acquiring the county of Lancaster for his successors and as the founder of ruling houses in 15th-century England, Portugal, Castile, and Aragon and even the Tudor dynasty. Gaunt died in 1399 and was buried (according to his will) beside his first and evidently favorite wife, Blanche, in St. Paul's Cathedral in London.

Bibliography

Armitage-Smith, Sydney. *John of Gaunt: King of Castile and Leon, Duke of Aquitaine and Lancaster, Earl of Derby, Lincoln, and Leicester, Seneschal of England.* New York: Barnes and Noble, 1964.

Dillon, Bert. "John of Gaunt." In *A Chaucer Dictionary: Proper Names and Allusions, Excluding Place Names.* Boston: G. K. Hall and Co., 1974.

Goodman, Anthony. *John of Gaunt: The Exercise of Princely Power in Fourteenth-Century Europe.* New York: St. Martin's Press, 1992.

Mehl, Dieter. *Geoffrey Chaucer: An Introduction to his Narrative Poetry.* A revised and expanded translation of *Geoffrey Chaucer, eine Einführung inseine erzä Dichturgen* by Erich Schmidt, Verlag Gmbh. 1973. Cambridge: Cambridge University Press, 1986.

Leslie Johnston

John of Salisbury (ca. 1115–1180)

John of Salisbury was a churchman and a scholar, a scholastic philosopher who was one of the premier Latinists of his age. He was a student of Peter ABELARD and was secretary, friend, and biographer of Thomas BECKET, but he is best remembered as author of the *Polycraticus* (The statesman's book).

John was born into a Saxon family near Salisbury in Wiltshire in the south of England. Not much is known about his early life, but in 1136 he traveled to France, where he spent 12 years studying in various cathedral schools. He studied under Abelard at his school at Mont St. Genevieve until the great man retired, then from 1138–40 studied grammar and the Latin classics at Chartres under William of Conches (who had written an important commentary on *The CONSOLATION OF PHILOSOPHY of BOETHIUS*) and the scientific curriculum of the LIBERAL ARTS, the *quadrivium* under Richard l'Evque. William and Richard were disciples of the great teacher Bernard of Chartres, who was known for his emphasis on Platonic philosophy and on the study of Latin literary classics, both of which play a role in Salisbury's writing. Ultimately he returned to Paris where he completed his education in theology between 1141 and 1145.

In 1148 Salisbury attended the Council of Reims, where he obtained, from St. BERNARD OF CLAIRVAUX, a letter of introduction to Theobold, archbishop of Canterbury. He also seems to have become part of the papal retinue, and spent the next several years at the court of Pope Eugenius III in Rome. In 1154 he returned to England, where he became secretary to Archbishop Theobald. It was at Canterbury that he wrote his two best-known works, the *Polycraticus* and the *Metalogion,* both of which he dedicated to Becket, then chancellor of England. About 1159, Salisbury fell into disfavor with King HENRY II, and although he remained as secretary to the new archbishop when Becket assumed the post in 1162, Salisbury was ultimately forced to leave England altogether in 1163, taking refuge in Reims with his friend Peter of La Celle, who was abbot of St. Remigius. Becket's own difficulties with Henry led him to follow Salisbury into exile at Reims, and Salisbury spent several years trying to promote a reconciliation between the archbishop and the king. In 1170, efforts apparently successful, Salisbury returned to England with Becket. Salisbury was probably present with the archbishop when, on December 29 of that year, he was murdered by Henry's agents in Canterbury Cathedral.

Following Becket's murder, Salisbury continued his career as statesman and churchman. He was made treasurer of Exeter Cathedral in 1174, and in 1176 was appointed bishop of Chartres. As bishop, he attended the third Lateran Council in 1179, and died the following year. He was buried near Chartres, at the monastery of St. Josaphat.

Salisbury was one of the most sophisticated scholars of his day, and his literary output reflects his wide learning and his facility with the Latin language. Some 300 of his letters survive, written to various scholars and leaders of his time, and give a vivid picture of intellectual life in the 12th century. He wrote a *Vita Sti. Anselmi* (Life of St. ANSELM) in 1163, and his *Vita Sti. Thomae Cantuar* (Life of Saint Thomas of Canterbury) in 1171. His *Historia pontificalus* (Pontifical history), composed ca. 1163, is an eyewitness history of the papacy during Salisbury's time in service in Rome, from 1148–52. The *Metalogicon* is a treatise in four books concerned with the correct use of logic. It contains information about education in the 12th century, and about the scholastic controversies of Salisbury's age. His best-known work, the *Polycraticus,* is a study in eight books concerned with the principles of government, providing an account of the ideals of feudal society. Salisbury's work in general is a model of elegant Latin prose and depth of learning.

Bibliography

John of Salisbury. *The Historia pontificalis of John of Salisbury.* Edited and translated by Marjorie Chibnall. Oxford: Clarendon Press, 1986.

The Letters of John of Salisbury. Edited by W. J. Millor and H. E. Butler. Revised by C. N. L. Brooke. Oxford: Clarendon Press, 1986.

———. *The Metalogicon of John of Salisbury: A Twelfth-Century Defense of the Verbal and Logical Arts of the Trivium.* Translated with an introduction and notes by Daniel D. McGarry. 1955. Westport, Conn.: Greenwood Press, 1982.

———. *Polycraticus: The Statesman's Book.* Abridged and edited with an introduction by Murray F. Markland. New York: F. Ungar, 1979.

Wilks, Michael J., ed. *The World of John of Salisbury.* Oxford: Published for the Ecclesiastical History Society by B. Blackwell, 1984.

Joinville, Jean, sire de (ca. 1224–1317)

Jean, sire de Joinville, is best known as the author of a lively and vivid biography of Louis IX (St. Louis), a narrative based on his personal memoirs of his friendship with the king and their exploits in the Seventh Crusade (1248–54). Joinville was a knight of Champagne who outlived Louis and three of his royal successors and who, in his 80s, composed his memoirs at the request of the royal family.

Jean was the son of the seneschal of Champagne, Simon de Joinville, and his second wife, Béatrix de Bourgogne. After his elder brother Geoffroy's early death in 1232 or 1233, Jean became the successor to the family estates, but his mother ruled in his stead from 1233 until 1245. In 1240 Jean married Alixe de Grandpré, to whom he had been engaged since 1230. She bore him two children. After his wife's death in 1261, Jean married Alixe de Reynel, who bore him six children. In 1248, Jean joined the Seventh Crusade, during which he met the French king Louis IX. The crusaders attacked Damietta and al-Mansourah in Egypt, but on the route to Cairo the army was defeated and both Louis and Jean were taken prisoners. Only after a heavy ransom had been paid were both freed in 1250, whereupon they left Egypt and sailed to Acre in Palestine, where they fortified towns and established order among the Christian barons. Finally in 1254, the French army returned home, but the whole enterprise proved to be a failure and very costly for everyone involved, including Jean, who lost a good part of his estates to his creditors. When Louis decided to go on a second crusade in 1267, Jean refused to accompany him again, but he continued in the king's service until the latter's death near Tunis in 1270. Jean himself lived until 1317. Between 1305 and 1309, Jean wrote the *Vie de saint Louis* (*Life of Saint Louis*), a most important prose memoir that sheds significant light on the aristocratic world of 13th-century France.

Although Jean enjoyed a close relationship with the king, in his *Vie* he did not refrain from expressing his criticism of some of Louis's decisions dictated by his religious idealism, but often in disregard of the military and political necessities. Queen Joan of Navarre commissioned Jean to write these memoirs as a model for her son, Louis

IX's grandson, the future King Louis X. Although several copies were made, the *Vie* was soon forgotten and not rediscovered until the 18th century. Today it is regarded as a major chronicle text that informs us about the deeply religious king, the crusade, and 13th-century aristocratic life in general. Between 1250 and 1251, Jean also composed a short treatise, *Li romans as ymages des poinz de nostre foi,* in which he offered a type of written and visual credo (explanation of one's belief) for the religious reader. We also have one letter from Jean that he wrote to King Louis X in 1315.

Bibliography

Corbett, Noel L., ed. *La vie de Saint Louis: le témoignage de Jehan, seigneur de Joinville: texte du XIVe siecle.* Sherbrooke, Québec: Naaman, 1977.

Friedman, Lionel J. *Text and Iconography for Joinville's Credo.* Cambridge, Mass.: Mediaeval Academy of America, 1958.

Monfrin, J., ed. *Vie de saint Louis.* Paris: Dunod, 1995.

Shaw, Margaret R. B., ed. and trans. *Chronicles of the Crusades.* Harmondsworth, U.K.: Penguin, 1983.

Slattery, Maureen. *Myth, Man, and Sovereign Saint: King Louis IX in Jean de Joinville's Sources.* New York: P. Lang, 1985.

Albrecht Classen

jongleur *(joglar)*

The jongleur (or *joglar,* in Provençal) was an itinerant professional entertainer known chiefly in medieval France and Occitan, but also in Spain, Italy, and Norman England. The particular term was used as early as the eighth century, though jongleurs seem to have been known in France from the fifth to the 15th centuries. In the beginning the term referred to a professional entertainer of any kind, including jugglers (a term derived from *jongleur*), acrobats, dancers, actors, and musicians. By the 10th century, however, the term was used exclusively for musical entertainers.

In Occitan, beginning in the 11th century, *joglars* would perform lyrics composed by the TROUBADOURS. Often the troubadour would mention the *joglar*'s name in the *tornada,* or ending envoi of the song, mentioning as well the song's intended recipient—often through a *senhal* or pseudonym—who might be expected to reward the *joglar* for delivering and performing the song. One of Jaufre RUDEL's lyrics ends:

Without any letter of parchment
I send this vers, which we sing
in our plain romance tongue,
to En Hugo Brun, by Filhol;

(Goldin 1973, 105, ll. 29–32)

Here Filhol is the *joglar,* who apparently was expected to memorize the song to perform for En Hugo, rather than carry it in written form. In another lyric *tornada,* BERNART DE VENTADORN writes:

Garsio, now sing my song
for me, and take it
to my Messenger, who was there.
I ask what counsel he would give.

(Goldin 1973, 145, ll. 61–64)

Garsio is the *joglar,* and the "Messenger" is the *senhal* for Bernart's friend or patron, the addressee of the song.

These kinds of *tornadas* became less and less frequent from the 12th through 13th centuries, which, as William Paden points out, may suggest that the means of delivery for the songs was changing from an oral to a written medium. The destruction of Occitan culture during the Albigensian Crusade in the 13th century may also have had something to do with this decline.

In northern France the *jongleur* was employed to sing and disseminate the songs of the TROUVÈRES, but in northern France jongleurs also recited ballads, told stories and saints' lives, and sang CHANSONS DE GESTE.

The importance of *jongleurs* is chiefly a function of their wandering. Relying on the compositions of others, such as troubadours, *jongleurs* traveled among various courts and countries, disseminating vernacular songs and lyric poetry throughout western Europe. They provided one vehicle for troubadour poetry, particularly lyrics in the COURTLY LOVE vein, to migrate from court to court and even country to country.

Bibliography

Goldin, Frederick, ed. and trans. *Lyrics of the Troubadours and Trouvères: An Anthology and a History.* Garden City, New York: Anchor, 1973.

Harvey, Ruth E. "Joglars and the Professional Status of the Early Troubadours," *Medium Ævum* 62 (1993): 221–241.

Paden, William D. "The Role of the Joglar." In *Chrétien de Troyes and the Troubadours: Essays in Memory of the Late Leslie Topsfield,* edited by Peter S. Noble and Linda M. Paterson. Cambridge: St. Catherine's College, 1984.

Judah Halevi (Yehuda Halevy) (ca. 1071–ca. 1141)

Judah Halevi was probably the most celebrated Hebrew poet of the Middle Ages. He was also a philosopher and theologian famous for his *Book of the Kuzari* in Arabic prose. A Spanish Jew by birth, Halevi planned a pilgrimage to the Holy Land late in his life, probably dying in Egypt without ever seeing Palestine.

Halevi was born either in the Muslim city of Tudela on the border of Christian Spain, or in Muslim Toledo just before the so-called Reconquest of that city by Christians in 1071. In his youth, Halevi traveled to the various scholarly centers maintained among Andalusian Jews. He formed a close friendship with fellow poet Moses ibn Ezra in Granada, and a friendly exchange of poems between the two has survived. Ultimately, Halevi settled in Christian Toledo, capital of Alfonso VI's Castile. He worked as a physician in Toledo, apparently under the direct patronage of the king. But when ill-feeling toward the Jews erupted into violence in 1108–09, violence that claimed the life of his close friend Solomon ibn Ferrizuel, Halevi elected to return to Muslim Spain, settling in Córdoba.

It was here that Halevi wrote what he called his *Book of Argument and Proof in Defence of the Despised Faith,* which was to become known as *The Book of the Kuzari,* because it is inspired by the historical conversion of the king of the Kazars to Judaism in the eighth century. Composed as a dialogue between a rabbi and the Kavar king, Halevi's treatise is the only important Jewish classic presented in the form of a Platonic dialogue. The book was translated from Arabic into Hebrew during the 12th century. Unlike other medieval Jewish philosophers such as MAIMONIDES, Halevi is not interested in reconciling Judaism with Aristotelian philosophy. He is chiefly interested in asserting the superiority of revealed truth to philosophical arguments, though he does employ philosophy to demonstrate the truth of revelation. The God of Abraham, for Halevi, is not the same as the God of Aristotle. His existence is shown through his working in Jewish history, and the Jews therefore are spiritually superior to the rest of humankind, and their prophetic mission is to bring God's word to the world.

It was shortly after his completion of the *Book of the Kuzari* that Halevi made his decision to emigrate. His experiences among Christians and Muslims in Spain and his philosophical explorations of his faith led him to the determination to live in Israel's promised land. He left Spain in 1140 bound for Egypt. According to legend, Halevi's literary reputation preceded him to Alexandria, where he was welcomed with great acclamation. Legend says he visited Damascus and Tyre before arriving in Palestine—where an Arab horseman trampled him to death as he recited his poem "Elegy for Zion" before the gates of Jerusalem. Documents recently discovered in Egypt, however, suggest that in fact Halevi died there and never reached Jerusalem.

Judah Halevi's poetry, like that of his friend Moses ibn Ezra, takes many of the forms and conventions of contemporary Spanish Arabic poetry such as meter and rhyme, and adapts them to classical Hebrew verse. Nearly 1,000 extant poems are attributed to Halevi, and they generally fall into three categories: The first is secular poetry, focusing on love or on friendship or sometimes even on wine; a second category is religious poetry, characterized by an intense love of God; and the third is national poetry, closely related to his religious poetry since for him the nation is the locus of

God's interaction in the history of his people. One of his poems, editorially entitled "To Israel, in exile," demonstrates this, using the voice of God speaking to his people:

O sleeper, whose heart is awake, burning
and raging, now wake
and go forth, and walk in the light of My
presence. . . . Let them not
exalt, those who say "Zion is desolate!" for
My heart is in Zion and
My eyes are there. I reveal Myself and I
conceal Myself, now I
rage, now I consent—but who has more
compassion than I have
for My children?

(Carmi 1981, 334–335)

It is only in Zion that the Jew can be completely united with God. Halevi's "Songs of Zion" are his best-known poems, and his realization of the theme of passionate love and longing for the Holy Land is the most effective since the Psalms themselves.

Bibliography

Carmi, T. *The Penguin Book of Hebrew Verse.* Harmondsworth, U.K.: Penguin, 1981.

Silman, Yochanan. *Philosopher and Prophet: Judah Halevi, the Kuzari, and the Evolution of His Thought.* Translated by Lenn F. Schramm. Albany: State University of New York Press, 1995.

Judas (ca. 1250)

The religious carol called *Judas* is preserved in a single manuscript from the 13th century, now at Trinity College of Cambridge University. The poem consists of 18 couplets in seven-beat lines that can be easily rewritten as the familiar alternating tetrameter/trimeter lines rhyming *abcb* that make up the English BALLAD stanza. This has led scholars to consider *Judas* the oldest extant written example (by some 200 years) of a popular English ballad.

Written in a Southwestern dialect of MIDDLE ENGLISH, the text includes the parallelism and incremental repetition as well as the quick-moving narrative and absence of transitions common to folk ballads. The subject matter, based largely on the New Testament but partly on medieval traditions concerning Judas Iscariot, is somewhat atypical of the later popular ballads. In fact the details of the narrative, particularly those concerning Judas's sister, are unique and remarkable, having no known source in any other text.

In the poem Christ sends Judas with 30 pieces of silver to procure the Maundy Thursday meal for himself and his disciples. On the way Judas meets his sister, who chides him for following a false prophet. He defends his master, but accepts his sister's invitation to sleep with his head in her lap. When he awakens his money is gone, and his sister nowhere to be found. He then meets a "rich Jew" named Pilate, who asks him if he will "sell" his master. Frantic to regain the 30 pieces of silver entrusted to him by Christ, Judas agrees. The scene shifts abruptly to the Last Supper, with Jesus announcing to the disciples that he has been bought and sold for their meat. Judas leaps up to ask whether he is the guilty one, and before an answer comes, Peter rises to vow his support of Christ though Pilate come with "ten hundred" knights. The poem ends with Christ saying Peter will forsake him three times before the cock crows.

The poem's amelioration of Judas's guilt is certainly extraordinary, though the invention of the apocryphal character of Judas's sister who becomes ultimately responsible for the betrayal of Christ is not terribly surprising given the atmosphere of misogyny so common among medieval clerics and their emphasis on Eve's responsibility for original sin. There is some question as to whether *Judas* can really be considered a popular ballad, but Child did include it as number 23 in his collection.

Bibliography

Boklund-Lagopoulou, Karin Margareta. " 'Judas': The First English Ballad?" *Medium Aevum* 62 (1993): 20–34.

Child, Francis James, ed. *The English and Scottish Popular Ballads.* 5 vols. 1882–98. New York: Cooper Square Publishers, 1965.

Judith (ca. 950)

Judith is an OLD ENGLISH poem retelling the story of the apocryphal Old Testament book of Judith as written in the Vulgate Bible. The anonymous poet applies the heroic style and attitudes of Anglo-Saxon heroic poetry to the story of the Jewish heroine Judith, who saves her people from the Assyrian army through her own courage and faith in God. The actively heroic female protagonist is unusual in Old English literature.

Judith immediately follows the text of *BEOWULF* in the famous COTTON VITELLIUS A.XV manuscript. The text as it survives is fragmentary. It begins with an incomplete line and runs another 349 lines. The numerals X, XI, and XII appear in the margins, suggesting that the original poem consisted of 12 divisions of "fits," and that we have only the last three and a small portion of fit IX. Scholars have suggested that the complete poem must have consisted of some 1,200 or 1,300 lines, with each fit containing 100 lines or so. But other scholars believe that we have very nearly the entire poem: The opening that we have is echoed in the closing lines of the poem, focusing on Judith's confidence in God's grace. Further, the poet's adaptation of the book of Judith focuses freely on episodes that conform easily to Old English poetic conventions, like battle scenes and scenes in the Assyrian general Holofernes's banquet, portrayed as in a Germanic mead hall. The parts of the source that detract from the pure narrative—the long exposition and background to the war with Assyria, and Judith's long hymn of thanksgiving to God that ends the book—are the parts that are missing from the extant poem. It is quite possible that the poet never included them.

The poem as we have it begins as Judith is invited to a feast in the Assyrian camp. After much carousing the Assyrian soldiers bring the beautiful virgin Judith to the tent of their general Holofernes, who, drunk with wine, falls into a stupor. At this point Judith, anachronistically invoking the Holy Trinity in her prayer for heaven's help, draws a sword she has concealed and with two blows hacks off the Assyrian's head. She and her maid conceal the head and make their way back to the besieged city of Bethulia. Here she shows her kinsmen the general's head and urges them to take arms and attack the Assyrian encampment. Stunned by the sudden attack, the Assyrian soldiers turn to their general and find his decapitated body, at which point they flee, and the poem ends with their destruction by the Jewish defenders of Bethulia.

The poet's style is vivid and focuses on action. Only two characters are named in the poem, thus emphasizing the diametric opposition of Judith and Holofernes. The poet expands details of the battle and portrays Holofernes as a degenerate version of a Germanic leader in his hall, entertaining his retainers. The internal rhyme and use of unusually long alliterative lines suggest that the poem was written late in the Old English period, probably in 10th-century Wessex. At that time the figure of Judith was commonly used as an example to Christian women to be chaste and to resist bravely the devil. But particularly in the later 10th century, during the period of increased Viking invasions under the reign of Ethelred "the Unready," Judith became a model of resistance, so that AELFRIC, for example, cites her as a figure of armed defense against heathen foreign invaders. It is likely the *Judith* poet had the same kind of encouragement in mind. Attempts to link the character of Judith to a historical woman, like Queen Aethelfled of Mercia (d. 918)—famed for victorious battles against the Danes—have not won widespread scholarly consensus. But the poet certainly hoped to arouse a similar martial spirit in his readers.

Bibliography

Beowulf and Judith. Edited by Elliot Van Kirk Dobbie. Vol. 4, The Anglo-Saxon Poetic Records. New York: Columbia University Press, 1953.

Godden, Malcolm. "Biblical Literature: The Old Testament," in *The Cambridge Companion to Old English Literature,* edited by Malcolm Godden and Michael Lapidge. Cambridge: Cambridge University Press, 1991, 206–226.

Harmann, J. P. "The Theme of Spiritual Warfare in Old English *Judith,*" *Philological Quarterly* 55 (1976): 1–9.

Kaske, R. E. "Sapientia et Fortitudo in the Old English Judith." In *The Wisdom of Poetry: Essays in Early English Literature in Honor of Morton W. Bloomfield,* edited by Larry D. Benson and Siegfried

Wenzel, 13–29. Kalamazoo: Medieval Institute Publications, Western Michigan University, 1982.

Nelson, Marie, trans. *Judith, Juliana, and Elene: Three Fighting Saints.* New York: Peter Lang, 1991.

Woolf, R. "The Lost Opening to the *Judith,*" *Modern Language Review* 50 (1955): 168–172.

Julian of Norwich (1342–ca. 1416)

The first woman writer in the English language whose name we know, Julian of Norwich was a late 14th-century mystic about whom we know very little beyond the autobiographical details she shares in the text of her *Showings,* sometimes called by later editors the *Revelations of Divine Love.*

She was born in 1342, probably in Norwich. At the age of 30 and a half, she says in her *Book of Showings,* on May 13, 1373, she was suffering from an illness that she thought would take her life. During that night she had a series of 16 visions. Shortly after her recovery, she wrote down what she remembered of these "showings." But over a period of 20 years, she says, she contemplated the revelations (she never had any other visions after that night), and she wrote a second, longer text that interprets the visions in a more thorough and sophisticated manner. Thus the *Showings* survive in two different versions: the shorter, earlier version, dated about 1373; and the later, longer version, from about 1393.

It is possible that Julian was in holy orders at the time of her illness, but there is no way to know. Her *Showings* do reveal that she was educated and familiar with religious writings in both English and Latin, but some of that familiarity could have been gained after the crisis of her illness. In any case she made the decision to become an anchoress—a religious recluse confined to an enclosed cell who takes a vow never to leave, but to devote her life to prayer. This decision may have been a response to her visions. Her cell was attached to the church of St. Julian in Norwich, which suggests that "Julian" may have been a name she adopted at the time of her enclosure. Four extant Norwich wills leave her money for her maintenance, the last of these dated 1416. Since she is mentioned in no documents after 1416, she must have died shortly after that date.

Julian is also mentioned in the *Book of Margery Kempe,* wherein Margery KEMPE seeks out the anchoress for advice in spiritual matters, in which Julian seems to have had a reputation as an expert.

Julian's *Showings* are written in a rather colloquial style full of vivid, concrete imagery. Her most memorable images are simple and natural, such as the image of God holding in his hand a ball the size of a hazelnut, and telling Julian this is "all that is made" (chapter 5), thereby implying the fragile and minute nature of the entire created universe as compared with the majesty of God. She can create powerful effects through simple repetition and parallelism, as when the Lord tells her that sin is necessary, but "all shall be well, and all shall be well, and all manner of thing shall be well" (chapter 27).

Theologically Julian is best known for her doctrine of the motherhood of Christ (chapters 58–59). While the doctrine of God as mother has its roots in the Bible itself and in other medieval theologians, Julian's expression of the second person of the trinity as female is distinctive. In her theology Christ is the person from whom we derive our human nature, so that Christ is our mother twice: He bears us and also redeems us, thereby giving us a second birth. Julian further associates "God our Mother" (the second person of the trinity) with wisdom. In this she follows the traditional association of Christ as the logos of John's Gospel (the "Word" of God—a term from Greek philosophy associated with reason) with the Jewish personification of Wisdom, who is female in the Old Testament.

Julian gives us a number of other profound theological insights, but the theme of the whole of her *Showings* and of God's revelations to her on that night in 1373 she sums up in one word: love. "Love was his meaning," she says at the conclusion of the *Showings* (chapter 86). Nothing, she insists, can separate us from God's love.

Bibliography

Baker, Denise Nowakowski. *Julian of Norwich's Showings: From Vision to Book.* Princeton, N.J.: Princeton University Press, 1994.

Dinshaw, Carolyn, and David Wallace, eds. *The Cambridge Companion to Medieval Women's Writing.* Cambridge: Cambridge University Press, 2003.

Julian of Norwich. *A Book of Showings to the Anchoress Julian of Norwich.* Edited by Edmund Colledge and James Walsh. 2 vols. Toronto: Pontifical Institute of Mediaeval Studies, 1978.

McEntire, Sandra J., ed. *Julian of Norwich: A Book of Essays.* New York: Garland, 1998.

Nuth, Joan M. *Wisdom's Daughter: The Theology of Julian of Norwich.* New York: Crossroads, 1992.

Junius Manuscript (The Caedmon Manuscript) (ca. 1000)

MS Junius 11 in Oxford's Bodleian Library (MS 5123) is one of the four major collections that contain virtually all extant OLD ENGLISH poetry. The manuscript, named for the 17th-century antiquarian Franciscus Junius (who donated it to the university), contains four lengthy Old English poems on Christian subjects: *GENESIS*, *EXODUS*, *DANIEL*, and *CHRIST AND SATAN*. The poems are difficult to date, but clearly were written between the seventh and the 10th centuries.

Junius had postulated that the author of these poems was the legendary poet CAEDMON, who according to the Venerable BEDE was the first to couple Christian subjects with Germanic poetic form. Modern scholarship no longer accepts the attribution to Caedmon, partly because it seems clear that the poems were not written by the same poet. But the poetry in the manuscript is still sometimes regarded as being in the "Caedmonian School."

Of all the Old English poetic codices, the Junius Manuscript is the most elaborately manufactured. It was produced by four distinct hands about the year 1000, at Christ Church in Canterbury according to some speculations. All half lines are carefully punctuated. Sections of the text are marked by elaborately illuminated initial capitals in animal forms. The manuscript is also illustrated by a number of line drawings.

Bibliography

Krapp, George Philip, ed. *The Junius Manuscript.* Vol. 1, *Anglo-Saxon Poetic Records.* New York: Columbia University Press, 1931.

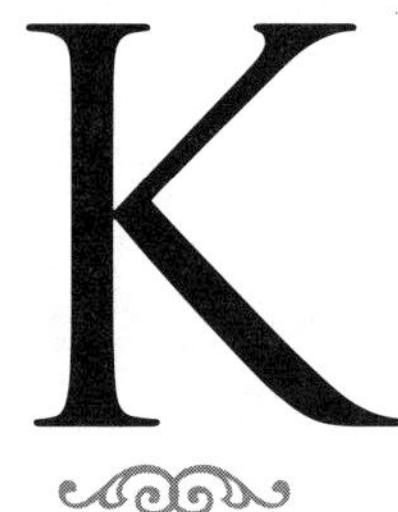

Kabir (fl. ca. 1450)

Kabir was a northern Indian poet and mystic, one of the most influential poet-saints of the bhakti movement—a spiritual movement that became popular in India between the 12th and 18th centuries. The bhakti focused on a passionate devotion to god, and stressed that this devotion was internal—independent of the traditional, external Hindu rituals or social mores. Kabir, who was raised a Muslim in the low social caste of weavers, condemned both Muslim and Hindu ritual, and opposed the institutionalized caste system as well. Presenting a mysticism that transcends religious sectarianism, Kabir's poetry has influenced Hindus and Muslims as well as Sikhs in India through the ages.

Details of Kabir's life are shrouded in mystery and legend. One tradition claims that he was of virgin birth, his Brahman mother having become pregnant while visiting a Hindu shrine. In any case he may have been illegitimate: Legend says he was adopted as an infant by a Muslim family in the city of Benares (Varanasi), and was raised as a part of a community of weavers recently converted to Islam—his name is a Muslim word meaning "the great," an epithet of Allah. Another legend says that he became a disciple of the famous Hindu guru Ramananda. While some say he studied Hindu texts, other traditions claim that he had no formal education and was illiterate, having learned only to write the word *Rama*—a Hindu name for god. His songs, in the Hindi language, were most likely performed before an audience of Muslims and Hindus from all social classes. The poems display an ecumenical fusion of Muslim and Hindu traditions, and present the divine power as an undifferentiated god with whom the human soul seeks to unite.

Legends of miracles surround Kabir's life. One tradition says he fed a great crowd of people through a divine miracle. Another legend has him walking on water. But the most famous legend concerns Kabir's death. He is rumored to have been banished from Benares for his unorthodox teaching, and to have spent many years wandering through the cities of northern India, finally dying at Maghar near Gorakhpur. Yet he is said to have had many disciples from both the Hindu and Muslim traditions, and upon his death the Hindus wanted his body for cremation, while the Muslims wanted it for burial. But before the heated argument could erupt into violence between the factions, it was discovered that a great heap of flowers had replaced Kabir's body under his shroud. The flowers were divided equally among Kabir's followers.

These legends suggest the reverence in which Kabir was held by subsequent generations. The poems of his most important collection, the *Bijak* (a name that probably means "account book"), reveal a universal mysticism characteristic of a particular branch of the bhakti movement called *nirgun* ("without qualities"), in which, like many other mystical traditions, god is perceived as unnamable and limitless. Human institutions like orthodox religions that involve external rituals, or the study of sacred texts, or the ascetic discipline associated with yoga, are all meaningless. God must be approached through the devotion of interior spiritual practice that spontaneously and mystically seeks unity with him.

Of the Hindus, Kabir says:

I've seen the pious Hindus, rule-followers,
early morning bath-takers—
killing souls, they worship rocks.

(Hess and Singh 1983, "Saints, I see the world is mad," ll.4–6)

The Muslims fare no better:

I've seen plenty of Muslim teachers, holy
men
reading their holy books
and teaching their pupils techniques.
They know just as much.

(Hess and Singh 1983, "Saints, I see the world is mad," ll.7–10)

The only real truth involves the disintegration of all such boundaries in the unity of god:

Kabir says, plunge into Ram!
There: No Hindu. No Turk.

(Hess and Singh 1983, "It's a heavy confusion," ll.11–12)

Kabir's poetry displays a reverential tone toward god, but an ironic and iconoclastic tone toward society. He uses a conversational vernacular that has made his songs accessible to generations of Indians of all classes. Some of his poems, epigrammatic couplets called *doha,* are so much a part of the popular culture in northern India that even today people will sometimes preface what they say with, "As Kabir says . . ." In recent decades his poems have been translated by American poet Robert Bly and earlier by the Indian Nobel Prize winner Rabindranath Tagore.

Bibliography

Kabir. *The Bijak of Kabir.* Translated by Linda Hess and Shuledev Singh. San Francisco: North Point Press, 1989.

———. *The Kabir Book: Forty-four of the Ecstatic Poems of Kabir.* Translated by Robert Bly. Boston: Beacon Press, 1977.

———. *Songs of Kabir.* Translated by Rabindranath Tagore. New York: S. Weiser, 1974.

Sethi, V. K. *Kabir: The Weaver of God's Name.* Punjab, India: Radha Soami Satsang Beas, 1984.

Vaudeville, Charlotte. *A Weaver Named Kabir.* Delhi: Oxford University Press, 1993.

Kaiserchronik (ca. 1146–1150)

An anonymous Middle High German author (or authors) composed, sometime between 1146 and 1150 in Regensburg, a versified world chronicle in 17,283 verses, with special emphasis on the Roman Empire, from the founding of the city of Rome by Romulus and Remus to the time of the German Hohenstaufen king Conrad III (d. 1151), creating an uninterrupted line of rulers far into the High Middle Ages. According to the *Kaiserchronik,* the establishment of the Roman Empire by Julius Caesar, the transformation of that empire into a Christian one by Constantine, and the foundation of Germany through CHARLEMAGNE were the highlights of the entire world history. The author(s) heavily relied on many legends and anecdotes about well-known Roman figures, such as Sylvester (pope from 314–335), who converted Emperor Constantine the Great to Christianity in 314 C.E.), St. Faustina (d. 580), and Crescentia (third- or fourth-century Christian martyr), to illustrate the individual emperors' moral and ethical character. The entire history of medieval Germany, however, is only briefly dealt with in the final 3,000 verses. The chronicle pursues the historical sequence of the emperors and, at the end, of many dukes and princes, although we observe numerous fabrications and gaps.

The author(s) clearly harbored negative sentiments against the Greeks from antiquity, and espoused the idea that both the German emperor and the pope shared the responsibility for the Christian empire. Many of the profound, historically documented conflicts between both the emperor and the pope are ignored, whereas the history of the German Empire is intimately connected with ancient Rome through an uninterrupted line of rulers. The combination of historical and fictional material in the *Kaiserchronik,* such as the foundation of the Frankish tribes by the Homeric Trojans after the destruction of their city at the hands of the Greeks, the inclusion of accounts about famous protagonists in Germanic epic poetry (Dietrich of Bern), and finally the blending of myths with facts (wrong identification of the Huns under Attila with the Hungarians), guaranteed its considerable popularity (more than 40 manuscripts). The author(s) drew much of the material from Latin and vernacular sources; the early Middle High German *Annolied* (ca. 1077) provided the crucial basis for the discussion of Caesar and the Germans.

Bibliography

Knape, Joachim. "Historiography as Rhetoric." In *The Medieval Chronicle II,* edited by Erik Kooper, 117–129. Amsterdam: Editions Rodopi, 2002.

Ohly, Ernst Friedrich. *Sage und Legende in der Kaiserchronik. Untersuchungen über Quellen und Aufbau der Dichtung.* Darmstadt, Germany: Wissenschaftliche Buchgesellschaft, 1968.

Schröder, Edward, ed. *Die Kaiserchronik eines Regensburger Geistlichen.* Monumenta Germaniae Historica. Deutsche Chroniken, I/1. 1895. Berlin: Weidmann, 1964.

Albrecht Classen

Kakinomoto no Hitomaro (Hitomaro) (fl. 689–700)

The acknowledged genius of the huge eighth-century Japanese poetry anthology called the MAN'YŌSHŪ, the court poet Hitomaro, as he is familiarly known, is widely regarded as master of the verse form called the *chōka,* or "long poem." The *Man'yōshū* contains 19 *chōka* and about 75 short poems (the 31-syllable *tanka*) directly attributed to Hitomaro. A number of the *tanka,* as was customary, function as envois (or *hanka*) appended to the longer *chōka.* There are, in addition, some 380 other poems in the collection, mostly *tanka,* that are said to derive from something called the *Hitomaro Kashū* (Hitomaro poem collection), but it is unclear how many of these poems are actually his (some are demonstrably not written by him) or what the relationship of these poems is to the poet.

Virtually nothing is known of Hitomaro's life, and no contemporary references to him exist outside of the headnotes to his poems in the *Man'yōshū.* It seems probable that he was a court official of minor status, without any real power or authority, and not significant enough to appear in any official histories of his time. Although in his society, anyone associated with the court was expected to be able to compose a short poem on occasion, Hitomaro was more of an official court poet. He may have been active during the reign of the emperor Temmu (672–686), but seems to have been essentially poet laureate for his widow, the empress Jitō, who officially reigned from 686 to 696, though she kept real power until her death in 702. Hitomaro documents the great events of Jitō's reign, whether a grand imperial procession to Yoshino or some other site, or the death of some member of the royal family. His earliest datable poem is a lament on the death of Prince Kusakabe in 689, while his latest is another lament, this time for the princess Asuka, written in 700. Hitomaro's devotion to the imperial family was deep, sincere, and religious. Many of his poems begin with a formula proclaiming the sovereignty and divinity of the empress, and his lament for Prince Kusakabe begins with an account of the divine ancestry of the imperial family, a tenet of the Shinto religion. It has been observed that Hitomaro's poetry is uniformly Shinto in its worldview, and does not evince any overt influence of the Buddhism that was becoming more prevalent in Japan during his lifetime. One can, however, see in several of his poems a general conviction of the impermanence of the physical world, a sentiment that might be borrowed from Buddhism.

It is customary to divide Hitomaro's poems into two categories: the "public poems," that he wrote in his role as court poet, and the "private poems" in which he deals with more personal and intimate moments. The most acclaimed of Hitomaro's public poems (and the longest poem in the *Man'yōshū* at 149 lines) is his *chōka* "Following the temporary enshrinement of Prince Takechi," who had died in 696 at the age of 42. Takechi had made his reputation fighting the Jinshin War in 672 for his father, the emperor Temmu. Afterward he was made prime minister and designated crown prince during the reign of his mother, the empress Jitō. The poem opens with a praise of the emperor Temmu, and ends with a description of the great palace that Prince Takechi had built on Mount Kagu, suggesting that although Takechi was gone, his works—like the palace—would live on. The central section of the poem is a stirring description of the battle in which Takechi made his reputation. It is unique in medieval Japanese poetry in its prolonged description of the battle, and proceeds generally by the depiction of basic human emotions amid highly visual images in the form of similes, as in these lines:

Frightful to hear was the bow-strings'
clang,
Like a whirlwind sweeping
Through a winter forest of snow.
And like snow-flakes tempest-driven
The arrows fell thick and fast.

(Nippon Gakujutsu Sinkōkai 1965, 40)

It is Hitomaro's private poems, however, that are most admired today, largely because of their elegant expression of universal human emotion. Among these is his famous poem on abandoning his wife in Iwami while leaving for the capital, expressing the profound loneliness of the parting in a famous image of tangled seaweed that he sees upon a rocky strand as he leaves. The image becomes for him the image of his love:

Like the sea-tangle, swaying in the wave
Hither and thither, my wife would cling to
me,
As she lay by my side.

(Nippon Gakujutsu Sinkōkai 1965, 32)

But left without him, he visualizes his wife not as tangled seaweed but as sagging, dry grass:

My wife must be languishing
Like drooping summer grass.

(Nippon Gakujutsu Sinkōkai 1965, 32)

Hitomaro's other well-known *chōka* include two poems on his wife's death, a contemplative poem on the transience of earthly glory inspired by his view of the ruined capital of Ōmi, and a complex poem on seeing the body of a man shipwrecked on the island of Samine that ends with sympathy for the man's wife who does not know he is dead.

While English readers of Hitomaro may appreciate his vivid depictions of the human condition, Hitomaro's technical mastery is impossible to translate. He is famous for his effective use of *makurakotoba* (literally "pillow-words"), or conventional epithets: These were often figurative words or phrases with conventionally fixed meanings, that modified the following word, such as *chihayaburu* ("mighty they are") for the gods, or *shirotae no* ("of white bark cloth or hemp") to modify "sleeves" (Miner, et al., 1985, 288). Hitomaro uses these with imagination, rather than simply mechanically as many other poets had before him, and he seems to have coined or at least altered half the pillow-words that he used. He also makes extensive use of what were technically called *jo* (prefaces)—these were lines early in a poem that foreshadowed later images or ideas—either by sound, by simile, or by logical connection (Miner, et al., 1985, 279). Further, Hitomaro uses parallelism and refrain as well as complex or ambiguous sentence structure to give his poetry a technical brilliance unknown before him and emulated afterward.

Within a few generations of his death, Hitomaro was revered as a legendary, semi-divine personage, called in the preface to the *KOKINSHU* (ca. 905) the "sage of poetry." So admired was he that one reason the circumstances of his life are so uncertain is that for centuries, his admirers guarded details like the supposed place of his birth as secrets known to only a few intimates. Hitomaro remains one of the greatest of Japanese poets, and one of the few with a worldwide reputation.

Bibliography

Keene, Donald. *Seeds in the Heart: Japanese Literature from Earliest Times to the Late Sixteenth Century.* A History of Japanese Literature, 1. New York: Columbia University Press, 1999.

Levy, Ian Hideo. *Hitomaro and the Birth of Japanese Lyricism.* Princeton, N.J.: Princeton University Press, 1984.

Miner, Earl, Hiroko Odagiri, and Robert E. Morrell. *The Princeton Companion to Classical Japanese Literature.* Princeton, N.J.: Princeton University Press, 1985.

Nipon Gakujutsu Shinkokai, trans. *The Manyoshu.* With a new foreword by Donald Keene. 1940. New York: Columbia University Press, 1965.

Kālidāsa (fl. between 375 and 415)

Kālidāsa is generally recognized as the most important poet of classical India, and as India's greatest dramatist. Little is known of his life: Even his birth date is controversial, with estimates ranging from 150 B.C.E. to 650 C.E. But most scholars believe he was active during the Gupta period, usually recognized as the high point of classical Indian culture, and Kālidāsa is generally associated with the northern Indian reign of Candragupta II (375–415), greatest of the Gupta monarchs. He is believed to have been born in Ujjain, and to have been of the Brahman caste (although one legend says he was a lowly cowherd). He seems to have traveled widely, since his works reveal a familiarity with the geography of most of the Indian subcontinent.

Kālidāsa is generally believed to be the author of two long lyrical poems, two epic poems, and three dramas. His poem *Ritusamhāra* is a lyrical composition in six books describing the Indian seasons in vivid imagery. His *Mēghadūta* (The cloud-messenger) is a lyrical love poem, purported to be a message sent through a cloud by Yaksha, an absent lover, to his beloved in a distant town. The epic *Kumārasambhava* (The birth of the war god) celebrates the god Siva's marriage to Parvati. *Raghuvamsa* (The house of Raghu) is an epic focusing on the lives of a number of kings, beginning with Rama, hero of the widely popular traditional epic *Rāmāyana.*

Perhaps Kālidāsa is best known as a dramatist. His earliest play was *Mālavikāgnimitra,* a drama concerning the second century B.C.E. hero Agnimitra. Kālidāsa's play *Vikramōrvasīya* (The king and the nymph) retells the ancient and popular Indian story of the virtuous King Pururavas and the beautiful nymph Urvasi. But Kālidāsa's most famous work, and India's most beloved classical play, is *Abhijñānaśākuntala* (*ŚĀKUNTALĀ AND THE RING OF RECOLLECTION*), often simply called *Śākuntalā*).

The plot of *Śākuntalā* is based on the first book of the epic *Mahābhārata,* telling of the birth of the epic's hero Bharata. Kālidāsa shapes the story as a heroic romance—a *nātaka* in Sanskrit, which denotes a play in which a noble hero loves a beautiful woman. The woman in this case is Śākuntalā, a child of nature living in an isolated place in the woods. King Dusyanta sees her and falls in love with her, and she returns his passion. They are forced to part, and are kept apart by the curse of a sage. The loss of Dusyanta's signet ring makes him forget to meet Śākuntalā. When the king finds the ring, he remembers his love, but does not know where to find her. As the play progresses, both lovers are changed and refined through their suffering. Ultimately, with supernatural intervention, the king is reunited with his beloved, and with their love child, Bharata.

Language is one of the more interesting aspects of this play. Kālidāsa has his noble male characters speak in Sanskrit poetry, while his women and lower-caste characters speak in prose, and in *Pankrits,* or vernacular languages. This kind of subtlety, and some of the technical aspects of Indian dramatic theory of which *Śākuntalā* is the prime example, are elements that are lost in any translation of the work. But the play has comic elements (particularly in the character of the Buffoon) and elements of supernatural wonder that come through even in translations. The English translation made by Sir William Jones in 1789 was very popular in Europe, and influenced the great German classical writers, including particularly Johann Wolfgang von Goethe.

Bibliography

Kālidāsa. *Theater of Memory: The Plays of Kālidāsa.* Translated by Edwin Gerow, David Gitomer, and Barbara Stoler Miller, edited by Barbara Stoler Miller. New York: Columbia University Press, 1984.

Kamakura period (1185–1336)

The Kamakura period refers to the late medieval era of Japanese history that saw the emergence of the warrior or samurai class, which replaced the elegant court culture of the HEIAN PERIOD that had flourished for more than 400 years. It was a period that also saw the emergence of Buddhism as the popular religion of Japan, and as a significant influence on the literary productions of the period, the most important of which were the legends that were ultimately collected to form the very influential *TALE OF THE HEIKE.*

By the 12th century, the power of the Heian imperial court, dominated by the Fujiwara clan, began to fall apart. The provincial governors were forming into a warrior class, the imperial bureaucracy was paranoid and inept, and retired emperors were attempting to control events from behind the throne. After the imperial succession of 1156, the new emperor sought the support of the two most powerful warrior clans in Japan: the Minamoto (or Genji) clan and the Taira (or Heike) clan. Before long the clans themselves began a power struggle, one that left the Taira in charge of Kyoto as de facto rulers of Japan, while the Minamoto retreated to the provinces east of the capital. For 20 years the Taira enjoyed their position of power, and created a court on a scale as grandiose as any the Heian rulers had ever envisioned. In a bloody civil war (called the "Gempei war") that raged throughout the country from 1180 to 1185, the Minamoto clan returned and ultimately destroyed the Taira clan completely. Having won political, economic, and military power, the Minamoto set up a government in Kamakura, east of Kyoto, dominated by samurai warriors that were to control Japanese society for 200 years.

The aristocracy was allowed to keep the capital at Kyoto, but without any real power. For the next two centuries, the aristocrats engaged in numerous plots to restore the ancient power of the Heian court. At the same time, they also tried to work with the military government to retain as many rights and privileges as they could from the old system. Because it was so integral to the identity of the Heian court culture and the aristocrats' sense of status, traditional *waka* (poetry in Japanese) was preserved and encouraged by the court. In 1202, the retired emperor Go-Toba commissioned five editors, led by the highly respected poet Fujiwara no Teika, to compile the *Shin Kokin waka-shū* (or *New Kokinshū*), a collection of 1,978 *waka* in 20 books, imitating the structure of the original *KOKINSHŪ.* To the classifications of the original *Kokinshū* (dominated by nature poetry and love poetry), the *New Kokinshū* added a section of Buddhist poems and a section of Shinto poems. Unlike the *Kokinshū,* the new anthology contained few anonymous poems, and included nearly all contemporary verse. Also, most of the poets included were professional poets. The days of gifted courtiers writing occasional poetry as a social expectation were gone.

While most of the warrior society outside of Kyoto had little use for the elegance of TANKA poems, there were a few exceptions. The poet Saigyō (Satō Norikiyo), a Buddhist priest whose 94 poems in the *New Kokinshū* were only a small fraction of the 1,552 poems he published in a collection of his own poetry, had been born into a samurai family. More surprisingly, Minamoto no Sanetomo, the third Kamakura shogun (chief samurai and practical ruler of Japan), married an aristocrat's daughter and studied *waka* poetry as well as music and other court arts. He wrote some

700 poems before being assassinated at 27 by his political enemies (led by his own nephew).

Outside of the Kyoto court, Buddhism proved to be an important influence on literature of the Kamakura period. Buddhism had been imported from China centuries earlier and was an important feature of the Heian court, but it was not until the Kamakura period that a new school of Buddhism was developed by Buddhist priests interested in appealing to the general population. The new Japanese Buddhism promised rewards to the faithful in a heavenly paradise after death (called the Pure Land), even for those who never achieved enlightenment in this life.

At the same time, a number of aristocrats took refuge from the tumultuous times by taking vows as Buddhist priests and renouncing the world, retreating to isolated areas outside the cities or the great monasteries in Nara and Kyoto. The result was a genre that became known as "recluse literature," the best-known example of which is "An Account of a Ten-Foot Square Hut," by Kamo no Chōmei. Kamo describes his retreat from the transient world, leaving behind the fallen capital and the world of suffering that accompanies human attachment to material things. Living in a small hermitage outside Kyoto and focusing on his ultimate rebirth, Kamo develops an attachment for the tranquil life he has created for himself, and ironically fears that this attachment will stand in the way of his enlightenment and his entry into the Pure Land.

Another form of Buddhist literature is seen in collections of what were called *setsuwa* tales, short stories with clear morals that may have been put together for use in Buddhist sermons. The last such collection, compiled between 1279 and 1283, was called the *Shasekishū* (Sand collection). It was assembled by the Buddhist priest Mujū Ichien, who, some critics claim, was more interested in the moral lessons than in a well-told story.

But the most important impact of Buddhism on late Kamakura letters was in the spread of *katarimono* (or ballads), particularly those called *heikyoku* (Taira songs), beginning in the 13th century. The *heikyoku* were poems concerned with incidents during the bloody Gempei war between the Taira and the Minamoto clans. The ballads were sung by blind Buddhist monks called *Biwa Hoshi*—so called because they were accompanied by a *biwa* or lute. These were wandering singers who traveled about the country, particularly to the homes of the new samurai warrior class, whose recent ancestors were the subjects of the ballads. Thus the narratives of the war were given a heavily Buddhist coloring by their narrators, who generally attributed the downfall of the Taira clan to the sins of its leaders. By 1371, these older tales had been collected and compiled into the considerable text that today is generally known as the *Tale of the Heike.*

Another period of bloody warfare from 1336 to 1392 finally destroyed the power of the aristocracy in Kyoto completely and brought to an end the Kamakura period. But the *Tale of the Heike* is the most important literary work to come from this period. It reflected the values of the new warrior culture: values of honor, loyalty, courage, and sacrifice. At the same time it reflected the new widespread Buddhist morality of its compilers.

Bibliography

Kato, Shuicho. *A History of Japanese Literature: From the Man-yōshu to Modern Times.* New abridged edition. Translated and edited by Don Sanderson. Richmond, U.K.: Curzon Press, 1997.

Keene, Donald. *Seeds in the Heart: Japanese Literature from Earliest Times to the Late Sixteenth Century.* Vol. 1. New York: Columbia University Press, 1999.

Miner, Earl, Hiroko Odagiri, and Robert E. Morrell. *The Princeton Companion to Classical Japanese Literature.* Princeton, N.J.: Princeton University Press, 1985.

Kampan (ca. 12th century)

Kampan was perhaps the most important Tamil poet of the Middle Ages. He probably lived in the 12th century, though some traditions put him as early as the ninth. While there are a number of legends about his life, very little is actually known. It is thought that Kampan was born in the Tanjore district of India, and that a chieftain named

Cataiyapan was his patron. His chief work is *Iramavataram* (The Descent of Rama), an epic poem of some 40,000 lines based on Valmiki's famous first-century Sanskrit epic *Ramayana.* Kampan's work is one of the great literary masterpieces in the Tamil language, and displays the poet's considerable rhetorical and technical skill as well as his scholarly erudition: He displays familiarity not only with Valmiki, but also with literary traditions in both Sanskrit and Tamil.

Kampan's story is not a translation of Valmiki's, but does follow the traditional story fairly closely. Rama is a prince of Ayodhya, the eldest and favored son of King Dasharatha. As a young man, Rama is able to win the hand of Sita, princess of Mithila, in an archery contest. The elderly king wants to name Rama as his successor, but through the machinations of his stepmother Kaikeyi, Rama is deprived of the throne in favor of Kaikeyi's son Bharata, and exiled to the wilderness for 14 years. Believing that his father's promises must be kept at all costs, Rama accepts his exile rather than wage a war for the throne, and travels to the wilderness with his wife Sita and his brother Lakshmana.

In the forest, however, Sita is kidnapped by Ravana, the demon king of Sri Lanka. Rama engages the help of an army of monkeys and bears to help search for her. Hanuman, the monkey god, pledges his service to Rama. He leaps across the ocean to the island of Sri Lanka where it is believed Sita has been taken. Rama and his army attack the island, kill Ravana, and rescue Sita. However, before the reunion is complete, Sita must prove her chastity in a trial by fire. When the fire will not burn her, Sita is seen as vindicated by the gods. She and Rama make a triumphant return to Ayodhya, and initiate a golden age known as Rama's rule.

Kampan's story is essentially the same as Valmiki's, but it has some distinctive features in terms of style and emphasis. Kampan seems more concerned with the emotional responses of characters, especially women. Kampan also clearly presents Rama as an incarnation of the Hindu god Vishnu. In doing so he is following a tradition that had originated among the Tamil saints a few centuries earlier.

Bibliography

Kampan. *The Forest Book of the Rāmayāna of Kampan.* Translated with anotation and introduction by George L. Hart and Hank Heifetz. Berkeley: University of California Press, 1989.

Richman, Paula, ed. *Many Ramayanas: The Diversity of a Narrative Tradition in South Asia.* Berkeley: University of California Press, 1991.

Kanze Kojirô Nobumitsu (1453–1516)

An important composer of Nō drama, Kanze Kojirô Nobumitsu was one of the last artists to produce a significant number of Nō plays. He was the grandnephew of ZEAMI, the most renowned composer of Nō drama. Nobumitsu was a writer, actor, and musician, and was leader of the Kanze school of Nō theater, the school with which Zeami had been associated. As such, he participated in the elite cultural circles of the late MUROMACHI PERIOD.

Nobumitsu began his career as a drummer (part of the *hayashi,* or instrumental chorus of musicians that played at Nō performances). He began composing relatively early, though, and rose to a leadership role in the theater that began to send Nō drama in a new direction, one that tends to make the plays more "realistic" and "dramatic" from a Western point of view. It has been suggested that the influence of shogun military leaders during the Edo period squelched this new direction in the drama in favor of the more conservative values of the older theater, and that those strictures have affected criticisms of Nō theater to the present day, making Nobumitsu's contributions undervalued, since they do not conform to the earlier aesthetic ideal. Some of Nobumitsu's better-known plays are *Funabenkei* (Benkei on board), *Momijigari* (Autumn excursion), and *Taisei Taishi* (Prince Taisei). But Nobumitsu's most famous play, an unusual example of Nō theater that seems especially "dramatic" by western standards, is *DOJOJI.*

Bibliography

Keene, Donald, ed. *Twenty Plays of the No Theatre.* Assisted by Royall Tyler. Records of Civilization: Sources and Studies, 85. New York: Columbia University Press, 1970.

Komparu, Kunio. *The Noh Theater: Principles and Perspectives.* New York: Weatherhill/Tankosha, 1983.

Katherine Group

The Katherine Group includes the Middle English hagiographies (SAINTS' LIVES) *Seinte Katerine* (*St. Katherine*), *Seinte Iuliene* (*St. Juliana*), and *Seinte Marherete* (*St. Margaret*), along with the devotional prose pieces HALI MEIDENHAD (*Holy Maidenhood; Letter on Virginity*), and SAWLES WARDE (*Care of the Soul; Custody of the Soul*). All of the hagiographies are directly adapted from Latin sources, and *Sawles Warde* is heavily dependent upon Latin sources as well. Of the group, only *Hali Meidenhad* appears to be substantively original, and it, too, relies upon a long history of related texts. The Katherine Group is so named because the legend of *Katerine* appears first in the primary manuscript. Also, of the virgin martyrs, Katherine is the one most directly committed to pure virginity, as the other women indicate they will marry their suitor if he converts. The group as a whole has gained attention from editors as well as scholars. *Seinte Katerine* is the most edited of the hagiographies, though overall, more modern editions of *Sawles Warde* have been produced.

In manuscript tradition, as well as in content, the Katherine Group is closely related to anchoritic literature, particularly ANCRENE WISSE and the WOOING GROUP. London, British Library MS Royal 17 A.xxvii includes four Katherine Group pieces (the three hagiographies and *Hali Meidenhad*), and one from the Wooing Group (a fragment of *Þe Lofsong of ure Lefdi*), while London, British Library, MS Cotton Titus D.xviii includes two incomplete versions of *Ancrene Wisse,* three Katherine Group texts (*Seinte Katerine, Sawles Warde,* and *Hali Meidenhad*), and one Wooing Group piece (the title piece, *Þe Wohunge of ure Laured*). Overall, all of these texts present virginity, and its natural progression of becoming a Bride of Christ, as the best choice—spiritually, physically, personally, and socially—for women. While *Ancrene Wisse* provides the regulations for a virginal life, and the Wooing Group illustrates the joys of *sponsae-brides Christi* (brides of Christ), the Katherine Group provides concrete examples of the superiority of chastity.

The three hagiographic pieces are similar in nature. They are composed in rhythmic prose that utilizes both alliteration and end-rhyme. All three virgin-martyr legends follow the standard paradigm of renunciation, testing, and consummation. In each, a beautiful, noble virgin living during the era of the Diocletian persecutions successfully resists marriage to a pagan, while also debating with devils and converting masses of bystanders. She is spectacularly and publicly tortured in graphic scenes that echo with overtones of sadomasochism, miraculously escaping unscathed until she is finally executed by beheading. Each of these saints is a legendary rather than historical figure, but this does not lessen the importance of these works. The legends illustrate contests of reason and strength, and instead of being designed to convert non-Christians, they are intended to reinforce existing faith. The heroic women on display in these texts skillfully elicit information from demons, and respond to them in kind, creating dialogues about the nature and state of Christian faith.

The theme of heroic virginity is carried on throughout both of the other two works included in the Katherine Group, particularly in *Hali Meidenhad,* which specifically recommends the lives of Katherine, Margaret, and Juliana as templates for living a holy life. *Hali Meidenhad* is described in one of the Katherine Group manuscripts, Oxford, Bodleian Library, MS Bodley 34, as "an epistle on maidenhood written for the comfort of maidens." Related to the early church tradition of treatises on virginity, a genre firmly established in the third and fourth centuries, *Hali Meidenhad* is a particularly graphic warning about the perils of sexual intercourse and the horrors of earthly marriage. Human men are described as rutting beasts who beat, starve, and sexually molest their wives. Children are presented as sources of both physical and spiritual pain. For instance, they cause pain, and perhaps even death, through childbirth, and they cause sadness through their own early deaths. The only way a woman can avoid the terrors of a carnal relationship is to preserve her virginity and turn all her emotions toward Christ, who is the perfect spouse. These descriptions are so lurid that Oswald Cockayne, an early editor of the text, referred to it as "coarse and repulsive." The primary sources of the text are ALANUS DE INSULIS's *Summa de arte praedicatoria (Art of the Preacher)*, GREGORY THE GREAT's *Patoral curalis (Pastoral Care)*, the sermons of St. BERNARD OF CLAIRVAUX, and Hildebert's letter to the recluse Athalisa. Some scholars also suggest Pope INNOCENT III's *De miseria humanae conditionis (On the Misery of the Human Condition)* as a possible source.

Sawles Warde is primarily an expansion of *De custodia interioris hominis (On the Keeping of the Inner Self)*, often attributed to St. ANSELM of Canterbury. However, other Latin sources may have contributed to its composition, too. In *Sawles Warde*, the body, which houses the soul, is described as a castle under siege. Wit (Reason) is in charge of the castle, whose gate (maidenhead) is being attacked by vices. The castle is also inhabited by the fickle Will (Desire), Wit's wife, and is guarded by the ineffective Five Senses. Wit calls upon the four Cardinal Virtues for assistance, and they, with additional help from Fear and Love of Life, manage to successfully stave off the vices. In form, *Sawles Warde* is an intricate verse homily in ALLEGORY that some scholars believe is a precursor to later medieval allegorical drama.

Bibliography

Hassel, Julie B. *Choosing Not to Marry: Women and Autonomy in the Katherine Group.* London: Routledge, 2002.

Facsimile of MS Bodley 34: Seinte Katerine, Seinte Marherete, Seinte Iuliene, Hali Meithhad, Sawles Warde. With an introduction by N. R. Ker. EETS o.s. 247. London: Published for the Early English Text Society by the Oxford University Press, 1960.

Millett, Bella, and Jocelyn Wogan-Browne. *Medieval English Prose for Women.* Oxford: Clarendon Press, 1992.

Price, Jocelyn. "Liflade Seint Iuliene," *Medeivalia et Humanistica* 14 (1986): 37–58.

Robertson, Elizabeth. *Early English Devotional Prose and the Female Audience.* Knoxville: University of Tennessee Press, 1990.

Tolkien, J. R. R. "*Ancrene Wisse* and *Hali Meiðhad*," *Essays and Studies* 14 (1929): 104–126.

Michelle M. Sauer

Kells, Book of (ca. 800)

The *Book of Kells* is one of the most famous and magnificent illuminated manuscripts in the world. It was produced around 800 somewhere in the British Isles. The vellum manuscript contains the four Gospels, with prefaces and the "Eusebian canons"—tables containing concordances to the Gospels. The manuscript comprises 340 vellum pages, each page containing 16 to 18 lines of text in a handwriting known as "insular majuscule." But the chief interest in the book lies in its lavish illuminations. Three elaborate full-page miniatures of the symbols for the evangelists Matthew, Mark, and John appear before the openings of those Gospels. Directly facing the opening texts of each Gospel are portraits of the four evangelists themselves. There are, in addition, full-page illuminations illustrating Christ in majesty, the Virgin and Child, the Temptation of Christ, and the Arrest of Christ. There is also a magnificent "Carpet Page"—a page of pure geometric symbols—and a much-admired "Chi Rho" page—a full page ornately decorating the first three letters of the name *Christ* where it first appears in Matthew's Gospel.

The manuscript was housed at the monastery of Kells in Meath, Ireland, from at least the year 1006, when it was reported stolen in the Annals of Ulster, and referred to as the Gospel of Columba. The book was recovered, though its highly wrought golden cover was lost. It remained at Kells for centuries, and is almost certainly the book that GIRALDUS CAMBRENSIS describes having seen at Kildare in the 12th century and declares must be the work of angels, not men. In 1653 it was sent to Dublin, and later in the 17th century Archbishop Ussher donated the manuscript to Trinity College there, where it remains to this day, displayed regularly in the Old Library.

This much is known. What experts cannot agree on is where the manuscript originated. The decorative plan of the manuscript (including the evangelist symbols, the carpet page, and the Chi Rho page) is similar to that of earlier insular (i.e., British Isles) manuscripts, such as the Book of Durrow and the famous Lindisfarne Gospels. Because of similarities in style, some scholars have suggested that the *Book of Kells* originated at Lindisfarne. Others have proposed that the foliate decoration in the manuscript connects it with the scriptoria, or monastic copying centers, at Wearmouth or Jarrow, the sister monasteries associated with the Venerable BEDE. But the very early association of the manuscript with St. Columba has led most scholars over the years to attribute the production of the book to the church of St. Columba on the Isle of Iona off Scotland. Viking raids of Iona during the ninth century probably forced the removal of the valuable manuscript to the safer monastery at Kells.

Examined with a magnifying glass, one square inch of design in a *Book of Kells* miniature revealed 158 ribbonlike interlacings, revealing the complexity of design that went into the illustrations. With their tightly coiled spirals and geometric patterns, their interlacing figures of animals, humans, and fantastic creatures, woven into incredibly intricate designs of various colors, the illuminations in the *Book of Kells* are universally recognized as the most impressive in medieval manuscript painting.

Bibliography

Alexander, Jonathan J. G. *Insular Manuscripts, 6th to the 9th Century.* London: Harvey Miller, 1978.

The Book of Kells. Fine Art Facsimile Volume. Lucerne: Faksimile Verlag Luzern, 1990.

Nordenfalk, Carl A. *Celtic and Anglo-Saxon Painting: Book Illumination in the British Isles 600–800.* New York: George Braziller, 1977.

Kempe, Margery (ca. 1373–ca. 1440)

Margery Kempe was born into a prosperous middle-class family in the Norfolk port of King's Lynn in ca. 1373. She was the daughter of John Brunham or Burnham, an influential burgess of Lynn who served, according to extant archives, as mayor and member of Parliament, and in numerous other positions of importance. Much of what we know about Kempe herself derives from what has been called the earliest autobiography in English, *The Boke of Margerie Kempe of Lynn.* Thus any attempt to summarize her life and work needs to take into account the version of events she represents in the *Boke.* The proem to the *Boke* reveals that the book is "not wretyn in ordyr, every thyng aftyr other as it wer don" (Windeatt 2000, ll. 134–35), yet it is possible to reconstruct a hypothetical chronology of Kempe's life based upon the information she includes in her *Boke.* Margery married John Kempe when she was approximately 20 years old (ca. 1393), and although she dates her first vision of and "conversation" with Christ to a period of illness following the birth of her first child (some critics have attributed her illness to post-partum depression), her full conversion into a life dedicated to Christ does not occur for another 20 years, 14 children, and various worldly enterprises including brewing and milling. Kempe is unsuccessful in her occupational attempts until she feels "the drawt [pull or attraction] of owyr Lord" (Windeatt 2000, 1. 252). After many years of spiritual growth and travels, Kempe enlists two priests to write her life and visions.

Although Kempe's account of her life, in which she refers to herself as a "creature," contains instances of spiritual doubt and backsliding, and temptations entered into, for the most part the narrative focuses on her particularly emotional form of piety, her teachings and preachings (a contested issue in the 14th and 15th centuries because women's teaching was associated with the LOLLARDS, and Margery is often accused of this specific heresy), and, in particular, the ways in which her community slanders her behavior and beliefs. This last is key: Slander becomes, for Kempe, the proof that she is Christ's beloved as he assures her over and over in her narrative that the more she is slandered, the more she suffers for him, and the more he loves her. Much of her narrative is concerned with her travels in England and abroad, her pilgrimages to holy shrines, and her interactions with lay and clerical figures during her travels. Kempe's disruptive behavior, which includes loud crying, excessive emotional responses to the Passion, a tendency to correct others, an often reiterated claim to a personal and singular relationship with Christ, and a disregard for clerical authority, invite slander from those around her. Yet the more she is slandered, the more certain she is of Christ's regard and her ultimate salvation. In addition to accounts of her travels and interactions (mostly negative) with others, Kempe recalls visions in which she participates in, variously, the Annunciation, the birth of Christ, and the Passion. These scenes, in which Kempe becomes a central figure in biblical narratives, can be read as a literalization of common spiritual injunctions to contemplate and figuratively participate in the life of Christ. Kempe takes the injunctions further than is usually encountered; however, there is precedence in the visions of continental mystics, with whose works Kempe shows familiarity. Realistic and fantastic in turn, Kempe's narrative is, at the least, a fascinating account of a late medieval woman's untraditional quest for spiritual vocation and validation in a culture barely tolerant of nonconformity.

For centuries what was known about Kempe was drawn from a seven-page quarto pamphlet, *A shorte treatyse of contemplacyon taught by our lorde Ihesu cryste, or taken out of the boke of Margerie Kempe of Lynn,* printed ca. 1501 by Wynkyn de Worde. This quarto pamphlet contains devotional extracts from Kempe's *Boke* and nothing of the somewhat idiosyncratic account of her life and behavior and visions. As a result, Kempe was thought to be either an anchoress or a woman of spiritual enlightenment in the tradition of JULIAN OF NORWICH. When the sole surviving manuscript of the complete book was discovered in 1934, scholars were forced to revise their opinion of her life and work, and much of the revision was ungenerous as scholars struggled to validate what seemed to be the product of a "queer, unbalanced creature." Learned discussions about hysteria, post-partum depression, degraded spiritual understanding, and excessive sexual obsessions were the commonplaces of critical discourse regarding Kempe and her narrative. In the last two decades, however, feminist scholars and others have offered interpretations and contextualizations that provide analyses of Kempe and her work without the negative adjudication of earlier scholars. One approach is to contextualize Kempe in the continental mystical tradition, and as her work shows clear derivation from this tradition, these arguments are sound and allow us to place her emotive spirituality within a specific historical trajectory of spiritual development. Another approach, and one that is increasingly the basis for other approaches, divides Kempe the author from Margery the character and claims that Kempe's character (Margery) is the means by which Kempe critiques her social community, lay and clerical. Lynn Staley's work in this area is astounding in its implications of authorial intentionality and craft, and has influenced many scholars who are currently working on Kempe and her narrative. Kempe's extraordinarily materialistic and realistic version of life and spirituality, including her failings and faults, is fundamentally, as the proem suggests, intended for "synful wrecchys," and may have been received more easily by an audience of similarly sinful folk than high-minded, elegant, and theologically accurate treatises. One thing we may be certain of is that Kempe's life and work will continue to be the focus of lively analyses for some time to come.

Bibliography

Aers, David. *Community, Gender, and Individual Identity.* London: Routledge, 1988.

Ashley, Kathleen. "Historicizing Margery: *The Book of Margery Kempe* as Social Text," *Journal of Medieval and Early Modern Studies* 28 (1998): 371–388.

Beckwith, Sarah. "A Very Material Mysticism: The Medieval Mysticism of Margery Kempe." In *Medieval Literature: Criticism, Ideology, and History,* edited by David Aers, 34–57. New York: St. Martin's Press, 1986.

Delany, Sheila. "Sexual Economics, Chaucer's Wife of Bath and *The Book of Margery Kempe.*" In *Writing Women: Women Writers and Women in Literature Medieval to Modern.* New York: Schocken Books, 1983, 76–92.

Kempe, Margery. *The Book of Margery Kempe.* Edited and translated by Lynn Staley. New York: W. W. Norton, 2001.

Lochrie, Karma. *Margery Kempe and Translations of the Flesh.* Philadelphia: University of Pennyslvania Press, 1991.

———. *The Book of Margery Kempe.* Edited by Barry Windeatt. Harlow: Longman, 2000.

Staley, Lynn. *Margery Kempe's Dissenting Fictions.* University Park: Pennsylvania State University Press, 1994.

Elisa Narin van Court

kenning

A kenning is a traditional figure of speech distinctive to OLD ENGLISH and Old Norse poetry. The term *kenning* seems to have derived from the Germanic word *kenna,* meaning to define or characterize—in other words, to name. Usually considered a kind of periphrasis or circumlocution, a kenning is essentially a metaphor in which a literal, single noun is replaced by a figurative compound of two words. Kennings always consist of a noun modified by the possessive form of another noun, sometimes fused together to form a single word. For example, the kenning *swanrade* ("swan's road") in *BEOWULF* refers to the sea: The analogy implied is that the sea is to a swan as a road is to a man or a horse.

Kennings in Old English poetry are generally simple, as the one cited above, or as "storm of swords" for a battle. In the SKALDIC POETRY of medieval Norway and later Iceland, however, kennings could become extremely complex, when one or both of the terms of the kennings contained kennings themselves. Peter Hallberg cites the skaldic line "the swan of the sweat of the thorn of the wounds" (*sára þorns sveita svanr*) as an example. Here, the "thorn of the wounds" is a kenning for *sword.* "The sweat of the sword" is a kenning for *blood.* "The swan of blood," then, is the raven, the bird of the battlefield (Hallberg 1975, 23). In some types of Old Icelandic courtly poetry, nothing is ever directly named, and all nouns are replaced by kennings. The understanding of such poetry becomes an intellectual challenge, akin to the popularity of such literary forms as RIDDLES in Old English.

Bibliography

Hallberg, Peter. *Old Icelandic Poetry: Eddic Lay and Skaldic Verse.* Translated by Paul Schach and Sonja Lindgrenson. Lincoln: University of Nebraska Press, 1975.

kharja

The term *kharja* derives from the Arabic word meaning "exit." A *kharja* was the end of a longer poem (the *muwashshah*) that was made up of several sections, or strophes, and was fashionable in Mozarabic Spain. While the *muwashshah* itself was written in classical Arabic and later imitated in Hebrew, the *kharja* (a final strophe, usually of three or four lines) was written in a spoken, vernacular dialect—either colloquial Arabic, Hebrew, or a Romance language, or even a mixture of these languages. Many of the *kharjas* seem to have been composed before the poems of which they are part, and were perhaps in oral circulation.

The *kharja* was generally a love song from the point of view of a lower-class woman longing for her absent lover. The *kharjas* that survive are thus the earliest extant love poems in any Romance vernacular, dating at least as far back as the early 10th century. Often they express the kind of idealization of romantic love that becomes common in the tradition of *fin amors* or COURTLY LOVE that arose in neighboring Provençe at the end of the 11th century and spread throughout Europe.

Some of the imagery of the *kharjas* is also reminiscent of the Provençal TROUBADOURS. The motif of love causing the lover physical pain, for example, is present, along with the assertion that only the beloved can cure the speaker's suffering: "my eyes languish, ah God,/ah they hurt me so!" (Dronke 1968, I, 29) says one *kharja,* and another laments "My beloved languishes with love of me./Who is there to cure him?/By my lover's soul, what thirst for my coming!" (Dronke 1968, I, 31).

Bibliography

Dronke, Peter. *Medieval Latin and the Rise of the European Love-Lyric.* 2nd ed. 2 vols. Oxford: Clarendon Press, 1968.

King Horn (ca. 1250–1300)

King Horn is probably the earliest surviving verse ROMANCE in MIDDLE ENGLISH. It consists of 1,544 very short, mainly three-stress lines in the form of couplets. Scholars in the past have dated the poem to about 1225, but more recent scholarship has suggested that more likely the poem was produced in the later 13th century, somewhere in the southern West Midlands. It is possible that the poem is based on an Anglo-Norman source: The rhymes suggest the influence of Norman French BALLAD meter, and there is an Anglo-Norman poem called *Horn et Rimenhild* that follows roughly the same plot as *King Horn*. Most scholars, however, believe that *King Horn* is based on a source that predates the Norman text. It has also been suggested that the meter of *King Horn*, which depends on strong stresses rather than measured syllables, is more closely related to English ALLITERATIVE VERSE. As with other early Middle English romances such as *HAVELOK* and *BEVIS OF HAMPTON*, *King Horn* derives from the folk traditions of the English people who survived the Norman Conquest, and therefore is part of what is called the "matter of England."

The story of *King Horn* is essentially same as that of the later—and generally inferior—romance *HORN CHILDE*. Here, Horn, son of the King of Suddene, is set adrift as a child by the Saracens who killed his father. He ends up in the kingdom of Westernesse (in northern England), where he is raised in the household of King Aylmer and where the king's daughter, Rymenhild, falls in love with him. The lovers are betrayed by Horn's friend Fikenhild, who reveals their affair to the king and claims that Horn is plotting to murder Aylmer. In consequence, Horn is exiled to Ireland. Here, he accomplishes marvelous feats of arms against invading Saracens, and is offered the hand of Reynild, daughter of King Thurston of Ireland—but Horn cannot forget Rymenhild. After seven years he returns to Westernesse, where Rymenhild is about to be forced to marry King Mody. Horn, in disguise, makes himself known to Rymenhild and then kills the would-be husband, and confronts King Aylmer, announcing that he will be back to claim Rymenhild after he has won back his own kingdom of Suddene. Horn goes off and defeats the Saracens, who killed his father, thus winning back his kingdom. When he returns to Westernesse for Rymenhild, he finds that once again she is about to be married, this time to the treasonous Fikenhild. Horn kills the traitor and marries his faithful love, Rymenhild. Meanwhile Reynild, the Irish princess, marries Horn's faithful companion Athulf, and the romance ends on a happy note.

As in many romances, the chief theme of the poem seems to be the development and maturity of Horn himself, his quest being essentially a quest for his own identity, established when at last he reclaims his birthright. The poem is told in a direct manner with a straightforward and symmetrical structure and a number of parallel episodes, without the digressions that often characterized earlier French romances that may have served as models for the poem. Nor does the poet make use of the conventions of COURTLY LOVE so common in French poetry, choosing instead to depict his heroine as a flesh-and-blood woman with natural desires. The Saracen villains no doubt are inspired by the crusading milieu of the 13th century, but their piracy in Ireland and England suggest that in the original tradition the villains may have been Vikings.

King Horn is significant in its preservation of native English literary traditions as it introduces the newer continental genre into English letters. It seems a poem to appeal to popular rather than courtly tastes, and thus seems an ancestor of the rhymed romances of the 14th century.

Bibliography

Allen, Rosamund S. "The Date and Provenance of *King Horn:* Some Interim Reassessments," in *Medieval English Studies Presented to George Kane.* Edited by Edward Donald Kennedy, Ronald Waldron, and Joseph S. Wittig. Suffolk, U.K.: St. Edmundsburg Press, 1988, 99–126.

———, ed. *King Horn.* New York: Garland Medieval Texts, 1984.

French, Walter H. *Essays on King Horn.* Ithaca, N.Y.: Cornell University Press, 1940.

Hearn, Matthew. "Twins of Infidelity: The Double Antagonists of *King Horn*," *Medieval Perspectives* 8 (1993): 78–86.

Hynes-Berry, Mary. "Cohesion in *King Horn* and *Sir Orfeo*," *Speculum* 50 (1975): 652–670.

Scott, Anne. "Plans, Predictions, and Promises: Traditional Story Techniques and the Configuration of Word and Deed in *King Horn*." In *Studies in*

Medieval English Romances: Some New Approaches, 37–68. Cambridge, U.K.: Brewer, 1988.
Speed, Diane. "The Saracens of *King Horn,*" *Speculum* 65 (1990): 564–595.

Kingis Quair, The (ca. 1424)

The Kingis Quair ("The King's Book") is an early 15th-century poem consisting of 197 RHYME ROYAL stanzas in a Northern dialect of MIDDLE ENGLISH. The poem survives in a single manuscript from about 1490 (Bodleian Library Arch. Selden B 24), which was discovered and printed only in 1783. The manuscript attributes the poem to King JAMES I of Scotland, although some scholars have questioned the attribution and suggest that it is based only on autobiographical similarities between the events of the text and James's life. Like the protagonist of the poem, James was a king kidnapped in his youth and held prisoner for 18 years, emerging from his captivity to marry the woman he had fallen in love with while imprisoned—in James's case, Lady Joan Beaufort. For most readers, however, these similarities and the manuscript attribution, plus the fact that the Scottish chronicler John Major claimed that James had written a poem about Joan prior to their marriage, give us good reason to assume that James is the poem's author, and that he wrote the poem while in England.

The Kingis Quair begins with a royal prisoner who, after reading BOETHIUS, thinks back on his abduction and 18 years in prison, and laments his fortune. He sees a beautiful woman walking in the garden below the tower in which he is kept, and falls in love with her (a scene clearly reminiscent of CHAUCER's *KNIGHT'S TALE*). The poem then becomes a DREAM VISION, as the speaker in a dream is whisked through the heavens to the palace of Venus, goddess of love, who agrees to help him attain the Lady. But first, guided by Good Hope, he must visit the house of Minerva, goddess of wisdom, who teaches him prudence, and then the goddess Fortune, who gives him a place on her wheel and promises him success in love. When he awakens, he goes to the window of his tower, not knowing whether to believe the dream, when a dove comes to him with a message from heaven that his sorrow over his love will soon end. The poem ends as the narrator gives thanks for everything that has contributed to his winning of his love (even his prison walls), and with an acknowledgement of his debt to Chaucer and to GOWER.

The northern dialect of the poem is interspersed with elements of London English, which may reflect James's long stay in England and his familiarity with the works of Chaucer and other Midland poets. The ALLEGORY of the poem's central part overwhelms the slender plot of the autobiographical frame, though in that sense the structure of the poem is not unlike Chaucer's dream visions, like *The BOOK OF THE DUCHESS* and *The PARLIAMENT OF FOWLS.* Perhaps the most significant contribution to later literature made by the poem is the term "Rhyme Royal," which came to be applied, in deference to the royal composer of *The Kingis Quair,* to the seven-line stanza Chaucer had used and apparently invented.

Bibliography

James I of Scotland. *The Kingis Quair.* Introduction, notes and glossary by John Norton-Smith. Oxford: Clarendon Press, 1971.
The Kingis Quair of James Stewart. Edited by Matthew P. McDiarmid. Totowa, N.J.: Rowman and Littlefield, 1973.
Scheps, Walter, and J. Anna Looney. *Middle Scots Poets: A Reference Guide to James I of Scotland, Robert Henryson, William Dunbar, and Gavin Douglas.* Boston: G. K. Hall, 1986.

Knight in the Panther's Skin, The (*The Man in the Panther's Skin, Vepkhistkaosani*) Shota Rustaveli (12th century)

Shota Rustaveli's poem *The Knight in the Panther's Skin* is considered by many to be the pinnacle of Georgian literature. Although little is known about its author's life (not even the dates of his birth and death), scholars do know that, as his name indicates, Rustaveli was probably born in Rustava, a city in Meskheti in south Georgia. He was apparently a prince and the treasurer and court poet during the reign of Queen Tamar of Georgia, and scholars believe he was well educated and that he traveled widely. Also it seems that Rustaveli was not only a talented poet, but was also a gifted visual artist who painted frescoes in the Georgian Monastery of the Cross in Jerusalem, where he was charged in the early 13th century with the restoration of the monastery after Muslims had driven the European crusaders out of Jerusalem in 1187.

Also translated as "The Man in the Panther's Skin" or "The Knight in the Tiger's Skin," *Vepkhistkaosani* was first printed in 1712 in the capital of Georgia, Tbilisi, and has since been translated into many languages by numerous authors including Arthur Leist and Marjory Wardrop, and most recently into English by Venera Urushadze. It was illustrated in the 20th century by the Georgian painter Sergo Kobuladze.

Legend says that Rustaveli was orphaned as a child and raised by his uncle, a monk, which may explain some of the religious and philosophical concerns in his epic. The poem is a tale of adventure and romance with philosophical and nationalistic undertones. It presents humanistic ideals such as love, friendship, philanthropy, and courage as well as horrific fighting scenes. The epic, in 1,600 four-line stanzas, is marked by its metrical pattern of flowing rhyme and understated alliteration.

The Knight in the Panther's Skin and its author are highly regarded in the Republic of Georgia. The poem is seen by some as Georgia's national epic although the nations of India, China, and Arabia also form the setting of the poem. Rustaveli is still regarded as the greatest Georgian poet: The highest prize in Georgian art and literature is the Shota Rustaveli State Prize, and the main street in Georgia's capital is named Rustaveli Road. Landmarks in Tbilisi include the Shota Rustaveli State Academic Theatre, the Shota Rustaveli Institute of Georgian Literature of the Georgian Academy of Sciences, and the Shota Rustaveli Underground Station.

Bibliography

Rustaveli, Shota. *The Knight in the Panther's Skin.* Translated by Venera Urushadze. Commack, N.Y.: Kroshka Books, 1998.

Leslie Johnston

Knight's Tale, The Geoffrey Chaucer (ca. 1381)

The Knight's Tale is the first of the *Canterbury Tales*. Probably written before the rest of the tales and incorporated later, the *Knight's Tale* is a courtly romance based on Boccaccio's *Teseida*. It concerns two Theban kinsmen, Palamon and Arcite, who both fall in love with Emelye, sister-in-law of Duke Theseus of Athens. Three major changes Chaucer made to Boccaccio's story are, first, reducing the length of the narrative to about a third of Boccaccio's text, and second, enhancing the role of Palamon to make the two knights more equal rather than focusing, as Boccaccio had, chiefly on Arcite; and third, adding a philosophical element to the poem through the influence of Boethius's *Consolation of Philosophy*, a text Chaucer was probably translating about the same time. One of Chaucer's more popular tales in the Renaissance, *The Knight's Tale* was the source for Shakespeare and Fletcher's play *Two Noble Kinsmen.*

The tale is divided into four parts. In part 1, Theseus discovers the wounded bodies of the two Theban youths among the dead after his successful assault on Thebes. Because they are of the "blood royal" of Thebes, he brings them back to Athens to perpetual imprisonment. From their prison cell, Palamon catches sight of Emelye walking in the garden and falls immediately in love with her. When Arcite looks out to see what has so affected his cousin, he is similarly love-struck. The two quarrel over Emelye for some time. But one day a guest of Theseus begs for Arcite's release from prison, and Theseus lets him go, but only on the condition that he never return to Athens. Thus the first part of *The Knight's Tale* ends with Palamon imprisoned but able to see Emelye, and Arcite free but exiled from Emelye's presence.

In part 2, Arcite, his looks altered over time by the anguish he feels at being unable to see his beloved, returns to Athens in disguise and becomes a servant in Theseus's court. Palamon is able to escape from prison, and by chance the two meet in a grove outside of Athens, where Palamon is hiding. Still quarreling over Emelye, the two agree to do battle the following day. Arcite brings arms from Athens and the two begin a deadly battle. At that point Theseus by chance rides by with his household and stops the fight. When he learns the cause of the pair's enmity, he remarks on the fact that neither of them has ever spoken to Emelye (she herself has been unaware of their existence, let alone their love for her); but he orders the cousins to postpone their battle for a year, during which time he promises to build a large arena for a great tournament to which they will each bring 100 knights, and promises Emelye as the prize for the victor in the tournament.

In part 3, Chaucer includes long descriptions of Theseus's great arena as well as of the knights accompanying each cousin as they arrive in Thebes for the tournament. The morning before the tournament begins, each of the chief characters prays at one of the gods' temples within the arena: Arcite prays to Mars for victory in the tournament; Palamon prays to Venus for Emelye; Emelye prays to Diana, asking that she not be required to marry, but that, if she must have one of the suitors, she go to the one that desires her most. On Olympus, each of the gods clamor to Jupiter to have their prayer answered, and Jupiter's old father, Saturn, says that he will ensure that all works out in a manner that satisfies the three prayers.

In the tournament, after long fighting, Palamon is taken captive and Arcite declared the winner. But as he rides toward a smiling Emelye, basking in victory, Arcite is thrown by his horse and is killed by the fall. As he dies Arcite tells Emelye not to forget Palamon if she should ever marry. Arcite is buried, and after several years' mourning, Theseus calls Palamon to Athens, and in a lengthy speech in which he says the greatest wisdom is to "make virtue of necessity," he arranges for Palamon to marry Emelye in order to ally the kingdoms of Athens and Thebes.

Critical attention has often focused on the two lovers, and each has his defenders as the more worthy of Emelye's attentions. For the most part, though, Palamon and Arcite are seen as essentially equal. Theseus has also been the subject of scholarly attention, and he is generally seen as a wise ruler concerned with justice. But justice and order in the face of what appears to be an unjust universe is the problem that has concerned the greatest number of scholars. This is also the question raised by Boethius in the *Consolation of Philosophy,* and the meditations on destiny, on love, and particularly on the "First Mover," whom Theseus credits in the end with seeing all of human destiny from an eternal vantage point we are not vouchsafed, give the poem a serious philosophical dimension unusual in a chivalric romance.

Bibliography

Benson, Larry, et al., ed. *The Riverside Chaucer.* 3rd ed. Boston: Houghton-Mifflin, 1987.

Bloom, Harold. *Geoffrey Chaucer's "The Knight's Tale."* New York: Chelsea, 1988.

Kolve, V. A. *Chaucer and the Imagery of Narrative: The First Five Canterbury Tales.* Stanford, Calif.: Stanford University Press, 1984.

Leicester, H. Marshall. *The Disenchanted Self: Representing the Subject in the* Canterbury Tales. Berkeley: University of California Press, 1990.

Muscatine, Charles. *Chaucer and the French Tradition: A Study in Style and Meaning.* Berkeley: University of California Press, 1957.

Kojiki (*Record of Ancient Matters*) (ca. 712)

The oldest surviving written text in Japanese, the *Kojiki* was first presented at the emperor's court in Nara in 712, two years after the founding of that imperial city. It is basically a chronicle in three parts, divided into 114 shorter sections, covering the gods and the mythological creation of the world (with particular attention to Japan itself) moving through the deeds of legendary emperors down to those of more recent history. In a preface written in Chinese prose, the apparent compiler of the chronicle, Ō no Yasumaro, says that the emperor Temmu required that such a work be assembled after his victory in the Jinshin War in 672. Yasumaro says that he recorded the text from material memorized and transmitted orally by Hieda no Are. Most scholars believe that Are, and probably Yasumaro as well, also had access to sixth-century written sources now lost, one being the *Teiki* (a genealogy of Japanese emperors), and the other the *Kyūji* (a compilation of stories and anecdotes of the imperial court). But it is also certain that the *Kojiki* contains some material that was in existence orally before the introduction of writing to Japan—in particular some of the many *uta,* or songs and poems, embedded in the text.

The Japanese text makes use of Chinese characters in ways that became conventional in later Japanese writing. Sometimes the Chinese characters are used as ideograms, the symbol standing for the concept, pronounced as a Japanese word rather than a Chinese word. Sometimes the symbols are used as phonograms, so that the sound associated with the symbol was what the writer intended, and a number of Chinese characters might be strung together to form a multi-syllable Japanese word. This occurs chiefly in the *uta* or songs. Sometimes a combination of the two styles is used, as when the name of a god is spelled out phonetically in the context of a prose anecdote made up mainly of ideograms.

The first part of the *Kojiki,* sections 1–46, depicts the age of the gods and the myth of creation. The heaven and the earth are created. Then Izanagi (the male principle) and Izanami (the female principle) are chosen by the gods to generate the world, an act depicted as procreation and described with a good deal of sexual imagery. Their coupling gives birth to the Japanese islands. The text moves on to explore the relationships among the gods. The second part of the text deals with the 15 legendary emperors, beginning with Jinmu in 600 B.C.E. and ending with Ōjin in 310 C.E. The third volume of the *Kojiki* begins with the reign of Nintoku in 313 and ends with the historical reign of the Empress Suiko, the 33rd sovereign, from 592 to 628. The second and third parts of the text follow a pattern of first presenting genealogical material in prose, then including *uta* associated with the time, then adding anecdotes or other stories that had been collected by the editors or handed down orally.

The third part of the text deals largely with the historical struggle in the fourth and fifth centuries between the Imperial Yamato clan and other local Japanese clans. The gods who are shown taking part in the action are basically clan gods. Thus the third part of the *Kojiki* presents what is essentially a political myth. The gods represented are gods of Izumo (from Japan itself) and the gods of *Takama-no-hara* (the "Plain of High Heaven"). The Izumo gods represent the clans who fought the Yamato and are ultimately subjugated by the high gods, chief among whom is the sun goddess Amaterasu, presented as the progenitor of the Yamato emperors.

With this it becomes clear that one of the chief purposes of the *Kojiki* is to legitimize imperial power, specifically the right of the Yamato to rule over other Japanese groups. Having broken their tributary relationship with China in the seventh century, the Japanese rulers were intent on establishing a new imperial worldview modeled on the Chinese system, and in order to do so they needed a myth that legitimized their sovereignty by tracing the ancestry of the Yamato emperor to the gods themselves.

The *Kojiki* was not well known in the early centuries of its existence, but since the 18th century in particular it has been seen as the sacred book of the Shinto religion. But its importance for Japanese culture goes far beyond that distinction. It preserves ancient Japanese stories and myths and provides valuable information about the reigns of some of the earliest historical emperors. Many more recent works of literature allude to the legends of the *Kojiki,* while the poems and stories it contains are also valuable and respected as early literary texts in their own right. The poems of the *Kojiki* are Japan's first recorded poetic expressions, and from them ultimately are developed the later forms of Japanese poetry or *waka.* Finally, the form of the text, containing prose interspersed with poetry, would be a typical feature of Japanese literature throughout the Middle Ages.

Bibliography

Keene, Donald. *Seeds in the Heart: Japanese Literature from Earliest Times to the Late Sixteenth Century.* Vol. 1 of *A History of Japanese Literature.* New York: Columbia University Press, 1999.

Kato, Shuichi. *A History of Japanese Literature: From the Man'yōshū to Modern Times.* New Abridged Edition. Translated and Edited by Don Sanderson. Richmond, U.K.: Japan Library, 1997.

Miner, Earl, Hiroko Odagiri, and Robert E. Morrell. *The Princeton Companion to Classical Japanese*

Literature. Princeton, N.J.: Princeton University Press, 1985.

Kokinshū (*Kokin Waka Shū*) (ca. 905–920)

The *Kokinshū,* literally the "Collection of Old and New Poetry," was the first imperially sanctioned anthology of Japanese poetry. Inspired perhaps by an earlier collection of poetry, the MAN'YŌSHŪ, the emperor Daigo ordered a group of court intellectuals to compile a collection that would include the best contemporary poetry they could find as well as the best poems they could collect from past generations. Working on the anthology from about 905 until perhaps as late as 920, and guided by the genius of the poet and critic Ki no Tsurayuki, the four editors put together a collection of 1,111 poems, nearly all in the form of the 31-syllable TANKA. This anthology was to be the touchstone for Japanese poetic composition for the next 1,000 years. For one thing, it established the brief, lyrical tanka as the preferred form for poetry. It set a precedent for imperial anthologies, 20 more of which were to be published by the year 1439. Through the example of its poetry and through Ki no Tsurayuki's Japanese preface to the collection, the *Kokinshū* established the canons of taste for Japanese poetry, based exclusively on the values of the noble class, since all of the writers represented in the anthology were minor aristocrats involved in the life of the court. Most important, the anthology was an announcement to the world that *waka* (that is, native Japanese) poetry was of value in itself, and that Japan was no longer dependent on China for its cultural models.

The poems of the older *Man'yōshū* had been composed in Japanese, but were recorded using Chinese characters or ideographs—thus the Japanese word was represented by the Chinese character for the same concept. By the time of the *Kokinshū,* the Chinese characters had been adapted to represent the sounds of syllables in the Japanese language, so that the poems were far easier to read, since the reader need no longer be familiar with thousands of Chinese characters, but only the limited number that represented the sounds of Japanese.

The collection contains two prefaces, one in Chinese (by Ki no Yoshimochi) and the more significant Japanese one, in which Ki no Tsurayuki gives birth to the critical analysis of Japanese verse. He makes the following declaration:

> Japanese poetry has its seed in the human heart and burgeons into many different kinds of leaves of words. We who live in this world are constantly affected by different experiences, and we express our thoughts in words, in terms of what we have seen and heard. . . . Poetry moves without effort heaven and earth, stirs the invisible gods and demons to pity, makes sweet the ties between men and women, and brings comfort to the fierce heart of the warrior.
>
> (Keene 1999, 246)

These qualities of poetry—that it is a reaction to an experience, that it comes from the heart, that it enhances male-female relationships—are qualities that would have been important to the intellectuals and officials at the HEIAN court. The composition of poetry was expected of every member of the aristocratic society, so that every educated person knew to commemorate important moments in verse. Indeed, one's status as a cultured aristocrat depended on the sensitivity and verbal dexterity manifested in the often introspective lyric form of the tanka. It was from the best of these kinds of poems that Ki no Tsurayuki, Ki no Yoshimochi, and their fellow editors drew their selections.

The most prominent subject for these poems was, by far, nature and observations on the seasons. The second most common theme was love. Of the 1,111 poems in the *Kokinshū,* 342 are seasonal poems and 360 are love poems. Part of the genius of the *Kokinshū* is the choice to arrange the poems not in order of chronology or by author, but rather by topic. The 20 books of the *Kokinshū* fall into two halves: The first half is dominated by nature poems, which fill the first six books; the second half by love poems, which fill books 11 through 15.

Within their topical sections, the poems are arranged in a way that outlines a loose narrative. The nature poems, for example, begin with poems on spring (Books 1 and 2), and move through summer (Book 3) to autumn (Books 4 and 5) and finally winter (Book 6). More inspired is the arrangement of the love poems, which are intended to follow the progression of a love affair: The earliest poems deal with first meeting and infatuation, and they progress through passion and courtship, consummation of the affair, then cooling or disillusionment, separation and loneliness, and painful memories.

Certainly the tanka poems of the *Kokinshū* are limited in their subject matter. There are no poems on war or poverty or ugliness, nothing to break the precious mood of the delicate poetry. Even the love poetry tends to be circumspect about the sex act itself—unlike the poems of the *Man'yōshu,* which tend to be much more frank. In the *Kokinshū,* the lover is generally presented only as someone the narrator is thinking of, or perhaps dreaming about.

Many of the tanka of the *Kokinshū* are anonymous, but the compilers did preserve the names of several poets with their poems. The most revered of these include Ki no Yoshimochi himself, the admired love poet Ariwara Narihara, and the women Ono no Komachi—author of perhaps the most passionate love poems in the collection—and the prolific Izumi Shikibu, the most admired poet of her day, who was lady in waiting to a royal consort.

The *Kokinshū* preserved countless polished gems of poetry. It began a tradition of royal anthologies that imitated it for 500 years, and began the conventions of brevity and suggestiveness in Japanese poetry that have continued into the haiku of today. It established aristocratic taste as the standard of poetry. And it gives us, even today, a glimpse into the refined courtly culture of Heian Japan as it existed, and as it saw itself.

Bibliography

Brower, Robert H., and Earl Miner. *Japanese Court Poetry.* Stanford, Calif.: Stanford University Press, 1961.

Keene, Donald. *Seeds in the Heart: Japanese Literature from Earliest Times to the Late Sixteenth Century.* Vol. 1 of *A History of Japanese Literature.* New York: Columbia University Press, 1999.

McCullough, Helen Craig. *Kokin Wakashū: The First Imperial Anthology of Japanese Poetry.* Stanford, Calif.: Stanford University Press, 1985.

———. *Brocade by Night: "Kokin Wakashū" and the Court Style in Japanese Classical Poetry.* Stanford, Calif.: Stanford University Press, 1985.

Rodd, Laura Rasplica, and Mary Catherine Henkenius. *Kokinshū: A Collection of Poems Ancient and Modern.* Princeton, N.J.: Princeton University Press, 1984.

Koran (Qur'ân) (610–632)

The most important text in the Arabic-speaking world and the ultimate inspiration for all literature written in Arabic, the Koran (al-Qur'ân or Qur'an) is the sacred Scripture of Islam and the direct revelation of God through his prophet Muhammad. Revealed to Muhammad over a 23-year period, the Koran was preserved orally by the Prophet's followers, who committed various portions to memory, and also in written form by some, like his secretary Zayd ibn Thabit, who became known as "scribe of the revelation." In 651, the various verses of the Koran were gathered together and put into their current arrangement for wider circulation: The text of the Koran consists of 114 chapters or *suras,* arranged not in any continuous narrative but rather according to length, roughly from the longest *sura* (286 verses) to the shortest (three verses).

For Muslims, the Koran is not merely a revelation of the word of God; it is in fact the literal word of God, revealed to Muhammad through the intermediary angel Gabriel. The earthly Koran is a duplicate of a divine Koran that exists for all eternity in the Seventh Heaven, uncreated and co-eternal with God himself. It is God's final revelation to human beings, spoken in Arabic through an Arab prophet. Thus the Koran cannot be translated. Although its sense might be rendered into another language for purposes of instruction or interpretation, the translated text is not the Koran in the sense that, for example, an English version of the Christian Bible is thought to be the true Bible.

In general, the *suras* can be categorized according to where they were written. The earlier *suras,* generally shorter, were written in Mecca, during the period when Muhammad was preaching and converting people to his new faith in that city. There are 85 Meccan *suras,* and typically they exhort people to believe in the one God. They speak of the coming day of judgment and the heavenly reward of those who believe in God, and damnation for those who do not. They also call for social justice, instructing believers to help those in need, like outcasts, widows, and orphans, and to give generously to the poor. The 29 Medinian *suras*, generally later than the Meccan ones, were written during the period of a growing Muslim community in Medina after Muhammad's flight to that city. They are generally legalistic and are concerned with the ethical organization and the daily life of the Muslim political and social community.

Literally, *al-Qur'an* means "the Recitation," a title that suggests the oral nature of the text. For the most part, the text has the rhythm of an oral dialogue, between God and Muhammad or one of the earlier prophets, and between the prophet and his often uncooperative community. Extended narratives are the exception in the Koran. The story of Noah in *sura* 71 gives a short narrative, but the acknowledged narrative masterpiece of the Koran is *sura* 12, the story of Joseph (Yusuf). The most important *sura* in the Koran is probably the Exordium of *sura* 1—a short poem praising God's power and mercy and asking for his guidance—that, according to Muslim law, must appear at the head of every formal document and every oral presentation.

The Koran, as the foundational document of Muslim education and the spiritual authority of Islam, ensures that written Arabic is identical throughout the Muslim world. Written in a kind of rhymed prose, the Koran set a stylistic standard for literature in Arabic that is imitated in poetry and prose throughout the Middle Ages and even to the present day. The Koran has also exercised a profound influence on the content of Arabic literature: Condemning poets and storytellers as purveyors of untruth, the Koran encouraged literature that was generally didactic, concerned with morality and spirituality, and denigrated fiction and folk literature within Islamic countries.

Bibliography

Cook Michael. *The* Koran: *A Very Short Introduction.* Oxford: Oxford University Press, 2000.

Quran: The Final Testament. Authorized English version, with the Arabic text translated from the original by Rashad Khalifa. Tucson, Ariz.: Islamic Productions, 1992.

Rahman, Fazlur. *Major Themes of the Qur'ân.* Minneapolis, Minn.: Bibliotheca Islamica, 1980.

Turner, Colin, ed. *The Koran: Critical Concepts in Islamic Studies.* New York: Routledge, 2004.

Kormak's Saga (ca. 1200–1250)

Kormak (or Cormac) Ogmundarson was an Old Icelandic SKALDIC poet who lived from about 930 to 970. Kormak is known to have worked as a court poet for both Earl Sigurd Hakonson (d. 962) and for Harald Gráfeldr (Harald Graycloak), king of Norway from 960 to 970, and he was respected enough as a poet that some of his official court verses survived and were included by SNORRI STURLUSON in his handbook of skaldic poetry, the *PROSE EDDA* (ca. 1225). However, *Kormak's Saga*, an early Icelandic family SAGA that focuses on the life of the poet, essentially ignores Kormak's official public life to concentrate on his lifelong obsession for the woman Steingerd. The saga, which survives in a single vellum manuscript called the *Moðruvallabók* (ca. 1340) plus a later fragment, is a prose narrative like all sagas, but contains nearly 80 skaldic poems as well, more verse than any other surviving saga (nearly a third of the entire text).

The plot of the saga focuses on Kormak's jealousy and his conflicts with Steingerd's two husbands, Bersi and Thorvald. Kormak loves Steingerd from the first time he sees her, catching a glimpse of her ankles. But while he is wooing her, he is cursed by a witch, who prophesies that he will never have any joy of her. The curse begins to manifest itself in his life, as he cannot quite bring himself to take the important step of marrying her—in fact, he fails to show up on the day of his wedding, and Steingerd's kinsmen marry her, against her will, to the widower Bersi. He loses a formal duel (a *Holmgang* or "battle-wager") with Bersi on a technicality (the details of the duel make fascinating reading for those interested in the early history of Iceland). But in a second duel Bersi is badly wounded in the thigh by Kormak's friend Steinar.

Steingerd takes the opportunity to divorce the crippled Bersi, but rather than return to Kormak, she weds Thorvald ("the Tinsmith") instead. Now Kormak goes out of his way to insult and provoke Thorvald, attacking him with satiric verses, publicly humiliating him through open misconduct with Steingerd, and even striking him with a tiller. But Thorvald does nothing until Kormak rescues Steingerd from pirates, after which Thorvald offers to give up his wife as a reward for Kormak's rescue of her. Freed from her husbands, Steingerd is now available to marry Kormak, but instead she rebuffs him completely. The rejected Kormak admits that fate is unlikely to allow the two of them to live together, and throws himself into a Viking expedition, only to be killed in Scotland fighting a giant, who falls upon him after Kormak has killed him.

One of the questions debated by scholars is the relationship between the poetry and the prose in the text. Most scholars have felt that the poetry in the text is Kormak's genuine verse, preserved in the oral tradition from the 10th century. There is some debate as to whether the romantic narrative was a tradition surviving from Kormak's life, or the imaginative creation of the saga writer. Some have suggested that both the poetry and the prose are creations of the saga writer; however, since there are a number of places in the text where the prose writer seems to misunderstand the point of the poem he quotes, this last suggestion seems unlikely. But there is a possibility that the narrative, and the poetry as well, was influenced by the story of TRISTAN AND ISOLDE, a love story that had been retold in an Old Norse version in 1226. Certainly Kormak betrays some of the typical characteristics of the courtly lover, including melancholy and inability to sleep.

Most of the poems in *Kormak's Saga* are in the form called *dróttvœtt,* one of the most difficult skaldic verse forms, which used both alliteration and complex rhyme. In the saga, Kormak is depicted reciting 64 stanzas of poetry, much of it love poetry. Bersi, also a poet, recites 14 poems, and Steingerd herself recites one expressing her determination to have Kormak. But Kormak himself is no prize. Not unlike the hero of *EGIL'S SAGA*, another skaldic poet, Kormak is quarrelsome and uncouth, rash and perverse, and not a particularly likable character—though his hopeless devotion to his beloved Steingerd does arouse some sympathy. But the narrative remains an unusually romantic family saga, containing a significant collection of memorable skaldic poetry.

Bibliography

Andersson, Theodore M. *The Icelandic Family Saga: An Analytic Reading.* Harvard Studies in Comparative Literature, 28. Cambridge, Mass.: Harvard University Press, 1967.

Hollander, Lee M., trans. *The Sagas of Kormak and the Sworn Brothers.* Princeton, N.J.: Princeton University Press, 1949.

Morris, William, and Eiríkr Magnússon. *The Story of Korkak, the Son of Ogmund.* Introduction by Grace J. Calder, and a note on the manuscript work of William Morris by Alfred Fairbank. London: William Morris Society, 1970.

O'Donaghue, Heather. *The Genesis of a Saga Narrative: Verse and Prose in Kormaks Saga.* Oxford: Clarendon Press, 1991.

lai

The term *lai* was originally applied to French poems of the 12th and 13th centuries. Some *lais* were lyric poems, but the best-known were short narrative ROMANCES, also called *contes.* Some of the earliest *lais* were those of MARIE DE FRANCE, who composed them for the French-speaking court of King HENRY II and his queen, ELEANOR OF AQUITAINE, probably in the 1170s. Marie's *lais* were often called "Breton *lais*" because they were generally based on earlier Celtic legends preserved and disseminated in the songs of Breton MINSTRELS. Some of these, including Marie's *lai LANVAL,* were based on legends surrounding King ARTHUR, the chief Breton hero.

The earlier French *lais,* like Marie's, were written in octosyllabic (eight-syllable) lines arranged in couplets. Some *lais* of the later Middle Ages developed more complex verse forms. This was particularly true of lyric *lais,* the earliest of which are Provençal lyrics by the poet Gautier de Dargies. These lyric *lais* were generally addressed to a courtly lady or to the Virgin Mary. However they were composed in stanzas that varied in both rhyme scheme and metrical pattern, and so differed from other such poems. By the 14th century, Guillaume de MACHAUT had standardized the form of the lyric *lai.* As described in DESCHAMPS's *Art de Dictier* (Art of writing poetry), the standard lyric *lai* consisted of 12 pairs of stanzas of differing meter, all looking at the same idea in different ways. In the 12th section, the meter returned to the same form as the first, so that a circular movement was created.

The variety of metrical form was also the case in England, where a number of 14th-century English poems were written in imitation of French narrative *lais,* and accordingly were called "Breton lays" in English. Some of these are in short couplets, but many are called TAIL-RHYME ROMANCES because of their distinct verse form. Some of the better-known Breton lays in English are *SIR ORFEO,* the *SIR LAUNFAL,* and CHAUCER's *FRANKLIN'S TALE.*

Since about the 16th century, the term *lay* in English has been used more generically to refer simply to a song, although this meaning seems to have been inherent in the term since the 14th century. Certainly the term *lay* (as opposed to *Breton lay*) seems to have had such a connotation for Chaucer, whose ideas about lyric poetry owe a great deal to Machaut: In his "Retraction" to the *CANTERBURY TALES,* Chaucer mentions his writing "many a song and many a lecherous lay," referring to his short lyric poems.

Bibliography

Burgess, Glyn S., ed. *The Lais of Marie de France: Text and Context.* Athens: University of Georgia Press, 1987.

Donovan, Mortimer J. *The Breton Lay: A Guide to Varieties.* Notre Dame, Ind.: University of Notre Dame Press, 1969.

Hanning, Robert, and Joan Ferrante, trans. *The Lais of Marie de France.* New York: Dutton, 1978.

Lancelot du Lac

Sir Lancelot du Lac was the greatest of King ARTHUR's knights, according to most late medieval Arthurian romances. Known for his strength, prowess, and bravery, Lancelot was even better known as the lover of Arthur's queen, GUENEVERE. Their affair became one of the major causes of the downfall of Arthur's Round Table, according to the very influential work of Sir Thomas MALORY at the end of the 15th century.

Lancelot's first appearance in literature is in the Old French *LANCELOT: THE KNIGHT OF THE CART* (ca. 1175), by CHRÉTIEN DE TROYES. Here, after the queen has been abducted by the evil Meleagant, Lancelot sets out to rescue her. When his horse dies and he is offered a ride in a cart—an act that would publicly shame a knight—he hesitates for only two steps before climbing in. After crossing a dangerous sword bridge, he does battle with Meleagant until he is persuaded by the queen not to kill the treacherous knight. But when Lancelot comes face to face with Guenevere, she snubs him, angry that he hesitated for two steps before getting into the cart to rescue her. Ultimately, after she has forgiven him, Lancelot tears the bars from the window of her chamber and the two spend the night together. From that point, Lancelot obeys everything that the queen tells him to do, even if it means his own shame, as happens when she tells him to "do his worst" in a tournament.

In ULRICH VON ZATZIKHOVEN's *Lanzelet* (ca. 1194–1204), Lancelot is carried off by a mermaid as a child, and is raised without knowledge of his royal parentage until he is 15. (This relates to one odd detail in Chrétien's story, where the poet mentions a magic ring that was given Lancelot by a fairy woman who raised him.) At 15 Lancelot sets out to win a place at Arthur's court. He conquers the lords of three castles, and wins the love of three separate maidens, one of whom (Yblis, daughter of Iweret) he marries. After finally discovering his true parentage, Lancelot hears word that Guenevere has been abducted, this time by Valerin of the Tangled Wood. Ultimately Lancelot, along with Arthur's other knights, rescues the queen.

It seems unlikely that Chrétien was Ulrich's source, since Ulrich does not include anything about Lancelot's affair with the queen. Rather the two poets may have had a common source, perhaps a Celtic story of abduction. Since Chrétien stated at the beginning of his romance that he had been given the material and treatment by his patron, MARIE DE CHAMPAGNE, it seems likely that Marie and Chrétien are responsible for turning what may have been an earlier story of Lancelot (one that more closely resembled Ulrich's) into one that incorporated the fashionable new concept of COURTLY LOVE.

The other major romance of which Lancelot is the protagonist is the voluminous early 13th-century *Prose Lancelot,* a part of the VULGATE CYCLE of Arthurian romances. In it, Lancelot is revealed as the son of King Ban of Benwick. When his father dies, he is carried off by the Lady of the Lake and raised by her, joined eventually by his cousins, Lionel and Bors. At the age of 18, Lancelot learns his true parentage from the Lady, and she takes him to Arthur's court. Here, he sees and falls in love with the queen, and it is she who knights him and gives him his sword—a ceremony that symbolized his divided loyalties. But his many adventures win him the reputation of the greatest knight in the world. He does learn, however, that because of his adultery with the queen, he will be prevented from achieving the greatest knightly quest of all, the HOLY GRAIL. Instead, that quest is reserved for his son, GALAHAD, whom Lancelot begets with Elaine, daughter of King Pelles, who tricks him into believing he is sleeping with Guenevere.

Lancelot continues as a major character in the two subsequent Vulgate Cycle romances, *The Quest of the Holy Grail* and the *Mort Artu* (Death of Arthur). In the *Quest,* Lancelot is repeatedly reminded of his sin with the queen, and on this spiritual quest, the skills of the secular warrior are of no use—it is purity that achieves the Grail, and in this, Galahad, Perceval, and Bors all exceed Lancelot. In the last romance of the cycle, Lancelot and the queen are discovered together. Lancelot escapes, but the queen is condemned to death. In rescuing her, Lancelot by chance kills two of Sir GAWAIN's brothers, and the war that ensues ultimately tears apart Arthur's kingdom.

The Vulgate Cycle romances were the major sources for Malory's *Le MORTE DARTHUR*. But Malory's sympathies remain solidly with his favorite knight, Sir Lancelot du Lac. While the Christian ideals that permeated chivalric romance in the Vulgate Cycle changed the perception of Lancelot as the great secular hero and lover, Malory was not willing to abandon the secular ideal. In his version of the Quest, Lancelot is convinced of his sin, but by his own penance he earns a glimpse of the Grail, and is clearly depicted as fourth among the Grail knights, and the greatest of all earthly knights. In an episode apparently invented by Malory, Lancelot is able to heal the Hungarian knight Sir Urry, who can only be made whole by the greatest knight in the world. In the end, the love of Lancelot and Guenevere is proof of their nobility, so that both lovers end their lives in sanctity in holy orders.

Lancelot generally does not fare as well in postmedieval versions of Arthurian legend, which often depict him as tormented by his dual loyalty. This kind of psychological "realism" is not characteristic of the medieval depictions of the knight, which were more concerned with what Malory calls his "worship," or his public image. For this, Malory's Lancelot is the high point.

Bibliography

Chrétien de Troyes. *Lancelot: The Knight of the Cart.* Translated by Burton Raffel. Afterword by Joseph J. Duggan. New Haven, Conn.: Yale University Press, 1997.

Lacy, Norris J., et al., eds. *Lancelot-Grail: The Old French Arthurian Vulgate and Post-Vulgate in Translation.* 5 vols. New York: Garland Publishing, 1993–1996.

Malory, Sir Thomas. *Le Morte Darthur, or the Hole Book of Kyng Arthur and of His Noble Knyghtes of the Rounde Table.* Edited by Stephen H. A. Shepherd. New York: Norton, 2004.

Ulrich von Zatzikhoven. *Lanzelet.* Translated by G. T. Webster. With an introduction by Roger Sherman Loomis. New York: Columbia University Press, 1951.

Walters, Lori J., ed. *Lancelot and Guinevere: A Casebook.* New York: Garland, 1996.

Lancelot: The Knight of the Cart Chrétien de Troyes (ca. 1176–82)

Probably the fourth of the five extant Arthurian verse ROMANCES by the French poet CHRÉTIEN DE TROYES, *Lancelot: The Knight of the Cart* is thought to have been written sometime close to the writing of Chrétien's *YVAIN: THE KNIGHT OF THE LION.* Incidents from the narrative of *Lancelot* are thrice referred to in *Yvain,* and some critics suggest that the poet's unusual references to episodes in one of his own compositions indicate a close chronology of composition and/or serve as thematic contrast in *Yvain*'s negation of adulterous love, which figures so prominently in *Lancelot.* Indeed it has been argued that Chrétien's discomfort with the unsanctified love of Lancelot and Guenevere leads him to give responsibility for the poem's "subject" and "meaning" (Chrétien 1997, ll. 26–27) to his patron, the Countess MARIE DE CHAMPAGNE, and to leave the poem to be completed by the otherwise unknown Godfrey of Lagny.

The central plot of *Lancelot* is fairly straightforward, although there are a series of seemingly disconnected episodes and adventures leading to the central action in the fashion of Arthurian romances. The poem opens at Arthur's court where the evil Méléagant (who holds many of Arthur's people captive) challenges Arthur to send one of his knights with Queen Guenevere to the woods where, if Arthur's knight defeats him in battle, the evil knight will free Arthur's people, but if Méléagant himself is the victor, Guenevere is the prize. By means of petulance and a rash promise, Kay is given the honor of accepting the challenge, which he promptly fails. Arthur is persuaded by Gawain to follow Méléagant, and they soon come upon Kay's riderless horse, which confirms their worst fears. Gawain rides ahead and comes upon an unnamed knight in need of a horse because he has ridden his to its death. Gawain gives the knight a horse (we later learn this is Lancelot, although the romance convention of disguise or failed recognition clearly suggests to the audience, if not to

Gawain, Lancelot's identity at this first meeting) and follows him, only to find the horse the knight had taken "dead in the road" (l. 306) and the signs of a "furious" fight with many knights (l. 310). Gawain rides on until he comes upon the "unknown" knight "alone and on foot," following a cart into which the knight climbs only after some moments of "hesitant shame" (l. 363).

The cart is, of course, the cart of the title, and Lancelot's hesitation is key to understanding one of the central tensions in the romance: the conflict between ideal knightly honor and duty (including the avoidance of shame and fealty to one's secular lord) and the ideals of COURTLY LOVE (including duty in the service of and submission to one's lady). Chrétien explores this conflict in his earlier *EREC AND ENIDE*, but here the conflict takes on additional significance: Here the lovers are involved in an adulterous affair, and the lack of balance or moderation will find no final resolution in a measured marriage of knightly and courtly values. Lancelot hesitates to enter the cart because it would shame his honor as a knight—carts being used to display the infamy of criminals, murderers, and other low-lifes; yet after his initial hesitation, Lancelot listens to Love which "hurriedly ordered him / Into the cart" (ll. 372–73), and thus sets in motion a series of adventures in which he must prove his devotion to women to redeem his sin against the courtly code of love. When Lancelot does finally rescue the queen, her coldness to him is not, as he thinks, because he shamed himself by riding in the cart, but because he hesitated to do so and thus put his knightly honor before his love. When Guenevere forgives Lancelot they manage to spend an adulterous interlude together in the midst of enemies and Arthurian knights. Méléagant discovers the adultery—though he believes the queen has been with Sir Kay—and brings a legal charge against the queen (in medieval legal documents adultery between a lady and one of her husband's knights is a felony). Lancelot defends her and, after further adventures, Lancelot defeats Méléagant in a trial by combat.

There are early- and mid-12th-century Welsh and Breton versions of Guenevere's abduction and rescue, yet Lancelot's role and the adulterous relationship seem to originate with Chrétien's romance. Critical commentary tends to focus either on the poet's distaste for his subject matter, and particularly the adultery (and to invoke this to explain Chrétien's unusual gesture of ascribing subject matter and meaning to his patron), or on the ways in which the poet may be validating courtly codes of love. Examples of those were found in the *Art of Courtly Love* (ca. 1185) of ANDREAS CAPELLANUS, an author not only contemporaneous with Chrétien, but writing for essentially the same courtly audience, including Marie, countess of Champagne. Chrétien's willingness to portray his romance characters as shamed or foolish seems to support those who would argue for the poet's discomfort with too strict an adherence to the principles of courtly love. Yet adultery is not a new issue in Chrétien's Arthurian romances: In *CLIGÈS* the poet presents an adulterous affair that, however many times the lovers claim they will not be TRISTAN AND ISOLDE, is very like that adulterous relationship without the excuse of a magic potion. Nonetheless it is worth noting the ambiguities and conflicts that arise from the adultery in *Cligès* seemingly expressed in the wholesale fragmentation of bodily and emotional integrity throughout the romance. If the moral conflicts in *Lancelot* are not easily resolved by modern critical analysis, they were immensely popular for their medieval audience, and *Lancelot* became one of the most influential romances of the Middle Ages. The adultery between Lancelot and Guenevere is the cause of the destruction of the Arthurian court in the 13th-century VULGATE CYCLE, which was the primary source for Sir Thomas MALORY's 15th-century *MORTE DARTHUR*, which is, in its turn, the source for most of the hundreds of retellings of the Arthurian legend into the 21st century.

Bibliography

Andreas Capellanus. *The Art of Courtly Love, by Andreas Capellanus.* Translated by John Jay Parry. New York: Ungar, 1941.

Chrétien de Troyes. *Lancelot: The Knight of the Cart.* Translated by Burton Raffel. Afterword by Joseph J. Duggan. New Haven, Conn.: Yale University Press, 1997.

Baldwin, John W. *The Language of Sex: Five Voices from Northern France Around 1200.* Chicago: University of Chicago Press, 1994.

Benton, John F. "The Court of Champagne as a Literary Center." In *Culture, Power, and Personality in Medieval France,* edited by Thomas N. Bisson, 3–43. London: Hambledon Press, 1991.

———. "Clio and Venus: A Historical View of Medieval Love." In *Culture, Power and Personality in Medieval France,* edited by Thomas N. Bisson, 99–121. London: Hambledon Press, 1991.

Cross, Tom Peete, and William Albert Nitze. *Lancelot and Guenevere: A Study on the Origins of Courtly Love.* Chicago: University of Chicago Press, 1930.

Frappier, Jean. *Chrétien de Troyes: The Man and His Work.* Translated by Raymond J. Cormier. Athens: Ohio University Press, 1982.

Kelly, Douglas. *"Sens" and "Conjointure" in the Chevalier de la Charette.* Studies in French Literature, 2. The Hague: Mouton, 1966.

———. *Medieval French Romance.* Twayne's World Authors Series, 838. New York: Twayne, 1993.

Noble, Peter S. *Love and Marriage in Chrétien de Troyes.* Cardiff: University of Wales Press, 1982.

Elisa Narin van Court

Land of Cockaygne, The (ca. 1275–1300)

The Land of Cockaygne is a MIDDLE ENGLISH poem in 190 lines of rough octosyllabic (eight-syllable) lines, probably written in Ireland in the late 13th century. The poem is a parody of the idea of the earthly paradise, and also a satire of monastic life. It survives in a single manuscript dated about 1330, containing Latin and French as well as English texts, and associated with the Franciscan abbey in Kildare.

The poem describes the paradisal Land of Cockaygne (the name, in French, probably means "Land of the Cakes"), which lies somewhere west of Spain. It is better than the recognized paradise, where the only thing to eat is fruit, and there is no alcohol at all. Cockaygne is a place where no one has to work and where the drinks flow free. There is an abbey in that land whose walls are formed out of pies, meat and fish, with shingles made of flour cakes, and nails formed from fat sausages. The monks can eat their fill without fear of recrimination. The wellsprings flow with wine, and the ground is made of gold and precious stones. The geese are roasted on a spit and then fly into the abbey crying out to be eaten. The monks themselves are able to fly, and wouldn't come to evensong at all if the abbot did not call them by spanking a young maiden's white buttocks like a drum to call them to prayers. The nuns from the convent near the monastery like to swim naked in the river of milk, and the young monks fly over them and pick out the ones with whom they want to have sex—they will have 12 different "wives" a year. Unfortunately, in order to reach this Paradise, one must go through an incredibly severe penance: walk through swines' dung up to the chin for seven years.

The poem is in a tradition that goes back to Lucian's satirical second century *True History,* which also describes a comic and licentious Paradise. It also draws, of course, on Christian traditions of the Earthly Paradise, as well as the GOLIARDIC VERSE celebrating food and drink. There are parallels to *The Land of Cockaygne* in Irish satire, in Old French and in Anglo-Norman, but the ribald anticlerical satire makes this poem unique. It appears that the poem is intended to satirically express a monk's vision of paradise, and ironically that vision is a place where he can engage in the sins of the flesh—sloth, greed, gluttony, and especially lust—without recrimination. He must only get through the penance of this world—perhaps his strict monastic life—to win the reward of an eternity of heavenly debauchery.

Bibliography

Jonassen, Frederick B. "Lucian's *Saturnalia,* the *Land of Cockaigne,* and the Mummers' Plays," *Folklore* 101 (1990): 58–68.

"The Land of Cokayne," in *Middle English Literature,* edited by Charles W. Dunn and Edward T. Byrnes. New York: Harcourt Brace Jovanovich, 1973, 188–192.

Vasvari, Louise O. "The Geography of Escape and Topsy-Turvy Literary Genres." In *Discovering New Worlds: Essays on Medieval Exploration and Imagination,* edited by Scott D. Westrem, 178–192. New York: Garland, 1991.

Langland, William (ca. 1330–ca. 1388)

Almost nothing can be said with certainty about the author of the popular and influential 14th-century DREAM VISION poem *PIERS PLOWMAN*. In the past, there was controversy as to whether a single author wrote all three versions of the poem, known by scholars as the A-, B-, and C-texts. As many as five different authors were projected at one time, but the current critical consensus is that a single author, named William Langland, is responsible for all three texts.

Two 15th-century manuscript notes attribute the poem to Langland, and a line in the B-text (Schmidt 1995, passus 15, l. 152) is apparently intended as a play on the author's name: It can be translated as "I have lived in the land, my name is Long Will." In one manuscript a Latin note identifies Langland as the son of Eustace de Rokayle, who was a supporter of Lord Despenser and held land from him in Oxfordshire at a place called Shipton-under-Wychwood. It seems likely Langland's father was a franklin rather than a member of the noble class. Some have conjectured that Langland may have been illegitimate, but it is not necessary to make that assumption: It was not uncommon in the 14th century for father and son to be known by different surnames.

Any other information about Langland's life can only be conjectured from the three texts of the poem. While it is certainly dubious to identify the narrator of a medieval text, particularly an ALLEGORY like *Piers Plowman,* with the author himself, it was customary for the narrator of a dream vision to be at least a parody of the author himself (as in CHAUCER's dream visions). Furthermore the specific detail of some of the "autobiographical" aspects of the Dreamer (named, allegorically and autobiographically, "Will") are specific enough to suggest they are personal details—like Chaucer's reference in *The HOUSE OF FAME* to his accounting practices as controller of customs.

Thus when, in the B-text, Langland refers to his age as 45 years, scholars have assumed that he must have been born in about 1330, since the B-text seems to have been completed about 1377 (judging from a reference in the prologue to the coronation of RICHARD II, which would have taken place in that year). Langland was certainly from the West Midlands, since he writes in that dialect, and it is assumed that he lived much of his early life in or near Malvern Hills, which forms the setting for the first two visions of the poem. It is believed he was born at Cleobury Mortimer in Shropshire, about eight miles from Malvern Hills.

Langland speaks in the C-text of attending school. Many believe he was educated at the priory of Great Malvern in Worcestershire, and perhaps later at Oxford. He certainly trained for the priesthood, but took only minor orders. Passages in his poem suggest that the reason for this was that he was forced to leave school by the death of his father and other financial supporters (perhaps during the BLACK DEATH, when Hugh Despenser III is known to have died). He also indicates that he—or at least Will the Dreamer—had a wife named Kitte and a daughter, Callotte. A married cleric could not advance in the church beyond the rank of subdeacon. These things led E. Talbot Donaldson (1965) to conjecture that Langland was an acolyte, a poor clerk without a benefice and no way to make a living within the church hierarchy. He certainly seems to have been poor.

In the C-text Will is shown excusing his shiftless lifestyle before the allegorical characters Reason and Conscience by arguing that his position as a tonsured clerk should exempt him from manual labor: His only tools to support himself are his prayer book and Psalms with which he prays and sings the office of the dead for anyone that would pay him. He may also have picked up occasional odd clerical jobs in the city of London, where, according to the C-text, he was living in the city at Cornhill with his wife and daughter.

The only other thing we know about Langland is that, in the midst of the poverty that seems to have followed him his entire adult life, he worked for some 25 to 30 years honing and revising his masterpiece. The A-text, whose character Lady Meed is believed to be modeled on the figure of Alice Perrers, mistress of King EDWARD III, for that reason must have been written in 1365 or soon after. The B-text, as already noted, must have been completed around 1377. Scholars generally agree that Langland was probably still at work on the C-text when he died. Though some independent evidence suggests that Langland may have been dead by 1387, his apparent allusions to a Statute of Laborers of 1388 make that date more likely the date of his death.

If Langland was anything like the character of Will in the poem—and it is possible that he creates a kind of exaggerated parody of himself there—he may have been a gaunt, tall fellow (nicknamed "Long Will"), who had wandered about a great deal and done some begging, had little use for the rich or powerful, and was impulsive and sometimes contentious. What we can be sure of is that he was an original and gifted poet whose single masterpiece continues to amuse, puzzle, and move readers even today.

Bibliography

Alford, John A. *A Companion to Piers Plowman.* Berkeley: University of California Press, 1988.

Donaldson, E. Talbot. *Piers Plowman: The C-Text and Its Poet.* Yale Studies in English, 114. Hamden, Conn.: Archon Books, 1966.

Du Boulay, F. R. H. *The England of Piers Plowman: William Langland and His Vision of the Fourteenth Century.* Cambridge, U.K.: Brewer, 1991.

Langland, William. *Piers Plowman: A New Translation of the B-text.* Translated by A. V. C. Schmidt. Oxford: Oxford University Press, 1992.

———. *The Vision of Piers Plowman: A Critical Edition of the B-text based on Trinity College Cambridge MS B.15.17.* Edited by A. V. C. Schmidt. 2nd ed. London: Everyman, 1995.

Wittig, Joseph S. *William Langland Revisited.* New York: Twayne, 1997.

Lanval Marie de France (ca. 1170)

In her collection *Lais,* MARIE DE FRANCE, an Anglo-Norman poet who obviously lived in England but originated from France, included the *LAI Lanval.* This verse narrative seems to be based on an oral Breton source, as the author insists on its historical veracity and yet does not refer to any written account of it.

The protagonist is a "very noble young man whose name in Breton is Lanval." We are immediately transported into the world of King Arthur, who is here involved in military conflicts with the Scots and Picts, whereas in most courtly ROMANCES, Arthur simply celebrates the arrival of spring or spends his time organizing court festivals. Only the oldest sources dealing with King Arthur, such as GEOFFREY OF MONMOUTH'S *HISTORIA REGUM BRITANNIAE* (ca. 1138) and its translations into French by Geffrei Gaimar (ca. 1140s) and by WACE (ca. 1155), depict the king as a military leader. In other words Marie draws from ancient accounts about this mythical figure to tell her story of the young protagonist Lanval, who has come from a country far away where his father rules as a king. Although he shines in every knightly virtue, many members of Arthur's court are jealous of him, and the king seems to overlook him entirely, never rewarding him for his many accomplishments. Soon Lanval runs out of money and faces poverty, not knowing how to ask for help.

Depressed about this situation, he leaves the court and rides into the countryside, where he encounters two damsels who take him to their lady, who is awaiting him in a most valuable tent that would find no parallel in the entire world, neither in the present nor in the past. Because of the summer heat the lady is hardly covered, and Lanval immediately falls in love with her. She reveals that she had been looking for him for a long time and would like to offer him her love if he proves to be worthy and courtly. Not surprisingly, Lanval does not hesitate to accept her conditions and pledges his love for her. Not only does she reward him with sexual pleasures, she also showers him with all the material wealth he can think of, although she warns him that their relationship has to remain an absolute secret, otherwise he would lose her—a traditional fairy-tale motif. But she promises him always to appear in his presence whenever he will ask for her, without being seen by anyone else. Then she sends him back to King Arthur's court, where he can suddenly demonstrate extreme hospitality and generosity to everyone.

His happiness, however, is soon shattered because the queen begins to desire him and offers herself to him as his mistress. Lanval rejects her because he does not want to break his oath of faith given to King Arthur, and because he enjoys the love of his invisible lady. The queen at first accuses him of being homosexual—a narrative motif often used in courtly romances, such as in the anonymous *Roman d'Eneas,* in HEINRICH VON VELDEKE's *Eneit,* in IPOMEDON, the *Roman de Silence,* the *Histoire de Gille de Chyn,* the *Roman de la Violette ou de Gerart de Nevers,* and in ULRICH VON LICHTENSTEIN's *Frauenbuch.* In his rush to defend himself, Lanval reveals his secret love and ridicules the queen as unworthy of comparison to his own lady.

In close parallel to the story of Potiphar's wife in the Old Testament (Genesis 39), the queen then resorts to the strategy of maligning Lanval and accusing him of having asked for her love, which she had refused, and then of having ridiculed and humiliated her by claiming that the lowest servant girl of his true beloved was worthier than the queen. King Arthur immediately takes his wife's side and wants Lanval to be tried by his barons who convene a court council. The barons decide that the accused must provide proof for his claim regarding his mistress's beauty and social rank, otherwise he would be dismissed from the king's service and banished from the court. Unfortunately Lanval knows that his lady would no longer come to him because he broke his oath never to talk about her in public and to reveal their love.

As soon, however, as the verdict is about to be given, two of the maidens of Lanval's lady appear in support of the young man and announce the arrival of their mistress. Gawain, loyal and trustworthy courtier as ever, approaches Lanval in the hope that one of the maidens would be his love, which would save the young man from being tried and expelled from court, but this is, of course, not the case. Nevertheless the appearance of the two maidens delays the court proceedings, and the barons return to their deliberations, when two more maidens appear, repeating the previous message. Once again Lanval's friends assume that one of them is the true lady, since they are more beautiful and worthy than King Arthur's queen. But the second delay of the verdict makes the queen angry, so the barons hasten to return to their duty, when finally Lanval's beloved appears, entirely defeating the queen's claims and demonstrating through her appearance that she is indeed much more beautiful and worthy than the queen. The young man is immediately acquitted, and when his lady leaves the court, he jumps onto the palfrey behind her and disappears with her into the utopian world of Avalon, never to be seen again.

The fairy-tale motif is obvious, but Marie clearly indicates that she transformed oral poetry derived from the old Bretons into a literary account in which many different discourses—mythic, legal, courtly, and always intertextual—intertwine. *Lanval* proves to be so intriguing because of its impressive interplay with literary and biblical sources. The interrupted court deliberations, for example, seem to be based on Marie's possible familiarity with the *Historia septem sapientum* (History of the seven sages), which, in turn, was a Latin translation of the Old French *Roman des sept sages de Rome,* and this again drew from a ninth-century Persian version, the *Book of Sindbad.* Moreover *Lanval* reveals Marie's intimate familiarity with the legal and political discourse of her time, and the narrative by itself indicates the extent to which 12th-century women could assume powerful political positions. Lanval's rescue by his lady appears as an ironic reversal of the traditional gender roles of knights rescuing damsels in distress, and whereas knights traditionally seem to have endless amounts of money available to them, here the young man, who is far away from home and, at first, without any friends, finds himself in financial distress from which he is relieved by his lady. In true fashion of all of her *lais,* Marie here projects a literary utopia where true happiness in love can be achieved in the unreality of fiction, but the short narrative also indicates the extent to which Marie indirectly criticized the courtly world where jealousy, envy, deception, rumors, and malignment seem to be the order of the day, and backstabbing is obviously a common and quite effective strategy for getting rid of an opponent.

Bibliography

Bloch, R. Howard. *The Anonymous Marie de France.* Chicago: University of Chicago Press, 2003.

Burgess, Glyn S., and Keith Busby, trans. *The Lais of Marie de France.* London: Penguin, 1986.

Burgess, Glyn S. *The Lais of Marie de France: Text and Context.* Athens: The University of Georgia Press, 1987.

Jambeck, Karen K. " 'Femmes et tere': Marie de France and the Discourses of 'Lanval.' " In *Discourses on Love, Marriage, and Transgression in Medieval and Early Modern Literature,* edited by Albrecht Classen. Tempe, Ariz.: MRTS, forthcoming.

Rychner, Jean, ed. *Les Lais de Marie de France.* 1966. Classiques Français du Moyen Age, 93. 2nd ed. Paris: Champion, 1981.

Albrecht Classen

Lapo Gianni (ca. 1250–ca. 1328)

Lapo Gianni was a lyric poet and, with his better-known friends DANTE and Guido CAVALCANTI, one of the *stilnovisti,* the Florentine poets of the *DOLCE STIL NOVO,* or "sweet new style," that revolutionized Italian vernacular poetry in the late 13th century.

Though it is not absolutely certain, it is assumed that Lapo the poet was the notary of the same name, who was a member of the Ricevuti family of Florence, and whose name appears on official acts between 1298 and 1328. Dante mentions him as a friend in his sonnet *"Guido, I' vorrei che tu e Lapo ed io,"* and Cavalcanti refers to him as well. Dante also praises Lapo in *De VULGARI ELOQUENTIA* as one of the few contemporary poets who have achieved eloquence in the Italian vernacular (the others being, not surprisingly, Cavalcanti and himself).

Lapo's poetry abounds in imagery familiar to the *stilnovisti.* The lady is like an angel from heaven. The lover possesses a "gentle heart." Lapo's imagery is often derived from new and unconventional sources: In one poem he is drawn toward his lady by love, just as the Magi were drawn to Christ by the star. In another the "spirits" of late medieval psychology explain how Love suddenly takes him:

In your face, like an angel's full of love,
I saw your beautiful eyes and the dark light
that bore like an arrow
through my eyes a tender spirit,

(Goldin 1973, 339, ll. 1–4)

At the same time, however, Lapo seems to take a great deal from the Provençal TROUBADOURS and their successors in the earlier Italian Sicilian school of GIACOMO DA LENTINO: Lapo's poems have a lighter and more joyous tone than much *stilnovist* poetry. The ending of his poem *"Dolc'è 'l pensier che mi notrica il core,"* for example, uses feudal terms and images more at home in the courts of southern France than the cities of Tuscan Italy:

How I am inscribed in the book of Love
you shall recount, my song, in courtesy,
when you see my lady:
for I have become her man, and serve.

(Goldin 1973, 341, ll. 25–29)

The direct address to the song, the virtue of "courtesy," the vassalage to the lady, all are pure troubadour. Lapo is a skilled poet who is able to combine both traditions in his poetry. Though he lacks the lofty reputation of his greater contemporaries, Lapo's contribution to Italian poetry of the 13th century is significant.

Bibliography

Goldin, Frederick, trans. *German and Italian Lyrics of the Middle Ages: An Anthology and a History.* New York: Doubleday, 1973.

lauda

A *lauda* (plural, *laude*) was a popular religious poem or "song of praise," adapted from the Christian liturgy and widespread in Italy in the 14th and 15th centuries. The earliest *laude* were 13th-century Latin hymns, the best known being the *Stabat Mater* and the *Dies Irae.* St. FRANCIS OF ASSISI wrote some of the first *laude* in the vernacular, called the *Cantico delle Creature.*

The popularity of the *lauda* was augmented by the rise of the religious Order of the Flagellants (a group devoted to public penance, whose members paraded through European cities, beating each other with ropes or chains). This group, originating in Umbria (in central Italy north of Rome) in about 1260, practiced fraternal singing of *laude* in their rituals, which helped spread the genre to Umbrian composers, the best known of whom was JACOPONE DA TODI, the most famous practitioner of the form.

Early *laude* followed no standard metrical form. However, as more came to be written, the *lauda* came to imitate the form of the *ballata*, an Italian dance song with a refrain. Most commonly Jacopone's *laude* were written in octosyllabic (or eight-syllable) lines. Sometimes seven- or 11-syllable lines are used. In the *ballata*, individual stanzas were sung by a soloist and the refrain by a chorus. This responsive format, coupled with the fact that the *laude* were often verse narratives of Christ, the Virgin, or one of the other saints, encouraged the development of the *laude* into a dramatic form. In many *laude*, an actual dialogue was created, rather than a simple alternating solo and chorus, so that singers took the parts of various characters.

By the 15th century, the *laude* had moved out of Umbria and become widespread throughout Italy. Such early Renaissance writers as Lorenzo de' Medici and Girolamo Savonarola were interested in the form. By the following century, however, the form had declined significantly in popularity.

Laxdaela Saga, The (*The Saga of the People of Laxardal*) (ca. 1245)

The Laxdaela Saga (Saga of the people of Salmon River Valley) is a 13th-century Icelandic saga telling the tragic story of eight generations of the descendents of Ketill Flatnose. Set in Norway, Scotland, and Iceland, the saga covers the period from the settlement of Iceland in the ninth century through the country's acceptance of Christianity in 1000. The saga is remarkable in its emphasis on strong woman protagonists, which has led to speculation that the anonymous author was a woman.

Laxdaela Saga begins as Ketill Flatnose flees Norway to escape the tyrannical policies of King Harald Fairhair. He settles in Scotland. His daughter, Unn the Deep-Minded, leaves Scotland for Iceland with her grandchildren a generation later, and there becomes established as matriarch of a large family and holds sway over a significant portion of land at Breidafjord in western Iceland. She dispenses land to her kinsmen and to others, who later quarrel over boundaries as Iceland becomes more settled.

The main action of the saga concerns three of Ketill's descendants in the seventh generation: Gudrun Osvifsdottir, Kjartan Olafsson, and Bolli Thorleiksson, whose love triangle has been compared with that of Brynhild, Sigurd, and Gunnar in the heroic tradition recounted in the *Elder Edda* and elsewhere. Gudrun loves Kjartan, but like Brynhild, she is denied his love. She marries Kjartan's foster brother Bolli, and (once again like Brynhild) plots vengeance on her former love with her new husband. Bolli ambushes Kjartan and kills him. Bolli himself is killed later in retribution for Kjartan's murder, and Gudrun ultimately urges her sons to take vengeance for their father's death. After this is accomplished, she marries again. In her old age, after the advent of Christianity in Iceland, Gudrun becomes the first nun and anchoress in the country. The saga ends with her death.

Laxdaela Saga is clearly based on historical events, as evidenced by the records in the 12th-century Icelandic *Landnamabok* (Book of settlements). However, the author's sense of chronology and historic detail is flawed. Still, the appeal of the saga is not its historicity but its presentation of Gudrun, the most memorable of all saga heroines, and the tragic conflicts that lead to familial enmity and a seemingly endless cycle of vengeance. These things are conventional in Icelandic family sagas. Less conventional are the author's interest in physical appearances, dress, and manners (suggesting an acquaintance with courtly ROMANCE), and the author's focus on strong female characters who are at the center of the action both in the opening chapters (with Unn) and the main body of the text (with Gudrun). Indeed the saga could be called the first biography of a secular woman in medieval Europe.

For this reason some scholars have suggested a woman author. Others, because of the scholastic learning evident in the text, have suggested a clerical author. In either case the turbulence and internecine feuds that form the subject matter of the saga may be intended to mirror the political situation of the author's own time, Iceland's infamous Sturlung Age (1230–64), a period of turbulence, treachery, and civil war.

Bibliography

Andersson, Theodore M. *The Icelandic Family Saga: An Analytic Reading.* Cambridge, Mass.: Harvard University Press, 1967.

Layamon (12th century)

Layamon is the author of *The Brut,* an English redaction of WACE's Old French *Roman de Brut,* chronicling the history of the legendary kings of Britain from the time of the founding of Britain by Brutus, great-grandson of the Trojan Aeneas, until the time of Cadwalader and the ultimate victory of the Saxons. Like Wace and his source, GEOFFREY OF MONMOUTH's *HISTORIA REGUM BRITANNIAE,* Layamon includes a long section on the exploits of King ARTHUR. Thus Layamon's *Brut* is the first English-language version of the Arthurian legend, and one of the most important texts in early Middle English literature.

Virtually nothing is known about Layamon's life. He says in his prologue that he was a priest, son of Leovenath, who lived in the village of Ernly on the Severn River, near Redstone Rock. His village has been identified as modern-day Areley Kings, some 10 miles from Worcester. Apparently Layamon had visited other parts of England, for he mentions traveling widely in his prologue. Judging from his text, he seems to have known southern and southwestern England and southern Wales fairly well.

In his prologue Layamon refers to Eleanor, who "was" Henry II's queen. This would suggest a date for the text after 1189, the year Henry died, and more likely after 1204, the year that Eleanor died. Despite his reference to Eleanor, though, Layamon seems to have been writing not for a courtly audience but for an audience familiar with English and with the traditions of pre-conquest poetry.

Thus Layamon writes with a deliberate attempt to use English vocabulary, even archaic English vocabulary, whenever possible. He also writes ALLITERATIVE VERSE, though he seems to have been only vaguely familiar with Old English poetic style: His lines imitate the half-lines of Old English meter, but often are too long and only occasionally follow the strict formulas of Old English prosody. Often, he uses rhyme and assonance as well, which would have been derived purely from French poetry. It seems likely that Layamon's acquaintance with the Old English alliterative tradition was through oral sources.

It is possible that he made some use of both oral and written sources that have not survived, but he refers explicitly in his prologue to three sources: an English book by BEDE that is almost certainly the Old English translation of Bede's *Ecclesiastical History of the English People;* a Latin text by Saints Albin and Augustine of Canterbury that has never been identified and likely no longer exists; and Wace, whom he calls a "French clerk."

Layamon's *Brut* is twice as long as Wace's poem, and differs in a number of ways. For one thing Layamon omits much of the material Wace had included to appeal to a French courtly audience, such as his interest in courtly love. But Layamon adds material that reflects an earlier, more brutal warrior society. When Arthur is told of how Guenevere has betrayed him with Modred, for example, Sir Gawain vows to have the queen torn apart by horses:

> "Lord God, Ruler of judgments, Protector of all the earth, why has my brother Modred wrought this evil? Today, here before these retainers, I disown him; God willing, I will kill him. I myself will hang him highest of all outlaws. Under God's law, I will have the queen torn asunder by horses. While I live I will never know happiness until I have avenged my uncle well."
>
> (Bzdyl 1989, 251)

Here the violent aspect of Layamon is clear, as is his debt to the old Germanic virtues of loyalty to one's lord and taking vengeance for a wrong.

Layamon also adds far more dialogue and more concrete detail to the incidents described by Wace. There are more than 500 direct speeches in Layamon's *Brut,* as opposed to only about 160 such speeches in Wace. Further, Layamon shows a significant interest in the supernatural and especially in prophecy, suggesting an underlying belief that actions in this world are controlled by fate. Just before news comes of the queen's betrayal, for example, Layamon gives Arthur a prophetic dream in which he sits astride a great hall, but is dashed down by the actions of Modred and the queen. Prophecy also underlines much of Merlin's part in Layamon's story: After the last battle, when Arthur has been carried off to Avalon, Layamon says this:

> The Britons believe that Arthur is still alive and dwells in Avalon with the fairest of all elves. They still look to when Arthur will return. No man nor woman can say truly more of Arthur except what the prophet Merlin himself once said—and his words are true: an Arthur will yet come to help the English.
>
> (Bzdyl 1989, 254)

Note here Layamon's reference to "the English." One difficult question in dealing with Layamon is why, when he does so much in his poetry to emulate the warrior society and English poetic style of the Anglo-Saxons, he nevertheless stresses the villainy of the Saxons in the Arthurian story. But the above quotation gives us an answer: Layamon's loyalty was to the land of Britain, and he supported the native inhabitants of the island against invaders. All who live on the island are English, he seems to say.

Layamon's poem survives in two manuscripts: Cotton Caligula A.ix and Cotton Otho C.xiii. Both were produced between 1250 and 1325. The Caligula text is generally considered to be closer to Layamon's original, since it includes more archaic language and more English vocabulary. It is written in an early South West Midland dialect.

Layamon remains an important writer because of his introduction into English of the Arthurian legend. He also demonstrates that an alliterative tradition of some sort survived, probably orally, after the Norman Conquest. And finally Layamon is interesting to read in his own right, because of his many dramatic scenes of vivid detail and lively dialogue.

Bibliography

Layamon. *Brut.* Edited by G. L. Brook and R. F. Leslie. 1963. Oxford: Oxford University Press, 1978.

———. *Layamon's Brut: A History of the Britons.* Translated by Donald G. Bzdyl. Medieval and Renaissance Texts and Studies, Vol. 65. Binghamton: State University of New York at Binghamton, 1989.

Le Saux, Françoise. *Layamon's "Brut": The Poem and Its Sources.* Woodbridge, Suffolk, U.K.: Boydell and Brewer, 1989.

Lay Le Freine ("Lai of the Ash Tree") (early 14th century)

The *Lay Le Freine* is an anonymous MIDDLE ENGLISH verse ROMANCE that survives only in the famous Auchinleck manuscript from the early 14th century. The story is based on one of the late 12th-century LAIS of MARIE DE FRANCE and, like Marie's poem, is written in octosyllabic (eight-syllable) couplets, though at only 408 lines it is briefer than Marie's 518-line poem. In two places (lines 121–133 and 341–408) the manuscript is damaged, and thus the poem is missing some lines that have been reconstructed in modern editions. It is written in a southern dialect, with some characteristic features of the East Midland dialect of London.

The story follows Marie's text fairly closely. In the beginning Le Freine's mother, envious of her neighbor's twin boys, begins a rumor that multiple births can only result from more than one father, and thus raises questions about her neighbor's faithfulness to her husband. When she herself delivers twins, Le Freine's mother has no choice but to destroy one of her children or face the consequences of her own vicious rumor. She gives one daughter to the midwife and tells her to kill the child and never to reveal the twin birth. But the midwife instead convinces her to abandon the child at a convent. She takes the baby to a nunnery, leaving her in a hollow ash-tree outside the convent walls.

The forsaken Le Freine is raised by the kind Abbess, who christens her "Le Freine" or "the Ash-Tree," and represents the child as her own niece. When the girl is grown Le Freine becomes the lover of a rich nobleman named Guroun. Under pressure from the church to abandon his lover and take a wife of noble blood to give him legitimate heirs,

Guroun breaks off the affair, though the generous and patient Le Freine volunteers to help prepare Guroun's castle for his wedding celebration. When Guroun's intended arrives with her mother, she turns out to be Le Codre (that is, "The Hazel Tree"), Le Freine's estranged twin sister. Her mother recognizes Le Freine by the rich embroidered cloth she had wrapped the baby in when she gave her to the midwife, and in the end, Le Freine is reunited with her family, and Guroun marries Le Freine—now revealed to be of the appropriate nobility and family. Le Codre, we are reassured, marries another gentle knight of that country.

The tale is in some ways reminiscent of the tale of patient Griselde, familiar from CHAUCER's *CLERK'S TALE* and as the last story in BOCCACCIO's *DECAMERON,* in which the patient woman is rewarded in the end after much suffering. Le Freine is a completely passive heroine, and nearly completely silent—the narrator allows her a direct speech only some 30 lines before the end of the story, when her act of generosity in adorning the bridal bed with her own rich blanket reveals to her mother who she really is. By contrast, her mother, the gossiping, garrulous woman, nearly loses her family through her own vile tongue. The folklore motifs of the abandoned twin child who is revealed in the end to be of noble blood suggest the tale's affinity with an oral tradition. Furthermore, the fact that the 22-line prologue to *Le Freine* also appears in two manuscripts as the prologue to another Middle English Breton *lai, SIR ORFEO* (which also is included in the Auchinleck manuscript), suggests some affinity between the authors and perhaps the audiences of those two poems.

Bibliography

Rumble, Thomas C. *The Breton Lays in Middle English.* Detroit: Wayne State University Press, 1965.

Donovan, Mortimer J. "Le Freine." In *The Breton Lay: A Guide to Varieties,* 126–139. Notre Dame, Ind.: University of Notre Dame Press, 1969.

Freeman, Michelle. "The Power of Sisterhood: Marie de France's *Le Fresne,*" in *Women and Power in the Middle Ages,* edited by Mary Erler and Maryanne Kowaleski. Athens: University of Georgia Press, 1988, 250–264.

Auchenlick Manuscript Web site, National Library of Scotland. "Lay Le Freine." Available online. URL: http://www.nls.uk/auchinleck/mss/freine.html. Accessed February 6, 2005.

"Lay le Freine." In *The Middle English Breton Lays,* edited by Anne Laskaya and Eve Salisbury. Kalamazoo, Mich.: Medieval Institute Publications, 1995.

Legend of Good Women, The Geoffrey Chaucer (ca. 1386)

CHAUCER's unfinished *Legend of Good Women* or, as he refers to it in the introduction to the *MAN OF LAW's TALE,* the "Seintes Legende of Cupide" (Legend of cupid's saints), is a collection of nine brief narratives of women martyred for love, set in the frame of a dream vision. Chronologically, the *Legend of Good Women* was composed immediately after *TROILUS AND CRISEYDE* and just before Chaucer began his more successful collection of stories, the *CANTERBURY TALES.*

Readers have generally found the prologue to be the most interesting part of the text. In it Chaucer presents himself as going out in May to do homage to the Daisy, and meeting the God of Love and his consort, Alceste (a classical Greek heroine who agreed to die in her husband's place). Love chastises Chaucer for having written of the faithless Criseyde, and translating the *ROMAN DE LA ROSE,* which he calls a "heresy" against his law. Alceste intercedes for the poet, listing his other, nonoffensive works, and it is agreed that as penance for his sins against the God of Love, he will write a series of narratives praising women who die while remaining true in love, often betrayed by their lovers. Nine tales are included in the Legend: Cleopatra, Thisbe, Dido, Hypsipyle and Medea in one tale, Lucrece, Ariadne, Philomela, Phylis, and Hypermnestra, whose tale Chaucer left unfinished.

Though it probably owes much to literary sources, particularly Guillaume de MACHAUT's *Jugement dou Roy de Navarre,* the prologue may reflect a literal commission Chaucer received from King RICHARD II and his queen, ANNE OF BOHEMIA, who may be allegorized as the God of Love and Alceste in the prologue. This conjecture is supported by the fact that Chaucer's fellow poet John

GOWER was given a similar commission about the same time to write his *CONFESSIO AMANTIS.* As Gower's poem presents the confession of a lover who has committed sins against Love, so Chaucer writes a Legend—a term associated with collections of saints' lives such as the 13th-century *GOLDEN LEGEND* compiled by Jacobus de Voragine—praising martyrs to Love. Both poems take part in an elaborate poetic game of a "religion of love," in which standard Christian language and customs are adapted and parodied in the COURTLY LOVE tradition.

This, however, does not explain why the prologue survives in two different versions, known as F (denoting the Fairfax manuscript in Oxford's Bodleian Library) and G (named for the Cambridge Gg manuscript). Clearly Chaucer revised the original F prologue at some point, removing much of the elaborate praise of the Daisy (which had been influenced by a popular current French fashion of "Madeleine" or Daisy poems), and also removed a command from Alceste to deliver the poem to the queen. Scholars have conjectured that Chaucer revised the poem in 1394, when Queen Anne died, and so removed the specific reference to her. If Anne was the force behind the poem, it would also explain why Chaucer never finished it. He is enjoined in the prologue to produce his legends "year by year," and if he did indeed produce one legend per year, then he would have been composing his ninth legend when Queen Anne died.

Critics have sometimes found the legends themselves to be uninteresting because of their formulaic qualities: All men in the tales are false deceivers, all women innocent victims. It has even been suggested that Chaucer himself grew bored with the sameness of the legends and therefore abandoned them. In addition critics have had difficulty with the tone of the tales, which at times seem ironic or include apparently incongruous humor. It has been suggested that these elements indicate Chaucer's tales are a parody of the sort of narrative that idealizes passive female victims—stories like Chaucer's own *Man of Law's Tale,* which mentions the *Legend.* Some have also suggested that the tales are not as uninteresting as they are made out to be: The Cleopatra and Dido stories contain vivid descriptive detail, for example, and the Lucrece story rises to a moving climax.

The Legend of Good Women seems inspired largely by Ovid's *Heroides,* a series of fictional letters supposedly written by classical or mythological heroines (including many heroines of Chaucer's legends) at moments of crisis. Also influential to Chaucer's conception was BOCCACCIO's *De Claris Mulieribus,* a catalogue of illustrious women of the past. Of course he was also inspired by genuine saints' lives, like that which inspired his own *SECOND NUN'S TALE* of Saint Cecilia—tales that depicted women in a light that may, by contrast, suggest that the virtue of women like Medea, for instance, falls short of the ideal. Still the faithfulness and real heroism of someone like Lucrece may well raise her to a kind of secular saintliness.

Bibliography

Delany, Sheila. *The Naked Text: Chaucer's "Legend of Good Women."* Berkeley: University of California Press, 1992.

Frank, Robert W., Jr. *Chaucer and the Legend of Good Women.* Cambridge, Mass.: Harvard University Press, 1972.

Hansen, Elaine. "Irony and the Antifeminist Narrator in Chaucer's *Legend of Good Women,*" *JEGP* 82 (1983): 11–31.

Kiser, Lisa J. *Telling Classical Tales: Chaucer and the Legend of Good Women.* Ithaca, N.Y.: Cornell University Press, 1983.

McMillan, Ann, ed. and intro. *The Legend of Good Women by Geoffrey Chaucer.* Houston: Rice University Press, 1987.

Payne, Robert O. "Making His Own Myth: The Prologue to Chaucer's *Legend of Good Women,*" *Chaucer Review* 9 (1975): 197–211.

Phillips, Helen, and Nick Havely, eds. *Chaucer's Dream Poetry.* Harlow, U.K.: Pearson Education, 1997.

Stone, Brian, trans. *Geoffrey Chaucer: Love Visions.* London: Penguin, 1983.

Lenten Is Come with Love to Toune
(ca. 1300)

One of the best-known of the HARLEY LYRICS—the group of MIDDLE ENGLISH poems in the British

Museum Ms. Harley 2253—is the short poem that begins "Lenten is come with love to toune." The lyric consists of three 12-line stanzas rhyming *aabccbddbeeb.* Thus the long stanza is divided into four triads, each forming an independent unit in itself but linked to the rest of the stanza through the *b* rhyme. There are four metrical feet in each line of the poem except the *b* rhyme lines, which contain three.

The first stanza of the poem is basically an extended REVERDIE, or lyric celebrating the return of spring. The poet praises the blossoms and the song of birds. By the end of the first stanza, he has injected a pathetic fallacy into the natural world, ascribing human emotions to the birds who rejoice at their good fortune. This continues to a greater extent in the second stanza, where the emphasis is less on description of spring and more on the response of the natural world to spring's arrival. The rose puts on her rosy complexion, and the leaves in the wood grow with desire, and even the moon puts on a radiant face. The animation of all natural objects emphasizes the feeling of abundant life introduced in the first stanza, but seems also to suggest that it is human participation in the natural phenomenon of spring that gives it meaning. In the final triad of the second stanza, the speaker introduces a human problem: He, like all men of passion, complains of unrequited love during the spring.

The most conventional way to begin a love poem was to introduce a spring setting and then contrast the lover's sorrow with the joy of the season. What is unusual about *Lenten Is Come* is that the springtime opening goes on for 21 lines before the lover introduces his situation. Moore said that the love theme in this poem was "intrusive" and that it disturbed "the unity of the nature study" (1951, 53). But the jarring juxtaposition of the harmonious natural world and the speaker's lovesickness seems deliberate.

In the final stanza, the speaker again praises the natural world, personifying the moon again as well as the *deores* (animals) with their *derne rounes* (secret songs) (Luria 1974, 6, l. 29). Then, as in stanza two, a sudden shift away from the natural world occurs with a juxtaposition of parallel lines:

Wormes woweth under cloude,
Wimmen waxeth wounder proude,

(Luria 1974, 6, ll. 31–32)

The parallelism invites a comparison of worms and women—and the women seem to get the worst of it. The worms make love underground, while the women simply grow overly proud. Worms, lowest of creatures in God's universe, follow natural law in their mating. But the arrogance of women—and here the speaker clearly has in mind his own beloved's disdain of him—causes them to behave in a distinctly unnatural manner.

In the final triad of the poem, the speaker says that if he does not obtain what he desires from his lady, he will run off—will forsake human society altogether and become a wild man of the woods. This may seem appropriate in a poem that has shown the harmony of the natural world in contrast with the discord of human love. But the wild man was an image of madness in medieval literature: The speaker's actions are as inappropriate as the disdainful lady's in the poem. To emulate the natural world, the man and woman must come together.

Bibliography

Brook, G. L. *The Harley Lyrics: The Middle English Lyrics of Ms. Harley 2253.* 4th ed. Manchester, U.K.: Manchester University Press, 1968.

Fein, Susanna, ed. *Studies in the Harley Manuscript: The Scribes, Contents, and Social Contexts of British Library MS Harley 2253.* Kalamazoo, Mich.: Medieval Institute Publications, 2000.

Luria, Maxwell S., and Richard Hoffman. *Middle English Lyrics.* New York: Norton, 1974.

Moore, Arthur K. *The Secular Lyric in Middle English.* Lexington: University of Kentucky Press, 1951.

Oliver, Raymond. *Poems Without Names: The English Lyric, 1200–1500.* Berkeley: University of California Press, 1970.

Ranson, Daniel J. *Poets at Play: Irony and Parody in the Harley Lyrics.* Norman, Okla.: Pilgrim Books, 1985.

Letters of Abelard and Heloise (Peter Abelard and Heloise) (ca. 1135)

Among the most admired texts documenting a real-life medieval love affair are the letters between Peter ABELARD, the renowned philosopher and cleric, and his one-time pupil HELOISE, abbess of the Benedictine convent of the Paraclete in Champagne at the time of the composition of the letters. The scandalous affair between the two had led to Abelard's castration at the hands of Heloise's family and to her ultimate taking of the veil. It became, however, the stuff of legend, and when JEAN DE MEUN alluded to their affair in his *ROMAN DE LA ROSE* in about 1280, Abelard and Heloise were immortalized. The three pairs of letters that have survived intact as part of their legacy are extant in nine manuscripts (one of which was owned by PETRARCH). But none of the surviving manuscripts predates 1350, a fact that has led many scholars to question their authenticity over the years. One theory is that the letters are the product of the literary imagination of some anonymous 14th-century author (or authors). Another holds that Abelard himself wrote all of the letters, attributing some of them to Heloise. But a growing number of scholars, epitomized by Barbara Newman (1995), now concur that the letters as we have them are the genuine epistles of the two 12th-century lovers.

The exchange of letters was provoked, apparently, by the publication of Abelard's *Historia calamitatum* (History of my calamities, ca. 1132), in which (among other things) he gives his own self-vindicating version of his affair with Heloise. It is she who initiates the correspondence, having read Abelard's version. She sends him a letter denouncing the treachery that befell him, and requesting that Abelard be with her again, if not physically then at least intellectually, through written correspondence. She challenges Abelard's portrayal of their affair as a private matter by claiming that everyone in Paris sang the love songs he wrote to her, and she accuses him of feeling only lust, not love for her. Yet she reminds him of his obligations to her, calling herself his wife, mistress, and whore, and says he became a nun only at his urging. She begs for "grace" from him in the form of a letter.

To this alternatingly accusatory and cajoling letter, Abelard responds formally and in the official capacity of a monk, transforming their passion into a holy friendship. He addresses the Abbess Heloise as his superior, but gives her a catalogue of "wifely virtues," mentioning as well his desire to be buried at Heloise's Paraclete—though only, he says, so that the nuns may pray at his tomb.

Heloise's reply is a model of spiritual anguish, in which she describes what she calls her hypocrisy, how she imagines even during the Mass the physical love for Abelard that she cannot expunge from her mind and heart. She recalls Abelard's castration and now feels herself wounded for their love, blaming God himself for her sorrow, but in the end applies to Abelard to be her healer, her spiritual guide. Abelard warns her to overcome her passions and to rely on reason. He reminds her that she is the bride of Christ, that she must turn her love into a spiritual love, and urges her to resist the temptation to blame God, an act that will lose her salvation. He also regrets his betrayal of Heloise's uncle (the canon Fulbert), and his sexual violence against Heloise herself when she had retreated to a convent to avoid him.

Heloise sends one more letter to Abelard, and he sends her two replies. In her final letter, Heloise requests that Abelard set out a formal Rule specifically for the nuns of her convent. It appears, at least, that Heloise has followed Abelard's direction, and sublimated her desire to her spiritual life—unless, of course, she is merely repressing what she has been forbidden to express explicitly. He answers with a Rule that focuses on the study of Scripture. The final letter in the collection contains Heloise's warm but official address to Abelard, followed by 42 questions from the nuns concerning specific biblical readings, and includes Abelard's answers to each of the questions.

While Abelard is certainly the only great medieval philosopher and theologian that has left such an intimate collection of correspondence, it is chiefly Heloise who becomes the focal point of any reading of the letters. What they reveal about her intelligence and rhetorical skill, her independence and outspoken views, make these letters a unique window into the personality of one of the most remarkable women of medieval Europe.

Bibliography

Baswell, Christopher. "Heloise." In *The Cambridge Companion to Medieval Women's Writing,* edited by Carolyn Dinshaw and David Wallace, 161–171. Cambridge: Cambridge University Press, 2003.

Dronke, Peter. *Abelard and Heloise in Medieval Testimonies,* Glasgow. The University of Glasgow Press, 1976.

The Letters of Abélard and Heloïse. Rev. ed. Translated with an introduction by Betty Radice. New York: Penguin, 2004.

Newman, Barbara. "Authority, Authenticity, and the Repression of Heloise," in *From Virile Woman to Woman Christ: Studies in Medieval Religion and Literature.* Philadelphia: University of Pennsylvania Press, 1995, 46–75.

Radice, Betty. "The French Scholar-Lover: Héloïse," in *Medieval Women Writers,* edited by Katharina M. Wilson. Athens: University of Georgia Press, 1984. 90–108.

Lewys Glyn Cothi (Llywelyn y Glyn) (fl. 1447–1486)

A wandering Welsh bard of the late 15th century, Lewys Glyn Cothi was known for his Welsh nationalism during a period of oppressive British laws, and also for his partisan verse composed during the War of the Roses, during which he supported the Lancastrian side, but even more zealously supported the cause of Jasper Tudor and of his nephew, Henry Richmond, who became Henry VII.

According to tradition, Lewys took his bardic name from the valley of Cothi in northern Carmarthenshire, where he was supposed to have been born. He grew up in a house called, no doubt satirically, Pwlltinbyd ("The Pit in the World's Backside"). As an adult, he seems to have spent a good deal of time enjoying the hospitality of the noble manor houses of Wales. He especially praised the warm welcome he received in the island of Anglesey. But he speaks of many other noble patrons. Late in his life, for example, he seems to have been the guest of Sir Roger Vaughan of Tretower, for whom he composed two poems that he copied into the famous manuscript of the Red Book of Hergest (source of *The* MABINOGION), which happened then to be in Sir Roger's possession. Lewys Glyn Cothi does seem to have returned to Carmathenshire to die at Abergwili, some time after 1486.

One of Lewys Glyn Cothi's recurring themes is his Welsh nationalism. He chafed against the English governors of his country, and at oppressive laws that the English had imposed. Outlawed, apparently for prophesying the ascension of Henry Tudor to the English throne, he fled to the city of Chester. Here he apparently married an English widow, in violation of a 1402 edict that forbade intermarriage between the English and Welsh. He was subsequently seized by the officials of the town, who confiscated and sold his property. The mayor banished him from the city, naked, he says, as a salmon. In a blistering attack on the men of Chester, Lewys laments his fate and begs for a blanket from his patroness Erin of Llwydiarth, who he fancies will send him a richly embroidered cover to keep him warm in bed through the winter.

Lewys Glyn Cothi was a master of the *awdl,* a kind of long Welsh ode that used both alliteration and internal rhyme in one of 24 traditional bardic meters. One such *awdl* is a lament on the death of Edmund Tudor (father of the future Henry VII) that makes use of heraldic symbols in a kind of beast-ALLEGORY typical of medieval political poetry. The expression of loss at the end of the poem is profound, as Lewys decries the emptiness of a land without its leader, comparing it to a house with no feast or a church with no priest. Another nationalistic *awdl* of Lwys's is devoted to Jasper Tudor, Edmund's brother and the earl of Pembroke, and to his nephew Henry, the future king.

Lewys also writes in the conventional bardic form of the *cywydd* (seven-syllable rhyming couplets with alliteration), as in his poem praising Niclas ap Gruffudd of the Shropshire town of Oswestry, whom he compares to Moses, to the Greek hero Jason, and to King ARTHUR's nephew and, in Wales, the most popular knight, Sir GAWAIN. Lewys also writes in praise of the town of Oswestry itself, which he refers to as "the London of Wales." He goes on to praise the town's most important citizen, Meredudd ap Hywel, also in hyperbolic terms, comparing him to Hector of Troy and to Emperor Macsen from the *Mabinogion.*

A comic poem, through which Lewys also satirizes the English, is one directed at the English citizens of Flint. In this poem, Lewys Glyn Cothi describes his attempt to entertain the revelers at an English wedding. The guests greet his song of praise with ridicule, and bring on one William the Piper to entertain instead. Lewys describes with disgust the noise of the bagpipes—which the guests seem to love—and when he is sent away with no payment, Lewys curses the town of Flint and its inhabitants.

Aside from poems praising his Welsh patrons and denigrating the English, Lewys Glyn Cothi also wrote a number of religious poems. Among the best known are a *cywydd* on John the Baptist and a long *awdl* in 120 stanzas on the Trinity. But perhaps Lewys's best-known poem among contemporary readers is his "Lament for Siôn y Glyn," a poignant and emotional poem about the death of a child from the father's point of view. Lewys enumerates the things that the boy loved—an apple, a bird, a bow made of a twig, and a wooden sword. Toward the end of the poem, the narrator recalls these images as he speaks of the boy himself:

My lark, my weaver of spells,
My bow, my arrow, my love,
My beggar, O my boyhood.
Siôn is sending his father
A sword of longing and love.

(Clancy 1977, 64, no. 39)

Lewys Glyn Cothi was a poet of many moods, of variety and of passion. He remains little known among English readers, but offers a great deal to those interested in late medieval Wales at the dawn of the Tudor era.

Bibliography

Breeze, Andrew. *Medieval Welsh Literature.* Dublin: Four Courts Press, 1997.

Clancy, Joseph P., trans. "Lament for Siôn y Glyn." In *The Oxford Book of Welsh Verse in English,* edited by Gwyn Jones, 62–64. Oxford: Oxford University Press, 1977.

Williams, Gwyn. *An Introduction to Welsh Poetry: From the Beginnings to the Sixteenth Century.* 1954; Freeport, N.Y.: Books for Libraries Press, 1970.

Li Bai (Li Po, Li T'ai-po) (701–762)

Li Bai was one of the greatest poets of the high TANG DYNASTY, the high point of medieval Chinese culture. In contrast to his great contemporaries DU FU, a Confucian spokesman for social responsibility, and WANG WEI, a Buddhist ascetic, Li Bai defied conventions—both aesthetic and social—and wrote Taoist-influenced poems of imagination, individuality, and indulgence.

In looking at Li-Bai's life, it is difficult to separate truth from legend, and many apocryphal stories have grown up about him because of the personae of his poems. But it is generally believed that he was born in Central Asia, probably Chinese Turkestan. It has been suggested that his family may have been of Turkish origin; another possibility is that one of his ancestors had been banished there from China proper. In any case at about the age of five Li Bai moved with his family to Sichuan (Szechuan), where he was probably raised as a gentleman would be, studying the Confucian classics, as well as how to use a sword and how to write a poem.

Li Bai does not seem to have had the family connections to attain an important position in society, nor to provide the training for the civil service examination that would have helped him obtain a position. He is said to have left home at the age of 19 to stay with a Taoist recluse and to travel extensively in northern and central China. He seems to have loved to travel all his life: He mentions a wide variety of places and describes scenic natural sites in verse, and many of his poems are written to thank friends for their hospitality. Around this time he became known as the "Old Wine Genius."

According to one story, he stopped wandering long enough to settle in Yun Meng as a young man, where he married the granddaughter of a former prime minister. After moving to Shanxi (Shansi), he is said to have testified for a young soldier named Guo Ziyi (Kuo Tzu-i), saving the soldier from a court-martial—an act that became significant later in his life. His marriage, however, was not so successful, and it is said his carousing with fellow poets as part of a group known as the "Six Idlers of the Bamboo Valley" eventually led to the end of his first marriage. He was to marry three more times in his life.

Li Bai became acquainted with a Taoist wizard named Sima Zhengshen (Si-ma Cheng-shen) and, through this contact, became an initiate into Taoism. As such, he experimented with drugs and with Taoist "elixirs," which were taken in hope of achieving immortality. His Taoism certainly, and possibly the associated substances as well, may have influenced the imagery of some of his poems, which often depict fantastic descriptions of Taoist heavens, as in the following poem with its flying Taoist immortal:

There was once one Undying on a crane
Who flew and flew up over Purest Ether

He raised his voice within sapphire clouds
And said that his name was An-qi.

(Owen 1996, "The Old Airs," 401)

Two other Taoist priests befriended by Li Bai in his travels were Wu Yun and He Jizhang (Ho Chi-chang), who gave him the name of "Banished Immortal," the Taoist name for a heavenly being that, for some violation, was banished from the heavens to live out a lifetime in the mortal realm. It was through Wu Yun that Li Bai was introduced to the imperial court.

At the age of 42, Li Bai met the Tang emperor Xuanzong (Hsuän-tsung), who seems to have been impressed by the eccentric genius and appointed him to the Hanlin Academy, a prestigious imperial establishment for intellectuals who had not risen through the normal channels. As a member of the academy, Li Bai was commissioned by the emperor to compose a variety of commemorative poems for state occasions. But in court Li Bai seems to have only added to his reputation as a drunk and an eccentric, and apparently offended enough powerful members of the court that after only three years in the emperor's service, he was dismissed in 744.

Li Bai returned to his life of wandering, this time through eastern and southern China, apparently using Shandong (Shantung) as a home base. He glorified his dismissal from the court by claiming it was an exile brought about by powerful enemies jealous of his genius. And though he had lost the support of the emperor, there were still a large number of intellectuals who admired his talent. Du Fu, his friend and fellow poet, referred to him as one of the "Eight Immortals of the Wine Cup."

In 755, during the revolt of An Lushan, Li Bai threw in his lot with one of the emperor's sons, the prince of Yun, who reportedly intended to set up an independent kingdom in southeast China. When the rebellion was put down, the prince was executed, and Li Bai was arrested. According to legend, Guo Ziyi, the soldier he had saved earlier, was now minister of war, and spared Li Bai's life. Instead the poet was exiled to southwestern China. An amnesty later allowed him to return from exile to travel again, this time along the lower Yangtze, where he died shortly thereafter in 762.

One legend claims that an intoxicated Li Bai died when he fell out of a boat while trying to embrace a reflection of the Moon in the water. This almost certainly is a myth stemming from his poetry, which so often talks about drinking and about the Moon. A more realistic guess is that he died of either pneumonia, cirrhosis of the liver, or mercury poisoning from one of his Taoist elixirs.

Li Bai has been called the most "romantic" of the Tang poets, and his ability to see everyday things in fresh ways, his delight in the natural world, and his emphasis on personal imaginative experience certainly have affinities with romantic poetry. But these are also Taoist concerns, as are his depictions of imaginary, otherworldly landscapes and his unusual familiarity with alchemy and its technical terms. He is best remembered for his championing of individual spontaneity against social conformity, and for his persona of the wild, intoxicated poet-genius.

Bibliography

Owen, Stephen, ed. *An Anthology of Chinese Literature: Beginnings to 1911.* New York: Norton, 1996.

Owen, Stephen. *The Great Age of Chinese Poetry: The High Tang.* New Haven, Conn.: Yale University Press, 1980.

Waley, Arthur. *The Poetry and Career of Li Po.* London: Allen and Unwin, 1950.

Libeaus Desconus (ca. 1375–1400)

Libeaus Desconus is a 14th-century poem written in MIDDLE ENGLISH but drawing heavily on the French *Le bel inconnu* by Renaut de Bâgé. Although authorship is uncertain, it has been attributed to Thomas Chestre, the author of *SIR LAUNFAL*. *Libeaus* employs the "fair unknown" motif that emerged as an occasional theme in medieval ROMANCES. The poem follows the trials of an unknown youth as he ascends to knighthood at King ARTHUR's court, and battles knights and giants in his quest to free an imprisoned maiden.

The poem opens by explaining that although the knight's name was Gyngalyn and he was the son of Sir GAWAIN, his mother called him *Beau-fis* due to his fair face, and he knew no other name. His mother is not identified but is said to have met Gawain by a forest side. Although some scholars have speculated that Dame Ragnell was his mother, in *The WEDDYNG OF SYR GAWEN AND DAME RAGNELL*, it is Arthur who meets Ragnell beside the forest, not Gawain, although the story does end with Gawain wedding Ragnell and freeing her from a curse.

Gyngalyn approaches Arthur's court and because he does not know his true name is named *Libeaus Desconus* by Arthur. After being knighted, he requests to be given the first fight asked of Arthur. Although Arthur has misgivings about Libeaus's youthful state and inexperience, he grants the request. The maid Elene next appears at court, seeking a knight to free the lady of Sinadoun from imprisonment. Keeping his word to Libeaus, Arthur offers the services of Libeaus, but Elene laments his untested abilities. Nevertheless, Arthur is not persuaded to send another and Libeaus is armed and departs with Elene and her dwarf. True to the "fair unknown" motif, the lady Elene rebukes Libeaus constantly as they travel, mocking his knightly abilities.

As the tale unfolds, Libeaus defeats two giants and numerous knights, granting mercy to the knights while dispatching them to Arthur's court to pay homage to the king. Eventually, after many adventures and an interlude with La Dame d'Amour (from whose sorcery he escapes only by heeding the advice of the maid Elene), Libeaus arrives at Sinadoun to rescue the lady from her prison. There, he defeats the steward of the castle, Sir Lambard, who recognizes in Libeaus's skill his relation to Gawain. The last two men that Libeaus must battle are the clerks, Mabon and Yrain, who have cast a spell over the lady and thus imprisoned her as a worm within the walls of the castle. Once the evil clerks are defeated, Libeaus falls to prayer, and the lady breaks free from the walls, winds her serpent body around Libeaus, and is transformed back to her female state.

In a typical "fair unknown" tale, the protagonist, dubbed a fair-unknown because he does not know his name or his lineage, embarks on knightly adventures with the blessing of King Arthur, and in the course of the tale, proves both his knightly skills and nobility, and discovers his true identity. Deviations from the conventional theme are prolific, though, and many tales contain some but not all elements, or include a protagonist who knows his identity but simply does not divulge it. One example of the form a deviation may take is that Libeaus's identity is not divulged at the conclusion of the tale.

As is typical in fair-unknown romances, Libeaus weds the lady in the end. Notably absent from this tale is the revelation of the protagonist's identity. Although he has proven himself a worthy knight, won the fair maiden he rescued, and the tale concludes with Libeaus wedding the lady and being properly revered in Arthur's court, there is no mention of a reunion with Gawain or divulgence within the court that they are father and son.

Other medieval romances employing the fair-unknown theme include the aforementioned *Le bel inconnu*, Robert de Blois's 13th-century *Beaudous*, the 13th-century German *Wigalois*, the 13th-century French verse fragment *Gogulor*, the 14th-century Italian *Cantari Di Carduino I*, and two tales from Thomas MALORY's *Le MORTE*

DARTHUR, "The Tale of Sir Gareth of Orkeney" and "The Tale of La Cote Male Tayle."

The text of *Libeaus* survives in one 17th- and five 15th-century manuscripts, including the British Library MS Cotton Caligula A.ii, in which the only extant text of *Sir Launfal* is also found. The stanzaic TAIL-RHYME poem has been translated into modern prose by Jessie L. Weston and Middle English versions are available.

Libeaus Desconus is unique in that it offers an early fair-unknown romance in Middle English, prior to more thorough treatment of the theme in English by Thomas Malory. In addition, Gawain scholars may be interested in points of the text that intersect with other Arthurian literature concerning Gawain, specifically, the tales in which Gawain, often a philanderer, marries and produces an heir.

Bibliography

Bâgé, Renaut de. *Le bel inconnu (Li biaus descouneüs; The Fair Unknown)*. Translated by Colleen P. Donagher. Edited by Karen Fresco. New York: Garland, 1992.

Mills, Maldwyn. "The Composition and Style of the 'Southern' *Octavian, Sir Launfal,* and *Libeaus Desconus,*" *Medium Ævum* 30 (1961): 88–109.

Sir Cleges; Sir Libeaus Desconus. Two Old English metrical romances rendered into prose by Jessie L. Weston, with designs by Caroline M. Watts. Translated by Jessie L. Weston. London: D. Nutt, 1902.

Michelle Palmer

liberal arts (seven liberal arts)

The seven liberal arts were the basis of a general secular education throughout medieval western Europe. Based on a system dating back to classical times, the liberal arts were made up of the *trivium*—essentially what contemporary educators might call the "humanities," consisting of grammar, rhetoric, and dialectic (i.e., logic)—and the *quadrivium*—basically the sciences, including arithmetic, geometry, astronomy, and music.

The history of the liberal arts probably begins with Isocrates, the leading rhetorician and Sophist of Athens in the fourth century B.C.E. He developed a system of education in the arts focusing on rhetoric, arguing that the purpose of the arts was to train good citizens, that an effective citizen must be able to persuade, and that the art of persuasion (or rhetoric) requires a broad educational background. Other Greek thinkers argued for the importance of other disciplines: Plato denigrated the study of rhetoric and emphasized the importance of mathematics, while Aristotle focused on logic as the most important basic study. For all of these classical thinkers, the liberal arts were chiefly preparation for the more advanced study of philosophy. Christian thinkers in Alexandria went further, considering the arts as preparation for philosophy, and the study of philosophy itself as preparation for theology. By the early fifth century, St. AUGUSTINE, himself a one-time rhetoric instructor, saw the arts as direct preparation for a study of the Scriptures. Further into the Middle Ages, it became common to see the seven liberal arts in themselves as encompassing all of philosophy, and therefore as essential for preparing clerics directly for the advanced study of theology. By the 12th century, the Virgin Mary was depicted as the queen of the Seven Liberal Arts, which in themselves embodied all human wisdom and were thought of as the "handmaids" of theology.

The definition of the liberal arts core as it came to be known throughout the Middle Ages occurs in the fifth-century *Marriage of Philology and Mercury,* composed by the Stoic philosopher Martianus Capella. The work of the sixth-century philosopher BOETHIUS also contributed significantly to the development of the liberal arts, as he translated into Latin a number of the most significant texts of Aristotle and of Euclid. Boethius's study of music was to become the basic textbook in medieval schools for centuries. Still, it was not until the time of ALCUIN (ca. 800), and the development of the system of education sparked by the Carolingian renaissance under CHARLEMAGNE, that the liberal arts were universally accepted as the basis of education throughout the Latin West.

The term *trivium* does not occur until the ninth century, though the arts it refers to had been recognized for more than 1,000 years. Grammar was essentially the study of the basics of the Latin language, for which the grammar texts of Donatus or of Priscian were most often used, but the subject also included the study of literature in Latin, including the Vulgate Bible and texts by the church fathers as well as classical texts. The discipline of rhetoric dealt with the art of persuasion but also included instruction in the composition (in Latin) of poetry and prose as well as, after the 10th century, letter writing. In addition, rhetoric might include some study of the law. Dialectic, the study of formal logic, was inspired chiefly by Aristotle.

The *quadrivium* was intended to follow the *trivium* in the school curriculum, the implication being that it comprised more difficult subjects, which might be taught only to more advanced students. Boethius first uses the term *quadrivium* itself in his treatise on arithmetic (a translation of an earlier work by Nicomachus of Gerasa). Boethius, basing his categories on earlier theories of Pythagoras, distinguishes "discrete" quantities (those that can be numbered) as those that can be studied in and of themselves through arithmetic (e.g., square numbers, perfect numbers) and those that can be studied through music (e.g., ratios); and "continuous" quantities (those known through line rather than number) as those that are fixed and studied through geometry, and those in motion that are studied in astronomy. Boethius himself saw these disciplines as useful to train the mind to think of abstract truths, and hence to prepare it for the study of philosophy.

How this system worked in practice depended, of course, on individual schools and instructors and on developments over time. While the *trivium* was supposed to be taught to all students, sometimes the only subject universally taught might be grammar (a situation from which we get the term "grammar school" for the primary grades). With the rise of scholasticism in the 12th century and the establishment of universities in the 13th, dialectic became a more important subject than grammar in northern Europe. In the south, rhetoric continued to be emphasized in the curriculum, and contributed to the development of Bologna as an important center for the study of law. In general, a master of arts degree at a medieval university was often the terminal degree in itself, or it was considered the foundation from which a student might go on to study the advanced professional disciplines like law, or medicine, or, most important, theology. However, by the time of Thomas AQUINAS in the later 13th century, the increasingly available variety of texts of Aristotle had become so much a part of the university curriculum that philosophy had come, again, to be seen as a separate discipline in itself, and Aquinas recommended what late classical theorists had felt: That the liberal arts should prepare one for the study of philosophy, and only then was one ready to study theology.

Bibliography

Curtius, Ernst Robert. *European Literature and the Latin Middle Ages.* Translated by Willard R. Trask. New York: Pantheon Books, 1953.

Hunt, Richard W. *The History of Grammar in the Middle Ages: Collected Papers.* Edited, with an introduction, a select bibliography, and indices by G. L. Bursill-Hall. Amsterdam: Benjamins, 1980.

Masi, Michael, ed. *Boethius and the Liberal Arts: A Collection of Essays.* Berne: P. Lang, 1981.

McKeon, Richard. "Rhetoric in the Middle Ages," *Speculum* 17 (1942): 1–32.

Stahl, William Harris, et al. *Martianus Capella and the Seven Liberal Arts.* 2 vols. New York: Columbia University Press, 1971–1977.

Li He (Li Ho) (790–816)

A Chinese poet of the late TANG DYNASTY, Li He was a child prodigy who died at the age of 26. Li He defied the norm of Chinese poetry—the classical balance, order, and harmony—in favor of an emotional, highly subjective style that focused on striking images of death and the supernatural. Though popular in his own day, Li He's poetry soon fell out of fashion, only to be revived in the 20th century, particularly among Western students of Chinese literature.

Born in Changgu (Ch'ang-ku) in modern Henan (Honan), Li He was from an impoverished family, but one that traced its ancestry to the Tang royal house. His father, Jinsu (Chin-su), was at one point magistrate of his county. From his early days, Li He was in somewhat delicate health, and he is described as having been exceedingly thin, with bushy eyebrows and long fingernails, and with hair that had turned white at the temples by the time he was 18.

A precocious child, Li He began writing poetry, according to legend, at the age of seven. Anecdotes about his youthful skills abound, at least two of which describe him at a very young age, astounding the famous poet HAN YU with his verse. By the age of 15, his reputation as a poet had spread even to the capital at Changuan (Ch'ang-an). He was known particularly for his poems in the *yuefu* (*yu'eh-fu*), or traditional ballad style.

His father probably died in 806, and at 21, spurred by his family's poverty and his own drive to achieve something worthy of his royal blood and his literary talent, Li He traveled to Henan to take the district examination to qualify him for the JINSHI (*chin-shih*) degree, the initial step in what he hoped would be an influential political career. After receiving outstanding marks on the district exam, Li He traveled to the capital at Chang-an to take the *ju* (*chü*) exam—the final step for the *jinshi* degree. He was sponsored by the poet Han Yu (then magistrate of Henan) and by Huang Fushi (Huang-fu Shih), another high-ranking official.

But Li He never got the chance to take the exam. Apparently one of his competitors in the examination had raised the charge that Li He, should he pass the examination and assume the title *jinshi*, would be breaking a "character taboo"—the "Jin" of his father's name or a homophone for the first character of "jinshi," and it was considered taboo for a man to have the same name as his father. While the taboo sounds absurd in modern times, such taboos were taken seriously during the Tang dynasty. Still it seems a technicality that could have been simply an excuse to deny Li He the chance to achieve *jinshi* status: He is known for having had an arrogant personality, and could easily have offended the wrong person. In any case Li He stayed in Chang-an until it became obvious he would never have a chance to take the exam, and then returned home in 811.

By virtue of his father's status, however, Li He was appointed to a minor position—that of supervisor of ceremonies—and in 812 he returned to Chang'an to take this post. He found it dull and disappointing, and his health was declining. He resigned his position in 813 and returned to Ch'ang-ku. He died there in 816.

Western readers have thrilled to the fantastic and intense images of the supernatural in Li He's poetry. In lines like the following, the supernatural and the macabre meet to create a striking, vivid image:

The witch pours the libation, clouds fill the
sky,
In the flaming coals of the jade brazier the
fumes of incense throb
. . .
She calls to the stars and summons the
demons to taste of her dish and cup:
Mankind shudders when the mountain
goblins feed.

(Graham 1965, "Magic Strings," ll. 1–8)

Li He's position in Chinese literature is unique. His literary output is small (some 240 poems) compared to the great Tang masters like LI BAI and DU FU. But in his special area of poetry of the supernatural, Li He stands alone.

Bibliography

Frodsham, J. D., trans. *The Poems of Li Ho.* Oxford: Clarendon Press, 1970.

Graham, A. C., trans. *Poems of the Late T'ang.* Baltimore: Penguin, 1965.

Tu, Kuo-ch'ing. *Li Ho.* Boston: Twayne 1979.

Lindsay, Sir David (David Lyndsay of the Mount) (ca. 1486–ca. 1555)

Sometimes called "the last Scottish Chaucerian," Sir David Lindsay had a career that straddled the late medieval and early modern periods. Like CHAUCER's, his verse is often satiric, and his persistent use of ALLEGORY is certainly inspired by medieval tradition; his attacks on the Catholic Church in Scotland were a factor in the Scottish Reformation. Lindsay was a poet, a courtier, and a diplomat who was closely attached to the court of the Scottish king James V. His best-known work is the drama *Ane Pleasant Satyre of the Thrie Estaitis* (1540), the only complete extant Scottish MORALITY PLAY.

Lindsay's father, also called Sir David Lindsay of the Mount, had estates near Cupar in Fife, and also near Haddington in East Lothian. Lindsay may have been born at either. He may have gone to school at Haddington, and is believed to have graduated from Saint Andrews University in 1508. He is believed to have entered the service of King James IV that same year. He is first mentioned as taking part in a play that was presented before the king and his wife, Margaret Tudor (sister of Henry VIII), at Holyrood in October of 1511, where he is described as wearing a colorful yellow and blue coat. He seems to have impressed the royal family, because the following year he was appointed usher to the newborn prince, the future James V. As usher his tasks were to be a companion, storyteller, and general playmate for the young prince.

On September 9, 1513, James IV was killed at the Battle of Flodden Field in an ill-advised attempt to invade England, leaving the 17-month-old James V as king of Scotland. But Lindsay continued in his position as usher to the new king until about 1524, when James fell under the power of the earl of Angus, his new stepfather, along with Angus's powerful family, the Douglases. Lindsay was expelled from the court, and Angus kept the child king confined as a prisoner in Edinburgh Castle until 1528, when the Queen Mother, Margaret, having divorced Angus, rescued the boy and the Douglas faction was overthrown. James, now 16, assumed power and began to rule in his own right.

Lindsay was restored to his position at court upon James's return to power, and was made herald of the court in 1529. At this point, Lindsay began his writing career, producing his first poem, *The Dreme,* in 1528. The poem is a DREAM VISION in which Dame Remembrance shows the poet earth, hell, and heaven, from which he can look down and see the troubled political situation of Scotland. The poem is in the "Mirror for Princes" tradition. Lindsay followed this poem with a *Compleynt to the King* (1529), written in octosyllabic (eight-syllable) couplets, wherein he focuses particularly on the corrupt state of the Scottish church. Lindsay blends humor with satire in his next work, *Testament and Complaynt of our Soverane Lordis Papyngo* (1530), which mixes advice to the king and satire of the clergy put into the mouth of a dying pet parrot. Lindsay again puts satire into the mouth of an animal in *The Complaynt and Publict Confession of the King Is Auld Hound* (ca. 1536), where the sage advice comes from a dog. This sense of humor that must have kept the young king entertained and sustained Lindsay's close personal relationship with him is evident in his *An Answer Quhilk Schir David Lyndsay Maid to the Kingis Flyting* (An answer which Sir David Lindsay made to the king's flyting [1536]), apparently part of an exchange of poetic abuse with the king himself (a practice called a *FLYTING*, popularized by William DUNBAR).

In the meantime Lindsay was engaged in diplomatic missions for the king. He visited the Hapsburg emperor Charles V in 1531. In 1536 he was part of a royal mission to France to negotiate a marriage alliance for the king. At some point before 1540, he was given the title Lyon king-at-arms, the chief herald of Scotland. Part of his duties involved entertainment and instruction of the court, and it is in this capacity that he seems to have written his *Pleasant Satyre of the Thrie Estaitis,* an entertainment for Epiphany produced before the king at court in 1540. Like most of his works, this morality play contains a good deal of ribald comedy, but is didactic in its intent, focusing particularly, once again, on abuses of the clergy.

After the untimely death of King James in 1542, his week-old daughter Mary was named Queen of Scots. Lindsay stayed on at court and continued his diplomatic role, visiting the court of Henry VIII in 1544 and the Danish court of King Christian III in 1548. Beyond this we know little of Lindsay's final years, except that his literary output continued: He wrote a "Tragedy" of the murdered Cardinal Beaton in 1547, in which the cardinal (assassinated by Protestant nobles hoping to topple the Catholic Church in Scotland) speaks his own warning, offering his life as an admonition to other powerful figures, whether of church or state. In 1542, he finished—in his role as Lyon king-at-arms—a document called the *Register at Arms of the Scottish Nobility,* still the most authoritative text on Scottish heraldry, though it was not published until 1821.

The Historie of Squyer Meldrum (ca. 1553) is part biography, part courtly ROMANCE, influenced somewhat by John BARBOUR's *BRUCE*. Of all Lindsay's works, it is the one most likely to please modern readers. In 1,594 lines of octosyllabic couplets, it follows the military and amorous exploits of an early 16th-century Scottish laird from Fife, Lindsay's own neighborhood.

Lindsay's last and longest poem is called *The Monarchie* (1554), otherwise known as the *Dialogue Between Experience and a Courtier*. This 6,000-line poem is a history of the world from the Creation through Doomsday, in which Lindsay focuses on four ancient empires and then discusses the spiritual empire of Christ—and, characteristically, the anti-Christian empire of the papacy. Six years after Lindsay penned this poem, the Church of Scotland was organized under Calvinist principles.

Bibliography

Happé, Peter, ed. *Four Morality Plays*. Harmondsworth, U.K.: Penguin, 1979.

Kinsley, James, ed. *Squyer Meldrum*. London: Thomas Nelson, 1959.

Lyall, Roderick, ed. *Ane Satire of the Thrie Estaitis*. Canongate Classics no. 18. Edinburgh: Canongate, 1989.

Li Shangyin (Li Shang-yin) (ca. 813–ca. 858)

Li Shangyin was one of the outstanding poets of the late TANG DYNASTY. Nearly 600 of his poems are extant. These include historical verses that are subtly satirical, and more accessible untitled love poems celebrating illicit love affairs. His poems include a good deal of sensual imagery, but also often contain obscure language, with cryptic quotations and political allusions that make his verse very difficult to understand and even more difficult to translate. He was also a master of the ancient prose style called *pianwen* or parallel prose, in which the complete text consisted of passages that were parallel or antithetical.

Li Shangyin was born in what today is China's Henan (Honan) province, and for a short time in his youth he seems to have been attached to the Taoist temple there. In 837, Shangyin successfully passed the highest imperial civil service examination, the *JINSHI* (*ch'in-shih*). However, he was never successful in advancing in his political career, largely because he entered public service just as two influential factions, the Niu and the Li, were struggling for power within the imperial bureaucracy, and Shangyin was caught in the middle. He held several minor posts, including editor of the Archival Office, deputy magistrate for a county close to the capital, scribe of the Archival Office in 842 and later a professor at the High School. In 851 he joined the staff of the powerful new governor of Sichuan (Szechuan), but he eventually resigned because of ill health and died in 858.

Li Shangyin never held a position of power in the bureaucracy, and was out of favor for much of his life. But his carefully structured poems, with their beautiful if obscure language, were highly influential on later generations of Chinese poets. Most appealing to Western readers is probably the intense emotion sometimes revealed in Li's untitled love poems, such as becomes apparent in lines like these:

> *The spring silkworm's thread will only end*
> *when death comes;*
> *The candle will not dry its tears until it*
> *turns to ashes.*
> *Before the morning mirror, she only grieves*
> *that her dark hair may change;*
> *Reciting poems by night, would she not feel*
> *the moonlight's chill?*

(Liu 1969, Poem 6, ll. 3–6)

Bibliography

Liu, James J. Y. *The Poetry of Li Shang-yin: Ninth Century Baroque Chinese Poet*. Chicago: University of Chicago Press, 1969.

litotes

From the Greek *litos*, meaning "small," litotes is a figure of speech that uses a specific kind of understatement for ironic purposes. In litotes a thing is indirectly affirmed by negating its contrary. In everyday language one might say, "He's not my favorite instructor," to indicate that in fact you do not like the instructor at all. Often litotes is expressed as a double negative, as when one says, "I'm not unsympathetic to your cause," to mean "I sympathize with your cause."

Litotes figures prominently in OLD ENGLISH poetry, where it is a favorite rhetorical device. In *BEOWULF*, for example, the poet introduces a grim irony into many scenes with the use of litotes. Late in the poem, as Beowulf leads his Geatish warriors to the lair of the dragon, the poet comments:

Næs þæt yðe ceap
to gegangennegumena ænigum!

(Heaney 2000, 162, ll. 2415–2416)

No easy bargain
Would be made in that place by any man.

(Heaney 2000, 163)

Typical of the *Beowulf* poet, the irony here borders on humor, as if anyone could conceive of fighting a fire-breathing dragon as an "easy bargain." Such is the effect of litotes in Old English poetry.

Bibliography

Heaney, Seamus. *Beowulf: A New Verse Translation.* New York: Farrar, Straus and Giroux, 2000.

Li Qingzhao (Li Ch'ing-chao) (ca. 1084–ca. 1151)

Li Qingzhao was the most important woman poet of medieval China and the outstanding composer of CI (*tz'u*) poetry—a genre of lyric poem that put new words to old song tunes. She was a scholar, an aristocrat, an art collector, and later a widow and refugee, in addition to being the outstanding poet of her time.

She was born into a scholarly family of government officials in what is today Jinan (Chi-nan), and her early life was spent in the lively intellectual atmosphere surrounding her parents and their friends. She learned to write poetry at a young age and already had something of a reputation as a poet when she married Zhao Mingcheng (Chao Ming-ch'eng) at about age 18. It was by all accounts a marriage of equals, as her husband shared her passion for scholarship and the arts. They became great collectors of early Chinese paintings, calligraphy, and inscriptions in bronze and stone. Zhao began a career in the bureaucracy of the Song (Sung) empire, and the couple moved to Shandong (Shantung) province in about 1108.

Upon the Jurchen invasion and occupation of northern China in 1127 and the fall of the Song capital at Kaifeng, Li and her family were forced to flee with the imperial court to the south. Li and her husband lost much of their famous art collection, and after they had reached JianKang (Chienk'ang; present-day Nanjing [Nanking]), Zhao died in 1129. Widowed and nearly destitute, Li spent much of the rest of her life wandering along with the constantly fleeing court, spending most of her last days in Hangzhou (Hangchow) and Jinhua (Chinhua).

There is a tradition that Li Qingzhao married again in about 1132, and that her husband, a military man, abused her so that she sued him for divorce. Though the suit was successful, the law required that any woman suing her husband must be confined, and Li was forced to spend time in prison. The evidence supporting this story, however, is considered by some scholars to be highly suspect. Though lonely and bereft, Li continued to write poetry until her death. She is known to have been writing poetry for the court in the 1140s, and the last official record of her is dated 1149.

One of Li's first acts after her husband's death was to publish his 30-volume *Jin shi lu* (*Chin shih lu;* Records on metal and stone), a study of ancient Chinese inscriptions that Chao had collected over the years. To this Li added an afterword, *Hou hsu.* Unlike the typical scholarly afterword, Li's was a remembrance of their happy marriage and a discussion of how the scholarship invested in Chao's work related to their marital life.

Of her own work, Li published some seven volumes of *shi* (or traditional) poems, and six volumes of *ci* (the newer style of song-lyric), plus the prose *Lan ci* (*Lun tz'u;* Discourse on lyric) providing a brief theoretical discussion of the new *ci* lyric. Only 50 of her *ci* poems and 17 *shi* (*shih*) are now extant. Her poems range in subject from the political turmoil of her time to her own intense emotions, and her style has been called simple, fresh, and natural. The *ci* poem generally focused on particular moments and the feelings they invoked, and Li's lyrics, as in the following lines, often evoke her sorrow at the loss of her husband:

The flute player is gone.
The jade tower is empty.
Broken hearted—we had relied on each other.
I pick a plum branch,
But my man has gone beyond the sky,
And there is no one to give it to.

(Rexroth and Chung 1979, "On Plum Blossoms," ll. 16–21)

Bibliography

Hu, Pinqing. *Li Ch'ing-chao.* New York: Twayne, 1966.

Jiaosheng, Wang. *The Complete Ci-poems of Li Qingzhao: A New English Translation.* Philadelphia: University of Pennsylvania Press, 1989.

Rexroth, Kenneth, and Ling Chung. *Li Ching-chao: Complete Poems.* New York: New Directions, 1979.

Llull, Ramón (Raymond Lull) (ca. 1232–1316)

Recent scholarship has discovered that this Catalan theologian, teacher, and mystic espoused one of the most open-minded attitudes toward the representatives of non-Christian religions during the Middle Ages, although he made great efforts throughout his life to missionize among Jews and Muslims. By the same token, Llull was essentially the founder of Catalan literature and the most important Catalan philosopher and theologian of his time composing in the vernacular.

Llull was born on Mallorca (Majorca) as the son of a nobleman and entered the service of King James I of Aragon in 1246. He married Blanca Picany in 1257 and had two children with her. In 1263, after a fairly comfortable life as a high-ranking courtier, Llull, having listened to a Franciscan preacher delivering a sermon, suddenly experienced a series of mystical visions of the crucified Christ. Consequently he accepted, as his divine mission, the task of writing "the best book in the world." Llull abandoned his family and his public function and became a Franciscan tertiary, accepting the lifestyle of a monk, though he was still married. For nine years he studied philosophy and theology, the Arabic language, and the Muslim religion. In 1272 he wrote a compendium of AL-GHAZĀLI's logic and the *Liber de contemplació en Déu* ("Book on the Contemplation of God"). Llull founded a school for the study of Arabic in Miramar on Majorca in 1276 and for his entire life pushed for this philological approach in missionary activities since he firmly believed that all interactions with members of other religions had to be based on a solid understanding of their language. This finally convinced the church at the Council of Vienne in 1311 to incorporate Arabic and Hebrew, among other Oriental languages, as important subjects for students of divinity. This practice was subsequently adopted at most of the major medieval universities. Llull himself went on many journeys to North Africa, Cyprus, and Sicily, where he studied intensively Arabic and the KORAN and tried to reach out to Muslims and Jews. He was a most prolific writer, composing approximately 300 works, of which some 268 are still extant, written in Latin, Catalan, Arabic, and perhaps in Provençal (none of the texts that Llull had allegedly written in Arabic have survived).

Llull was deeply convinced that human reason would be the fundamental catalyst to convert non-Christians who only needed to pay close attention to the logical arguments presented by their dialogue partners to abandon their old faith and to turn to Christianity. In 1299 he began his *Principia philosophiae* (First principles of philosophy) in which he attempted to combine Aristotelian philosophy with Christian teachings. Llull also composed poetry in Catalan, then a treatise on chivalry, and a kind of autobiographical verse romance, *Libre de Evast e Blanquerna* (1282 and 1287), in which he himself is personified as the Court Fool, or Lover. In his much later prose work *Phantasticus* (1311), he depicted himself as "Ramon lo Foll." In his *Llibre d'amic e amat* (*Book of the Lover and the*

Beloved), Llull offers religious-poetic reflections for every day of the year. Llull is, however, most famous for his enormously popular and often translated *Llibre del gentil e los tres savis* (*The Book of the Gentile and the Three Wise Men*), written between 1275 and 1277, in which he portrays a gentile (an unbeliever) discussing with representatives of the three major world religions—Christianity, Islam, and Judaism—about the truth of their belief. Although they all argue against each other, in a remarkably tolerant fashion they ultimately agree to disagree with each other and to continue with their discussions at a later time.

Between 1295 and 1296, Llull created an enormous encyclopedia, his *Arbre de ciència* (*Tree of Science*). In his *Liber praedicationis contra Judaeos (et Saracenos)* (*Liber de trinitate et incarnatione*) from 1305 Llull outlines his methodological approach in preaching to and converting Jews. His last major composition was his *Ars magna* (*The Great Art*), composed in 1308, in which he tried to summarize all of human knowledge, reducing it to one basic principle, applying profound scholastic teachings adopted from Aristotle, Thomas Aquinas, and other contemporary thinkers. Llull also produced several preaching handbooks, such as his *Rhetorica nova* (1302), *Liber de praedicatione* (1304), *Ars brevis praedicationis* (1313), and, most important, his *Summa sermonum* (1312–13), a vast collection of sermons.

In 1315 Llull traveled to North Africa again to missionize there, but according to legend he was stoned to death in Bourgie, Algeria. Most likely, however, he was only expelled and died a year later in 1316 either on his way home or in Majorca. In Paris, one of Llull's admirers had already written a biography of his master in 1311, the *Vita coetanea*. Llull exerted strong influence on the philosophies of Nicholas of Cusa, Giordano Bruno, and Gottfried Wilhelm Leibnitz. His works had also a great impact on late-medieval and early-modern alchemy.

Bibliography

Classen, Albrecht. "Toleranz im späten 13. Jahrhundert, mit besonderer Berücksichtigung von Jans von Wien und Ramón Llull." Forthcoming in *Mediaevistik*.

Hames, Harvey J. *The Art of Conversion: Christianity and Kabbalah in the Thirteenth Century*. Leiden: Brill, 2000.

Johnston, Mark D. *The Spiritual Logic of Ramon Lull*. Oxford: Clarendon Press, 1987.

Llull, Ramón. *Raimundi Lulli Opera Latina*. 18 vols. Turnholt: Brepols, 1975–1989.

———. *Selected Works of Ramon Llull (1232–1316)*. Edited by A. Bonner. 2 vols. Princeton, N.J.: Princeton University Press, 1985.

Peers, E. Allison. *Ramón Lull: A Biography*. 1929. Reprint, New York: B. Franklin, 1969.

Albrecht Classen

Lollards

The Lollards were members of a controversial English reform movement that began in the 14th century. The word *Lollard* was a derogatory term, perhaps from the Dutch word *lollaert* meaning "mumbler." They were also sometimes referred to as Wycliffites because of the movement's following of the unorthodox doctrines of the Oxford Franciscan John WYCLIFFE.

In his works Wycliffe emphasized the importance of a personal spiritual connection with the deity and of looking at the Bible as the literal word of God. Wycliffe, with the help of John Purvey and Nicholas of Hereford, translated the Bible into English in order to make it more accessible to the common people. The 1390 edition became known as the Lollard Bible and was widely available until it was banned in 1407.

Wycliffe denied the need for confession to a priest, the use of religious images, and prayers for the dead. He questioned the veracity of the doctrine of transubstantiation (that is, the belief that the bread and wine literally became the body and blood of Christ). Wycliffe also criticized pilgrimages. Later Lollards such as the priest William THORPE advanced the argument that pilgrimages were no longer taken for spiritual enlightenment, but instead for bodily pleasure or earthly achievement. Perhaps the most incendiary criticism was Wycliffe's condemnation of the wealth and power of church authority and the clergy.

Wycliffe's death in 1384 did not slow the growth of the Lollard movement. By 1395, almost half of England was considered Lollard (Lambdin 2000, 358). Support came from all backgrounds, including the wealthy under the reign of Richard II (1377–99) whose land had been confiscated by the church. Even Richard's queen, ANNE OF BOHEMIA, had a Lollard Bible; however, she may have used it exclusively to learn English.

Noble support, including that of John of Gaunt, waned when Wycliffe sympathizers were active in the PEASANTS' REVOLT of 1381. Court support also diminished under Henry IV (1399–1413) when the Roman church became more influential in England and Lollard intolerance increased. The persecution took place on both the intellectual and legislative fronts. Church authorities such as Reginald PECOCK wrote texts disputing the beliefs of the Lollards. New statutes were also passed. In 1406, an anti-Lollard statute was enacted to aid in the trials of the so-called heretics. Thorpe's account of his examination is especially edifying with respect to the content of the trials. In 1410, trials became more consequential when the *De heretico comburendo* statute was made to introduce the burning of heretics in England. Those burned included John Purvey and Nicholas of Hereford.

In 1414 Sir John Oldcastle, Lord Cobham (c. 1370–1417), tried to dethrone Henry V (1413–22) in Oldcastle's Uprising. In 1415, Oldcastle was convicted of heresy and sent to the Tower of London. He escaped, but was captured and executed as the last Lollard martyr in 1417.

The Council of Constance under Pope John XXIII (in the wake of the execution of John HUS for heresy) condemned Wycliffe's writings as heretical in 1415. In 1428, the council exhumed his remains, cremated them, and threw them into the River Swift.

Although there were resurfacings of Lollards into the 16th century, the momentum had died out of the movement after the suppression of Oldcastle's Uprising. Most Lollards had been driven underground. The ideas of the movement prevailed, however, and influenced the Hussites in Bohemia in the 15th century. The Hussites' ideology influenced Martin Luther; thus there is a direct connection between Lollardy and the Protestant Reformation.

Bibliography

Copeland, Rita. *Pedagogy, Intellectuals, and Dissent in the Later Middle Ages: Lollardy and Ideas of Learning.* Cambridge: Cambridge University Press, 2001.

Lambdin, Robert T., and Lambdin, Laura Cooner, eds. *Encyclopedia of Medieval Literature.* Westport, Conn.: Greenwood Press, 2000.

Powell, Susan. "Lollards and Lombards: Late Medieval Bogeymen?" *Medium Aevum* 59, no. 1 (1990): 133–139.

Rex, Richard. *The Lollards.* Houndmills, U.K.: Palgrave, 2002.

Malene A. Little

López de Ayala, Pedro (1332–1407)

The most important Castilian literary figure of the 14th century was the historian, poet, and statesman Pedro López de Ayala. Ayala was a nobleman who served in the courts of four Castilian kings, rising to the rank of chancellor of the realm. He is also the author of a famous *Chronicle* that gives firsthand accounts of some of the events of those kings' reigns, and a lengthy poetic miscellany called the *Rimado del palaçio* that is the last great poem in the *cuaderna vía* verse form.

Ayala was born in Vitoria to Fernán Pérez de Ayala, a wealthy member of the noble class. He was educated by his uncle, Pedro Gomez Barrosa, a cardinal of the church. In 1353, Ayala became a page in the household of King Pedro I (called "The Cruel"). He became so valuable to the king that he was put in charge of the Castilian navy in Pedro's war against Aragon. He fled with the king when Castile was invaded by Enrique de Trastamara, but subsequently deserted Pedro and joined Enrique's supporters in 1366. He served the new sovereign when he became King Enrique II, being captured by the Black Prince and quickly ransomed in 1367. Ayala was made governor of Toledo in 1375, and ambassador to Aragon in 1376. At other times he represented Castilian kings at the courts of Portugal and Paris, and at the papal court in Avignon. He served Enrique's successor, Juan I, being captured in battle with the Portuguese and spending two years in captivity. During the years of Enrique III's minority after Juan's death in 1390, Ayala served as a member of the Regency Council. But when Enrique decided to rule in his own right in 1393, Ayala retired from court life to write. But in 1399, Ayala was named royal chancellor of Castile.

Ayala's direct experiences with four Castilian kings make his *Chronicle* a valuable eyewitness account of the reigns of those kings between 1350 and 1406. Unlike many of his contemporary chroniclers, Ayala eschews the use of unreliable legendary material and focuses on firsthand knowledge. His history has also been praised for its insightful analyses of his principal characters and their motives. He remains more objective than most medieval chroniclers as well: Although some critics have called his treatment of Pedro the Cruel slanted, probably to help justify his own desertion of Pedro's cause, it can be argued that Ayala is not blind to the faults of any of his royal patrons, condemning Enrique II for his mistreatment of Jews, for example. Influenced by the Roman historian Livy, whose work he translated into Castilian, Ayala seems to have consciously emulated Livy's dramatic prose style. It has also been demonstrated that Ayala borrowed some of his more vivid descriptions of events from some popular ballads of his time.

Ayala's major poetic text is the *Rimado del palaçio* (ca. 1400), an 8,200-line miscellany written largely in the old four-line *cuaderna vía* stanzas, the lines ranging from 14 to 16 syllables and the stanzas linked by a single rhyme: *aaaa.* The poem falls into three separate parts. The first section, of about 700 stanzas, is a treatise on morality, discussing the Ten Commandments, the Seven Deadly Sins, the acts of mercy, the five senses, the estates of society, and the Four Cardinal Virtues (justice, temperance, fortitude, and prudence). Ayala ends the first section of the poem by discussing the temptations of the court and of the uses of power, and speaks of how kings can make the right use of power. Part two of the poem consists of 200 lyric stanzas in a number of different forms, dealing with a variety of subjects, ranging from the Virgin Mary to the Great Schism of the Western church (with one pope in Avignon and a rival pope in Rome). The final section of the poem returns to another 1,250 stanzas of *cuaderna vía,* and is a versification of many passages from GREGORY THE GREAT's *Moralia of Job,* a text that Ayala had previously translated into Castilian prose. Ayala's poem on the whole is a satire of the sins and corruption typical in the courts he knew so intimately, and an argument for peace and for moral government.

Ayala, often called the Great Chancellor, produced a number of other texts as well, particularly translations. In addition to the translations of Livy and Gregory already mentioned, Ayala was responsible for the Castilian versions of BOETHIUS's *CONSOLATION OF PHILOSOPHY,* of the works of ISIDORE OF SEVILLE, and of BOCCACCIO's *De casibus,* or *The Fall of Illustrious Men,* the latter translation proving largely responsible for the vogue of Italian influence in Spanish literature that lasted well into the Renaissance. Despite his busy life during decades of Castilian politics, through his history, his poetry, and his translations, Ayala made himself the most important man of letters in 14th-century Spain.

Bibliography

Clarke, Dorothy Clotelle, comp. *Early Spanish Lyric Poetry: Essays and Selections.* New York: Las Americas, 1967.

Joset, Jacques, ed. *Libro rimado del palaçio.* 2 vols. Madrid: Alhambra, 1978.

Wilkins, Constance L. *Pedro López de Ayala.* Boston: Twayne Publishers, 1989.

Lord Randal (15th century)

The earliest extant English version of the popular ballad *Lord Randal,* as it appears in Francis Child's edition, is as recent as the 18th century. However, there are earlier German versions, and Italian analogues existed in the early 17th century. Because the ballad was originally English (and perhaps based on the fate of the 13th-century Ranulf, earl of Chester), it may date as far back as the 15th century.

The poem tells the story of a young man who has been poisoned by his lover. (A variant is a young boy who has been poisoned by his stepmother.) His mother discovers the treachery after a series of questions. She then proceeds to ask how he wants to divide his estate. The last person she asks about is the lover to whom he leaves "hell and fire" (Morgan 1996, 22). Alternately he leaves her "the rope and the halter that/do hang on yonder tree/And there let her hang for the/poisoning of me" (Carthy 2003, 72).

The repetition of lines like the opening ("Oh where ha' you been, Lord Randal my son?/And where ha' you been, my handsome young man?") functions to drive the ballad forward while simultaneously giving the background story. The melancholy mood of the ballad and pragmatic questioning of the mother about her son's bequests make *Lord Randal* a haunting piece.

The ballad is very popular and versions of it can be found throughout Britain, America, Canada, and Europe. Scored versions, dating back to the 18th century, can even be found for those who wish to sing the tragic ballad. A British version changes the murderer into "gypsies" and the eels into "snakes." This version functions not only as a ballad, but also as a tale of warning to 20th-century children about the dangers of wandering from home.

Bibliography

Bird, S. Elizabeth, " 'Lord Randal' in Kent: The Meaning and Context of a Ballad Variant," *Folklore* 96 (1985): 248–252.

Carthy, Martin. "Lord Randal (Child #12)," *Sing Out!* (Winter 2003): 72.

Child, Francis James, ed. *The English and Scottish Popular Ballads*. 1882–98. Reprint, New York: Cooper Square Publishers, 1965.

McCarthy, Terence. "Robert Graves and 'Lord Rendal,' " *Tennessee Folklore Society Bulletin* 45, no. 2 (1982): 48–52.

Morgan, Gwendolyn A., ed. and trans. *Medieval Ballads: Chivalry, Romance, and Everyday Life: A Critical Anthology*. New York: Peter Lang, 1996.

Malene A. Little

Love, Nicholas (fl. 1410)

Nicholas Love was a prior in Yorkshire who translated the influential *Meditationes vitae Christi* into his work *The Mirror of the Blessed Life of Jesus Christ*. It was significant not only because of its spiritual value, but also as a rebuttal of LOLLARD attacks on the church.

Little is known about Love's life, not even the dates of birth and death. His translation of *Meditationes vitae Christi* was done while he was prior of the newly established Carthusian house of Mount Grace in north Yorkshire. After *The Mirror of the Blessed Life of Jesus Christ*, he produced nothing more, presumably due to time constraints from the responsibilities of running the monastery.

Meditationes vitae Christi was originally thought to be written by St. BONAVENTURE, but is actually a 14th-century Italian work by the Franciscan Johannes de Caulibus. The intent of the work was to allow the reader to identify with Christ's humanity and thus feel more empathy for his sacrifice and our redemption. The text is separated into seven days of Christ's life; this way the material would correspond with the seven days of Holy Week. The text for Friday, the day of the Passion, is also divided into seven parts, representative of the canonical hours, and was often circulated by itself. The entire text became a source of inspiration for numerous mystery plays, songs, and poetry.

Love's translation, *The Mirror of the Blessed Life of Jesus Christ*, was approved by Archbishop Arundel in 1410. It was in part used to challenge Lollard views. It included numerous incidental attacks on Lollard beliefs as well as an additional chapter that reaffirmed the orthodox view of the Eucharist. Love's translation was especially successful; his fluency and expressiveness were powerful and allowed people to personalize their relationships with Christ.

Bibliography

Oguro, Shoichi, Richard Beadle, and Michael G. Sargent. *Nicholas Love at Waseda: Proceedings of the International Conference, 20–22 July 1995*. Rochester, N.Y.: D. S. Brewer, 1997.

Salter, Elizabeth. *Nicholas Love's "Myrrour of the blessed lyf of Jesu Christ."* Salzburg, Austria: Institut Für Englische Sprache und Literatur, Universität Salzburg, 1974.

Sargent, Michael G., ed. and introduction. *Nicholas Love's Mirror of the Blessed Life of Jesus Christ: A Critical Edition Based on Cambridge University Library Additional mss 6578 and 6686.* New York: Garland, 1992.

Malene A. Little

Lydgate, John (ca. 1370–ca. 1449)

John Lydgate was a Benedictine monk from Bury Saint Edmunds who wrote more poetry than any other known medieval English poet. He was much praised by his contemporaries and by writers in the years immediately following his death, but his reputation declined rapidly after the late 16th century. For example, in the famous poem "Lament to the Makers" (1502), William DUNBAR lists the "Monk of Bury" among the three greatest English poets (along with John GOWER and Geoffrey CHAUCER), but by the beginning of the 19th century, the encyclopedist Joseph Ritson dismisses Lydgate as "a voluminous, prosaic and drivelling monk" (1802).

Lydgate's work is indeed voluminous, encompassing some 145,000 lines of poetry, which is three times the known work of Chaucer and twice the amount written by William Shakespeare. Lydgate's poems cover a wide range of religious, historical, and moral subjects, written in a similarly wide range of verse forms. His works include both original pieces and expanded translations of works originally in Latin, French, and Italian.

Much of the modern reader's dissatisfaction with Lydgate comes from the length of his poems and their difficult language. Critic Derek Pearsall defends Lydgate's leisurely style as one appropriate to a culture in which works were read aloud, making repetition and use of conventional language strategies welcomed by listeners. The difficulty of Lydgate's language stems largely from his desire to promote English as a serious literary language by using English to imitate the rhetorical flourishes common to classical Latin poetry. In fact, Lydgate is credited with having introduced more than 800 Latin-based words into the English language.

Much of Lydgate's work was commissioned for important patrons in the nobility and royal family. Under a patronage system, a poet produces works on demand when requested by a particular patron. The patron might specify the occasion for which a poem was composed, and he or she might further specify the subject matter of the poem. Rather than being stifled by the patron's requests, Lydgate used the occasions of the commissioned poems to pursue his own agendas of poetic theory and moral guidance.

For example, when Prince Hal, later Henry V, commissioned a poem about the fall of Troy, Lydgate spent eight years producing the *TROY BOOK* (1420), based on a translation of GUIDO DELLE COLONNE's *Historia Troians* (1287) as well as other works on the Trojan legends, including Chaucer's *TROILUS AND CRISEYDE*. Lydgate uses the examples of the classical heroes to demonstrate his belief that yielding to passion risks destruction and that dedication to chivalry leads to success. In the closing lines, he stresses the vanity of worldly affairs, affirms Henry's French conquests, and wishes blessings on Henry's reign.

Another of Lydgate's reworkings of classical material is his *SIEGE OF THEBES* (ca. 1420–22), which retells the destruction of Thebes. As with the *Troy Book,* Lydgate is able to show how the classical past is relevant to understanding life in the modern world. Here Lydgate moralizes the Thebes story to show the advantage of words over swords, perhaps as another message to Henry V. *The Siege of Thebes* is often associated with the Chaucer canon because of the interpretation it gives of Chaucer's work. Because Chaucer's *KNIGHT'S TALE* begins with the destruction of Thebes, Lydgate's poem is a prequel to Chaucer's story. Lydgate makes the Chaucer connection more explicit with a frame tale in which the pilgrims from Chaucer's *CANTERBURY TALES* are preparing to leave Canterbury for London. When invited to join the pilgrims' tale-telling contest, Lydgate tells his story about Thebes. Early printed editions of Chaucer's work included *The Siege of Thebes* as late as 1598.

Not surprisingly for a monk, Lydgate wrote a number of religious poems in which he worked deliberately to use elevated English as a means of moving people to religious devotion, thus creating a new standard of English religious poetry. The religious poems include religious instruction, prayers, lyrics, SAINTS' LIVES, and other religious narratives, as well as translations of various hymns and psalms. Perhaps the best known of the religious materials is his *Life of Our Lady* (ca. 1409–11), a tribute to the Virgin Mary.

Lydgate also contributed to the development of English drama through a series of seven so-called "mumming poems." These works were commissioned for various holidays and provide a kind of narration to be read aloud during performances of pantomimes. For example, in the *Mumming at Eltham* (1424), written as entertainment for the king and queen's Christmas residency at Eltham Palace, the characters of Bacchus, Juno, and Ceres present gifts of wine, wheat, and oil to the king. Lydgate's commentary assures the king and queen that through the intervention of these gifts, the kingdom shall have peace.

Another of Lydgate's famous works is the *Fall of Princes* (ca. 1431–39), an encyclopedic collection of people of high position who fell from power. Lydgate surveys biblical, historical, and legendary materials to consider examples ranging from Adam and Eve all the way to France's King John. The tradition of cataloging the unfortunate was well established in Lydgate's time. BOCCACCIO had produced a well-known similar work, *De Casibus virorum illustrium* (1358), and Chaucer had adapted Boccaccio for his *MONK'S TALE* in the *Canterbury Tales.* Lydgate's work exceeds these examples in scope and in his emphasis that a wise reader can benefit from these examples. Individual moral choices as much as fortune determine fate. *Fall of Princes* is also interesting because of its patronage history. The work was commissioned by Humphrey, duke of Gloucester and younger brother of Henry V. In the early sections of *Fall of Princes,* Lydgate praises Humphrey for his generosity and contributions to humanistic learning in England, but by the end of the poem, Lydgate incorporates several hints about his poverty and need for money. Apparently, Humphrey was more generous in theory than in fact.

Lydgate was born around 1370 in the village of Lidgate or Lydgate. By 1382 he entered the Benedictine abbey in the nearby town of Bury St. Edmunds. This abbey was one of the largest, wealthiest, and most powerful abbeys in England. Even though Lydgate's parents were probably peasants, he advanced rapidly in the monastery. He was ordained in 1389, made a deacon in 1393, and reached the full order of priesthood in 1397. The abbey library was reputed to house over 2,000 books, one of the largest collections in England. With access to this collection, Lydgate developed an encyclopedic learning. And, through his role in the abbey, Lydgate was brought into contact with important political figures, including members of the royal family.

Part of Lydgate's life was spent away from the abbey. He apparently read theology at Gloucester College, Oxford, a college tied to Bury St. Edmund's abbey. He spent time in the English royal courts of London, Windsor, and in Paris. He also served as the prior of the Benedictine house at Hatfield Regis from 1423–34. Most of his long life, however, was spent in Bury St. Edmunds. He died, presumably at the abbey, in 1449. The location of his tomb is not known. Tradition held that he was buried in the abbey, but the abbey was destroyed during Henry VIII's dissolution of English monasteries (1539) and only scant ruins remain.

Few modern readers consider Lydgate an author read for pleasure, but he remains an important literary figure for several reasons. His volume of poetry and the popularity that poetry achieved reveal much about aesthetic taste of the 15th and 16th centuries. Because the critical movement known as New Historicism has paid special interest to ways literary culture and history intersect, recent critics concentrate on ways Lydgate used his role as poet to address social and political concerns, even in commissioned works. Finally, Lydgate did much to promote the acceptance of formal poetry written in English.

Bibliography

Ebin, Lois. *John Lydgate.* Twayne's English Authors, 407. Boston: Twayne, 1985.

Pearsall, Derek. *John Lydgate.* Charlottesville: University of Virginia Press, 1970.

Renoir, Alain. *The Poetry of John Lydgate.* Cambridge, Mass.: Harvard University Press, 1967.

Schirmer, Walter. *John Lydgate: A Study in the Culture of the XVth Century.* Translated by Ann E. Keep. Berkeley: University of California Press, 1961.

David Sprunger

Ma'arri, Abu al-'Ala al-

See AL-MA'ARRI, ABU AL-ALA.

Mabinogion, The (ca. 11th century)

The *Mabinogion* includes 11 tales in Middle Welsh that are grouped together because of their common characters and themes. The main tales of the *Mabinogion* are divided into Four Branches, or related adventures: *Pwyll Prince of Dyfed, Branwen Daughter of Ll^yr, Manawydan Son of Ll^yr,* and *Math Son of Mathonwy.* The title itself, *Mabinogion,* has long been interpreted as an indication that the stories concern the boyhood of key figures in the medieval Welsh literary pantheon, the Welsh word for "boy/son" being *mab.* Other scholars argue that the tales in the Four Branches all include references to the activities of Pryderi, a figure with striking similarities to the ancient British god Maponos. Regardless, all the heroes and heroines of the Four Branches are of divine origin and exhibit superhuman traits.

The First Branch relates how the king of the Otherworld changes places with Pwyll, the mortal king of Dyfed (southwestern Wales), in order to father a divine child with a human mother. The enterprise comes to naught, and Pwyll is allowed to return to Dyfed, where he meets his future wife, Rhiannon, through a magical horse. Together they have a special son, Pryderi, who is abducted shortly after birth. Rhiannon is accused of murdering him and is forced to perform years of penance until the boy is found in the fosterage of a nearby family. The Second and Third Branches mention Pryderi only in passing and instead focus on the marriage of Branwen to Matholwch, the king of Ireland, and the heroics of her brother, Bran. When Matholwch treats Branwen discourteously, Bran rescues Branwen and her son Gwern. After much negotiating the married couple reach a compromise, but during the ensuing celebration, Gwern is killed and a battle begins in which Bran is mortally wounded.

In the Third Branch, Pryderi is imprisoned in the Otherworld through magic, and as a result there are bad harvests throughout Dyfed until his return. In the Fourth Branch Pryderi dies in battle, but the real action centers around Llew and his hunt for a wife. Due to his unseemly birth, Arianrod, Llew's mother, resents her son and curses him so that he can never have a human wife. Llew's cohorts, Math and Gwydion, form a beautiful bride for him out of flowers, Blodeuwedd. Despite being created for Llew, Blodeuwedd takes a lover, whom Llew then kills. Blodeuwedd is changed into an owl as punishment for her faithlessness.

The main themes in the literature of the *Mabinogion* concern the origins of both place-names and personal names, instances in which a wife has either been falsely or rightly accused of wrongdoing or infidelity, and journeys to and from the Otherworld. Key events in the lives of important Welsh mythological personages dominate the

Mabinogion and related literature, which describe births, childhood events, marriages, battles, exiles, and deaths. These themes can be found in most early Celtic literature, including one of Ireland's earliest medieval epics, the ULSTER CYCLE.

The stories of the *Mabinogion* are found in two medieval manuscripts, the *White Book of Rhydderch* (ca. 1300–25), which is held in the National Library of Wales, Aberystwyth, and the *Red Book of Hergest* (ca. 1400), which is housed at Jesus College, Oxford. Additional fragments of the tales can be found in many manuscripts, the earliest of which dates from the beginning of the 13th century. Although the stories evolved over centuries, most Celtic scholars agree that linguistic evidence in the texts indicates that the Four Branches and the earlier tales were committed to writing before the Norman Conquest of 1066.

Also considered part of the *Mabinogion* mythology is the story of *CULHWCH AND OLWEN*, the earliest Arthurian tale in Welsh, and three later Arthurian ROMANCES heavily influenced by contemporary Norman-French literature: *OWAIN* or *The Lady of the Fountain*, *PEREDUR*, and *GEREINT AND ENID*. The Arthur of *Culhwch and Olwen* is far removed from the King ARTHUR of French romance, but rather is a commanding but crude figure who wields both conventional weapons and magic. Rather than continually exhibiting omnipotent traits himself, it is his followers whose strength and deeds redound to Arthur's credit and demonstrate his power. Hearty and honorable warriors, such as Bedwyr (Bedivere) and Cei (Kay), serve as his reliable right-hand men. While many elements found in the medieval Welsh tales are recognizable in the subsequent retellings of Arthurian legend by GEOFFREY OF MONMOUTH and Thomas MALORY, there are some notable departures. For example, the Cei of Welsh mythology bears little resemblance to the bumbling fool portrayed in later literature.

Bibliography

Ford, Patrick K., ed. and trans. *The Mabinogi and Other Medieval Welsh Tales.* Los Angeles: University of California Press, 1977.

Jones, Gwyn, and Thomas Jones, ed. and trans. *The Mabinogion.* London: J. M. Dent, 1996.

Koch, John T., and John Carey, ed. *The Celtic Heroic Age: Literary Sources for Ancient Celtic Europe and Early Ireland and Wales.* New York: David Brown, 2003.

Parry, Thomas. *A History of Welsh Literature.* Oxford: Oxford University Press, 1955.

Williams, Ifor. *The Beginnings of Welsh Poetry.* Cardiff: University of Wales Press, 1990.

Diane Korngiebel

Machaut, Guillaume de (ca. 1300–1377)

Machaut was the most prolific and most influential 14th-century French poet and composer, setting an example with his narrative *dits* (narratives with interspersed lyric poems) that was followed by poets both in France and England for the next 200 years. With his *Messe de Nostre Dame*, he created the earliest polyphonic Mass Ordinary in the Middle Ages. He also composed 20 motets. Representative of his age, but also at the forefront of a new trend, Machaut had his collected works copied down several times in carefully edited manuscripts, organized according to the genres, and with all his poems in each genre arranged chronologically. The illustration programs in his manuscripts are highly elaborate, and Machaut himself seems to have determined the specific themes of individual images that served to better explain his narratives. In his compositions Machaut created difficult *LAIS* with music, many of them of considerable length, often requiring more than 30 minutes in performance. In his more mature works Machaut incorporated melismas (successions of notes on a single syllable) for textless tenor and contratenor, a practice that was subsequently copied far into the 15th century.

Machaut was born in the village of Machault near Reims and was educated in Paris, where he received his master's degree (*magister*). Because of his low social status, we can only outline his life on the basis of self-references in his works. He served from ca. 1323 to the late 1330s as personal secretary and clerk to Jean l'Aveugle (John the Blind) of Luxembourg, king of Bohemia and father of the German emperor Charles IV. Probably as a form of payment for his services, Machaut received a canonry at Reims in 1333, which secured him a solid income. In his role as secretary, Machaut accompanied the king on military expeditions through Poland, Russia, and Lithuania in 1329, and to northern Italy in 1330–31. After Jean's death in 1346 in the Battle of Crécy, Machaut found other patrons, such as Jean's daughter, Bonne of Luxembourg, and her two sons Charles, duke of Normandy, and John, duke of Berry. His last major patron was King Charles the Bad of Navarre, for whom he composed the verse chronicle *Prise d'Alexandrie* (ca. 1369–71). Many other princes paid him respect and asked him to compose works for them. Machaut died in April of 1377 in Reims.

Machaut's earliest narrative poem, the *Dit du vergier* (late 1330s), closely follows the allegorical dream poem the *ROMAN DE LA ROSE* by GUILLAUME DE LORRIS. Here the God of Love appears with six young men and six young women and promises to help the lover achieve his goal if he proves worthy. The *Jugement du roy de Behaigne* (late 1330s) is a love debate. Judging from the many subsequent allusions to this text and from the large number of manuscripts (20 manuscripts from the 14th and 15th centuries), we can be certain that this was one of Machaut's most popular allegorical poems. In his *Remede de Fortune* (ca. 1340), the lover tells of his long but silent service to his lady. He composes many poems and passes them to his friends, until one day his lady comes across one of his poems. Although she asks him about the poet, the lover cannot tell her the truth and withdraws into a park, lamenting his self-induced misfortune. But Lady Hope appears and encourages him to return to his lady who then indeed accepts him as her lover and exchanges rings with him. But because of the need for discretion and secrecy in love within the context of the court, she soon forgets him again.

The *Dit du lyon* (1342) tells the allegorical story of a lion who leads the narrator into a grove where he observes the lion's love experiences. Whenever his lady removes her gazes from him, other hostile beasts attack the lion. The narrator intervenes on behalf of the lion and then returns to his manor. The *Jugement du roy de Navarre* (1349) is another love debate, dedicated to Charles the Bad. Here the judgment is in favor of the lady, but the most important aspect proves to be the poet's examination of his own role as a writer. Here Machaut also includes a reference to the BLACK DEATH, which he himself survived while hidden behind a convent's wall during the years 1348–49. In his narrative comments he also describes the chaotic circumstances of that time, including the persecution of the Jews, the appearance of the flagellants, the mass burials of the dead, and the depopulation of the entire country. The *Dit de l'alerion* (early 1350s) is a bird allegory that creates direct analogies between women and birds of prey, or between hawking and *fin'amors* (or COURTLY LOVE). The *Fointeinne amoureuse* (1360–62) is another dream vision in which the Narrator overhears a lover bemoaning that he has to go into exile—which is a direct reflection of John, duke of Berry's trip to England in 1360 as a hostage during the Treaty of Brétigny. But in the dream Venus arrives and assures the lover of his lady's fidelity during his long-term absence. The *Voir dit* (1363–65), a kind of epistolary novel in verse, might well be an autobiographical account of a love affair. In 1356–57 Machaut composed *Confort d'ami* to offer consolation to Charles the Bad in his imprisonment since 1356, and in 1369–71 he wrote his *Pris d'Alexandrie* as a literary document of the career of Pierre de Lusignan, king of Cyprus.

Machaut also achieved great mastery in musical composition, focusing on motets, fixed-form lyrics, and on the Mass. Both his disciples and the general posterity expressed great respect for him. His literary and musical *œuvre* exerted great influence on the subsequent generations of poets and musical composers, such as Eustache DESCHAMPS, Jean FROISSART, CHRISTINE DE PIZAN, and Geoffrey CHAUCER. Machaut's greatest literary contribution consisted of his love poetry in which he idealized the three elements of "Dous Penser" (Sweet Thought), "Souvenir" (Memory), and "Espoir de joïr" (Hope for Joy).

Bibliography

Brownlee, Kevin. *Identity in Guillaume de Machaut.* Madison: University of Wisconsin Press, 1984.

Butterfield, Ardis. *Poetry and Music in Medieval France: From Jean Renart to Guillaume de Machaut.* Cambridge: Cambridge University Press, 2002.

De Looze, Laurence. *Pseudo-Autobiography in the Fourteenth Century: Juan Ruiz, Guillaume de Machaut, Jean Froissart, and Geoffrey Chaucer.* Gainesville: University Press of Florida, 1997.

Earp, Lawrence M. *Guillaume de Machaut: A Guide to Research.* New York: Garland, 1995.

Kelly, Douglas. *Medieval Imagination: Rhetoric and the Poetry of Courtly Love.* Madison: University of Wisconsin Press, 1978.

Machaut, Guillaume de. *Comfort for a Friend.* Edited and translated by R. Barton Palmer. New York: Garland, 1992.

———. *The Fountain of Love.* Edited and translated by R. Barton Palmer. New York: Garland, 1993.

———. *The Judgment of the King of Bohemia.* Edited and translated by R. Barton Palmer. New York: Garland, 1984.

———. *The Judgment of the King of Navarre.* Edited and translated by R. Barton Palmer. New York: Garland, 1980.

———. *Œuvre de Guillaume de Machaut.* Edited by Ernest Hoepffner. 3 vols. Paris: Didot, 1908–1921.

———. *The Taking of Alexandria.* Edited and translated by R. Barton Palmer. New York: Routledge, 2002.

———. *The Tale of the Alerion.* Edited and translated by Minnette Gaudet and Constance B. Hieatt. Toronto, Buffalo, and London: University of Toronto Press, 1994.

Albrecht Classen

Macrobius (Macrobius Ambrosius Theodosius) (ca. 360–ca. 435)

Macrobius was a late Latin grammarian, a Neoplatonic philosopher, and the author of three known late classical texts. He may also have been an important statesman of the Roman Empire. For 1,000 years, throughout the Middle Ages, Macrobius was one of the most widely read and influential of all classical writers—particularly through his enormously popular *Commentary on the Dream of Scipio.*

Next to nothing is known with any certainty about Macrobius's life. He lived during a turbulent era, in which the Roman Empire was threatened in turn by the Visigoths, the Huns, and the Vandals. Yet he was able to obtain a remarkable education. His own work reveals a knowledge of some 90 Greek writers (most prominently Plato and Homer) and an additional 115 Latin authors (Virgil and Cicero in particular, but also many of the only surviving fragments of the otherwise unknown poet Ennius). He says at one point that he hopes he may be forgiven for writing in Latin, since he was born "under a different sky." Thus he was not born in Italy. Some scholars have suggested that he was from a Greek-speaking part of the empire (his name is Greek). Most scholars believe he must have been from northern Africa. Possibly he was from a Greek-speaking community in Egypt. It is possible that the writer was the same Macrobius who was prefect of Spain in 399–400, proconsul of Africa in 410, and ultimately grand chamberlain of the empire in 422. One argument against the writer's identification with the statesman is that, in order to achieve the post of grand chamberlain, the statesman must have been a Christian. The writer, however (in his *Saturnalia*), seems to admire some of the most outspoken contemporary critics of Christianity.

One other detail of Macrobius's life that he discusses himself is his love for his son, Eustachius. Macrobius dedicates each of his three extant works to Eustachius, and they seem intended in part to teach the young man. What is probably Macrobius's earliest work, *On the Differences and Similarities Between Greek and Latin Verbs,* is a grammar textbook that might have been intended for Eustachius's early education. The text survives today only in a summary made sometime in the Middle Ages, once attributed, on no good evidence, to Johannes Scotus.

Macrobius's longest work (though missing several passages at various points in the text) is his *Saturnalia,* a dialogue in seven books in the manner of Plato, set during the three days of the great Roman festival of Saturn, and involving 12 different speakers. The text is a compendium of pagan lore, antiquarianism, quotations of numerous poets, and, in books 3 through 6, a long commentary of Virgil. His discussion of Virgil adds nothing to our appreciation of Virgil's poetic skills; rather, it presents the poet as a kind of oracle whose verses, rightly understood, have the authority of infallible wisdom. It was an attitude toward Virgil that was to pervade the Middle Ages.

Macrobius's best-known work, however, is certainly his *Commentary on the Dream of Scipio.* The dream itself had been the conclusion of Cicero's *De republica,* and was the only part of that text known in the Middle Ages, simply because it was included in Macrobius's popular commentary. Macrobius uses Cicero's story as a starting point for a detailed discussion of Neoplatonic philosophy, in particular Neoplatonic theories concerning arithmetic, geometry, music, and astronomy, the four subjects of the *quadrivium,* the scientific portion of the LIBERAL ARTS curriculum—indeed, Macrobius's work, perhaps written again to teach his son, became a standard school text in those subjects in the later Middle Ages. But perhaps even more influential was his discussion of the nature of dreams. Known in medieval times as *somniorum interpres* ("interpreter of dreams"), Macrobius classified dreams into five categories. The *visum,* or apparition, was a kind of hallucination when one is half asleep. The *insomnium,* the nightmare, was a dream induced by physical or mental distress. The *oraculum,* or oracular dream, was a meaningful dream in which a parent or other revered person appears to us and tells us what will or will not occur. The *visio,* or prophetic vision, is a dream of events that actually come to pass. And finally, the *somnium,* or enigmatic dream, was defined as a meaningful dream that shows us symbolically or in some ambiguous way an important truth. Such dreams are most interesting because they require interpretation. And such dreams provided the inspiration for the medieval tradition of the DREAM VISION poem, which presents events in a symbolic manner that the reader must interpret.

Macrobius influenced generations of medieval European writers. In his *PARLIAMENT OF FOWLS* (ca. 1381), Geoffrey CHAUCER presents his narrator as falling asleep reading the *Dream of Scipio,* and having his own dream vision. But in a more general sense, Macrobius's Neoplatonism influenced medieval thought on a deep level, and his writing was one of the major vehicles through which classical culture was passed to the Middle Ages.

Bibliography

Cameron, A. "The Date and Identity of Macrobius," *Journal of Roman Studies* 56 (1966): 25–38.

Kelly, Douglas. *The Conspiracy of Allusion: Description, Rewriting, and Authorship from Macrobius to Medieval Romance.* Leiden, The Netherlands: Brill, 1999.

Macrobius. *Commentary on the Dream of Scipio.* Translated with an introduction and notes by William Harris Stahl. New York: Columbia University Press, 1952.

———. *The Saturnalia.* Translated with an introduction and notes by Percival Vaughan Davies. New York: Columbia University Press, 1969.

Māhadēviyakka (Mahadevi) (12th century)

Māhadēviyakka was one of the poet-saints of the Virashaiva bhakti community, a spiritual movement particularly devoted to Siva, one of the three great gods of Hinduism. The *-akka* in her name means "elder sister," suggesting a preeminent position in the spiritual family of bhakti devotees. This movement opposed the traditional Hindu caste system and what they saw as the mechanical rituals of the priesthood. is one of a number of women involved in the movement. Although Māhadēviyakka was married to a king, and although BASAVANNA (the apparent leader of the bhakti movement) was a Brahmin (the highest caste), many members of the movement came from the lower castes, who were generally illiterate. Māhadēviyakka, like the other Virashaiva poet-saints, wrote in the Kannada language of southern India, and typically composed short poems called *vacanas* (literally "sayings" or "utterances"). *Vacanas* tended to be colloquial and direct, rather than learned or obscure.

Tradition says that Māhadēviyakka was born in Udutaki in Sivamogga, and that a *guru,* or spiritual teacher, initiated her into the worship of Śiva at the age of 10. She is said to have grown into a beautiful woman with long tresses. She was apparently forced into a marriage with the local king, Koushika—

some say only to save her parents' lives—but she never considered it to be a true marriage, because, as she said, she was already married to Śiva, whom she calls Cenna Mallikarjuna ("Lord white as jasmine"). She even says in one poem that she intends to "cuckold her husband with Śiva."

Clearly unhappy in the marriage, Mahadeviyakka ran away from her husband. Tradition says that she wandered naked in the countryside after leaving her marriage, covered only with her long hair. In defiance of societal norms, she discarded the material trappings of society and opened herself to total communion with Śiva. In a poem about her nakedness, she declares:

To the shameless girl
wearing the White Jasmine Lord's
light of morning,
you fool,
where's the need for cover and jewel?

(Ramanujan 1973, 124)

Eventually Māhadēviyakka came to the bhakti community at Kalyanna, where a group like herself was advocating the radical reform of the Hindu caste system and the rejection of elaborate ritual in order to emphasize a more personal religion of the heart. This personal quest for religious truth was particularly important for Māhadēviyakka. Her spiritual attitude was certainly a mystical one, one that stressed a personal experience of God. For her, the total immersion in the love of God and the transcendence of the physical world was the ultimate religious experience. "I burn/desiring what the heart desires," she says in one poem: "Cut through, O lord,/my heart's greed,/and show me/your way out,/O lord white as jasmine" (Ramanujan 1973, 17).

She is said to have lived the final years of her life in a cave and to have died young, in her twenties. Yet her 350 poems have left a remarkable record of female spirituality in medieval India.

Bibliography

Ramanujan, A. K., ed. and trans. *Speaking of Siva.* Harmondsworth, U.K.: Penguin, 1973.

Maiden in the mor lay (early 14th century)

Maiden in the mor lay is an enigmatic and haunting Middle English lyric popular in the early 14th century. The text consists of four stanzas of seven short lines each, full of repetitions (the first two lines of each stanza are repeated in lines five and six, while line three is repeated in line four). The final, slightly longer line completes the focus of the verse, in all but the first stanza answering a question asked in the first line: What did the maiden eat? The *primerole* (i.e., primrose) and the violet. What did she drink? The cold water of the well-spring. What was her bower? The red rose and the lily flower.

Between 1317 and 1360, Richard de Ledrede, the Franciscan bishop of Ossory in Ireland, complained that the minor clergy of his cathedral spent their time singing scandalous secular lyrics in English and French. He composed some 60 Latin lyrics to be sung to the tunes of the secular verses, some of whose titles were preserved to indicate which tunes the Latin lyrics were intended to use. One of these was "Maiden in the mor." The text of the English lyric is preserved, apparently somewhat serendipitously, on a narrow strip of parchment that preserves 12 short pieces, including several dance songs (among them the lyric *Ich am of Irelaund* that inspired Yeats's poem "I am of Ireland"). The parchment scrap was attached to the Bodleian manuscript Rawlinson D 913, and the short poems contained thereon are known as the "Rawlinson lyrics."

Though almost all readers are charmed by the incantation-like tone of *Maiden in the mor,* interpretations of the text have varied widely. Robertson (1951) interpreted the poem as religious allegory, claiming that the moor represented the wilderness of the world before the coming of Jesus Christ, while the cold water of the well symbolized the grace of God. The maiden was the Virgin Mary, the primrose a symbol of her earthly beauty, and the violet a figure of humility, while the rose and the lily had their conventional medieval connotations of charity and purity—all qualities associated chiefly with the Virgin.

Other scholars, however, like the bishop of Ossory, have seen the poem as secular, even pagan. Speirs describes the maiden as a faery being, the

Spirit of the well-spring. He speculated that the poem was connected with fertility dances aimed at magically influencing the forces of nature. Peter Dronke (1966) sees a relationship between the Moor Maiden and a water sprite of Germanic legend who, according to myth, appeared at dances and charmed men, but had to return to the moor at a preordained time lest she die.

No single interpretation is accepted by a consensus of scholars. The poem remains suggestive and ambiguous, which is part of its fascination.

Bibliography

Davies, R. T., ed. *Middle English Lyrics: A Critical Anthology.* Evanston, Ill.: Northwestern University Press, 1964.

Dronke, Peter. *The Medieval Lyric.* New York: Harper and Row, 1966.

Speirs, John. *Medieval English Poetry: The Non-Chaucerian Tradition.* London: Faber and Faber, 1957.

Robertson, D. W., Jr. "Historical Criticism." In *English Institute Essays: 1950,* edited by A. S. Downer, 3–31. New York: Columbia University Press, 1951.

Maimonides, Moses (1135–1204)

Moses ben Maimon, known as Maimonides throughout Europe, was the most important Jewish philosopher of the Middle Ages, one of the most important thinkers in the entire history of Judaism, and one of the most influential religious scholars of any time period. He wrote most of his works in Arabic, except for the *Mishneh Torah,* his great codification of the Jewish Law, written in Hebrew. His GUIDE FOR THE PERPLEXED (*Dalālat al-Ha'irin*) was known to Jewish, Muslim, and Christian philosophers, and influenced the thought of St. Thomas AQUINAS.

Maimonides was born in Córdoba in Islamic Spain in 1135, and received a thorough early training in rabbinical tradition as well as the sciences and philosophy. When the fanatical Almohads came to power in 1148, Maimonides and his family fled to Morocco and subsequently to Palestine before finally settling in Egypt in 1165. Maimonides continued his studies, with his older brother David supported the family through merchant activities. But when David's ship went down in the Indian Ocean, Maimonides turned to medicine to earn money. His renown as a physician became widespread, and he was eventually named court physician to the great Egyptian vizier, the famous Saladin (Muslim hero of the Third Crusade). But his fame as a rabbinical scholar was even more widespread, as Jews from throughout the world addressed questions to him. He was ultimately named head, or *Nagid,* of all the Egyptian Jews. He died in 1204, and was buried in the city of Tiberius in Palestine.

Maimonides composed a number of medical treatises and one philosophical work on logic, but his earliest important work, his *Book of Illumination,* is a commentary on the basic rabbinical text, the Mishneh. Begun when he was 23 and completed a decade later in 1168, the text includes Maimonides' famous 13 principles of the Jewish faith. His second major work was the *Mishneh Torah,* in which Maimonides codified the whole of Jewish law, a task no one had undertaken before. Although conservative Jews worried that Maimonides' code would discourage ordinary Jews from studying the Talmud any more, the *Mishneh Torah* became a standard guide, and later served as the basis for the 16th-century code called the *Shulkhan Arukh,* which Orthodox Jews still consider authoritative today. Nonetheless, *Guide for the Perplexed* is probably Maimonides' most important work.

For modern Jews, Maimonides is probably the most widely studied of scholars. In Hebrew he is known as the "Rambam," from the acronym of "Rabbi Moses ben Maimon." It was commonly said of him that from Moses the prophet until Moses ben Maimon, there had been no one like him.

Bibliography

Buijs, Joseph A. *Maimonides: A Collection of Critical Essays.* Notre Dame, Ind.: University of Notre Dame Press, 1988.

Diamond, James Arthur. *Maimonides and the Hermeneutics of Concealment: Deciphering Scripture and Midrash in The Guide of the Perplexed.* Albany: State University of New York Press, 2002.

Dobbs-Weinstein, Idit. *Maimonides and St. Thomas on the Limits of Reason.* Albany: State University of New York Press, 1995.

Fox, Marvin. *Interpreting Maimonides: Studies in Methodology, Metaphysics, and Moral Philosophy.* Chicago: University of Chicago Press, 1990.

Herschel, Abraham Joshua. *Maimonides: A Biography.* Translated from the German text by Joachim Neugroschel. New York: Farrar, Straus, Giroux, 1982.

Leaman, Oliver. *Moses Maimonides.* London: Routledge, 1990.

Maimonides, Moses. *The Guide for the Perplexed.* Translated with an introduction and notes by Shlomo Pines. With an introductory essay by Leo Strauss. Chicago: University of Chicago Press, 1963.

———. *The Guide for the Perplexed.* Abridged with introduction and commentary by Julius Guttmann. Translated from the Arabic by Chaim Rabin. With a new introduction by Daniel H. Frank. Indianapolis, Ind.: Hackett, 1995.

———. *Maimonides' Introduction to the Talmud: A Translation of the Rambam's Introduction to his Commentary on the Mishna.* Translated and annotated by Zvi L. Lampel. New York: Judaic Press, 1975.

Russell, H. M., and J. Weinberg, trans. *The Book of Knowledge: From the Mishneh Torah of Maimonides.* New York: Ktav, 1983.

Malory, Sir Thomas (ca. 1410–1471)

Thomas Malory is the supposed author of *Le* MORTE *D*ARTHUR, the last medieval English version of the Arthurian chivalric romances, which was published by William CAXTON in 1485. What we know of Malory's life has been gleaned from his book and from scanty court records. For many years, it was believed that the only accurate biographical statement was found at the end of *Le Morte Darthur,* which states that the book was finished in prison in the ninth year of the reign of Edward IV (March 1469–March 1470), a statement that provides little direction. Critical controversy over the exact identity of Malory continues to plague scholars; however, in 1934, another version of the *Morte* besides Caxton's was discovered. It contained not the seamless 21 books presented by Caxton, but rather eight separate ROMANCES to which were appended personal remarks. At the end of the first of these, the author identifies himself as "knight presoner Sir Thomas Malleore," thus lending credence to the identification discussed below.

Thomas Malory (the standardized modern spelling) of Newbold Revell, Warwickshire, was born anywhere between 1405 and 1416 into an established East Midlands gentry family. His father, John Malory, was an esquire who owned land not only in Warwickshire, but also in Northamptonshire and Leicestershire. John served as sheriff twice and also as a member of Parliament and a justice of the peace. He married Philippa Chetwynd, and records indicate that besides a son, Thomas, they also had at least three daughters.

Nothing more is known of young Thomas. At the age of 23, records indicate that he was a respected landowner who was increasingly interested in politics. By 1441, he had been knighted. Sometime in these years, he also married Elizabeth Walsh of Wanlip, with whom he had a son, Robert. During these years, he also served in the retinue of Richard Beauchamp, the earl of Warwickshire (known as the "Father of Courtesy"), perhaps at Calais, but certainly in France. Malory was also elected a member of Parliament for Warwickshire in 1445, serving primarily on the tax-exemption commission.

Prior to his election, Malory had experienced his first brush with the law. In 1443, he was accused of wounding and imprisoning Thomas Smith, although the charges were soon dismissed. This began a pattern that would haunt Malory for the rest of his life, and from 1450 onward, he was often either in prison or on the run. His first major crime seems to have been taking part in a plot to ambush and murder the duke of Buckingham early in 1450. In May 1450, Malory was accused, for the first time, of raping Joan Smith. The actual charges leveled against Malory are intriguing. Instead of being accused of abduction, which was fairly standard in rape cases, the records read *cum ea carnaliter* ("he lay with her carnally"), and the complaint was not filed by Joan, but rather by her husband, Thomas. Three months later, in August

1450, Malory is once again accused of raping Joan Smith, and also of stealing 40 pounds of items from her husband.

Besides rape and ambush, Malory was also accused of various forms of extortion and theft throughout 1450–51, including personal assault, breaking and entering, cattle rustling, and poaching. In mid-1451, he was arrested and imprisoned at Coleshill in Warwickshire, but quickly escaped by swimming the moat. He then supposedly broke into an abbey (Abbey Coombe), assaulted the abbot, tormented the monks, stole much of the treasury, and trashed the monastery. By 1452, he was once again in prison, this time in London, awaiting trial.

Malory pled "not guilty" to each and every charge, yet mostly remained in prison. In 1456, under the protectorship of the duke of York, Malory received a royal pardon, but it was ignored until 1460 when the Yorkists actually took the throne. Malory appears to have changed sides frequently during the Wars of the Roses, and in 1468, he was specifically excluded from the general amnesties issued by Edward IV.

In October 1470, the Lancastrians returned to power and freed the members of their party still imprisoned. Six months later, Thomas Malory died. He was buried in Greyfriars, Newgate, one of the most fashionable churches of its day. Originally his grave bore a great marble tombstone, now destroyed. However, the inscription was preserved in parish records. It names Malory a *valens miles* ("valiant knight"). It also lists the date of his death as March 14, 1470, which under the present-day calendar would be 1471.

Malory supposedly wrote *Le Morte Darthur* while he was in prison, perhaps as quickly as within two years. It is a varied composition, based on French prose romances and ancient Welsh legends, all filtered through Malory's own perspective. It is this final point that is, perhaps, the most offensive to many.

There are other candidates that have been suggested as the Malory who wrote *Le Morte Darthur,* and for a long time, scholars and fans alike strove to uncover a different identity for Thomas Malory than the habitual felon from Newbold Revell whose life seems so inconsistent with the chivalry he extols in his book. For example, John Bale conjectured that the author of the *Morte,* Malory or not, was Welsh, primarily because many of the Arthurian adventures take place there. The variant spellings of his surname, including Maleore and Mallorie, also provided hope, mostly unfounded after the 1934 discovery. A Thomas Malory from Yorkshire has been discovered, but he was probably too young to have written the text. Another Thomas Malory, from Cambridgeshire, has been suggested, but this Malory never seems to have been imprisoned. The Warwickshire Malory seems the candidate most likely to have been the author. Overall, it seems that many are offended that the man who wrote the most enduring version of the great chivalric romances was himself such a scoundrel. However, sifting through the charges brings a new understanding—many of the accusations and prison terms appear to be political side effects from the Wars of the Roses, and the "rape" charges appear to have been the result of a longstanding extramarital affair. Both of these situations are reflected in the *Morte* itself, perhaps explaining in part why it has become the standard source for later versions of the Arthurian legend.

Bibliography

Archibald, Elizabeth, and A. S. G. Edwards, eds. *A Companion to Malory.* Cambridge: D. S. Brewer, 1996.

Field, P. J. C. *The Life and Times of Sir Thomas Malory.* Cambridge: D. S. Brewer, 1993.

Matthew, William. *The Ill-Framed Knight: A Skeptical Inquiry into the Identity of Sir Thomas Malory.* Berkeley: University of California Press, 1966.

McCarthy, Terence. *An Introduction to Malory.* Rev. ed. Woodbridge, Suffolk, U.K.: Boydell and Brewer, 1991.

Riddy, Felicity. *Sir Thomas Malory.* Leiden: Brill, 1987.

Michelle M. Sauer

Manciple's Tale, The Geoffrey Chaucer (ca. 1396)

Chaucer's *Manciple's Tale* is the last fictional text in *The Canterbury Tales,* in most manuscripts coming immediately before the Parson's sermon on the Seven Deadly Sins that ends the collection. A BEAST FABLE like *The NUN'S PRIEST'S TALE,* the Manciple's has neither the charm nor the joy in linguistic play apparent in that tale of Chaunticleer and the fox. But it does raise significant questions, particularly about the use of language. Though it uses a widespread folklore motif of the "tell-tale bird," the immediate source of Chaucer's tale may have been the very popular book of the *SEVEN SAGES OF ROME,* a text Chaucer mentions in the prologue to *The WIFE OF BATH'S TALE.* But Chaucer also knew a version of the story told in GOWER'S *CONFESSIO AMANTIS,* and probably the original version in Ovid's *Metamorphoses* as well.

The Manciple's Tale is the story of Phoebus (Apollo), described in the tale as a great archer who killed the serpent Pithoun, and as the greatest singer and musician on earth. He owns a beautiful white crow with a magnificent singing voice and the ability to speak. He also has a beautiful new wife. The jealous Phoebus keeps his wife under close scrutiny, but the narrator of the tale comments that anyone who thinks he can guard a woman will find himself mistaken. The wife takes a lover, despite Phoebus's watchful eye, and it is the crow that tells him of his wife's betrayal. In rage, Phoebus kills his wife. Then, in grief-stricken repentance, he breaks his musical instruments as well as his bow. Then he turns on the crow, cursing it so that it loses its beautiful song as well as its ability to speak, and its feathers turn to black. The tale ends with the moral, "Kepe wel thy tonge, and thenk upon the crowe" (Benson 1987, 286, l. 362).

Critics have not always thought highly of *The Manciple's Tale,* though more recent scholars have seen a good deal of irony in the tale—for example, in the 54 lines that recommend verbal restraint. Others, considering more specifically the Manciple narrator (a Manciple was a low-level official that purchased provisions for a college), have suggested the story reflects a servant's dilemma of how to speak the truth without getting into trouble. But others have seen the tale, coming as it does near the end of the *Canterbury Tales,* as revisiting the theme of proper and improper uses of language, and the "sentence and solaas" (instructiveness and entertainment) that were initially proposed as criteria for judging the tales.

Bibliography

Benson, Larry, et al. *The Riverside Chaucer.* 3rd ed. Boston: Houghton Mifflin, 1987.

Ginsberg, Warren. "Chaucer's Canterbury Poetics: Irony, Allegory, and the *Prologue* to *The Manciple's Tale,*" *Studies in the Age of Chaucer* 18 (1996): 55–89.

Grudin, Michaela Paasche. "Chaucer's *Manciple's Tale* and the Poetics of Guile," *Chaucer Review* 25 (1991): 329–342.

Storm, Mel. "Speech, Circumspection, and Orthodontics in *The Manciple's Prologue* and *Tale* and the Wife of Bath's Portrait," *Studies in Philology* 96 (1999): 109–126.

Mandeville, John (fl. 1357)

Although most people in the 14th and 15th centuries who were familiar with MARCO POLO'S *Travels* (*Le divisament dou Monde,* 1299) decried his account as fantastic and as a pack of lies, the much more imaginary and fanciful *Travels* by the English author John Mandeville enjoyed a considerably higher reputation and was regarded as deeply authoritative for centuries despite its almost entirely fictional nature. Even Christopher Columbus consulted Mandeville in preparation for his journey to the West. We know very little of Mandeville, except what he tells us himself in his book. He claims to have been an English knight from St. Alban who traveled to Egypt, served under the sultan, and then made his way to the Far East, where he served the great khan from 1322 to 1356. Modern English scholars generally discount his claim of English origin, whereas Belgian and French scholars mostly assume that he was an Englishman who lived at Liège.

Mandeville wrote the account of his travels in Anglo-Norman, a variant of medieval French spoken in England after William the Conqueror had established his authority over that country in 1066. Mandeville's *Travels,* first composed sometime between 1356 and 1366, but probably published first in 1357, were extraordinarily popular and were translated until 1400 into practically every European language, including Czech, Danish, Dutch, French, German, Irish, Latin, and Spanish. Counting all language versions, there are some 300 copies extant today (Polo's *Travels* have survived only in about 70 copies). After the invention of the printing press ca. 1450, Mandeville's *Travels* were also printed many times all over Europe because readers simply enjoyed, as the author states himself, "newe thinges and newe tydynges ben plesant to here" (228).

The huge number of manuscripts can be divided into two groups—an insular, English group, and a continental version. The latter group connects the author with two people, Jean de Bourgogne (d. 1372) and Jean d'Outremeuse (1338–1400), but it has remained unclear what the relationship between them and Mandeville might have been. The continental version, today still extant in 32 manuscripts, originates from a French manuscript compiled in 1371 by the Paris stationery Raoul d'Orléans for Gervaise Crétain (or for Charles V of France); it was first printed in 1480. The insular group, extant in 23 manuscripts, began quite some time before 1390 when a Latin translation was written at Abington Abbey. This English version was used by CHAUCER and the poet of *CLEANNESS*. The third version, the Liège version, is extant in seven manuscripts and originated at Liège in 1373. In his prologue, however, Mandeville claims that he translated his text from Latin into French, and then again from French into English so that he could reach out to the widest audience and appeal to their curiosity.

Mandeville's *Travels* heavily depend on a long and ancient tradition of monster lore (*teratology*), deriving much material from Pliny, Aethicus, Solinus, and Herodotus. He also drew from other travel accounts, such as those by the monks Odoric of Pordenone and John of Plano de Carpini, and the merchant Balducci Pegolotti. In fact, considering the large number of sources apparently used by John Mandeville, such as Albert of Aix's *Historia Hierosolymitanae expeditionis* (1125), the *Letter of Prester John* (ca. 1165), Jacopo de Voragine's GOLDEN LEGEND (*Legenda aurea*, ca. 1275), William von Boldensele's *Itinerarius* (1337), Caesarius of Heisterbach's *Dialogus Miraculorum* (ca. 1223), and Brunetto Latini's *Li Livres dou Trésor* (ca. 1264), John Mandeville's *Travels* prove to be an inspired agglomeration of fictional and nonfictional texts that indeed appealed to a large audience all over medieval and early-modern Europe. Surprisingly, Mandeville did not resort to Bartholomaeus Anglicus's encyclopedic *De proprietatibus rerum* (ca. 1245) and Ranulf HIGDEN's *Polychronicon* (ca. 1347), both highly popular, more or less scientific texts from late medieval England, which might suggest that Mandeville did not live in England when he composed his *Travels*. Overall, however, Mandeville created his influential text on the basis of vast library holdings, summarizing the current knowledge of world geography. In all likelihood they were not the results of real travel experiences.

The travel account takes the reader from England to Constantinople, from there to the Holy Land, Cyprus, Babylon, Egypt, Sicily, then back to Mount Sinai, Jerusalem, the Dead Sea, the River Jordan, Syria, Albania, and Libya, then to India (with a separate chapter on the alleged apostle St. Thomas), Java, and finally to Cathay in the Far East (perhaps China), ruled by the great khan. Mandeville's greatest interest focuses on the organization of the court of that ruler, and the religion and customs of the Tatars, but he does not hesitate quickly to switch to Persia and fanciful countries beyond Cathay. We also hear of the mythical Prester John and his Christian kingdom somewhere in the middle of Asia, of places associated with paradise and hell, and outlying posts in the earthly sphere, not overlooking the enigmatic country of the Amazons. Marco Polo in essence had attempted to relate his personal experiences as accurately as possible and to provide concrete information for merchants and other businessmen interested in the trade with the East. By contrast, John Mandeville created a most fanciful and highly effective fictional blend of theological, geographical, literary, and chronological accounts about the Holy Land, Egypt, Tatary, and China, which deeply appealed to popular interests in the exotic and enigmatic Orient. Directly appealing to widespread curiosity about the wonders of the East and relying on a large number of learned treatises dealing with the East, Mandeville wrote one of the most successful best sellers of his time and found avid readers such as Jean, duke of Berry (1340–1416), CHRISTINE DE PIZAN (1364–1430), Leonardo da Vinci (1452–1519), Martin Behaim (1459–1507), Martin Frobisher (1535?–94), and Richard Hakluyt (1552?–1616).

Bibliography

Mandeville, Sir John. *The Travels of Sir John Mandeville.* Translated with Introduction by C. W. R. D. Moseley. Harmondsworth, U.K.: Penguin, 1983.

Seymour, M. C. *Sir John Mandeville.* Aldershot, U.K.: Variorum, 1993.

———, ed. *Mandeville's Travels.* Oxford: Clarendon Press, 1967.

———. *Mandeville's Travels: The Defective Version.* Oxford: Oxford University Press, 2002.

Tzanaki, Rosemary. *Mandeville's Medieval Audiences: A Study on the Reception of the Book of Sir John Mandeville (1371–1550).* Aldershot, U.K.: Ashgate, 2003.

Albrecht Classen

Mankind (ca. 1465)

With the exception of *EVERYMAN, Mankind* is probably the best-known and most often studied late medieval MORALITY PLAY. A verse drama in 914 lines, *Mankind* is written in the East Midland dialect of MIDDLE ENGLISH, and is known to have been performed in East Anglia, both in Cambridgeshire and in Norfolk. With *The CASTLE OF PERSEVERANCE* and *Wisdom, Mankind* is one of a group of dramas called the "Macro Plays," so named after the Reverend Cox Macro (1683–1767), the earliest known owner of the single manuscript in which they survive. There is no indication that the play was particularly popular in its own time, nor was it much performed or printed in the ensuing centuries, not because of any lack of quality but because of a good deal of vulgar and even obscene language that permeates the play. In recent decades, however, appreciation of the play has grown, and nowadays it is admired for its liveliness, its psychological "realism," and its incorporation of popular theatrical elements that contribute to its unified dramatic effect.

As in most morality plays, the characters of *Mankind* are personified abstractions presenting an ALLEGORY of human salvation—of vices and virtues in conflict over a human soul. Mankind, the protagonist, clearly represents the individual human being. The other main character of the play is Mercy, depicted not, as in other allegories, as one of the daughters of God, but rather as Mankind's father confessor—hence, the character does not properly represent the quality of mercy itself but rather the means by which human beings may attain God's mercy. Mercy opens the play with a sermon on repentance, during which Mischief, the play's chief VICE, enters and ridicules Mercy's speech. The manuscript is missing a leaf at this early point, but when the story resumes, three minor vices—New Guise ("latest fashion," or "the pride of life"), Nowadays (apparently the desire for instant gratification), and Nought (that is, vanity)—are dancing around Mercy and mocking him mercilessly and spewing out blasphemies and vulgarities. The three are chased off, after which Mercy provides Mankind with several precepts for his spiritual guidance: Live a life of moderation, he is told—like a knight of Christ, Mankind must fight against the temptations of the flesh, the world, and the devil. This advice apparently strengthens Mankind's resolve. He goes to till his land, his agricultural labor suggesting a physical remedy to the sin of sloth (and no doubt also representing a spiritual labor), but also typologically recalling Adam, and reinforcing Mankind's identification with all of fallen humanity. When New Guise, Nowadays, and Nought reappear, Mankind chases them off with his spade.

Having failed to tempt Mankind by the attractions of vice, Mischief switches to a strategy designed to convince Mankind of the difficulty of achieving virtue, despite his hard work. First, he advises New Guise, Nowadays, and Nought to conjure up a true devil, Titvillius. The devil appears and sends his three conjurers off to steal money and horses. Meanwhile, Mankind has gathered seeds for sowing his land, but Titvillius, invisible to Mankind, puts boards in the earth to make it impossible for Mankind to plant his seeds. Titvillius also interrupts Mankind's prayers, and puts it into his head that Mercy is not to be trusted, calling him a married priest, a fugitive criminal, and a horse thief. The devil then advises Mankind to go sport himself with a prostitute, and then to beg pardon of New Guise, Nowadays, and Nought for chasing them off with his shovel. The scene shifts to a mock-court established by Mischief. Mankind appears in new, fashionable garb furnished by New Guise, and is made to swear in court that he will become a thief and a killer. To depict his protagonist's fall, the playwright now has Mankind speak in the language of the vices, rather than in Mercy's style as he had previously. Now Mischief tries to push Mankind to despair, hoping to tempt him to suicide. Mankind, preparing to hang himself, is ultimately rescued by Mercy, who has the last word in the text, urging mankind to confession and to reconciliation with God.

There is no known source for the play, but, particularly in its emphasis on labor as an antidote to sloth, *Mankind* clearly draws heavily from the Old Testament book of Job, and to some extent from William LANGLAND's *PIERS PLOWMAN* as well. Some scholars have also compared its style with 15th-century Dominican and Franciscan preaching style. Furthermore, the playwright was conscientious about the meter of his verse, particularly in the lines of Mercy and Mankind, who speak in four-line stanzas rhyming *abab*.

Mankind calls for very simple staging: All that is needed for the set is a stage wide enough to represent Mankind's plot of land, and the only prop necessary is Mankind's spade. The simplicity of the production has led scholars to speculate that a professional touring troupe acted the play, though there is some debate as to whether the play was performed outdoors or in a great hall of similar space indoors. The play was most likely performed as a part of the carnivalesque Shrovetide celebration on the eve of Lent—such a context would explain the broad humor of the play. The fact that the vices at one point make the audience sing an obscene Christmas song does not preclude a Shrovetide performance, since the medieval Christmas celebration extended until the beginning of Lent.

The interplay between actors and audience is important for the effect of this play. As Pamela King points out, when the audience sings with the vices, they have sinned through "idleness of the tongue," anticipating the fall of Mankind. When before calling up the devil, the vices take up a collection from the audience, they themselves have engaged in the ritual of a black mass that helps bring about Mankind's overthrow (250–251). As Mankind allegorically represents all humankind, the audience, as a part of mankind, participates in the fall into sin. In the end, the conventional Christian themes of the play—the danger of demonic temptation (especially for an idle mind), the importance of reason controlling bodily passions, the infinite mercy of God—are likely less moving and effective for the audience than their participation in the performance itself, a participation that makes very real the abstract themes.

Bibliography

Bevington, David, ed. *Medieval Drama.* Boston: Houghton-Mifflin, 1957.

Coogan, Mary P. *An Interpretation of the Moral Play, "Mankind."* Washington, D.C.: Catholic University Press, 1947.

Wickham, Glynne. *The Medieval Theatre.* Cambridge: Cambridge University Press, 1987.

Mannyng, Robert, of Brunne (Bourne) (ca. 1283–ca. 1340)

All we know about Robert Mannyng is the little he tells us in his two major poems—*Handlyng Synne* (1303–17), the first confessional manual in English, and *The Story of England,* a verse chronicle extending through the reign of Edward I. Mannyng was born at Brunne (or Bourne) in Lincolnshire, and studied at Cambridge between about 1298 and 1302. Shortly thereafter he entered the priory at Sempringham (six miles from Brunne), the founding house of the Gilbertine order. Mannyng was probably a canon there. Almost immediately he began work on *Handlyng Synne,* which he completed about 1317. After that, we know only that at some point he left Sempringham to reside at the Gilbertine Priory of Sixhills, because he claims that as his residence in his *Story of England.* That poem, according to the author's own testimony, was finished in 1338, after which we know nothing of Mannyng's life.

Of the two works, *Handlyng Synne* is by far the better known. The poem, in 12,638 lines of octosyllabic (eight-syllable) rhyming couplets, is essentially a translation of an Anglo-Norman text, *Le Manuel des Péchés,* composed in Mannyng's Lincolnshire in about 1260. (The French poem was originally attributed to William of Waddington, but most likely he was merely the scribe.) These poems are part of a proliferation of such texts in the wake of the Fourth Lateran Council of 1215 and subsequent bishops' decrees, which admonished all Christians to make regular confession to their priests. A number of writers responded by producing guides to the meaning and practice of confession. *Handlyng Synne* is aimed at the laity (thus its composition in English) with the intent of giving them instruction on the recognition of sin in preparation for confession. In the prologue to the work, Mannyng explains his title by describing our "handling" of sin in three ways: His text will demonstrate how we all "handle" sin in our daily lives without always realizing it; how we need to examine our sins, or "handle" them, by reflecting upon them, so that we can then "handle" them in confession and thereby free ourselves of their taint. Mannyng goes on to structure his text according to the Ten Commandments, the Seven Deadly Sins, the specific sin of sacrilege, the seven sacraments, the 12 points of "shrift" (or confession), and the 12 graces that proceed from those points. The poem ends with a caution against despair: Mannyng makes it clear that one who makes a full and proper confession can be assured of God's forgiveness. Mannyng's poem says nothing about penance—he makes it clear that one must confess to a priest to receive the proper penance. His only task is to help the audience recognize sin.

It seems clear that Mannyng wanted his work to be read aloud to laymen, mainly to instruct them, but also to provide an alternative to what he thought of as profane tales that they might typically hear at social gatherings. Accordingly Mannyng adds to his source by including a large number of often quite entertaining exempla or illustrations for the various sins he discusses, which he gleans from other texts, from folklore, and from other oral sources. His best-known story is the "Dancers of Colbek." In this story, a group of carolers on Christmas Eve are dancing in a churchyard. Despite warnings and threats from the priest, the carolers refuse to stop dancing and attend Mass. For their sacrilege the priest curses them and condemns them to continue dancing for an entire year. The priest finds to his chagrin, however, that one of the dancers is his own daughter, Ave. When the girl's brother attempts to pull her from the endless dance, he pulls her arm off. The curse finally abates after a year, and the dancers are able to return to normal—all except the priest's daughter, who dies. In grief the priest dies shortly thereafter. It is typical of Mannyng, who displays a genuine antipathy to social injustice, that his story of the carolers raises our sympathies for the dancers far more than for the self-righteous priest who curses them.

Mannyng's other major work, *The Story of England,* is also a close translation (in some 17,000 lines) of an Anglo-Norman text, a chronicle by Peter of Langtoft, a canon from Bridlington. In his prologue Mannyng says that he was commissioned by Robert of Malton to translate Langtoft. The text, which outlines the history of England from the time of Noah through the reign of Edward I (d. 1307), is also addressed to a lay audience, whom Mannyng intends to instruct on the history of their native land. For the first part of the chronicle, however, Mannyng relies less on Langtoft than on WACE's *Roman de Brut,* which he finds more detailed and lively. He also uses Wace's source, GEOFFREY OF MONMOUTH, as well as the Venerable BEDE and other Latin sources. But for the second part of his poem, Mannyng relies almost exclusively on Langtoft.

Bibliography

Crosby, Ruth. "Robert Mannyng of Brunne: A New Biography," *PMLA* 57 (1942): 15–28.

Mannyng, Robert. *Robert Mannyng of Brunne: Handlyng Synne.* Edited by Idelle Sullens. Medieval and Renaissance Texts and Studies 14. Binghamton: State University of New York Press, 1983.

Robertson, D. W., Jr. "The Cultural Tradition of *Handlyng Synne,*" *Speculum* 22 (1947): 162–185.

Man of Law's Tale, The Geoffrey Chaucer (ca. 1390)

One of CHAUCER's *CANTERBURY TALES, The Man of Law's Tale* relates the story of Dame Constance, a creature of pathos whose life is a series of trials to her Christian faith, through all of which she remains steadfast and from all of which she is miraculously saved through God's providence. Chaucer based his tale on an Anglo-Norman story by Nicholas TRIVET, but also seems clearly to have been aware of John GOWER's version of the story in his *CONFESSIO AMANTIS.*

Chaucer's tale is divided into three parts. In part one a group of Syrian merchants are so impressed by the beautiful Constance, daughter of the Roman emperor, that they extol her virtues to their Sultan. In true COURTLY LOVE fashion, the Sultan falls in love with Constance purely through her reputation, and sues for her hand in marriage. On the condition that the Sultan agree to be baptized along with all who owe him fealty, the Emperor agrees to let his daughter marry the Syrian prince. But the Sultan's mother, angered at her son's betrayal of Islam, stirs up enmity toward him and his new bride.

Through the Sultaness's machinations, the Sultan and all his court are massacred at the banquet welcoming Constance, and she herself is set adrift on the sea in a rudderless boat. She drifts all the way to Northumbria, where she is befriended and sheltered by the constable and his wife, Hermengild, whom she converts to Christianity. But Constance spurns the advances of a lustful knight, and in retaliation he cuts Hermengild's throat while she sleeps, leaving the knife next to Constance, thus framing her for the murder. When the king, Alla, holds court to investigate the matter, the evil knight is struck dead. Recognizing her virtue, Alla marries Constance. But when she bears a son, Maurice, in Alla's absence, her mother-in-law Donegild sends forged letters to the king saying that Constance has borne a monster. Through Donegild's plotting, Constance and her son are set adrift, again, in the rudderless boat.

In the third part of the tale, Constance is nearly raped by a steward who comes aboard her boat, but God protects her and the villain is thrown overboard. She is ultimately rescued by a Roman senator returning from Syria, where the Romans have taken revenge for the Sultaness's treachery. The senator brings Constance and Maurice to Rome, where Alla has come on pilgrimage as penance for killing his mother to avenge Constance. Catching sight of Maurice, Alla sees his resemblance to Constance, and the three are reunited, after which Constance is also restored to her father. She returns to Northumbria with Alla, and when he dies, returns to her father in Rome. When the emperor dies, Maurice inherits the Roman throne.

The Man of Law's Tale has been called a secular saint's life, a romance with Constance as a passive romantic heroine, and also a story with clear folktale elements, particularly the motif of the "calumniated wife," complete with not one but two wicked stepmothers. Most accurately it is probably what Derek Pearsall has called it: "an extended exemplum of God's grace granted to patience and constant faith" (Pearsall 262). But what is most distinctive about *The Man of Law's Tale,* and what sets it apart from the Trivet and Gower analogues, is its highly rhetorical style. Like his other religious tales (*The PRIORESS'S TALE, The SECOND NUN'S TALE, The CLERK'S TALE*), *The Man of Law's Tale* is written in RHYME ROYAL stanzas, a form Chaucer seems to have equated with highly serious work. But more than that, Chaucer uses a highly emotional tone, full of apostrophes and other figures recommended by medieval rhetoricians designed to appeal to the reader's emotions, evoke pity for his heroine, and provide moral commentary. Before her murder trial, the narrator addresses her and calls on Christ to defend her: "Allas! Custance, thou hast no championn," he says (Benson 1987, l. 631), except for him who died for our redemption.

Bibliography

Benson, Larry, et al., ed. *The Riverside Chaucer.* 3rd ed. Boston: Houghton-Mifflin, 1987.

Cooper, Helen. *Oxford Guides to Chaucer: The Canterbury Tales.* Oxford: Clarendon Press, 1989.

Delaney, Sheila. "Womanliness in 'The Man of Law's Tale,' " in *Writing Woman: Women Writers and Women in Literature Medieval to Modern,* edited by Sheila Delany. New York: Schocken Books, 1983, 36–46.

Edwards, A. S. G. "Critical Approaches to the 'Man of Law's Tale.' " In *Chaucer's Religious Tales,* edited by C. David Benson and Elizabeth Robertson, 85–94. Cambridge, U.K.: Brewer, 1990.

Pearsall, Derek. *The Canterbury Tales.* London: Allen and Unwin, 1985.

Raybin, David. "Custance and History: Woman as Outsider in Chaucer's 'Man of Law's Tale,' " *Studies in the Age of Chaucer* 12 (1990): 65–84.

Robertson, Elizabeth. "The 'Elvyssh' Power of Constance: Christian Feminism in Geoffrey Chaucer's *The Man of Law's Tale.*" *Studies in the Age of Chaucer* 23 (2001): 143–180.

Manrique, Jorge (1440–1479)

Jorge Manrique, son of a distinguished Castilian family, was a military man by vocation and a lyric poet by avocation. He is best known for his *Coplas por la muerte de su padre don Rodrigo* (Verses on the death of his father, Don Rodrigo, 1476), an elegy that is considered one of the classics of Spanish poetry.

He was probably born at Paredes de Nava in about 1400. The father for whom Manrique composed his greatest poem was Rodrigo Manrique, count of Paredes and grand master of the Order of Santiago. Rodrigo was a renowned general, and his fourth son, Jorge, followed his father in that profession. Like his father, Jorge opposed the weak king of Castile and León, Henry IV, and supported the king's half-brother, the Infante Don Alfonso. When the young Alfonso died in 1468, the Manriques threw their support behind the other claimant to the throne, Henry's half sister Isabella "the Catholic." When civil war broke out after Henry's death in 1474, the Manriques fought for Isabella and her new husband, Ferdinand of Aragon, against supporters of rival claimants to the throne. After his father's death in 1476, Manrique continued his active support of Isabella, and distinguished himself in several conflicts, finally falling in her service doing battle against one of her chief enemies, the marqués of Villena, before the castle of Garci-Muñoz in 1479.

Manrique wrote some 50 extant lyrics, most of them undistinguished to modern tastes—they tend to be clever but conventional, though his contemporaries saw Manrique as one of the major Spanish love poets of the time. His poems also deal with religion and with the vicissitudes of Fortune. Many of these are collected in the *Cancionero general,* a large collection of verses published by Hernando del Castillo in 1511.

But the one poem on which Manrique's reputation rests is the elegy on his father, written immediately after the general's death in 1476. The poem consists of 43 stanzas of 12 lines, rhyming *abcabcdefdef.* The verse form is called *pie quebrado:* In it, most lines are eight syllables long, but every third line (that is, each *c* and *f* line) is only four syllables. In the poem Manrique laments his father's passing, celebrating his major victories and comparing him to great figures of the classical world, but puts his death into a universal context by contemplating the brevity and vanity of earthly life and giving examples of the great Spanish kings and soldiers who had passed away before. The poem ends with a climactic allegorical dialogue between Death and Don Rodrigo.

There is nothing particularly original in the elegy. The form seems to be influenced by the poetry of Jorge's uncle, Gomez Manrique (also a lesser-known lyric poet), and sentiments from the Bible, BOETHIUS, and other sources. But Manrique gives memorable expression to these commonplace sentiments. Many scholars have seen the complex tone of the elegy—which combines the medieval *contemptu mundi* (contempt for the world) tradition with the humanistic pride in personal achievement associated with the Renaissance—as evidence that Manrique was a transitional figure between the medieval and early modern periods. Manrique's influence has been widespread and lasting: His poetry has influenced writers like Lope de Vega and Pedro Salinas, and his elegy was translated into eloquent English by Longfellow in 1833.

Bibliography

Dominguez, Frank A. *Love and Remembrance: The Poetry of Jorge Manrique.* Studies in Romance Languages, no. 33. Lexington: University Press of Kentucky, 1988.

Manuel, Don Juan (1282–1348)

The most important writer of prose in 14th-century Spain was the nobleman Don Juan Manuel, prince of Castile and *adelantado mayor* (hereditary governor) of Murcia. Don Juan was the nephew of King ALFONSO X (1221–84), known as *El Sabio,* or "The Learned." He spent much of his life in political squabbles with the kings of Castile, attempting to maintain and expand his own power and influence. But he is best remembered for his prose works, in particular *El conde Lucanor* ("Count Lucanor"), a collection of 51 moral fables and folk-stories drawn from a variety of sources.

Don Juan was the grandson of King Ferdinand III, and his father Prince Manuel (Alfonso X's younger brother) died when Don Juan was only two years old. The death of his mother, Beatriz of Savoy, left the young Don Juan an orphan six years later. He was educated at the court of King Sancho IV, his cousin. In 1294, at the age of 12, Don Juan fought in his first military engagement when his territory in Murcia was attacked by a Moorish army. It was his entry into the political life of Castile, which would consume more than 40 years of Don Juan's life.

Sancho died in 1295, and his widow Dona Maria de Molina, queen mother of Castile, was regent for her nine-year-old son Ferdinand IV. Don Juan supported his uncle Prince Juan's claim to the throne, but voiced open conflict with Ferdinand and Dona Maria until, in negotiations with King James II of Aragon, Don Juan was successful in securing a promise of marriage to Constanza, James's three-year-old daughter. At that point Don Juan and James II formed an alliance against Ferdinand IV, who subsequently pronounced a death sentence on Don Juan. When Aragon and Castile formed an alliance against the Moors in 1309, Don Juan refused to join them, and instead engaged in raids on Ferdinand's territory of León. In 1312, Don Juan was finally able to marry the 12-year-old Constanza. But in that same year, Ferdinand died, replaced on the throne by his infant son Alfonso XI. In 1319, Don Juan was made one of the co-regents of Castile during the king's minority, and for six years acted essentially with royal power as the king's guardian, while a kind of anarchy raged in Castile as the various regents fought one another. In 1325, Alfonso assumed power at the age of 14, and promptly quelled any further ambitions on Don Juan's part by appointing Don Juan's political rivals to be his closest advisers.

While Don Juan began to form new alliances against Alfonso, the new king made peace by offering to marry Don Juan's young daughter, Constanza. For two years, Don Juan supported Alfonso, but when the king repudiated Constanza and broke off their engagement in 1327, imprisoning her and contracting to marry the daughter of the king of Portugal, Don Juan retaliated ferociously. He began by forming an alliance with Mahomet III, the Moorish ruler of Granada, and together they made war on Alfonso. Don Juan lost his Muslim allies after 1329 but was successful in finding a new ally in Pedro IV of Aragon, and he gained Portugal's support by betrothing the now-available Constanza to the young heir to the Portuguese throne. But when Alfonso refused to allow Constanza to travel to Portugal for her wedding in 1336, Don Juan renewed his attacks on the Castilian monarch. Defeated, Don Juan was forced into exile at Valencia until 1338. The Pact of Seville, signed by Don Juan and Alfonso in 1340, made peace between the parties, and Constanza was finally allowed to travel to Portugal.

Reconciled with Alfonso, Don Juan joined with him in wars against the Moors, and led the victorious Castilian army into Algeciras in 1344. But after that engagement, Don Juan decided to retire to his castle at Peñafiel, where he had founded a Dominican monastery and where he spent his last years peacefully, in study and in writing, until his death in 1348.

Don Juan wrote 14 literary works that we know of, and was conscientious in having accurate texts produced and kept at the Peñafiel monastery. Still, none of these original manuscripts survive, and only eight of Don Juan's 14 known works are extant at all. One of these, *Libro de los estados* (Book of the estates), is a discussion of the medieval theory of the estates, or classes of society. It contains a version of the popular story of *BARLAAM AND JOSAPHAT*, and includes Don Juan's personal recollections of his own experiences. His *Libro de las armas* tells of Don Juan's visit, at the age of 12, to the deathbed of his cousin Sancho IV, and relates Sancho's dying recollections of his violent life. But by far his best-known work is *El conde Lucanor* (also called the *Libro de Patronio*). Probably influenced by the earlier *Libro de* CALILA E DIGNA, this collection of tales is framed by a narrative in which Patronio, a servant and tutor to the young Count Lucanor, tells 51 tales as responses to questions from Lucanor about the kinds of things that might typically concern a young nobleman—how much to trust powerful neighbors, or unsupportive allies, for example. The tales—drawn from animal fables, folktales, and historical anecdotes—illustrate Patronio's practical advice on matters of diplomacy and politics, and, in the end, spiritual matters. But Don Juan's practical morality in political matters, illustrating how a statesman may need to use deceit at times, or violence at other times, has led some to see Don Juan as a precursor of Machiavelli. The fact that Don Juan was the earliest prose stylist in vernacular Castilian has also led to comparisons with other vernacular artists of the 14th century, like DANTE and CHAUCER. While a comparison with those artists may be something of a stretch, it is certainly true that, while Alfonso X had established Castilian as a language for serious literary texts, Don Juan developed it into a vehicle for a distinctive individual style.

Bibliography

Dunn, Peter N. "Don Juan Manuel: The World as Text," *Modern Language Notes* 106 (1991): 223–240.

Manuel, Don Juan. *The Book of Count Lucanor and Patronio.* Translated by John E. Keller, L. Clark Keating, and Barbara E. Gaddy. New York: Peter Lang, 1993.

Sturcken, H. Tracy. *Don Juan Manuel.* New York: Twayne, 1974.

Man'yōshū ("Collection of Ten Thousand Leaves," "Collection for Ten Thousand Generations") (eighth century)

The *Man'yōshū* is the oldest and, according to most critics, the greatest anthology of Japanese poetry. The ambiguous title may mean either "Collection of 10,000 Leaves [pages]" or "Collection for 10,000 Generations," suggesting that the editors thought the huge collection (actually 4,516 poems) would stand for many ages. The exact date of its compilation is unknown, though the latest datable poem in the collection was written in 759. The final compiler of the collection is thought to have been Ōtomo Yakamochi, one of the poets best represented in the later pages of the anthology.

According to some scholars, the impetus to form such a collection may have come from Japan's attempts to "modernize" under the threat of Chinese invasion during the TANG DYNASTY. With the Taika Reform of 645–646, Japanese emperors were attempting to reform provincial government, taxation, and land tenure to weaken the power of local chieftains and create an absolute monarchy on the model of China. The fear was that unless Japan transformed itself along Chinese lines, the Tang emperors would view Japan as a barbarous state and engage in "civilizing" missions to the Japanese mainland, possibly including invasion. In 660, the Chinese invaded the kingdom of Paekche on the Korean Peninsula—an event that worked in Japan's favor, since a number of Korean refugees fled to Japan, many of them well versed in Chinese learning. Some of these refugees became tutors for Japanese nobility, and this tutoring included conventions of Chinese poetry. One product of this influx of Chinese learning seems to have been the encouragement of the kind of poetry collected in the *Man'yōshū.*

The *Man'yōshū* does contain a good number of earlier poems, though the time period from which most of the poetry comes is 600–759. The collection is divided into 20 books, arranged roughly chronologically, though some of the books have been organized by topic. But it is customary among critics to divide the collection according to four time periods. The earliest period includes poems that go as far back as the fifth century, and ends with poetry from the reign of Emperor Tenji (668–671). Some of the poems from this period are anonymous, but the poets named are all members of the highest nobility (such as Empress Kōgyoku or Emperor Tenji himself), possibly because only they were literate or cultured enough at the time to compose such poetry, or possibly because their importance led to their poems being preserved before any others. The second period of the *Man'yōshū,* from about 672 (the date of the Jinshin War) to 710 (the date the capital was moved to Nara), is dominated by a single major figure, Kakinomoto HITOMARO, one of Japan's greatest poets. Hitomaro was court poet to Empress Jitō, and writes poems that are often longer than others in the collection, dealing with a variety of both public and private topics. The third period includes the decades from 710 to 733 (the date of the poet Yamanoue no Okura's death), and includes the largest number of important poets, such as Okura, Yamabe Akahito, and Otomo Tabito. Okura was known for incorporating Buddhist and Confucian elements in his poetry, under the influence of the Chinese. Tabito, under a similar influence, introduces Taoist elements. Only Akahito seems purely Japanese in outlook. The fourth and final period of the *Man'yōshū* includes the years between 733 and 759. This period is dominated by Yakamochi, the last important poet of the collection, and the one credited with the final compilation of the *Man'yōshū.* While some critics admire his poetry highly, many regard his productions as undistinguished by comparison with the other major poets in the collection.

Nearly all of the poems in the *Man'yōshū* are *CHŌKA* ("long poems") or TANKA (short poems). The *chōka* might be any length (though the longest in the *Man'yōshū* is 149 lines), and alternated lines of five and seven syllables, ending with a couplet of seven-syllable lines. The tanka was a poem of 31 syllables in five lines, falling into a pattern of five, seven, five, seven, and seven syllables. The vast majority (4,207) of the poems in the collection are *tanka,* although the 265 *chōka,* particularly those of Hitomaro, tend to be the most admired poems in the collection.

It is also customary to categorize poems in the collection by subject matter as *zōka, sōmon,* or *banka.* The *zōka* is a poem on a "miscellaneous" subject. The *sōmon* is a poem on personal or family concerns, like a love poem, or like Hitomaro's *chōka* on leaving his wife as he traveled to the capital. A *banka* (the term literally means "coffin pulling song") was a poem lamenting a death, and would include a number of Hitomaro's poems concerning the deaths of members of the royal family.

The poetry of the *Man'yōshū* is also characterized by three particular rhetorical devices. One of these is the *makurakotoba* (literally "pillow-words"): These were formulaic conventional epithets that were placed before words and modified them. The second device was called the *jo* or "preface." This was generally a phrase at the beginning of a poem or section of a poem that connected with a later part of the poem figuratively or logically. The third device was the "binary measure"—a form of parallelism inspired by Chinese poetry and often involved formulaic phrases that paired spatial or temporal concepts like night and day, land and sea, or heaven and earth. Such rhetorical figures are generally lost in translation, but are part of the artistry of the poems of the *Man'yōshū.*

Despite the profound influence of Chinese and Korean thought on the collection, many Japanese think of the *Man'yōshū* as the product of a pure Japanese culture. Certainly it is predominantly Shinto in its spiritual outlook, unlike later collections. It also includes some 2,000 anonymous poems, some of which seem to come from older folk traditions, or are written by poets outside the noble class, such as some purportedly by frontier guardsmen. But it seems likely that these have in general been rewritten or heavily edited by

Yakamochi or other poet-editors. Perhaps the main thing that can be said of the *Man'yōshū* is that its enormous variety has given readers of all generations something to admire and to relate to, and has given subsequent generations of Japanese poets the forms and traditions that were to become the basis of Japanese verse.

Bibliography

Keene, Donald. *Seeds in the Heart: Japanese Literature from Earliest Times to the Late Sixteenth Century.* Vol. 1, *A History of Japanese Literature.* New York: Columbia University Press, 1999.

Levy, Ian Hideo. *Hitomaro and the Birth of Japanese Lyricism.* Princeton, N.J.: Princeton University Press, 1984.

The Manyoshu. Translated by Nipon Gakujutsu Shinkokai. With a new foreword by Donald Keene. 1940. New York: Columbia University Press, 1965.

Miner, Earl, Hiroko Odagiri, and Robert E. Morrell. *The Princeton Companion to Classical Japanese Literature.* Princeton, N.J.: Princeton University Press, 1985.

Map, Walter (ca. 1140–ca. 1210)

Walter Map was a courtier and writer, a favorite in the English court of HENRY II, whose best-known work, *De nugis curialium* (*Courtiers' Trifles*), is a witty, entertaining, and often satirical collection of miscellaneous anecdotes, observations, fairy stories, and gossip written in Latin prose. Map, whose road to preferment was guaranteed by his religious education, ended his career as the archdeacon of Oxford.

Map was born in Wales and at the age of 14 went to Paris to study with Gerard Pucelle, an expert on canon law who was later bishop of Coventry. Map returned to England in 1162, and became attached to Henry II's court. His wit and intelligence apparently made him a favorite of the king, with whom he traveled on occasion and served for a time as an itinerant justice. He was also selected clerk of the king's household, an appointment that suggests he had received holy orders, or was about to do so.

In 1179, Map attended the Third Lateran Council in Rome as the king's representative. Here he was specifically appointed to dispute with the Waldensians, a recently established proto-Protestant heretical sect that denied the value of intercession by saints or the Virgin, denied the existence of purgatory, and denied all sacraments but baptism and the Eucharist. He continued to receive royal preferments and by 1186 had been made chancellor of Lincoln. In 1197, he was named archdeacon of Oxford. In about 1210, his friend and fellow Welshman GIRALDUS CAMBRENSIS speaks of him as having passed away sometime earlier.

De nugis, composed probably between 1181 and 1192, is the only text attributed with certainty to Map. It is filled with a fascinating variety of material. Its first book laments the corruption in orders like the Carthusians, the Templars, and the Hospitallers, but particularly the Cistercians, or White Monks, whom Map seems to have especially abhorred. Map also attacks heretics, such as the Waldensians he had previously disputed at Rome. Book 2 of *De nugis* includes a number of fairy stories and other Welsh anecdotes, including a close analogue of the romance of SIR ORFEO, concerning a man who rescues his wife from death when he finds her in the company of a fairy host. The third book contains a number of romantic stories, while the fourth, amid more tales, includes a famous text usually called "The Epistle of Valerius to Ruffinus." This treatise, often erroneously attributed to St. JEROME or St. AUGUSTINE, was popular in the later Middle Ages and was widely circulated independently in manuscript form. Nicholas TRIVET, the English Dominican, even wrote his own commentary on it in the 14th century. Later, CHAUCER refers to the text in the prologue to *The WIFE OF BATH'S TALE.* The epistle, descried by the Wife of Bath as an antifeminist tract, condemns men who seek pleasure with women rather than wisdom. Map's fifth book provides a history of the Anglo-Norman court.

Map was highly regarded in the later medieval period, and was for a long time believed to be the author of most of the satiric extant GOLIARDIC VERSE, and was as well the purported author of a Latin original of the prose Lancelot, part of the vast French VULGATE CYCLE of Arthurian ROMANCE. Neither of these attributions is accepted any longer by modern scholars. Even so, Map's *De nugis* provides a multivalent picture of an intelligent man with broad and varied interests, and with certain bitter enmities: Giraldus Cambrensis claims that when Map took the oath as king's justice, he swore to dispense justice fairly to all men except Jews and Cistercians, whom Map claimed were just to no one themselves.

Bibliography

Hanna, Ralph, III, and Traugott Lawlor. *Jankyn's Book of Wikked Wyves.* Using materials collected by Karl Young and Robert A. Pratt. Athens: University of Georgia Press, 1997.

James, M. R., trans. *De Nugis Curialium: Courtier's Trifles.* Revised by C. N. L. Brooke and R. A. B. Mynors. Oxford: Clarendon Press, 1983.

Levine, Robert. "How to Read Walter Map," *Mittellateinisches Jahrbuch* 23 (1988): 91–105.

Marcabru (Marcabrun) (ca. 1105–1150)

Marcabru was one of the earliest of the Provençal TROUBADOURS. He was born in Gascony, in the city of Auvillar, in the first decade of the 12th century. Unlike most other troubadours, he was not of noble birth, but he seems to have been educated, perhaps as a cleric. He found patronage among the high nobility of Provençe and Spain, including Guillaume X of Aquitaine (son of the first troubadour) and Alfonso VII of Castille. Some 42 of his lyrics survive, including four with their musical settings.

Marcabru is the first practitioner of what is called the *TROBAR CLUS*, the deliberately obscure, hermetic troubadour style. In one of his lyrics, "Per savi·l tenc ses doptanssa," he begins with the lines "I say he's a wise man, no doubt about it/who makes out, word for word,/what my song signifies,/and how the theme unfolds:/for I myself take pains/to cast some light on the obscurity" (Goldin 1973, 83, ll. 1–5).

Most often his lyrics deal with the corruption and depravity of the noble class, for which he blames the troubadours in part for their glorification of lust, which Marcabru calls *amars,* or bitter love. This he contrasts with *amors,* the good love that he extols: a love that does not cause pain but brings joy; that is not selfish but responsible. His style is often satiric, as he depicts false lovers with bitter irony. He categorizes those in his courtly audience who practice or uphold *amars* as false lovers, jealous ones, gossipmongers, and spies. Those who respect *amors* he calls his friends. In the same lyric cited above, Marcabru says that "whoever settles down with Lust [amars]/wars against himself" (Goldin 1973, 83, ll. 15–16), and later asserts:

> *It fills me with anger and grief*
> *to hear that pack of perjurers telling us*
> *that Love deceives and tortures*
> *a man by cooling down his lust.*
> *They are liars, for the happiness of lovers is*
> *Joy, Patience, Restraint.*
>
> (Goldin 1973, 83, ll. 19–24)

Marcabru significantly influenced later poets, particularly those writing in the *trobar clus* style. His categories of groups like "talebearers" and "jealous ones" among the courtly audience were also taken up by a number of later poets.

Bibliography

Goldin, Frederick, ed. and trans. *Lyrics of the Troubadours and Trouvères.* New York: Anchor, 1973.

Marco Polo (ca. 1254–1324)

Medieval Europe's greatest explorer and travel writer, Marco Polo, probably was born in Venice about 1254. He may have been about six years old when his father, Niccolò, and his uncle Maffeo traveled to the East, where they became the first Europeans to reach China, or as they called it, Cathay. They returned to Venice in 1269, with a request from the great khan, Kublai, written in Turkish and addressed to the pope, expressing the khan's interest in Christianity and inviting 100 learned men to visit his empire and provide instruction in Western religion and science.

In 1271 the 17-year-old Marco set out with his father and uncle on their return trip to China, though instead of 100, they were able to convince only two Dominican friars to make the arduous trek across Asia with them. The timid friars quickly deserted the expedition, but the three Polos pressed on, reaching China in three and a half years after a 6,000-mile journey through Armenia, Persia, Afghanistan, and along the trade route known as the "Silk Road" into China.

In May of 1275 they reached the khan's summer palace in his original capital of Chengdu. Marco was quite taken by the luxury and splendor of the palace, and his description of it in his memoirs as the greatest palace ever constructed later inspired Coleridge to write his poem about Xanadu (i.e., Chengdu). The newly built capital, called Khanbalig or Cambalic, "The City of the Khan" (modern Beijing), Marco described as the greatest city in the world.

Kublai, who adopted the Polos as favorites in his court, was particularly fond of Marco, and employed him as a diplomat. Sent on missions to Burma, India, and remote parts of China, Marco witnessed and wrote about places that no Westerner would see again until the 19th century.

In 1292, the Polos left the elderly khan in order to escort a Mongol princess to Persia, and while there, received news that Kublai had died. Realizing that in the struggle for power in the wake of the khan's death his close advisers may be in a very dangerous position, the Polos decided the time had come for them to return to Venice. After a difficult trip home, they arrived in Venice in 1295, after a journey of 24 years.

Three years after returning home, Marco commanded a galley in a Venetian sea-battle with rival Genoa. Captured and imprisoned in Pisa, Marco met a Pisan writer of romances named Rusticiano. At the urging of Rusticiano, Marco sent to Venice for his papers, and worked with the Pisan writer to produce the memoirs of his journey, known to his contemporaries as *The Travels of Marco Polo* or *The Description of the World.* The text quickly became one of the most popular books in Europe—hundreds of manuscripts of the *Travels* appeared throughout the West within a century of its first publication, and Marco's adventures exerted a powerful influence on the European imagination.

Released from prison after a year, Marco returned to Venice, married, and had three children. He seems to have lived contentedly with his business affairs in Venice until his death in 1324. He was famous, though most readers considered the wonders described in his book as mere fabrications, traveler's tall tales, of the sort made famous by writers like John MANDEVILLE. His *Travels* became popularly known as *Il Milione,* "The Million Lies." It is said that on his deathbed, his friends called upon him to revise his book and remove the sections he had made up, to which he angrily responded "I did not tell half of what I saw!"

Still, parts of the *Travels*—a section in which giant birds drop elephants from the sky, for example—must indeed have been products of Marco's imagination. Other questions have arisen about the authenticity of the *Travels:* Marco never mentions the Great Wall, for instance. Nor does he speak of things like women's foot binding, which must have seemed remarkable to a European visitor. These things, plus the fact that the Polos are never mentioned in the Annals of the Yuan (Mongol) Empire recorded during Kublai's reign, have led some to doubt that Marco ever actually visited China at all.

Still, much of what Marco wrote was confirmed by travelers during the 18th and 19th centuries, and his geographical descriptions have been shown to be remarkably accurate. His accounts of some important events of Kublai's reign are more detailed than extant Chinese accounts. Though it may be difficult at times to separate with absolute certainty fact from fiction in the *Travels,* the text has been remarkably influential and fascinating in its rich, detailed pictures of parts of Asia through the eyes of the first European to see them.

Bibliography

Larner, John. *Marco Polo and the Discovery of the World.* New Haven, Conn.: Yale University Press, 1999.

Polo, Marco. *The Travels of Marco Polo.* Edited by Manuel Komroff. New York: Norton, 2002.

Power, Eileen. *Medieval People.* New York: Barnes and Noble, 1963.

Spence, Jonathan D. *The Chan's Great Continent: China in Western Minds.* New York: Norton, 1998.

Marie de Champagne (1145–1198)

In his *Art of Courtly Love* (ca. 1180–1290), ANDREAS CAPELLANUS several times refers to Marie de Champagne. She was the daughter of ELEANOR OF AQUITAINE (1121–1204, daughter of Guillaume X, duke of Aquitaine, and granddaughter of the first troubadour, GUILLAUME IX) and King Louis VII of France (1120–1180). Eleanor's second husband, King HENRY II (1133–1189) of England, demonstrated, like his wife, great interest in courtly poetry. Eleanor's daughter Marie married Henry I, count of Champagne (1127–1181), also known as "the Liberal," who transformed his territory from a fairly backward country into one of the richest and strongest French principalities. Their court at Troyes became a center of literary patronage. After Henry's death on a crusade, Marie ruled as a fairly independent regent from 1181 until 1187 when her son Henry II of Champagne (1166–97) assumed his inherited authority (he also became king of Jerusalem in 1191 through marriage with Isabella, the daughter of Amalric I of Jerusalem; Henry died under mysterious circumstances in 1197).

From a variety of accounts we know that Marie was a highly learned person to whom lovers appealed, asking for a judgment in contested cases of love. Andreas might have made up this story, but the historical circumstances suggest that Marie, along with her mother, Eleanor, with whom she seemed to have enjoyed a friendly relationship, had established a literary center at her court in Troyes and was considered an authority in the area of COURTLY LOVE. In Andreas's treatise Marie consistently argues that true love is possible only outside of marriage. Both Marie and her mother Eleanor obviously exerted a considerable influence on the standard, formalistic image of *fin' amors* prevalent at the French courts of their time. CHRÉTIEN DE TROYES (fl. 1165–91) seems to have created several of his courtly ROMANCES on behalf of Marie de Champagne. Above all in the prologue to *LANCELOT, The Knight of the Cart,* Chrétien credits Marie for having provided him with both "the matter and the meaning" of his romance, but he seems to have disagreed with the idealization of adultery in the tale, leaving his text as a fragment, which then was completed by Godefroi de Leigni. Many other 12th-century poets, such as RAIMBAUT D'ORANGE and Gautier d'Arras, frequented Marie's court where they received her patronage. It seems very likely that another TROUBADOUR, BERTRAN DE BORN, spent time at Marie's court and dedicated some of his poems to her, and so did CONON DE BÉTHUNE, GACE BRULÉ, and Aubouin de Sézanne. We can also infer from a variety of literary sources that the famous troubadour BERNART DE VENTADORN (ca. 1147–ca. 1170) wrote some of his poetry for Marie de Champagne. The troubadour Rigaut de Barbezieux's (fl. 1175–1215) poem "Pros comtess'e gaia, ab pretz valen,/que tot'avetz Campaigna enluminat" has traditionally been associated with Marie de Champagne, who served as his patron. However recent scholars have seriously questioned this connection.

Marie was also interested in religious literature and asked Evrat, cleric at the Church of Saint-Etienne, for a verse translation of the Old Testament book Genesis into French. Although the first part seems to reconfirm traditional male misogyny, in the second part, which might have been influenced by Marie herself, the role of women is painted in much more positive terms.

Bibliography

Andreas Capellanus. *The Art of Courtly Love.* With introduction, translation, and notes by John Jay Parry. 1941. Reprint, New York: Norton, 1961.

Hall-McCash, June. "Marie de Champagne and Eleanor of Aquitaine: A Relationship Reexamined," *Speculum* 54 (1979): 698–711.

———. "Marie de Champagne's 'Cuer d'ome et cors de fame': Aspects of Feminism and Misogyny in the Twelfth Century." In *The Spirit of the Court: Selected Proceedings of the Fourth Congress of the International Courtly Literature Society, Toronto 1983,* edited by Glyn S. Burgess and Robert A. Taylor, 234–245. Cambridge, U.K.: Brewer, 1985.

Henderson, Jane Frances Anne. "A Critical Edition of Evrat's *Genesis:* Creation to the Flood." Ph.D. diss., University of Toronto, 1977.

Albrecht Classen

Marie de France (ca. late 12th–early 13th centuries)

The author known as Marie de France was one of the first highly educated women writers; she lived and wrote in England in the late 12th century. The royal court at the time was Anglo-Norman, as was the language of literature and the nobility, and Marie's connections with the court are demonstrated both in her use of Anglo-Norman and in her dedications (one of her works seems to be dedicated to King HENRY II). Although there is no reliable record to testify to Marie's identity and her life, three extant works are attributed to her, including a collection of *LAIS*, short romances that focus on emotion, rather than action (*see* LANVAL); a collection of fables after Aesop (*Isopet*), short tales where animals are used to exemplify moral lessons for humans; and *St. Patrick's Purgatory*, a translation of a Latin hagiography into Norman French. In a fairly unconventional gesture, particularly for women writers at this time, Marie signs each of her works to assert her authorship. The most famous example of this occurs in the epilogue of her collection of *Fables* where she writes: "I'll give my name, for memory:/I am from France, my name's Marie" (Marie de France 1987, ll. 3–4). Marie's claim to be "from France" (or, more accurately, "of France" ["si sui de France"]), may mean that she was born in France or that she was of the French royal family. The latter supposition, suggested by some scholars, is probably incorrect and Marie only intends "of France" to indicate her place of birth. This would make sense, especially if she were writing in England, for the Anglo-Norman aristocracy.

Scholars have long speculated concerning her identity and have suggested figures as various as MARIE DE CHAMPAGNE, the daughter of ELEANOR OF AQUITAINE; Marie of Boulogne, King Stephen's daughter; or the Abbess of Shaftesbury, sister to King Henry II. Unfortunately, we will probably never know who she was, and what we do know is limited to what we can glean from her writings. That Marie moved in aristocratic circles, including the royal court of Henry II and Eleanor, seems clear. Equally clear is Marie's status as a noblewoman: Her education, the people she knew, and the subject matter of much of her writings testify to her nobility. Marie's education naturally included the Bible and the classics, French and Anglo-Norman literature, and most probably an assortment of moral or didactic treatises. In addition to French, Marie knew Latin and English, and was able to translate from these languages for her *Purgatory* and the *Fables*.

Marie de France is often considered one of the finest writers of short fiction before CHAUCER, and her *Lais* and *Fables* reflect the milieu in which they were produced: secular, sophisticated, aristocratic, didactic, and, at times, political. In the *Lais*, Marie draws on Breton tales either read or heard, although few of the 12 *lais* have direct literary antecedents. And while Marie's *Lais* enjoy wide popularity today, the number of extant manuscripts (23 of the *Fables* and 5 of the *Lais*), suggests that her collection of *Fables* was more widely disseminated and probably the more popular of the two collections in the Middle Ages. The *Lais* are concerned with love, particularly COURTLY LOVE, and are filled with passions and potions, magic and symbolism. Attuned to courtly tastes in literature, Marie's *Lais* celebrate love (and adultery) in all their guises, but most especially love that is impassioned and outside social boundaries. Thus, the *Lais* are fantastic, entertaining, and secular in focus and theme. Nonetheless the *Lais*, for all their entertainment value, do contain lessons or didactic elements. The morality of adultery may not be questioned, but the immorality of cruelty or lovelessness certainly finds full expression. And notwithstanding the secular nature of the *Lais*, spiritual or Christian readings are possible, especially in *lais* such as *Yonec*, where eucharistic imagery, Christian ritual, and allusions to the Trinity give complex meaning to a tragic and adulterous affair.

While political concerns are sometimes an allusive element in the *Lais*, politics and the critique of court and aristocratic life are easily found in the *Fables*. Indeed, some of the *Fables* are overt in their political commentary, and it may be this aspect of their composition that accounts for their popularity. Marie's *Fables* are particularly critical of abuses of power engaged in by the Norman aristocracy against the feudal underclass, and if the *Lais* were popular with the courtly inner circles, the *Fables* possibly attracted a wider and more diverse readership. Unlike the *Lais,* the *Fables* have well-developed realistic aspects and unlike fables in general, whose moralism is often abstract, Marie's works are moral and didactic in specific and often satiric ways. Unfortunately, without a fuller knowledge of Marie's identity and life, scholars can only speculate about the pointed observations in her critical and political *Fables.*

The works of Marie de France draw on conventions of genre and translation, but manage to transcend the limitations of both. If the author is unconventional in the assertions of authorship we find in all of her works, she is similarly unconventional in her treatment of familiar materials. Marie de France is aware of the moral responsibilities inherent in authorship and her works reflect her idea of the ideal rhetorical balance between entertainment and enlightenment.

Bibliography

Burgess, Glyn S. *The "Lais" of Marie de France: Text and Context.* Athens: University of Georgia Press, 1987.

———. *Marie de France: An Analytical Bibliography.* London: Grant and Cutler, 1977.

Finke, Laurie A. *Women's Writing in English: Medieval England.* London: Longman, 1999.

Marie de France. *Fables.* Edited and translated by Harriet Spiegel. Toronto: University of Toronto Press, 1987.

———. *The Lais of Marie de France.* Translated by Robert Hanning and Joan Ferrante. Michigan: Baker Books, 1978.

Thiébaux, Marcelle, trans. *The Writings of Medieval Women: An Anthology.* 2nd edition. New York: Garland, 1994.

Elisa Narin van Court

Masnavi-ye ma'navi (*Mathnawī-i Ma'nawī, Spiritual Couplets*) Rumi (ca. 1270)

Jalaloddin RUMI's best-known text is his vast, six-volume compilation of Sufi thought known as the *Masnavi-ye ma'navi,* or Spiritual Couplets. Composed of numerous anecdotes or parables drawn from a variety of Persian, Arabic, and other sources (somewhat in the manner of Faridoddin ATTAR), the *Masnavi* is revered by Sufis as second only to the KORAN itself in importance and influence. Indeed, in Persian it is sometimes popularly called the Koran.

The *Masnavi* was inspired by and dedicated to Rumi's disciple and close companion Celeb Humam al-Din Hasan, who lived with Rumi the last 10 years of the poet's life and who succeeded Rumi as head of the Sufi order called Mawlawi that Rumi had founded. The text is made up of some 26,000 long couplets in Persian verse. The *Masnavi* is a learned work, the culmination of Rumi's years of study and teaching, and so is rich in allusions to the Koran and the life of Muhammad. But it is also a creative and original text, full of deep emotion and admirable wit. The intent of Rumi's parables and allegories is to lead his reader in the path of spiritual perfection, in the tradition of Islamic Sufi mysticism.

In general, Rumi's Sufi thought has been compared with Neoplatonism. For Rumi, ultimate reality, that is real existence, is an attribute that belongs solely to God. The image of God is fixed on all created things, since they were formed by him. The final destiny of all things is to return to God, if in fact they are not already a part of him. The mystic's desire is to achieve unity with the Godhead—to return to him even in this world. Thus the accumulation of worldly goods is futile. Learning gleaned from books can only give one knowledge of the physical world, not of ultimate reality. To achieve this higher knowledge, one must transcend the self, the *nafs.* This is for Rumi the mystery of love—"to die before dying."

But the *Masnavi* gives no straightforward or systematic guide to mystical practice. Instead, it seems at times a rather random collection of thoughts, images, and poetry—a story will grow out of another story, which may lead to a dazzling lyrical section, followed by a digression, which may ultimately lead back to the original anecdote, from which Rumi may veer away again. Rumi's own comments in parts of the *Masnavi* imply that his original readers were frustrated by this storytelling method, and by his refusal to provide any clear instruction in the Sufi path. Rumi answers these objections by asserting that the tales (sometimes apparently irrelevant, sometimes even bawdy) were not included merely for the sake of entertainment, but must be understood for their didactic significance—readers must learn, he says, to separate "the grain from the husk." In response to the common Muslim attitude that fiction was a disreputable form of literature, Rumi responds that even the Koran itself used illustrative stories.

The opening passage of the *Masnavi,* a poem recited in the ritual of the Mawlawi dervishes, is called "The Song of the Reed," and illustrates some of these precepts. The reed flute (the instrument used in the dervishes' ritual dancing) becomes in the poem a symbol of the Sufi adept: Torn from the reed bed that is its natural home, the reed flute plays music expressing its longing to return. In the same way the soul of the Sufi, knowing its place of origin is in God and feeling the love that draws it to its first home, expresses its own song of longing. Later in book II of the *Masnavi,* Rumi discusses the pitfalls of mistaking the transient things of this world for the highest good and loving those things rather than the ultimate reality. It is, he says, like mistaking lightning for the sun:

A lack of knowledge cannot discern;
it mistakes a flash of lightning for the sun.
Lightning is transient and faithless;
without clearness you will not know
the transient from the permanent.
Why is lightning said to laugh?
It is laughing at whoever
sets his heart upon its light.

(Helminski 1998, 44)

The *Masnavi* has always been revered by Persian readers, and many have committed it to memory. But by the mid-14th century it was translated into Turkish and eventually into Arabic, and thus became popular throughout Islam, and hundreds of commentaries on Rumi's text in many languages are extant. His work became influential in 19th-century Germany and impressed Hegel. Rumi's enormous recent surge of popularity in the English-speaking world rests on translations of parts of the *Masnavi* as well as of the short lyrics of Rumi's other major work, his *Divân-e Shams-e Tabrizi* (Collected Poems of Shams Tabrizi), but translations fail to do justice to the rhythm and imagery of the verse.

Bibliography

Keshavarz, Fatemah. *Reading Mystical Lyric: The Case of Jalal Al-Din Rumi.* Studies in Comparative Religion. Columbia: University of South Carolina Press, 1998.

Rumi, Jalaloddin. *The Essential Rumi.* Translated by Coleman Barks. San Francisco: Harper, 1997.

———. *Rumi: The Book of Love: Poems of Ecstasy and Longing.* Translated by Coleman Barks. San Francisco: Harper, 2003.

———. *The Rumi Collection.* Edited by Kabir Helminski. Brattleboro, Vt.: Threshold Books, 1998.

Schimel, Annemarie. *The Triumphal Sun: A Study of the Works of Jalaloddin Rumi.* Persian Studies Series, 8. Albany: State University of New York Press, 1980.

Mechthild von Magdeburg (ca. 1207–1282)

Mechthild was born around 1207 as the daughter of a noble family of lower rank; she lived near Magdeburg and apparently received a good courtly education. There in 1230, she moved into a house of Beguines (a kind of voluntary convent for women without the strict rules and the vows of a traditional convent). As a 12-year-old Mechthild had already experienced religious visions, but she waited until 1250 before writing them down in response to a request from her confessor, Heinrich von Halle. This huge collection of visions, her *Licht der fließenden Gottheit* (*Flowing Light of the Godhead*), became one of the most important contributions to medieval mystical literature because of the intricate combination of the erotic and the religious. In many visions Mechthild reports intimate encounters with Christ, who asks that her soul come to bed with him to make love. During the 1260s, Mechthild suffered from many setbacks, caused both by severe illness and the public opposition against Beguines, especially by the church authorities. In 1270, Mechthild joined the Cistercian women's convent Helfta, near Eisleben. Helfta was, at that time, a major center of women's learning under the famous abbess Gertrud the Great. Mechthild inspired Gertrud and also the nun Mechthild von Hackeborn to write down their own mystical visions. Mechthild von Magdeburg died in 1282.

The original Middle Low German text of her *Licht der fließenden Gottheit* is lost today. In its place we have a Middle High German translation written sometime between 1343 and 1345 in Basel, probably by Heinrich von Nördlingen (extant in only one manuscript). Unusual for a woman's mystical text, Mechthild's book was also translated into Latin. Mechthild relied on many different sources to express her visions, such as texts by AUGUSTINE, Bernard of Clairvaux, Hugh and Richard of St. Victor, Pseudo-Dionysius, and Joachim of Fiore. Drawing from her literary education in her youth, she also utilized erotic courtly poetry to formulate the religious experiences in her visions.

Bibliography

Andersen, Elizabeth A. *The Voices of Mechthild of Magdeburg.* Oxford: Peter Lang, 2000.

Mechthild von Magdeburg. *'Das fließende Licht der Gottheit'. Nach der Einsiedler Handschrift in kritischem Vergleich mit der gesamten Überlieferung.* Edited by Hans Neumann. 2 vols. Munich: Artemis, 1990.

———. *The Flowing Light of the Godhead.* Translated by Frank Tobin. With a preface by Margot Schmidt. New York: Paulist Press, 1998.

Albrecht Classen

Meogo, Pero (Pero Moogo, Peter the Monk) (fl. 1250)

Beyond his own verses, we know nothing certain about Pero Meogo, not even the meaning of his surname. Derived from the Latin *monachu,* it appears to imply that Pero was, in fact, a monk, though it is apparent that at least at the time he wrote his extant poetry, he was a Galician *jogral* (the equivalent of a JONGLEUR). He is known mainly for his nine *CANTIGAS DE AMIGO,* all of which concern a girl, her lover, and the girl's mother, and nearly all of which take place in a setting involving a fountain and deer. Scholars have traced the association of the deer with the fountain to imagery in the Old Testament, and for that reason speculation has arisen that Pero was a converted Jew—though his familiarity with the Scriptures might be explained just as well if he were, indeed, a monk.

The nine lyrics, taken together, can be read as forming a linked narrative in which the girl keeps trying to meet her lover at the fountain, the mother tries to prevent it, and the lover may or may not be able to make the tryst. Praised for their attention to detail, the poems often suggest a symbolic level behind the simple narrative. The stag seems clearly a symbol of the lover himself, in particular his male sexuality, while the fountain seems a symbol of fertility, or perhaps of female sexuality. The stag is wounded in one poem, paralleling the wound of love that the lover may be feeling. In another poem the stag muddles the water in the fountain, perhaps symbolically suggesting a sexual encounter. In another the daughter returns home with a torn dress—possibly suggesting a loss of innocence or virginity. The mother's disapproval, it may go without saying, implies, as well, the social norms that the girl may be violating.

A brief look at a few verses from one of these lyrics may suffice to give a sense of Pero's style. Frede Jensen points out that the lyric *Levou-s' a louçana* (The beautiful girl arose) is, in fact, an *alvorada,* a subgenre popular in Iberian poetry related to the Provençal *ALBA,* but rather than portray the sorrowful parting of lovers at dawn, it is instead a dawn song in which a joyous meeting of lovers is anticipated:

The beautiful girl arose, the fair girl arose:
She goes to wash her hair in the cold
fountain.
So joyously in love, in love so joyously.

The fair girl arose, the beautiful girl arose:
She goes to wash her hair in the fountain so cold.
So joyously in love, in love so joyously.

(Jensen 1992, 50.1, ll. 1–6)

Noteworthy in this poem, as well, is the use of parallelism, both within each line and between the two stanzas, as the same idea is presented in a parallel manner to give it a slightly different emphasis each time. Seven of Pero's nine extant poems make use of this kind of parallelism. Such "parallelistic" elements, like the *cantiga de amigo* genre in general, suggest the influence of a popular, indigenous tradition rivaling the pervasive influence of the Provençal TROUBADOURS in late medieval Portuguese poetry.

Bibliography

Bell, Aubrey. "The Hill Songs of Pero Meogo," *MLR* 17 (1922): 258–262.

Flores, Angel, ed. *An Anthology of Medieval Lyrics.* New York: Modern Library, 1962.

Jensen, Frede, ed. and trans. *Medieval Galician-Portuguese Poetry: An Anthology.* Garland Library of Medieval Literature, 87. New York: Garland, 1992.

Merchant's Tale, The Geoffrey Chaucer (ca. 1394)

The Merchant's Tale is one of several *CANTERBURY TALES* in which CHAUCER explores the institution of marriage. The story follows *The CLERK'S TALE* of patient Griselda, and the Merchant narrator tells it largely to contrast the deceitful May, the "real life" spouse, with the saintly Griselda. The narrator, disillusioned with his own marriage after all of two months, presents a bitter and cynical look at marriage, though the effect of the tale is an indictment more of foolish attitudes and motives concerning marriage than of the institution itself.

The Merchant's Tale follows a FABLIAU plot involving adultery and trickery. Its style, however, is far more formal and elaborate than a typical fabliau, and its diction, aristocratic characters, and use of the supernatural are more characteristic of a ROMANCE. The ironic contrast between subject and style make *The Merchant's Tale* one of the most striking of *The Canterbury Tales.*

As the story begins, January, a Lombard knight who has lived a life of debauchery and lechery for 60 years, has decided it is time to marry. He wants an heir, but he also claims to be concerned about his mortal soul, and wants a wife so that he can allay his lust in a manner sanctioned by the church. He therefore determines to marry a young wife. He asks his courtiers to advise him on his proposal, and the flattering sycophant Placebo tells him he has made a wise decision, but Justinus calls it a foolish plan.

Nevertheless January has made up his mind, and marries the youthful May. The Merchant narrator describes the wedding in gruesome detail, highlighting with disgust January's rough whiskers and sagging neck. We are not told how May feels. However January's young squire, Damian, is attracted to May, and passes her a note declaring his love. She begins to look for a way to satisfy him.

January has a private garden built in which he and May can walk. In the course of time, however, he loses his sight, and May hatches a plot with Damian to meet him in a pear tree in the garden. As she and January walk in the garden, she feigns hunger for the fruit, and climbs the tree. She and Damian have sex in the tree above January's head.

At the climax of the tale, the gods Pluto and Proserpine come walking in the garden and witness the cuckolding. The indignant Pluto restores January's sight, but Proserpine gives May the skill to convince January not to believe the evidence of his own eyes. She says that she was told if she "struggled with a man in a tree," her husband's sight would be restored. The tale ends with the willfully blinded January stroking May's womb, believing he has begotten an heir.

Scholarly comment on the tale has focused on the question of whether it was originally intended for the Merchant; since there are two lines that imply a clerical narrator, one conjecture is that it was initially meant for *THE FRIAR'S TALE* or *THE MONK'S TALE.* This has also led to a division of opinion as to the tone of the tale: If it is closely identified with the bitter Merchant of the tale's prologue, it is a dark and heavy tale. But taken by itself, some critics argue, it is a lighter satire, like most fabliaux. The variety of genres on display and Chaucer's generic experiments in the tale have also been of interest to scholars.

Bibliography

Brown, Emerson, Jr. "Chaucer, the Merchant, and Their Tale: Getting Beyond Old Controversies: Part I," *Chaucer Review* 13 (1978): 141–156.

Brown, Emerson, Jr. "Chaucer, the Merchant, and Their Tale: Getting Beyond Old Controversies: Part II," *Chaucer Review* 13 (1979): 247–262.

Edwards, A. S. G. " 'The Merchant's Tale' and Moral Chaucer," *Modern Language Quarterly* 51 (1990): 409–426.

Hagen, Susan K. "Chaucer's May, Standup Comics, and Critics." In *Chaucer's Humor: Critical Essays*, edited by Jean E. Jost, 127–143. New York: Garland, 1994.

Middle English (ca. 1100–ca. 1500)

The Middle English period is essentially a transitional period in the history of the English language between the basically Germanic character of OLD ENGLISH and the language of the earliest printed books that record what is essentially modern English in the early 16th century. It was a period of tremendous change in the language, sparked by developments that had begun in late Old English times (particularly the influence of Old Norse) and new, cataclysmic transformations brought by the Norman Conquest of 1066. It was also a period of tremendous variety of creative activity in literature, as writers drew from the influence of French and Latin texts as well as from the old native tradition.

When considering anything as fluid as the history of a language, precise dates separating one "period" from another must be somewhat arbitrary. However, when William the Conqueror, the duke of Normandy, defeated Harold, the last Anglo-Saxon king, at the Battle of Hastings in 1066 and brought to England a new French-speaking noble class, it began a period of significant developments in the language of the conquered English. A huge influx of French vocabulary was the most obvious direct result of the conquest. The grammar of English also underwent major changes, when the vowels of unstressed final syllables—whether *a, e, o,* or *u*—all came to be pronounced in the same way, as an unstressed schwa (ə). Thus the distinct inflections of Old English were lost, and ultimately inflected endings disappeared almost completely in Middle English, leaving a number of words with an unstressed final *–e*. English became a language that depended more on word order and function words like prepositions than on word endings or inflections, as it had in the Old English period. Other extensive changes occurred in pronunciation: A process known as the "Great Vowel Shift" took place at the end of the Middle English period, through which the vowels of English lost their former "European" pronunciation, and came to be pronounced as we say them in modern English. By the time the Middle English period ended—after the Tudor monarchs established a strong central government and William CAXTON had brought the printing press to England in the late 15th century—the language would have been unrecognizable to King Harold.

After the Norman Conquest, England was in effect a trilingual country, with the nobility speaking their dialect of French (called Anglo-Norman), the clergy speaking the Latin characteristic of the medieval church, and the common people speaking English. Since for the most part the nobility and the clergy were the literate classes, written literature in English all but disappeared for some time, though a native English literary tradition must have been kept alive orally. A few English texts appear in the 13th century, but the 14th century saw a great outpouring of literary texts in English. By this time, the Hundred Years' War (begun in 1337) was loosening the English ties to France and creating more of a sense of English nationalism, so that by the early 14th century, most of the noble class was bilingual, and by mid-century children of the nobility and the merchant class were studying French as a second language. The BLACK DEATH, which killed nearly half the English population, created a labor shortage that the nobles tried to counter by keeping wages at preplague levels, ultimately causing the PEASANTS' REVOLT of 1381. International trade was increasing at the same time, giving the merchant class more income and therefore more power, and King EDWARD III, to fund his French war, found himself having to negotiate with the House of Commons to enact taxes—and addressing Parliament in English by 1363. The reformer John WYCLIFFE, questioning some of the secular powers of the church in a manner that foreshadowed the Protestant Reformation, was responsible for an English translation of the Bible by 1384.

The time was ripe, therefore, for an upsurge of literature written in English. At the court, Geoffrey CHAUCER (ca. 1342–1400), the most important and influential poet in medieval England, established English as a courtly language, writing at first in imitation of French poets like Guillaume de MACHAUT and JEAN DE MEUN, but later influenced by the great Italian poets of the 14th century—DANTE, PETRARCH, and especially BOCCACCIO, who inspired Chaucer's great love story *TROILUS AND CRISEYDE* (1385). Chaucer's friend John GOWER (ca. 1330–ca. 1408), whose first two major poems had been in Latin and in French, chose to write his *CONFESSIO AMANTIS* in English, in part at least because of Chaucer's success in the medium. The influence of Chaucer and of Gower on poets of the 15th century was profound and enduring, so that John LYDGATE and Thomas HOCCLEVE, for example, are to a large extent imitators of Chaucerian verse, and the "Scottish Chaucerians" like HENNRYSON and DUNBAR, though more admired by modern readers, are no less inspired by the court poetry of Chaucer and Gower.

The theme of COURTLY LOVE apparent in Chaucer's *Troilus* was one of the most important general influences on Middle English literature. A significant number of ROMANCES, usually dealing with a knight who proves himself worthy of his beloved by accomplishing a quest of some kind, often to save his lady, abound in Middle English literature. Some of these texts may have been written for the provincial courts of English-speaking nobles; others (in particular those called TAIL-RHYME ROMANCES) were part of the repertoire of traveling MINSTRELS, and so may have been intended for a middle-class audience. Many such romances are concerned with the court of King ARTHUR, and often have the traditional English hero GAWAIN as their protagonist, rather than a French knight like Sir LANCELOT. Ultimately these romances culminate in the late 15th-century text of *Le MORTE DARTHUR* by the knight Thomas MALORY (and published by Caxton in 1485), though for the most part Malory relied on French sources for his definitive compilation of the medieval legend of King Arthur.

One of the most significant literary developments of the late 14th century was the phenomenon known as the ALLITERATIVE REVIVAL: a movement in the west and north of England to create poetry in the old Anglo-Saxon style of ALLITERATIVE VERSE—a tradition that must have been kept alive orally through the years. Some of these texts also dealt with Arthurian subjects, like the *ALLITERATIVE MORTE ARTHURE*, a poem on the tragic downfall of Arthur that was one of Malory's sources. William LANGLAND's *PIERS PLOWMAN*, which exists in three versions and scores of manuscripts, was the most popular of all these texts: It is a poetic ALLEGORY that ranges across the social and religious landscape of the late 14th century and depicts the turmoil of Langland's society. But generally the most admired poet of the alliterative revival is the "Pearl poet," author of the four poems of the Cotton Nero A.x. manuscript (including *SIR GAWAIN AND THE GREEN KNIGHT* and *PEARL*). The poet's technical virtuosity, brilliant detail, and thematic emphasis on "courtesy" in both its chivalric and moral senses make this author the alliterative poet most admired among modern readers.

It is essential to remember that religion, specifically the Roman Catholic Church, was at the center of people's lives throughout the Middle English period, and that the majority of writers were in some way connected professionally with the church. Therefore much of the literature from this period is religious in tone and substance. The middle to late 14th century was a period of flowering for the English mystical tradition, and a number of mystical writers flourished during this time, including Richard ROLLE, Walter HILTON, JULIAN OF NORWICH (the first known woman writer in the English language), and the anonymous author of the treatise The CLOUD OF UNKNOWING. Margery

KEMPE, the author (or narrator) of the first autobiography in English, was also active at this time (late 14th and early 15th centuries) and speaks of herself as a mystic. The cycle of MYSTERY PLAYS, produced by craft guilds for the common citizens of English cities in the late 14th and 15th centuries, were also religious in intent, depicting the story of human salvation from Creation to Doomsday. MORALITY PLAYS, more likely professional dramatic productions, were concerned with salvation within the individual human psyche, and were often presented in the form of an allegorical *PSYCHOMACHIA*. These dramatic productions formed the foundation from which developed the great English dramatic tradition of the Renaissance.

There were five dialects of Middle English: Northern (spoken north of the Humber River), East Midland (the area that included East Anglia, Essex, and bordering areas to the west), West Midland (essentially the western half of what had been called Mercia in Old English times), Southern (corresponding to ALFRED THE GREAT's kingdom of Wessex), and Kentish. The reader of Middle English literature will note that Middle English authors all wrote in their own dialects, so that, for example, Langland and the Pearl poet write in the West Midland dialect, while John BARBOUR, author of *The BRUCE*, writes in a distinctly Northern dialect. The author of the *ANCRENE WISSE* composes in a Southern dialect, while Dan Michel of Northgate's *AYENBITE OF INWYT* is in Kentish. The so-called "London standard"—the East Midland dialect—did not become standard English until the end of the Middle English period, probably because it was the language of the country's largest population center, of the center of government, and of the two major seats of higher learning (Oxford and Cambridge). The fact that Chaucer, the greatest writer in the language, had written in the East Midland dialect was probably no coincidence.

Bibliography

Benson, Larry D., ed. *The Riverside Chaucer.* 3rd ed. Boston: Houghton-Mifflin, 1987.

Burrow, J. A., and Thorlac Turville-Petre. *A Book of Middle English.* 3rd ed. Malden, Mass.: Blackwell, 2004.

Dalrymple, Roger. *Middle English Literature: A Guide to Criticism.* Malden, Mass.: Blackwell, 2004.

Horobin, Simon, and Jeremy Smith. *An Introduction to Middle English.* New York: Oxford University Press, 2002.

Iglesias-Rabade, Luis. *Handbook of Middle English.* Munich: Lincom, 2003.

Lambdin, Laura Cooner, and Robert Thomas Lambdin. *A Companion to Old and Middle English.* Westport, Conn.: Greenwood Press, 2002.

Machan, Tim William. *English in the Middle Ages.* Oxford: Oxford University Press, 2003.

Miller's Tale, The Geoffrey Chaucer (ca. 1392)

The second of the *CANTERBURY TALES*, the *Miller's Tale* is a bawdy FABLIAU put into the mouth of the drunken Miller, who claims to tell the story to repay the Knight for his courtly romance. A story of the rivalry between two clerics lusting after a carpenter's wife, the *Miller's Tale*'s plot parallels that of the *KNIGHT'S TALE;* but as a comic tale of middle-class characters, the Miller's fabliau undercuts the chivalric values of the Knight's courtly ROMANCE. Long considered indecent, the tale is today considered one of CHAUCER's greatest achievements and the premier example of its genre.

The tale is perhaps the best-known of all literary fabliaux, combining naturalistic description with a complex plot involving two widespread folklore patterns: the "second flood" and the "misdirected kiss" motifs. In the tale a rich old carpenter named John weds a young wife, Alison, whom he jealously guards. His boarder, the student Nicholas, propositions Alison, who readily yields to his advances. Meanwhile the fastidious parish clerk, Absalon, also woos Alison, but the lady prefers Nicholas.

Nicholas is able to convince John that he has foreseen a second great flood, and persuades him to hang three kneading tubs from his ceiling in which Alison, John, and Nicholas can sleep the night of the flood and float safely away in the morning. They climb into the tubs that evening, and when John falls asleep, Nicholas and Alison climb down and frolic in the carpenter's bed.

Absalon, the parish clerk, interrupts them, begging at the window for a kiss. When he agrees to leave if she kisses him, Alison puts her backside out the window. In the dark, Absalon kisses it, and when he hears derisive laughter as the window closes, he realizes what he has done. He returns to the window with a red-hot plowshare borrowed from a blacksmith, and, seeking revenge, asks for another kiss. This time Nicholas puts his posterior out the window, and Absalon brands it with the plowshare. As Nicholas screams in pain for "water," John awakens, believes the flood has come, and cuts the rope holding his tub. He crashes to the floor, breaking his arm, and when the neighbors come to see what the noise is about, Alison and Nicholas convince them the carpenter is mad.

The humor of the story lies not only in the comic situations, but also in Chaucer's arrangement of the two plots to make them converge in the unexpected ending. This complexity of plot, as well as Chaucer's carefully developed characters, elevates the *Miller's Tale* well above the conventional medieval fabliau.

In addition to Chaucer's transformation of the fabliau genre, scholars have been interested in the *Miller's Tale*'s ironic parody of COURTLY LOVE and of the *Knight's Tale.* Other themes of scholarly interest have included the idea of justice in the story, the various allusions to the MYSTERY PLAYS, and the related problems of class raised in the tale.

Bibliography

Benson, Larry, et al., ed. *The Riverside Chaucer.* 3rd ed. Boston: Houghton-Mifflin, 1987.

Brewer, D. S. "Class Distinction in Chaucer," *Speculum* 43 (April 1968): 290–305.

Kolve, V. A. *Chaucer and the Imagery of Narrative: The First Five Canterbury Tales.* Stanford, Calif.: Stanford University Press, 1984.

Mann, Jill. "Speaking Images in Chaucer's 'Miller's Tale.' " In *Speaking Images: Essays in Honor of V. A. Kolve,* edited by R. F. Yeager and Charlotte C. Morse, 237–254. Asheville, N.C.: Pegasus Press, 2001.

Patterson, Lee. *Chaucer and the Subject of History.* Madison: University of Wisconsin Press, 1991.

Minnesang

German courtly love poetry, or *Minnesang,* emerged around 1170, produced both by GOLIARDIC singers who wandered from court to court looking for patrons of their art, and also by members of the highest aristocratic circles. The first signs of profound changes affecting *Minnesang* occurred around 1200 with the appearance of great poets such as WALTHER VON DER VOGELWEIDE and NEIDHART, who either challenged the traditional premises of the erotic ideals of their predecessors or satirized the social conditions. The poems of this "classical" period of *Minnesang* are contained in the famous edition of *Des Minnesangs Frühling.*

Minnesang was mostly supported by members of the Hohenstaufen family, but the songs were not copied down until the early 14th century on behalf of the famous Zürich family Manesse. The earliest poets, such as DER VON KÜRENBERG, Meinloh von Sevelingen, Der Burggraf (Castellan) von Regensburg, Spervogel, and DIETMAR VON AIST, seem to have been influenced by autochthonous (indigenous) sources, but later poets, such as HEINRICH VON VELDEKE, FRIEDRICH VON HAUSEN, Rudolf von Fenis, Albrecht von Johansdorf, and HEINRICH VON MORUNGEN, reflect clear influences from Provençal TROUBADOUR and French TROUVÉRE poetry. Research has also detected influences from the Dutch and the Italian areas. Latin poetry, such as those collected in the *CARMINA BURANA,* seem to have exerted additional influence in the shaping of *Minnesang.*

Most of these *Minnelieder* (love songs) commonly explore the problems of unrequited love and the subsequent love pains that will last forever (Ulrich von Gutenburg). This "negative" experience of love allows the singer to examine his own self and to question the true meaning of the erotic emotion. Modern scholarship has mostly identified the ultimate purpose of *Minnesang* as ritual or performance, that is, as a ludic form of courtly self-confirmation for the male members of chivalry. The beloved lady is never identified by name or social status, though she always appears to enjoy a higher rank than the singer. *Minnesang* knows many different types of genres, one of which was the *Tagelied* ("dawn song," see *ALBA*). Here the lovers wake up early in the morning because a bird or a watchman has alerted them about the coming of daylight, and lament the fact that he has to depart from her (examples appear in Dietmar von Aist and Heinrich von Morungen). They join in lovemaking one more time and express their deep sorrow.

In the so-called "crusade song," perhaps best represented by Friedrich von Hausen, the poet formulates his grief over the dilemma between the love for his lady and the love for the Godhead who has called upon him to go on a crusade. Some poets utilize a female voice to create so-called women's stanzas (REINMAR DER ALTE), which were often integrated in an intricate dialogue poem, or *Wechsel* (as in Albrecht von Johansdorf, Henry VI, Reinmar, Heinrich von Morungen). The creators of the famous Middle High German courtly romances, HARTMANN VON AUE, GOTTFRIED VON STRASSBURG, and WOLFRAM VON ESCHENBACH, also composed some *Minnelieder* (love songs). Women, however, seem to have been excluded from the creation of German courtly love poetry.

Bibliography

Gibbs, Marion E., and Sidney M. Johnson. *Medieval German Literature: A Companion.* New York: Garland, 1997.

Heinen, Hubert. "Minnesang (12th–13th c.)," In *Medieval Germany: An Encyclopedia,* edited by John M. Jeep, 525–532. New York: Garland, 2001.

Moser, Hugo, and Helmut Tervooren, eds. *Des Minnesangs Frühling.* 38th ed. Vol. 1, *Texte.* Stuttgart: Hirzel, 1988.

Sayce, Olive. *The Medieval German Lyric, 1150–1300: The Development of Its Themes and Forms in Their European Context.* Oxford: Clarendon Press, 1982.

Wesley, Thomas J., trans. *Medieval German Lyric Verse in English Translation.* UNC Studies in Germanic Languages and Literatures, 60. Chapel Hill: University of North Carolina Press, 1968.

Albrecht Classen

minstrel

Minstrels were originally traveling professional entertainers of late medieval Europe in the tradition of the earlier SCOP or JONGLEUR. While some minstrels were clearly attached at least semipermanently to noble houses, most typically they were itinerant musicians, singers, storytellers, magicians, or jugglers who wandered from court to court and from town to town, performing wherever they were likely to find patronage. They do seem to have performed for all classes of society, from kings and nobles to priests, burgers, and laborers. As singers and storytellers, minstrels were likely to circulate love lyrics, folk BALLADS, old legends like the CHANSONS DE GESTE, and newer tales in the form of ROMANCES. Some of the popular MIDDLE ENGLISH romances, such as *HAVELOK THE DANE,* seem to have been the kind of tales popularized by minstrels. Rather than writing their songs or tales down, however, most minstrels seem to have relied on memory and improvisation as central to their art.

Minstrels flourished from the later 13th century through the early 15th. As time went on, more and more minstrels became associated with music rather than poetry and more often were attached permanently to noble houses or settled in towns, and during the 14th and 15th centuries, minstrel guilds began to develop throughout Europe. These guilds required that minstrels be trained by other members of the guild, ensured that there was work in the town for guild members, and protected guild members from competition by wandering musicians—the group from whom minstrels sprang to begin with. With the development of printing in the late 15th century, the art of minstrelsy, particularly as the wandering storyteller, declined significantly throughout Europe.

Bibliography

Southworth, John. *The English Medieval Minstrel.* Woodbridge, Suffolk, U.K.: Boydell, 1989.

Mirk, John (ca. 1355–after 1414)

John Mirk was an English Augustinian canon and the author of three devotional texts, two in English and one in Latin. His anthology of sermons in English, the *Festial* (ca. 1382–90), was one of the earliest printed books in England, and became one of the most widely read texts of the late 15th century.

Mirk was probably born and raised in Yorkshire. It is unknown whether or not he attended one of the universities, but he was well educated in Latin and in theology. He became a canon of the Lilleshall Abbey, near Shrewsbury close to the Welsh border, and apparently regularly preached at the nearby church of Saint Alkmund's in Shrewsbury. Ultimately he was appointed prior of his monastery.

Mirk's *Festial,* his most popular text, was an anthology of a full year's worth of sermons, filled with entertaining and vivid exempla for each homily. The *Festial* comes out of Mirk's early years of preaching and a direct knowledge of the state of parish ministry in the years following the BLACK DEATH. Augustinian monasteries like Lilleshall often had to supply their own pastors to parish churches that they controlled. But the plague, which had hit the clergy at a proportionally higher rate than the laity, had wiped out a generation of parish priests. New priests pressed into service after the Black Death were often untrained, and had no formal education. Thus Mirk's intent in the *Festial* was to provide these new underprepared clergy with help and support—in English, since the new priests knew no Latin.

The same impulse was doubtlessly behind Mirk's other major work in English, the *Instructions for Parish Priests,* probably also written during those unsettled years between 1382 and 1390. Possibly intended as a companion volume to the *Festial,* the *Instructions* provide details to priests on how they might deal with a variety of practical situations (what to do about mice chewing communion wafers, for instance), as well as advice on proper conduct for priests and parishioners. Its arrangement follows the seven sacraments, beginning with a discussion of baptism and ending with extreme unction. This is followed by translations and explanations of the Our Father, the Hail Mary, the creed, and articles of faith. The text is loosely based on an earlier Latin text by William of Pagula called *Oculus sacerdotis* (ca. 1320–28).

Pagula is also the source for much of Mirk's Latin work, the *Manuale sacerdotis* (ca. 1414). This, too, is a handbook for priests, but Mirk's purpose is different. Intended for a more learned audience of priests and probably written after Mirk's promotion to prior, the *Manuale* gives modern readers a firsthand look at the life of a priest in rural England. Like the *Instructions,* much of the *Manuale* is concerned with the proper moral conduct of priests, but in this case Mirk is probably reacting to the challenge to the church posed by the LOLLARD faction in England. As Fredel points out (1994), Mirk's way of fighting Lollardy was not to directly attack the Lollard heretics, but rather to point out the common abuses among the clergy in England that fed the heresy in the first place—and to do it in Latin, so that his chastisement was kept within the circle of priests themselves, rather than spread among the laity and the heretics.

Details of Mirk's death are unknown, but undoubtedly he died not many years after 1414 at the abbey of Lilleshall, where he had spend most of his life. Late in the 15th century, his *Festial,* originally intended for a clerical audience, became popular among middle-class and noble readers, whose preferences ran toward devotional texts in English, especially ones illustrated with vivid and interesting tales like Mirk's exempla. Caxton printed the text in 1483, and it was reprinted several times well into the next century.

Bibliography

Fletcher, Alan J. "John Mirk and the Lollards," *Medium Aevum* 56 (1987): 217–224.

———. "Unnoticed Sermons from John Mirk's *Festial,*" *Speculum* 55 (1980): 514–522.

Powell, Susan. "John Mirk's *Festial* and the Pastoral Programme," *Leeds Studies in English,* n.s., 25 (1991): 85–102.

Mirour de l'Omme (*Speculum hominis, Speculum meditantis*) John Gower (ca. 1376–1379)

The *Mirour de l'Omme (The Mirror of Mankind)* is a lengthy moral treatise in French verse. It is the earliest significant work of the major English poet John Gower, and, while lacking in unity and focus due in large part to its sprawling length, it introduces the themes of the moral degeneration of contemporary society and the importance of individual responsibility for virtue that were to dominate Gower's later works.

Lost for centuries, the *Mirour de l'Omme* was discovered in 1895 by Gower's modern editor G. C. Macaulay in a single manuscript, Cambridge University Library Addition MS. 3035. The manuscript contains 26,603 lines of verse. It is missing four leaves in the beginning, a few at the end, and seven more at various points throughout the text, so that the complete poem must originally have been some 31,000 lines. Gower uses a stanza of 12 octosyllabic lines (known as a Héliland Strophe) rhyming *aabaab/baabaa.* Most often the stanzas contain a pause midway through, and a moral tag or summary in the last two or three lines. It was a form common to French moral poets of the time, and Gower's versification is extremely polished and regular.

Calling sin the cause of all the world's evil, Gower opens the *Mirour de l'Omme* with a discussion of the origin of sin. After his fall Lucifer gives birth to Sin, and drawn to his own vile creation, he couples with her and gives birth to Death. Driven by the same unnatural lust as his father, Death engenders with Sin seven more hideous daughters—the Seven Deadly Sins. The ALLEGORY is unmistakably reminiscent of John Milton's *Paradise Lost* (1667), but it is unlikely that Milton could have known the *Mirour de l'Omme* (since we know of no extant manuscript other than the one found by Macaulay). Still, no common source has ever been found for the allegory.

As the poem continues, the Devil sets his sights on ruining God's creation. Because Man is initially inclined to follow the tenets of Reason, the Devil cannot corrupt him, and decides to reinforce his party. He marries the seven sins to his ally, the World, pledging Hell as their dowry. Gower gives a lengthy description of the procession of the seven sins, drawn from conventional iconography: from Pride riding her Lion and dressed in elaborate attire to Lechery riding her goat and carrying her dove, the sins marry World and each of them begets five more daughters, personifying the different branches of each sin. Man is overcome by the attack of so many sins, and to aid Man, God sends seven Virtues to marry Reason and beget their own daughters as antidotes to the variety of vices. This section is reminiscent of the catalogues of virtues and vices found in confessional manuals like CHAUCER'S *PARSON'S TALE.*

In the next 8,000 lines, Gower goes on to show the effects of the various sins in the world through an ESTATES SATIRE in which he considers the three estates of humankind—clergy, nobility, and common people—and their various occupations, and finds them all corrupted by sin. In many ways this is the most interesting part of the *Mirour de l'Omme* because of its depiction of life in late 14th-century London; this section might be compared to the GENERAL PROLOGUE of Chaucer's *CANTERBURY TALES.* Many stock complaints about the various professions form part of the descriptions here, including that of a monk devoted to food and to hunting, a corrupt friar who uses the confessional for personal gain, and a tavern keeper who cheats customers by providing every wine in Europe from a single cask.

In the last 3,000 lines of the poem, Gower looks for the solution to the world's corruption. In the bygone former age, human beings were in harmony with the law of love that held the world in order. But now man's rebellion against Reason has thrown the world into chaos. Human beings—not God or the Devil or the stars—are responsible for the condition of the world, and to set it right, man must follow the law of nature. The poem ends with a life of the Virgin as an example of how human beings should live in accordance with God's law of love.

The *Mirour de l'Omme* is most interesting in relation to Gower's other major works, the Latin *VOX CLAMANTIS* (1379–82) and the English *CONFESSIO AMANTIS* (1386–90), with both of which it shares a moral tone, a concern with the corruption of society, and an emphasis on human responsibility. In order to suggest the parallels among the three works, Gower sought later in his life to give the early poem a Latin title parallel to the other two, changing his original French title of *Mirour de l'Omme* to *Speculum hominis* and ultimately to *Speculum meditantis.* The poem is also valuable for its picture of London life and for its rhetorical sophistication. Its first English translation was made available only in 1992.

Bibliography

Fisher, John H. *John Gower: Moral Philosopher and Friend of Chaucer.* New York: New York University Press, 1964.

Gower, John. *Mirour de l'Omme.* Translated by William Burton Wilson. Revised by Nancy Wilson Van Baak. With a foreword by Robert F. Yeager. East Lansing, Mich.: Colleagues Press, 1992.

Macaulay, G. C., ed. *The Complete Works of John Gower.* 4 vols. Oxford: Clarendon Press, 1899–1902.

Yeager, Robert F. *John Gower: Recent Readings.* Kalamazoo: Western Michigan University Press, 1989.

monarchia, De Dante Alighieri (ca. 1313)

De monarchia is a Latin treatise on political philosophy composed by DANTE ALIGHIERI in the early 14th century. The tract is chiefly an argument for the need of a universal temporal monarch who would balance the universal spiritual power of the papacy. Essentially Dante's political ideals were forged during the corrupt pontificate of Boniface VIII, whose perpetual meddling in the temporal affairs of Italy had contributed to political unrest in Dante's native Florence, and had resulted in Dante's own exile in 1302.

De monarchia is (unlike Dante's other post-exilic texts, *De VULGARI ELOQUENTIA* and *CONVIVIO*) a completed work, consisting of three books. The first makes the case that for the good of the world, a universal monarch is necessary. The second book, looking back upon the glorious imperial power of Rome, argues that the Roman people's assumption of the imperial office was warranted. In the third book, Dante asserts that the authority of the emperor comes directly from God, and not through any intermediary, such as, a pope.

The date of *De monarchia*'s composition is a matter of some scholarly debate. Suggested dates range from some time prior to Dante's exile in 1302, to late in Dante's life—1317 or later. Many scholars associate the text with the advent of the Holy Roman Emperor Henry VII of Luxembourg, who was Dante's best hope for an emperor of the sort he advocated in *De monarchia.* Henry was born in the 1270s and was named king of Germany (with the support of Pope Clement V) in 1308. His announced intention of being crowned emperor in Rome—the first such coronation since Frederick II in 1220—apparently galvanized his enemies against him. He led an army of 5,000 across the Alps in 1310 and was crowned in Milan on Epiphany. But the powerful Guelf party (traditionally associated with support of the temporal power of the pope) resisted his more significant coronation at Rome. He was finally crowned at the church of St. John Lateran in June of 1312. But by this time the opposition of the Guelfs was making his attempts to pacify Italy more difficult. Supported by the Ghibelline party (made up to a large extent of old aristocratic families who traditionally backed the emperor), Henry led his army to Florence, the main Guelf stronghold in northern Italy, and in September laid siege to the city, an act that must have inspired Dante's emulation and support. But the siege was unsuccessful, and Henry retired to Pisa for the winter. In the summer of 1313, he changed his plans and decided to attack Naples, the seat of Guelf influence in the south. But Henry's Italian campaign came to an abrupt end on August 24, when he died in Buonconvento, near Siena—apparently of malaria contracted at his coronation in Rome the year before.

BOCCACCIO alleges that Dante wrote *De monarchia* during Henry's campaign in Italy. But Boccaccio is notoriously inaccurate about historical details. Further, it is hard to imagine why Dante would not mention Henry by name anywhere in *De monarchia* if he was writing it while the emperor was active. There are probably allusions to Henry in the *Inferno* and the *Purgatorio,* the first two canticles of the *DIVINE COMEDY,* on which Dante was working during Henry's activities in Italy—why, then, not do the same kind of thing in *De monarchia?* Perhaps the best argument is that Dante wrote his text late in 1313, after Henry's death. One problem with this date is the passage in the first book of *De monarchia* that almost certainly alludes to lines from canto 5 of the *Paradiso* (the last part of the *Comedy*), suggesting that the text was not written until 1317. However, that passage may be a scribal interpolation, or Dante may have revised the text in about 1317.

Dante's Latin text was translated into Italian twice by the end of the 15th century, and survives in several manuscripts, three from the 14th century. It was printed twice in the 16th century. These figures suggest that the text was fairly popular, despite the fact that in 1328, it was condemned as heretical by Cardinal Bertrando del Poggetto. The hostile response of the church hierarchy to the text is not surprising, given Dante's rejection of the subordinate role of the emperor and his advocating limiting the temporal power of the papacy. But it could be claimed that history has ultimately vindicated Dante's point of view.

Bibliography

Dante. *Monarchia.* Translated and edited by Prue Shaw. Cambridge: Cambridge University Press, 1995.

Mancusi-Ungaro, Donna. *Dante and the Empire.* New York: P. Lang, 1987.

Monk's Tale, The Geoffrey Chaucer (ca. 1373–1386)

CHAUCER's *Monk's Tale* is one of the lesser-known *CANTERBURY TALES.* It takes the form of a series of vignettes illustrating the fall of important figures in history, beginning with Lucifer and Adam, and extending through 15 more notables from biblical or classical times, or in a few cases from near-contemporaries, like Pedro the Cruel, king of Castile (d. 1369), and Ugolino of Pisa (d. 1289). The stories range from one stanza for Lucifer or Adam to 16 in the case of Zenobia, third-century queen of Palmyra. The point of the stories is to illustrate the power of Fortune in human affairs and, at least implicitly, to remind the reader that the only true stability lies not in this world but in the world to come.

Such collections were popular in the Middle Ages. Chaucer's was inspired chiefly by BOCCACCIO's Latin text *De Casibus Virorum Illustrium* (*The Fall of Illustrious Men*), and in the 15th century the English poet John LYDGATE wrote a poem of 36,000 lines on the subject called *The Fall of Princes.* It seems likely that Chaucer was also drawing on a section of the *ROMAN DE LA ROSE,* wherein Reason condemns Fortune for her role in the downfall of a number of historical personages.

A number of scholars have suggested that *The Monk's Tale* is an early work, from the early 1370s, after Chaucer's first Italian journey (1372–73). The stories of some of the contemporary figures cannot have been written before 1385, but it has been suggested that Chaucer added them when he revised the earlier poem to include among the *Canterbury Tales.* However, since he does not mention the collection when he lists his own works in the prologue to *The Legend of Good Women,* and since the influence of Boccaccio doesn't become pervasive in his poetry until after his second visit to Italy in 1378, some have argued that Chaucer wrote *The Monk's Tale* later, even while he was beginning the *Canterbury Tales.*

The tale ends when the Knight interrupts the Monk, saying he has had enough of the gloomy stories (the Monk has said that he has 100 such stories to tell, and the threat of that many more seems too much for the Knight). The Host agrees that the tales are monotonous, and many readers have likely concurred. However, the individual short narratives with which Chaucer is experimenting in *The Monk's Tale* are often quite powerful in their brevity. The collection is also interesting as an illustration of the medieval concept of tragedy, which is quite different from the classical sense. As the Monk explains:

> *Tragedie is to seyn a certeyn storie,*
> . . .
> *Of hym that stood in greet prosperitee*
> *And is yfallen out of heigh degree*
> *Into myserie, and endeth wrecchedly.*
>
> (Benson 1987, 241, ll. 1973–77)

That is, tragedy is defined as a fall from prosperity, through the whims of Fortune—something outside of human control.

Of interest, as well, is the stanza used in *The Monk's Tale:* a stanza of six decasyllabic (10-syllable) lines rhyming *ababbcbc*—it is a form that Chaucer uses nowhere else in his narrative poetry, and may be utilized here specifically because the couplet in the middle of the stanza suggests the high point of Fortune's wheel, and the end of the stanza falls off from its climax as Fortune's wheel turns down from its height.

Bibliography

Benson, Larry, et al. *The Riverside Chaucer.* 3rd ed. Boston: Houghton Mifflin, 1987.

Knight, Stephen, et al. "Colloquium: The Monk's Tale," *Studies in the Age of Chaucer* 22 (2000): 379–440.

Ruud, Jay. " 'In Meetre in Many a Sondry Wyse': Fortune's Wheel and *The Monk's Tale,*" *English Language Notes* 26 (1989): 6–11.

morality play

Morality plays were popular dramatic entertainments in late medieval England. In contrast with the MYSTERY PLAYS, which retold the universal biblical history of salvation from the Creation of the world to Doomsday, morality plays focused on the salvation of an individual human being (whose name—"Mankind," "Everyman," or the like—indicates that he represents all human individuals). Whereas the mystery plays were set in the physical world, including earth, heaven, and hell, the setting of the morality play was most often the individual psyche, and the characters' personifications of abstract qualities, attributes, sins, and virtues that play a part in the spiritual health and salvation of the individual soul. Where mystery plays took their inspiration from Scripture, morality plays took theirs from sermons and from allegorical texts like PRUDENTIUS's well-known *PSYCHOMACHIA,* a fourth-century poem describing a struggle between personified sins and virtues within the psyche.

The medieval morality plays dealt with one of three themes: the *psychomachia* in which Virtues and Vices vie for the man's soul; the summoning of Death, wherein the Mankind figure is summoned to his judgment where he must give an accounting of his life; and the debate by the daughters of God—Mercy and Peace against Justice and Truth—over the salvation of the deceased. The earliest extant complete morality play, *The CASTLE OF PERSEVERANCE* (ca. 1425), contains all three elements in a long script of some 3,600 lines. That play is known to have been performed on a stationary stage made up of separate platforms (as opposed to a movable pageant wagon characteristic of the mystery plays).

The earliest morality play we have any record of was called *Pater Noster* and was performed in York in the late 14th century. There is some speculation that it may have been written by John WYCLIFFE, but it has not survived. Five medieval morality plays are extant: The fragmentary *Pride of Life* (late 14th century) and the well-known *EVERYMAN* (ca. 1485), both of which concern the confrontation of Death; and the so-called Macro play—named for the owner of their manuscripts—including the aforementioned *Castle of Perseverance* along with *Wisdom* (ca. 1460) and *MANKIND* (ca. 1473), the last two of which essentially follow the *psychomachia* pattern of temptation and resistance.

Clearly the purpose of morality plays was didactic and gravely serious, but the plays were also highly theatrical and often entertained their audiences with a folksy kind of humor. Particularly popular was the character called the VICE, a demonic trickster figure who became a favorite stage figure. The pageantry of something like a parade of the Seven Deadly Sins, personified and costumed, was also a popular feature. As morality plays continued to be performed well into the Tudor period, the influence of some of these characters extended to Elizabethan drama: Marlowe includes a pageant of deadly sins in *Doctor Faustus,* while the Vice character survives in the countless clowns that appear in Elizabethan plays.

Although the initial impetus of morality plays was the promulgation of orthodox Catholic doctrine, morality plays continued to be written well into Reformation England. Often the subject of these later moralities (or "interludes" as some later allegorical plays were called) was political rather than religious, or had to do with the conflict between Catholicism and Protestantism. Some of these later moralities include John Skelton's *Magnyfycence* (ca. 1516), Sir David LINDSAY's *Ane Pleasant Satyre of the Thrie Estaitis* (1540), and John Bale's *King John* (ca. 1548). The late survival and the popularity of the morality play genre made it a vital link in the development of Renaissance drama in England.

Bibliography

Davenport, W. A. *Fifteenth-Century English Drama: The Early Moral Plays and Their Literary Relations.* Cambridge, U.K.: Brewer, 1982.

King, Pamela M. "Morality Plays." In *The Cambridge Companion to Medieval English Theatre,* edited by Richard Beadle, 240–264. Cambridge: Cambridge University Press, 1994.

Potter, Robert. *The English Morality Play.* London: Routledge and Kegan Paul, 1975.

Morte Darthur, Le Sir Thomas Malory (ca. 1469–1470)

Beside CHAUCER's *CANTERBURY TALES, Le Morte Darthur* is perhaps the most enduringly popular of all English texts written in the Middle Ages, and it is certainly the most famous of all English treatments of Arthurian legend. Only one manuscript of the text survives (the "Winchester Manuscript"), copied sometime before 1483, after Malory's death in 1471, but the first printer in England, William Caxton, produced an edition in 1485, which formed the basis of nearly all subsequent editions that were to appear through the first half of the 20th century.

Early critiques of Sir Thomas MALORY's work were not always positive: The great Renaissance scholar Roger Asham, for instance, found that "the whole pleasure of [the] booke standeth in two speciall poyntes, in open mans-slaughter, and bold bawdrye (*ribaldry*)" (*The Scholemaster,* 1570); Nathaniel Baxter, Puritan author, and tutor in Greek to Sir Philip Sydney, found it comprised of "the horrible actes of those whoremasters, Launcelot du Lake (LANCELOT DU LAC), Tristram de Liones, Gareth of Orkney, Merlin, the Lady of the Lake, with the vile and stinking story of the Sangreall (*Holy Grail*)" (Baxter's dedicatory epistle to the translation of Calvin's sermons on Jonas, 1577); and the historian William Oldys claimed that the work "seems to have been kept in print, for the entertainment of the lighter and more insolid readers" (*Biographia Britannica,* 1748).

Approval of Malory is, however, more plentiful—evident, for instance, in his influence on such writers as Sir Philip Sydney (*Defense of Poesie,* ca. 1579, and *Arcadia,* 1578–83), Edmund Spenser (*View of the Present State of Ireland,* 1596, and the *Faerie Queene,* 1590–1596), Shakespeare (*2 Henry IV,* 1597–98), John Milton (*Paradise Lost,* 1667), William Wordsworth ("The Egyptian Maid," 1828), William Morris (*The Defence of Guenevere and Other Poems,* 1858), Alfred, Lord Tennyson (the *Idylls of the King,* 1859–85), and Mark Twain (*A Connecticut Yankee in King Arthur's Court,* 1889), not to mention a host of writers of modern fantasy and science fiction.

Le Morte Darthur is conventionally understood to have eight separate "books" or sections: 1, the birth of Arthur, his rise to the throne, the tale of Balyn and Balan, Arthur's wedding, early adventures of knights of the Round Table; 2, Arthur's war with Lucius, emperor of Rome; 3, early adventures of Sir Launcelot du Lake; 4, the story of Sir Gareth of Orkney; 5, tales of Sir Trystrams de Lyones; 6, the quest for the Holy Grail (Sankgreal); 7, the story of the love between Launcelot and Guenevere; and 8, the destruction of the court of Arthur, and the death of Arthur. For most of these, Malory translated from French prose sources, though book 2 is derived from an accomplished English poem, the ALLITERATIVE *MORTE ARTHURE.* Book 4 appears to be largely of Malory's own invention, and books 7 and 8 combine French sources with another English poem, the STANZAIC *MORTE ARTHUR.* Malory tends to use one source in particular as a kind of template for the plan of each book, a procedure that may indicate a serial borrowing of source manuscripts not inconsistent with his famous claim that, while writing, he was a "knyght presoner."

In handling his sources Malory typically engaged in extensive abbreviation, suppressed moments of sentimentality and introspection, and reduced passages of religious and doctrinal expression and accounts of magical phenomena; he enhanced accounts of martial endeavor and chivalric values, and drew greater attention to the heroism of certain characters—especially Launcelot. It is generally agreed that books 7 and 8 present Malory at his most innovative and challenging, and where his prosody is most liberated from that of his sources. The characterizations of Launcelot, GUENEVERE, ARTHUR, GAWAIN, and Mordred all achieve unprecedented degrees of moral, emotional, and expressive nuance, and Malory's own extemporaneous comments show an intensity of personal engagement and cumulative thematic insight not matched in earlier books. For example, in the midst of his account of the cataclysm resulting from the discovery of Guenevere's adulterous relationship with Launcelot, Malory questions not Guenevere, but the practices of his own age:

> . . . ryght so faryth the love nowadayes, sone hote, sone colde: thys ys no stabylyté. But the olde love was nat so; for men and women coude love togydirs seven yerys, and no lycoures (*lecherous*) lustis was betwyxte them—and than was love trouthe and faythefulnes.
>
> And so in lyke wyse was used such love in Kynge Arthurs dayes. Wherefore I lykken love nowadayes unto sommer and wynter: for, lyke as the tone (*one*) ys colde and the othir ys hote, so faryth love nowadayes. And therefore all ye that be lovers, calle unto youre remembraunce the monethe of May, lyke as ded (*did*) Quene Gwenyver, for whom I make here a lytyll mencion, that whyle she lyved she was a trew lover, and therefor she had a good ende.

Critical receptions of Malory were affected dramatically after 1934, when the Winchester Manuscript was discovered. Compared against Caxton's edition, the manuscript provides extra autobiographical information, divides and decorates the text differently, and has thousands of variant readings. Further complications arose in 1977 when it was discovered that the Winchester Manuscript had been in Caxton's printing shop when he was preparing his own edition. Much discussion has ensued about which aspects of which version are more authentic, and, although Winchester has emerged as the more authoritative, the high degree of forensic scrutiny now being applied to Caxton's text promises a finer appreciation of Malory's intentions. Also providing new contexts for a finer appreciation are studies of Malory's life records, especially those which suggest something about the reasons for Malory's periods of extensive imprisonment; theft, battery, rape, and attempted murder are all alleged in the records, and imprisonment for political affiliations or severe debt cannot be ruled out. That all of these are important subjects in *Le Morte Darthur* makes the prospects for further research especially exciting.

Bibliography

Archibald, Elizabeth, and A. S. G. Edwards, eds. *A Companion to Malory.* Woodbridge, U.K.: D. S. Brewer, 1996.

Field, P. J. C. *The Life and Times of Sir Thomas Malory.* Woodbridge, U.K.: D. S. Brewer, 1993.

Kato, Takako. *Caxton's Morte Darthur: The Printing Process and the Authenticity of the Text.* Oxford: Clarendon Press, 2002.

McCarthy, Terence. *An Introduction to Malory: Reading the Morte Darthur.* Woodbridge, U.K.: D. S. Brewer, 2002.

Sutton, Anne F. "Malory in Newgate: A New Document," *The Library.* Seventh Series, no. 1 (2000): 243–262.

Takamiya, Toshiyuki, and Derek Brewer, eds. *Aspects of Malory.* Woodbridge, U.K.: D. S. Brewer, 1981.

Vinaver, Eugène, ed. *The Works of Sir Thomas Malory.* 3rd ed. Revised by P. J. C. Field. 3 vols. Oxford: Clarendon Press, 1990.

Wheeler, Bonnie, Robert L. Kindrick, and Michael Salda, eds. *The Malory Debate: Essays on the Texts of "Le Morte Darthur."* Woodbridge, U.K.: D. S. Brewer, 2000.

Stephen H. A. Shepherd

Mum and the Sothsegger (*Richard the Redeles*) (15th century)

Mum and the Sothsegger is an early 15th-century English alliterative poem in the *PIERS PLOWMAN* tradition of social commentary. The poem survives in a single manuscript (British Museum MS Additional 41666), from which are missing the beginning and ending of the poem. The extant text includes 1,751 lines. The poem was formerly known by scholars as *Richard the Redeles.*

Allusions in the text to contemporary events during the reign of Henry IV suggest that the poem was written shortly after 1409. The title, conferred by the scribe, names the poem after its two chief personified abstractions: Mum (the personification of self-interested silence), and Sothsegger (one that speaks out and tells the truth).

The main action of the poem begins with a debate between the two: Truthtelling is necessary within the state, so that honest criticism can be heard. But Mum argues that flattering those in power is much more profitable. Clearly the Sothsegger is in the right, while Mum, embodying self-interest and hypocrisy, represents everything that is wrong in society. Yet the narrator is undecided about which path to choose, and wanders off to examine the world and find which of the two qualities is best. He discovers that while Mum is easy to find everywhere, it is much more difficult to find truthtellers. The poem turns into an example of ESTATES SATIRE, as the narrator visits with personified Liberal Arts at the university, with the friars, a parish priest, and finally the town.

Like *Piers,* the poem also involves a DREAM VISION. Here, the narrator is shown a hive of bees that represent the perfect commonwealth, in which the beekeeper (in the role of sovereign) exterminates those who do not contribute to the good of the hive.

Ultimately the poem criticizes the religious establishment in ways that suggest the author held some LOLLARD sympathies, and it suggests that in a well-run kingdom, a good king will listen to the constructive criticism of his subjects. Interestingly, the poem's Narrator presents himself, finally, as one of those truthtellers so hard to find.

Bibliography

Dean, James M., ed. *Richard the Redeless and Mum and the Sothsegger.* Kalamazoo, Mich.: Western Michigan University for TEAMS, 2000.

Barr, Helen, ed. *The Piers Plowman Tradition: A Critical Edition of Pierce the Ploughman's Crede, Richard the Redeless, Mum and the Sothsegger, and The Crowned King.* London: J. M. Dent, 1993.

Muqaddimah, The Ibn Khaldūn (1377)

The important Islamic jurist, philosopher, and historian IBN KHALDŪN is best known for his *Muqaddimah* (Introduction). What we think of as the *Muqaddimah* is the preface and first book of his *Kitāb al-'Ibar,* or "Universal History." Its well-deserved reputation rests on the fact that it is the world's first attempt to find a rational explanation for the historical changes in human society, outside of religious myth or conventional cliché. Ibn Khaldūn's revolutionary methods have led subsequent generations to call him the first sociologist, or the first true philosopher of history.

Ibn Khaldūn begins by considering the effect of the physical environment on human beings, and concludes that the middle or temperate latitudes, away from the extremes of the northern and southern climates, provide the ideal setting for human civilization. He then considers the nature of the human species, in an Aristotelian manner: God has given us the gift of rational thought, so we realize that we need to cooperate with others because it is impossible for us to produce everything we need by ourselves. However, we are animals, Ibn Khaldūn says, so we must be governed by someone with the power to prevent our harming one another if we are to live in a cooperative society. Once this cooperative society is formed, the result is what Ibn Khaldūn calls *'umrân,* or "civilization." As the organization becomes more populous, *'umrân* increases until the state is formed, the highest form of *'mrân.*

What enables some groups to achieve this advanced state more readily than others is a quality Ibn Khaldūn calls *'asabîyah,* a word meaning something like "group consciousness." Generally one feels this *'asabîyah,* toward one's family or tribe, with whom one has a blood relationship, but in the more advanced civilization the attitude is broadened to include the larger political entity of the nation. Certain groups with a very strong sense of *'asabîyah.* are able to dominate other groups, and further, within the dominant group the leading family, founder of a dynasty, will be the one with the strongest *'asabîyah.* For Ibn Khaldūn, the word *dawlah* means both "dynasty" and "state," for he sees the two as inseparable—when the dynasty falls, so does the state itself.

It is under a dynasty that human cultural achievement reaches its apex. In the large cities and towns necessary for the *'umrān* of the dynasty, human needs are more easily met and the excess labor available goes into the production of arts, crafts, and sciences. But the desire for luxuries on the part of the ruling dynasty encourages them to seek higher and higher taxes to pay for the luxuries they desire, and to consolidate their power as their *'asabîyah* decreases. They are forced to rely on outside military support from a group whose own *'asabîyah* is stronger. Ultimately, this group overthrows the reigning dynasty and founds its own state, only to succumb ultimately to the same fate in what Ibn Khaldūn describes as the cyclical pattern of history.

Despite the constant rise and fall of states, Ibn Khaldūn sees that the arts and sciences, the higher aspects of civilization, are maintained and advanced through what he calls *malakuh* or "habit." The new rulers generally keep the things they admired in the previous dynasty, and individuals who have learned the arts and sciences will educate those of the new order willing to learn them. Thus Ibn Khaldūn argues that, despite historians who claim that the world has declined from a previous golden age, and that the current civilization is inferior to that of the past, the only difficulty with the present civilization is a decline in political organization. In the cycle of history, it will rise again.

Bibliography

Al-Azmeh, Aziz. *Ibn Khaldûn: An Essay in Reinterpretation.* London: Routledge, 1990.

Baali, Fuad. *Social Institutions: Ibn Khaldûn's Social Thought.* Lanham, Md.: University Press of America, 1992.

Ibn Khaldûn. *The Muqaddimah: An Introduction to History.* Translated by Franz Rosenthal, abridged and edited by N. J. Dawood, with a new introduction by Bruce B. Lawrence. Princeton, N.J.: Princeton University Press, 2005.

Mahdi, Muhsin. *Ibn Khaldûn's Philosophy of History: A Study in the Philosophic Foundation of the Science of Culture.* London: G. Allen and Unwin, 1957.

Murasaki Shikibu (fl. 978–1014)

Lady Murasaki Shikibu, recognized as Japan's greatest author, wrote *The* TALE OF GENJI (*Genji Monogatari*), the world's first novel and one of the best. Her reputation parallels that of Shakespeare: Her obscurity and her family's low position in the medieval HEIAN aristocracy have led a few to question the authenticity of her authorship of the *Genji*, a masterpiece that has wielded immeasurable influence over subsequent writers from her time to the present.

The few details available about her life derive mostly from her diary, *Murasaki Shikibu Nikki*, and from official records. Like CHRISTINE DE PIZAN and SEI SHŌNAGON, she was a daughter of a court scholar. In the diary she claims that as a child she mastered, much more quickly than her brother, such subjects as Chinese (the official language, much as Latin was for medieval Europe) so that her father regretted "she was not born a man" (Bowring 1982, 139). In 999, she became wife to the older Fujiwara Nobutaka, who died two years later, leaving her with a daughter. It is believed she began writing her masterpiece, the *Genji*, shortly after she was widowed; approximate dates for the novel's composition are 1001–10. She apparently never remarried, but her diary suggests that the powerful Fujiwara Michinaga took a romantic interest in her, and a court chronicler states she was his concubine, although scholars dispute that claim.

Even though the exact relationship between the two is unclear, her diary implies that Michinaga invited her to tutor his daughter Shōshi, a consort of Emperor Ichijō. Her diary recounts life at court during the years 1008–10, the period of the pregnancy of Shōshi and the birth of her son. Michinaga may have asked Murasaki to write the diary as a record of the glorious birth of Prince Atsuhira, a victory over the rival royal consort, Teishi, whose entourage included the author of *The Pillow Book*, Sei Shñagon.

One piece of information gleaned from the diary is the origin of her pen name Murasaki. She tells that one evening a drunken nobleman approached the women hidden behind their screens—as custom dictated—and asked if

"Murasaki" was present, in reference to the favorite concubine of Genji in the author's famous novel. The author replied, "I cannot see the likes of Genji here, so how could she be present?" (Bowring 91)—an insinuation that court nobles fall short of the ideal set by her fictional Genji. Lady Murasaki's given name remains unknown, since propriety demanded that ladies' private names not be publicly revealed. Shikibu, which serves as her given name, alludes to her father's rank at the Bureau of Rites.

Her diary also reveals that the emperor was impressed with her erudition when the *Genji* was read to him and that, to her horror, Michinaga took drafts of her masterpiece from her room without her permission. These events serve as indicators that *Genji* was recognized as a superior piece of literature in her own time, and its reputation as a monumental work survives to this day. Shortly after completing the diary, Murasaki disappears, and nothing is known about her final years (although in later eras strict Buddhists will claim she is in hell, suffering for the "sins" she penned).

The one other remaining text by Murasaki is *Murasaki Shikibu Shū,* a collection of *waka* poetry, mostly extracted from the *Genji* and the diary. But her towering stature as an author rests upon her supreme achievement of the *Genji* narrative.

Bibliography

Miner, Earl, Hiroko Odagiri, and Robert E. Morrell. *The Princeton Companion to Classical Japanese Literature.* Princeton, N.J.: Princeton University Press, 1985.

Murasaki Shikibu. *Murasaki Shikibu: Her Diary and Poetic Memoirs.* Translated by Richard Bowring. Princeton, N.J.: Princeton University Press, 1982.

Barbara Stevenson

Muromachi period (1336–1572)

The late medieval period of Japanese history (1336–1572) is generally called the Muromachi age, named after the district of Kyoto where the seat of power lay. The political center of Japan shifted from Kamakura back to Kyoto as a new military government, the Ashikaga shogunate, gained power and ruled Japan for more than 200 years. Unlike their predecessors during the KAMAKURA PERIOD, the Ashikaga shoguns were never able to extend their power to the whole country. But the period saw significant aesthetic accomplishments, the most important of which was the development of NŌ DRAMA.

The era began in turmoil. The emperor Go-Daigo was briefly successful in restoring the old imperial power by overthrowing the Kamakura government in 1334 in a period called the Kemmu restoration. But he was not able to gain the support of the wealthy landowners, and the administrative machinery of the imperial government was not capable of maintaining him in power. The warrior Ashikaga Takauji, who at first supported the new emperor, turned against Go-Daigo and drove him from the capital in 1336. A new emperor was appointed, clearly subordinate to Takauji, who made himself shogun in 1338, while Go-Daigo set up a rival imperial court at Yoshino in the south. For more that 50 years, the two imperial courts were at odds, the northern court generally having the upper hand, though on several occasions the southern emperor was able to retake Kyoto for brief periods. Under the third shogun, Ashikaga Yoshimutsu (r. 1363–94), the southern court was finally eliminated and a single imperial succession restored. Yoshimutsu solidified the power of the shogunate, and was able to establish power over all the central provinces, though the outer regions remained outside his control. Yoshimutsu established trade with China, made improvements in agriculture that increased domestic production, and improved the economy. He also became a powerful and generous patron of the arts.

In the outer provinces, however, local warlords known as *daimyo* held sway. Their power increased over the years while the shogunate's power waned, and rivalries between the warlords eventually culminated in the Ōnin War (1467–77), during which Kyoto was destroyed, the shogunate defeated, and the nation forced into a century and a half of civil war called the *Sengoku* (Age of the country at war), which lasted until the second half of the 16th century. Portuguese traders arrived in 1542, and the

Jesuit missionary Francis Xavier in 1549. Over the objections of the Buddhist establishment, many of the warlords welcomed the visitors, anticipating an economic trade boom with the West. Meanwhile Oda Nobunaga, most powerful of the warlords, captured Kyoto in 1568 and overthrew what was left of the Muromachi government.

Despite the turbulence of the times, Japanese literature flourished during the Muromachi period. One important form of literature was the war chronicle, the most influential of which was *The Taiheiki* (Record of great peace), a 40-book chronicle narrating the events of the Kemmu Restoration and its aftermath, a 50-year period. Written in a combination of Japanese and Chinese, it is famous for its depiction of heroes who supported the imperial cause. The text seems to have been influenced significantly by *The TALE OF THE HEIKE.* Another significant war tale from this period is the *Meitokuki,* telling of the rebellion of the powerful Yamana family against the Ashikaga shogunate in 1391. Though the author, most likely a priest, is clearly a partisan of the shogun, the most memorable parts of the text are those that describe the deaths of the Yamana warriors.

More important than the war chronicles, drama flourished during the Muromachi period. Through the direct patronage of the Ashikaga shoguns, the Nō drama reached its period of maturity under its most important and innovative playwright and actor, ZEAMI (1363–1443). Applying the aesthetic principles first formulated in HEIAN court poetry to the creation of drama, Zeami also changed the subject matter of *Nō* plays from stories of the gods associated with local shrines around Kyoto to stories drawn from classical literature of Heian Japan, like the *TALE OF GENJI.* He also drew heavily on the more recent *Tale of the Heike,* a story of warriors that appealed to the new samurai culture of the Ashikaga military elite. Zeami developed the warrior play, whose protagonist was the spirit of a warrior whose resentment at his traumatic death prevented him from detaching himself from this world. The most popular of Zeami's warrior plays was *Atsumori,* concerning the young Heike warrior killed in the ninth chapter of the *Tale of the Heike.*

Another form of drama, the *kyōgen,* or comic drama, also became popular in the Muromachi period. With the turmoil in the capital, cultured aristocrats fled to the provinces, and as a result, later medieval literature shows a new interest in life among common people. This may explain the relationship of Nō drama with *kyōgen,* whose plays were performed alongside the Nō drama and in the same venue. In *kyōgen* plays, the common people, such as servants, are able to overcome obstacles for happy endings.

The warrior elite also sponsored a new type of poetry called *renga,* or "linked poetry," made up of sequences of stanzas in the form of the 31-syllable tanka poems. The sequences were of varying length, and might be composed by one, two, or three poets or more. Various complex rules governed the composition of such poems, including conventions of language and rhythm, and the classification of stanzas by topics. The most famous *renga* poet was Sōgi (1421–1502), who came from an obscure background and who lived through the Ōnin War to achieve great reputation and influence as the greatest poet of his times.

Another type of literature characteristic of Muromachi Japan was what has been called "outsiders' literature." Members of the establishment, whether aristocrats or Buddhist priests, might leave the court or the capital (either by choice or necessity) for a more isolated place, and may ultimately write their own observations as "outsiders." One of the earliest of these is Yoshida KENKŌ (ca. 1283–ca. 1350), whose *Essays in Idleness* include 243 fragments on various subjects, pertaining to, as he says "trivial things that came into my head." Another "outsider" was the Zen Buddhist priest Ikkyū (1394–1481), whose *Kyōunshū* (Mad cloud collection) consists of more than 1,000 poems written in Chinese. His poems are composed in four lines, with seven words per line, and are of three types: poems of Zen philosophy; poems decrying the depravity of contemporary times; and love poems, apparently addressed to Ikkyū's blind female attendant.

Another literary trend in Chinese-language poetry during the Muromachi age was the rise of *Gozan* literature. *Gozan* means "Five Temples" (there were five Buddhist temples each in Kyoto and in Kamakura), and literature written by Zen priests or monks associated with those temples became common late in the Kamakura period and continued into the Muromachi age. This literature might be in Japanese, Chinese, or a combination. By the later Muromachi period, *Gozan* poetry began to include the theme of love. No women were allowed in the Zen temples of Muromachi Japan, and some recent scholars have been interested in the theme of homosexual love in poets like Shinden Shōban (1380–1452), Tōshō Shūgen (fl. ca. 1460), and San'eki Eiin (fl. ca. 1520)—a theme that seems to have influenced the later Japanese warrior culture.

The Muromachi period produced a great deal of artistic innovation in poetry, drama, and prose. There was still a strong Buddhist influence on the literature, and a courtly influence as well, with Heian aesthetics clearly governing such developments as Nō drama. At the same time, the tastes and influence of the military elite as well as those outside the establishment, including influences from popular entertainment, began to have some impact during this era.

Bibliography

Chance, Linda H. *Formless in Form: Kenko, "Tsurezuregusa" and the Rhetoric of Japanese Fragmentary Prose.* Stanford, Calif.: Stanford University Press, 1997.

Japanese Nō Dramas. Edited and translated by Royall Tyler. London: Penguin, 1992.

Kato, Shuicho. *A History of Japanese Literature: From the Man-yōshu to Modern Times.* New abridged edition. Translated and edited by Don Sanderson. Richmond, U.K.: Curzon Press, 1997.

Keene, Donald. *Seeds in the Heart: Japanese Literature from Earliest Times to the Late Sixteenth Century.* Vol. 1 of *History of Japanese Literature.* New York: Columbia University Press, 1999.

Miner, Earl, Hiroko Odagiri, and Robert E. Morrell. *The Princeton Companion to Classical Japanese Literature.* Princeton, N.J.: Princeton University Press, 1985.

Rimer, J. Thomas, and Yamazaki Masakazu, trans. *On the Art of Nō Drama: The Major Treatises of Zeami.* Princeton, N.J.: Princeton University Press, 1984.

Muset, Colin (ca. 1200–ca. 1250)

Colin Muset was a JONGLEUR, a professional musician active in northern France in the second quarter of the 13th century. His status as jongleur is clear from the references in his lyrics to the instruments he plays, including the *viele* (an early type of fiddle) and the *flageolet* (a kind of duct flute related to the recorder). Colin is of particular interest because, unlike many jongleurs, he was not simply a performer but also composed his own lyrics; but unlike most of the well-known TROUVÈRES, he was not a member of the noble class and so was not educated in traditional classical rhetoric.

Nothing specific is known of Colin's life. He is thought to have been born in the area of Lorraine or Champagne, and to have performed in the noble houses of the Upper Marne Valley. Critics have praised Colin for his originality, for he touches on themes uncommon in the courtly tradition. In general these are a reflection of his socioeconomic status: He praises generous patrons and chastises stingy ones; he longs for good food and the good life. He gives us a glimpse of the life of the wandering musician in 13th-century France. In one poem he says:

When I see winter coming again,
then I'd like to settle down,
if I could find a host
who was generous and not anxious to count,
and had pork and beef and mutton,
mallards, pheasants, and venison,
fat chickens and capons
and good cheeses in straw,

and the lady were as full
as the husband of solicitude,
and always tried to please me

(Goldin 1973, 439, ll. 1–11)

Colin is also known for his casual attitude toward the technical aspects of his composition: He will use identical words to rhyme, or assonance instead of rhyme, or will compose lines that do not fit the meter he is using. Perhaps this unconcerned attitude stems from his lack of courtly education.

In addition his music is simple in style and form, similar to folk songs. Despite these things Colin is one of the most admired of the trouvères. Fifteen of his lyrics survive, along with eight melodies, preserved in eight manuscripts.

Bibliography

Bédier, Joseph. *De Nicolao Museto.* Geneva, Switzerland: Slatkine Reprints, 1973.

Goldin, Frederick, ed. and trans. *Lyrics of the Troubadours and Trouvères: An Anthology and a History.* Garden City, N.Y.: Doubleday, 1973.

Tischler, Hans, ed. *Trouvère Lyrics with Melodies: Complete Comparative Edition.* Neuhausen, Germany: Hänssler-Verlag, 1997.

van der Werf, Hendrik. *The Chansons of the Troubadours and Trouvères: A Study of the Melodies and Their Relation to the Poems.* Utrecht, Netherlands: A. Oosthoek, 1972.

My lefe is faren in londe (14th century)

One of the many anonymous MIDDLE ENGLISH lyrics dating from the 14th century is "My lefe is faren in londe" (that is, "My love has gone [traveled] far away [into the country]"). Like many Middle English lyrics, the poem deals with a conventional love theme—that of the narrator's longing caused by a separation from his beloved—but does so in a simple, fresh, and spontaneous way.

The lyric is a single stanza of seven trimeter (three-stress) lines, rhyming *ababcbc.* The speaker says he is parted from his lover, and simply asks "Why is she so?" (Davies 1964, l. 2). He is not able to go to her because he is cruelly bound where he is. But his heart, he says, is bound to her, wherever she is (literally wherever she rides or walks). He ends by saying he has true love for her, a "thousandfold" (l. 7). Like many such lyrics, it is generalized, with only the broad outlines of a situation behind the emotion of the speaker, so that the poem might be seen to have a universal application to anyone separated from the one he or she loves.

Some Middle English lyrics were set to music, and it is quite possible that "My lefe is faren in londe" was sung as early as the 14th century. Although the text of the lyric survives in a late 15th-century manuscript (Trinity College Cambridge, MS. R. 3. 19), it is almost certainly older than that document. Presumably it is the song that CHAUCER has his cock and hen, Chaunticleer and Pertelote, sing "in sweet accord" (i.e., harmony) in the *NUN'S PRIEST'S TALE.* The song must have been popular enough that Chaucer expected his audience to recognize it and possibly even know the melody.

Bibliography

Davies, R. T., ed. *Medieval English Lyrics: A Critical Anthology.* Evanston, Ill.: Northwestern University Press, 1964.

mystery plays

The most widespread and popular form of drama in medieval Europe was the mystery play, which retold a story from the biblical narrative. While extremely popular in France and in Germany, these plays were most widespread in England, where they took the form of a long series of relatively short plays depicting the traditional biblical history of the world from creation through Doomsday. These plays, which might be called *sacre representazzione* in Italy or *auto sacramentale* in Spain, derive their English name mystery plays (an 18th-century coinage) from the French term *mystère,* denoting a trade or craft. What is known of the production of mystery plays in England indicates that the craft guilds, the most powerful political and economic organizations of the medieval towns, took responsibility for the staging of the various plays. Mystery plays were known to have been performed in England during CHAUCER's lifetime (late 14th century), and continued well into the Elizabethan period, with productions recorded in the 1570s, during Shakespeare's youth. Most extant English mystery plays belong to one of four cycles—the YORK CYCLE (which comprises 48 plays), the CHESTER CYCLE (with 24 plays), the TOWNELEY CYCLE (sometimes called the Wakefield Cycle, with 32 plays), and the N-TOWN PLAYS (also known as the *Ludus Coventriae,* with 42 plays). Only the first two of these seem to be the surviving scripts of actual cycle dramas as performed in Chester and in York, although it is clear from medieval archives that many English towns (notably Coventry, Norwich, Newcastle, Lincoln, and others) staged such plays.

The English mystery plays are particularly associated with the festival of CORPUS CHRISTI, a holiday honoring the sacrament of the Eucharist and the real presence of the body of Christ in the sacrament. Falling on the Thursday after the movable feast of Trinity Sunday, Corpus Christi could be celebrated on any date between May 23 and June 24. As an early summer festival, Corpus Christi was perfect for an outdoor celebration, and this may have influenced the development of outdoor dramatic entertainment. The fact that Corpus Christi was initially celebrated, beginning in 1311, with a procession of the host (the communion wafer) through the town may have influenced the staging of the plays, so that they were produced in a procession as well.

The production of mystery places varied from place to place and from year to year, so any generalization about them is dubious, and most scholars prefer to speak of specific local customs. Nevertheless, in at least some towns (such as York), the plays were staged on large wagons (called pageants), which were drawn to a series of preordained stops in the city, where audiences would be waiting, so that each play might be performed several times during the course of the day, and any given audience would see the entire cycle as a series of plays as one wagon followed another to the staging area.

Obviously, staging a cycle would have been a huge community effort, in terms of time, manpower, and expense. Yet participating in the festival was a matter of civic pride, and each guild was responsible for furnishing the pageant wagon, actors, props, and scenery for its own play. Individual guilds laid claim to particular plays that they kept from year to year. Sometimes these assignments made logical sense, as in the assigning of the York Noah play to the shipwrights' guild, the play of the Last Supper to the bakers' guild, or the play of the Magi to the goldsmiths' guild. Sometimes there was no particular connection, as in the assignment of the York HARROWING OF HELL play to the saddlers' guild. The guilds very likely also commissioned the script of the play, perhaps from a learned local priest or from their guild chaplain.

The purpose of the mystery cycles was certainly basically didactic—to present the biblical salvation history to an audience that for the most part could not read the Scriptures themselves. But the character of the English mystery plays reflects their audience and their various authors' efforts to popularize the text and appeal to the broad range of medieval burghers. Characters are clearly good or evil, and the evil are more often than not comic in their futile defiance of the Almighty. The language of the characters is the language of their audience—the language of the marketplace or the farm, with its colloquialism, its occasional bawdiness or coarseness, full of everyday anachronistic expressions that allowed the audience to identify with the characters.

Mystery plays were enormously entertaining, as authors added numerous comic elements to the traditional stories to appeal to the audience of common people. Noah's wife, for example, became a favorite shrewish character in more than one of the cycles. The most admired of all mystery plays is the famous *SECOND SHEPHERDS' PLAY* from the Towneley Cycle, in which the comic plot concerning the shepherds and the sheep-stealing Mak dominates a play purportedly about the Nativity.

Still, it was the allegorical MORALITY PLAYS that exerted the greatest influence on the development of Elizabethan drama, and not the more realistic mystery plays. Associated as they were with the Roman Catholic festival of Corpus Christi and with veneration of the Virgin Mary, whose life served as the background for a number of the dramas, the mystery plays were suppressed during Elizabeth's reign and the triumph of Protestantism.

Bibliography

Beadle, Richard, ed. *The Cambridge Companion to Medieval English Theatre.* Cambridge: Cambridge University Press, 1994.

Kolve, V. A. *The Play Called Corpus Christi.* Stanford, Calif.: Stanford University Press, 1966.

Robinson, J. W. *Studies in Fifteenth-Century Stagecraft.* Kalamazoo: Western Michigan University, Medieval Institute Publications, 1991.

Woolf, Rosemary E. *The English Mystery Plays.* London: Routledge and Kegan Paul, 1972.

Nara period (710–794)

The Nara period is a relatively short period of Japanese history in which Chinese culture remained influential while, at the same time, Japan began to advance its own unique cultural identity. Empress Gemmei established the capital at Nara (Heijo kyo), a planned city laid out on a grid in imitation of the TANG capital of Changan. Modeling Chinese Confucian practice, the Japanese launched a highly centralized government explained in Prince Shotoku's *Seventeen-Article Constitution.* Concentrated efforts by the imperial court to record and document itself produced the first works of Japanese history, the *Kojiki* (712) and the *Nihon Shoki* (720). Chinese Buddhism continued to be promoted, and Emperor Shomu (724–749) erected the Todai-ji, a huge wooden temple that houses an especially impressive Buddha. Because most of Japanese society was rural and practiced Shinto, it was at this time that the urban Buddhist ruling class became alienated from the common people.

A number of distinctly Japanese achievements occurred during the Nara Period. *MAN'YOSHU* (*Anthology of a Myriad Leaves*) (759) is the first collection of native poetry in Japanese literature. It is written using a syllabary in which Chinese characters serve as phonetic symbols of syllables rather than of words. Chinese characters were used to express sounds of Japanese until the Kana script was invented in the later Nara Period. With the spread of written language, the distinctly Japanese poetic form, the *waka,* appeared. The traditional methods of hanging and horizontal Japanese scroll painting, which incorporated both image and word, were established as well.

Bibliography

Keene, Donald. *Seeds in the Heart: Japanese Literature from Earliest Times to the Late Sixteenth Century.* New York: Henry Holt and Co., 1993.

Sansom, George B. *A History of Japan to 1334.* Stanford, Calif.: Stanford University Press, 1958.

Cynthia Ho

Neidhart (ca. 1180–ca. 1240)

The poetic generation after WALTHER VON DER VOGELWEIDE is clearly dominated by the Austro-Bavarian poet Neidhart (only in his poetry he calls himself, with tongue-in-cheek, *von Reuenthal,* or "of the dale of sorrow"). In his songs he mentions many names of places and towns in Austria, and there are references in his poems to Duke Frederick II of Austria (1230–46) as his patron, to political events in the 1230s, and to a Crusade. This Crusade could have been the expedition of Leopold of Austria in 1217 and 1218, or Emperor Frederick II's Crusade in 1228 and 1229. WOLFRAM VON ESCHENBACH mentions Neidhart in his *Willehalm* epos (ca. 1220) as a well-known singer, whereas Wernher der Gartenære talks in his *Meier Helmbrecht* (ca. 1260–70) about Neidhart as already dead. This gives us a framework for his life from ca. 1180/1190 to ca. 1240. The *Manessische Liederhandschrift* (ms. C, early 14th century) includes a fictionalized portrait of the poet standing between some peasants.

Neidhart is famous for the introduction of two specific types of love songs, the Summer song and the Winter song. Whereas in the former the figure Neidhart is highly successful in winning the love of the country girls (by itself a grotesque parody of traditional COURTLY LOVE poetry), in the latter his economic woes prove to be his greatest hindrance as the rich peasant lads (many are named) are the clear winners in the competition for the village girls. Neidhart also offers remarkable mother-daughter dialogue poems, describes winter sport, formulates harsh criticism of peasants, and satirizes old women who display uncontrollable sexual desires. Neidhart projects humorous, but also very negative images of peasant life, but it seems that the true target of his criticism is the lower nobility, here cast in the image of peasants. Neidhart enjoyed tremendous popularity, documented not only by 25 manuscripts and three early-modern prints, but also by a large number of pseudo-Neidhart songs, grotesque and obscene verse novellas about the Neidhart figure, and Neidhart-Shrovetide plays from the later Middle Ages. Remarkably the melodies of many of his songs have been preserved in several 15th-century manuscripts.

Bibliography

Shockey, Gary. " 'Gein wem solt ich mich zâfen?': The Peasant Lady Speaks in Summer Lay 14 of Neidhart," *Neuphilologische Mitteilungen* 102, no. 4 (2001): 469–481.

Simon, Eckhard. *Neidhart von Reuental.* Boston: Twayne, 1975.

Traverse, Elizabeth. *Peasants, Season and Werltsüeze: Cyclicity in Neidhart's Songs Reexamined.* Göppingen, Germany: Kümmerle, 1997.

Wießner, Edmiund, ed. *Die Lieder Neidharts.* Fortgeführt von Hanns Fischer. 4th rev. Edited by Paul Sappler. Altdeutsche Textbibliothek, 44. Tübingen, Germany: Niemeyer, 1984.

Albrecht Classen

Nennius (fl. 800)

Nennius is the purported author of the *Historia Brittonum* (History of the Britons), an early ninth-century compilation containing the first literary reference to Arthur (later called King ARTHUR) as hero of the British people.

Of Nennius himself we know next to nothing. Clearly he was Welsh, said to be a monk from Bangor in north Wales, and wrote in the early ninth century. The *Historia Brittonum* seems to have been inspired by a resurgence of Welsh nationalism, and Arthur is described as a heroic warlord.

The *Historia* itself is something of a mishmash, cobbled together from the earlier texts of GILDAS, BEDE, St. JEROME, and oral tradition. Nennius says that he "made one heap" of everything that he found. It begins with a section on the "Six Ages of the World," beginning with the Creation and ending at Doomsday. A geographical description of Britain follows, with references to Scots, Picts, and Britons. Nennius mentions, for the first time in literature, the tradition that Britain is named for Brutus, descendent of the Trojan Aeneas. There is an account of the Roman occupation of Britain, a discussion of the British king Vortigern's folly allowing the Saxon invasion, and mention of Vortigern's dread of his rival and ultimate successor, Ambrosius. This section relies mainly on Gildas and Bede. It is interspersed with largely irrelevant lives of St. Germanus and of St. Patrick in Ireland, and is followed by the discussion of Arthur.

Nennius makes Arthur *dux bellorum,* or "leader of battles," and describes his defeating the Saxons in 12 battles, including the Battle of Mount Badon, at which Arthur is said to have killed 960 Saxons by his own hand. Many scholars believe that this list of battles is based on a lost Welsh poem.

Following these accounts is a series of Anglo-Saxon genealogies, a section on northern British history, and a fascinating section on "Marvels of Britain and Ireland." The marvels contain two specific accounts of Arthurian interest: a stone near Builth Wells said to display the paw print of Arthur's dog, Cabal; and the tomb of Arthur's son, named Amr. The tomb is said to change its length every time it is measured—a phenomenon Nennius claims to have witnessed himself. But of chief interest in this story is not the elastic tomb but the legend surrounding it: that Arthur killed his own son—a motif that forms the seed of the Arthur-Mordred rivalry that becomes a vital part of later versions of the Arthurian legend.

The *Historia Brittonum* survives in some 35 manuscripts, to the earliest of which (Harley MS 3859) is appended the *Welsh Annals* (*ANNALES CAMBRIAE*).

Bibliography

Alcock, Leslie. *Arthur's Britain.* London: Penguin, 1971.

Bengle, Richard L. *Arthur King of Britain: History, Chronicle, Romance and Criticism.* New York: Appleton-Century-Crofts, 1964.

Morris, John, ed. and trans. *Nennius: British History and The Welsh Annals.* London: Phillimore, 1975.

New Council, The (*Nová rada*) Smil Flaška (ca. 1394)

Nová rada (The new council) is a BEAST FABLE in verse, intended as a political satire on the reign of Wenceslas IV (1361–40), king of Bohemia and sometime Holy Roman Emperor. Its author, Smil Flaška of Pardubice, was a Czech noble writing in defense of the traditional rights and privileges of the nobility against the crown.

Smil's father was a powerful aristocrat, and his uncle, Ernest of Pardubice, was archbishop of Prague. Smil was educated at Prague University and inherited his father's lands upon the elder's death ca. 1389. Ultimately, however, he lost or sold his estates. By the mid-1390s, he had joined the Lords' Union, a baronial faction opposed to King Wenceslas. The nobles engaged in military action against the king in an attempt to stop the erosion of their rights, particularly regarding inherited property. From 1394 until his death in 1403 at the siege of the king's city of Kutná Hora, Smil was chief notary of the land court for the Lords' Union. It was early in this period, about 1394, that he wrote *The New Council.*

Smil's poem is a series of 44 counsels presented by birds and other animals who have been drawn together to advise the Lion King. The Lion is clearly representative of Wenceslas, whose coat of arms was the Lion of Bohemia. The animal's speeches are framed by the Eagle and the Swan, probably representing the Empire and the Church respectively—though the Eagle was also the heraldic symbol of Jošt of Luxembourg, Wenceslas's younger brother who led the first baronial rebellion against the king in 1394. Other speakers—the Horse, Wolf, Peacock, Beaver, Nightingale, and so on—are more difficult to identify. It is also sometimes difficult to determine whether the speeches are intended to give the king good advice or to satirize his reign. Accordingly many scholars believe that the text of 1394 is a reworking of an earlier text, perhaps called simply *The Counsel,* written by the younger Smil and intended as a benevolent "Mirror of Princes" manual for the young King Wenceslas. The extant text, according to this theory, has been added to and revised for the purposes of satirizing the reign of the older King Wenceslas.

The text as we have it focuses on three major baronial complaints about Wenceslas's reign: first, that the king had allowed outsiders, foreigners, to become part of his council; second, that he had allowed men to purchase positions in government, particularly in the land courts; and finally, perhaps most significantly, that he had claimed his traditional feudal right to reversion, seizing the property of nobles who had apparently died without legitimate heirs. The third complaint was one that affected Smil's own family, and he alludes to it in *The New Council* in the counsel of the Wolf.

In addition to these major complaints, the animals' counsels also allude to allegations about very specific personal shortcomings of the king's, such as his laziness, his drunkenness, his alienation of the church, his penchant for spending time with common people and dressing below his station, and his strange fondness for frequent hot baths (with female bath attendants). Whether or not there was an earlier version of the text, clearly the one that we have is the work of a courtier who has lost faith in a king he believes has forfeited his political and moral authority to rule.

Bibliography

Thomas, Alfred. *Anne's Bohemia: Czech Culture and Society, 1310–1420.* Minneapolis: University of Minnesota Press, 1998.

Nibelungenlied (ca. 1200)

Although we know of several heroic epics that were composed in Middle High German before 1200, the anonymous *Nibelungenlied* is the most famous representative of this genre, sharing many of its monumental, tragic elements with epics like BEOWULF and CANTAR DE MÍO CID. Composed and later copied down around 1200, probably in Passau on behalf of Bishop Wolfger of Erla, the *Nibelungenlied* reflects historical events dating back to the fifth century when the Huns under Attila attacked western Europe. In a battle against Roman and Hunnish forces around 436/437, the Burgundian kingdom in the Rhine Valley under King Gundahari was destroyed. The king and thousands of his troops were killed, and the remaining Burgundians were settled by the Romans in the area now known as Burgundy. After the Western Roman Empire ultimately collapsed in 476, the Ostrogothic king Theodoric (called Dietrich in the epic) established his rule over Italy with the approval of the Eastern emperor Zeno in 493 and ruled until 526, but his successors could not maintain control and were eventually defeated by Byzantine forces.

The *Nibelungenlied* poet combined many of these historical elements to create a mythical account, best reflected by the initial stanza, which also indicates that he drew from oral sources: "We have been told in ancient tales many marvels of famous heroes of mighty toil, joys, and high festivities, of weeping and wailing, and the fighting of bold warriors." The epic consists of two major portions connected through the figure of Kriemhild, sister of the three Burgundian kings Gunther, Gernôt, and Giselher, and wife of the hero Siegfried.

Siegfried, whose father Sigemunt is king of the Netherlands, arrives in Worms to woo Kriemhild, whom he has never seen before but whose beauty is famous. Gunther's court steward, Hagen, relates that Siegfried has accomplished many heroic deeds, especially the slaying of a dragon. Siegfried bathed in its blood and acquired an impenetrable skin, except for one spot on his shoulder blade where a leaf from a linden tree had fallen. Siegfried at first demands that Gunther hand over his lands, but the young hero, pacified by the thoughts of Kriemhild, is soon mollified and inducted into the courtly lifestyle. Nevertheless Hagen becomes his mortal enemy, out of envy and fear of Siegfried's superior strength as displayed in warfare and at hunting. Despite his glamorous appearance, Siegfried quickly demonstrates an irrational and weak character, easily influenced by others and blind in the machinations in his surroundings. In order to win Kriemhild's hand, Siegfried foolishly assists Gunther in winning the Icelandic queen Brunhild by resorting to deception and cunning, utilizing his magical cloak of invisibility.

Brunhild, who thought she was to be Siegfried's, distrusts her husband and rejects him on the wedding night, humiliating him by binding his hands and feet and hanging him on a nail. Again, Siegfried's help is requested, and again he takes Gunther's place, using the magical cloak to defeat Brunhild. Having subdued her, Siegfried takes her ring and belt, symbolically raping her, and practically robbing her of all her superhuman strength. Siegfried gives these two objects to his wife. Later when the couple has returned to Worms for a visit, Kriemhild and Brunhild quarrel over their ranks while arranging their Mass procession. Brunhild assumes that Siegfried is nothing but Gunther's vassal, which would give her the superior rank over her sister-in-law. But Kriemhild produces Brunhild's ring and belt. Calling her opponent Siegfried's whore, she triumphantly walks into the church ahead of her competitor. Brunhild, deeply upset, appeals to Hagen, who convinces Gunther that Siegfried has become a liability and must be killed. During a hunting episode, he stabs Siegfried in the back at the only spot where he is vulnerable, unwittingly revealed to him by Kriemhild. Although Kriemhild immediately realizes who killed her husband and proves Hagen's guilt when Siegfried's wound begins to bleed again in Hagen's presence, she has no means to avenge herself, especially after Hagen takes from her Siegfried's famous Nibelung treasure and sinks it into the Rhine.

After 13 years of mourning, Kriemhild is wooed by the Hunnish king Etzel (Attila), and although he is a heathen, finally accepts his offer of marriage. Her motives, however, are transparent: She hopes Etzel will provide her the military and monetary means to realize her revenge. Most important, her relative, Margrave Rüedeger, Etzel's vassal, secretly negotiates to protect her and to take revenge on anyone who might threaten Kriemhild (1256–57). Seven years later, Kriemhild invites her Burgundian family to visit and insists that Hagen accompany them.

Gunther and his men accept the invitation and travel to Hungary, but after they have crossed the Danube, Hagen destroys their boat to ensure that no coward among them dare flee for home. This is in response to the "water nixes'" prophecy that none but their chaplain will return alive. Hagen tests the prophecy by throwing the chaplain overboard into the Danube. When the latter reaches shore despite his inability to swim, Hagen knows the warning is accurate.

Although King Etzel tries to treat his guests hospitably, Kriemhild incites hostilities, quickly leading to massive slaughters on both sides. Finally Kriemhild reminds Etzel of his promise, and after killing many warriors Rüedeger is confronted by Gernôt: Tragically, they slay each other, although Rüedeger's daughter and Gernôt's brother Giselher had been engaged. Finally Kriemhild incites Dietrich, another exiled Germanic warrior at Etzel's court, to assist her, but all his men are killed except his master-at-arms, Hildebrand. Ultimately Dietrich himself battles the sole survivors among the Burgundians, Hagen and Gunther, taking both prisoners without slaying them. Kriemhild, in her insatiable desire for revenge, has Gunther killed, and decapitates Hagen with her own hand when he refuses to return the Nibelung treasure, a metonymic symbol of Siegfried. Hildebrand, witnessing this horrible scene, leaps at her and cuts her into pieces.

The *Nibelungenlied* poet gravely laments the catastrophic outcome, but he refrains from telling us anything about the subsequent events. An anonymous poet later picked up this narrative thread and composed a lengthy poem, *Die Klage* (*The Lament*), which describes the enormous grief affecting all survivors, their relatives, and friends, until Gunther's son is crowned as his successor. Many other heroic poems in various languages later drew from the *Nibelungenlied*, demonstrating its enormous popularity and powerful literary messages regarding the consequences of violence, revenge, hatred, jealousy, irrational discourse, lack of communication, and the tragic implications of absolute bonds of blood fealty.

Since the publication of its first modern edition in 1782, the *Nibelungenlied* has been a major source for mythical reflections about the Middle Ages and was abused as a treasure house for modern nationalistic, even Nazi ideology, especially when concepts such as honor, supreme loyalty, leadership, and absolute heroism in the name of the fatherland were evoked. Hermann Göring's perverse comparison of the Battle of Stalingrad in 1943 with the Burgundians' final battle at the court of King Etzel stands out. More spiritual approaches informed Friedrich Hebbel's drama *Nibelungen* (1862) and Richard Wagner's *Der Ring des Nibelungen* (1876). The profound and continuous influence of the poem can be documented by a vast number of modern retellings, translations, movies, paintings, and dramatizations.

Bibliography

Classen, Albrecht. "The Downfall of a Hero: Siegfried's Self-Destruction and the End of Heroism in the *Nibelungenlied*," *German Studies Review* 26, no. 2 (2003): 295–314.

Das Nibelungenlied. After the edition by Karl Bartsch. 22nd ed. by Roswitha Wisniewski. Mannheim, Germany: Brockhaus, 1988.

Gentry, Francis G., Winder McConnell, Ulrich Müller, and Werner Wunderlich, eds. *The Nibelungen Tradition: An Encyclopedia*. New York: Routledge, 2002.

Hatto, A. T., trans. *The Nibelungenlied*. London: Penguin, 1965.

Haymes, Edward R., and Susann T. Samples. *Heroic Legends of the North: An Introduction to the Nibelung and Dietrich Cycles*. New York: Garland, 1996.

McConnell, Winder, ed. *A Companion to the Nibelungenlied.* Columbia, S.C.: Camden House and Boydell and Brewer, 1998.

Albrecht Classen

Nine Worthies (Worthies of the World)

The Nine Worthies were a group of historical and legendary figures popular in the late Middle Ages and Renaissance that became a common theme in literature and in art. The Worthies were intended to represent all aspects of the perfect chivalric knight. Known as conquering heroes and powerful warriors, as well as displaying the knightly virtues of loyalty, integrity, generosity, etc., the Worthies served as exemplars for contemporary knights who, in the anachronistic view of their era, conceived of knighthood as an institution dating back to ancient times. Thus as William CAXTON puts it in the prologue to his edition of MALORY's *Le MORTE DARTHUR* (1485), the Worthies comprise "three Paynims, three Jews, and three Christian men." The three pagans were Hector of Troy, Alexander the Great, and Julius Caesar; the three Jews were Joshua, King David, and Judas Maccabeus; and the three Christians were King ARTHUR, CHARLEMAGNE, and Godfrey of Bouillon, the leader and hero of the First Crusade, who was credited with the conquest of Jerusalem.

This is the configuration proposed by the Frenchman, Jean de Longuyon, in his *Voeux du Paon* (Vows of the peacock, ca. 1312), the earliest extant literary treatment of the Nine Worthies theme, and the list remained quite standard—whether in literature, painting, tapestries, stained glass, sculpture, or woodcut—for hundreds of years. Occasionally there was some variation. A 10th "Worthy" might be proposed: Some French texts include Bernard du Guesclin, who was the greatest French soldier of the 14th century and was responsible for winning much of France back from England in the Hundred Year's War. But Gueslin was never accepted outside of France itself. Occasionally substitutions are made: The ROMANCE hero GUY OF WARWICK is substituted for Godfrey of Bouillon in some configurations. In *Love's Labour's Lost* (Act V, scene 2), Shakespeare includes Pompey and Hercules among the Worthies, and in his incomplete list leaves off several others more commonly included. Sometimes, for the sake of symmetry, a list of nine worthy women might also be included, though there was never a standard list of women as there was of men.

Most often the theme of the Nine Worthies was used to demonstrate chivalric ideals as embodied in these figures. The anonymous author of the late 14th-century MIDDLE ENGLISH poem *The PARLIAMENT OF THE THREE AGES,* however, uses the Worthies as examples of the transience of worldly glory in the face of Fortune's ever-turning wheel. The French poet Eustache DESCHAMPS uses the Worthies, heroes of the past, to contrast with the degenerate, unchivalric present in a *BALLADE* written in 1386. Caxton's use of the tradition in his edition of Malory is not unlike Deschamps's: In the wake of the Wars of the Roses, Caxton points to the noble deeds done in Arthur's day and to the justice and virtue of his knights, and exhorts the readers of his own time to follow their example.

Bibliography

Caxton's Malory. Edited with an introduction and critical apparatus by James W. Spisak. Based on work begun by the late William Matthews. With a dictionary of names and places by Bert Dillon. Berkeley: University of California Press, 1983.

Ginsberg, Warren, ed. *Wynnere and Wastoure and the Parlement of the Three Ages.* Kalamazoo, Mich.: Published for TEAMS by the Medieval Institute, 1992.

Njal's Saga (*The Story of Burnt Njal*) (ca. 1280)

Njal's Saga is the best-known and most admired of the Old Icelandic sagas. At 400 pages in modern editions, it is also by far the longest, and with some 600 characters, the most complex as well. Like most family sagas, its action concerns a blood-feud, this one extending over a period of 50 years. Events in the saga take place from about 930 to 1020. Thus they overlap the conversion of Iceland to Christianity in 1000, which plays a significant part in the story. At the center of the action is the lawyer, farmer, and sage Njal Thorgeirsson of Bergthorsknoll, who is burned alive in his own home, along with most of his family.

The saga is divided into two main sections, telling two separate but related stories. Chapters 1–81 are concerned with Njal's friend Gunnar of Hlidarend, a hero who, through the malevolence and envy of his wife, Hallgirth, drives away his own friends (all but the loyal Njal) and commits acts that bring upon him a sentence of outlawry. When he refuses to leave Iceland, he is attacked in his home by a horde of his enemies. He defends himself heroically, killing many of his attackers, but when his bowstring is destroyed and he begs Hallgirth for strands of her hair to repair it, she refuses out of revenge for a slap he had once given her. Ultimately Gunnar is killed.

Much of the first half of the saga is also the story of Njal, Gunnar's wise and generous friend. Chapters 82–159 tell Njal's own story, and that of his quarrelsome sons. After a dispute with Thrain Sigfusson, Njal's sons attack and kill Thrain. Njal tries to head off a feud by adopting Thrain's son Hoskuld as his own foster son. But Njal's sons quarrel with Hoskuld and kill him as well. Flosi Thordarson, the uncle of Hoskuld's widow, takes up the feud, refuses any settlement, and ultimately leads an assault on Njal's farm at Bergthorsknoll, where he burns Njal and his sons alive. Kari Solmundarson, Njal's son-in-law and the only surviving male member of his family, prosecutes the burners and kills some of them before finally reconciling with Flosi in the final chapter of the saga.

More than 50 manuscripts of *Njal's Saga* are extant, the earliest of which date from the late 13th century. Written around 1280, it is one of the later sagas, and its style suggests its author was well-educated and highly literate. Many scholars believe the author used a number of written sources, but others argue that the saga is a traditional narrative based mainly upon oral sources. As with all sagas, the historicity of *Njal's Saga* is difficult to determine. Both Gunnar's death and the burning of Njal at Bergthorsknoll are corroborated by the historical text *Landnamabok* (Book of settlements), but there are a number of anachronisms and other errors in fact, so the story must be assumed to be an imaginative retelling of historical events.

One problem for scholars of *Njal's Saga* has been the unity of the text. The two disparate halves, as well as the length of the saga, have suggested to some that the text we have is in fact a combination of two separate sagas. Others, however, have pointed to thematic parallels in the two parts. Both halves deal with tension between the old, pagan violence of feuds and the new, Christian values of peace and settlement of disputes by law. Njal, who accepts Christianity, is constant in his opposition to the old culture's demand for revenge, and although Gunnar strives to be like Njal, he gives in to the old ways. Both ultimately die in blood feuds, but the new ethic seems to prevail in the end, with the peaceful settlement between Flosi and Kari.

Bibliography

Allen, Richard F. *Fire and Iron: Critical Approaches to Njal's Saga.* Pittsburgh: University of Pittsburgh Press, 1971.

Jón, Karl Helgason. *The Rewriting of Njal's Saga: Translation, Ideology, and Icelandic Sagas.* Buffalo, N.Y.: Multilingual Matters, 1999.

Lönnroth, Lars. *Njal's Saga: A Critical Introduction.* Berkeley: University of California Press, 1976.

Magnusson, Magnus, and Hermann Palsson, trans. and introduction *Njal's Saga.* Harmondsworth, U.K.: Penguin, 1960.

Sveinsson, Einar Olafur. *Njal's Saga: A Literary Masterpiece.* Edited and translated by Paul Schach. Lincoln: University of Nebraska Press, 1971.

Nō (Noh theater)

The oldest form of drama performed in Japan, Nō developed in the later 14th and early 15th century from an earlier form of drama known as *sarugaku.* It was developed to a large extent from innovations made by the famous playwright Kan'ami (1333–84) and his even more influential son, the playwright and theorist ZEAMI (ca. 1363–ca. 1443), whose plays gained the recognition and support of the Ashikaga shōguns. One of the changes Zeami made was to choose protagonists not from popular tradition, as earlier *sarugaku* plays had done, but rather from HEIAN culture or from classical Japanese literature, particularly the *TALE OF THE HEIKE*. Zeami also led Nō theater away from realism and emphasized subtle internal conflict in his characters.

Nō plays are traditionally performed by an all-male cast. There are four conventional roles in the drama: the lead role (*shite*), the chief supporting role (*waki*) (opposite to, but not necessarily the opponent of, the lead role—he provides the impetus for the inner drama of the *shite*), the lead role's companion and the secondary character's companion. The plays are divided among five types, based on the role of the protagonist. The first category, *Wakinō,* comprises plays about gods. The second, *Nibanmemono,* is made up of warrior plays. The third category, *Sambanmemono,* consists of plays about women. The fourth, *Yobanmemono,* is a category in which the *shite* is a mad person, or a person from "modern" times—essentially the category includes the plays that are not part of any other group. The fifth group, *Gobanmemono,* are plays about demons or other supernatural characters.

Most of the actors wear masks, except for children and actors portraying living male characters. The secondary character and his companion, who are always living male characters, never wear masks. But the chief characters, often ghosts or women, are typically masked. The language of the plays varies from verse to prose, and involves varied degrees of chanting, from something close to ordinary speech using prose to something approaching singing. It is impossible to know precisely about the style of acting during the 14th century, but traditional Nō acting today is highly stylized and all movement is slow and choreographed—all body movements are classified as *shimari,* or "performance dance." There are traditional subtle clues in the Nō actor's movement, particularly in the walk, that indicate the character's gender, age, and social position.

Nō plays also conventionally contain a chorus (the *jiutai*), consisting of from six to 10 members. Unlike the chorus of a Greek tragedy, the Nō chorus does not assume a specific role in the play. They remain motionless throughout the play, sitting on the right of the stage and chanting in unison, sometimes acting as a narrator and sometimes repeating the characters' lines, particularly the lines of the *shite* when he is dancing. Four musicians sometimes accompany the chanting with a flute and three drums (one a hip drum, one a stick drum, and one a shoulder drum). The characters at times perform dances as well, often to indicate heightened emotion, and these dances are also accompanied by the musicians, and sometimes also by the chanting of the chorus.

The stage for Nō plays is a 19-foot square with a bridgeway (from the dressing room to the left side of the stage) that can sometimes serve as a second performing area. The stage contains no scenery, so that the dialogue itself must indicate the play's setting. Props are also rare, with an occasional prop taking on symbolic meanings during the play. Costumes, however, are beautiful and elaborate, often to the point of obscuring the body and face of the performer, so that even with those not wearing masks, the audience must focus on the subtle and graceful movements of the actor rather than on facial expressions.

Most of the 250 or so Nō plays still being performed are ghost dramas, a type of play made popular by Zeami in the 14th century. In such plays, a wandering monk meets a ghost who has taken the form of a local peasant or other figure in the first act. In the second act the monk dreams of the ghost in its true form, who in the dream reenacts its death or whatever incident in its earthly life has prevented it from resting in peace. In many plays the monk's prayers bring about the pacification of the restless spirit.

Subtlety, suggestion, simplicity, and internal conflict characterize Japanese Nō theater. Westerners experiencing the plays for the first time are likely to be confused and put off by the lack of "action." But like most drama, a Nō play is a sensual experience involving sound, color, and movement, and so cannot be defined simply by the words on a page: It must be experienced.

Bibliography

Japanese Nō Dramas. Edited and translated by Royall Tyler. London: Penguin, 1992.

Miner, Earl, Hiroko Odagiri, and Robert E. Morrell. *The Princeton Companion to Classical Japanese Literature.* Princeton, N.J.: Princeton University Press, 1985.

Rimer, J. Thomas, and Yamazaki Masakazu, trans. *On the Art of Nō Drama: The Major Treatises of Zeami.* Princeton, N.J.: Princeton University Press, 1984.

Sekine, Masaru. *Zeami and His Theories of Noh Drama.* Gerrards Cross, U.K.: C. Smythe, 1985.

Terasaki, Etsuko. *Figures of Desire: Wordplay, Spirit Possession, Fantasy, Madness, and Mourning in Japanese Noh Plays.* Ann Arbor: Center for Japanese Studies, University of Michigan, 2002.

Notker Balbulus ("the Stammerer") (ca. 840–912)

Notker, called Balbulus (Stammerer), was a monk of the Benedictine Abbey of St. Gall near Zurich, Switzerland. He is known as a composer, a poet, a biographer, and a theorist.

Notker was born about 840 of prominent Swiss parents, who sent him as a child to study with the monks of St. Gall. St. Gall was a very influential monastery with a valuable musical library. Notker remained as a monk in the abbey for the rest of his life, and aside from being a revered teacher at the school, he is mentioned as holding the offices of librarian, master of guests, and precentor, or choirmaster.

Notker was reputed to have been of frail health and to have stammered, but he seems to have had a significant talent for music, and popularized the sequence, a new type of liturgical hymn. This was a hymn sung after the *Alleluia* and before the Gospel in the Latin mass. Notker composed music and lyrics for these hymns, and in about 880, created a book of hymns containing a number of these sequences.

In addition to lyrics for hymns, Notker also is known to have written some lives of saints, poems, and letters, and is generally thought to be the anonymous "Monk of St. Gall," who in 883–84, wrote the anecdotal and idealized biography of CHARLEMAGNE entitled *Gesta Caroli* (The deeds of Charles). The book, composed for the Holy Roman Emperor Charles the Fat, helped glorify Charles's great-grandfather Charlemagne as a legendary hero among the German-speaking people.

Notker died in 912. Always venerated by the monks of St. Gall, Notker was beatified by the Catholic Church in 1512.

Bibliography

Murdoch, Brian O. *Old High German Literature.* Boston: Twayne, 1983.

Thorpe, Lewis, trans. *Two Lives of Charlemagne.* Harmondsworth, U.K.: Penguin, 1969.

N-Town Plays (*Ludus Coventriae,* Hegge Cycle) (late 15th century)

One of the four extant compilations of late medieval MYSTERY PLAYS, the N-Town Plays survive in a single manuscript, British Library MS Cotton Vespasian D.viii. Richard James, librarian to the antiquarian book collector Sir Robert Bruce Cotton, obtained the manuscript from Robert Hegge of Corpus Christi College in Oxford in about 1630, and therefore the plays are sometimes referred to as the "Hegge Cycle." James labeled the manuscript *Ludus Coventriae* on its flyleaf, which led early scholars to consider it the cycle performed at Coventry on the festival of CORPUS CHRISTI. While that identification was debunked in the 19th century, it is not clear where the plays were actually performed. Scholars agree that it was somewhere in East Anglia, but the manuscript's introductory "Proclamation" claims that the plays were performed in "N [*nomen*] town" on a Sunday. The name of the town, in other words, is left as a generic *nomen* or "name." But the fact that the festival of Corpus Christi always fell on a Thursday indicates that this was not a Corpus Christi cycle.

Thus it is not even clear that the N-Town plays are truly a cycle in the same sense as the CHESTER CYCLE or the YORK CYCLE—that is, a group of discrete plays telling a coherent salvation history from Creation until Doomsday, produced for the festival of Corpus Christi by the craft guilds of a major English city. The "Proclamation" declares that the plays will be performed at six o'clock on the following Sunday, and for some time it was believed that the manuscript represented the repertory for a troupe of touring players. But more recent scholars look at the possibility that the proclamation was simply intended to alert the townspeople to come to a particular location for the performance. Copious stage directions in the text suggest that some of these plays (later additions to the manuscript) were performed at a fixed place on a scaffold, and some may have been performed with wagons. It does appear that the main compiler behind the manuscript may have been a cleric, possibly a monk or friar: The plays make use of liturgical music, and several of the plays emphasize preaching (as in the *Woman Taken in Adultery*) or scholarly learning (such as *Christ and the Doctors*). Thus scholars have suggested that the manuscript originated in the Benedictine monastery at Bury St. Edmunds. Other suggestions include the Thetford Priory in East Anglia, the towns of Great Yarmouth or Bishops Lynn (where plays are known to have been performed), and the great cathedral city of Norwich. But it is impossible to know precisely where the manuscript was produced, or where the plays were performed.

The collection in the manuscript seems to have been compiled from several different sources, and the plan of the manuscript seems to have changed over time. The motives of the main scribe are a matter of some scholarly dispute: It may be that he was collecting plays to deliberately create something along the lines of civic cycles like the York plays. It may be that he was collecting plays for something he hoped to turn into a printed text. Whatever its maker's intent, the manuscript consists of a basic cycle and five additions to the original collection. The plays of the cycle portion are all written in 13-line stanzas, and they begin with seven Old Testament plays or episodes (the Creation, the Fall, Cain and Abel, Noah's Ark, Abraham and Isaac, Moses, and a "Tree of Jesse" play focusing on the prophets). Two unusual plays dealing with apocryphal legends of Mary are included (*Joseph's Trouble about Mary* and the *Trial of Mary and Joseph*), followed by four traditional Nativity plays (the Nativity, the Shepherds, the Magi, and Herod's Slaughter of the Innocents). Five plays deal with the life and ministry of Christ (*Christ and the Doctors, The Baptism, The Temptation, The Woman Taken in Adultery,* and *The Raising of Lazarus*), and six plays concern Christ's passion and the end of the world (concerning the Marys at the Tomb, Christ's appearance to Mary Magdalene and a later appearance play, a play of the Ascension, of Pentecost, and an incomplete play of Doomsday). Later plays of Lamech, the Burning Bush, and the Cherry Tree Miracle were added to this cycle.

To this basic cycle, the original scribe seems to have added five more plays in eight-line stanzas concerning Saint Anne and the Virgin Mary, four of which are not mentioned in the manuscript's "Proclamation." These plays (concerning the Conception of Mary, the Presentation of Mary at the Temple, the Parliament of Heaven, the Annunciation, and Mary's visit to Elizabeth) appear to have been performed together on scaffold stages on a single day (perhaps on St. Anne's Day, July 26). Subsequently a play on the purification of Mary was added to the manuscript. Later was added a Passion play, focusing on Judas's betrayal of Christ; and later still a second Passion play was included, beginning with the trial of Christ before Caiaphas and ending with the Resurrection. It seems likely these plays were added to fill in the gaps of the original cycle, or were included to replace the passion narrative that the manuscript originally contained. Finally, a substantial play concerning the Assumption of the Virgin was inserted.

The sources of the N-Town plays were, of course, the Christian Bible (particularly the Gospel of Matthew), and some apocryphal gospels, including the *Nativity of Mary,* as well as Marian stories from the *GOLDEN LEGEND* and the *Meditationes* of Pseudo-Bonaventure. More than any other cycle, the N-Town plays focus on the Virgin Mary. Several of its Marian plays are unique in English drama, including the scene of Christ's post-Resurrection appearance to his mother (a Franciscan tradition) and the trial of Joseph and Mary, depicting the couple before a late medieval ecclesiastical court challenging Mary's virtue because of her premarital pregnancy. One explanation for such unusual content is the relationship of the N-Town plays to the continental dramatic tradition: Emphases on the Virgin, plays concerning Lamech, the Parliament in Heaven, and the Jesse Tree, and the use of the fixed stage, all are more typically found in Continental drama than in the English tradition. The close economic ties that East Anglia shared with northern Europe (especially Flanders) because of its cloth industry may explain the cultural context that would account for such similarities.

Certainly the most unusual and the most eclectic of the extant collections of mystery plays, the N-Town cycle has in recent years become a favorite manuscript for postmodern critics interested in resisting the idea of a text as a finished product, preferring to think of it rather as a continuing process. In that way, this text is certainly the most contemporary of the mystery cycle codices.

Bibliography

Coletti, Theresa. "Devotional Iconography and the N-Town Marian Plays," *Comparative Drama* 11 (1977): 22–44.

———. "Sacrament and Sacrifice in the N-Town Passion," *Mediaevalia* 7 (1981): 239–264.

The Corpus Christi Play of the English Middle Ages. Edited by R. T. Davies. Totowa, N.J.: Rowman and Littlefield, 1972.

Forrest, M. Patricia. "Apocryphal Sources of the St. Anne's Day Plays in the Hegge Cycle," *Medievalia et Humanistica* 17 (1966): 38–50.

———. "The Role of the Expositor Contemplacio in the St. Anne's Day Plays of the Hegge Cycle," *Medieval Studies* 28 (1966): 60–76.

Gibson, Gail McMurray. "Bury St. Edmunds, Lydgate, and the N-Town Cycle," *Speculum* 56 (1981): 56–90.

Meredith, Peter. *The Passion Play from the N-Town Manuscript.* London: Longman, 1990.

The N-Town Play: Cotton MS Vespasian D.8. Edited by Stephen Spector. 2 vols. EETS, ss 11 and 12. Oxford: Published for the Early English Text Society by the Oxford University Press, 1991.

Steven, Martin. *Four Middle English Mystery Cycles: Textual, Contextual and Critical Interpretations.* Princeton, N.J.: Princeton University Press, 1987.

Núñez, Airas (fl. 1280–1290)

Airas Núñez was one of the most important and innovative of the medieval Galician-Portuguese lyric poets. His 15 extant lyrics display a broad generic variety—there are seven *cantigas de amor* (love songs), three CANTIGAS DE AMIGO (songs with women speakers), one *pastorela* (or PASTOURELLE), and four *cantigas de escarnho* (satirical poems). They also evince an innovative technical virtuosity and a thematic originality.

Núñez was probably born in Galicia, sometime in the mid 13th century. He writes in Galician-Portuguese, but scatters some passages of vernacular Provençal through his lyrics, a fact that has led some scholars to speculate that he may have been educated in France. Some documents append the title *clérigo* to his name, and some have thought therefore that he was a priest, though it seems more likely that his reputation for learning inspired the title. What little we know of Nuñez's life is gleaned from a few references to him in documents from the court of Sancho IV of Castile, who seems to have been Núñez's patron in the decade from 1280–90, and one of Núñez's poems suggests that he traveled to Santiago on pilgrimage with King Sancho in 1284. A most interesting chancery document from the Castilian court is one granting Núñez money to buy clothing and an animal. Since one of his poems tells the story of how thieves set upon him and took his mule and his clothing, it seems likely that the grant of funds was related to that incident.

In his love songs, Núñez distances himself from the conventions of Galician-Portuguese lyrics by adopting a tone more in line with that of the Provençal TROUBADOURS than with the tradition as it had developed in Portugal: Núñez emphasizes the hope and *joi* of love rather than the despair emphasized by his fellow countrymen. He also, like the troubadours, sees the spring as a season of true inspiration to sincere feelings of love.

Even more unusual is his treatment of the mother-daughter relationship in his *cantiga de amigo* entitled *Bailad' og', ai filha, que prazer vejades* (*Dance today, oh daughter, and may it give you pleasure*). Here, rather than acting as a strict guardian of the daughter's behavior, the mother encourages her daughter to dance before her "friend"—advice that makes the daughter suspicious:

—Dance today, oh daughter, and may it give you pleasure,
in front of your friend, whom you love sincerely.
—I shall dance, mother, since you are asking me to,
yet I gather one thing from you:
you are very happy if he were to live only a short time,
since you are asking me to dance well in front of him.

(Jensen 1992, 6.5, ll. 1–6)

In Núñez's *pastorela* entitled *Oí oj eu ũa pastor cantar* (Today I heard a shepherdess singing), he breaks with tradition again, not only by using snatches of other lyrics in his refrains, but in reversing the expectations of the genre. Rather than attempting to seduce the young shepherdess, the speaker merely listens to her song in secret, and then moves on without making his presence known:

After the shepherdess had made the garland,
she went away singing, moving away softly;
and I returned quickly to my road,
for I had no desire to trouble her.

(Jensen 1992, 6.6, ll. 25–28)

Such breaks with tradition make Airas Núñez's lyrics fresh and vivid, and make him one of the most important of medieval Galician-Portuguese poets.

Bibliography

Flores, Angel, ed. *An Anthology of Medieval Lyrics.* New York: Modern Library, 1962.

Jensen, Frede, ed. and trans. *Medieval Galician-Portuguese Poetry: An Anthology.* Garland Library of Medieval Literature, 87. New York: Garland, 1992.

Nun's Priest's Tale, The Geoffrey Chaucer (ca. 1395)

One of the most widely read and admired of CHAUCER's *CANTERBURY TALES, The Nun's Priest's Tale* is a BEAST FABLE in which a fox tricks a cock named Chaunticleer into closing his eyes to sing in order to seize him and carry him away, and the cock subsequently tricks the fox into letting him go. But the tale is told in a mock-heroic style that treats Chaunticleer and his favorite wife, Pertelote, as if they are a knight and lady in a courtly ROMANCE. The tale is also full of fascinating digressions and rhetorical displays that effectively divert the reader from the simple plot.

Chaucer's tale seems to be drawn from the *ROMAN DE REYNART,* an epic-length compilation of the fables of Reynart the Fox. The ultimate source of the story was probably a fable by MARIE DE FRANCE called "Del cok e del gupil," or "The Cock and the Fox."

In the tale the rooster Chaunticleer lives like a king with his seven wives in the barnyard of a poor widow. Sleeping next to his beloved Pertelote, Chanticleer awakes in a great fright. He tells Pertelote that he has dreamt of being attacked by a strange, red beast. Pertelote, vowing that she cannot love a coward, tells Chaunticleer that his dream was likely caused by indigestion, and offers to mix up a laxative for him. But Chaunticleer, declaring that he defies laxatives, defends the prophetic power of dreams. He recounts several examples of dreams that proved accurate in foretelling disastrous events. Yet despite besting her in a long debate, Chaunticleer ends up following Pertelote's advice to pay no heed to the dream.

As Chaunticleer struts about the yard later in the day, he is startled by a fox, who through flattery gets the cock to close his eyes, stand on his toes, and crow loudly. But as soon as Chaunticleer blinks, the fox seizes him and makes for the woods. The widow, her household, and all the animals on the farm, even down to the buzzing bees, pursue the fox. The narrator goes through a number of digressions at this point, including a meditation on free will and predestination, a diatribe against taking women's advice, a complaint about the evils that occur on Fridays that parodies a lament on the death of RICHARD I by GEOFFREY OF VINSAUF, and a catalogue of all those who join in the chase. Ultimately Chaunticleer saves himself by convincing the fox to taunt the pursuing crowd once he has reached the safety of the woods.

When the fox opens his mouth to do so, Chaunticleer flies to the safety of a tree. As the tale ends Chaunticleer draws the moral that one should not blink when one ought to keep his eyes open, and the fox answers with the moral that one shouldn't speak when one ought to keep silent. The narrator concludes that the reader should take the fruit of the tale and leave the chaff.

This last direction has been difficult for scholars to follow, since almost all of the tale is "chaff"—that is, digressions that have little to do with the basic plot or any morals drawn from it. Like the rest of the tale, that final advice is probably a joke, since in it Chaucer invites us to dismiss nearly all of the tale. Scholars have noted the appropriateness of the tale to a priest narrator, especially one that served a nunnery. The tale's relationship with *The MONK'S TALE,* which precedes it, has also been explored, particularly the way the tale parodies the "fall of a great man," the theme of the tragedies that make up *The Monk's Tale.* Other scholars have seen relationships between this tale and other tales in Fragment VII of *The Canterbury Tales,* including *The PRIORESS'S TALE,* whose moral "murder will out" is echoed when Chaunticleer describes his dream. Perhaps most fruitfully, the tale has been interpreted as a parody of rhetorical excess, so that the tale's style is, in fact, its central point. Some have seen the narrator as losing control of his material through his unchecked rhetorical flights. But all agree that this is one of the most entertaining of all Chaucer's tales—a masterwork of comedy.

Bibliography

Benson, Larry, ed. *The Riverside Chaucer.* 3rd ed. Boston: Houghton Mifflin, 1987.

Bloomfield, Morton W. "The Wisdom of the Nun's Priest's Tale." In *Chaucerian Problems and Perspectives: Essays Presented to Paul E. Beichner, C.S.C.,* edited by Edward Vasta and Zacharias P. Thundy, 70–82. Notre Dame, Ind.: University of Notre Dame Press, 1979.

Gallick, Susan. "Styles of Usage in the *Nun's Priest's Tale,*" *Chaucer Review* 11 (1978): 232–247.

Johnson, Lynn Staley. " 'To Make in Som Comedye': Chaunticleer, Son of Troy," *Chaucer Review* 19 (1985): 225–244.

Wheatley, Edward. "Commentary Displacing Text: *The Nun's Priest's Tale* and the Scholastic Fable Tradition," *Studies in the Age of Chaucer* 18 (1996): 119–141.

Ockham, William (William of Occam) (ca. 1288–1347)

One of the most significant theologians and philosophers of late medieval Europe, William of Ockham is generally considered to be the first "nominalist" thinker, so called because his position on universals held that they were only names, or terms, and unlike specific individuals, did not exist in reality. Ockham is also famous for his writings on logic, wherein he formulated the famous "Ockham's razor"—the dictum that the simplest explanation is likely the truth. Though his philosophical contributions are significant, it should be remembered that Ockham thought of himself as a theologian first, and specifically as a Franciscan theologian, since he belonged to that order. He spent much of the latter part of his life in conflict with the pope over ideas of ecclesiastical poverty, a doctrine of some interest to followers of St. FRANCIS.

Born around 1288, most likely in the village of Ockham in Surrey, William joined the Franciscan order as a teenager. He was ordained a subdeacon in 1306, and in about 1309 went to study at Oxford. He began giving lectures on PETER LOMBARD's *Sentences* in 1317, and quickly achieved an international reputation in the field of logic, developing the formula that became his "razor": "plurality should not be assumed without necessity" (Adams 1987, I, 156). His opinions were controversial, however, and he was never awarded a chair at Oxford. After 1321, he seems to have left Oxford to teach in London. Probably all of his nonpolitical writings were written before 1324, when he was summoned to Avignon to answer charges of heresy, chiefly in his famous commentary on the *Sentences*. In 1326, a papal commission censured 51 of Ockham's propositions, though none was ever officially condemned by the pope.

The papacy had been located at Avignon since the beginning of the century, and Ockham found it a den of corruption. While waiting for his own case to be decided, he met the general of the Franciscan Order, Michael of Cesena, who was involved in a controversy with Pope John XXII over belief in the poverty of Jesus and his disciples, and its implication for the church—a doctrine the pope was planning to condemn. Ockham joined Cesena in defending the doctrine of ecclesiastical poverty. In 1328, he and Cesena fled from Avignon and joined the court of the Holy Roman Emperor Louis of Bavaria in Munich. From here the excommunicated Ockham wrote a number of attacks on the pope, accusing him of seven separate heresies and a number of other errors, including claiming more power than God ever intended for a single person.

For the last two decades of his life, Ockham remained under the emperor's protection and continued to publish political treatises against the power of John XXII and subsequent popes. He died in Munich on April 10, 1347, and was buried at the Franciscan church there. Some believe that he died of the BLACK DEATH, though most scholars now find that unlikely.

Ockham's most important works are his commentary on the *Sentences,* called the *Ordinatio* (1321–23), his chief work on logic, called the *Summa logicae* (ca. 1323), and the *Quodlibeta septum* (ca. 1323). His chief political works, written mainly from Munich, include the *Opus nonaginta dierum* and the *Dialogus.* It is important to remember that in all of his writings, Ockham was working within the Franciscan tradition. This is obvious in his political writings, stemming from the controversy over ecclesiastical poverty. But his philosophical and theological tracts are equally Franciscan in their concerns, often building upon or reacting to his great Franciscan predecessor DUNS SCOTUS.

In general Ockham bases his theology and philosophy on two basic principles: first, that God's power is absolute, and cannot be limited by anything but his own will. This is God's *potentia absoluta,* his power considered in and of itself. God's power in creation—his creation of natural laws, for instance—is God's *potentia ordinata,* his power as exercised in the world. But Ockham insists that all creation is contingent on God, and that God is not limited by the laws of his creation except as far as he himself wills it. The second chief principle is that nothing actually exists except individuals and their qualities, and all human experience consists of our knowledge of these individuals—the chief feature of nominalism. It is important to note that the *via moderna,* the chief school of Western philosophy for the two centuries following Ockham, is based essentially on these principles. Further, in his political writings, Ockham's insistence on the separation of church and state anticipates modern political philosophy. In short, his influence on late medieval thinkers, writers as well as theologians, was profound, and a number of scholars have recently examined the influence of nominalism on texts like Chaucer's *CLERK'S TALE* and other writings. Ockham also influenced reforming theologians who followed him, particularly those who advocated general councils to govern the church in the early 15th century.

Bibliography

Adams, Marilyn McCord. *William Ockham.* 2 vols. Notre Dame, Ind.: University of Notre Dame Press, 1987.

Boehner, Philotheus, ed. and trans. *William of Ockham: Philosophical Writings: A Selection.* Edinburgh: Nelson and Sons, 1962.

Courtenay, William J. *Schools and Scholars in Fourteenth-Century England.* Princeton, N.J.: Princeton University Press, 1987.

Peck, Russell A. "Chaucer and the Nominalist Questions," *Speculum* 53 (1978): 745–760.

Ruud, Jay. "Chaucer and Nominalism: *The Envoy to Bukton,*" *Mediaevalia* 10 (1984): 199–212.

Spade, Paul Vincent. *The Cambridge Companion to Ockham.* Cambridge: Cambridge University Press, 1999.

Utz, Richard J. *Literary Nominalism and the Theory of Rereading Late Medieval Texts: A New Research Paradigm.* Medieval Studies, 5. Lewiston, N.Y.: Edwin Mellen Press, 1995.

ogham (*ogam*)

Ogham (called *beithe-luis-nin* by the Irish) is an ancient Celtic alphabet used for writing in Irish. The alphabet consisted of 20 letters made from one to five parallel grooves or notches cut across a vertical line, usually the edge of a stone with two faces. The 15th-century manuscript treatise *The Book of Ballymote* explains that the 20 *ogham* letters were grouped into four categories, each with five letters. The categories differed according to the direction of the slashes made, and the letters were distinguished by the number of slashes. Thus the *ogham* symbol for the *b* sound, for example, was one slash to the right of the center line, while the symbol for *c* was four slashes to the left of the line. In later centuries, five more letters were added to the alphabet, designating diphthongs and other sounds not common to the ancient Irish tongue.

Etymologically, the term *ogham* seems to be related to Ogma, the name of the Celtic god of learning and culture. Nearly 400 *ogham* inscriptions have been found, all carved on *gallán,* or standing stones and read from the bottom up. Based on allusions in early Irish literature, it is assumed that such inscriptions were also made on wooden staves, though none of these has survived. The inscriptions date from the fourth century through the eighth, though most predate the seventh century. The vast majority are found in Ireland, concentrated in the southwestern part of the island (especially Kerry and Cork). However, *ogham* inscriptions have also been found in Wales, Cornwall, Scotland, and the Isle of Man, left perhaps by Irish raiders in the early medieval period or by settlers from Ireland who migrated there.

The stone inscriptions offer little linguistic information, since they are quite brief and nearly all consist of a proper name in the genitive case followed by a patronymic, in a form like "[the stone] of Noísiu the son of Uisliu." It seems likely that most of the stone pillars have a funerary function. Others may define property boundaries. It has been conjectured, and *The Book of Ballymote* confirms, that *ogham* was a secret and ritualistic alphabet, not unlike Old Norse runes, and that therefore some of the inscriptions on wood were magic incantations or used for divination. However, there is no physical evidence of such uses. But the inscriptions we do have are in a form of ancient Gaelic much older that the Old Irish we have in manuscripts.

The origin of *ogham* is uncertain. Certainly the inscriptions predate the fifth-century conversion of the island to Christianity and the introduction of Latin, though many believe that the letters are based to some extent on the Latin alphabet. Others have suggested a connection between *ogham* and the runic alphabet, though this theory has little support. The fact that the *ogham* symbols all derive their names from trees or other plants, and that not all of these plants grow in Ireland, does suggest that the *ogham* alphabet may be much older than is generally supposed, possibly going back to the continental origins of the Gaelic people of Ireland.

Bibliography

Daniels, Peter T., and William Bright. *The World's Writing Systems.* New York: Oxford University Press, 1996.

Lehmann, R. P. M., and W. P. Lehmann. *An Introduction to Old Irish.* New York: Modern Language Assn., 1975.

Ointment Seller, The (*Unguentarius, Mastičkář*) (ca. 1340)

The 14th-century Czech-Latin play known as *Mastičkář*, or *The Ointment Seller,* is an Easter mystery play concerned with the visit of the three Marys to a seller of balms and spices, from whom they purchase the ointments with which they intend to embalm the body of Christ on Easter morning. Probably composed during the reign of John of Luxembourg (1310–46), the farce may have been performed as a part of a Central European Easter festival known as the *risus paschalis.* The play, written in Czech with Latin passages and snatches of pseudo-Hebrew as well as broken German, contains raucous farcical and scatological elements that parody the resurrection and satirize the "outsiders" in Czech society: Jews, Germans, and women.

The text is preserved in two extant manuscripts: The longer and earlier of these (431 lines) is in the Czech National Museum, while the shorter (298 lines) is known by the name of the Austrian town in which it was discovered, Schlägel.

The plot of the irregular verse drama has the Marys come to the shop of an ointment seller and quack doctor named Severin. Before dealing with the women, he performs a mock resurrection: A Jew named Abraham approaches him, asking for an ointment for his dead son Isaac. Severin promises to revive Isaac, and tells his apprentices to concoct the suitable ointment. The chief apprentice, the Jewish clown Rubin, deliberately replaces the proper ointment with human feces which, when used to anoint the dead Isaac's buttocks, seems to bring him back to life. Severin tells the boy to stand up and praise God, Christ, and the Blessed Virgin. Now the Marys approach and offer to buy the ointment with which to anoint the body of Christ. Moved by their grief, Severin is willing to give them a discount on the ointments, but his wife interrupts with shrewish protestation, calling the Marys whores, and she is ultimately beaten by her husband. This is followed by another quarrel and beating of the apprentices, further delaying the Marys' obtaining of the necessary ointments.

Scholars have noted how some of the farcical elements in the play seem to derive from folk tradition, evinced, for example, by the parallel between the plot of *The Ointment Seller* and the English mummers' play, in which a quack doctor performs a pseudo-resurrection. More controversial is the use of obscenity and scatological humor in the play. One suggestion is that the farcical or "carnival" elements in the play are intended to satirize or to deride the oppressive hegemony of the church. Alfred Thomas, the most recent scholar to comment on the play, believes the opposite is true: The objects of satire, he claims, are not those in power but rather the outsiders in Czech society, including Jews (like the obscene Rubin as well as Abraham and Isaac, who make use of the excremental balm); Germans (whose participation in knightly tournaments is satirized, and whose language is occasionally mocked by some of the characters' use of broken German words that sound like obscene Czech ones); and women, who are all depicted as either hags or whores (until the Marys become part of the holy Easter story and speak and sing in Latin).

Bibliography

Jakobson, Roman. "Medieval Mock Mystery (The Old Czech *Unguentarius*)," in *Selected Writings, VI, Early Slavic Paths and Crossroads, Part Two, Medieval Slavic Studies.* Berlin: Mouton, 1985, 666–690.

Thomas, Alfred. *Anne's Bohemia: Czech Culture and Society, 1310–1420.* Minneapolis: University of Minnesota Press, 1998.

Veltrusky, Jarmila F. *A Sacred Farce from Medieval Bohemia—Mastičkář.* Michigan Studies in the Humanities, no. 6. Ann Arbor: Horace H. Rackham School of Graduate Studies, The University of Michigan, 1985.

Old English (ca. 450–ca. 1100)

Old English is the name given to the language spoken by the Anglo-Saxons from the time of their conquest of Britain in the fifth century until their own conquest by the Normans in 1066, after which the influence of Norman French on the language helped produce some of the changes that resulted in the development of Old English into MIDDLE ENGLISH. Old English literature includes a complex and sophisticated poetic tradition that preserves some of the prehistoric heroic tradition of the Anglo-Saxon people, as well as a rich prose tradition of texts concerned chiefly with Christian themes. Old English is the earliest written vernacular literary tradition in Europe.

The Old English language was a Germanic language, and like modern German was highly inflected, relying on case endings that designated the function of nouns in sentences. Nouns were categorized as masculine, feminine, and neuter, and the grammatical genders were inflected differently. Adjectives were also inflected, agreeing with the nouns they modified in case, number, and gender. Some verbs had a weak conjugation that formed its past tenses by a dental suffix (like -ed in modern English), but most fell into one of seven classes of "strong" verbs (as in modern German) that give us "irregular" verbs like *write, wrote, written* in modern English. Written Old English used three characters unknown in modern English: the thorn (þ) and the eth (ð), which indicated the sounds spelled as *th* in modern English, and the *æsc*—pronounced "ash"—(æ), which indicated the sound in modern English called the short *a*.

According to the Venerable BEDE (d. 735), the chief historical source for the period, three Germanic tribes—the Angles, Saxons, and Jutes—began their invasion of Celtic Britain in 449 C.E. They came from the southern part of the Jutland peninsula, from northwestern Germany, and from the Low Countries and spoke mutually intelligible but somewhat distinct dialects of Germanic that developed eventually into four Old English dialects: Kentish (spoken by the Jutish people who presumably settled Kent), West Saxon (spoken by the Saxon people who settled in the southwestern part of Britain), and the more closely related Mercian and Northumbrian (spoken by the Angles who settled the rest of the island). By the time the Christian missionary St. Augustine arrived in Kent in 597, there were seven established Anglo-Saxon kingdoms. Christianity brought the Latin alphabet and with it the potential to produce written texts. By the eighth century, the monasteries of Anglo-Saxon England had become the most important centers of intellectual culture in Europe, and Bede, a Benedictine monk from the monastery at Jarrow, was probably the most learned man on the continent—a scientist, grammarian, theologian, and historian. By the end of the century, CHARLEMAGNE was to turn to ALCUIN OF YORK (735–804), the product of this English monastic system, to direct the renaissance of learning in the Carolingian empire. Viking invasions in the ninth century colonized much of northeast England and threatened to put an end to this vital Anglo-Saxon civilization, but the military genius of the king of Wessex, ALFRED THE GREAT (r. 871–899), prevented that destruction.

Alfred also fostered a renaissance of learning in England, which had declined since the time of Alcuin. He wrote and translated a number of texts himself, and also encouraged the production of other texts, including the *ANGLO-SAXON CHRONICLE* (a record of events in England from the eighth century through his own reign) and a translation of Bede's most important work, his *Ecclesiastical History of the English People,* into Old English. Alfred and his descendents, who further limited Viking incursions into England (though many Norsemen settled on the island peaceably), were the first monarchs able to call themselves kings of all England. But by the time of Ethelred the Unready (as he is commonly known—actually the Old English adjective usually attached to his name means "unadvised"), Viking raids had increased again, and Danish influence in England grew so strong that after Ethelred's death in 1016, the Danish king Canute became king of England. After his death, the line of Wessex was restored and Edward the Confessor became king in 1042, but upon his death the claim to the throne by his successor Harold was challenged by Duke William of Normandy, who successfully invaded England, killed Harold in battle, and was crowned king of England on December 25, 1066, effectively bringing the Old English period to an end.

There are only some 189 extant manuscripts containing a significant amount of writing in the Old English language, and of these, 125 are essentially ecclesiastical collections. As a result of his work to revitalize learning in England, almost all of these manuscripts are in the late West Saxon dialect of King Alfred's Wessex. The most admired genre of Old English literature in modern times has been poetry, yet nearly all Old English poetry survives in only four manuscripts, known as the JUNIUS MANUSCRIPT, the EXETER BOOK, the VERCELLI BOOK, and Ms. COTTON VITELLIUS A.xv, the manuscript containing the great epic *BEOWULF.* There are 140 poems in these four manuscripts, and another 45 scattered among other texts. Like Germanic poetry in general, Old English verse was based on stress and alliteration: Each line contained four stressed syllables (plus an unspecified number of unstressed syllables). The line was divided into two half-lines by a caesura between the second and third stressed syllable. The two half-lines were linked by alliteration: The initial sound of the first stressed syllable in the second half line is also used in either or both of the stressed syllables of the first half line. Other characteristics of Old English poetry include the use of KENNINGS—truncated metaphors that refer to common nouns in figurative terms, as "whale's road" for the sea, and LITOTES, or understatement—in which the poet ironically understates a condition or emotion, saying perhaps "with few companions" to mean "alone."

The earliest surviving poem in English is a seventh-century lyric known as *CAEDMON'S HYMN.* A poem praising God for the creation of the world, *Caedmon's Hymn* adapts the Germanic heroic poetic tradition to Christian themes, and in doing so establishes a pattern that most Old English poetry would follow. There are SAINTS' LIVES and prayers, for example, as well as long narrative retellings of Old Testament stories in poems like *GENESIS, EXODUS* and *DANIEL,* as well as the impressive Old English version of the apocryphal book *JUDITH.* The best-known of all Old English religious poems is the *DREAM OF THE ROOD,* a retelling of the crucifixion of Christ from the point of view of the Cross itself.

Other Old English poems generally fall into three categories: ELEGAIC poems, heroic poems, or GNOMIC VERSE. Well-known elegiac lyrics like *The WANDERER, The SEAFARER* and *The WIFE'S LAMENT* deal with the experience of loss and the transience of earthly goods and power. Gnomic verses include a number of maxims that survive in two short collections, as well as a large number of RIDDLES in the Exeter Book. The heroic tradition continues in poems like *The* BATTLE OF BRUNNANBURH—a celebration of a great English victory in 937 by King Alfred's grandson Aethelstan over an alliance of invaders that survives in the *Anglo-Saxon Chronicle,* and *The* BATTLE OF MALDON—a poem celebrating the old Germanic heroic customs by lauding the courage of retainers who go down to glorious defeat after the death of their lord in a battle with Vikings in 991.

Beowulf, whose 3,182 lines make it the longest poem in Old English (with 10 percent of the entire body of Old English verse), also celebrates the Germanic warrior code, but does so from the view of a Christian poet who sees it as glorious but flawed, and invokes a kind of elegiac mood for the lost glory of those heroic days. Thus *Beowulf* is a compendium of all the most important themes of Old English poetry.

Of course, far more Old English prose survives than poetry, much of it of literary significance. Aside from the *Anglo-Saxon Chronicle* itself and the Old English translation of Bede, a number of Alfred's translations are much admired, including his English version of Saint GREGORY THE GREAT's *Cura pastoralis* and his translation of BOETHIUS's CONSOLATION OF PHILOSOPHY. But the most popular genre of Old English prose is the sermon. The two most admired prose stylists in Old English, WULFSTAN and AELFRIC, both active around the year 1000, in the period of Viking invasions under the ill-advised Ethelred, are both known for their sermons. Wulfstan's famous *Sermon of Wolf to the English* in 1014 attributes the Viking atrocities to the punishment of a just God for the English sins. Aelfric, the greatest scholar of his age and the most admired Old English prose writers, left two large collections of sermons for use during two seasons of the Christian year.

When the Normans displaced the Anglo-Saxon nobility and ended the Old English culture that was superior to their own, they effectively ended written literature in English for 200 years. It was not until the 14th century that English literature regained the heights it had reached in the Old English period. Indeed, European vernacular literature begins with Old English texts.

Bibliography

The Anglo-Saxon Chronicle. Translated and edited by M. J. Swanton. New York: Routledge, 1998.

Dobbie, Elliott van Kirk, ed. *Beowulf and Judith.* Anglo-Saxon Poetic Records, IV. New York: Columbia University Press, 1953.

Godden, Malcolm, and Michael Lapidge, eds. *The Cambridge Companion to Old English Literature.* Cambridge: Cambridge University Press, 1991.

Greenfield, Stanley B., and Daniel G. Calder. *A New Critical History of Old English Literature.* New York: New York University Press, 1986.

Heaney, Seamus. *Beowulf: A New Verse Translation.* First bilingual ed. New York: Farrar, Straus, and Giroux, 2000.

Hogg, Richard M. *The Cambridge History of the English Language.* Vol. 1: *The Beginnings to 1066.* Cambridge: Cambridge University Press, 1992.

Krapp, George Philip, and Elliott van Kirk Dobbie, eds. *The Exeter Book.* Anglo-Saxon Poetic Records, III. New York: Columbia University Press, 1936.

Krapp, George Philip, ed. *The Junius Manuscript.* Anglo-Saxon Poetic Records, I. New York: Columbia University Press, 1931.

———, ed. *The Vercelli Book.* Anglo-Saxon Poetic Records, II. New York: Columbia University Press, 1932.

Smyth, Alfred P. *King Alfred the Great.* Oxford: Oxford University Press, 1995.

Swanton, Michael, ed. *Anglo-Saxon Prose.* London: Dent, 1975.

Omar Khayyām (Ghiyāth al-Dīn Abū al-Fath 'Umar ibn Ibrāhīm al-Nīsābūrī al-Khayyāmī) (1048–1131)

Omar Khayyām was a Persian scientist and mathematician famous in his own day for his contributions in the fields of algebra and astronomy. Although his occasional verse was little known in the Middle Ages, the publication in 1859 of Edward FitzGerald's *Rubā'iyāt of Omar Khayyam* made him the most widely known Persian poet in the world, at least until the recent popularity of RUMI. Of course only a few of FitzGerald's translated verses can with any confidence be attributed to Omar.

Omar Khayyām (the name means "Omar, Son of the Tent-maker") was probably born and educated in Nishapur, and grew to manhood in an Iran newly conquered by the Seljuk Turks. It was a time in which scholars were not likely to find much employment unless they could attract the patronage of the rich or powerful. In 1070, Omar moved to the ancient city of Samarkand in Central Asia (now Uzbekistan), where he was supported by a wealthy jurist named Abu Tahir, and was able to gain the favor of Shams al-Mulk Nast ibn Ibrahim, the Qarakhanid ruler of Transoxiana. By the age of 25, Omar had produced a treatise on arithmetic and one on music, and had also composed two treatises on algebra, in which, among other things, he presents the first general theory of cubic equations. Shams's rival, the Seljuk sultan Jalāl al-Dīn Malikshāh (r. 1072–92), lured Omar to his own court in Isfahan and became the mathematician's patron and friend for some 18 years. In Malikshāh's service Omar was asked to take part in the establishment of a new solar calendar in 1079. Omar measured the length of the year at 365.24219858156 days, an astoundingly accurate calculation. As the chief scholar of the court, he prepared new astronomical tables and wrote a number of treatises on philosophy and theology, and he also began making plans for a new observatory.

But Malikshāh's death put an end to Omar's favored position at court, and plans for his observatory were abandoned. Omar also came under fire at this point from conservative Muslims who thought his studies were contrary to Islam. Omar spent several years trying to return to favor at court, and when, in 1118, Malikshāh's third son, Sanjar, became overall Seljuk ruler, Omar became part of a new center of learning in Sanjar's new capital of Merv, Turkmenistan, and there continued to work on mathematical studies.

Early biographers of Omar Khayyām mention nothing about his verse, and there is no contemporary witness to his poetic ability. But in his day it was common for educated Persians to compose occasional verse, typically in quatrains called *rubā'i* (plural *rubā'iyāt*). These epigrammatic poems included four half-lines, of which the first two and the fourth rhymed. Thus the quatrain introduced and developed a theme in the first two half-lines, and reached a climax in the fourth after a suspenseful pause in the third half-line. Like the roughly contemporary Japanese TANKA, such quatrains were composed by virtually every literate Iranian as a social expectation and circulated privately and by word of mouth. Certainly they were never collected into a *dīwān,* the anthology of a professional poet.

A manuscript dated 1161 cites some of Omar's verses, and he is first mentioned as a poet about 1177. The first extant manuscript containing a complete quatrain of Omar's is dated 1209. By the end of the 14th century, there were some 60 poems attributed to him, and as his reputation as a poet grew, more and more verses were credited to Omar. Clearly there were a number of anonymous quatrains that were produced in medieval times, and as Omar's reputation grew, so did the number of verses he was supposed to have written. By the late 15th century, more than 300 *rubā'iyāt* were ascribed to him, and that number had grown to some 1,200 by the time FitzGerald made his translation.

FitzGerald includes about 600 quatrains in his *Rubā'iyāt,* a number of which were never attributed to Omar himself, but were borrowed from other Sufi poets as they contributed to the picture FitzGerald was trying to paint of Omar as a skeptical and melancholy sensualist. Even today determining which poems might genuinely be attributed to Omar Khayyām is extremely difficult, and made an even thornier task by the fact that literary Persian changed very little over the centuries, so that poems written hundreds of years after Omar lived might still be passed off as his. At this point scholars have succeeded in narrowing down to about 100 the poems considered Omar Khayyām's genuine work. But given the nature of the evidence, a consensus among scholars would be hard to achieve. Most, appropriately, take a very conservative view about what may be accepted as genuine. It is simply difficult to know what Omar himself wrote, and difficult to separate the real Omar from the one created by FitzGerald's compilation.

Bibliography

Dashtī, Alī. *In Search of Omar Khayyam.* Translated by L. P. Elwell-Sutton. New York: Columbia University Press, 1971.

Edward FitzGerald's The Rubaiyat of Omar Khayyam. Edited and with an introduction by Harold Bloom. Philadelphia: Chelsea House Publishers, 2004.

Kasra, Parichehr, ed. and trans. *The Rubā'iyāt of Umar Khayyām.* Delmar, N.Y.: Scholars' Facsimiles and Reprints, 1975.

Rashed, R., and B. Vahabzadeh. *Omar Khayyam, the Mathematician.* New York: Bibliotheca Persica Press, 2000.

Ormulum, The (ca. 1200)

The Ormulum is an early MIDDLE ENGLISH poetic text of some 20,000 short, unrhymed lines, produced in the North East Midlands (possibly in the abbey of Bourne in southern Lincolnshire) late in the 12th century. Its author, who was apparently also the scribe of the poem's surviving manuscript (Oxford Bodleian ms. Junius 1), identifies himself as *Orm* (an Old Norse name meaning "Serpent"), and says that he is an Augustinian canon. He addresses his manuscript to his brother and fellow Augustinian Walter, who seems to have been in an administrative position in the abbey in which Orm lived and worked. At Walter's request, Orm says in his dedication, he is producing an English translation of the entire year's gospel texts as listed in the Mass book, with each text accompanied by an interpretive homily in English verse. Perhaps the book was intended to be of use to preachers in the vernacular.

Orm lists 242 texts and homilies in his table of contents. The extant manuscript, however, contains only 32 entries. Possibly part of the manuscript has been lost, but most scholars believe that the prodigious task Orm set for himself was never finished. The text is arranged chronologically around the life of Christ as presented in the chosen Gospel texts, except for a few intended homilies on Peter and Paul that were to have appeared near the end of the manuscript. It is possible that those particular saints had some special connection to Orm's and Walter's abbey. At any rate, Orm must have worked on this major project for many years, perhaps decades, and the manuscript shows signs of both large-scale revisions and smaller corrections. It may have been abandoned upon the death of Walter, or Orm may have grown too old or weak to finish the task.

Readers are generally agreed that *The Ormulum* is a very tedious work. But whatever its shortcomings as a literary text, *The Ormulum* is of great interest to linguists, especially because of the spelling system adopted by Orm, who consistently doubles consonants after short vowels.

Bibliography

Fulk, Robert D. "Consonant Doubling and Open Syllable Lengthening in the *Ormulum,*" *Anglia* 114 (1996): 481–513.

Mancho, Guzmán. "Is *Orrmulum's* Introduction an Instance of an Aristotelian Prologue?" *Neophilologus* 88 (2004): 477–492.

The Ormulum. Edited by Robert Holt, with notes and glossary by R. M. White. 2 vols. 1878. New York: AMS Press, 1974.

Parkes, M. B. "On the Presumed Date and Possible Origin of the Manuscript of the 'Ormulum': Oxford, Bodleian Library, MS. Junius 1," in *Five Hundred Years of Words and Sounds: A Festschrift for Eric Dobson,* edited by E. G. Stanley and D. Gray. Cambridge: Brewer, 1983, 115–127.

Worley, Meg. "Using the *Ormulum* to Redefine Vernacularity," in *The Vulgar Tongue: Medieval and Postmedieval Vernacularity,* edited by Fiona Somerset and Nicholas Watson. University Park: Pennsylvania State University Press, 2003, 19–30.

ottava rima

Ottava rima is a verse form originating in late medieval Italy, consisting of stanzas of eight hendesyllabic (or 11-syllable) lines rhyming *abababcc.* The form was popularized by BOCCACCIO, who first used it in his *Il FILOSTRATO* (ca. 1339) and *TESEIDA*(ca. 1341).

The form was in existence prior to Boccaccio, however: It may have developed from stanza forms used in certain *CANZONI* or *SIRVENTES;* or it may have come from an earlier Italian genre called the *strambotto,* which was a single stanza of six or eight lines used generally for sentimental love poems. The *strambotto* took a variety of forms, but one form popular in Tuscany did use the *abababcc* rhyme scheme. It has also been conjectured that MINSTRELS were using this particular *strambotto* verse form for composing long narrative poems by the early 14th century. Whether or not that is true, it is certain that ottava rima appears in religious poems from the late 13th century.

Although Boccaccio did not invent the form, he refined it and popularized it for use in long narrative texts. Part of Boccaccio's immense influence on CHAUCER included his use of the narrative verse stanza: Chaucer developed his RHYME ROYAL stanza after reading Boccaccio's narratives and deciding to drop the final *a* rhyme from the form, creating a seven-line stanza rhyming *ababbcc.* Subsequent Italian writers, however, made greater use of Boccaccio's ottava rima itself, notably Ariosto and Tasso in the Renaissance. Thomas Wyatt is credited for introducing ottava rima into English in the 16th century (using iambic pentameter rather than hendesyllabic lines), and it was later used by Spenser, Milton, and most effectively by Lord Byron in his mock epic *Don Juan.*

Owain (*The Lady of the Fountain*) (13th century)

Owain is a Middle Welsh prose ROMANCE, one of three romances included in some manuscripts of the *MABINOGION* (the others being *PEREDUR* and *GERAINT AND ENID*). *Owain* tells essentially the same story as CHRÉTIEN DE TROYES's French verse romance *YVAIN* or *The Knight with the Lion.* While many believe that Chrétien's poem is the source of the Welsh *Owain,* others believe that both texts come from a common source, either Welsh or Breton. Since the Welsh poem shows some French influence, notably in its concern with courtliness, it seems likely that the Welsh writer had some familiarity with the French text.

Owain begins with one of King ARTHUR's knights, Cynon, relating the story of his encounter with a magic fountain and his defeat at the hands of the Knight of the Fountain. Owain decides to retrace Cynon's steps. He finds the fountain and defeats the Knight of the Fountain, chasing him into a city where Owain is trapped behind a portcullis that falls and kills his horse. He is saved by Luned, serving woman to the Lady of the Fountain, when Luned gives him a ring of invisibility that enables him to hide undetected in the castle. While invisible, Owain falls in love with the Lady of the Fountain, and Luned is able to convince her lady to accept Owain as her new husband. He marries the Lady and becomes the Knight of the Fountain himself for three years.

Meanwhile Arthur sets out to find Owain. He and his knights come to the fountain, where Sir Cei is defeated by the disguised Owain. Other knights challenge Owain, but he defeats all but Gwalchmei (the Welsh name for GAWAIN), whom he fights until the two recognize one another, after which they all rejoice. Owain obtains leave of his wife to go back to Arthur's court for three months, but when that time period is up and Owain has forgotten to return, a damsel comes to the court and berates Owain, snatching his mistress's ring from his finger.

The loss of his lady drives Owain mad, and he runs wild in the forest for some time until cured by a balm from a widowed countess. Restored to reason, he comes upon a lion in mortal combat with a serpent. Owain helps the lion and slays the serpent, after which the lion becomes his devoted companion. With the aid of his lion, Owain defeats a cruel giant and rescues the sons of an earl who hosts him in his castle. Then he succeeds in saving Luned, who is about to be burned at the stake. Ultimately he regains the love of his lady, and lives with her until she dies. Upon her death he leaves his role as Knight of the Fountain, continues his adventures, which include the rescue of 24 maidens from their oppressor, and returns at last to Arthur's court.

The romance's theme of developing maturity and self-awareness (enabling Owain to redeem his life) is essentially the same as that of Chrétien's poem, and unusual in Welsh narrative of this time. It appears that the goal of the writer was to adapt the concerns of French courtly romance to the tradition of Welsh narrative. Certainly the tale also contains elements of Celtic folklore, in particular the motif of the magic fountain and the beautiful lady who chooses her consort, which seems a dramatization of Celtic sovereignty myth. Thus the relationship between *Owain* and *Yvain* is complex, suggesting either a common Celtic source for both texts but the Welsh writer's familiarity with the French text, or an earlier Celtic influence on Chrétien's French romance.

Bibliography

Breeze, Andrew. *Medieval Welsh Literature.* Dublin: Four Courts Press, 1997.

Jarman, A. O. H., and Gwilym Rees Hughes. *A Guide to Welsh Literature.* Swansea, U.K.: C. Davies, 1976.

Jones, Gwyn, and Thomas Jones, trans. *The Mabinogion.* 2nd ed. London: Dent, 1974.

Thomson, R. L., ed. *Owain.* Dublin: Dublin Institute for Advanced Studies, 1970.

Owl and the Nightingale, The (ca. 1189–1216)

The Owl and the Nightingale is a DEBATE POEM in early MIDDLE ENGLISH, written in a southeastern dialect in 1,794 lines of octosyllabic (eight-syllable) couplets. The poem survives in two late 13th-century manuscripts, but was probably composed in the late 12th or very early 13th century. In the poem, the narrator overhears a comic debate between a serious Owl and a lively Nightingale over the relative benefits each brings to mankind.

The date of the poem has been a matter of some scholarly dispute. It appears, from a reference to the late "King Henry" in the text, that the poem was written sometime between 1189, when HENRY II died, and 1216, when Henry III succeeded to the throne—since had the poem been written after 1216 it would have been necessary to specify which King Henry was being referenced. The authorship of the poem has also been debated. Because the poem ends with the argument unresolved, and the two birds flying off to present their case to one "Nicholas of Guildford" to judge, some scholars have suggested that Nicholas was himself the author. Nicholas is praised as an accomplished man in the poem, and it is possible that he was a learned priest capable of writing a poem such as *The Owl and the Nightingale,* full of wit and learning. Other scholars suggest that Nicholas was the poet's patron, or that the poem was presented to Nicholas by an anonymous clerical friend or, according to one author, by the nuns of Shaftesbury Abbey. The question of the poem's authorship remains unsolved.

Many scholars have interpreted the poem as ALLEGORY: The Owl and the Nightingale have been seen as representing the worldly vs. the ascetic life, or the minstrel vs. the preacher, or art vs. philosophy. Most often the birds have been seen as spokespersons for love poetry and religious poetry. In the end such interpretations are unsatisfactory, since the birds' argument extends to a wide variety of topics that make all of these suggestions possible, but never focuses seriously on any one of them. The birds discuss the characteristics of their respective species, they argue about music, about papal missions, and about theological and philosophical questions like the necessity for confession, and man's free will vs. God's foreknowledge. But what is ultimately most memorable in the poem is the characterization of the two protagonists.

The Owl is presented as self-important, melancholy, ascetic, and irascible; the Nightingale as optimistic, jovial, unreflective, and a bit shallow. The two of them harangue one another about a variety of topics in a haphazard manner, dealing with them in a rather superficial way. They are more interested in either attacking one another (with name-calling, innuendo, and lampoon) or exaggerated self-aggrandizement. Thus the Nightingale berates the Owl for her ugliness, and the Owl retaliates by criticizing the Nightingale's scrawniness. The Nightingale compares the Owl to a lunatic, and the Owl complains of the Nightingale's "crazy cacklings" in the forest. They accuse one another of being unclean. The Owl denounces the Nightingale for having only one talent—singing—while the Owl herself has many talents, including doing the practical work of ridding barns of mice. This last argument seems to impress the Nightingale.

The poet-narrator appears to favor the Owl's case, though that support is never explicit. However, since the tone of the poem is mildly satiric, it may well be that the poet is simply, like the Nightingale, comically impressed by the self-importance of the Owl, who is herself a ludicrous character because of her egotism and her black-and-white certainty of her own views. Ultimately the poem seems chiefly a send-up of the very human tendency to become contentious. *The Owl and the Nightingale* is the first of what became a popular subgenre in Middle English literature, the bird-debate. Later poems like *The* THRUSH AND THE NIGHTINGALE and John CLANVOWE's *Cuckoo and the Nightingale,* and perhaps even CHAUCER's *PARLIAMENT OF FOWLS,* may owe their inspiration largely to *The Owl and the Nightingale.*

Bibliography

Barratt, Alexandra. "Flying in the Face of Tradition: A New View of *The Owl and the Nightingale,*" *University of Toronto Quarterly* 56 (1987): 471–485.

Cartlidge, Neil, "The Date of *The Owl and the Nightingale,*" *Medium Aevum* 65 (1996): 230–247.

———, ed. *The Owl and the Nightingale.* Exeter, U.K.: University of Exeter Press, 2001.

Cawley, A. C. "Astrology in *The Owl and the Nightingale,*" *Modern Language Review* 46 (1951): 161–174.

Coleman, Janet. "*The Owl and the Nightingale* and Papal Theories of Marriage," *Journal of Ecclesiastical History* 38 (1987): 517–567.

Holsinger, Bruce. "Vernacular Legality: The English Jurisdictions of *The Owl and the Nightingale.*" In *The Letter of the Law: Legal Practice and Literary Production in Medieval England,* edited by Emily Steiner and Candace Barrington, 154–184. Ithaca, N.Y.: Cornell University Press, 2002.

Hume, Kathryn. *The Owl and the Nightingale: The Poem and Its Critics.* Toronto: Toronto University Press, 1975.

Jacobs, Nicolas. "*The Owl and the Nightingale* and the Bishops." In *Medieval Literature and Antiquities: Studies in Honour of Basil Cottle,* edited by Myra Stokes and T. L. Burton, 91–98. Cambridge: D. S. Brewer, 1987.

Stone, Brian, trans. *The Owl and the Nightingale, Cleanness, St Erkenwald.* 2nd ed. London: Penguin Classics, 1988.

P

Pardoner's Tale, The Geoffrey Chaucer (ca. 1395)

The most often anthologized of CHAUCER's *CANTERBURY TALES, The Pardoner's Tale* is a sermon on greed that contains a grim exemplum (or illustrative story) demonstrating the theme that "avarice is the root of all evil." Ironically the Pardoner narrator—a charlatan who displays phony saints' relics to lend credibility to his selling of indulgences, or pardons for sin—freely admits to his pilgrim audience that he is himself guilty of the very sin he preaches against.

In a revelatory, confessional prologue similar to that of *The WIFE OF BATH*, the Pardoner tells his audience about the tricks he uses when preaching to get his listeners to contribute more generously to the offertory. The text of his sermon, he says, is always the same: *radix malorum est cupiditas* ("the root of evil is cupidity," or greed). Thus, he brags, he preaches against the same vice of which he is himself guilty. He then delivers his sermon, which consists largely of an exemplum of three revelers—young men who spend all of their time drinking, gambling, and swearing in the local taverns of Flanders during a period of plague. When they learn that one of their comrades has been taken by Death, they swear an oath of brotherhood to track down this Death and kill him.

As they search for Death, they come upon a mysterious old man whom they irreverently threaten and accuse of being in league with Death. They order him to show them where Death is, and the old man points down a crooked way, claiming that they will find Death under a tree at the end of that path. The three rioters follow the path, but what they find is a large treasure under the tree. They immediately stop looking for Death. The three decide to split up the gold and take it away by night, so as not to be observed. In the meantime the youngest of them is sent into town for something to eat and drink. Thinking to have the gold to himself, the young rioter poisons two of the bottles of wine that he brings back. The other two rioters have plotted to murder the youngest when he returns. This they do, and then they drink the wine, and die as well. The Pardoner concludes with a condemnation of greed and other sins, and then offers to let the Host come kiss his relics and obtain his pardon in exchange for a cash contribution. The Host vehemently rejects the offer with a coarse insult, and the Knight is forced to step in and make peace between the two before the pilgrims can move on.

For the Pardoner's prologue, Chaucer made use of the speech of *Fals Semblant* (False seeming) in the *ROMAN DE LA ROSE*. The exemplum is based on a folktale pattern and has analogues in ancient Buddhist, Persian, and African tales, as well as more modern retellings such as the film *The Treasure of the Sierra Madre*. Chaucer's closest analogues are two Italian short stories or novellas, but neither of these is likely to be a direct source.

Scholars have written voluminously on the Pardoner and his tale. One favorite topic has been the Pardoner's sexuality. In the GENERAL PROLOGUE, the narrator speculates that the Pardoner is "a gelding or a mare"—that is, presumably, a eunuch or a homosexual. Scholars have often been interested in the relationship of this sexuality to the Pardoner's spiritual sterility. Another area of debate has been the identity of the strange old man in the tale—he has been identified with Death, Old Age (the harbinger of death), the *vetus homo,* or fallen man, discussed by St. Paul, the legendary "Wandering Jew," or simply an old man.

Perhaps the most debated critical problem in the text is the motivation of the Pardoner at the end of the tale: Why, after telling the pilgrims in the beginning that he is a hypocrite and a cheat, would he propose that the pilgrims come up and pay to kiss his relics at the end? Is it a joke? Part of the entertainment? Forgetfulness? Is he carried away by his own rhetoric? Is he motivated by an arrogant belief in his own ability to move his hearers even after telling them he is a fake? Or is he motivated by an unconscious (or a conscious) desire for punishment for his sins? All of these, and more, have been suggested, and there is no firm agreement.

Bibliography

Benson, Larry, et al. *The Riverside Chaucer.* 3rd ed. Boston: Houghton Mifflin, 1987.

Kittredge, George Lyman. "Chaucer's Pardoner," *The Atlantic Monthly* 72 (1893): 829–833.

McAlpine, Monica. "The Pardoner's Homosexuality and How It Matters," *PMLA* 95 (1980): 8–22.

Miller, Robert P. "Chaucer's Pardoner, the Scriptural Eunuch, and the Pardoner's Tale," *Speculum* 30 (1955): 180–189.

Patterson, Lee. "Chaucerian Confession: Penitential Literature and the Pardoner," *Medievalia et Humanistica* 7 (1976): 153–173.

Pearsall, Derek. "Chaucer's Pardoner: The Death of a Salesman," *Chaucer Review* 17 (1983): 358–365.

Rowland, Beryl. "Chaucer's Idea of the Pardoner," *Chaucer Review* 14 (1979): 140–154.

Sturges, Robert S. *Chaucer's Pardoner and Gender Theory: Bodies of Discourse.* The New Middle Ages. New York: St. Martin's Press, 2000.

Paris, Matthew (ca. 1200–1259)

Matthew Paris was an English monk and Latin chronicler, whose influential account of the early part of the reign of Henry III is admired for its lively narration and for its use of eyewitness accounts, including his own personal knowledge.

Matthew joined the Benedictine abbey of Saint Albans in Hertfordshire in 1217. While it has been suggested that his surname may indicate he attended the University of Paris, there is no need for such an assumption, since the name was a common one in England in the 13th century, particularly in Lincolnshire. Thus Matthew may well have completed his education in the abbey. He was, in any case, quite learned. When the abbey's official historiographer, Roger of Wendover, died in 1236, Matthew took over Roger's position, and completed the work that was to become his most important composition, the *Chronica majora* ("Great Chronicle"). The first part of the chronicle is Matthew's reworking of Roger's text. The second part is Matthew's original composition, covering the period from 1235 to 1259. The work is unusual in its incorporation of world history, including events in continental Europe and the East. It appears by the history that Matthew was personally acquainted with Henry III, and may have been present at his marriage to Eleanor of Provence in 1236. At any rate the details of the text have led scholars to speculate about Matthew being in the king's favor. Matthew's negative portrayal of Henry's father, King John, however, has been influential on historians' views of that monarch and has only recently come into question.

Matthew was important enough in his own day to be sent in 1248 on a papal mission to the Benedictine monastery of Holm (Trondheim) in Norway. In the meantime Matthew was writing other historical works, including his *Chronica minora* (Minor chronicle), also called the *Historia Anglorum* (History of England). This is a shorter history focused on England from 1200 to 1250, mainly summarizing the major chronicle, but with some additional material. Matthew also produced his *Vitae abbatum S. Albani* (Lives of the abbots of Saint Albans), which compiles biographies of the first 23 abbots of Matthew's home monastery.

Only the last three, ending in the year 1255, are likely Matthew's completely original compositions.

Matthew also wrote in French, and is generally acknowledged to be the author of four SAINTS' LIVES in Anglo-Norman verse: one on the Saxon king Edward the Confessor, one on St. Edmund, one on St. Albans, and one on Thomas BECKETT, which survives only in fragmentary form. At one time Matthew was believed to be the author of the *Vitae duorum offarum* (Lives of the two offas), a text found in some manuscripts of the *Chronica majora,* but scholars no longer believe he wrote those lives. Matthew was apparently a skilled artist as well as a historian, and is credited with illustrating some of his manuscripts with drawings, diagrams, maps, and miniature painting.

Bibliography

Lewis, Suzanne. *The Art of Matthew Paris in the Chronica majora.* Berkeley: University of California Press in collaboration with Corpus Christi College, Cambridge, 1987.

Paris, Matthew. *The Illustrated Chronicles of Matthew Paris: Observations of Thirteenth-Century Life.* Translated, edited, and with an introduction by Richard Vaughan. Cambridge: Corpus Christi College, 1993.

———. *The Life of St. Edmund.* Translated, edited, and with a biography by C. H. Lawrence. Oxford: A. Sutton, 1996.

Vaughan, Richard. *Matthew Paris.* Cambridge: Cambridge University Press, 1958.

Parliament of Fowls, The Geoffrey Chaucer (ca. 1382)

The Parliament of Fowls is one of CHAUCER's earlier DREAM VISION poems, written as a celebration of Valentine's Day—a day, we are told in the poem, when every bird chooses its mate. It has also been suggested that the poem was written to commemorate the adolescent RICHARD II's betrothal to ANNE OF BOHEMIA. This reading would identify the three tercel eagles in the poem with the three noble rivals for Anne's hand: Richard himself, Charles of France, and Friedrich of Meissen.

If that is the poem's intent, it would date the text to about 1380–82. This would place the poem soon after Chaucer's second Italian journey, and the poem reflects the influence of BOCCACCIO in particular. Abandoning the short, octosyllabic (eight-syllable) couplets of the earlier dream visions *The BOOK OF THE DUCHESS* and *The HOUSE OF FAME,* here, under the Italian influence, Chaucer adopts a longer decasyllabic (10-syllable) line and invents the stanza form called RHYME ROYAL. Rhyming *ababbcc,* the rime royal stanza is strikingly similar to Boccaccio's OTTAVA RIMA (which rhymed *abababcc*): Chaucer simply eliminated the fifth line to create a stanza with two equal parts (lines 1 through 4 and lines 4 through 7), both including the *b*-rhyme of the central fourth line. Thus the structure supports the fourth line as a turning point in the stanza.

The Parliament of Fowls begins with a comic persona of Chaucer avidly reading in order to learn "a certeyne thing," presumably about love. The narrator tells of his experience reading Cicero's "Dream of Scipio," summarizing Africanus's journey into the heavens with the younger Scipio to view the insignificant earth. When the narrator falls asleep reading, Africanus comes to him and guides him through a gate reminiscent of DANTE's infernal one. But this gate leads not to hell but into a garden of love, an idealized landscape surrounding a dark Temple of Venus. Much of the description is adopted from a similar one in Boccaccio's *TESEIDA.* Ultimately the dreamer emerges into the light where the Goddess Nature is supervising a great meeting of birds, who have all gathered on Valentine's Day to choose their mates. Nature holds on her hand a beautiful formel (female) eagle, to which three tercel (male) eagles lay claim. Each tercel eagle makes his case, and Nature says that the formel must choose among them. Meanwhile the birds hold a noisy parliament to debate the issue of just whom the formel should choose. A variety of opinions is expressed by representatives of the different classes of birds—the "birds of ravine," probably suggesting the nobility; the seed fowl, representing the clergy; the waterfowl, representing the commoners; and the worm fowl, suggesting the middle class.

Ultimately the formel postpones her decision for a year, and Nature tells the other birds that they are free to choose their own mates. Before they leave, the birds sing a harmonious song in the form of a *roundel* (or RONDEAU). The noise of the birds awakes the dreamer, who goes back to his books to keep looking for answers.

If there is an answer to his question in the parliament, the Narrator hasn't seen it. Scholars have debated themselves as to whether the theme of the poem is love and love's complexities, or whether the theme is politics: Africanus discusses the importance of acting for the "common profit" in the beginning, and the birds' song at the end returns their own chaotic society to harmony at the end. Many recent critics have suggested that the poem is really about the nature of knowledge and truth and how we know what we know: The birds' song seems to suggest that we can have certainty in this world, while the final stanza that shows the dreamer still searching for something suggests that he, at any rate, has not been able to find any certain knowledge.

The Parliament of Fowls is a pivotal text in Chaucer's career: It is the most mature of his early dream visions, and its rime royal verse form looks forward to his great love poem *TROILUS AND CRISEYDE*, while the ESTATES SATIRE of the bird parliament itself looks forward to the GENERAL PROLOGUE to the *CANTERBURY TALES*.

Bibliography

Aers, David. "*The Parliament of Fowls:* Authority, the Knower, and the Known," *Chaucer Review* 16 (1981): 1–17.

Brewer, D. S., ed. *The Parliament of Fowls.* London: Thomas Nelson, 1960.

Leicester, Marshall, Jr. "The Harmony of Chaucer's *Parlement:* A Dissonant Voice," *Chaucer Review* 9 (1974): 15–34.

Ruud, Jay. "Realism, Nominalism, and the Inconclusive Ending of the *Parliament of Fowls,*" *Geardagum* 23 (2002): 1–28.

Parliament of the Three Ages, The (The Parlement of the Thre Ages) (ca. 1370–90)

The Parliament of the Three Ages is a late 14th-century alliterative poem of some 660 lines, composed somewhere in the north Midlands. The poem survives in two manuscripts, and is part of the ALLITERATIVE REVIVAL, a trend among MIDDLE ENGLISH poets of the west and north to write in the alliterative style that had characterized poetry in OLD ENGLISH. The *Parliament* presents a DREAM VISION in which the narrator witnesses a dispute among Youth, Middle Age, and Old Age.

The poem begins with a youthful narrator riding into the woods on a May morning in search of deer to poach. He brings down a great stag, and a detailed description follows in which he butchers and dresses the dead deer, a description not unlike the hunting scenes in the contemporary *SIR GAWAIN AND THE GREEN KNIGHT.* Tired from his exertion, the narrator falls asleep. In his dream he sees three figures: a bold knight on his horse, a wealthy man dressed in gray, and a white-haired man clad in black. The first man, representing Youth, vows to fight in a tournament to prove himself worthy of his Lady's love. The second man, representing Middle Age, begins immediately to upbraid Youth and to advise him to acquire some land, wealth, and security. Their argument is cut short by Old Age or "Elde," who dominates the last two-thirds of the poem. Asserting the inevitability of death and loss through the turning of Fortune's wheel, Elde asserts the transitory nature of all things worldly, and so the futility of both the pleasures of Youth and prudence of Middle Age.

The greatest part of Elde's monologue is taken up by a lengthy account of the NINE WORTHIES—world conquerors from the pagan era (Hector of Troy, Alexander, and Caesar), from the biblical Jewish era (Joshua, David, and Judas Maccabeus), and from the medieval Christian world (King ARTHUR, CHARLEMAGNE, and Godfrey de Bouillon). Elde describes how each of these great figures lost everything through the turning of Fortune's wheel. He then more briefly lists the wisest men of history (Aristotle, Virgil, Merlin, and Solomon) and the greatest lovers (IPOMADON, Amadas, Samson, TRISTAN, Dido, Guenevere, and others), and shows how these, too, were destroyed in the end. The tone and subject of Elde's speech recall those of CHAUCER's *MONK'S TALE* with its relentless focus on tragedy and loss. The poem ends as the dreamer awakens and gives a brief prayer to God and to Mary to amend his sins.

Scholars have sometimes faulted the poem for the disproportionate speech of Elde, which seems tangential to the initial and somewhat undeveloped argument between Youth and Middle Age. But the poem is only apparently a DEBATE POEM. In fact Death shuts down all debate and Elde is its messenger. Parallels have been drawn between *The Parliament of the Three Ages* and a similar Middle English alliterative dream vision/debate poem, *WINNER AND WASTER*. Both appear in the same British Library manuscript, and the frugal Middle Age and prodigal Youth seem representations of "Winner" and "Waster" respectively. It has even been suggested that the same author wrote both poems. That view is not generally accepted, however, and in any case the emphases of the poems are different: While *Winner and Waster* focuses on the reform of the political and economic world, *The Parliament of the Three Ages,* with its gloomy concentration on Fortune, focuses on the transience of all worldly things.

Bibliography

Gardner, John, trans. *The Alliterative Morte Arthure, The Owl and the Nightingale, and Five Other Middle English Poems.* Carbondale: Southern Illinois University Press, 1971.

Ginsberg, Warren, ed. *Wynnere and Wastoure and the Parlement of the Thre Ages.* Kalamazoo, Mich.: Published for TEAMS by the Medieval Institute, 1992.

Offord, M. Y., ed. *The Parlement of the Thre Ages.* EETS 246. Oxford: Oxford University Press, 1959.

Parson's Tale, The Geoffrey Chaucer (ca. 1395)

CHAUCER's *Parson's Tale* is the final section of *The Canterbury Tales,* as they are arranged in the two earliest and most important manuscripts of the *Tales,* the HENGWRT and the ELLESMERE manuscripts. The "tale" is a lengthy prose treatise on penance, including a sermon on the Seven Deadly Sins, and is not entirely in keeping with the pilgrim Parson's promise in the prologue to the tale to tell a "merry tale in prose" that will "knit up" the tale-telling contest that provides the overall structure of Chaucer's text. This discrepancy has led some readers to speculate that Chaucer did not intend *The Parson's Tale* as the conclusion of *The Canterbury Tales,* but regarded it as a separate text altogether. Others have argued that the tale is perfectly appropriate and provides an effective ending for Chaucer's tales: The Parson sees the earthly pilgrimage to Canterbury as a figure of the ultimate pilgrimage to the heavenly Jerusalem, and for him the sacrament of penance is necessary before it is possible to enter the heavenly city.

The speaker begins the tale by defining penance and discussing types of contrition. He talks about the difference between venial and deadly sins. Then in part 2 of the tale, the speaker deals with three parts of penance. First, and at greatest length, he considers the recognition of sin, discoursing on the seven deadly sins (lust, gluttony, greed, sloth, wrath, envy, and pride), and details different varieties of each major sin, as well as the remedies for these sins, such as humility for pride or chastity for lust. The second part of penance is confession, and the speaker describes how to make a full and true confession. Finally he discusses satisfaction. The tale ends as the speaker invites all those who seek the heavenly Jerusalem to repent, confess their sins, and make appropriate satisfaction for them. In the end it appears that Chaucer himself seems to have responded to the call for repentance, as the tale, and the *Canterbury Tales* as a whole, ends with a "Retraction" in Chaucer's own voice, in which the writer expresses his repentance for writing many of his greatest works, including *The Canterbury Tales* themselves.

The Parson's Tale seems to use a number of sources, including mainly 13th-century Latin and French treatises on penance and on the seven deadly sins. Critical commentary on the tale has focused on its relationship with the rest of the tales, and with the question of how it contributes to the unity of the *Canterbury Tales* text, with most critics seeing the moral view of *The Parson's Tale* providing a comment on the world and values of the pilgrim narrators. Critics who have discussed the "Retraction" have seen it as either the narrator's response to the Parson's sermon, or as Chaucer's participating in a literary convention that gives him a chance to list the works for which he wants to be remembered.

Bibliography

Baldwin, Ralph. *The Unity of the Canterbury Tales.* Copenhagen: Rosenkilde and Bagger, 1955.

Benson, Larry, et al. *The Riverside Chaucer.* 3rd ed. Boston: Houghton Mifflin, 1987.

Little, Katherine. "Chaucer's Parson and the Specter of Wycliffism," *Studies in the Age of Chaucer* 23 (2001): 225–253.

McGerr, Rosemarie P. "Retraction and Memory: Retrospective Structure in the *Canterbury Tales,*" *Comparative Literature* 37 (1985): 97–113.

Owen, Charles A., Jr. "What the Manuscripts Tell Us about the Parson's Tale," *Medium Aevum* 63 (1994): 239–249.

Patterson, Lee. "The 'Parson's Tale' and the Quitting of the *Canterbury Tales,*" *Traditio* 34 (1978): 331–368.

Wenzel, Siegfried. "The Source of Chaucer's Seven Deadly Sins," *Traditio* 30 (1974): 351–378.

———. "Notes on the *Parson's Tale,*" *Chaucer Review* 16 (1982): 237–256.

Parzival Wolfram von Eschenbach (ca. 1205)

For many medieval and modern readers WOLFRAM VON ESCHENBACH's Middle High German *Parzival* (ca. 1205) represents one of the most important courtly ROMANCES of the entire Middle Ages. In part based on CHRÉTIEN DE TROYES's *PERCEVAL* (ca. 1180–90), in part the result of Wolfram's own literary invention (Wolfram's work is about twice as long as Chrétien's), this romance draws from many different literary traditions (Asian, Celtic, Latin, French, and German); combines a multitude of political, religious, ethical, moral, erotic, and anthropological issues; and projects, almost in a utopian manner, a new universal human community where racial and religious conflicts are reduced, though not completely eliminated, to an astonishing degree.

Parzival is divided into 16 books, but from a narrative point of view into four major sections. The first deals with Parzival's father, Gahmuret, and his first wife, the black Queen Belakâne, then with Gahmuret's second wife, Queen Herzeloyde, followed by Gahmuret's death while in the military service of a mighty military ruler in the East, and the birth of Parzival. The second part deals with Parzival's upbringing in the wilderness of Soltâne, where his mother tries to shield him entirely from the dangers of knighthood, then his entering the world of chivalry at the court of King ARTHUR, his marriage with Condwîr âmûrs, his encounter with the Grail kingdom at Munsalvaesche, and his ultimate failure to meet the challenges presented to him there because he is only schooled according to standard chivalric teachings by the knight Gurnemanz that do not apply to the Grail. This section concludes with Parzival being cursed by the grail messenger Cundrie for his failure, which makes him depart from King Arthur's court. The third part represents a major shift in narrative focus. Parzival's friend Gawan is equally challenged in his chivalry by another knight, and, like Parzival, he now departs from King Arthur to pursue his own destiny. After several erotic and knightly adventures, he meets the Duchess Orgelûse, a woman whose husband had been killed by King Gramoflanz. Distrustful of all men, she now gives Gawan the cold shoulder. He falls in love with her, however, and has to undergo many difficult and also embarrassing, if not humiliating, adventures before she begins to accept his wooing. Finally, Gawan risks his life to liberate Castle Schastel Marveile from a magic spell, thereby freeing many women from a sorcerer's power, among them his two sisters, his mother, and his grandmother. As a final act he promises to fight King Gramoflanz, which then paves the way for Gawan to win Orgelûse's love.

King Arthur, however, manages to settle the conflict between Gramoflanz and Gawan, foreshadowing the happy outcome of Parzival's quest. The latter, who had revoked his belief in God after he had been cursed by the Grail messenger Cundrie for his failure at Munsalvaesche, comes across Christian pilgrims who show him the way to the hermit Trevrezent. The latter, who turns out to be Parzival's own uncle, reintroduces him to Christianity and teaches him the full meaning of the Gospel. In his discussions with Trevrezent, the truth about Parzival's terrible failures and crimes committed throughout his life is revealed: When Parzival left his mother without turning back to her even once, she died of grief. Outside of King Arthur's court he killed his relative, the knight Ither, whose red armor he claimed for himself. And, as Parzival has to admit shamefully, he did not ask the crucial question of the Grail king concerning his suffering although he had observed the liturgical procession, the appearance of the Grail itself, and the lamentation of the entire court. Trevrezent, however, assumes, like a priest, Parzival's guilt and seeks God's forgiveness on his behalf, which allows his nephew to return to the world of chivalry and to seek out Munsalvaesche once again.

At this point he runs into his half-brother Feirefiz, son of Gahmuret and Belacane, who is checkered in black and white as a result of his hybrid nature. Since they do not recognize each other, they engage in a deadly battle. At one point Parzival would have killed Feirefiz if God had not made his sword (originally Ither's) break apart, so Feirefiz, observing this and being the perfect knight, offers peace and reveals his own identity, a gesture normally expected from the defeated knight first. They ride together to King Arthur's court, and soon Cundrie arrives and announces that Parzival has been chosen as the successor of the Grail king, contingent, of course, upon his asking the crucial question. Once Anfortas has been released from his suffering and so from his office and has his wound healed quickly, Parzival assumes the throne at Munsalvaesche. Feirefiz is baptized, though rather quickly and without any real religious indoctrination because he wants to marry Anfortas's sister, Repanse de Schoye. Both return to Feirefiz' kingdom in the East where their son, John, rises to the position of the mythical Prester John, the vastly powerful ruler and missionary of the Eastern world. Parzival, on the other hand, now reunited with his wife Condwîr âmûrs and his two sons, stays behind and rules the Grail kingdom. Wolfram's *Parzival* concludes open-endedly as the narrator only indicates that Parzival's son Loherangrîn was later appointed as the husband of the duchess of Brabant, but then left her again when she asked him, against his explicit ban, about his origin.

Without fully embracing religious and racial tolerance, Wolfram's narrative still offers most amazing perspectives regarding the relationship between various peoples and religions. Cundrie, the ugliest woman on earth, emerges as the most learned person, commanding knowledge of Arabic, lapidary sciences, astronomy and astrology, and so forth. Violence, which erupts at many points in the romance, is viewed very negatively, especially violence against women. Feirefiz's love for Repanse is treated as more important than what a true conversion to Christianity would normally require. His quick baptism proves to be enough for him to enter the otherwise closely guarded Grail community, especially as he partly belongs to that world anyway through his father. Most important, Wolfram projects a new, religiously inspired Grail kingdom that supersedes the world of King Arthur. The Grail world, in turn, assumes a global position, sending out its knights to wherever a country is in need of a royal husband. Feirefiz and later his son John connect the European world with the Asian world. Though certainly under Christian rule, this new universal perspective proves to be highly innovative for the Middle Ages.

Bibliography

Bumke, Joachim. *Wolfram von Eschenbach.* 7th rev. ed. Stuttgart: Metzler, 1997.

Wolfram von Eschenbach. *Parzival.* Studienausgabe. Translated by Peter Knecht, with an introduction by Bernd Schirok. Berlin: de Gruyter, 1998.

Wolfram von Eschenbach,. *Parzival.* Translated by A. E. Hatto. Harmondsworth, U.K.: Penguin, 1980.

Wynn, Marianne. "Wolfram von Eschenbach." In *German Writers and Works of the High Middle Ages: 1170–1280,* edited by James Hardin and Will Hasty, 185–206. Detroit: Gale Research, 1994.

Albrecht Classen

Paston Letters, The (ca. 1422–1504)

The Paston Letters are a collection of more than 1,000 items of personal and business correspondence documenting three generations or about 90 years (ca. 1422–1504) of the wealthy Paston family of Norfolk. The letters, many of which were written during the War of the Roses (1455–85), have long been valued as a source for the political history of that turbulent period. The fact that most of the letters deal with everyday lives of the household also makes them an important source for the domestic lives of people of the Pastons' class. Furthermore, the letters are of great linguistic value, providing important illustrations of written English immediately before and after the development of the printing press.

The documents begin with the career of the judge William Paston, who makes the family fortune through marrying Sir Edmund Berry's daughter, Agnes. Their son, John, marries the lady Margaret Mauteby, and becomes a gentleman with significant political connections. Some 60 percent of the documents in the *Paston Letters* date from 1440 to 1466, the year of John's death. While there are letters dealing with Yorkist lords trying to recruit John to their faction in 1454, and letters dealing with the long mental illness of the Lancastrian king Henry VI, the most notable letters concern Sir John Fastolf, famous soldier, Knight of the Garter, and reputed LOLLARD, who was cousin to John's wife, Margaret. When Fastolf died in 1459, he left vast estates in Norfolk to John Paston. Litigation concerning the estates carried over into the time of John's son, John II, when two of Fastolf's executors sold the manor of Caister, where the Pastons lived, to the duke of Norfolk, who besieged the estate in 1469.

But aside from these political events, domestic affairs take up a good portion of the letters. Often these involve marriages, which for an upwardly mobile middle-class family like the Pastons were all-important in consolidating land, money, and influence. We learn, for instance, of John II's engagement to Anne Haute, cousin to the queen, and the subsequent annulment of the engagement in 1477. We also learn of the marriage of Margery Paston to the family's head bailiff, Richard Calle—a match never condoned or recognized by the family. The letters also demonstrate the effective management of the great estate by women, such as Margaret Paston, who are consistently left in charge when their husbands are away from home for long periods of time. Margaret deals with terms for tenants on the Pastons' land and arranges marriage as well, though it has been pointed out that her own letters are in many different handwritings—the women of the Paston estate seem to have dictated their letters, which some scholars have suggested shows an inability to write, or at least to write well. However, these women most certainly could read, as evidenced by mention of books in their possession. In fact, the variety of people who wrote the letters contained in the Paston documents indicates a high literacy rate among the nonlaboring classes of England in the 15th century.

The *Paston Letters* stayed in the family until the 18th century, when they ultimately came into the possession of James Fenn, who published them in 1787 and 1789. A third volume of the letters came out in 1823. However, the originals of the letters were lost until 1865, when many of them resurfaced. Four separate parts of the collection were acquired by the British Museum between 1875 and 1933, and that is where the bulk of the original documents are held today.

Bibliography

Colin, Richmond. *The Paston Family in the Fifteenth Century.* Cambridge: Cambridge University Press, 1990.

Davis, Norman. "The Language of the Pastons." In *Middle English Literature,* edited by J. A. Burrow, 45–70. Oxford: Oxford University Press, 1989.

Paston Letters and Papers of the Fifteenth Century. 2 vols. Edited by Norman Davis. Oxford: Clarendon Press, 1971–1976.

Pastourelle (*pastorela*)

The *pastourelle* was a medieval lyric genre that took the form of a dialogue between a shepherdess and a noble suitor (a knight or occasionally a cleric). The term *pastourelle* comes from the Old French term for "little shepherdess." In the classic form of the genre, the knight recounts his meeting with the shepherdess and his attempts to woo her, but she rebuffs his advances and the suitor generally fails in his attempts to seduce her. Thus the poem depicts an idealized country setting free from the constrictions of the court, and a situation between persons of unequal social class. But invariably the shepherdess, the suitor's social inferior, proves to be his intellectual equal.

The genre is found most frequently in Old French poetry, where nearly 200 examples survive, though it originated with the Old Provençal TROU-

BADOURS, where the genre was called *pastorela.* The earliest examples come from the poet MARCABRU. In Marcabru's lyric *"L'autrier jost' una sebissa,"* the high-born suitor creates a romantic fantasy that the shepherdess wittily demolishes. She tells him:

"Master, a man hounded by madness
promises and pledges and puts up security:
that's how you would do homage to me,
Lord," said this peasant girl;
"but I am not willing, for a little
entrance fee, to cash in my virginity
for the fame of a whore."

(Goldin 1973, 75, ll. 64–70)

The *pastourelle* was very popular in Old French by the 13th century, and the genre spread to Spain, Portugal, Germany, and Italy, where new twists might be added and where some of the most memorable examples of the genre were written. In WALTHER VON DER VOGELWEIDE's *"Nemt, frowe, disen kranz,"* the poet is enamored of the shepherd girl until he awakens to find that the meeting was a dream. He ends the poem searching for the dream girl:

She has stirred me so
that this summer, with every girl I meet,
I must gaze deep in her eyes:
perhaps one will be mine: then all my cares
are gone.

(Dronke 1996, 202)

In Guido CAVALCANTI's poem *"In un boschetto,"* the shepherdess consents to make love with the poet, and the Arcadian scene becomes a paradise:

She took me by the hand, to show her love,
and told me she had given me her heart.
She guided me to a fresh little grove,
where I saw flowers of every colour bloom;
and I felt so much joy and sweetness there,
I seemed to see the god of love descending.

(Dronke 1996, 201)

Thus occasionally the suitor is successful in his wooing of the shepherdess. Sometimes, however, the knight attempts to use force—in nearly one out of five Old French *pastourelles,* the lyric ends with a rape or attempted rape. THIBAUD DE CHAMPAGNE's poem *"L'autrier par la matinée"* ends with an interesting twist to this situation, in which the knight is humiliated after an attempted rape:

So then I tried to use a little force,
and she starts to rant and rave:
"Perrinet, help! He's raping me!"
The shouts start coming from the woods.
I dropped her one-two-three
and took off on my horse.

When she saw me running away,
she called out to embarrass me,
"Noble knights are very brave."

(Goldin 1973, 477, ll. 44–53)

The *pastourelle* may have its true origins in the classical pastorals of Theocritus, particularly his *Idyll* number 27, which presents a similar situation. But it also seems related to popular folk traditions and when performed may have involved dancing. The influence of the genre survived the Middle Ages and can be seen, for example, in Elizabethan dialogue lyrics.

Bibliography

Dronke, Peter. *The Medieval Lyric.* 3rd ed. Cambridge: D. S. Brewer, 1996.

Goldin, Frederick, ed. and trans. *Lyrics of the Troubadours and Trouvères: An Anthology and a History.* Garden City, N.Y.: Doubleday, 1973.

Paden, William D., ed. and trans. *The Medieval Pastourelle.* 2 vols. New York: Garland, 1987.

Patience (ca. 1375)

Patience is one of four major narrative poems preserved in a single manuscript (British Museum Cotton Nero A.x) by the late 14th-century author known as the "Gawain poet" or the "Pearl poet." Like the other poems in the manuscript (*SIR*

Gawain and the Green Knight, Pearl, and *Cleanness*), *Patience* is written in a northern West Midland dialect. It is structured in stanzas of four alliterative lines—like all of the poems of the Gawain poet, *Patience* is part of the ALLITERATIVE REVIVAL of the later 14th century.

Patience is a MIDDLE ENGLISH verse retelling, in 531 lines, of the Old Testament story of Jonah. It begins with a 60-line passage extolling the virtue of patience, and then offers Jonah's story as an illustration of human impatience contrasted with the patience of God. The poet's conception of patience is far more complex and varied than a modern reader is likely to suspect. In a vivid and detailed narrative, the poet considers patience as endurance of misfortune, but also as self-control in all circumstances—essentially it is obedience to truth or to ultimate reality, to the will of God.

The Jonah story follows the chronology of the biblical narrative, though the poet adds a good deal of concrete detail. The belly of the whale, which the poet compares with hell, is so slimy that Jonah must stumble about, looking for a clean nook to lodge in while praying to God for three days. After the whale has spit him up on dry land, the poet mentions how badly his clothes need washing. When God spares the city of Nineveh after Jonah's preaching, the prophet is angry and blames God for his "courtesy"—a word with profound significance for all of the poems in the Cotton Nero A.x manuscript. Courtesy is behavior in accordance with charity: By the end of the poem God's courtesy includes his mercy and patience that preserves human beings in the world.

In effect the poem is organized like a medieval sermon, specifically a sermon on the eighth beatitude ("Blessed are they which are persecuted for righteousness' sake: for theirs is the kingdom of heaven," Mt. 5.10), to which the poet alludes in the prologue. Thus like a sermon, it begins with a statement of the theme followed by an illustration of the theme with a detailed exemplum (not unlike *The Pardoner's Tale* by the Gawain poet's contemporary Geoffrey CHAUCER). The author's source was, of course, chiefly the book of Jonah in the Vulgate Bible, but he may also have known a hymn on Jonah by the late Latin poet PRUDENTIUS, as well as another Latin poem, *De Jona et Ninive,* attributed to the early Christian theologian Tertullian. Still the depiction of Jonah in *Patience* owes little to any earlier source. None of the traditional exegetic interpretations of the Jonah story (Jonah as an allegorical type of Christ, for instance) occur in the poem, and the poet is unique in applying the notion of patience to Jonah 's story. Also unusual is the poet's playing up the comic aspects of Jonah and his encounters with God. It is certainly one of the most entertaining and effective scriptural paraphrases in medieval English, and is more tightly crafted than the Gawain poet's most similar poem, *Cleanness.*

Bibliography

Bowers, R. H. *The Legend of Jonah.* The Hague: Nijhoff, 1971.

Brewer, Derek, and Jonathan Gibson, ed. *A Companion to the Gawain-poet.* Woodbridge, U.K.: D. S. Brewer, 1997.

The Complete Works of the Pearl Poet. Translated with an introduction by Casey Finch; Middle English texts edited by Malcolm Andrew, Ronald Waldron, and Clifford Peterson. Berkeley: University of California Press, 1993.

Gardner, John, trans. *The Complete Works of the Gawain-poet.* Woodcuts by Fritz Kredel. Chicago: University of Chicago Press, 1965.

Schleusner, Jay. "History and Action in *Patience,*" *PMLA* 86 (1971): 959–965.

Williams, David J. "The Point of *Patience,*" *Modern Philology* 68 (1970–71): 127–136.

Paul the Deacon (ca. 720–799)

Paul the Deacon was a Lombard chronicler originating from a noble family in Friuli in northern Italy. His father, Warnefrid, sent him to the royal court of Ratchis of Pavia for his education, and later he lived at the court of Duke Archis of Benevent (763), until he joined the convent of St. Peter near Civate on the Lake Como. In about 780, he entered the Benedictine convent of Monte Cassino. In 782, Paul secured his brother Arichis's release from prison—he had rebelled against Charlemagne—by means of an elegy dedicated to Charlemagne, who subsequently invited him to his court. Paul stayed in

Francia from 781 until 784 or 785 and composed a history of the bishops of Metz for the king (*Liber de episcopis Mettensibus*, or *Liber de ordine et numero episcoporum in civitate Mettensi*), along with a collection of homilies, or sermons. In 785, he returned to Monte Cassino, where he continued with the composition of important chronicle accounts and religious narratives.

In 787, he began with the work for which he is most famous today, the *Historia gentis Langobardorum* (*History of the Langobards*), which provides a chronological overview of the years 568 until 744. He based his chronicle on both oral and written sources, and included a number of Langobardian legends. The large number of extant manuscripts and excerpts (more than 100 still exist today) demonstrates that Paul enjoyed a wide-reaching popularity with his detailed and well-written chronicle. Shortly before 774, Duchess Adalperga of Benevent commissioned him to continue the *Historia Romana* (Roman history) originally written by Eutropius (d. ca. 610), taking the reader from the emperorship of Valentinian I (364–375) to the times of Emperor Justinian (527–565). Both here and in his *Historia Langobardorum*, Paul places particular emphasis on the role that women played in history. Paul also wrote a *vita* of Pope GREGORY THE GREAT (590–604), a commentary of the Rules of St. Benedict, an account of miracle narratives concerning St. Benedict, a collection of homilies (*Homiliarium*), grammatical studies, riddles, epigrams, poetry, and letters.

Bibliography

Goffart, Walter. *The Narrators of Barbarian History (A.D. 550–800): Jordanes, Gregory of Tours, Bede, and Paul the Deacon.* Princeton, N.J.: Princeton University Press, 1988.

Paul the Deacon. *History of the Lombards.* Translated by William Dudley Foulke. 1907. Philadelphia: University of Pennsylvania Press, 1974.

———. *Pauli Historia Langobardorum.* Edited by Ludwig Bethmann and Georg Waitz. 1878. Hannover: Hahnsche Buchhandlung, 1987.

———. *Pauli Historia Romana.* Edited by Hans Droysen. 1879. Munich: Monumenta Germaniae Historica, 1978.

Pearl (ca. 1375)

Pearl is an important Middle English DREAM VISION poem preserved in a single late 14th-century manuscript known as Cotton Nero A.x, the same manuscript in which survive three other long poems: *SIR GAWAIN AND THE GREEN KNIGHT, CLEANNESS*, and *PATIENCE*. On the basis of vocabulary and style, most scholars attribute all four poems to the same writer. All four poems are written in the same Northwest Midland dialect, and all belong, to some extent, to the ALLITERATIVE REVIVAL that characterized much English poetry of the time.

Interpretation of the poem has varied. Many consider the poem to be autobiographical, concerned with the death of the poet's own infant daughter. Others see the dead girl, the Pearl-maiden, as a literary device enabling the poet to teach a number of important doctrinal truths. Essentially the poem moves from the narrator's inconsolable grief for the loss of his precious pearl, to the real understanding of Christian precepts that he had previously known in his mind but had not embraced with his heart.

The poem begins with the narrator despondent over losing a pearl, and he searches in vain the grass in which the jewel has been lost. His inordinate grief suggests something more than a literal gem, and it is only gradually that the reader becomes aware that what has been lost is the dreamer's two-year-old daughter, who now, in his dream, appears to him as a grown woman bedecked in pearls. The Dreamer sees her across a stream in a paradisal land, and slowly comes to realize she is the adult, spiritual version of his lost child. He is overjoyed to see her, and she convinces him that his excessive grief is inappropriate—that she lives a blessed life now as Queen of Heaven and Bride of Christ. Against the Dreamer's fears about infant salvation, the Pearl maiden reveals that baptism is sufficient for a child to attain salvation, and when the Dreamer fears that she was too young to have received the reward she describes, the maiden recounts for him the parable of the vineyard from Matthew 20.1–16: All are exalted equally in heaven. Excessive grief over his daughter must be assuaged by faith and patience, and the Dreamer must be taught that the real pearl he needs to be seeking is the "pearl of great price" of Matthew 13.45–46: the Kingdom of Heaven. The Dreamer's obstinacy and ignorance are gradually, through the patient teaching of the pearl-maiden, somewhat satisfied, and he wishes to have a glimpse of the heavenly Jerusalem itself. Thus the last fifth of the poem is devoted to a lengthy description of the heavenly city as described in Revelation 20–21, and of his beloved Pearl in the train of 144,000 virgins that pass before the throne of the Lamb in Revelation 14. Overcome by longing and a desire to reunite with his Pearl, the Dreamer impulsively attempts to cross the stream and enter the heavenly city, at which he immediately awakens. Presumably a more patient man after his vision, the Dreamer awakes better able to cope with his loss.

But Pearl is admired not only for its content but also for its complex form. The poem is written in four-stress, octosyllabic (eight-syllable) lines that generally also use alliteration. The lines form 101 12-line stanzas, rhyming *ababababbcbc*. These are arranged into 20 groups of five stanzas each (except section 15, which contains six). The c-rhymes are the same in all five stanzas, and the final word of the last line is identical in all five stanzas of any given section. In addition, the first line of the last four stanzas in each section contains this same repeated word somewhere in the line, and that word is used in the first line of the succeeding section, linking the sections together. The final line of the poem ends with the word "paye" (roughly translated as "content"), which is also the final word of the first line. Thus line 1212 of the poem links to line 1, and the poem forms a complete, perfect circle—a pearl.

This elaborate rhyme scheme is used elsewhere in Middle English in shorter poems, but to attempt it in a poem of 1,212 lines was a remarkable undertaking. There is some question as to why the poet broke the pattern in section 15 with an extra stanza. Some scholars believe that the poet intended to eliminate one of the stanzas from this section, though there is no agreement as to which. Others suggest that the poet meant to demonstrate that nothing of man's making is perfect, and deliberately introduced a defect in the poem. Still others believe that, unlike 1,200, 1,212 lines suggests the multiple 12 x 12, or 144, reflecting the 144,000 virgins among whom the Pearl maiden is now counted.

Whatever the cause, readers have found little to criticize in the elaborate structure of the poem, and much to admire in its skillful depiction of a man whose dream reveals to him the answers to the theological questions that have added to his grief.

Bibliography

Andrew, Malcolm, Ronald Waldron, and Clifford Peterson, ed. *The Complete Works of the "Pearl" Poet.* Translated by Casey Finch. Berkeley: University of California Press, 1993.

Bishop, Ian. *Pearl in Its Setting: A Critical Study of the Structure and Meaning of the Middle English Poem.* Oxford: Blackwell, 1968.

Boroff, Marie, trans. *Pearl.* New York: Norton, 1977.

Brewer, Derek, and Jonathan Gibson, ed. *A Companion to the Gawain-Poet.* Woodbridge, U.K.: D. S. Brewer, 1997.

Gordon, E. V., ed. *Pearl.* Oxford: Clarendon Press, 1953.

Kean, P. M. *"The Pearl": An Interpretation.* London: Routledge and Kegan Paul, 1967.

Prior, Sandra Pierson. *The Pearl Poet Revisited.* New York: Twayne, 1994.

Peasants' Revolt of 1381

The Peasants' Revolt was an uprising of laborers, urban workers, and peasants that occurred in southern England in the 14th century. It was the culmination of tensions caused by several social factors. The depopulating effects of the BLACK DEATH had given tenants and laborers greater economic power with regard to the landholding class. Landlords, caught between the financial difficulties caused by a dearth of workers and shrinking markets, pushed statutes through Parliament in 1349 and 1351 that would protect their rights by establishing wages at the levels they were before the outbreak of plague.

The ill-will this freezing of wages generated was increased soon after by further legal measures. Between 1377 and 1381, Parliament imposed a series of taxes levied by head count, called poll taxes. The burden of most parliamentary subsidies usually fell on those who had the most wealth, but the poll taxes were levied on both rich and poor without regard to a person's ability to pay. The poll tax of 1381 was imposed to help fund England's ongoing war with France and was the heaviest tax to date. The fact that the revenue raised was in support of the war effort only exacerbated matters. From an English perspective, the war with France was a succession of failures. Edward III had presented the war as necessary to England's future, but the lack of substantial victories led the common people to believe that incompetent military leaders and administrators were wasting their tax money. Huge numbers of peasants and other workers sought to evade this latest levy, and as a result, the government attempted to forcibly collect the tax. This highhandedness was the immediate cause of the Peasants' Revolt.

The uprising itself was short-lived, lasting from the end of May until the end of June. It began in Essex and Kent and spread to other areas in central and southeastern England. While many men were involved in its leadership, the most prominent were Wat Tyler, from Kent, and John BALL, a former priest. A couplet, composed by rebel leader John Ball, encapsulates the questioning of social inequality: "When Adam dug and Eve span, who was then the gentleman?" Fortified by the preaching of their leaders, the rebels marched toward London in mid-June, behaving in an orderly and disciplined manner. Upon reaching the city, the rebels killed two men they identified with the spate of unjust taxes and the lack of success in the war with France. They also attacked the Savoy, the London palace of JOHN OF GAUNT, the noble most heavily involved in the war effort. The majority of the royal court took refuge in the formidable Tower of London.

Although agitating for social change, most of the rebels remained respectful of the English monarchy. The royal court capitalized on this sentiment by sending the 14-year-old king, RICHARD II, to negotiate with the rebels in a series of talks over the course of two days. The most important of the rebels' demands was the abolition of legal serfdom (called villeinage) and the limiting of rents. They also stipulated their inclusion in the "community of the realm" with a voice in political decision-making. With his court trapped in the Tower of London, the young king had little choice but to acquiesce to rebel demands.

The rebels were so joyous over the victories of the first day's negotiations that many celebrated that evening, indulging copiously in food and drink. The rebel contingent for the second day's meeting was much reduced as a result. Some felt that the victory was already won, while many others suffered the effects of severe hangovers. The inglorious end to the negotiations of the second day remains shrouded in mystery, but it would appear that Wat Tyler brandished his dagger at a member of the king's retinue. The Lord Mayor of London responded by killing Tyler, and the king was forced to calm the rebels by offering himself as their new leader. Exhibiting a remarkable presence of mind, Richard II led the rebels outside London where they dispersed, no doubt believing that their adventure had ended in victory.

The revolt lost much of its impetus, and any real momentum that remained was quickly crushed by the subsequent actions of Richard II. According to the evidence of contemporary chronicles, the king ordered the rebel leaders hunted down, captured, and summarily executed. None of the concessions were honored. However, it would be wrong to assume that the Peasants' Revolt had no lasting effect. The government ceased to impose poll taxes on the entire population, but most important, a large segment of English society had come to view itself as part of a larger nation, the community of the realm. The questioning of the orders of society as well as issues of equality and justice can be found in medieval literature composed in the turbulent period before the outbreak of the uprising, most notably in the works of Geoffrey CHAUCER (c. 1343–1400) and in *PIERS PLOWMAN*, the literary masterpiece of William LANGLAND (ca. 1330–ca. 1388).

Bibliography

DeWindt, Edwin Brezette, ed. *A Slice of Life: Selected Documents of Medieval English Peasant Experience.* Kalamazoo, Mich.: Medieval Institute Publications, 1996.

Dobson, R. B., ed. *The Peasants' Revolt of 1381.* London: St. Martin's Press, 1982.

Hanawalt, Barbara A. *The Ties that Bound: Peasant Families in Medieval England.* Oxford: Oxford University Press, 1986.

Hilton, R. H. *Bond Men Made Free: Medieval Peasant Movements and the Rising of 1381.* London: Routledge, 2003.

Diane Korngiebel

Pecock, Reginald (ca. 1395–ca. 1460)

Reginald Pecock was a theologian whose works were controversial not only for their contents, but also because they were written in the then vulgar English. His most important work, *The Repressor of Over Much Blaming of the Clergy* (ca. 1449), was written as an argument against LOLLARD ideology, but proved to be the work that resulted in his ultimate ruin with the orthodox church.

Pecock was born in or near St. David's in Wales around 1395. He was educated at Oriel College, Oxford, where he became a fellow in October 1417. He was ordained a subdeacon in 1420, and deacon and priest in 1421. He earned his bachelor of divinity degree in 1425, and proved himself to be so brilliant that Humphrey, duke of Gloucester, took notice of him and introduced him to the court in London. In 1431, he was elected master of Whittington College, London, and rector of St. Michael's in Riola. In 1444, he was promoted to bishop of St. Asaph. In 1450, he became bishop of Chichester, and in 1454, he was made a member of the Privy Council.

Because his writings were so controversial, Pecock was expelled from the Privy Council just three years after he was made a member. At the same time his works were examined before Archbishop Bourchier. It was found that he was guilty of "[setting] natural law above the scriptures, disregarding the authority of the pope and the saints, and . . . writing on these important matters in English" (Kunitz 1952, 398). The latter was deemed a transgression because it allowed lay people, who were not theologically trained, to consider difficult spiritual questions, which could lead them into heresy. Pecock was condemned for heretical opinions and given the choice of public recantation or burning at the stake. He gave a public recantation at St. Paul's Cross on Sunday, December 4, 1457. He chose to abjure his works and delivered 14 of his books to be burned. He was stripped of his bishopric and sentenced to Thorney Abbey, Cambridgeshire, to spend the rest of his life in seclusion and deprived of books and writing materials.

Pecock's works were written in defense of the orthodox church that ultimately condemned him. In his earliest extant work, *The Reule of Crysten Religoiun,* Pecock tries to use persuasion to convince the Lollards that natural law is higher than that of the Scriptures. Even in this early work, Pecock offended orthodox believers, but because of his connections to the house of Lancaster, there was no immediate retaliation.

His two best-known works were the *Donet* (ca. 1440) and its supplement, *The Follower to the Donet* (ca. 1454). They were written as a dialogue between father and son and served as an introduction to the chief truths of the Christian religion.

The Repressor of Over Much Blaming of the Clergy (ca. 1449) was arguably Pecock's most important work and was written as a defense against the Lollardist arguments. He states he will examine 11 of their objections, but only analyzes six and refers to other works for the other five. In this work, some of the points he considers include the Lollardist oppositions to "images, pilgrimages, clerical endowment, ecclesiastical hierarchy, papal authority, and the religious orders" (Pearsall 1999, 423).

In the *Book of Faith* (1456), Pecock examines "faith and the roles of reason and scriptural authority" (Ousby 1993, 728). He came close to stating that faith can be established by rational argumentation. This was the work that culminated in his examinations by church authorities.

Pecock spent his life writing religious works in defense of orthodox religion. Ironically it was this devotion that forced him to make the decision between his life's work and his life.

Bibliography

Brockwell, Charles W. *Bishop Reginald Pecock and the Lancastrian Church: Securing the Foundations of Cultural Authority.* Lewiston, N.Y.: Edwin Mellen Press, 1985.

Brockwell, Charles W., Jr. "The Historical Career of Bishop Reginald Pecock, D.D.: *The Poor Scholeris Myrrour* or a Case Study in Famous Obscurity," *Harvard Theological Review* 74, no. 2 (April 1981): 177–201.

Kunitz, Stanley J., and Haycraft, Howard, eds. *British Authors Before 1800: A Biographical Dictionary.* New York: The H. W. Wilson Company, 1952.

Ousby, Ian. *The Cambridge Guide to Literature in English.* Cambridge: Cambridge University Press, 1993.

Pecock, Reginald. *The Reule of Crysten Religioun.* Edited by William Cabell Greet, ed. EETS, o.s. 171. London: Oxford University Press, 1927.

Pearsall, Derek, ed. *Chaucer to Spenser: An Anthology of Writings in English 1375–1575.* Oxford/Malden, Mass.: Blackwell Publishers, 1999.

Malene A. Little

Peire d'Alvernhe (fl. 1150–1180)

Peire d'Alvernhe was a well-known TROUBADOUR, a contemporary of BERNART DE VENTADORN and GUIRAUT DE BORNELH. Nineteen of his songs are extant, in addition to a *TENSO*, or DEBATE POEM, he wrote with Bernart. In his verse he claims that wisdom acquired through the joy of love as well as a gift of eloquence combine to make him a great poet. One of his dominant themes is the moral effect of love.

As with most of the troubadours, little is known with certainty about Peire's life. According to his *VIDA*, he was from central France, born in Clermont in Auvergne. Peire seems to have visited several courts in southern France and in Spain, and there is some evidence that Ramon V of Toulouse was one of his patrons. Bernart Marti, a contemporary poet, claims that Peire was a canon of the church who abandoned his vows to become a troubadour. There is no way to tell whether this claim is true, but Peire did write some of the earliest religious verse in the Provençal language, and also seems to indicate in his later poetry that he is abandoning COURTLY LOVE altogether in order to pursue the love of the Holy Spirit.

Peire was strongly influenced by MARCABRU, and thus chose to write much of his verse in *TROBAR CLUS*, the obscure, difficult troubadour style. He was one of the first poets to actually use the term *clus* in regard to his poetry. But he seems to have preferred the term *vers entiers* (literally "whole songs"), by which, according to Linda Paterson, he means "'songs in which the [high] level of style is faultlessly maintaine,' and its opposite indicates works in which too high a style has been attempted, resulting in laboriousness and obscurity" (Paterson 1975, 67). That is, Peire preferred the highest possible style, but believed that lesser poets should not attempt to write such verse. Essentially his was an elitist view of a kind of poetry appreciated by the select few.

Peire's best-known poem is his famous satire on the troubadours, in which he lampoons a dozen other poets, including Bernart, Giraut (who "looks like a goatskin dried out in the sun" [l. 14]), Guillem de Ribas (whose "singing sounds like hell" [l. 34]), and RAIMBAUT D'ORANGE (whose poetry has "neither warmth nor cheer" [l. 58]). Peire ends his satire with a boast (or *GAP*) about his own superiority, but then undercuts the boast with a poke at his own obscure style:

Peire d'Alvernhe, now he has such a voice
He sings the high notes, and the low (and the in-between),
And before all people gives himself much praise;
And so he is the master of all who here convene;
If only he would make his words a little clearer,
For hardly a man can tell what they mean.

(Goldin 1973, 175, ll. 79–84)

It has been conjectured that the 12 other poets were present at this song's first performance, and that the tone is intended as good-natured joking, as the self-mockery at the end would suggest.

Peire was highly esteemed in his own day, particularly for his outstanding melodies, as his *vida* makes clear. But DANTE also admired him for his poetic skill and his erudition, and lauds him in *De VULGARI ELOQUENTIA*.

Bibliography

Goldin, Frederick, ed. and trans. *Lyrics of the Troubadours and Trouvères: An Anthology and a History.* Garden City, N.Y.: Doubleday, 1973.

Paterson, Linda M. *Troubadours and Eloquence.* Oxford: Clarendon Press, 1975.

Perceval: The Story of the Grail (*Conte du Graal*) Chrétien de Troyes (ca. 1190)

The French poet CHRÉTIEN DE TROYES's longest (at 9,200 lines) and most puzzling ROMANCE is his last, the unfinished *Perceval,* or *Le Conte du Graal* (The story of the Grail). The poem contains a dedication to Count Philip of Flanders, who was Chrétien's patron after the poet had left the service of the Countess MARIE DE CHAMPAGNE, for whom his other romances were probably written. Chrétien says that he is putting into verse the story of the Grail (*see* HOLY GRAIL), which he found in a book given him by the count. The truth of that assertion is unclear, but the story itself is a bildungsroman, following the young, naïve Perceval on a quest for his identity, out of adolescence and into maturity and adult responsibility. More important for most readers, Chrétien also introduces the Grail motif into the literary tradition of King ARTHUR.

The romance of Perceval falls into three sections: the early, mostly comic, adventures of the woefully ignorant protagonist; the episodes surrounding Perceval's experiences at the Grail castle and their aftermath; and the curious adventures of GAWAIN (*Gauvain* in Chrétien's French). The poem begins when Perceval, raised in the wild forest by his overprotective mother, encounters five knights of Arthur's court. Their shining coats of mail lead Perceval to think he has met God and his angels. When he learns the truth, his interest in the knights is insatiable, and he determines to go to Arthur's court and be made a knight. His mother mourns, saying she had kept him from the world because his brothers, both knights, had been killed in combat. But Perceval insists on leaving, and his mother tries to give him some useful instruction: Help maidens in distress, she tells him; he may accept a kiss or ring from a maiden, but nothing else; he should not be long with a man without learning his name; and above all else, his mother says, he should visit churches to pray. As he rides away, he sees his mother fall to the ground, but is too eager to leave to go back and see what has happened to her.

Perceval is not gone long before he finds a rich pavilion, which he mistakes for a church. When he enters and finds a maiden there, he kisses her seven times and takes a ring from her finger, comically misapplying his mother's advice. When he gets to Arthur's court at Carlisle, Perceval finds Arthur in distress over being insulted by a knight in red arms who has stolen his golden cup and threatened to take his lands. Perceval pursues the knight, kills him with a javelin throw, and dresses in his arms. He believes he is now a knight because he has the outward trappings, but must learn the ethical and social responsibilities of knightly status. He rides off in his new armor and meets a kindly lord named Gornemant, who welcomes Perceval to his castle and takes the time to instruct him in horsemanship and the use of knightly arms, dubs him a knight, and gives him more advice: Grant mercy to any knight who requests it, the lord tells him; don't talk too much, so as not to appear foolish; support women or orphans who are in trouble; and finally, the lord repeats Perceval's mother's advice in telling him to go to church.

Perceval next meets the beautiful Blancheflour, whom he discovers in distress because her knights have been captured and her castle besieged by the army of Clamadeu, who wants Blanchefleur for himself. The town will surrender the next day, and the lady will kill herself, unless Perceval can intervene. But Perceval succeeds in defeating first Clamadeu's seneschal and then the lord himself. After several days with his new love, Perceval leaves her out of belated concern for his mother, whom he decides to visit.

This brings Perceval to the Grail adventure, and with these episodes the tone of the romance changes from comic to more serious, as Perceval's failures have more dire consequences. Perceval comes upon a nobleman fishing in a river, who invites the knight to his castle. When Perceval arrives, he finds the Fisher King already seated in his hall, and while they converse, a strange procession passes before them: First, a squire holding a lance trickling a drop of blood passes by, followed by two more squires holding candelabra. Next, a maiden walks by holding a golden, bejeweled Grail (a wide, deep dish), and she is followed by another young woman carrying a silver carving platter. While Perceval marvels at this, he says nothing, remembering Gornemant's advice not to talk too much. An ivory table is placed before them, and Perceval and the king enjoy a rich feast, though before every new course the Grail procession passes before them again. The disabled king is carried to bed and Perceval sleeps in the castle hall, but when he awakes, the castle is deserted and he rides away in wonder.

But this failure to ask the question is the turning point of the story. Perceval soon discovers that the Fisher King, maimed in battle by a spear thrust through his thighs, is king of the Waste Land, and that the king would have been healed and fertility returned to the land had Perceval asked about the Grail procession. Further, Perceval is told that, when he left his mother, he caused her death. The chastised Perceval rides on to Arthur's court, where a loathly lady messenger arrives on a mule and shames Perceval before the court, cursing him for his silence during the Grail procession. Perceval leaves the court, vowing not to sleep two nights in the same place until he discovers who is served from the Grail.

At this point Perceval's story is interrupted abruptly by a long section following the adventures of Gawain, who leaves Arthur's court at the same time to rescue a besieged damsel. A number of rather insignificant adventures surrounding Gawain follow; so irrelevant to the Perceval story are they that a number of scholars have suggested that the Gawain section was originally intended to be a separate romance, but that the incomplete condition of the Perceval manuscript upon Chrétien's death caused the confusion. But most scholars see in Gawain's adventures parallels to Perceval's, and consider the Gawain section of the romance as a commentary and deliberate contrast with the first section.

But Gawain's adventures are interrupted by a 300-line interlude in which Perceval, after five years of searching unsuccessfully for answers, encounters a hermit on Good Friday who proves to be his own uncle. In the romance's third "instruction" scene, the hermit tells Perceval that the Grail contained a Mass wafer, used to sustain the life of the Fisher King's invalid father for 15 years. It is his own sin—his failure of charity in not returning to his mother when he saw her fall—that caused his failure at the Grail Castle. Now Perceval makes his first confession, to his uncle on Good Friday, and on Easter Sunday receives the Eucharist for the first time.

The poem then returns to Gawain's story. Gawain himself sets out to seek the bleeding lance (a part of the Grail procession not explained by the hermit), which somehow is connected with the fate of Arthur's kingdom, but the romance leaves off before reaching a conclusion. It is assumed that Chrétien died before completing his poem. The rich suggestiveness of the text, however, inspired in the decades following Chrétien's death four different continuations of the Perceval story, by authors trying to bring it to a satisfactory conclusion—bringing the length of the text to more than 45,000 lines.

The origin of the Grail motif has been the most widely discussed aspect of Chrétien's poem. Its origin has been suggested in ritualistic survivals of the cult of Adonis, in magic vessels of Celtic myth, in religious legends of Persia, or in Christian allegory. There is no scholarly consensus for any of these explanations, and it may be wisest to simply accept the Grail for what Chrétien makes of it: a plot device that underscores Perceval's failures and need for growth, which is the focus of the romance.

Bibliography

Chrétien de Troyes. *Li Contes del Graal.* Edited by Rupert T. Pickens, translated by William W. Kibler. New York: Garland, 1990.

Holmes, Urban T. *Chrétien de Troyes.* New York: Twayne, 1970.

Kelly, Douglas, ed. *The Romances of Chrétien de Troyes: A Symposium.* Lexington, Ky.: French Forum, 1985.

Lacy, Norris J. *The Craft of Chrétien de Troyes.* Leiden, Netherlands: Brill, 1980.

Topsfield, L. T. *Chrétien de Troyes: A Study of the Arthurian Romances.* Cambridge: Cambridge University Press, 1981.

Peredur *(Historia Peredur vab Efrawc)* (ca. 1200)

Peredur is a Welsh prose ROMANCE retelling the story of King ARTHUR's knight PERCEVAL. It is one of three romances (with *OWAIN* and *GERAINT AND ENID*) regularly included in texts of the *MABINOGION*. The earliest complete version of *Peredur* dates from the end of the 13th century, but the romance was most likely originally composed in the late 12th or early 13th century. Some Welsh scholars hold that the text was written in the early 12th century, and therefore predates CHRÉTIEN DE TROYES's *PERCEVAL*. The vast majority of scholars, however, believe Chrétien's poem to be the source of the Welsh romance.

The story begins with Peredur's father, Efrawg, a northern earl who supports himself by holding tournaments. When he and Peredur's six brothers are killed in knightly combat, the boy's mother takes him to raise in the wilderness. But one day Peredur meets three knights who awaken his innate interest in chivalry, and he sets out for Arthur's court to be dubbed a knight himself. At court a strange knight insults the Queen, and Peredur rides off to avenge her, killing the knight with a javelin and taking his armor.

Seeking knightly adventures, Peredur comes to the castle of an uncle who is lame, and who instructs him on some of the finer points of chivalry, advising him not to be too inquisitive. Riding on to another castle, Peredur finds that it belongs to another of his uncles. Here Peredur witnesses a strange procession of a bleeding lance followed by a platter on which is held a severed head in a pool of blood. But Peredur, following his first uncle's advice, does not ask what it means.

To this point the plot has followed that of Chrétien fairly closely, although Chrétien's grail (the inspiration for what was to become the HOLY GRAIL in later versions of the legend) is replaced by the severed head. But now a number of different adventures ensue, including a period of instruction in arms by the witches of Caer Loyw (the Welsh name for Gloucester). Peredur then returns to Arthur's court, where he is accosted by Sir Cei, whom he easily bests and injures. After some time at court, he leaves again for a series of adventures, including competition in a tournament before the Empress of Constantinople. He wins her love and he rules at her side for 14 years. Back again at Arthur's court, a loathly maiden on a yellow mule enters the court and courteously greets all except Peredur. Him she berates for failing to ask the meaning of the procession at his uncle's castle. Had he asked the question, he learns, he would have healed the lame king and restored the land. After more adventures Peredur learns that the witches of Caer Loyw had crippled his uncle and had killed his cousin, whose head is carried on the platter. Peredur learns that he is fated to avenge his family. With the help of Arthur and Gwalchmei (the Welsh name for GAWAIN), the witches are destroyed.

Peredur has not been admired for its aesthetic quality. Critics have called it "confused" and "chaotic." In particular it seems weak where it deviates from Chrétien's story—the years in Constantinople seem irrelevant to the plot, and the replacement of the mysterious grail with the severed head, turning *Peredur* into a story of family revenge, takes away the wonder and mystery of Chrétien's tale. But the question of sources has been one that has fascinated scholars, particularly the sources for material not found in Chrétien. Most interesting has been the suggestion that the marriage to the Empress is a manifestation of the mythic Celtic sovereignty ritual, in which the beautiful goddess/queen, who represented sovereignty, chose her own mate.

Bibliography

Barber, Richard. *The Holy Grail: Imagination and Belief.* Cambridge, Mass.: Harvard University Press, 2004.

Bromwich, Rachel, A. O. H. Jarman, and Brynley F. Roberts, eds. *The Arthur of the Welsh: The Arthurian Legend in Medieval Welsh Literature.* Cardiff: University of Wales Press, 1991.

Goetinck, Glenys. *Peredur: A Study of Welsh Tradition in the Grail Legends.* Cardiff: University of Wales Press for the Language and Literature Committee of the Board of Celtic Studies, 1975.

Peredur. Introduction and English translation by Meirion Pennar. With illustrations by James Negus. Facsimile of the Welsh text edited by J. Gwenogvryn Evans. Felinfach, U.K.: Llanerch, 1991.

Peterborough Chronicle

The *Peterborough Chronicle* is the most recent and the longest sustained of the seven extant manuscripts of the ANGLO-SAXON CHRONICLE. Each manuscript of the *Anglo-Saxon Chronicle* records the "common stock"—the original account of the history of Britain from 60 B.C.E. until the reign of King ALFRED THE GREAT in 891. That original manuscript was apparently copied at Winchester and sent throughout England to important centers of regional culture, where local scribes received regular updates from the capital, but also began recording events of local interest, so that after about 915 the several manuscripts begin to diverge significantly. What scholars refer to as "Manuscript E" of the *Anglo-Saxon Chronicle* (catalogued in Oxford's Bodleian Library as MS. Laud 636) is also called the *Peterborough Chronicle,* after the monastery in which the text was copied and maintained up until 1154, when its last entry records the death of King Stephen. No other manuscript of the *Anglo-Saxon Chronicle* is maintained after the year 1080.

Scholars have conjectured that the extant manuscript was a copy made after a fire destroyed the original manuscript kept at Peterborough in 1116. The scribe that copied the manuscript to that point continued making entries in the *Chronicle* until 1131, after which a second scribe took over the task until the final entry in 1154.

This later part of the *Chronicle* contains a number of memorable entries. Particularly poignant is the entry for 1083, describing the slaughter of the monks at Glastonbury. The entry for 1087, containing a biography of William the Conqueror, is the longest entry in any part of the *Anglo-Saxon Chronicle.* But the most famous section of the *Peterborough Chronicle* is that containing the entries for 1135–54, describing the civil wars and brutality during the disastrous reign of King Stephen. Most notable is the entry for 1137, which describes the robbing and burning of villages and of churches, the destruction of fields resulting in starvation, and the reduction of once-thriving people to begging or to emigration. The chronicler asserts that these things went on for the entire 19 years of Stephen's reign, and became progressively worse.

In addition to its historical interest, the *Peterborough Chronicle* is a valuable text for linguists. Since it covers the period from before the Norman Conquest (1066) to almost 100 years later, the *Chronicle* is a written record of the transition of English from the OLD ENGLISH period into the early MIDDLE ENGLISH.

Bibliography

Clark, Cecily, ed. *The Peterborough Chronicle 1070–1154.* 2nd ed. Oxford: Clarendon Press, 1970.

Rositzke, Harry A., trans. *The Peterborough Chronicle.* New York: Columbia University Press, 1951.

Whitelock, Dorothy, ed. *The Peterborough Chronicle.* Copenhagen: Rosenkilde and Bagger, 1954.

Peter Lombard (ca. 1105–ca. 1160)

Peter Lombard was an important Italian scholastic theologian whose *Sententia* (Sentences) became the principle theology text in university education until well into the Renaissance. He was acquainted with St. BERNARD and studied in Paris under Bernard's archenemy, Peter ABELARD, and gained fame as a teacher in his own right before serving as bishop of Paris. But it is as *Magister Sententiarum* (Master of the sentences) that he is best known.

Peter was called "the Lombard" from his birthplace in Lumellogno or possibly Novara in Lombardy. He was from a poor family and his early education was accomplished in Italy, until Humbert, the bishop of Lucca, sent him to Bernard of Clairvaux asking for his support of Lombard's continued education in France. Bernard made it possible for Peter to study theology at Reims, and then gave him a letter of introduction to Gilduin, the abbot of Saint Victor in Paris. While in Paris, Lombard seems to have attended the lectures of Abelard, the most renowned teacher of his time. He also became familiar with the legal works of the great canonist Gratian. By 1144, he was celebrated as a theologian in his own right, and about the same time was made a canon in the Cathedral Church at Notre Dame, where he lectured on theology.

Lombard was called to take part in the consistory of Pope Eugenius III, convened in Reims in 1148 to discuss the controversial opinions of Gilbert of Poitiers. In 1154 he traveled to Rome, and there became familiar with John Damascene's *De fide orthodoxa* (*The Orthodox Faith*), which had just been translated into Latin. Since Lombard makes use of this text in his *Sentences,* it seems likely that he compiled his great work between 1155 and 1157. Some time before 1157, he was ordained a priest and a subdeacon, and in 1159 he was elected bishop of Paris. He held that post only a short time, being replaced by Maurice de Sully (who built the present Notre Dame Cathedral) in about 1160. Perhaps Lombard was replaced because of failing health—he died shortly thereafter.

Lombard's *Sentences* set out ambitiously to present Christian doctrine in its entirety. Book 1 is devoted to the existence of God, the Trinity, divine foreknowledge, and predestination. Book 2 is concerned with the Creation, the existence of angels, human nature, free will, and grace. Book 3 focuses on Christ—his incarnation, his sacrifice and human atonement, and his virtuous life as a model for human virtue. The fourth and last book is concerned with the sacraments of the church (Lombard seems to have been the first to establish them as seven) and with eschatology—death and judgment.

What made the *Sentences* so widely read and influential was not Lombard's authoritative proof of Christian doctrine, supported by biblical texts and by the opinions of the church fathers—this had been the method of previous theologians. The popularity stemmed instead from Lombard's organization and conciseness, and his application of the new scholastic methods of dialectic that had been introduced and popularized by Abelard and by Gratian. The *Sentences* are essentially a compilation of previous influential works on theology, including St. AUGUSTINE, Julian of Toledo, Ivo of Chartres, Hugh of St. Victor, the Bible itself, and of course Abelard, Gratian, and John Damascene. The opinions are presented, sometimes as conflicting, and are sometimes left unreconciled.

Perhaps the most influential of Lombard's teachings were those on the sacraments. The Roman Church adopted as its official doctrine his argument that the sacrament is both a symbol and a vehicle for grace, and that the appropriate number of sacraments is seven. On the other hand, despite a generally cautious approach, Lombard's opinions were sometimes controversial. For example, he was accused of arguing that the divine essence was something separate from the divine persons, and of therefore holding that there were actually four persons, not three, in the trinity. Lombard's teaching on this topic, however, was approved by the Fourth Lateran Council in 1215. He was also accused of holding the doctrine of "christological nihilism," that the human aspect of Christ has no substantial reality. But despite these and other objections to its orthodoxy, Peter Lombard's *Sentences* became the standard text for the study of theology in universities of the 13th century, and it became a common practice for every master of theology—from Thomas AQUINAS to BONAVENTURE to DUNS SCOTUS to William OCKHAM—to compose a commentary on the *Sentences.*

Lombard wrote other extant works in addition to the *Sentences,* including a gloss or commentary on the Psalms of David and one on the Epistles of Paul. But his enduring reputation remains that of *Magister Sententiarum.*

Bibliography

Colish, Marcia L. *Peter Lombard.* 2 vols. Brill's Studies in Intellectual History 41. Leiden, Netherlands: Brill, 1994.

Petrus Lombardus. *Sententiae in IV libris distinctae.* 3rd ed. 2 vols. Grottaferrata, Italy: Editiones Collegii S. Bonaventurae ad Claras Aquas, 1971–1981.

Rogers, Elizabeth Francis. *Peter Lombard and the Sacramental System.* Merrick, N.Y.: Richwood Publishing, 1976.

Rosemann, Philipp W. *Peter Lombard.* Oxford: Oxford University Press, 2004.

Petrarch, Francis (Francesco Petrarca) (1304–1374)

Petrarch is universally acknowledged as one of the greatest Italian writers, and is generally recognized as the founder of the movement that came to be known as humanism—a movement that aimed to revive the study of the Greek and Roman classics, and that promoted an attitude about human beings that extolled achievement in this world, rather than considering this world a mere pilgrimage to the next, as medieval Christianity often advised. Petrarch was one of the most famous writers of his time, and significantly influenced his contemporaries (particularly BOCCACCIO). Even more, Petrarch influenced his successors, not, as he would have desired, through his voluminous writings in Latin, but chiefly through his lyric poetry in the vernacular, which popularized the SONNET form and the language and conventions of the "Petrarchan" love that pervaded the Renaissance.

Petrarch was born in 1304 in Arezzo. His father, a native Florentine, had been exiled in 1302 along with DANTE and other White Guelfs (the party that opposed Pope Boniface VIII). In 1314, Petrarch's family moved to Avignon, the new seat of the papacy, where his father worked as notary for the French pope Clement V. His father intended Petrarch to enter the legal profession, and accordingly sent him to study law at Montpellier (1319–23) and Bologna (1323–25), but Petrarch was uninspired by the law and devoted much of his time to the study of classical literature and culture. Petrarch returned to Avignon in 1326, after his father's death, and entered the service of the powerful Cardinal Giacomo Colonna, who employed him as a diplomat and gave him the opportunity to follow his scholarly pursuits. Petrarch made use of the huge library at Avignon, and devoted most of his time to the study, collection, and transcribing of manuscripts of classical antiquity. He also traveled a good deal in Colonna's service, so that he began to move in the influential circles of European courts. In the late 1320s, he published his first scholarly work, an edition of Livy's history of Rome that coherently organized the scattered manuscripts of the Latin historian. Perhaps more important, on Good Friday of 1327 he is supposed to have seen for the first time, in a church in Avignon, the unattainable lady he called Laura, the inspiration for his most famous poetry. It is possible, as some have suggested, that Laura is a literary fiction, a character created by Petrarch to be the object of his love poetry. Others believe that she was the wife of Hugues de Sade and that she died in the BLACK DEATH of 1348, and that Petrarch's love for her was strictly platonic for more than 20 years. In either case, from 1327 on, Petrarch began writing vernacular love poetry addressed to a woman named Laura.

In about 1330, Petrarch seems to have tired of Avignon and began a period of wandering. Petrarch also traveled through France and Germany in 1333, a journey recorded in a number of his surviving letters. He returned to Avignon in 1336, and took minor orders, as canon of the Cathedral of Lombez, which provided him with an income and demanded little of his time beyond a daily reading of his office. In 1337 he traveled to Rome with members of the Colonna family. Later that year, he began spending a good deal of time at a house he bought in Vaucluse in southern France, where he wrote many of his literary works of the 1330s and early 1340s, beginning work on his epic poem *Africa,* a work in Latin hexameters recounting the story of the Roman hero Scipio Africanus and his victory over Carthage in the Second Punic War. Here Petrarch also finished his *De viris illustribus,* a collection of the lives of famous men. And he continued to work on his lyric poems.

One of the things that drove Petrarch was a desire for personal achievement and a quest for individual fame, a motive that many scholars see as characteristic of Renaissance humanism. Renowned through Italy for his Latin scholarship, Petrarch, in one of the great public-relations coups in history, was crowned poet laureate by the Roman Senate on Easter Sunday of 1341. It was an act that helped make him the most famous man of letters in Europe—a reputation he was able to sustain throughout his life. In 1345, in his manuscript studies, he discovered Cicero's letter to Atticus. These personal letters inspired him to compose letters of his own as a literary form, letters to his contemporaries as well as to some of the ancient writers. During this decade he also wrote his *Secretum,* presented as a dialogue between himself and St. Augustine, who chides him for his excessive love of Laura, showing him that such love is idolatrous, and that he is self-deceived in thinking of it as idealistic. But the decade ended in disaster with the advent of the Black Death, which took not only Petrarch's beloved Laura, but also his longtime patron, Cardinal Colonna.

Looking for a new patron, Petrarch moved to Milan in 1353 and spent some time acting as a diplomat for the powerful and autocratic Visconti family. He also lived in Venice for a while, and eventually was granted land in Arqua near Padua in 1368. He continued working on his personal letters, revisions of his lyric poems, and his transcriptions of classical texts, eventually building up the largest private library in Europe. He also studied Greek, though he admits he did not learn it well. Most important, these were the years of his friendship with his great contemporary, Giovanni Boccaccio. Petrarch convinced Boccaccio to abandon writing in the vernacular and to take up the study of classical culture, and the composition of texts in Latin. It was under Petrarch's influence that Boccaccio began his work on the Latin text of his *Genealogy of the Gentile Gods.* And Petrarch, who first met Boccaccio in Florence in 1350 and admired his *DECAMERON,* made a Latin verse translation of the story of Patient Griselde, the last tale of the *Decameron*—a translation that CHAUCER used for his version of the story in *The CLERK'S TALE.* Even after his retirement to Padua, Petrarch spent a good deal of time on diplomatic missions. He died at his home in July of 1374, purportedly with his head resting on an opened manuscript of Virgil.

It is clear that Petrarch thought his ultimate literary reputation would be based on his Latin works, in particular his epic *Africa,* which he left unfinished in draft form upon his death. But despite the enormous efforts he put into his study and recovery of classical literature, and the inspiration it gave to his own Latin compositions, modern readers have not been moved by them, and Petrarch's posthumous fame rests almost solely on his vernacular verse. His *CANZONIERE* (Scattered rhymes), a collection of 366 lyrics, are deeply introspective lyrics that explore the poet's psyche as affected and transformed by his love for the unattainable woman, Laura—both before and after her death. In these lyrics, Petrarch perfected and popularized the sonnet form. He also drew largely on the tradition of COURTLY LOVE as it had developed for two centuries throughout Europe and, particularly, as it had been refined by Dante, CAVALCANTI, and other poets of the Italian *DOLCE STIL NOVO,* who had elevated the lady to an angelic position. But however much they owe earlier poetry, Petrarch's lyrics focus to a greater extent on sexual frustration (he never actually meets Laura) and on the contrary emotions of his own psyche. Thus the images and vocabulary of Petrarch's poetry abound in paradox: Love is both a joy and a torment; the Lady is both friend and enemy. His lyrics also employ conventional catalogue descriptions of his lady's beauties—eyes like the sun, hair like gold wires, lips like coral. In this sense his poetry is original, and its influence on the next 300 years of European verse was so powerful that his successors gave his name—"Petrarchan"—to both the Italian sonnet form he refined and the love conventions he transformed. English poets like Wyatt, Surrey, and Spenser used Petrarch as a model, as did Shakespeare, who also parodied Petrarchan conventions in works like his sonnet "My mistress' eyes are nothing like the sun."

Bibliography

Bernardo, Aldo S. *Petrarch, Scipio and the "Africa": The Birth of Humanism's Dream.* Baltimore: Johns Hopkins University Press, 1962.

Bloom, Harold, ed. and intro. *Petrarch.* New York: Chelsea House, 1989.

Foster, Kenelm. *Petrarch: Poet and Humanist.* Edinburgh: Edinburgh University Press, 1984.

Mann, Nicholas. *Petrarch.* Oxford: Oxford University Press, 1984.

Petrarch, Francis. *The Canzoniere, or, Rerum vulgarium fragmenta.* Translated with notes and commentary by Mark Musa. Introduction by Mark Musa with Barbara Manfredi. Bloomington: Indiana University Press, 1996.

———. *Letters of Old Age.* Translated by Aldo S. Bernardo, Saul Levin, and Reta A. Bernado. Baltimore: Johns Hopkins University Press, 1992.

———. *The Secret by Francesco Petrarch.* Edited with an introduction by Carol E. Quillen. Boston: Bedford/St. Martin's, 2003.

Quillen, Carol Everhart. *Rereading the Renaissance: Petrarch, Augustine, and the Language of Humanism.* Ann Arbor: University of Michigan Press, 1998.

Roche, Thomas P., Jr. *Petrarch and the English Sonnet Sequences.* New York: AMS Press, 1989.

Trinkaus, Charles. *The Poet as Philosopher: Petrarch and the Formation of Renaissance Consciousness.* New Haven, Conn.: Yale University Press, 1979.

Philippe de Thaon (or Thaün) (fl. early 12th century)

The Anglo-Norman cleric Philippe de Thaon was the author of the first BESTIARY in a European vernacular language, and thus was largely responsible for the popular vogue of such pseudo-scientific discussions of animals (real and imaginary) in France and western Europe for the next 200 years.

Philippe must have had some connection with the Norman-English court. The earliest text of his *Bestiaire*, preserved in the British Museum Cotton Nero A.v. manuscript, bears a dedication to Aélis (or Adela) de Louvain, second wife of King Henry I of England. This dates the manuscript to sometime within a few years of 1121, when Henry married Adela. A later manuscript of the text, preserved at Oxford, includes a different dedication, this time to ELEANOR OF AQUITAINE, who had married the future King HENRY II in 1152. Thus Philippe's connection to the court seems to have continued well into the mid-12th century.

Interested in other forms of science or pseudoscience than merely animal lore, Philippe also wrote a *Comput*, a poetic treatise on the calendar intended mainly for ecclesiastical purposes. The text consists of 1,090 lines of hexasyllabic (six-syllable) couplets. Apparently written before he had a connection to the English court, the work is dedicated to Philippe's uncle, Honfroi de Thaon, who had the position of chaplain to Eudo Dapifer, royal steward of France who died in 1120. Thus the *Comput* dates from before 1120, possibly (based on internal evidence) as early as 1113, which makes it essentially the earliest extant scientific treatise in vernacular French. In addition to the *Comput*, Philippe is also known to have written a *lapidary*, which would have contained descriptions of the properties of precious stones and their uses in medicine and other pseudo-scientific areas.

But Philippe's most influential work was his *Bestiaire*. The bestiary tradition in Latin goes back to a second-century Greek original, the *Physiologus* (Natural philosopher), and includes the *Etymologies* by the seventh-century Spanish saint and encyclopedist ISIDORE OF SEVILLE. Philippe's source was probably a later Latin text that had made use of Isidore as well as the *Physiologus* tradition. The text is 3,194 lines of hexasyllabic couplets, though a few hundred lines from the end, he shifts to eight-syllable lines. The text comprises 38 chapters: The first 23 deal with beasts, beginning, as was customary, with the lion. Chapters 24–34 are concerned with birds, beginning with the partridge (curiously, in Philippe's arrangement, preceding the eagle, who would more traditionally have been accorded the primary position). Chapters 35–38 deal with precious stones, and are themselves more of a lapidary appended to the bestiary—and it is here that Philippe switches to the eight-syllable lines.

The three extant manuscripts of Philippe's *Bestiaire* (the British Museum and Oxford manuscripts, and an incomplete later manuscript located in Copenhagen) all contain a Latin prologue and Latin rubrics in the margins throughout that either summarize the text or give instruction to the illustrator as to the nature of the picture that should be included. The authorship of these Latin rubrics is a matter of scholarly debate, but Florence McCulloch believes they are Philippe's, so that they indicate his interest in the production of his own manuscript.

The popularity of bestiaries is explained partly by their moralizing tendencies: From the time of the earliest Greek *Physiologus*, the descriptions of the animals were accompanied by allegorical interpretations that indicated a moral lesson to be learned from the beast described. For example, in Philippe's description of the Phoenix, we learn that the bird originated in Arabia, and that it destroys itself by burning on a pyre of its own construction. But after its fiery immolation, the Phoenix becomes a worm. The priest of Heliopolis finds the worm, which, on the third day, is reborn as an adult bird. The conclusion, of course, is that the Phoenix, by his resurrection, symbolizes Christ. Philippe does not invent this idea, nor does he add a great deal to it that is different, but he is important for having given new life to the ancient tradition of the bestiary by popularizing it in the vernacular.

Bibliography

McCulloch, Florence. *Mediaeval Latin and French Bestiaries.* Studies in the Romance Languages and Literatures, 33. Rev. ed. Chapel Hill: University of North Carolina Press, 1962.

Short, Ian, ed. *Comput: MS BL Cotton Nero A.V.* London: Published by the Anglo-Norman Text Society from Birkbeck College, 1984.

Physician's Tale, The Geoffrey Chaucer (ca. 1386)

The Physician's Tale is one of the least admired of CHAUCER'S *CANTERBURY TALES*. Coming directly before the universally admired *PARDONER'S TALE* in what is generally called "Fragment VI" of the *Tales*, the *Physician's Tale* may suffer by comparison. It is a short and rather disturbing story of a father who kills his daughter to protect her virginity, first told by the classical Latin historian Livy, and retold in various versions during the Middle Ages, including a brief version in the *ROMAN DE LA ROSE* and a version by Chaucer's friend John GOWER in his *CONFESSIO AMANTIS*. Chaucer's tale seems to have been written prior to Gower's, but Chaucer probably knew Livy's account as well as that in the *Roman*.

In the story the evil judge Appius lusts after 14-year-old Virginia, the beautiful and virtuous daughter of Virginius. Appius hatches a plot with his lackey Claudius, in which Claudius brings a suit against Virginius, saying that Virginia is not his daughter but rather Claudius's slave. After a travesty of justice in court, during which Appius awards Virginia to Claudius, Virginius perceives the plot and its motive. He goes home and informs Virginia that he must kill her to protect her chastity. She laments, but sees there is no other way. Virginius strikes off her head, and brings the head to Appius. The people, who learn of the atrocity, rebel. Appius is thrown in prison where he commits suicide, while Claudius, condemned to hang, is saved when Virginius pleads for his life. The narrator expresses the moral of the story as "forsaketh synne, er synne yow forsake" (Besnon 1987, 193, l. 285).

Most readers have found the tale unsatisfying, and have been confused by the "moral" at the end. In other medieval versions of the tale, it has been used to illustrate the results of bad government, but Chaucer sidesteps this implication. Some have suggested that Chaucer deliberately avoided the political themes, especially anything involving popular uprising, in a tale written so soon after the PEASANTS' REVOLT. Others have suggested that the narrator displays a spiritual blindness, and oversimplifies the moral, not realizing the complexity of the tale he tells. Further, Chaucer may have seen the tale as far more problematic than previous authors—indeed, he deliberately complicates things by expanding the character of Virginia, and thus our sympathies for her, in a scene of utmost pathos with her father. Nor is Virginius depicted in a particularly positive way—he is, after all, a child murderer. Thus the narrator's own oversimplification of the moral may reflect Chaucer's belief in the inadequacy of previous interpretations of the morally complex story.

Bibliography

Collette, Carolyn P. " 'Peyntyng with Greet Cost': Virginia as Image in the 'Physician's Tale,' " *Chaucer Yearbook* 2 (1995): 49–62.

Delany, Sheila. "Politics and the Paralysis of the Poetic Imagination in the Physician's Tale," *Studies in the Age of Chaucer* 3 (1981): 47–60.

Fletcher, Angus. "The Sentencing of Virginia in the Physician's Tale," *Chaucer Review* 34 (2000): 300–308.

Ramsey, Lee C. " 'The Sentence of It Sooth Is': Chaucer's *Physician's Tale*," *Chaucer Review* 6 (1972): 185–197.

Ruud, Jay. "Natural Law and Chaucer's 'Physician's Tale,' " *Journal of the Rocky Mountain Medieval and Renaissance Association* 9 (1988): 29–45.

Pierce the Ploughman's Creed (ca. 1393–1401)

Pierce the Ploughman's Creed is a MIDDLE ENGLISH poem of 850 lines in ALLITERATIVE VERSE from the southern West Midlands. It is a social and political satire in the tradition of LANGLAND'S *PIERS PLOWMAN*, like *MUM AND THE SOTHSEGGER*, *RICHARD THE REDELESS*, and *The CROWNED KING*. The poem is more clearly LOLLARD (i.e., in sympathy with WYCLIFFE'S views) in its sympathies than the other texts it is grouped with. It is also the only poem in the *Piers Plowman* tradition that exists in more than one manuscript, surviving in two 16th-century manuscripts and a 15th-century fragment, as well as a black-letter printed edition from 1553.

In the poem, the narrator, like *Piers Plowman*'s Will, sets out on a spiritual quest. In this case, the quest is simple: The narrator wants to learn the Apostle's Creed, and is searching for someone to teach him. He first visits each of the four orders of friars, assuming that such holy men must be able to teach him such a basic lesson in the faith. He finds that the friars are unable to give him what he calls the plain truth—they do not seem to know what it is, or at least are uninterested. His first visit is to a Franciscan, to whom he reveals that a Carmelite friar has promised to teach him the creed, and asks the Franciscan's opinion. The Franciscan laughs, saying that the Carmelites are all lechers and liars, who follow no rule of obedience and preach easy penance for the people. They travel about with their harlots and claim they are their sisters. It is the Franciscans, says the friar, who live like the apostles of old. The Franciscan tells him of the Franciscans' elaborate chapel, and tells the narrator that, for a contribution, he will absolve him of his sins, whether he knows the creed or not. The narrator agrees but as he leaves the Franciscan feels that something is wrong, and remembers Christ's command to "judge not, lest ye be judged." Uneasy with the Franciscan, the narrator next finds a sumptuously rich Dominican abbey, and finally finds a friar in the refectory who is "fat as a barrel" and richly attired. When the narrator mentions that an Austin friar had promised to teach him the creed, the Dominican berates the order of Austins, saying that they associate with whores and thieves. He goes on to boast of the prominence of his own order, but the narrator, realizing that pride is a great sin, leaves the Dominican and seeks out an Austin friar.

The narrator tells the Austin that he seeks someone who can teach him his creed, mentioning that a "Minor" (that is, a Franciscan) had promised to show him the way to salvation. The Austin begins by cursing the Franciscans for their great riches, their luxurious fur-lined habits and their hypocrisy and greed, pointing out as well how far they were from the original ideal of St. FRANCIS. The Austin friar then invites the narrator to become a lay brother of his order, saying that if he gives enough goods to the friars, they will absolve him of his sins, whether he knows his creed or not. The narrator leaves, thinking to himself that the only creed here is one of covetousness. He seeks out a Carmelite and begs him to teach him the creed. When he tells the Carmelite that a "preacher" (that is, a Dominican) has promised to help him, the Carmelite attacks Dominicans for their pride and concern with worldly honors. The Carmelite claims priority over the other orders, saying that Carmelites date back to Elijah. For a contribution, the Carmelite says he will teach the narrator, but the narrator says he has no money, and asks the Carmelite to teach him for the sake of God's love. The friar first chides the narrator, telling him point blank that he is a fool for expecting something without payment. Finally, he can't be bothered with the narrator's problem because he must go meet a housewife who plans to leave money to the Carmelites.

Despairing that he cannot find someone to teach him the creed, the narrator finds a poor plowman. It is Piers, who, with his wife and three small children, is described in vivid detail in what is perhaps the starkest bit of social commentary of its time. Piers is dressed in threadbare attire, and his wife has no shoes yet walks with bloody feet on the bare ice. She goads the oxen attached to Piers's plow, which are so feeble that one could count every one of their ribs. The children are crying off to the side, perhaps from hunger or cold, as Piers works in the field. But when the narrator approaches and Piers sees his sorrow, the poor Plowman offers to give him food—in stark contrast with the wealthy friars.

Piers is the moral authority of the poem—a position he achieves because of his unwavering acceptance of God's will in his life. Although he praises the virtues of St. Francis and St. Dominic, he condemns their contemporary followers, the hypocritical and greedy friars whom the narrator has just visited. Piers goes on, finally, to teach the narrator the creed, which he recites in simple, direct language. The narrator ends the poem by claiming that he writes only in order to amend the targets of his satire, and prays that God will forgive anything he has said amiss, that God will save all faithful friars, and that He will through grace bring other friars to repentance and amendment of their lives. Scholars have commented upon how the antifraternal sentiments of the poem owe a great deal to Lollard views of the late 14th century. Friars had been the targets of satire for decades, partly because they usurped the rights to preaching, hearing confession, and burial that more properly belonged to the secular clergy, but partly, certainly, because some of them truly were hypocritical, greedy, and power seeking, as they characterize one another in *Pierce the Plowman's Creed.* In the mid-14th century, Richard FitzRalph, archbishop of Ireland, attacked friars, upheld Christ's poverty (the state that gives Piers his moral authority), and called on the pope to strip the friars of their privileges. Wycliffe reiterated FitzRalph's call for the revocation of friars' privileges.

In his criticism of the four orders, Piers specifically mentions his approval of Wycliffe for denouncing friars' behavior. Piers also approves of the Welsh Lollard Walter Brut, who had been condemned as a heretic by the friars and put on trial by Bishop Trefnant of Hereford in 1393 (thus the poem must be later than that date). But the author of *Pierce the Plowman's Creed* was not fully a Wycliffite, since he includes in the creed as Piers recites it lines that support the doctrine of transubstantiation, a doctrine Wycliffe had notoriously denied late in his career.

Bibliography

Barr, Helen, ed. *The Piers Plowman Tradition: A Critical Edition of Pierce the Ploughman's Crede, Richard the Redeless, Mum and the Sothsegger, and The Crowned King.* London: Dent, 1993.

Dean, James, ed. *Piers the Plowman's Crede,* in *Six Ecclesiastical Satires.* Kalamazoo, Mich.: Medieval Institute Publications, 1991.

Kane, George. "Some Fourteenth-Century 'Political' Poems," in *Medieval English Religious and Ethical Literature: Essays in Honour of G. H. Russell,* edited by Gregory Kratzmann and James Simpson. Cambridge: D. S. Brewer, 1986, 82–91.

Lampe, David. "The Satiric Strategy of *Peres the Ploughmans Crede,*" in *The Alliterative Tradition in the Fourteenth Century,* edited by Bernard S. Levy and Paul E. Szarmach. Kent, Ohio: Kent State University Press, 1981, 69–80.

Lawton, David. "Lollardy and the Piers Plowman Tradition," *Modern Language Review* 76 (1981): 780–793.

von Nolcken, Christina. "Piers Plowman, the Wycliffites, and *Pierce the Plowman's Creed,*" *The Yearbook of Langland Studies* 2 (1988): 71–102.

Pier della Vigna (ca. 1190–1249)

As Frederick II's chancellor and one of the most powerful statesmen of his time, PIER DELLA VIGNA was also an important literary figure, one of the poets of the "Sicilian school" of lyric poetry, a group responsible for the first court poetry in the Italian vernacular. His apparent suicide inspired DANTE to immortalize him in Canto XIII of the *Inferno.*

Pier was born in Capua. His family was apparently connected with the judicial system, but was of modest means, so that Pier had to make sacrifices to study law at the University of Bologna. In 1220, the archbishop of Palermo introduced him to the Holy Roman Emperor, Frederick II, and shortly thereafter Pier joined Frederick's court at Naples as a notary. Once at the court, Pier became one of the emperor's most trusted advisers. He became a judge in 1225 and "protonotary" of Sicily in 1246, and ultimately Frederick's chancellor in 1249. During the intervening years he was sent on a number of delicate diplomatic missions for the emperor. In 1230 he signed the Treaty of Ceprano, which ended a period of hostilities between Frederick and Pope Gregory IX. In 1231, he also was deeply involved in the composition of the Constitutions of Melfi—a law code that centralized imperial power in Sicily and served as the kingdom's fundamental law code until Napoleonic times.

At Frederick's court Pier also became acquainted with fellow notary and poet GIACOMO DA LENTINO, and with him was instrumental in adopting the style and themes of the Provençal TROUBADOURS into Italian vernacular poetry. Three of his *CANZONI,* one SONNET, and part of a *tenzone* (*see* TENSO) with Giacomo are extant. All display the influence of the troubadours' COURTLY LOVE tradition. Pier's official letters are also an important literary achievement: Written in an eloquent Latin, the letters are one of the most important primary documents for historians studying Frederick's reign.

Shortly after Pier's elevation to chancellor, he was accused of treason—apparently on trumped-up charges lodged by rival courtiers jealous of his influence with the emperor. Convicted and condemned by Frederick, Pier was dragged in chains through the towns of Tuscany as an example to traitors, and ultimately blinded with a red-hot iron. He may have died under torture, but was widely held to have committed suicide in April 1249. He is best remembered as Dante portrayed him: Speaking in the form of a tree in the wood of suicides, the shade of Pier della Vigna proclaims his undying loyalty to Frederick II.

Bibliography

Goldin, Frederick, trans. *German and Italian Lyrics of the Middle Ages: An Anthology and a History.* New York: Doubleday, 1973.

Jensen, Frede, ed. and trans. *The Poetry of the Sicilian School.* New York: Garland, 1986.

Piers Plowman William Langland (ca. 1367–1387)

One of the great religious poems in the English language, *Piers Plowman* is a text from the late 14th century ALLITERATIVE REVIVAL in England's West Midlands. One of the most popular poems of the late Middle Ages with 51 surviving manuscripts, the poem is an ALLEGORY in the form of a DREAM VISION in which the narrator, Will, experiences a series of visions that take him from an overview of 14th-century English society to an exploration of his own psyche to a vision of the Crucifixion and the Harrowing of Hell and, ultimately, a vision of the coming of Antichrist and a besieged church. The Dreamer, Will, seems to be both the allegorical personification of the human Will itself, and the persona of the poem's purported author, William LANGLAND.

Langland is named as the poem's author in one early 15th-century manuscript. In addition, the author seems to pun on his name at one point (in passus 15) when he says that he has lived in the "land" and that his name is "long Will." But virtually nothing is known of the poet beyond what can be gleaned from the text of his poem itself. He may have been born in about 1330 near Malvern Hills in Worcestershire. If we can read the figure of Will autobiographically (and that is questionable), Langland mentions living in London with his wife "Kit" and his daughter, and implies that he had taken minor orders and makes a living by singing psalms. One manuscript claims that Langland was the son of a gentleman of Oxfordshire named Stacy de Rokayle. In another manuscript, a certain John But says that Langland had died suddenly sometime before 1387.

There are three separate versions of *Piers Plowman,* and the general scholarly consensus is that Langland is the author of all three. The earliest, known as the A-text (ca. 1367), comprises 10 chapters, or passus ("steps") as Langland calls them. In some 2,500 lines Langland explores the need for reform in the Christian commonwealth. In about 1377 or shortly thereafter, Langland added nine more passus and 4,700 more lines, nearly tripling the length of the poem and turning the dreamer's quest inward, a version known as the B-text. Finally, Langland revised the poem again in about 1386, making some structural revisions and hundreds of other minor editorial changes, aimed apparently at clarifying the poem and at altering sections that had been read by the rebels in the 1381 PEASANTS' REVOLT as calls for radical change in society—the C-text. While the C-text is clearly the poet's final version of the poem, literary scholars over the years have generally preferred the B-text as the superior literary achievement.

The poem presents 10 separate dreams (sometimes dreams within dreams), separated by brief waking passages. It opens with Will's first vision of a "fair field full of folk"—a brief ESTATES SATIRE in which Langland presents the Christian community, with its three estates, and the individuals who fall short of their obligations to the commonwealth. The prologue is followed by the appearance of Holy Church, personified as a woman, who gives Will the rudiments of the Christian faith. In a sense, the remainder of the poem follows from Will's question to Holy Church in this first passus: What must I do to be saved?

A first-time reader of *Piers Plowman* is generally confused and bewildered by the rapid shifting of scenes, the abrupt comings and goings of characters, the apparently illogical sequences of events. In part this may be explained as the logic of a dream. In part, as well, it may be that the poem is not intended as a narrative that would follow a cause and effect series of events, but rather is more like a sermon whose unifying theme is that initial question about salvation.

Overall the poem falls into two sections—the first part, known as the *Vision of Will concerning Piers Plowman* (or the *Visio*), introduces the main themes of the poem and shows Will a vision of the contemporary world as it is; the second part, the *Lives of Dowel, D-bet, and Dobest* (called the *Vita*). The first part gets under way when Will asks Holy Church how to tell truth from falsehood, and is shown a series of visions involving Lady Meed. "Meed" is money or reward, whose influence in the king's court threatens society. The king wishes to marry her to Conscience, but she is ultimately driven from the court by Conscience and Reason. It appears that society may be back on the right track, if led by Conscience without greed. Reason gives a sermon calling for repentance, and this is followed by Langland's justly famous passage describing the confessions of the seven deadly sins, which are personified and described as individuals engulfed in the sins they represent. In response to the sermon, the people all begin a pilgrimage to find Truth (the allegorical representation of God). But they do not know the way, and a simple plowman, Piers, offers to guide them to Truth, once they help him plow his half-acre. The pilgrimage falls apart when Truth sends Piers a pardon, but a priest tells Piers it is no pardon at all, and in anger Piers tears the pardon and vows to leave off his plowing and spend his life in prayer and penance, searching for Dowel (i.e., "Do well").

This begins the *vita* section of the poem, consisting of three parts: Dowel, Dobet, and Dobest. There is no consensus as to what these three lives represent, but one suggestion is that Dowel focuses on one's own individual needs, Dobet on the physical needs of others, and Dobest on the spiritual needs of others (Gasse 1994, 230). In the Dowel section, Will, guided by Clergy, Scripture, and Study, explores his own interior faculties of Imagination, Intelligence, and Thought. In a dream within a dream, Will follows Fortune for 45 years, before meeting Patience, Conscience, and Haukyn (the Active Man) in a new vision. But when this vision ends, Will enters a new vision, concerning the life of Dobet. This time Will is chided by Anima for seeking knowledge rather than engaging in charity. In another dream within the dream, Will sees Piers Plowman guarding the Tree of Charity, from which the devil steals fallen fruit, and then sees Abraham, Moses, and the Good Samaritan as the allegorical personifications of Faith, Hope, and Charity. This section climaxes in the famous HARROWING OF HELL scene in passus 18, wherein Christ comes to Jerusalem to joust in the arms of Piers Plowman, is crucified, and descends into hell, from which he snatches back all souls from the devil.

In the final two passus Langland presents his last two visions, which comprise the life of Dobest, presented as a history of the church. Piers is now the vicar of Christ on earth—apparently in the role of Peter, the first pope (the name Piers is a variant of Peter). Piers receives the Holy Spirit and organizes the plowing of the field of the world—the allegorical representation of the ideal Christian society. But in the face of the onslaught of Antichrist, Conscience has a fortress built called Unity, the church itself. But when Conscience allows a friar into Unity, he begins to corrupt the people through easy confessions, and Conscience, seeing the fortress crumbling, turns pilgrim in the end and goes on a quest to seek Piers Plowman, at which point the Dreamer awakens.

The poem, in all its apparent disorder and difficulty, is held together by recurring themes, such as the nature of sin, the nature of God's love, the ideal of the perfect society, and the way to personal salvation. It is also unified by the figure of the Dreamer, whose search for salvation leads him on the whole roller-coaster ride of visions within visions. And the poem is unified by the motif of Piers Plowman himself, the most enigmatic of allegorical figures: He is a simple laboring plowman and a friend of Truth who knows the way to find Him. He establishes an ordered society in the world. He preaches the primacy of charity, is the guardian of the Tree of Life, and lends his arms to Christ. Finally he is God's vicar on earth. While he seems identified at times with Saint Peter and with Christ himself, and at other times is a simple, poor workingman, it may be that Piers represents unfallen human nature—the image of God in man that was marred by the Fall and restored by Christ.

Langland's poem is a record of a deep spiritual quest filled with very human doubts, contempt for hypocrisy (particularly among the religious), concern for economic hardships, and a deep anger at corruption in the institutions of church and state. The 15 surviving manuscripts from the 14th century alone attest to the poem's popularity, which probably extended to an audience of parish priests and local clergy, and to a growing and conservative lay public of middle-class readers who enjoyed didactic literature. *Piers Plowman*'s four printed versions before 1561 are evidence of the poem's continued popularity into the 16th century, explained by the view of Langland as a precursor of the Reformation because of his anticlerical satire. The poem has enjoyed a revival of popularity in recent decades, perhaps because the indeterminacy of the text appeals to postmodern poetics. But whatever critical perspective one brings to the poem, *Piers Plowman* is one of the most remarkable achievements of MIDDLE ENGLISH literature.

Bibliography

Aers, David. *Chaucer, Langland, and the Creative Imagination.* London: Routledge and Kegan Paul, 1979.

Alford, John, ed. *A Companion to Piers Plowman.* Berkeley: University of California Press, 1988.

Benson, C. David. *Public Piers Plowman: Modern Scholarship and Late Medieval English Culture.* University Park: Pennsylvania State University Press, 2004.

Carruthers, Mary. *The Search for St. Truth: A Study of Meaning in Piers Plowman.* Evanston, Ill.: Northwestern University Press, 1973.

Davlin, Mary Clemente. *A Game of Heuene: Word Play and the Meaning of Piers Plowman B.* Cambridge: D. S. Brewer, 1989.

Godden, Malcolm. *The Making of Piers Plowman.* London: Longman, 1990.

Harwood, Britton J. *Piers Plowman and the Problem of Belief.* Toronto: University of Toronto Press, 1992.

Kerby-Fulton, Kathryn. *Reformist Apocalypticism and Piers Plowman.* Cambridge: Cambridge University Press, 1990.

Langland, William. *Piers Plowman: The Donaldson Translation.* Edited by Elizabeth Robertson and Stephen H. A. Shepherd. New York: W. W. Norton, 2004.

Simpson, James. *Piers Plowman: An Introduction to the B-text.* London: Longman, 1990.

———. *The Vision of Piers Plowman: A Critical Edition of the B-Text Based on Trinity College Cambridge MS B.15.17.* Edited by A. V. C. Schmidt. 2nd ed. London: Dent, 1995.

Pillow Book, The (*Makura no Sōshi*) Sei Shōnagon (ca. 1002)

The Pillow Book is considered by contemporary scholars to be one of the two great literary monuments of the Japanese HEIAN PERIOD (the other being MURASAKI SHIKIBU's *TALE OF GENJI*). SEI SHŌNAGON, author of *The Pillow Book,* was a lady in waiting at the court of Teishi, royal consort of the emperor Ichijō from about 990 until her death in childbirth in 1000. In *The Pillow Book,* Sei presents a curious and idiosyncratic picture of life in Teishi's court, focusing on the years 993–994.

The work's title derives from Sei's description of how she came to write the book. Tradition holds that Teishi, having received a surplus of paper (a scarce commodity at the time), asked her ladies how they should make use of the surplus, and Sei responded that it would make a perfect pillow. Apparently she intended to keep scraps of paper close to where she slept in order to jot down observations, impressions, or random thoughts in the evening before she drifted off in slumber.

This mode of composition gives *The Pillow Book* its highly unusual form, unlike any genre of Western literature. It is autobiographical and owes something to the *nikki,* or diary, genre of Heian literature. But it is much more than a diary. The text is made up of some 300 short occasional pieces, mostly prose, but with 16 *waka* (or poems in Japanese) intermixed. The randomly arranged pieces give the impression of being spontaneously created, and Sei's text give birth to a new literary genre that became known as *zuihitsu,* a term meaning "following the writing brush," and thus implying casual, random observation. Sei's most important medieval successor in this genre was KENKŌ, but the form remains an important influence in Japanese literature to the present time.

The prose passages of *The Pillow Book* fall roughly into three categories. There are the diary-like entries, consisting of anecdotes of the court, including stories of Teishi's cat and dog. There are essaylike entries, in which Sei expresses her personal observations and opinions in a highly outspoken manner. And perhaps most famously, there are 164 lists of various matters, such as "Depressing things" (which include having to take a hot bath upon waking up in the morning). "Hateful things" (which include a man who snores after a woman has invited him to spend the night with her), and "Pretentious things" (which include the title "doctor of literature").

But a simple categorization of entries cannot do justice to this varied and enigmatic work. Chiefly it is admired for its tone and style, and for the strong personality of its author (or at least her persona) that shines through on every page. Sei uses a lively and varied sentence structure that is atypical of medieval Japanese prose, contrasting sharply with the more verbose and romantic style of *Genji.* The witty and humorous tone of most of *The Pillow Book* also contrasts with the somber *Genji* and other Heian pieces that tend to focus on the Buddhist notion of the transience of life. Sei herself comes across as a rather haughty aristocratic and highly opinionated satirist who sees herself as the arbiter of all things proper; she lampoons anyone or anything that does not meet her standards of refinement, beauty, intelligence, or behavior. In that vein, she is occasionally a vivid realist (again in contrast to the romantic *Genji*), focusing at one point on fleas under ladies' skirts. But it should be noted that Sei is just as hard on herself as anyone else, depicting herself as unattractive and abrasive, and a poor poet.

Admired for her subjectivity and her individualism, Sei is sometimes criticized for her work's lack of structure. In part this may be due to a confused textual tradition, in which two distinct versions of the text have survived, differing from each other in their ordering of the material. In part, however, this apparent lack of organization reflects precisely the randomness Sei sought to convey in her text.

Bibliography

Bowring, Richard, trans. *Murasaki Shikibu: Her Diary and Poetic Memoirs.* Princeton, N.J.: Princeton University Press, 1982.

Miner, Earl, Hiroko Odagiri, and Robert E. Morrell. *The Princeton Companion to Classical Japanese Literature.* Princeton, N.J.: Princeton University Press, 1985.

Sei Shōnagon. *The Pillow Book of Sei Shōnagon.* Translated by Ivan Morris. New York: Columbia University Press, 1971.

Poetic Edda, The (Elder Edda) (ca. 1280)

The Poetic Edda is a collection of some 38 anonymous poems in Old Norse, drawn together in late 13th-century Iceland into a single manuscript, called the Codex Regius, the most famous manuscript in Old Norse. A second manuscript fragment, Arnamagnaean 748 (ca. 1300), contains six poems also in the Codex Regius, plus one additional poem, *Baldrs draumar* (Balder's dream). Sometimes called the "Elder Edda," this compilation of poems is actually more recent than the *PROSE EDDA* of SNORRI STURLUSON (ca. 1225); many of the poems it contains were written down between 1225 and 1240, during the revival of interest in the old mythology stimulated by Snorri's *Edda.* The history of the Codex Regius manuscript after its production ca. 1280 is unclear, but it was discovered in 1643 by the scholar Brynjólfur Sveinsson, bishop of Skálholt, who presented it to the king of Denmark in 1662. The manuscript was in the Royal Library of Copenhagen until 1971, when it was returned to Iceland.

On the assumption that the Eddic poems must be older than Snorri's *Edda,* because Snorri quotes from older versions of some of them, Bishop Sveinsson inexplicably attributed the manuscript to the famous Icelandic scholar Sæmundr Sigfusson the Wise (d. 1133). Scholars no longer seriously attribute the *Poetic Edda* to Sæmundr, but contend that the various poems in the collection were composed by multiple authors over a long period of time. In addition, many of the poems must have been circulating in the late 10th century, since, for example, the poet Eyvindr Skaldaspillir cites some of them in his own work from about that time. Since many of the poems deal with pagan myth and show no influence of Christianity, it seems likely that some of them were composed before the 11th century, when Iceland was Christianized. The term "Edda" itself seems to have been coined by Snorri for his own text, a handbook for SKALDIC poets including a compendium of Norse mythology. Perhaps as a collection of mythic poems, the Codex Regius invited a title that linked it with the other most famous collection of Norse myths.

The Eddic poems, however, are not nearly as complex as skaldic poems are. Like virtually all Germanic poetry, they use alliterative lines. In general, however, the lines are arranged into simple strophes. There are two basic types of Eddic meter: The first, called *fornyrðislag* ("old lore meter"), is virtually the same as ALLITERATIVE VERSE common to all Germanic languages—it consists of long alliterative lines of four stressed syllables separated by a caesura. In Eddic verse, however, these lines are also arranged into four-line stanzas. The other chief type of Eddic meter is called *ljóðaháttr* (chant meter). Peculiar to Old Norse, this meter also uses four-line stanzas, but while the first and third lines of these are conventional long alliterative lines, the second and fourth are two- or three-stress lines. This type of meter was almost exclusively used for recording characters' direct speeches.

The poems of the *Poetic Edda* fall into two groups: mythological poems and heroic poems. The 15 mythological poems all concern the gods. Some of these are humorous tall tales, like *Thrymskvida,* or the "Lay of Thrym." In this poem one of the giants, Thrym, is able to steal Thor's hammer, and will only restore it to the gods if he is allowed to marry the beautiful goddess Freya. Freya refuses to go through with the marriage, and so Thor is forced to dress as a woman himself and travel to the wedding feast in the land of the giants with Loki as his attending handmaiden. When Thor gets his hands on his hammer, the disguise comes off and he uses the weapon on the giants themselves. *Thrymskvida* is a fairly late poem in the collection, dated 1150–1300, when paganism was an antiquarian interest rather than a living religion. Other poems are more solemn, and clearly take the gods more seriously, as does the opening poem, *Völuspá,* or the "Prophecy of Vala" (the Wisewoman). In this, perhaps the most important of the Eddic poems, Odin brings a Wisewoman (a *volva*) back from the dead, and she chants to him a song of the cosmos, describing the history and composition of the universe, as well as its future. The poem gives us our most striking and complete view of pagan Norse cosmology. It is thought to be a very early poem, dating from 850–1030. In another more serious poem, *Baldrs Draumr* (Balder's dream), nightmares haunt the god Balder, and Odin travels to the underworld to consult another volva, who reveals Balder's impending death, an event that will trigger the ultimate fall of the gods and the end of the world. Although this is a later poem, likely from the 13th century, it is thought to be a reworking of an earlier text.

There are, in addition, 23 heroic poems of lays in the *Poetic Edda,* generally concerning different episodes in the famous story of Sigurd the dragon slayer and his family and contemporaries, a story also related in the Norse *VOLSUNGA SAGA* (ca. 1270) and the Middle High German *NIBELUNGENLIED* (ca. 1200). Other characters involved in the story told by the Eddic poems as a whole are Atli (Attila), king of the Huns, and Jormunrekr (Ermanaric), king of the Visigoths. These poems, as a group, tell the story of Sigurd's death at the hands of his brothers-in-law, a revenge plotted by the jealous Brynhild, who also kills herself. Many poems deal with Sigurd's widow Guðrún, who marries Atli. Guðrún's brother Gunnarr dies at Atli's hands, and Guðrún ultimately takes terrible revenge on Atli. Later, when Guðrún's daughter Svanhildr is killed by her own husband, Jormunrekr, Guðrún's clamor for revenge ultimately dooms her sons, the only surviving members of her family. The bulk of this Sigurd-Guðrún story seems to have been written down in the 13th century.

It seems certain that Eddic poetry was essentially an oral phenomenon, like skaldic poetry but probably predating it, as the chief vehicle for the preservation of the old traditions. We owe a great debt to the antiquarian scholar or poet responsible for the compilation of the Codex Regius, who preserved the tradition in the written form that has kept it alive to this day.

Bibliography

Archer, Paul, and Carolyne Larrington, eds. *The Poetic Edda: Essays on Old Norse Mythology.* New York: Routledge, 2002.

Glendinning, Robert J., and Haraldur Bessason, eds. *Edda: A Collection of Essays.* Manitoba: University of Manitoba Press, 1983.

The Poetic Edda. Edited with translation, introduction, and commentary by Ursula Dronke. 2 vols. Oxford: Clarendon Press, 1969–1997.

Terry, Patricia A., trans. *Poems of the Elder Edda.* With an introduction by Charles W. Dunn. rev. ed. Philadelphia: University of Pennsylvania Press, 1990.

Prioress's Tale, The Geoffrey Chaucer (ca. 1385)

One of the more disturbing and controversial of CHAUCER's *CANTERBURY TALES,* the tale of the Prioress is a "Miracle of the Virgin" story that, like many such narratives, is full of pathos involving the suffering of an innocent child, and full as well of the virulent anti-Semitism that often characterized Christian attitudes toward Jews in the late Middle Ages, even in places like Chaucer's England, from which all Jews had been exiled 100 years before (in 1290).

In the tale a young boy of seven living in a city in Asia is exceptionally devoted to the Virgin, and from an older boy learns by rote the hymn *Alma redemptoris mater* after discovering that it is a hymn in praise of Mary. The child regularly walks through the Jewish ghetto on his way to school, singing the hymn as he goes. The Jews, enraged by this behavior, hire a thug who cuts the boy's throat and throws him into a privy. The boy's distraught mother searches for him anxiously throughout the ghetto, but is unable to find the child until, miraculously, he begins to sing the *Alma redemptoris mater* from the privy in which he is hidden. The provost of the town is called, and he has those responsible for the murder tortured, drawn, and hanged. The child is brought to the church, where he reveals that, though his throat is cut to his "nekke boon," he was still able to sing because the Virgin Mary had appeared to him and placed a grain upon his tongue. After the Abbot removes the grain, the child dies and is buried as a holy martyr.

Some critics have focused on the tale's expression of "affective piety"—the new highly emotional religiosity that had become widespread in the late 14th century. But the bulk of the criticism has concentrated on the tale's anti-Semitism. One could argue that Chaucer was simply a man of his time, but in repeating the "blood libel" (the charge that Jews murdered Christian children), he would surely have been aware of papal condemnations of that libel and its promulgation. It could be argued that for the Prioress narrator, who would have never seen a Jew in 14th-century England, Jews existed only as literary "villains" in Marian miracles. Some have argued that Chaucer is emphasizing the shallow intellect of the Prioress by depicting her unthinking cruelty juxtaposed to her unthinking sentimentality. How close the Prioress narrator's attitude comes to Chaucer's own, however, remains a difficult question for readers and scholars of Chaucer's work.

Bibliography

Alexander, Philip S. "Madam Eglentyne, Geoffrey Chaucer and the Problem of Medieval Anti-Semitism," *Bulletin of the John Rylands Library of Manchester* 74 (1992): 109–120.

Benson, C. David. *Chaucer's Drama of Style: Poetic Variety and Contrast in The Canterbury Tales.* Chapel Hill: University of North Carolina Press, 1986.

Collette, Carolyn P. "Sense and Sensibility in the *Prioress's Tale,*" *Chaucer Review* 15 (1980): 138–150.

Despres, Denise. "Cultic Anti-Judaism and Chaucer's Litel Clergeon," *Modern Philology* 91 (1994): 413–427.

Patterson, Lee. " 'The Living Witness of Our Redemption': Martyrdom and Imitation in Chaucer's Prioress's Tale," *Journal of Medieval and Early Modern Studies* 31 (Fall 2001): 507–560.

Pigg, Daniel F. "Refiguring Martyrdom: Chaucer's Prioress and Her Tale," *Chaucer Review* 29 (1994): 65–73.

Robertson, Elizabeth. "Aspects of Female Piety in the 'Prioress's Tale,' " in *Chaucer's Religious Tales,* edited by C. David Benson and Elizabeth Robertson. Cambridge: D. S. Brewer, 1990, 146–160.

Prose Edda (*Snorra Edda, Younger Edda*)

Snorri Sturluson (ca. 1225)

The *Prose Edda,* or the *Edda* of SNORRI STURLUSON (*Snorra Edda*), is a 13th-century handbook of mythology and of poetics, written in part to instruct and support young poets in the practice of SKALDIC POETRY, the extremely complex Old Norse court poetry of the late Middle Ages. Snorri's *Edda* is made up of four parts: a prologue, an outline of mythology called the *Gylfaginning,* a rhetorical handbook called *Skáldskaparmál,* and an exemplary poem and metrical commentary called the *Háttatal.* The text survives in four manuscripts and several fragments, and is the only medieval source containing the whole of Norse mythology. Often mistakenly referred to as the "Younger" *Edda,* Snorri's text was apparently actually written before the *POETIC EDDA* or "Elder" *Edda,* the compilation of which was probably inspired by the interest in older Norse verse sparked by Snorri's text.

The sections of the *Edda* were probably composed in reverse order from where they occur in the text. Probably the first written, in the early 1220s, the *Háttatal* is a poem of 102 strophes or stanzas, and is a rather conventional poem of praise addressed to King Hakon Hakonarson of Norway and his kinsman Jarl Skúli, whom Snorri had met on his visit to Norway in 1218–20. But the poem is remarkable in that each strophe is written in a different skaldic meter, or variation of some meter or use of language. The poem is accompanied by Snorri's prose commentary explaining the various aspects of versification illustrated in the poem.

Snorri probably next wrote the longest section of the *Edda,* the *Skáldskaparmál* (Poetic diction). This section is devoted mainly to the devices of KENNING (the conventional truncated metaphor of Germanic poetry, so highly complex and allusive in skaldic verse), and the *heiti* (names) or poetic synonyms that were so much a part of this poetry. Snorri enumerates kennings for Norse gods and goddesses, poetry, gold, men, battles, weapons, ships, Christ, and kings. He also lists *heiti* for gods and aspects of the universe, animals, the sea, kings, men, and women. Because the kennings in particular are so highly allusive, Snorri includes a number of mythological stories in the *Skáldskaparmál* to explain the point of those kennings. Thus, for example, Snorri explains why gold is referred to as "Kraki's seed" by recounting the legend of the Danish king Hrolf Kraki, who, being pursued by the Swedish king Adils and his warriors, eluded them by sowing the ground with gold in order to entice the Swedes into stopping to pick it.

Having completed his discussion of rhetorical figures in the *Skáldskaparmál,* Snorri apparently decided that a full review of Norse mythology was necessary for a skaldic poet to be effective, and therefore composed the *Gylfaginning* (The deluding of Gylfi). In this section, the Swedish king Gylfi confronts three wizards, wagering his head in a contest of the knowledge of mythic lore. As they ask one another questions, a comprehensive narrative summary of Norse mythology emerges, from the origins of the universe and the identity of the gods and goddesses, to a description of Odin's great hall Valhalla, to adventures of the gods Thor and Freyr, to the death of the god Baldr and *ragnarok,* the downfall and death of the gods.

The part of the *Edda* that Snorri probably wrote last is the prologue. Possibly in anticipation of disapproval from the Icelandic church, Snorri downplays Norse mythology in his prologue, asserting the truth of the Christian account of Creation, but explaining that, having lost sight of the true religion, the northern European pagans derived their view of the gods from ancient legendary kings and heroes (named Odin, Thor, and the like) who emigrated into Europe from Asia, and hence were called *Aesir* (the Old Norse word for "gods"). There is no historical basis for Snorri's account, but it served his purpose of disavowing any serious belief in the myths he related.

Much of what we know about skaldic poetry and about the complex metrics and metaphors involved in its practice come from Snorri's *Edda.* In addition, poems, or fragments of poems, by some of the very early Norse poets, including the first known skald, Bragi the Old, survive—sometimes exclusively—in Snorri's text. The *Prose Edda* is one of the most valuable literary texts of Old Norse literature—perhaps of all medieval European literature.

Bibliography

Ciklamini, Marlene. *Snorri Sturluson.* Boston: Twayne, 1978.

Ross, Margaret Clunies. *Skáldskaparmál: Snorri Sturluson's Ars Poetica and Medieval Theories of Language.* Odense, Denmark: Odense University Press, 1987.

Sturluson, Snorri. *Edda.* Edited and translated by Anthony Faulkes. London: Dent, 1987.

Prose Merlin (*Vulgate Merlin*) (ca. 1210)

The *Prose Merlin* is a ROMANCE focusing on the history of Merlin, the seer and magician of the court of King ARTHUR. The text is a prose redaction of a poem attributed to ROBERT DE BORON, a poem that is extant only in a 504-line fragment. Robert's name appears twice in the prose text, so that the *Prose Merlin* has also been attributed to him, but Robert's connection with the prose text is unclear.

The *Merlin* is a sequel to another prose romance, the *Joseph d'Arimathie,* a prose version of another poem of Robert de Boron's called the *Estoire dou Graal* (History of the Grail). It was also intended to precede the romance called the *Didot-Perceval,* a text concerned with the Arthurian quest for the Holy Grail. Thus the *Prose Merlin,* in this earliest of Arthurian cycles, is intended to be a bridge between the story of the Grail's origins and the quest by Arthur's knights to find the Grail.

Before long the *Prose Merlin* was included in another, longer cycle of Arthurian prose romances, the VULGATE CYCLE (also called the Lancelot-Graal cycle), where it follows a prose *Estoire del Saint Graal* and where it is continued by a text known as the *SUITE DE MERLIN.* The text was apparently in a constantly evolving state, as additions or revisions were made to the original text to adapt it to the later Vulgate Cycle.

The *Prose Merlin* begins with Merlin's conception—he is begotten by a demon who seduces a virgin as part of the devil's plot to emulate Mary's conception of Christ. His mother's faith and the child's baptism enable him to frustrate any demonic control of his life, but he does inherit from his demonic father a knowledge of the past, and God gives him the ability to see the future. He is thus able to become the adviser of kings. He first helps depose the evil king Vortigier, then advises King Uther Pendragon as he fights against the invading Saxons. He introduces the Round Table during Uther's reign, explaining that the table recalls and parallels, first, the table from the Last Supper, and second, the Grail Table (itself a recreation of the Last Supper). At the Round Table, Merlin introduces the "Judas Seat" or the "Perilous Seat"—a chair that was to remain empty until the knight destined to achieve the Grail was to come to court. This would be, Merlin tells Uther, during the reign of his son and successor. Merlin arranges for Uther to beget Arthur upon Ygerne, then takes the infant child and delivers him to be fostered by the wise Antor. Ultimately Arthur will be revealed as the true king by his ability to pull a sword from a stone in a magical test. Merlin dictates the story of Uther's reign to his master and scribe Blaise, and intends for the story to become a part of the whole story of the Grail, but apparently abandons it when he becomes enamored of, and imprisoned by, the lady Viviane.

The fact that the *Merlin* and its companion romances are in prose is perhaps a result of medieval attitudes toward poetry and prose: Verse was the vehicle for imaginative fiction, while prose was the medium for serious treatment of history: Thus the prose of *Merlin* implies its historical truth. The story was influenced by the pseudo-history of GEOFFREY OF MONMOUTH and by WACE's *Roman de Brut,* but to a very large extent, it adds material about Merlin that was completely new to the Arthurian tradition. It became quite popular in the later Middle Ages—there are 55 surviving texts of the *Prose Merlin*—and had a tremendous impact on the subsequent development of Arthurian legend, because it served as one of the major sources for Thomas MALORY'S enormously influential *LE Morte DARTHUR* (ca. 1470).

Bibliography

The Story of Merlin. Translated by Rupert T. Pickens. Vol. 1 of *Lancelot-Grail: The Old French Arthurian*

Vulgate and Post-Vulgate in Translation, edited by Norris J. Lacy. New York: Garland, 1993–1996.

Proverbs of Alfred (ca. 1150–1180)

The *Proverbs of Alfred* are a collection of 35 early MIDDLE ENGLISH maxims compiled in a 600-line poem and attributed, imaginatively, to King ALFRED THE GREAT. The poem survives in three 13th-century manuscripts, but appears to have been composed somewhat earlier, probably in the late 12th century. The poem begins with a discussion of Alfred himself, and then provides a list of sayings, each of which begins with the formula "Thus quath Alfred." The verses are written in imitation of the ALLITERATIVE VERSE of OLD ENGLISH poetry, though they do not follow the classical rules of Anglo-Saxon verse and are quite irregular.

The proverbs deal with a wide variety of topics. Some are simply kernels of popular wisdom. Some are maxims that have a strongly Christian element, while others are precepts of conduct that a parent might pass along to a child. Still others, concerning women and marriage, embody the sort of antifeminist attitude prevalent among late medieval clerical writers.

The sources for the *Proverbs* seem to be chiefly the wisdom books of the Old Testament and the very popular Latin text called the *Distichs of Cato.* They also seem in line with the native English tradition of GNOMIC VERSE that would have been known in King Alfred's time. However, there is no actual connection between the proverbs and King Alfred himself. It seems clear that Alfred, like King Solomon of biblical times, had achieved such a reputation for wisdom during his reign that his countrymen for generations attributed wise sayings to him. No collection of Alfred's proverbs exists in Old English, but Alfred's reputation for wise sayings is alluded to in the well-known Middle English poem *The OWL AND THE NIGHTINGALE* (ca. 1200) as well as other places. It would have been natural, therefore, to assign such a collection to Alfred.

Bibliography

Arngart, O. S., ed. *The Proverbs of Alfred: An Emended Text.* Lund: LiberLäromedel-Gleerup, 1978.

Pearsall, Derek, ed. *Old English and Middle English Poetry.* London: Routledge, 1977.

South, Helen Pennock. *The Proverbs of Alfred: Studied in the Light of the Recently Discovered Maidstone Manuscript.* 1931. New York: Haskell House, 1970.

Prudentius (Aurelius Prudentius Clemens) (348–after 405)

Prudentius was the first great Christian poet in Latin. He wrote SAINTS' LIVES, hymns (some of which are still sung today), and the first narrative poem in Europe written entirely as an allegory—the *PSYCHOMACHIA* (War within the soul). His works became classics of Roman Christianity, and he is the only layperson considered to be a father of the Roman Church.

Prudentius was born in Spain in 348, probably to a Christian family since he never mentions his conversion. The exact place of his birth is uncertain: Calahorra seems most likely, but Saragossa and Tarragona have also been suggested. He was from a noble family, and he received a classical Roman education. After practicing as a lawyer, he held administrative offices in two provinces before he was called to the capital and appointed to a fairly high post under the emperor Theodosius. According to a brief biographical note introducing an edition of his works in 405, Prudentius decided to retire from public life to pursue a contemplative life devoted to Christianity and poetry.

Prudentius revolutionized Latin poetry by using the classical verse forms for Christian subjects. Among his works are the *Cathemerinon* (Book of the hours), which is made up of 12 hymns, six of which are for hours of the day and six of which are for particular church festivals. The hymns are remarkable for their use of light and dark imagery, and in many cases can still be found in contemporary Christian hymnals—including "Of the Father's Love Begotten" for Christmas and "Earth Has Many a Noble City" for Epiphany. Another work, the *Peristephanon* (Crowns of martyrdom), is a series of 14 poems on the lives of martyrs like St. Agnes and St. Lawrence. The *Apotheosis* is a long didactic poem in hexameters (six-foot lines) concerned with supporting the doctrine of the Trinity. Its companion piece, *Hamartigenia* (The origin of sin), is concerned with the nature of evil, and specifically argues against the doctrine of dualism propounded by the Gnostic theologian Marcion and his disciples. Prudentius's two-volume *Contra symmachum* was written to condemn the pagan Roman religion. It also argues that Christianity's function within the empire was to complete the civilizing function begun by Roman law and institutions—that is, to fulfill Rome's ultimate destiny.

But certainly Prudentius's most influential poem was the *Psychomachia.* The poem presents an allegorical battle between personified virtues and vices, wherein the soul, assisted by the virtues, rescues the body from the vices that attack it. The poem was extremely popular and highly influential throughout the medieval period, sparking a vital tradition of medieval allegorical poetry.

Prudentius gleaned his theology from the Bible and from Christian thinkers like St. Ambrose and Tertullian. His works, particularly the *Psychomachia,* were popular throughout the Middle Ages and were studied in monastic schools from the ninth century on.

Bibliography

Eagan, Sister M. Clement, ed. *Prudentius, Poems, Volume 1 and Volume 2.* The Fathers of the Church: A New Translation, vols. 43, 52. Washington, D.C.: Catholic University of America Press, 1962, 1965.

Haworth, Kenneth R. *Deified Virtues, Demonic Vices, and Descriptive Allegory in Prudentius' Psychomachia.* Amsterdam: A. M. Hakkert, 1980.

Smith, Macklin. *Prudentius' Psychomachia: A Reexamination.* Princeton, N.J.: Princeton University Press, 1976.

Thomson, H. J., ed. and trans. *Prudentius.* 2 vols. Loeb Classical Library. Cambridge, Mass.: Harvard University Press, 1947–1953.

van Assendelft, Marion M. *Sol ecce surgit igneus: A Commentary on the Morning and Evening Hymns of Prudentius (Cathemerinon 1, 2, 5, and 6).* Groningen, Netherlands: Bouma's Boekhuis, 1976.

Psychomachia Prudentius (ca. 405)

PRUDENTIUS's poem *Psychomachia* (War within the soul) was one of the most influential poems of the Middle Ages, initiating a vogue for ALLEGORY that lasted in European literature for 1,000 years. The *Psychomachia,* the first completely allegorical poem in Europe, is the story of the battle between virtues and vices over the possession of the human soul.

Perhaps Prudentius's theme was suggested by Ephesians 6.10–20, in which St. Paul speaks of the Christian's battle against spiritual forces, allegorizing the "armor of God." But at the same time, Prudentius was highly influenced by Virgil's *Aeneid,* and adapts the epic language and imagery of that poem to his moral allegory.

The poem, written in 915 lines of Latin dactylic hexameters (six-foot lines), begins with a preface retelling the story of Abraham rescuing his nephew Lot from his imprisonment by pagan kings, as told in Genesis 14. Prudentius sees this story as a symbol of our hearts' need to struggle against the vices that hold our bodies captive. This leads into Prudentius's depiction of personified female Virtues and Vices doing battle in a mental landscape over the prize of the soul.

His method of presentation is a series of single combats, recalling the style of epic poems like the *Aeneid* and the *Iliad.* Thus Faith begins the fray by doing combat with Idolatry. Chastity then fights Lust, and Patience vies with Anger. Pride rides onto the field on a high horse to rally her comrades, and tries to trample down Humility and her supporter, Hope. But Pride falls, and Sensuality enters the fray. She is almost able to entice the Virtues to yield to her, when Sobriety takes the field and defeats her. Avarice next challenges Reason, but ultimately switches sides and disguises herself as Frugality. Trying to pass herself off as a Virtue, she begins to lead others astray, until Mercy exposes her for what she really is, and advocates generosity to the poor. Finally Peace takes the field, and drives the war away.

Just when the strife seems over and the Virtues begin to retire, Concord is treacherously stabbed by the disguised figure of Discord, or Heresy, whose intent is to stir up dissension among the unified community of Faith. Faith executes Heresy, who is subsequently dismembered by the other Virtues. Concord and Faith then address the Virtues, urging them not to allow Discord to destroy their unity. Faith proclaims that a temple should be raised up, as Solomon built his temple in Israel when peace and security had been achieved there. In language echoing the description of the New Jerusalem in Revelation 21, Prudentius describes the construction of the Temple, a dwelling place for Christ within the human soul cleansed of sin.

Prudentius's poem is of interest on more than theological grounds. His Virtues and Vices are more than simple personified abstractions. They are described in ways that depict them as human beings with the qualities of the virtue or vice they allegorize. Patience, for instance, does nothing aggressive to defend herself against Anger's attacks. She simply stands firm, and her armor cannot be pierced. In the end Anger, in her rage, kills herself. Similarly Sensuality is described as having "scented locks, slow voice, and wandering eyes;/Lost in delights, she lived to pamper flesh" (Eagen 1965, ll. 312–13), and she comes drunk to the battle.

Prudentius varies the individual duels enough to avoid monotony, but all of the single combats contain similar elements. In each case the Virtue is described, and is challenged by her opposite Vice, who is described in some detail as well. Thus Patience, for example, is challenged to battle by Anger. The Virtue inevitably wins the battle, and is allowed to give a speech of triumph, not unlike the kind one might find in epic poetry, in which the particular Vice is condemned and the Virtue upheld. In this speech or elsewhere in the description of the combat, biblical figures are used as examples of the virtue—or the vice—in question (Job, for example, is used to illustrate Patience).

Prudentius, as the first important Latin poet of Christendom, became a standard author read in the monastic schools of Europe from the ninth century onward. More than 300 manuscripts of his works survive from the Middle Ages, some of them containing illuminated copies of the *Psychomachia.* Such popularity attests to the widespread influence of this text.

Bibliography

Haworth, Kenneth R. *Deified Virtues, Demonic Vices, and Descriptive Allegory in Prudentius' Psychomachia.* Amsterdam: A. M. Hakkert, 1980.

Prudentius. *Prudentius.* 2 vols. Translated and edited by H. J. Thomson. Loeb Classical Library. Cambridge, Mass.: Harvard University Press, 1947–1953.

———. *Prudentius, Poems, Volume 1* and *Volume 2.* Edited by Sister M. Clement Eagan. *The Fathers of the Church: A New Translation,* vols. 43, 52. Washington, D.C.: Catholic University of America Press, 1965.

Smith, Macklin. *Prudentius' Psychomachia: A Reexamination.* Princeton, N.J.: Princeton University Press, 1976.

qasída

The *qasída* is a classical genre of Arabic verse that seems to have originated in the oral poetry of pre-Islamic Bedouin society in the early sixth century. The written genre became a standard poetic form throughout the Muslim world, and was used by Arabic, Persian, Turkish, and Urdu poets. *Qasídas* ran from about 30 to 120 lines or so—sometimes longer in Turkish, though in other traditions the *qasída* rarely exceeded 100 lines. *Qasídas* dealt with a variety of themes, from elegy to panegyric to satire. Later *qasídas* almost always were formal praise poems. In form, *qasídas* commonly opened with a line containing a pair of rhyming half lines, and continued with that rhyme repeated at the end of every line.

The typical *qasída* in its early form consisted of two main sections. The first section was quite formulaic: The poem begins with reference to a place—usually an abandoned campsite in the desert—that recalls the speaker's former love. In a mood of nostalgia and melancholy, the poet recalls details of the love affair, generally including a detailed catalogue of the lady's attributes. Finally the speaker of the poem resolves to leave off his dismal brooding, mount his camel, and ride away. At this point the poet typically includes another detailed catalogue—this time listing the attributes of the camel. It has been suggested that these parallel descriptions imply a contrast, the lady representing a life of ease, the camel one of action and striving (Hamori 1974).

The second part of the *qasída* was far more variable. It might contain a list of the poet's merits or accomplishments, or those of his tribe. It might celebrate the great deeds or qualities of the poet's patron, or the one he hoped would become his patron. It might, in contrast, satirize an enemy of the poet's.

Later *qasídas* were written almost exclusively as praise poems, so the second part of the poem chiefly extolled the virtues of one's patron. In those poems the structure of the poem consisted of, first, the description of the amorous affair (a section called *nasib*); second, a description of the poet's journey across the desert until he reaches the safe haven of the patron's headquarters; and third, a section of fairly conventional praise for the patron.

The importance of the *qasída,* however, certainly goes beyond the mere praising of patrons. Even from the beginning of the Islamic period, the *qasída* had what Hamori calls a "ritualistic" quality, recalling and somewhat idealizing the mythic time of origins in the desert. Doubtless this explains why, even when the poem's intent was largely panegyric, the amorous *nasib* and the journey by camel remain significant parts of the genre. But the genre continued to develop—by the 12th and 13th centuries, religious themes were introduced. The genre has persisted in Islamic societies to the present day, with modern themes, but such modern poems are part of a literary tradition dating back 1,500 years to the pre-Muslim deserts.

An important writer of *quasídas* was IBN AL-'ARABI.

Bibliography

Hamori, Andras. *On the Art of Medieval Arabic Literature.* Princeton, N.J.: Princeton University Press, 1974.

Sperl, Stefan, and Christopher Shackle, eds. *Qasída Poetry in Islamic Africa and Asia.* 2 vols. Leiden, Netherlands: E.J. Brill, 1996.

Quem Quaeritis trope (10th century)

The three-line trope (a passage inserted into the authorized service) that begins *Quem quaeritis* (Whom are you seeking?) was first inserted into the introit (the opening of the service) of the Mass for Easter in the early 10th century. Around this brief dialogue sung between a singer impersonating the Angel and singers impersonating the three Marys at the tomb of Christ grew a whole tradition of what is generally called "liturgical drama," that is, short dramatizations of biblical events performed as part of formal church services. Antiphonal singing (in which parts of the choir sang responsively) during the Mass was a dramatic practice by nature. Adding words to the singing of wordless vowel sequences created a genuine dialogue.

In the three lines of the trope, translated from the Latin, the Angel begins by asking "Whom do you seek in the sepulcher, oh followers of Christ?" The Marys answer "Jesus of Nazareth who was crucified, oh heavenly one." To this the Angel responds "He is not here; he is risen, just as he foretold. Go and announce that he is risen from the sepulcher." The lines have their ultimate source in the synoptic Gospel accounts of Easter morning, though the words of the trope are not the same as any of the Gospel stories.

The trope survives in 14 manuscripts, the earliest of which is dated to about 930–35. In 970, a text called the *Regulis Concordia,* produced at Winchester, describes a reenactment of the sepulcher scene, including an exchange of the *Quem quaeritis* type and apparently making use of a makeshift "sepulcher" to create the scene. This dramatization was not a part of the Mass itself, however, but was performed at matins. At that time, the office of matins would have ended at sunrise, and the association of Christ's resurrection with sunrise on Easter morning may account for the shift of the dialogue out of the Mass itself.

The precise origin of this kernel of medieval drama is debated. Some believe that it occurred originally in the Abbey of St. Martial at Limoges (source of the earliest manuscript), while others have claimed that honor for the Benedictine abbey of St. Gall in Switzerland. More recent scholars have suggested other sources for the trope. Some have argued that the Easter vigil service in the Roman rite shows elements of the dialogue and was probably where it originated. Others have suggested a dramatic element in the Gallican liturgy, used in northern Europe until the Roman rite replaced it in the eighth and ninth centuries. Still others have shown that drama was encouraged at the court of CHARLEMAGNE more than 100 years prior to the *Quem quaeritis* trope, and that these dialogues may have had their source in the earlier ritual of the Byzantine church.

Whatever its origin, it is clear that the *Quem quaeritis* trope is the earliest extant example of what became a widespread practice. By the 11th century, a Christmas version of the trope was developed, in the form of a dialogue between Shepherds and Midwives beginning "Whom are you seeking in the manger?" Between the 11th and 13th centuries, both the Christmas and Easter versions of the trope were expanded and varied to a large extent, and other tropes were developed for other important Christian feast days, like Ascension Day and the Feast of the Assumption of the Virgin. By the later Middle Ages, more complex liturgical drama was in existence. Critics have often suggested that these liturgical dramas were the immediate inspiration, or ancestors, of the highly developed MYSTERY PLAY cycles of the later medieval period, though no direct connection between the two has ever been proven. Still, the practice of dramatizing biblical events common to liturgical drama certainly paved the way for the popularity of the reenactments made in the mystery plays.

Bibliography

Goldstein, Leonard. *The Origin of Medieval Drama.* Madison, N.J.: Fairleigh Dickinson University Press, 2004.

Hardison, O. B., Jr. *Christian Rite and Christian Drama in the Middle Ages: Essays in the Origin and Early History of Modern Drama.* 1965. Westport, Conn.: Greenwood Press, 1983.

Raimbaut de Vaqueiras (ca. 1155–ca. 1207)

Raimbaut de Vaqueiras was a Provençal TROUBADOUR whose exploits on the battlefield were at least as interesting as his poetry. He was born in humble circumstances, rose to the rank of knight through his military service, left some 36 lyrics of significant merit, and was probably killed during the Fourth Crusade.

Raimbaut was born to a very poor family in the area of Vaucluse in Provence. As a young man he traveled into northern Italy, where at the court of Montferrat he was befriended by Boniface, the future margrave of Montferrat. In the later 1180s, he traveled back to Provence and, by 1189, was probably attached to the court of Hugues I of Baux. Raimbaut returned to Italy in about 1190, and when Boniface succeeded his father to become Boniface I, margrave of Montferrat in 1192, Raimbaut joined his court. Boniface welcomed and patronized a number of poets, including probably Peire VIDAL and the noted TROUVÈRE, CONON DE BÉTHUNE, but it was Raimbaut who stayed with him the longest.

Raimbaut supported Boniface in Sicily during the margrave's campaign there in service of the emperor Henry VI. It was in Sicily that Raimbaut is said to have saved Boniface's life and, as a result, was knighted by his patron. When Boniface was chosen as one of the leaders of the Fourth Crusade, Raimbaut decided to return to Provence as Boniface left from Venice in 1202, but by 1203, Raimbaut had joined Boniface in Constantinople. Here he wrote one of his best-known works, an epic letter to Boniface, in which Raimbaut details his life and campaigns with his patron.

On September 4, 1207, near Messiaple, Boniface was killed in a skirmish with Bulgarian forces allied with the Byzantines. Most scholars have assumed that Raimbaut died alongside his patron. However, it is possible that he survived the attack and returned to Provence. A certain Raimbaut de Vaqueiras is mentioned in a document from 1243, and some have suggested this is the same man—though realistically, he would have been nearly 90 years old at the time.

Raimbaut wrote a number of lyrics, some bilingual or multilingual texts. His best-known lyric is his *Kalenda Maya* (May Day), which he calls an *estampida.* It is the first known example of this lyric genre—a dance song with lyrics expressing love and devotion to a lady, written in four stanzas with a refrain, followed by one or two envois set to a different melody.

But certainly Raimbaut's most important literary contribution is no single poem but rather his introduction of the vernacular Provençal lyric tradition into the courts of Italy. Through his influence, and to a lesser extent some of the other troubadours who visited Italian courts, the future course of Italian literature was set, ultimately culminating in the great poets of the 13th and 14th centuries, including DANTE and PETRARCH.

Bibliography

Goldin, Frederick, ed. and trans. *Lyrics of the Troubadours and Trouvères: An Anthology and a History.* Garden City, N.Y.: Doubleday, 1973.

Linskill, Joseph. *The Poems of the Troubadour Raimbaut de Vaqueiras.* The Hague: Mouton, 1964.

McPeek, Gwynn S. " 'Kalenda Maia': A Study in Form." In *Medieval Studies in Honor of Robert White Linder,* edited by Brian Dutton, J. Woodrow Hassell, Jr., and John E. Keller, 141–154. Valencia: Castalia, 1973.

Raimbaut d'Orange (Raimbaut d'Aurenga) (ca. 1130–1173)

Raimbaut III, count of Orange, was a TROUBADOUR from the region of Provence. He was lord of the town of Omelas, west of Montpellier, and held the castle of Cortezon between Orange and Avignon. Here he kept a lavish court, and here he also seems to have entertained other troubadours, like MARCABRU, PEIRE D'ALVERNHE, and GIRAUT DE BORNELH, with whom he composed a famous *TENSON,* or DEBATE POEM, on styles of poetry, Giraut defending the clear and easy *TROBAR LEU* style, and Raimbaut rather arrogantly defending the difficult, closed style called *TROBAR CLUS.* He does not care, Raimbaut says in that poem, if his songs are widely known, for "cheap abundance never/had great worth:/that is why you set a higher price on gold than salt,/and it is the same with any song" (Goldin 1973, 205, ll. 31–35).

It is said that Raimbaut squandered much of his inheritance on gambling and high living. When he died Giraut wrote a lament for him that mourned the death of folly and games of dice. Early tradition also linked him romantically with the famous *trobairitz,* the COUNTESS OF DIA, but that connection is likely to be spurious. In fact very little is known with certainty about his life.

His poetry, however, reveals a man of high intelligence, admirable technical skill, a taste for irony, and a persistent sense of humor. He had little sympathy with the conventions of the COURTLY LOVE lyric, nor, as an aristocrat, did he need to follow convention for the sake of a patron. Like GUILLAUME IX, the first troubadour and another nobleman, he has a mischievous streak. Sometimes he parodies the conventions of love, or adopts a persona that ironically undercuts courtly attitudes. As Simon Gaunt points out, Raimbaut's poems are often *GAPS,* or boasting poems, or can be seen as inverse *gaps,* in which he boasts about his sexual deprivation, pushing the courtly tradition, as Gaunt says, to "its most absurd limits" (Gaunt 1989, 141). In his "Escotatz, mas no say qus' es," for instance, Raimbaut parodies the frustrated lover and manages to stand religion on its ear as well by asking his lady for sex in the name of the Father, Son, and Holy Ghost:

It's been a good four months—that's more
than a thousand years to me, yes,
since she promised me and swore
to give me what I long for most.
Lady, my heart is your prisoner,
therefore sweeten my bitterness.
Help me, God, in nominee Patriis et Filli et Spiritus
sancti! Madam, how will it all turn out?

(Goldin 1973, 181, ll. 22–28)

There is much variety as well as humor in Raimbaut's 39 extant lyrics. Though he defends the *trobar clus* style (possibly learned from Marcabru) in his early verse, he seems to have composed more in the clearer *trobar leu* style later on, perhaps through Giraut's influence. Later he seems to have become interested in the highly ornate *trobar ric* style, with its complex rhyme schemes and rare vocabulary. In this he may have influenced the technical virtuosity of ARNAUT DANIEL.

Bibliography

Gaunt, Simon. *Troubadours and Irony.* Cambridge: Cambridge University Press, 1989.

Goldin, Frederick, ed. and trans. *Lyrics of the Troubadours and Trouvères: An Anthology and a History.* Garden City, N.Y.: Doubleday, 1973.

Pattison, Walter T. *The Life and Works of the Troubadour Raimbaut d'Orange.* Minneapolis: University of Minneapolis Press, 1952.

Ralph of Diceto (Radulph de Diceto, Ralph of Diss) (ca. 1130–1202)

Ralph of Diceto was dean of Saint Paul's Cathedral in London in the late 12th century, and the author of two important chronicles. An advocate of the Angevin royal line, Ralph supported HENRY II in his controversy with Thomas BECKETT, and served the royal court of RICHARD I as well. His best-known work, the *Ymagines historiarum* (Outlines of histories), is an important primary source for the last years of Henry's reign, and for the reign of Richard.

Scholars do not agree on the location of "Diceto." Most believe that Ralph was from France originally. He apparently studied at the University of Paris as a young man, and by 1152 seems to have obtained a degree and was made archdeacon of Middlesex, a position he held for some 28 years. He may have returned to the University of Paris for further study, as well, after his appointment.

In 1166, Ralph was chosen by the English bishops to act as their envoy when they protested a series of excommunications launched by Beckett as archbishop of Canterbury. Generally, however, he seems to have preferred to work behind the scenes, and he never mentions this appointment in his chronicles. Ralph was named dean of Saint Paul's in 1180, and while he worked hard to reform the administration of the chapter and to initiate new building, and while he is known to have written a number of commentaries on the Scriptures, it is for the historical writings he composed after 1180 that he is remembered.

Diceto was in a position to be acquainted with nearly all of the most powerful people of his time, and as a result had access to eyewitness as well as written sources unavailable to most writers. His two major works are the *Abbreviationes chronicorum* (which records the history of the world from the birth of Christ until 1147) and the *Ymagines historiarum* (which begins with the knighting of the future Henry II in 1148 and continues the history until 1201). Ralph relies heavily on a previous chronicler, Robert of Torigny (or Robert de Monte), for events up until about 1272. After that date, and particularly after 1280, Ralph's chronicle becomes a firsthand contemporary history, and this section of the chronicle is especially valuable to historians.

Diceto has not been admired for his literary style, and occasionally his chronology is unreliable. But his insights into character and into the political ramifications of events are astute, and despite his Angevin sympathies, he is generally balanced and fair in his presentation of events, even in his account of Henry II's feud with Beckett, perhaps the most politically charged controversy of his time.

Bibliography

Stubbs, William, ed. *Radulfi de Diceto decani Lundoniensis opera historica. The Historical Works of Master Ralph de Diceto, Dean of London.* 2 vols. Rolls Series, 68. London: Longmans, 1876.

razo

Like the VIDAS, *razos* were preserved mainly in 13th-century Italian manuscripts of TROUBADOUR poetry. While the *vidas* provided short biographies of individual troubadours and were included in lyric anthologies as an introduction to each author, the *razos* (from the Provençal word for "reason" or "explanation") would relate the circumstances under which specific lyrics were composed. *Razos* tend to be a bit longer than *vidas,* though none exceeds 2,500 words. Fewer *razos* than *vidas* are extant; *razos* exist for only about two dozen troubadours. But evidence suggests that the *razos* were probably originally composed prior to the more numerous *vidas.*

It is likely that the extant *razos* were originally recited by JONGLEURS prior to the performance of individual songs. The stylistic similarities among most written *razos* and *vidas* are indicative of a single author. Some scholars believe that the jongleur Uc de Saint-Circ (mentioned in some manuscripts) collected *razos* from other jongleurs in the mid-13th century, and wrote them down in the form included in the manuscripts.

Biographical information in the *razos* is factually suspect. It seems clear that most of the *razos* are fictionalized stories drawn from the poems they introduce. Often they describe lovers' quarrels, reflecting the attitude of the typical CANSOS or love poems. Some, as Elizabeth Poe has pointed out, are so outlandish as to suggest a deliberately humorous effect. Poe mentions a *canso* by Peire VIDAL, written for a lady named Loba. Punning on the name, Peire compares his treatment at this lady's hands to that of a wolf beaten by shepherds. In the *razo* for this poem, Uc describes Peire as trying to sneak into his lady's castle dressed in a wolf skin, and being chased by dogs and shepherds.

One of the most important legacies of the *razos* is their influence on DANTE. Inspired by the examples of the troubadour anthologies, he structured his first important poetic work, the *VITA NUOVA*, to include authentic *razos* introducing each poem, where he gives his own version of how the poems came to be written. Dante saw the *razos* for what they were: the first form of "literary criticism" of European vernacular poetry.

Bibliography

Martinez, Ronald. "Italy." In *A Handbook of the Troubadours*, edited by F. R. P. Akehurst and Judith M. Davis, 279–294. Berkeley: University of California Press, 1995.

Poe, Elizabeth W. "The Vidas and Razos." In *A Handbook of the Troubadours*, edited by F. R. P. Akehurst and Judith M. Davis, 185–197. Berkeley: University of California Press, 1995.

Reeve's Tale, The Geoffrey Chaucer (ca. 1392)

The Reeve's Tale is the third of CHAUCER's *CANTERBURY TALES*. The tale is a FABLIAU offering a cynical but comic view of human beings at their worst. It employs a common folklore motif called the "cradle trick," and Chaucer may have based it directly on a French fabliau. But as with his other fabliaux, Chaucer expands the genre in *The Reeve's Tale*, with his naturalistic detail and animated characterization of the proud Miller and his family.

Oswald the Reeve, described as thin and choleric in the GENERAL PROLOGUE, seethes with anger after *The MILLER's TALE*, in which a carpenter is cuckolded after marrying a young wife. The Reeve sets out to "quite," or repay, the Miller, and tells his own story of an arrogant and thieving Cambridge miller named Symkyn, his wife (proud of her elevated lineage as illegitimate daughter of the town parson), and their rather unattractive daughter.

Two students from Cambridge (John and Aleyn) bring Symkyn business from the college, and are determined to watch the miller carefully so that he doesn't cheat them. But Symkyn has his wife turn the clerks' horse loose, and while they chase down the animal, Symkyn steals a good part of their grain. When the students return, Symkyn is forced to let them stay the night because of the late hour. Aleyn, knowing they have been cheated, determines to take revenge on the Miller by lying with his daughter. In the dark he sneaks into her bed. John, afraid of being called a fool by his classmates when they hear of Aleyn's conquest, decides to have sex with the Miller's wife. When she gets up during the night, John moves a cradle from the foot of Symkyn's bed to his own. When she returns, the wife, feeling for the cradle in the dark, gets into bed with John.

As dawn approaches, Aleyn leaves Malyne and, fooled by the cradle, climbs into her father's bed. When he boasts about the time he has had with Malyne, a slapstick brawl breaks out, and ultimately the clerks beat Symkyn and steal back their own grain.

Critical response to *The Reeve's Tale* has generally found its comedy inferior to *The Miller's Tale*. However scholars have found it useful to compare the cynical narrator's view of sex with that of the joyful narrator of *The Miller's Tale*. The parody of courtly language, especially in Aleyn's farewell to Malyne, which parodies the traditional *ALBA*, or dawn-song, of love poetry, has also interested scholars. Also worth noting is Chaucer's use of northern dialect in his portrayal of the two clerks' language: This is the first extended use in English of dialect for comic effect.

Bibliography

Benson, C. David. *Chaucer's Drama of Style: Poetic Variety and Contrast in the Canterbury Tales*. Chapel Hill: University of North Carolina Press, 1986.

Benson, Larry, et al., eds. *The Riverside Chaucer*. 3rd ed. Boston: Houghton-Mifflin, 1987.

Cowgill, Bruce Kent. "Clerkly Rivalry in The Reeve's Tale." In *Rebels and Rivals: The Contestive Spirit in The Canterbury Tales,* edited by Susanna Freer Fein, David Raybin, and Peter C. Braeger, 59–71. Studies in Medieval Culture, 29. Kalamazoo, Mich.: Medieval Institute Publications, 1991.

Pigg, Daniel E. "Performing the Perverse: The Abuse of Masculine Power in the Reeve's Tale." In *Masculinities in Chaucer: Approaches to Maleness in the Canterbury Tales and Troilus and Criseyde,* edited by Peter G. Beidler, 53–61. Cambridge, U.K.: Brewer, 1998.

Reinmar der Alte (ca. 1150–ca. 1210)

Next to WALTHER VON DER VOGELWEIDE, Reinmar der Alte has always been viewed as the most important Middle High German courtly love poet. GOTTFRIED VON STRASSBURG, for instance, in his *TRISTAN* (ca. 1210), laments Reinmar's death: "the leader of them all, is thus silenced to the world" (4,478–79), and Walther von der Vogelweide, though somewhat with tongue-in-cheek, praises his great art (L. 83, 1). There might have been some rivalry between Walther and Reinmar, but this did not diminish the latter's tremendous reputation throughout the German Middle Ages.

In one of his songs Reinmar indirectly mourns the death of his patron, Duke Leopold V of Austria (1194). He himself might have originated from Austria, though Gottfried seems to locate him in Alsace (Hagenau). Reinmar was probably born between 1150 and 1160 and died before 1210. He is depicted in the *Manessische Liederhandschrift* (ms. C, early 14th century), where he is identified with the unusual appellate *"der Alte"* ("the Old One"). Apart from 60 songs clearly attributable to Reinmar, there is also a considerable corpus of so-called "pseudo-Reinmar" songs. Whereas he gained greatest respect for his esoteric, spiritual love poetry (*hohe Minne*), those songs of questionable authenticity treat love in a much more material and erotic manner. According to recent scholarship, however, they might simply have been part of Reinmar's repertoire, more or less repressed by 19th- and early 20th-century scholarship.

The traditional corpus of Reinmar's *Minnelieder* is determined by the male voice's emotional but ritualized suffering resulting from the distant lady who is elevated into an abstract, almost absolute state of womanhood. Women's love appears as the ultimate reward for men's life here in this world, but since courtly ladies are basically unapproachable, Reinmar strongly emphasizes love pains, which subsequently elevate the man to a higher ethical level. Consequently the wooer must unswervingly demonstrate loyalty and patience, and never show a sign of doubt about his lady's triumphant virtues. This does not imply that Reinmar never even mentions the erotic goal of his wooing, as he states on several occasions that happiness and sexual fulfillment are also on his mind (nos. 14 and 15). Sometimes Reinmar resorts to the genre of *Wechsel,* or exchange poem, where the wooing man and his lady enter a dialogue (songs no. 2, 3, and 4). Significantly Reinmar employs women's stanzas where he utilizes a female voice in a skillful dramatic setting. His song, "Si jehent, der sumer der sî hie" (They say that summer has arrived, song no. 16), is a widow's lament, a song put into the mouth of the wife of the deceased Leopold V of Austria. Two songs, nos. 30 and 31, are Crusade songs in which he explores, similarly to HARTMANN VON AUE, the emotional conflict between the call of God to liberate the Holy Land and his desire to stay with his lady back home.

Apart from song no. 12, which demonstrates some textual links with a poem by GACE BRULÉ, Reinmar does not seem to have borrowed much at all from French TROUBADOUR or TROUVÈRE poets. His lyrical œuvre represents the epitome of Middle High German courtly love poetry prior to Walther von der Vogelweide and NEIDHART, as Reinmar still pursues the absolute ideals of traditional courtliness, whereas his successors seriously began to question the esoteric concept of love advocated by Reinmar and his contemporaries.

Bibliography

Jackson, William E. "Reinmar der Alte and the Woman as Courtly Victim." In *New Images of Medieval Women: Essays Towards a Cultural Anthro-*

pology, edited by Edelgard E. DuBruck, 73–101. Lewiston, N.Y.: Edwin Mellen Press, 1989.

Des Minnesang Frühling. Edited by Hugo Moser and Helmut Tervooren. 38th ed. Stuttgart, Germany: Hirzel, 1988.

Albrecht Classen

reverdie

Specifically, a *reverdie* was a late medieval dance song that welcomed the coming of spring. The form of the song was generally the same as a chanson (or CANSO): five or six stanzas with no refrain. A *reverdie* might express joy at the newly growing buds and flowers, the singing of the returning birds, and the rekindling of thoughts of love associated with the spring.

Later *reverdies* in German, Latin, and Provençal extended the praise of spring's rebirth of natural life to praise of the Easter season and the rebirth of spiritual life. Other TROUBADOURS used the form of the *reverdie* to praise other seasons as well as spring.

The term *reverdie* is also sometimes broadened to refer to any poetic passage celebrating the return of spring. Thus a large number of medieval love poems in the COURTLY LOVE tradition begin with a *reverdie,* putting the speaker's love in the context of the joy in the natural world's renewal. Sometimes the speaker's love is in concord with this rebirth, as in these lines from the troubadour BERNART DE VENTADORN:

When the new grass and the leaves come forth
and the flower burgeons on the branch,
and the nightingale lifts its high
pure voice and begins its song,
I have joy in it, and joy in the flower,
and joy in myself, and in my lady most of all;

(Goldin 1973, 137–39, ll. 1–6)

At other times, the speaker's love is unrequited, or causes him pain, and so the new season only depresses him, as it does the speaker of these lines from RAIMBAUT DE VAQUEIRAS, separated from his beloved:

I have no pleasure in winter or spring,
the season of brightness, the oak leaf,
my advancement seems like my undoing,
and my greatest joy my grief.

(Goldin 1973, 269, ll. 1–4)

But perhaps the best known *reverdie* in all medieval poetry occurs in the opening lines of Geoffrey CHAUCER'S *CANTERBURY TALES:*

Whan that Aprill with his shoures soote
The droghte of March hath perced to the roote,
And bathed every veyne in swich licour
Of which vertu engendred is the flour;
Whan Zephirus eek with his sweete breeth
Inspired hath in every holt and heeth
The tendre croppes, and the yonge sonne
Hath in the Ram his half cours yronne,
And smale foweles maken melodye,
That slepen al the nyght with open ye
(So Priketh hem Nature in hir corages),
Thanne longen folk to goon on pilgrimages,

(Benson 1987, 23, ll. 1–12)

Chaucer was certainly thinking about the centuries of poets that had used the introductory spring celebration to introduce love poems, but gives the *reverdie* a twist in the end by relating it to spiritual regeneration. However, as has been noted above, this was not atypical of *reverdies* in other languages.

Bibliography

Benson, Larry, et al., eds. *The Riverside Chaucer.* 3rd ed. Boston: Houghton-Mifflin, 1987.

Diehl, Patrick S. *The Medieval European Religious Lyric: An Ars Poetica.* Berkeley: University of California Press, 1985.

Goldin, Frederick, ed. and trans. *Lyrics of the Troubadours and Trouvères: An Anthology and a History.* Garden City, N.Y.: Doubleday, 1973.

rhyme royal

Rhyme royal, or the "Chaucerian stanza," is a verse form invented by Geoffrey CHAUCER consisting of seven decasyllabic (10-syllable) lines rhyming *ababbcc.* Chaucer found the stanza valuable and flexible for use in narrative poetry.

He first used it in *The PARLIAMENT OF FOWLS,* and used it again in *TROILUS AND CRISEYDE* and some of the *CANTERBURY TALES,* particularly the more serious ones like *The CLERK'S TALE* and *The PRIORESS'S TALE.* Other late medieval poets, including LYDGATE, DUNBAR, and HENNRYSON, later used the stanza and it was given the name "rhyme royal" because it was used in *The KINGIS QUAIR,* a poem attributed to King JAMES I of Scotland.

The stanza also remained popular in the Renaissance, and was employed by Skelton, and Spenser, and by Shakespeare as well in his narrative poem *The Rape of Lucrece.*

Chaucer adapted the rhyme royal form from BOCCACCIO'S OTTAVA RIMA stanza—an eight-line stanza rhyming *abababcc.* Boccaccio's stanza consists of six lines of description or narration and a concluding couplet that might comment on or sum up the stanza. Chaucer eliminated Boccaccio's fifth line, creating a stanza form that invited more flexibility by creating a turning point in the fourth line, the middle of the stanza: The *b* rhyme in line four completes the *abab* quatrain that starts the stanza, and also begins the *bbcc* pair of couplets that ends the stanza. The following famous stanza from *Troilus* illustrates the rhyme royal form:

> *Ye knowe ek that in forme of speche is chaunge*
> *Withinne a thousand yeer, and wordes tho*
> *That hadden pris, now wonder nyce and straunge*
> *Us thinketh hem, and yet thei spake hem so,*
> *And spedde as wel in love as men now do;*
> *Ek for to wynnen love in sundry ages,*
> *In sundry londes, sundry ben usages.*
>
> (Benson 1987, 489, ll. 22–28)

Here, the first four lines describe how strange to us is the speech of those that lived in bygone times. But a shift occurs in line four, and the final four lines describe how much those people were like us after all, particularly in matters of love.

Bibliography

Benson, Larry, et al., eds. *The Riverside Chaucer.* 3rd ed. Boston: Houghton-Mifflin, 1987.

Rhyming Poem, The (10th century)

The Rhyming Poem is an OLD ENGLISH poem of 87 lines included in the 10th-century manuscript known as the EXETER BOOK. Like many of the other poems in the Exeter Book (including such well-known texts as *The WANDERER, The SEAFARER, The RUIN,* and *The WIFE'S LAMENT*), *The Rhyming Poem* is ELEGAIC—that is, a poem with a somber and meditative mood, usually occasioned by the speaker's misfortune, exile, and loneliness. In *The Rhyming Poem,* the speaker, apparently a former king who has lost his power, yearns for his past glory as he laments his fallen condition and the changeableness of earthly fortune. The first part of the poem (lines 1–42) describes the speaker's happy past, while the second half speaks of his gloomy present condition. The speaker's own decline parallels that of the world in general, as the speaker realizes the transient nature of physical creation, and the poem ends with a gruesome description of mortal decay and the hope that the saved will dwell eternally in a blissful Christian heaven.

The poem's use of rhyme has been attributed to a familiarity with rhyming Latin hymns, and hence with a learned, clerical environment. It is therefore possible that the author was familiar with BOETHIUS's famous *CONSOLATION OF PHILOSOPHY*—certainly the theme of the poem is consistent with that text. Some scholars have even suggested *The Rhyming Poem* is intended as a loose paraphrase of the 29th and 30th chapters of the Old Testament Book of Job.

What is remarkable about *The Rhyming Poem* is not its elegiac mood, which is fairly commonplace, but its remarkable display of technical virtuosity. Most unusual is the use of rhyme: While some later poems in Old English employ rhyme along with the conventional form of ALLITERATIVE VERSE, this poem displays the earliest and most consistent exploitation of rhyme. Here, each half-line of the alliterative verse rhymes with the second half line. In some cases, two lines have the same rhyme scheme. There are even two occasions (lines 13–16 and 51–54) where four consecutive lines utilize the same rhyme. The metrical pattern becomes even more intense in lines 29–37, where the poet uses essentially the same sound (*-ade*) at the end of each of these eight consecutive lines. The poet's aesthetic virtuosity is particularly evident in the rather astonishing line 77, where the poet breaks the rules of classical alliterative verse and includes a half-line with only one stressed syllable—the single word *an,* meaning "alone," is in fact alone in its half-line: *oþæt beoþ þa ban an*— "Until there is just the bone, alone" (Greenfield and Calder 1986, 291). These and other features, such as the consistent use of parallel phrases and clauses without transitional words (a device, called "asyndetic parataxis," fairly common in Old English poetry), make the details of the poem very difficult to decipher at some points, though the overall elegiac theme is clear and, ultimately, the craft of the poem is noteworthy.

Bibliography

Greenfield, Stanley B., and Daniel G. Calder. *A New Critical History of Old English Literature.* New York: New York University Press, 1986.

Krapp, George Philip, and Elliott van Kirk Dobbie. *The Exeter Book.* Anglo-Saxon Poetic Records, 3. New York: Columbia University Press, 1936.

Richard I (Richard Plantagenet) (1157–1199)

Although Richard I was born in Oxfordshire, England, on September 8, 1157, and reigned over England from 1189 to 1199, he grew up in Aquitaine, in southern France, spoke native French and very little English, and only spent six months of his kingship in England (he spent the rest of the time on his interests in France and on his crusading activities); thus, he is often referred to as "the absent king." Perhaps, however, a better testimony to this king's character is the legendary nickname given to him because of his courage and bravery on the battlefield, Richard "the Lionheart," as he is referred to in the 14th-century ROMANCE *RICHARD COEUR DE LYON,* in the legend of ROBIN HOOD, and in Sir Walter Scott's *Ivanhoe.* As a handsome soldier who stood approximately six feet four inches tall, Richard's physical disposition also suited his nickname.

The third of HENRY II's legitimate sons and the favorite of ELEANOR OF AQUITAINE's eight children with Henry, Richard became duke of Aquitaine in 1168, and duke of Poitiers in 1172, while his older brother Henry the Young King was named his father's successor and crowned king of England. Along with Henry and his other brother Geoffrey, duke of Brittany, Richard revolted against his father in 1173–74. Later, in 1183, he joined forces with his father and fought against those same brothers when they supported a rebellion against Richard in Aquitaine. Finally, in 1188, Richard allied himself with King Philip of France to fight for Aquitaine, which he believed he (rather than Henry's youngest son John) should rightly inherit; Richard defeated his father in 1189. Upon his father's death (caused by a fever in 1189), Richard became duke of Normandy, count of Anjou, and, on September 3, 1189, king of England.

Shortly after he inherited the throne, Richard joined the Third Crusade, which led him to capture Messina and Cyprus. In 1191, he met Berengaria of Navarre, and married her later that year; the marriage produced no heirs, perhaps, some argue, because of his homosexuality. On April 6, 1199, Richard signed a treaty with Saladin, the Muslim sultan who commanded the Egyptian troops, that granted Christians access to the holy places in Jerusalem. On his way back to England, in 1192, Richard was shipwrecked, captured, and imprisoned by Leopold V of Austria. Legend has it that while he was imprisoned, he was discovered by a troubadour and turned over to the custody of Holy Roman Emperor Henry VI, who demanded a 150,000-mark ransom from England for the king's return. The ransom, which was raised through heavy taxation of the British people, was eventually met, and Richard regained his freedom in February of 1194. The king returned to England to suppress the revolt raised against him by his brother John and to participate in a second coronation ceremony in April of 1194, to reestablish his control over the country. Shortly after he was crowned for the second time, he left for France to fight Philip to retain control of Normandy, and thereafter he never returned to England.

One of the many contradictions of Richard's life was that he and Philip II were close allies when they were young, but they eventually became enemies. Richard joined forces with Philip Augustus in order to preserve his right to succeed to the throne, but Philip eventually became one of his greatest rivals—some say this is because they once shared an intimate relationship that ended bitterly; others say it is because of Philip's sister, Alice, whom Richard was supposed to marry but could not after she and Richard's father, HENRY II (another man Richard shared an inconsistent relationship with), shared a romantic love affair.

While Richard was in France or fighting in the Crusades, his ministers, William of Longchamp and Hubert Walter, carried on the administration set up by Henry II and ruled the kingdom quite effectively. While the king was actually in England, he impressed the people with his charisma and talent—besides being generous and chivalrous, he was skilled in music, poetry, and martial arts—and with his ability to come up with copious funds and troops for the Third Crusade. He was a patron of poets like the TROUBADOUR BERTRAN DE BORN, as well as the TROUVÈRE BLONDEL DE NESLE, and he also seems to have written verse himself, including one on his imprisonment beginning "*Ja nus hons pris ne dira sa reson*" (No prisoner will ever speak his mind) (Goldin 1973, 377–379).

Richard died of an arrow wound inflicted during the siege of Chaluz in France—the castle was supposedly filled with a treasure trove of gold that one of his subjects had failed to turn over to him. It is believed that if Richard had been properly armed, the wound that killed him would not have hurt him at all. Upon Richard's death, his brother, called John "Lackland" because he never received an inheritance from his parents, inherited the English crown. Although Richard might have been the "Absent King," he is fondly remembered for his chivalric nature and bravery in battle. These characteristics have been recorded in the previously mentioned romance, in the legend of Robin Hood and Sir Walter Scott's *Ivanhoe,* as well as Scott's *The Talisman,* Cecil B. DeMille's 1935 film of *The Crusades,* and James Goldman's play and later film *The Lion in Winter* (1968), starring Katherine Hepburn with Anthony Hopkins portraying Richard.

Bibliography

Broughton, Bradford B. *The Legends of King Richard I, Coeur de Lion: A Study of Sources and Variations to the Year 1600.* The Hague: Mouton, 1966.

Brundage, James A. *Richard Lion Heart.* New York: Scribner, 1974.

Gillingham, John. *Richard I.* Yale English Monarchs. New Haven, Conn.: Yale University Press, 2000.

Goldin, Frederick, ed. and trans. *Lyrics of the Troubadours and Trouvères: An Anthology and a History.* Garden City, N.Y.: Doubleday, 1973.

Reston, James. *Warriors of God: Richard the Lionheart and Saladin in the Third Crusade.* New York: Doubleday, 2002.

Richard II (1367–1400)

Richard II was born to Edward, the Black Prince, and Joan, the "Fair Maid of Kent," on Epiphany in 1367. Ten years later, in 1377, Richard succeeded his grandfather, King EDWARD III, to the throne. Until Richard turned 22 years old, his uncle, JOHN OF GAUNT, duke of Lancaster, along with a council of magnates, exercised power for Richard. The young king was pale and blond with delicate features, and he appeared weak to many—it was not until the PEASANTS' REVOLT in 1381 (the peasants' outcry against poll taxes, low wages, and feudal laws), when Richard was age 14, that the young king showed extraordinary bravery and courage when he met the rebelling peasants, addressed them in a friendly manner, said that he was their lord and king and wished to know what they wanted, and, finally, agreed to their demands. Although Richard's promise was never met and the leaders of the rebellion were ultimately executed, the uprising asserted the peasants' power and endeared the young king to them.

Richard married ANNE OF BOHEMIA in 1382, and the couple's relationship was one of mutual love and admiration. Her sudden death in 1394, childless at the age of 27, prompted Richard to demolish the palace where she died; some believe he never fully recovered from the anguish brought on by her death.

King Richard prized peace, and perhaps peace with France (although short-lived) was Richard's greatest contribution to England. He allied the two countries by marrying the seven-year-old daughter of the king of France, Isabelle Valois, in 1396. In 1394 and again in 1399, Richard led armies to subjugate Ireland, but the task saw very little success.

Beginning in 1386, during a period when Gaunt was out of the country, Richard's power was curtailed by powerful elements within the nobility, led by his uncle, Thomas of Woodstock, the Duke of Gloucester. Angered by Richard's promotion of unprepared cousellors from the lower ranks of the nobility to positions of great influence—most particularly the despised Robert de Vere, earl of Oxford—the nobles focused on eliminating the king's bad advisers. In 1388, Parliament placed many of Richard's dearest friends and supporters on trial under the accusation of treason. Richard had the distress of presiding over what became known as the "Merciless Parliament" while his friends were tried, and of knowing there was nothing he could do to prevent their fates—some were ruthlessly hanged, drawn, and quartered. The Lords Appellant who brought the charges forth were led by Gloucester, and included his cousin, Henry Bolingbroke, son of John of Gaunt; they went on to rule the country until Richard II regained control the following year. Eventually, in retaliation, Richard had three of the five Lords Appellant arrested and executed and the remaining two, including Bolingbroke, exiled. When John of Gaunt died in 1399, Bolingbroke became duke of Lancaster. But before Henry could return from exile, Richard seized his possessions thus, when Henry returned, he had the support of the nobility, who saw Richard as overstepping his bounds by seizing nobles ancestral lands. He also was supported by the common folk, who objected to what they saw as the waste and extravagance of Richard's court; the heavy taxes he imposed even during peacetime; and his arrogant advisers, whom they saw as perverting the legal system. Henry angrily usurped the throne. Richard surrendered to the future King Henry IV in August of 1399, and abdicated from the throne in September.

Richard died in January of 1400, at the age of 33, while in prison at Pontrefact Castle. His death was unquestionably a slow, miserable one; while in prison he was denied basic necessities and suffered from neglect, probably finally dying of starvation. He was buried at the favorite residence of Edward II, the (equally incompetent) king he had sought to have canonized. Richard was the last king of the Plantagenet dynasty, and his overthrow marks the split of the family into two lines, the Houses of Lancaster and York, and anticipates the War of the Roses, which broke out in the 1450s—some go so far as to say that his death was the first casualty of the 85-year-long English civil war.

Richard valued art and culture, and he was a lavish spender. His interests had much to do with stimulating an English cultural renaissance. He was a patron of the arts, and, specifically, the patron of CHAUCER, his clerk of the works. Richard possessed a library of French and English illuminated manuscripts. His list of accomplishments also includes the invention of the handkerchief and the restoration of Westminster Hall. English literature flourished during Richard's reign, when writers including GOWER, LANGLAND, and the *PEARL* poet were producing their finest works. Later, during the Elizabethan era, his own life made great material for Shakespeare, whose *Richard II* is relatively accurate in its depiction of Richard as regal in appearance and manner yet, ultimately, an inadequate ruler.

Bibliography

Gillespie, James L., ed. *The Age of Richard II.* New York: St. Martin's Press, 1997.

Richard II: The Art of Kingship. Edited by Anthony Goodman and James Gillespie. Oxford: Clarendon Press, 1999.

Saul, Nigel. *Richard II.* Yale English Monarchs Series. New Haven, Conn.: Yale University Press, 1997.

Senior, Michael. *The Life and Times of Richard II.* With an introduction by Antonia Fraser. London: Weidenfeld and Nicolson, 1981.

Leslie Johnston

Richard Coeur de Lyon (ca. 1300–1325)

Richard Coeur de Lyon (Richard the Lion Heart [or Lionhearted]) is a MIDDLE ENGLISH verse ROMANCE of some 7,136 lines, composed in the southeastern part of England at the very beginning of the 14th century. The anonymous text is written in rhymed octosyllabic (eight-syllable) couplets and mixes chronicle with pure legend in telling the story of RICHARD I, king of England, and his adventures on the Third Crusade. The text survives in seven manuscripts and several fragments, and is believed by some to be based on an Anglo-Norman original from the mid-13th century, though no such source has survived.

Popular tradition has turned the protagonist of this romance into a mythic character bearing little resemblance to the historical personage of Richard I. The charismatic quality of Richard's character, presented by the patriotic writer as a point of national pride, is attributed in the romance to the fact that his mother is not the historical ELEANOR OF AQUITAINE but a supernatural elf-woman who is daughter of the infidel king of Antioch. In the romance, Richard proclaims a tournament on the day of his coronation. Jousting in his own tournament in disguise, Richard determines that Sir Thomas Multon and Sir Fulk Doyly are the worthiest knights in the realm, and chooses them to visit the Holy Land with him on a pilgrimage, in order to become familiar with the land prior to the intended Third Crusade. Returning in disguise from the pilgrimage, they insult a minstrel in a tavern. In retaliation, the minstrel (an Englishman who has recognized the king) visits Richard's enemy Modard, king of Almayn, and betrays Richard to him. Modard arrests and imprisons the three travelers. Challenged by Modard's arrogant son, Richard strikes the prince dead with a single blow of his fist. Modard wants Richard put to death, and sends a lion to kill him in his prison chamber. But Richard destroys the lion by reaching down its throat and pulling out its heart. He then carries the heart into Modard's hall and eats it raw before the king's eyes. Thus he earns his nickname, and Modard allows him to be ransomed.

Upon his return to England, Richard plans his crusade, and much of the poem is devoted to his exploits against the Saracens in the Holy Land. There are detailed descriptions of battles, as well as gruesome depictions of Richard's slaying of numerous Saracens, whose heads he cooks and dines upon with relish, serving them as well to visiting "pagan" ambassadors. In the romance, Richard is successful in conquering Babylon and Jaffa, and agrees to a three-year truce, after which the poem breaks off, unfinished.

The romance of *Richard Coeur de Lyon,* while popular in medieval England, is seldom read today: It is without merit as history, and is not a distinguished literary text, being in addition too grisly for most tastes. It has been suggested that the author was the same poet who wrote the contemporary romances *Of Arthour and of Merlin* and *King Alisaunder,* but there is no way to prove such a conjecture. Perhaps the most valuable impact of the poem is its influence on Sir Walter Scott's early 19th-century novel *The Talisman.*

Bibliography

Ambrisco, Alan S. "Cannibalism and Cultural Encounters in Richard Coeur de Lion," *Journal of Medieval and Early Modern Studies* 29 (1999): 499–528.

Broughton, Bradford B. *The Legends of King Richard I, Coeur de Lion: A Study of Sources and Variations to the Year 1600.* The Hague: Mouton, 1966.

Chapman, Robert L. "Notes on the Demon Queen Eleanor," *Modern Language Notes* (June 1995): 393–396.

Heng, Geraldine. "The Romance of England," in *The Postcolonial Middle Ages,* edited by Jeffrey Jerome Cohen. New York: St. Martin's Press, 2000, 132–172.

Richard the Lion-Hearted, and Other Medieval English Romances. Translated, edited, with an introduction by Bradford B. Broughton. New York: Dutton, 1966.

Richard the Redeles (ca. 1400)

Richard the Redeles (Richard the Unadvised) is a satirical ALLITERATIVE VERSE poem in MIDDLE ENGLISH dealing with the disastrous reign of King RICHARD II and his deposition by Henry IV in

1399. The poem, written in an East Midland dialect, emulates the style and some of the ideas of William LANGLAND's very popular poem, *PIERS PLOWMAN.* Indeed, in the single manuscript in which *Richard the Redeles* survives (Cambridge University Library MS LI iv 14), dating from the second quarter of the 15th century, it follows the B-text of *Piers Plowman* itself. The premise of the poem is that, first, Richard (at age 11) was too immature to have been thrust into the royal office, and that, second, he failed because of his lack of wise counsel from the poorly prepared upstart favorites with whom he surrounded himself. The poem seems intended as a book of "advice to princes," using the story of the misrule of Richard II as an exemplum as the poet makes his case for how current and future princes should rule.

The poem is divided into four passus, in the manner of *Piers,* though it is unclear whether the divisions are by the author or the scribe. Passus 1 begins as the Narrator declares his intent to write a treatise for Richard's benefit. He portrays himself in Christ Church in Bristol, where he claims to overhear people arguing the merits of Richard and of Henry. From this point, it is clear that the Narrator is a persona created by the poet, since the poem's references to events early in Henry IV's reign indicate that the poem was written well after Richard's deposition. The Narrator catalogues the myriad accusations against the king: Richard's disregard for law, and the fiscal irresponsibility (including waste and extravagance) of his court along with heavy taxation even in peacetime. He goes on to castigate the king specifically for the same abuses of which Parliament had accused him: appointing, and failing to correct or punish, unworthy advisers who failed to consider his people's welfare. In passus 2, the Narrator specifically condemns the manner in which Richard bestowed his livery of the "white hart" on his favorites. The bestowal of livery was a sign of the king's acceptance of these retainers into his "maintenance." Legally, this indicated that the king would support his retainers in all causes, including legal ones. Parliament had actually outlawed this custom in 1390, though the king continued the convention. In practice this led to serious abuses of the legal system by Richard's retainers. The Narrator speaks of the 1399 return from exile of Henry Bolingbroke (the future Henry IV), and of his welcome by the people as one who would redress these wrongs. The passus ends with the execution of three of Richard's closest advisers.

In passus 3, the poem (following no chronological order) deals with Richard's execution in 1397 of the duke of Gloucester, the earl of Arundel, and the earl of Warwick, three of the "Lords Appellant" who had been responsible for the acts of the "Merciless Parliament" that had executed Richard's closest supporters in 1388. Halfway through the passus, the poet turns his focus to Richard's unwise choices of counselors—young men who cared more for fashionable clothing than serious consideration of political problems. Passus 4 begins to describe a session of Parliament, satirically depicting Richard's last Parliament of 1398. The Narrator takes the opportunity to lament Richard's excessive taxation and to portray the incompetence of Parliament itself. After 93 lines, passus 4 breaks off, and the poem is apparently incomplete in the manuscript.

One of the strategies of the poem is the allegorical use of animal imagery, often based on the liveries or coats of arms of the major figures. Richard and his retainers are Harts. His uncle and chief of the Lords Appellant, the duke of Gloucester, is represented as the Swan, while Arundel is the Horse and Warwick the Bear. Henry Bolingbroke is variously the Eagle, the Falcon, or the Greyhound. This sort of beast ALLEGORY was not uncommon in such satirical poetry in the Middle Ages, and one of the things it suggested was the discrepancy between the events of human society and the laws of the natural world—that is, attention is drawn to the ways in which Richard has strayed from divinely ordained natural law. The commonwealth will prosper in ordered harmony only if the individuals in the commonwealth, most especially those in positions of power, rule by natural reason, what Langland had called "Kynde Wit" in *Piers Plowman.*

We know nothing of the anonymous author of *Richard the Redeles,* other than his familiarity with Langland's poem. His poem has often been linked with another alliterative satire in the tradition of *Piers Plowman* called *MUM AND THE SOTHSEGGER,* and at one time it was suggested that the two incomplete texts were in fact part of the same poem. Most scholars do not accept that connection any longer, though it has been recently suggested that the two poems are written by the same author, and that *Mum* is the later poem, in which the poet expands on the ideas he introduced in *Richard* (Barr 1993, 15–16). The poet does evince an intimate knowledge of the workings of Parliament and the events of the Shrewsbury Parliament of 1398. He is interested in legal matters and in the king's financial dealings, and he uses a good deal of legal vocabulary. Some scholars have suggested he may have been a clerk in the 1398 Parliament. It is unlikely that he was university-educated, and he seems not to have been a member of the clergy, for his political advice, though intended for Christian kings, is more practical than theoretically moral: The welfare of the commonwealth depends on mature, considered, wise counsel, and the king must surround himself with dependable, experienced, counselors—and listen to them.

Bibliography

Barr, Helen, ed. *The Piers Plowman Tradition: A Critical Edition of Pierce the Ploughman's Crede, Richard the Redeless, Mum and the Sothsegger, and The Crowned King.* London: J. M. Dent, 1993.

Eberle, Patricia J. "The Politics of Courtly Style at the Court of Richard II," in *The Spirit of the Court,* edited by Glyn S. Burgess and Robert A. Taylor. Cambridge: D. S. Brewer, 1985, 168–178.

Richard the Redeless and Mum and the Sothsegger. Edited by James M. Dean. Kalamazoo, Mich.: Medieval Institute Publications, 2000.

riddles (Old English riddles) (eighth–10th centuries)

Among the poems of the OLD ENGLISH collection known as the EXETER BOOK are some 95 short poems, all written in traditional Old English ALLITERATIVE VERSE, that take the form of riddles. They appear in three groups in the Exeter Book: Numbers 1–59 are preserved together; number 60, along with a second version of number 30, occurs later; and numbers 61–95 occur at the end of the manuscript. Related to the kind of "wisdom literature" common in Anglo-Saxon times, such as the GNOMIC VERSES also included in the Exeter Book, these riddles deal with a wide variety of subjects, from the natural world to the battlefield to the scriptorium to the kitchen and farmyard, and seem intended for a learned audience, though they do convey a kind of folk wisdom as well. As with most riddles worldwide, the solution to the riddle is an intellectual challenge, since in the riddle a subject is described in such a way that the different elements of the description might be referring to any number of subjects, but when completely put together make sense only when applied to one.

Though they were at one time attributed to CYNEWULF, the differences in tone, style, and subject matter have led modern scholars to conclude that the riddles were written by a variety of poets, probably over a long period of time. While it is difficult to date them with any precision, it is known that riddles were popular in English monasteries of the eighth century. Building on the 100 riddles or enigmas produced by the late classical poet Symphosius (ca. fourth century), the famous English scholar Aldhelm, bishop of Serborne, wrote in the late seventh century his own collection of 100 riddles in Latin, utilizing them chiefly for didactic purposes in a treatise on prosody. This was followed by a collection of 40 Latin riddles by Tatwine, archbishop of Canterbury in the early eighth century—a collection brought to the traditional 100 by 60 more riddles of "Eusebius," thought to be Hwætberht, abbot of Wearmouth and friend of the Venerable BEDE. Eusebius's riddles, like Aldhelm's, seem to have been intended for the classroom, as exercises for teaching grammar.

It seems likely that the Old English riddles were begun about this time. The 95 poems in the manuscript suggest that perhaps there was some attempt on the editor's part to assemble 100 riddles, as in the Latin collections, though the Old English poems differ from the Latin riddle collections significantly in their intent. There seems to be no didactic intent in the Old English riddles; rather the point seems to be entertainment and pure intellectual stimulation. Unlike the Latin enigma, the Old English riddles do not include titles containing the solution to the riddle. As a result, modern readers must puzzle over the riddle unaided. Indeed, in some cases, no solution has been found to these 1,100-year-old brainteasers. In the case of some of the later riddles there are problems because the manuscript has been damaged in its last pages. In any case, the precise relationship between the Latin and Old English riddles is unclear. Certainly the Latin texts influenced the English ones to some degree: Three riddles (on the "Bookworm," the "Reed-Pen," and the "Fish in the River") derive from Symphosius, and two others (on a "Coat of Mail" and on "Creation") are based on Aldhelm. But the majority of riddles seem to be independent productions.

Some of the Exeter Book riddles are in the first person—that is, the subject itself speaks; others are in the third person—the poem's speaker describes the subject from outside. Both types have formulaic beginnings and endings: A first-person riddle will begin with "I am . . ." and end with a challenge like "Say what I am called." The third-person riddle will begin with a phrase like "I saw . . ." and end with another kind of challenge, such as "Explain, if you can." Some of the riddles, such as number 42, on "The Cock and Hen," contain runes as clues to the poem's solution. Some, like number 12, on the Ox, include descriptions of the subject in various states of existence—in this case, the living ox and the uses of the dead ox's skin. Still other riddles are famous because of their double entendres, like number 25 on the Onion, number 61 on the Ornamented Shirt, and number 44 on the Key: Here, an apparently obscene description turns out, in the end, to be completely innocent.

Some of the riddles, finally, are indecipherable; others are so obscure or quirky that they are virtually impossible for most readers to decipher. Consider, for example, riddle number 85, wherein is described:

> *Two ears it had, and one eye solo,*
> *two feet and twelve hundred heads,*
> *back, belly, a brace of hands*
> *a pair of sides and shoulders and arms*
> *and one neck.*
>
> (Alexander 1966, 102)

It is unlikely that, without assistance, a typical reader would be able to identify the subject as a One-Eyed Garlic Seller.

Though amusement seems to be a major purpose of the riddles, they are also in general serious poetry. One like riddle number 1, on the Storm, is easily solved, but develops the theme at length in a stirring description. Even the briefest of riddles are related closely to the Old English poetic device of the KENNING, since the riddles are essentially extended metaphors with one term missing. They play with language in a variety of ways, and they force the reader to see the familiar through new eyes. As Andrew Welsh says, "the fundamental techniques of riddle making are also fundamental techniques of poetry making" (Welsh 1994, 104).

Bibliography

Adams, John F. "The Anglo-Saxon Riddle as Lyric Mode," *Criticism* 7 (1965): 335–348.

Alexander, Michael, trans. *The Earliest English Poems.* Harmondsworth, U.K.: Penguin, 1966.

Greenfield, Stanley B., and Daniel G. Calder. *A New Critical History of Old English Literature.* New York: New York University Press, 1986.

Hacikyan, Agop. *A Linguistic and Literary Analysis of Old English Riddles.* Montreal: Casalini, 1966.

Krapp, George Philip, and Elliott van Kirk Dobbie, eds. *The Exeter Book.* Anglo-Saxon Poetic Records, 3. New York: Columbia University Press, 1936.

Lendinara, Patrizia. "The World of Anglo-Saxon Learning." In *The Cambridge Companion to Old English Literature,* edited by Malcolm Godden and Michael Lapidge, 264–281. Cambridge: Cambridge University Press, 1991.

Nelson, Marie. "The Rhetoric of the Exeter Book Riddles," *Speculum* 49 (1974): 421–440.

Rinaldo d'Aquino (early 13th century)

Rinaldo d'Aquino was one of the poets of the "Sicilian school" of lyric poetry, a group associated with the Sicilian court of the Holy Roman Emperor, Frederick II, and responsible for introducing the conventions of the COURTLY LOVE lyric in the tradition of the Provençal TROUBADOURS into Italian vernacular poetry. Among his fellow poets were GIACOMO DA LENTINO and PIER DELLA VIGNA.

There is no consensus as to the identity of this poet. Three possible candidates with the name Rinaldo d'Aquino have been suggested. One was a page or a falconer in Frederick's household who eventually was granted a benefice in 1270. A second is mentioned in a document from 1242 where he is called *magister*, a title that would suggest he was an academic. The third candidate is the most interesting: The poet may have been the brother of St. Thomas AQUINAS, who, according to one story, kidnapped Thomas in about 1243 with the help of Pier della Vigna, and held him in the family castle of San Giovanni in an attempt to prevent Thomas from joining the Dominican order.

Whichever candidate was in fact the poet, he was admired if not for his innovation, at least for his deft handling of the conventional themes of the courtly tradition. Dante twice praises one of his *CANZONI* in *De VULGARI ELOQUENTIA*. Of Rinaldo's roughly dozen extant poems, perhaps his best-known is "Già mai non mi conforto," a Crusade song in the voice of a woman whose lover is leaving her to fight. The poem is simple, direct, and moving. Some critics have seen the influence of popular Italian lyrics in the poem. Here the speaker explores the irony of the cross as the symbol of her grief rather than her comfort:

The cross saves humanity
and makes me lose the way.
The cross fills me with grief,
I get no help
praying to God.
O pilgrim cross,
why have you destroyed me?

(Goldin 1973, 31, ll. 25–30)

Bibliography

Goldin, Frederick, trans. *German and Italian Lyrics of the Middle Ages: An Anthology and a History.* New York: Doubleday, 1973.

Jensen, Frede, ed. and trans. *The Poetry of the Sicilian School.* New York: Garland, 1986.

Riquier, Guiraut (ca. 1230–ca. 1300)

Guiraut Riquier is known as the last of the TROUBADOUR poets of southern France. Although, unlike the other better-known troubadours, Guiraut has no surviving *VIDA*, much of his biography can be inferred from his 89 extant lyrics. Born in Narbonne near the Spanish border, Guiraut seems to have spent much of his life searching for a generous patron.

One of Guiraut's earlier poems is *Ples de Tristor*, a *planh*, or lament, for Amalric IV, who was viscount of Narbonne until his death in 1270. It was perhaps after Amalric's death that Guiraut sought the patronage of the king of Castile, Alfonso el Sabio. In 1274, Guiraut addressed a letter to Alfonso, requesting better treatment for troubadours and JONGLEURS at court. Whether Alfonso responded or not we do not know. In any case, by 1279, Guiraut had left Castile and seems to have been in the service of Henry II, the count of Rodez. Although Guiraut probably made some later journeys, it is likely that he died in the vicinity of Rodez, probably some time near the end of the 13th century.

All of Guiraut's poems survive in a single manuscript, apparently based on his own manuscript copy. In his poems he satirizes the decadent nobility of his age, and longs for the poetic tradition of the past. He also is known for adapting some of the traditional images of the COURTLY LOVE tradition to poetry in praise of the Virgin Mary. Perhaps most remarkably, the music for some 48 of Guiraut's lyrics is extant. This is more than twice the number surviving from any other troubadour. Perhaps this is the result of his compiling his own manuscript copy of his poems.

Bibliography

Aubrey, Elizabeth. *The Music of the Troubadours.* Bloomington: Indiana University Press, 1996.

Bossy, M. A. "Cyclical Composition in Guiraut Riquier's Book of Poems," *Speculum* 66 (1991): 277–293.

Robert de Boron (fl. 1180–1190)

As in so many cases in the Middle Ages, practically nothing is known about this important Old French poet. Robert de Boron only mentions his own name and the name of a companion or his lord, Gautier de Montbéliard, in the epilogue to his *Joseph d'Arimathie* (Joseph of Arimathea), also called *Roman de l'estoire dou Graal* (ROMANCE of the quest of the Grail). Boron is located in northern Franche-Comté (south of Champagne and Alsace). Gautier is known to have gone on a Crusade in 1201, and stayed in Palestine until his death in 1212.

Robert composed his grail romance under the influence of CHRÉTIEN DE TROYES's *Conte du Graal* (The story of the Grail, also called PERCEVAL) sometime after 1180, but some scholars date the work to the early 1190s. *Joseph d'Arimathie* consists of 3,500 octosyllabic (eight-syllable) verses and relates the history of the HOLY GRAIL, connecting it with the Last Supper and Christ's descent from the cross. In particular here Joseph, one of Pontius Pilate's soldiers and a secret follower of Christ, is said to have collected Christ's blood and arranged the interment of the body. When Joseph is imprisoned because the body has vanished, Christ appears and comforts him with the holy vessel, the Grail. Joseph was the first to establish the motif of the Grail society and its function to send out representatives into the world to bring help wherever needed. Later Joseph's brother-in-law, Bron, the Rich Fisher, takes the Grail to England, which provides the narrative basis for the combination of the eucharistic character of the Grail with the world of King ARTHUR and the sorcerer Merlin. The only truly common element of Robert's romance and Chrétien's *Conte du Graal* consists of this figure, whom the latter calls *riche roi Pescheor* (rich Fisher King). Since clever business-oriented monks of Glastonbury claimed in 1191 that they had discovered King Arthur's grave *in valle Avaloniae juxta Glastoniam* ("in the vale of Avalon near Glastonbury"), Robert's reference to the "Vales of Avalon" to which the figure Petrus in his *Estoire* moves is often interpreted as an indication that the romance can be related to the area of Somerset. *Joseph d'Arimathie* concludes with some comments by the narrator about further adventures that he would relate in Latin if he were to find time.

Robert's romance has survived in only one manuscript (B.N. fr. 20047), which continues with a fragmentary text of a *Merlin* romance (504 verses). A later writer created a prose adaptation of *Joseph* where the history of the Grail and the history of Britain are intimately intertwined. This literary myth obviously appealed to the audience, demonstrated by 46 surviving manuscripts and some fragments. Two manuscripts contain a prose romance, the so-called *Didot-Perceval,* which draws from narrative allusions in Robert's *Joseph* and logically concludes the trilogy.

Robert was the first to inject Christian theology into the Grail myth, identifying the Grail with Christ's cup of the Last Supper and thus outlining the *translatio* (transfer) of the most sacred Christian reliquary to the medieval West. His greatest contribution to the history of Arthurian romance literature was that he inspired many subsequent writers of the VULGATE CYCLE to pursue the religious interpretation of the King Arthur and the Grail myth.

Bibliography

Bryant, Nigel, trans. *Merlin and the Grail: Joseph of Arimathea, Merlin, Perceval.* Cambridge: D. S. Brewer, 2001.

O'Gorman, Richard. "The Middle French Redaction of Robert De Boron's *Joseph d'Arimathie,*" *Proceedings of the American Philosophical Society* 122 (1978): 261–285.

———. "Robert de Boron's Joseph d'Arimathie and the Evolving Doctrine of the Immaculate Conception," *Romance Notes* 37, no. 1 (1996): 23–30.

Rittey, Joanne. *Amplification as Gloss in Two Twelfth-Century Texts: Robert de Boron's Joseph d'Arimathie and Renaut de Beaujeu's Li Biaus Descouneüs.* New York: Lang, 2002.

Robert de Boron. *Le roman du Graal.* Edited by Bernard Cerquiglini. Paris: Union Générale d'Editions, 1981.

Albrecht Classen

Robert of Gloucester (fl. 1260–1300)

Robert of Gloucester is credited with writing a late 13th-century MIDDLE ENGLISH verse chronicle of England that, in its full version, begins with the legendary founding of the island by Brutus and comes to an end with the death of Henry III and the ascension of Edward I in 1272. It is certain that at least three writers are responsible for the chronicle, which survives in two different versions, each with seven extant manuscripts. Robert was responsible probably only for the later material in the longer version of the text.

Some scholars have suggested that Robert was a secular clerk, partly because none of the 14 extant manuscripts of the chronicle appear to have been produced at a monastic scriptorium. Most scholars, however, assume that Robert was a monk at the monastery of St. Peter's in Gloucester, and that the text of the entire chronicle was ultimately compiled there. What is called the early version of the chronicle includes some 12,000 lines; the later or shorter version is 10,000 lines of verse. The author uses couplets of 14-syllable lines, with caesuras or breaks generally after the eighth syllable of each line.

Both versions of the chronicle begin with the text of an earlier, apparently anonymous chronicle starting with the story of Brutus and running through the death of King Henry I (1135). This portion of the text relies heavily on the pseudohistory of GEOFFREY OF MONMOUTH, and supplements this with information from the Latin history of HENRY OF HUNTINGDON. The chronicle spends a good deal of time on the story of King ARTHUR, and has the distinction of being the second text in English, after LAYAMON's *Brut,* to deal with the Arthurian story. In doing so, the writer seems to have made some use of Layamon's text as well, and appears to have had some acquaintance with Arthurian ROMANCES, since he emphasizes Sir GAWAIN as the flower of courtesy.

The portion of the text probably written by Robert of Gloucester is the continuation of the history after the death of Henry I, from the reign of King Stephen down through the death of Henry III, in the longer version of the text. This is the most significant portion of the chronicle, since it seems to contain firsthand accounts of some historical events, especially the town and gown riots that took place in Oxford in 1263, and the Battle of Evesham in 1265, at which Simon de Montfort was killed.

The shorter version of the history, which also begins with the reign of Stephen and ends with the ascension of Edward in 1272, appears to be by a different hand than Robert's longer text. It also adds some new material from Geoffrey of Monmouth and from Layamon to the earlier history.

The chronicle was popular through the Middle Ages and into the early modern period, and was widely influential on other historians through the 18th century. Its description of Simon de Montfort's death has been long admired, as has its loving praise of England. In addition to his chronicle, Robert of Gloucester was once proposed as the author of the SOUTH ENGLISH LEGENDARY, with which the chronicle has some stylistic and linguistic similarities, but that attribution is no longer seriously considered.

Bibliography

Gransden, Antonia. *Historical Writing in England, c. 550 to c. 1307.* London: Routledge and Kegan Paul, 1974.

Robert of Gloucester. *The Metrical Chronicle of Robert of Gloucester.* Edited by W. A. Wright. 2 vols. London: Eyre and Spottiswoode, 1887.

Robin Hood

With the possible exception of King ARTHUR, Robin Hood remains the most popular character from medieval English literature. Originally a mythological character connected with pre-Christian nature rites and folk dramas, the name became attached over the course of time to a variety of social conflicts. Although specific features of Robin Hood's character and even particular plot episodes have become fixed, the historical flexibility of his story has allowed the heroic outlaw to remain a "living" character long after the Middle Ages.

Robin Hood predates the written records of him. Many attempts have been made to identify a specific historic individual who inspired the legend, but there are too many candidates. Robert Hood was a fairly common name in medieval England, and legal records from the 13th century refer to several who ran afoul of the law. But the same records also report that "Robynhod" or "Hobbehod" was a surname in use at the time, suggesting that the character was even older and had become a sobriquet for outlaws or foresters. At the same time, hundreds of place names such as Robin Hood's Field or Robin Hood's Well are spread across the length and breadth of England, suggesting an early and broad distribution of the story.

Popular poems about Robin Hood are first mentioned in William LANGLAND'S ALLEGORICAL POEM *PIERS PLOWMAN*, written in the late 1370s. Langland's reference to "rymes of Robyn Hood" doesn't tell us much about the outlaw or the sorts of poems that were composed about him, but he was probably thinking of ballads like "Robin Hood and Guy of Gisbourne," "Robin Hood and the Monk," or "Robin Hood and the Potter," all of which survive in forms from about a century later. Since these poems were composed, memorized, and performed without being written down, they are probably much older than the surviving written copies but may also have changed frequently in ways that have not been preserved. The author of the *GEST OF ROBYN HODE*, a poem from the mid-15th century, appears to have woven together three or four independent poems in order to create a longer and more complex narrative about the outlaw.

These early ballads are vigorous and violent. Not only men at arms, but monks, a page boy, and the sheriff of Nottingham are killed, and the bounty hunter Guy of Gisbourne is grotesquely disfigured. Robin Hood waylays the rich and takes their money, but he does not pass it on to the poor. Rather he embodies the freedom, solidarity, fidelity, and hospitality of the Greenwood, the imagined arboreal refuge from the social economy of town, court, and church. Robin is generous to his companions, devoted to the Virgin Mary, and keeps his word rigorously. All of this puts him at odds with the sheriff and various members of the clergy, who exploit the law to enrich and empower themselves. The goal in these early poems is to embarrass these authorities of state and church and to preserve the outlaw's own skin, although Robin himself is not immune from making mistakes and requiring the help of his men, especially Little John, to restore his fortunes.

The dramatic action of the ballads has a clear affinity with performance. It is difficult to determine, however, which came first, the poem or the play. Performances of Robin Hood plays and games and festivals are recorded widely across England and Scotland in the 15th and 16th centuries and surely represent a much older tradition. These were originally connected with midsummer celebrations of the seasonal cycle and the new genesis of flocks and crops. Prominent members of the community underwrote the performances, and the festivals were frequently used to raise funds for parish expenses. The papers of the Paston family of Norfolk from 1473 refer to a servant who played the part of Robin Hood (*see* PASTON LETTERS).

Only a few "scripts" of these dramas survive. One, referred to as "Robin Hood and the Sheriff," seems to tell the same story found in the ballad "Robin Hood and Guy of Gisbourne." This text consists of 24 lines of dialogue without stage directions and, in fact, without even a clear indication of who is speaking. This text suggests that the chief interest in this drama was the sword fighting, wrestling, shooting, and throwing, and the actors had a great deal of freedom in choreographing this physical action. Indeed the violence and the antiauthoritarian character of the outlaw also led the plays to be condemned by churchmen and eventually to be banned.

From an early date, historians made an attempt to place Robin Hood at a particular point in English history. The plays and ballads are almost silent about Robin's historical situation, but the *Gest of Robyn Hode* places him in the reign of "Edward oure comely kyng," probably Edward III (1327–77). Early chroniclers, however, worked the outlaw into their historical narratives. Andrew of Wyntoun wrote in his *Orygynale Chronicle* (ca. 1420) that in 1283 Little John and Robin Hood were living in Inglewood, a royal forest near Carlisle, and Barnsdale. This is substantially earlier than the period suggested by the *Gest*, but coincides with the rebellion of William Wallace and a period of antiauthoritarian feeling in Scotland. One hundred years later, another Scottish historian, John Major, placed Robin Hood in the historical situation where he is most often depicted now, the 1190s. This shifted the outlaw's activity to a period when the king, RICHARD I, was absent and the authority of the ruler, John, was questionable.

Major's dating also allowed later writers to make social conflict between Saxons and Normans a central issue of the Robin Hood story as well. Of course none of these dates have historical grounding, but they reveal a consistent desire to make Robin Hood real and to make his rebellious actions historically understandable.

Of course the story of Robin Hood has continued to grow and adapt after the Middle Ages. During the 17th century, several writers created entire biographies of the hero, some including elaborate genealogies to verify his historical existence. Late in the 18th century, the medieval ballads were rediscovered as part of nationalist and romantic movements, and Robin Hood was reconceived as representative of both Englishness and egalitarianism. In the 20th century, television and film have recognized the dramatic potential in Robin Hood and adapted him to embody freedom versus fascism, communalism versus corporate greed, individual conscience versus organized religion, and other social and cultural issues. Because he has proved to be such a resilient character, consistently appealing and continually adapting, Robin Hood remains a vital figure in the cultural imagination nearly 1,000 years after his first appearance.

Bibliography

Dobson, R. B., and J. Taylor, eds. *Rymes of Robin Hood: An Introduction to the English Outlaw.* 3rd ed. Stroud: Sutton, 1997.

Fowler, David C. *A Literary History of the Popular Ballad.* Durham, N.C.: Duke University Press, 1968.

Gray, Douglas. "The Robin Hood Poems," in *Robin Hood: Anthology of Scholarship and Criticism,* edited by Stephen Knight. Cambridge: Brewer, 1999, 3–37.

Holt, J. C. *Robin Hood.* 2nd ed. London: Thames and Hudson, 1990.

Knight, Stephen. *Robin Hood: A Complete Study of the English Outlaw.* Oxford, U.K.: Blackwell, 1994.

———. *Robin Hood: A Mythic Biography.* Ithaca, N.Y.: Cornell University Press, 2003.

Knight, Stephen, and Thomas Ohlgren, eds. *Robin Hood and Other Outlaw Tales.* Kalamazoo, Mich.: Medieval Institute Publications, 1997.

Matthews, John. *Robin Hood: Green Lord of the Wildwood.* Glastonbury, U.K.: Gothic Image, 1993.

Potter, Lois, ed. *Playing Robin Hood: The Legend and Performance in Five Centuries.* Newark: University of Delaware Press, 1998.

Wiles, David. *The Early Plays of Robin Hood.* Cambridge: Brewer, 1981.

Timothy S. Jones

Rolle, Richard (Richard Hermit of Hampole) (ca. 1300–1349)

The first of the great English mystical writers of the 14th century was the hermit Richard Rolle of Hampton. A prolific writer in both Latin and English, both poetry and prose, Rolle was renowned in his own day and immediately after his death for his pious life and stature as a spiritual adviser. Criticized by many for his intemperate attitude toward his detractors, his disregard of papal authority, and his impetuous nature, Rolle was also admired for his passionate descriptions of the mystical experience of God and the lyric presentation of the suffering of Christ.

Rolle was born in about the year 1300 in Thornton Dale, near Pickering in Yorkshire. His parents gave him his early education, after which he was sent to Oxford by Thomas Neville, who was Lord of Raby and later Archdeacon of Durham. But Rolle, anxious for the life of a hermit, left Oxford at the age of 18 without taking any degree or minor orders. It was once believed that he later spent time studying at the Sorbonne, but this has been discredited. For some time he lived in the woods near his home at Thornton, where he adopted a hermit's garb made up of two of his sister's gowns and his father's rain hood.

On the eve of the Feast of the Assumption, probably in 1326, Rolle wandered into a chapel in a village near Thornton, where, after spending the night keeping vigil, he preached a sermon at Mass the following morning. It was apparently a very effective sermon, and one of the parishioners present for it was John de Dalton, bailiff of Pickering. Dalton was so moved by Rolle's sermon that he became his patron, providing him with a suitable habit and a private cell in Dalton's own home.

In his private cell, Rolle was able to devote himself freely to meditation, contemplative prayer, and writing. After several years he seems to have had something of a falling out with Dalton. In any case he left his cell there and began a life of wandering, eventually settling at Hampole, near the Yorkshire town of Dorcaster. Here he settled as a hermit in a cell in the woods near a nunnery. The rest of his life was spent meditating, writing, and acting as spiritual adviser to the Cistercian nuns in the house near his cell, and to an anchoress (a female contemplative shut away from the world) named Margaret Kirkby who had a cell nearby in Anderby. It was in Hampole that Rolle died, tradition says on Michaelmas (September 29) in 1349. Since this was the time of the BLACK DEATH in Yorkshire, it is likely that Rolle died of the plague.

After his death a cult grew around Rolle, particularly among the nuns of the neighboring convent, extolling his visionary writings and his virtue as a spiritual mentor. The nuns even put together a legend of his life, in preparation for his becoming a saint; however, he was never canonized. It is likely that one of the things that kept Rolle from such consideration was his tendency to lash out in his writings at anyone who disagreed with him or questioned his vocation. He called such people his "persecutors," and his defensiveness often reads as anticlericalism, anti-intellectualism, and sheer arrogance. Later English mystical writers, including Walter HILTON and the anonymous author of *The CLOUD OF UNKNOWING,* were wary of Rolle's writings, and considered him to be an immature and undisciplined thinker whose observations were not likely to be helpful as spiritual guides.

At his best, however, Rolle gives dramatic descriptions of mystical experience. His best-known text is probably the Latin tract *Incendium amoris,* or "The fire of love." Here, against his detractors, Rolle writes a defense of his life as a solitary hermit. But he also describes how his persistent solitary prayer, after a period of many years, ultimately resulted in his mystical experience of God. He describes this in three stages, which he calls *calor* (warmth), a heat that consumed his heart in love; *dulcor* (sweetness), a sweetness that engulfed his entire being; and *canor* (melody), divine melodies that he alone could hear from the throne of God.

In addition to his Fire of Love, Rolle wrote a 10,000-line English poem, probably for Margaret Kirkby, called "The Pricke of Conscience." In its seven books, Rolle discusses the trials of earthly life as well as the soul's fate after death. Rolle also wrote a commentary on the Psalms, several lyric poems among which the best known is "A Song of the Love of Jesus," and in 1348, shortly before his death, a treatise on disciplined spiritual life called "The Form of Perfect Living."

Role's passionate spirituality, his focus on the love of Christ and on the experience of unity as a gift of God's grace, and his pioneering use of English as a language of contemplative literature make Rolle one of the most important formative stimuli on the flowering mystical tradition in late medieval England.

Bibliography

Horstmann, Carl, ed. *Yorkshire Writers: Richard Rolle of Hampole and His Followers.* Rochester, N.Y.: University of Rochester Press, 1999.

Knowlton, Sr. Mary Arthur. *The Influence of Richard Rolle and of Julian of Norwich on the Middle English Lyrics.* The Hague: Mouton and Co., 1973.

Rolle, Richard. *The English Writings.* Edited and translated by Rosamund S. Allen. Classics of Western Spirituality Series. New Jersey: Paulist Press, 1999.

———. *The Fire of Love.* Translated by Clifton Wolters. London: Penguin Books, 1972.

———. *Prose and Verse.* S. J. Ogilvie-Thomson, ed. London: EETS/Oxford University Press, 1988.

Watson, Nicholas. *Richard Rolle and the Invention of Authority.* Cambridge Studies in Medieval Literature 13. Cambridge: Cambridge University Press, 1991.

romance (chivalric romance)

The chivalric romance was the most popular literary form of the later European Middle Ages. The term *romance* originally referred to anything written in the Old French language, thus categorizing it as composed in a language derived from Latin, or "Roman," rather than something in Latin itself.

Eventually the term came to refer to a particular kind of story—one concerned with courtly knights who, motivated by love or by religious fervor, went in search of adventure. Romance plots almost always involve a quest, in which a single knight sets forth to accomplish some task—to rescue a lady in distress, to answer a question, to meet an opponent's challenge, to obey his Lord's command, or to seek an artifact like the HOLY GRAIL. On the journey, the knight meets with numerous adventures, sometimes completely unrelated to the quest. Ultimately he achieves the quest and his honor and worth as a knight is established, or renewed.

The romance was established as a distinct genre in the mid-12th century, particularly with the works of CHRÉTIEN DE TROYES and MARIE DE FRANCE. Romances quickly replaced in popularity the older CHANSONS DE GESTE, with their epic and heroic values, by presenting more fashionable and contemporary chivalric protagonists. Whereas the epic stressed the virtues of strength, courage, loyalty to one's Lord, and a simple Christian piety, the romance added the importance of courtly manners and behavior as a sign of genuine nobility. The epic focused on war and on the fate of nations; the romance was more often concerned with COURTLY LOVE and with the fate of the individual hero. The epic plot was simple and straightforward, while the plot of romances was often episodic and even rambling. The epic hero was almost always static; the romance hero was dynamic—his quest was often ultimately a quest for his own identity, since in achieving the quest he established his name. Character is presented through action and dialogue in the epic, while in romance characters are presented as having an interior life and engage in interior monologues to an extent that does not occur in earlier literature. Further, romances display a fascination with magic and a sense of wonder and fantasy that is absent from the epic, which deals with the supernatural only in the form of God or the gods.

Medieval romances have traditionally been categorized according to their subject matter. Some romances, especially in France, built on the earlier CHARLEMAGNE legends made popular by the chansons de geste. The well-known romances of *FERUMBRAS* and *VALENTIN ET ORSON* are examples of these. This narrative material is generally referred to as the "matter of France." Classical history and literature provided another major source for narrative romance, in particular the legends of ALEXANDER THE GREAT and the myths surrounding the siege of Thebes (like CHAUCER's *KNIGHT'S TALE*) and the Trojan War (including Chaucer's great romance *TROILUS AND CRISEYDE*). Since most medieval knowledge of Greek culture came through classical Latin sources, this legendary material was known collectively as the "matter of Rome." In England, a group of romances grew up around traditional English heroes and older Germanic legends, including romances like *KING HORN*, *GUY OF WARWICK*, and *HAVELOCK THE DANE*. This legendary stock came to be called the "matter of England."

But by far the most popular material for romance, the source from which Chrétien de Troyes drew his initial inspiration, is traditional Celtic lore, or the "matter of Britain." This material comprises the legends of King ARTHUR and his knights of the Round Table, and includes the exploits of Sir LANCELOT, whose love for Arthur's Queen Guenevere is the subject of one of Chrétien's earliest romances. Arthurian romances incorporate as well the adventures of Sir GAWAIN, the most popular knight in MIDDLE ENGLISH romances, including the highly admired *SIR GAWAIN AND THE GREEN KNIGHT*, and those of Sir PERCEVAL and Sir GALAHAD, whose quest leads them to the Holy Grail. Sir TRISTAN, once a Celtic legend in his own right and hero of his own romances, most notably that of the German poet GOTTFRIED VON STRASSBURG, ultimately becomes associated with the court of King Arthur as well, and by the time of Sir Thomas MALORY's 15th-century compilation of Arthurian lore, *Le MORTE DARTHUR*, is himself a knight of the Round Table.

The romance genre had spread into Germany by the last years of the 12th century, and into Italy, Spain, and even Scandinavia by later in the Middle Ages. The earliest romances in English appeared in the 13th century, and flourished by the 14th and 15th centuries. Most romances are in verse, though prose romances began to appear in France in the

13th century, the most notable being those included in the VULGATE CYCLE of Arthurian romances. In English, romances might be composed in ALLITERATIVE VERSE, in rhymed couplets similar to the French, or in six- or 12-line units that came to be known as TAIL-RHYME stanzas. The romance continued to thrive well into the 16th century, until the genre was disparaged by Renaissance humanists and lampooned in Cervantes's *Don Quixote.*

Bibliography

Bruckner, Matilda Tomaryn. *Shaping Romance: Interpretation, Truth, and Closure in Twelfth-Century French Fictions.* Philadelphia: University of Pennsylvania Press, 1993.

Green, D. H. *The Beginnings of Medieval Romance: Fact and Fiction, 1150–1220.* Cambridge: Cambridge University Press, 2002.

Ker, W. P. *Epic and Romance: Essays on Medieval Literature.* 1897. New York: Dover Publications 1957.

Krueger, Roberta L. *The Cambridge Companion to Medieval Romance.* Cambridge: Cambridge University Press, 2000.

Loomis, Robert Sherman. *The Development of Arthurian Romance.* New York: Norton, 1963.

Roman de la Rose Guillaume de Lorris and Jean de Meun (first part, ca. 1237; second part, ca. 1264–1274)

GUILLAUME DE LORRIS (fl. 1220–40) created the first part of the *Roman de la Rose,* leaving it unfinished by ca. 1237. JEAN DE MEUN (ca. 1235/40–1305) continued the fragment by ca. 1264, and completed this first major allegorical verse ROMANCE in Old French several years later. Guillaume's portion consists of 4,058 verses, followed by a brief conclusion of 78 verses composed by an anonymous poet. Jean de Meun's portion includes a total of 17,721 verses and offers a much more satirical, at times more realistic treatment of the theme, concluding with a very graphic description of the sexual act. Guillaume develops a beautiful dream allegory in which a young man (the Lover, or the *Amant*), once he has become a servant of the God of Love, shyly attempts to win the Rose hidden in a garden, but he faces many forces resisting his efforts, such as Pride, Villainy, Shame, Despair, and Faithlessness. This portion of the *Roman de la Rose* proves to be a virtual *Ars d'Amors* (or Art of love, v. 28), based on a deep psychological understanding of courtly love. Jean, on the other hand, utilizes this allegorical framework to explore the whole gamut of human emotions involved in erotic passion, and many general philosophical issues as well. Jean examines, above all, the conflicts between love and reason, between free will and destiny, and the conflict between art and nature; then he discusses the impact of the stars on human life, the role of (mis)fortune, and man's inability to control it—a direct reflection of BOETHIUS's *De consolatione philosophiae* (*CONSOLATION OF PHILOSOPHY*)—and the depravity of human society, which regularly breaks the rules of nature. But then he also investigates the properties of glasses and mirrors, among other issues. At the end the Lover succeeds, with the help of False Seeming, a go-between (Duenna), Venus, Genius, and the God of Love, to break down all barriers, to win the Rose, and to deflower her, but there is no more word of love; instead the entire quest suddenly appears to have been completely sex-driven. Unabashedly the Lover admits that he entirely forgot the recommendations by Reason and that sexuality will always triumph over all religious and philosophical teachings. Once the Lover has awakened from his dream, the *Roman* comes to an abrupt end.

The *Roman de la Rose* was one of the most popular literary texts from the entire Middle Ages, as documented by the vast number of manuscripts (more than 250). In fact no other medieval secular literary text has survived in so many manuscripts. There are also countless literary adaptations, translations into English, Dutch, Italian, and possibly also into German (Hugo von Montfort [1357–1423]), and early-modern printed editions in the 15th and 16th centuries. Most manuscripts are lavishly illuminated and offer beautiful full-page miniatures. A majority also contain rubrics, sometimes in rhymed couplets, helping the reader to follow the thematic and narrative development. The enormous appeal exerted by the *Roman* is also indicated by the numerous marginal glosses and annotations in the various manuscripts.

Gui de Mori created a remarkable revision, or *remaniement,* of the text in the late 13th century, suppressing the allusions to pagan mythology, adding more didacticism, and developing a more straightforward narrative sequence. Both Jean Molinet (1433–1507) and Clément Marot (ca. 1496–1544) published a prose version each, transforming the original theme of foolish (earthly) love into an allegory of divine love. The *Roman de la Rose* gained the most attention when in 1401 CHRISTINE DE PIZAN (ca. 1364–ca. 1430) entered a public debate about the text's intrinsic values and protested against its misogynistic orientation. Her opponents were high-ranking personalities, such as the royal secretaries Jean de Montreuil and Pierre and Gontier Col, whereas the chancellor of the University of Paris, Jean Gerson, supported Christine's criticism of the *Roman* and published vitriolic sermons against the *Roman de la Rose.*

Many of the most famous late-medieval poets such as DANTE, BOCCACCIO, GUILLAUME DE MACHAUT, Geoffrey CHAUCER, John GOWER, Thomas HOCCLEVE, John LYDGATE, Thomas USK, Gavin DOUGLAS, and Jean FROISSART were deeply influenced by the *Roman.* Others composed imitations, such as the anonymous author of *Echecs amoureux* (late 14th century), for which Evrart de Conty provided an extensive prose commentary (ca. 1400). Most 15th-century French poets indicated their thorough familiarity with the *Roman de la Rose* through references and allusions to the verse narrative, truly a milepost of medieval French literature.

Bibliography

Arden, Heather. *The Romance of the Rose.* Boston: Twayne, 1987.

Brownlee, Kevin, and Sylvia Huot. *Rethinking the "Romance of the Rose": Text, Image, Reception.* Philadelphia: University of Pennsylvania Press, 1992.

Classen, Albrecht. "Hugo von Montfort: A Reader of the *Roman de la Rose,*" *Monatshefte* 83, no. 4 (1991): 414–432.

Dahlberg, Charles, trans. *The Romance of the Rose.* Princeton, N.J.: Princeton University Press, 1971.

Fleming, John F. *The Roman de la Rose: A Study in Allegory and Iconography.* Princeton, N.J.: Princeton University Press, 1969.

Guillaume de Lorris and Jean de Meun. *Le roman de la Rose.* Edited by Félix Lecoy. 3 vols. Paris: Champion, 1965–1970.

Nouvet, Claire. "Reversing Mirror: *Guillaume* de Lorris' *Romance of* the *Rose,*" in *Translatio Studii. Essays by His Students in Honor of Karl D. Uitti for His Sixty-Fifth Birthday.* Edited by Renate Blumenfeld-Kosinski, Kevin Brownlee, Mary B. Speer, and Lori J. Walters. Amsterdam: Rodopi, 2000, 89–205.

Robbins, Harry W. *The Romance of the Rose.* New York: E. P. Dutton, 1962.

White, Hugh. *Nature, Sex, and Goodness in a Medieval Literary Tradition.* Oxford: Oxford University Press, 2000.

Albrecht Classen

Roman de Renart (ca. 1174–1250)

Despite its title, the *Roman de Renart* represents only an agglomeration of episodic narratives. They have been preserved in 26 branches composed by more than 20 different authors between 1174 and 1250. The *Roman* has survived in 13 major manuscripts, all of which tell the basic tale of the fox Renart as an incredibly witty and resourceful protagonist who is constantly looking for sexual adventures and food and ruthlessly takes whatever he can find, easily triumphing over such opponents as Tibert the cat, Chantecler the rooster, and Tiecelin the crow. One of Renart's victories is the rape of the she-wolf Hersent, which leads to the perennial enmity between the wolf Isengrin and the fox Renart. The king of the animals, the lion Noble, summons Renart to court, but the fox always outsmarts everyone and comes out of the trial as the king's most favored subject. Each branch of these narratives adds and expands on the original account, but the overall design remains the same. Some of the most important branches are *Branches* 6, (the judicial duel between Reynart and Isengrin), 8 (the pilgrimage of the animals), and 10 (the cure of the lion).

Renart incorporates the most basic instincts in man, and he pursues them with a vengeance, living out his dreams of uninhibited sexuality, violence, and accumulation of wealth. By the same token, Renart demonstrates extraordinary skills in assuming varying roles and masks that allow him to transgress all social norms and taboos. Although the *Roman* situates the events in the world of animals, the narratives are clearly meant as critical allusions to the world of feudalism. Curiously, however, although Renart's brutal behavior ought to raise a sense of outrage and disgust, all branches of the *Roman* contain strong elements of humor, and the fox's witty maneuvers to outsmart his mostly evil-minded and mean-spirited opponents prove to be hilarious and impressive. Often the reader/listener feels forced to sympathize with the protagonist who only pursues his simple drive for sexual fulfillment and wants to meet his basic need for food and drink. Ultimately, despite his mostly "criminal" behavior, Renart demonstrates that life and nature are the strongest forces in this world, and that social norms often tend to serve only the interests of special groups whose power is regularly undermined by the fox's operations. Significantly, whereas Renart seems to break the laws all the time, his opponents do not demonstrate any better moral and ethical principles and often prove to be nothing but vengeful, stupid, and gullible enemies. Although the fox often victimizes the other animals—the wolf above all—the audience hardly ever feels sympathy with them and cheers Renart's triumphs over the evil and mighty ones in this world. Undoubtedly the many different authors and adaptors of the *Roman de Renart* intended to ironize and satirize the contemporary courtly culture, and they revealed its material underpinnings in an almost grotesque, but certainly highly hilarious, manner.

The earliest versions of the *Roman* were composed by clerics, a few of whom we know by name: Pierre de Saint-Cloud, Richard de Lison, and the priest of La Croix-en-Brie. They obviously drew much material from classical antiquity and the early-medieval literature (Aesop's fables in prose and verse; *Ecbasis captivi,* and Magister Nivardus's *Ysengrimus,* the latter two from the middle of the 12th century). But there are also obvious literary parallels to the TRISTAN material, to MARIE DE FRANCE'S *LAIS,* and reminiscences of the *Mort Artu.*

Many of the branches change the structure and material of earlier branches, so the *Roman de Renart* really represents a large corpus of texts that were constantly rewritten. The *Roman* was adapted for their own purposes by late-medieval French poets such as RUTEBEUF (*Rénart le bétourné*), the anonymous author of the 13th-century *Couronnement de Renart,* Jacquemart Gielée (*Renart le nouvel,* late 13th century), the Priest of Troyes (*Renart le contrefait,* two redactions, 1319–28), and Jean Tenessax (*Livre de maistre Renart,* 15th century). The *Roman de Renart* was also translated into many other European languages. A Latin version by Balduinus (*Reinardus Vulpes*) appeared before 1280. The Alsatian poet Heinrich der Glîchezâre composed a Middle High German verse epic, *Reinhart Fuchs,* by the late 12th century. The poet Arnout-Willem created a Flemish version ca. 1250 (*Van den vos Reynaerde*), which was reworked in a western Flemish version ca. 1375. Geoffrey CHAUCER drew his material for *The NUN'S PRIEST'S TALE* (ca. 1387) from the French source, followed by Hinrek van Alkmar's Dutch translation in 1480, and an English translation published by William CAXTON in 1481. A Low German version appeared in 1498 (*Reinke de Vos*), which in turn was translated into High German in 1650, and many times thereafter. Numerous new editions and translations have been published since then, the most famous being, perhaps, Johann Christoph Gottsched's *Reineke Fuchs* (1752) and Johann Wolfgang von Goethe's hexametric (six-foot line) verse epic *Reineke Fuchs* (1794) with its satirical allusion to the French Revolution.

Bibliography

Owen, D. D. R., trans. *The Romance of Reynard the Fox.* Oxford, U.K.: Oxford University Press, 1995.

Varty, Kenneth, ed. *Reynard the Fox: Cultural Metamorphoses and Social Engagement in the Beast Epic from the Middle Ages to the Present.* New York: Berghahn Books, 2000.

———. *The Roman de Renart: A Guide to Scholarly Work.* Lanham, Md.: Scarecrow Press, 1998.

Albrecht Classen

rondeau (roundel)

The rondeau began as one of the fixed forms of French lyric poetry characterized by the use of repetition and only two rhymes, as discussed by GUILLAUME DE MACHAUT in the *Remède de Fortune* (ca. 1340) and EUSTACHE DESCHAMPS in *Art de dictier* (1392). Machaut's rondeaux, like most earlier lyrics, were set to music.

The form generally was a vehicle for the expression of the conventional sentiments of *fin amor*, or COURTLY LOVE, though it was also adopted by church musicians for spiritual purposes.

Most often the literary rondeau consisted of 15 lines (either octosyllabic or decasyllabic) divided into three sections—a quintet, quatrain, and sestet. The first line of the poem also serves as a refrain and is repeated as the last line of the second and third sections of the poem, so that the typical rhyme scheme is *aabba aabR aabbaR* (where *R* is the refrain).

CHAUCER introduced the form into English poetry (as he introduced the French courtly tradition into English in general). He mentions in the prologue to the *LEGEND OF GOOD WOMEN* that in his youth he had written "many an ympne for [the God of Love's] halydayes,/Than highten balades, roundels, virelayes" (Benson 1987, 600, F 422–23). His best-known example of what he calls a "roundel" is the concluding lyric of *The PARLIAMENT OF FOWLS:*

Now welcome somer, with thy sonne softe
That hast thes winters wedres overshake,
And driven away the longe nyghtes blake!

Saynt Valentyn, that art ful hy on-lofte,
Thus syngen smale foules for thy sake;
Now welcome, somer, with thy sonne
  softe,
That hast thes wyntres wedres overshake.

Wel han they cause for to gladden ofte,
Sith ech of hem recovered hath hys make,
Ful blissbul mowe they synge when they
  wake:
Now welcome, somer, with thy sonne softe,
That hast thes winters wedres overshake,
And driven away they longe nyghtes blake!

(Benson, 394, ll. 680–92)

Note that in Chaucer's handling of the form, the three parts have three, four, and six lines, and the refrain consists of the first two lines for part 2, and the entire first section for part 3, so that the rhyme scheme (still consisting of two rhymes) is *abb abAB abbABB*. Another lyric generally attributed to Chaucer, "Merciles Beaute," is a triple roundel in precisely the same form.

Bibliography

Benson, Larry, et al., ed. *The Riverside Chaucer.* 3rd ed. Boston: Houghton Mifflin, 1987.

Rudel, Jaufré (fl. 1125–1148)

Jaufré Rudel was one of the earliest TROUBADOURS, composers of love songs in the vernacular Provençal language of southern France. He seems to have been a nobleman, and tradition says he was lord of Blaye. Only seven of his songs survive, and in them he created the persona of the hopeless lover whose lady is unattainable, a persona that became so conventional that it turned into cliché in the late medieval courtly love tradition.

Next to nothing is known of Jaufré's biography. Certain details have been gleaned from his poetry, but none of these has any real evidence to support it. He is believed to have joined the Second Crusade in 1147, mainly because in one of his poems, Jaufré says that he intends to do so. MARCABRU addresses one of his songs to "Lord Jaufré Rudel beyond the sea," which also indicates that he had made a journey, most likely on a crusade.

In the *VIDA*, or short biography of Rudel that was written toward the end of the 13th century, the famous story of his love for the lady of Tripoli appears. According to the *vida,* Jaufré heard so many good things about the countess of Tripoli from pilgrims returning from Antioch that he fell in love with her without ever having seen her. He wrote many love songs to her, and purely out of a burning desire to see her he joined a crusade and crossed the sea. But he became so ill during the journey that he was nearly dead when he arrived in Tripoli. He was taken to an inn, and his story was told to the Countess. She came to see him and took him in her arms, whereupon he recovered enough to thank God for giving him the joy of seeing her; then he died in her arms. He was buried with great honor by the Templars, and the lady became a nun out of grief for her lover's death.

There is no reason to believe that any part of the *vida* is true, since all such *vidas* were written well after the deaths of their subjects and their stories gleaned not from facts but legends that had grown out of images in the poems. But the romantic idea of the distant lover is one that Jaufré cultivates in his poetry, as he does, for example, in the first stanza of his best-known poem, *Lanquan li jorn son lonc en may,* where the new season of spring fails to lift the poet's mood because he is so far from his lady:

When days are long in May,
I enjoy the sweet song of the birds far away,
And when I am parted from their song,
And parting reminds me of a love far away:
I go bent with desire, head bowed down;
Then neither the song nor the hawthorn's flower
Pleases me more than the winter's ice.

(Goldin 1973, 105, ll. 1–7)

Bibliography

Goldin, Frederick, ed. and trans. *Lyrics of the Troubadours and Trouverès: An Anthology and a History.* Garden City, N.Y.: Doubleday, 1973.

Pickens, Rupert T. *The Songs of Jaufré Rudel.* Studies and Texts, 41. Toronto: Pontifical Institute of Mediaeval Studies, 1978.

Wolf, George, and Roy Rosenstein, eds. *The Poetry of Cercamon and Jaufre Rudel.* Garland Library of Medieval Literature, 5. New York: Garland, 1983.

Ruin, The (10th century)

The Ruin, a brief OLD ENGLISH poem found in the 10th-century collection known as the EXETER BOOK, is an unusual poem in the Old English canon: Rather than presenting a dramatic situation or a focus on the narrator's condition, the speaker of *The Ruin* presents a meditation on the crumbling walls of an ancient Roman city.

Although the text is badly damaged by a fire, the lines that survive skillfully create the melancholy mood associated with Old English ELEGAIC POETRY. In this case the loss mourned is the general loss of human civilization ravaged by time. The subject of the poem is likely the Roman city of Bath in England. As the Anglo-Saxons generally did, the speaker refers to the stone works of the Romans as "the work of the Giants." The Saxons did not build with stone, but even the Romans, the speaker muses, had passed into nothingness, and these wasted ruins are all that is left. Where are they who built the walls, the speaker asks:

Earthgrip holds them—gone, long gone,
fast in gravesgrasp while fifty fathers
and sons have passed.

(Alexander 1966, 30)

Although at 45 lines *The Ruin* is one of the shorter Old English elegies, it remains, nevertheless, one of the most moving.

Bibliography

Alexander, Michael, trans. *The Earliest English Poems.* Harmondsworth, U.K.: Penguin, 1966.

Krapp, George Philip, and Elliott Van Kirk Dobbie, eds. *The Exeter Book.* The Anglo-Saxon Poetic Records, 3. New York: Columbia University Press, 1936.

Renoir, Alain. "The Old English 'Ruin': Contrastive Structure and Affective Impact," in *Old English Elegies: New Essays in Criticism and Research,* edited by Martin Green. Rutherford, N.J.: Fairleigh Dickinson University Press, 1983, 148–173.

Ruiz, Juan (ca. 1283–ca. 1350)

While his work, the *Libro de buen Amor* (*BOOK OF GOOD LOVE*), is perhaps the most important long poetic text surviving from medieval Spain, Juan Ruiz remains a mystery, our only knowledge of him coming from certain autobiographical portions of his text. A miscellany of 12 poems, each focused on a different love affair, the *Book of Good Love* comprises fables, picaresque adventures in the first person, adaptations of Arab and classical tales, anticlerical satire, religious poems, and a vivid depiction of daily life in medieval Spain. For the variety, realism, and the earthiness of his work, Ruiz has sometimes been called "the Spanish CHAUCER."

According to his text, Ruiz was born in Alcalá de Henares, and was educated in Toledo. Here he likely became acquainted with the Muslim culture that profoundly influenced his book. He became a cleric and wrote lyrics to be sung by JONGLEURS. He is believed to have written the first version of his great work by 1330 while serving as archpriest in the village of Hita, some 30 miles east of his hometown of Alcalá. However, for some reason he ran afoul of his superior Gil de Albornoz, the archbishop of Toledo, who imprisoned him for some 13 years. The cause of his imprisonment is unknown, though if there is any truth behind the autobiographical sections of the poem suggesting Ruiz's love affairs with nuns, the sentence may not have been unmerited. During his imprisonment, tradition has it, Ruiz composed the second, expanded version of the *Book of Good Love,* completed in or around 1343.

All of this assumes that the autobiographical passages in the text are to be taken at face value. But modern scholars have raised doubts about their accuracy, and it has even been suggested that they are interpolations. The Ruiz of the text may be a persona, may even be a pseudonym for the real author. It has even been suggested that the imprisonment mentioned in the text is intended metaphorically, that the author never languished in an actual prison cell but may have been in a "prison" of old age or some such figurative place.

Questions of authorship are only part of the ambiguity surrounding the text of the *Book of Good Love.* The work survives in three manuscripts, two of which preserve the 1330 version and one the 1243 version. The poem contains 1,728 verses, with a prevailing *cuaderna vía* meter (lines of 14 syllables), though various lyrics are interspersed in the text representing some 15 other verse forms. It seems likely that the lack of unity in the *Libro* is an indication that Ruiz had written the various parts of the text at different times and ultimately assembled the somewhat disparate sections into the final work as we have it.

Bibliography

Zahareas, Anthony N. *The Art of Juan Ruiz, Archpriest of Hita.* Madrid: Edtudios de Literatura Española, 1965.

Rumi, Jalaloddin (1207–1273)

The most popular and influential of all Muslim poets, Rumi was a well-known Persian theologian and mystic. Rumi was a master of two kinds of poetry: the mystical lyric (in the form of both *GHAZAL* or short lyric, and *robai* or quatrain) and the didactic narrative (in the form of the *masnavi* or couplet). His poetry is known for its musical qualities of rhyme and meter, for its ecstatic tone, and for its everyday imagery that deepens into many layers of meaning. He is known as the founder of the Mawlawi or Mevlevi Order, a fraternal organization of mystics known for its so-called whirling dervishes, that exerted a wide influence in Turkey for hundreds of years and remains active today.

Rumi was born in the city of Balkh in what is now northern Afghanistan, and was the son of the teacher and theologian Bahaoddin Valad. Forced to flee from their native city, perhaps to escape a Mongol attack, the family eventually settled in Konya, the Seljuk capital in present-day Turkey. Rumi was a student of his father until Valad's death in 1231, and then was taught Muslim law and Sufism by his father's disciples. He also seems to have spent some years studying in Damascus and Aleppo before ultimately receiving a teaching appointment at the Muslim university in Konya.

A respected scholar and mystic, Rumi did not become a poet until he came under the influence of the itinerant dervish Shamsoddin (Shams) Tabrizi in 1244. A dervish was a radical ascetic in the Sufi tradition, who gave up all worldly goods and wandered about as a mendicant teacher. Rumi was so enamored of Shams that he invited him into his home and arranged his marriage to a young woman who was Rumi's ward. Rumi saw Shams as the spokesperson for God himself, and became so devoted a disciple of Shams that his own students, jealous of the relationship, drove Shams away from Konya in 1246. Shams returned, but disappeared again in 1247, either driven away permanently by Rumi's disciples, or, some believe, murdered by them.

But it was his spiritual friendship with Shams that transformed Rumi from a respected teacher into an ecstatic mystical poet. He compiled, over the next few years, a huge collection of lyric poems, largely on the theme of his search for his beloved Shams. He wrote the poems in the voice of Shams, as if trying to recreate his friend and teacher within himself. His first great work is called *Divân-e Shams-e Tabrizi* (Collected poems of Shams Tabrizi); it consists of some 6,000 Persian lyrics in 40,000 verses.

Apparently needing a close spiritual companion for poetic inspiration, Rumi later befriended an illiterate goldsmith named Salâhoddin Zarkub. Determined to avoid a repeat of the situation with Shams, Rumi was able to convince his disciples and family to accept Zarkub, who stayed with Rumi for many years.

Rumi's third and last mystical partner was Chelebi Husamoddin Hasan, who lived with Rumi for the last 10 years of his life. It was Husamoddin that inspired Rumi's *Masnaviye ma'navi* (Spiritual couplets), a long didactic encyclopedia of Sufi mystical thought, containing stories and parables introduced from many sources (somewhat in the tradition of ATTAR). It consists of some 26,000 couplets in Persian. Among the Sufis the *Masnaviye* is considered second only to the KORAN in importance. By the middle of the 14th century, the *Masnavi* was being read throughout the Muslim world. Eventually it was translated into Turkish, Sindhi, Pashto, and, of course, Arabic.

Upon Rumi's death, Husamoddin became his successor and, with Rumi's son Soltan Valad, became leader of the Mevleviya order of mystics, the whirling dervishes whose ritual dance, the *sema*, was designed to put the dancer into an ecstatic state of mystical union with the divine.

As a mystic Rumi presents the reader with no coherent system of thought in his poetry. Rather he expresses traditional Sufi themes. He symbolically expresses the yearning for mystical union with God, and emphasizes the need to withdraw from the world to engage in deeper and deeper states of meditation. For Sufi mystics, the place to find God is within oneself, and Rumi's poetry is intended to guide the reader on that inward journey. Such themes have struck a responsive chord in the contemporary world, and Rumi's popularity has extended into the West, with a plethora of translations into English, while he still remains the greatest of mystical poets in the Muslim world.

Bibliography

Keshavarz, Fatemah. *Reading Mystical Lyric: The Case of Jalal Al-Din Rumi.* Studies in Comparative Religion. Columbia: University of South Carolina Press, 1998.

Rumi, Jalaloddin. *The Essential Rumi.* Translated by Coleman Barks. San Francisco: Harper, 1997.

———. *Rumi: The Book of Love: Poems of Ecstasy and Longing.* Translated by Coleman Barks. San Franciso: Harper, 2003.

Schimel, Annemarie. *The Triumphal Sun: A Study of the Works of Jalaloddin Rumi.* Persian Studies Series 8. Albany: State University of New York Press, 1980.

Rutebeuf (Rutebuef, Rustebeuf) (fl. 1254–1285)

Rutebeuf was a 13th-century French poet best known for his satirical verse and COMPLAINTS about his personal troubles as an impoverished JONGLEUR. Since there are no contemporary references to him, it is widely assumed that "Rutebeuf" was a pen name. Thus nothing is known of Rutebeuf's life beyond what might be gleaned from his apparently autobiographical poems. If these can be relied upon, it appears that he was probably born in Champagne, but spent most of his life in Paris. His poems are clearly not intended for noble audiences, but are either religious in nature or seem to reflect the voice of the common people of Paris.

Of some 56 extant poems attributed to Rutebeuf, the most frequently read today are the lyrics concerned with his own troubles. Among these are *Le Mariage de Rutebeuf* (ca. 1461), where he claims to have married an old, mean, and ugly wife with no dowry; and the *Complainte de Rutebeuf,* in which he recounts the unfortunate events that have brought him to the state of penury in which he finds himself. He addresses his complaint to the count of Poitiers, Alphonse—brother of King Louis IX (Saint Louis).

Rutebeuf wrote a wide variety of other poems, from Hymns to the Virgin Mary and a SAINT'S LIFE concerning St. Elizabeth, to five FABLIAUX and numerous biting satires. The most common targets of Rutebeuf's satire are the mendicant orders, regularly lampooned for their corruption in the later Middle Ages. He was a strong advocate for the University of Paris, particularly the scholar Guillaume de Saint-Amour, in its mid-13th-century quarrel with the religious orders. But in addition to friars, Rutebeuf provides biting commentary on King Louis himself for his support of religious orders, on the pope, and on the nobility. But Rutebeuf concentrates not only on those in power. He satirizes merchants and lazy workers as well, and is particularly hard on women.

Rutebeuf's *Dit de l'Herberie* is a dramatic monologue spoken by a quack doctor, and was probably intended for performance before a popular audience. This interest in dramatization also seems to have led Rutebeuf to write one of the earliest dramas in the French theater, *Le Miracle de Théophile.* The first play with the word *miracle* in the title, this short (700-line) theatrical piece is an early version of the Faust legend. In the play, Théophile is a materialistic priest who is cheated out of his fortune by an acquisitive bishop. Furious at the church, Théophile forsakes his allegiance to God and makes a contract with the devil in order to regain his wealth. Seven years later, Théophile repents his bargain, and through the miracle of the Blessed Virgin's intercession he is restored to God's grace.

Rutebeuf wrote in a variety of different verse forms and was a technical master of prosody, especially in the popular French eight-syllable or octosyllabic lines. He was ruthless in exposing the failings of all social classes, and in attacking anything he saw as social abuses. In his satiric tone and his autobiographical complaints, Rutebeuf has most often been compared with the later, 15th-century French poet François VILLON.

Bibliography

Medieval French Plays. Translated by Richard Axton and John Stevens. New York: Barnes and Noble, 1971.

Regalado, Nancy Freeman. *Poetic Patterns in Rutebeuf: A Study in Noncourtly Poetic Modes of the Thirteenth Century.* New Haven, Conn.: Yale University Press, 1970.

S

Saadia Gaon (Saadia ben Joseph, Said al-Fayyumi) (882–942)

Saadia ben Joseph, known as Saadia Gaon, was a medieval Jewish scholar, philosopher, and polemicist, whose rational defense of the Jewish faith at a time of skepticism and doubt made him the father of medieval Jewish philosophy. Using the methods of rationalist Muslim theologians, Saadia's great work *The* BOOK OF DOCTRINES AND BELIEFS (*Kitāb al-'Amānāt wa-al-I'tiqādāt, Sefer ha-Emunot we-ha-De'ot*) became the basis for all subsequent Jewish philosophy.

Saadia was born in Egypt, where he received his early training. Later he moved to Palestine to continue his education. When a controversy broke out between the Palestinian and Babylonian Jewish authorities concerning the Jewish calendar, Saadia argued vigorously for the Babylonian side. His arguments carried the day and essentially ensured that control over Jewish life would rest with the Babylonians. Saadia was appointed head, or *gaon*, of the rabbinical school at Sura near Baghdad in 928, and under his leadership the school became the premier academy in the Jewish world. He suffered a setback in his public life in 930, when he declined to support a judgment coming from the court of the exilarch, David ben Zakkai, who was the secular head of the Jewish people in Babylon. Saadia questioned the honesty of the decision, and as a result, he lost his position at Sura and, for seven years, lived in Baghdad as an exile. Even without his post, Saadia was still universally considered the most important authority in the Jewish world on matters of Talmud and Jewish law. He also continued to write, completing his major philosophical work by about 933. He was finally reconciled with the exilarch and restored to his post in 937, but he held it for only five more years, dying, according to his son Dosa, of "melancholia" after a series of illnesses.

Saadia's contributions to Jewish letters are myriad and significant. Early in his career, he composed the *Agron* (Collection), the first Hebrew dictionary, which was to become the foundation of all subsequent Hebrew lexicography. He also wrote a book of Hebrew grammar. Recognizing that his fellow Jews were becoming more and more assimilated into the majority Muslim culture of his time and place, Saadia made the first translation of the Hebrew Scriptures into Arabic, with his own commentary. He put together the first comprehensive and systematic *Siddur,* or prayer book, including the ritual Hebrew prayers for weekdays, festivals, and sabbaths, and also including Saadia's own liturgical poetry plus his own commentary in Arabic. He also wrote a number of treatises on problems of Jewish law, as well as a commentary on the mystical work called *Sefer Yetzirah,* which he tried to make more accessible by applying a rational and philosophical approach to the text. *The Book of*

Doctrines and Beliefs is undoubtedly his greatest work.

For many scholars Saadia's most important contribution to Judaism is his lengthy and heated polemical battle against the Karaite sect. The Karaites accepted the Hebrew Scriptures, but refused to accept the teachings of rabbinical authorities, and so denied the authority of the Talmud. Only the Torah comes from God, the Karaites claimed—the Talmud was the work of men. In books, letters, and articles written in Arabic, Saadia defended the traditional view that the Talmud was the oral Torah, given by God at Sinai but not written until hundreds of years later in the Babylonian academies. While the Karaites launched their own counterattacks, armed with poorer philosophical training and less fluent Arabic, their arguments were far less effective, and ultimately Saadia, more than anyone else, was responsible for the defeat and decline of the Karaites.

It is impossible to overestimate the importance of Saadia's contribution to Jewish thought and culture. Reemphasizing Jewish life and belief at a crucial moment in the history of the faith, Saadia established the foundations for the future direction of Jewish thought. The greatest of Jewish philosophers, Maimonides himself, said that if it had not been for Saadia, "Torah would have been forgotten in Israel."

Bibliography

Efros, Israel Isaac. *Studies in Medieval Jewish Philosophy.* New York: Columbia University Press, 1974.

Helm, Paul, ed. *Referring to God: Jewish and Christian Philosophical and Theological Perspectives.* New York: St. Martin's Press, 2000.

Hyman, Arthur, and James J. Walsh, eds. *Philosophy in the Middle Ages: The Christian, Islamic, and Jewish Traditions.* 2nd ed. Indianapolis: Hackett, 1983.

Rosenthal, Erwin I. J., ed. *Saadya Studies.* New York: Arno Press, 1980.

Saadia Gaon. *The Book of Beliefs and Opinions.* Translated by Samuel Rosenblatt. New Haven, Conn.: Yale University Press, 1948.

———. *The Book of Doctrines and Beliefs.* Translated by Alexander Altman. Abridged. Indianapolis: Hackett, 2002.

Skoss, Solomon Leon. *Saadia Gaon: Earliest Hebrew Grammarian.* Philadelphia: Dropsie College Press, 1955.

Sa'di, Moslehoddin (Saadi) (ca. 1200–1292)

Sa'di, one of the most widely read writers in the Muslim world, is the author of two major works, *Bustan* (The orchard) and *Golestan* (The rose garden), the latter of which is second only to the KORAN in its popularity among Muslim readers, and was the first Persian text translated into a European language. Like Shakespeare in English, Sa'di's works are so well known that he is often quoted in everyday speech.

Sa'di was born in the city of Shiraz in what today is southern Iran. Not much is known about his life, but it is generally accepted that he spent some time studying in Baghdad and probably Damascus. Certainly the knowledge of the Koran, Islamic law and society, and Arabic and Persian literary history evident in his works indicates he was well educated. It is certain that he made pilgrimages to Mecca and probably to Medina more than once, and it can be conjectured from anecdotes he includes in his works that his extensive travels may have taken him as far as Morocco, Abyssinia, Byzantium, and India, and, at one point, put him into contact with European crusaders. He also seems to have become acquainted with wandering Sufi mystical teachers, or "dervishes," for whom he formed a deep sympathy.

After some 30 years of travel as a student and a teacher, Sa'di returned to Shiraz in 1256, when he began his writing career. His first important text, *Bustan*, was completed in 1257, and dedicated to the Zangid caliph of Shiraz, whom he admired for keeping a peaceful and ordered city. The *Bustan* consists of 4,100 rhymed couplets, and includes a number of stories illustrating the virtues all Muslims were expected to demonstrate.

Sa'di completed his best-known text the following year: *Golestan* consists mainly of prose passages interspersed with occasional short lyric poems. The work is in the *adab* tradition, the ideal of Muslim literature that combines moral instruction with a beautiful and vivid poetic style. Muslims did not consider pure fiction a form of true literature, but found it permissible to include stories, as Sa'di does, to illustrate moral points.

The *Golestan* is made up of an introduction followed by eight books, each on a different topic: the first two, "On the Nature of Shahs" and "On the Morals of Dervishes," focus on those whom Sa'di saw as representing political and religious authority. Stories included in these and the other six books sometimes only loosely or tangentially relate to the subject. Sa'di includes a huge range of topics, from the mystical to the erotic, and gives good, commonsense counsel on proper moral behavior in virtually any given situation.

Sa'di's minor works include a few panegyrics in praise of the caliph of Shiraz and other Persian rulers, as well as a series of *GHAZALS*. Sa'di is probably the first Persian poet to use the *ghazal* as a vehicle for love poetry.

After about 1260, the city of Shiraz came under the rule of the Mongols, and Sa'di is thought to have spent the last years of his life in a Sufi religious community in Shiraz. He died in about 1292, at approximately 90 years of age.

Sa'di's influence and popularity have been enormous. For centuries *Golestan* has been the primary text in Persian reading classes. It was translated into Turkish as early as the 14th century, and was translated into German in 1654. French, Latin, Dutch, and English translations soon followed, and the *Bustan* was translated into English in the 17th century as well. And although in recent years tastes have moved away from it somewhat, for 700 years the *Golestan* was considered to be the ideal model of prose style in the Persian language.

Bibliography

Sa'di, Moslehoddin. *The Bostan of Saadi* (*The Orchard*). Translated by Barlas Mirza Aquil-Hussain. New York: Octagon Press, 1998.

———. *The Gulistan, or Rose Garden, of Sa'di.* Translated by Edward Rehatsek. London: Allen and Unwin, 1964.

———. *Morals Pointed and Tales Adorned: The Bustan of Sa'di.* Translated by G. M. Wickens. Toronto: University of Toronto Press, 1974.

saga

The term *saga* is an Icelandic word meaning "saying" or "telling." For medieval Icelanders, it simply referred to anything written in prose, whether it told a story or simply related information. Modern scholars have applied it more specifically to any of a large number of narrative prose tales written in medieval Iceland (or occasionally in Norway), beginning in the 12th century and running through the 15th. These narratives are generally anonymous, and written in an objective, unadorned style by writers who saw themselves as simply recorders of traditions rather than as self-conscious literary artists. The sagas range in length from brief stories to novel-length narrative.

Sagas developed and changed during the later Middle Ages in Iceland, and therefore fall into a number of different categories, based mainly on their subject matter, style, and intent. The earliest sagas were historical accounts in the form of biographies of Icelandic bishops and of Norwegian kings. *Olaf's Saga*, the story of King Olaf Tryggvason, may be the first of these, composed perhaps as early as 1180. SNORRI STURLUSON's collection of kings' sagas, *HEIMSKRINGLA* (ca. 1225), contains many of the most famous examples of this genre.

The most important and admired narratives are the family sagas, or the "sagas of the Icelanders." These texts are the major contribution of Iceland to world literature. Only 30-odd family sagas are extant. Writing during a period of social decline and lawlessness, the authors of the family sagas focused on significant Icelanders from what they perceived as a golden age of the building of their country, the so-called saga age of about 900 to 1050. They display a real interest in recording Icelandic history. Usually the protagonists of the sagas were the ancestors of the writers' own influential contemporary Icelanders.

The family saga generally told a tragic story, often involving legal disputes and blood vengeance. A conventional family saga would begin with a concise but important introduction of the main characters and their family backgrounds, focusing on certain character traits and behaviors that would become significant for the action of the narrative. A typical saga plot would pit a noble or virtuous man against a belligerent antagonist, whose willingness to bully or to take advantage of the better qualities of his victim most often has tragic consequences for the nobler protagonist. Revenge may be taken by the family of the wronged individual, and ultimately the two parties are usually reconciled.

The most admired family sagas are usually about individuals, like the tragic *NJAL'S SAGA* and the fascinating *EGIL'S SAGA* about a cantankerous SKALDIC poet that may have been written by his descendent, Snorri Sturluson. Sometimes, however, they concern groups, such as *LAXDAELA SAGA*, which tells the sweeping story of the people of the region of Laxdaela over a 150-year period.

Later in the 13th century, another type of historical saga developed dealing with contemporary events, known as the *Sturlunga Saga*, or the saga concerning the Sturlung Age. Named after the dominant Icelandic family of the period, the Sturlung Age (1200–64) was known for its civic turmoil, its greed, and its disregard for rule of law. The *Islendinga Saga*, the best known example of this genre, was composed by Snorri Sturluson's nephew Sturla Thordarson, and features Snorri himself as an important character.

Other sagas are *fornaldarsögur*, or legendary sagas, dealing with mythic or legendary heroes from Norse myth and folklore. Such tales were full of supernatural elements and thus formed a real contrast with the essentially realistic and historical family sagas. The best-known of these narratives is *VOLSUNGA SAGA*, a story of the Norse hero Sigurd, the famous dragon-slayer. Another later type of saga was the *riddararsögur*, or the saga based on foreign sources, most often ROMANCES or CHANSONS DE GESTE. The result of the influence of the European vogue for chivalric stories, these prose romances were composed in imitation of traditional sagas. The earliest was probably *Tristram's Saga:* Based on the *Tristram* of THOMAS OF BRITAIN by a certain Friar Robert, it was composed at the request of the Norwegian king Hakon Hakonsarson in about 1226.

By the 14th century, the romances and the legendary heroic sagas were indistinguishable and dominated Icelandic literature. Such texts, however, are generally seen as inferior to the family sagas. When critics or readers speak of Icelandic sagas, inevitably they are speaking specifically about the family sagas.

Bibliography

Andersson, Theodore M. *The Icelandic Family Saga: An Analytic Reading.* Cambridge, Mass.: Harvard University Press, 1967.

———. "The Icelandic Sagas," in *Heroic Epic and Saga*, edited by Felix J. Oinas. Bloomington: Indiana University Press, 1978, 144–171.

Bykock, Jesse L. *Feud in the Icelandic Saga.* Berkeley: University of California Press, 1982.

Clover, Carol J. *The Medieval Saga.* Ithaca, N.Y.: Cornell University Press, 1982.

Miller, William Ian. *Bloodtaking and Peacemaking: Feud, Law, and Society in Saga Iceland.* Chicago: University of Chicago Press, 1990.

Schach, Paul. *Icelandic Sagas.* Boston: Twayne, 1984.

Saint Erkenwald (ca. 1400)

Saint Erkenwald is a poem in ALLITERATIVE VERSE, written in the late 14th or early 15th century in a north West Midland dialect of MIDDLE ENGLISH. The poem of 352 lines survives in a single manuscript (British Museum MS Harley 2250), in which it occurs amid a number of SAINTS' LIVES from the *SOUTH ENGLISH LEGENDARY*, but *Saint Erkenwald* differs from those conventional saints' lives in many ways, ignoring the lineage, calling, passion, or martyrdom of the saint, and focusing only on a single miraculous incident in the saint's career—an incident that appears in no other work associated with Erkenwald.

The historical Erkenwald was first described by the Venerable BEDE in his eighth-century *Ecclesiastical History of the English People* as a revered bishop of London and the first of the city's saints. He was born in 630, and was purportedly the son of Offa, king of East Anglia. A pious young man, he founded two monastic houses—one for nuns at Barking in Essex, to be headed by his sister Aetehlburgh, and the other for monks at Chertsey in Surrey, which he entered himself. He was consecrated bishop of London in 675 at the age of 45, and died at Barking Abbey in 693. For some 450 years, his shrine stood in St. Paul's Cathedral and was reputed to work miracles of healing. In 1148 his body was moved to the wall above the high altar in St. Paul's, and in 1386, during a rebuilding project for the cathedral, Bishop Robert Braybrooke proclaimed that the feasts of St. Erkenwald (the dates of his burial and his reinterment) would be celebrated as major festival days in the cathedral.

It may have been the contemporary interest in St. Erkenwald's festivals and in the rebuilding of the cathedral that led the anonymous poet to compose the poem of *Saint Erkenwald,* but the poet chose to use neither Bede or the two more recent, 12th-century Latin saint's lives of Erkenwald as sources for his own poem. Instead, he used a popular legend associated with St. GREGORY THE GREAT: According to this legend, Gregory, upon hearing of the acts of justice attributed to the righteous pagan emperor Trajan, shed tears for Trajan's soul. God, witnessing Gregory's compassion, released Trajan from his place among the unbaptized in hell.

The *Saint Erkenwald* poet tells a similar story, but makes the protagonist the renowned English bishop. The poem begins with a 32-line section that situates the story in its historical context—another time of rebuilding of St. Paul's Cathedral, as early English Christians transform it from a pagan building to a consecrated one. Workmen examining the foundations of the building discover an elaborate tomb. The mayor of the city has them open the tomb, and inside they find a richly dressed and perfectly preserved corpse—here the poem draws on the tradition that the bodies of the sanctified will not undergo corruption. As the people examine the tomb, they can find no indication of who the corpse is. Word of the mystery comes to Bishop Erkenwald in Essex, and he returns to London, where he spends the night praying that God will show him the truth. In the morning he first says Mass in the cathedral, then goes down to the vault, with the people of the city pressing behind him. Told by the mayor and dean of the cathedral that they have not been able to discover anything about the corpse, Erkenwald observes that this shows the limits of human reason. This ends Part 1, halfway through the text at line 176.

In Part 2, Erkenwald addresses the corpse itself, conjuring it to speak in the name of God. The corpse reveals that he was a pagan judge, who lived some 350 years before the birth of Christ. So renowned was he for his just decisions that when he died the people buried him like a king. In death, though he believes in God and had led a just life, he is doomed to spend eternity in Limbo. Erkenwald is so moved by the righteous pagan's story that he expresses a wish to be able to baptize him—and just as he says the words that he would say in baptism, a tear falls from his eye onto the face of the corpse.

In the final 32 lines of the poem, the corpse describes what happened to his soul the moment Erkenwald's tear fell: Instantly, it was transported to heavenly bliss. Having described this, the corpse falls into corruption and disintegrates. The poem ends as Erkenwald leads a procession from the cathedral, with all the people following.

The poem is clearly intended as an illustration of the infinite mercy and the incomprehensible grace of God. The poet was aware of current 14th-century debate concerning the fate of virtuous pagans, and may have been specifically aware of the way William LANGLAND dealt with the issue, as well as with the story of the Emperor Trajan in *PIERS PLOWMAN,* where Langland had described baptism by fire and grace as equal in value to baptism by water. The *Saint Erkenwald* poet provides a kind of compromise position, in which the pagan judge is saved, but only after an unconventional baptism—but still a baptism of water.

One question that scholars have debated about the poem is its authorship. For many years, it was believed by a good number of scholars that the same poet who wrote *SIR GAWAIN AND THE GREEN KNIGHT* and *PEARL* was the author of *Saint Erkenwald.* In recent decades that theory has been convincingly dismissed by critics (notably L. D. Benson) who have argued that the subject matter, date of the manuscripts, dialect, and vocabulary of the poems are too different to suggest common authorship. More recently, a certain John Massey of Cheshire has been suggested as a candidate, based on the fact that the name "Massey" appears in the manuscript, and that Thomas HOCCLEVE speaks of a poet by that name being active in the right area of England at the time the poem was probably written. But any such identifications remain pure conjecture. Ultimately, the poem stands on its own merits, and the authorship question is merely a sidelight to the thematic interest and artistry of the poem.

Bibliography

Benson, L. D. "The Authorship of 'St. Erkenwald,'" *Journal of English and Germanic Philology* 64 (1965): 393–405.

Davidson, Arnold. "Mystery, Miracle and Meaning in *Saint Erkenwald*," *Papers on Language and Literature* 16 (1980): 37–44.

Kamkowski, William. "Saint Erkenwald and the Inadvertent Baptism: An Orthodox Response to Heterodox Ecclesiology," *Religion and Literature* 27, no. 3 (Autumn 1995): 5–27.

Morse, Ruth, ed. *St. Erkenwald.* Cambridge: D. S. Brewer, 1975.

Peterson, Clifford, ed. *Saint Erkenwald.* Philadelphia: University of Pennsylvania Press, 1977.

Stone, Brian, trans. *The Owl and the Nightingale; Cleanness; Saint Erkenwald.* Harmondsworth, U.K.: Penguin, 1971.

saint's life (saint's legend, hagiography)

One of the most popular literary genres in medieval Europe was the saint's life. These were short narrative biographies of holy men and women, most often martyrs, whose stories were intended to reveal the active presence of God in their lives, and therefore to inspire the reader or audience to follow the saint's example, to persevere under adversity, or to remain steadfast in the faith. Or, on a more practical level, saints' lives might be written to advance the reputation of the patron saint of a particular monastery, or to extol the powers of the relics of a particular saint that might be housed in a particular church or cathedral. What most interests the hagiographer (or writer of a saint's life) are the miracles surrounding the saint that provide the irrefutable proof of the saint's sanctity. In a way the saints' lives were a kind of Christian ROMANCE, in which the saint, like the romance hero, accomplishes his or her quest for God's ultimate reward against overwhelming odds in the form of worldly obstacles.

From early medieval times, a portion of the life of a saint would be read in a church before the daily service, or during a Mass performed for the saint's feast day (the day commemorating the saint's death). As time went on, by the 12th century, saints' lives became popular entertainment for pious laypersons as well. The most popular and influential collection of saints' lives was Jacobus de Voragine's *GOLDEN LEGEND*, a Latin compilation from the mid 13th century. The term *legend* comes from the Latin word *lectio* ("lesson" or "reading"), alluding to the custom of using the saint's life as a reading in the divine office. Eventually, of course, "legend" took on the connotation of a "tall tale," presumably because of the miraculous events depicted in the saints' legends. But that connotation seems to have come about in postmedieval times. There is certainly no irony in the title of the most popular collection of saints' lives in MIDDLE ENGLISH, the early 14th-century *SOUTH ENGLISH LEGENDARY.*

Saints' lives generally followed a very conventional pattern. Often they would begin with a fanciful explanation of the etymology of the saint's name or the name of his or her birthplace. The saint would generally have gained a significant reputation for faith and goodness, even at an early age, so that he or she would have come to the attention of some powerful and corrupt figure, most commonly a pagan judge or governor. If the saint is female, it is common for the corrupt official to have lustful designs on her virtue. Brought before the official, the saint engages in a debate or argument about Christianity and paganism, in which the saint's arguments always best the pagan official's. The saint generally argues that the pagan's gods are merely stone idols, that the earthly torments at the official's disposal are as nothing compared with the eternal torments of the damned that await him, and that the pagan official has no real power except what the omnipotent grants him—in this last, particularly, the saint's confrontation of the pagan official recalls the gospel scene of Christ before Pilate, and therefore demonstrates the saint's emulation of Christ, a model for what the reader should do.

Having been bested in the verbal contest, the pagan judge usually follows by unleashing torture on the saint. These torments are such that under normal circumstances, the victim would find them unbearable, but through the miraculous action of God the saints survive or even thrive under the torture. In the AELFRIC'S OLD ENGLISH *Life of Saint Agatha,* for example, the saint is twisted on the rack and has her breast hacked off, but God sends Saint Peter to her cell as a physician to heal her wounds. In CHAUCER'S *SECOND NUN'S TALE,* which is the Life of St. Cecilia, Cecilia is nearly beheaded, then boiled for three days in a cauldron, but all the while she remains perfectly comfortable and continues to preach to all who can hear her. Ultimately the saint dies, and is welcomed into paradise, but there may first be some supernatural sign that demonstrates God's disapproval of the pagan judge's actions. In St. Agatha's legend, an earthquake interrupts the last torment that the governor has planned for her. Often the end of the tale includes marvelous stories of miracles wrought by the saint's remains, or relics. St. Agatha's tomb, for instance, saved her city from the eruption of Mount Etna. In the *Golden Legend,* St. Christopher's blood brings sight to a blinded judge, who converts in response to his miraculous healing.

Saints' lives seem to have sprung ultimately from such roots as apocryphal Gospels and Acts of the Apostles, and also to some extent from classical, Oriental, Celtic, and Germanic myths that provide elements like battles with dragons (St. George) or protagonists who are 12-foot giants (St. Christopher). Some of the earliest real saint's lives were in Eusebius of Caesarea's fourth-century *History of the Martyrs of Palestine.* St. JEROME also wrote some fourth-century saints' lives that were imitated by ISIDORE OF SEVILLE in the early seventh century. In sixth-century Gaul, GREGORY OF TOURS wrote several lives of local saints, and about the same time, Pope GREGORY THE GREAT wrote a number of lives of the saints of Italy. In the eighth century, the Venerable BEDE included the lives of a number of English and Irish saints in his *Ecclesiastical History of the English People.* During the Carolingian period in France, a number of earlier legends were rewritten with an eye toward improving their literary style, and hagiographic activity increased as the Middle Ages advanced. By the 13th century compilations of saints' lives were appearing, including the *Speculum historiale* of Vincent of Beauvais and the *Speculum sanctorale* of Bernard of Gui, in addition to the hugely popular *Golden Legend* already mentioned.

The widespread popularity of saints' lives led to their imitation in other, more secular kinds of medieval literature, such as the depiction of Sir GALAHAD in *The Quest of the Holy Grail* and other romances, or in the creation of a kind of "secular saint" in tales of pathos like Chaucer's *CLERK'S TALE* of Patient Griselda. They also served as models for later collections like John Foxe's *Book of [Protestant] Martyrs* in the English Reformation. They remained popular to some extent until the 18th century, and still provide some of the earliest accounts of the biographies of some Catholic saints.

Bibliography

Bjork, Robert E. *The Old English Verse Saints' Lives: A Study in Direct Discourse and the Iconography of Style.* Toronto: University of Toronto Press, 1985.

Jacobus de Voragine. *The Golden Legend.* Translated by Christopher Stace. London: Penguin, 1998.

Kitchen, John. *Saints' Lives and the Rhetoric of Gender: Male and Female in Merovingian Hagiography.* New York: Oxford University Press, 1998.

Noble, Thomas F. X., and Thomas Head, eds. *Soldiers of Christ: Saints and Saints' Lives from Late Antiquity and the Early Middle Ages.* University Park: Pennsylvania State University Press, 1995.

Robertson, Duncan. *The Medieval Saints' Lives: Spiritual Renewal and Old French Literature.* Lexington, Ky.: French Forum, 1995.

Szarmach, Paul E., ed. *Holy Men and Holy Women: Old English Prose Saints' Lives and Their Contexts.* Albany, N.Y.: State University of New York Press, 1996.

Whatley, E. Gordon, Anne Thompson, and Robert Upchurch, eds. *Saints' Lives in Middle English Collections.* Kalamazoo, Mich.: Published for TEAMS (The Consortium for the Teaching of the Middle Ages) in association with the University of Rochester by Medieval Institute Publications, 2004.

Wogan-Browne, Jocelyn. *Saints' Lives and Women's Literary Culture c. 1150–1300: Virginity and Its Authorizations.* Oxford: Oxford University Press, 2001.

Śakuntalā and the Ring of Recollection

Kālidāsa (ca. 400)

Abhijñānaśākuntala (usually translated as "The recognition of Śākuntalā" or "Sākuntalā and the ring of recollection," but often simply called *Sākuntalā*) is the best-known play by India's acknowledged greatest master of classical Sanskrit, Kālidāsa. The play is an example of the genre known as *nātaka* in Sanskrit, which denotes a heroic romance, a play in which a noble hero loves a beautiful woman, but in an epic world in which the hero is a royal sage and the heroine roughly symboic of the forces of nature. The source of the play is the story of Duhsanta Paurava and Śāuntalā as told in the first book of the classic Sanskrit epic *Mahābhārata* (ca. fourth century B.C.E.), wherein Duhsanta and Sākuntalā give birth to the epic's hero, Bhārata.

Kālidāsa retells this familiar story in seven acts. The play opens in a summer setting as Sākuntalā, revealed to be the daughter of a warrior sage and a nymph, is living with her adopted father, Kanva, in a rustic grove that serves as an ascetic hermitage. Kanva is absent, having gone on pilgrimage seeking to prevent a vague threat to Sākuntalā that he has become aware of. In his absence, the king Dusyanta finds his way to the ascetic grove, and, captivated by her beauty, watches the young virgin from behind a tree while she and her companions water the trees. When Sākuntalā is threatened by a bee, Dusyanta steps out to rescue her.

When the king discovers that Sākuntalā is not, as he had assumed, the daughter of the Brahman ascetic (and therefore unavailable), but rather of a warrior, he begins to press his suit. At first Sākuntalā resists him, but eventually the two succumb to an overwhelming passion and marry in secret—a *gāndharva* or marriage of "mutual consent." Once they have consummated their love, the king must return to his city, but he gives Sākuntalā a ring as a token of their marriage, and tells her he will send for her.

Dusyanta, however, is not able to keep that vow. In the fourth act of the drama—the central act, considered the *garbha* (or "womb") of the play—comes the major turning point, for Sākuntalā, preoccupied by her passion and her departed lover, neglects her duties in the hermitage and incurs the wrath of the sage Durvāsas, who places a curse upon her. As a result of the curse, the king forgets her.

But Sākuntalā, now pregnant with the king's child, can no longer stay in the hermitage, and her adoptive father Kanva sends her to the capital to seek her husband. Disaster befalls Sākuntalā on the journey, for when she pauses on her way to pray at a river shrine sacred to Śaći, consort of the Hindu god Indra, she loses her signet ring in the water. Thus when she reaches the capital, Dusyanta fails to recognize her and spurns her. The devastated Sākuntalā prays to the earth to open and swallow her up, but at that point she is carried off by a light formed like a woman.

Ultimately, a fisherman finds Sākuntalā's ring in the river, and brings it to the king. When Dusyanta recognizes the token of his love for the faithful Sākuntalā, the curse is broken and he realizes what he has done, and burns with love for her. In the world of the play, this love is able to transform and refine the king, making him capable of attacking and destroying demonic beings who menace the gods themselves.

Having proven himself in this cosmic battle, the king, riding in the chariot of Indra himself, is taken to a paradisal hermitage on a holy mountain, where he sees a young boy (Bhārata) whom he gradually realizes is his own son, and where, ultimately, he is reunited with his great love, Sākuntalā.

Barbara Stoler Miller discusses the dramatic theory behind a play like *Sākuntalā and the Ring of Recollection:* The action of the play depicts a conflict between the cosmic forces of *kāma* (sensual passion) and *dharma* (sacred duty). Sākuntalā, the woman associated with the generative powers of the natural world, is both the object and representation of desire. Dusyanta learns that his passion must be curbed by duty, but his duty is awakened by his passion (Miller 1984, 27–29). The king is inspired to true heroism by his love, and his heroic feats make him worthy of the love that he gains at the end of the play, when he is reunited with his beloved Sākuntalā and their son, Bhārata.

Sākuntalā is the most popular of Kālidāsa's three surviving plays, admired for its beautiful love poetry as well as for the humor Kālidāsa includes throughout the play (and whose common characters speak in *Pankrit,* the local vernacular dialect, rather than in the Sanskrit of his noble characters). It was the first of Kālidāsa's dramas to be translated into English, and an 18th-century German translation was influential on Goethe, whose prologue to *Faust* was inspired by *Sākuntalā.*

Bibliography

Gerow, Edwin. "Plot Structure and the Development of Rasa in the *Śākuntalā,*" parts 1 and 2. *Journal of the American Oriental Society* 99 (1979): 559–582; 100 (1980): 267–282.

Kālidāsa. *Theater of Memory: The Plays of Kālidāsa.* Edited by Barbara Stoler Miller, translated by Edwin Gerow, David Gitomer, and Barbara Stoler Miller. New York: Columbia University Press, 1984.

Santillana, Iñigo López de Mendoza, marqués de (1398–1458)

The Marqués de Santillana was a Spanish poet, soldier, statesman, literary critic, and patron. Profoundly influenced by the great Italian writers DANTE, BOCCACCIO, and especially PETRARCH, Santillana is often seen as a humanist and transitional figure between medieval and renaissance Spain. He wrote long allegories influenced by the Italians, and he was the first poet to write SONNETS in the Castilian language, but his best-known works are his lyric poems in the style of the Provençal TROUBADOURS.

Santillana was born Iñigo López de Mendoza in Carrión de los Condes, Palencia. His father was Diego Hurtado de Mendoza, the grand admiral of Castile, a title Iñigo inherited. His father died in 1404, after which the young Mendoza went to live with his wealthy and cultured grandmother, Doña Mencia de Cisneros. Between 1412 and 1418, he served at the royal court of Aragon, where in 1416, he seems to have met and married Catalina de Figueroa, the daughter of the grand master of Santiago. He began making a name for himself as a soldier in 1420, by supporting the Infante Don Enrique, heir to the Castilian throne. He fought in support of King Juan II of Castile (1405–1454) in several battles, gaining the king's gratitude in particular for his victories at Huelva in 1436, and in the Battle of Olmedo in 1445, after which Juan conferred upon him the title Marqués de Santillana and Conde del Real de Manzanares.

With other Castilian nobles, Santillana took part in a struggle with the royal favorite, the constable Álvaro de Luna, who was executed in 1453. When King Juan died the following year, Santillana largely withdrew from public affairs, and after the death of his wife and son shortly thereafter, he spent the final years of his life in seclusion at his palace in Guadalajara, where he died in 1458.

Santillana was a highly educated man, able to read Italian, Catalan, Galician-Portuguese, and French. Although he does not seem to have known Greek or Latin himself, he collected numerous classical manuscripts. He also commissioned Spanish translations of the *Iliad,* the *Aeneid,* and Seneca's tragedies. Having befriended the Spanish poet and scholar Enrique de Villena, Santillana commissioned him to translate DANTE's *DIVINE COMEDY* as well (completed in 1428). By his reading, collecting, and literary patronage, Santillana was able to build up the greatest private library of his day, now part of the Biblioteca Nacional in Madrid.

Santillana's *Prohemio,* or preface to a collection of his own poetry, which he prepared to be sent to Don Pedro of Portugal in 1449, is generally considered the first work of literary criticism in Spanish. In it Santillana expresses his preference for strict classical models of literature, praises the Italian poets as well as the Provençal-inspired Galician-Portuguese lyrics, and denigrates popular and folk songs. He categorizes poetry into three styles; The sublime style (referring to Greek and Latin poets), the middle style (by which he refers to learned poetry in the vernacular), and the low style (in which he includes ballads and other folk songs). Finally Santillana extols the role of literary patrons.

Santillana's own poetry shows a remarkable variety. He introduced the sonnet form into Spanish literature, composing some 42 sonnets in the Petrarchan style. His longer poems are generally written in a form called *arte mayor*, consisting of eight-line stanzas with 11- or 12-syllable lines rhyming *abbaacca*. These tend to be ALLEGORICAL and to show the influence of Italian poets as well, particularly of Dante. Perhaps his best-known allegorical poem is *Comedieta de Ponza* (1436), which deals with the defeat of Alfonso V of Aragon and his Navarrese allies by the Genoese navy in battle off the island of Ponza in 1435. His *Diálogo de Bías contra Fortuna* (1448) was written apparently to comfort the Conde de Alba, Santillana's cousin who had been imprisoned by his enemy, de Luna. The text, owing something to BOETHIUS, portrays a debate between the Stoic philosopher Bías and the figure of Fortuna. Another of Santillana's longer poems, the *Doctrinal de prìvados*, celebrates the downfall of de Luna, represented in the form of a public confession of the royal favorite's sins. Another didactic work is Santillana's *Proverbios de gloriosa doctrina e fructuosa enseñanza*, a rhymed collection of proverbs originally written, it is presumed, for the Infante Don Enrique. The collection became well known and was translated into English in 1579.

But despite these more ambitious projects, Santillana is best remembered today for his short lyric poems, influenced to a large extent by Portuguese and French lyrics, and owing something to the troubadour tradition, in particular his pastoral songs called *serranillas*. Santillana's lyrics have been praised for their elegant simplicity. It is on these simple songs that his contemporary reputation rests.

Bibliography

Foster, David William. *The Marqués de Santillana.* New York: Twayne, 1971.

Trend, John Brande. *Marqués de Santillana: Prose and Verse.* London: Dolphin Bookshop, 1940.

Sawles Warde (ca. 1220)

Sawles Warde (Care of the soul, or Custody of the soul), which was most likely composed ca. 1220, is considered a part of the MIDDLE ENGLISH text grouping known as the KATHERINE GROUP. An ALLEGORICAL verse homily written in alliterative prose, *Sawles Warde* is primarily an expansion of *De custodia interioris hominis* (On the keeping of the inner self), often attributed to St. ANSELM of Canterbury. However, other suggested sources include the *Vision of the Monk of Eversham*, and three chapters from Hugh of St. Victor's *De anima* (*On the soul*), though this latter source has been somewhat discredited. In turn, *Sawles Warde* itself possibly had an impact on two later works, *Þe Holy Boke Gratia Dei* (The holy book of the grace of God) and the *AYENBITE OF INWIT* (The remorse of conscience), though neither influence has been proven conclusively. *Sawles Warde* demonstrates notable alterations of its source materials: It focuses more on concrete sensual descriptions than on philosophical interpretations; it advocates *temperantia* (moderation) as the key to survive evil; it adds characters, including Will. Some scholars have also argued that *Sawles Warde* is a precursor to later medieval allegorical drama such as *The CASTLE OF PERSEVERANCE*, which features a similar motif.

Allegorically, *Sawles Warde* represents the body, the dwelling-place of the soul (the treasure), as a castle. As such, it joins a lengthy tradition that was utilized in the Middle Ages by St. Anselm of Canterbury, St. BERNARD OF CLAIRVAUX, and Hugh of St. Victor, among others. In the text, Wit (Reason) is the lord of the castle, and thus constable of the soul. The castle, populated by various allegorical figures, is being attacked by vices. One of these is Will (Desire), Wit's wife and lady of the castle. Will is impulsive and often self-absorbed. The Five Senses also dwell within the castle, and are difficult to rule as well. They are partially responsible for guarding the castle, but prove to be incompetent. Another group of servants employed by Will to guard the castle are the "inner servants." Though not as clearly delineated as other characters, the inner servants correspond to the inward human emotions brought about by the five senses—desires of the flesh (carnality) and emotional entanglement (*cupidas*). Together these servants are supposed to safeguard the castle, or more specifically, the entrance gate (maidenhead). However, they are losing ground. Wit requires help, and gets it from the four Cardinal Virtues—Justice, Prudence, Strength, and Temperance. Their progress toward good behavior is aided by the appearance of two visitors, Fear, who details the terrors of hell, and Love of Life, who describes the joys of heaven. At the end, Fear is asked to leave, though he can always be recalled, and Love of Life is invited to remain.

Sawles Warde has been popular with modern scholars, and nine editions of the text exist. The earliest of these was produced in 1868, and the most recent was compiled in 1990. As is typical with medieval works, most early scholarship focused on linguistic features, questions of authorship, and source materials. More recent criticism has focused on gender and feminist issues surrounding the text. For instance, by adding the character Will and fleshing out the characters of the Cardinal Virtues, the *Sawles Warde* author may have been designing a specific appeal to the female audience.

Because of its inclusion in the Katherine Group, as well as its content and manuscript tradition, *Sawles Warde* is often considered to be an anchoritic text. It survives in London, British Library, MS Cotton Titus D.xviii, appearing immediately after ANCRENE WISSE, and with *St. Katherine*, HALI MEIDENHAD, and *þe Wohunge of Ure Laured. Sawles Warde* also survives in Oxford, Bodleian Library, MS Bodley 34, with the rest of the Katherine Group, and London, British Library, MS Royal 17 A.xxvii, with *St. Juliana, St. Katherine, St. Margaret,* and *þe Oreisun of Seinte Marie.*

Bibliography

Becker, Wolfgang. "The Source Text of *Sawles Warde*," *Manuscripta* 24 (1980): 44–48.

Eggebroten, Anne. "*Sawles Warde:* A Retelling of *De Anima* for a Female Audience," *Mediaevalia* 10 (1984): 27–47.

Millett, Bella, and Jocelyn Wogan-Browne. *Medieval English Prose for Women.* Oxford: Clarendon Press, 1992.

Wilson, R. M. *Sawles Warde: An Early Middle English Homily.* Leeds School of English Language Texts and Monographs 3. Leeds, U.K.: Printed by T. Wilson for members of the School of English Language in the University of Leeds, 1938.

Michelle M. Sauer

Scivias Hildegard von Bingen (ca. 1151)

The *Scivias* (a contraction, presumably, of *Sci vias Domini,* or "Know the ways of the Lord") is the best-known work of the 12th-century abbess, mystic visionary, composer, prophetess, and preacher Hildegard von Bingen. Written in Latin over a 10-year period, the *Scivias* records a series of Hildegard's visions concerning God and Creation, the Fall of man and his Redemption, and the end of the world. It is a lengthy text of some 150,000 words, divided into three main sections or books, the first containing six visions, the second (twice the length of the first) containing seven, and the last (as long as the first and second combined) containing 13 visions. For each revelation, Hildegard first describes what she has seen, and then explains the vision in words that she portrays as coming to her through a voice from heaven. These explanations may be only a few chapters long, but may extend to more than a hundred for the more complicated visions, and are often supported by direct references to Scripture. Both the vision and its explanation are concluded with a kind of formulaic sentence that is different for each of the three books and acts as a kind of refrain.

In a preface to the *Scivias,* Hildegard describes a vision she had at the age of 42, in which she is commanded by heaven to write down the instruction she has received through her many visionary experiences, to share it with others—both her own nuns and the wider church—so that they, too, could experience the understanding she has gained. At first she balks at the thought, believing herself to be unworthy, but when she is struck down by illness, she obeys the divine directive and spends the next 10 years composing her *Scivias.*

In general, book 1 of the *Scivias* is concerned with the Creation of the world, the fall of Lucifer and mankind, and the subsequent breaking of the perfection of God's cosmos; book 2 describes the redemption of humankind, particularly through the church; and book 3 is concerned with salvation and the coming end of the world.

More specifically, book 1 opens with a vision of the perfect kingdom of God. This is followed by Lucifer's introduction of sin into Creation and his subsequent fall, followed by the fall of Adam and Eve. The fifth vision depicts *Synogoga,* the blind personification of the Jewish faith, in contrast with *Ecclesia,* the Christian Church, figuring the redemption that will come through Christ. The first book ends with a catalogue of the orders of angels in heaven.

Book 2 opens with a vision of Christ's incarnation, followed by a vision of the Holy Trinity. The remainder of book 2 comprises interconnected visions of the church, focusing on the redemption of humanity through the sacraments of baptism, confirmation, communion, holy orders, and penance. The focus is on God's plan to redeem his fallen world through the church.

The lengthier and more complex book 3 traces again Christ's incarnation and resurrection, deals with the importance of the virtues for the salvation of the individual human soul, and gives, in the 11th and 12th visions, a description of the apocalypse, the Antichrist, and the last judgment. The final vision is in fact a musical play called *Ordo virtutum* (Order of virtue), an original composition of Hildegard's, perhaps figuring the blessed harmony of heaven.

In her own time, Hildegard was best known for her apocalyptic visions, in particular the 11th vision of book 3 of the *Scivias,* on the last days and the fall of Antichrist. This vision first depicts five beasts (a dog, wolf, lion, pig, and horse) symbolizing five evil ages to come. The beasts come from the north, the realm of Satan. These are followed by the coming of Antichrist, pictured as a parodic mirror image of Christ: the Antichrist is born of a whore who pretends to be a virgin, and is possessed by the devil from his birth. He preaches and converts many through false miracles, and he disseminates false scriptures. Opposed by God's two "witnesses," Enoch and Elijah, the Antichrist ultimately succeeds in destroying them. He rejects all forms of continence and indulges his own lusts until, in Hildegard's most striking image, he rapes Ecclesia, the female personification of the church itself, who is ultimately redeemed by her true bridegroom, Christ, as Antichrist is struck down by God's thunderbolt.

It is chiefly for memorable visions like these that Hildegard is remembered. The *Scivias* is not intended to be a logical presentation of theological arguments, like those of Hildegard's contemporaries St. ANSELM and Peter ABELARD, although she does weigh in on some important questions. Concerned with the problem of why God would allow Satan to cause the fall of humanity, Hildegard asserts a version of the "paradox of the fortunate fall": God permitted the loss of Eden, Hildegard says, in order that he could provide human beings with the infinitely better dwelling in heaven. But in general, Hildegard presents pictorial ALLEGORIES that suggest truths, but she implies that God's purposes cannot be fully understood in this world. Her book is intended more as a prophetic text: she describes her call at the beginning of the *Scivias* in a manner reminiscent of the biblical calls of Isaiah or Ezekiel, and like the prophets her main purpose seems to be to castigate her society and advocate for God's laws. Against the Catharists of her own day (who rejected the physical world as evil), she extols the sanctity of the flesh when limited to God's plan of marriage. But she also condemns all forms of sexual vices, and prescribes remedies like special diets, fasting, mortification of the flesh, and even beatings for lustful thoughts.

Concerned at all times with orthodoxy, Hildegard submitted an unfinished copy of her manuscript for scrutiny by St. BERNARD OF CLAIRVAUX and Pope Eugenius III, who after reading the manuscript at the council of Trier in the period 1147–48 sent her a command that she was to continue to write down whatever visions God sent her. She was thus recognized as a seer in her own lifetime, and validated by the pope himself. It was from this recognition that Hildegard went on to become a major public figure throughout Europe, sought out by political and ecclesiastical figures and the luminary of four major preaching tours before her death in 1179 at the age of 82.

Bibliography

Flanagan, Sabina. *Hildegard of Bingen, 1098–1179: A Visionary Life.* London: Routledge, 1989.

Hildegard von Bingen. *Scivias.* Translated by Columba Hart and Jane Bishop. New York: Paulist Press, 1990.

Maddocks, Fiona. *Hildegard of Bingen: The Woman of Her Age.* New York: Doubleday, 2001.

Newman, Barbara. *Sister of Wisdom: St. Hildegard's Theology of the Feminine.* Berkeley: University of California Press, 1987.

Scogan, Henry (ca. 1361–1407)

Henry Scogan was an English poet and friend of Geoffrey CHAUCER. He was an esquire in the household of King Henry IV, and was tutor to the king's sons, to whom he addressed his only surviving poem, *A Moral Balade* (ca. 1406). But Scogan is perhaps best known as the subject of Chaucer's comic short poem, the *Envoy to Scogan.*

In addition to being an esquire of the king, Scogan was lord of the manor of Haviles, a property he inherited upon the death of his brother in 1391. He became tutor to Henry IV's sons: Henry the Prince of Wales, Thomas (later duke of Clarence), John (later duke of Bedford), and Humphrey (later duke of Gloucester), all born between 1388 and 1391. Thus the princes would have been between 15 and 18 years of age when Scogan wrote his poem, if Skeat's suggestion of 1406–07 for the poem's date is accurate—though that was based merely on Scogan's reference to "old age" catching up to him in the poem. According to the copyist John SHIRLEY, the poem was first read at a supper organized by London merchants at which the four princes were guests of honor.

A Moral Balade is a poem of 189 lines, made up of 21 eight-line stanzas rhyming *ababbcbc.* Between the 13th and 14th stanzas of his poem, Scogan inserts Chaucer's short poem, the BALLADE *Gentilesse* (often subtitled, in manuscripts "A moral ballade," like Scogan's poem), which stands out because of its seven-line RHYME ROYAL stanzas. Scogan accuses himself in conventional ways of a misspent youth, says he is now old (though he couldn't have been more than about 46), and gives the princes advice similar to that contained in Chaucer's poem—that true nobility was not a matter of birth but rather of character. The poem, sometimes mistaken as Chaucer's, was often printed in early editions of Chaucer's works.

But most readers will be better acquainted with Scogan through the poem that Chaucer addresses to him. That poem, usually dated 1393 because its allusion to torrential rains seems appropriate for that year, humorously takes Scogan to task for having abandoned his Lady because she would not return his love. Chaucer claims that Venus is weeping uncontrollably over the situation, and thus Scogan is responsible for the rains. It seems likely that Scogan had sent an equally humorous poem to Chaucer declaring his intention of giving up his love, and that Chaucer was responding with this poem. But that must remain conjecture, since the only extant work of Scogan's that we have is the *Moral Balade.*

Bibliography

Ruud, Jay. "Chaucer's *Envoy to Scogan:* 'Tullius Kyndenesse' and the Law of Kynde," *Chaucer Review* 20 (1986): 323–330.

Scogan, Henry. "A Moral Balade," in *The Complete Works of Geoffrey Chaucer.* Vol 7, *Chaucerian and Other Pieces,* edited by Walter W. Skeat. Oxford: Clarendon Press, 1897, 238–244.

scop

The OLD ENGLISH *scop* (pronounced "shope") was a professional poet and singer, both the reciter of old legends and the creator of new ones. The name seems to be the preterite form of the verb *scieppan* (to shape or create), thus the scop was the tribe's "shaper," or "creator." No mere entertainer, the scop was the living keeper of the oral history and heroic tradition of his people. While many *scopas* seem to have been permanently attached to royal households (as the scop character in *BEOWULF* seems a fixture at the court of the Danish king Hrothgar), some *scopas* no doubt wandered from court to court, seeking a patron who would employ them. The Old English poem *WIDSITH* (far traveler) illustrates the life of one such poet. A lord had much to gain from the employment of a good scop, since in addition to retelling old legends, part of the scop's responsibility was to create new songs, sometimes extemporaneously, that glorified his patron or his patron's family. The scop in *Beowulf*, for example, is depicted as composing an impromptu lay immediately after Beowulf's battle with the monster Grendel.

The scop seems generally to have performed before his lord and guests in the lord's hall, singing or chanting to a harp—a seventh-century Anglo-Saxon harp was discovered among the artifacts of the Sutton Hoo ship burial recovered in 1939. He would have known a great number of stories concerning the ancient Germanic heroes. Much he may have memorized, though many of his stories may have been told through oral formulas that could be adopted to various situations.

The tone of the poems created by *scopas* was formal and somber, and poets used a specialized vocabulary more formal and more ancient than everyday speech. He was respected as the keeper of the traditions that united his people, so that his function was not unlike that of a priest. After the conversion of the Old English people to Christianity, Old English poets adopted their poetic traditions and language to the service of the new religion, as the story of CAEDMON's Hymn illustrates. It seems likely that while the *scopas* survived in later Anglo-Saxon times, they began to sing songs with Christian themes. Certainly most of the written Old English poetry that survives deals with Christian matter, and it is not unreasonable to assume that the oral performers of poetry were singing similar songs.

Bibliography

Alexander, Michael, trans. *The Earliest English Poems.* Harmondsworth, U.K.: Penguin, 1966.

Seafarer, The (10th century)

The Seafarer is an OLD ENGLISH poem of 124 lines preserved in the 10th-century EXETER BOOK manuscript, which contains a wide assortment of Anglo-Saxon poetry. Like *The WANDERER*, the poem most often associated with it, *The Seafarer* describes the life of a *wraecca*, or exile, far from his home. But unlike the Wanderer, the speaker of this poem is in self-imposed exile, traveling by sea to some unspecified destination. The text of the poem has apparently become corrupted in transmission, and in any case, the language is obscure enough to make this poem one of the most difficult in the Old English canon.

Much of the difficulty comes from the fact that the poem has three distinct divisions. In the first 33 lines, the speaker describes the adversity he has endured in his many winters at sea. In a middle section, the speaker describes a new journey he has yet to make and his apprehension with regard to that new voyage. But he then seems to reverse his previous attitude toward seafaring and to embrace the new journey. In the third part of the poem, lines 64–124, the speaker launches into a didactic meditation on human existence. The speaker laments the impermanence of human existence in this world: Lords, mead halls, gold, and brave warriors all inevitably vanish. The poem concludes with the consolation that with God, eternal life is possible.

Difficult critical questions surround the poem: Why does the speaker apparently change his attitude toward his seafaring exile after line 33? What is the relationship between the first, descriptive half of the poem, and the second, meditative half? Earlier criticism suggested that there were two speakers in the poem: an old sailor and a young one. Another early suggestion was that everything after line 64 of the poem was a later addition by a monastic scribe. Neither of these suggestions is taken seriously any longer.

Clearly the connection between the two halves of the poem comes from the traditional Christian image of life as a pilgrimage through which we must travel en route to our eternal heavenly home. With this in mind, the first 33 lines represent the difficulties of human life on that spiritual journey, while lines 33–64 show the Christian soul's willingness to take that final step on the pilgrimage to God. The remainder of the poem is a meditation on the theme of life's pilgrimage.

Other scholars have suggested that the sea journey is not allegorical at all, but represents the speaker's willingness to become a *peregrinus*, that is, a hermit who deliberately takes to the sea, often in a rudderless boat, to endure exile and privation for the sake of a closer relationship with God. Such pilgrim hermits were known to Anglo-Saxon society, and are described in the *ANGLO-SAXON CHRONICLE* in the entry for the year 891.

Despite the difficulties in its interpretation, *The Seafarer* is a powerful poem, and its description of the transience of human life is justly famous. The poem inspired Ezra Pound to make his own translation (leaving off the didactic ending), and thus it continues to speak to readers even today.

Bibliography

Alexander, Michael, trans. *The Earliest English Poems.* Harmondsworth, U.K.: Penguin, 1966.

Krapp, George Philip, and Elliott Van Kirk Dobbie, eds. *The Exeter Book.* Vol. 3, The Anglo-Saxon Poetic Records. New York: Columbia University Press, 1936.

Orton, Peter. "The Form and Structure of *The Seafarer*," *Studia Neophilologica* 63 (1991): 37–55.

Whitelock, Dorothy. "The Interpretation of *The Seafarer.*" In *Early Cultures of Northwest Europe,* 261–272. H. M. Chadwick Memorial Studies. Cambridge: Cambridge University Press, 1950.

Second Nun's Tale, The Geoffrey Chaucer (ca. 1380)

CHAUCER's "Legend of Saint Cecilia," attributed to the Second Nun in Fragment 8 of *The CANTERBURY TALES,* is a saint's life that Chaucer is known to have written before the *Canterbury Tales* project was begun, and incorporated into the *Tales* later. Chaucer refers to the story as a separate text in a catalogue of his works included in the prologue to *The LEGEND OF GOOD WOMEN* (ca. 1386). The fact that the pilgrim narrator refers to herself at one point as an "unworthy son of Eve" suggests that Chaucer had not completely revised the tale for inclusion in the later work. *The Second Nun's Tale* has, however, been praised recently as an example of an intellectual and tough Christianity within the *Tales,* as contrasted with the emotional, even sentimental, "affective piety" of *The PRIORESS'S TALE.*

The tale begins with a prologue in three parts. The first part is a condemnation of idleness, a sin for which Cecilia, constantly working to convert souls to Christianity, provides a clear contrast. The second part of the invocation is a prayer in praise of the Virgin Mary, which Chaucer based on a passage in the final canto of the *Paradiso* section of DANTE's *DIVINE COMEDY,* where it is put into the mouth of St. BERNARD. The third part of the prologue, taken like the rest of the tale from the *GOLDEN* LEGEND, a widely read collection of saints' lives, gives a long etymology of the name Cecilia.

In the tale proper, Cecilia, a well-born Roman woman, marries another noble Roman, Valerian. She informs Valerian on their wedding night, however, that she is defended by a guardian angel who protects her virginity and will destroy Valerian if he touches her. The skeptical Valerian demands to see this angel, but Cecilia says he must first be baptized. Valerian consents to this, is baptized by Urban (anachronistically called "Pope"), who, like the other Christians in Rome, leads a clandestine existence. Once Valerian is baptized, he can see the angel as well as the flowered crown of martyrdom prepared for him. He eagerly embraces the new religion, and, with the help of Cecilia's theological arguments about such things as the Trinity, convinces his brother Tiburce to join him in his newfound faith.

The crisis of the story occurs when the Roman prefect Almachius orders all citizens to sacrifice to an image of the god Jupiter, condemning to death any who will not do so. Valerian and Tiburce refuse, and when Almachius sends the officer Maximus to seize them, they eventually convert him as well. Ultimately Valerian and Tiburce are beheaded for refusing to worship the idol, and are followed in their martyrdom by Maximus. Finally Cecilia is brought before Almachius, and in a climactic debate demonstrates the foolishness of Almachius's religion and of his belief in his own power. She is condemned to be boiled in a "bath of flames" in her own house, but she survives for a day, and is further condemned to beheading. But when her executioner strikes her neck three times and is unable to behead her completely, she continues for three days to preach before she dies of her wounds. The narrator ends by declaring that the Church of St. Cecilia in Rome is on the site of the house wherein she was martyred, and that pilgrims may visit it even to this day.

Scholars have noted how faithful Chaucer remains to his source, following the popular saint's life much more closely than was his general practice. Some have considered this a result of the tale's being an early work, though it may simply be a sign of how much respect Chaucer had for the legend. In any case the tale is probably not particularly early, since its borrowing from Dante and its composition in RHYME ROYAL stanzas (a form Chaucer probably developed after reading BOCCACCIO) makes it likely to have been written in the middle of his career, after he had begun to feel the influence of the great Italian writers. In addition to comparing this with the more emotional *Prioress's Tale,* recent critics have also discussed the relationship of *The Second Nun's Tale* to *The Canon's Yeoman's Tale,* its companion in Fragment 8, comparing Cecilia's busy labors for God and burning in God's holy fire with the alchemists' fruitless work of false creation and the hellish fires of their experiments.

Bibliography

Benson, C. David. *Chaucer's Drama of Style: Poetic Variety and Contrast in The Canterbury Tales.* Chapel Hill: University of North Carolina Press, 1986.

Grennen, Joseph E. "Saint Cecilia's 'Chemical Wedding': The Unity of the *Canterbury Tales,* Fragment VIII," *JEGP* 65 (1966): 466–481.

Kolve, V. A. "Chaucer's Second Nun's Tale and the Iconography of Saint Cecilia," in *New Perspectives on Chaucer Criticism,* edited by Donald M. Rose. Norman, Okla.: Pilgrim Books, 1981, 137–174.

Reames, Sherry L. "The Cecilia Legend as Chaucer Inherited It and Retold It: The Disappearance of an Augustinian Ideal," *Speculum* 55 (1980): 38–57.

Second Shepherds' Play (*Towneley Secunda pastorum*) (ca. 1475)

The *Second Shepherds' Play* is the best known and most highly regarded of the popular MYSTERY PLAYS of medieval England. The play is one of several in the TOWNELEY CYCLE (associated with the town of Wakefield in Yorkshire) written by an anonymous artist known as the "Wakefield Master," whose plays are identifiable by their use of a 13-line stanza rhyming *ababababcdddc. The Second Shepherds' Play,* so named because it is the second play in the Towneley Cycle concerning the Nativity, is unusual among mystery plays in the complexity of its comic subplot and its development of character. Particularly notable is the character of the sheep-stealing Mak, one of the great comic characters of medieval theater.

The play opens on the night of Christ's birth. A shepherd enters and complains about the weather, sounding remarkably like an English shepherd from the Yorkshire moors. He continues to complain about injustices in the social order. He is joined by a second shepherd who also grumbles about the weather and then moans about his relationship with his wife. A third shepherd, an employee of the others, continues the grousing about the weather, but goes on to complain about his relationship with his employers. Ultimately the three shepherds assuage their sorrows by singing a song in three-part harmony—a musical resolution of the earlier discord. Thus the reconciliation of the shepherds to their human relationships at the beginning of the play prefigures the reconciliation of the world to God through the birth of his Son.

At the close of the song, Mak enters. His reputation as a thief makes the shepherds disinclined to trust him, but when he tells them he is hungry and not welcome at home, the shepherds relent and allow Mak to spend the night with them. Mak waits until the shepherds fall asleep, then rises, steals one of their ewes, and takes it home to his wife, Gill. He returns to the shepherds' camp before they awake to avoid suspicion.

In the morning Mak awakes with the shepherds and takes his leave. At that point they notice the missing sheep, and visit Mak's house to look for the sheep. Gill pretends that she has delivered a child that night, so that she and Mak can disguise the ewe as a child and hide it in a cradle. Having found no sign of their ewe, the shepherds apologize and leave, but they remember the new baby, and decide they should present the child with gifts. When they return and discover the sheep hidden in the cradle, Mak and Gill try to brazen it out, swearing that some elf must have altered the child's appearance. The shepherds, forgoing any more severe punishment, decide to let Mak off with a simple blanket-tossing, and they leave with their sheep.

It is doubtless that the shepherd's acts of basic human charity—their allowing Mak to spend the night with them, their desire to present the baby with gifts, and their forgiveness of Mak for his theft—are what make them worthy recipients of the angelic message. And that message comes immediately after the shepherds finish with Mak. An angel directs them to the Christ child, and when they arrive in Bethlehem, they find the child with Mary in the stable. The first shepherd gives the baby a bob of cherries; the second gives him a small bird to play with; the third offers a ball, saying he hopes the baby will grow up to play tennis. The play ends as the shepherds sing another song.

At first glance it seems that the actual story of Christ's nativity is merely an afterthought appended to the comic "subplot" of Mak and the sheep, which is four times as long. But it is not difficult to see the parallel between the stolen sheep in Mak's cradle and the Lamb of God in Mary's manger. Aside from inviting us to compare the fallen world of the first part of the play (a world whose anachronistic shepherds make it very much like the contemporary world of the audience) with the restored world of Christ's nativity, the shepherds' charity demonstrates the appropriate frame of mind necessary for human beings to accept God's grace.

Bibliography

Gardner, John. *The Construction of the Wakefield Cycle.* Carbondale: Southern Illinois University Press, 1971.

Meredith, Peter. "The Towneley Cycle," in *The Cambridge Companion to Medieval English Theatre,* edited by Richard Beadle. Cambridge: Cambridge University Press, 1994, 134–162.

Stevens, Martin. "Language as Theme in the Wakefield Plays," *Speculum* 52 (1977): 100–117.

Stevens, Martin, and A. C. Cawley, eds. *The Towneley Plays.* 2 vols. Oxford: Published for the Early English Text Society by the Oxford University Press, 1994.

Sege off Melayne, The (*The Siege of Milan*) (ca. 1350–1400)

The Sege off Melayne is a fragmentary late 14th-century ROMANCE of CHARLEMAGNE, written in a northern dialect of MIDDLE ENGLISH and surviving in a single manuscript (British Museum MS Additional 31042, known as the "London Thornton" manuscript) dating from about 1450. The 1,599-line poem is written in 12-line TAIL-RHYME stanzas rhyming *aabccbddbeeb,* the form of many popular romances of the time. Unlike most Charlemagne romances, however, *The Sege off Melayne* has no known source, and, although the narrator refers to "the chronicle" as his source, the poem may even have originally been composed in English, particularly since its theme seems less the glorification of the French king than it is the exaltation of the religious ideal of the crusade. The protagonist of the poem is clearly the archbishop, Turpin, rather than Charlemagne himself or one of the 12 peers of France (such as Roland or Oliver).

The theme of the poem is the defense of the faith against the Saracen infidel, the great goal of the late medieval crusading mentality. It begins as the sultan Arabas leads his armies into Tuscany, conquering many cities. He burns the crucifixes in the churches and sets up Mohammedan "idols" in their place, and martyrs many Christian women and children. Sir Alantyne, the lord of the city of Milan, is confronted by the conquering army, and given the choice of death or conversion to Islam. He spends the night in prayer, and an angel appears to him, telling him to go to Charlemagne, king of France, and tell him that God bids him to rescue Milan from the heathen. The same night, Charlemagne also receives a vision in which an angel gives him a sword, symbolizing a holy sanction for a war on the Saracens.

In a council of Charles's retainers, Ganelon advises Charles not to go to the war, but to let Roland lead an army there instead—as in *The SONG OF ROLAND* and other CHANSONS DE GESTE, Ganelon is depicted as a treasonous knight. Roland's army rides to Milan and engages the Saracen army but suffers a terrible defeat. Roland is taken prisoner, with Oliver and two other peers, but the other

40,000 Christian warriors are slain. The poet, calling the French troops "our knights," focuses specifically on the death of the duke of Normandy, who has a dying vision of French knights being welcomed into heavenly bliss.

In the second fitt (or section), the sultan tries to persuade the four French knights to forsake Christianity by burning a crucifix in order to demonstrate the powerlessness of the Christian God. As an answer to the knights' prayers, not only does the crucifix fail to burn, but fire flashes from it and blinds the Saracens, enabling the four knights to kill their captors (including the sultan Arabas) and escape on white horses, which appear at the precise moment they are needed. When Bishop Turpin hears of the slaughter, he laments to the Virgin Mary, complaining to her that had she not been born and given birth to Christ, these 40,000 knights would not have been killed. Charles is disturbed by the news, and Ganelon advises him to make himself vassal to the new sultan, Garcy. Turpin curses Ganelon and his advice, and urges Charles to take vengeance for the knights he has lost. The bishop himself sends throughout Christendom for an army of priests, 100,000 strong, who come to fight for the faith under his guidance. But once again, under Ganelon's advice, the king refuses to take part in the battle. At this, Turpin calls the king a coward, and excommunicates both him and Ganelon. He then leads his huge army against the city of Paris, and Charles decides to relent, ask the bishop's forgiveness and absolution, and go himself to Milan. Within three weeks he has raised another army, and they set out for Lombardy.

In fitt three, the final battle begins. Turpin essentially directs the battle. He goads the others on to do their duty to their God. When his squire despoils the body of a dead Saracen, Turpin beats him with his sword and declares that there should be no spoils until victory is won. Wounded twice, Turpin still fights on. He vows not to eat or drink or have his wounds tended to until Milan is taken back by the Christians. He urges Charlemagne to fight on against superior odds even as reinforcements arrive from Brittany. But the manuscript breaks off at this point, before what was clearly to be an ultimate victory for the Christian forces.

The Sege off Melayne is a lively and readable romance, of particular interest for its focus on Turpin and the moral values he represents. In addition, the poem provides a clear view of Christian attitudes toward Muslims in the late medieval period.

Bibliography

Barron, W. R. J. *English Medieval Romance.* London: Longman, 1987.

Mehl, Dieter. *The Middle English Romances of the Thirteenth and Fourteenth Centuries.* London: Routledge and Kegan Paul, 1968.

Three Middle English Charlemagne Romances. Edited by Alan Lupack. Kalamazoo, Mich.: Medieval Institute Publications, 1990.

Sei Shōnagon (fl. 966–1017)

Sei Shōnagon lived during the early medieval period in the HEIAN dynasty in Japan, an era that witnessed an extraordinary production of literary works. For instance Sei's contemporaries include MURASAKI SHIKIBU, author of *The TALE OF GENJI,* the greatest Japanese masterpiece. Sei's own contributions are *waka* (native Japanese) poetry and, most significantly, *The PILLOW BOOK (Makura no Sōshi).*

Since custom prevented revealing in public the private given names of women, we do not know her true name. "Sei" derives from the first letter of her family name, and "Shōnagon" refers to her position, a middle rank known for its learning. Her father was a Chinese scholar, and she appears to have been one as well. She married in 983, but little is known about her marriage. About that time she entered the court service of Teishi, a consort of the emperor. When her patron died in 1000, she left court and apparently remarried.

The most famous observation about Sei comes from Murasaki Shikibu, her rival at the court of Empress Shōshi: "She thought herself so clever, and littered her writings with Chinese characters, but if you examined them closely, they left a great deal to be desired" (Bowring 1982, 131). It confirms the impression that Sei creates in *The Pillow Book* of herself as an author who can write in Chinese as well as in Japanese. Though women dominate the canon of Heian Japanese literature, in general it was men who studied and wrote in the official Chinese (a language that has its counterpart in Latin in the medieval West).

Most of the knowledge and impressions we have of Sei come from the persona she creates for herself in *The Pillow Book.* The work—and by extension its author—are unique. This original collection of personal observations and memoirs, interspersed with poems, is made up of pieces presumably written at night and placed in the drawers of wooden pillows—hence the name "pillow book."

Sei created the genre for *The Pillow Book,* a genre later called *zuihitsu*—often translated as "prose miscellany." Much discussion has centered upon how Sei invented her unique masterpiece. Since it is autobiographical, it shares characteristics of the Heian diary (*nikki*). Yet it is more than a memoir; it includes 164 lists and poetry. Its textual history is complex. Although Sei focuses upon her life at the court of Empress Teishi and she began the work while at court, she completed it after Teishi's death and her own subsequent departure from court. Furthermore there is disagreement over the original order Sei imposed upon her text.

Sei's persona and writing style often provide ironic contrasts to major Heian literary conventions. Instead of the Buddhist theme about the tragic ephemeral nature of this world, her work is witty and lighthearted. For instance she tells anecdotes about the empress's pet cat and dog. Under her list of "hateful things," she complains of clumsy lovers who stumble as they get out of bed and fumble getting dressed the next morning. Also Sei describes herself as the antithesis of the ideal Heian court lady: She claims that she is unattractive and writes poor poetry. And, as Murasaki's comment attests, Sei flaunts her Chinese frequently, something proper modest women would never do.

But even through careful omission and a light tone, Sei cannot fully disguise the fact that Teishi's court was in disarray as the emperor Ichijō more and more favored his other wife, Shōshi (Murasaki's patron). Eventually Teishi died in childbirth, and Sei departed from the court. Little is known about the final years of Sei's life, but later strict Buddhists claim that she died impoverished and alone, punishment for the "sins" revealed in *The Pillow Book.*

The Pillow Book is recognized as a great masterpiece because of its wit and originality, its clear insights into life in Heian Japan, and its "linguistic purity" (Morris 1971, 13).

Bibliography

Bowring, Richard, trans. *Murasaki Shikibu: Her Diary and Poetic Memoirs.* Princeton, N.J.: Princeton University Press, 1982.

Miner, Earl, Hiroko Odagiri, and Robert E. Morrell. *The Princeton Companion to Classical Japanese Literature.* Princeton, N.J.: Princeton University Press, 1985.

Sei Shōnagon. *The Pillow Book of Sei Shōnagon.* Translated by Ivan Morris. New York: Columbia University Press, 1971.

Barbara Stevenson

Seven Sages of Rome, The (ca. 1300–1325)

The Seven Sages of Rome is a MIDDLE ENGLISH verse ROMANCE that exists in several versions, ranging from roughly 2,500 lines to about 4,300 lines. The earliest known version was written in Kent in the early 14th century, but that text is based on a French text from about 1150 called *Les Sept Sages de Rome.* That French source is itself derived from a long and complex tradition going back, through either Latin sources derived from Byzantine or Hebrew traditions, or through Spanish sources derived from Arabic, to an Eastern source called the *Book of Sindbad.* A Syrian version of the *Book of Sindbad* from the 10th century is extant, and it is possible that this parent text dates back to the fifth century, and may have originated in India.

Like *The* CANTERBURY TALES or the THOUSAND AND ONE NIGHTS, *The Seven Sages of Rome* is structured as a frame narrative, in which 15 stories are integrated effectively with the frame tale. The story opens as Diocletian, emperor of Rome, sends his son to be educated by seven sages. The young man's stepmother is jealous of his influence with the emperor, and fearful that he will succeed his father in the imperial office, and she determines to have the boy executed. She attempts to seduce the boy and, failing that, goes to

Diocletian and accuses the son of attempting to rape her. The young man does not defend himself but remains completely silent, and the stepmother takes advantage of this silence by telling the emperor a story each night for seven nights. All of her stories illustrate the danger of sons displacing their fathers. The emperor reacts to each of her tales by condemning his son to death, but every morning is persuaded by one of the seven sages to spare the boy's life, as each of them tells him a tale illustrating the lying ways of women. Ultimately the boy is able to speak for himself, and tells the truth about his stepmother's actions, forcing her to confess the truth. In the end, the empress is burnt.

The complex relationships between the Middle English *Seven Sages of Rome* and the huge number of variants in other medieval languages have been of most interest to scholars. There are some 40 different versions of the Seven Sages story, and about 100 different tales distributed within the frames of the different versions. The most common English-language version is from a tradition called Version A, and there are also French, Italian, Swedish, and Welsh renderings of this version. This complex background and the skillful interweaving of frame text and framed narrative make the English *Seven Sages of Rome* far more than simply just another antifeminist medieval text.

Bibliography

Runte, Hans R., J. Keith Wikeley, and Anthony J. Farrell, eds. *The Seven Sages of Rome and The Book of Sindbad: An Analytical Bibliography.* New York: Garland, 1984.

The Seven Sages of Rome (Southern Version). Edited by Karl Brunner. EETS, o.s. 191. London: Published for the Early English Text Society by Oxford University Press, 1933.

Shem Tov (Rabbi Shem Tov ben Yitzhak Ardutiel, Sem Tob, Santo, Santob de Carrión) (ca. 1290–ca. 1369)

Shem Tov ("Good Name" in Hebrew) was a 14th-century Castilian Jew who composed poetry in both Spanish and Hebrew during the reigns of Alfonso XI (1312–50), and his son and successor Pedro I (1350–69). He was born and lived in the town of Carrión de los Condes in Castile. In his *Proverbios morales* (Moral proverbs), his best-known work, he uses the Spanish-sounding name of Santob de Carrión, and presents the text as counsel from a "white-haired poet" to King Pedro, known as "the Cruel." Pedro was a monarch particularly known for his tolerance of Jews, and therefore an appropriate audience for Shem Tov's verse.

The *Proverbios morales* is written in 686 stanzas of four heptasyllabic (seven-syllable) Spanish lines rhyming *abab.* As such it is the first Jewish literary text written in Spanish. Inspired by the biblical genre of wisdom books like Proverbs and Ecclesiastes, Shem Tov's *Proverbios morales* represent the first verse treatment in Spanish of the wisdom genre (known in Hebrew as *musar*). Shem Tov drew some of his inspiration from the Bible, from the Talmud, and from the 11th-century Spanish Jewish philosopher Avicebron, but he seems to have based a number of his proverbs on his own philosophy. The work deals with questions of ethics and philosophy, and survives in five manuscripts. The rabbi rather conventionally promotes work and study in his proverbs, and warns of the harm that a king might cause through injustice and profligate living. But more radically Shem Tov also expresses a deep skepticism and relativism concerning philosophical and religious questions, most of which he sees as inherently subjective. Only God, the king, and the law are beyond question for Shem Tov.

Several Hebrew works are also attributed to Shem Tov. In about 1345, he composed a rhymed prose narrative (a form called a *maqāma*). Two of his other texts are intended for the liturgy—a hymn called *Vidui Gadol* (Confession on Yom Kippur) and a prayer of supplication (or *bakkashah*). Shem Tov also translated a liturgical work by Israel ben Israel into Hebrew. But it is the enigmatic *Proverbios morales* upon which his modern reputation rests. Shem Tov's proverbs influenced a number of subsequent Spanish poets, including SANTILLANA, who imitated them. The work is unusual for the Middle Ages, and in many ways looks forward to the Renaissance.

Bibliography

Santob de Carrión. *Proverbios morales.* Edited by Theodore A. Perry. Madison, Wisc.: Hispanic Seminary for Medieval Studies, 1986.

———. *The Moral Proverbs of Santob de Carrión: Jewish Wisdom in Christian Spain.* Translated by Theodore A. Perry. Princeton, N.J.: Princeton University Press, 1987.

Shepard, Sanford. *Shem Tov: His World and His Works.* Miami: Ediciones Universal, 1978.

Shipman's Tale, The Geoffrey Chaucer (ca. 1390)

The Shipman's Tale is one of several FABLIAUX included in CHAUCER's *CANTERBURY TALES.* As such it is a comic tale of deception and adultery lampooning the licentiousness of the clergy, the deviousness of women, and the blind materialism of the merchant class. Most scholars agree that Chaucer originally intended the tale for *The WIFE OF BATH,* but reassigned it to the *Shipman* when he found a more appropriate tale for the *Wife.* Thus there is little in the tale to link it particularly to the pilgrim Shipman narrator.

The tale tells the story of a wealthy merchant from St. Denis and his beautiful wife, though the narrative suggests the merchant is far more focused on his business than on his spouse. A monk, Dan John, visits the merchant's lavish estate frequently, and is thought to be the merchant's cousin. One day the monk visits when the merchant is busy in his counting house. He and the wife engage in thinly veiled flirtatious banter, during which the monk reveals an attraction to the wife, while she in turn complains that her husband neglects her and that he will not even give her the 100 franks she needs to pay a debt. She hints that she will show her gratitude in every way imaginable if the monk will give her the 100 franks. Dan John promises to help her, helping himself to a foretaste of his reward by stroking her "flanks."

The merchant is about to travel to Flanders on a business trip when the monk asks him for a loan of 100 franks. Having obtained the loan, the monk goes to see the wife. After paying her the money, he enjoys her sexual favors. When the merchant returns from Flanders, his financial situation forces him to ask the monk for the repayment of his loan. The monk informs the merchant that he has already repaid the debt, having given the money to the merchant's wife during his absence. The merchant mentions the matter to his wife that evening, expressing his embarrassment at having asked Dan John to repay the loan when he had already paid her. He asks his wife what has happened to the money, and she tells him she has already spent it on rich attire for herself, claiming that for the merchant's own honor, he should ensure that his wife is fashionably dressed. As for the money, she tells the merchant he can "Score it on my tail [tally]"—with the double meaning that he can put it on her tab as something she owes him, or she can pay him back by giving him her "tail."

The story is based on the motif of the "lover's gift regained"—an extremely popular plot device that appears in numerous medieval analogues, including one from BOCCACCIO's *DECAMERON* (the first story of the eighth day), and remains popular in the oral tradition of jokes even to the present time. The French milieu of the tale (as opposed to the very English setting of *The MILLER'S TALE* and *The REEVE'S TALE* in Oxford and Cambridge) might suggest that this story is earlier than those, perhaps Chaucer's first attempt in the fabliau genre, and therefore closer to the French fabliaux that Chaucer used as models. Critical views of the tale have examined it as a comment on the bourgeois ethos of the merchant class, and have seen the imagery making as the equation of sex and money, of human relationships and financial transactions. *The Shipman's Tale* has also been considered as the first tale in Fragment 7 of the *Canterbury Tales,* the largest collection of coherently linked tales in the text, and one with a tremendous variety of literary genres, retrospectively drawn together through ironic commentary in *The Nun's Priest's Tale* that concludes the fragment.

Bibliography

Benson, Larry, and Theodore Andersson, eds. *The Literary Context of Chaucer's Fabliaux: Texts and Translations.* Indianapolis: Bobbs-Merrill, 1971.

Benson, Larry, et al., ed. *The Riverside Chaucer.* 3rd ed. Boston: Houghton Mifflin, 1987.

Howard, Donald. *The Idea of The Canterbury Tales.* Berkeley: University of California Press, 1976.

Silverman, Albert H. "Sex and Money in Chaucer's Shipman's Tale," *Philological Quarterly* 32 (1953): 329–336.

Shirley, John (ca. 1366–1456)

Remembered mainly as a scribe whose manuscript attributions are important for establishing the authorship of some of CHAUCER's shorter poems, John Shirley was also important for his manuscript copies of many of LYDGATE's poems and for his translations of some French and Latin texts into English.

Though he was born as early as 1366, possibly in Worcestershire, virtually nothing is known of Shirley's early life until he appears in 1403, in the retinue of Richard Beauchamp, the earl of Warwick. Shirley became Warwick's secretary, and apparently accompanied the earl to Wales during Henry IV's Welsh wars and to France under Henry V. Warwick is known to have traveled widely, to Jerusalem on pilgrimage, through Lithuania, Prussia, and Germany, and to the Council of Constance in 1414. It is unknown whether his secretary accompanied him on any of these journeys, but Shirley did have the reputation of traveling to various countries. Eventually Shirley became undersheriff of Worcestershire. By the late 1420s, however, Shirley had married his second wife, a woman from a London family, and was living in London himself, apparently no longer in Warwick's service. It is likely that he copied most of his manuscripts during his time in London. He died in 1456, and his tomb in London says that he had 12 children and that he died in his 90th year.

Some 20 surviving manuscripts are associated with Shirley, but three are particularly important: in London, British Library MS. Additional 16165; in Cambridge, Trinity College Library MS. R.3.20; and in Oxford, Bodleian Ashmole MS. 59. These are large anthologies of vernacular poetry, mainly in English, but with a few texts in French or Latin. Important for the transmission of some of the work of Lydgate and Chaucer, these manuscripts help to establish Chaucer's authorship of poems like his *Complaint unto Pity,* the *Complaint to His Lady, Adam Scriveyn,* the *Complaint of Mars,* the *Complaint of Venus,* and *Lak of Stedfastnesse.* Indeed in the case of *Adam Scriveyn,* Shirley's is the only extant manuscript copy. In addition Shirley often included rubrics with the poems he copied, explaining something of the context in which the poem was written, at least from what he had heard. Recent scholars have been interested in how these comments contributed to the construction of Chaucer's reputation as a "social poet" of the court. Of course many of Shirley's guesses are simply wrong: He thought that *TRUTH* was a deathbed poem, and that Chaucer had sent *Lak of Stedfastnesse* to RICHARD II during his last years, both of which are almost certainly false. Shirley says, too, that Chaucer's *Complaint of Mars* concerns the affair between the king's half brother, John Holland, and Isabel of York (sister-in-law of JOHN OF GAUNT), and that the *Complaint of Venus* was written as an answer to *Mars.* Again neither of these speculations seems likely; thus many of the stories Shirley passed along seem to have been popular—but unfounded—rumors attached to the poems.

At one time it was thought that Shirley was a book dealer who copied his manuscripts to sell. Modern scholars see no evidence of this. It seems likely that Shirley copied his manuscripts mainly for his own use, but was certainly generous in loaning his books widely to friends and acquaintances. He even composed what is known as his "bookplate poem"—a single RHYME ROYAL stanza appearing at the beginning of two of his large manuscripts, in which Shirley claims ownership of the books and admonishes the reader to return the book to its proper owner. In addition he composed two "Verse Prefixes" that appeared at the beginnings of his manuscripts, each of which is 104 lines of rhymed couplets and acts as a kind of table of contents and short commentary on the poems contained in each volume.

Shirley's translations included *The Boke of Gode Maners* (translated from Jacques Legrand's French *Le livre de bons meurs*), *Le secret des secres* (The secrecy of secrecies, a book of moral axioms, also from the French), and *A full lamentable Cronycle of the dethe and false murdure of James Stearde, lat kynge of Scotys,* a translation of a Latin chronicle on the death of the Scottish king James I. The original of the latter is not extant, so Shirley's text is the only witness to this contemporary account of the king's murder.

Bibliography

Boffey, Julia, and A. S. G. Edwards. " 'Chaucer's Chronicle,' John Shirley, and the Canon of Chaucer's Shorter Poems," *Studies in the Age of Chaucer* 20 (1998): 201–218.

Connolly, Margaret. *John Shirley: Book Production and the Noble Household in Fifteenth-Century England.* Aldershot, U.K.: Ashgate, 1998.

Lerer, Seth. *Chaucer and his Readers: Imagining the Author in Late Medieval England.* Princeton, N.J.: Princeton University Press, 1993.

Siege of Jerusalem, The (ca. 1370–1390)

The Siege of Jerusalem is a long (1,334 lines) ALLITERATIVE VERSE poem in MIDDLE ENGLISH, probably composed in the last decades of the 14th century in far west Yorkshire. This production of the so-called ALLITERATIVE REVIVAL tells the story of the Roman siege and destruction of Jerusalem in 70 C.E., and the subsequent dispersion of the Jews. The nine surviving manuscripts testify to a wide popularity, and the medieval collations that situate the poem variously in scriptural, romance, Crusade, or historical contexts indicate that the reception of the poem was diverse, complicated by the poem's complex retelling of a popular and well-known story.

Drawing on chronicles and legendary materials, including Josephus's first-century account of the *Jewish War,* the apocryphal *Vindicta salvatoris,* RANULPH HIGDEN'S *POLYCHRONICON,* the *Bible en françois* of Roger d'Argenteuil, and the *Legenda Aurea,* the poem relates how Titus and Vespasian, Roman leaders and recent converts to Christianity, embark upon a crusade against the Jews of Jerusalem to avenge Christ's death (and to punish the Jews for ceasing to pay taxes to the Roman emperor). The Romans lay siege to Jerusalem and after a graphic and bloody battle in which many Jews are slain, the Jews retreat within the city walls and the Romans assail the town. The poetic narrative of the two-year siege of Jerusalem by the Romans is filled with diverse and disturbing details of both Roman and Jewish actions, including detailed scenes inside the city walls, where hundreds die daily for lack of food and water, the gruesome murder of the Jewish high priest that leads hundreds of Jews in Jerusalem to take their own lives, and a Jewish woman killing and eating her own child. The siege ends with the surrender of the Jews and their sale into slavery by the Romans.

The Siege of Jerusalem is formed and informed with a variety of sensibilities, religious, political, economic, and social. Regarding the religious, the Roman crusade against the Jews and Jerusalem is framed in Christian justifications, and medieval expressions of anti-Semitism are given voice when the Jews are referred to as the "faithless," the "heathen," and Christ-killers. Political issues of empire and rule are played out within the Roman camp and between the Romans and the Jews. Because the Jews have refused to pay tribute to Rome, the economics of revenge activate, in part, the original decision to besiege the city. The social dimensions of the work range from the semi-chivalric Roman knights hunting and hawking outside the city walls (a ROMANCE element at odds with its own setting) to relations within the city and relations between individual Jew and Christian. Unlike the less-nuanced *Titus and Vespasian* concerning the same events, *The Siege of Jerusalem* has proved fertile ground for a variety of interpretations and readings.

Marginalized for years from critical consideration due to its seemingly unambiguous anti-Semitism and violence, *The Siege of Jerusalem* is in the process of being reassessed by scholars of Middle English literature and culture. Although the author remains anonymous, there is some consensus (based on manuscript evidence and theological influences) that the poet was an Augustinian canon writing at Bolton Priory. The composition and reception of the poem are widely debated, and the debate primarily revolves around the nature of the poem's anti-Semitism. Where some scholars read *The Siege of Jerusalem* as expressing the anti-Semitism considered to be an inevitable and universal commonplace of medieval thinking and writing, others find a more subtle representation of Jews and Judaism that includes both anti-Semitic and sympathic gestures. Written approximately 100 years after the expulsion of the Jews from England in 1290, the poem is increasingly the cause of discussions about the nature of medieval anti-Semitism and the ways in which Jews (absent or present) define the Christian community.

Bibliography

Chism, Christine. "*The Siege of Jerusalem:* Liquidating Assets," *Journal of Medieval and Early Modern Studies* 28 (1998): 309–340.

Hanna, Ralph. "Contextualizing *The Siege of Jerusalem,*" *Yearbook of Langland Studies* 6 (1992): 109–121.

Hamel, Mary. "*The Siege of Jerusalem* as a Crusading Poem." In *Journeys Toward God: Pilgrimage and Crusade,* edited by Barbara N. Sargent-Baur, 177–194. Kalamazoo, Mich.: Medieval Institute Publications, 1992.

Kölbing, E., and Mabel Day, eds. *The Siege of Jerusalem.* EETS o.s. 188. London: Published for the Early English Text Society by H. Milford, Oxford University Press, 1932.

Lawton, David, and Ralph Hanna III, eds. *The Siege of Jerusalem.* EETS o.s. 320. Oxford: Published for the Early English Text Society by the Oxford University Press, 2003.

Millar, Bonnie. *The Siege of Jerusalem in Its Physical, Literary and Historical Contexts.* Dublin: Fourcourts, 2000.

Narin van Court, Elisa. "*The Siege of Jerusalem* and Augustinian Historians: Writing About Jews in Fourteenth-Century England," *Chaucer Review* 29 (1995): 227–248.

———. "Socially Marginal, Culturally Central: Representing Jews in Late Medieval English Literature," *Exemplaria* 12 (2000): 293–326.

Elisa Narin van Court

Siege of Thebes, The (*The Destruction of Thebes*) John Lydgate (ca. 1420)

The Siege of Thebes (called in some manuscripts *The Destruction of Thebes*) is a long MIDDLE ENGLISH poem by the 15th-century poet John LYDGATE, finished in about 1420, and presented as a continuation of CHAUCER's *CANTERBURY TALES.* The prologue to Lydgate's poem is modeled after the GENERAL PROLOGUE to Chaucer's work, and presents Chaucer's pilgrims, having reached the holy shrine of Thomas BECKETT at Canterbury, meeting the monk Lydgate. Having visited the shrine himself, Lydgate now becomes a member of their party and tells the first tale on the pilgrims' trip back to London.

Lydgate presents himself as the new poet-narrator of the text, Chaucer having been dead for some 20 years. Certainly it was Lydgate's sincere admiration for Chaucer that led him to frame his tale as he did, and also to imitate Chaucer's style by writing his tale in the decasyllabic (or 10-syllable) couplets that Chaucer had introduced into English verse. Most readers find Lydgate's use of the form less skillful than Chaucer's, and they find his tale somewhat tedious by comparison. Indeed at 9,400 lines, *The Siege of Thebes* is more than four times as long as *The KNIGHT'S TALE,* Chaucer's longest Canterbury tale in verse. The centerpiece of the tale is a three-part, 4,540-line exemplum illustrating Thebes's fate under three disastrous rulers: Edippus (Oedipus), the incestuous patricide; his sons Ethyocles and Polymyte, whose enmity and thirst for power lead to the siege of the city; and finally Creon, whose unnatural rule leads to the destruction of the city itself by the forces of the Athenian king Theseus. Lydgate, conscious of the relationship between his tale (the first on the return trip from Canterbury) and *The Knight's Tale* (the first on the trip to Canterbury), is careful to end his tale in a way that dovetails with the beginning of Chaucer's, which picks up the narrative immediately after the events of *The Siege of Troy.* Lydgate even borrows phrases from Chaucer's tale to make the transition smooth.

Lydgate's debt to Chaucer in the poem is clear throughout. He also alludes to Boccaccio's influence, and seems to have based the plot of the story on the French *Roman de Thèbes* (ca. 1175), but also used some classical Latin writers, such as Seneca and Martianus Capella. One of his best-known works, the poem was written about midway in Lydgate's long career, which spanned the entire first half of the 15th century. The English king Henry V seems to have been the intended audience of Lydgate's poem, and the poem's allusion to the Treaty of Troyes, which named Henry heir to the French throne in 1420, suggests that *The Siege of Thebes* must have been written between 1420 and 1422, when Henry died. There are 29 extant manuscript versions of the poem, five of which actually appear at the end of texts of the *Canterbury Tales*. Even one of the early printed versions of Chaucer's work—John Stowe's from 1561—appends Lydgate's text to the *Tales*. One of the tale's most authoritative early manuscripts (British Museum Arundel 119) is known to have belonged to William de la Pole, the duke of Suffolk—husband of Chaucer's only known grandchild, Alice Chaucer.

Bibliography

Allen, Rosamund S. "*The Siege of Thebes:* Lydgate's Canterbury Tale." In *Chaucer and Fifteenth-Century Poetry,* edited by Julia Boffey and Janet Cowen, 122–142. London: King's College, Centre for Late Antique and Medieval Studies, 1991.

Bowers, John M., ed. *The Canterbury Tales: Fifteenth-Century Continuations and Additions.* Kalamazoo, Mich.: Published for TEAMS in association with the University of Rochester by Medieval Institute Publications, Western Michigan University, 1992.

Lydgate, John. *Lydgate's Siege of Thebes.* Edited by Axel Erdmann and Eilert Ekwall. 2 vols. EETS e.s. 108 and 125, 1911 and 1930. London: Published for the Early English Text Society by the Oxford University Press, 1960.

———. *The Siege of Thebes.* Edited by Robert R. Edwards. Kalamazoo, Mich.: Medieval Institute Publications, 2001.

Schirmer, Walter F. *John Lydgate: A Study in the Culture of the XVth Century.* Translated by Ann E. Keep. London: Methuen, 1961.

sijo

The *sijo* is a Korean verse form that developed in the 13th and 14th centuries, toward the end of the Koryŏ period (935–1392), although it did not reach the peak of its development until the 16th-century emergence of major poets in the genre like Chŏng Ch'ŏl. Previously, there was a distinction between the poetic forms used by aristocratic writers and those used by common people, but the *sijo* came to be used by all classes. The *sijo* has dominated Korean poetry since the late medieval period, somewhat as the TANKA form did in Japan—and like the tanka, its ultimate roots are probably in Chinese poetry. Still practiced in Korea, and imitated by poets in other languages, the *sijo* is probably Korea's most important contribution to world literature.

The term *sijo* means "melody of the times." These poems were originally sung or chanted, probably to a well-known tune and with instrumental accompaniment. Thus the poems were originally part of performances, and were either memorized or composed spontaneously by the singer. Early *sijo* were not recorded in written form until the 18th century, and the music has been lost. Still, the basic conventions of the *sijo* are clear from the beginning.

A complex verse form, the conventional *sijo* has three lines. Each line contains four phrases or groups of syllables. In each of the first two lines, the first phrase was made up of three syllables, the second of four, the third of either three or four syllables, and the last phrase of four syllables. Thus each of the first two lines might contain 14 or 15 syllables. The third line of the poem more strictly included phrases of three, five, four, and three syllables. Thus the entire poem comprised from 43 to 45 syllables, and there was a natural break in the poem after the first and the middle lines. Because of the groups of syllables within the lines, there was also a lesser break after the second phrase of each line (thus translations of Korean *sijo* are often printed as six lines).

Typically the first line of the *sijo* will introduce a theme, while the second line will develop or will counter that theme in what is sometimes called a "turn." The third line provides a resolution of the tensions introduced in the first two lines, or it introduces a judgment or a paradox, or a contrasting theme. Thus the third line gives the *sijo* a twist that provides a strong conclusion for the poem. This twist may take the form of a surprising twist of phrasing or of sound or tone, rather than simply of meaning—and such effects are very difficult to translate, but generally are the demonstration of the poet's genius and originality.

An early example of a *sijo* is the following late medieval poem by Hwang Hŭi (1363–1452). Like most classic *sijo,* it is untitled:

Spring has come to a country village;
How much there is to be done!
I knit a net and
A servant tills the fields and sows:
But who will pluck the sweet herbs
That grow on the back-hill?

(Lee 1994, 774)

Here the theme of spring introduced in line one (translated here as the first two lines) is developed with concrete images of specific tasks in the second line, while the twist at the end introduces a task that may be overlooked, and one that smacks less of frenetic activity than leisurely enjoyment of nature.

While *sijo* might be written on a broad range of subjects, nature and love are by far the most common themes, as they are with Japanese *tanka.* Korean poets, occupying a kind of central ground between the more powerful Chinese and Japanese, make use of both Buddhism and Confucianism in their poems.

Bibliography

Hungguyu, Kim. *Understanding Korean Literature.* Translated by Robert J. Fouser. New Studies in Asian Culture. Armonk, N.Y.: M. E. Sharp, 1997.

Kim, Kichung. *An Introduction to Classical Korean Literature: From Hyangga to P'ansori.* New Studies in Asian Culture. Armonk, N.Y.: M. E. Sharp, 1996.

Lee, Peter H., trans. *Anthology of Korean Literature: From Early Times to the Nineteenth Century.* Honolulu: University Press of Hawaii, 1981. Reprint in *The HarperCollins World Reader: Antiquity to the Early Modern World,* edited by Mary Ann Caws and Christopher Prendergast. Vol. 1. New York: HarperCollins, 1994, 774.

———, ed. *The Columbia Anthology of Traditional Korean Poetry.* New York: Columbia University Press, 2002.

McCann, David R. *Early Korean Literature: Selections and Introductions.* New York: Columbia University Press, 2000.

Sir Degaré (ca. 1300–1325)

Sir Degaré is a MIDDLE ENGLISH verse ROMANCE of about 1,100 lines, written in a southwest Midland dialect in the early 14th century. The poem, composed in couplets, survives in six manuscripts and in three early printings, suggesting it was relatively popular in its own day. Some scholars believe it was based on a lost Breton *LAI.* Certainly it has many qualities of the Breton *lai,* including the interaction with the fairy world and its setting in Brittany.

Degaré is conceived under bizarre circumstances: His princess mother, visiting her own mother's grave in the woods, wanders from her ladies-in-waiting and is ravished by a scarlet-robed fairy-knight in the forest. The mysterious knight then announces that the princess will give birth to a male child, and leaves the woman his sword, the tip of which is broken off. The princess must hide her pregnancy and her newborn from her possessive father, whose incestuous desire for his daughter is strongly implied. The fatherless infant is abandoned at the door of a hermitage along with gold and silver, the broken sword, and his mother's gloves. Growing up as an orphan in the hermitage, the boy has no status in society and no family identity, and the kind hermit names him Degaré, or "the Lost One." When Degaré is grown, he leaves the hermitage on a quest for his identity, to learn his true parentage. Beginning his adventures, Degaré defeats a dragon with a club and is knighted by the earl that he rescues. He then comes to Brittany, his mother's kingdom, where she is being offered as a prize to the knight who can defeat her father in single combat. Defeating the king, Sir Degaré wins his mother's hand. Fortunately Degaré still has the glove with him, and before the marriage is consummated, she tries on the gloves, which fit perfectly, and Degaré realizes he has found his mother. He flees the incestuous union and goes off to search for his other parent. Along the way he wins a beautiful damsel by defeating her unwanted suitor, but he says that he cannot marry her until he has found his father. Finally, he engages in a climactic battle with a potent knight who, recognizing the sword in Degaré's hand, reveals that he is the young man's father and proves it by producing the sword's lost tip. The two are reunited, and ultimately, the tale ends happily as Degaré's parents marry, and he weds his own lady.

Sir Degaré has had its share of detractors as well as defenders. Certainly the poem's characters are purely conventional, but the suspense created by the well-constructed plot goes far in sustaining reader interest. The plot suggests the influence of some later manifestation of the Oedipus myth, possibly the Legend of Pope GREGORY THE GREAT contained in the *Gesta Romanorum.* The folktale or fairy-tale atmosphere of the romance is part of its popular appeal.

Bibliography

Faust, George Patterson. *Sir Degaré: A Study of the Texts and Narrative Structure.* Princeton, N.J.: Princeton University Press, 1935.

Rosenberg, Bruce A. "The Three Tales of Sir Degaré," *Neuphilologische Mitteilungen* 76 (1975): 39–51.

Sir Degaré. Edited by Anne Laskaya and Eve Salisbury, in *The Middle English Breton Lays.* Kalamazoo, Mich.: Medieval Institute Publications, 1995.

Slover, Clark H. "*Sire Degarre:* A Study of a Medieval Hack Writer's Methods." *University of Texas Studies in English* 11 (1931): 6–23.

Stokoe, W. C., Jr. "The Double Problem of Sir Degaré," *PMLA* 70 (1955): 518–534.

Sir Gawain and the Green Knight
(ca. 1375–1400)

Often considered the most elegantly written and stylistically perfect ROMANCE in MIDDLE ENGLISH, *Sir Gawain and the Green Knight* survives in only one copy and is found with three other poems in MS Cotton Nero A.x, Art. 3, in the British Library. The four poems are thought to have been written at the end of the 14th century, and all are generally considered to be the work of one author, although there are substantive differences between the poems. Of the four, *Gawain* alone is romance in genre; two are moral exempla with overt didactic intents, and the third is a DREAM VISION whose moral and spiritual ethos connects it with the exempla poems. As a romance, and a fashionably chivalric romance, *Gawain* seems at some remove from its companion poems. Yet it shares with them a common dialect and composition tradition—they all belong to the native ALLITERATIVE VERSE tradition in which the structure of the poems is determined by alliteration rather than rhyme. This form of verse was more common in the West and North during the later medieval period, and we can speculate that the poems were composed outside the court circles in which poets such as Geoffrey CHAUCER were writing. Nonetheless, the poems should not be read as unsophisticated productions—they are highly stylized in form and content, and none more so than *Gawain.* In addition to their shared alliterative form, the poems also share thematic concerns and moral beliefs, and the links (both verbal and thematic) between the four are a strong argument for common authorship.

As the one representative of romance in the manuscript, *Gawain* may be less overtly didactic, but under cover of fashionable romance the poem offers a moral ethos as highly developed as that found in its companion poems. If there are differences in moral tone, the differences may be found in the nature of the narrative: *Gawain* is an Arthurian romance, and, as such, courtly concerns (love, social life, fine arts, details of clothing) are ever present. Additionally, while *Gawain* clearly demonstrates a spiritual dimension in its moral exposition, the moral and spiritual testing that transpires in the poem, and from which the reader is to learn, is located in real events and in tests located in real-life situations. Nonetheless, whereas the three other poems seem more concerned with moral certitudes, *Gawain* deals less with certitude than with uncertainty and the ways in which moral failing may be open to interpretation.

In *Gawain* the poet has artfully combined numerous folklore motifs such as "the exchange of blows," "the exchange of winnings," and "the sexual temptation of a knight by his host's wife," and the interlocking of these motifs is echoed in the very structure of the poem itself. Divided into four fitts or chapters, the poem is also structured in stanzas of varying lengths but all ending with a "bob and wheel," which consists of a short line (the "bob," which is usually two words in length) followed by a four-line stanza rhyming *abab* ("the wheel"). Similar in some ways to the couplet of a Shakespearean sonnet, the wheel often reflects back on the stanza it concludes. In Fitt 1, the poem opens with an invocation of the Fall of Troy, a very popular theme, and an allusion to the mythic foundation of Britain by Brutus, the great-grandson of Aeneas. The invocation of the Troy story is also found at the poem's end, and thus the poem is framed by allusions that are mythic and subtly convey the issues of identity with which the romance is concerned.

The action of Fitt 1 opens in King ARTHUR's court during the Christmas holidays where Arthur has vowed not to feast until he has seen some marvel or wondrous thing. The king's desire is fulfilled when a very large and very green knight rides into the hall on an equally green horse. Arthur and his knights are astonished into silence and the Green Knight declares that he has not come to fight but to beg a game of the court: He will allow a knight to behead him with an axe on the condition that the knight will meet him a year hence to accept a blow in return. Although Arthur is eager to take on this exchange, his nephew, Gawain, convinces the king that Gawain should be the one to accept the challenge. Gawain cuts off the Green Knight's head, and the now-headless Green Knight mounts his horse, picks up his head from the floor, and before he rides out, addresses the court in words that confirm the exchange of blows agreement he has been granted.

Fitt 2 begins with the passing of the seasons until almost a year has passed and Gawain needs to make ready for his quest to find the Green Knight and fulfill his oath by allowing the knight his axe blow. There is an elaborate "arming of the knight" scene, the highlight of which is the description of the pentangle on Gawain's shield and how it represents all the virtues, chivalric and Christian, that are embodied in Gawain. Gawain sets off and, after many adventures barely alluded to, takes winter refuge in a castle where he is warmly greeted by his host and his host's wife and court. In the sociable atmosphere of the court, Gawain agrees to stay for a while and during the stay he will exchange with his host, at the end of each day, whatever they received that day. This "exchange of winnings" seems innocent enough, until Gawain (and we) realize in Fitt 3 that what Gawain will receive each day are the very obvious sexual advances of his host's wife. As a true, chivalric knight, Gawain's days pass in exquisite agony: He cannot insult a woman, but he also cannot betray his host. The elegance and perfection of the poem's structure is showcased in the account of the next three days: Each day the host goes out to hunt, leaving Gawain in his bed and susceptible to the host's wife. And the poem goes back and forth between descriptions of the host's "real" hunting endeavors and the seduction scenes played out between Gawain and the host's wife. At the end of the first and second days, Gawain and the host exchange their winnings: The host gives Gawain the animal (a deer and a boar) he has hunted, and Gawain gives the host the kisses he has received. The moral dilemma in which Gawain finds himself is complicated on the third day when the host's wife offers him a belt that protects the wearer from harm or injury. Knowing he will be leaving soon to keep his bargain with the Green Knight, Gawain accepts the belt. Yet at day's end, when the host gives him the fox he has hunted, Gawain repays him with kisses, and says nothing about the belt.

Fitt 4 opens with Gawain setting out from the hospitable castle to seek the Green Knight. Wearing the lady's green belt, Gawain meets with the Green Knight but flinches at the first blow of the axe. The second blow is a feint, and with the third and last blow, Gawain is lightly nicked. The Green Knight then reveals who he is (the host of the hospitable castle), the plot (to trick and test an Arthurian knight), and why he nicked Gawain with the third blow (on the third day at the castle Gawain did not, with perfect honesty, exchange his winnings with his host). Gawain is mortified and shamed when the plot and his own behavior are revealed and returns to Arthur's court wearing the green belt as a reminder of his chivalric failure. The perfect interdependence of action and motifs is made manifest when Gawain, and we, realize that the real test was not the beheading game but the exchange of winnings. Yet the poem ends having raised more questions than it answers, and one of the key uncertainties is just what constitutes Gawain's moral and chivalric failure.

The critical writings concerning *Sir Gawain and the Green Knight* are vast and varied. Some look at the folklore origins of the plot and the figure of the Green Knight; some discuss chivalry and morality, while others discuss the impossible ideals of the chivalric code as it is written into romances. The artistry of the poem has long been the focus of many critics, yet more recent criticism involves historical, feminist, and cultural readings of characters, plot, and moral lessons. Issues of identity, both personal and national, are the focus of some current readings of the poem, as are the homosocial possibilities latent in the exchange of winnings motif. The poem is a masterpiece of the ALLITERATIVE REVIVAL, an elegant romance within which we find essential moral issues raised and only partially resolved in a tale of a flawed, but very human, Arthurian knight.

Bibliography

Andrew, Malcolm, and Ronald Waldron, eds. *The Poems of the Pearl Manuscript.* York Medieval Texts, 2nd ser. Berkeley: University of California Press, 1978.

Benson, Larry D. *Art and Tradition in Sir Gawain and the Green Knight.* New Brunswick, N.J.: Rutgers University Press, 1965.

Bercovitch, Sacvan. "Romance and Anti-Romance in *Sir Gawain and the Green Knight,*" *Philological Quarterly* 44 (1965): 30–37.

Green, D. H. *Irony in the Medieval Romance.* Cambridge: Cambridge University Press, 1979.

Narin, Elisa. " 'əat on . . . əat oəer': Rhetorical Descriptio and Morgan le Fay in *Sir Gawain and the Green Knight,*" *Pacific Coast Philology* 23 (1988): 60–66.

Tolkien, J. R. R., and E. V. Gordon, eds. *Sir Gawain and the Green Knight.* 2nd ed., revised by Norman Davis. Oxford: Clarendon Press, 1967.

Elisa Narin van Court

Sir Gowther (ca. 1400)

Sir Gowther is a MIDDLE ENGLISH verse ROMANCE in 12-line TAIL-RHYME stanzas. It is composed in a northeast Midland dialect, and tells the popular story known generally as "Robert the Devil"—the story of the violent deeds of a man sired on a mortal woman by a devil. The best-known and earliest written version of the story is a 12th-century French poem of 5,000 lines called *Robert le Diable,* which is associated with the father of William the Conqueror, Robert, the sixth duke of Normandy—a man whose violence and cruelty were legendary. While some have assumed the French poem to be the source of the English one, the story existed in a number of languages in chronicles, miracle plays, sermon exempla, romances, and in oral and written folktales. *Sir Gowther* is known as one of the Middle English "Breton *LAIS,*" though it also bears some similarities to the genre of SAINTS' LIVES.

In the poem Gowther's mother is unable to have a child with her husband, and prays desperately for a baby. The Devil hears her prayer, and engenders Gowther with her, apparently in the guise of her husband. But Gowther's demonic heritage manifests itself quickly: He grows teeth as an infant. He also grows prodigiously, and his voracious appetite kills nine wet nurses, before he ultimately bites off his own mother's nipple. As he grows up, he engages in a series of barbarous acts, including raping a convent of nuns. His father, in an effort to rein in his wild lawlessness, has him baptized and makes Gowther a knight, but the chivalric code means nothing to Sir Gowther, and he continues his evil ways until, one day, an old earl reveals to Gowther that his father was thought to be a demon. The shock of this leads Gowther to confront his mother at knifepoint to discover the truth.

It is the truth that sets Gowther on the road to redemption. After first going to Rome and confessing his sins, he begins a long period of penance. He is made mute, cut off from humanity in the wilderness, and condemned to eat only the food brought to him by dogs. From here he enters the emperor's court, where he assumes the role of Hobbe the Fool, taking a position under the table with the dogs, who continue to bring him food, now from the hand of the emperor's mute daughter, with whom Gowther carries on a chaste relationship despite their mutual silence. During a three-day tournament between the forces of the emperor and the Saracen forces of a sultan who is a suitor for the hand of the emperor's daughter, Gowther prays each day for a shield, horse, and armor to fight the Saracens. His mute prayers are answered, and on three successive days, he defeats his foes on the battlefield in disguise, and returns each night to his position under the table. Only the daughter knows of his exploits. But when he is wounded in the shoulder, the lady is so distressed that she leaps from a tower. She lies comatose for three days, but finally awakens and, miraculously, is able to speak. She absolves Gowther, and in doing so ends his penance, restoring him to his full humanity. The two marry. Gowther ends up inheriting the German Empire, marrying his mother to a new husband, and building an abbey to atone for his sins against the nuns.

Sir Gowther survives in two 15th-century manuscripts—British Museum Royal MS 17 B.43, and the National Library of Scotland MS Advocates 19.3.1. While the manuscripts are substantially the same, the British Museum manuscript (which is the younger of the two) leaves out the description of Gowther's ravishing of the nuns. It also adds a section identifying Gowther with the eighth century English saint Guthlac, who founded Croyland Abbey. It seems likely that the two manuscripts were intended for different audiences—that the audience of the British Museum manuscript was more refined, less interested in the violent or scurrilous details, and more interested in hearing a saint's life. Clearly the popular folktale had a broad appeal across different social classes.

Bibliography

Hopkins, Andrea. *The Sinful Knights: A Study of Middle English Penitential Romances.* Oxford: Clarendon Press, 1990.

Marchalonis, Shirley. "*Sir Gowther:* The Process of a Romance," *Chaucer Review* 6 (1971): 14–29.

Sir Gowther, in *The Middle English Breton Lays*, edited by Anne Laskaya and Eve Salisbury. Kalamazoo, Mich.: Medieval Institute Publications, 1995.

Sir Isumbras (ca. 1320)

The MIDDLE ENGLISH poem *Sir Isumbras* is a brief ROMANCE of 771 lines in 12-line TAIL-RHYME stanzas rhyming *aabccbddbeeb,* written in the northeast Midlands early in the 14th century. It was well-known by 1320, when William of Nassington disparaged the story as "vanity" in his *Speculum Vita.* One of the most popular of all Middle English romances, *Sir Isumbras* survives in nine manuscripts and five early printed editions. There is no known source for the poem, but it employs the widespread motif of the man tried and chastened by misfortune. Ultimately, the roots of the story are in the biblical book of Job, but scholars have noted parallels between Sir Isumbras and the popular legend of St. Eustace, so that in some ways *Sir Isumbras* turns material more typical of a SAINTS' LIFE into a romance.

This may explain why *Sir Isumbras* appears to undercut the usual themes of romance: While Isumbras is a noble and courteous knight, he suffers tribulation because his wealth and power make him forget about God. The tale is told in a brisk and unadorned style, and there is no elaborate description of the wealth and pageantry of the court. Nor is there an emphasis on COURTLY LOVE; rather it is Isumbras's family—his wife and three children—who matter most to him. Sir Isumbras is about sin and redemption through penitence, but these issues are depicted in the poem through the gain or loss of material wealth and social prestige. The poem is essentially in two parts, which mirror one another: The first depicts Isumbras's losing everything, the second shows him gaining it back.

Isumbras is a knight with wealth, a beautiful wife, and three fine sons. But pride has made him forget Christ. One day in the forest a bird delivers a message from God: Because of his pride, Isumbras must choose to be afflicted either in his youth and his age. He chooses youth, and as the bird flies off, his hawks and hounds run off and his horse dies under him. As he walks toward home, a boy tells him his buildings have been burned and his men killed—only his wife and children are left alive, and for that Isumbras is grateful. He meets his herdsmen, who tell him all of his livestock have been stolen. Patiently, he comforts his family and advises that they leave that country and go on pilgrimage to Jerusalem, in sign of which he carves a cross into his shoulder with a knife.

As the family travels toward the sea, a lion makes off with their oldest son, and a leopard steals the second. Isumbras, his wife, and their youngest son reach the sea, where they find an invading Muslim armada. When they beg the sultan for food, he has Isumbras beaten and steals his wife. She, preparing to be sent back to be queen of the sultan's homeland, gains permission to see her husband. She feeds him and gives him gold, telling him to come after her. But when he leaves the ship, a great bird flies off with his gold, and a unicorn steals away with his youngest son. Destitute and alone, Isumbras prays for guidance, and from this point his fortunes take a different turn.

Isumbras meets a group of ironworkers and begs for food, but they propose that instead he work for food, as they do. He spends seven years with the smiths, working up to the status of a craftsman, at which point he forges himself a suit of armor. He rides off in this armor to do battle against the sultan, who has been ravaging Christian lands for seven years. He fights well and is able to kill the sultan. But he slips off before the Christian king can knight him, and continues his pilgrimage, finding his way to the Holy Land.

Outside Jerusalem, Isumbras is visited by an angel, who brings him food and drink and tells him that his sin is forgiven. He continues to wander until he reaches a rich castle, where he hears there is a magnificent queen who gives handouts to the poor each day at her gate. The starving Isumbras waits at the gate, and is invited in to eat in the queen's hall. He sits beside the queen and tells her of his travels, but for sorrow cannot eat a thing. The queen offers to allow the palmer to stay in her castle as her man, and arranges a tournament in which he defeats all the Saracen knights.

The tale's ending takes a number of improbable twists. One day in the woods, Isumbras discovers his wife's gold that the bird had stolen. Later, squires search his room and find the gold, which the queen recognizes as the gold she had given her husband. They are reunited and Isumbras is made king. But when he requires that all his subjects become Christian, the Saracen knights rise against him. He arms his wife like a knight and the two of them ride against 30,000 Saracens. But just as the battle begins, three strange knights join them, riding a lion, a leopard, and a unicorn. Together they defeat the army, and Isumbras learns that the three knights are his own children, come to help him by the grace of God. Isumbras thus ends restored to his family, and with more wealth than he began.

Thus Isumbras works his way back from destitution through his own hard work and the merit of his seven years of penance. He also realizes the most valuable things in life are his wife and children, and is able to recover them as well as his status. *Sir Isumbras* is a brief and unusual romance, but is quite lively and readable.

Bibliography

Braswell, L. "Sir Isumbras and the Legend of Saint Eustace," *Medieval Studies* 27 (1965): 128–151.

Crane, Susan. *Insular Romance: Politics, Faith, and Culture in Anglo-Norman and Middle English Literature.* Berkeley: University of California Press, 1986.

Hudson, Harriet. *Four Middle English Romances.* Kalamazoo, Mich.: Medieval Institute Publications, 1996.

Mehl, Dieter. *The Middle English Romances of the Thirteenth and Fourteenth Centuries.* London: Routledge and Kegan Paul, 1968.

Sir Launfal (*Launfalus Miles*) (ca. 1375–1400)

Sir Launfal is a late 14th-century ROMANCE in a southeastern dialect of MIDDLE ENGLISH, generally categorized (like *SIR ORFEO* and the *LAI LE FREINE*) as a Breton *LAI*. The poem contains 1,044 lines in 12-line TAIL-RHYME stanzas, and is the best known of several Middle English retellings of MARIE DE FRANCE's well-known 12th-century *lai* of *LANVAL*. *Sir Launfal* is the only identified production by the poet who calls himself Thomas Chestre, of whom nothing else is known. Based on style and language, some scholars have suggested that Chestre is also the author of the romance called *LIBEAUS DESCONUS*, but this is only conjecture.

Sir Launfal follows the general plot outline of Marie's *Lanval*, but with some alterations that show the Middle English poem to be less a courtly than a bourgeois entertainment. It begins by introducing the protagonist, Launfal, as a very courteous knight of King ARTHUR's Round Table. Launfal, however, is slighted by Queen GUENEVERE, and leaves the court, taking up lodging with the mayor of the city of Caerleon. Here, his natural generosity eventually impoverishes him, so that he does not even have decent clothing to wear. One day he rides off by himself into the woods, where he is surprised to be invited by two beautiful ladies-in-waiting into the pavilion of a fairy princess named Tryamour. She promises to be his love, provides him with a purse with an endless supply of cash, promises to make him victorious in any knightly battles, and pledges to come to him whenever he calls to her—but all on the condition that their love remain completely secret. Should Launfal reveal her existence to anyone, he will forfeit her love and all her gifts.

From this point, Launfal regains his noble reputation, and he returns to Arthur's court as a prosperous and respected knight. The queen, however, becomes attracted to Launfal and makes sexual advances to him. When he rebuffs her, Guenevere becomes angry, declares he must not be attracted to women at all, and accuses him of homosexuality. The incensed Launfal answers that he has a mistress whose lowliest maid is more beautiful than the queen. Stung, the queen goes to King Arthur and accuses Launfal of treason. She tells the king that Launfal tried to seduce her and repeats his insulting words.

Launfal is brought to trial and ordered to produce his mistress so that the court can judge her beauty compared with that of the queen. But Launfal has lost his love. She will no longer appear to him because he has broken his vow not to boast of her. But at the last moment, Tryamour appears at the trial. She reveals the truth of Guenevere's guilt, and when she breathes on the queen's eyes, Guenevere becomes blind. In the end Tryamour rides off with Launfal to the fairy land of Olyroun, where they live happily forever.

Scholars speculate that Sir Launfal was based not directly on Marie's *Lanval* but on a lost intermediary translation. Some of the changes, such as Guenevere's ill treatment of Launfal in the beginning and her blinding in the end, are intended simply to further vilify the queen and provide for her a "just" punishment. Some additions, like the tournament scene and Launfal's battle with Sir Valentine, seem added to appeal to a romance audience expecting adventure and feats of arms. But the biggest change from Marie's courtly *lai* is the bourgeois sensitivity displayed in the narrator's fascination with unlimited wealth and possessions. Launfal's lodging with the wealthy burgesses of Caerleon is just another indication of the poet's appropriating a courtly genre for a middle-class audience.

Bibliography

Anderson, Earl R. "The Structure of *Sir Launfal*," *Papers on Language and Literature* 13 (1977): 115–124.

Martin, B. K. "*Sir Launfal* and the Folktale," *Medium Ævum* 35 (1966): 199–210.

Miles, M. "The Composition and Style of the 'Southern' *Octavian, Sir Launfal,* and *Libeaus Desconus,*" *Medium Ævum* 31 (1962): 88–109.

Nappholz, Carol J. "Launfal's 'Largesse': Word-Play in Thomas Chestre's *Sir Launfal,*" *English Language Notes* 25 (1988): 4–9.

Spearing, A. C. "Marie de France and Her Middle English Adapters," *Studies in the Age of Chaucer* 12 (1990): 117–156.

Sir Orfeo (ca. 1300)

Sir Orfeo is a short ROMANCE in a southeastern dialect of MIDDLE ENGLISH, composed in the very early 14th century. The poem consists of 603 lines in octosyllabic couplets and survives in three manuscripts, two of which contain a short prologue categorizing the poem as a Breton *LAI* and defining the genre as a short verse romance characterized by the central element of *ferly* or the marvelous, and told originally in the Briton language. Since the same prologue begins the *LAY LE FREINE* in the famous Auchenlick manuscript, some scholars believe that the same author may have written both poems. No Breton source is known for *Sir Orfeo* (although there are references in Old French to a non-extant romance called the *Lai d'Orphey*). The ultimate source for the story is the tale of Orpheus, as told in books 10 and 11 of Ovid's *Metamorphoses.*

The tale turns Ovid's Orpheus and Eurydice into Sir Orfeo and his wife Heurodis. Orfeo, a magnificent harper, is king of Thrace (which the poet identifies with Winchester) and Heurodis is his queen. In a dream the king of Fairy appears to Heurodis and tells her he will abduct her despite anything she or Orfeo can do. Orfeo and 1,000 of his troops guard the queen, but she magically disappears from under a grafted tree notwithstanding their efforts. Orfeo, in despair over the loss of his wife and his inability to protect her, leaves his kingdom in the charge of his Steward. He shoulders his harp and wanders off into the wilderness in beggar's rags, where he lives as a wild man—a conventional medieval depiction of madness.

For 10 years he wanders in the forest, playing his harp in a way that charms the beasts, until one day he happens to catch sight of Heurodis herself, among 60 ladies who are out hawking in the woods. He follows the ladies right through a mountainside into a level, green land with a castle. Pretending to be a minstrel, he gains entrance to the castle, where he sees people who had been drowned, burned, wounded, all thought to be dead but actually snatched by the king of Fairy. There, too, he sees Heurodis sleeping beneath the grafted tree. Orfeo comes before the king and entertains him with his harp. The king is so moved that he grants Orfeo any boon he asks for, and he asks for Heurodis. The two are allowed to leave.

The English poet omits the tragic ending of Ovid's story, in which Orpheus loses Eurydice when he looks back at her. Instead, the two arrive back in Winchester, where Orfeo, still in disguise, meets his Steward on the street. The Steward, believing him to be a minstrel, invites Orfeo to the castle, where he says all harpers are welcome for his lord's sake. At the castle, Orfeo takes out his harp to play, and the Steward instantly recognizes the harp. He asks Orfeo where he obtained it, and Orfeo tells him he took it off a man who had been torn in pieces by lions. The Steward swoons in sorrow when he hears this, after which Orfeo reveals his true identity, and rewards the Steward for his loyalty by making him heir to the throne.

It is likely that one of the poet's sources for his story was BOETHIUS's brief summary of Ovid's tale in book 3 of his *CONSOLATION OF PHILOSOPHY*. Here, Boethius uses the story as an ALLEGORY of how humankind's desire for God's light is thwarted by our attachment to earthly things that draw our thoughts toward hell. Some modern critics of the poem have used Boethius's ideas to justify an allegorical reading of *Sir Orfeo*, suggesting that Orfeo's rescue of Heurodis depicts human reason saving the flesh from hell. But it seems clear that the poet resisted the Boethian interpretation of the tale when he omitted the tragic ending, and specifically resisted identifying fairyland with hell—depicting it, in fact, like Orfeo's own Winchester.

A more pertinent question for the poem is why the poet chose to change the end of the story, and why he added the test of the Steward. Perhaps the point is a reinforcement of the main tale's theme of long-term devotion rewarded. One thing that seems clear is the poet's emphasis on the importance of treating minstrels well: In what was probably a poem in the repertoire of traveling minstrels, there is almost certainly some self-interest evident in the text.

Bibliography

Bliss, A. J., ed. *Sir Orfeo*. 2nd ed. Oxford: Clarendon Press, 1966.

Dorena, Allen. "Opheus and Orfeo: The Dead and the Taken," *Medium Aevum* 33 (1964): 102–111.

Friedman, John Block. *Orpheus in the Middle Ages*. Cambridge, Mass.: Harvard University Press, 1970.

Gros Louis, Kenneth R. R. "The Significance of Sir Orfeo's Self-Exile," *Review of English Studies* n.s. 18 (1967): 245–252.

Hanson, Thomas B. "*Sir Orfeo*, Romance as Exemplum," *Annuale Mediaevale* 13 (1972): 135–154.

Hill, D. M. "The Structure of Sir Orfeo," *Medieval Studies* 23 (1961): 136–153.

Lerer, Seth. "Artifice and Artistry in *Sir Orfeo*," *Speculum* 60 (1985): 92–109.

Liuzza, Roy Michael. "*Sir Orfeo:* Sources, Traditions, and the Poetics of Performance," *Journal of Medieval and Renaissance Studies* 21 (1991): 269–284.

O'Brien, Timothy D. "The Shadow and Anima in *Sir Orfeo*," *Mediaevalia* 10 (1984): 235–254.

Sir Patrick Spens (ca. 15th century)

Sir Patrick Spens is one of the most famous medieval ballads and it believed to have been composed in the late 14th or early 15th century. Its popularity is such that is was revived in British popular song in the 19th century. Although there has been no widely accepted identification of a historical Patrick Spens, most critics agree that the poem refers to the death of the Scottish child-queen Margaret, the "Maid of Norway," in 1290. Granddaughter of the Norwegian king Eric II, she drowned on her way back to Scotland from Norway to marry the English king Edward I's eldest son.

Sir Patrick Spens tells the story of a Scottish king who wishes to send a ship across the North Sea to Norway. Under the advice of "an eldern knicht," the king designates Sir Patrick Spens to head the voyage. Because of the dangerous time of year and a calamitous harbinger of "the new moone/ wi the auld moone in hir arme," Spens realizes the voyage will be ill-fated, but proceeds out of a sense of duty. It is precisely these celestial and meteorological details that prove the ballad's historical accuracy. The ballad ends with the drowning of the lords and the endless wait by their women back home.

Gwendolyn Morgan (1996) suggests that the ballad was composed by commoners who mocked the aristocratic values of chivalric duty as stupid and judged the aristocracy to be lazy. This is apparent in the perceived treachery to Sir Patrick Spens and the idle mannerisms of the nobles and ladies.

Sir Patrick Spens is an enduring poem not only because it acts as an elegy for a poignant event, but also because it stands as an affecting narrative on its own. Generally dated to the 15th century, it has been suggested that the poem may be an 18th century invention, since it is unknown prior to its inclusion in Percy's *Reliques* (1765).

Bibliography

Child, Francis James, ed. *The English and Scottish Popular Ballads.* New York: Cooper Square Publishers, 1965.

Representative Poetry Online, University of Toronto English Library. Sir Patrick Spence. Available online. URL: http://eir.library.utoronto.ca/rpo/display/poem63.html. Accessed on June 30, 2003.

Morgan, Gwendolyn A., ed. and trans. *Medieval Ballads: Chivalry, Romance, and Everyday Life, A Critical Anthology.* New York: Peter Lang, 1996.

Percy, Thomas, ed. *Reliques of Ancient English Poetry.* London: J. Dodsley, 1763.

Malene A. Little

Sir Perceval of Galles (ca. 1300–1340)

Sir Perceval of Galles is an early 14th-century MIDDLE ENGLISH ROMANCE composed in the northern dialect. The protagonist, young Perceval, is raised in the forest by his mother, and then later enters Arthurian society in search of knighthood. The plot surpasses the theme typical of a bildungsroman (a story of the protagonist's maturing process) by focusing on familial connections. Not only does Perceval prove his knightly worth, wed the maiden he saves, and become lord of his own land, he returns to the forest to retrieve his mother.

The poem includes 2,288 lines in TAIL-RHYME stanzas of 16 lines (rhyming *aaabcccbdddbeeeb*). The author also utilizes the literary device known as stanza-linking, wherein a key word in the last line of a stanza is repeated in the first line of the next stanza; occasionally, the entire line is repeated. The only extant version of the poem survives in the Thornton Manuscript (Lincoln Cathedral A.5.2. fol. 161r–76r).

The poem opens praising the deeds of Perceval's father, who married King ARTHUR's sister, Acheflour (a sister whose name is unique to this poem). When Percyvell is killed by the "Rede Knyghte," his grieving widow flees to raise her son in the forest, far from the knightly life. Perceval dwells there for more than 15 years until a chance encounter with GAWAIN, Yvain, and Kay. Perceval is so impressed by the knights that he determines to seek knighthood from Arthur. After a farewell scene with his mother in which she imparts a ring as a token of their relationship, Perceval departs but, before reaching the court, stops at a castle where he finds a sleeping maiden with whom he exchanges rings.

Perceval's introduction to court is comical, as are many of the scenes depicting his naiveté. He advances so near the king that his mare practically touches the king's nose as Perceval demands to be knighted. The feast is interrupted by the Red Knight, who killed Perceval's father and who not only drinks from Arthur's cup, but takes possession of it. Upon learning that the court had been plagued by this intruder and thief for five years, Perceval pledges to retrieve the cup, and in the ensuing battle, Perceval defeats the Red Knight and dons his armor. Even at this early point in the poem, Perceval's decisions rather unwittingly lead to his success (i.e. the defeat of the Red Knight also avenges his father's death) so that these successes appear providential.

In Perceval's next quest, he travels to Maidenland to defeat an evil sultan and free the imprisoned Lady Lufamour. He defeats numerous knights surrounding the castle and eventually defeats the sultan, Golrotherame. In so doing, he becomes lord of Lady Lufamour's lands, and they wed. These narratives are laced with uncommon glimpses into the interiority of the strategizing of the characters, which serves to underscore Perceval's advancement into the society and gradual understanding after his isolated youth in the woods. The text acknowledges Perceval's inexperience but cites his strength: "Thofe he couthe littill insighte, / The childe was of pith" (Braswell 1995, ll. 1639–1640).

Perceval dwells with Lufamour in Maidenland for 12 months after their marriage, but returns to the forest to see his mother. This return marks the first circular turn back to events from the poem's beginning as Perceval encounters the maiden who was asleep in the first castle where he found sustenance. The maiden is no longer asleep but bound as a captive of the Black Knight. Perceval learns that she was imprisoned for a "fault" and then she explains that while asleep, her ring was exchanged for another by an unknown person. Her lost ring provides safety for the wearer, and thus, the purported invulnerability of Perceval is exposed to be false in that he was protected by the ring. Perceval recognizes his responsibility for the maiden's captivity and loosens and frees her. The restoration of the maiden's freedom, though, coincides with the return of the Black Knight, who challenges Perceval. Perceval defeats the Black Knight, and in his first merciful act, at the supplication of the maiden, he frees the Black Knight as he promises to forgive her.

However, when Perceval attempts to exchange rings again, he discovers that the ring from his mother is now in the hands of a giant. To reclaim the token of their relationship, Perceval must conquer the giant, who wields an iron club weighing more than 300 pounds. He not only defeats the giant, but strikes off his hand and foot and reclaims his ring. With his ring in his possession, he continues his search for his mother, whom he finds so crazed from her grief that she does not recognize him. Perceval brings his mother out of the wilderness, and once she has been revived, returns with her to his own kingdom. The poem's last stanza is succinct in its explanation of the remainder of Perceval's life, saying only that he went to the Holy Land and was killed there.

As a character, Perceval is most thoroughly treated by CHRÉTIEN DE TROYES in *PERCEVAL*, or *Conte del Graal*. Chrétien's Perceval differs so radically from the Perceval of this poem that scholars initially thought that the two were not connected, and that the English author had not read Chrétien. However, more recent scholars assert that the poem is an adaptation.

In *Sir Perceval of Galles*, the author is cognizant of the characters and devices in the beginning of the poem and carefully returns not only to the mother left in the wilderness but to the maiden whose magic ring sustained Perceval, the circular pattern lending itself to a restorative theme that some scholars say replaces the grail motif (*see* HOLY GRAIL). The emphasis on family also adds an additional layer to the romance that invites further analysis and interpretation.

Bibliography

Barron, W. R. J. *English Medieval Romance.* London: Longman Publishing, 1987.

Baswell, Mary Flowers. *Sir Perceval of Galles and Ywain and Gawain.* Kalamazoo, Mich.: Medieval Institute Publications, 1995.

Eckhardt, Caroline D. "Arthurian Comedy: The Simpleton-Hero in *Sir Perceval of Galles*," *Chaucer Review* 8 (1974): 205–220.

Fowler, David C. "*Le Conte du Graal* and *Sir Perceval of Galles*," *Comparative Literature Studies* 12 (1975): 5–20.

Michelle Palmer

sirventes

The *sirventes* was a special genre of TROUBADOUR poetry that was written in stanzas but that was concerned with politics or moralizing rather than love, the subject of the better-known *CANSO*.

Politics or current events were often the subject matter of the *sirventes*, as, for example, in the poem by the troubadour BERTRAN DE BORN, beginning "Miei sirventes vuolh far de.ls reis amdos" ("I shall make a half *sirventes* about both kings") (Goldin 1973, 233), in which he looks forward to a coming conflict between Alfonso VIII of Castile and RICHARD I of England.

Most often the tone of the *sirventes* was satiric, and the poet did not shy from reviling the object of his satire. In the following poem, Peire VIDAL exhorts the cities of Italy to unite against an invasion by the Holy Roman Emperor Henry VI in 1194–95, and spends some time berating the Germans themselves:

> *The Germans, I find, are gross and vulgar,*
> *and when one of them gets it into his head he's*
> *a courtly man,*
> *it is a burning mortal agony, an insult,*
> *and that language of theirs sounds like the*
> *barking of dogs.*

(Goldin 1973, 263, ll. 9–12)

Typically, along with the satire, a *sirventes* contained a moral or didactic message. The troubadour Peire CARDENAL was the master of this type of poem, particularly in his attacks on the venality of the clergy. In one of his lyrics, for example, he says that all power is now in the hands of the clergy, who are characterized by "stealing, betrayal, hypocrisy, violence, and sermons" (Goldin 1973, 291, ll. 19–21).

Other common subjects for *sirventes* were praise of individuals, literary satire, or the Crusades. The word *sirventes* means "servant" in Provençal, but could also mean "mercenary" or "foot soldier." The connection between the term and the genre is unclear, but certainly the point of view of a poem like Bertran de Born's above is that of a mercenary.

It could also be said that the *sirventes* came to be considered an inferior and less original genre in troubadour poetry, one that did not require the same amount of creative energy as the *canso*. Many *sirventes* were written to the tune, and with the same rhyme schemes, as popular *cansos*. Though the genre eventually came to be seen as imitative, its greater practitioners produced some remarkably effective and original poetic satires.

Bibliography

Goldin, Frederick, ed. and trans. *Lyrics of the Troubadours and Trouvères: An Anthology and a History.* Garden City, N.Y.: Doubleday, 1973.

skaldic poetry

Of the two chief forms of Old Norse poetry, "Eddic" poetry (the sort found in the *POETIC EDDA*) was comparatively simple, following the basic conventions of most Germanic verse, like that of OLD ENGLISH. It was anonymous ALLITERATIVE VERSE, was relatively simple in diction, and related traditional mythological material. Skaldic poetry, by contrast, was highly intricate and complex in its structure and diction, composed by identifiable self-conscious literary artists in the employ of Scandinavian kings and princes. Today more than 40,000 lines of skaldic poetry are extant, dating from between 850 and 1400. The names of 250 skaldic poets, mainly Icelandic, have also come down to us. Though it seems likely that skaldic poetry was composed in all Scandinavian countries, only poems composed by Norwegian and, to a much larger extent, Icelandic poets (working in the courts of Norwegian princes) have survived.

The first known skald was Bragi Boddason, called "the Old" (ca. 835–900). The emergence of the earliest skalds corresponds with the consolidation of royal power in Norway (under King Harald Fairhair) and the concomitant expansion of the royal court. Most of the skaldic poetry that survives was written to celebrate some royal figure. The king needed the skald to commemorate his heritage, his great victories, and his generosity—it was on the skald that his fame depended. In contrast with praise poems, a skald could also produce what was called a *níð* (an insult or derision), which was thought to have particularly dire consequences.

The predominant form of skaldic verse was the *dróttvætt* ("heroic meter"—verse appropriate for the *drótt,* or royal retainers). A stanza in this meter comprised eight lines, each with six syllables. Each line has three stressed syllables and uses internal rhyme. The basic unit of composition is a couplet, in which two syllables of the first line alliterate with the first syllable of the second line. A caesura separates the internal rhyming syllables of each line, and of necessity also separates the alliterating syllables of the first line of each couplet. In addition, there were at least 48 different variations of this verse form, demonstrated in SNORRI STURLUSON's *Háttatal,* included as a tour de force in his *PROSE EDDA* (ca. 1225). In order to conform to this incredibly complex pattern, the syntax of skaldic poetry is often very free, so that segments of different sentences are intertwined in a way that often makes for ambiguity of meaning.

Rhetorical complexity is also an integral part of skaldic verse. Poets use a great number of *heiti* ("names"), or synonyms often used only in poetic contexts, for a large number of concepts (the gods, warriors, weapons, animals, ships, the sea) that are common in Norse poetry of the court. Each of these *heiti* has a slightly different connotation, so that a poet can choose precisely the right term from the 150 *heiti* for the god Odin that fits his meter, alliteration, internal rhyme, and the sense of his line.

Even more challenging is the skaldic use of KENNINGS. The poets do use simple kennings at times—truncated metaphors by which a subject is spoken of as if it were something else (a ship as the "horse of the sea" for example). A kenning generally consists of two terms—a basic term (the horse) and a second term with which the basic term is related in the metaphor (the sea). But in skaldic verse, each individual term of the kenning might be expressed by a kenning—so that if the sea might be called the "swan's road," a kenning for a ship might be "horse of the swan's road"—and so on. And if this does not complicate matters enough, many kennings are based on mythological allusions, so that gold might be called "Sif's hair" because of a myth that Loki had cut off all of Sif's hair (she was Thor's wife), and was forced to make her new hair out of gold. Thus, understanding the skaldic poem involved appreciation of its convoluted syntax, puzzling through its riddle-like kennings, and knowing the myth that the kennings alluded to.

Only a small portion of Old Norse skaldic poetry has survived, and much of the earlier verse has survived embedded in prose works from the 13th century and later—such as, for example, the poems of the ninth-century Icelandic skaldic poet and warrior Egil Skallagrimsson quoted in the 13th-century *EGIL'S SAGA*. There is some debate as to whether these embedded poems are genuine or later compositions by the saga writers themselves, but Snorri Sturluson does assert in the prologue to his *HEIMSKRINGLA* (ca. 1235) that poems by the skalds of Harald Fairhair were still remembered verbatim. But any comments made by the saga writers about the circumstances of the poems' compositions are probably not to be trusted, being in general imaginative guesses about the inspiration for each poem. Still, our best knowledge of how skaldic poetry works comes from prose treatises of the 13th century, the best known of which is Snorri's *Prose Edda.* Anyone exploring the specific aspects of skaldic poetry should begin with Snorri.

Bibliography

Nordal, Guðrún. *Tools of Literacy: The Role of Skaldic Verse in Icelandic Textual Culture in the Twelfth and Thirteenth Centuries.* Toronto: University of Toronto Press, 2001.

Ross, Margaret Clunies. *Skáldskaparmál: Snorri Sturluson's Ars Poetica and Medieval Theories of Language.* Odense, Denmark: Odense University Press, 1987.

Sturluson, Snorri. *Edda.* Edited and translated by Anthony Faulkes. London: Dent, 1987.

Turville-Petre, E. O. G. *Scaldic Poetry.* Oxford: Clarendon Press, 1976.

Snorri Sturluson (1179–1241)

Snorri Sturluson was Iceland's best-known medieval writer. He was a historian, a poet, and perhaps a saga writer as well. He wrote *HEIMSKRINGLA* (a history of the kings of Norway), the *PROSE EDDA* (a handbook of Norse mythology and SKALDIC POETRY), and is thought to be the author of *EGIL'S SAGA* (one of the finest of the Old Icelandic family SAGAS). Embroiled in the politics of his day in Norway, Snorri fell afoul of the Norwegian king, and was murdered in what was probably a political assassination in 1241.

Snorri was born in Hvamm in the western part of Iceland in 1179. He was from the powerful Sturlung family, which attained unprecedented influence in the period 1200–64, and after whom this turbulent period of the 13th century is named. The Sturlung Age was known for its lawlessness and violence that became so tumultuous that the Norwegian king stepped in to govern and by 1264, Iceland had lost its independence.

Snorri grew up as the foster son of Iceland's most powerful chieftain, Jón Loftsson, and was educated at Oddi, Iceland's premier center for learning, located at Jón Loftsson's farmstead. Here he learned law and history, as well as the arts of poetry and saga writing. Snorri was ambitious, grew to be a powerful man of the time, and accumulated a great deal of wealth, becoming chieftain of several judicial districts. He was made lawspeaker of the Althing (the Icelandic parliament) in 1215–18 and again in 1222–31. As lawspeaker, he recited the whole body of Icelandic law at the beginning of the session, and acted as arbiter in legal disputes.

He also visited Norway twice. After his first visit (1218–20), he left with great honor, having ingratiated himself with both King Hakon Hakonarson and his regent, Jarl Skúli. Snorri returned to Iceland at the height of his power, and by the mid-1220s was the richest man in Iceland. But violent squabbles with rival members of his Sturlung family and their allies reduced his influence by 1235, and in 1237 he left Iceland again for Norway. There he became involved in the political battle surrounding the Norwegian throne. King Hakon Hakonarson was being challenged by Jarl Skúli. Snorri supported Skúli's rebellion, and when Skúli was killed in 1240, Snorri was ordered by Hakon not to return to Iceland. Against the king's wishes, Snorri sailed home. In 1241, Snorri was murdered at his home in Skalholt by his former son-in-law, Gizurr Thorwaldsson, on Hakon's orders.

But it is for his literary achievements that Snorri is remembered. And this is unusual: Prose texts in Iceland were almost always anonymous, prose being seen as simply the retelling of traditional stories. Snorri is the chief exception to this rule. Known in his own day as a respected skaldic poet, it is Snorri's prose works that have made his posthumous reputation. His prose voice is witty, intelligent, and objective, perhaps in contrast with the sometimes ruthlessly ambiguous figure that appears in his biography. His *Heimskringla* (The disk of the world, ca. 1235) is a collection of sagas on the kings of Norway, beginning with the *Ynglinga saga,* an account of the legendary ancestors of the Norwegian kings, dating back to Odin himself, the chief Norse god. Snorri then tells of King Harald Fairhair about 850, and includes sagas of the various kings from Harald's time to his own age. Snorri's *Edda* (called the *Prose Edda,* or the *Younger Edda,* to distinguish it from the *POETIC EDDA,* mistakenly thought to be older) is something of a textbook describing the various meters and types of KENNINGS found in skaldic verse. This poetic guide is linked to a handbook of Norse mythology. As for *Egil's Saga,* if Snorri did in fact write it, as the style suggests, it is a brilliant picture of a complex poet-chieftain who was, in fact, one of Snorri's own ancestors.

The tale of Snorri's stormy life is told in the *Islendinga Saga,* composed by Sturla Thordarson (1214–84), Snorri's own nephew and apparently the heir of his literary talent, though the saga mentions little of Snorri's cultural achievements. To appreciate those, we need to read Snorri himself.

Bibliography

Bagge, Sverre. *Society and Politics in Snorri Sturluson's Heimskringla.* Berkeley: University of California Press, 1991.

Ciklamini, Marlene. *Snorri Sturluson.* Boston: Twayne, 1978.

Egil's Saga. Translated with an introduction by Hermann Palsson and Paul Edwards. Harmondsworth, U.K.: Penguin, 1976.

Sturlunga Saga. Translated by Julia H. McGrew. With an introduction by R. George Thomas. 2 vols. New York: Twayne, 1970–1974.

Sturluson, Snorri. *Edda.* Edited and translated by Anthony Faulkes. London: Dent, 1987.

———. *Heimskringla: History of the Kings of Norway.* Translated with an introduction by Lee M. Hollander. Austin: Published for the American-Scandinavian Foundation by the University of Texas Press, 1964.

Somadeva (11th century)

Somadeva was a Sanskrit poet known for his late 10th-century collection of tales called the *Kathasaritsagara* (The ocean to the rivers of story). Little is known of his life, but he seems to have been of the Brahman caste, and he does mention in his text that Queen Suryamati of Kashmir was his patron and that he wrote the *Kathasaritsagara* for her, to take her mind off the study of the sciences. Somadeva based his work on a much older collection of stories called the *Brhathatha* (The great romance), attributed to Gunadhya. The *Brhathatha* is no longer extant, but Somadeva's rescension is a worthy aesthetic creation in its own right, and preserves a good deal of ancient Indian folklore.

The *Kathasaritsagara* contains some 350 tales, including some collections of stories that have been brought in from a variety of sources. Clearly Somadeva did not create any of these tales, but retold them in an entertaining way. The tales are not unlike European fairy tales in their emphasis on adventure and on the supernatural. A number of them are somewhat bawdy. They are told in a relatively simple narrative style and with details that appeal to the reader's imagination.

The *Kathasaritsagara* is structured as a framed narrative, not unlike the *THOUSAND AND ONE NIGHTS* or CHAUCER's *CANTERBURY TALES.* The largest frame explains how the *Brhathatha* came to be written after two goblins were tossed out of paradise for listening to the tales the god Siva told his wife Parvati. Required to tell all of Siva's stories to someone on earth in order to win their way back to heaven, one of the goblins relates the stories to a troll, who later conveys them to Gunadhya, who tells them to the world.

Within this tale is the main frame of the *Kathasaritsagara,* in which Prince Naravahanadatta acquires a great deal of wealth and magical powers that make him king of the spirits of the air. In the meantime he has a number of amorous encounters with a princess and other beautiful women. Many of the stories in the collection are told by characters within the narrative of this frame to entertain lovers and friends, just as Siva's original tales were told to entertain his wife.

Since the stories of the *Kathasaritsagara* most often deal with the acquisition of wealth, and have middle-class protagonists who focus on material gain, it has been suggested that the stories reflect the materialist values of cosmopolitan areas of 11th-century India. Somadeva's book is a valuable historical source for the social customs of the time, as well as an entertaining collection of colorful characters and powerful, imaginative stories.

Bibliography

Somadeva. *Tales from the Kathasaritsagara.* Translated by Arshia Sattar. With a foreword by Wendy Doniger. New Delhi: Penguin, 1994.

van Buitenen, J. A. B., trans. *Tales of Ancient India: Translated from the Sanskrit.* Chicago: University of Chicago Press, 1959.

Song of Roland (*Chanson de Roland*) (end of 11th century or early 12th century)

The Old French *Chanson de Roland* is one of the most famous epic poems from the Middle Ages and inspired a number of medieval imitations, such as the Priest Konrad's Middle High German *Rolandslied* (ca. 1170), The Stricker's *Karl der Große* (ca.

after 1220), and many other Old Norse, Middle English, Welsh, Dutch, and Latin versions. It also spawned a whole group of similar epic poems in French, known as CHANSONS DE GESTE (Songs of Deeds). Whereas the later Middle High German *Rolandslied* emphasized the nationalistic aspect of the story, the Old French *Chanson de Roland* underscored the religious motif above all. The anonymous Old French poet—the name of Turoldus, who is mentioned in the last line of the text, cannot be trusted as a biographical reference—relied on concrete historical events and transformed those into a literary masterpiece apparently in the immediate aftermath of the First Crusade (1096–99).

In 777, a group of Saracen (Arabic) princes traveled from Spain to the court of CHARLEMAGNE asking for his military assistance against some of their Muslim opponents. Although the king was already involved in military operations against the Saxons, he agreed and soon marched into Spain, using two armies, the first crossing the Pyrenees in the direction of Gerona, the second crossing the Basque Pyrenees in the direction of Pamplona. Both armies then joined and they besieged Saragossa, but to no avail. When new hostilities broke out in Saxony, Charlemagne had to return, but during the passage through the Pyrenees, his rear guard was ambushed by Basque troops on August 15, 778, and all men were killed, including Anselm, the king's seneschal, and Roland, duke of the Marches of Brittany.

About 200 years later, the many legends concerning these events were transformed into a major epic, the *Song of Roland.* Here Charlemagne, who had been 38 at the time of the expedition, is described as a 200-year-old ruler who represents all of Christendom in its historical struggle against the Saracens, who have replaced the historical Basques and are depicted as evil-spirited, treacherous, and monstrous opponents who resort to the most unethical strategy to conclude a seven-year war against the Christians. Anselm does not figure in the epic, whereas Roland emerges as Charlemagne's nephew and as a warrior with superhuman strength, accompanied by Oliver and 10 other peers, the paragons of French chivalry. The Saracens under Marsile attack with 400,000 men and rely on the betrayal of the 20,000 Frankish troops by Count Ganelon, Roland's own stepfather, who is jealous of the protagonist and is bent on destroying his nephew and his peers. Despite his prophetic dreams, Charlemagne moves out of Spain, leaving the rear guard behind, unknowingly clearing the way for the slaughter. When the Saracens approach, Roland refuses to call his uncle back with the help of his horn, Olifant, afraid of damaging his own honor. His friend Oliver seriously criticizes him for his failure to use Olifant, but when the Frankish army has been reduced to 60 men, he then rejects Roland's suggestion finally to use the horn. Archbishop Turpin, however, points out that the dead need to be buried, whereupon Roland blows the horn, but in the process the arteries of his temples burst, causing his own death. The Saracens flee when they hear the sound, but Charlemagne arrives too late to save any of his men.

The king carries their corpses back to *dulce France* (sweet France), when he is suddenly confronted by the army of Marsile's overlord, the emir Baligant. Charlemagne defeats him and conquers Saragossa, before he then returns to his capital at Aix-la-Chapelle. Oliver's sister Aude, Roland's fiancé, dies from grief over the tragic news, and Ganelon, after a difficult trial with an ordeal, is tried and condemned to death by quartering.

The anonymous French poet, who obviously drew from a variety of oral sources, created a remarkably consistent and compact epic narrative that is divided into individual *laisses,* or stanzas. The *Chanson* is characterized by many dialogues, clearly identified characters, and concrete motivations. Scholars are divided about the proper interpretation of Roland's decision not to call back Charlemagne when the rear guard is first attacked. Whereas some perceive this as a personal failure due to his hubris and false sense of heroism, others argue that this forces the king to return to his war efforts and to defeat the Saracens once and for all. This epic contains detailed discussion of honor, military discipline, chivalry, loyalty, friendship, treason, jealousy, wisdom, the conflict between Christians and Muslims, revenge, the question of faith, martyrdom, bravery, leadership, the significance of dreams as messages from God, the fundamental decision-making process in life, and the absolute conflict between good and evil.

The text has been preserved in a number of manuscripts, the oldest from the second half of the 12th century (Oxford, Bodleian, Digby 23 [O]). The corpus of manuscripts is divided into a group of Old French versions and a group of Franco-Italian versions, best represented by the early 14th-century manuscript V in the Codex IV in the Biblioteca di S. Marco in Venice. The *Chanson de Roland* was first rediscovered in the early 19th century by Francisque Michel, who published the *editio princeps* in 1837, which inspired generations of medievalists and others to pursue their interest in the heroic world of the Middle Ages.

Bibliography

Brault, Gerard J., ed. and trans. *The Song of Roland: An Analytic Edition.* 2 vols. Philadelphia: Pennsylvania State University Press, 1978.

Burgess, Glyn, trans. *The Song of Roland.* Harmondsworth, U.K.: Penguin, 1990.

Cook, Robert Francis. *The Sense of the Song of Roland.* Ithaca, N.Y.: Cornell University Press, 1987.

Jones, George Fenwick. *The Ethos of the Song of Roland.* Baltimore: Johns Hopkins University Press, 1963.

Vance, Eugene. *Reading the Song of Roland.* Englewood Cliffs, N.J.: Prentice Hall, 1970.

Albrecht Classen

sonnet

The sonnet is a 14-line lyric poem that has its origins in medieval Italy. The term comes from the Italian *sonnetto,* meaning "little sound or song." While the sonnet has become a prevalent literary form in a number of languages and has acquired different forms (most notably the Shakespearean or English sonnet form), the first sonnets followed what is now known as the Italian or Petrarchan form, consisting of hendecasyllabic (or 11-syllable) lines arranged into an octave (or eight-line section) followed by a sestet (or six-line part). Typically there is a turn of thought or *volta* beginning with the sestet, so that a conventional sonnet might ask a question in the octave to be answered in the sestet, or introduce a situation in the octave to be interpreted in the sestet, or express a desire or complaint in the octave that is assuaged in the sestet—any two-part progression that involves a pivotal change that can occur in the sestet of the poem.

The earliest extant sonnets are credited to GIACOMO DA LENTINO, a notary attached to the imperial court of Frederick II in Sicily, who flourished between 1215 and 1233. Giacomo's sonnets rhymed *abababab cdecde;* the following is Frederick Goldin's translation of one of Giacomo's earliest:

The basilisk before the shining mirror
dies with pleasure;
the swan sings with greatest rapture
when it is nearest death;
at the height of its pleasure the peacock
gets upset when it looks at its feet;
the phoenix burns itself all up
to return to be reborn.
I think I have become much like these
creatures,
I who go gladly to death before her beauty
and make my song lusty as I approach the
end;
in merriment I suddenly despair,
burning in fire I am made new again in joy
because of you, whom I long to return to,
gentlest one.

(Goldin 1973, 219, ll. 1–14)

Like most of the later Italian sonnets, this one is about love, and plays on the COURTLY LOVE convention of dying for love of one's lady. The turn of thought accompanying the sestet's change of rhyme involves the speaker's comparison of himself with the fantastic animals he has introduced in the octave.

The sonnet form was picked up and used by many later poets of the Italian Middle Ages. In particular the Tuscan poet GUITTONE D'AREZZO altered the form in the later 13th century to create the *abbaabba* rhyme scheme for the octave, a pattern that became standard in all later Italian sonnets. The great Tuscan poets Guido GUINIZELLI and Guido CAVALCANTI utilized this form, and DANTE included love sonnets in both his *Rime* and his *VITA NUOVA*. But it was Francis PETRARCH whose influence spread the sonnet form across Europe and gave his name to the traditional Italian sonnet form.

CHAUCER was the first to translate a Petrarchan sonnet into English, in the *Canticus Troili* embedded in the first book of his courtly ROMANCE, *TROILUS AND CRISEYDE*, but Chaucer did not copy Petrarch's form. The marquis de Santillana (1398–1458) introduced the sonnet form into Spain, and it became popular in France and England during the Renaissance, with Sir Thomas Wyatt first imitating Petrarch's form and style in English the early 16th century.

Bibliography

Goldin, Frederick, ed. and trans. *German and Italian Lyrics of the Middle Ages: An Anthology and a History.* Garden City, N.Y.: Doubleday, 1973.

Kleinhenz, Christopher. *The Early Italian Sonnet: The First Century (1220–1321).* Lecce, Italy: Milella, 1986.

Wilkins, Ernest Hatch. *The Invention of the Sonnet, and Other Studies in Italian Literature.* Rome: Edizioni de Storia e letteratura, 1959.

Sordello (Sordel) (ca. 1200–ca. 1270)

Sordello is the best-known of the Italian TROUBADOURS. He is famous now largely because of his significant position in DANTE's *DIVINE COMEDY*, where in cantos 6 and 7 of the *Purgatorio*, he shows Dante and Virgil into the Valley of Princes. Dante saw Sordello as a figure representing an elevated and admirable political morality.

What we know of Sordello's life hardly seems to warrant Dante's lofty opinion of him. Born a minor nobleman from Goito near Mantua, Sordello became embroiled in two serious scandals involving his relationships with women: He secretly married Otta, daughter of the Strasso family with whom he was staying in Ceneda. He fled with her to Treviso in 1227, and sought refuge from the tyrant Ezzelino II da Romano. But it seems he then began an affair with Ezzelino's sister, Cunizza, wife of the Count Ricciardo di San Bonifazio. Fleeing the wrath of the lady's brother and husband, Sordello left Italy in 1229, and spent some years wandering in Spain and Portugal.

Eventually Sordello came to Provence, where he found a patron, Blacatz, lord of Aups. Blacatz was head of an ancient noble family, and between 1194 and 1236 was patron of numerous poets, as well as the composer of 12 extant songs. Perhaps because of Blacatz's death, Sordello became attached in the mid-1230s to the court of Raimon Bérenger IV, count of Provence, whom he served until about 1245.

After 1245, Sordello was a knight in the service of Charles of Anjou. He followed Charles into Italy in 1265 as part of Charles's expedition to wrest the kingdom of Sicily from the Hohenstaufen king Manfred. Apparently Sordello was taken prisoner in Naples in 1266. Following Charles's successful campaign, Sordello took part in the distribution of fiefs in the new Angevin kingdom in 1269. He received lands and six castles in Abruzzi for his loyal service. But he seems to have died shortly thereafter. Some say he died back in Provence; some say he died a violent death. But nothing about his death is known for certain.

Some 40 of Sordello's poems are extant, all written in Provençal. Only 12 of these are *cansos,* or love poems. But when Sordello does speak of love, it is with an extreme and almost platonic delicacy and deference to his lady: In one poem he says that he would rather serve his lady hopelessly for years than to serve another lady who would be so loose as to invite him to her bed. In another he says that he will write in the simple, clear *TROBAR LEU* style, because that is what pleases his lady.

But Sordello is better known for his *SIRVENTES,* or political songs. His best-known poem, and the one that aroused Dante's praise, is his *planh* or lament on the death of Blacatz, written about 1237. In this poem Sordello takes to task eight major political leaders of Europe, and charges them to eat the heart of the dead man, in order to inspire them to courageous action. To his own lord, Raimon Bérenger, he says:

And the Count of Provence, it is well that
he eats if he remembers
A man's worth nothing living robbed of his

inheritance,
And for all his effort to hold his ground and defend himself,
He must eat of this heart for the heavy burden he bears.

(Goldin 1973, 315, ll. 37–40)

This *planh* (or COMPLAINT) must have given Sordello the reputation for political principles that inspired Dante to use him in the *Purgatorio.* In Dante's story Sordello embraces Virgil as a native from his own home in Mantua, then delivers a prophetic diatribe on the political corruption in Dante's Italy. Ultimately he leads Dante and Virgil into the Valley of Princes in canto 7.

In addition to Dante, Sordello also provided poetic inspiration for Robert Browning in the 19th century, whose long poem *Sordello* appeared in 1840. Browning focuses not on Sordello's political philosophy, but rather on his amorous affairs, particularly with the sister of Ezzelino.

Bibliography

Goldin, Frederick, ed. and trans. *Lyrics of the Troubadours and Trouvères: An Anthology and a History.* Garden City, N.Y.: Doubleday, 1973.

Wilhelm, James J. *The Poetry of Sordello.* New York: Garland, 1986.

South English Legendary, The (*Early South English Legendary*) (ca. 13th–15th centuries)

A collection of SAINTS' LIVES in MIDDLE ENGLISH verse (mainly seven-syllable couplets), *The South English Legendary* was a very popular text, surviving in 63 manuscripts, no two of which are identical. The number of legends included varies from manuscript to manuscript, from 55 to 135 in those that are more or less complete. The earliest known manuscript (Oxford Bodleian Library ms. Laud Misc. 108)—which is clearly not the original—is dated about 1270, while the latest was compiled around 1500. The original version was probably produced in southwest England in the mid-13th century, and ultimately was copied throughout the South and the Midlands. At one time the work was attributed to the monk ROBERT OF GLOUCESTER, but that attribution is no longer accepted. Its original author, audience, and purpose are unknown.

The textual history of *The South English Legendary* is incredibly complex. Copied by scribes throughout England for a variety of audiences, each manuscript received some revision or alteration, whether in the form of the addition of a favorite local saint, the alteration of vocabulary because of differences in dialect, the revision of the order in which the lives are presented, or the wholesale reworking of some of the lives: Some lives (like that of St. Agnes) survive in two versions that merely differ in length; others (Saint Benedict, for example) exist in two radically different versions because of completely different sources.

Most of the lives included in the *South English Legendary* probably have their sources in Latin originals (it is possible that the *GOLDEN LEGEND,* compiled about 1260, was an inspiration for the *South English Legendary*), though most were probably known to their audiences through long oral and written traditions. Saints' lives in general tend to contain certain generic formulas, whatever the details of the original legend, so that many of the legends in this collection have similar features. For example, because the ideal of physical virginity had become synonymous in Christian theology with spiritual purity, nearly all of the female saints included in the collection are depicted as virgin martyrs who reject the material world, most often marriage in particular, as representing the lusts of the flesh. Virginity is less of an emphasis for male saints, but there are formulaic aspects to their lives as well: The martyrs are all persecuted by zealously anti-Christian emperors or their surrogates, and all are tortured in a dramatic manner. Later male saints are all admired for miraculous events that surround their lives as a result of their holiness.

Still, there is some interesting variety in the text. The collection includes lives of New Testament figures (such as Mary Magdalene and John the Baptist), of early Christian martyrs (St. Agnes and St.

Cecilia), of important church figures (St. Francis and St. Gregory), of Irish saints (St. Patrick and St. Brendan), and of popular English saints (like Thomas Beckett and Saint Frideswide). It also includes a variety of other miscellaneous material, such as information about feast days and Old Testament history, as well as a detailed account of medieval cosmogony. Two different prologues, one longer than the other, survive in the extant manuscripts. Both declare that the *Legendary* is made up of the lives of holy men and women, and that the lives should be read on the feast days appropriate for the individual saints. Thus the chief concern of the compilers of the manuscripts was to collect lives for use chronologically throughout the church year—in some manuscripts the lives are arranged according to the calendar year, from January through December, in some according to the Liturgical Year, beginning with Advent in November.

Certainly this desire of a text for festival days contributed to the widespread textual tradition of the *South English Legendary*. But the popularity of the text in its own time undoubtedly owes something as well to its colloquial use of language and its often humorous or even satirical narrative voice. What could be a rather tedious didactic exercise often becomes, in the *Legendary*, fascinating and entertaining reading.

Bibliography

Boyd, Beverly. "A New Approach to the *South English Legendary*," *Philological Quarterly* 47 (1968): 494–498.

Görlach, Manfred. *The Textual Tradition of the South English Legendary*. Leeds Texts and Monographs, New Series 6. Leeds: University of Leeds, 1974.

Klaus, Jankofsky, ed. *The South English Legendary: A Critical Assessment*. Tübingen, Germany: Francke, 1992.

The South English Legendary. Edited from Corpus Christi College Cambridge MS 145 and British Museum MS Harley 2277. Edited by Charlotte d'Evelyn and Anna J. Mill. 3 Vols. EETS, 235, 235, and 244. London: Oxford University Press, 1956.

Thompson, Anne B. "Narrative Art in the *South English Legendary*," *JEGP* 90 (1991): 20–30.

Spoils of Annwfn, The (*Preiddeu Annwfn*) (ca. 900)

The Spoils of Annwfn is a brief but puzzling poem in Welsh, preserved in the 13th-century book of TALIESIN. Though structurally similar to other poems in that manuscript, it was certainly not written by the sixth-century bard Taliesin. Most likely the poem was composed between the eighth and 12th centuries, probably around the year 900. *The Spoils of Annwfn* is interesting chiefly as an early text dealing with the legend of King ARTHUR.

In the poem Arthur (not yet called king) leads his men in a raid on Annwfn, the mythic dwelling place of the Celtic deities. Annwfn is depicted here as both an underworld city and an island in the sea to which Arthur and his host must travel in his ship Prydwen ("Fairface"). Arthur's goal is to obtain a magic cauldron in the possession of the lord of Annwfn. The cauldron is guarded by nine maidens, and it has the property of measuring the courage of warriors: A coward could not cook with it.

The expedition proves to be dangerous and costly for Arthur—only seven men return alive, including the poem's narrator, who uses that fact as a kind of refrain after each section of the poem, repeating "apart from seven, none came back." With each refrain, the narrator also calls Annwfn by another name: "Faerie," for example, or "Fortress of Revelry." These various epithets have led to some confusion in the poem, since some readers have taken them to refer to different destinations, and suggested that the poem is about several different journeys, from each of which only seven warriors returned. This seems less likely than the poet's using various epithets for the underworld. But the difference in interpretation does illustrate the difficulty of understanding or translating this poem. Other difficulties arise from the many allusions to traditional Celtic legend that are incomprehensible to modern readers.

Scholars have recognized similarities between this poem and another Welsh text, the tale of Branwen in the second branch of the *MABINOGION*. Though that text does not involve Arthur and describes a voyage to Ireland rather than the underworld, it does concern a magic cauldron that can raise the dead. It is possible that these magic Celtic vessels are early versions of what was to become the legend of the HOLY GRAIL in later texts.

Bibliography

Breeze, Andrew. *Medieval Welsh Literature.* Dublin: Four Courts Press, 1997.

Loomis, Roger Sherman. *The Development of Arthurian Romance.* New York: Norton, 1963.

Williams, Gwyn. *An Introduction to Welsh Poetry.* 1954. Freeport, N.Y.: Books for Libraries Press, 1970.

Squire of Low Degree, The (*The Squyr of Lowe Degre*) (ca. 1450–1500)

A late MIDDLE ENGLISH verse ROMANCE of 1,130 lines in octosyllabic (eight-syllable) couplets, *The Squire of Low Degree* was written in the East Midlands late in the 15th century. There is no extant manuscript of the entire poem, which is preserved in a 1560 printed text and fragments of a 1520 printed edition by the famous early printer Wynkyn de Worde. The 1520 text bears the title "Undo Your Door," a phrase drawn from one of the poem's episodes.

The romance tells the story of a poor young squire's love for the daughter of the king of Hungary. The princess agrees to accept the squire's suit, but insists that before she can marry him he must distinguish himself as a knight. A slanderous steward sees the squire and princess together, and reports the tryst to the king. When the king still trusts the squire, the steward sets a trap to ambush the squire on his way to see the princess. The squire manages to kill the steward in the ambush, but is taken prisoner. The princess, believing her lover dead, is beside herself with grief. Her father attempts to console her by reminding her of all there is to enjoy in the world, describing courtly feasts, music, and sports. But it is to no avail; the princess is inconsolable. At last the king relents and sets the squire free from his imprisonment, but the young man still must leave the court to prove himself a knight worthy of the princess. He rides out on his quest, and has his share of knightly adventure. When he returns after seven years, the princess is about to take vows as an anchoress. But he claims his beloved, her father gives them his blessing, and the two are wed.

The Squire of Low Degree is a late romance that seems to be made up of a number of motifs from earlier romances. Its theme of an inborn nobility even in someone of a lower social status, and its vivid descriptions of courtly life and manners, make this poem one of the more accessible of English verse romances.

Bibliography

Hudson, Harriet E. "Construction of Class, Family, and Gender in Some Middle English Popular Romances," in *Class and Gender in Early English Literature: Intersections,* edited by Britton J. Harwood and Gillian R. Overing. Bloomington: Indiana University Press, 1994, 76–94.

Sands, Donald B., ed. *Middle English Verse Romances.* New York: Holt, Rinehart and Winston, 1966.

Seaman, Myra J. "The Waning of Middle English Chivalric Romance in 'The Squyr of Lowe Degre,'" *Fifteenth-Century Studies* 29 (2004): 174–199.

Spearing, A. C. "Secrecy, Listening, and Telling in The Squyr of Lowe Degre," *Journal of Medieval and Renaissance Studies* 20 (1990): 273–292.

Wright, Glenn. "'Other Wyse Then Must We Do': Parody and Popular Narrative in the Squyr of Lowe Degre," *Comitatus: A Journal of Medieval and Renaissance Studies* 27 (1996): 14–41.

Squire's Tale, The Geoffrey Chaucer (ca. 1390)

The Squire, presented in the GENERAL PROLOGUE as the fashionable and charming son of the more sober Knight, presents what promises to be a chivalric ROMANCE of the sort then popular in France, with an interlaced structure involving several characters and plot threads. Thus *The Squire's Tale* would have been more complex, more full of wonder and supernatural elements, than any other story in *The CANTERBURY TALES.* The tale breaks off after some 664 lines, though both Edmund Spenser and John Lane wrote continuations of the story later. Lane's continuation runs to 7,000 lines, which may be the chief reason CHAUCER chose not to finish it—it would have been far too long to include in *The Canterbury Tales* as they were conceived.

No direct sources for *The Squire's Tale* have been found, though clearly Chaucer was inspired by contemporary French romances, themselves influenced by Oriental models that had come through Moorish Spain. Accordingly Chaucer uses Oriental-sounding names in the tale, including "Cambyuskan," the Latinized form of "Genghis Khan."

In the first part of the tale, Cambyuskan, king of Tartary, has a great birthday feast. During the meal's third course a knight rides in to deliver wondrous, magical gifts for Cambyuskan sent by the kings of Arabia and India. One is the brass steed on which the knight sits—the horse can bear its rider anywhere in the world within 24 hours. The second is a magic ring that grants its wearer the ability to understand the language of the birds. The third gift is a sword that is able to cure any wound that it makes. And the final gift is a magic mirror in which one can see coming dangers. The mirror and the ring, we are told, are gifts for Cambyuskan's daughter, Canacee.

In part 2 Canacee rises the next morning and goes for a walk. She finds a wounded falcon, crying piteously in a tree above her. Because her ring allows her to understand the falcon's speech, Canacee learns that the falcon has been betrayed by her lover. Taking pity on the bird, Canacee brings the falcon home in order to nurse her back to health.

As the second part of the tale ends and the third begins, the Squire narrator promises to tell about Cambyuskan's wars, about the adventures of Cambyuskan's sons Cambulus and Algarsif, and about how Cambalo fought against her brothers to win the love of Canacee. But the tale breaks off abruptly after the first two lines of the third part, and what follows is the Franklin's enthusiastic response to the Squire's tale, that leads into his own story.

Critics have speculated about whether *The Squire's Tale* is intended as a satire of the immaturity and excessive rhetoric of its teller. Others have argued that the tale was intended to be interrupted by the Franklin, who tactfully stops the Squire from running on indefinitely.

Bibliography

DiMarco, Vincent. "The Dialogue of Science and Magic in Chaucer's 'Squire's Tale,'" in *Dialogische Strukturen/Dialogic Structures: Festschrift fur Willi Erzgraber zum 70. Geburtstag,* edited by Thomas Kuhn and Ursula Schaefer. Tübingen, Germany: Gunter Narr, 1996, 50–68.

Edwards, Robert R. "The Failure of Invention: Chaucer's 'Squire's Tale.'" In *Ratio and Invention: A Study of Medieval Lyric and Narrative,* edited by Robert R. Edwards. Nashville, Tenn.: Vanderbilt University Press, 1989, 131–145.

Goodman, Jennifer. "Chaucer's 'Squire's Tale' and the Rise of Chivalry," *Studies in the Age of Chaucer* 5 (1983): 127–136.

Pearsall, Derek. *The Canterbury Tales.* London: George Allen and Unwin, 1985.

Stanzaic Morte Arthur, The (14th century)

The *Stanzaic Morte Arthur* is a MIDDLE ENGLISH poem composed probably in the North Midlands area of England in the middle of the 14th century. As the title suggests, the poem narrates the events leading up to the death of King ARTHUR and is an important link in the Arthurian tradition, drawing on a French source, *Mort Artu,* and ultimately influencing Thomas MALORY in the final two tales of his 15th-century *Le MORTE DARTHUR.*

The poem comprises 3,969 lines and survives in one manuscript, Harley 2252 in the British Library. The manuscript is a miscellany, and the section containing the poem can be dated between 1460 and 1480. Generally, the poem's eight-line stanzas have four-stress iambic lines, with a rhyme scheme of *abababab,* although the number of lines in the stanzas varies at points, as does the rhyme scheme.

The poem's beginning positions the action after the quest of the Holy Grail, as Arthur is urged by the queen to host a tournament to boost what she alleges is the waning honor of the Round Table. The tournament at Winchester brings the Lord of Ascolot and results in his daughter's falling in love with LANCELOT. Ultimately, her love goes unrequited as Lancelot can only love Queen GUENEVERE ("Gaynor" in this poem), but before the maid's death resulting from the discovery that Lancelot could not love her, the queen is so distraught by the appearance of a relationship between the two that she sends Lancelot away. Consequently, when the queen is falsely accused of poisoning a knight, she has no one to champion her against the charges of the dead knight's brother, Sir Mador. Her piteous appeal to the knights whom she had served is an example of the dramatic scenes that pervade this poem. Although Bors pledges to fight for her should no other knight offer, Lancelot returns and defeats Sir Mador, grants him mercy, and Sir Mador forgives his brother's death for the sake of Lancelot, who, given his reputation as a knight, honors him by fighting with him. At this point, the court considers how the poisoning could have occurred, and upon torture, one squire who served that day admits his guilt, and Guenevere is therefore exonerated.

Lancelot's restoration to the Round Table is short-lived, however, as the poem progresses and Agravain and Mordred plot to expose to Arthur the affair of Guenevere and Lancelot. Brothers GAWAIN, Gaheriet, and Gaheries disagree, but Agravain and Mordred are determined and they disclose it to Arthur. They set a trap for the lovers by purporting to leave them alone in the castle, and when Lancelot is caught within the queen's bower without his armor, he attacks one knight, arms himself, then defeats the remaining knights and flees. A pivotal part of the poem occurs next when the court determines to burn the queen for her disloyalty to Arthur. Reluctantly, Gaheriet and Gaheries obey the king's orders to stand guard over her and are thus, unwittingly, slain by Lancelot when he returns to rescue Guenevere. It is this unintentional double murder that turns Gawain irrevocably against Lancelot and is the underlying impetus for the remainder of the action of the poem. Gawain's relentless determination to avenge his brothers death by either killing Lancelot or dying in the process results in multiple battles and Lancelot's exile to the Continent.

Subsequent warring with Lancelot in France leaves Arthur's kingdom in the hands of his son, Mordred, who, unaccountably in this poem, betrays Arthur, acts as ruler in his absence and attempts not only to depose him and usurp the kingdom, but to marry his queen as well. Guenevere escapes to a tower where she barricades herself against Mordred, Arthur returns to fight Mordred and reclaim his land, and Gawain is struck dead in the penultimate battle. Arthur mourns Gawain and is motivated by a dream vision to appeal to Mordred for peace until Lancelot can arrive to battle alongside Arthur. In the meeting to discuss a truce, however, a knight strikes at an adder and the two sides, both deeply distrusting one another, believe the other has attacked, and they begin to fight. Arthur kills Mordred and barely escapes with his own life. After Bedivere returns Excalibur to the sea as Arthur directs, Arthur is transported to Avalon by three ladies. Bedivere discovers a grave he believes to be Arthur's based on the report of the hermit and mourns the loss of his lord.

The poem does not end with the death of Arthur, however. The poem follows Lancelot as he arrives in England to find the Round Table in ruin, and charts his meeting with Guenevere, their joint repentance of their sin, and his penance at a chapel for seven years. He is eventually joined by Bors and other knights. Thus the Round Table is dissolved and the knights dedicate their service, in the absent of their king, to God. When Lancelot dies, the remaining knights are joined by Ector, Lancelot's brother, who mourns Lancelot in another dramatic scene. In hermit's clothes, they advance to Aumsbury where they find Queen Guenevere dead. She is buried beside the grave purported to be Arthur's and the poem thus ends with her death.

Scholars have previously commented on the absence of Fortune in the *Stanzaic Morte Arthur* and its focus instead on the impetus for the action of individual deeeds, as well as the psychological ramifications of the events upon its characters. Human error plays a role, as well, in Lancelot's unintentional killing of Gawain's brothers, and the presence of the adder at the battle.

The *Stanzaic Morte Arthur* is an important work for Arthurian scholars in that it, along with the *ALLITERATIVE MORTE ARTHURE,* represents part of the English tradition of Arthurian literature prior to the works of Sir Thomas Malory, which synthesized so many of both the French and the English texts. Malory drew heavily from the *Stanzaic Morte Arthur* and the French prose *Mort Artu* (last romance of the VULGATE CYCLE and the source for the stanzaic poem, which condensed much of it) in constructing the books of "Launcelot and Gwenyvere" and "The Death of Arthur." Like the author of the *Stanzaic Morte Arthur,* Malory also condensed much of his French romance sources, possible evidence that he was influenced by the example set by the stanzaic *Morte.* Because Malory shaped the Arthurian tradition and influenced subsequent writers, the effect of the *Stanzaic Morte Arthur* on him and his last two tales in *Le Morte Darthur* demonstrates the poem's importance in literary history, in addition to the appeal of the text itself.

Bibliography

Barron, W. R. J. *English Medieval Romance.* London: Longman, 1987.

Benson, Larry Dean, ed. *King Arthur's Death: The Middle English Stanzaic Morte Arthur and Alliterative Morte Arthure.* Indianapolis: Bobbs-Merrill, 1974.

Knopp, Sherron E. "Artistic Design in the Stanzaic *Morte Arthur,*" *ELH* 45 (1978): 563–582.

Wertime, Richard A. "The Theme and Structure of the Stanzaic *Morte Arthur,*" *PMLA* 87 (1972): 1075–1082.

Michelle Palmer

Story of Ying-ying, The Yuan Zhen (Yüan Chen) (ca. 804)

The most popular and important work of prose fiction from medieval China's TANG DYNASTY was written by the Confucian scholar, poet, and statesman YUAN ZHEN. Originally entitled *Hui-chen chi* (Meeting with an immortal)—the title of a lengthy poem embedded in the narrative—the story has become known as *Yingying zhuan* (*Ying-ying Chuan; The Story of Ying-ying*), after its female protagonist.

The Story of Ying-ying belongs to a new narrative genre called *chuanqi* (*ch'uan ch'i*) (literally "transmissions of the marvelous") introduced into Tang literature during the eighth century. Prior to this development, Chinese prose fiction had been largely undeveloped, existing mainly of short anecdotes and fables, or short supernatural tales often illustrating Buddhist or Taoist concepts. But with the development of *chuanqi,* writers became more serious about structure and literary style in fiction.

This new genre seems to have built not on previous Chinese fiction but rather on historical narratives. The *chuanqi* tales are strongly influenced by earlier historical narrative. Typically the action of the story is presented as a specific event occurring at specific historical time and place. In *The Story of Ying-ying,* Yuan Zhen even inserts himself into the story as a minor character, increasing the impression of historical veracity. In addition these stories often contained what might be considered primary historical documents—letters from the characters, for example, or poems composed by them—that help create the impression that the narrative is the result of historical research.

The genre grew rapidly, though traditionalists still considered it a vulgar form of entertainment rather than true literature. Still many scholars wrote and read such stories for their own enjoyment, and by the early ninth century, it had become a common practice for candidates for the civil service examinations to present their sponsors or examiners original *chuanqi* compositions prior to their exams, as an indication of their own literary aptitude. It has been conjectured that *The Story of Ying-ying* was such a composition, and that the young Yuan Zhen composed it prior to his examination in 806.

In *The Story of Ying-ying,* a young scholar named Chang, on his way to the capital to take his civil service examination, stops for lodging at a monastery, where he meets the beautiful but enigmatic Ying-ying, a distant relative. They engage in an illicit affair. Once at the capital, Chang loses interest in Ying-ying and abandons her. She writes him a long letter, included in the narrative—a letter he shows to his friends, some of whom write poems about it—including a 60-line poem by Yuan Zhen himself.

Most modern readers see Chang's action as heartless and sympathize with Ying-ying, but Chang does present an argument that his breaking off the affair is a matter of duty to his family and to the Confucian ideal of public service. The narrator appears to agree with him. Ying-ying, on the other hand, seems capricious and manipulative, and, despite her protests of eternal love, marries someone else fairly quickly. For that matter Chang's moral rectitude doesn't stop him from trying to see Ying-ying when he passes through her town, an opportunity she refuses him. In the end neither character is especially sympathetic, and the story may be read as an ironic view of how human beings, perhaps insincerely, play roles expected of them (romantic heroine, dedicated public servant) in conventional situations. Some critics have conjectured that the tale is really a semiautobiographical expression of regret by Yuan Zhen himself over an early affair and his treatment of the lady involved, but such guesses must always remain in the realm of speculation.

The Story of Ying-ying was tremendously popular in its own time and for generations after, and was retold in various forms in verse, prose, and drama. One of the best-known versions of the tale was a play called *Xixiangji* (*Hsi-hsiang chi; The Romance of the Western Chamber*) by the 13th-century dramatist Wang Shihfu. Despite his voluminous output of serious lyric poetry, Yuan Zhen remains famous for his achievement in what he would have probably considered an inferior genre, narrative fiction.

Bibliography

Hightower, James R., trans. "The Story of Ying-ying." In *Traditional Chinese Stories: Themes and Variations,* edited by Joseph S. M. Lau and Y. M. Ma. New York: Columbia University Press, 1978.

Palandri, Angela C. Y. Jung. *Yüan Chen.* Boston: G. K. Hall, 1977.

Wang Shihfu. *The Romance of the Western Chamber.* Translated by S. I. Hsiung. New York: Columbia University Press, 1968.

Sumer is icumen in (13th century)

Sumer is icumen in is occasionally known as *The Cuckoo Song* because of its chorus. This song, celebrating the joy of spring (MIDDLE ENGLISH often used "summer" in this sense), is often assumed to have been written between 1230 and 1240, but the complexity of the music suggests that a date of about 1300 might be more likely. It has two stanzas and a two-line refrain with the following rhyme scheme: *abcbb abcbbb bb.*

The poem celebrates the effects of spring and lists numerous indications of its presence. The first stanza has the images of seeds, leaves growing on trees, and blossoming flowers. The second stanza addresses animal life and celebrates the birth of lambs and calves.

The poem is the only English lyric found in a 13th-century commonplace book, compiled by Reading Abbey monks, with numerous contemporary Latin and French musical pieces. The lyric contains singing instructions in Latin that explain the *rota* or round form. Because of the deceptively simple lyrics linked with the complex music, written for four voices accompanied by two additional voices, it appears this poem may be a learned, religious adaptation of a popular secular tune.

Twentieth-century poet Ezra Pound wrote a parody of *Sumer is icumen in* that he entitled *Winter is icumen in* and in which he described the frustrations associated with winter.

Bibliography

Davies, R. T., ed. *Medieval English Lyrics: A Critical Anthology.* Evanston, Ill.: Northwestern University Press, 1964.

Moore, A. K. *The Secular Lyric in Middle English.* Lexington: University of Kentucky Press, 1951.

Reiss, Edmund. *The Art of the Middle English Lyric: Essays in Criticism.* Athens: University of Georgia Press, 1972.

Summa Theologica (*Summa Theologiae*)

Saint Thomas Aquinas (1265–1272)

The most successful medieval attempt to compile an integrated and systematic Christian philosophy is Saint Thomas AQUINAS's *Summa Theologica* (Summa [or Compilation] of theology). Aquinas began the *Summa* in about 1265, and left it unfinished upon his death. In it, he attempts to reconcile Christian theology with Greek philosophy, in particular the philosophy of Aristotle. For this task, he was able to rely on new Latin translations of the philosopher made by his fellow Dominican friar William of Moerbecke.

Aquinas indicates that his *Summa Theologica* is intended as an orderly synthesis for beginning students of Christian theology (thus it is not intended, for example, as an argument addressed to nonbelievers). It reiterates some of the ideas from his earlier and less systematic *Summa Contra Gentiles.* To some extent, Aquinas is countering some of the issues raised at the University of Paris in the 13th century by the study of the Muslim philosopher AVERROËS's commentaries on Aristotle. These ideas, particularly Averroës's denial of individual immortality, had led to the doctrine of the "double truth," that certain things might be proved true by reason, but that their opposite should be believed true as a matter of faith. For Aquinas, truth was indivisible, and the truth of philosophical reason must be in accord with the truth of divine revelation. The *Summa* demonstrates that human reason can prove some of the tenets of faith, such as, for Aquinas, the existence of God; reason can also illuminate some of the truths of faith that cannot be proven; and sometimes, the assumptions of philosophers that contradict those of faith can be shown to be unsupported by reason.

Thomas divides the *Summa* into four major sections: part one deals with questions of sacred doctrine, the unity of God, the holy Trinity, the created world, angels, the six days of Creation, man, and on divine government. The first part of the second part considers questions of man's end, human actions, passions, habits, vices, and sins, followed by questions of law and of grace. The second part of the second part reflects on the theological virtues of faith, hope, and charity, the cardinal virtues of prudence, justice, fortitude, and temperance, and finally acts pertaining to certain men. The incomplete third part looks at the incarnation and the life of Christ, the sacraments of baptism, confirmation, communion, penance, extreme unction, holy orders, and matrimony, and ends by considering the resurrection. The complete *Summa* comprises 38 tracts divided into 631 questions, subdivided into about 3,000 separate articles.

Each individual article of the *Summa* follows the dialectic method advocated by the scholastic philosophers of the high Middle Ages. The article is worded as a question, such as, for example "Whether the Natural Law Can Be Changed?" (the fifth article of Question 94 in the first part of the second part). For each article Aquinas first enumerates some "objections," or arguments against his own position, such as "the slaying of the innocent, adultery and theft are against the natural law. But we find these things changed by God: as when God commanded Abraham to slay his innocent son" (Thomas Aquinas 1947, I, 1011). He then says "On the contrary," and cites a quotation that supports his own view, usually from the Scriptures, from Aristotle, or from one of the church fathers like St. AUGUSTINE. In this particular article, he cites the *Decretals* (the most influential work of medieval canon law) as saying "The natural law dates from the creation of the rational creature. It does not vary according to time, but remains unchangeable" (Thomas Aquinas 1947, I, 1012). He always follows this assertion by the main body of his argument, beginning with the phrase "I answer that. . . ." Finally, he ends the article by explicitly countering each of the opposing arguments with which he had begun the question; for example, his reply to the above objection, while somewhat lengthy, ends with the contention that "in natural things, whatever is done by God is, in some way, natural" (Thomas Aquinas 1947, I, 1012).

Although several of its conclusions were officially condemned by the church in 1277, shortly after Aquinas's death, in subsequent centuries the *Summa Theologica* became essentially an expression of the official theological position of the Roman Catholic Church. It remains to this day the most influential book of its kind ever written.

Bibliography

Clark, Mary T., ed. *An Aquinas Reader.* Rev. ed. New York: Fordham University Press, 2000.

Davies, Brian. *Aquinas.* London and New York: Continuum, 2002.

Eco, Umberto. *The Aesthetics of Thomas Aquinas.* Translated by Hugh Bredin. Cambridge, Mass.: Harvard University Press, 1988.

Thomas Aquinas, Saint. *Summa Theologiae.* Cambridge: Blackfriars, 1964ff.

———. *Summa Theologica.* Translated by the Fathers of the English Dominican Province. 3 vols. New York: Benziger Brothers, 1947.

Malene A. Little

Summoner's Tale, The Geoffrey Chaucer (ca. 1390)

The Summoner's Tale is the most scatological of CHAUCER'S *CANTERBURY TALES.* Fittingly attributed to the pilgrim Summoner, the most physically disgusting of the pilgrims described in the GENERAL PROLOGUE, the *Summoner's Tale* is presented as the Summoner's revenge on the pilgrim Friar, who has just told a tale critical of Summoners (officers whose job was to summon offenders to ecclesiastical courts). The tale has no known analogues and was probably Chaucer's own invention. Because of its contemporary setting, bourgeois characters, and comic emphasis on trickery, the tale has often been called a FABLIAU, but it lacks the focus on sexual escapades generally characteristic of that genre. Chiefly the tale is a satire of the greed and hypocrisy of friars.

The tale begins with an anecdote in which a friar, visiting hell, is shown the final resting place of all friars in Satan's hindquarters—a perversion of a popular tale in which the Virgin reveals the heavenly home of friars to be under her protective skirts. Then begins the tale proper, in which a Yorkshire friar, begging from door to door, calls at the household of the bedridden old Thomas, whose wife tells the friar how bad-tempered her ill husband is. The friar preaches an impromptu sermon against anger, and then asks Thomas for a financial contribution. Despite Thomas's protestations that he has given all he can, the friar continues pressing him, until Thomas promises to give him a rich gift if he will swear to share it equally among his 12 convent brothers. The friar agrees, and Thomas tells him to reach down under his backside where the treasure is hidden. When the friar does so, Thomas farts in his hand.

The friar storms out of Thomas's house and angrily complains to the local lord. Rather than focus on punishing Thomas, the lord becomes fascinated with the arithmetic or "ars-metrike" problem of how to divide the fart 12 ways. His squire suggests that the 12 friars assemble around a cartwheel, with their noses at the ends of the spokes. The complaining friar may be in the center, at the hub of the wheel. Thomas may then be invited to sit on the hub of the wheel and break wind, so that the fart will travel along the spokes of the wheel and be distributed evenly to the waiting friars. The squire is handsomely rewarded for his ingenuity, and the friar is silenced.

Scholarly interest in the tale has often looked at the characterization of the friar, who is the epitome of con man, hypocrite, glutton, and false comforter. He says he can't eat a bite but orders a gourmet meal; he was absent when the couple's child died but claims to have had a vision of him in heaven; and he condemns the very sin he is most guilty of himself. Biblical and iconographic allusions have also interested scholars, particularly the image of the wheel and its relation to Pentecost, as well as allusions to the Abraham story and other biblical events. These elements suggest a serious satirical intent for the tale, despite its surface coarseness.

Bibliography

Fleming, John V. "Anticlerical Satire as Theological Essay: Chaucer's 'Summoner's Tale,' " *Thalia* 6, no. 1 (1983): 5–22.

Olsen, Glending. "The End of The Summoner's Tale and the Uses of Pentecost," *Studies in the Age of Chaucer* 21 (1999): 209–245.

Ruud, Jay. " 'My Spirit Hath His Fostering in the Bible': The Summoner's Tale and the Holy Spirit," in *Rebels and Rivals: The Contestive Spirit in The Canterbury Tales,* edited by Susanna Greer Fein, David Raybin, and Peter C. Braeger. Studies in Medieval Culture, 29. Kalamazoo, Mich.: Medieval Institute Publications, 1991, 125–148.

tail-rhyme romances

A tail-rhyme stanza might take many forms, but most typically it consists of a rhyming pair of long lines followed by a shorter line (the "tail"). The three-line pattern is repeated, with the third lines rhyming, to form a six-line stanza sometimes known as a "romance six." This stanza might rhyme *aabaab* or *aabccb,* with the b-rhyme lines having three stressed syllables and the other lines having four. A stanza might also contain 12 lines, basically combining the romance sixes into a longer stanza rhyming *aabaabccbddb,* or *aabccbddbeeb.* The term "tail-rhyme" itself is an English translation of the Latin *rythmus caudatus* (in French it was called *rime couée*).

Tail-rhyme stanzas were common in a large group of MIDDLE ENGLISH metrical ROMANCES from the 14th and 15th centuries. While some English romances were written in ALLITERATIVE VERSE, and others in rhymed octosyllabic (eight-syllable) couplets, many are tail-rhyme romances. A number of these seem to have been composed or circulated by wandering MINSTRELS, and so may have been intended for an audience of the middle class or the lower gentry, rather than the more courtly audience of a more sophisticated poet like CHAUCER or GOWER. Some of the better-known tail-rhyme romances are *SIR ISUMBRAS, BEVIS OF HAMPTON, HORN CHILDE,* and *GUY OF WARWICK* from the early 14th century, the last two found in the famous Auchinleck manuscript, which may once have been in the possession of Chaucer. Late 14th-century tail-rhyme romances include *The EARL OF TOULOUSE, LIBEAUS DESCONUS, SIR LAUNFAL,* and *IPOMADON*—the longest of the romances at 8,890 lines. Tail-rhyme romances from the 15th century include *The TURKE AND SIR GAWAIN* and *The WEDDYNG OF SYR GAWEN,* both from the northern part of England. Most of these are in 12-line stanzas.

The best known tail-rhyme romance in Middle English is Chaucer's parody of the genre, *The TALE OF SIR THOPAS,* an unfinished romance in six-line stanzas, some rhyming *aabaab* and others rhyming *aabccb.* Chaucer found much to burlesque in the genre, and made particularly effective use of the romance of *Guy of Warwick,* but he seems to have been familiar with all of the romances from the Auchinleck manuscript and several others as well.

At least a few dozen tail-rhyme romances have survived from Middle English, and it has been suggested that there was actually a school of minstrels in 14th-century East Anglia producing tail-rhyme romances. In any case, the popularity of these kinds of romances waned after the 15th century, although most modern poets have still made use of varieties of the tail-rhyme stanza, as, for example, Shelley does in his poem "To Night."

Bibliography

Benson, Larry D., ed. *The Riverside Chaucer.* 3rd ed. Boston: Houghton-Mifflin, 1987.

Trounce, A. McI. "The English Tail-Rhyme Romances," *Medium Aevum* 1 (1932), 87–108, 168–82; 2 (1933), 34–57; 3 (1934), 30–50.

Táin bó Cuailnge (*The Cattle Raid of Cooley*) (ca. sixth century)

The central narrative of the Old Irish ULSTER CYCLE (a heroic cycle of tales concerned with the deeds of the great hero CUCHULAIN), the *Táin bó Cuailnge* is the closest thing in Old Irish to a traditional national epic. Though made up of alternating passages of prose and verse, and though the textual state of the tale does not give a complete and unified early version of the narrative, nevertheless the *Táin* holds in Irish literature status and influence comparable to the Homeric epics in Greek.

The earliest extant text of the *Táin* dates from an 11th-century manuscript called the *Book of the Dun Cow.* This text seems to be based on an earlier, ninth-century written version. Ultimately the story probably had a long oral tradition, preserving features from the Irish heroic age, including the use of chariots and the practice of headhunting. Although a late 12th-century manuscript (the *Book of Leinster*) preserves a later, more coherent version of the story, it is the earlier version, known as Recension 1, that has been the focus of scholarly attention.

The complex narrative begins when Mebd, queen of Connacht, determines with her husband Ailill to raid Ulster in order to win a marvelous, magical, prized black bull. An army is assembled from all over Ireland to make war on Conchobar, king of Ulster. At its head rides Fergus, a great Ulster hero who, along with Conchobar's son Cormac, wants revenge on the king for deceiving them into luring the sons of Uisliu to death (*see* EXILE OF THE SONS OF UISLIU). Fergus, feeling compassion for his homeland, leads the army by a circuitous route while sending a warning to Ulster. But Conchobar and the men of Ulster are unable to respond. They are all afflicted with an illness caused by the goddess Macha, whom they had insulted. Only the young warrior Cuchulain is immune, and is left to defend Ulster single-handedly against Mebd's entire army.

Cuchulain begins by leaving an OGHAM warning on a twisted oak tree. When this is not heeded, he kills four warriors and mounts their heads on the fork of a tree. Fergus recognizes that this is the work of Cuchulain, his foster son. As the army advances, Cuchulain continues a kind of guerrilla warfare, picking off warriors on a regular basis. When the army reaches Cualnge, the river rises and wipes out 100 chariots, and Cuchulain attacks and kills another 100 warriors.

Cuchulain continues to kill 100 soldiers every night and will accept no terms from Queen Mebd. But Fergus proposes that Cuchulain agree to the challenge of single combat: Every night a new warrior will be sent to do battle with Cuchulain—and the army will advance only so long as the combat lasts. Cuchulain agrees, and this goes on until Fer Diad, Cuchulain's own foster brother, is chosen to fight him. For three days the two heroes do battle, until on the fourth day Cuchulain chooses to fight in the ford of the river. Here Cuchulain is most invulnerable, for here he can use his mysterious weapon, the *gae bolga*—a kind of spear that makes 30 wounds. He releases it in the water and it destroys Fer Diad, and Cuchulain laments his foster brother's death in a moving poem.

While Cuchulain recovers from his wounds, the recovered Ulster army finally comes to face the army of Queen Mebd, and Fergus does battle with Conchobar himself. But now the wounded Cuchulain rises and enters the battle. Fergus, who has sworn never to do battle with his foster son, retires from the field, and with him go all but the men of Connacht. Cuchulain defeats this entire army himself, and forces Mebd and Ailill to surrender. The saga ends with a climactic battle between the great black bull of Cualnge and the champion bull of Connacht, in which both are killed, and a peace is established for seven years.

Cuchulain is certainly a hero of epic status, his strength holding up the kingdom of Ulster. His superhuman powers suggest that in pre-Christian Ireland he had something of a divine status, though that is played down in written versions of the text, necessarily produced under the Christianity that had brought Roman writing to Ireland. Aside from its epic dimensions, and the fascinating window it provides on ancient Irish heroic society, the *Táin* is worth reading because of its intriguing characters with complex motives—people like the apparently amoral Queen Mebd and the conflicted hero Fergus. For people like William Butler Yeats and the founders of the Irish literary renaissance, the *Táin* was a text of prime significance in the national literature of Ireland.

Bibliography

Dillon, Myles. *Early Irish Literature.* Chicago: University of Chicago Press, 1948.

Kinsella, Thomas, trans. *The Táin.* London: Oxford University Press, 1970.

Taiping guangji (*Taiping kuang-chi*) (ca. 978)

The *Taiping guangji* (Extensive records of the Taiping era) is a collection of some 7,000 tales and anecdotes compiled by government fiat during the early years of the Song (Sung) dynasty—a period (976–983) known as the *Taiping* or "Reign of Great Tranquility." The collection was made from some 500 sourcebooks, more than two-thirds of which are no longer extant. Most of the tales were composed during the preceding TANG DYNASTY and earlier, and a large number of them are concerned with supernatural elements: There are gods and other deities, Taoist magicians, marvelous animals and plants, fairies and magic spells, portents from heaven, and, of course, ghosts. The collection remains quite a popular source for fantastic tales.

The *Taiping guangji,* however, were very nearly lost to posterity, despite the good work of the efficient editor Li Fang, who had compiled the collection in some 18 months. Prose fiction was not considered a serious form of literature in medieval China, since fiction was thought of as misleading and likely to lead to vice and dishonesty. Fiction was known as *xiaoshuo* (*hsiao shuo;* insignificant tellings). Prose tales could only gain credibility if they were purported to be historical. The fantastic tales of the *Taiping guangji* were beyond such a designation.

The *Taiping guangji* had been one of three large compilation projects initiated by order of Emperor Taizong (T'ai-tsung) during the early Song years, but when objections were raised to the collection, claiming that the compendium would be useless to students, plans to publish the collection were abandoned, despite the fact that printing blocks for the collection had already been produced. The text was preserved in manuscript, however, and the collection was finally printed during the Ming dynasty.

Bibliography

Idema, Wilt, and Lloyd Haft. *A Guide to Chinese Literature.* Ann Arbor: Center for Chinese Studies, the University of Michigan, 1997.

Tale of Beryn, The (*Second Merchant's Tale, History of Beryn*) (ca. 1410–1420)

The Tale of Beryn is a late MIDDLE ENGLISH verse tale that survives in a single mid-15th-century manuscript of *The* CANTERBURY TALES, although it is clearly not the work of CHAUCER. It is also clearly somewhat earlier than the manuscript, perhaps about 1410 (as linguistic parallels with the contemporary *MUM AND THE SOOTHSEGGER* suggest), or as late as 1420, which would have been a jubilee celebration in Canterbury (the 250th anniversary of Thomas BECKETT's murder in the cathedral), which might have been a logical time for a revival of interest in Chaucer's story of a Canterbury pilgrimage. The anonymous author was thoroughly familiar with *The Canterbury Tales,* and displays his knowledge of the GENERAL PROLOGUE as well as *The* MILLER'S TALE, *The* REEVE'S TALE, *The* FRIAR'S TALE, *The* SUMMONER'S TALE, *The* PARDONER'S TALE and *The* CANON'S YEOMAN'S TALE. The tale is preceded by a lengthy prologue in which Chaucer's pilgrims arrive in Canterbury, visit the shrine, engage in other exploits, and begin their homeward journey. *The Tale of Beryn,* presented as the second tale of the Merchant, follows. The prologue and tale include 4,022 lines of rhymed couplets; however, only a few of these can be construed as decasyllabic (10-syllable) lines in the manner of Chaucer. Generally the lines contain 12 to 14 syllables, and (perhaps under the influence of popular English ALLITERATIVE VERSE) seem to be six-stress lines with a pause or caesura in the middle. Thus the poem begins:

When all this fresh feleship were com to
Caunterbury,
As ye have herd tofore, with tales glad and
mery,

(Bowers 1992, 60, ll. 1–2)

The compiler of the manuscript (Northumberland MS 455, dated ca. 1450–1470) apparently wanted to complete Chaucer's plan from the General Prologue, wherein the Host describes a tale-telling contest that would be held on the way to Canterbury and on the way back. In virtually all other manuscripts of *The Canterbury Tales,* it is clear that Chaucer abandoned that original idea and intended the pilgrimage to end with *The Parson's Tale,* at the gates of the city. In the Northumberland manuscript, however, *The Tale of Beryn* is assigned to the Merchant as the first tale to be told on the journey back to London. It is followed by Chaucer's *TALE OF MELIBEE, The MONK'S TALE, The Nun's Priest's Tale, The MANCIPLE'S TALE,* and the *PARSON'S TALE,* all displaced from their normal positions. Since there are some leaves missing from the end of the manuscript, it is unknown whether the compiler included a section on the pilgrims arriving back at the Tabard Inn and Harry Bailey's selection of a winner in the storytelling competition.

In the prologue, the pilgrims reach the city and visit the shrine of St. Thomas Beckett in the cathedral. The various pilgrims interact with one another and explore the city, and they stay at one of the local inns for the night. Much time is spent on a FABLIAU-like escapade involving the Pardoner. The poet depicts the Pardoner as a lustful heterosexual with a keen interest in a bartender named Kit (ignoring implications of homosexuality or castration in the General Prologue that modern readers have emphasized). The Pardoner convinces Kit to meet him privately, and gives her money to buy them supper. When he reaches her room, however, he is locked out and she is supping with her lover, who beats the Pardoner with a staff. Kit and her love convince the Innkeeper that the Pardoner is a thief, and he winds up spending the night out in the cold in a kennel with a fierce dog who continually threatens to bite him.

When morning comes, the pilgrims reassemble and start their homeward journey, and the Host calls upon the Merchant to start the trek back to London with a tale. The tale is perfectly suited to the Merchant: It is a comic story whose noble young protagonist decides he would rather be a merchant than a knight. He sets sail for foreign parts with his merchandise, but a storm drives him to an unknown land. The natives of the strange land are thieves and tricksters who ensnare the young merchant in complex legal maneuvers. But he meets a lame man named Geffrey, who reveals that he, too, is a foreigner and has been faking his handicap for years in order to study how to take revenge upon the men of that land. Geffrey shows the young merchant how to win his law case by using tricks even more outrageous than those used on him.

The poet's interest in legal matters has led some scholars to speculate that he may have been a lawyer himself, or may have written the tale for an audience at one of the Inns of Court (the schools in London that trained lawyers). It is true that the French source of the tale, called *Bérinus,* does not emphasize the legal aspects quite so much. However, there is a Latin couplet following the tale in the manuscript that identifies the author as a "son of the church of St. Thomas." This, plus the fact that the language of the text shows clear evidence of a Kentish origin for the tale, and the fact that the poet evinces an unusual familiarity with pilgrim rituals at St. Thomas's shrine, all point to an author who was a monk connected with the cathedral shrine and the cult of St. Thomas.

The Tale of Beryn and its prologue provide an interesting look at how one 15th-century reader of Chaucer understood the master's text. It is also an interesting satire of legal practices and an amusing comic story in its own right.

Bibliography

Bowers, John M., ed. *The Canterbury Tales: Fifteenth-Century Continuations and Additions.* Kalamazoo, Mich.: Published for TEAMS by Medieval Institute Publications University, 1992.

———. "*The Tale of Beryn* and *The Siege of Thebes:* Alternative Ideas of *The Canterbury Tales,*" *Studies in the Age of Chaucer* 9 (1985): 23–50.

Brown, Peter. "Journey's End: The Prologue to *The Tale of Beryn.*" In *Chaucer and Fifteenth-Century Poetry,* edited by Julia Boffey and Janet Cowan, 143–174. King's College London Medieval Studies 5. London: King's College, 1991.

Darjes, Bradley, and Thomas Rendall. "A Fabliau in the *Prologue to the Tale of Beryn,*" *Mediaeval Studies* 47 (1985): 416–431.

Green, Richard Firth. "Legal Satire in *The Tale of Beryn,*" *Studies in the Age of Chaucer* 11 (1989): 43–62.

Winstead, Karen A. "The *Beryn*-Writer as a Reader of Chaucer," *Chaucer Review* 22 (1988): 225–233.

Tale of Gamelyn, The (ca. 1370)

Gamelyn is a vigorous tale of family rivalry and corrupt justice composed during the later 14th century in the northeast Midlands of England. It is written in MIDDLE ENGLISH at a time when this was becoming a more popular language for writing ROMANCES, but *Gamelyn* has more in common with a folktale like Cinderella than with stories of knights errant, COURTLY LOVE, or military exploits. In its directness the tale is akin to the BALLADS, but it is written in rhymed couplets in poetic lines with seven stressed syllables and irregular feet. Moreover it has at its center issues of property, inheritance, and justice that were the preoccupation of the nobility. As a result the poem seems to be a transitional work, evidence of the diverse forms that romance could take outside the continentally influenced tastes of the royal court.

On his death bed, a knight setting his affairs in order commands his friends to divide his property among his three sons and not to neglect the youngest, Gamelyn. But after the knight passes on, his eldest son, John, takes Gamelyn into his own house, treats him poorly, and neglects his farms, forests, and livestock. When Gamelyn comes of age, he looks at his property and becomes enraged with his brother. After winning a wrestling match, Gamelyn invites the crowd of onlookers home for a party, infuriating his brother. John, in turn, tricks Gamelyn into allowing himself to be bound while John throws a party for his own friends. When the taunting becomes more than Gamelyn can bear, he breaks loose and beats the guests with a staff before running to the woods and joining a band of outlaws. While Gamelyn is in the forest, John is appointed sheriff of the county and makes it his objective to try Gamelyn in court. He forces Gamelyn to appear by threatening to try the third brother, Sir Ote, in his place, and then bribes the jury to deliver a guilty verdict. When Gamelyn sees that the court is corrupt he throws the judge out of his seat and takes his place. He then pronounces judgment on his brother John, the judge, and the 12 jurors: All are guilty, all are hanged.

Gamelyn has much in common with ballads of ROBIN HOOD and other stories of medieval English outlaws. Like the *Romance of Fouke le fitz Waryn* and the *Gesta Herewardi,* the story is concerned with property rights, although it takes place at a lower social level. Gamelyn, too, becomes an outlaw as the only means of achieving justice when faced with powerful and unscrupulous adversaries. In this, he is unlike Robin Hood, who is a perpetual inhabitant of the forest and the outlaw status. But like Robin Hood, and unlike many displaced youthful heroes of romance, Gamelyn achieves his goal through physical skill and his innate sense of justice rather than due to the accident of noble birth. Thus *Gamelyn* stands in a middle ground between the tastes and politics of chivalric romance and those of the popular ballad.

The tale has connections to two great figures of English poetry, Geoffrey CHAUCER and William Shakespeare. *Gamelyn* was preserved only in manuscripts of the *CANTERBURY TALES,* where it is sometimes identified as "The Cook's Tale of Gamelyn." In fact, the language and style are unlike Chaucer's and there are no good grounds for identifying him as the author. Some scholars, however, have speculated that he may have known the story and considered adapting it for one of the Canterbury pilgrims. If so, it is tempting to think of him assigning it to the Yeoman, a member of the rural gentry who would appear to have been the audience for Gamelyn, rather than to the urban Cook.

Gamelyn was not included in the earliest printed editions of the *Canterbury Tales,* but it was read and adapted by Thomas Lodge as his prose romance *Rosalynde* or *Euphues Golden Legacie* (1590). This work transferred the action to the home of a French knight in Bordeaux and exchanged the exclusively masculine interests of the Middle English poem for a plot centered on love. Shakespeare, in turn, subdued the violence further, removed the outlaws, and further transformed the forest exile into a pastoral idyll in *As You Like It* (1599).

Bibliography

Kaeuper, Richard. "An Historian's Reading of *The Tale of Gamelyn,*" *Medium Aevum* 52 (1983): 51–62.

Keen, Maurice. *The Outlaws of Medieval Legend.* London: Routledge, 1961.

Knight, Stephen, trans. "The Tale of Gamelyn." In *Medieval Outlaws: Ten Tales in Modern English,* edited by Thomas H. Ohlgren, 168–186. Stroud: Sutton, 1998.

Scattergood, John. "*The Tale of Gamelyn:* The Noble Robber as Provincial Hero," in *Readings in Medieval English Romance,* edited by Carol M. Meale. Cambridge: Brewer, 1994, 159–194.

Skeat, W. W., ed. *The Tale of Gamelyn from the Harliean Ms. No. 7334, Collated with Six Other Mss.* Oxford: Clarendon, 1884.

Timothy S. Jones

Tale of Genji, The (*Genji Monogatari*)

Murasaki Shikibu (ca. 1001–1010)

The monumental masterpiece *The Tale of Genji (Genji Monogatari)* was written by Lady MURASAKI SHIKIBU, circa 1001–1010, in HEIAN Japan. The most treasured classic of Japan, this extensive work is the world's first novel and one of its greatest. This early medieval Japanese classic is as complex as DANTE's *DIVINE COMEDY* and just as difficult to summarize and to generalize about. The work falls under the genre of *monogatari*—a romance tale in prose, but it is interspersed with nearly 800 poems. Ostensibly the protagonist is Genji (son of the emperor), but there is an enormous cast of characters, many of whom play central parts, and after Genji's death, attention shifts to subsequent generations.

By the 13th century the work's 54 chapters had been categorized into three major sections. Chapters 1 through 33 cover the birth and early life of Genji. His beautiful but low-ranking mother, Kiritsubo, was the emperor's favorite concubine, and his excessive attentions to her provoke the jealousy of the First Wife and other higher women, who harass Genji's mother to an early death. Thus set into action is a complex, karmic sequence of cause and effect, which shapes the novel.

As a young man, Genji discusses love and women with his friends, a discussion that foreshadows the many love affairs to come. There is the Locust Shell Lady, the one woman who resists the irresistible Genji. His family arranges his marriage with Aoi, but the two prove incompatible. After being warned by his father not to snub the proud, high-ranking Lady Rokujō, Genji jilts her in favor of a younger, obscure, low-ranking beauty (echoing his father's marriage and relationship with his mother). In a jealous rage, the Rokujō Lady's murderous spirit leaves her body at night while she is sleeping to possess and kill her rival, Yūgao—a horror witnessed by Genji. Genji witnesses it again when the same spirit possesses and kills Genji's wife, Aoi.

Although the novel has a tragic tone, derived from the Buddhist recognition of the ephemeral nature of this world, the author nevertheless tends to alternate serious episodes with comic ones. For instance Genji pursues the Safflower Princess, who he assumes is a great beauty (following Heian custom, she would be hidden behind screens). To his horror he finds out too late that she is the antithesis of the idealized noble beauty: She is so shy that she cannot speak, she cannot sing, nor write poetry, nor engage in any of the other activities expected of such a woman. And finally, when she does reveal her face, it has a large bulbous nose—so she is ugly as well.

Other notable affairs from the first section include his egregious error of fathering a child by his father's now favorite consort, Fujitsubo, who gives birth to a son that everyone assumes is the emperor's and who will grow up to be emperor himself—until he learns of his misconception and retires. Genji's affair with Oborozukiyo will anger her powerful relatives, who will demand that he be sent into exile as punishment. While in exile he fathers with the Akashi Lady a daughter that he will give to his childless primary consort, Murasaki, upon his return from exile. Of his many women, he favors Murasaki (the author's nickname derives from this character), and as Genji ages, he spends more and more time with her.

In the second section, Genji ages and dies, and the tone of the novel darkens. Genji agrees to marry Nyosan, who fathers a son with Kashiwagi, the son of Genji's best friend, Tō-no-chūjō (an incident reminiscent of Genji's own affair with Fujitsubo). Murasaki dies, apparently brokenhearted and worn down by Genji's many affairs. Genji's son by his first wife, Yūgiri, emerges as a major character, as Genji prepares to die after burying Murasaki.

The last section of the novel is dominated by Ukifune (the granddaughter of Yūgao), who is loved by Kaoru (Genji's supposed son by Nyosan) and Niou (Genji's grandson).This love triangle resembles the love affair of Genji and Yūgao, who had a daughter by Tō-no-chūjō. Despondent over her concurrent relationship with them both, Ukifune attempts to commit suicide by plunging into a river. She is washed ashore where she is discovered and then lives with Buddhist monks and nuns. The novel ends with her decision to become a nun, even though she is still a beautiful, young woman. (In Heian Japan, conversion to the monastic life usually occurred late in life, as death approached; it provided a means of learning how to forego the ephemeral things of this world to focus on the next.)

There is much to admire about this great novel. Although Genji is nicknamed "the shining one," Murasaki's careful characterization avoids reducing Genji to an idealistic, stereotypical hero, as Genji's flaws lead to mistakes that he must atone for. Aside from the interesting psychology of her characters, Murasaki develops central themes drawn from her Buddhist beliefs: Karma and impermanence are two major ones. The novel's detailed descriptions provide insights into life during Heian Japan and illustrate the power politics of the time (many scholars believe she models Genji, other characters, and some episodes after the lives of members of the powerful Fujiwara clan). Although a voluminous novel with countless characters, the careful plotting in *Genji* brings coherence and unity to the work. The story, for the most part, is chronological with time as a motif—references to the four seasons abound.

This novel has wielded tremendous influence over subsequent writers from Murasaki's own time up to today. For example Murasaki's niece, who wrote the *Sarashina Diary (Sarashina Nikki),* describes spending her youth reading the *Genji* and dreaming of a life similar to the heroines of the novel. Then in the KAMAKURA era, NŌ DRAMA was inspired by the enactment of episodes from the *Genji.* Even today popular culture in Japan is filled with *Genji* influences, as comic books and animation illustrate.

Bibliography

Miner, Earl, Hiroko Odagiri, and Robert E. Morrell. *The Princeton Companion to Classical Japanese Literature.* Princeton, N.J.: Princeton University Press, 1985.

Morris, Ivan. *The World of the Shining Prince: Court Life in Ancient Japan.* New York: Alfred A. Knopf, 1969.

Murasaki Shikibu. *The Tale of Genji.* Translated by Royall Tyler. New York: Viking, 2001.

Stevenson, Barbara, and Cynthia Ho, eds. *Crossing the Bridge: Comparative Essays on Medieval European and Heian Japanese Women Writers.* New Middle Ages Series, edited by Bonnie Wheeler. New York: Palgrave/St. Martin's, 2000.

Barbara Stevenson

Tale of Melibee, The Geoffrey Chaucer (ca. 1390)

After the Host, Harry Bailey, has interrupted the Pilgrim CHAUCER's recitation of his burlesque *TALE OF SIR THOPAS,* the poet's persona responds with a lengthy moral allegory in prose known as *The Tale of Melibee.* In the past critics of *The* CANTERBURY TALES saw Melibee as a deliberately bad tale, one chosen specifically to bore the Host in revenge for the interruption of *Thopas.* More recent scholars have seen little sense in this interpretation—why should Chaucer's readers suffer through a bad tale so that the fictional pilgrim may avenge himself on the fictional Host? In fact the Host is not bored with the tale at all, but rather wishes his wife Goodelief had heard it, an intimidating shrew who seems to be the opposite of Melibee's wife, Prudence.

In the tale a band of his enemies breaks into Melibee's house, where they attack and beat his wife, Prudence, and daughter Sophie, leaving the daughter with five mortal wounds. The furious Melibee wants vengeance, but his wife counsels him to receive his suffering in patience. She says he should call a council of his friends, which he does, and they advise him to go to war to avenge himself.

Though Melibee agrees to their advice, Prudence once again steps in and speaks for patience. Overcoming his initial reluctance to listen to a woman, she delivers a long admonitory speech on the proper use of counsel, as well as of wealth and power. Though concerned with the harm it will do to his reputation and his honor, Melibee finally is convinced by his wife to seek peace. He ultimately thanks God for sending him a wife of such "discretion," and on her advice, he summons his enemies and forgives them openly, praying at the same time that God will forgive all of his own trespasses.

Chaucer's tale is a rather close (by medieval standards) translation of Renaud de Louens's French work, the *Livre de Melibée et de Dame Prudence* (ca. 1336), itself a freer translation of the earlier Latin *Liber consolationis et consilii* by Albertanus of Brescia (1246). Renaud's text was popular, and was included in the book of the *Ménagier de Paris* (1392–94), compiled as a manual of advice for the Ménagier's young wife. The tale's contemporary popularity, then, suggests that more recent critics' contempt for *Melibee* hardly reflects the tastes of Chaucer's own age. Though the tale has not been a critical favorite, some scholars who have seriously considered *Melibee* have seen it as a pacifist political tract, applying possibly to JOHN OF GAUNT's proposed war in Spain, or a generally pacifist warning to the English nobility to use caution and seek wise counsel rather than act rashly. Others have seen it as a distinctly religious tale, relating consciously to other tales in Chaucer's text, particularly those concerned with marriage, and those (like *The* KNIGHT'S TALE) that glorify war.

Bibliography

Benson, Larry, et al., eds. *The Riverside Chaucer.* 3rd ed. Boston: Houghton Mifflin, 1987.

Collette, Carolyn. "Heeding the Counsel of Prudence: A Context for the *Melibee,*" *Chaucer Review* 29 (1995): 416–433.

Cowgill, Jane. "Patterns of Feminine and Masculine Persuasion in the *Melibee* and the *Parson's Tale.*" In *Chaucer's Religious Tales,* edited by C. David Benson and Elizabeth Robertson, 171–183. Chaucer Studies 15. Cambridge, U.K.: Brewer, 1990.

Owen, Charles A., Jr. "The Tale of Melibee," *Chaucer Review* 7 (1973): 267–280.

Stillwell, Gardiner. "The Political Meaning of Chaucer's *Tale of Melibee,*" *Speculum* 19 (1944): 433–444.

Strohm, Paul. "The Allegory of the *Tale of Melibee,*" *Chaucer Review* 2 (1967): 32–42.

Tale of Sir Thopas, The Geoffrey Chaucer (ca. 1390)

When the Pilgrim CHAUCER is asked by the Host to tell a tale of his own, the poet's persona launches into a rollicking, singsong burlesque of popular English TAIL-RHYME ROMANCE, a recitation so apparently incompetent that the Host stops the performance in mid-narrative. Many readers of *The* CANTERBURY TALES have since been disappointed not to see the completion of this brilliant parody of MINSTREL literature created by the courtly Chaucer (who at the same time displays no little affection for the popular genre).

The verse form of *The Tale of Sir Thopas* is unique in Chaucer: six-line stanzas rhyming *aabaab,* the *a*-rhyme lines having four metrical feet, and the *b*-lines having three. Five stanzas include a third *aab* tercet, appended to the main stanza by a two-syllable transition line or "bob." Such appendages seem to be completely random, and are, with the verse form generally, part of Chaucer's parody.

The tale begins by introducing Sir Thopas, a brave and chaste knight of Flanders, adored by all the young maidens in his hometown of Poperyng. He is handsome—"He hadde a semely nose" (Benson 1987, 213, l. 729)—well attired—his robes "coste many a jane" (Benson 1987, 213, l. 735)—and good at archery and wrestling (not exactly aristocratic sports). But Thopas himself is in love with an elf-queen whom he has seen only in a dream. Riding off to seek his love, he encounters the ominous giant Sir Olifaunt. The giant orders Thopas to be off, saying he cannot come near because the elf-queen dwells there. Sir Thopas leaves, promising to return to fight the following day, after he has got his armor, and the giant chases him off with stones. The second *fitt* (*fitts* were common divisions of minstrel romances) begins in proper minstrel fashion, with the narrator's call of "Listeth, lordes to my tale" (Benson 1987, 215, l. 833), and continues with a lengthy and clichéd description of the arming of Sir Thopas. As the third *fitt* opens with a parody of the minstrel's call for attention, "Now holde youre mouth, *par charitee*" (Benson 1987, 215, l. 891), Thopas sets off again on his adventure, but before the pilgrim Chaucer can get to the climactic battle, the Host, Harry Bailey, interrupts him, calling his rhyming "drasty" (crappy) and "rym dogerel" (Benson 1987, 216, ll. 923–925), and asking for something in prose if the pilgrim Chaucer can do no better in verse. Chaucer responds with a nearly interminable moral allegory, *The* TALE OF MELIBEE.

Specific ways that *Sir Thopas* parodies existing tail-rhyme romances like BEVIS OF HAMPTON and the English *Sir Tristrem* are outlined in J. A. Burrow's notes to the tale in the *Riverside Chaucer* (Benson 1987, 917–923). Perhaps the most interesting of recent critical approaches to *Sir Thopas* is that which views it as a significant part of Fragment VII of the *Tales*—a long, coherent section of the unfinished *Canterbury Tales* text that seems particularly concerned with the act of storytelling. At the beginning of the frame story, the Host called for tales with "the best sentence" (i.e., wisdom, moral significance), and "moost solaas" (solace, or pleasure). Sir Thopas may be seen as a tale of pure *solaas*, virtually without any kind of *sentence* at all.

Bibliography

Benson, Larry, et al. *The Riverside Chaucer*. 3rd ed. Boston: Houghton Mifflin, 1987.

Burrow, J. A. "*Sir Thopas:* An Agony in Three Fits," *Review of English Studies* 22 (1971): 54–58.

Gaylord, Alan T. "The Moment of *Sir Thopas:* Towards a New Look at Chaucer's Language," *Chaucer Review* 16 (1982): 311–329.

———. "Chaucer's Dainty 'Dogerel': The 'Elvish' Prosody of *Sir Thopas*," *Studies in the Age of Chaucer* 1 (1979): 83–104.

Jones, E. A. " 'Loo, lordes myne, heere is a fit!': The Structure of Chaucer's *Sir Thopas*," *Review of English Studies* 51 (2000), 248–252.

Patterson, Lee. " 'What Man Artow?': Authorial Self-Definition in *The Tale of Sir Thopas* and *The Tale of Melibee*," *Studies in the Age of Chaucer* 11 (1989): 117–175.

Tale of the Bamboo Cutter, The (*Taketori monogatari*) (ca. 900–920)

The Tale of the Bamboo Cutter is the first extant Japanese *monogatari*, or work of literary fiction. Its precise date of composition is unknown: Though some scholars say it cannot be later than 909, others claim it may be as late as 920. Most agree, however, that the current text dates from around 960. Long recognized for its primacy, the tale is referred to in the classic TALE OF GENJI as the parent and first to come of all tales. However, some changes may have occurred from the earlier version of the story, because there are allusions in *The Tale of Genji* to incidents in the tale that do not occur in the surviving text. Written in *kana majiri* (a combination of ideographs from the Chinese and native Japanese syllabary), the text displays the influence of Chinese literature as well as Buddhist scriptures. The text includes 15 *waka* (native Japanese poems), beginning the convention of including *waka* in narratives, a convention that became typical in future *monogatari*, in particular *The Tale of Genji* itself. The story of *The Tale of the Bamboo Cutter* follows a fairy tale–like plot.

Indeed, some scholars believe that there was a "Bamboo Cutter" *setsuwa* (or folklore motif). Others, however, believe that the tale came into Japanese from Chinese, and point to other versions of the story popular throughout Asia.

The tale is not really the story of the Bamboo Cutter, who provides an opening and closing for the narrative. The real protagonist is the girl Kaguya-hime. As the story opens, the old Bamboo Cutter and his wife are childless, but one day he discovers, hidden in a bamboo stalk, a tiny girl some three inches tall. He brings her home, and within three months she has matured into a full-grown woman. She is the most beautiful woman in the land, and her reputation spreads so that she is pursued by various suitors. Kaguya-hime resists the idea of marriage, until the Bamboo Cutter convinces her that it is customary for men and women to be married. She relents, and decides to give the suitors a chance. But she will only marry one who can accomplish an impossible task that she will assign.

Five suitors agree to accept the challenge. Two of the suitors are princes and three are high-ranking noblemen. The first prince must find and bring back the original stone bowl of the Buddha. But the prince, unenthusiastic about traveling to India on what was sure to be a fruitless quest, attempts to pass off a counterfeit bowl on Kaguya-hime, which she immediately recognizes. The second prince is assigned to bring back a gold and silver branch from the Taoist land of paradise. He is more successful in fooling Kaguya-hime, and nearly gets away with it, but he is interrupted in the midst of describing the hardships he endured on his quest by the craftsmen he hired to manufacture the branch, looking for payment.

The last three suitors more honestly attempt to accomplish the tasks set for them, but with no more success than the princes. The first nobleman is sent to obtain the fireproof hide of a firemouse, but is tricked into buying a false fur. The second nobleman is sent to obtain a valuable jade from around the neck of a dragon, but a storm at sea makes him seasick and he fails to find the dragon—he returns home to be mocked by his other wives. The last suitor is assigned to retrieve a priceless shell from a swallow's nest on the side of a cliff, but finds only bird droppings in the nest, faints, and falls to his death. Thus all five suitors fail, but Kaguya-hime is not disappointed, since she had no desire to be married in the first place.

After the suitors' fiasco, the emperor himself seeks Kaguya-hime's hand, but she is unmoved by his suit. Seeking the Bamboo Cutter's support in the matter, the emperor promises the old man a court position if he can persuade his adopted daughter to accept the sovereign. But when he comes to visit her and press his suit, the young maid turns herself into a shadow and disappears. The emperor is forced to give up his pursuit of her.

After three more years, Kaguya-hime begins to act strangely, spending much of her time gazing up at the moon. She reveals to the Bamboo Cutter the truth about her origins: She has come, she says, from the palace of the moon people, and her time on earth is nearly over. Her people will soon come to take her back. The Bamboo Cutter refuses to let her go, and vows to fight off the moon people when they come to fetch her. The emperor sends a company of soldiers to help him keep Kaguya-hime on earth, but when the moon people arrive in a flying chariot, no one can prevent them from taking Kaguya-hime. She offers a jar of the elixir of immortality to her adopted parents, but they refuse to taste any of it, saying that life has no appeal without their daughter. The moon people have brought a robe of feathers to garb her for her ascent into the sky—a robe that will cause her to forget all ties to the earth. Before donning the robe, however, the young maid pauses long enough to write a final poem to the emperor. Then she slips on the robe and is gone. The tale ends when the Bamboo Cutter and his wife send the elixir of life to the emperor, who refuses it because he can never see Kaguya-hime again, and orders it to be burnt on the top of Mount Fuji—which explains the smoke that perpetually comes from the mountain.

There are many unanswered questions regarding *The Tale of the Bamboo Cutter.* Who was the original audience of the tale? It seems likely to have been a noble one, and a number of candidates have been suggested as its author, but none has won wide scholarly support. Was the author's intent to satirize the aristocrats of the HEIAN court? Or was it simply to tell a fairy tale? The tale is indeed fantastic, but there are concrete realistic details in the descriptions of the suitors. The author seems to have been well-educated, but the tale is told in a simple, straightforward style. The Bamboo Cutter himself is simple and rather foolish, but sympathetic. Kaguya-hime, however, is a cold and unfeeling protagonist, who elicits little sympathy. But the most remarkable thing about *The Tale of the Bamboo Cutter* is its tight structure and its concise narrative. The plot follows the logical, cause-effect organization that many medieval Japanese tales lack, which makes it entertaining reading for a Western audience.

Bibliography

Kato Shuicho. *A History of Japanese Literature: From the Man-yōshu to Modern Times.* New abridged ed. Translated and edited by Don Sanderson. Richmond, U.K.: Curzon Press, 1997.

Keene, Donald. *Seeds in the Heart: Japanese Literature from Earliest Times to the Late Sixteenth Century.* Vol. 1 of History of Japanese Literature. New York: Columbia University Press, 1999.

Miner, Earl, Hiroko Odagiri, and Robert E. Morrell. *The Princeton Companion to Classical Japanese Literature.* Princeton, N.J.: Princeton University Press, 1985.

The Tale of the Bamboo Cutter. Translated by Donald Keene. Japan: Kodansha International, 1998.

Tale of the Heike, The (*Heike Monogatari*) (1371)

The Tale of the Heike is an important Japanese narrative that has its origins in the KAMAKURA PERIOD and deals with the turbulent times of the Gempei Wars at the end of the 12th century. Covering the 60-year span from 1131 and 1191, the text tells the story of the struggle between the Heike (or Taira) clan and the Genji (or Minamoto) family for political, economic, and military supremacy over Japan. The stories in the *Tale of the Heike* have been compared with the legend of King ARTHUR in Europe in terms of their popularity and influence. With the exception of the *TALE OF GENJI*, *The Tale of the Heike* is the most admired prose text in Japanese literature.

Specifically what is meant by the "Tale of the Heike" is somewhat ambiguous. There were versions of the story composed within a few decades of the end of the Gempei Wars (1185). These seem to have been of three different types: Some were intended to be historical records of events. Some were intended for use in sermons by itinerant preachers. Still others were ballads (called *heikyoku* or "Taira songs"), sung by blind wandering Buddhist monks called *Biwa Hōshi*—so called because they accompanied themselves on a *biwa* or lute. By the early 14th century there were some 100 variants of the story. The text that is generally implied by the title *Tale of the Heike* is one associated with the reciter Kakuichi (ca. 1300–71), who seems to have compiled the work from the productions of earlier writers, so that it is impossible to tell what precisely is the work of Kakuichi himself.

The Kakuichi text is divided into 12 numbered chapters, each including a number of episodes bearing individual titles. The main text is followed by an epilogue. There is some scholarly disagreement about the structure of the text. However, looked at as a whole, the text seems to fall into three main divisions. The first section begins with justly famous opening lines called *Gion Shōja* (the Japanese term for the Jetavana Temple), which set a thematic tone for the rest of the text: The lines are a testament to the transience of mortal life and a reminder that the rich and powerful will all ultimately come to nothing. The teak trees shed their flowers and the animals shed tears at the death of Shakamuni, who in these lines enters Nirvana at the Jetavana Temple. Following this, the text recounts the power and courtly qualities of the Heike, focusing on the ruthless Kiyomori, whose evil reign ends in his fall and death. His son and successor, Shigemori, is virtuous and admirable, a foil to his father, but his death leaves the Heike without a moral center.

Among the other Heike leaders presented in the text are Koremori, a family man possessed of courtly virtues who is made commander of the Heike forces in the north. Defeated and discouraged, he leaves the battle. Torn between a desire to go home to his family, to renounce the world as a Buddhist recluse, or to accept the realities of war, he ultimately commits suicide. Another Heike military commander, Tadanori, leaves the burning capital of Kyoto and braves enemy lines in order to bring his poetry to the editor Fujiwara Shunzei, who is compiling an anthology of *waka* (Japanese poems), because he wants to be remembered as a poet, not a warrior. When he is killed in battle, even his enemies mourn the death of Tadanori the poet.

One of the recurring themes of the *Tale* is the contrast between the cultured Heike and the somewhat boorish Genji, who, though more impressive warriors than the Heike, are inferior to them culturally. In the second part of the text, the Heike, without their leader Kiyomori, are thrown into disorder. Now the Genji begin to dominate the narrative. The chief figure becomes Yoshinaka—a violent and brutish, yet courageous and proud leader who is ultimately doomed. A more generally sympathetic character is Yoshinaka's youthful successor, the heroic Yoshitsune (the ultimate Genji victor, Yoshinaka's more ruthless brother Yoritomo, plays a peripheral role in the story). Under Yoshitsune, the Genji rout the Heike at Ichi-no-tani, and finally destroy them completely in the sea battle at Dan-no-ura, where not only the Heike warriors but the emperor and Kiyomori's widow are all killed.

One of the well-known episodes in this third section of the text is the death at Ici-no-tani of the young Heike warrior Atsumori, whose story became the source of dramatic treatments in both kabuki and Nō theater. Another is the story of Yokubue (one of many significant women in the text), whose separation from her lover depicts an idea of love as a desire for what cannot be attained, an attitude related to the Buddhist concept of the transience of the physical world and the futility of such desire.

The ending, or epilogue, to the main text is set far from the battlefield and focuses on Kenrei Mon'in, the mother of the emperor, who has become a cloistered recluse at Ohara, in the mountains north of Kyoto. From here, she prays for the soul of her dead son. In many ways, *The Tale of the Heike* as a whole can been seen as an offering to appease the spirits of the dead Heike, gone but restless, and the text grants the Heike sympathy in their defeat. Certainly they are in general more sympathetic than the stern warriors of the victorious Genji (with the exception of Yoshitsune).

This is not to say that the Taira or Heike are viewed uncritically. The Buddhist compilers of the story recognized the sins of the Heike, and their serious mistakes, including their arrogance, and saw those things as the causes of their downfall. But it did not necessarily follow that the Genji were therefore better. What the authors focus on is the tragic glory of the doomed Heike—the magnificent fall of the heroes and the pity of their suffering.

Recent scholars have examined *The Tale of the Heike* as the Japanese national epic. Certainly its focus on the warrior class, its epic scope, and its historical basis are reason to categorize the text as an epic. Its nonheroic episodes that deal with women, children, romance, and natural beauty, seem less typical of epic. The point of view of the text, as most scholars now believe, is the aristocratic point of view of the people of Kyoto, rather than the warrior class itself. The text is, finally, an epic-like text, but a purely Japanese creation unlike anything produced in Western literature.

Bibliography

Kato, Shuicho. *A History of Japanese Literature: From the Man-yōshu to Modern Times.* New abridged ed. Translated and Edited by Don Sanderson. Richmond, U.K.: Curzon Press, 1997.

Keene, Donald. *Seeds in the Heart: Japanese Literature from Earliest Times to the Late Sixteenth Century.* Vol. 1 of History of Japanese Literature. New York: Columbia University Press, 1999.

McCullough, Helen C. *The Tale of the Heike.* Stanford, Calif.: Stanford University Press, 1988.

Miner, Earl, Hiroko Odagiri, and Robert E. Morrell. *The Princeton Companion to Classical Japanese Literature.* Princeton, N.J.: Princeton University Press, 1985.

Taliesin (late sixth century)

Taliesin is the name of the earliest known Welsh poet, believed to have been a court poet to the late sixth-century King Urien and his son Owain of

Rheged (an area around the Solway Estuary, southwest of Scotland). Like that of his near-contemporary ANEIRIN, Taliesin's poetry deals mainly with the northern British Celts' struggle against the Saxon invaders. His reputation was considerable: With Aneirin, he is one of five British poets mentioned in the *Historia Brittonum* (ca. 800), attributed to NENNIUS, and he is, with Aneirin, one of only two of these poets whose name is attached to extant poems.

The poetry attributed to Taliesin survives in a 13th-century manuscript called the *Book of Taliesin.* Probably copied from an earlier, 10th-century text, the *Book of Taliesin* includes 58 poems: Some of these are religious, some purport to be prophetic, some are riddles, some are poems praising mead and beer. These poems are likely all of 10th-century origin. But 12 historical poems in the text appear to be earlier, and are generally believed to be Taliesin's.

These 12 poems all are set in northern Britain and all deal with late sixth-century events: Urien is known to have died ca. 590. Most are praise poems honoring King Urien and King Owain, chiefly dealing with their military exploits against the English. Also included is an elegy on Owain's death, indicating that Taliesin survived both of his major royal patrons. The poems are brief and simple, lacking any excessive rhetorical ornamentation or figurative language. They praise Urien and Owain for their heroism in battle, their generosity to their friends, and their defense of the Christian faith—the Celtic Britons, it should be remembered, retained their Christianity from Roman times, while the Anglo-Saxons still followed the pagan Germanic religion. Another historical poem is on the death of Uthyr Pendragon, reputed in later texts to be the father of King ARTHUR himself.

Taliesin also appears as a character in a 15th-century narrative attributed to Gruffyd Elis. Possibly based on surviving oral legends of Taliesin, the story follows a youth named Gwion Bach, who pilfers three magical drips from a witch. She chases him as both of them transform from one shape to another, until the witch, in the form of a hen, swallows the youth, who has taken the form of a seed. Eventually the witch gives birth to the boy again. This time he is Taliesin. At the age of 13 he joins the retinue of King Maelgwyn, becoming his court poet and, eventually, the most famous bard in the world. The tale, mythic as it is, demonstrates the aura surrounding the name of Taliesin in later centuries, and suggests, as well, the respect with which the bard was held in Welsh society, as a being possessed of special, even supernatural, genius.

Bibliography

Breeze, Andrew. *Medieval Welsh Literature.* Dublin: Four Courts Press, 1997.

Evans, Stephen S. *The Heroic Poetry of Dark-Age Britain: An Introduction to Its Dating, Composition, and Use as a Historical Source.* Lanham, Md.: University Press of America, 1996.

Ford, Patrick K., ed. *The Mabinogi and Other Medieval Welsh Tales.* Berkeley: University of California Press, 1977.

Gruffyd Elis. *Ystoria Taliesin.* Edited by Patrick K. Ford. Cardiff: University of Wales Press, 1992.

Matthews, John. *Taliesin: The Last Celtic Shaman.* Rochester, Vt.: Inner Traditions, 2002.

Williams, Gwyn. *An Introduction to Welsh Poetry: From the Beginnings to the Sixteenth Century.* 1954. Freeport, N.Y.: Books for Libraries Press, 1970.

Williams, J. E. Caerwyn, trans. *The Poems of Taliesin.* Edited by Ifor Williams. Dublin: Institute for Advanced Studies, 1968.

Tang dynasty (618–906)

After the fall of China's powerful Han Dynasty in 220 C.E., the empire fell apart, and for some 350 years China experienced a rapid succession of short-lived rulers, including some non-Chinese peoples who invaded the country from the north and the west. Finally in 589, the Sui dynasty succeeded in reunifying the empire, though the Sui administration rapidly became overextended and in 618 was ousted by the northern Tang dynasty. The Tang dynasty went on to rule China for nearly three centuries. The first half of the Tang dynasty was a period of political stability, of military expansion particularly to the north and west, and of economic growth with the reopening of trade routes to the west. It was also a period of creative accomplishment in the arts, most notably in figure painting, porcelain (with the introduction of new cobalt blue glazes), silver and gold ornaments, and especially in poetry.

The Tang capital was in the northern city of Changan, located near modern-day Xi'an. At the height of Tang power, during the reign of Emperor Xuangzong (712–756), Changan was a walled city 30 miles square that was home to 1 million people. Governing an empire that stretched for 1,000 miles from the Great Wall to the southern island of Hainan and with a population of some 50 million souls, the government bureaucracy working in the capital and in the provinces was immense. Changan stood at the end of the great caravan route known as the Silk Road, through which the Tang dynasty formed close ties with India and Persia, and foreign influences in the form of music and exotic goods poured into the capital from the West. In addition, students, Buddhist monks, and diplomatic representatives from Korea and Japan commonly stayed in the capital for extended periods. Both Buddhism and Taoism remained important spiritual forces in Tang China among both the elite and the common people. But Confucianism also experienced a resurgence as a philosophy of social and political organization in the empire. More than any other court in the world, Changan was truly a cosmopolitan center.

In order to find talented individuals to staff its huge administrative bureaucracy, and to conform to the Confucian ideal of government by the meritorious, the Tang emperors reinstituted the civil service examinations that had begun under the Han rulers centuries earlier. The Tang government instituted five examinations, each conferring a different degree, but the most competitive and prestigious of the examinations was the *jinshi* (*chin-shih* or "presented scholar") exam, so-called because the degree pronounced one suitable for presentation before the emperor. Only about 1 percent of the candidates tested passed this test. This exam had three parts: One tested the candidate's rote knowledge of one of the Confucian classics, one required him to write an essay on a contemporary problem, and the third required him to compose a poem and a piece of rhymed prose after being assigned a topic and a particular rhyme scheme.

It would be a mistake to assume that the civil service system opened government service to the humble classes: In practice, only wealthier families would have generally had the means to provide their sons with the education needed to succeed on the exams. But some scholars from outside the circle of the wealthy were able to make lives for themselves within the bureaucracy. And since poetic talent was a major criterion for the degree of "presented scholar," many of the most admired poets of Tang China (including WANG WEI, LI HE, and YUAN ZHEN) consequently earned their living as government employees.

At court, the emperor or any member of the imperial family might set a topic for courtiers, who would have to respond with a poem. Typically the poems would then be assessed and one of them judged to be of highest quality. In imitation of the emperor, officials in the provinces also sponsored poetic competitions, and even patronized literary salons for poets, many of whom thrived under these provincial governors. But the importance of poetry as a conventional medium of social exchange in everyday life, perhaps as an outgrowth of its importance on the civil service examinations, distinguishes Tang China from almost every other civilization in world history (with the possible exception of HEIAN Japan, which modeled itself largely on Tang China). Poems might be written upon meeting an old friend, or taking leave of one who is being sent to a post in the provinces. A courtier or other bureaucrat might write a poem and leave it for a friend who was not at home when the poet called, or might write a cheerful poem about a homecoming. Collections of the works of major Tang poets are full of incidental poems concerning incidents of the poet's public and private life. Probably for this reason, many of the major Tang poets are known to subsequent generations by their personalities, in particular the exuberant Taoist LI BAI and his friend, the socially conscious Confucian poet DU FU.

The form of Chinese poetry as refined by the poets of the high Tang was fairly prescriptive. The language of these poems is spare and understated and often deliberately ambiguous. The form called "recent style" or "regulated verse" was regulated by length restrictions on both the entire poem (the poems were four or eight lines) and on the individual lines (which were to be of either five or seven syllables). The verses followed a pattern that rhymed every even line of the text, and a pattern of parallelism of word order in the middle couplets. In addition, there were untranslatable alternating patterns in the tones of the Chinese words. Toward the end of the Tang period another kind of poetry appeared, a kind of free verse set to music, perhaps influenced in part by foreign elements entering the capital. Some of these poems were sung to accompany dramatic productions (an early development on the road to the later creation of opera). The poems were also sung or read in the tea houses that began to appear in Tang China at the end of the eighth century.

By the mid-eighth century, military leaders guarding the frontiers of the empire began to grow in power and influence while the central government weakened. In 755 a general from the northeast named Al Lu-shan moved on the capital, capturing the city of Changan and forcing the emperor to flee. Although Al Lu-shan died two years later, the rebellion continued for some time. The rebellion is immortalized in some of the verses of Du Fu and Li Bai, as well as in the court poet BO JUYI's "Song of Unending Sorrow," a narrative poem telling the story of the emperor's flight with his concubine. After the rebellion, the administrative structure of the empire began to crumble. There were internal power struggles, a falling off of tax revenues as provincial governors kept much of what was collected to finance their own armies, and foreign trade diminished. Ultimately a series of peasant revolts beginning in 860 brought about the collapse of the Tang dynasty. But the cultural and artistic legacy of the period remains, especially in the verse of its major poets, particularly Du Fu, Li Bai, Wang Wei, Li He, Bo Juyi, Yuan Zhen, HAN SHAN, DU MU, HAN YU, and LI SHANGYIN.

Bibliography

Idema, Wilt, and Lloyd Haft. *A Guide to Chinese Literature.* Michigan Monographs in Chinese Studies, 74. Ann Arbor: University of Michigan Press, 1985.

McMullen, David. *State and Scholars in T'ang China.* Cambridge: Cambridge University Press, 1998.

Owen, Stephen, ed. *Anthology of Chinese Literature: Beginnings to 1911.* New York: Norton, 1996.

———. *The Great Age of Chinese Poetry: The High Tang.* New Haven, Conn.: Yale University Press, 1980.

tanka

The tanka is a Japanese poetic form that became the dominant genre in medieval Japan by the time of the HEIAN PERIOD in the late eighth century. The Japanese prized brevity and suggestiveness in their poetry, and the tanka showcases those qualities. It is a five-line poem of 31 syllables, containing lines of five, seven, five, seven, and seven syllables. A tanka was divided into the *kami no ku* (the "upper poem" or first three lines) and the *shimo no ku* (the "lower poem" or last three lines). The third line usually contained an image that united the two halves of the poem, which addressed different subjects.

The agglutinative nature of the Japanese language, in which a simple verb, for example, may trail several suffixes indicating things like probability and mood, complements this kind of a poem. A single verb, for example, may be seven syllables long, and therefore take up an entire line of a tanka.

The *KOKINSHŪ*, completed about 905, contains 1,111 of these short poems. The poems are all composed by members of an aristocratic class that considered the ability to create a poem in response to any given social situation essential for good breeding. Most often these poems deal with human relationships, particularly love, or are a response to or appreciation of the beauties of nature. Ideally the tanka should express *yojo*, a kind of deep yearning that involved all of the emotions. At their best tankas express universal human emotions in understated but striking and memorable images, as, for example, does this anonymous poem (number 746 in the *Kokinshu*). Note how the third line links the keepsake, subject of the upper poem, with the expressed emotion, subject of the lower poem:

This very keepsake
is now a source of misery,
for were it not here
there might be fleeting moments
when I would not think of you.

(McCullough 2002, 2171)

Bibliography

McCullough, Helen Craig, trans. *The Kokinshu.* In *The Norton Anthology of World Literature,* 2nd ed. Vol. B, edited by Susan Lawall et al., 2,160–2,174. New York: Norton, 2002.

Tao Qian (T'ao Ch'ien, T'ao Yüan-ming) (365–427)

Born in the turbulent period of the late Qin (Chin) dynasty, Tao Qian became the most important writer of his age. He gave up a career in the imperial bureaucracy to live a simple rural life, and has been admired ever since for choosing a life of poverty over one that demanded he sacrifice his principles as well as his own contentment.

T'ao Chian was born in Xinyang (Hsinyang) in what is now (Jiangxi Kiangsi) province, to a poor family of provincial bureaucrats, and seemed destined to follow that career path himself. But political turmoil had followed in the wake of barbarian invasions that forced the imperial court to move south to Nanjing. Tao Qian spent 10 years in various official posts, none of which he kept long. For a time, he was part of the retinue of one of the powerful noblemen who had usurped the political authority of the emperor. In his last post, he was magistrate of P'eng-tse, not far from his home, but even this post he kept for a mere two months before he left public service altogether and retired to the simple life of a farming community for the last 22 years of his life.

There had been a tradition in Chinese poetry, not unlike European poetry of the Renaissance, that idealized and even sentimentalized the pastoral life. But when Tao Qian writes of that life, it is from the point of view of someone actually living it. It would be misleading to think of Tao Qian's retreat to a rural community as mere escapism. There were a number of motives behind it. One was certainly the internal struggle that weighed a desire for wealth and power against a life of peace and integrity. Another was a Taoist love of nature and commitment to a "natural" kind of life. At a time when Confucianism was in decline and the new Buddhist religion was on the rise alongside the more traditional Taoism, Tao Qian based his personal philosophy largely on Taoist principles. For Tao Qian happiness could be found only in following one's inherent nature, and one satisfied that nature not by accumulating wealth or property, but in a private world, performing simple labor and having no more than is necessary to meet basic needs: Life is brief and must be lived happily—that is, naturally—or it is wasted.

Tao Qian is the author of one of the most influential short texts in Chinese prose literature, *The Peach Blossom Spring,* in which a fisherman, after following a trail of peach blossoms in the water, is led to an idyllic rural community of peace and happiness. Though he enjoys the village, the fisherman prepares to return to the outside. The inhabitants of the village, appalled at what they hear about the turbulence and violence of the fisherman's world, tell him there is no reason to mention their existence to anyone else. But after the fisherman returns to his own city, he tells the magistrate about the village. But no one is ever able to find the way back to that utopian community. The tale has been compared to Tao Qian's own life and his poetry: His poems, like the fisherman, tell of the possibility of contentment in the simple life, but the likely audience of those poems—that is, the literate populace, mainly members of the government bureaucracy—are unlikely ever to find such contentment.

Tao Qian is best known as a poet, and his most famous poem is called *The Return,* most likely written at the time of his abandonment of official life and return to his rural village. In this long poem, he bluntly states: "The world and I shall have nothing more to do with one another" (Hightower 1970, "The Return," l. 35). He goes on to elaborate on why such a break was necessary:

So little time are we granted human form
in the world!

Let us then follow the inclinations of the heart:
Where would we go that we are so agitated?
I have no desire for riches
And no expectation of Heaven.
Rather on some fine morning to walk alone
Now planting my staff to take up a hoe,

(Hightower 1970, "The Return," ll. 49–55)

Bibliography

Davis, A. R. *Tao Yüan-ming: His Works and Their Meaning.* Cambridge: Cambridge University Press, 1983.

Kwong, Charles Yim-tze. *Tao Qian and the Chinese Poetic Tradition: The Quest for Cultural Identity.* Ann Arbor: Center for Chinese Studies, University of Michigan, 1994.

Hightower, James Robert, trans. *The Poetry of T'ao Ch'ien.* Oxford, U.K.: Clarendon Press, 1970.

Hinton, David. *The Selected Poems of T'ao Ch'ien.* Port Townsend, Wash.: Copper Canyon Press, 1993.

tenso (*tenson, tenzone*)

The *tenso* was a form of poetry originating in 12th-century Occitan in the poetry of the Provençal TROUBADOURS. Eventually the form spread to poets in Italy and in Sicily. The term, meaning "dispute" or "rivalry" in Provençal, was applied to poems that consisted of a dialogue or debate between two poets, or sometimes between a poet and a fictional opponent. The poets occasionally included incentive against one another, and the subjects of the *tenso* could vary from love to politics to poetry itself.

In one of the earliest *tensos,* MARCABRU and a poet named Ugo Catola engage in a debate on the nature and value of love. Ugo begins, "Marcabru, my friend, let us compose/a *vers* about love, for I have it in my heart," (Goldin 1973, 89; ll. 1–2), and Marcabru answers him, "Ugo Catola, right, let's do it now,/but I denounce false love/for never, since the serpent came down from the bough,/have there been so many women full of tricks" (Goldin 1973, 89; ll. 5–8). The poets alternate stanzas in this manner for 56 lines.

In another well-known *tenso,* GIRAUT DE BORNELH and RAIMBAUT D'ORANGE debate the relative merits of two styles of troubadour poetry, the simple *TROBAR LEU* and the complex *TROBAR CLUS.* Raimbaut begins by asking, "Now, Giraut de Bornhelh, I would like/to know why you go denouncing/our difficult style" (Goldin 1973, 203; ll. 1–3), to which Giraut answers, "it seems to me/the song is better loved/and more applauded/when you make it easy and open to all" (Goldin 1973, 203; ll. 10–13).

Eventually two specialized types of *tensos* developed. One was called the *partimen.* In this poem one poet would propose a question for dispute, usually containing hypothetical alternatives, such as whether it was better to love and serve a lady without ever achieving her love, or to be too easily granted the lady's love. A second poet decides which position to defend, and makes a case. The first poet answers with an argument in favor of the other alternative. A typical *partimen* would alternate between three identical stanzas from each poet, and, in the end, would be submitted to an arbiter to choose between them. Occasionally three poets might take part in such a dispute, but that was rare. And though such poems give the impression of spontaneous debate, they were almost certainly composed over time and sometimes distance between poets, who might then perform them or have them performed at some noble court that could serve as arbiter.

The other specialized type of *tenso* was the *jeu parti,* developed in the 13th century. This poem might have two characters arguing over a proposition, most often, again, concerning love. The characters alternate stanzas and, as in the *partimen,* submit the poem to an arbiter in the end.

Bibliography

Goldin, Frederick, ed. and trans. *Lyrics of the Troubadours and Trouvères: An Anthology and a History.* Garden City, N.Y.: Doubleday, 1973.

terza rima

Terza rima is a verse form invented by DANTE for use in his *DIVINE COMEDY* in the early 14th century. The form consists of a series of tercets (three-line stanzas) rhyming *aba bcb cdc ded* etc., all in hendecasyllabic, or 11-syllable, lines. That is, the tercets are interconnected in that each succeeding stanza takes the rhyme for its first and third lines from the second line of the previous stanza. Thus *The Inferno* (first part of the *Divine Comedy*) begins with these nine lines:

Nel mezzo del cammin di nostra vita
Mi ritrovai per una selva oscura,
Ché la diritta via era smarrita.
Ahi quanto a dir qual era è cosa dura
Esta selva selvaggia e aspra e forte
Che nel pensier rinova la paura!
Tant' è amara che poco è più morte;
Ma per trattat del ben ch'i' vi trovai,
Dirò de l'altre cose ch'i v'ho scorte.

At the midpoint in the journey of our life
I found myself astray in a dark wood
For the straight path had vanished.
A dread thing it is to tell what it was like,
This wild wood, rugged, intractable,
Which, even as I think of it, brings back my fear.
So bitter it is that scarcely worse is death.
But, to expound the good which there I met with,
I will speak of other things I witnessed there.

(Creagh and Hollander 1989, xviii–xix)

Such a series of interlinked stanzas could go on indefinitely, until brought to an end by a single line that rhymed with the second line of the immediately preceding tercet. This is the way in which Dante ends each of the cantos of his *Comedy.*

For Dante the terza rima form held significant symbolic meaning. The three-line stanza, of course, reflects the holy Trinity. But it has also been suggested that the potentially endless pattern of the lines evokes a long and arduous journey, as Dante the pilgrim takes through the three realms of the afterlife. Further, the interconnected stanzas might have suggested the interconnectedness of all God's creation.

It is possible that Dante found the pattern for the terza rima in tercets used in an earlier kind of satirical poem called the *SIRVENTES.* But it is Dante who really forged the verse form. Later in the 14th century it was copied by BOCCACCIO in a poem called *Amorosa visione,* and by PETRARCH in *I Trionfi.* CHAUCER experimented with its use in one portion of his *Complaint to His Lady,* but seems to have abandoned it. Ultimately it was introduced into English by Thomas Wyatt in the 16th century, and later used with some success by Milton, Shelley, and T. S. Eliot.

Bibliography

Bernardo, Aldo S., and Anthony L. Pellegrini, eds. *Dante, Petrarch, Boccaccio: Studies in the Italian Trecento in Honor of Charles S. Singleton.* Binghamton, N.Y.: Center for Medieval and Early Renaissance Studies, State University of New York at Binghamton, 1983.

Boyde, Patrick. *Dante's Style in His Lyric Poetry.* Cambridge: Cambridge University Press, 1971.

Creagh, Patrick, and Robert Hollander, ed. and trans. *Inferno.* In *Lectura Dantis Americana: Inferno I* edited by Anthony K. Cassell. Philadelphia: University of Pennsylvania Press, 1989.

Teseida, Il (*Teseida delle nozze d'Emilia,* "The Theseid of the Marriage of Emilia") Giovanni Boccaccio (ca. 1341)

The *Teseida,* or the "Story of Theseus," is one of BOCCACCIO's early works, begun probably in the late 1330s, when he was still living on his own in Naples, but not completed until after he had been forced to return to Florence as a result of the economic crisis of the early 1340s. Boccaccio conceived of the *Teseida* as an epic poem in the vernacular, and probably wrote it as a conscious response to DANTE's call (in *DE VULGARI ELOQUENTIA*) for a classical epic in Italian. Emulating the classical masterpieces most admired by his age, Virgil's *Aeneid* and Statius's *Thebaid,* Boccaccio planned a poem in 12 books. He chose to write in a verse form that had previously been used in Italian lyrics and folk literature, the OTTAVA RIMA: a stanza of eight 11-syllable lines rhyming *abababcc* that he had used previously in *Il* FILOSTRATO. But despite its epic aspirations, *Il Teseida* is essentially an elaborate ROMANCE, in which Teseo (Theseus) plays a secondary role, and the chief interest is the love triangle between Emilia, Teseo's sister-in-law, and her two admirers—the Theban kinsmen Arcita and Palemone. It was this love story that caught the attention of CHAUCER, who used Boccaccio's poem as the chief source for his chivalric romance *The* KNIGHT'S TALE (ca. 1382).

The poem certainly begins in epic style, following Teseo, duke of Athens, in his wars with the Amazons. When he wins the war, Teseo weds the Amazon queen Ippolita, and returns to Athens with his Ippolita and Emilia, her beautiful sister. But he is immediately called to war again, this time against the tyrant Creonte of Thebes. He finally returns home with a number of prisoners from the Theban war, including the noble Palemone and Arcita. The martial deeds of Teseo thus constitute the first two books of the poem. Beginning in book 3, the love then moves to center stage.

From their prison cell, Arcita and Palemone catch sight of Emilia walking in her garden, and both fall instantly and irrevocably in love with her. When Teseo eventually releases Arcita and frees him under the condition that he never return to Athens on pain of death, Arcita reenters Athens in disguise and serves in Teseo's court in order to be close to Emilia. One day he is overheard lamenting his love by an informant of Palemone, and Palemone escapes from his prison, seeks out Arcita, and challenges him to single combat in the forest. They are discovered and separated by Emilia and Teseo, who convince them to resolve their dispute by taking part in a tournament that the duke himself shall arrange, the champion to be awarded the hand of Emilia as his prize. Ultimately Arcita is victorious in the tournament, but dies after he falls from his horse at the tournament's conclusion.

In the last two books of the poem, Boccaccio moves at a leisurely pace, stretching his narrative to conform to the 12-book epic structure. Arcita's funeral and the funeral games (a conventional aspect of the classical epic) take up book 11, while book 12 is concerned with Emilia's internal conflict between marrying Palemone and remaining a virgin devoted to the goddess Diana. The poem ends as she yields to Teseo's persuasion and marries Palemone.

After the poem's initial composition, Boccaccio added a dedication to Fiammetta, his secret name or *senhal* for his nominal lover Maria d'Aquino (though it is debatable whether such a woman ever actually existed). He also added sonnets to introduce each book and somewhat pedantic glosses to imitate a well-known commentary on the *Thebaid* by Lactantius. It was all designed to give his poem the tone and grandeur of a true epic. While Boccaccio and many of his admirers may have thought he had written an Italian epic, most more modern readers have been less certain of that designation. When Chaucer retold the story, he shortened it by some two-thirds, and it is specifically the epic trappings—the first two books and the last two—that Chaucer found easiest to cut.

Bibliography

Anderson, David. *Before the Knight's Tale: Imitation of Classical Epic in Boccaccio's Teseida.* Philadelphia: University of Pennsylvania Press, 1988.

Boccaccio, Giovanni. *Theseid of the Nuptials of Emilia (Teseida delle nozze di Emilia).* Translated with an introduction by Vincenzo Traversa. New York: Peter Lang, 2002.

McGregor, James H. *The Shades of Aeneas: The Imitation of Vergil and the History of Paganism in Boccaccio's Filostrato, Filocolo, and Teseida.* Athens: University of Georgia Press, 1991.

Testament François Villon (1461)

The major work on which the reputation of the great French poet François VILLON chiefly rests is his 2,000-line poem *Testament.* The poem, written (we are told in its first lines) in 1461 when the poet was 30 years old, comprises 186 eight-line stanzas, into which Villon has inserted several short fixed-form lyrics including 16 *BALLADES*, two RONDEAUX, and a chanson. Essentially the poem purports to be a last will and testament, in which Villon's primary purpose is to bequeath his possessions to his friends and acquaintances before what he suggests may be his imminent death.

Immediately prior to his composition of the *Testament,* Villon had been arrested and imprisoned at Meung on the orders of Thibaud d'Aussigny, bishop of Orléans. He was released from imprisonment by order of King Louis XI in 1461. Accordingly, Villon begins the poem with a bitter invective against the bishop, praying that God will do to the bishop what the bishop has done to Villon. This is followed by praise for the king who freed him, and from here moves to a consideration of what he has learned through his suffering. Although he is a sinner, Villon tells us, God desires his conversion and reformation, not his death.

In several stanzas, Villon laments his lost youth and blames his poverty for forcing him into a life of crime. He includes an anecdote about Alexander and a Pirate, in which the Pirate tells Alexander that he is a criminal because he has only one ship—if he had a fleet, he would be an emperor. From here, Villon moves to a lament on the impermanence of worldly things—in particular Villon bemoans the transience of beauty, particularly in the deaths of beautiful women, and inserts his famous "Ballade des dames du temps jadis" ("Ballade of the Ladies of Bygone Days"), which includes the famous refrain most often translated "Where are the snows of yesteryear?"

Villon goes on to consider the ravages of age on both men and women, and includes another *ballade* in the voice of an old woman advising young ones to make the most of their youth. But Villon continues to focus on women in general, and then on women's love, inserting a double *ballade* on the unfortunate consequences of love. Ultimately he repudiates love itself, giving it up forever.

Now considering his own broken body, Villon returns to his tirade against the bishop of Orléans, and curses the bishop as he describes the tortures to which he was subjected in Meung. Finally, Villon moves on to the bequests that make up the testament. He begins by bequeathing his soul to God and his body to the earth, then moves on to his father, to whom he leaves his books. He has nothing to give his mother except a prayer for her to recite to the Virgin, which he includes as a *ballade.* He follows these with a variety of other bequests, some somewhat serious in the form of individual lyric poems, some outlandish, some apparently based on topical or private references that are incomprehensible to us.

Villon moves on to a discussion of Parisian women, and includes a well-known and graphically ribald *ballade* about "Fat Margot" and her sexual appetite. Ultimately, he makes some requests about his burial; forgoing any appeal for a tomb, he writes a verse for his own epitaph, asking for eternal rest after a life of hard knocks. He then names his executors—rich men with whom he was never acquainted—and adds a *ballade* in which he pardons everyone he can think of, including whores and swindlers and fools, but denies his pardon to those who made his life difficult—for them, he wishes a hammer would crush their ribs.

Overall, the *Testament* shows a technical mastery of form and meter. However, its overall structure seems formless: As the above summary shows, the poem is organized around an association of ideas and images rather than by any logical progression. Villon focuses repeatedly on the transience of earthly things, and employs the traditional *ubi sunt* ("Where are they?") topos of classical literature: Where are the years of my youth, he asks? Where are the beautiful women gone? Where are my old companions? Where, indeed, are the snows of yesteryear? But Villon, a master of many styles, also includes mocking satire in his repeated attacks on those who he believes have wronged him in life. What makes the *Testament* a classic of medieval French poetry is its variety of language, style, and tone, moving from the somber to the satirical, from the moving to the mocking, sometimes within the same stanza. The poem has made Villon one of the most admired poets in the French language.

Bibliography

Burl, Aubrey. *Danse Macabre: François Villon, Poetry, & Murder in Medieval France.* Stroud, Gloucestershire, U.K.: Sutton, 2000.

Fein, David. *François Villon Revisited.* New York: Twayne, 1997.

Sargent-Baur, Barbara N. *Brothers of Dragons: Job Dolens and François Villon.* New York: Garland, 1990.

Taylor, Jane H. M. *The Poetry of François Villon: Text and Context.* Cambridge and New York: Cambridge University Press, 2001.

Villon, François. *Complete Poems.* Edited with English translations and commentary by Barbara N. Sargent-Baur. Toronto: Toronto University Press, 1994.

Testament of Cresseid Robert Henryson (late 15th century)

The most important poem by the Scottish poet Robert Henryson is his *Testament of Cresseid,* Henryson's alternative ending to CHAUCER's *TROILUS AND CRISEYDE.* A 616-line poem in rhyme royal stanzas emulating the text that inspired it, the poem begins as do Chaucer's own dream visions, *The BOOK OF THE DUCHESS* and *The PARLIAMENT OF FOWLS,* with the narrator reading a book—in this case the *Troilus* itself. Noting that Chaucer had left Cresseid's fate untold, Henryson declares his intention to write his own tragedy of Cresseid's end.

The story begins as Diomede has tired of Cresseid and forsaken her. An alien "fallen" woman in an enemy camp, she is forced to move in with her father Calchas, and there blasphemously complains against Cupid and Venus, blaming them for her problems. The gods, in their function as planets, meet in council as they do in Chaucer's *KNIGHT'S TALE,* and decide that Saturn and the Moon must inflict punishment on Cresseid for her blasphemy. Saturn takes away her beauty and her joy, while the Moon strikes her with leprosy—a disease that in Henryson's day would have been equated with syphilis. In the leper house, Cresseid delivers a memorable COMPLAINT on the common theme of the transience of earthly happiness.

One day, as Cresseid sits on the side of the road begging, Troilus rides by and, though he fails to recognize her, is reminded of his lost love when he sees her, and throws a handful of gold and jewels in her lap. After he leaves, another leper tells her that her benefactor was Troilus himself. Cresseid, realizing at last Troilus's true love for her, a love that she forsook to follow her own lusts and therefore subjected herself to the vicissitudes of Fortune, is moved to make her last will and testament. Here, she accepts responsibility for her downfall, leaving her worldly fortune to the lepers and sending Troilus a ring he had given her.

Ultimately the poem uses Chaucer's *Troilus* as its background, but alters the ending, leaving off Troilus's death at the hands of Achilles. In his 1532 edition of Chaucer, William Thynne printed Henryson's poem as Book 6 of *Troilus and Criseyde.* That custom continued through several later editions of Chaucer.

Testament of Love, The Thomas Usk (ca. 1387)

The Testament of Love is the only surviving work of the London tradesman and political figure Thomas Usk. Usk says at the beginning of the text that it will be concerned with Philosophy and the Law, both of which must accord with Love. The allegory in three books begins with Usk as the speaker, imprisoned, bemoaning his separation from "Margaret," whom he says he has served faithfully for seven years. He prays to Margaret, who is spoken of as a woman but eventually is revealed to be the "Pearl of great price" of Matthew 13, and perhaps an emblem of divine grace. At this point appears the figure of Love (the personification of divine love), to whom Usk describes his involvement in London politics, apparently to excuse his abandonment of Northampton. But Love, sounding very much like BOETHIUS's Lady Philosophy, convinces him that earthly fame is transient, and that God is powerful and merciful. Book 2 deals with grace, and here Usk rejects LOLLARDY, having become interested in the heresy, he says, through Northampton. Book 3 is particularly concerned with the Bethink theme of free will and predestination, and also includes a well-known passage praising CHAUCER as the true servant of Love.

No manuscripts of Usk's *Testament* are extant. The text survives only in William Thayne's 1532 printed edition of the works of Chaucer. For several hundred years the work was attributed to Chaucer, until the great 19th-century scholar Walter Skeat found that the first letters of each section of the poem form the acrostic MARGARET OF VIRTU HAVE MERCI ON THIN USK (that is, "Thine Usk"). The work does owe a great deal to Chaucer, borrowing from *Troilus and Criseyde* and from *The House of Fame,* and possibly from his translation of Boethius's *Consolation.* Usk also seems to have made use of the C-text of William Langland's *Piers Plowman,* as well as a treatise on free will and providence by St. Anselm. Usk's *Testament* is an important example of 14th-century English prose, and while it has some particularly effective passages, others are quite obscure for modern readers.

Thibaut de Champagne (1201–1253)

One of the most popular and prolific of the trouvères, Thibaut IV, count of Champagne and Brie, wrote more than 60 poems that are extant—the largest number of any of the trouvères. He was the grandson of Marie de Champagne and thus the great-grandson of Eleanor of Aquitaine and King Louis VII.

Thibaut was born in Troyes in 1201. His father, Thibaut III, had died before he was born, and in order to gain the favor of King Philip II Augustus, his mother Blanche of Navarre made the king guardian of the child. Still, because of the circumstances of his birth, Thibaut's claim to the lordship of Champagne was challenged twice before he secured his position.

In support of Louis VIII, Thibaut fought the English at La Rochelle in 1224. He also supported the king in the Crusade against the Albigensians, though he abruptly left the king's service in 1226 and returned to Champagne. Three months later Louis died, and his wife, Blanche of Castile, became regent during the minority of her son. Thibaut at first joined a group of powerful nobles opposed to Blanche's regency, but later switched allegiance and became one of the queen's chief supporters during her regency of 1228–32. His vacillation, however, angered his former allies, who attacked Champagne and were forced to retreat only when the queen threatened to intervene.

Thibaut's relationship with Queen Blanche has been the subject of a good deal of controversy. He was accused of being the queen's lover, and even of poisoning Louis VIII to advance his own love. The fact that many of his love poems were dedicated to the queen only served to lend weight to these accusations, but they appear to be pure fabrication.

Thibaut became king of Navarre in May of 1234 after the death of his uncle, Sancho VII, called "Sancho the Strong." Thibaut seems not to have concerned himself much with the administration of Navarre, however, simply letting his deputies run the country. He was unpopular in Navarre, and was criticized by the troubadour Sordello in his lament for Blacatz. In 1239, he was one of the leaders of the crusade organized by Pope Gregory IX. His army was unsuccessful in several battles, and Thibaut returned to Champagne the following year, either because of his lack of success or, according to some sources, his disillusionment with the bickering among the other leaders of the crusade.

Back in France Thibaut joined the French in renewed battles against the English in 1242 and, in 1244, was defeated in Gascony by the English commander Nicolas de Molis. In 1248, Thibaut made a pilgrimage to Rome to be released from an interdiction he had suffered because of ill relations with the clergy. Beyond that not much is known about Thibaut's later years. When he died in 1253, he was one of the most admired poets of northern France.

Thibaut's poems are in the courtly love vein of the Provençal troubadours, and often depict the paradoxical nature of love as joy and suffering. One of the distinguishing marks of Thibaut's verse is his use of extended metaphors: the lover as a pelican, for example, or as the prisoner of love. In the following passage from one of his best-known poems, he borrows the figure of the unicorn as a metaphor for the lover:

I am like the unicorn
astonished as he gazes,
beholding the virgin.
He is so rejoiced by his chagrin,
he falls in a faint in her lap;
then they kill him, in treachery.
Now Love and my lady
have killed me just that way:
they have my heart, I cannot get it back.

(Goldin 1973, 467, ll. 1–9)

Thibaut is also known for his versatility: His extant lyrics include at least 36 chansons (or CANSOS), some 14 *jeux-partis* (or debate poems; see TENSO), eight *serventois* (or SIRVENTES), a few PASTOURELLES, and four crusading songs, written to raise support for the crusade. One begins:

Lords, be sure of this: whoever does not now
depart
for that land where God died and lived,
and does not take the cross of the Holy
Land,
will hardly go to Paradise.

(Goldin 1973, 477–479, ll. 1–4)

Regarded as one of the most important lyric poets of the 13th century, Thibaut is praised by DANTE in his *De* VULGARI ELOQUENTIA, where he is ranked with Guido GUINIZELLI and the troubadour GIRAUT DE BORNELH.

Bibliography

Brahney, Kathleen J. *The Lyrics of Tibet de Champagne.* New York: Garland, 1989.

Goldin, Frederick, ed. and trans. *Lyrics of the Troubadours and Trouvères: An Anthology and a History.* Garden City, N.Y.: Doubleday, 1973.

Pensom, Roger. "Thibaut de Champagne and the Art of the Trouvère," *Medium Aevum* 57 (1988): 1–26.

Tischler, Hans, ed. *Trouvère Lyrics with Melodies: Complete Comparative Edition.* Neuhausen: Hänssler-Verlag, 1997.

van der Werf, Hendrik. *The Chansons of the Troubadours and Trouvères: A Study of the Melodies and Their Relation to the Poems.* Utrecht, Netherlands: A. Oosthoek, 1972.

Thomas à Kempis (ca. 1379–1471)

The assumed author of *The Imitation of Christ,* after the Bible the most popular spiritual work in Christian history, Thomas à Kempis was a 15th-century writer of devotional works, sermons, and saints' lives, and a member of the Augustinian order of Canons Regular. Thomas is considered the outstanding representative of the late medieval spiritual movement known as *Devotio Moderna* (Modern devotion).

Thomas was born Thomas Hemerken in the town of Kempen in the Rhineland, from which he took the surname "à Kempis." His father was a blacksmith and his mother a schoolmistress who probably gave the young Thomas his earliest education. In 1393 he began studying in Deventer in the Netherlands, at a school established by the Brethren of the Common Life. This group, founded by the Dutch mystic and priest Geert (or "Gerard") de Groote (1340–84), was a community of secular priests and lay persons who, though they took no vows, focused on their interior spiritual lives through meditation, reading, and education. The Brethren were instrumental in popularizing the *Devotio Moderna,* a movement that discounted the highly intellectual, scholastic theology of the 13th and early 14th centuries and limited the importance of external rituals of the church in favor of meditation and the inner life. After spending some time living among the Brethren, Thomas surprisingly chose to join the Augustinian order rather than stay with the Deventer community. Thomas entered the monastery of Mount St. Agnes near Zwolle in 1399, shortly after his brother John had become prior of the monastery.

Thomas spent the rest of his life in the monastery at Mount St. Agnes. He was professed in 1407 (after an unexplained delay of eight years) and ordained a priest in 1413 or 1414. He served as a scribe in the monastery, copying many manuscripts, including one of the Bible. He served twice as subprior and was, for some time, master of novices. He is also known to have written a number of works, including a collection of *Sermones ad novicios* (Sermons to novices), biographies of both Geert de Groote and of his successor, Florentius Radewijns (whom Thomas had known during his years with the Brethren of the Common Life), and the *Chronica Montis Sanctae Agnetis,* a history of the monastery at Mount St. Agnes. He also wrote two mystical treatises (*The Little Garden of Roses* and *The Valley of the Lilies*), and several works of devotional counsel, the best known of which is *Soliloquy of the Soul* (a practical spiritual guide in the manner of the Brethren of the Common Life).

Thomas died at Zwolle in 1471, having lived well into his 90s.

The Imitation of Christ was first issued anonymously in about 1425. An early manuscript from about 1441 cites Thomas à Kempis as its author, but over the years some have disputed Thomas's authorship, suggesting St. BERNARD, St. BONAVENTURE, Pope INNOCENT III, Walter HILTON, and even Thomas's brother John as possible authors. Others have suggested that Thomas composed the text of the *Imitation of Christ* from manuscripts originally composed by Geert de Groote. But there seems no good reason to doubt Thomas's authorship. The doctrine of the book is clearly in line with the beliefs of the Brethren of the Common Life, and Thomas's other writings are consistent with the content of the *Imitation.*

The book is written in a colloquial Latin style, and is intended to instruct the reader in Christian perfection, focusing on Christ as the model of behavior and stressing, particularly, self-renunciation and the superiority of following Christ over all the learning one can obtain. It is divided into four books dealing with, first, freedom from desire for worldly goods, meditation and preparing the soul for prayer, the comfort of prayer life, and the importance of the sacrament of communion in the spiritual life of the Christian. In the many manuscripts of the *Imitation of Christ,* the four books do not always occur in the same order; nor do all manuscripts contain all four books. The text was translated into German by 1434, into French by the 1440s, and into English in 1502. *The Imitation of Christ* has since been translated into hundreds of languages and gone through thousands of editions. Thomas à Kempis's text and the spirituality of the Brethren of the Common Life continue to inspire readers to this day.

Bibliography

Becker, Kenneth Michael. *From the Treasure-House of Scripture: An Analysis of Scriptural Sources in De imitatione Christi.* Turnhout, Belgium: Brepols, 2002.

Thomas à Kempis. *The Imitation of Christ in Four Books: A Translation from the Latin.* Translated by Joseph N. Tylenda. Rev. ed. New York: Vintage, 1998.

Thomas Aquinas, Saint (ca. 1224–1274)

St. Thomas Aquinas is generally considered the most important philosopher in the scholastic tradition that had begun with St. ANSELM more than a century earlier. He was associated most often with the University of Paris, though he maintained ties with his native Sicily throughout his life. His *SUMMA THEOLOGICA,* left unfinished upon his death, remains his greatest achievement, and perhaps the high point of scholasticism. Its goal is no less than the reconciliation of Aristotelian rationalism with Christian doctrine.

Thomas was born in his family's castle in Aquino. His family had ties to Frederick II, the Holy Roman Emperor. In 1231, Thomas began school at the Benedictine monastery of Monte Cassino, where he learned Latin and studied the church fathers. But he was forced to return home in 1239, when hostilities broke out between the emperor and the pope. Back in Sicily he attended the University of Naples from 1239 to 1244. The university was the first in Europe founded independently of the church, and it had ties to Frederick's court, where translations of Aristotle and his Muslim and Jewish commentators in Arabic and Greek texts were revolutionizing the way people thought about intellectual inquiry.

In about 1242 Thomas joined the Dominican order. His family opposed the move, wishing to have him named abbot of Monte Cassino, but Thomas was drawn by the Dominican commitment to teaching and preaching, and he soon left to complete his studies at the University of Paris with the most important thinker of his day, Albertus Magnus.

When the Dominicans started an international college in Cologne in 1248, Albert was sent to Germany to take charge of the college, and he took Thomas with him as his assistant. It is likely that Thomas began teaching there, and that he was made priest about 1250. In 1252 he returned to Paris to lecture on the Scriptures and on PETER LOMBARD's *Sentences,* the most common university textbook of the time. In the *Sentences* Peter had put in one volume all of the most important opinions of the church fathers on various theological questions. But Aquinas saw that these opinions raised a number of problems, and wrote a commentary on the *Sentences* in which he tried to apply the new Aristotelian method to theological questions.

In 1256 Thomas received his appointment to a major divinity chair at the University of Paris. At the time he was working on a major text, the *Summa contra Gentiles*, which was intended to be a handbook for missionaries. The Dominicans were establishing a center in Barcelona to train missionaries to the Jews and Muslims, and Thomas's work, intended to prove the truth of the Christian faith, was meant to help them in their work—particularly the first three of its four books, which explore the basic principles available to Christians and nonbelievers alike.

Thomas finished this *Summa* in 1259, and in that same year he was sent to Italy, where he taught at Anagni, then at Rome and Viterbo. It was in Italy that Thomas did most of his writing. Here he produced several works and wrote the bulk of the *Summa Theologica*. The structure of the *Summa* is a model of scholastic dialectic method: Thomas divides the work into hundreds of related questions. For each question he first gives several arguments against his own position. He then gives a quotation that supports his stance, usually from "The Philosopher" (i.e., Aristotle) or from one of the church fathers like St. AUGUSTINE. He then gives his argument, and finishes by specifically countering each of the opposing arguments with which he had begun the question.

Thomas was in Paris again from 1268 to 1272, though, and here he took part in an intellectual debate with Siger of Brabant, the chief exponent of Averroism in Paris. The theories of AVERROËS (Ibn Rushd) had been causing a stir in Paris since the 1230s, and some of these theories—notably Averroës's doctrine that the passive intellect (the individuating portion of the human soul) does not survive death (and therefore there is no individual immortality)—were incompatible with Christian doctrine, and Thomas wrote a number of commentaries on Aristotle aimed chiefly at disputing this Averroist doctrine.

Ultimately Thomas returned to Naples in 1272 where he began the third part of his huge *Summa Theologica*. However, on the evening of December 6, 1273, Thomas had a life-changing experience that he said rendered everything he had previously written meaningless. Most believe it was a mystical vision of some kind, but Thomas never returned to his writing. Then, invited by Pope Gregory X to take part in the Council of Laon, Thomas fell ill on the way to the council and died.

Thomas remains indisputably the greatest Christian philosopher and theologian of the 13th century. Although some of his doctrines were condemned in 1277 in a general crackdown on philosophical "errors" made by scholastic philosophers, the Dominicans themselves officially adopted his methods at about the same time. His opinions ultimately came to represent the solid expression of Roman Catholic orthodoxy. He also seems to have been particularly influential on DANTE, who places him in a lofty position in paradise. The fourfold method of scriptural exegesis that Thomas discusses (an idea that goes back to St. Augustine) is one that Dante applies to his *DIVINE COMEDY* as well. Thomas was canonized in 1323 as "Doctor Angelicus."

Bibliography

Aquinas, Thomas, Saint. *Summa Theologiae*. Cambridge, U.K.: Blackfriars, 1964ff.

Clark, Mary T., ed. *An Aquinas Reader*. Rev. ed. New York: Fordham University Press, 2000.

Davies, Brian. *Aquinas*. London and New York: Continuum, 2002.

Eco, Umberto. *The Aesthetics of Thomas Aquinas*. Translated by Hugh Bredin. Cambridge, Mass.: Harvard University Press, 1988.

Thomas of Britain (Thomas de Bretagne) (late 12th century)

Very few facts are known about Thomas of Britain except that he wrote in Anglo-Norman and probably lived in England at the court of King HENRY II and ELEANOR OF AQUITAINE. He composed his *Tristran* romance sometime after 1155, when WACE had completed his *Roman de Brut*, which seems to have provided inspiration for a number of motives and narrative elements in Thomas's text. Another possibility is that both Wace and Thomas were influenced by GEOFFREY OF MONMOUTH's chronicle

Historia Regum Britanniae (1136–39). When Chrétien de Troyes wrote his *Cligès* (1176–77), he made satirical references to the love concept developed by Thomas, which implies that the *Tristran* must have been well known by that time.

Thomas's *Tristran* has survived in 10 fragments from six manuscripts, which were all prepared with great care and (calligraphic) artistry, occasionally illustrated (like the Carlisle fragment, discovered in 1995). Thomas's version deeply impressed his posterity, as documented not only by the many manuscripts, but also by Gottfried von Strassburg's comment in the prologue to his *Tristan* (ca. 1210), where he lavishly praises Thomas for having created the only true account of the love affair between Tristan and Isolde (Gottfried's spelling; vv. 149–171). The Norwegian Brother Robert closely followed Thomas's *Tristran* in his *Tristramsaga* of 1226.

The various fragments mostly relate different aspects in the lives of the two lovers. The Cambridge fragment, for instance, presents the orchard scene where Tristran and Ysolt (Thomas's spelling) are surprised by King Marc while sleeping there. When they awake, they catch sight of the departing king, and Tristran decides to leave. In the Sneyd fragment, Tristran, in a lengthy monologue, explores his dilemma in feeling love both for Queen Ysolt and his own wife, Ysolt of the White Hands. In the Turin fragment, Tristran creates a hall of statues where he reveals his love pangs and fears of losing Ysolt to the sculpture of Brangvein (Ysolt's companion). Other fragments concentrate on different narrative elements, such as Tristran's disguise as a leper and major knightly battles (Douce). Most important, Thomas tells us the end of the love story, with Tristran near his death and waiting for rescue through his beloved Ysolt. The latter arrives indeed, but Tristran's jealous wife deceives her husband, pretending that the ship's sail is black, indicating that Ysolt is not coming, though Ysolt actually had ordered a white sail to be set to signal her arrival. Because of his profound love pains, Tristran dies, and when the Irish princess finds him, she laments vehemently and passes away as well, stretched out at the side of her lover. Thomas, as all other poets working with the Tristran material, relies on the concept of a love potion that the two lovers drink by accident and that ultimately bring them infinite love pains. Tristran's attempt to mollify these by marrying another Ysolt fails, but this allowed the poet to incorporate a whole new string of narrative elements involving his wife's brother, Kaerdin, and his love for Brengvein, companion and tutor of the Irish princess. In contrast to other versions, Thomas emphasizes both the love between Tristran and Ysolt and between these two and their respective spouses.

Bibliography

Adams, Tracy. "Archetypes and Copies in Thomas's Tristan: A Re-examination of the Salle aux Images Scenes," *Romanic Review* 90, no. 3 (1999): 317–332.

Bédier, Joseph, ed. *Le roman de Tristan par Thomas.* 1905. 2 vols. New York: Johnson Reprint, 1968.

Gottfried von Strassburg. *Tristan: With the Surviving Fragments of the Tristran of Thomas.* Translated by A. T. Hatto. 1960. Harmondsworth, U.K.: Penguin, 1984.

Grimbert, Joan Tasker, ed. *Tristan and Isolde: A Casebook.* Arthurian Characters and Themes. 1995. New York: Routledge, 2002.

Hunt, Tony. "The Significance of Thomas's *Tristan,*" *Reading Medieval Studies* 7 (1981): 41–61.

Albrecht Classen

Thomas of Celano (d. 1260)

Born into a noble family in the Abruzzi, the Franciscan friar Thomas of Celano is best known as the first biographer of St. Francis of Assisi and as an eyewitness to the early world of Francis's followers. No contemporary biography of Thomas exists, but references in his own writings and in those of others allow a reconstruction of the important elements of his life. Thomas's exceptional writing ability, his theological acumen, and his knowledge of the monastic literary tradition indicate that he was well educated in both the liberal arts and theology. Thomas probably refers to himself in *The Life of Saint Francis* when he describes Francis's return from Spain in 1215: "some literate men and nobles gladly joined him. He [Francis] received such men with honor and dignity, since he himself was very noble and distinguished in spirit, and respectfully gave to each his due. In fact since he was endowed with outstanding discernment, he wisely considered in all matters the dignity of rank of each one" (*Early Documents* 2001, Vol. 1, 231).

During the Franciscan Chapter of 1221, Thomas was chosen for the mission to Germany, where he subsequently became vicar. He probably returned to Italy by 1228 for Francis's canonization. For the occasion Pope Gregory IX commissioned Thomas to write the first official account of Francis's life, *The Life of Saint Francis* (conventionally called *Celano I*), which was completed in 1229. His vivid description of the canonization events in Book 3 implies that he was present. Next, in 1230, Thomas completed a set of nine lessons on Francis's life for the liturgical celebration of the divine office, *The Legend for Use in the Choir.* Thomas's second life of Francis was commissioned by the Franciscans themselves, at the command of the minister general. *The Remembrance of the Desire of Soul* (conventionally called *Celano II*) was completed in 1247, and reflects a fuller portrait of the saint with a shift from biography to an exploration of the way of life that Francis founded. Besides Francis, three other historical figures are honored in the text: Clare of Assisi, Elias Buonbarone (the first minister general), and Hugolino dei Conti Segni (Pope Gregory IX). At about the same time Thomas also composed *The Tract on the Miracles of St. Francis.*

Thomas is also an important source for the life of St. Clare, who appears in *Celano I and II.* Because he was present at many of the events involving her, it is assumed that shortly after her death in 1253, he wrote *The Legend of Saint Clare,* a text used for her canonization. Perhaps Thomas is also the author of *Dies irae,* the plainsong of the requiem Mass, which describes Judgment and Jesus' prayer for mercy based in part on Zephaniah 1.14–16.

Bibliography

Celano, Thomas. *St. Francis of Assisi: First and Second Life of St. Francis with Selections from the Treatise on the Miracles of Blessed Francis.* Translated with introduction and footnotes by Placid Hermann. Chicago: Franciscan Herald Press, 1988.

Clare of Assisi. Early Documents. Edited and translated by Regis J. Armstrong. New York: Paulist Press, 1988.

Francis of Assisi. The Early Documents. Edited by Regis J. Armstrong, J. A. Wayne Hellman, and William Short. 3 vols. New York: New City Press, 2001.

Cynthia Ho

Thorpe, William (fl. 1407)

William Thorpe was a LOLLARD priest who was arrested on April 17, 1407, for preaching Lollard ideology. Thorpe wrote an account of his resulting examination by Archbishop Thomas Arundel, chancellor to Henry IV. Thorpe's description of the events gives a unique insight into the proceedings of Lollard interrogation.

Little is known about the life of William Thorpe. He was educated at Oxford and influenced by the teachings of John WYCLIFFE and his followers. It was probably through mutual Oxford contacts that he met John Pollyrbache, the man with whom Thorpe was arrested. Pollyrbache is an alias and there is reason to believe he was also known as John Pulverbatch, John Pollerpage, and John Pullerbach (Jurkowski 2002).

Thorpe's account is interesting in part because of the political environment in which it occurred. Arundel was hostile toward the Lollards and influential in the 1402 statute that allowed the burning of heretics. Thorpe and Pollyrbach were arrested in Shrewsbury, a town in no position to oppose the will of the powerful chancellor. Although Thorpe and Pollyrbach had been given permission to preach at the church, Shrewsbury was in a precarious situation with the civil authorities. Affected by the Welsh Revolt, the Battle of Shrewsbury, and flooding, which led to erosion of the town's walls, the town had requested full tax exemption until the end of the war. When the opportunity to oblige Arundel in his heretic hunt arose, they quickly turned over Thorpe and Pollyrbache to the authorities under the 1406 anti-Lollard statute (Jukowski 2002).

The account itself is important as a religious tract because it gives additional written information on the various beliefs of Lollardy. Thorpe willingly admitted he preached the following:

> þat þe sacrament of þe auter aftir þe consecracioun was material breed; and þat ymagis schulden in noo wyse be worschippid; and þat men schulden not goon in pilgrimage; and þat preestis haue now no titil to tiþis; and þat it is not leeful to swere in ony maner
>
> (Hudson 1993)

> That the Sacrament of the Altar after the consecration was material bread; and that images should in no wise be worshipped; and that men should not go on pilgrimage; and that priests have now no title to tithes; and that it is not lawful to swear in any manner.

Although Arundel threatened Thorpe with burning, Thorpe not only refused to recant his beliefs, but he also said the people who had done so did it at the peril of their souls and reputations.

William Thorpe's account of his examination under Archbishop Arundel is beneficial in its elucidating the atmosphere of Shrewsbury during this time of political turmoil, and, particularly, in its presentation of a Lollard trial. As such, it also helps illuminate Margery KEMPE's depiction of her own examination for Lollardy in her autobiography. No one knows the details of Thorpe's death, but he is purported to have fled to Bohemia to join the Hussites, since there are two Latin manuscripts of his *Testimony* that were produced in Bohemia ca. 1420.

Bibliography

Jurkowski, Maureen. "The Arrest of William Thorpe in Shrewsbury and the Anti-Lollard Statute of 1406," *Historical Research: The Bulletin of the Institute of Historical Research* 75 (August 2002): 273–295.

Hudson, Anne, ed. *Two Wycliffite Texts: The Sermon of William Taylor 1406; The Testimony of William Thorpe 1407.* EETS 301. Oxford: Oxford University Press, 1993.

Malene A. Little

Thousand and One Nights, The

Like CHAUCER'S *CANTERBURY TALES* or BOCCACCIO'S *DECAMERON*, *The Thousand and One Nights* (*Alf Layla wa-Layla*) is a collection of stories within a frame narrative; the frame creates a context for the telling of tales within the larger tale, and makes for a highly entertaining text. The most popular work of medieval Arabic literature, both in Islamic countries and in the West, *The Thousand and One Nights* has never been recognized by Arab literary scholars as a serious literary text or part of the Arabic literary canon. Still its tales of fantasy, magic, romance, violence, and lust continue to ensure its place in popular, if not learned, literary circles.

By the 10th century, the Arabic scholar al-Nadim called the work "foolish" and "vulgar." His opinion remains widespread among Arabic scholars today—Egypt banned the *Nights* as immoral as recently as 1989. Partly this antipathy is based on a general Islamic mistrust of fiction—the KORAN condemns all fiction as lies. In addition the colloquial language of the *Nights* is a barrier to its acceptance: Serious literature in medieval Arabic was written in what was called the *adab* style, a courtly form characterized by wide learning and complex poetic forms.

Despite this official rejection, *The Thousand and One Nights* has flourished as folk literature since its beginnings. Those origins, however, are murky. Clearly the tales began as oral stories, but modern scholarship has managed to trace their textual origin to a collection in Persian called the "Thousand Stories," produced during the Sassanid period (226–652), the last pre-Islamic dynasty in Persia. That Persian text seems to have been a translation from an original collection in Sanskrit that had come into Persia from India.

During the ninth and 10th centuries, Persian texts of all kinds were translated into Arabic, and like many other texts, *The Thousand and One Nights* was probably translated at the court of the caliph in Baghdad. The inclusion of a number of tales set in the Baghdad of the caliph Haroun al-Rashid (763–809) indicates how translators and scribes felt perfectly free to add new tales to the *Nights* even as they sought to transmit the text—a practice that stemmed, most likely, from an impulse to try to fill the fanciful "thousand and one" tales of the title.

From Baghdad the core of tales spread through the Islamic world, apparently becoming particularly popular in Syria and in Egypt, where two different branches of the *Nights* developed. The earliest extant manuscript of the *Nights* was produced in Syria in the 14th century. Manuscripts related to this one are more conservative, consisting of a core of tales most of which came, ultimately, from the original Arabic translation.

In Egypt the *Nights* were particularly popular during the Mamluk period (1250–1517). Here, new tales were added from Egyptian, Turkish, Indian, Persian, and Jewish sources. This Egyptian branch of manuscripts contains the most famous stories in the *Nights*—the tales of the seven voyages of Sinbad (added early in the Mamluk period), Ali Baba and the 40 Thieves, and a very late addition, the tale of Aladdin—none of which appear in the earliest texts of the *Nights.*

Because of its Iranian personal and place names, one part of the text that can be definitely traced to the Persian-Indian source is the frame narrative. This is the familiar story of Shahrazad (Scheherazade), daughter of King Shahrayar's vizier. The king, whose wife has proved spectacularly unfaithful, decides that all women are therefore untrustworthy, and hatches the mad plan of ensuring his wives' fidelity by marrying a new bride every night and executing her every morning. Shahrazad, witty and well read, resolves to save the women of her land by volunteering to marry the king. She forestalls her own execution by telling Shahrayar stories, which she breaks off each night at the climactic moment. In order to hear the end of the story, the king must keep her alive until the following evening. This open format allowed translators and scribes to insert new stories at will. The frame ultimately ends with the king's sparing Shahrazad's life, presumably after a thousand and one tales, and accepting her as his faithful wife.

The Thousand and One Nights is a highly unusual literary classic, having been composed over many centuries by a wide variety of contributors in several countries. In modern times, the *Nights* became popular in western Europe when Antoine Galland translated the text into French (1704–08), and Richard Burton made a popular English translation (1885–88). Both Galland and Burton added new tales (much as earlier Arab scribes and translators had done), and, curiously, these western texts were translated back into Arabic, with the new tales added. Because of this complex textual history, a definitive scholarly edition of the "original" manuscript of the *Nights* was not available until 1984.

Bibliography

Bettelheim, Bruno. *The Uses of Enchantment: The Meaning and Importance of Fairy Tales.* New York: Knopf, 1976.

Gerhardt, Mia Irene. *The Art of Story-Telling: A Literary Study of the Thousand and One Nights.* Leiden, Netherlands: Brill, 1963.

Ghazoul, Ferial Jabouri. *The Arabian Nights: A Structural Analysis.* Cairo: Cairo Associated Institution for the Study and Presentation of Arab Cultural Values, 1980.

Haddawy, Husain, trans. *The Arabian Nights.* Based on the text of the fourteenth-century Syrian manuscript edited by Muhsin Mahdi. New York: Knopf, 1992.

———, trans. *The Arabian Nights II: Sinbad and Other Popular Stories.* New York: Norton, 1995.

Three Ravens, The (ca. 15th century)

The Three Ravens is one of the best known of the English and Scottish popular BALLADS of the late Middle Ages. It may be one of the earliest extant ballads, though it was first printed only in Thomas Ravencroft's *Melismata* (1611). In any case the apparent metamorphosis of the lover into a doe is characteristic of ancient songs (Morgan 1996, 119).

The ballad is an analogue to *The Twa Corbies* and some believe also to the *CORPUS CHRISTI CAROL*. The formation of such analogues is easy to understand when one takes into account the oral tradition of balladry. There is argument as to whether *The Twa Corbies* or *The Three Ravens* is the earlier of the two ballads. It now appears that the more cynical *Twa Corbies* was the original and *The Three Ravens* may be aristocratic adaptation.

Like many ballads the main image of *The Three Ravens* is tragic. Three Ravens discuss what they are going to have for breakfast. One spies a fallen knight that lies under his shield. Another raven notices that the knight's hawk and hound protect him. A pregnant deer buries the knight and dies that evening of a broken heart. Most commentators assume that the doe is the knight's lover, transformed into a deer.

Other interpretations of the poem have suggested that the knight is Christ and the deer the bride of Christ, the Christian soul. Another suggestion is that the knight is the Maimed King, of the Grail tradition. Certainly much is made in the poem of the knight's bloody wounds, kissed by the doe. There may be an allusion in this to the Eucharist, the consumption of the body and blood of Christ. This is the chief aspect of the poem that connects it to the *Corpus Christi Carol.*

Bibliography

Child, Francis James, ed. *The English and Scottish Popular Ballads.* New York: Cooper Square, 1965.

Morgan, Gwendolyn A., ed, and trans. *Medieval Ballads: Chivalry, Romance, and Everyday Life: A Critical Anthology.* New York: Peter Lang, 1996.

Malene A. Little

Thrush and the Nightingale, The

(ca. 1275)

The Thrush and the Nightingale is a MIDDLE ENGLISH poem from the last quarter of the 13th century. Written in the West Midlands, the work is a DEBATE POEM in which the two birds argue the merits of women. As such, it is of the same "beast debate" genre as the earlier *OWL AND THE NIGHTINGALE* and CLANVOWE's 14th-century *Cuckoo and the Nightingale.*

The poem is made up of 32 six-line stanzas, rhyming *aabccb.* The *a* and *c* lines are tetrameter (four feet), while the *b* lines are trimeter (three feet). The Nightingale may be chosen as advocate of one point of view because of her conventional association with love or, as Owen and Owen suggest (1971, 271), her connection, in medieval BESTIARIES, with motherhood and thus the tender aspects associated with women. The Thrush is chosen, perhaps, because the beauty of its song rivals that of the Nightingale, making him a worthy opponent.

The first line of the poem, "Somer is comen with love to towne" (Owen and Owen 1971, 272), echoes the well-known HARLEY LYRIC, *LENTEN IS COME WITH LOVE TO TOUNE.* As in that poem and conventionally in medieval poetry, the return of spring is harbinger of new thoughts of love. The poem's speaker, having introduced the idea of love, abruptly introduces the poem's subject: He once heard two birds arguing—the Nightingale contending that women are admirable, the Thrush that they are despicable.

Until the end of the poem, it seems a kind of love debate: The Thrush, apparently male, sounds like a wronged lover who wants nothing more to do with women. And for most of the debate, the Thrush has the best of the argument. Each of his points is supported by a concrete example—Adam and Samson, led astray by wicked women, along with Alexander, Gawain, and Constantine. The Nightingale defends women by discussing general "female" nurturing qualities, and seems to be getting the worst of the argument until the end, when she gives her single culminating example, the Virgin Mary. The poem shifts from a love poem to a religious one. As the epitome of comfort and nurture, the Virgin trumps all of the Thrush's negative examples, and he admits defeat, vowing never again to disparage woman, after which he leaves the forest in shame and a kind of self-imposed exile.

The poem is fairly close in style to conventional French and Latin debate poems, in which arguments are given in self-contained stanzas. The sentiments expressed are quite conventional. The poem has often been compared with *The Owl and the Nightingale,* and it is possible that the earlier poem influenced *The Thrush and the Nightingale.* However, as Gardner points out (1971, 266), the later poem has "no connective narrative, few personal touches, and no humor"—all significant characteristics of *The Owl and the Nightingale.* It seems likely that the relationship between the two poems is not as close as was once thought.

Bibliography

Gardner, John. *The Alliterative Morte Arthure, The Owl and the Nightingale, and Five Other Middle English Poems: In a Modernized Version with Comments on the Poem and Notes.* Carbondale: Southern Illinois University Press, 1971.

Owen, Lewis J., and Nancy H. Owen. *Middle English Poetry: An Anthology.* Indianapolis: Bobbs-Merrill, 1971.

Tournament of Tottenham, The (ca. 1400–1440)

The Tournament of Tottenham is a poem of 234 lines surviving in two manuscripts, written in the Northern dialect of MIDDLE ENGLISH, although its setting is in the south, near London. It is a rollicking burlesque of a courtly tournament as performed by country peasants competing for the hand of the local reeve's daughter. Ultimately, it is difficult to determine whether the poet's intent was to satirize the elaborate conventions of chivalry and ROMANCE, or to mock the churlish behavior of the country peasants trying to imitate their social betters.

Like many courtly romances, this poem begins with a feast, but the feast takes place in a tavern and concerns not knights like Sir GAWAIN or Sir LANCELOT, but rather "treue drinkers" with names like Hawkin, Gib, Hud, Dudman, Terry, and Tomkyn. The poem's protagonist, Perkyn the Potter, announces his love for Tyb, the daughter of Randal the Reeve, but a number of the carousers express their own desire for the fair maiden. A tournament is declared at which Tyb is to be the prize, though the other prizes offered—a cow, hen, mare, and sow—undercut Tyb's status as the courtly romance heroine. A description of the arming of the warriors follows, and includes the participants' use of good black bowls for helmets and wicker fans for shields. When Tyb rides into the tournament, she is greeted not by a trumpet blast but by a trumpeting fart from Gyb's horse.

Before the battle begins the chief combatants all swear ludicrous oaths, including Terry's oath that he intends, unheroically, to sneak off with Tyb while the others are fighting. The heraldic devices used for the combatants' coats of arms—a dough-trough and baker's shovel for the cowardly Terry, for example, and a sieve, rake, and three pieces of cake for Hud—are equally absurd travesties of serious coats of arms. Perkyn, given the honor of the final boast, swears to defeat them all and capture the best horses among them to give to Tyb. The battle itself is a chaotic free-for-all, with Perkyn emerging as the victor, though the horses he captures are too tired to be brought to Tyb. After his victory, Perkyn and Tyb rush to bed unceremoniously, and the poem ends the next day with another feast, though this time the defeated combatants all limp to the feast with broken heads and shoulders.

The poem is made up of 26 stanzas in a very complex form, beginning with four long alliterative lines rhyming *aaaa,* followed by five shorter (roughly three-stress) lines rhyming *bcccb.* The stanza form recalls that of some of the better-known heroic romances of the north, including texts like *The AWNTYRS OFF ARTHURE* and even *SIR GAWAIN AND THE GREEN KNIGHT,* but is here used for comic effect as the shorter "bob and wheel" stanza endings bring each individual stanza to a ludicrous conclusion.

It is clear that the *Tournament of Tottenham* travesties many elements of the courtly romance. But it has been suggested (*see* Jones) that the poem may reflect a historical Shrovetide custom in 15th-century Germany and Switzerland in which bourgeois actors presented a mock tournament for the amusement of the nobility. The poem may parody that kind of event.

Bibliography

Jones, George F. "The Tournaments of Tottenham and Lappenhausen," *PMLA* 66 (1951): 1123–1140.

The Tournament of Tottenham, in *Middle English Poetry: An Anthology,* edited by Lewis J. Owen and Nancy H. Owen. Indianapolis: Bobbs-Merrill, 1971, 326–335.

Wright, Glenn. "Parody, Satire, and Genre in *The Tournament of Tottenham* (1400–1440)," *Fifteenth-Century Studies* 23 (1997): 152–170.

Towneley Cycle (Wakefield Cycle)

One of four surviving manuscripts containing collections of MYSTERY PLAYS—short plays or "pageants" relating the salvation history of humankind from the Creation of the world through Doomsday—is the late 15th-century Huntington MS. HM 1, better known as the Towneley manuscript. The manuscript is named for the Towneley family who owned it from the 17th to the 19th centuries, and its history prior to that is unknown. The collection was once called the Wakefield Cycle in the belief that it comprised a cycle of plays performed for the CORPUS CHRISTI festival in the West Riding town of Wakefield in Yorkshire, but there are serious questions that make that connection unlikely: Wakefield was too small to have had a guild structure that would have supported a full-scale Corpus Christi pageant like the nearby YORK CYCLE—a festival in which individual craft guilds supported the production of specific plays each year.

One area of scholarly discussion concerning these plays is where and under what circumstances they were performed. There are a few references in the town records of Wakefield from the late 16th century suggesting that plays were regularly performed in Wakefield that were associated with Corpus Christi, but it is not clear that these were the plays in question, or that an entire cycle was performed there. Some scholars completely reject the idea that the Towneley plays were performed as a complete cycle by local townspeople at the feast of Corpus Christi. Others say that there is really not enough evidence to say for sure one way or another.

It seems clear that the Towneley plays could not have been performed on pageant wagons of the sort used to stage the plays in the streets of York. Although the manuscript lacks stage directions, some of the plays obviously would have needed a larger acting space, or two or three playing areas, in order to be performed. The Cain and Abel play, for instance, would need a plow and a team to pull it. The *SECOND SHEPHERDS' PLAY* would have needed three separate acting areas—the heath for the shepherds, Mak's house, and the stable of the nativity.

Certainly some plays may be associated with Wakefield: The name *Wakefield* is written at the beginning of two plays in the manuscript, which may in fact indicate that they originated or were intended for an acting troupe from Wakefield. The dialect of the plays indicates specifically that they were performed in West Riding in Yorkshire. But the manuscript lacks the kind of thematic and stylistic unity characteristic of the York Cycle or the CHESTER CYCLE. Five of the plays are direct borrowings from the York Cycle: the play of the Exodus from Egypt, Jesus and the Doctors in the Temple, the Harrowing of Hell, the Resurrection, and the fragmentary Last Judgment play. Two other Towneley plays are revised versions of York pageants. Thus it appears that the plays were collected from various sources rather than composed as a single unit, in a manner more reminiscent of the N-TOWN PLAYS. It has been suggested that the Towneley manuscript is a compilation of "clerks' plays" from which a troupe might choose individual plays or pageants for production, a practice that is known to have occurred in the Netherlands (Davidson 1994, 433).

The chief genius behind the most admired plays in the collection is still generally called the Wakefield Master. Of the 32 pageants contained in the extant manuscript, the Wakefield Master is the author of six, and seems to have had a hand in revising two of the borrowed York pageants, as well as four other plays. The Wakefield Master is known to have been a clergyman because of his in-depth knowledge of religious matters, and he may have written specifically for a skillful troupe of amateur Wakefield actors. He can be identified by his characteristic use of a nine-line stanza rhyming *aaaabcccb,* in which the first four long lines rhyme, and the fifth line is a "bob" or short three-syllable line leading to a "wheel" of shorter lines at the end. The fact that the long opening lines contain internal rhyme as well leads some modern editors to print the verses as 13-line stanzas, rhyming *ababababcdddc.* Other characteristics of the Wakefield Master's style include an extensive and varied vocabulary, an interest in characters as individuals rather than as types, a bent for social criticism, and a sense of comedy that appears particularly in his most famous composition, the *Second Shepherds' Play.* This comic tale of the sheep-stealing Mak and the three disgruntled shepherds on the eve of Christ's nativity is the most popular and anthologized of all medieval mystery plays, and deservedly so. But the Wakefield Master's other plays are also of interest: He also wrote the Towneley versions of the *Mactatio Abel* (the Cain and Abel play), *Prcessus Noe cum Filiis* (the play of Noah and the flood), *Prima Pastorum* (the first shepherds' play), *Magnus Herodes* (Herod the Great and the Slaughter of the Innocents), and *Coliphizacio* (the buffeting).

It may be that the Wakefield Master's plays formed a core around which a later compiler assembled the group of pageants from a variety of sources. However, since none of the Wakefield Master's plays have been revised or altered in any way, it may be that he himself made the last revision of the entire cycle. However, the manuscript was definitely marred later by Protestant reformers determined to eradicate aspects of the pageants that most clearly reflected their Roman Catholic origins. Thus a number of leaves are missing from the manuscript, including sections both before and after the Doomsday pageant that it is believed contained plays of the Assumption and the Coronation of the Virgin. Whether those kinds of changes were made in the manuscript after the English Reformation to allow the continued performance of the plays (as certain "corrective" marginal notes suggest), or were made later by a zealot trying to cleanse the manuscript of its doctrinal impurities, is difficult to say. In either case, mystery plays in general disappeared from English town life during Elizabeth's reign, relics of England's Catholic past.

Bibliography

Davidson, Clifford. "Jest and Earnest: Comedy in the Work of the Wakefield Master," *Annuale Mediaevale* 22 (1982): 65–83.

Helterman, Jeffrey. *Symbolic Action in the Plays of the Wakefield Master.* Athens: University of Georgia Press, 1981.

Johnston, Alexandra F. "Evil in the Towneley Cycle." In *Evil on the Medieval Stage,* edited by Meg Twycross, 94–103. Lancaster, U.K.: Medieval English Theatre, 1992.

Meredith, Peter. "The Towneley Cycle." In *The Cambridge Companion to Medieval English Theatre,* edited by Richard Beadle, 134–162. Cambridge: Cambridge University Press, 1994.

Meyers, Walter E. *A Figure Given: Typology in the Wakefield Plays.* Pittsburgh: Duquesne University Press, 1968.

Palmer, Barbara D. " 'Towneley Plays' or 'Wakefield Cycle' Revisited," *Comparative Drama* 21 (1988): 318–348.

Rose, Martial, trans. *The Wakefield Mystery Plays.* Garden City, N.Y.: Doubleday, 1962.

Stevens, Martin. "The Missing Parts of the Towneley Cycle," *Speculum* 45 (1970): 254–265.

The Wakefield Pageants in the Towneley Cycle. Edited by A.C. Cawley. Manchester, U.K.: Manchester University Press, 1958.

Trevisa, John (ca. 1342–ca. 1402)

John Trevisa was influential in making the English language an acceptable vehicle for important written works. His translations of the Latin texts of Ranulf HIGDEN's *Polychronicon* (ca. 1385–87) and Bartholomaeus Anglicus's *De proprietatibus rerum* (On the properties of things) (1398) gave common people access to important works.

Trevisa was born at Crocadon, St. Mellion, in Cornwall around 1342. He was a fellow at Exeter College, Oxford, from 1362–69 and at Queen's Hall from 1369–79. In 1379 he was expelled, along with two other students, for "unworthiness," but later reinstated. It has been speculated that the expulsion was due to their sympathies with the doctrines of John WYCLIFFE. (Kunitz, 522)

Prior to 1387 he became vicar of Berkeley in Gloucestershire, as well as chaplain to Thomas, Lord Berkeley. He also acted as a nonresidential canon at Westbury-on-Trym, near Bristol. Lord Berkeley and his two sons remained Trevisa's patrons until his death at Berkeley circa 1402.

It was Lord Berkeley for whom Trevisa translated the *Polychronicon,* the *De proprietatibus rerum,* and the *De regimine principum.* In the preface to the *Polychronicon,* he wrote *A Dialogue in Translation Between a Lord and a Clerk,* in which he describes how he overcame Berkeley's reluctance about translating books into the "vulgar tongue" and thus making them accessible to the common people.

Trevisa finished his translation of Ranulf Higden's *Polychronicon* in the period 1385–87. Higden

(d. 1364) was a monk in Chester whose book was a history of the world from Creation to medieval times. Trevisa not only translated the work, but also annotated it and updated the history through 1385–87. Additionally he included a famous description of the English language and its various dialects as of the year 1385.

Trevisa completed his annotated translation of the Latin encyclopedia *De proprietatibus rerum* in February 1398. It was originally written by Bartholomaeus Anglicus (Bartholomew the Englishman) in the early 12th century. It was a 19-book work, each volume of which dealt with a different facet of living, such as spirituality or the natural world.

The *De regimine principum* (Concerning the rule of princes) was a translation of a 1280s Latin work by the Augustinian friar, Aegidius Romanus (Giles of Rome). It was meant as an all-inclusive guide to rulers. Although the translation cannot be exactly dated, the length suggests it was written between his other major translations. His translation of *De regimine principum* was one of the sources for Thomas HOCCLEVE's most famous work, the *Regiment of Princes.*

Trevisa's translations are brilliant not only in their ease of reading, but also in the conscientiousness he showed in making them. He was careful to translate the works as exactly as he could, and when two interpretations were possible, he would include both translations. Trevisa would also include translations of entries he did not understand with the notation "God wot what this is to mean" (Kunitz 1952, 522–523).

Trevisa remains an important translator and popularizer of Latin texts. His English versions of Higden's *Polychronicon* and Bartholomaeus Anglicus's *De proprietatibus rerum* were instrumental in raising the perception of English as a language for learned discussion.

Bibliography

Babington, Churchill, and Lumby, J. R., eds. *Polychronicon Ranulphi Higden Monachi Cestrensis; Together with the English Translations of John Trevisa and of an Unknown Writer of the Fifteenth Century.* 9 vols. London: Longman, Green, Longman, Roberts and Green, 1865–1886.

Fowler, David C. *The Life and Times of John Trevisa, Medieval Scholar.* Seattle: University of Washington Press, 1995.

Kim, H. C., ed. "*The Gospel of Nichodemus,* translated by John Trevisa." Ph.D. diss., University of Washington, 1963.

Kunitz, Stanley J., and Howard Haycraft, eds. *British Authors Before 1800: A Biographical Dictionary.* New York: H. W. Wilson, 1952.

Seymour, M. C., et al., eds. *On the Properties of Things: John Trevisa's translation of Bartholomaeus Anglicus De Proprietatibus Rerum.* 3 vols. Oxford, U.K.: Clarendon Press, 1975–1988.

Waldron, Ronald. "Trevisa's Original Prefaces on Translation: A Critical Edition," in *Medieval English Studies Presented to George Kane,* edited by Edward Donald Kennedy, Ronald Waldron, and Joseph S. Wittig. Woodbridge, Suffolk, U.K.: D. S. Brewer, 1988, 285–299.

Malene A. Little

Tristan Gottfried von Strassburg (ca. 1210)

GOTTFRIED VON STRASSBURG's version of the TRISTAN story sets in with a highly significant prologue in which the narrator characterizes true love as a quasi-eucharistic experience, possible only for those with a noble heart, a spiritual form of nobility. The ROMANCE begins with Tristan's parents, Rivalin and Blanscheflûr, who beget their child outside of wedlock. Whereas Rivalin soon dies in battle, Blanscheflûr succumbs during labor. The young orphan is raised in hiding by the country's marshall, Rual li foitenant, and his wife, Floræte, and receives the best possible education, soon proving to be a child prodigy, excelling particularly in music and foreign languages. When Norwegian merchants try to kidnap him, a wild storm forces them to drop him at a distant coast. From there he finds his way to the court of King Mark, whom he does not yet recognize as his uncle, until his tutor Rual arrives four years later and explains the relationship. Subsequently Tristan frees his deceased father's country, Parmenie, from King Morgan's suppression by killing his opponent, but he quickly returns to his uncle, leaving Parmenie in Rual's and his sons' hands. In Cornwall Tristan proves his outstanding chivalric abilities when he kills the Irish knight Morold, who tried to collect tribute from Mark, but Tristan is poisoned in the process. He finds healing only with the Irish queen Isolde, who asks him to instruct her daughter, Isolde the Fair, in the arts. After Tristan has returned home, he faces serious envy on the part of Mark's barons, and to protect himself from their enmity he promises to win Isolde the Fair's hand for Mark. Tristan accomplishes his goal by killing a dragon that had ravaged Ireland, and so he gains the right to ask for Isolde's hand on behalf of Mark. However, while traveling back to Cornwall, the two young people drink a love potion—clearly to be understood metaphorically—that her mother had brewed for her daughter and her future husband. Thus begins their lifelong love affair that occupies the rest of the romance.

Tristan and Isolde soon fall under suspicion of committing adultery, but they manage to hide their affair for a while until bloodstains—Tristan had jumped to Isolde's bed to make love with her right after a blood-letting session—on both their beds betray them. Isolde denies the charges yet must undergo an ordeal with the hot iron to prove her innocence. Swearing to God, however, that she lay in no other man's arms than her husband's and those of a poor pilgrim who had carried her from the ship to the shore and then had fallen, she tells the "truth" and does not burn herself because she had asked Tristan to pretend to be a pilgrim. In the meantime Tristan wins, as a gift for Isolde, a magical dog, Petitcrîu, whose bell hanging from its neck produces music that makes every listener completely happy. Nevertheless Isolde, realizing the deceptive quality of this music, tears off the bell and destroys the magic to protect her true love for Tristan. Mark, however, clearly recognizes that his wife and nephew love each other and expels both from his court.

Tristan and Isolde retire into a love cave where they enjoy each other as in an erotic utopia, until one day Marke happens to discover the cave and observes both sleeping next to each other in bed. Yet even here he is deceived by Tristan, who makes him believe that a strategically placed sword between them confirms their innocence. Consequently Mark allows them to return to his court, but they cannot contain their love and are finally caught *in flagrante.*

This time Tristan leaves for good and traverses various countries until he comes across another young woman called Isolde (Whitehand). A new love relationship develops, but it seems to be only one-sided, as Tristan always longs for Isolde the Fair, yet misleads Isolde Whitehand by apparently wooing her. Since Gottfried's text breaks off at this point, we don't know how he would have concluded his romance. Both the Old French versions and the 13th-century German *Tristan* romances suggest a number of variant conclusions, each of them leading up to Tristan's and Isolde's deaths. Ultimately Isolde emerges as the true heroine, fully capable of manipulating her environment to her profit, maintaining extraordinary self-control, and demonstrating the highest degree of loyalty to her lover, whereas Tristan begins to waver in his love and seems torn between Isolde the Fair and Isolde Whitehand. While Isolde has to go through a lengthy learning process and then achieves the triumphs of a true lover with a noble heart, Tristan hardly needs any development and seems to pale as a character at the end of the narrative in comparison with Isolde.

Bibliography

Bekker, Hugo. *Gottfried von Strassburg's Tristan: Journey Through the Realm of Eros.* Columbia, S.C.: Camden House, 1987.

Chinca, Mark. *Gottfried von Strassburg: Tristan.* Cambridge: Cambridge University Press, 1997.

Gottfried von Straßburg. *Tristan.* Edited by Karl Marold. Werner Schröder, 1906. 3rd revised edition, Berlin: de Gruyter, 1969.

———. *Tristan and Isolde.* Edited and translated by Francis Gentry. New York: Continuum, 1988.

Grimbert, Joan Tasker, ed. *Tristan and Isolde: A Casebook.* Arthurian Characters and Themes, 2. New York: Routledge, 2002.

Albrecht Classen

Tristan and Isolde

The mythical account of the two lovers Tristan/Tristrant/Tristrem and Isolde/Iseut/Isotta deeply influenced the entire history of European literature from the early Middle Ages to the present, originating in ancient Irish, Cornish, and Scottish sagas, as confirmed by various references to "Drustan/Drvstavs" and "Eselt" from the sixth to the eighth centuries. It gained a solid foothold in the middle of the 12th century with the Old French version by an otherwise unknown BÉROUL (*Tristan*) and with the fragments by Thomas d'Angleterre (including one recently discovered in Carlisle). The narrative of the adulterous love affair—Isolde being married to Tristan's uncle Mark but in love with Tristan only—quickly spread through oral channels and is already reflected by MARIE DE FRANCE in her *lai* "Chevrefeuil," in CHRÉTIEN DE TROYES's *CLIGÈS,* and songs by BERNART DE VENTADORN, RAIMBAUT D'ORANGE, CHÂTELAIN DE COUCY, REINMAR DER ALTE, and others (all written ca. 1170–90). Comic and grotesque elements were explored by the anonymous Old French authors of the *Folie Tristan de Berne* and the *Folie Tristan d'Oxford,* and the 13th-century Middle High German author of *Tristan als Mönch.* EILHART VON OBERGE composed a highly influential Middle High German *Tristrant* romance at around 1190, and the Alemannic poet GOTTFRIED VON STRASSBURG wrote his version, probably the most famous one, in ca. 1210. The early 13th century witnessed the emergence of the most influential text, *Tristan en prose,* which was translated into most European languages throughout the following centuries, such as Middle English, Medieval Spanish, Medieval Italian, Old Norse, Old Czech, Greek, and Serbo-Russian. By the end of the 16th century the literary myth of this love affair seems to have fallen into oblivion, but the medieval texts were rediscovered by the end of the 18th century, leading to a remarkable revival of the myth in a myriad of forms, including translations, retellings, poems, dramas, operas (Richard Wagner, 1867–69), scholarly studies (Denis de Rougemont, 1939), films (Jean Cocteau, 1943; Yvan Lagrange, 1972), and novels (John Updike, 1965).

Bibliography

Classen, Albrecht, et al., eds. *Tristania. A Journal Devoted to Tristan Studies.* 20 vols. Lewiston, N.Y.: Edwin Mellen Press, 1975–2004.

Albrecht Classen

Trivet, Nicholas (Nicholas Trevet) (ca. 1258–ca. 1334)

Nicholas Trivet was an English Dominican friar best known as a chronicler, though his story of Constance became the source of CHAUCER's *MAN OF LAW'S TALE,* and his commentary on BOETHIUS's *CONSOLATION OF PHILOSOPHY* was one of the texts Chaucer used in making his own translation of Boethius, known as the *Boece.*

Trivet was the son of a judge named Thomas Trivet, who lived either in Norfolk or Somerset. Nicholas became a Dominican in London, and studied at Oxford and later in Paris, and it may have been there where he became interested in chronicles, both in English and French. He wrote commentaries on a number of classical texts, including one on Boethius and significant commentaries on Seneca and on St. AUGUSTINE's *CITY OF GOD.* He also composed theological tracts on the Bible and the Mass, and commentaries on other medieval theologians. His scholarly reputation enabled him to secure a position teaching at Oxford, while his competence and theological wisdom helped him become prior of his Dominican order in London.

But Trivet's reputation rests chiefly on his three chronicles: the *Historia ab orbe Condita ad Christi Nativitatum* (History from the creation of the world to the birth of Christ) (1327–28), a worldwide encyclopedic chronicle (a precursor of HIGDEN's *POLYCHRONICON*) based largely on Vincent of Beauvais; the *Annals of Six Kings of England* (ca. 1320), for which he was best known and which covers the period 1135–1307—from Stephen through Edward I, the latter of whose reign is a particularly important part of Trivet's book; and the *Anglo-Norman Chronicle* (ca. 1320), a history from the creation of the world to 1285. The latter survives in some eight manuscripts, and contains the story of the saintly Constance, whose constant faith in the face of persistent adversity made hers an inviting story to retell in verse for both John GOWER, who includes it in his CONFESSIO *AMANTIS,* and Chaucer, whose *Man of Law's Tale* is certainly the best-known version, though his ultimate source for the story was Trivet's chronicle.

Bibliography

Block, Edward A. "Originality, Controlling Purpose, and Craftsmanship in Chaucer's *Man of Law's Tale*," *PMLA* 68 (1953): 572–616.

Paull, Michael R. "The Influence of the Saint's Legend Genre in the *Man of Law's Tale*," *Chaucer Review* 5 (1971):179–194.

trobar clus

Trobar clus is a style of TROUBADOUR poetry that is characterized by deliberate obscurity, metrical complexity, allusive and difficult language, and intricacy of rhyme schemes. It is a closed or hermetic style of writing practiced by poets who wished to communicate mainly with those in the courtly audience they deemed intelligent, initiated, and therefore worthy of the troubadour's song. The term combines the Provençal words *trobar,* or the composition of poetry, and *clus,* meaning "closed."

The invention of the *trobar clus* style is often credited to the early 12th-century Provençal poet MARCABRU, though the term was not known in his time. The attitude toward the audience implied by the style goes back even further to the first troubadour, WILLIAM IX, duke of Aquitaine, who ends one of his poems with the comment:

> *Concerning this vers, I tell you a man is all*
> *the more noble*
> *As he understands it, and gets more praise*
>
> (Goldin 1973, 39, ll. 37–38)

But RAIMBAUT D'ORANGE is probably the key figure in the development and definition of the *trobar clus* style. In a famous *TENSO,* or DEBATE POEM, with his contemporary GIRAUT DE BORNELH, concerning the relative merits of different poetic styles, Raimbaut defends his use of the *clus* style by saying that many among his listeners are uneducated, and that to write in a style that pleases all of them would be to lower his standards:

> *I do not want my songs turned*
> *into such a lot of noise; . . .*
> *fools will never*
> *be able to praise them,*
> *for such have no taste and no concern*
> *for the worthiest and most precious things.*
>
> (Goldin 1973, 203, ll. 15–21)

It was a matter of pride, then, for the poet to write in a style inaccessible to the vulgar. Giraut, on the other hand, defends the easier style called the *TROBAR LEU.*

In a study of troubadour eloquence, Paterson generalizes that, after looking at what a number of the troubadours actually say about *trobar clus,* it is impossible to give a very specific definition of the style: "*trobar clus* is flexible and treated differently by different poets" (Paterson 1975, 93). But the exclusive nature of the verse was influential on DANTE, who speaks with Arnaut Daniel in the *Purgatorio,* and on later poets like Pound and Eliot.

Bibliography

Goldin, Frederick, ed. and trans. *Lyrics of the Troubadours and Trouvères: An Anthology and a History.* Garden City, N.Y.: Doubleday, 1973.

Paterson, Linda M. *Troubadours and Eloquence.* Oxford: Clarendon Press, 1975.

trobar leu

Trobar leu was a style of TROUBADOUR poetry that was characterized by simple, natural, and accessible diction and relatively simple verse forms. It was a style intended to appeal to the broadest possible audience. The term comes from the Provençal words *trobar,* or the art of composing verse, and *leu,* meaning "light" or "easy."

Perhaps the best-known troubadour in the *leu* style is BERNART DE VENTADORN, whose wide popularity probably owed much to his composition in a style that appealed to a broad audience. The term itself, however, seems to have been invented by GIRAUT DE BORNELH, who was more concerned than Bernart with developing a theory of composition, and who discusses the style in seven different songs. Giraut seems to have developed the theory of the *leu* style in reaction to the *TROBAR CLUS.*

For Giraut *trobar leu* describes verse that is "easy to sing and understand, light and entertaining, apparently carefree, smooth and polished with obscurity planed away" (Paterson 1975, 208). But he insists that it takes as much skill and effort to produce verse that is smooth and polished as it does to compose something obscure, and therefore the *trobar leu* style should not be considered inferior to the *trobar clus,* even though it seems easier.

In a well-known *TENSO,* or DEBATE POEM, with RIMBAUT D'ORANGE, Giraut engages in an argument over the relative merits of the two styles, suggesting that there may have been a controversy on the matter among troubadours in about 1170. Rimbaud cares nothing for popularity, but wants to be appreciated only by those with the most intelligence and the best taste. But Giraut, applying reasoning comparable to that of rhetoricians like GEOFFREY OF VINSAUF (Paterson 1975, 113–14), argues that he is making his verse appropriate to his audience. Since he is writing for a broader segment of the courtly audience, including those whom Rimbaut calls "fools," he will use his skills to shape his verse to the tastes and understanding of that audience. Thus Giraut says:

I have no complaint
if each man writes the kind of song that
suits him,
but it seems to me
the song is better loved
and more applauded
when you make it easy and open to all

(Goldin 1973, 203, ll. 8–13)

Trobar leu, then, is a style more popular, more appealing for a general audience, than the more obscure and exclusive style of the *trobar clus.*

Bibliography

Gaunt, Simon. *Troubadours and Irony.* Cambridge: Cambridge University Press, 1989.

Goldin, Frederick, ed. and trans. *Lyrics of the Troubadours and Trouvères: An Anthology and a History.* Garden City, N.Y.: Doubleday, 1973.

Paterson, Linda M. *Troubadours and Eloquence.* Oxford: Clarendon Press, 1975.

trobar ric (*trobar car, trobar prim*)

The term *trobar ric* describes a style of TROUBADOUR poetry that made use of elaborate technical contrivances and ornate language, but whose sense was clear to the audience. The phrase combines the Provençal *trobar* (the composition of verse) and *ric* ("precious," "noble," "valuable"). Some scholars have seen the style as a deliberate sort of middle ground between the *TROBAR CLUS* and the *TROBAR LEU,* but it seems likely that the troubadours themselves used the term more loosely, and seem to have used it interchangeably with the terms *trobar car* or *trobar prim.*

Peire VIDAL was one of the first troubadours to use the term *trobar ric.* In one of his songs he says:

I can put together and inter-
lace words and music with such skill
in the noble art of song
no man comes near my heel,
when I have a good subject.

(Goldin 1973, 255, ll. 1–5)

Here the term is translated as "noble art of song." Peire claims to be the premier practitioner of the style. But here it seems simply a general way of describing what he sees as a high style.

ARNAUT DANIEL writes probably the best examples of what are loosely called *trobar ric* lyrics. Arnaut is sometimes considered a writer in the *trobar clus* style, but generally he seems to separate the technical aspects of *trobar clus,* including elaborate rhyme and stanza structure, from the deliberately obscure meaning of the *trobar clus,* thereby combining ease of understanding with complexity of form. Arnaut invented the complex verse form, the *sestina,* in which the same six words appear in an alternating pattern at the ends of the lines of six six-line stanzas, and a three-line concluding stanza repeats all six words, two per line. The complexity of this stanza form owes something to the *trobar clus* style, but the clear sense of Arnaut's poems put them into the category of *trobar ric.*

But the category remains vague. As Linda Paterson notes, it is convenient to call *trobar ric* all poems, like Arnaut's, that search for complex or ornate forms without the obscure sense of the *clus* style, "but it is doubtful whether the troubadours themselves ever did so" (Paterson 1975, 184). Still *trobar ric* remains a convenient category in considering the variety of troubadour styles.

Bibliography

Goldin, Frederick, ed. and trans. *Lyrics of the Troubadours and Trouvères: An Anthology and a History.* Garden City, N.Y.: Doubleday, 1973.

Paterson, Linda M. *Troubadours and Eloquence.* Oxford: Clarendon Press, 1975.

Troilus and Criseyde Geoffrey Chaucer (ca. 1385)

Troilus and Criseyde is Geoffrey CHAUCER's longest complete poem, at 8,239 lines of RHYME ROYAL stanzas, divided into five books. Written in the mid- to late-1380s, soon after *The KNIGHT'S TALE* and his translation of BOETHIUS's *CONSOLATION OF PHILOSOPHY* (the *Boece*) and immediately prior to his *LEGEND OF GOOD WOMEN*, *Troilus* is Chaucer's most polished composition, much more so than the unfinished *CANTERBURY TALES*, and is the mature and serious poetic work on which Chaucer probably thought his reputation would ultimately rest. The work tells the unhappy story of Troilus, prince of Troy, and his failed love for the beautiful young widow Criseyde, presented against the background of the Trojan War.

The kernel of the story of *Troilus and Criseyde* was included in BENOÎT DE SAINTE-MAURE's 12th-century poem, the *Roman de Troie*. Benoît's ROMANCE was translated into a Latin prose version called *Historia destructionis Troiae* by Guido della Colonne (1287), a text that inspired BOCCACCIO to turn the Troilus story into a complete tale of its own. Chaucer's immediate source for the tale was Boccaccio's youthful poem called *Il FILOSTRATO* (The love-struck, ca. 1338). Boccaccio's story is shorter and less complex than Chaucer's: In it Troilo falls in love with Criseida, and the lady's cousin, Troilo's friend Pandaro, easily convinces Criseida to become the prince's lover. Forced to leave Troy in the end to join her father, who has defected to the Greek camp, Criseida betrays Troilo, falling in love with the Greek warrior Diomede.

Chaucer deepens and fleshes out the story, partly by including serious philosophical reflections drawn from Boethius, and partly by creating much more complex characters for Criseyde and for Pandarus in particular, but also for the Narrator himself, who appears as a fourth major character in the poem. Criseyde is an intelligent, articulate, and independent woman, but one whose fears for her own safety compel her to choose the easiest path; she is one whose love is real, but who chooses self-preservation over unflinching fidelity. Pandarus, still Troilus's friend but made by Chaucer into the uncle and guardian of Criseyde, has more complex responsibilities and loyalties than Boccaccio's Pandaro. Pandarus is a master of persuasive sophistry, of self-deprecation and good humor, who seems to want the best for both lovers. His banter is the chief source of humor in the poem, but his motives are complex and ambiguous. The Narrator presents himself as an unsuccessful lover who tells this story to help other lovers. Constrained to follow the story as told by his imaginary source called Lollius, the Narrator is enamored of his own creation in Criseyde, and labors to put everything she does in the best light. As for Troilus himself, he is the character that Chaucer changes the least: He is a noble and scrupulously true lover, the servant of his lady in the manner of a COURTLY LOVER, but he is indecisive, fatalistic, passive, and self-pitying, and hence easily manipulated by others. One of the most admired aspects of Chaucer's poem is what critics have, somewhat anachronistically, considered the psychological realism of its characters. For many scholars, Chaucer's poem is one of the important forerunners of the modern novel.

Book I of the poem begins as the astrologer Calchas, Criseyde's father, foresees the doom of Troy, and in fear leaves the city. Left alone and the daughter of a traitor, Criseyde begs Prince Hector for his protection, which he grants. Later, at a festival, the younger prince Troilus scoffs at all lovers, until, catching sight of Criseyde, he is instantly overcome by love of her. Suffering from the pains of love, he goes to bed, where he remains frozen by lovesickness. Pandarus visits him and discovers the truth, promising to visit Criseyde himself.

Book 2 is perhaps the most admired section of the poem. It begins with Pandarus's visit and conversation with Criseyde, a brilliant dialogue in which we see each trying to outwit and outguess the other in a dazzling verbal sparring match. This is followed by a remarkable interior monologue in which Criseyde weighs her options, trying to decide whether to accept Troilus's attentions. When she inclines toward acceptance, Pandarus creates an elaborate ruse by which, playing on her fears, he convinces Criseyde that she is in danger and needs the protection of some powerful nobles of the town, including Troilus. When she meets with Troilus in Book 3, she agrees to accept his service. After some time, through another of Pandarus's machinations, the lovers are finally brought to bed together in Pandarus's own house—Troilus, swooning at the critical moment, must be picked up and placed in Criseyde's bed by Pandarus.

Book 3 ends with Troilus on top of Fortune's Wheel; in Book 4, the wheel begins its downward turn. During a prisoner exchange, the Greeks, in gratitude for Calchas's encouraging support and at his request, demand Criseyde in exchange for the Trojan Antenor. Devastated, the lovers meet one last time. Rejecting Pandarus's ignoble plan to run away with Criseyde, Troilus is hesitant to accept Criseyde's alternative—her promise that she will find a way to escape her father and return to Troy within 10 days. As Book 5 opens, Troilus is present at the formal exchange of prisoners, and the Greek Diomede acts as Criseyde's escort to the enemy camp. Diomede immediately begins to woo Criseyde. While Troilus pathetically awaits his beloved at the gates of the city through the 10th day, Criseyde has essentially determined not to try to escape: Her fears and her instinct for self-preservation above all have overcome her love and good intentions, and she eventually accepts Diomede as her new lover—though the Narrator will not go so far as to say she gave him her heart. When Troilus sees a broach on Diomede's armor that had been his gift to Criseyde, he realizes her betrayal. He enters battle ferociously, hoping to either kill Diomede or die himself to end his misery. But Achilles quickly puts an end to his life.

The poem ends with a long passage called the Palinode, in which Troilus ascends to the eighth sphere, from which he looks back upon the earth and laughs at his own attachment to the vain things of the physical world. The Narrator advises his readers to learn from Troilus's lesson, and to place their faith not in the fickle Fortune that governs this world, but in the stability of God. Critical discussions of Chaucer's poem have often centered on the appropriateness of this ending to the rest of the poem, since it seems to contradict much of the poem's emphasis on the value of earthly love. Scholars have also discussed the nature of love in the story, and Chaucer's apparent attitude toward the medieval idea of courtly love: Most would hold that Chaucer was more interested in the reality of the psychological complexities of love than in the artificial "codes" of conventional courtly love poetry. Of course, the characters of Criseyde and Pandarus have also excited a good deal of critical commentary.

Another important question raised by many critics concerns the pervasiveness of Fortune, fate, and predestination in the poem. This concern is reinforced by many of the Boethian passages in the text, most notably a long soliloquy by Troilus in Book 4 in which he concludes that "all that comes comes by necessity." Even the Narrator feels the pressure of this determinism, as he bemoans the fact that he is forced to follow his source and present Criseyde's unfaithfulness. And all is set against the backdrop of a Troy the reader knows to be doomed to fall. The question of how much free will was involved in Troilus and Criseyde's love may itself be answered in the controversial Palinode, which does imply that human beings have the freedom to turn from worldly vanity.

Troilus and Criseyde was popular in its own time, surviving in 16 manuscripts and a number of fragments, plus three early printed editions. One of the manuscripts (Corpus Christi College, Cambridge, MS. 61) contains a remarkable miniature frontispiece of Chaucer reading the poem to the court of RICHARD II and ANNE OF BOHEMIA. The poem remains the most widely read and admired of Chaucer's poems after *The Canterbury Tales.*

Bibliography

Barney, Stephen A., ed. *Chaucer's Troilus: Essays in Criticism.* Hamden, Conn.: Archon Books, 1980.

Bloomfield, Morton W. "Distance and Predestination in Troilus and Criseyde," *PMLA* 72 (1957): 14–26.

Grady, Frank. "The Boethian Reader of *Troilus and Criseyde,*" *Chaucer Review* 33 (1999): 230–251.

Huppe, Bernard F. "The Unlikely Narrator: The Narrative Strategy of the *Troilus.*" In *Signs and Symbols in Chaucer's Poetry,* edited by John P. Hermann and John J. Burke, Jr., 174–191. Tuscaloosa: Alabama University Press, 1981.

Kellogg, Laura D. *Boccaccio's and Chaucer's Cressida.* New York: P. Lang, 1995.

Kirby, Thomas. *Chaucer's Troilus: A Study in Courtly Love.* Louisiana State University Studies 40. University, La.: Louisiana State University Press, 1940.

Mann, Jill. "Troilus' Swoon," *Chaucer Review* 14 (1980): 319–345.

McAlpine, Monica E. *The Genre of "Troilus and Criseyde."* Ithaca, N.Y.: Cornell University Press, 1978.

Meech, Sanford B. *Design in Chaucer's Troilus.* Syracuse, N.Y.: Syracuse University Press, 1959.

Pearcy, Roy J. " 'And Nysus doughter song with fresshe entrente': Tragedy and Romance in *Troilus and Criseyde,*" *Studies in the Age of Chaucer* 24 (2002): 269–297.

Salu, Mary, ed. *Essays on "Troilus and Criseyde."* Chaucer Studies, 3. Cambridge: D. S. Brewer: 1979.

Shoaf, R. A., and Catherine S. Cox, eds. *Chaucer's Troilus and Criseyde: Subgit to Alle Poesye: Essays in Criticism.* Binghamton, N.Y.: Medieval and Renaissance Texts and Studies, 1992.

Steadman, John M. *Disembodied Laughter: "Troilus" and the Apotheosis Tradition, A Reexamination of Narrative and Thematic Concerns.* Berkeley: University of California Press, 1972.

Vitto, Cindy L., and Marcia Smith Marzec, eds. *New Perspectives on Criseyde.* Fairview, N.C.: Pegasus Press, 2003.

Wetherbee, Winthrop. *Chaucer and the Poets: A Essay on "Troilus and Criseyde."* Ithaca, N.Y.: Cornell University Press, 1984.

Windeatt, Barry. "Chaucer and the *Filostrato.*" In *Chaucer and the Italian Trecento,* edited by Piero Boitani, 163–183. Cambridge: Cambridge University Press, 1983.

troubadours (12th and 13th centuries)

In the early 12th century, a group of courtly poets emerged in the south of France (the area known as Provence) composing love songs in Old Occitan. The basic concept of their poetry was the idea of *fin'amors:* a cultured, sophisticated form of love that aimed for the exploration of emotions, courtly behavior, and the playful interaction of men and women within an erotic context (often called, in modern times, COURTLY LOVE). The troubadours often allude to their sexual desires, but they seldom imply any sexual fulfillment because their poetry was predicated on the notion of unrequited love inspired by fear, hope, longing, and desire.

There are many theories regarding the origin of troubadour poetry, but no conclusive evidence has ever answered this complex question. No antecedents are known to us, unless we consider early medieval Latin poetry by Baudri of Bourgueil and Marbode of Rennes, for instance, as a decisive source of influence. Another possibility might have been the Mozarabic poets in Spain, who also composed so-called *KHARJAS,* vernacular strophes in Romance dialect (Hispano-Arabic) that conclude their love songs in classical Arabic. Scholars have also pointed to the renewed and intensive interest in the Virgin Mary from the early 12th century on, whom the troubadours might have had in mind when they sang songs of adulation of their beloved ladies. Moreover, in 12th-century Provence many courts were nearly deserted because a large percentage of noblemen had joined the crusades to the Holy Land and often never returned from the wars. It could have been that the large number of ladies left behind invited the remaining aristocratic poets to embark on a new cult of courtly love to fill the void. Possibly the crusaders were inspired by Arabic love poetry that they had heard of in Palestine and began to create their own songs after their return home. But it is equally possible that troubadour poetry emerged indigenously because, due to improved climatic, economic, and hence financial conditions, the higher aristocracy was being transformed into a leisure class with a taste for a new type of sophisticated erotic entertainment.

Etymologically the troubadour is a male poet who composes a song (*trobar*) or finds a melody. We also know of a small group of female poets, the *trobairitz*, who joined their male counterparts in the game of creating courtly love poetry. Whereas courtly love was first practiced in the south, by the late 12th century this cultural development had reached central and northern France, where the poets were called trouvères. The ideals of courtly love were concurrently and subsequently explored by the Middle High German *MINNESÄNGer* and, by the early 13th century, by south Italian and Sicilian poets.

The first known troubadour was GUILLAUME IX, duke of Aquitaine and count of Poitiers (1071–1127), who already demonstrated an amazing versatility in his poetry, composing both a song of *fin'amors*, about striving for unrequited love, and a downright bawdy love song, then a nonsense poem, and a religious song dealing with the departure from this world. MARCABRU, who belongs to the following generation, created the prototype of the *PASTOURELLE*, in which a male wooer tries to seduce—though unsuccessfully—a shepherdess who knows how to confound the man rhetorically. Marcabru also introduced a variety of different love scenes, perhaps even the topic of conjugal love. Some of the best-known 12th-century troubadours were Jaufre RUDEL, PEIRE D'ALVERNHE, RAIMBAUT D'ORANGE, BERNART DE VENTADORN, BERTRAN DE BORN, GIRAUT DE BORNELH, ARNAUT DANIEL, FOLQUET DE MARSEILLE, RAIMBAUT DE VAQUEIRAS, Peire VIDAL, and Peire CARDENAL. Many troubadours introduced their poems with images of nature, either winter or summer, depending on the theme of the song, whether the lover feels happy or sad, such as in the case of CERCAMON's "Qant la douch'aura s'amarcis" ("When the sweet breeze turns bitter") or Jaufré Rudel's "Lanquan li jorn son lonc en mai" ("When the days are long in May").

In the middle of the 12th century, Peire d'Alvernhe and Raimbaut d'Orange idealized the concept of *TROBAR CLUS* (closed composition, or arcane poetry) versus *TROBAR LEU* (easy composition, or light poetry). By the end of the 12th century, the Catalan Raimon Vidal wrote a treatise explaining the nature of troubadour poetry, the *Règles de trobar* (Rules of composition). In the 12th century, many of the traditional troubadours were so admired that other poets created more or less fictional biographical *VIDAS* (lives) and *RAZOS* (reasons), which were appended to the text collections and stated the poet's birth date and social rank, and described the type of poetry he wrote. While the earliest troubadour poems prove to be highly refreshing and innovative, the vast number of subsequent compositions by the 13th century tend to be very formalistic, rhetorically styled, repetitive, and obviously intended for public performance for courtly audiences.

During the first 140 years these courtly love poems were mostly handed down orally; the first manuscript with troubadour poetry dates from as late as 1254. The vast popularity of troubadour poetry is testified by 95 manuscripts still extant from the late Middle Ages. Only four of these manuscripts contain musical notation, and the melodies are copied down only nonmensurally, ignoring the rhythm and duration of each individual note. The entire tradition of troubadour poetry was anchored in an oral culture, and its preservation in manuscripts was only the result of a preservation effort by later generations. The earliest troubadours called their poems simply *cansos*, or *vers* (songs). Later poets differentiated between *CANSOS*, dealing with the ideal of *fin'amors*, and *SIRVENTES*, satires of personal, political, and moral shortcomings. Subcategories of troubadour poetry were the *pastourelle;* the *ALBA*—a dawn song in which man and woman, after they have spent a night together, are awakened in the morning and have to separate; the Crusade song—the lover has to go on a Crusade and laments the need to leave his mistress behind; the *planh*—funeral lament; and the *TENSO*—a DEBATE POEM in which man and woman explore the meaning of love or argue against each other about the significance of courtly love. Troubadour poetry comprises 2,542 compositions by about 450 poets; about 250 of these songs are accompanied by music.

Bibliography

Akehurst, F. R. P., and Judith M. Davis, eds. *A Handbook of the Troubadours.* Berkeley: University of California Press, 1995.

Gaunt, Simon, and Sarah Kay, eds. *The Troubadours: An Introduction.* Cambridge: Cambridge University Press, 1999.

Goldin, Frederick, ed. and trans. *Lyrics of the Troubadours and Trouvères: An Anthology and a History.* Garden City, N.Y.: Doubleday, 1973.

Hill, Raymond Thompson, and Thomas Goddard Bergin, eds. *Anthology of the Provençal Troubadours.* 2nd ed. Revised by T. G. Bergin with Susan Olson et al. New Haven, Conn.: Yale University Press, 1973.

Jensen, Frede, ed. and trans. *Troubadour Lyrics: A Bilingual Anthology.* New York: Peter Lang, 1998.

von der Werf, Hendrik. *The Chansons of the Troubadours and Trouvères: A Study of the Melodies and Their Relation to the Poems.* Utrecht, Netherlands: Oosthoek, 1972.

Wilhelm, James J., trans. *Lyrics of the Middle Ages: An Anthology.* New York and London: Garland, 1990.

Albrecht Classen

trouvères (fl. ca. 1150–late 13th century)

Once the rich TROUBADOUR poetry had developed in Provence in the south of France during the first half of the 12th century, formulated in the *langue d'oc* (the Provençal language), Old French poets in central and northern France also adopted the ideals and values associated with COURTLY LOVE, expressing themselves in the *langue d'oïl* or French vernacular. CHRÉTIEN DE TROYES, famous for his introduction of the Arthurian material in French literature, also composed the earliest trouvère poetry as early as 1160.

One crucial moment of cross-fertilization between the cultures of the south and north might have been the marriage of ELEANOR OF AQUITAINE with the Capetian king Louis VII of France in 1137. Her great interest in Occitan poetry—her grandfather had been the first troubadour poet GUILLAUME IX—carried over to her court in Paris, where she assumed the role of patron for many artists and writers. The social background of the trouvère poets was highly diverse, some being clergy, others nobles, clerks, bourgeois, and JONGLEURS. They composed mostly love poetry fairly similar to that created in Provence. Some of the best known trouvère poets were Chrétien de Troyes, Huon d'Oisi, CONON DE BÉTHUNE, GACE BRULÉ, BBLONDEL DE NESLE, le CHÂTELAIN DE COUCI, THIBAUT DE CHAMPAGNE, Colin MUSET, Gautier d'Epinal, Renaut de Beaujeu, Gautier de Dargies, Richart de Semilli, Guiot de Provins, and RUTEBEUF, but still the majority of trouvère poetry has come down to us anonymously.

Their themes were not particularly innovative; instead they dealt with a wide range of conflicts in love, mostly unrequited, but in contrast to the troubadour poetry, the French poets pursued less esoteric and metaphysical ideals and reflected upon concrete, socially identifiable situations. An unusual phenomenon proves to be the 13th-century school of poets, or poetic guild (*puy*), in Arras (*Puy d'Arras*), a town of 20,000 inhabitants. Here newfound wealth, based on trade and commerce, sparked the emergence of some 200 poets who composed courtly love poetry, although they intended it for a bourgeois audience. In clear contrast to troubadour poetry, however, a large number of trouvère poems were copied down in manuscripts along with their melodies (about 1,500 out of more than 2,500 songs). As in the case of the Occitan lyric poetry, we do not know what sources the trouvères used, except for some general remarks included in their own texts. One of their favorite themes was to raise an issue regarding the fundamental meaning of love, expressed in a *jeu parti,* or DEBATE POEM, that concludes with an appeal to a judge. Generally the trouvères explored the complex topic of love from a personal perspective, creating *chansons d'amour,* or *grand chants courtois.* In the *TENSO* (another type of debate poem) two persons exchange their opinions about the meaning and relevance of their poetry. Nevertheless the topic of unrequited, rejected, and unfulfilled love dominated the entire corpus of trouvère poetry, in which the singers mostly reflect upon their own feelings. Whereas the troubadour poets tended to imply their sexual desires more or less openly, their northern counterparts were rarely that explicit and limited their desires to lofty ideals of love. Some trouvère poets, such as Thibaut IV, count of Champagne and king of Navarre (1201–53), openly displayed their great delight in animal images and in references to classical mythology and to medieval literary figures, including Roland and Oliver, TRISTAN, and Merlin.

Most trouvère poems begin with an introductory stanza reflecting on nature or the desire to sing a song. The concluding stanza is also clearly marked, often followed by a partial stanza (envoi) in which the poet "sends" the song to the beloved or to someone in the audience. In a surprisingly large number of cases the poets adopt female voices who discuss issues of love (*CHANSON DE TOILE*). They also enjoyed political and other types of satire (*sotte chanson*), and often intended their songs for dances (*ballette, rondet, rotrouenge, estampie, motet*). Poets such as Rutebeuf (ca. 1230–ca. 1285) and ADAM DE LA HALLE (fl. 1277–88) introduced moral and ethical issues in their works. By the 14th century, trouvère poetry experienced a considerable revival through composers such as Guillaume de MACHAUT (ca. 1295–1377) and Eustache DESCHAMPS (1346–ca. 1407) who developed new musical forms, such as the RONDEAU, the BALLADE, and the *chanson.* Nevertheless by the 15th century, courtly love poetry became increasingly idealizing and artificial, perhaps best represented by CHARLES D'ORLÉANS's (1394–1465) compositions, dominated by melancholy.

Bibliography

Akehurst, F. R. P., and Judith M. Davis, eds. *A Handbook of the Troubadours.* Berkeley: University of California Press, 1995.

Goldin, Frederick, ed. and trans. *Lyrics of the Troubadours and Trouvères: An Anthology and a History.* Garden City, N.Y.: Doubleday, 1973.

Holmes, Urban T. *A History of Old French Literature from the Origins to 1300.* New York: Crofts, 1948.

Rosenberg, Samuel N., and Hans Tischler, eds. *Chanter m'estuet: Songs of the Trouvères.* Bloomington: Indiana University Press, 1981.

von der Werf, Hendrik. *The Chansons of the Troubadours and Trouvères: A Study of the Melodies and Their Relation to the Poems.* Utrecht, Netherlands: Oosthoek, 1972.

Albrecht Classen

Troy Book John Lydgate (1420)

The *Troy Book* by John LYDGATE is a 30,000-line narrative poem about the destruction of Troy. It is notable as an example of the way Lydgate (ca. 1370–ca. 1449), a Benedictine monk from the abbey of Bury St. Edmunds, used classical materials to comment on contemporary events.

The *Troy Book* was commissioned by Prince Hal, later Henry V, at 4:00 P.M. on Monday, 31 October 1412. Working on the task for eight years, Lydgate obviously reviewed many tales of Troy, including the French *Roman de Troie* (1160) by BENOÎT DE SAINTE-MAURE; the Latin *Historia Traoians* (1287) by GUIDO DELLE COLONNE; and the English *TROILUS AND CRISEYDE* by Geoffrey CHAUCER. Using Guido as the central framework for his version, Lydgate expanded and shaped the source materials to make a distinctly English version of the legend.

While it is impractical to summarize the entire poem in this brief entry, the main points follow: The poem is divided into five parts, framed by a prologue and an envoi. Part one deals with background on Troy, including the stories of Jason and the Argonauts, Hercules and the golden fleece, Medea's faithful love, and Hesione's abduction. The section ends with the destruction of old Troy. Part two begins with the rebuilding of Troy and then moves to Paris's mission of retaliation for the kidnapping of Hesione, which culminates in Paris's capture of Helen and their return to Troy with the Greek army in pursuit. Parts three and four cover the various battles between armies and individual heroes. Tangential stories include the love stories of Troilus and Criseyde and of Achilles and Polyxena. In part five, Troy surrenders to the Greeks and the poem follows the fate of the survivors, particularly Aeneas and Odysseus. Concluding comments that span the end of part five and the envoi warn against the vanity of worldly affairs and invoke blessings on Henry.

In language, the *Troy Book* demonstrates Lydgate's fondness for a flowery English style based on conventions of classical Latin poetry. In fact, of the more than 800 words that Lydgate is said to have introduced to English from Latin and the Romance languages, more than 200 appear for the first time in the *Troy Book.*

The *Troy Book* survives in 23 manuscripts and two pre-1600 printed editions. At least five of the known manuscripts include an illustration of a monk, presumably Lydgate, presenting the finished work to a king, presumably Henry. A stylized woodcut version of the presentation scene appears in one of the early printed editions. Other manuscripts may have included similar pictures, but the first leaves have been cut out of the manuscripts, presumably by someone who valued the picture more than the poem.

Bibliography

Bergen, Henry. *Lydgate's Troy Book: Edited from the Best Manuscripts with Introductions, Notes, and Glossary.* 4 vols. EETS, e.s. 97, 103, 106, and 126. London: Kegan Paul, Trench, Trübner, 1906–1935.

Ebin, Lois. *John Lydgate.* TEAS 407. Boston: Twayne, 1985.

Pearsall, Derek. *John Lydgate.* Charlottesville: University of Virginia Press, 1970.

Renoir, Alain. *The Poetry of John Lydgate.* Cambridge, Mass.: Harvard University Press, 1967.

Schirmer, Walter. *John Lydgate: A Study in the Culture of the XVth Century.* Translated by Ann E. Keep. Berkeley: University of California Press, 1961.

David Sprunger

Truth (*Balade de Bon Conseyl*) Geoffrey Chaucer (ca. 1386)

The lyric poem *Truth,* also called the *Balade de bon conseyl* or the "Ballade of Good Counsel," is one of CHAUCER's so-called "Boethian" lyrics, a set of short poems concerned with moral and philosophical subjects (which also includes *Gentilesse, Lak of Stedfastness,* and *The Former Age*), written in the 1380s, when Chaucer was involved with his translation of BOETHIUS's *CONSOLATION OF PHILOSOPHY.* It is one of the best known of Chaucer's lyrics, and, in his own time, seems to have been the most popular, surviving in 24 manuscripts.

The poem is a *BALLADE* of three RHYME ROYAL stanzas, concerned with the moral principle of "truth," a term that in the 14th century implied not only fidelity, but personal integrity and devotion to God—and, as a corollary to that, ethical right conduct in the world. Chaucer's "good counsel" consists chiefly of not following the crowd or becoming overly concerned with the baubles offered by Fortune, but keeping one's eyes on the heavenly reward. Each stanza ends with the refrain "And trouthe thee shal delivere, it is no drede"—that is, "truth shall free you, there is no fear," a clear allusion to Christ's words in John 8.32, that "the truth shall set you free."

In one manuscript the poem contains a final stanza, an envoi addressing a certain "Vache," a word that means "cow" but likely refers to the courtier Sir Philip de la Vache, who had lost his position in court about 1386. Puns on Vache's name, including the line "Forth, beste, out of thy stal!" (l. 18), add a typically Chaucerian humorous undertone to this profoundly serious poem.

Bibliography

Benson, Larry D., et al., eds. *The Riverside Chaucer.* 3rd ed. Boston: Houghton Mifflin, 1987.

Ruud, Jay. *"Many a Song and Many a Leccherous Lay": Tradition and Individuality in Chaucer's Lyric Poetry.* Garland Studies in Medieval Literature, 6. New York: Garland, 1992.

Scattergood, V. J., ed. *Oxford Guides to Chaucer: The Shorter Poems.* Oxford: Oxford University Press, 1995.

Turke and Sir Gawain, The (ca. 1500)

The Turke and Gawain is a late 15th-century ROMANCE in MIDDLE ENGLISH that is preserved in a 17th-century manuscript called the Percy Folio, along with three other late romances focusing on Sir GAWAIN, always the favorite of King ARTHUR's knights in medieval English literature. Along with *The Grene Knight, The Carle off Carlile,* and *The Marriage of Sir Gawain, The Turke and Gawain* is extant in a manuscript that appears to have been mutilated by household servants of the manuscript's owner, who tore half-pages from the text, apparently to light fires. Thus the surviving text of *The Turke and Gawain* has a number of large gaps, the 335 extant lines being only perhaps half of the original text. Thus much of the reconstructed plot of the story must be conjectured. Although the manuscript is late, the language and orthography of the text suggest that it was originally produced in the North or the North Midlands area of England. It is written in TAIL-RHYME stanzas—that is, in this case, stanzas rhyming *aabccb,* with the couplets in four-stress lines and the repeated *b* rhyme (the "tail") in three stress lines. It was a popular MINSTREL stanza, and the audience of this poem probably consisted of middle- or lower-class listeners likely to be found in the tavern or marketplace, as opposed to a very courtly audience.

The plot as we have it is an unlikely combination of the head-chopping game familiar from *SIR GAWAIN AND THE GREEN KNIGHT* and the folktale motif of three impossible tasks. As in many Arthurian romances, the peace of Arthur's court is disturbed by the arrival of an outsider, the Turke of the poem's title, who issues a challenge, demanding a champion from the court to exchange blows with him. Gawain accepts the challenge and gives the Turke a strong blow—apparently without weapon—but the Turke postpones his return blow, requiring Gawain to accompany him on a journey before deigning to complete his part of the challenge. The inordinately courteous Gawain agrees, and the Turke leads him through violent storms to a mysterious castle, where Gawain is fed. Gawain asks to receive the blow from the Turke that will fulfill his bargain, but instead the Turke requires Gawain to follow him to the Isle of Man, where they enter the castle of the king, a powerful giant. The Turke tells Gawain he will be tested, but that he will receive help from the Turke. Gawain is first forced to play a game of tennis against 17 giants who use a heavy brass ball that no one in England would be able to strike. With the help of the Turke, Gawain defeats the giants. The Turke then successfully accomplishes the second challenge—lifting a great chimney over his head and twirling it. The final challenge is a cauldron of molten lead into which the giant king intends to hurl Gawain. But the Turke, through the ruse of a cloak of invisibility, is able to burn the giant in the cauldron instead. After the tasks have been accomplished, rather than returning the blow he owes to Gawain, the Turke surprisingly bows his neck and asks Gawain to strike off his head. The decapitated Turke turns into the noble Sir Gromer, who had been enchanted in that alien form. Sir Gromer becomes the new king of the Isle of Man, and a number of enchanted captives are released as Gawain returns to Arthur's court.

The motifs of the story suggest a number of issues common to romance. Here the archetypal "other," the pagan Turk or Saracen, is converted to Christianity through a death and rebirth ritual that enables him to be resurrected as a Christian and a valuable member of Christian society. Meanwhile Sir Gawain, who is first offered the throne of Man but refuses it, remains the popular embodiment of chivalric virtues as the late medieval English audience sees him: one who is free to ride anywhere in search of adventure, rather than be tied to the responsibility of governing.

Bibliography

Hahn, Thomas, ed. *Sir Gawain: Eleven Romances and Tales.* Kalamazoo, Mich.: Medieval Institute Publications, 1995.

Jost, Jean E. "The Role of Violence in Aventure: 'The Ballad of King Arthur and the King of Cornwall' and 'The Turke and Gowin,' " *Arthurian Interpretations* 2, no. 2 (1988): 47–57.

Lyle, E. B. "*The Turk and Gawain* as Source of *Thomas of Ercledoune,*" *Forum for Modern Language Studies* 6 (1970): 98–102.

Ulrich von Liechtenstein (ca. 1200–1275)

We are surprisingly well informed about Ulrich von Liechtenstein's biography. He was born at the beginning of the 13th century, near Judenburg in Styria (modern Austria), and died on January 26, 1275. His name often appears in historical documents between 1227 and 1274, especially because he was appointed to important political posts in Styria, such as lord high steward from 1244 to 1245, court marshall from 1267 to 1272, and supreme provincial judge of Styria in 1272.

Ulrich has gained considerable fame in modern scholarship for his more or less fictional autobiography in verse, his *Frauendienst* (Service of ladies, ca. 1255), in which he provides many insights into his life as a knight and lover of courtly ladies. Foreshadowing significant developments in the literature of the early Renaissance, Ulrich here combines prose with verse, and letters with courtly love songs within the framework of his autobiography. Fitting for an esquire and subsequently for a knight, tournaments play the most significant role for Ulrich and his compatriots, and a major section of the *Frauendienst* discusses his organization of a series of tournaments while in disguise as Lady Venus, dressed in most impressive women's clothes (1227). On a second tour of tournaments (1240), Ulrich assumes the role of King ARTHUR and achieves similar success both as actor and as knight. Most of the names of the tournament participants can be verified historically.

Around 1257, Ulrich composed his *Frauenbuch* (Women's book) in which a lady and a knight, deploring the decline of courtly virtues, discuss with each other who might be responsible for it, what to do with homosexuality, and how to help women find sexual satisfaction within marriage. In the latter part the knight makes a number of suggestions on how to return to ideal courtly behavior. Here the traditional distinction between love and marriage is removed in favor of the latter, though Ulrich still embraces the traditional concept of wooing a courtly lady, which would inspire the young man to aspire to the highest ideals.

In his *Frauendienst,* Ulrich emphasizes that he composed 58 melodies for his songs, which do not differ remarkably from traditional courtly love poetry. However, when he reflects upon composing a dawn song (1987, stanzas 1622–1632; see *ALBA*), Ulrich sharply criticizes the reliance on castle guardians to protect lovers from being discovered early in the morning, which constitutes the basic framework for a dawn song; he suggests that such lovers should rely only on their own precaution.

Bibliography

Heinen, Hubert. "Ulrich von Lichtenstein: homo (il)literatus or Poet/Performer?" *Journal of English and Germanic Philology* 83 (1984): 159–172.

Spechtler, Franz Viktor, and Barbara Maier, eds. *Ich—Ulrich von Liechtenstein. Literatur und Politik im Mittelalter.* Klagenfurt, Austria: Wieser, 1999.

Ulrich von Liechtenstein. *Frauendienst.* Edited by Franz Viktor Spechtler. Göppingen, Germany: Kümmerle, 1987.

Thomas, J. W., trans. *Ulrich von Liechtenstein's Service of Ladies.* Chapel Hill: University of North Carolina Press, 1969.

Albrecht Classen

Ulrich von Zatzikhoven (late 12th century)

Ulrich von Zatzikhoven composed his Middle High German version of the LANCELOT romance, the *Lanzelet,* after 1194 or 1195. He seems to have been closely connected with the imperial court of the Hohenstaufen. According to linguistic evidence, Ulrich originated in southwest Germany and based his German translation, as he states, on Huc of Morville's *Lanzelete,* which does not exist today and which is not identical with CHRÉTIEN DE TROYES's *LANCELOT.* Ulrich claims that he did not alter his source at all when he translated it into Middle High German, but there are clear signs of influence from Chrétiens's and HARTMANN VON AUE's *Erec* and *Yvain* (*Iwein*) and WOLFRAM VON ESCHENBACH's *PARZIVAL.*

Although the *Lanzelet* has survived in only five manuscripts (ms. S. burnt in 1870), Ulrich's posterity remembered him with great respect. In the *Manessische Liederhandschrift* (ms. C), the fictionalized portrait of Waltram von Gresten shows the latter and his lady reading Ulrich's *Lanzelet.* The romance deals with a young prince whom a mermaid kidnaps and raises in her fairyland. When he is 15, he wants to become a knight and learn his name. This will be revealed to him, however, only once he has defeated Iweret von Belforet. Many of the subsequent events bear great similarity to those experienced by Parzival in Wolfram's romance, except that Lanzelet participates in a grand tournament and wins the prize. He rejects King ARTHUR's invitation to his court, however, because he does not know his own name. Only once he has learned his identity does he travel to Arthur, but many battles and serious conflicts erupt, which Lanzelet overcomes all the time. At one point he is made prisoner, but can escape with the help of Walwein, Tristant, Erec, and Karjet. Subsequently a mighty sorcerer has to be defeated, and finally the triumphant protagonist can assume the government of his inherited kingdom.

Bibliography

McLelland, Nicola. *Ulrich von Zatzikhoven's Lanzelet: Narrative Style and Entertainment.* Cambridge: Brewer, 2000.

Ulrich von Zatzikhoven. *Lanzelet.* Translated by Kenneth G. T. Webster. With an introduction by Roger Sherman Loomis. New York: Columbia University Press, 1951.

———. *Lanzelet: Eine Erzählung.* Edited by K. A. Hahn. Frankfurt am Main, Germany: Brönner, 1854. Reprinted with afterword and bibliography by Frederick Norman. Berlin: de Gruyter, 1965.

Albrecht Classen

Ulster Cycle

The tales of the Ulster Cycle belong to the genre of heroic legend and mythology and represent some of the finest examples of the medieval Irish epic that have survived. Rather than being presented as single tales, Irish mythology is organized into story groups, each of which concerns the adventures of a set of characters. There are four main story groups, or cycles, in Irish mythology: the Mythological Cycle, the Historical Cycle, the FENIAN CYCLE, and the Ulster Cycle. While it is tempting to view each cycle as a discrete entity, there are themes and main characters that appear frequently in several cycles. All offer details of early Irish society as a world dominated by warriors and cattle raids in which abductions and violence figure prominently. Most of the stories describe the significant life events of Irish heroes and heroines, mainly births, training, battles, feastings, marriages, and deaths. These men and women are presented not as gods, but as humans with superhuman abilities.

The oldest of the four cycles is the Ulster Cycle, which describes the actions of the heroes of Ulster from about 200 B.C.E. through the fourth century C.E. The action itself is contained geographically within the two Irish kingdoms of Ulster and Connacht that encompass the northwestern quadrant of Ireland. The tales of this cycle revolve around the activities of the king of Ulster, Conchobor Mac Nessa, and the adventures of his nephew, CUCHULAIN, particularly as they fight against the queen of the neighboring kingdom of Connacht, Medb, her husband, Ailill, and her lover, Fergus (who also happens to be an exiled former king of Ulster).

The central narrative is the *TÁIN BÓ CUAILNGE* (The cattle raid of Cooley), in which the conflicts between the kingdoms of Ulster and Connacht climax when Queen Medb invades Ulster in order to steal the Brown Bull of Cooley, a magnificent beast with magical properties. In the great battle that ensues, the young Cuchulain engages in a series of bloody single combats that always end in the death of his opponents. Although seemingly invincible, Cuchulain is eventually mortally wounded in a later story, but in typical heroic style, he has himself tied to a post so that he might die still standing.

The earliest extant version of the *Táin Bó Cuailnge* is contained in *The Book of Leinster,* which dates from the early 12th century. *The Yellow Book of Lecan* contains a later recension of the story from the late 14th or early 15th centuries. Both manuscripts are housed in Trinity College, Dublin. Despite the late dates of surviving manuscripts, linguistic evidence within the texts points to a much earlier composition date, certainly by the eighth century and perhaps as early as the fifth or sixth century. Like many literary works compiled over time from written and oral sources, the *Táin* bears the marks of several different scribes in the form of seemingly irrelevant glosses, major inconsistencies, plot repetition, and no single narrative voice.

Although the escapades of various heroes and heroines define the action of the tales, place-names in the Ulster Cycle are as central to the narratives as are the characters themselves. Many of the stories exist solely to provide the history behind the naming of particular physical features. In the final scenes of the *Táin,* almost more important than the fatal wounding of the prized bull of Cooley is its wandering across Ireland naming places as it limps along to its eventual death. The same focus on topographical elements and the origin of placenames is found throughout the Ulster Cycle and is a major element in medieval Irish and Celtic literature generally.

While the *Táin* is the single most important tale in the Ulster Cycle, there are about 100 other stories included in the Ulster grouping, most of which are preliminary to the action of the *Táin* and serve to introduce several of its main characters. One such story is *The EXILE OF THE SONS OF UISLIU,* the story of Derdriu (Deirdre), a beautiful young woman who is betrothed to the much older King Conchobor. Derdriu falls in love with one of Conchobor's knights, who must then choose between his loyalty to his king and his love of Derdriu with tragic results. This same theme of love vs. loyalty is explored in medieval Welsh literature, particularly in the tales of the *MABINOGION,* and becomes an important element in the tales of Arthurian legend.

Bibliography

Dillon, Myles. *Early Irish Literature.* Dublin: Four Courts Press, 1994.

Gantz, Jeffrey. *Early Irish Myths and Sagas.* London: Penguin Books, 1981.

Haywood, John, and Cunliffe, Barry. *Atlas of the Celtic World.* London: Thames and Hudson, 2001.

Kinsella, Thomas, ed. and trans. *The Tain.* Translated from the Irish epic *Táin Bó Cuailnge.* Dublin: The Dolmen Press, 1969.

Koch, John T., and Carey, John, eds. *The Celtic Heroic Age: Literary Sources for Ancient Celtic Europe and Early Ireland and Wales.* New York: David Brown, 2003.

Diane Korngiebel

Usk, Thomas (ca. 1350–1388)

Thomas Usk was embroiled in the tumultuous London political scene of the 1380s, gaining some notoriety for switching parties and betraying his former leader. He was, however, supported by the king, RICHARD II, until Usk's arrest and ultimate execution at the hands of the "Merciless Parliament" of 1388. At some point in the mid-1380s, Usk wrote his only surviving work, *The TESTAMENT OF LOVE,* a prose ALLEGORY based to a large extent on BOETHIUS's *CONSOLATION OF PHILOSOPHY.*

Usk was born in London. His father was a cap maker, and, like other tradesmen, Usk became a part of the political life of the city that was dominated by the trade guilds. Usk was a close supporter of the mayor John of Northampton, a leader of the Mercer's Guild that controlled London economically until 1383, when Northampton was defeated for reelection by Nicholas Brembre, supported by the Victualers' Guilds. When Northampton supporters rioted in London in early 1384, Brembre came down hard on the rioters, and arrested Northampton's followers. Usk fled London, but was caught and arrested in 1384.

It was at this point that Usk reversed his loyalties. It is possible that a private interview with the king himself ultimately swayed Usk's decision. While neither Brembre's nor Northampton's parties seems to have been innocent of corruption, Brembre was a strong supporter of the king; Usk apparently decided that he was wrong to have supported Northampton, and issued what is called his "Appeal," in which he details Northampton's plots against Brembre, and suggests that he had also conspired with members of the court opposed to the king. Usk's testimony helped to convict Northampton when he was brought to trial for treason in August of 1384, and when Northampton was condemned to death, he was saved only when the queen, ANNE OF BOHEMIA, stepped in and pleaded for clemency. Meanwhile Brembre put Usk in protective custody for three months, to keep him from possible retaliation by Northampton's disciples. It seems likely that Usk wrote most of his *Testament* during this period of confinement, in part to justify his apparent betrayal of Northampton—though he probably continued to work on it at least until his final arrest in 1387.

His shifting loyalties certainly worked in Usk's favor from 1385 to 1387, as he benefited from Richard's royal patronage. He became sergeant of arms to the king in 1385, and, in September of 1387, was appointed under-sheriff of Middlesex (including London). Fortune took a severe turn for Usk, however, when the king's uncle, the duke of Gloucester, seized power and began to weed out the king's advisers. Usk was arrested in late 1387.

Following the execution of Nicholas Brembre, Usk was brought to trial before what became known as the "Merciless Parliament" on March 3, 1388. He was quickly convicted of treason and sentenced to be hanged, drawn, and beheaded the following day. *The Testament of Love* is Usk's only literary legacy.

Bibliography

Shoaf, R. Allen, ed. *Thomas Usk: The Testament of Love.* Kalamazoo: Medieval Institute Publications, 1998.

Valentin et Orson (ca. 1498)

Valentin et Orson is a late medieval French prose text attached to the CHARLEMAGNE cycle of ROMANCES. It was apparently written during the reign of King Charles VIII (1483–98) and printed at Lyons about 1489. The story, essentially a folktale about twin brothers raised apart and reunited, was artificially attached to the court of Charlemagne's father, King Pepin, and after its popular French version appeared, it was translated into a number of European languages.

The romance tells the story of Bellisant, King Pepin's sister, who is wed to the Byzantine emperor, Alexander. She is falsely slandered by the archpriest of Constantinople and subsequently exiled by the emperor. In the forest she gives birth to twin boys. One of the children (Orson) is seized by a bear and carried off to be raised among the animals, and eventually becomes a wild man of the woods. The other twin (Valentin) is found by King Pepin himself and brought to court, where he is raised as a courtier and a knight.

Years later Valentin comes across Orson in the woods. With the special empathy of twins, the two recognize one another. Valentin overcomes his brother, brings him to court, and there domesticates and educates the wild man. Together the two have a number of adventures and, ultimately, rescue their imprisoned mother from a wicked giant named Ferragus. They are able to accomplish this with the help of the dwarf Pacolet, a servant of the giant who owns a fantastic wooden horse that instantaneously transports its rider wherever he desires.

There may have been an earlier French source for the 15th-century romance. But there are also Italian, Icelandic, German, and Dutch versions of the *Valentin et Orson* story. An English translation, entitled *The History of two Valyannte Brethren, Valentyne and Orson,* was made by Henry Watson and printed in 1550. There are a number of later English versions, including a BALLAD on the subject included in Thomas Percy's *Reliques* in the 18th century.

Bibliography

Dickson, Arthur. *Valentine and Orson: A Study in Late Medieval Romance.* 1929. New York: AMS Press, 1975.

Valentine and Orson. Translated by Henry Watson. Edited by Arthur Dickson. EETS, o.s. 204. London: Published for the Early English Text Society by the Oxford University Press, 1937.

Vercelli Book, The (*Codex Vercellensis*) (10th century)

Codex CXVII of the chapter library of the cathedral in Vercelli, Italy, is a manuscript generally known as The Vercelli Book. This is one of four manuscripts containing virtually all the extant poetry in OLD ENGLISH. The manuscript seems to have been copied in the late 10th century by a monastic scribe, possibly at Worcester, and is made up of 135 folios containing 23 sermons interspersed with six poems on religious subjects. The best known of these are *The DREAM OF THE ROOD* and two poems attributed to CYNEWULF, named *ELENE* and *The FATES OF THE APOSTLES* by modern editors.

The scribe seems to have constructed the text from a number of different pieces that came to him, with no particular plan in mind. This is apparent, in part, because he also seems to have copied the dialects of each of the different texts. It has been suggested that there is some thematic connection between the sermons and the poems that occur between them—for example the poems *Soul and Body* and *Falseness of Men* are placed immediately following a group of sermons dealing with penitence and Judgment Day. But such connections are rather loose.

How this manuscript of Old English religious prose and poetry came to belong to a cathedral in Italy is something of a mystery. It was discovered in Vercelli in 1822, by a German jurist, Friedrich Blume, while he was browsing for legal manuscripts. One suggestion is that it had belonged to a hospice for English pilgrims that had been founded in Vercelli in the 13th century.

Bibliography

Krapp, George Philip, and Elliott van Kirk Dobbie. *The Vercelli Book.* Anglo-Saxon Poetic Records, 2. New York: Columbia University Press, 1942.

Vice, The

The Vice is the generic name for a stock character in late medieval MORALITY PLAYS. Composed mainly as ALLEGORIES, these plays often presented a kind of psychomachia in which personified abstractions, representing aspects of the human mind, engaged in a battle for the soul of the play's hero, often called Mankind or Everyman, a character representative of all humankind. Sometimes this plot took the form of a battle between personified Virtues and Vices. The play might have a chief Vice, called something like Myscheff (Mischief), as in the play *MANKIND*, or Sensuality in the play *Mary Magdalene.* Later writers referred to the character simply as the Vice.

The Vice was typically a sinister but often comic tempter in the service of the Devil. He was a boisterous mischief-maker whose part, as the morality play developed as a genre, became chiefly farcical. He might be dressed as a fool, and ride upon the Devil's back. Typically, he engaged in puns and practical jokes, playing them on everyone in the play, even the Devil himself, in whose service he was nominally engaged. He had a tendency to introduce himself to the viewers and announce baldly that he was a villain, to make side comments to the audience, and to comment on the action. He might disguise himself as a Virtue, and so might have an enigmatic name such as Ambidextrous. But he engaged in a good deal of slapstick comedy, and he was, therefore, a very popular figure—one that audiences enjoyed seeing well into the 16th century. It seems likely that certain characters in Elizabethan drama—the ironic and cynical villains like Iago and Richard III who consistently address the audience—are later developments of the Vice figure from medieval drama. Very likely the same is true for Shakespeare's Falstaff, the comical corrupter of young Prince Hal, who is even called "that reverend vice" at one point (*1 Henry IV*.2.3.458).

Bibliography

Chambers, E. K. *The Mediaeval Stage.* London: Oxford University Press, 1903.

Cushman, L. W. *The Devil and the Vice in the English Dramatic Literature Before Shakespeare.* New York: Humanities Press, 1970.

Vicente, Gil (ca. 1465–1536)

Gil Vicente was a major Portuguese-born playwright and lyric poet who composed plays in a variety of genres and wrote in both the Portuguese and Castilian languages. A court poet who wrote some 44 extant plays, Vicente is considered by some critics to be the last and best representative of medieval Portuguese drama, and by others to be the first important Renaissance dramatist in Portugal.

Little is certain in our knowledge of Vicente's life. He may have been born in Lisbon, but some believe he was born in the country, perhaps the province of Beira Alta. It has been suggested that he studied law at the University of Lisbon, but it would appear by the evidence in his plays that he was self-educated. He may have been a goldsmith and financial adviser to the Portuguese court, but there are those who believe the goldsmith Vicente was the poet's relative. If the playwright was in fact the goldsmith, he was made master of the Royal Mint from 1513 to 1517. It is certain that the poet was an actor and director of court pageants as well as a playwright during the reigns of the Portuguese kings Manuel I and Juan III, so that a number of his plays appear to have been written as occasional pieces for courtly entertainment. He produced his plays between 1502 and 1536—therefore, it is assumed he died shortly after 1536.

Of Vicente's 44 plays, 16 are written in Portuguese, 11 are in Castilian Spanish (which was becoming the preferred language among Portuguese court poets), and 11 are bilingual. His first play is called the *Visitação* (Visitation), and was written to commemorate the 1502 birth of King Manuel and queen Maria's heir, Prince Juan. In it a shepherd visits the queen's bedchamber to congratulate her on the prince's birth. Another play clearly written to flatter the court, specifically regarding Portugal's new overseas adventures, is the allegory *Auto da Fama* (Play of fame, 1515), in which Fame is courted by France, by Italy, and by Spain in turn, but rejects them all in favor of Portugal.

Vicente's other plays comprise a variety of genres, including farce, comedy, tragicomedy, chivalric play, and religious play. His best-known religious plays are the trilogy of "ship" plays: the *Auto da barca do Inferno* (Ship of hell, 1517), the *Auto da barca do Purgatorio* (Ship of purgatory, 1518), and the *Auto da barca da Glória* (Ship of glory, 1519). These allegorical plays deal with human vices and with the judgment of souls after death. They include bitterly satiric portraits of royal and clerical souls expressing their outrage at being consigned to hell. Another of Vicente's well-known religious plays is the *Auto da Sibila Casandra* (Play of the prophetess Casandra, ca. 1509), in which a shepherdess named Casandra refuses marriage because she believes herself to be the virgin destined to become the mother of the Messiah. After being reproved for her pride, Casandra is finally depicted worshipping at Christ's actual nativity.

Vicente's chivalric plays, both written in Castilian, are more complex than his other works. *Dom Duardos* (ca. 1522), his longest play, presents scenes from the Palmerín cycle of ROMANCES, focusing on the episode in the story where Dom Duardos, disguised as a gardener, courts Flérida, princess of Constantinople. *Amadis de Gaula* (ca. 1523) is, of course, based on a few episodes in the Amadis cycle. Some of Vicente's other plays include two farces based on the very popular *CELESTINA*. One of his last plays, *The Auto da Mofina Mendes* (1534), has drawn some scholarly attention for the apparent influence of Erasmus suggested by its opening scene, which satirizes friars and scholasticism—a scene that resulted in the play's condemnation by the Spanish Inquisition.

Vicente's works were published by his son, Luis, in Lisbon in 1562, with royal sponsorship that saved the book from the censorship of the Inquisition. His plays depict a wide assortment of characters and portray a range of Portuguese society. The tone of the plays varies from the devoutly religious to the bitingly satirical. He does not spare the corrupt clergy or the arrogant nobility. Apparently an accomplished musician, Vicente also included a number of songs in his plays. He is called by some the Portuguese Plautus, emphasizing his seminal role in Portuguese drama, particularly comedy. Vicente is universally recognized as one of the major influences on Renaissance drama in Spain and Portugal.

Bibliography

Bell, Aubrey F. G., ed. and trans. *Four Plays of Gil Vicente.* Cambridge: Cambridge University Press, 1920.

Garay, René Pedro. *Gil Vicente and the Development of the Comedia.* Chapel Hill: University of North Carolina Department of Romance Languages, 1988.

Parker, Jack Horace. *Gil Vicente.* New York: Twayne, 1967.

Stathatos, Constantin C. *A Gil Vicente Bibliography (1925–2000).* Kassel, Germany: Edition Reichenberger, 2001.

vida

The scribes that compiled some of the earliest anthologies of TROUBADOUR poetry in the 13th and 14th centuries prefaced the work of each poet with a short biography in prose, known as *vidas.* These accounts are seldom more than a few sentences long, and usually give such information as the poet's parentage and where he was born, what class he belonged to and who his patrons were, who his great loves were, what kind of person he was, the kind and quality of poetry he wrote, and where he died. There are *vidas* for about 100 troubadours, surviving in some 20 manuscripts, mostly produced in northern Italy; five of these date from the 13th century. *Vidas* are to be distinguished from *RAZOS*, which are generally longer prose introductions to individual troubadour poems in the anthologies.

The *vidas* are the largest source of biographical information we have concerning the troubadours, and also one of the least reliable. While many of the historical and geographical facts found in the *vidas* are verifiable, the information in the *vidas* comes from a variety of nonbiographical sources, including popular folktales, *SAINTS'* LIVES, and even FABLIAUX. But the single largest source of information for the *vidas* is the troubadours' own body of poetry. Thus the *vida* for Jaufré RUDEL, famous for his poetry extolling his "love far away," includes the fanciful notion that he fell in love with the countess of Tripoli without ever having seen her, and that he traveled to find her only to die in her arms. None of this is verifiable, but it is a fanciful extrapolation from Jaufré's poetry.

Recently some attention has been paid to the prose *vidas* as literary creations in their own right. Recent studies have argued that there are stylistic similarities in most of the earlier *vidas* and *razos,* enough to suggest that they were all originally composed by a single writer. Two manuscripts contain references to an author named Uc de Saint-Circ, and, according to Elizabeth W. Poe, "we can take as a working assumption that all of the *vidas* and *razos* pertaining to events before 1257 or so were the work of Uc" (1995, 188). Uc, a JONGLEUR educated at Montpellier, seems to have collected *vidas* and *razos* already current among other jongleurs, added historical and geographical details he may have researched, and composed the *vidas* all in his own style.

Poe describes characteristics of Uc's style, noting that humor and wordplay are common in the *vidas.* For example Uc will sometimes ironically juxtapose incongruous items using the conjunction "and," as when he calls GUILLAUME IX "one of the most courtly men in the world and one of the greatest deceivers of women" (Poe 1995, 194). Uc will also sometimes add things as unexpected afterthoughts in a manner that creates a humorous effect, as in the *vida* of Peire de Valeira: "His songs did not have much value," Uc says, and then adds "and neither did he" (Poe 1995, 194).

Bibliography

Egan, Margarita. *The Vidas of the Troubadours.* Garland Library of Medieval Literature, 6. New York: Garland, 1984.

Poe, Elizabeth W. "The Vidas and Razos." In *A Handbook of the Troubadours,* edited by F. R. P. Akehurst and Judith M. Davis, 185–197. Berkeley: University of California Press, 1995.

Vidal, Peire (ca. 1160–ca. 1205)

One of the best known and most accessible of the Provencal TROUBADOURS is the poet and musician Peire Vidal. Peire traveled extensively through France, Italy, Spain, Cyprus, Malta, Palestine, and Hungary, and his verses abound with references to these places. He also names a number of noblemen in these various places with whom he was acquainted and some of whom were his patrons, including such great lords as King Alfonso II of Aragon, Vicomte Barral of Marseille, Count Roman V of Toulouse, and by some accounts King RICHARD I of England.

Peire was born in Toulouse, the son of a furrier. He led an adventurous life and was apparently something of an eccentric character, though some of his escapades, taken seriously in his *VIDA*, are based on humorous boasts he makes in his poetry, and were never intended to be taken seriously. But his lively interest in the politics of his time as well as in the writing of love poetry makes him interesting for modern readers, as does his cultivation of the *TROBAR RIC* style, which joined elaborate verse forms to clear, straightforward themes. Some 40 of his poems are extant, 13 of them with surviving melodies.

Perhaps the most remarkable aspect of Peire's lyrics is his creation of "hybrid" forms that combine elements of the *CANSO*, or love song, with elements of the *SIRVENTES*, or political song, sometimes within the same stanza of a poem, as in the following:

> *God and Saint Julian shelter me now*
> *in this sweet land of Canavès;*
> *for I shall never go back to Provence,*
> *Lanerio and Aglaiano make me welcome here.*
>
> *And if I could have her, whom I have so long entreated,*
> *let the valiant King En Alfons remain up there,*
> *and I would make my poetry and songs right here,*
> *for the gentlest lady ever begged for love.*
>
> *And since Milan is at the crest,*
> *I wish it were at peace with Pavia,*
> *and Lombardy defending itself*
> *from vicious brutes and murderous bandits.*
>
> (Goldin 1973, 265, ll. 25–36)

Here Peire makes a political statement, supporting the Lombards against the emperor; praises the land he is in and his lady; and acknowledges his lord Alfonso of Aragon, who is lord of Provence—and he does it all within 10 lines of the same poem. This kind of combination was unprecedented in troubadour poetry, and has led Frederick Goldin to call Peire "a performer who does not limit himself to the traditional roles but mixes them up and so surprises his audience" (1973, 248).

Another fascinating aspect of Peire's poetry is his use of outrageous boasts, a habit he seems to have picked up from the poetry of GUILLAUME IX. These suggest a poet on close terms with his audience—an audience that knows when the poet is engaging in self-mockery. In one of his poems, Peire says:

> *there never was a man so pleasing in chamber*
> *or so savage and excellent in armor,*
> *and so I am loved and dreaded by such as do not even*
> *see me or hear my words.*
>
> (Goldin 1973, 251, ll. 22–24)

Peire remains one of the most popular of the troubadours, his poetry full of passion, adventure, and eccentricity.

Bibliography

Goldin, Frederick, ed. and trans. *Lyrics of the Troubadours and Trouvères: An Anthology and a History.* Garden City, N.Y.: Doubleday, 1973.

Vidyāpati (ca. 1352–ca. 1448)

Vidyāpati was a Brahman court poet serving the kings of Mithila, just west of modern Bengal, probably in the late 14th and early 15th centuries. His poetry, though written in the local dialect, displays a scholar's knowledge of Sanskrit. Other facts of his biography are uncertain, though there are many traditions concerning his life. Most important, he wrote some of the most popular poems associated with the Vaishnava sect (those devoted to the worship of Vishnu as god), a group particularly devoted to Vishnu's incarnation as Krishna. As such, he was involved in the widespread spiritual movement called bhakto (sharing [in god]) that characterized the Hindu religion of the 12th through 18th centuries, though some have questioned whether he was himself a bhakta poet-saint.

According to tradition Vidyāpati was born in northeast Bihar in a village in Madhubani called Bisapi. A member of the Brahman caste, he would have studied Sanskrit as a youth. He is said to have received a commission from the Mathili king Kirti Simha to write a poem in praise of the king, and then to have become court poet under Kirti's son Deva Simha. One legend says that when his king was captured by the mogul leaders of Delhi, Vidyāpati was able to obtain Simha's release by winning over the mogul king through his poetry. There is, however, no real certainty to any of these biographical details.

Indeed there is no certainty as to Vidyāpati 's authorship of the more than 500 love poems attributed to him and reputed to have been written between 1380 and 1406. Although Vaishnava poems conventionally include what is called a *bhanitā* or signature line, the question of authorship in these poems is complex. For one thing it was customary for devotees to assume a religious name, and it was not uncommon for many people to have the same religious name. Poets were futher inclined to adopt the name of an earlier, well-known poet who may have inspired them as a tribute or as a means of lending authority to their own religious stance. Thus we cannot be sure that the same Vidyāpati wrote all the poems attributed to him. The matter is complicated by the fact that some poems attributed to Vidyāpati appear in other manuscript collections ascribed to someone named Sekhara.

The Vidyāpati poems, though, speak for themselves, whoever their author was. The poems show a familiarity with the tradition of Sanskrit court poetry of love, but focus chiefly on the myth of Krishna's love affair with the *gopī*, or herdswoman, Rhādhā, which had become popular with the Bengal Vaishnava saints. The myth of their erotic love became a metaphor for the passionate desire existing between god and the human soul (represented by Rhādhā). The ending of one such poem might serve as an example of the desired unity between god and the soul:

As wing to bird,
water to fish,
life to the living—so you to me.
But tell me,
Madhava, beloved,
who are you?
Who are you really?
Vidyāpati says, they are one another.

(Dimock and Levertov 1965, 15)

Bibliography

Bhattacharya, Deben, trans. *Love Songs of Vidyapati.* Edited with notes and introduction by W. G. Archer. New York: Grove Press, 1970.

Dimock, Edward C., and Denise Levertov, ed. and trans. *In Praise of Krishna.* Garden City, N.Y.: Doubleday, 1967.

Villehardouin, Geoffroi de (ca. 1150–before 1218)

Geoffroi composed, in prose, one of the two French eyewitness accounts of the conquest of Constantinople by the Christian crusaders in 1204, *La Conquête de Constantinople,* famous for its detailed and precise descriptions. He was the son of a noble Champenois family and served the count of Champagne, Thibaut III, as marshal (beginning in 1185) and gained a reputation for his mediating skills. Thibaut, who was one of the organizers of the Fourth Crusade, heavily relied on Geoffroi for the diplomatic preparations. He sent him, along with CONON DE BÉTHUNE, to Venice in 1201, to negotiate the sea voyage on Venetian ships. In return for his diplomatic and, more important, his military services, Geoffroi was appointed marshal of Romania in 1205. In the same year Geoffroi led an expedition against the Bulgarians, and he was involved in securing the retreat to safety after the defeat of the crusaders in the Battle of Adrianople the same year. In 1208 he was appointed the commander of the royal guard in Constantinople. The historical records last mention him in 1212, and in 1218, his son arranged a memorial for him.

Geoffroi wrote his chronicle of the Fourth Crusade after the actual events and insists that he is telling nothing but the truth, though this has been questioned in modern times. He begins with the preaching of the Crusade by Foulques de Neuilly during the tournament of Ecry on November 28, 1199, and closes during the year 1207, with the death of Boniface of Montferrat. Geoffroi's intention seems to have been the defense of the Crusade against the criticism that only the two Christian cities of Zara and Constantinople had been attacked and conquered, whereas the crusaders never made it to Jerusalem. He justifies this by the lack of support from European knighthood to pay the Venetians for the passage, which forced the crusaders to take Zara to extort the money, and by the fact that many knights later deserted the army. Moreover Geoffroi identifies the greed and sinfulness of the Cistercians—who condemned the attack against Christian cities—and of the crusaders as responsible for the failure of the Fourth Crusade, whereas he tends to whitewash the noble leaders, especially Thibaut (who died in 1201), and later Boniface de Montferrat, who conquered Constantinople. Geoffroi's chronicle circulated in a number of manuscript copies, six of which are still extant, and in two early printed editions, which are lost today. Two fragments of the *Conquête* are also extant, as is a copy in the popular 13th-century *Chronique de Baudouin d'Avesnes.* It was translated into Latin in 1573, then into Italian, English, German, and Bulgarian.

Bibliography

Beer, Jeanette M. A. *Villehardouin: Epic Historian.* Geneva: Droz, 1968.

Geoffroi de Villehardouin, *La conquête de Constantinople,* edited by Edmond Faral. 2 vols. 2nd ed. Paris: Les Belles Lettres, 1937.

Lock, Peter. *The Franks in the Aegean, 1204–1500.* London: Longman, 1995.

Marzials, Frank, trans. *Memoirs of the Crusades.* Westport, Conn.: Greenwood Press, 1983.

Noble, Peter. "Villehardouin, Robert de Clari and Henri de Valenciennes: Their Different Approaches to the Fourth Crusade," in *The Medieval Chronicle,* edited by Erik Kooper. Amsterdam and Atlanta: Editions Rodopi, 1999, 202–211.

Shaw, Margaret R. B., ed. and trans. *Chronicles of the Crusades.* Harmondsworth, U.K.: Penguin, 1983.

Albrecht Classen

Villon, François (1431–1463)

Since medievalists have rediscovered the 15th century as a fertile period in the history of late medieval literature, they have always celebrated the provocative, often outrageous, poems by François Villon. His contemporaries, however, did not seem to have had much respect for him, and he obviously failed in his plans to achieve the status of a court poet and to secure a patron. Although he was once a guest at CHARLES D'ORLÉANS's court and wrote several poems for him, this did not translate into public recognition of his poetic art. Villon was of humble origin, as he tells us in his rhymed *TESTAMENT* (vv. 273–75) (composed in 1431). Because of financial woes his mother entrusted the child to her relative, Guillaume de Villon, chaplain of the Parisian church of Saint-Benoît-le-Bétourné. François's original name was Montcorbier, or des Loges, but he adopted the name of the chaplain, who made sure that Villon gained a solid education, which led to a university baccalaureate degree in 1449, and the degree of *magister* (master) in 1452. But Villon, as we call him now, could not find steady employment, and soon got into conflict with the law. In 1455 he killed a priest in a quarrel, fled from Paris, and later pleaded that he had acted in self-defense, a plea that was subsequently accepted. In 1456, he committed burglary and fled from Paris once again. At this time he began the long cycle of his *Lais.* In 1457, Villon visited Charles d'Orléans in Blois, and wrote three poems for him. In 1461, Villon was a prisoner in Meung-sur-Loire, but the recently enthroned King Louis XI granted him and other prisoners amnesty. Villon immediately returned to Paris, where he began a collection of poems under the title *Testament.* In the fall of that year the poet was again charged with burglary, but was soon released. Only a few days later Villon was involved in a street brawl in which a notary was stabbed. This time Villon was sentenced to be executed, but his appeal to the secular court of Parlement was successful, since they converted the death penalty to banishment from Paris for 10 years. Villon left us several poems about this incident, and beyond that, we have no police records or further poems by Villon.

In his *Lais* (320 verses grouped into octaves in which he metaphorically says good-bye to all his friends, his mistress, and his own property), in his *Testament* (more than 2,000 verses), and also in his many miscellaneous poems, Villon talks much about himself, his miserable life, his failures, and his misfortunes in love. The poet also voices sarcastic criticism of the church, the university, and the general social ills of his time. The more we can identify Villon as a man without any career or family life, the more we must credit him with an astonishing creativity and innovative quality in his poetry. Being free of any literary patronage—which was, of course, to his personal disadvantage—Villon was independent enough to explore a wide range of topics and poetic forms with which he left his unique mark on 15th-century French poetry. More than any other contemporary poet—perhaps with the only exception of the German poet Oswald von Wolkenstein from South Tyrol (1376/77–1445)—Villon projects a poetic autobiography without following the rigid framework of a narrative autobiography. In his individual poems he addresses himself, his friends, his enemies, then an imaginary reader, and he constantly combines ironic comments with crude jokes, and incorporates learned references, gibes, and puns.

Villon openly admitted his disappointment with life and regularly tried to find a scapegoat for his many failures, and although he often blamed the church for many of his own problems, the poet still firmly embraced the Christian faith in a manner typical for his time. Villon repeatedly resorted to the topos of the *ubi sunt* formula, reflecting upon the transitoriness of life in general and of his personal situation in particular. In formal terms Villon heavily relied on the traditional genres of the *BALLADE* and the RONDEAU. In contrast to GUILLAUME DE MACHAUT (the most influential French poet of the previous century), Villon did not set his poems to music, but intended them to be read aloud. A few examples will quickly illustrate the richness of Villon's poetic discourse. When he laments about his poverty (*Testament* no. 36), he assures himself that it is better to be poor than once to have been a rich lord and "now to rot in a rich tomb" (Villon 1994, l. 288). Considering the deaths of all the famous and wealthy people before him, Villon wonders about his own destiny. He knows that he will die as well, but he places all emphasis on his own life at the present: "Provided I've enjoyed myself / I do not mind a decent death" (ll. 419–20). Proud of his advanced education, the poet includes references to Orpheus and Narcissus (ll. 633–640), but he always reminds his readers that he sees himself in the center of life: "About poor me I want to speak, / Beaten like laundry at a stream" (ll. 657–658). Villon admits that he failed in love (ll. 713ff.), and also alludes to a water torture he was exposed to during his imprisonment (ll. 737–738). The *Testament* concludes with an epitaph for his own tomb and then some ballads in which he sarcastically expresses his forgiveness to all those who hurt him in his life.

Although it would be inappropriate to identify Villon's poems as autobiographical in the narrow sense, they clearly stand out for their highly individualized perspectives and the directness with which he approaches his readers and listeners, although in one of his *ballades,* he also admits: "I know all things except myself" (VI, 8). He never expresses any respect for political and philosophical authorities and argues, for example, that he gained more understanding of life through wandering the world than from reading AVERROËS's commentaries on Aristotle (*Testament,* 89–96). This refreshing individualism that pokes fun at everything and everyone represents the decisive rupture that was to separate the Middle Ages from the Renaissance.

Villon's works were preserved in some manuscripts and quite a number of early modern prints, but his true recognition did not come until 1832, when Jean Henri Romain Prompsault published his complete works for the first time, based on a solid examination of the relevant manuscripts.

Bibliography

Burl, Aubrey. *Danse macabre: François Villon, Poetry, & Murder in Medieval France.* Stroud, Gloucestershire, U.K.: Sutton, 2000.

Fein, David. *François Villon Revisited.* New York: Twayne, 1997.

Sargent-Baur, Barbara N. *Brothers of Dragons: Job dolens and François Villon.* New York: Garland, 1990.

Taylor, Jane H. M. *The Poetry of François Villon: Text and Context.* Cambridge and New York: Cambridge University Press, 2001.

Villon, François. *Complete Poems.* Edited with English translations and commentary by Barbara N. Sargent-Baur. Toronto: Toronto University Press, 1994.

Albrecht Classen

Vinland Sagas (13th century)

Two 13th-century Icelandic family SAGAS that relate independent traditions concerning the Norse exploration of the North American continent around the year 1000 are known collectively as the *Vinland Sagas,* taking their title from the name the Icelanders gave to the area of North America they discovered—a name that means "Wineland," referring to the vines that were found growing naturally. The two accounts, known as *Grœnlendnga saga* (*The Greenlanders' Saga*) and *Eiríks saga rauða* (*Eirik the Red's Saga*), both detail several voyages from Norse Greenland to Vinland, though the two versions differ in many of the details regarding these voyages. In both sagas Leif Eiriksson, son of Eirik the Red, first settler of Greenland, is the driving force for the exploration of the new land, and his family members take a major role in the voyages. In particular the role of Leif's sister-in-law Gudrid and her husband Thorfinn Karlsefni is important in both texts. Both sagas describe the attraction of Vinland—its vines and abundant wheat growing wild, but both suggest that Norse attempts to settle in Vinland were abandoned because of fierce resistance from the native peoples of the land, called Skraelings in the sagas.

Most scholars think that the *Greenlanders' Saga* is the earlier of the two, dating from shortly after 1200. The saga survives only as interpolations in a saga concerning Norway's King Olaf Tryggvason preserved in a 1388 manuscript called the *Flateyarbók. The Greenlanders' Saga* is somewhat rough and episodic, but is likely to be closer to historical fact than *Eirik's Saga. Eirik's Saga* is extant in two manuscripts, one from the early 1300s and the other from about 1400. Scholars have determined that *Eirik's Saga* must have been written after 1264. Its literary style is more sophisticated, and the narrative more coherent, but scholars believe that a number of incongruous Christian elements, such as the suggestion that Leif Eiriksson was on a mission to Christianize Greenland, make *Eirik's Saga* less reliable historically than the *Greenlanders' Saga.*

It was once thought that *Eirik's Saga* was a later writer's attempt to refine and polish the story of *The Greenlanders' Saga,* but there is little evidence of that: The differences in the tales are simply too great. First, while in both sagas Eirik's discovery and settlement of Greenland in 985 is a vital first step to Vinland, in the *Greenlanders' Saga* it is Bjarni Herjolfsson who first sights land to the west, having been blown off course while trying to visit his father in Greenland. Leif Eiriksson, faulting Bjarni for his lack of curiosity, sets out deliberately to explore those lands, and names them Helluland (Flat-Rock Land), Markland (Forest Land), and Vinland (Wineland). In *Eirik's Saga* it is Leif, after visiting Norway and receiving a charge from King Olaf Tryggvason to Christianize Greenland, who goes off course and accidentally discovers Vinland.

Secondly, according to the *Greenlanders' Saga,* Leif's brother Thorvald Eiriksson makes a separate voyage to Vinland, but is killed by a Skraeling's arrow after provoking battle with the natives. In *Eirik's Saga* Thorvald goes along on the expedition of Thorfinn Karlsefni, and is killed by an arrow from the bow of a Uniped, a fantastic one-footed creature.

In both sagas Thorstein Eiriksson, another of Leif's brothers, makes an unsuccessful attempt to find Vinland. In the *Greenlanders' Saga* he marries Gudrid before setting out. He brings her on the voyage, but they go off course and wind up stranded at Lyusfjord, where he dies. In *Eirik's Saga*

Thorstein marries Gudrid after returning from his fruitless voyage, and they settle in Lyusfjord. But in both stories his corpse sits up and prophesies that Gudrid will marry again and have an illustrious family.

Further, Leif's half sister Freydis is portrayed differently in the two sagas. In the *Greenlanders' Saga,* she takes her own expedition to Vinland, where she brutally murders her partners (killing the women with an axe), and is cursed by Leif when she arrives back in Greenland. In *Eirik's Saga* she is a part of Karlsefni's expedition, where the pregnant Freydis distinguishes herself for her ferocity by beating her naked breast with a sword to frighten off Skraeling attackers.

A final difference in the sagas is the amount of space devoted to Thorfinn Karlsefni's voyage in *Eirik's Saga,* where it clearly dominates the story. Thorfinn, who has married Gudrid, Thorstein Eiriksson's widow, takes a large expedition to Vinland in an attempt to trade with the natives and set up a permanent settlement. Here Gudrid gives birth to their son, Snorri, the first European born on the North American continent. Ultimately internal quarrels among the Norsemen and the antagonism of the Skraelings force them back to Iceland. In both sagas Thorfinn and Gudrid settle in the north of Iceland at Skagafjord, and Gudrid's descendants include three prominent Icelandic bishops.

The differences in the sagas and their inclusion of supernatural or marvelous incidents have made their historical value questionable and for some time raised doubts about whether such voyages actually took place. There is some independent corroboration of the tales, however: The German historian Adam of Bremen wrote, in ca. 1075, that he learned of Norse voyages to "Wineland" from the Swedish king Swen Estrithsson. Later historical references also suggest that, though the Greenlanders gave up trying to colonize Vinland, they still made occasional trips there to gather timber, even through the 14th century. The similarities of the sagas—their focus on Leif Eiriksson as well as on Karlsefni and Gudrid and the Skraelings—suggest that the details of an original oral account of the Vinland voyages, passed down through two and a half centuries to two separate authors, was distorted by oral tradition but retained some basic historical facts.

Attempts to locate the actual site of Vinland on the east coast of North America were fruitless until 1961, when the Norwegian archaeologist Helge Ingstad discovered an unquestionably Norse site at the northern tip of Newfoundland, called L'Anse aux Meadows. Ingstad's discovery proved that the accounts in the sagas were not simply romantic fabrications, but memories of real events. But there are no grapes in Newfoundland, and in all medieval accounts it is the naturally occurring grapevines that gave the place its Norse name. This suggests that Leif's Vinland must have been further south—but Ingstad's site remains the only Norse site ever discovered in the Americas.

Bibliography

Ingstad, Helge. *Westward to Vinland: The Discovery of Pre-Columbian Norse House-sites in North America.* Translated by Erik J. Friis. London: Cape, 1969.

Jones, Gwyn, trans. *Eirik the Red and Other Icelandic Sagas.* Oxford: Oxford University Press, 1980.

———. *The Norse Atlantic Saga: Being the Norse Voyages of Discovery and Settlement to Iceland, Greenland, and North America.* 2nd ed. Oxford: Oxford University Press, 1986.

Magnusson, Magnus, and Hermann Palsson. *The Vinland Sagas.* Harmondworth, U.K.: Penguin, 1965.

The Sagas of Icelanders: A Selection. With a preface by Jane Smiley and an introduction by Robert Kellogg. New York: Viking, 1997.

virelai (virelay)

The *virelai* was one of the fixed forms of French verse of the 13th, 14th, and 15th centuries. Usually set to music, one form of the *virelai* used short lines and was divided into stanzas, each using only two rhymes. In general the last rhyme of one stanza became the first rhyme of the next stanza, so that the *virelai* might rhyme *aabaab bbcbbc ccdccd* etc., with no determinate length. This sort of *virelai* might also have two opening lines that would occur intermittently as a refrain. A second form of the *virelai* alternated longer and shorter lines within stanzas, with the shorter lines of one stanza providing the rhyme for the longer lines of the next stanza. Such a *virelai* might rhyme *abab bcbc cdcd,* where the first and third lines of each stanza are long and the second and fourth are short. Again this kind of *virelai* could be any length.

Like other fixed forms, including the RONDEAU and the *BALLADE,* the *virelai* was generally used as a vehicle for conventional expressions of love, although another type of *virelai* was called the realistic type, and was intended to describe vividly some active scene.

The *virelai* was never a popular form in England, though in his prologue to *The LEGEND OF GOOD WOMEN,* CHAUCER claims to have written some in his youth. But the best known French poets of the 14th and 15th centuries, including MACHAUT, DESCHAMPS, and CHRISTINE DE PIZAN, wrote a number of *virelais.* Perhaps the best-known example is this one by Eustache Deschamps:

Sui je, sui je, sui je belle?

Il me semble, à mon avis,
Que j'ay beau front et doulz viz

Et la bouche vermeillette;
Dittes moy se je suis belle.

J'ay vers yeulx, petits sourcis,
Le chief blont, le nez traitis,

Ront menton, blanche gorgette;
Sui je, sui je, sui je belle?

J'ay dur sain et hault assis,
Lons bras, gresles doys aussis,

Et par le faulz sui greslette;
Dittes moy se je suis belle.

(Wilkins 1969, 79)

And so on, for some 45 lines. Deschamps's poem (an unusual example of the first form of *virelai* mentioned above) uses only two rhymes throughout, plus the refrain. An example of the second form is this one by Christine de Pizan:

En ce printemps gracieux
D'estre gai suis enviex
  Tout à l'onnour
De ma dame, qui vigour
  De ses doulz yeulz
Me donne, don't par lesquielx
  Vifs en baudour.
Toute riens fait son atour
De mener joye à son tour,
  Bois et prez tieulx
Sont, qu'ilz semblent de verdour
Estre vestus et de flour
  Et qui mieulx mieulx.

(Wilkins 1969, 93)

Note how varied is the line length of these opening stanzas of Christine's poem. But note that the last short line of the first stanza does provide the rhyme for the first long line of the second.

Bibliography

Wilkins, Nigel, ed. *One Hundred Ballades, Rondeaux and Virelais from the Late Middle Ages.* Cambridge: Cambridge University Press, 1969.

Vita nuova (*New life*) Dante Alighieri (1295)

The *Vita nuova* is a collection of 31 of DANTE's earlier lyric poems, introduced, connected, and explained by 41 prose passages that narrate the story of his love for the woman he called Beatrice ("Bringer of Blessings"), and of her death in 1290, and its devastating effect on the poet. Dante says he began gathering his earlier poems about Beatrice and putting them together to create what is essentially a fictionalized autobiography when he was 27, that is, in 1292. Sometimes the poems recapitulate the events narrated in the prose sections; sometimes they present emotional reactions or ideas generated by the narrated experiences. The arrangement of the poems reflects the development of the young narrator's attitudes about poetry, love, and his lady, from an early self-centeredness through a focus on the perfections of the Lady herself, to a vision of the Lady as the embodiment of heavenly attributes and the symbol of heavenly love.

The form of alternating poetry and prose passages was not invented by Dante. It had been used by BOETHIUS in his early sixth-century *CONSOLATION OF PHILOSOPHY*, a text with which Dante was certainly familiar. What is new in the *Vita nuova* is the way that the prose passages keep the continuous story going, while at the same time not only explaining the occasion for the poems included, but interpreting the poems from a technical perspective. This technical preoccupation is related to Dante's concern with structure and with numbers so evident in the *Vita nuova*. The number 9, for example, appears no less than 22 times in the book: Dante first meets Beatrice in his ninth year; he doesn't see her again until nine years later, in the ninth hour; he begins to write the *Vita nuova* after nine more years. Nine as the square of 3, number of the holy Trinity, would suggest for Dante's medieval audience the harmony of the divinely created universe. A look at the book's overall structure emphasizes this order and harmony: The poems fall into three groups, each attached to one of three *CANZONI*, the longer thematic poems in the text. The second group of poems has a *canzone* in the middle with four shorter poems (mainly SONNETS) on either side. The first and third groups each contain 11 poems, the first having 10 short poems and a *canzone*, the third having a *canzone* followed by 10 short poems. The symmetry is inescapable.

Part of the effect is to focus attention on the central poem of the book—the *canzone* beginning *"Domna pietosa e di novella etate"* (A lady of tender years, compassionate). The poem introduces the poet's premonition of Beatrice's death, the central event of the narrative. In addition this *canzone* speaks of that death in language and imagery recalling the crucifixion of Christ, thereby suggesting the ultimate end toward which Dante's poetry is developing. Dante, looking back at his love affair and recreating it based on his new perspective and understanding, wants to demonstrate the development of his own attitudes as they are shaped by his experiences. As he tells it, the early stages of his love show him preoccupied with his own suffering, focused on his own emotions and exploring them at length, mainly in private, his lady being not much more than a mirror to reflect back his view of himself. At one point, denied a greeting by Beatrice, the young Dante returns to his room where, he says, "I fell asleep like a little boy crying from a spanking" (Musa 1973, 17).

When he is later convinced by certain unnamed ladies of the town that his true happiness lay in praising his lady rather than focusing on himself, he writes the first of the major *canzoni* in the book, the poem in section 19 beginning *"Donne, ch'avete intelletto d'amore"* (Ladies, who have intelligence of love). This poem, presented here legitimately as a turning point in Dante's career, concentrates on Beatrice's perfections, rather than Dante's own emotions. The angels of heaven desire to have Beatrice with them, since heaven lacks perfection without her. On earth her power is able to ennoble those who look on her and, if they are worthy, to bring them God's salvation. Beatrice has thus become the mediator between the poet and God himself, and when he later has the premonition of Beatrice's death, the crucifixion imagery implies her Christ-like nature: Just as the love of Christ leads us heavenward and cannot be selfish, so (the poem implies) the same must be said of Dante's love of Beatrice.

How much of the text reflects Dante's real experience and how much reflects his reinterpretation of events years after Beatrice's death is a moot question; all we can do is look at the literary text as he created it. Here the new attitude toward his love is what ultimately enables him, after some time, to accept her death and continue to see her as a mediatrix for God's love. The concluding sonnet of the *Vita nuova*, beginning *"Oltre la spera che più larga gira"* (Beyond the sphere that makes the widest round), depicts the lover's sigh ascending into heaven, where it sees his lady Beatrice in splendor. Returning to the earth, however, the sigh is unable to express the sight in a way Dante can understand. He only hears the name of "Beatrice" being uttered many times. But the *Vita nuova* ends with the poet's own "miraculous vision" that inspires him to write about Beatrice in a nobler way. He ends by vowing to write of her "that which has never been written of any other woman" (Musa 1973, 86). Nor does Dante write of her again until she becomes the embodiment of Grace in his *DIVINE COMEDY:* Ultimately Beatrice has become what is promised at the end of the *Vita nuova,* a conception made possible by the poet's development in the text of this little book from the egotism typical of earlier COURTLY LOVE poetry to the deification of the beloved typical of what Dante called his own *DOLCE STIL NOVO,* his "sweet new style" of poetry.

Bibliography

Ahern, John. "The New Life of the Book: The Implied Reader of the *Vita nuova,*" *Dante Studies* 110 (1992): 1–16.

Baranski, Zygmunt G. "The 'New Life' of 'Comedy': The Commedia and the *Vita Nuova,*" *Dante Studies* 113 (1995): 1–29.

Harrison, Robert Pogue. "Approaching the *Vita nuova,*" in *The Cambridge Companion to Dante,* edited by Rachel Jacoff. Cambridge: Cambridge University Press, 1993, 34–44.

Martinez, Ronald. "Mourning Beatrice: The Rhetoric of Threnody in the *Vita Nuova,*" *Modern Language Notes* 113 (1998): 1–29.

Musa, Mark, trans. *Dante's Vita Nuova: A Translation and an Essay.* Bloomington: Indiana University Press, 1973.

Volsunga Saga (Saga of the Volsungs) (ca. 1270)

The *Volsunga Saga* is the best known of the *fornaldar sogur* (Legendary sagas) to come out of medieval Iceland. Whereas the family sagas, such as the much admired *EGILS'S SAGA* and *NJAL'S SAGA,* deal with historical persons and their descendants, the sagas of legend were written later, and imitate the narrative prose style of the family sagas but take Old Norse legend as their subject matter. The saga survives in one manuscript from about 1400, and in later paper manuscripts, though it seems clear that the saga was written between 1250 and 1300. The theme of the *Volsunga Saga* is the story of Sigurd, Brynhild, and the ancient wars among the Burgundians, Huns, and Goths—a story that had been popular among the Germanic tribes for centuries and that had been told, earlier in the 13th century, by an anonymous German poet in the *NIBELUNGENLIED.* There is no evidence that the author of the Old Norse text knew the *Nibelungenlied;* however, it is clear that the writer based his saga on the earlier poems in the Old Norse *POETIC EDDA,* where the events he describes have their first Norse expression. Indeed, the author includes a number of poetic passages in his text, including nearly the complete text of one of the poems from the *Edda.*

The saga is complex and somewhat sprawling. It might be divided into six major parts. The first section of the text, depicting the birth of Volsung, has no source in the *Poetic Edda.* Here Rerir, king of the Huns, cannot beget an heir, and his prayers are answered by a golden apple delivered to him by the gods. His wife conceives after tasting the apple, but Rerir dies before his child is born. His queen remains pregnant for six winters, then dies, asking that the child be cut from her womb. Thus Volsung is born nearly a full-grown man. Volsung succeeds his father as king of the Huns, marries Hljod, and fathers 10 powerful sons, including Sigmund.

The second part of the saga, the story of Sigmund and his twin sister, Signy, has no counterpart in the Edda either, and may be from a lost poem. Here Signy marries Siggeir, the treacherous king of the Goths. During the wedding feast, the god Odin visits in disguise, and plunges the magic sword *Gram* into the great oak tree in the center of Volsung's hall. The sword gives its wielder the power to win all battles, but only Sigmund is able to draw the sword from the tree. Siggeir tries to buy the sword from Sigmund, but when he is denied, he plots revenge. That revenge involves an ambush of Volsung and his sons as they come to visit Siggeir's palace, and the death of all but Sigmund, who escapes with Signy's help. For years they plot revenge on Siggeir, and when Signy's sons by Siggeir prove too weak to help them, she insists they be killed. Then in disguise, she visits her brother and is impregnated by him. She gives birth to Sinfjotli, who ultimately helps Sigmund kill Siggeir and burn his palace. Signy comes to them and reveals the fact that Sinfjotli is Sigmund's son. At that point, Signy, who ordered the deaths of her own children, turns and enters the burning palace to die with her husband.

The third section of the poem, based on Eddic poems, concerns Sigmund's son Helgi. The complex fourth section deals with the Sigurd, Brynhild, and Gudrun story, told in six poems of the Edda. Sigmund marries Hjordis, but is killed in battle with King Lyngi, her former suitor, after breaking his magic sword. He gives the pieces of the sword to Hogni and tells her to have their child reforge it and take revenge. Hjordis bears Sigurd, who is raised in Denmark by his stepfather, King Alf. After reforging his father's magic sword, Sigurd helps his tutor Regin obtain a magic ring and cursed treasure from the dragon Fafnir (Regin's brother), and upon eating the heart of the dragon, Sigurd learns to understand the talk of birds, who warn him that Regin plans to betray him and keep the treasure for himself. Sigurd kills Regin, but he also learns from the birds of a sleeping Valkyrie placed within a ring of fire by Odin. Intrigued, Sigurd rides through the ring of fire, makes love to the Valkyrie Brynhild, and gives her the cursed ring, promising to return for her. Meanwhile Sigurd travels to Burgundy, where, as a result of a magic potion, he forgets Brynhild and marries Gudrun, daughter of the king. He swears an oath to Gudrun's brother Gunnar, and on Gunnar's bidding he wins Brynhild while disguised as his brother-in-law. After the potion wears off, he reveals the whole truth to Gudrun, who, in a quarrel with Brynhild, reveals to her who really won her. The enraged Brynhild tells Gunnar that Sigurd took advantage of her and demands he kill Sigurd or she will leave him. Sigurd is murdered by Gunnar's brother Guttorm, after which Brynhild kills herself, asking that she be burned on Sigurd's funeral pyre, since she had always loved him.

The fifth part of the story uses the Eddic poems *Atlakviða* and *Atlamál,* and depicts Gudrun's marriage to Attli (Attila), king of the Huns. Having learned of Sigurd's treasure, Attli invites Gunnar and his brother Hogni to Hunland to try to get the secret of the treasure from them. Distrusting Attli, the brothers sink Sigurd's treasure into the Rhine and vow never to reveal its location. At Attli's palace, the Burgundians are attacked, and all are killed but Gunnar and Hogni, who are captured. Both brothers refuse to reveal the treasure's location, though Gunnar tells Attli that he will give him the treasure if Attli cuts out his brother's heart. When Attli does so, Gunnar laughs and says that now that the only other person who knows where the treasure was is dead, he will never reveal it. Gunnar is then killed by snakes. In revenge, Gudrun secretly cuts the throats of the sons she bore to Attli and serves him their hearts, after which she runs Attli through with a sword.

The final section of the story, based on the Eddic poem Jamðismál, concerns Gudrun's later life and that of Svanhild, her daughter with Sigurd. King Jormunrek sends his son Randver to woo Svanhild, but on the advice of the evil counselor Bikki, Randver marries her himself. When Jormunek discovers this, he hangs his son and has Svanhild trampled to death by horses. Gudrun's sons are killed trying to avenge their sister.

The *Volsunga Saga* is valuable in a number of ways. For one thing, it preserves the story of Sigmund and Signy, which has not survived elsewhere. Further, the saga was based on a complete text of the *Poetic Edda,* and therefore preserves the contents of two central poems on Sigurd that are missing or fragmentary in the surviving text of the *Edda.* In addition, the saga was one of the major sources for Wagner's Ring cycle operas in the 19th century, and events in the saga (the reforged sword, the magic but cursed ring) inspired Tolkien's perennially popular *Lord of the Rings* in the 20th.

Bibliography

Finch, Robert G. "*Atlakviða, Atlamál* and *Volsunga Saga:* A Study in Combination and Integration." In *Speculum Norroenum: Norse Studies in Memory of Gabriel Turville-Petre,* edited by Ursula Dronke, 123–138. Odense, Denmark: Odense University Press, 1981.

———. "The Treatment of Poetic Sources by the Compiler of *Völsunga saga*," *Saga-book* 16 (1962–1965): 315–353.

The Saga of the Volsungs: The Icelandic text according to MS Nks 1824 b, 4°. Translation, introduction, and notes by Kaaren Grimstad. Saarbrücken, Germany: AQ-Verlag, 2000.

The Saga of the Volsungs: The Norse Epic of Sigurd the Dragon Slayer. Introduction and translation by Jesse L. Byock. Berkeley: University of California Press, 1990.

Vox clamantis John Gower (ca. 1381–1400)

John Gower's second important work, *Vox clamantis* (The voice of one crying), is a poem of 10,265 lines of Latin elegiac verse. The title is taken from Isaiah and from John the Baptist, and implies the prophetic nature of the poet's words that call for the reform of society. Less adept at Latin than he was at French or English, Gower includes in his text extensive borrowings (some 1,300 lines) from Ovid, Godfrey of Viterbo, Alexander Neckam, Peter Riga, and other medieval Latin writers. The poem survives in 10 manuscripts, four produced in Gower's lifetime. The manuscript tradition demonstrates that Gower revised the poem at least twice to reflect changing political conditions in England.

Gower must have been nearly finished with *Vox clamantis* when the PEASANTS' REVOLT occurred in 1381. At that time he added an introductory book to the poem that takes the form of an allegorical description of the revolt. In a DREAM VISION, the narrator sees bands of people changed into beasts marching across the land. For Gower, failure to follow the dictates of Reason is the cause of sin and turns human beings into beasts, and this introductory book shows the chaotic consequences for society of individual sins. Wat Tyler is presented as a jackdaw whose speeches upset the divinely ordained order of the world, and the book depicts the subsequent sacking of London and murder of the archbishop. The narrator, fleeing the chaos, takes refuge aboard a ship, perhaps representing Faith.

The Narrator's ship lands in England, where the inhabitants have rejected the law and love of God, which holds the universe in harmony and which *should* do the same for society. In book 2, the original opening of the poem, Gower deals with the question of how society has reached this chaotic state. Some would blame Fortune, he says, but this is merely failure to take moral responsibility: Human beings themselves are responsible. Gower follows this beginning with four books of ESTATES SATIRE, in which he criticizes the greed, lechery, and other vices that characterize the three estates (clergy, nobility, and common people) in a manner very similar to the final section of his earlier French poem, the *MIROUR DE L'OMME*.

Book 6 turns to the responsibilities of the king to keep the peace and to rule justly in accordance with God's law and love. But Gower concludes the poem, in book 7, with an apocalyptic vision beginning with the statue described in Nebuchadnezzar's dream representing the degeneration of human society after the Golden Age and moving into a discussion of the Seven Deadly Sins that have corrupted the three estates discussed earlier. This is capped by a striking discussion of how the decay of the human body after death parallels the Seven Deadly Sins. Thus death, sin, and corruption are brought together, and Gower, the prophet crying in the wilderness, predicts an apocalypse for the English nation if order and justice are not restored. Each individual must reform, but the reform must take place from the top down. Thus the king's responsibility is the greatest.

It is in Gower's attitude toward the king, RICHARD II, that his progressive revisions of *Vox clamantis* can be seen. In the early version of 1381, Gower shows an inclination to excuse the 14-year-old monarch for the chaos of society. In about 1393 Gower revised the poem to remove any excusing of Richard and to suggest the king's responsibility for the unrest of his realm. In 1400, Gower appended to *Vox clamantis* another Latin poem, the *Cronica tripertita.* Here Gower sees Richard's 1399 deposition by Henry IV as a direct result of Richard's own sins. Gower's interest in royal responsibility and the necessity of the king to rule in accordance with the natural law of God would continue to be apparent in his next and most important work, the English poem CONFESSIO *AMANTIS.*

Bibliography

Fisher, John H. *John Gower: Moral Philosopher and Friend of Chaucer.* New York: New York University Press, 1964.

Macaulay, G. C., ed. *The Complete Works of John Gower.* 4 vols. Oxford: Clarendon Press, 1899–1902.

Stockton, Eric W., trans. and introduction. *The Major Latin Works of John Gower: The Voice of One Crying, and The Tripartite Chronicle.* Seattle: University of Washington Press, 1962.

Yeager, Robert F. *John Gower: Recent Readings.* Kalamazoo: Western Michigan University Press, 1989.

vulgari eloquentia, De (Eloquence in the vernacular tongue) Dante Alighieri (ca. 1304–1305)

DANTE's *De vulgari eloquentia* is an unfinished Latin treatise in which the poet argues that it is appropriate to write literature concerning serious topics—such as war, love, and virtue—in the vernacular Italian language. Thus it is an important text in Dante's attempt to give theoretical justification for his use of Italian, rather than Latin, to compose his *magnum opus,* the DIVINE COMEDY. While this may seem of little importance to a modern reader, it must be remembered that in the European Middle Ages, a literary work with aspirations to high aesthetic seriousness would, prior to Dante, almost certainly be composed in Latin.

Along with his CONVIVIO, one of the first important works Dante produced after his exile from Florence in 1302, *De vulgari eloquentia* was conceived of as a study in four books dealing with the origin and the history of language and then discussing the poetic forms and literary styles possible in the vernacular language. He chose to write the thesis in Latin to persuade the more conservative elements in his audience.

The theme of *De vulgari eloquentia* is one that had concerned Dante for some time. In the 25th chapter of his VITA NUOVA (1295), itself written in the vernacular, he had defended the use of Italian for love poetry, and claimed for the vernacular poet the legitimate use of the same rhetorical figures common to writers in Latin. In the first book of the *Convivio,* a philosophical work written in Italian, Dante announces his intention of writing a small treatise concerning eloquence in the vernacular language. This suggests that Dante had not yet written *De vulgari eloquentia* by the time he had started the *Convivio;* however, it is likely that he began work on *De vulgari eloquentia* while he worked on the *Convivio.* He seems to have abandoned both works by 1307, devoting himself more fully to his *Divine Comedy.*

Thus, of the four projected books of *De vulgari eloquentia,* only two exist, and the second is incomplete, breaking off in the middle of a discussion of the structure of a poetic stanza. In Book 1 Dante first makes a distinction between what he calls *locutio prima* or natural language, and *locutio secundria,* or *gramatica,* the language studied in school (Latin). He asserts that the nobler language is the primary one, because it is more natural, it is universal (everyone has one, whether they have attended school or not, and because it would have been the language spoken by human beings in paradise). This leads Dante to consider the origins of language, and he goes on to claim that Adam (not, as the Bible would have it, Eve) spoke the first word, and that it must have been the name of God. Dante sees the destruction of linguistic unity that occurred at the Tower of Babel as still going on, and he discusses the 14 different dialects of Italian spoken in his own day. He considers, as well, vernacular literature in French and Provençal, discussing some of the more impressive TROUBADOUR poets. He asks what language is best for literary composition, and argues that the ideal language does not exist, but must be forged by poets themselves in their verse, and he gives some guidelines for this ideal language that he refers to as the "illustrious vernacular."

In the second book of *De vulgari eloquentia,* Dante provides an incomplete treatise on the "art of poetry." Here Dante argues that the highest form of poetry, and the most appropriate for lofty literary subjects, is the long lyric form called the *CANZONE.* In the midst of his discussion of metrical aspects of the *canzone,* Dante breaks off, and never completes his text.

Dante abandoned his treatise on the "vulgar tongue," just as he abandoned the *Convivio*, on which he was apparently working at the same time, in favor of his *Comedy*, the first installment of which (the *Inferno*) was completed in 1307. Though he seems not to have intended the incomplete text to be widely circulated, it has survived in four manuscripts, one from the 14th century, and an Italian translation of the text was printed in the early 16th century. Just why Dante never finished his text is a matter for debate, but it is true that in the *Comedy*, Dante's prime example of sublime poetry in the vernacular, he breaks many of the rules for the "illustrious vernacular" that he had proposed in *De vulgari eloquentia*—he uses a number of words in the comedy that he had advised against in the earlier work, words that were quite appropriate for the style of "comedy" as opposed to tragedy.

Bibliography

Dante Alighieri. *De Vulgari Eloquentia.* Edited and translated by Steven Botterill. Cambridge: Cambridge University Press, 1996.

Shapiro, Marianne. *De Vulgari Eloquentia: Dante's Book of Exile.* Lincoln: University of Nebraska Press, 1990.

Vulgate, The Saint Jerome (ca. 405)

The Vulgate (meaning "common language") is the Latin version of the Bible produced mainly by St. JEROME. It was the text that became the standard version of the Christian Scriptures in western Europe from the fifth century until the time of the Protestant Reformation in the 16th, and therefore had a profound and widespread influence on European culture for the entire medieval period.

During the fourth century, a number of older Latin translations of Scripture were in circulation throughout Europe, but these were for the most part unreliable and manifested great discrepancies. At the request of Pope Damasus, Jerome undertook the creation of a new, scholarly, and accurate rendering of the Christian Bible into Latin, the common language of the entire western Roman Empire. Within two years, Jerome had completed a new translation of the four Gospels from their original Greek.

Moving to the Old Testament after 384, Jerome began with the Psalms, significant because of their regular use in the Christian liturgy. Jerome completed what became known as the Gallican Psalter in about 392. As his source, he used the text of the Septuagint (named for the "70 elders"), a Greek translation of the Hebrew Scriptures made in Hellenic Alexandria that had been in circulation since the third century B.C.E. and had been the version most familiar to the early church. But as Jerome continued his work on the Old Testament over the next 15 years, he came to believe that for a true translation he needed to work directly from the Hebrew texts of the Scriptures. This decision was controversial at the time, since the church had from its beginning relied on the Septuagint, which many believed to be divinely inspired, and Jerome's revision of the Psalms, called the "Hebrew Psalter," never gained the popularity that his Gallican Psalter had. But the rest of his Old Testament, on the basis of its undeniable excellence, gradually became the standard version used in the West.

It was not until (most likely) the early seventh century that the Vulgate as we now know it was assembled into a single text, comprising Jerome's Old Testament, the Gallican Psalter, Jerome's Gospels, and newly revised translations of the remainder of the New Testament by an unknown author who followed Jerome. The text also contained Jerome's translations of the Apocryphal books of Judith and Tobit, as well as older Latin versions of the rest of the Apocrypha.

Jerome's Vulgate became the first mass-produced printed book in Europe when Gutenberg printed it in 1454. Over the centuries, many errors had crept into Jerome's text as it was copied and recopied by scribes, and a critical edition of the Vulgate was published in 1528. At the height of the Counter-Reformation in 1560, the Council of Trent declared the Vulgate the authoritative text of Bible. A corrected edition (purging some 3,000 textual errors) produced under Pope Clement VIII in 1592 (known as the "Clementine edition") became the standard Catholic Bible. It was the Vulgate version that Martin Luther translated into German at the beginning of the Reformation, and it is the Vulgate version that remains the text on which today's standard Catholic Douay-Confraternity English translation of the Bible is based. Even contemporary Bible translators look at Jerome's Vulgate text as an important authority, because they realize that he had access to manuscripts in the original Hebrew that predate most surviving Hebrew texts by nearly 1,000 years.

Bibliography

Kamesar, Adam. *Jerome, Greek scholarship, and the Hebrew Bible: A Study of the Quaestiones Hebraicae in Genesim.* Oxford: Clarendon Press, 1993.

Vulgate Cycle (Lancelot-Grail Cycle, Pseudo-Map Cycle) (ca. 1210–1235)

The Vulgate Cycle is the name given to a collection of five substantial ROMANCES in French prose, concerning the legends of King ARTHUR and the HOLY GRAIL. It was the major source for Thomas MALORY's *Le MORTE DARTHUR,* and itself draws from the earlier verse romances of CHRÉTIEN DE TROYES, in particular his *LANCELOT* and *PERCEVAL.* Previously, French prose had been used mainly for vernacular translations of Latin theological texts or for sermons. By the 13th century, it began to be used for historical texts in the vernacular as well, like those of JOINVILLE and VILLEHARDOUIN. The prose romances written in the early 13th century, beginning with the Vulgate Cycle, manifested some elements of both of these prose genres, being more overtly Christian in tone and more full of narrative detail in the manner of a prose chronicle.

An earlier cycle of three Grail romances had been composed in French verse by the Burgundian poet ROBERT DE BORON. His romances—*Joseph d'Arimathie, Merlin,* and a poem generally known as the Didot-Perceval—were immediately adapted into prose by an anonymous writer, and those prose romances were the immediate inspiration for the longer Vulgate Cycle.

The first of the Vulgate romances in the sequence of the plot (though one of the last to be written) is the *Estoire del Saint Graal* (The history of the Holy Grail), which continues the story of Robert's Joseph of Arimathea, who in the romance possesses Christ's cup from the Last Supper—in which he had caught the blood of Christ after the Crucifixion. In the *Estoire,* Joseph's son Josephe, who in the romance becomes the first Christian bishop, ultimately brings the Grail to England. Upon his death, Josephe bequeaths the Grail to the first "Fisher King," Alain, who houses it in Corbenic Castle, where it will await the eventual coming of the Grail knight.

The second romance, also written late, is the prose adaptation of the story of Robert's *Merlin.* Here, Merlin, the wonder worker and seer, helps King Uther Pendragon sire Arthur by disguising him as the Duke of Cornwall to allow him to lay with the duchess Igerne. Merlin creates the test of the sword in the stone by which Arthur establishes his royal legitimacy, and then helps Arthur in the wars by which he secures his empire. Arthur's nephew Gauvain (GAWAIN) is a major character of the romance, as hero of his uncle's military campaigns, as he is in the chronicle tradition begun by GEOFFREY OF MONMOUTH. The *Merlin* also looks forward to later romances in the cycle by its introduction of the Round Table as an image of the earlier Grail Table, which is itself the image of the table of the Last Supper. It also introduces GUENEVERE as Arthur's queen, and tells of the birth of LANCELOT.

The prose *Lancelot,* which follows Merlin, is a huge work that in itself is half the length of the entire Vulgate Cycle. In keeping with the Grail story, Lancelot is a descendant of King David, and is baptized Galahad. The greatest hero of Arthurian tradition, LANCELOT is raised by the Lady of the Lake. But when he comes to Arthur's court, he falls in love with Guenevere, and, as is typical of the COURTLY LOVE tradition, he embarks on a series of adventures that will establish him as the greatest knight and prove him worthy of the queen's love. The long narrative includes the exploits of other knights as well, interwoven with those of Lancelot in a technique of romance known as *enterlacement.* As in Chrétien's Lancelot, the hero delivers the prisoners of Logres in the kingdom of Gorre, though he fails a test involving a tombstone in the cemetery on his adventure, a failure that is attributed to his sinful love of the queen. That love also leads him to father GALAHAD, believing he is sleeping with the queen—an act that will have a profound effect on subsequent parts of the cycle. Galahad, descended from King David and Joseph of Arimathea on his father's side, and from the Grail kings on his mother's, is the chosen knight destined to achieve the quest of the Holy Grail.

The *Queste del Saint Graal* is the story that made Sir Galahad a significant figure in world literature, and established the quest of the Holy Grail as central to the Arthurian tradition. The tale describes the mysterious appearance of the Grail vessel before the knights of the Round Table and the knights' decision to seek the Grail. While Galahad has already proven himself the chosen Grail knight by pulling a sword from the stone and by sitting in the Perilous Seat at the Round Table, the innocent Perceval and Lancelot's kinsman Bohoret (Bors) are also successful in finding the Grail because of their virtue and chastity. The narrative follows these three successful knights and interweaves their stories with those of the secular knights, particularly Lionel, Hector, and Gauvain, who fail consistently through their misunderstanding of the quest, the true nature of which is interpreted and explained regularly by pious hermits who inhabit much of the romance's landscape. Lancelot's adventures are interwoven as well, as he tries to atone for his adulterous relationship with the queen that prevents him from achieving the Grail—he is the greatest secular knight, but this is a spiritual quest, and thus Galahad, the embodiment of the spiritual knight, eclipses Lancelot's prowess on this quest.

The final romance of the cycle is the *Mort Artu* (The death of Arthur), relating the downfall of the Round Table, and the passing of Arthur and his world. Lancelot's love for the queen is finally exposed by the jealousy of Gauvain's brothers, and when Lancelot rescues the queen from execution, he accidentally kills Sir Gaheriet (Gareth), Gauvain's favorite brother. This begins a war in which Arthur and Gauvain besiege Lancelot and his supporters in France. But the king's natural son, Mordred, left in charge of the kingdom during the war, usurps the throne, forcing Arthur to return home to fight a bloody battle on Salisbury plain, in which Mordred is killed and Arthur mortally wounded. Arthur has his squire Girflet throw his sword Excalibur into the lake, where it is caught by a hand coming out of the water, after which a mysterious boat carrying Morgain and other women comes to take Arthur away. He is expected to return one day, like the Second Coming of Christ.

The Vulgate Cycle was at one time attributed to Walter MAP, who was attached to the court of England's King HENRY II, but Map died well before the romances of the Vulgate Cycle were composed. While there is no scholarly consensus about authorship, many believe that one writer conceived of the plan for the *Lancelot,* the *Queste del Saint Graal,* and the *Mort Artu,* but that a series of other writers completed the romances, and that the *Estoire del Saint Graal* and *Merlin* were added subsequently to complete the story. The cycle was highly influential throughout the later Middle Ages, inspiring a number of imitations and sequels, including the prose *Tristan* and the *Suite du Merlin.* Most important, the Vulgate romances were the sources from which Malory compiled his seminal treatment of Arthurian legend as the Middle Ages drew to an end.

Bibliography

Burns, E. Jane. *Arthurian Fictions: Re-reading the Vulgate Cycle.* Columbus: Ohio State University Press, 1985.

Kennedy, Elspeth. *Lancelot and the Grail: A Study in the Prose Lancelot.* Oxford: Clarendon Press, 1986.

Kibler, William W., ed. *The Lancelot-Grail Cycle: Text and Transformations.* Austin: University of Texas Press, 1994.

Lacy, Norris J., ed. *Lancelot-Grail: the Old French Arthurian Vulgate and Post-Vulgate in Translation.* 5 vols. New York: Garland, 1993–1996.

Wace (ca. 1110–ca. 1175)

Wace was a Norman French poet best known for writing the *Roman de Brut,* a poem of some 15,000 octosyllabic couplets in Old French that chronicles the legendary history of the kings of Britain, including a large section on King ARTHUR.

Wace's story is largely a translation and redaction of GEOFFREY OF MONMOUTH's Latin prose chronicle *HISTORIA REGUM BRITANNIAE* (1138), the work that introduced the Arthurian legend into the mainstream of European literature. Wace is largely responsible for popularizing that legend in French. His *Brut,* completed, he says in its conclusion, in 1155, was dedicated (according to Wace's later English translator, LAYAMON) to HENRY II's queen, ELEANOR OF AQUITAINE. Wace reshaped his material probably to suit his patron: He eliminates some of the graphic violence of Geoffrey's story, as well as some of the more fantastic portions, like the prophesies of Merlin. Wace also plays up the elements of COURTLY LOVE in the story, in particular the story of Uther Pendragon's love for the Lady Ygerne that results in Arthur's begetting. He also is the first writer to mention King Arthur's Round Table—a wedding gift from Guenevere's father. Also of interest are Wace's comments about the existence, in the mid-12th century, of an oral tradition about Arthur among Breton storytellers—a tradition that included the "Breton hope": the legend among the Celtic people that Arthur would return again from the Isle of Avalon.

Not much is known about Wace's life, but he does give a few pieces of autobiographical information in his later work, the *Roman de Rou.* He says that he was born in the early 12th century on the Isle of Jersey. He was educated at Caen in Normandy and later in the Ile de France, probably either in Paris or Chartres. He later returned to Caen between 1130 and 1135, where he was appointed *clerc lisant* (reader) to King Henry I. About this time he also began to write, apparently to supplement his income. He wrote at least three early texts: a "Life of St. Margaret," a "Life of St. Nicholas," and "The Conception of Our Lady," all of which are translations from Latin into the Old French vernacular. After the success of his *Brut,* Henry II commissioned Wace to write a verse chronicle of his own ancestors, the dukes of Normandy. Wace began the work, entitled the *Roman de Rou,* around 1160. Germane to this enterprise, he is said to have accompanied Henry II to Fécamp in 1162, where the remains of Dukes Richard I and Richard II were reburied. About this time Henry also made him canon of the church at Bayeux. By 1175, he had composed 16,000 lines of his history. But for reasons unknown, Henry replaced Wace as court historian with BENOÎT DE STE.-MAURE (author of the *Roman de Troie*), who was assigned the task of finishing the work. That is the last we know of Wace, though it is likely that he died at Bayeux about this time.

Wace's contribution to the popularization of Arthurian legend is enormous. His French text certainly influenced MARIE DE FRANCE and CHRÉTIEN DE TROYES, as well as subsequent French writers in the Arthurian tradition. But also, as the source of Layamon's *Brut,* his influence on the history of the Arthurian legend in English was equally strong.

Bibliography

Foulon, Charles. "Wace." In *Arthurian Literature in the Middle Ages,* edited by Roger Sherman Loomis, 94–103. Oxford: Clarendon Press, 1959.

Mason, Eugene, trans. *Arthurian Chronicles: Wace and Layamon.* Medieval Academy Reprints for Teaching 35. Toronto: University of Toronto Press, 1996.

Weiss, Judith, trans. *Wace's Roman De Brut: Text and Translation.* Exeter Medieval Texts and Studies. 2nd ed. Exeter, U.K.: University of Exeter Press, 2003.

Walafrid Strabo ("The Squinter") (ca. 809–849)

Walafrid was a German cleric of the Carolingian period known for his polished and elegant Latin style. He was the author of SAINTS' LIVES, religious treatises, religious verse, introductions to historical works, and theological commentaries.

Walafrid was born in Swabia about 809. He was educated at Reichenau Abbey on Lake Constance. At the age of 17, he moved to Fulda. He wrote of feeling cold and homesick at Fulda, but received an excellent education under Hrabanus Maurus. He wrote his first major work at the age of 18, when he put into verse an apocalyptic vision (the *Visio Wettini*) of the realms of the afterlife as experienced by Wetti, one of his former teachers at Reichenau. He dedicates the poem to Wetti's brother Grimwald. In the vision, CHARLEMAGNE is pictured being tormented in hell—an ironic detail since Walafrid later wrote an introduction to EINHARD's biography of Charlemagne.

In 829, Walafrid went to the court of the king Louis the Pious, where he was employed as tutor to his son, the future king Charles the Bald. He remained in this position until 838, when he returned to Reichenau with an appointment as abbot. However, when Louis died in 840, Walafrid supported the king's son Lothar as Louis's successor. But when Lothar was defeated by his brothers, Louis the German and Charles the Bald, Walafrid was forced to abandon Reichenau and go into exile at Speyer (Spires).

Through the offices of his former colleague Grimald, now chaplain to Louis the German, Walafrid was pardoned and reinstated as abbot of Reichenau in 842. He died while in France on a visit to his former pupil Charles, on August 18, 849. His teacher Hrabanus wrote his epitaph, praising him for his contributions to the church and to letters.

Walafrid's most influential work was a great compilation of biblical commentary (mostly collected from patristic sources) known as the *Glosa ordinaria,* a text that remained for more than 500 years the most important collection of exegesis in existence. It was still being printed as late as the 17th century. He also wrote a poetic life of St. Gall and several other saints' lives. Perhaps his best-known poem is the *Hortulus,* also dedicated to his old patron Grimald. It describes a garden Walafrid kept, and discusses the medicinal herbs and other plants that the abbot tended with his own hand.

Walafrid remains important because of his highly influential *Glosa,* for the picture he gives us of medieval horticulture, and for his early *Visio Wettini,* seen by many as a forerunner to DANTE's *DIVINE COMEDY.*

Bibliography

Godman, Peter. *Poets and Emperors: Frankish Politics and Carolingian Poetry.* Oxford: Clarendon Press, 1986.

Raby, F. J. E. *A History of Christian-Latin Poetry.* 2nd ed. Oxford: Clarendon Press, 1953.

Walahfrid Strabo's Visio Wettini. Edited and translated by David A. Traill. Bern, Switzerland: H. Lang, 1974.

Waldere (ninth or 10th century)

The *Waldere* is a fragmentary OLD ENGLISH poem preserved on two pages today kept in the Royal Library of Copenhagen (Ny Kgl. s. ms. 167b), comprising 63 verses in which two, perhaps three, speeches are given; the first by Hidgyth (Hildegund), the second by Hagano, the third by Waldere (Walther). The poem reflects upon the Latin *Waltharius* poem composed by Ekkehard I of St. Gall ca. 825, or it derives from a source common to both.

In the Latin epic, Waltharius (accompanied by his beloved Hildegund) escapes from the Hunnish king Attila to whom they both had been sent as hostages from their native countries, Aquitaine and Burgundy, respectively. When they arrive in the kingdom of the Burgundians, King Guntharius, out of greed for the treasures that Waltharius had taken with him from the Hunnish court, attacks the two with 12 of his men. However, Waltharius has positioned himself in a mountain pass where only one warrior can approach the hero at a time. Waltharius defends himself valiantly and kills 10 of Guntharius's men, including Hagano's nephew. At the end, having lured Waltharius out of his refuge, both the Burgundian king and his liege man Hagano enter the fray, and in this battle Guntharius loses a leg, Waltharius a hand, and Hagano one eye. As soon as they realize this tragic outcome, they strike a friendship, laughing about their disfigurements. This is possible especially because Hagano had also been a hostage at Attila's court before Waltharius managed to escape, and greatly respects Waltharius as a warrior. Afterward Waltharius and Hildegund return home and are married. Waltharius ascends to the throne of his father Elfhere's kingdom and reigns for 30 years.

In the first speech contained in *Waldere,* Hidgyth encourages Waldere to fight courageously with his trustworthy sword Mimming. The second fragment seems to begin with a short speech by Hagano, who praises the quality of Mimming, which had been sent by Theoderic the Great as a gift to Widia. The last section consists of Waldere's speech in which he taunts Guthhere.

The Anglo-Saxon *Waldere* demonstrates that Germanic heroic poetry was also known in England. Scholars now assume that *Waldere* and the Latin epic *Waltharius* developed separately out of a Germanic heroic epic lay. Other versions of the *Waltharius* are extent in Italian, Old Norse, and Polish.

Bibliography

Anderson, Theodore M. "The Speeches in the *Waldere* Fragments." In *De Gustibus: Essays for Alain Renoir,* edited by John Miles Foley, J. Chris Womack, and Whitney A. Womack, 21–29. New York: Garland, 1992.

Crossley-Holland, Kevin, trans. *The Anglo-Saxon World: An Anthology.* 1982. Oxford: Oxford University Press, 1999.

Langosch, Karl. *"Waltharius": Die Dichtung und die Forschung.* Darmstadt, Germany: Wissenschaftliche Buchgesellschaft, 1973.

Norman, Frederick. "The Old English *Waldere* and Some Problems in the Story of Walther and Hildegunde." In *Mélanges pour Jean Fourquet: 37 essais de linguistique germanique et de littérature du Moyen Âge français et allemand,* edited by Paul Valentin and Georges Zink, 261–271. Paris: Klincksieck, 1969.

Waldere. Edited by Arne Zettersten from Royal Library, Copenhagen NY Kgl. S. Ms. 167 b. Manchester, U.K.: Manchester University Press, 1979.

Albrecht Classen

Walther von der Vogelweide (ca. 1175–ca. 1230)

Both contemporaries and posterity have always recognized Walther von der Vogelweide as the most influential Middle High German poet of erotic, political, and religious songs. Although many towns in Austria and Germany today claim to be Walther's birthplace, no definite information about his biography is available. We know, however, that he was active as a GOLIARD (wandering poet/singer dependent on generous patrons) sometime between 1190 and 1230, and that he seems to have originated in Austria. In his song L. 32, 14, he confirms that he learned the art of poetry from the famous REINMAR DER ALTE at a court in Austria, undoubtedly Vienna. The 14th-century notary Michael de Leone claimed that Walther died in his city of Würzburg, but even this is uncertain despite a modern tomb erected in his honor behind the Würzburg cathedral. Two important manuscripts, the *Manessische Liederhandschrift* (C) and the *Weingartner Liederhandschrift* (B), identify Walther by the German title *her* (lord), which suggests that he might have been of lower nobility, but his poetic complaints about poverty and social misery speak a different language. In 1220, Emperor Frederick II gave him a small estate which he hailed jubilantly because it would keep the frost away from his toes (L. 28, 31).

Walther is the first medieval German poet also to address political events and to reflect upon their consequences for his own life. He often spent time at the various royal courts in Germany and clearly took sides in the political struggles on the highest level, which also included heavy criticism of the pope and the church. We know that Walther stood in the service of Bishop Wolfger of Erla, the later patriarch of Aquileia, who gave him five shillings to buy a fur coat in 1203, the only concrete reference in any historical document confirming the biographical dates both of Walther and many of his contemporaries who refer to him. He also seems to have served as a political emissary for high-ranking lords. Walther's particular praise of his various patrons extends to the Hohenstaufen kings Philipp and Frederick II, the Thuringian margrave Hermann, and Duke Leopold VI of Austria.

Walther is particularly famous for his innovative COURTLY LOVE poetry in which he clearly projects fulfilled love relationships, such as in his best-known "Under der linden" (L. 39, 1). Moreover he critically discusses the traditional value of unrequited love and rejects the poems of his predecessors for their artificial projection of love pain. In "Herzeliebez frowelîn" (L. 49, 5) Walther skillfully contrasts the glass ring on the hand of his beloved, who has obviously accepted his wooing, with the golden ring on the hand of a distant queen, who would not even pay attention to his words of love. Walther also raises the significant question of what the meaning of courtly love (*minne*) might be and insists that love should lead to happiness (L. 69, 1). In a political song he sings a praise of Germany (L. 56, 14), then he criticizes the widespread decline of courtly culture (L. 65, 31), and positions himself as courtly love poet in the center of all cultural activity (L. 72, 31). Surprisingly Walther also addresses the question of how to educate children properly (L. 87, 1), reflects upon the problems with old age (L. 124, 1), and ruminates about fundamental ethical and political questions (L. 8, 4).

Considering the enormous appeal exerted by Walther, the innovative nature of his poetry, and the boldness with which he dealt with many hotly disputed issues of his time, there is little surprise that his songs have been preserved in 36 manuscripts that were created all over the German-speaking lands.

Bibliography

Walther von der Vogelweide. *Leich, Lieder, Sangsprüche.* Edited by Christoph Cormeau. 14th rev. ed. Berlin: de Gruyter, 1996.

Zeydel, Edwin H., and Bayard Quincy Morgan, trans. *Walther von der Vogelweide: The Poems.* Ithaca, N.Y.: Thrift, 1952.

Albrecht Classen

Wanderer, The (10th century)

The OLD ENGLISH poem *The Wanderer,* like *THE SEAFARER* with which it is often linked, is one of the best-known examples of ELEGAIC POETRY, poetry in which the speaker laments some great loss. The poem survives only in The EXETER BOOK, a manuscript from about 975 that contains the largest surviving collection of poetry in Old English.

The poem is divided into two main sections. According to an unnamed Narrator, the first part of the poem is spoken by an "Earth walker" (*eardstapa*), or Wanderer, who, for 57 lines, laments his state of exile. He has lost his lord, and with him his companions and place in society, and now wanders in hope of finding some new lord to take him in. In particularly poignant lines, he describes dreaming of the old days and the gifts of his lord in the mead hall, only to wake and find himself still wandering on the sea.

The second part of the poem, lines 58–110, expand the theme of loss and isolation from the specific case of the Wanderer himself to the world in general. The speaker, here called the Wise Man, asserts that all things on earth are transient, and will be lost to violence and the ravages of time. Where are the horse, the young warrior, the gold-giving lord, the mead hall? All will vanish, the Wise Man concludes. The poem ends with a very Christian exhortation to put one's faith in heaven, the only place where joy is not transitory.

Critical issues in *The Wanderer* have revolved around the relationship of the two parts of the poem, and questions about the number of speakers involved. At one time it was suggested that the poem was actually an amalgam of two or more separate poems. It has also been suggested that the final lines, urging the reader to focus on heaven, were added later by a monastic scribe to an otherwise completely pagan poem. But most scholars today consider the poem a unified whole. Still scholars do not necessarily agree on who is speaking in each part of the poem. If the Wise Man is in fact the Wanderer whose exile has made him philosophical, then one can see a growth in the Wanderer's outlook. If the second speech, or even the final five lines of the poem, are attributed instead to the Narrator, then we learn something from the Wanderer's example, but the Wanderer himself is left in his bleak and melancholy existence.

Bibliography

Alexander, Michael, trans. *The Earliest English Poems.* Harmondsworth, U.K.: Penguin, 1966.

Green, Martin, ed. *The Old English Elegies: New Essays in Criticism and Research.* Rutherford, N.J.: Fairleigh Dickinson University Press, 1983.

Krapp, George Philip, and Elliott Van Kirk Dobbie, eds. *The Exeter Book.* The Anglo-Saxon Poetic Records, 3. New York: Columbia University Press, 1936.

Wang Wei (ca. 699–761)

Wang Wei was an imperial court poet during the greatest period of Chinese poetry in the TANG DYNASTY. He was known not only for his poetry, but also for his landscape painting, his music, and his calligraphy. Unlike his two great contemporaries, LI BAI (Li Po; a Taoist) and DU FU (Tu Fu; a Confucian), Wang Wei was a Buddhist who often described the illusory and transient nature of the created universe.

Wang Wei was born to an aristocratic family in what is now Shansi province, the eldest of five brothers. He is reputed to have been a child prodigy, composing poetry at the age of nine. At 21 he passed the imperial *jinshi* (*chin-shih*) (presented scholar) examination and was appointed to the post of assistant secretary for music. But he was exiled from court shortly thereafter for some minor indiscretion and demoted to a provincial office in Jizhou, where he remained for four years. He spent another six years traveling through the eastern provinces and became acquainted with Taoism.

More important when Wang Wei's wife died sometime after 730, he began to study Buddhism seriously with Chan Master Dao-guang. Beginning about 737, he spent intermittent periods of retreat in the mountains of Zhongnan (Chung-nan). His devotion to Buddhism ultimately led him to remain celibate and never to remarry.

He did not return to the capital until 733. Over the next 25 years, he held a variety of official positions in the capital and in the provinces, including grand secretary of the Imperial Chancery in 754. During the An Lu-shan rebellion of 755, he was captured and imprisoned in the Bodhi Temple in Chang'an, where he is said to have attempted suicide. Eventually he was released and briefly compelled to work for the rebel government. With the restoration of the emperor, however, he was pardoned—largely through the efforts of his brother Wang Chin, who was vice president of the Ministry of Justice at the time. He was restored to public office in 758 and finally appointed assistant secretary of state on the right, his highest political office.

Wang Wei could write celebratory courtly poetry on command, but is better known for more personal poems in which he contemplates nature. Wang Wei inherited a poetic tradition that idealized the contemplative life of a recluse living in a bucolic setting. In fact he does seem to have particularly loved his mountain estate at Wang Stream, south of the Tang capital at Chang'an, and dedicates much of his verse to his life there. He also celebrates the estate in his paintings. His delicate black ink landscape paintings often depict water and mist, and through them Wang Wei became one of the founders of Chinese landscape art.

During the last few years of his life, however, Wang Wei seems to have withdrawn from public life, visited his Wang Stream estate only infrequently, and stopped writing nature poetry, preferring to stay isolated in the capital reading Buddhist tracts. He died in 761 and was buried at his estate.

His poetic reputation is, once again, largely due to the efforts of his brother Wang Jin, who upon his death presented Wang Wei's collected poems to the emperor Taizong (Tai-tsung). Scholars consider about 370 extant poems to be genuinely his. Typically the poems deal with one of three themes: life at the court, Buddhist philosophy, or scenes from nature. Many critics have seen in Wang Wei's poetry, especially the nature poems, a painter's sensitivity to the arrangement of objects in space, and to how the observer's moving point of view can create changes in the scene observed. Others remark that his poems, like his paintings, are not full of detail, but create the atmosphere of a scene with a few suggestive strokes. The following poem (called "North Cottage") is one of a series of 20 quatrains Wang Wei wrote about his Wang Stream estate, and might well serve as an illustration of his technique:

> *North cottage, north of lake waters,*
> *Mixed trees half hide its red railings.*
> *South river's waters wind far away,*
> *Appear and vanish at the green forest's*
> *edge.*
>
> (Owen 1996, 395)

Here the scene is created with a few well-chosen details—the variety of trees, the half-hidden red railings. The perspective of the viewer turned one way allows the glimpse of only part of those railings, and turned the other way allows a glimpse of the river through the forest. Further, the Buddhist notion of the world as illusion is suggested in the poem: One only half sees the railings, only half sees the water of the river. The river, continually flowing, vanishes altogether, as do all things in this transient world. Thus Wang Wei's celebration of the landscape is not merely for its beauty or for the serene context of retirement it creates for the poet, but also for its demonstration of a Buddhist worldview. Even in four lines, the complexity of Wang Wei's poetry can be observed.

Bibliography

Owen, Stephen, ed. and trans. *An Anthology of Chinese Literature: Beginnings to 1911.* New York: Norton, 1996.

Wagner, Marsha L. *Wang Wei.* Boston: Twayne, 1981.

Yu, Pauline. *The Poetry of Wang Wei: New Translations and Commentary.* Bloomington: Indiana University Press, 1980.

Weaver, The (*Tkadleček*) (ca. 1407)

One of the more important and unusual works of Czech narrative prose from the early 15th century is the text called *Tkadleček* (The Weaver). Like the DEBATE POEMS popular in western Europe, *The Weaver* takes the form of a dispute between a lover named Ludvík and the allegorical figure of Misfortune, who has deprived the Lover of his lady, Adlička. Ludvík refers to himself as the "weaver," suggesting his ability to weave words of love. Essentially the dispute concerns the value of COURTLY LOVE, which Misfortune, speaking like a cleric trained in scholastic argument, condemns. Like most medieval literary debates, the winner of the debate is predetermined, so that in this case it is Misfortune who wins the debate and apparently holds the view sanctioned by the author.

Scholarly consensus holds that the anonymous author of *The Weaver* was himself a cleric, most likely graduated from Prague University—his education is demonstrated by some 90 references to Aristotle in his text. He was also most likely a member of the royal court. He would therefore have been a representative of a new breed of scholar-courtier becoming prevalent in the court of the Bohemian king and sometime Holy Roman Emperor Wenceslas IV (1378–1419). He may have written *The Weaver* for Wenceslas's Queen Sophia of Bavaria, perhaps at her own regional court of Hradec Králové.

Czech society of the early 15th century was characterized by a growing conflict between scholars and preachers on the one hand and the established church and court, whom the preachers condemned for their excesses, on the other. It was the same spirit of reform that gave rise to Jan HUS and the Hussite movement. The author of *The Weaver,* it has been suggested, represents in his debate the conflict between his own clerical training and the fashions of the court, represented by the lover. The text examines the arguments for and against courtly love, with the clear purpose of undermining the courtly love conventions in favor at the royal court. It also concerns the relative merits of courtly and scholastic writing: Where Misfortune sees the love allegories characteristic of the written text of courtly poetry as hindrances to truth, the Lover sees truth as veiled alluringly by the ALLEGORY, like a female body.

Ultimately Misfortune has the final word, a long and rhetorically effusive rejection of courtly traditions. *The Weaver* is notable for its elaborate rhetoric, its sexual puns, and its clerical misogyny that marks it as the product of a late medieval clerical male.

Bibliography

Thomas, Alfred. *Anne's Bohemia: Czech Literature and Society, 1310–1420.* Minneapolis: University of Minnesota Press, 1998.

The Weddyng of Syr Gawen and Dame Ragnell for Helpying of Kyng Arthoure (ca. 1450)

The Weddyng of Syr Gawen and Dame Ragnell is a 15th-century poem of the Arthurian tradition. While hunting, King ARTHUR finds himself alone in the forest and is confronted by Sir Gromer-Somer Jour who alleges that Arthur has appropriated his lands for Sir Gawen (*see* GAWAIN). In retaliation, he intends to cut off Arthur's head in 12 months unless Arthur can answer a riddle: What do women love best? Arthur agrees and returns home. He confides in Gawen and they ride out separately to poll the population in an attempt to solve the riddle. Arthur meets a horrible hag who claims to have the answer but her price of disclosure is marriage to Gawen. Arthur declines to promise but indicates he will counsel Gawen, and the foul woman, Dame Ragnell, tells Arthur that women love sovereignty best. Freed from the bargain with Gromer-Somer Jour (who happens to be Ragnell's brother), Arthur returns home, and Gawen and Ragnell are married. Ragnell tells Gawen that she can be beautiful either during the day when others see them together, or during the night when they are in bed, and Gawen asks her to choose what would be best. This act of yielding to Ragnell's decision gives her the sovereignty she seeks, and having found a knight who will treat her according to the riddle's solution, Ragnell is subsequently freed from the curse of hideousness and is beautiful both day and night. Gawen and Ragnell live happily together until she dies five years later.

The transformation from the ugly to the beautiful is part of a folktale tradition, the "loathly lady" motif. Analogues to the poem include CHAUCER'S *WIFE OF BATH'S TALE* (in which the errant knight is burdened with solving the same riddle as *The Weddyng*'s Arthur), GOWER'S "Tale of Florent" from the CONFESSIO *AMANTIS,* and the later 15th-century *Marriage of Sir Gawaine.* Neither *The Weddyng* nor *The Marriage* is as complex as *The Wife of Bath's Tale.* The riddle itself may have grown out of the tenets of the COURTLY LOVE tradition, which dominated ROMANCE literature. Poets in this genre were frequently courtiers writing for their female audience and the traditional chivalrous knight was often emasculated while carrying out mandatory sacrifices for the love of his lady. It has also been asserted that the motif has Celtic origins and was influenced by Irish, Welsh, Breton, and French tales.

Another detail in the poem is also found in (the roughly contemporary) *AWNTYRS OFF ARTHURE AT THE TERNE WATHELYNE,* wherein a visiting knight alleges that Arthur confiscated his lands and distributed them to Gawen, then challenges Arthur's court to battle. In *The Weddyng,* Gromer-Somer

Jour threatens to behead Arthur because Arthur took his lands and gave them to Gawen. It is Arthur's prideful and covetous nature that provoked Gromer's challenge. In the *Awntyrs,* Gawen battles the knight on Arthur's behalf, while in the *Weddyng,* Gawen aids Arthur in his quest for the riddle's solution and ultimately acts as Arthur's savior by promising to marry Ragnell. One notable difference in the two tales is that Gromer's lands are not restored to him in this poem.

As the tale relates to Arthurian literature, it is consistent with the English tradition that recognizes Gawen as the premier knight in Arthur's court, as opposed to Lancelot in the French tradition. In *The Weddyng,* Arthur is often more shrewd and thoughtful than the impetuous and rash character encountered in some (particularly French) Arthurian texts. For instance, when he initially meets Gromer, he claims to be unprepared for battle as he was hunting and had no war weaponry, and thus avoids battle.

The poem's one extant manuscript dates from either the very late 15th century or early 16th century, while the poem's date of composition is believed to be no earlier than the middle of the 15th century. Its rhyme scheme is six-line TAIL-RHYME stanzas with an *aabccb* scheme, and at least 64 lines are omitted from the scene describing the wedding banquet, as one page of the manuscript has been lost.

The poem provides an alternative to the traditional Gawain character, who often has the reputation of a philanderer, but in this text, he marries happily and sires a son. The poem is also useful in considering the frequently transforming relationship between the faithful knight, Gawain, and his lord, King Arthur.

Bibliography

Shenk, Robert. "The Liberation of the 'Loathly Lady' of Medieval Romance," *Journal of the Rocky Mountain Medieval and Renaissance Association* 2 (1981): 69–77.

Shepherd, Stephen H. A., ed., *Middle English Romances.* New York: Norton, 1995.

Michelle Palmer

Widsith (seventh century)

Widsith is a 142-line OLD ENGLISH heroic poem preserved in the late 10th-century manuscript called the EXETER BOOK. Most scholars believe that the poem predates the manuscript by hundreds of years, and is probably the oldest poem in the English language—quite possibly the oldest extant poem in any Germanic tongue. R. W. Chambers believed the poem was written in seventh-century Mercia. Essentially *Widsith* is a wandering MINSTREL's catalogue of heroes, tribes, and places important in the cultural memory of the Germanic peoples in the heroic age prior to their conversion to Latin Christianity.

The poem is made up of seven rather distinct parts. It begins with a prologue in which the poet Widsith (the name means "far traveler") introduces his journey with Ealhhild, sister of the Lombard king Aelfwine, as she travels to marry Eormanric the Ostrogoth. Precise historians might object that the fourth-century Eormanric was dead 200 years before the sixth-century Aelfwine, but others who see a good bit of folk memory in the poem suggest that here is preserved the memory of late sixth-century Lombard migration from northern Germany through the lands of the Huns and Goths into northern Italy.

The second section of the poem is a catalogue, or *thula,* of Germanic tribes and their illustrious founders, all of whom Widsith claims to have visited. It becomes clear that Widsith is not an actual minstrel, but rather a generic, ideal "poet" who transcends time. He moves from Attila the Hun through various other tribes, devoting the most time to the Anglian king Offa and the Danes, Hrothwulf and Hrothgar, familiar to modern readers of *BEOWULF.* Like the digressions in *Beowulf,* the intent of the list seems to be to evoke heroic stories familiar to the original audience through oral history.

A second catalogue follows, in which Widsith lists the vast number of tribes he has visited. Within this section is a passage (ll. 75–87) most scholars believe to be a later interpolation, wherein the poet claims a knowledge of Saracens, Romans, Egyptians, and others, expanding Widsith's knowledge beyond the Germanic realms to the entire known world.

Following this, Widsith continues the story he had begun in his prologue, and describes how Eormanric gave him a precious ring that he, in turn, passed on to his lord, Eadgils, chief of the Myrgings. Widsith says that Ealhhild also gave him a ring, and that in return he sang her praises throughout the world. Widsith then catalogues the most famous of Eormanric's descendents, alluding to the strife between Goths and Huns. He concludes this section by declaring that in all his travels, he has found that the best men are those God has made lords.

In the poem's epilogue, Widsith makes some observations about the role of the SCOP, or poet, in society. He decides that the scop is valuable because he is able to bring lasting fame and therefore immortality to his patrons.

In fact the poem itself demonstrates this conclusion, as it catalogues some 140 tribes and heroes of the Germanic world from the third to the sixth centuries, many of which the modern world would know nothing about, save through this poem and others like it. Certainly the poet's claim to have made the generosity of Ealhhild known through the world is true—without this poem no one would know of her. Many critics have seen the value of *Widsith* as a historical record. It has also been suggested that the poem, with its emphasis on the generosity of patrons and the poet's ability to immortalize the lord's reputation, is, in fact, a begging poem, in which Widsith is asking for a gift from his patron. Certainly it is also a poem about the power of poetry and of the poet himself.

Bibliography

Alexander, Michael, trans. *The Earliest English Poems.* Harmondsworth, U.K.: Penguin, 1966.

Chambers, R. W. *Widsith: A Study in Old English Heroic Legend.* Cambridge: Cambridge University Press, 1912.

Creed, Robert P. "Widsith's Journey through Germanic Tradition." In *Anglo-Saxon Poetry: Essays in Appreciation for John C. McGalliard,* edited by Lewis E. Nicholson and Dolores Warwick Frese, 376–387. Notre Dame, Ind.: Notre Dame University Press, 1967.

Krapp, George Philip, and Elliott Van Kirk Dobbie, eds. *The Exeter Book.* The Anglo-Saxon Poetic Records, 3. New York: Columbia University Press, 1936.

Malone, Kemp, ed. *Widsith.* London: Methuen, 1936.

Rallman, David A. " 'Widsith' as an Anglo-Saxon Defense of Poetry," *Neophilologus* 66 (1982): 431–439.

Wife of Bath's Prologue and Tale, The

Geoffrey Chaucer (ca. 1394)

CHAUCER's Wife of Bath, Alisoun, is perhaps his most original and memorable creation. Her prologue and tale form a pivotal point in the *CANTERBURY TALES,* inspiring responses in *The CLERK'S TALE* and *The MERCHANT'S TALE,* and imitation in *The PARDONER'S TALE.* That the character and her tale were well known in the circle of Chaucer's immediate audience is clear from the passing reference to the Wife in Chaucer's lyric "Envoy to Bukton" (1396). In the *Wife of Bath,* Chaucer creates an outspoken and independent woman who embodies all of the antifeminist stereotypes of medieval theologians even as she attempts to refute them through her powerful rhetoric.

In the prologue, Chaucer has combined a variety of sources, most important, St. JEROME's argument for virginity in *Adversus Jovinianum,* which Alisoun opposes vigorously and JEAN DE MEUN's section of the *ROMAN DE LA ROSE,* particularly the section in which La Vieille, the old woman, describes her life and the wiles of women, which seems to have been the model for Alisoun's confession. The Wife's prologue is a spirited vindication of her way of life—that is, of marriage and sexuality, in the face of the misogynist commonplaces of medieval clerics. She presents her defense somewhat in the form of a scholastic argument that might occur among clerics, citing experience and authority to support her defense of her own life.

Alisoun reveals that she has had five husbands, the first when she was only 12 years old. She also makes it clear that she would welcome a sixth. From authority she argues that Christ never specified how many times a woman could marry, and that while St. Paul preferred virginity he did not condemn marriage. Paul also said that the husband and wife owed one another the "marriage debt" (that is, sexual pleasure), and Alisoun makes it clear that she is more than willing to both pay and collect that debt.

For her argument from experience, Alisoun describes her marriages. She claims that three of her husbands were good and two were bad. The "good" husbands were her first three—all old men whom she lumps together without distinction. They were "good" because she could easily manipulate them, and could control and ultimately inherit their wealth. Her fourth husband, however, was younger and not so easily controlled, and had a mistress as well. Alisoun claims to have made him jealous by feigning unfaithfulness. In any case she was already interested in a young clerk named Jankyn before her fourth husband died, and she mentions how during the funeral, she couldn't keep her eyes off Jankyn's attractive legs as he acted as pallbearer for husband number four.

Alisoun married Jankyn for love, and admits that even though he beat her, she still loved him best. She describes how he would read to her daily from a "Book of Wicked Wives" until she could no longer stand it and tore a page from the book. In response Jankyn gave her a blow on the side of the head from which she is still deaf in one ear. She pretended to be dying until Jankyn begged her forgiveness and gave over to her the "sovereignty" in the marriage. After that, Alisoun claims, the marriage was happy and the two were true and faithful to one another.

Alisoun moves into her tale, which is a short Arthurian romance concerning a young knight and an old hag. Its source seems to be in the folklore motif of the "loathly lady." Analogues of the tale may be found in John GOWER's "Tale of Florent" from his CONFESSIO *AMANTIS*, and in the later 15th-century romance *The* WEDDYNG OF SYR GAWEN. But Chaucer shapes the tale to serve as a kind of psychological wish-fulfillment for Alisoun.

In the tale a young Knight of Arthur's court rapes a maiden, and is condemned to death by the King. The Queen intervenes and convinces the King that the ladies of the court should judge the Knight. She gives the Knight a reprieve and imposes a quest on him: He must return to court in a year and a day with an answer to the question, "What do women most desire?" If he fails to answer the question satisfactorily, he will die. The Knight wanders about, finding no definitive answer until, on his way back to court, he meets an old hag who says she will give him the answer if he will grant her whatever she asks. The Knight agrees, and returns to court with the hag. He answers the Queen that what women desire most is sovereignty in marriage. The ladies of the court all agree that the Knight has saved his life, and the old hag demands her reward. In return for saving his life, she demands that she become the young Knight's bride.

Reluctantly the Knight marries her. When he turns from her in disgust on their wedding night, the hag asks him what is bothering him. He replies that she is old and ugly, and of low birth. She takes each of these points and refutes it by rational argument. She then offers the Knight a choice: He can have her old and ugly but be assured of her virtue and faithfulness, or he can have her young and beautiful and take his chances on her chastity. Unable to choose between her two means of making him miserable, the Knight leaves the choice up to the hag. When she asks whether this means he has granted her sovereignty, he answers in the affirmative. In response she turns into the most beautiful woman he has ever seen, and promises she will be faithful as well, and the two live in marital bliss from that moment on.

Thus the tale is, for the Wife, a wish-fulfillment fantasy in which she not only gains mastery over a young husband, but also regains her own youth and beauty. The tale illustrates what Alisoun believes is the chief point of her prologue: that a happy marriage is one in which the woman has "sovereignty." But a careful reader might notice that, in fact, both Alisoun's prologue and tale illustrate that a happy marriage actually occurs when there is mutual love, respect, and kindness.

The Wife of Bath has been the subject of more critical commentary than any other figure in the Chaucer canon. Much attention has been paid to the character of Alisoun—whether she is sympathetic or monstrous, whether she is a character at all in the modern sense. Feminist critics have looked closely at her and at Chaucer and speculated about whether she provides a truly female perspective and about Chaucer's own attitude toward women. Others have seen her tale as beginning a "marriage debate" that includes the tales of the Merchant, Clerk, and FRANKLIN. Most would agree that in *The Wife of Bath's Tale,* Chaucer most clearly finds a perfect fit between tale and teller.

Bibliography

Beidler, Peter G., ed. *Geoffrey Chaucer: "The Wife of Bath": Complete Authoritative Text with Biographical and Historical Contexts, Critical History and Essays from Five Contemporary Critical Perspectives. Case Studies in Contemporary Criticism.* Boston: Bedford-St. Martin's, 1996.

Beidler, Peter G., and Elizabeth M. Biebel, eds. *Chaucer's Wife of Bath's Prologue and Tale: An Annotated Bibliography, 1900 to 1995.* Toronto: University of Toronto Press, 1998.

Carruthers, Mary J. "The Wife of Bath and the Painting of Lions," *PMLA* 94 (1979): 209–222.

Delaney, Sheila. "Strategies of Silence in the Wife of Bath's Recital," *Exemplaria* 2 (1990): 49–69.

Dinshaw, Carolyn. *Chaucer's Sexual Poetics.* Madison: University of Wisconsin Press, 1989.

Fleming, John V. "Sacred and Secular Exegesis in the Wyf of Bath's Tale." In *Retelling Tales: Essays in Honor of Russell Peck,* edited by Thomas Hahn and Alan Lupack, 73–90. Woodbridge, Suffolk, U.K.: Brewer, 1997.

Hansen, Elaine Tuttle. *Chaucer and the Fictions of Gender.* Berkeley: University of California Press, 1992.

Leicester, H. Marshall. "The Wife of Bath as Chaucerian Subject." In *Studies in the Age of Chaucer, Proceedings 1,1984,* edited by Paul Strohm and Thomas J. Heffernan, 201–210. Knoxville, Tenn.: New Chaucer Society, 1985.

Robertson, D. W., Jr. " 'And for My Land Thus Hastow Mordred Me?': Land Tenure, the Cloth Industry, and the Wife of Bath," *Chaucer Review* 14 (1980): 403–420.

Wood, Chauncey. "The Wife of Bath and 'Speche Daungerous.' " In *Chaucer and Language: Essays in Honour of Douglas Wurtele,* edited by Robert Myles and David Williams, 33–43, 191–192. Montreal: McGill-Queen's University Press, 2001.

Wife's Lament, The (*Wife's Complaint*) (10th century)

The Wife's Lament is an OLD ENGLISH poem of 53 lines found in the EXETER BOOK, a 10th-century manuscript that is the largest single compilation of Old English poetry. Like *WULF AND EADWACER, The Wife's Lament* has a female speaker who is pained by the absence of her man, in this case her husband rather than her lover.

The situation of the poem's speaker is rather obscure. Clearly she was married to a noble husband outside of her own tribe. It can be conjectured that the marriage was intended to bring peace between warring tribes, as was common in Germanic society—one might compare Hrothgar's queen Wealtheow in *BEOWULF.* In this poem the speaker's husband is separated from her, apparently because his kinsmen have hatched a plot to keep them apart. She is left alone among hostile enemies, she says, and apparently has been forced to live alone in a cave in the wilderness. She imagines her husband alone on some rocky shore, suffering the same friendless exile as she endures.

Because the details are sketchy, scholars have interpreted the poem quite differently. Some believe that the husband, swayed by his kinsmen's enmity, has himself banished the wife. Others believe that the husband has been exiled because of some feud, and so left the wife alone with his hostile family. In that case her picture of him in the end may be reality rather than her imagining.

The language of *The Wife's Lament* is very similar to that of other Old English poems like *The WANDERER* and *The SEAFARER,* and the mood of loss is very similar, making it appropriate to include *The Wife's Lament* in the genre of ELEGAIC POETRY.

Bibliography

Alexander, Michael, trans. *The Earliest English Poems.* Harmondsworth, U.K.: Penguin, 1966.

Krapp, George Philip, and Elliott Van Kirk Dobbie, eds. *The Exeter Book.* The Anglo-Saxon Poetic Records, 3. New York: Columbia University Press, 1936.

Wentersdorf, Karl P. "The Situation of the Narrator in the Old English *Wife's Lament*," *Speculum* 56 (1981): 492–516.

William of Malmesbury (ca. 1095–1143)

William of Malmesbury was one of the most important historians of medieval England. His best-known works, the *Gesta regum Anglorum* (Deeds of the kings of England) and its sequel *Historia novella* (Recent history), tell the story of English history from the Anglo-Saxon invasion of 449 until his own present (1142). Known for his critical assessment of primary sources, his concern with the relationship of physical features like geography and architecture on historical events, his lively and colorful style, and his interest in the motivations for human actions, William in unquestionably the most valuable and readable historian of his age.

William was born in Wiltshire in approximately 1095, the son of a Norman father and an English mother. He was apparently educated at the Benedictine Abbey of Malmesbury in Wiltshire, where he subsequently became a monk. In his education William became particularly interested in history, and was especially impressed by the work of the Venerable BEDE, whom he emulated. In 1125, William finished his *Gesta regum Anglorum,* which deals with English history until 1127. Some of the more interesting passages of this text deal with King ARTHUR, whom William depicts as assisting Ambrosius Aurelianus in fighting off the Anglo-Saxon invasions. William repeats as history the legend of the Battle of Mount Badon in which Arthur, bearing on his armor the image of the Virgin Mary, personally slaughtered 900 of the enemy—a story apparently derived from the *Historia Brittonum* attributed to NENNIUS. Further, William discusses the finding of the tomb of Arthur's nephew Walwen (GAWAIN), and dismisses British "fables" about Arthur, who he says needs to be appreciated for his authentic historical contributions. Another significant section of the *Gesta regum Anglorum* is William's account of the Norman invasion. William finds King Harold praiseworthy, but sees the invasion as just retribution for the "sins of the flesh" committed by the English.

William indicates that he had the opportunity to become abbott of Malmesbury, but preferred the role of librarian, where he could indulge his scholarly pursuits. He was a prolific writer, and the same year he completed the *Gesta regum* he also finished the *Gesta pontificum Anglorum* (Deeds of the pontiffs of England), an ecclesiastical history owing much to Bede. Over the next 10 to 15 years, he worked on a history of the saints of Glastonbury, where some scholars have speculated he may have been living at the time (1129–39). Among his other works are a life of St. Dunstan and a collection of Miracles of the Virgin. He compiled, as well, a collection of legal and historical documents now housed at Oxford's Bodleian Library.

About 1140, William began writing his final work, the *Historia novella* (Recent history), a sequel to the *Gesta regum Anglorum,* dealing with history from 1125 to 1142. William was apparently writing under the patronage of Robert, earl of Gloucester, a major figure in the civil war between King Stephen and the empress Maude. William's account of Stephen's reign (the years following 1135) is a significant and authoritative contemporary source for that epoch. The text of the *Historia novella,* however, is unpolished, suggesting the draft of a manuscript William never completed. It is assumed he died around 1143, before completing the history.

Bibliography

Gransden, Antonia. *Historical Writing in England, c. 550 to C. 1307.* London: Routledge and Kegan Paul, 1974.

Preest, David, trans. *The Deeds of the Bishops of England.* Woodbridge, U.K.: Boydell Press, 2002.

Scott, John, ed. and trans. *The Early History of Glastonbury.* Rochester, N.Y.: Boydell Press, 2001.

Thomson, R. M. *William of Malmesbury.* Rev. ed. Rochester, N.Y.: Boydell Press, 2003.

William of Malmesbury. *Gesta regum Anglorum: The History of the English Kings.* Completed by R. M. Thomson and M. Winterbottom. Edited and translated by R. A. B. Mynors. Oxford: Clarendon Press, 1998–1999.

Winterbottom, M., and R. M. Thomson, eds. *Saints' Lives: Lives of SS. Wulfstan, Dunstan, Patrick, Be-*

nignus and Indract. Oxford: Clarendon Press, 2002.

William of Palerne (ca. 1340–60)

William of Palerne is a lively, fantastical, and lengthy (over 5,500 lines) 14th-century MIDDLE ENGLISH alliterative adaptation of a French ROMANCE, *Guillaume de Palerne.* The date of composition is believed to be between 1340 and 1360, during the reign of EDWARD III, and there are two references in the narrative to the patron who commissioned the poem, Humphrey de Bohun, earl of Hereford. *William of Palerne* is preserved in a single manuscript (King's College Cambridge 30) with a copy of the *SOUTH ENGLISH LEGENDARY.* Although the two works were originally separate manuscripts, evidence indicates that they were probably connected as early as the 15th century. The writing of the romance of *William of Palerne* was undertaken, according to the narrative, "in ese of Englysch men" (l. 66), and "for hem that knowe no Frensche, ne never understo[n]" (1. 5538), and follows the comprehensive medieval definition of translation in which a narrative not only is rewritten in another language but is revised and shaped according to the poet-translator's interpretation. While remaining considerably faithful to his source, the English poet changes scenes, characters, courtly sensibility, and political behaviors. As a production of the so-called ALLITERATIVE REVIVAL, many narratives of which depict world historical and social concerns, the use of the alliterative form here could signal the ways in which the poet represents political concerns under cover of fashionable romance.

The fantastic plots and subplots of this romance do not lend themselves to a brief and coherent summary account, and much of the romance's humorous delight is lost in abstracting the basic story line. Nonetheless the romance narrative of exile and return begins when the king and queen of Sicily have a son named William whose death is plotted by the king's brother. A werewolf (who is really the son of the king of Spain bewitched by his stepmother) saves the child William and escapes with him to Italy, where the child is adopted by a cowherd. One day the emperor of Rome comes upon William and is so struck by his gentility and beauty that he takes him back to Rome. At the palace William is put under the care of the emperor's daughter, Meliors, and they fall in love. When she is betrothed against her will to another, Meliors and William escape dressed in bear skins with the guidance of the faithful werewolf. They go to Sicily, which is under siege by the king of Spain, and dressed now as hind and hart, take refuge in the queen's garden. In a wonderful revelation scene William is discovered to be the queen of Sicily's long-lost son; he battles the king of Spain, his inheritance is regained, the good are rewarded, the bad are forgiven, the werewolf regains his human form, and all live happily under the wise rule of William and Meliors.

William of Palerne creates a fantastic and humorously idealized realm in which personal and political ideals are both espoused and achieved. The world of the romance is utterly improbable in its presentation of unfailing courtesy and courtly behaviors, and predicated upon an ideology in which personal behavior becomes a political model. Yet embedded in its fantastic improbability are lessons of conduct and right rule that are as realistic, morally relevant, and conventional as those found in more conventional "mirrors for princes." The didacticism of *William of Palerne* is particularly concerned with individual happiness and social harmony, where exemplary personal behavior translates into exemplary political relations. It is worth noting that those sections of the poem most expanded from its source are scenes in which lessons of ideal rule and personal and political behavior are examined.

Critical engagement with *William of Palerne* has been slight, and, more often than not, the poem is discussed only briefly in surveys of Middle English romances. Some critics suggest that the poem was intended for an unsophisticated audience, while others discuss aristocratic patronage for alliterative revival works in general, and for this romance in particular. The amplification (from its source) of the ideals of wise rule and the exercise of kingship indicates a concern with political didacticism that may be key for future critical analyses.

Bibliography

Bunt, Gerrit Hendrik, ed. *William of Palerne: an Electronic Edition.* Ann Arbor: University of Michigan Press, 2002.

Calin, William. *The French Tradition and the Literature of Medieval England.* Toronto: University of Toronto Press, 1994.

Crane, Susan. *Insular Romance: Politics, Faith, and Culture in Anglo-Norman and Middle English Literature.* Berkeley: University of California Press, 1969.

Dalrymple, Roger. *Language and Piety in Middle English Romance.* Cambridge, U.K.: Brewer, 2000.

Diamond, Arlyn. "Loving Beasts: The Romance of *William of Palerne.*" In *The Spirit of Medieval English Popular Romance,* edited by Ad Putter and Jane Gilbert, 142–156. London: Longman, 2000.

Dunn, Charles W. *The Foundling and the Werewolf: A Literary-Historical Study of Guillaume de Palerne.* Toronto and Oxford: Oxford University Press, 1960.

Mehl, Dieter. *The Middle English Romances of the Thirteenth and Fourteenth Centuries.* London: Routledge and Kegan Paul, 1969.

Ramsay, Lee C. *Chivalric Romances: Popular Literature in Medieval England.* Bloomington: University of Illinois Press, 1983.

Elisa Narin van Court

William of Shoreham (fl. 1327)

William of Shoreham was a MIDDLE ENGLISH lyric poet of the early 14th century who authored seven extant poems, all of which have survived in a single manuscript (British Museum Additional MS. 17,376). A colophon (or scribal notation) to the manuscript mentions Simon, the archbishop of Canterbury—a fact that dates the manuscript to the beginning of the reign of King EDWARD III (1327–77) and suggests that William was active at that time. Little is known of William's life, other than his association with the village of Shoreham, near Sevenoaks in Kent (perhaps he was born there). He was made vicar of Chart Sutton in Kent in 1313, and because that position was connected with Leeds Priory, it has been suggested that William was an Augustinian canon at that priory.

William's seven poems are all religious and didactic, and deal with some of the favorite topics of medieval preachers. Four of them are concerned with Christian doctrine and theology, and include lyrics on the seven sacraments of the Catholic Church, on the Ten Commandments, and on the Seven Deadly Sins. A longer poem, the final poem in the manuscript, is a more substantial treatment of topics like the nature of the Trinity, the fall of Satan, and the Fall of Man, and apparently would have dealt with the Redemption as well, but is incomplete, as the manuscript breaks off after the temptation. One of William's other lyrics concerns the five joys of the Virgin, and another is a hymn to Mary apparently translated from a Latin text by Robert GROSSETESTE. The latter is perhaps William's best-known poem, appearing in anthologies of medieval English lyrics. It is made up mainly of conventional allegorical symbols of Mary. Its first stanza gives a good illustration of William's lyric style:

Marye, maide, milde and fre [noble],
Chamber of the Trinite,
One while lest [listen] to me,
Ase ich thee grete with songe.
Thagh my fet [vessel] unclene be,
My mes [meal] thou onderfonge [receive].

(Davies 1964, 103, ll. 1–6)

Generally writing in six- or seven-line stanzas, William's versification is often somewhat rough. But the sometimes difficult theological concepts he discusses are communicated clearly and simply, and his poetry's melancholy focus on the transience of earthly life is typical of medieval lyric religious verse.

It was once believed that William was also the author of a prose translation of the Psalms that appears in the same manuscript as his lyrics and is written in the same hand. But because the lyrics are in William's native Kentish dialect, while the Psalm translation is in a Midland dialect, it seems unlikely that William wrote the English Psalms.

Bibliography

Davies, R. T., ed. *Medieval English Lyrics: A Critical Anthology.* Evanston, Ill.: Northwestern University Press, 1964.

Konrath, M., ed. *The Poems of William of Shoreham.* London: Published for the Early English Text Society by K. Paul, Trench, Trübner and Co., Limited, 1902.

Winner and Waster (*Wynnere and Wastour*) (ca. 1352–1353)

Winner and Waster is a DREAM VISION poem of 503 extant lines, written in a Northwest Midland dialect of MIDDLE ENGLISH. The poem is a political ALLEGORY composed during the reign of King EDWARD III, who appears as a character in the poem. Its verse form marks it as part of the ALLITERATIVE REVIVAL popular in the west and north of England in the 14th century, and as such it is related to poems like *SIR GAWAIN AND THE GREEN KNIGHT, The ALLITERATIVE MORTE ARTHURE*, and particularly *The PARLIAMENT OF THE THREE AGES*, with which it has often been compared. Some scholars have suggested that the author of *Winner and Waster* is the same poet who wrote the *Parliament,* but most think the common authorship unlikely. *Winner and Waster* survives in a single 15th-century manuscript in the British Library (Additional MS 31042), which also contains the *Parliament of the Three Ages.* But the manuscript is incomplete and the text faulty in places due to scribal error.

The poem begins with the narrator falling asleep near the bank of a river in the west country. In his dream he sees two opposing armies approach one another on a great plain. One army, led by Winner, includes the pope and cardinals and a number of friars, as well as lawyers and merchants. With Waster, leader of the other host, are the nobility and the military—knights, squires, and bowmen. On a hill above the plain is the pavilion of the king—identified as Edward III by the motto of the Order of the Garter ("Evil be to him who evil thinks"). The king sends a great baron (presumably his son the Black Prince) to forbid the armies to do battle, and to require their leaders to come before the king and explain themselves. Winner and Waster do so in a series of eight speeches alternating between the two. Thus the text becomes a DEBATE POEM of the sort popular in the later Middle Ages. Winner, who represents those who work to create and to attain wealth, speaks first. He defends the need for producers of wealth in society, and condemns those who, like Waster, squander resources. The figure of Waster in the poem, however, represents not only profligates, but anyone who consumes what has been manufactured. Thus while the laziness and prodigality of Waster may be condemned in the poem, so too is the miserliness and selfishness of Winner. Both groups, though mortal enemies, are necessary in society. In the end the king seems to realize this. As in most debate poems, the argument has no clear victor, and the king settles the dispute by sending Winner to live with the pope in Rome (where he is most popular) and Waster to visit the shops of London, apparently to stimulate the economy. The manuscript breaks off before the end of the king's speech.

The poem may reflect class struggle between the bourgeoisie (as "winners") and the nobility (as "wasters") in the economic crisis following the BLACK DEATH. It also seems influenced by Aristotle's view of wastefulness and miserliness as extreme vices, with ideal moral behavior being the mean, the courtly virtue of liberality. In either case, the poet suggests that wise government is needed to solve the economic problems of society. The poem may reflect political events after the Black Death, when the Statute of Laborers (1351) and the Treason Statute (1352) were enacted to curb societal unrest, and the poet may be writing to urge the king to take decisive action to ensure order. However, the manuscript as we have it was hardly intended for a courtly audience, since it is interrupted periodically by a call to drink, as at a tavern. Such interruptions would be consistent with a MINSTREL performance for a middle-class audience, and it is possible that what has survived is a transcription of a minstrel's copy of a poem originally intended for a noble patron. How well known the poem was in its own day is hard to judge, given the single manuscript that survives, but some scholars believe that *Winner and Waster* was influential on another

Northwest Midland alliterative poem, William LANGLAND'S *PIERS PLOWMAN.*

Bibliography

Gardner, John, trans. *The Alliterative Morte Arthure, The Owl and the Nightingale, and Five Other Middle English Poems.* Carbondale: Southern Illinois University Press, 1971.

Ginsberg, Warren, ed. *Wynnere and Wastoure and the Parlement of the Thre Ages.* Kalamazoo, Mich.: Published for TEAMS by the Medieval Institute, 1992.

Trigg, Stephanie, ed. *Wynnere and Wastoure.* EETS 297. London: Oxford University Press, 1990.

Wolfram von Eschenbach (ca. 1180–ca. 1220)

Being the author of one of the most important courtly romances in Middle High German literature, *PARZIVAL* (ca. 1205), Wolfram also gained great respect for his Crusade epic *Willehalm* (ca. 1218) and his dawn songs (*see ALBA*). No historical document speaks about him, but on the basis of internal evidence and references to him by other poets, we know that he lived from ca. 1170 to ca. 1225. He identifies himself as a Bavarian, but obviously hailed from a little town near Ansbach in Franconia, Ober-Eschenbach, which renamed itself Wolframs-Eschenbach in 1917, in honor of the poet. In his *Parzival* Wolfram mentions his family several times in a satirical fashion, but nothing concrete is known about them. The *Manessische Liederhandschrift* (MS. C, early 14th century) offers a fictionalized portrait of Wolfram, entirely covered by knightly armor, which implies that he might have been of noble origin. He confirms this observation by stating in his *Parzival* that he descended from an aristocratic family and belonged to the knightly class. Although he repeatedly emphasizes that he is illiterate (*Parzival* 115, 27–30; *Willehalm* 2, 19–22), this comment can only be meant as satirical with respect to Latin and learned literature, whereas the vast number of sources utilized by Wolfram demonstrates his extensive schooling. He was certainly familiar with the basic disciplines taught at the universities, the *trivium* and the *quadrivium* (*see* LIBERAL ARTS), but we do not know whether he ever received formal training. Insofar as he based both his *Parzival* and his *Willehalm* on Old French sources (CHRÉTIEN DE TROYES), he must have had very good knowledge of French.

Late-medieval myths allude to a major competition between Wolfram and contemporary authors during a poetic tournament at the Castle Wartburg in Eisenach, Thuringia, but we only know for sure that Wolfram spent some time there, sponsored by his patron, Landgrave Hermann I of Thuringia (1190–1217). In his *Parzival,* Wolfram refers to a war between Hermann and King Philipp of Swabia, during which a vineyard near Erfurt was destroyed in 1203, giving us a verifiable date *post quem* (a date only after which the romance could have been composed). Wolfram also wrote a short fragmentary piece, *Titurel* (ca. 1220), in which he picked up narrative elements that he had left undeveloped in his *Parzival.*

Wolfram's four dawn songs prove to be highly sophisticated representatives of this genre, especially as he was the first one to introduce the figure of the castle guardian who alerts the lovers to the approaching dawn and the need to separate. In his dawn song "*Der helnden minne ir klage*" (no. IV), Wolfram advocates marriage as a preferable alternative to illicit love affairs. He also composed three more traditional courtly love songs. In his *Willehalm,* Wolfram explores, probably for the first time in the Middle Ages, concepts of religious and ethnic tolerance within the context of a highly bloody battle poem. In his *Parzival* we come across, for the first time in medieval literature, the idea of interracial marriage, as Parzival's father Gahmuret marries the beautiful black Queen Belakane. He leaves her again, but not because of their racial or religious differences, as he pretends in a letter to her, but because of his irrepressible desire to pursue his knightly career.

In his *Titurel,* finally, Wolfram experiments with the potentials of a literary fragment, the first medieval poet to do so. Not only has this text come down to us in two fragments, which would be a very common phenomenon, but the author also develops the idea of a fragment within his own text where an enigmatic and highly fascinating text is written on a dog leash. At the end the dog escapes the female protagonist, Sigune, who then forces her lover, Schionatulander, to recapture the dog and so the text; otherwise, he would never enjoy her love. Unfortunately, as we know from *Parzival,* the young man will die in his pursuit of the dog, unable to return either the dog or the text to his beloved. By the mid-century, a very little known poet, Albrecht (von Scharfenberg), composed a continuation of the *Titurel* text, today called the *Jüngere Titurel,* in which Schionatulander wins the dog and eventually gives a communal reading of the text on the leash, transforming it into a quasi-liturgical statement. This enormously popular text (56 manuscripts, one print) was long thought to have been Wolfram's own creation, and Albrecht's authorship was not recognized until the early 19th century.

Bibliography

Bumke, Joachim. *Wolfram von Eschenbach.* 7th ed. Stuttgart: Metzler, 1997.

Hasty, Will, ed. *A Companion to Wolfram's Parzival.* Columbia, S.C.: Camden House, 1999.

Poag, James F. *Wolfram von Eschenbach.* New York: Twayne, 1972.

Wynn, Marianne. "Wolfram von Eschenbach," in *German Writers and Works of the High Middle Ages: 1170–1280,* edited by James Hardin and Will Hasty. Detroit: Gale Research, 1994, 185–206.

Albrecht Classen

Wooing Group *(Wohunge Group)*

The Wooing Group (*Wohunge Group*) includes the title piece, *Þe Wohunge of ure Laured (The Wooing of Our Lord), On Lofsong of ure Loured (A Song of Praise Concerning Our Lord), On wel swuðe God Ureisun of God Almihti (An Exceedingly Good Orison to God Almighty), On Lofsong of ure Lefdi (A Song of Praise Concerning Our Lady),* as well as the two fragmentary renditions of the final two pieces, *On Ureisun of ure Lourede (An Orison to Our Lord),* and *Þe Oriesun of Seinte Marie (An Orison to Saint Mary).* All are 13th-century pieces written in the West Midlands dialect J. R. R. Tolkien christened the "AB" language (a standard written—rather than spoken—dialect, characterized by French and Norse loanwords, colloquial expressions, conservative spelling, and similarities to Old English syntax). Only one direct source has been found for any member of the Wooing Group: *On Lofsong of ure Lefdi* has its origins in an 11th-century Latin prayer by Marbod of Rennes, *Oratio ad sanctum Mariam.* While the other texts certainly share correlations with other prayers of the same era, they appear to be substantially original in composition.

Þe Wohunge survives in only one manuscript, London, British Library, MS Cotton Titus D.xviii (ff. 127r–133r), and the other three pieces of the *Wooing Group* are not found with it; instead, they are found at the end of ANCRENE WISSE in London, British Library, MS Cotton Nero A.xiv. While there is no general agreement among scholars as to authorship, *Ancrene Wisse,* the KATHERINE GROUP, and the Wooing Group are often combined, albeit loosely, into a confederation of texts. They are connected by manuscript tradition, as many of the texts appear and reappear in manuscripts in various combinations. Perhaps most significantly, there exist numerous thematic parallels among the group, including a focus on a suffering human Christ who has a personal relationship with the primarily female audience, and a connection to anchoresses. Anchoresses were women who completely withdrew from earthly life by having themselves enclosed in small cells attached to churches, from which they could never depart. They communicated with servants and visitors through a window that looked out on the churchyard, and observed Mass and received communion through a window that was directed towards the high altar. As contemplatives, the anchoresses' primary purpose was to pray, seeking complete union with God.

The pieces are written in lyrical prose, and combine COURTLY LOVE imagery of Christ as the perfect lover-knight with more earthy eroticism. Similarly, the texts combine nuptial metaphors with crucifixion imagery, blending divine marriage with shared divine pain. Jesus is at once the desired spouse and the suffering savior. In particular, the title piece outlines all the qualities that Christ has that make him the perfect spouse, and these are all defined in human terms. Christ is handsome, kind, noble, wealthy, generous, and loving. The other members of the Trinity make only rare appearances. For instance, God the Father is referred to only in the context of providing Jesus with a kingdom. Similarly, the Virgin Mary is invoked as a pure, unstained advocate for the female speaker's cause, but not fleshed out as an individual figure.

W. Meredith Thompson, an early editor of Wooing Group, put forth the claim that it was written by a woman for other women, probably anchoresses, and that *þe Wohunge* itself was written with one specific anchoress in mind. While this view is appealingly optimistic, it is rather unlikely, as the works appear more performative and directive than personal. Other scholars have suggested attributing common, but unknown, authorship to *Ancrene Wisse,* the Katherine Group, particularly *HALI MEIDENHAD,* and the Wooing Group.

Related to the Wooing Group, but not technically a part of it, is the 14th-century text *A Talkyng of the Loue of God (A Discussion of the Love of God).* This work, extant in two different manuscripts, is composed of large portions of *On Uriesun of ure Lourede* and *þe Wohunge of ure Laured,* along with SAINT ANSELM of Canterbury's *Liber meditatio et orationum* and original work. Though the primary source materials for this treatise were composed for women, evidence suggests that *A Talkyng* was intended for a male monastic audience.

To a great extent, traditional scholarship has overlooked the Wooing Group in favor of its more prominent companions, especially *Ancrene Wisse.* The few early investigations focused primarily upon philology, diction, and vocabulary. More recently, scholars have begun investigating the implications of gender and sexuality found in the Wooing Group as well as its place in the anchoritic context and the culture of late medieval piety. More investigation into these texts is needed in the future. These endeavors should be aided by the recent translations of Wooing Group and *A Talkyng* into modern English, making the texts accessible to a wider audience.

Bibliography

Innes-Parker, Catherine. "*Ancrene Wisse* and *þe Wohunge of ure Lauerd:* The Thirteenth-Century Female Reader and the Lover-Knight," in *Women, the Book, and the Godly: Selected Proceedings of the St. Hilda's Conference, 1993,* edited by Lesley Smith and Jane H. M. Taylor. Vol. 1 of 2. Cambridge: Brewer, 1995.

Sauer, Michelle M. *The* Wohunge Group *and* A Talkyng of the Loue of God: *Translated from the Middle English with introduction, notes, and interpretive essay.* Library of Medieval Women Series. Woodbridge, Suffolk: Boydell and Brewer, forthcoming.

———. " 'Prei for me mi leue suster': The Paradox of the Anchoritic 'Community' in Late Medieval England," *Prose Studies* 26 (2003): 153–175.

Thompson, W. Meredith, ed. *þe Wohunge of Ure Laured.* Edited from British Museum MS Cotton Titus D.xviii, together with *On Uriesun of Ure Lourerde; On Wel Swuðe God Ureisun of God Almihti; On Lofsong of Ure Louerde; On Lofsong of Ure Lefdi; þe Oreisun of Seinte Marie.* EETS 241. London: Published for the Early English Text Society by the Oxford University Press, 1958.

Westra, Salvina, ed. *A Talkyng of the Loue of God. Edited from MS Vernon (Bodleian 3938) and Collated with MS Simeon (Brit. Mus. Add. 22283).* The Hague: Martinus Nijhoff, 1950.

Michelle M. Sauer

Wulf and Eadwacer (10th century)

Wulf and Eadwacer is a very obscure OLD ENGLISH poem from the EXETER BOOK. At 19 lines, the lyric appears fragmentary at first, but the sketchy images do suggest a complete dramatic situation.

The poem's speaker is a woman longing for her lover, Wulf, who is apparently an outlaw living in exile. Eadwacer, whom she taunts contemptuously in the poem, appears to be her husband, though she seems never to have considered theirs a true marriage. Despite her intense longing, she fears for Wulf's safety if he returns. In the end the speaker mocks Eadwacer because Wulf has come back and apparently has carried off his child by her, whom she calls, with a punning reference to the father's name, "our cub," or *hwelp,* in the original.

Peter Dronke has suggested that *Wulf and Eadwacer* is the type of song that CHARLEMAGNE banned from any nunneries in his kingdom in 789. He had called them *winileados* ("songs for a friend")—songs composed by women to express their longing for absent lovers. Dronke believes that there were many such songs in Germanic languages that have not survived. The poem is also unusual in the Old English corpus because of its division into strophes and its use of a refrain, translated as "our fate is forked." *DEOR* is the only other poem in Old English with a similar structure.

Bibliography

Alexander, Michael, trans. *The Earliest English Poems.* Harmondsworth, U.K.: Penguin, 1966.

Baker, Peter S. "The Ambiguity of 'Wulf and Eadwacer.' " In *Old English Shorter Poems,* edited by Katherine O'Brien O'Keeffe, 409–426. New York: Garland, 1994.

Dronke, Peter. *The Medieval Lyric.* 3rd ed. Woodbridge, U.K.: Boydell and Brewer, 1996.

Krapp, George Philip, and Elliott Van Kirk Dobbie, eds. *The Exeter Book.* Vol. 3 of The Anglo-Saxon Poetic Records. New York: Columbia University Press, 1936.

Pulsiano, Philip, and Kirsten Wolf. "The 'Hwelp' in 'Wulf and Eadwacer,' " *English Language Notes* 28 (1991): 1–9.

Wulfstan (ca. 960–1023)

Wulfstan was an important scholar, statesman, and prelate of the early 11th century. A Benedictine monk, he was the product of the great Benedictine Revival of learning that had been promulgated by St. Dunstan, St. Athelstan, and especially Wulfstan's friend AELFRIC. Nothing is known of his early life, but Wulfstan was made bishop of London from 996 until 1002, when he became archbishop of York and bishop of Worcester. The dual appointment was probably granted because, with the Danes ravaging the northern part of England, it was only by having the see of Worcester that Wulfstan could have enough income to maintain his see at York. He held the joint appointment until 1016, when he dropped the Worcester Bishopric. From 1008 onward, he acted as an adviser to King Ethelred II (often called "the Unready," though the OLD ENGLISH epithet *unrœd* actually means "ill-advised" or "foolish"). Later he also advised the Danish king Cnut. Embroiled in the affairs of state, Wulfstan still had time to write a number of sermons as well as legal codes. His *Institutes of Polity* is admired as the first treatise on political theory in English, but Wulfstan is best remembered for the fiery sermon *Sermo Lupi ad Anglos,* produced, like all his sermons, under the pseudonym *Wulf* (wolf).

Born sometime in the late 10th century, Wulfstan lived during a period of instability and turmoil. Beginning in the 990s, Viking raids devastated the country. Some time after Christmas 1013, the hapless Saxon king Ethelred was forced into exile in Normandy, allowing the Danish king Svein Forkbeard to take the English throne. Though Svein died the following year, allowing Ethelred to regain the crown, Ethelred himself died in 1016, upon which Svein's son Cnut became king of England. As adviser to Cnut, Wulfstan is often credited with influencing the Dane to reign as a Christian king and to maintain the virtues of Anglo-Saxon civilization. Wulfstan continued to play an important role in English politics and jurisprudence during the reign of the Danish king until his death in York on May 23, 1023. At his request he was buried at the monastery at Ely.

Much of Wulfstan's literary effort is related to his work as a jurist under both Ethelred and Cnut. He drew up the so-called *Canons of Edgar* (concerned with ecclesiastical law and reform), and drafted a legal code for Ethelred as well as laws for King Cnut. *The Institutes of Polity* was not only the most admired Anglo-Saxon legal tract, but also is a document discussing the proper relationship between church and state, making it the first text to deal with political theory in Old English.

But Wulfstan's most revered contributions to Old English literature have been his sermons. Dozens of sermons are attributed to Wulfstan in manuscript, though scholars doubt the attribution in most cases. At least five, perhaps 20, are definitely from his hand. Of these, several deal with the impending Judgment Day, a theme common to sermons of his time (the close of the first millennium of the Christian era). Wulfstan's most famous sermon, the *Sermo Lupi ad Anglos* (Sermon of Wolf to the English), was delivered in the dark year of 1014, when Ethelred had fled the country and the Danes were taking over the kingdom, a kingdom full of social disorder and anxiety. In impassioned, sometimes alliterative language, Wulfstan sees the Viking invasions as chastisement for the sins of the English people, and appeals to all classes of England to repent and reform before the coming day of judgment, which the Danish atrocities merely foreshadow. It is one of the most powerful sermons of the Anglo-Saxon period.

Bibliography

Berthurum, Dorothy, ed. *The Homilies of Wulfstan.* Oxford: Clarendon Press, 1957.

Fowler, Roger, ed. *Canons of Edgar.* London: Oxford University Press for the Early English Text Society, 1972.

Gatch, Milton McCormick. *Preaching and Theology in Anglo-Saxon England: Aelfric and Wulfstan.* Toronto: University of Toronto Press, 1977.

Whitelock, Dorothy, ed. *Sermo Lupi ad Anglos.* 3rd ed. New York: Appleton-Century-Crofts, 1966.

Wycliffe, John (Wyclif) (ca. 1330–1384)

John Wycliffe was an English theologian, Oxford master, and religious reformer, who challenged papal control of the English church, condemned clerical greed and immorality, and defied the power of the medieval church hierarchy. He is also responsible for the first English translation of the Bible. Although his teachings were officially condemned and he was forced into retirement, Wycliffe's numerous followers, known as LOLLARDS, formed a religious movement that spread his ideas for generations after his death. His works also influenced the reforming activities of Jan HUS in early 15th-century Prague.

Wycliffe was probably born at the Yorkshire village of Hipswell, near Richmond, into a wealthy family. In 1354, he began his studies at Oxford, receiving a bachelor of arts degree from Merton College in 1356. He became master of Balliol College by 1360, but left that post in 1361, when he was made rector of Fillingham in Lincolnshire. He was appointed canon at Westbury-on-Trym in Gloucestershire in 1362, but was studying theology at Oxford in 1363, renting a room at Queen's College. Wycliffe was appointed rector of Ludgershall in Buckinghamshire in 1368, but that same year was back at Oxford studying theology. In 1371 he was made canon of Lincoln, and finally, in 1374, the king appointed Wycliffe rector of Lutterworth in Leicestershire, a living he kept until his death. Though appointed to several clerical positions, Wycliffe clearly spent the majority of his time between 1354 and 1381 at Oxford, where he lectured in philosophy and, after 1371, in theology, becoming a doctor of theology in 1372.

Beginning in the early 1370s, Wycliffe appears to have gained the favor of the royal house, in particular of Edward the Black Prince, his wife Joan of Kent, and his brother JOHN OF GAUNT. In 1376 Gaunt enlisted Wycliffe's aid in a campaign against the so-called Good Parliament, which had appointed royal councilors to advise the Crown, including Gaunt's enemy William of Wykeham, bishop of Winchester. Prior to this, in 1374, Wycliffe was sent to Brugge, Belgium, as a representative of King EDWARD III to negotiate with envoys from the pope concerning the payment of tribute to Avignon (the papal see). It can be assumed that Wycliffe was dissatisfied with the negotiations, because from 1374 onward, he began to attack papal authority over the English church. Wycliffe asserted that Christ was the only true sovereign of the church, and that the power of popes, bishops, and priests was dependent upon their state of grace. In a time of widespread clerical abuses, Wycliffe's doctrines seemed an attack on all religious authority. Wycliffe held that no official could claim legitimate authority based simply on the fact that he occupied a certain position, but must be in a state of grace.

Wycliffe promulgated his doctrines through treatises in Latin and through his own preaching in English, basing his arguments chiefly on Scripture but also on St. AUGUSTINE, GREGORY THE GREAT,

ROBERT GROSSETESTE, and to some extent Marsilius of Padua and William OCKHAM. Over the years, his anti-papal stance became more and more pronounced. He argued that the Scriptures were the chief authority for Christians, and believed that the Bible should be available to people in the vernacular. Accordingly, his followers initiated a project of translating the Bible from St. JEROME's Latin Vulgate into English. Wycliffe himself may have been responsible for an incomplete translation of the New Testament, but the bulk of the work on the translation was done by his disciples Nicholas Hereford and, in its final form in about 1395, John Purvey.

If the Bible was the only source of Christian doctrine, Wycliffe argued, then any aspect of the contemporary church that had no basis in Scripture was unjustified. For Wycliffe, this included the wealth of the clergy, the monastic life (which he saw as separating individuals from the life of the Church), pilgrimages, and indulgences. Wycliffe further argued that sacraments performed by priests in a state of sin were not valid, and this led to his assertion that the sacraments of the church were not in fact absolutely requisite for God's grace. Finally, he denied the doctrine of transubstantiation (the belief in the "real presence" of the body and blood of Christ in the Eucharist). These and similar doctrines brought the wrath of the orthodox church down upon him.

In 1377, Pope Gregory XI condemned 18 of Wycliffe's conclusions as "erroneous," and asked for his arrest, but Wycliffe's royal protectors prevented any formal action against him at that time. However, a commission in Wycliffe's own Oxford condemned him as a heretic and threatened him with excommunication because of his teaching on the Eucharist. Wycliffe also lost the support of John of Gaunt when some of his more radical followers were embroiled in the PEASANTS' REVOLT of 1381. In 1381, Wycliffe retired from Oxford to live quietly in Lutterworth, though he continued to write. The following year William Courtenay, archbishop of Canterbury, condemned 24 of Wycliffe's arguments as heresies, though in particular Wycliffe's teaching on the Eucharist was denounced. But Wycliffe himself was never physically threatened, and continued writing at Lutterworth until he succumbed to a stroke on December 31, 1384.

The great number of followers Wycliffe had created in Oxford soon developed into a radical movement of "Lollards," who subsequently spread throughout England and, ultimately, linked Wycliffe's doctrines to the English Reformation under Henry VIII. Through his influence on Jan Hus, Wycliffe also had an impact on the continental Reformation via Hus's Moravian followers and Martin Luther. In terms of literature, perhaps Wycliffe's most important contribution is his encouragement of the production of the Lollard Bible, the first complete Bible in the English language.

Bibliography

Hall, Louis Brewer. *The Perilous Vision of John Wyclif.* Chicago: Nelson-Hall, 1983.

Kenny, Anthony. *Wyclif.* Oxford: Oxford University Press, 1985.

Lahey, Stephen E. *Philosophy and Politics in the Thought of John Wyclif.* Cambridge: Cambridge University Press, 2003.

Levy, Ian Christopher. *John Wyclif: Scriptural Logic, Real Presence, and the Parameters of Orthodoxy.* Milwaukee: Marquette University Press, 2003.

Stacey, John. *John Wyclif and Reform.* Philadelphia: Westminister Press, 1964.

Wyclif, John. *On Simony.* Translated by Terrence A. McVeigh. New York: Fordham University Press, 1992.

———. *On the Truth of Holy Scripture.* Translated with an introduction and notes by Ian Christopher Levy. Kalamazoo: Published for TEAMS (The Consortium for the Teaching of the Middle Ages) by Medieval Institute Publications, Western Michigan University, 2001.

Yi Chehyon (1287–1367)

Yi Chehyon was a Korean statesman and scholar who became known, as well, as a painter and writer. Yi Chehyon was an official in the late Koryo dynasty (918–1392), which had instituted a State Civil Service examination in emulation of the Chinese system during the TANG DYNASTY. He won first place in the examination in 1301, at the age of 14, and began a government career that lasted some 60 years under five sovereigns and culminated in the important post of chief minister of the Chancellery for State Affairs.

As a government diplomat, Yi Chehyon made at least six trips to China, accompanying Korean kings who spent time in residence at the Yuan or Mongol court in Dadu. In China in 1314, he became acquainted with a number of important Chinese intellectuals, including the influential painter Zhao Mengfu, whose style of calligraphy Yi Chehyon is credited with introducing into Korea.

Like most Korean writers of the Koryo period, Yi Chehyon wrote poetry and prose in *hanmun* (letters of Han), or classical Chinese characters, since Korea did not have its own vernacular alphabet until the following century. Among his works are the *Tales of Yogong* (1342), a collection of notes and anecdotes about the people and events in his own life. This text is thought to have influenced the development of the *yadam*, a Korean genre of simple short story written in classical Chinese.

In his verse Yi Chehyon emulated the classical poetry of China and had studied Chinese versification. Perhaps his best-known poems, however, are Korean folk songs that he translated into Chinese and called *A Small Collection of Folk Songs.* These brief lyrics are fresh and charming, and some have female speakers, like the following:

A magpie chatters in a flowering bough by
the hedge,
A spider spins a web above the bed.
Knowing my heart, they announce his
return—
My beloved will be back soon.

(Lee 2002, 226)

Yi Chehyon's collected works were first published immediately after his death, in 1368. They were popular enough to be reprinted in 1432, 1693, and 1814.

Bibliography

Hungguyu, Kim. *Understanding Korean Literature.* Translated by Robert J. Fouser. New Studies in Asian Culture. Armonk, N.Y.: M. E. Sharp, 1997.

Lee, Peter H., ed. *The Columbia Anthology of Traditional Korean Poetry.* New York: Columbia University Press, 2002.

Yi Kyubo (1168–1241)

Yi Kyubo was a Korean scholar, statesman, literary critic, poet, and prose writer of the Koryo Period (918–1392). His *Collected Works of Minister Yi of Korea* (1251) was among the earliest texts by a Korean writer printed under official sponsorship.

Yi Kyubo left an estimated 1,500–2,000 poems and numerous prose works written in *hanmun*—that is, "letters of Han," the Korean term for Chinese characters. Korea did not develop a native writing system until the 15th century, so medieval Korean poets and writers, much influenced by Chinese culture and traditions, learned and used literary Chinese as their mode of expression.

The Koryo dynasty, emulating the TANG DYNASTY of China, instituted a State Civil Service Examination in 958, grounded in the classics of Confucian thought. Yi Kyubo passed the examination in 1190 and eventually rose to the influential post of first privy counselor under the ruling Ch'oe family. During the period of invasion and devastation wrought by the Mongol invasions from China that began in 1231 and culminated in the 1250s, Yi Kyubo accompanied the royal court to Kanghwa Island, where they lived in comparative luxury and comfort while thousands of Koreans were dying. Yi Kyubo seems to have felt some sympathy for the peasants' lot, however, as he composed poems that describe the struggles of the farmers during the Mongol atrocities.

Perhaps Yi Kyubo's best-known work is a long poem called the "Lay of King Tongmyong," which retells the mythic story of the founding of the Kingdom of Koguryo (one of the Three Kingdoms of Korea before the unification of the peninsula under the earlier Silla dynasty). The poem, with its emphasis on local Korean history, legend, and cultural achievements, is a kind of nationalistic statement in the face of a Chinese-dominated historical tradition in Korea and the political dominance of the Mongol dynasty.

Yi Kyubo also wrote prose works in the aristocratic genre known as *kajon,* or "fictitious biography." In the tradition of a form that had originated with the Chinese author HAN YU during the Tang dynasty, these stories took everyday objects and turned them into fictitious characters, giving them a history and a family. Among Yi Kyubo's works in this genre are the *Tale of the Turtle in Clear Water* and *The Story of Mr. Yeast.*

As a literary theorist, Yi Kyubo was involved in a debate current in Korean letters of the time, concerned with the relative importance of form (or *yongsa*) vs. creativity (or *shinui*) in poetry. Yi came down strongly on the side of creativity, emphasizing sincerity in particular. His own poetry expresses this concern. His poems dealing with nature or everyday events are characterized by closely observed sense images and an expressed empathy for other people. His striking imagery may be illustrated by the quatrain from a memorable poem called "Two Verses on the Moon in a Well":

> *From deep in the clear well by the mossy*
> *green rock,*
> *the newly risen moon shines straight back.*
> *In the water bottle I filled, the half moon*
> *sparkles.*
> *I carry back only one half of the moon*
> *round as a mirror.*

(McCann 2000, 81)

Other poems concern his family and himself, and these are often humorous with a touch of melancholy, such as this verse from a poem "To Sambek, My Son, Drinking Young":

> *You know already how to tip the wine jar;*
> *before many years pass you may bust a gut,*
> *so stop.*
> *Don't follow your father's example, always*
> *tipsy.*
> *All your life, people will be calling you a*
> *crazy fellow.*

(McCann 2000, 80)

Bibliography

Hungguyu, Kim. *Understanding Korean Literature.* Translated by Robert J. Fouser. New Studies in Asian Culture. Armonk, N.Y.: M. E. Sharp, 1997.

Kim, Kichung. *An Introduction to Classical Korean Literature: From Hyangga to P'ansori.* New Studies in Asian Culture. Armonk, N.Y.: M. E. Sharp, 1996.

Lee, Peter H., ed. *The Columbia Anthology of Traditional Korean Poetry.* New York: Columbia University Press, 2002.

McCann, David R. *Early Korean Literature: Selections and Introductions.* New York: Columbia University Press, 2000.

York Cycle

The cycle of MYSTERY plays performed at York is one of only four extant cycles from the late Middle Ages, out of at least 12 that are known to have existed. (Others are the CHESTER and TOWNELEY CYCLES, and N-TOWN, or *Ludus Coventriae,* PLAYS). Performed at the festival of CORPUS CHRISTI in early summer, these cycles were made up of a series of short plays drawn from the Bible and from legend, depicting Christian salvation history from the Creation of the world until Doomsday. The York Cycle may be the oldest of the four surviving collections, with records mentioning performances as early as 1376. York is also the largest cycle, with 48 plays in the single 15th-century manuscript that contains the text of the cycle (British library Additional MS 35290). That manuscript, discovered only in the 19th century, was produced for the corporation of the city of York sometime in the 1460s or 1470s as the master copy, or register, of the texts of the plays.

Production of the individual Corpus Christi plays was in the hands of the city's craft guilds. Plays were sometimes assigned to guilds on the basis of some logical connection with the subject matter—as, for instance, the Shipwrights' guild was assigned the play on *The Building of the Ark:* Apparently the actors actually constructed a scaled-down version of Noah's ship on stage during the performance of the play, to the astonishment of the assembled audience. But in general the guild assignment appears to have been random. Producing a play was an expensive project—money must be spent on costumes and props, as well as the storage and maintenance of a pageant wagon—the elaborate wagons that served as movable stages for the productions, sometimes with mechanical devices for raising or lowering supernatural characters, or for other special effects. But the guilds seem to have born the expense gladly, as a matter of civic pride. Professional actors were hired for major roles, but other parts were played by guild members themselves. Since no actor could appear in more than one play, some 700 actors must have been involved in a single Corpus Christi pageant, in addition to hundreds of other costume designers, stagehands, and other production helpers. The festival created an atmosphere of celebration that was one of the highlights of the city's year.

Some scholars have expressed doubt that an entire cycle of 48 plays could be produced on a single day, yet contemporary documents attest that it is so. In 1415, records show that 54 plays were performed in York on the day observing Corpus Christi. Plays were short—no play is much over 500 lines. In York, the pageant wagons progressed single-file through the city streets following a route with 12 individual stations at which each wagon stopped to perform. Thus each particular guild produced its play 12 times during the long day. To ensure time for the entire cycle, the first play was performed at 4:30 in the morning, and the last production took place after midnight. It was a grueling schedule, but an audience watching the complete cycle would be treated to a good deal of entertainment as well as a coherent Christian history of the world.

In addition to the special effects made possible by the pageant wagons, part of the entertainment included the costumes, which apparently could be quite ornate. While ordinary characters might be dressed in contemporary fashion, chief characters were dressed, it may be assumed, like the characters pictured in stained-glass windows of the time. Women's parts were played by men with wigs and costumes. Supernatural beings, like God, Satan, or angels, would wear masks and particularly lavish costumes. Comic lines and characters were written into the plays as well—as, for example, Noah's shrewish wife, who refuses to get on board the ark. Such comic relief provided a break from the overwhelmingly serious salvation history of the rest of the plays.

The Christian history of the plays provided the audience with a spiritual lesson as well. The York pageant includes a particular emphasis on the Nativity of Christ (with seven plays, from the Annunciation to the Magi and the Slaughter of the Innocents), and on the Passion of Christ (with nine plays depicting Christ's last hours in great specificity). The Old Testament plays chosen for inclusion in the cycle are all stories that a medieval audience would have recognized as allegorically prefiguring events of the New Testament, so that, for example, Noah's flood prefigures the Last Judgment, as Abraham's willingness to sacrifice Isaac prefigures God's ultimate sacrifice of his own son for human salvation. That such an interpretation was intended is clear from the words of the York Cycle's Noah, who predicts that God will not destroy the world by water again, but that he will ultimately bring the world to a close by fire. While scholars doubt that the entire cycle could have been written by a single author, and point to the continual revision of individual plays, deleting of old plays, and adding of new plays that must have taken place over the 200-year life of the York cycle (it is known, for example, that specific plays concerning the Virgin Mary were added at the end of the 15th century), still nothing is known with any certainty about the plays' authorship, and there are patterns of imagery that extend throughout the cycle, as well as an overall unity of conception that gives the cycle a kind of coherence: An audience watching the plays would experience Lucifer's enmity with God and his fall, and the Fall of Adam and Eve, Christ's birth and suffering and ultimate defeat of Satan, his HARROWING OF HELL and his Resurrection. Finally, having seen Christ's sacrifice for their sake, the audience would be forced to consider how they fit into God's overall plan for the world, by contemplating their own individual destiny during the play of the *Last Judgment.*

The last recorded performance of the York Cycle took place in 1569, after which it was suppressed, along with the other Corpus Christi cycles, by the Protestant ecclesiasts under Elizabeth's reign. The festival of Corpus Christi, established to celebrate the "real presence" of the body of Christ in the Eucharist, was suppressed in Protestant England, and the doctrine of many of the other plays—particularly the later additions dealing with the Virgin Mary—was clearly Catholic. In recent decades, however, beginning in 1951, the plays have been restored, and are performed once again in York every few years, reviving the sense of community pride they brought to the city in late medieval times.

Bibliography

Beadle, Richard. "The York Cycle: Texts, Performances, and the Bases for Critical Enquiry." In *Medieval Literature: Texts and Interpretation,* edited by Tim W. MacHan, 105–119. Binghamton, N.Y.: State University of New York Press, 1991.

Collier, Richard J. *Poetry and Drama in the York Corpus Christi Play.* Hamden, Conn.: Archon, 1978.

Davidson, Clifford. *From Creations to Doom: The York Cycle of Mystery Plays.* New York: AMS Press, 1984.

Johnston, Alexandra F. "The York Cycle and the Chester Cycle: What Do the Records Tells Us?" In *Editing Early English Drama: Special Problems and New Directions,* edited by A. F. Johnson, 121–143. New York: AMS Press, 1987.

Kolve, V. A. *The Play Called Corpus Christi.* Stanford, Calif.: Stanford University Press, 1966.

Stevens, Martin. "The York Cycle: City as Stage." In *Four Middle English Mystery Cycles: Textual, Contextual, and Critical Interpretations,* edited by Martin Stevens, 17–87. Princeton, N.J.: Princeton University Press, 1987.

Willis, Paul. "The Weight of Sin in the York *Crucifixio,*" *Leeds Studies in English* 15 (1984): 109–116.

The York Plays. Edited by Richard Beadle. London: Arnold, 1982.

Yoshida Kenkō (Urabe Kaneyoshi) (ca. 1283–ca. 1352)

Urabe Kanayoshi, known generally by his Buddhist name of Yoshida Kenkō, was a poet and essayist who lived during a turbulent era of Japanese history. He seems to have served the imperial court but withdrew at some point from public life to write his *Tsurezuregusa* (*Essays in Idleness*), a text that continues to be perused with pleasure by Japanese readers even after 700 years.

Kenkō was born into an influential family that for many years had been connected with the Shinto shrine of Yoshida in Kyoto. His father was an official at the imperial court. Yoshida himself served the emperor Go-Nijō, who reigned from 1301 to 1308. Sometime after the emperor's death, probably about 1313, he became a priest, spending about two years at the Buddhist temple on Mount Hiei, but afterward returning to Kyoto. He became known as a poet of what was called the Nijō school, a conservative, unimaginative group of poets following a pattern established a century before. Yoshida's reputation as a poet seems to have been much greater in his own time than subsequently. Still, he seems to have taken part in regular poetic gatherings in the capital even during the troubled times when emperors and shoguns were competing for power and when civil war threatened. In 1331, the figurehead emperor Go-Daigo led a revolt against the real power in the country, the warrior Hōjō family, but was defeated and sent into exile. In 1333 Go-Daigo returned and overthrew the Hōjōs, establishing what became known as the Kemmu Restoration, but in 1336 was driven once more into exile. Yoshida, with no personal ambitions himself, seems to have been able to survive in the capital no matter who was in control. There is even a story about his writing love letters for the powerful Kō no Moronao (d. 1351), one of the shoguns in power after the Emperor Go-Daigo's final banishment. Some, however, believe that Yoshida left the court sometime around the Kemmu Restoration and became a wandering monk; still others believe he was a recluse.

Certainly Yoshida was in a position to observe the ambition and the corruption of the nobility of his day, and he is able to put some of these observations into his masterpiece, the *Essays in Idleness.* This text is most often dated between 1330 and 1333, though that is not certain. It is a compilation of 243 miscellaneous fragments on a wide variety of topics, arranged in an apparently random manner, although some scholars have argued that Yoshida's arrangement is based on some associative plan, sometimes grouped around a similar moral theme, sometimes around a particular figure. It was a genre known in Japanese letters as *zuihitsu,* a term that means literally "following the writing brush," implying that the writer casually set down a variety of observations, anecdotes, reflections, maxims and meditations with no logical plan. In *Essays in Idleness,* these fragments are often contradictory. Sometimes they are irreverent or controversial, as when Yoshida declares that human behavior, not the stars, determines our destiny. Yoshida reinforces the impression of randomness by his brief prologue, in which he claims to have jotted down every "trivial" thing that occurred to him. These trivial matters included pronouncements on taste and etiquette, as well as observations about women, birds, flowers, the moon, the afterlife, and both martial and culinary arts. The closest parallel in extant Japanese literature is probably the much earlier *Pillow Book* of SEI SHŌNAGON, the 11th-century lady in waiting of the HEIAN court.

Yoshida's text has been recognized over the years as the first rather definitive statement of Japanese aesthetics and taste. Yoshida extols the aesthetic ideals of simplicity and of suggestion, two of the most important aspects of Japanese poetry from its beginning and clearly apparent in the dominant TANKA verse form. He also mentions irregularity or asymmetry as an aesthetic virtue preferred by the Japanese over the more classical virtues of symmetry or parallelism. For Yoshida, and for Japanese taste in general, absolute uniformity is less desirable or interesting than something that is incomplete or imperfect. This is related to the emphasis on suggestiveness, but is related, as well, to the most important aspect of beauty for Yoshida: transience.

Traditionally part of the Buddhist outlook, the impermanence and mutability of the world and human life was even more palpable to Yoshida given the political circumstances of his world. Reading the *Essays in Idleness,* one cannot avoid the overriding impression of transience, of decay, of the presence of death and the incomplete nature of human life. But Yoshida does not bewail this condition; rather he sees in it the ultimate source of aesthetic beauty. Things are valuable and they are beautiful because of their very impermanence. Such is the nature of the human experience. To expect anything else is to chase an illusion.

Yoshida became something of a legend through the popularity of his *Essays in Idleness,* and as a result a number of other works were attributed to him, none with any real evidence. One legend about him was that, after he had left the court and resided in a rustic cottage, he got into the habit of jotting down ideas as they occurred to him on scraps of paper that he then stuck on the walls of his house. According to this story, a later poet gathered the scraps from Yoshida's cottage walls and randomly compiled them into a book. Such a story is almost certainly apocryphal, but it does suggest the random feeling created by the *zuihitsu* genre. Still, the text of Yoshida's great work is not so random that it lacks an overriding theme: The most precious and beautiful thing in human life, Yoshida tells us, is uncertainty.

Bibliography

Chance, Linda H. *Formless in Form: Kenko, "Tsurezuregusa" and the Rhetoric of Japanese Fragmentary Prose.* Stanford, Calif.: Stanford University Press, 1997.

Keene, Donald. *Seeds in the Heart: Japanese Literature from Earliest Times to the Late Sixteenth Century.* Vol. 1 of *A History of Japanese Literature.* New York: Columbia University Press, 1999.

———, trans. *Essays in Idleness: The Tsurezuregusa of Kenkō.* New York: Columbia University Press, 1967.

Miner, Earl, Hiroko Odagiri, and Robert E Morrell. *The Princeton Companion to Classical Japanese Literature.* Princeton, N.J.: Princeton University Press, 1985.

Yuan Zhen (Yüan Chen) (779–831)

A brilliant and powerful statesman of the TANG DYNASTY, Yuan Zhen strove to reform the governments of two emperors, only to be twice banished from the imperial court for his efforts. With his friend and fellow poet BO JUYI, he advocated a new kind of poetry, simple in style and having as its chief aim social and political reform. While his poetry has declined in popularity over the centuries, Yuan Zhen is best known today as the author of one of the most influential works of prose fiction in Chinese literature, *Yingying zhuan* (*The STORY OF YING-YING*).

Yuan Zhen was born in Xi'an, the imperial capital of Tang China, in 779. His father, Yuan Yuan Kuna, died seven years later, and his mother took the family to live with relatives at Fengsiang in Shensi, a frontier town where the young Yuan Zhen was able to observe firsthand the suffering that military skirmishes and corrupt provincial government imposed on the common people. In the meantime Yuan Zhen's mother had taken over the boy's education, and he was learning, among other things, the art of poetry.

In 793, Yuan Zhen passed the first civil service examination, called *ming-ching* ("explication of the classics"). He moved back to Xi'an the following year. In 802, he was married, achieved first place in the next civil service examination, and was appointed to his first official post in the imperial library. Here he met fellow poet and bureaucrat Bo Juyi, who became his lifelong friend. Shortly after this, it is believed, Yuan Zhen composed his *Story of Ying-ying.* In 806, Yuan Zhen received an outstanding score on the *chih-k'e tui-ts'e* ("palace examination"), the highest of the civil service examinations, monitored by the emperor Hsien-tung himself. As a result he was given a position close to the emperor, as "Censor of the Left." Later that same year, however, he was banished from the capital, chiefly because of his presentation of a 10-point plan for reform of the government that angered some of his enemies at court—Yuan Zhen's Confucian concept of government for the benefit of the people was not always popular among the less idealistic elements in the imperial court. He was sent to take a minor position in Henan; however, when his mother died about this time, Yuan Zhen decided instead to retire and to observe a period of mourning.

By the time Yuan Zhen emerged from mourning in 809, elements friendlier to him were in power at court, and he was immediately appointed "Inspecting Censor" and sent to investigate allegations of corruption in Tung Ch'uan (in eastern Szechwan). Here he found evidence of rampant corruption in the administration of the military governor, but the officials he accused received only minor reprimands and he was transferred to another provincial post. When he removed a corrupt mayor from office without first consulting the court, Yuan Zhen was finally banished from the court for 10 years. Though his friend Bo Juyi and others appealed to the emperor, the banishment stood.

Languishing in minor posts in the provinces, Yuan Zhen spent much of his time editing his own poems (a collection of more than 800) that he completed in 812, and also wrote a number of additional lyrics in the simple style that he and Bo Juyi had adopted. In 821, with the advent of a new emperor, Muzong (Mu-tsung), who had been impressed by his poetry, Yuan Zhen was appointed secretary of the Ministry of Rites, and placed in charge of drafting official proclamations. In 822, he was made chief minister. However, his rivalry with the military leader P'ei Tu, with whom he shared the title of chief minister, ultimately led to his dismissal from office and banishment, once again, to minor posts in the provinces.

During these years Yuan Zhen compiled an edition of his collected works, and the following year added an edition of the works of his friend Bo. In 830, he was appointed governor of Wuchang, where he died the next year. His body was returned to Xianyang for burial, and in death Yuan Zhen was given the honorary title of minister of state.

While Yuan Zhen's ardent desire for reform met largely with indifference and opposition at the imperial court, resulting in a series of banishments, his poetry—simple in style but aimed just as directly at reform—was extremely popular in his own day. He was nicknamed "Yuan the Genius" because of his verse, and was especially admired for his use of rhyme. But his poetic reputation has since waned, and it is as a fiction writer that he is best remembered. *The Story of Ying-ying,* a masterpiece of the new genre of short stories in classical Chinese called *chuanqi* (*ch'uan-ch'i*), is a romantic tale of a young woman wooed and then deserted by an ambitious young man, who ultimately wants her again, once she has married someone else. Yuan Zhen would probably have seen the tale as unworthy, since it fails to stress a social purpose. But that, perhaps, is what has made the tale more universally appealing than his poetry.

Bibliography

Hightower, James R., trans. "The Story of Ying-ying." In *Traditional Chinese Stories: Themes and Variations,* edited by Joseph S. M. Lau and Y. M. Ma. New York: Columbia University Press, 1978.

Palandri, Angela C. Y. Jung. *Yüan Chen.* Boston: G. K. Hall, 1977.

Yvain: The Knight of the Lion Chrétien de Troyes (ca. 1177)

Yvain was probably the third of CHRÉTIEN DE TROYES's five extant ROMANCES, written sometime before or after the author's unfinished *LANCELOT.* Unlike the more complex and morally ambivalent *CLIGÈS,* in which Chrétien begins with a bibliography of his works, followed by a diptych (or double) structured romance of considerable thematic complexity, the narrative and thematics of *Yvain* are relatively straightforward, and the didactic elements are accessible to modern and medieval audience and reader alike. This is not to suggest that *Yvain* is entirely without complexity or depth of narrative and thematics; Chrétien was a masterful poet and social commentator and all of his extant romances testify to his deft handling of the balance between entertainment and education—the two elements required of all good literature. The clarity of *Yvain* is one of its strengths and we see this both in its clear narrative line and in the various tests with which the protagonist is challenged. One of the more popular of Chrétien's romances, *Yvain* was adapted into German, Norwegian, and Swedish versions, and there is a 14th-century Middle English romance, *YWAIN AND GAWAIN,* which is a slightly revised version of the French romance. Although critical conclusions may vary widely as to the significance of various episodes, the didactic elements are undeniable, and relevant to a medieval aristocratic audience.

After an introduction in which the poet, having set the scene in the fabled Arthurian court, laments the lost days when "true" love flourished, he proceeds to tell a story from those lost days, from that past time of idealized love and idealized knighthood. This kind of introduction is a convention in its nostalgia for a time that never was, and acts to set the scene for a romance in which honor, loyalty, nobility, and true service to the god of love reigned supreme. But it is important to keep in mind that the idealized introduction often functions as the template against which the action of the romance unfolds. In *Yvain,* this is certainly the case, and as we follow the story we are conscious of the ways in which characters do or do not fulfill the ideals set out in the introduction.

The romance literally begins in Arthur's court with a group of knights telling stories. One story in particular catches the attention of the Arthurian knight Yvain: a story in which the knight Calgrenant tells of an elaborate adventure of a magic fountain that raises a fantastic storm which, in its turn, provokes a challenge from an unknown knight whose property is damaged in the unearthly storm. Calgrenant fails in the hand-to-hand battle, and thus is shamed. This is not the normal fare of tales told by knights who usually emphasize their prowess and success, and his cousin, Yvain, vows to avenge his honor by seeking out the adventure himself. Unfortunately the king hears of the adventure and vows to go with all the court to see the magic fountain and storm, and the mysterious knight. When Yvain learns of this he knows that the right of combat will fall to others (in the knightly hierarchy Kay and Gawain are above him), so he resolves to leave at night, in secret, and pursue the adventure alone.

Not only does Yvain find the adventure but he prevails in every way. He withstands the storm, withstands the hand-to-hand combat, and kills the knight. Unfortunately in killing the knight, Yvain has followed him into his castle without a means of escape. A young serving girl, Lunette, offers him a ring to make him invisible, and so he survives the vengeance of the dead knight's men and, after a period of time, succeeds in winning the heart and hand of the dead knight's widow, Laudine. All of this action is prelude to the central substance of the romance: the oft-told story of the tensions inherent in balancing private and public, or marital and martial endeavors. This theme had been explored at length in Chrétien's first romance, *EREC AND ENIDE,* and the poet returns to it here in a somewhat more complex form. After his marriage to Laudine, Yvain is delighted with the arrival of Arthur and the court, so delighted that he lets Gawain talk him into leaving Laudine to pursue knightly feats of arms and honor. Laudine gives Yvain leave to depart on the condition that he will return within the year. Of course the year passes in a series of fabulous jousts in which Yvain prevails, wins honor and acclaim, and becomes more than a little prideful. He is repaid for this lack of knightly courtesy when Lunette finds him to reclaim the Lady Laudine's ring because Yvain, in his pride and success, has stayed away beyond the agreed-upon year. When he realizes his uncourtly disregard for Laudine, "such a storm broke / in his skull that he lost his senses" (2,805); like Lancelot's madness over Guenevere, the love anger of Laudine "breaks" Yvain and he wanders like a wild man in the forest.

Yvain is finally recognized and saved, and in this second part of the romance, his redemption back into the world of courtesy and honor takes the form of a series of adventures in which women need his help for various reasons. Accompanied now by a lion, whose qualities of loyalty and selflessness are both commentary on Yvain's earlier behavior and indications of the qualities he begins to acquire, Yvain takes the name "The Knight of the Lion" and in this guise provides true and disinterested service to women in need. At tale's end, having learned lessons of right conduct, courtesy, and the true balance between chivalric and marital duties, Yvain is reconciled with Laudine and all live happily ever after.

Critical commentary ranges widely over this romance and its concerns: the balance between public and private lives; the knightly ideal and how it succeeds or falters in realistic settings; gender issues as they are played out in the various female characters, and most specifically in the subtle psychology of the characters of Lunette and Laudine. While Lunette is shown to be smart, calculating (in the best sense), and a lively and persuasive debater, the exploration of Laudine's interiority or consciousness continues the focus on the interior lives of his characters that Chrétien first explored in *Erec and Enide.* The romance is rich in its comprehensive scope, and Chrétien does not neglect social issues. The position of women in his culture is thoroughly examined in Yvain's redemptive adventures, including an adventure that leads to the liberation of women forced to work in what we would consider "sweatshop" conditions. The Celtic and mythic elements upon which this romance is constructed are also a fruitful area for commentary.

In some ways a coming-of-age tale, *Yvain* is notable for its focus on courtly behavior, the nature of love and fidelity, and the ways in which social relations work. Less morally ambiguous than other works by Chrétien, *Yvain* (under the cover of a fashionable romance) offers a series of lessons and models for his 12th-century audience that has found a wide reception in many countries from the medieval period into the modern.

Bibliography

Boase, Roger. *The Origin and Meaning of Courtly Love.* Manchester, U.K.: Manchester University Press, 1977.

Chrétien de Troyes. *Yvain: The Knight of the Lion.* Translated by Burton Raffel. With an afterword by Joseph J. Duggan. New Haven, Conn.: Yale University Press, 1987.

Duby, Georges. *The Knight, the Lady, and the Priest: The Making of Modern Marriage in Medieval France.* Translated by Barbara Bray. New York: Pantheon Books, 1983.

Frappier, Jean. *Etude sur "Yvain ou le Chevalier au lion."* Paris: Société d'Edition d'Enseignement Supérieur, 1969.

Gantz, Jeffrey, trans. *Early Irish Myths and Sagas.* Harmondsworth, U.K..: Penguin Books, 1981.

Kelly, Douglas. *The Art of Medieval Romance.* Madison: University of Wisconsin Press, 1992.

Maddox, Donald. *The Arthurian Romances of Chrétien de Troyes: Once and Future Fictions.* Cambridge Studies in Medieval Literature, 12. Cambridge: Cambridge University Press, 1991.

Elisa Narin van Court

Ywain and Gawain (ca. 1325–1350)

The one extant copy of the MIDDLE ENGLISH ROMANCE *Ywain and Gawain* is found in the British Museum manuscript Cotton Galba E. IX, a large parchment manuscript whose contents range from romance to a verse treatise on the Seven Deadly Sins. There is little internal or external evidence concerning the date of composition, but with reference to details of clothing and language, scholars usually date the poem sometime between 1325 and 1350. This anonymous Arthurian romance is a translation of CHRÉTIEN DE TROYES's *YVAIN: THE KNIGHT OF THE LION;* indeed, it is the only surviving English version of one of Chrétien's romances. But as is common with medieval translations (the full sense of the phrase medieval *translatio* encompasses interpretation), the Middle English version, while faithful to the general plot and structure of its French source (the Middle English poet reduces Chrétien's 6,818 lines to 4,032), is not particularly faithful in its rendering of language, thematic focus, or sensibility. The English poet never names Chrétien as his source, and *Ywain and Gawain* is often unfavorably compared to its more polished and courtly French model; yet the transformations effected by the English poet are skillful and serve a purpose in their emphasis on personal responsibility and truth.

While the story remains essentially the same, from the very beginning of the Middle English poem, the poet situates his characters in a realm considerably less concerned with the conventions and conceits of COURTLY LOVE. In both versions the poets set the scene in the fabled Arthurian court. But where in Chrétien's original the knights and ladies speak of love and service to the god of love, and the poet laments the lost days when "true" love flourished, in the Middle English version the English knights and ladies speak of "dedes of armes and of veneri / and of gude knightes flat lyfed flen" (Friedman and Harrington 1964, ll. 26–27), and the poet is nostalgic for the days when truth, honor, and men's word and faith were trusted and true. The English poet is less concerned with the "fabled" refinements of cultivated and courtly society than he is with adventure and love of a more realistic and less studied form. Nonetheless, like the French version, the Middle English *Ywain and Gawain* has a clear narrative line and didactic elements accessible to modern and medieval audience and reader alike.

In the romance Ywain's cousin relates an adventure of a magic fountain, a fantastic storm, and a challenge from an unknown knight, a challenge in which Ywain's cousin fails and is shamed. Ywain silently vows to avenge his cousin, but before he can set out, Arthur has learned of the adventure and plans to take the court to witness the marvels and challenge the unknown knight. Ywain, desiring the adventure for himself, sets out alone, meets the unknown knight, kills him in battle, and then woos and wins the knight's widow.

In the love scenes between Ywain and Alundyne (the knight's widow), the English poet's transformations are particularly striking: He dispenses with Chrétien's extended Ovidian descriptions of Love's wounds and Love's rule, and much of the rhetoric of courtly love is excised in favor of a simple statement that "Luf, flat es so mekil of mayne, / Sare had wownded Sir Ywayne" ("Love that is so great in power, / Sore had wounded Sir Ywain" [871–72]). The elaborate rhetorical formulations and figures of the French version are either seriously cut or omitted altogether in this and in other scenes, and if the English romance loses metaphoric flights of fancy and subtle disputations, it gains a kind of realism and specificity that is one of the Middle English romance's strengths. One of the more striking examples of how the English poet's redaction of the French original adds to, rather than subtracts from, the poem's meaning is the scene in which, after the marriage of Alundyne and Ywain, when Ywain plans to go with Gawain and the court to tournaments and thus leave his new bride, Alundyne gives Ywain a ring to remind him of his promise to return within a year. The ring is magic, and when worn by a true lover, that lover cannot come to harm. In the French version, Laudine (Alundyne in the English version) tells Ywain: "No true love and faithful lover, if *he* wears it, / can be imprisoned or lose any blood, / nor any ill befall *him*" (italics added); in the Middle English the third-person pronoun ("he," "him"), and the generalized, formalized standard of behavior thus delineated, is replaced with the second-person pronoun and the effect is both immediate and specific: "An ay, whils *3e* er trew of love, / Over al sal 3*e* be above" (ll. 1,539–40, italics added). With the emphasis on "3e" ("you"), the romance, particularly in its dialogue, loses the courtly distance that tends to present relations as formalized style over content.

Like its French source, the Middle English version shows Ywain's unthinking betrayal of his lady, the tensions between fealty to one's lady and fealty to one's knightly endeavors, and the adventures Ywain must undertake before, at the romance's end, he is reconciled with his bride; but throughout, the poet edits, omits, and tightens the narrative, particularly in his seeming indifference to his source's elaborate discussions of courtly love and courtly behavior. Some scholars attribute the lack of emphasis on the courtly to the poet's focus on the essentials of his story and his tailoring the romance to the sensibilities of his audience (perhaps provincial and baronial). What the poem loses in the way of elaborate conceits and disquisitions on love, it gains in narrative force, powerful language, and a lively and controlled story line, all of which contribute to the poem's being considered one of the more successful of the Middle English romances.

Bibliography

Friedman, Albert B., and Norman T. Harrington, eds. *Ywain and Gawain.* London: Oxford University Press, 1964.

Bollard, John K. "Hende wordes: The Theme of Courtesy in *Ywain and Gawain,*" *Neophilologus* 78 (1994): 655–670.

Calf, Berenice-Eve S. "The Middle English Ywain and Gawain: A Bibliography, 1777–1995," *Parergon* 13 (1995): 1–24.

Hamilton, Gayle. "The Breaking of the Troth in *Ywain and Gawain,*" *Mediaevalia* 2 (1976): 111–135.

Matthews, David. "Translation and Ideology: The Case of *Ywain and Gawain,*" *Neophilologus* 76 (1992): 452–463.

Elisa Narin van Court

Z

zajal (*Zéjel*)

The Arabic *zajal* (known in Spanish as the *zéjel*) was a popular verse form that originated in Muslim Spain in the 12th century. Like the *muwashshah* (*see* KHARJA), the *zajal* was a strophic form—that is, it was built of several stanzas, usually five to six or more. The opening stanza introduced a theme that was developed in subsequent stanzas, and the poem ended with a repetition of the rhyme scheme of the opening stanza. A *kharja,* or refrain, might also be part of the poem. What particularly distinguished the *zajal* from the *muwashshah* was that the latter was written in classical Arabic, while the *zajal* was in colloquial Arabic, and therefore also included Spanish vocabulary, particularly in the *kharja.*

The *zajal,* therefore, was influenced by the non-Arab speech of the poet's everyday world. The name *zajal* seems to derive from a word meaning "to utter a cry or happy noise." The inventor of the genre, at least as a literary rather than a purely popular oral form, was the wandering singer Ibn Quzman (ca. 1078–1160), who used the form for all kinds of poetry, including eulogizing his patrons. The *zajals* were composed to be sung, and the earliest *zajal* music manuscripts date from the 13th century. The form eventually became popular throughout the Arab world. It also became a popular Spanish form of the late Middle Ages, where it was called the *zéjel.* It was imitated, as well, by Hebrew poets in Spain and elsewhere.

Bibliography

Irwin, Robert, ed. *Night and Horses and the Desert: An Anthology of Classical Arabic Literature.* Woodstock, N.Y.: Overlook Press, 1999.

Stern, Samuel Miklos. *Hispano-Arabic Strophic Poetry.* Edited by L. P. Harvey. Oxford: Clarendon Press, 1974.

Zeami (Seami, Kanze Motokiyo) (ca. 1364–ca. 1443)

Zeami is generally recognized as the most important playwright in the tradition of Japanese Nō theater. He became so well known that at one time, half of the 240 extant Nō plays were attributed to him, though modern scholarship has identified between 30 and 40 plays as indisputably his. He was also chief actor of his company and the foremost theorist of Nō art, having written some 21 treatises on the subject, most of which have been recovered only in the 20th century.

Much of Zeami's success came to him as a result of his association with the Ashīkaga shogunate, the most powerful force in the Japan of his lifetime. At the age of 11, while performing for the acting company of his father Kan'ami at the Imakumano Shrine in Kyoto, Zeami was observed and admired by the 17-year-old shogun Ashīkaga Yoshimutsu, and quickly became the young shogun's favorite and companion. Zeami became head of his troupe at the age of 20 upon the death of his father, but the patronage and protection of Yoshimutsu gave Zeami's troupe financial security and a permanent residence in the capital. Writing specifically to appeal to Yoshimutsu's refined tastes, and those of other educated aristocrats in the capital, rather than to the preferences of the masses, Zeami revolutionized Nō theater, changing it from a popular entertainment to an elegant art form.

When Yoshimutsu died in 1408, Zeami's privileged position began to deteriorate. He continued to write in the style he had developed under Yoshimutsu, but subsequent shoguns did not share Yoshimutsu's tastes. Under the next shogun, Yoshimochi, Zeami lost some prestige, but was fortunate in that his daughter married the successful playwright Komparu Zenchiku, whose success enabled him to support his father-in-law as Zeami's fortunes declined. Under the succeeding shogun, Yoshinori, Zeami's nephew Motoshige became the shogun's favorite, and Zeami incurred Yoshinori's wrath when he refused to assist his nephew in his new position. Zeami's decline continued when, at the age of 70, he was ordered to two years of exile on Sado Island, for reasons that are unclear. Zenchiku is known to have looked after his affairs while Zeami was in exile. Precisely when Zeami returned from his banishment is not known, but one legend claims that he died in a Zen temple upon his return.

Several innovations separated Zeami's plays from those of his predecessors. Instead of traditional popular heroes, he chose his protagonists from classical Japanese literature, such as the *TALE OF THE HEIKE* or figures from classical HEIAN culture. Zeami's plays are less realistic than previous plays, relying on unrealistic masks and costumes, a virtually empty stage with only a few insignificant props. More important, his plays achieve their dramatic tension not from the confrontation of characters so much as from the chief character's internal anguish. In a typical Zeami play, a monk or other secondary figure encounters an old man, who may relate the story of an ancient battle that occurred at the spot where they are standing. In the second part of the play, the monk realizes that the old man is the ghost of some dead warrior. The ghost begins a dance—a symbol of his inner turmoil—as he relates and works through an ancient obsession that prevents him from leaving the mundane world and achieving final enlightenment.

Zeami's plays are still performed today. His most anthologized play is *ATSUMORI,* a drama of the type in which the protagonist (or *shite*) is a warrior. The play, based on chapter 9 of *The Tale of the Heike,* opens with an encounter between the ghost of Atsumori, disguised as a grass cutter, and the monk Renshō, who had killed the 16-year-old Atsumori in battle, and had become a monk to leave behind that life of killing. The ghost, fixated on his defeat and death and obsessed with the man who killed him, has the opportunity to avenge himself but in the end lets the obsession go.

Izutso (The well-curb) is another of Zeami's most admired plays. In the genre called *kazuramono,* or "wig piece"—that is, a play with a female *shite*—this play focuses on the daughter of Aritsune from the 17th episode of the *ISE MONOGATARI* (Tale of Ise). The woman in the play struggles with her feelings for her lost love Narihira, and relates her love and memories of him. Ultimately she appears in Narihira's clothing. She goes to view her reflection in the well, and imagines her lost lover returning to her.

Zeami's critical writings may have sprung from a need to justify the new direction he was taking the drama. In any case, of his 21 critical treatises, Zeami's best-known is his earliest, *Fūshikaden* (Teachings in style and the flower), written about 1400–02. On the practical level, he emphasizes the bare stage and simple props, and regarding acting style, insists that actors should underplay their emotions, advocating very subtle gesture and movement. In terms of theory, Zeami is extremely difficult to translate, as many of the terms he introduces are quite ambiguous. He borrows language from the classic treatise on Japanese poetry (*waka*), Ki no Tsurayuki's Japanese preface to the *KOKINSHŪ.* Tsurayuki had declared that Japanese poetry has as its seed (*tane*) the human heart (*kokoro*). Zeami declares that in Nō theater, the *tane* or cause was the performance, while the *kokoro* was what he called the "flower." What he meant by "flower" is complex, but basically he seems to mean the effect that the actor produces in the audience.

Zeami's most difficult critical term is *yūgen,* his chief criterion for the art of Nō. The term refers to elegance and beauty but also to mystery and depth. Thus the quality of *yūgen* denoted emotion so subtle and profound that it could only be implied. The value of implication expressed in the concept of *yūgen* permeated Japanese poetry as well as drama, and, in fact, was an aesthetic ideal in all Japanese arts, from painting to calligraphy. Thus the change in the course of Nō theater under Zeami was ultimately a change that was in line with the direction of classic Japanese aesthetics since the time of the *Kokinshū.*

Bibliography

Hare, Thomas Blenman. *Zeami's Style: The Noh Plays of Zeami Motokiyo.* Stanford, Calif.: Stanford University Press, 1986.

Japanese Nō Dramas. Edited and translated by Royall Tyler. London: Penguin, 1992.

Rimer, J. Thomas, and Yamazaki Masakazu, trans. *On the Art of Nō Drama: The Major Treatises of Zeami.* Princeton, N.J.: Princeton University Press, 1984.

Sekine, Masaru. *Zeami and His Theories of Noh Drama.* Gerrards Cross, U.K.: C. Smythe, 1985.

Terasaki, Etsuko. *Figures of Desire: Wordplay, Spirit Possession, Fantasy, Madness, and Mourning in Japanese Noh Plays.* Ann Arbor: Center for Japanese Studies, University of Michigan, 2002.

Zorro, Joan (fl. ca. 1250–1300)

Known as "Foxy John," this humble *jogral* (i.e., JONGLEUR) was doubtlessly Portuguese, judging from his apparent familiarity with Lisbon and with the Tagus River. One of the earlier Lisbon *trovadores* or courtly singers, Zorro may have been active during the reign of Alfonso III (1248–79) or, more likely his son and successor King DINIS (1279–1325), a well-known patron of the arts and himself a poet.

Of Zorro's 11 extant compositions, 10 are *CANTIGAS DE AMIGO* (lyrics in which a woman speaks of her lover or "friend"), all of which manifest the popular, folk origins of that genre: They tend to be simple and lyrical, utilizing a parallel structure with a refrain, and sometimes using archaic diction. Seven of these poems are *marinhas,* or sea-poems, set on the estuary of the Tagus known as the *rio forte,* where the shipyards of Lisbon are located. Typical of these poems is "*Jus' a lo mar e o rio*" (Down to the sea and the river), which begins:

Down to the sea and the river
I shall go, for I am in love,
to where the king is building his ship;
my beloved, I shall go with you.

(Jensen 1992, 28.3, ll. 1–4)

The fourth line here is the refrain. In another poem, *Per ribeira do rio* (Along the bank of the river), the speaker sees her lover leaving and rejoices because she knows he wants to take her with him:

I saw the boat rowing
On it my beloved is leaving,
And the river-bank fills me with joy.

On it my friend is leaving,
He wants to take me with him,
And the river-bank fills me with joy.

(Jensen 1992, 28.5, ll. 10–15)

Here the parallelism is apparent as the second line of the first stanza is paralleled in the first line of the second stanza—a pattern that runs through the poem, where the third line is always the refrain.

One of Zorro's poems is a dance song, or *bailada,* beginning "*Bailemos agora, por Deus, ai velidas*" (Let us dance now, for the sake of God, oh beautiful girls) (Jensen 1992, 28.8), in which the speaker invites her friends to dance beneath the hazel trees with her. The lyric was famous enough that Airas NÚÑEZ wrote his own version, *Bailemos nós ja todas tres, ai amigas* (Let us dance now all three of us, oh friends) (Jensen 1992, 6.4), a poem generally conceded to be inferior to Zorro's. The relationship of these two poems, however, suggests the respect with which Zorro was regarded by other poets.

Bibliography

Bell, Aubrey F.G. "The Eleven Songs of Joan Zorro," *MLR* 15 (1920): 58–64.

Flores, Angel, ed. *An Anthology of Medieval Lyrics.* New York: Modern Library, 1962.

Jensen, Frede, ed. and trans. *Medieval Galician-Portuguese Poetry: An Anthology.* Garland Library of Medieval Literature, 87. New York: Garland, 1992.

SELECTED BIBLIOGRAPHY

Reference Works

Bondanella, Peter, and Julia Conaway Bondanella, eds. *Dictionary of Italian Literature.* Westport, Conn.: Greenwood Press, 1979.

Braun, Sidney D., ed. *Dictionary of French Literature.* Westport, Conn.: Greenwood Press, 1971.

Cross, F. L., ed. *Oxford Dictionary of the Christian Church.* Oxford: Oxford University Press, 1997.

Drabble, Margaret, ed. *The Oxford Companion to English Literature.* Rev. ed. Oxford: Oxford University Press, 1998.

Lambdin, Robert Thomas, and Laura Cooner Lambdin. *Encyclopedia of Medieval Literature.* Westport, Conn.: Greenwood Press, 2000.

Ousby, Ian, ed. *The Cambridge Guide to Literature in English.* Cambridge: Cambridge University Press, 1993.

Preminger, Alex, et al., eds. *Encyclopedia of Poetry and Poetics.* Princeton, N.J.: Princeton University Press, 1965.

Sadie, Stanley, and John Tyrrell, eds. *The New Grove Dictionary of Music and Musicians.* 2nd ed. 29 vols. New York: Grove, 2001.

Strayer, Joseph, ed. *The Dictionary of the Middle Ages.* 13 vols. New York: Scribner's, 1982.

Ward, Philip, ed. *The Oxford Companion to Spanish Literature.* Oxford: Clarendon Press, 1978.

Primary Texts

Alexander, Michael, trans. *The Earliest English Poems.* Harmondsworth, U.K..: Penguin, 1966.

Aquinas, St. Thomas. *Summa Theologiae.* Cambridge: Blackfriars, 1964ff.

Barks, Coleman, trans. *The Essential Rumi.* San Francisco: Harper, 1997.

Barr, Helen, ed. *The Piers Plowman Tradition: A Critical Edition of Pierce the Ploughman's Crede, Richard the Redeless, Mum and the Sothsegger, and The Crowned King.* London: Dent, 1993.

Benson, Larry D., ed. *The Riverside Chaucer.* 3rd ed. Boston: Houghton-Mifflin, 1987.

Bettenson, Henry, trans. *Augustine: The City of God.* Introduction by David Knowles. Harmondsworth, U.K.: Penguin, 1972.

Boccaccio, Giovanni. *The Decameron.* Translated by Mark Musa and Peter Bondanella. Introduction by Thomas G. Bergin. New York: New American Library, 1982.

Boethius. *The Consolation of Philosophy.* Translated by P. G. Walsh. Oxford: Oxford University Press, 2000.

Bogin, Meg. *The Women Troubadours.* Scarborough, U.K.: Paddington Press, 1976.

Brault, Gerard J., ed. and trans. *The Song of Roland: An Analytic Edition.* 2 vols. Philadelphia: Pennsylvania State University Press, 1978.

Brough, John, trans. *Poems from the Sanskrit.* Harmondsworth, U.K.: Penguin, 1968.

Carmi, T., ed. and trans. *The Penguin Book of Hebrew Verse.* Harmondsworth, U.K.: Penguin, 1981.

Child, Francis James, ed. *The English and Scottish Popular Ballads.* 1882–98. Reprint, New York: Cooper Square Publishers, 1965.

Chrétien de Troyes. *Arthurian Romances.* Translated by William W. Kibler and Carleton W. Carroll. Introduction and notes by William W. Kibler. New York: Penguin, 1991.

The Complete Works of the Pearl Poet. Translated with an introduction by Casey Finch; Middle English texts edited by Malcolm Andrew, Ronald Waldron, and Clifford Peterson. Berkeley: University of California Press, 1993.

Dahlberg, Charles, trans.: *The Romance of the Rose.* Princeton, N.J.: Princeton University Press, 1971.

Dante Alighieri. *The Divine Comedy.* Edited and translated by Charles Singleton. 3 vols. Bollingen Series, 80. Princeton, N.J.: Princeton University Press: 1970–1975.

Dante's Vita Nuova. Translated by Mark Musa. Bloomington: Indiana University Press, 1973.

Davies, R. T., ed. *Middle English Lyrics: A Critical Anthology.* Evanston, Ill.: Northwestern University Press, 1964.

Dimock, Edward C., and Denise Levertov, ed. and trans. *In Praise of Krishna.* Garden City, N.Y.: Doubleday, 1967.

Dobbie, Elliot Van Kirk. *Beowulf and Judith.* The Anglo-Saxon Poetic Records, 4. New York: Columbia University Press, 1953.

Goldin, Frederick, ed. and trans. *German and Italian Lyrics of the Middle Ages: An Anthology and a History.* New York: Doubleday, 1973.

———. *Lyrics of the Troubadours and Trouvères: An Anthology and a History.* Garden City, N.Y.: Anchor, 1973.

Gottfried von Strassburg. *Tristan und Isolde.* Translated by Francis Gentry. New York: Continuum, 1988.

Haddawy, Husain, trans. *The Arabian Nights.* Based on the text of the 14th-century Syrian manuscript edited by Muhsin Mahdi. New York: Knopf, 1992.

Hatto, A. T., trans. *The Nibelungenlied.* London: Penguin, 1965.

Heaney, Seamus, trans. *Beowulf: A New Verse Translation.* New York: Farrar, Straus and Giroux, 2000.

Irwin, Robert, ed. *Night and Horses and the Desert: An Anthology of Classical Arabic Literature.* Woodstock, N.Y.: Overlook Press, 1999.

Jensen, Frede, ed. and trans. *Medieval Galician-Portuguese Poetry: An Anthology.* Garland Library of Medieval Literature, 87. New York and London: Garland, 1992.

Japanese Nō Dramas. Edited and translated by Royall Tyler. London: Penguin, 1992.

Kinsella, Thomas, trans. *The Táin.* With brush drawings by Louis Le Brocquy. London: Oxford University Press, 1970.

Klaeber, Friedrich, ed. *Beowulf and the Fight at Finnsburg.* 3rd ed. Boston: D.C. Heath, 1950.

Knight, Stephen, and Thomas Ohlgren, eds. *Robin Hood and Other Outlaw Tales.* Kalamazoo, Mich.: Medieval Institute Publications, 1997.

Krapp, George Philip. *The Junius Manuscript.* Anglo-Saxon Poetic Records, 1. New York: Columbia University Press, 1931.

Krapp, George P., ed. *The Vercelli Book.* Anglo-Saxon Poetic Records, 2. New York: Columbia University Press, 1932.

Krapp, George Philip, and Elliott van Kirk Dobbie, eds. *The Exeter Book.* Anglo-Saxon Poetic Records, 3. New York: Columbia University Press, 1936.

Lacy, Norris J., general ed. *Lancelot-Grail: The Old French Arthurian Vulgate and Post-Vulgate in Translation.* 5 vols. New York: Garland Publishing, 1993–1996.

Langland, William. *The Vision of Piers Plowman: A Critical Edition of the B-text Based on Trinity College Cambridge MS B.15.17.* 2nd ed. Edited by A. V. C. Schmidt. London: Dent, 1995.

Lee, Peter H., ed. *The Columbia Anthology of Traditional Korean Poetry.* New York: Columbia University Press, 2002.

Malory, Sir Thomas. *Le Morte Darthur.* Edited by Stephen H. A. Shepherd. New York: Norton, 2004.

Moser, Hugo, and Helmut Tervooren, eds. *Des Minnesangs Frühling.* 38th ed. Stuttgart: Hirzel, 1988.

Murasaki Shikibu. *The Tale of Genji.* Translated by Royall Tyler. New York: Viking, 2001.

Owen, Stephen, ed. *An Anthology of Chinese Literature: Beginnings to 1911.* New York: Norton, 1996.

Percy, Thomas, ed. *Reliques of Ancient English Poetry.* 3 vols. 1765. Edinburgh: James Nichol, 1858.

Peterson, Indira Viswanathan. *Poems to Śiva: The Hymns of the Tamil Saints.* Princeton, N.J.: Princeton University Press, 1989.

Petrarch, Francis. *The Canzoniere, or, Rerum vulgarium fragmenta.* Translated with notes and commentary by Mark Musa. Introduction by Mark Musa with Barbara Manfredi. Bloomington: Indiana University Press, 1996.

Pope, John Collin, ed. *Eight Old English Poems.* 3rd ed. Prepared by R. D. Fulk. New York: Norton, 2001.

Ramanujan, A. K., ed. and trans. *Speaking of Śiva.* Harmondsworth, U.K..: Penguin, 1973.

The Sagas of Icelanders: A Selection. Preface by Jane Smiley and introduction by Robert Kellogg. New York: Viking, 2000.

Shepherd, Stephen H. A., ed. *Middle English Romances: Authoritative Texts, Sources and Backgrounds, Criticism.* New York: Norton, 1995.

Sperl, Stefan, and Christopher Shackle, eds. *Qasída Poetry in Islamic Africa and Asia.* 2 vols. Leiden, Netherlands: E.J. Brill, 1996.

Sturluson, Snorri. *Edda.* Edited and translated by Anthony Faulkes. London: Dent, 1987.

Thiébaux, Marcelle, trans. *The Writings of Medieval Women: An Anthology.* 2nd edition. New York: Garland, 1994.

Walsh, P. G., ed. and trans. *Love Lyrics from the Carmina Burana.* Chapel Hill: University of North Carolina Press, 1993.

Wilhelm, James J., and Laila Zamuelis Gross. *The Romance of Arthur.* New York: Garland, 1984.

Wolfram von Eschenbach. *Parzival.* Translated by A. E. Hatto. Harmondsworth, U.K.: Penguin, 1980.

Secondary Sources

Akehurst, F. R. P., and Judith M. Davis. *A Handbook of the Troubadours.* Berkeley: University of California Press, 1995.

Barber, Richard. *The Holy Grail: Imagination and Belief.* Cambridge, Mass.: Harvard University Press, 2004.

Beadle, Richard, ed. *The Cambridge Companion to Medieval English Theatre.* Cambridge: Cambridge University Press, 1994.

Benson, C. David. *Public Piers Plowman: Modern Scholarship and Late Medieval English Culture.* University Park: Pennsylvania State University Press, 2004.

Breeze, Andrew. *Medieval Welsh Literature.* Dublin: Four Courts Press, 1997.

Brewer, Derek, and Jonathan Gibson, ed. *A Companion to the Gawain-Poet.* Woodbridge, U.K., and Rochester, N.Y.: D. S. Brewer, 1997.

Butterfield, Ardis. *Poetry and Music in Medieval France: From Jean Renart to Guillaume de Machaut.* Cambridge: Cambridge University Press, 2002.

Clarke, Dorothy Clotelle, comp. *Early Spanish Lyric Poetry: Essays and Selections.* New York: Las Americas, 1967.

Cook, Michael. *The* Koran: *A Very Short Introduction.* Oxford: Oxford University Press, 2000.

Cooper, Helen. *Oxford Guides to Chaucer: The Canterbury Tales.* 2nd ed. Oxford: Oxford University Press, 1996.

Curtius, Ernst Robert. *European Literature and the Latin Middle Ages.* Translated by Willard R. Trask. New York: Pantheon Books, 1953.

Dalrymple, Roger. *Middle English Literature: A Guide to Criticism.* Malden, Mass.: Blackwell, 2004.

Dillon, Myles. *Early Irish Literature.* Chicago: University of Chicago Press, 1948.

Dronke, Peter. *Medieval Latin and the Rise of the European Love-Lyric.* 2nd ed. 2 vols. Oxford: Clarendon Press, 1968.

———. *The Medieval Lyric.* 3rd ed. Woodbridge, U.K..: Boydell and Brewer, 1996.

Fowler, David C. *A Literary History of the Popular Ballad.* Durham, N.C.: Duke University Press, 1968.

Gibbs, Marion E., and Sidney M. Johnson. *Medieval German Literature: A Companion.* New York: Garland, 1997.

Godden, Malcolm, and Michael Lapidge, eds. *The Cambridge Companion to Old English Literature.* Cambridge: Cambridge University Press, 1991.

Greenfield, Stanley B., and Daniel G. Calder. *A New Critical History of Old English Literature.* New York: New York University Press, 1986.

Hamori, Andras. *On the Art of Medieval Arabic Literature.* Princeton, N.J.: Princeton University Press, 1974.

Hasty, Will, ed. *A Companion to Gottfried von Strassburg's "Tristan."* Rochester, N.Y.: Camden House, 2003.

Howard, Donald R. *Chaucer: His Life, His Works, His World.* New York: Dutton, 1987.

Hungguyu, Kim. *Understanding Korean Literature.* Translated by Robert J. Fouser. New Studies in Asian Culture. Armonk, N.Y.: M. E. Sharp, 1997.

Hyman, Arthur, and James J. Walsh, eds. *Philosophy in the Middle Ages: The Christian, Islamic, and Jewish Traditions.* 2nd ed. Indianapolis, Ind.: Hackett, 1983.

Idema, Wilt, and Lloyd Haft. *A Guide to Chinese Literature.* Ann Arbor: Center for Chinese Studies, University of Michigan, 1997.

Jacoff, Rachel, ed. *The Cambridge Companion to Dante.* Cambridge: Cambridge University Press, 1993.

Kato, Shuicho. *A History of Japanese Literature: From the Man-yōshu to Modern Times.* New abridged edition. Translated and edited by Don Sanderson. Richmond, U.K..: Curzon Press, 1997.

Keene, Donald. *Seeds in the Heart: Japanese Literature from Earliest Times to the Late Sixteenth Century.* History of Japanese Literature, 1. New York: Columbia University Press, 1999.

Kelly, Douglas. *Medieval Imagination: Rhetoric and the Poetry of Courtly Love.* Madison: University of Wisconsin Press, 1978.

Kennedy, Robert Peter, and Kim Paffenroth. *A Reader's Companion to Augustine's Confessions.* Louisville, Ky.: Westminster John Knox Press, 2003.

Keshavarz, Fatemah. *Reading Mystical Lyric: The Case of Jalal Al-Din Rumi.* Studies in Comparative Religion. Columbia: University of South Carolina Press, 1998.

Kim, Kichung. *An Introduction to Classical Korean Literature: From Hyangga to P'ansori.* New Studies in Asian Culture. Armonk, N.Y.: M. E. Sharp, 1996.

Kolve, V. A. *The Play Called Corpus Christi.* Stanford, Calif.: Stanford University Press, 1966.

Krueger, Roberta L. *The Cambridge Companion to Medieval Romance.* Cambridge: Cambridge University Press, 2000.

Leaman, Oliver. *Moses Maimonides.* London: Routledge, 1990.

Lewis, C. S. *The Allegory of Love: A Study in Medieval Tradition.* New York: Oxford University Press, 1936.

Loomis, Roger Sherman, ed. *Arthurian Literature in the Middle Ages.* Oxford, U.K.: Clarendon Press, 1959.

McCann, David R. *Early Korean Literature: Selections and Introductions.* New York: Columbia University Press, 2000.

McMullen, David. *State and Scholars in T'ang China.* Cambridge: Cambridge University Press, 1998.

Miner, Earl, Hiroko Odagiri, and Robert E. Morrell. *The Princeton Companion to Classical Japanese Literature.* Princeton, N.J.: Princeton University Press, 1985.

Moser, Charles A., ed. *The Cambridge History of Russian Literature.* Cambridge: Cambridge University Press, 1989.

Newman, F. X., ed. *The Meaning of Courtly Love.* Albany: State University of New York Press, 1968.

O'Daly, Gerard. *Augustine's City of God: A Reader's Guide.* Oxford: Clarendon Press, 1999.

Olson, Glending. *Literature as Recreation in the Later Middle Ages.* Ithaca, N.Y.: Cornell University Press, 1982.

Orchard, Andy. *A Critical Companion to Beowulf.* Rochester, N.Y.: D. S. Brewer, 2003.

Owen, Stephen. *The Great Age of Chinese Poetry: The High T'ang.* New Haven, Conn., and London: Yale University Press, 1981.

Pearsall, Derek. *The Canterbury Tales.* London: George Allen and Unwin, 1985.

———. *The Life of Geoffrey Chaucer: A Critical Biography.* Oxford, U.K.: Blackwell, 1992.

Rexroth, Kenneth. *Women Poets of Japan.* New York: New Directions, 1982.

Sayce, Olive. *The Medieval German Lyric 1150–1300. The Development of Its Themes and Forms in Their European Context.* Oxford, U.K.: Clarendon Press, 1982.

The Selected Writings of Christine de Pizan. Translated by Renate Blumenfeld-Kosinski and Kevin

Brownlee. Edited by Renate Blumenfeld-Kosinski. New York: Norton, 1997.

Simpson, James. *Piers Plowman: An Introduction to the B-Text.* London: Longman, 1990.

Stevenson, Barbara, and Cynthia Ho, eds. *Crossing the Bridge: Comparative Essays on Medieval European and Heian Japanese Women Writers.* New Middle Ages Series, edited by Bonnie Wheeler. New York: Palgrave/St. Martin's, 2000.

Thomas, Alfred. *Anne's Bohemia: Czech Literature and Society, 1310–1420.* Minneapolis: University of Minnesota Press, 1998.

Tolkien, J. R. R. "*Beowulf:* The Monsters and the Critics," *Proceedings of the British Academy* 22 (1936): 245–295.

Valency, Maurice. *In Praise of Love.* New York: MacMillan, 1958.

Wallace, David. *Giovanni Boccaccio: Decameron.* Cambridge: Cambridge University Press, 1991.

Wilhelm, James J. *Seven Troubadours: The Creators of Modern Verse.* University Park: Pennsylvania State University Press, 1970.

Williams, Gwyn. *An Introduction to Welsh Poetry: From the Beginnings to the Sixteenth Century.* Freeport, N.Y.: Books for Libraries Press, 1970.

Wimsatt, James I. *Chaucer and His French Contemporaries: Natural Music in the Fourteenth Century.* Toronto: University of Toronto Press, 1991.

CONTRIBUTORS

Editorial Assistants

Leslie Johnston
University of Central Arkansas

Malene A. Little
Northern State University

Michelle Palmer
University of Central Arkansas

Contributing Scholars

Albrecht Classen
University of Arizona

Chris Craun
University of Central Arkansas

Cynthia Ho
University of North Carolina, Asheville

Timothy S. Jones
Augustana College

Diane Korngiebel
University of Central Arkansas

John Parrack
University of Central Arkansas

David Raybin
Eastern Illinois University

Michelle M. Sauer
Minot State University

Stephen H. A. Shepherd
Southern Methodist University

David Sprunger
Concordia College

Barbara Stevenson
Kennesaw State University

Elisa Narin van Court
Colby College

INDEX

Page numbers in **boldface** indicate main entries.

B

H

I

J

K

L

M

N

Q

R

S

T